P9-BHU-276

Contemporary Literary Criticism

Guide to Gale Literary Criticism Series

For criticism on	Consult these Gale series
Authors now living or who died after December 31, 1959	*CONTEMPORARY LITERARY CRITICISM (CLC)*
Authors who died between 1900 and 1959	*TWENTIETH-CENTURY LITERARY CRITICISM (TCLC)*
Authors who died between 1800 and 1899	*NINETEENTH-CENTURY LITERATURE CRITICISM (NCLC)*
Authors who died between 1400 and 1799	*LITERATURE CRITICISM FROM 1400 TO 1800 (LC)* *SHAKESPEAREAN CRITICISM (SC)*
Authors who died before 1400	*CLASSICAL AND MEDIEVAL LITERATURE CRITICISM (CMLC)*
Black writers of the past two hundred years	*BLACK LITERATURE CRITICISM (BLC)*
Authors of books for children and young adults	*CHILDREN'S LITERATURE REVIEW (CLR)*
Dramatists	*DRAMA CRITICISM (DC)*
Hispanic writers of the late nineteenth and twentieth centuries	*HISPANIC LITERATURE CRITICISM (HLC)*
Poets	*POETRY CRITICISM (PC)*
Short story writers	*SHORT STORY CRITICISM (SSC)*
Major authors from the Renaissance to the present	*WORLD LITERATURE CRITICISM, 1500 TO THE PRESENT (WLC)*

ISSN 0091-3421

Volume 82

Contemporary Literary Criticism

Excerpts from Criticism of the Works of Today's Novelists, Poets, Playwrights, Short Story Writers, Scriptwriters, and Other Creative Writers

James P. Draper
EDITOR

Jennifer Brostrom
Brigham Narins
ASSOCIATE EDITORS, CLC

Jeffery Chapman
Jennifer Gariepy
Christopher Giroux
Margaret Haerens
Drew Kalasky
Thomas Ligotti
Jennifer Mast
Sean René Pollock
Brian St. Germain
Janet Witalec
ASSOCIATE EDITORS

Gale Research Inc. • DETROIT • WASHINGTON, D.C. • LONDON

STAFF

James P. Draper, *Editor*

Jennifer Brostrom, Jeffery Chapman, Jennifer Gariepy, Christopher Giroux, Margaret Haerens, Drew Kalasky, Thomas Ligotti, Jennifer Mast, Brigham Narins, Sean René Pollock, Brian St. Germain, Janet Witalec, *Associate Editors*

Martha Bommarito, Nancy Dziedzic, Kelly Hill, Lynn M. Spampinato, *Assistant Editors*

Jeanne A. Gough, *Permissions & Production Manager*
Linda M. Pugliese, *Production Supervisor*
Donna Craft, Paul Lewon, Maureen A. Puhl, Camille P. Robinson, Sheila Walencewicz, *Editorial Associates*

Sandra C. Davis, *Permissions Supervisor (Text)*
Maria L. Franklin, Josephine M. Keene, Michele Lonoconus, Shalice Shah, Kimberly F. Smilay, *Permissions Associates*
Jennifer A. Arnold, Brandy C. Merritt, *Permissions Assistants*

Margaret A. Chamberlain, *Permissions Supervisor (Pictures)*
Pamela A. Hayes, Arlene Johnson, Keith Reed, Barbara A. Wallace, *Permissions Associates*
Susan Brohman, *Permissions Assistant*

Victoria B. Cariappa, *Research Manager*
Mary Rose Bonk, *Research Supervisor*
Reginald A. Carlton, Frank Vincent Castronova, Robert S. Lazich, Andrew Guy Malonis, Mary Beth McElmeel, Donna Melnychenko, Tamara C. Nott, Jaema Paradowski, Norma Sawaya, *Editorial Associates*
Laurel Sprague Bowden, Maria Bryson, Dawn Marie Conzett, Eva Marie Felts, Shirley Gates, Julie A. Kriebel, Sharon McGilvray, Stefanie Scarlett, Dana R. Shleiffers, Amy B. Wieczorek, *Editorial Assistants*

Mary Beth Trimper, *Production Director*
Deborah Milliken, *Production Assistant*

Cynthia Baldwin, *Product Design Manager*
Barbara J. Yarrow, *Graphic Services Supervisor*
Sherrell Hobbs, *Desktop Publisher*
Willie F. Mathis, *Camera Operator*

Library of Congress Catalog Card Number 76-38938
ISBN 0-8103-4990-6
ISSN 0091-3421

Printed in the United States of America
Published simultaneously in the United Kingdom
by Gale Research International Limited
(An affiliated company of Gale Research Inc.)
10 9 8 7 6 5 4 3 2 1

Contents

Preface

A Comprehensive Information Source on Contemporary Literature

Named "one of the twenty-five most distinguished reference titles published during the past twenty-five years" by *Reference Quarterly*, the *Contemporary Literary Criticism (CLC)* series provides readers with critical commentary and general information on more than 2,000 authors now living or who died after December 31, 1959. Previous to the publication of the first volume of *CLC* in 1973, there was no ongoing digest monitoring scholarly and popular sources of critical opinion and explication of modern literature. *CLC*, therefore, has fulfilled an essential need, particularly since the complexity and variety of contemporary literature makes the function of criticism especially important to today's reader.

Scope of the Series

CLC presents significant passages from published criticism of works by creative writers. Since many of the authors covered by *CLC* inspire continual critical commentary, writers are often represented in more than one volume. There is, of course, no duplication of reprinted criticism.

Authors are selected for inclusion for a variety of reasons, among them the publication or dramatic production of a critically acclaimed new work, the reception of a major literary award, revival of interest in past writings, or the adaptation of a literary work to film or television.

Attention is also given to several other groups of writers—authors of considerable public interest—about whose work criticism is often difficult to locate. These include mystery and science fiction writers, literary and social critics, foreign writers, and authors who represent particular ethnic groups within the United States.

Format of the Book

Each *CLC* volume contains about 500 individual excerpts taken from hundreds of book review periodicals, general magazines, scholarly journals, monographs, and books. Entries include critical evaluations spanning from the beginning of an author's career to the most current commentary. Interviews, feature articles, and other published writings that offer insight into the author's works are also presented. Students, teachers, librarians, and researchers will find that the generous excerpts and supplementary material in *CLC* provide them with vital information required to write a term paper, analyze a poem, or lead a book discussion group. In addition, complete bibliographical citations note the original source and all of the information necessary for a term paper footnote or bibliography.

Features

A *CLC* author entry consists of the following elements:

- The **Author Heading** cites the author's name in the form under which the author has most commonly published, followed by birth date, and death date when applicable. Uncertainty as to a birth or death date is indicated by a question mark.

- A **Portrait** of the author is included when available.

- A brief **Biographical and Critical Introduction** to the author and his or her work precedes the excerpted criticism. The first line of the introduction provides the author's full name, pseudonyms (if applicable), nationality, and a listing of genres in which the author has written. Previous volumes of *CLC* in which the author has been featured are also listed in the introduction.

- A list of **Principal Works** notes the most important works by the author.

- The **Excerpted Criticism** represents various kinds of critical writing, ranging in form from the brief review to the scholarly exegesis. Essays are selected by the editors to reflect the spectrum of opinion about a specific work or about an author's literary career in general. The excerpts are presented chronologically, adding a useful perspective to the entry. All titles by the author featured in the entry are printed in boldface type, which enables the reader to easily identify the works being discussed. Publication information (such as publisher names and book prices) and parenthetical numerical references (such as footnotes or page and line references to specific editions of a work) have been deleted at the editor's discretion to provide smoother reading of the text.

- Critical essays are prefaced by **Explanatory Notes** as an additional aid to readers. These notes may provide several types of valuable information, including: the reputation of the critic, the importance of the work of criticism, the commentator's approach to the author's work, the purpose of the criticism, and changes in critical trends regarding the author.

- A complete **Bibliographical Citation** designed to help the user find the original essay or book follows each excerpt.

- A concise **Further Reading** section appears at the end of entries on authors for whom a significant amount of criticism exists in addition to the pieces reprinted in *CLC*. Cross-references to other useful sources published by Gale Research in which the author has appeared are also included: *Children's Literature Review, Contemporary Authors, Something about the Author, Dictionary of Literary Biography, Drama Criticism, Poetry Criticism, Short Story Criticism, Contemporary Authors Autobiography Series,* and *Something about the Author Autobiography Series*.

Other Features

CLC also includes the following features:

- An **Acknowledgments** section lists the copyright holders who have granted permission to reprint material in this volume of *CLC*. It does not, however, list every book or periodical reprinted or consulted during the preparation of the volume.

- A **Cumulative Author Index** lists all the authors who have appeared in the various literary criticism series published by Gale Research, with cross-references to Gale's biographical and autobiographical series. A full listing of the series referenced there appears on the first page of the indexes of this volume. Readers will welcome this cumulated author index as a useful tool for locating an author within the various series. The index, which lists birth and death dates when available, will be particularly valuable for those authors who are identified with a certain period but whose death dates cause them to be placed in another, or for those authors whose careers span two periods. For example, Ernest Hemingway is found in *CLC,* yet a writer often associated with him, F. Scott Fitzgerald, is found in *Twentieth-Century Literary Criticism.*

- A **Cumulative Nationality Index** alphabetically lists all authors featured in *CLC* by nationality, followed by numbers corresponding to the volumes in which the authors appear.

- A **Title Index** alphabetically lists all titles reviewed in the current volume of *CLC.* Listings are followed by the author's name and the corresponding page numbers where the titles are discussed. English translations of foreign titles and variations of titles are cross-referenced to the title under which a work was originally published. Titles of novels, novellas, dramas, films, record albums, and poetry, short story, and essay collections are printed in italics, while all individual poems, short stories, essays, and songs are printed in roman type within quotation marks; when published separately (e.g., T. S. Eliot's poem *The Waste Land*), the titles of long poems are printed in italics.

- In response to numerous suggestions from librarians, Gale has also produced a **Special Paperbound Edition** of the *CLC* title index. This annual cumulation, which alphabetically lists all titles reviewed in the series, is available to all customers and is published with the first volume of *CLC* issued in each calendar year. Additional copies of the index are available upon request. Librarians and patrons will welcome this separate index: it saves shelf space, is easy to use, and is recyclable upon receipt of the following year's cumulation.

Citing *Contemporary Literary Criticism*

When writing papers, students who quote directly from any volume in the Literary Criticism Series may use the following general forms to footnote reprinted criticism. The first example pertains to material drawn from periodicals, the second to material reprinted in books:

[1]Anne Tyler, "Manic Monologue," *The New Republic* 200 (April 17, 1989), 44-6; excerpted and reprinted in *Contemporary Literary Criticism,* Vol. 58, ed. Roger Matuz (Detroit: Gale Research Inc., 1990), p. 325.

[2]Patrick Reilly, *The Literature of Guilt: From 'Gulliver' to Golding* (University of Iowa Press, 1988); excerpted and reprinted in *Contemporary Literary Criticism,* Vol. 58, ed. Roger Matuz (Detroit: Gale Research Inc., 1990), pp. 206-12.

Suggestions Are Welcome

The editor hopes that readers will find *CLC* a useful reference tool and welcomes comments about the work. Send comments and suggestions to: Editor, *Contemporary Literary Criticism,* Gale Research Inc., Penobscot Building, Detroit, MI 48226-4094.

Acknowledgments

The editors wish to thank the copyright holders of the excerpted criticism included in this volume, the permissions managers of many book and magazine publishing companies for assisting us in securing reprint rights, and Anthony Bogucki for assistance with copyright research. We are also grateful to the staffs of the Detroit Public Library, the Library of Congress, the University of Detroit Mercy Library, Wayne State University Purdy/Kresge Library Complex, and the University of Michigan Libraries for making their resources available to us. Following is a list of the copyright holders who have granted us permission to reprint material in this volume of ***CLC.*** Every effort has been made to trace copyright, but if omissions have been made, please let us know.

COPYRIGHTED EXCERPTS IN *CLC,* VOLUME 82, WERE REPRINTED FROM THE FOLLOWING PERIODICALS:

permission of the author.—***Encounter,*** v. LXVII, December, 1986 for "Appreciating Milosz" in Leopold Labez. © 1986 by the author. Reprinted by permission of the author.—***Esquire,*** v. 100, December, 1983. Copyright © 1983, Esquire Associates. Used by courtesy of the magazine.—***Extrapolation,*** v. 23, Spring, 1982. Copyright 1982 by The Kent State University Press. Reprinted by permission of the publisher.—***The Georgia Review,*** v. XXXV, Summer, 1981. Copyright, 1981, by the University of Georgia. Reprinted by permission of the publisher.—***The Guardian Weekly,*** v. 102, March 14, 1970. Copyright © 1970 by Guardian Publications Ltd. Reprinted by permission of the publisher.—***The Hudson Review,*** v. XVIII, Summer, 1965. Copyright © 1965, renewed 1993 by The Hudson Review, Inc. Reprinted by permission of the publisher.—***The Idol,*** October 16, 1968. Reprinted by permission of the publisher.—***The Listener,*** v. 118, July 9, 1987 for "In Search of Liberation" by Linda Taylor. © British Broadcasting Corp. 1987. Reprinted by permission of the author.—***London Review of Books,*** v. 11, March 2, 1989 for "Taking Leave" by Mark Edmundson. Appears here by permission of the *London Review of Books* and the author.—***Los Angeles Times Book Review,*** March 27, 1983; March 25, 1990; January 31, 1993. Copyright, 1983, 1990, 1993, *Los Angeles Times*. All reprinted by permission of the publisher.—***Magill's Literary Annual,*** 1977. Copyright, ©, 1977, by Frank N. Magill. All rights reserved. Reprinted by permission of the publisher.—***MELUS,*** v. 9, Summer, 1982; v. 14, Spring, 1987. Copyright, *MELUS,* The Society for the Study of Multi-Ethnic Literature of the United States, 1982, 1987. Both reprinted by permission of the publisher.—***Modern Age,*** v. 30, Spring, 1986. Copyright © 1986 by the Intercollegiate Studies Institute, Inc. Reprinted by permission of the publisher.—***The Nation,*** New York, v. 203, October 17, 1966; v. 205, November 27, 1967; v. 249, November 27, 1989; v. 253, July 1, 1991. Copyright 1966, 1967, 1989, 1991 *The Nation* magazine/The Nation Company, Inc. All reprinted by permission of the publisher./ v. 20, November 8, 1965. Copyright 1965, renewed 1993 *The Nation,* magazine/The Nation Company, Inc. Reprinted by permission of the publisher.—***National Review,*** v. XXIV, May 12, 1972. © 1972 by National Review, Inc., 150 East 35th Street, New York, NY 10016. Reprinted with the permission of the publisher.—***New Literary History,*** v. II, Winter, 1971. Copyright © 1971 by *New Literary History*. Reprinted by permission of the publisher.—***The New Republic,*** v. LXIV, October 22, 1930. Copyright 1930 The New Republic, Inc. Renewed 1958 by Harrison Blane Inc. Reprinted by permission of *The New Republic.*/v. 201, July 31, 1989; v. 206, March 16, 1992; v. 207, December 21, 1992. © 1989, 1992 The New Republic, Inc. All reprinted by permission of *The New Republic.*—***New Statesman,*** v. 74, November 3, 1967. © 1967 The Statesman & Nation Publishing Co. Ltd. Reprinted by permission of the publisher.—***New Statesman & Society,*** v. 1, October 21, 1988; v. 2, December 8, 1989. © 1988, 1989 Statesman & Nation Publishing Company Limited. Both reprinted by permission of the publisher.—***New York Herald Tribune Books,*** August 9, 1936. Copyright 1936, renewed 1964, New York Herald Tribune Inc. All rights reserved. Reprinted by permission.—***The New York Quarterly,*** n. 27, Summer, 1985. Copyright © 1985 by The National Poetry Foundation. Reprinted by permission of the publisher.—***The New York Review of Books,*** v. XXXII, November 21, 1985 for "Global Villager" by Harry Levin; v. 35, June 2, 1988 for "Witness" by A. Alvarez. Copyright © 1985, 1988 Nyrev, Inc. Both reprinted by permission of the respective authors./ v. XIX, October 5, 1972; v. XXXVI, January 18, 1990. Copyright © 1972, 1990 Nyrev, Inc. Both reprinted with permission from *The New York Review of Books.*/ v. 5, November 11, 1965; v. V, November 25, 1965. Copyright © 1965, renewed 1993 Nyrev, Inc. Both reprinted with permission from *The New York Review of Books.*—***The New York Times,*** June 20, 1966; October 8, 1969. Copyright © 1966, 1969 by The New York Times Company. Both reprinted by permission of the publisher./ February 13, 1938, February 18, 1948. Copyright 1938, renewed 1966; copyright 1948, renewed 1976 by The New York Times Company. Both reprinted by permission of the publisher.—***The New York Times Book Review,*** November 2, 1969; March 4, 1973; October 21, 1973; March 24, 1974; June 26, 1988; June 11, 1989; March 4, 1990; November 25, 1990; July 26, 1992; September 20, 1992; February 14, 1993; September 26, 1993. Copyright © 1969, 1973, 1974, 1988, 1989, 1990, 1992, 1993 by The New York Times Company. All reprinted by permission of the publisher./ January 24, 1965, September 12, 1965. Copyright © 1965, renewed 1993 by The New York Times Company. Both reprinted by permission of the publisher.—***The New Yorker,*** v. LXV, August 28, 1989 for "North of the Future" by George Steiner. © 1989 by the author. Reprinted by permission of Georges Borchardt, Inc. on behalf of the author.—***Newsweek,*** v. LXXIV, October 6, 1969. © 1969, Newsweek, Inc. All rights reserved. Reprinted by permission of the publisher.—***The Observer,*** November 22, 1992. Reprinted by permission of the Observer Limited, London.—***Parnassaus: Poetry in Review,*** v. 15, 1989 for "Grave Combats" by Baron Wormser. Copyright © 1989 Poetry in Review Foundation, NY. Reprinted by permission of the author./v. 15, 1989. Copyright

© 1989 Poetry in Review Foundation, NY. Reprinted by permission of the publisher.—***P. N. Review,*** v. 14, 1988 for "'Into Your Narrowest Being': The Poetry of Paul Celan" by Lesley Chamberlain. Reprinted by permission of the author.—***Partisan Review,*** v. LVIII, 1991 for "Uttering the Unutterable" by Peter Filkins. Copyright © 1991 by Partisan Review. Reprinted by permission of the author./ v. XI, Fall, 1944 for "Between Shall-I and I-Will" by Wylie Sypher; v. XII, Fall, 1945 for "The Forest and the Trees" by Isaac Rosenfeld. Copyright 1944, renewed 1971; copyright 1945, renewed 1972 by *Partisan Review.* Both reprinted by permission of the publisher and the respective authors.—***Poetry,*** v. CXXVIII, September, 1976 for "Asylum" by Alfred Corn. © 1976 by the Modern Poetry Association. Reprinted by permission of the Editor of *Poetry* and the author./ v. LXV, January, 1945 for "Bishop Berkeley and the Whales" by Jeremy Ingalls. Copyright 1945, renewed 1973 by the Modern Poetry Association. Reprinted by permission of the Editor of *Poetry* and the author.—***Prairie Schooner,*** v. XL, Winter, 1966. © 1966 by University of Nebraska Press. Reprinted from *Prairie Schooner* by permission of the University of Nebraska Press.—***Publishers Weekly,*** v. 234, July 1, 1988; v. 234, December 2, 1988. Copyright 1988 by Reed Publishing USA. Both reprinted from *Publishers Weekly,* published by the Bowker Magazine Group of Cahners Publishing Co., a division of Reed Publishing USA.—***The Review of Contemporary Fiction,*** v. 5, Fall, 1985; v. 9, Fall, 1989. Copyright 1985, 1989, by John O'Brien. Both reprinted by permission of the publisher.—***Salmagundi,*** v. 80, Fall, 1988. Copyright © 1988 by Skidmore College. Reprinted by permission of the publisher.—***The Saturday Review,*** New York, v. XLIX, June 25, 1966; v. L, October 21, 1967. © 1967 *Saturday Review* magazine./ v. XXX, August 23, 1947. Copyright 1947, renewed 1975 *Saturday Review* magazine; v. XLVIII, September, 1965. © 1965, renewed 1993 *Saturday Review* magazine.—***The Saturday Review of Literature,*** August 10, 1946. Copyright 1946, renewed 1974 *Saturday Review* magazine.—***The Sewanee Review,*** v. LXXV, Autumn, 1967. © 1967 by The University of the South. Reprinted with the permission of the editor of *The Sewanee Review.*/ v. LIV, Spring, 1946. Copyright 1946, renewed 1974 by The University of the South. Reprinted with the permission of the editor of *The Sewanee Review.*—***The Small Press Review,*** v. 19, February, 1987. © 1987 by Dustbooks. Reprinted by permission of the publisher.—***The Southern Literary Journal,*** v. XIX, Spring, 1987. Copyright 1987 by the Department of English. University of North Carolina at the Chapel Hill. Reprinted by permission of the publisher.—***The Southern Literary Journal,*** v. XXI, Spring, 1989. Copyright 1989 by the Department of English, University of North Carolina at Chapel Hill. Reprinted by permission of the publisher.—***Studies in the Novel,*** v. XI, Summer, 1979. Copyright 1979 by North Texas State University. Reprinted by permission of the publisher.—***Studies in Short Fiction,*** v. 27, Fall, 1990. Copyright 1990 by Newberry College. Reprinted by permission of the publisher.—***Texas Studies in Literature and Language,*** v. IV, Spring, 1962 for "Voice in the 'U.S.A' Biographies" by George Knox. Copyright © 1962, renewed 1990 by the University of Texas Press. Reprinted by permission of the publisher and the author.—***The Threepenny Review,*** v. 38, Summer, 1989. © copyright 1989 by The Threepenny Review. Reprinted by permission of the publisher.—***Time,*** New York, v. 85, March 19, 1965. Copyright 1965, renewed 1993 Time Warner Inc. All rights reserved. Reprinted by permission from *Time.*—***The Times Literary Supplement,*** n. 4328, March 14, 1986 for "Memoirs of an Intellectual Fidget" by Frederic Raphael. © The Times Supplements Limited 1986. Reprinted by permission of the author./ n. 3550, March 12, 1970; n. 3560, May 21, 1970; n. 3597, February 5, 1971; n. 3771, June 14, 1974; n. 3795, November 29, 1974; n. 4391, May 29, 1987; n. 4506, August 11-17, 1989; n. 4545, May 11, 1990; n. 4681, December 18, 1992. © The Times Supplements Limited 1970, 1971, 1974, 1987, 1989, 1990, 1992. All reproduced from *The Times Literary Supplement* by permission.—***TriQuarterly 67,*** Fall, 1986. © 1986 by TriQuarterly, Northwestern University. Reprinted by permission of the publisher.—***Unisa English Studies,*** v. XVI, May, 1978. Reprinted by permission of the Editor and the University of South Africa.—***The Village Voice,*** v. XIX, November 14, 1974 for "Underground Press Review" by Donald Newlove; v. XX, April 7, 1975 for "Spotwrites" by Eliot Fremont-Smith. Copyright © The Village Voice, Inc., 1974, 1975. Both reprinted by permission of *The Village Voice* and the respective authors./ v. XXXVII, June 30, 1992 for "Outward Bound" by Maurice Berger. Copyright © News Group Publications, Inc., 1992. Reprinted by permission of *The Village Voice* and the author.—***The Virginia Quarterly Review,*** v. 64, Summer, 1988. Copyright, 1988, by The Virginia Quarterly Review, The University of Virginia. Reprinted by permission of the publisher.—***The Washington Post,*** April 2, 1967; February 11, 1993. © 1967, 1993, Washington Post Co. Both reprinted with permission of the publisher.—***World Literature Today,*** v. 62, Winter, 1988; v. 65, Autumn, 1991. Copyright 1988, 1991 by the University of Oklahoma Press. Both reprinted by permission of the publisher.—***Western American Literature,*** v. XXV, November, 1990. Copyright, 1990, by the

Western Literature Association. Reprinted by permission of the publisher.—*The Yale Review,* v. LVI, December, 1966 for "Malcolm X: Mission and Meaning" by Robert Penn Warren. Copyright 1966, by Yale University. Reprinted by permission of William Morris Agency, Inc., on behalf of the Estate of the author.

COPYRIGHTED EXCERPTS IN *CLC,* VOLUME 82, WERE REPRINTED FROM THE FOLLOWING BOOKS:

Beach, Joseph Warren. From ***American Fiction: 1920-1940.*** The Macmillan Company, 1941. Copyright, 1941, renewed 1968 by Macmillan Publishing Company. All rights reserved. Reprinted by permission of the Literary Estate of Joseph Warren Beach.—Butterfield, Stephen. From ***Black Autobiography in America.*** University of Massachusetts Press, 1974. Copyright © 1974 by The University of Massachusetts Press. All rights reserved. Reprinted by permission of the author.—Cady, Joseph. From "Immersive and Counterimmersive Writing about AIDS: The Achievement of Paul Monette's 'Love Along,'" in ***Writing AIDS: Gay Literature, Language, and Analysis.*** Edited by Timothy F. Murphy and Suzanne Poirier. Columbia University Press, 1993. Copyright © 1993 Columbia University Press, New York. All rights reserved. Reprinted with the permission of the publisher.—Castronovo, David. From ***Thornton Wilder.*** Ungar, 1986. Copyright © 1986 by The Ungar Publishing Company. All rights reserved. Reprinted by permission of the publisher.—Colin, Amy. From ***Paul Celan: Holograms of Darkness.*** Indiana University Press, 1991. © 1991 Amy D. Colin. All rights reserved. Reprinted by permission of the publisher.—Courser, G. Thomas. From ***American Autobiography: The Prophetic Mode.*** Amherst: The University of Massachusetts press, 1979. Copyright © 1979 by The University of Massachusetts Press. All rights reserved. Reprinted by permission of the author.—Cowley, Malcolm. From "John Dos Passos: The Poet and the World," in ***Dos Passos: A Collection of Critical Essays.*** Edited by Andrew Hook. Prentice-Hall, 1974. © 1974 by Prentice-Hall, Inc., Englewood Cliffs, New Jersey. All rights reserved. Used by permission of Prentice-Hall/A Division of Simon & Schuster, Englewood Cliffs, NJ.—Dos Passos, John. From ***U.S.A.*** Harcourt Brace Jovanovich, 1937. Copyright 1930, 1932, 1933, 1934, 1935, 1936, 1937 by John Dos Passos. Copyright 1946 by John Dos Passos and Houghton Mifflin Company. Copyright © renewed 1958, 1960 by John Dos Passos. All rights reserved—Fox, Hugh. From ***Charles Bukowski: A Critical and Bibliographical Study.*** ABYSS Publications, 1971. © 1969 by ABYSS Publications. All rights reserved. Reprinted by permission of the publisher.—Gurko, Leo. From "John Dos Passos' 'U.S.A.': A 1930's Spectacular," in ***Proletarian Writers of the Thirties.*** Edited by David Madden. Southern Illinois University Press, 1968. Copyright © 1968 by Southern Illinois University Press. All rights reserved. Reprinted by permisson of the author.—Haberman, Donald. From ***The Plays of Thornton Wilder: A Critical Study.*** Wesleyan University Press, 1967. Copyright © 1967 by Wesleyan University. Reprinted by permission of the author.—Haley, Alex. From an epilogue to ***The Autobiography of Malcolm X.*** By Malcolm X and Alex Haley. Grove Press, 1965. Copyright © 1964, renewed 1992 by Alex Haley and Malcolm X. Copyright © 1965, renewed 1993 by Alex Haley and Betty Shabazz. All rights reserved. Reprinted by permission of Random House Inc.—Hatcher, Harlan. From ***Creating the Modern American Novel.*** Farrar & Rinehart, Incorporated, 1935. Copyright 1935, renewed 1962, by Harlan Hatcher. All rights reserved. Reprinted by permission of the author.—Kavan, Anna. From ***Julia and the Bazooka, and Other Stories.*** Edited by Rhys Davies. Alfred A. Knopf, 1970. Copyright © 1970 by Rhys Davies and Raymond Marriott. All rights reserved.—Kazin, Alfred. From an introduction to ***The 42nd Parallel.*** By John Dos Passos. A Signet Classic, 1969. Introduction copyright © 1969 by New American Library, a division of Penguin Books USA Inc. All rights reserved. Reprinted by permission of the publisher.—Kuner, M. C. From ***Thornton Wilder: The Bright and the Dark.*** Thomas Y. Crowell Company, 1972. Copyright © 1972 by Mildred Kuner. All rights reserved. Reprinted by permission of HarperCollins Publishers, Inc.—Lindbergh, Anne Morrow. From ***Listen! The Wind.*** Harcourt Brace Jovanovich, 1938. Copyright 1938 by Anne Morrow Lindbergh.—Lydenberg, John. From "Dos Passos's 'U.S.A.': The Words of the Hollow Men," in ***Essays on Determinism in American Literature.*** Edited by Sydney J. Krause. Kent State University Press, 1964. Copyright 1964, renewed 1992 by Kent State University. Reprinted by permission of the publisher.—Mayer, Elise F. From ***My Window on the World: The Works of Anne Morrow Lindbergh.*** Archon Books, 1988. © 1988 Elise F. Mayer. All rights reserved. Reprinted by permission of Archon Books, an imprint of The Shoe String Press, Inc.—McCarthy, Mary. From "The Skin of Our Teeth," in ***Sights and Spectacles: 1937-1956.*** Farrar, Straus and Cudahy, 1956. Copyright 1943, renewed 1970 by Mary McCarthy. Reprinted by permission of the author.—McNally, T. M. From ***Until Your Heart Stops.*** Villard Books, 1993. Copyright © 1993 by T. M. McNally. All rights reserved.—Monette, Paul. From ***Borrowed Time: An AIDS Memoir.*** Harcourt Brace Jovanovich, 1988. Copyright © 1988 by Paul Monette.—Pizer, Donald. From ***Dos Passos' 'U.S.A': A Critical Study.*** University Press of Virginia, 1988. Copyright © 1988 by the Rector and Visitors of the University of Virginia. Reprinted by permission of the publisher.—Rosen, Robert C. From ***John Dos Passos: Politics and the Writer.*** University of Nebraska Press, 1981. Copyright © 1981 by the University of Nebraska Press. All rights reserved. Reprinted by permission of the publisher.—Saint-Exupéry, Antoine de. From ***Wind, Sand and Stars.*** Translated by Lewis Galantiére. Reynal & Hitchcock, 1939. Copyright, 1939, by Antoine de Saint-Exupéry. Renewed 1966 by Lewis Galantiére. Reprinted by permission of Harcourt Brace Jovanovich, Inc.—Schroeder, Patricia R. From ***The Presence of the Past in Modern American Drama.*** Fairleigh Dickinson University Press, 1989. © 1989 by Associated University Presses, Inc. All rights reserved. Reprinted by permission of the publisher.—Vaughan, David Kirk. From ***Anne Morrow Lindbergh.*** Twayne, 1988. Copyright 1988 by G. K. Hall & Co. All rights reserved. Reprinted with the permission of Twayne Publisher, an imprint Macmillan Publishing Company.—Wilson, Edmund. From ***The Shores of Light: A Literary Chronicle of the Twenties and Thirties.*** Farrar, Straus and Giroux, 1952. Copyright 1952 by Edmund Wilson. Renewed 1980 by Helen Miranda Wilson. All rights reserved. Reprinted by permission of Farrar, Straus and Giroux, Inc.

PHOTOGRAPHS AND ILLUSTRATIONS APPEARING IN *CLC*, VOLUME 82, WERE RECEIVED FROM THE FOLLOWING SOURCES:

© Michael Montfort: **p. 1;** Photograph by Samuel Cherry: **pp. 10, 21;** © Lutfi Özkök: **p. 31;** Illustration by Edgar Jené from ***Der Traum vom Traume***, by Paul Celan: **pp. 44, 50;** Drawing by Adolph Dehn: **p. 63;** Drawing by Reginald Marsh: **pp. 69, 82, 92;** Courtesy of Mrs. Rose Knox-Peebles, the McFarlin Library at Tulsa, Oklahoma, and Mr. Peter Owen: **pp. 115, 120, 125;** © Jerry Bauer: **pp. 127, 232;** Photograph by Richard W. Brown, reproduced by permission of Smith College Archives, Smith College: **p. 147;** UPI/Bettmann: **p. 158;** AP/Wide World Photos: **pp. 162, 169, 394;** Reproduced by Special Permission of ***Playboy*** magazine. Copyright © 1963, 1994 by Playboy: **p. 208;** UPI/Bettmann Newsphotos: **p. 224;** Photograph by Jill Levine: **p. 262;** Dust jacket of ***Until Your Heart Stops***, by T.M. McNally. Villard Books, 1993. Copyright © 1993 by T.M. McNally. Jacket design by Richard Aquan. Jacket photograph by H & M Tavetian. Reprinted by permission of Random House, Inc.: **p. 268;** © Rollie McKenna: **p. 272;** Photograph by Tom Bianchi: **p. 313;** Photograph by Paul S. Conklin: **p. 336;** Courtesy of Charles Newton: **p. 374.**

Charles Bukowski

1920-1994

(Full name Henry Charles Bukowski, Jr.) German-born American poet, short story writer, novelist, and screenwriter.

The following entry provides an overview of Bukowski's career. For further information about Bukowski's life and works, see *CLC,* Volumes 2, 5, 9, and 41.

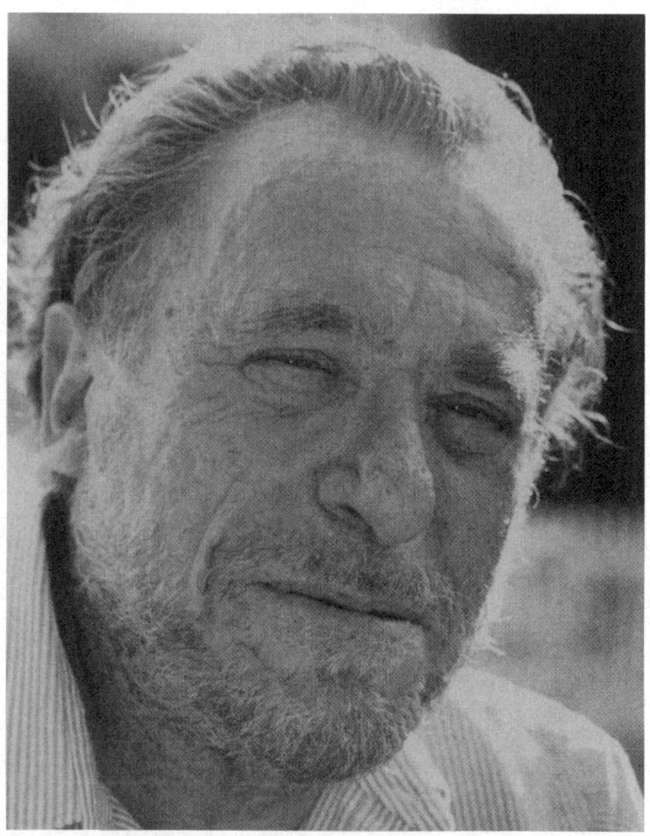

INTRODUCTION

A prolific and seminal figure in underground literature, Bukowski is best known for poetry and fiction in which he caustically indicts bourgeois society while celebrating the desperate lives of alcoholics, prostitutes, decadent writers, and other disreputable characters in and around Los Angeles. While Bukowski's works—which were initially published by small presses, literary magazines, and underground journals—have failed to generate extensive scholarship, his vernacular style and unsentimentalized treatment of unpleasant social realities have influenced several generations of writers. Hugh Fox called Bukowski "Henry Miller's successor on the American literary scene, just as iconoclastic, as sentimental, as profane—and as full of life and reality."

Born in 1920 in Andernach, Germany, Bukowski emigrated to Los Angeles in 1922 with his father, an American soldier, and his German mother. As an adolescent he was distanced from his peers by a disfiguring case of acne and he resisted the attempts of his abusive and uncompromising father to instill in him the American ideals of hard work and patriotism. Following high school, Bukowski attended Los Angeles City College from 1939 to 1941 but left without obtaining a degree. He began writing hundreds of unsuccessful short stories while drifting from city to city in a succession of low-paying jobs—including work as a mailman, post office clerk, Red Cross orderly, and laborer in a slaughterhouse and a dog biscuit factory. Although he published his first short story, "Aftermath of a Lengthy Rejection Slip," in a 1944 issue of *Story* magazine at the age of twenty-four, Bukowski virtually stopped writing for a decade, choosing instead to live as an alcoholic on skid row. After being hospitalized with a bleeding ulcer in 1955, Bukowski began writing poetry and resolved to drink less heavily. During this period he discovered the literature of Upton Sinclair, Sinclair Lewis, and especially Ernest Hemingway, which offered him an alternative to alcoholism and aided in the development of his own concise, realistic prose style.

Bukowski published his first collection of poetry, *Flower, Fist, and Bestial Wail,* in 1960. He quickly produced a series of poetry chapbooks, including *Longshot Pomes for Broke Players* and *Run with the Hunted,* featuring surreal verse that expresses sentimentality for the West's Romantic past as well as disgust for the vacuousness of modern culture. While these poems garnered him a small but loyal following over the next decade, Bukowski's work in the short story genre first gained him a wide readership and established his literary reputation. Beginning in 1967, when the antiwar and counterculture movements flourished in the United States, Bukowski began contributing a weekly column, "Notes of a Dirty Old Man," to the Los Angeles alternative newspaper *Open City,* and later, to the Los Angeles *Free Press.* Combining journalism, fiction, and philosophy in a rambling, disjointed style, these pieces established his philosophy and defiant, anarchic persona. Perceiving American culture as hypocritical, Bukowski censured American films and television as escapist wish-fulfillment, morality as organized hypocrisy, patriotism as conformism, and academic writers, scholars, and intellectuals as self-righteous charlatans who attack American society while reaping its benefits.

Bukowski began his career writing poetry critical of American bourgeois institutions while disclaiming the title of writer: "To say I'm a poet puts me in the company of versifiers, neontasters, fools, clods, and skoundrels [sic] masquerading as wise men." In *Longshot Pomes for Broke Players,* Bukowski introduces his characteristic outsider protagonist: the unstudied, self-exiled poet who provokes public enmity through his apparent rudeness to writers and other socialites, and maintains his freedom and uniqueness as a writer by rejecting the public literary world. In "Letter from the North," for example, the narrator responds to a despondent writer's request for sympathy with the question: "write you? about what my friend? / I'm only interested in poetry." In ensuing collections such as *It Catches My Heart in Its Hands* and *Crucifix in a Deathhand,* Bukowski's narrator retains his hostility to the outer world while revealing a paradoxical inner gentleness. In "Fuzz," the unsteady protagonist unexpectedly empathizes with a group of children who are taunting him: "when I go into the liquor store / they whirl around outside / like bees / shut out from their nest. / I buy a fifth of cheap / whiskey / and / 3 / candy bars." Much of Bukowski's subsequent poetry, collected in such volumes as *Poems Written before Jumping out of an 8-story Window, The Days Run Away Like Wild Horses over the Hills,* and *Fire Station,* deals in concrete, realistic terms with acts of rape, sodomy, deceit, and violence, particularly focusing on sexual relationships characterized by physical and emotional abuse in which women seek to enslave men through marriage and men attempt to avoid such enslavement through the equally imprisoning pursuit of wealth and material pleasures.

Many of the events described in Bukowski's poetry recur in the autobiographical short stories and novels he began writing in the 1970s. While his earlier stories, many of which were published in men's pornographic magazines, generally employ stock formulas, Bukowski's later fiction, published in *Erections, Ejaculations, Exhibitions, and General Tales of Ordinary Madness* and *South of No North: Stories of the Buried Life,* is more sophisticated, philosophical, and pointedly critical of American society. Many of these stories focus on sexual relationships that feminist and other critics have faulted as misogynistic. Other critics, however, believe these works expose the short-sightedness, pettiness, and spiritual bankruptcy of a dysfunctional society.

During the 1970s Bukowski began writing semiautobiographical novels featuring the first-person narrator Henry ("Hank") Chinaski, a hard-boiled, alcoholic survivor who trades a mediocre, normal life for a position that allows for unromanticized self-awareness in the socially unrestricted environment of the ghetto. Bukowski's first novel, *Post Office,* contrasts the mindlessness and monotony of Chinaski's work life as an employee of the United States Post Office with the varying degradation and vitality of his unconventional personal life. *Factotum* chronicles Chinaski's experiences as a young man before the events related in *Post Office,* while *Ham on Rye* recounts his adolescent years and conflicts with his tyrannical father. *Women* details Chinaski's sexual exploits after the events chronicled in *Post Office* and his eventual desire for a monogamous relationship. Chinaski is also a central character in Bukowski's novel *Barfly,* which he adapted into a screenplay for the film directed by Barbet Schroeder and starring Mickey Rourke and Faye Dunaway. Bukowski's encounters with California's film industry are also detailed in *Hollywood,* another novel featuring Chinaski. Bukowski died of leukemia in Los Angeles in 1994.

PRINCIPAL WORKS

"Aftermath of a Lengthy Rejection Slip" (short story) 1944; published in journal *Story*
Flower, Fist, and Bestial Wail (poetry) 1960
Longshot Pomes for Broke Players (poetry) 1962
Poems and Drawings (poetry and drawings) 1962
Run with the Hunted (poetry) 1962
It Catches My Heart in Its Hands: New and Selected Poems, 1955-1963 (poetry) 1963
Grip the Walls (poetry) 1964
Cold Dogs in the Courtyard (poetry) 1965
Confessions of a Man Insane Enough to Live with Beasts (poetry) 1965
Crucifix in a Deathhand: New Poems, 1963-1965 (poetry) 1965
All the Assholes in the World and Mine (poetry) 1966
The Flower Lover (poetry) 1966
The Genius of the Crowd (poetry) 1966
The Girls (poetry) 1966
Night's Work (poetry) 1966
On Going Out to Get the Mail (poetry) 1966
To Kiss the Worms Goodnight (poetry) 1966
True Story (poetry) 1966
The Curtains Are Waving (poetry) 1967
2 by Bukowski (poetry) 1967
At Terror Street and Agony Way (poetry) 1968
Poems Written before Jumping out of an 8-story Window (poetry) 1968
The Days Run Away Like Wild Horses over the Hills (poetry) 1969
If We Take . . . (poetry) 1969
Notes of a Dirty Old Man (short stories) 1969
Another Academy (poetry) 1970
Fire Station (poetry) 1970
Post Office (novel) 1971
Erections, Ejaculations, Exhibitions, and General Tales of Ordinary Madness (short stories) 1972; also published as *Life and Death in the Charity Ward* [abridged edition], 1974; selections also published in two volumes: *Tales of Ordinary Madness* and *The Most Beautiful Woman in Town, and Other Stories,* 1983
Me and Your Sometimes Love Poems (poetry) 1972
Mockingbird, Wish Me Luck (poetry) 1972
Love Poems to Marina (poetry) 1973
South of No North: Stories of the Buried Life (short stories) 1973
While the Music Played (poetry) 1973
Burning in Water, Drowning in Flame: Selected Poems, 1955-1973 (poetry) 1974
Africa, Paris, Greece (poetry) 1975
Factotum (novel) 1975

Weather Report (poetry) 1975
Winter (poetry) 1975
Scarlet (poetry) 1976
Love Is a Dog from Hell: Poems, 1974-1977 (poetry) 1977
Maybe Tomorrow (poetry) 1977
Legs, Hips, and Behind (poetry) 1978
Women (novel) 1978
A Love Poem (poetry) 1979
Play the Piano Drunk Like a Percussion Instrument until the Fingers Begin to Bleed a Bit (poetry) 1979
Dangling in the Tournefortia (poetry) 1981
Ham on Rye (novel) 1982
Horsemeat (novel) 1982
The Last Generation (poetry) 1982
Bring Me Your Love (short stories) 1983
The Bukowski/Purdy Letters: A Decade of Dialogue, 1964-1974 [with Al Purdy] (letters) 1983
Hot Water Music (short stories) 1983
Sparks (poetry) 1983
**Barfly* (novel) 1984
There's No Business (short stories) 1984
War All the Time: Poems, 1981-1984 (poetry) 1984
The Roominghouse Madrigals: Early Selected Poems, 1946-1966 (poetry) 1988
Hollywood (novel) 1989
Septuagenarian Stew (short stories and poetry) 1990
The Last Night of the Earth Poems (poetry) 1992

*This work was the basis for the film *BarFly* (1987); Bukowski's screenplay was published in 1987 as the *The Movie "BarFly."*

CRITICISM

Thomas R. Edwards (review date 5 October 1972)

[*In the following review of Bukowski's short story collection* Erections, Ejaculations, Exhibitions, and General Tales of Ordinary Madness, *Edwards applauds Bukowski's uncompromising stance as an author of "unregenerate lowbrow" prose.*]

Charles Bukowski never did escape from California. Certainly he is quite unimaginable anywhere else, and he is still out there on the West Coast, writing poems and stories about his five decades of drinking, screwing, horseplaying, and drifting around, proving defiantly that even at the edge of the abyss language persists. "A legend in his own time," the cover of his new collection of stories calls him, and that seems fair.

Erections, Ejaculations, Exhibitions and General Tales of Ordinary Madness is a mixed lot. Bukowski's main market, the underground press and the girlie mags, casts a long shadow here—as he says himself, "To get rid of a story you gotta have fucking, lots of it, if possible," and the little formulas of commercial pornography ("one of the best fucks I ever had," etc.) recur on cue. There are some heavy attempts at satiric fantasy, and a tendency to end stories with the kind of peek at the reader ("What would you do?") usually reserved for high-school composition classes.

But Bukowski is more fun to read than that. He writes as an unregenerate lowbrow contemptuous of our claims to superior being. Politics is bullshit, since work is as brutalizing and unrewarding in a liberal order as in any totalitarian one; artists and intellectuals are mostly fakes, smugly enjoying the blessings of the society they carp at; the radical young are spiritless asses, insulated by drugs and their own endless cant from any authentic experience of mind or body; most women are whores, though *honest* whores are good and desirable; no life finally works, but the best one possible involves plenty of six-packs, enough money to go to the track, and a willing woman of any age and shape in a good old-fashioned garter belt and high heels.

He makes literature out of the unfashionable and unideological tastes and biases of an average Wallace voter. And that sense of life is worth hearing about when it takes the form not of socko sex-and-*schmerz* but of blunt, unembarrassed explanation of how it feels to be Bukowski, mad but only north-north-west, among pretentious and lifeless claims to originality and fervor. Here he is in an underground press editorial office:

> I had been given the idea . . . that since it was the first anniversary of *Open Pussy* the wine and the pussy and the life and the love would be flowing.
>
> But coming in very high and expecting to see fucking on the floor and love galore, I only saw all these little love-creatures busily at work. They reminded me very much, so humped and dismal, of the little old ladies working on piecework I used to deliver cloth to, working my way up through rope-hauled elevators full of rats and stink, one hundred years old, piecework ladies, proud and dead and neurotic as all hell, working to make a millionaire out of somebody.

He comes off best at anarchist satire in a plastic world—drinking and foul-mouthing himself into disgrace in cocktail lounges, on airliners, and at college poetry readings, showing up at a high-society Zen wedding as the only guest who's put on a tie and brought a present (he resentfully gets drunk, tries to remove the Zen master's marvelously translucent ears, and is felled by a karate chop), mistaking long-haired boys for girls, caught between secret pleasure and horror at the knowledge that his poems are known and admired by some of the *cognoscenti.* For all his dedication to the old role of the macho artist, the boozing, tough-talking writing phallus we knew and loved so well, Bukowski has a bit of the softy, the man of sentiment, the gull in him, happily for his art; he knows as well as we do that history has passed him by and that his loss is ours too, and in some of these sad and funny stories his status as a relic isn't wholly without its sanctity. (pp. 21-2)

Thomas R. Edwards, "News from Elsewhere," in The New York Review of Books, *Vol. XIX, No. 5, October 5, 1972, pp. 21-3.*

Donald Newlove (review date 14 November 1974)

[*Newlove is an American novelist and critic whose works often deal with alcoholism. In the following favorable review of* Mockingbird Wish Me Luck, *Newlove deems Bukowski "the only* beloved *underground poet I've ever heard of."*]

Now 54, Bukowski is a militantly unregenerate alcholic, who started writing at 35 and whose poems celebrate degeneracy, bimbos, beating-off, gambling on the nags, with an occasional sigh for his baby daughter and a vast snort at his publishers, poetry readings, and people who lead straw lives ("I was born to hustle roses down the avenue of the dead."). Tough and direct, he often drifts into self-parody; tearfully black passages, lashes out in self-hatred at dead horses, sees Jello-bright colors, seldom hangs together for a whole poem, but is the only *beloved* underground poet I've heard of; I collect him, with great hope that his best lies before him. [***Mockingbird Wish Me Luck***] is stronger than his magnificently-titled earlier collection ***The Days Run Away Like Wild Horses over the Hills.*** My favorite piece in ***Mockingbird*** is also the funniest and raunchiest:

* drunk
ol' bukowski
* drunk
I hold to the edge of the table
with my belly dangling over my
belt.

and I glare at the lampshade
the smoke clearing
over
North Hollywood

The boys put their muskets down
lift high their fish-green beer

as I fall forward off the couch
kiss rug hairs like cunt
hairs

close as I've been in a
long time

(p. 45)

Donald Newlove, "Underground Press Review," in The Village Voice, *Vol. XIX, November 14, 1974, pp. 44-5.*

William Feaver (review date 29 November 1974)

[*In the following review, Feaver commends the humor and prose style of Bukowski's stories in* Life and Death in the Charity Ward.]

In the sonsobitches school of writing you talk as you speak, but more so. Short sentences. Expletives. "Oh shit, oh shit", your characters say nearly every time they achieve climax. Life is a balling, boozing, brawling merry-go-round and the tears show through the vomiting. Charles Bukowski treads the streets and pads of Los Angeles where many others trod before him: Philip Marlowe, for one, and the Kerouac crowd when they weren't in San Francisco or on the road. He writes evidently from experience, tightened up. His way of life veers between the campus poetry-reading and the charity ward where things reach bottom. It consists of shocking the folks one side of the tracks, letting rip the other side, and looking back to see how it all goes down in the world of books.

There's any amount of fresh, raging agony and ecstasizing in this set of short stories [***Life and Death in the Charity Ward***]. They are mostly very short and one-shot. As a rule, the author acts as guide, though other personae are sometimes created and given precedence—and in any case it's impossible to tell when Mr Bukowski is writing about himself or someone more so. He does three-line sentences every now and again, takes the reader by the nose and pulls him through apartments, warehouses and bars, talking all the while in a Marlowe-on-the-skids monotone.

Two things save the collection from being simply idiomatic-romantic. First, it's persistently funny, in a *Guys and Dolls* turned bums and asses way. The other quality is its intermingling of *Howl* and Spillane. As the monologue gathers pace and is brought to bear fully, ferociously on its targets, it sets up a tirade admirable in its intensity, strong enough to blow others, such as Hunter Thompson, who have tried venting all in this spirit, right off the Los Angeles map.

William Feaver, "LA Low-Life," in The Times Literary Supplement, *No. 3795, November 29, 1974, p. 1336.*

Gerald Locklin (review date July-August 1982)

[*Locklin is an American poet, fiction writer, educator, and critic. In the following review, he offers high praise for* Dangling in the Tournefortia *and suggests reasons for critical neglect of Bukowski's work.*]

Let me at once admit my bias: I think Bukowski is a writer of at least the stature of a Henry Miller. I also think he has been mistreated—or treated to a conspiracy of silence—by the American literary establishment and by factions outside the establishment as well. But he hasn't gone away. To the contrary, he and his American and European publishers have prospered. Films of his work are beginning to appear in Europe, where he seems to have become one of the best known, if not *the* best known, of contemporary American writers. A best-selling underground (or dirty old) man—talk about your oxymorons! Those who despised him as a drunken bum, now despise him as a drunken *rich* bum.

I am not a Bukowski idolater. Even Bukowski (maybe Bukowski most of all) knows that his work is uneven. His defense is that it's his job to write and the job of others to edit and evaluate.

Those who enjoy Bukowski do not have to be persuaded to read everything of his that appears, but I would not have recommended to the uninitiated a couple of his most recent collections because a reader could hit a run of second-rate offerings before encountering vintage Bukowski. I would have recommended ***The Days Run Away Like Wild Horses Over the Hills,*** for poetry, and his novel ***Post Office*** or one of the City Lights collection of stories. Or one might find a library with back issues of the *Worm-*

wood Review and follow his development in its pages over the past twenty years. I wouldn't hesitate to recommend to neophyte or jade [***Dangling in the Tournefortia***] though. I was sixty or seventy pages into it before I realized I hadn't read a poem that was not outstanding. I put the book down happy for Bukowski and happy for all of us who love books that live and will continue to live.

Of course, I've never understood why anyone finds Bukowski depressing. I've always found him a survival story. If he's come through, why can't the rest of us? George Orwell called Henry Miller the proletarian given a voice, and I'd say the remark is even truer of Bukowski. I like him best when he is being funny and dirty and conveying life at the infrared base of the socioeconomic spectrum. He's one of our few naturalists to possess a sense of style and a sense of humor. I like him least when he's waxing pseudopoetic or pseudophilosophical or stacking the deck to favor himself. What seems to bother people most about him, his *attitude* or *attitudes,* doesn't bother me. As just about everyone knows, Bukowski drinks a bit, and he can be unfair, in person and in print, at certain levels of the bottle, but there is also a purity in his unsparing view of humanity.

It's difficult to illustrate Bukowski's craft with excerpts because his poems tend to reach a certain length and the best are often the longest. While others debated how best to restore narrative and dramatic structures to verse, Bukowski just sat down and did it. He has the sense of timing and construction (and the voice) of a W. C. Fields, which is one reason why his infrequent readings, no matter what his state of inebriation, continue to draw throngs. To quote a line here and there makes as much sense as to tell a punch line without the build-up. In what is perhaps my favorite poem in this collection, the seriocomic **"yeah, man?"** the white protagonist pulls a knife on a Latin whose car is blocking his. Later the white returns to find his apartment in a shambles. His walls are spray-painted. His radio, television and electric clock are gone, as are his pillows and sheets. His mattress has been slashed; his faucets are running. His kitchen floor has been pissed on; eggs have been broken on it; garbage is dumped there. Missing are his knives, forks and spoons, the salt and pepper, the bread and coffee, everything in the refrigerator. The toilet paper is gone, and the mirror is broken, and the cabinet has been emptied of razor, shaving cream, Band-Aids, aspirins:

> and then he looked
> in the toilet
> and down in the bowl
> was a freshly-cut
> cat's tail
> furry and still
> bleeding
> in the water
> Larry hit the lever
> to flush it away
> and got an
> empty click
> lifted the lid
> looked inside
> and all the toilet parts
> were gone.

After a couple hits of the beer he has brought back with him, Larry decides

> that it was about time
> he moved
> further west.

This is not simply a nightmare tale of one man's misguided race relations; it is the demographic and demonological saga of white flight. Bukowski may or may not be characterized as a revolutionary; but he is undeniably a chronicler of politically significant phenomena.

His language is the product of a movement towards the spoken idiom that is at least as old as Wordsworth's preface to the second edition of the *Lyrical Ballads* and that weaves its way through, among others, Whitman, Robinson, Frost, Masters, Lindsay, Williams, Oppen, Reznikoff, Rakosi and Edward Field to become one of the dominant modes among young poets today, probably *the* dominant mode in Southern California. A special and striking influence upon the young Bukowski was the recently rediscovered Southern California fiction writer, John Fante, to whom this volume is dedicated. . . .

So why is Bukowski only now beginning to receive his due in his own country? One can only speculate, but he seems to have been perceived for a time, incorrectly I think, as an enemy of women and gays. Actually he is simply an abhorrer of orthodoxies. He has not given people used to respect—professors, for instance—the respect that they are used to. He is sparing in his praise of other writers. He not only knows that the literary world is rife with charlatanism, self-promotion, and mutual back-scratching, but he hasn't hesitated to say so. He proclaims his literary superiority. Frankly, a lot of people seem just plain jealous of him. And he has been his own worst enemy at times, espe-

Bukowski on Bukowski:

Sitting with a bottle at the typewriter is not the easiest way to cut through terror. I dreamed a lifetime of being a writer and now the demons are upon me. Writing heightens the feelings to such an extent that we are at the mercy of all happenings. A blade of grass becomes a sword; an affair of love claws the guts out. With the few people I know I pretend to be the tough guy, but I don't fool anybody. One of the saving graces (there's a platitude) is the ability to laugh now and then. Without that, going on might be impossible. The average man puts in his 8 hours, comes home beaten and satisfied. With the writer there is never satisfaction, there is always the next piece of work to be done. We are honed by our words. My gal friend says to me, "My God, you're touchy. You remind me of one of those fish at Marineland. They've got these points sticking out all over them. Touch one and that fish goes crazy. I'm going to take you down there and show you one of those fish."

"O.K., take me down there. I want to see one of those fish."

Charles Bukowski, in his "Notes of a Dirty Old Man" in NOLA Express, *1972.*

cially when the elixir has elicited his Doppelganger. But it must be admitted that Bukowski seldom initiates a relationship.

Bukowski has just finished his fourth novel [***Ham on Rye***], based on his childhood, a book that should go a long way towards making it obvious why he is the way he is and maybe even why we should be glad he is.

Gerald Locklin, "Dangling in the Tournefortia," in The American Book Review, *Vol. 4, No. 5, July-August, 1982, p. 6.*

Charles Bukowski with *The New York Quarterly* (interview date Summer 1985)

[*In the following interview, Bukowski discusses his writing technique.*]

[*New York Quarterly*]: *How do you write? In longhand, on the typewriter? Do you revise much? What do you do with worksheets? Your poems sometimes give the impression of coming off the top of your head. Is that only an impression? How much agony and sweat of the human spirit is involved in the writing of one of your poems?*

[Bukowski]: I write right off the typer. I call it my "machinegun." I hit it hard, usually late at night while drinking wine and listening to classical music on the radio and smoking mangalore ganesh beedies. I revise but not much. The next day I retype the poem and automatically make a change or two, drop out a line, or make two lines into one or one line into two, that sort of thing—to make the poem have more balls, more balance. Yes, the poems come "off the top of my head," I seldom know what I'm going to write when I sit down. There isn't much agony and sweat of the human spirit involved in doing it. The writing's easy, it's the living that is sometimes difficult.

When you're away from your place do you carry notebooks with you? Do you jot down ideas as they come to you during the day or do you store them in your head for later?

I don't carry notebooks and I don't consciously store ideas. I try not to think that I am a writer and I am pretty good at doing that. I don't like writers, but then I don't like insurance salesmen either.

Do you ever go through dry periods, no writing at all? If so how often? What do you do during these periods? Anything to get you back on the track?

A dry period for me means perhaps going two or three nights without writing. I probably have dry periods but I'm not aware of them and I go on writing, only the writing probably isn't much good. But sometimes I do get aware that it isn't going too well. Then I go to the racetrack and bet more money than usual and come home and drink much more than usual and scream at and abuse my woman. And it's best that I lose at the track without trying to. I can almost always write a damn near immortal poem if I have lost somewhere between 150 and 200 dollars.

Need for isolation? Do you work best alone? Most of your poems concern your going from a state of love / sex to a state of isolation. Does that tie in with the way [*you*] *have to have things in order to write?*

I love solitude but I don't need it to the exclusion of somebody I care for in order to get some words down. I figure if I can't write under all circumstances, then I'm just not good enough to do it. Some of my poems indicate that I am writing while living alone after a split with a woman, and I've had many splits with women. I need solitude more often when I'm not writing than when I am. I have written with children running about the room having at me with squirt guns. That often helps rather than hinders the writing: some of the laughter enters. One thing does bother me, though: to overhear somebody's loud tv, a comedy program with a laugh track.

When did you begin writing? How old? What writers did you admire?

The first thing I ever remembered writing was about a German aviator with a steel hand who shot hundreds of Americans out of the sky during World War II. It was in long hand in pen and it covered every page of a huge memo ringed notebook. I was about 13 at the time and I was in bed covered with the worst case of boils the medics ever remembered seeing. There weren't any writers to admire at the time. Since then there has been John Fante, Knut Hamsun, the Celine of *Journey;* Dostoevsky, of course; Jeffers of the long poems only; Conrad Aiken, Catullus . . . not too many. I sucked mostly at the classical music boys. It was good to come home from the factories at night, take off my clothes, climb on the bed in the dark, get drunk on beer and listen to them.

Do you think there's too much poetry being written today? How would you characterize what you think is really bad poetry? What do you think is good poetry today?

There's too much bad poetry being written today. People just don't know how to write down a simple easy line. It's difficult for them; it's like trying to keep a hard-on while drowning—not many can do it. Bad poetry is caused by people who sit down and think, Now I am going to write a Poem. And it comes out the way they *think* a poem should be. Take a cat. He doesn't think, well, now I'm cat and I'm going to kill this bird. He just does it. Good poetry today? Well, it's being written by a couple of cats called Gerald Locklin and Ronald Koertge.

You've read most of the NYQ craft interviews we've published. What do you think of our approach, the interviews you've read. What interviews have told you something.

I'm sorry you asked that question. I haven't learned anything from the interviews except that the poets were studious, trained, self-assured and obnoxiously self-important. I don't think that I was ever able to finish an interview; the print began to blur and the trained seals vanished below the surface. These people lack joy, madness and gamble in their answers just as they do in their work (poems).

Although you write strong voice poems, that voice rarely extends beyond the circumference of your own psychosexual concerns. Are you interested in national, international affairs, do you consciously restrict yourself as to what you will and will not write about?

I photograph and record what I see and what happens to

me. I am not a guru or leader of any sort. I am not a man who looks for solutions in God or politics. If somebody else wants to do the dirty work and create a better world for us and he *can* do it, I will accept it. In Europe where my work is having much luck, various groups have put a claim on me, revolutionaries, anarchists, so forth, because I have written of the common man of the streets, but in interviews over there I have had to disclaim a conscious working relationship with them because there isn't any. I have compassion for almost all the individuals of the world; at the same time, they repulse me.

What do you think a young poet starting out today needs to learn the most?

He should realize that if he writes something and it bores him it's going to bore many other people also. There is nothing wrong with a poetry that is entertaining and easy to understand. Genius could be the ability to say a profound thing in a simple way. He should stay the hell out of writing classes and find out what's happening around the corner. And bad luck for the young poet would be a rich father, an early marriage, an early success or the ability to do anything very well.

Over the last few decades California has been the residence of many of our most independent voice poets—like Jeffers, Rexroth, Patchen, even Henry Miller. Why is this? What is your attitude towards the East, towards New York?

Well, there was a little more space out here, the long run up the coast, all that water, a feeling of Mexico and China and Canada, Hollywood, sunburn, starlets turned to prostitutes. I don't know, really, I guess if your ass is freezing some of the time it's harder to be a "voice poet." Being a voice poet is the big gamble because you're putting your guts up for view and you're going to get a lot more reaction than if you're writing something like your mother's soul being like a daisy field.

New York, I don't know. I landed there with $7 and no job and no friends and no occupation except common laborer. I suppose if I had come in from the top instead of the bottom I might have laughed a little more. I stayed 3 months and the buildings scared the shit out of me and the people scared the shit out of me, and I had done a lot of bumming all over the country under the same conditions but New York City was the Inferno, all the way. The way Woody Allen's intellectuals suffer in N.Y.C. is a lot different than what happens to my type of people. I never got laid in New York, in fact, the women wouldn't even speak to me. The only way I ever got laid in New York was to come back 3 decades later and bring my own with me, a terrible wench, we stayed at the Chelsea, of course. The *New York Quarterly* is the only good thing that has happened to me out there.

You've written short stories, novels. Do they come from the same place your poems come from?

Yes, they do, there's not much difference—line and line length. The short story helped get the rent and the novel was a way of saying how many different things could happen to the same man on the way to suicide, madness, old age, natural and unnatural death.

You have a fairly distinct persona in most of your poems, and your strong voice seems to come out of that persona. It's the mask of a bored, dirty old man who's boozing it up in Li Po manner because the straight world isn't worth taking seriously. Usually there's an hysterical broad banging your door down while the poem is taking shape. First do you admit to this persona in your poems, and then to what extent do you think it reflects Bukowski the man? In other words are you the person you present to us in your poems?

Things change a bit: what once was is not quite what it is now. I began writing poetry at the age of 35 after coming out of the death ward of the L. A. County General Hospital and not as a visitor. To get somebody to read your poems you have to be noticed, so I got my act up. I wrote vile (but interesting) stuff that made people hate me, that made them curious about this Bukowski. I threw bodies off my court porch into the night. I pissed on police cars, sneered at hippies. After my second reading down at Venice, I grabbed the money, leaped into my car, intoxicated, and drove it about on the sidewalks at 60 m.p.h. I had parties at my place which were interrupted by police raids. A professor from U.C.L.A. invited me to his place for dinner. His wife cooked a nice meal which I ate and then I went over and broke up his China closet. I was in and out of drunktanks. A lady accused me of rape, the whore. Meanwhile, I wrote about most of this, it was my persona, it was me but it wasn't me. As time went on, trouble and action arrived by itself and I didn't have to force it and I wrote about *that* and this was closer to my real persona. Actually, I am not a tough person and sexually, most of the time, I am almost a prude, but I am often a nasty drunk and many strange things happen to me when I am drunk. I'm not saying this very well and I'm taking too long. What I am trying to say is that the longer I write the closer I am getting to what I am. I am one of those slow starters but I am all hell in the stretch run. I am 93 percent the person I present in my poems; the other 7 percent is where art improves upon life, call it background music.

You refer to Hemingway a lot, seem to have a love/hate thing for him, what he does in his work. Any comment?

I guess for me Hemingway is a lot like it is for others: he goes down well when we are young. Gertie taught him the line but I think he improved upon it. Hemingway and Saroyan had the line, the magic of it. The problem was that Hemingway didn't know how to laugh and Saroyan was filled with sugar. John Fante had the line too and he was the first who knew how to let passion enter in, emotion in, without letting it destroy the concept. I speak here of moderns who write the *simple* line; I am aware that Blake was once around. So when I write about Hemingway it's sometimes a joke thing but I'm probably more in debt to him than I'd care to admit. His early work was screwed down tight, you couldn't get your fingers under it. But now I get more out of reading about his life and fuckups, it's almost as good as reading about D. H. Lawrence.

What do you think of this interview and what question do you wish we'd asked you? Go ahead and ask it of yourself and then answer it.

I think the interview is all right. I suppose that some people will object that the answers lack polish and erudition, then they'll go out and buy my books. I can't think of any questions to ask myself. For me to get paid for writing is like going to bed with a beautiful woman and afterwards she gets up, goes to her purse and gives me a handful of money. I'll take it. Why don't we stop here? (pp. 19-25)

Charles Bukowski and The New York Quarterly, *in an interview in* The New York Quarterly, *No. 27, Summer, 1985, pp. 19-25.*

Ernest Fontana (essay date Fall 1985)

[*In the essay below, Fontana places Bukowski's novels in the tradition of the Los Angeles novel and delineates his characteristic concerns in* Ham on Rye.]

In a recent article on "California Writing and the West," Charles Bukowski is not once mentioned. This is not surprising since Bukowski's fiction does not present Southern California from the characteristic point of view of the immigrant or exile, for whom it is seen as mythically other to the territory of the writer's origins. Although Bukowski and the fictive persona of his novels, Henry Chinaski, were born in Germany, their families moved to Los Angeles when Bukowski-Chinaski was only two years of age. Thus for Bukowski-Chinaski, Los Angeles is not the chosen territory of exile as it is for Fitzgerald's Monroe Stahr, West's Tod Hockett, Didion's Maria, John Fante's Arturo Bandini, Isherwood's George, and Ann Nietzke's first-person narrator-observer, in her recent *Windowlight* (1981). The concept of regional literature implies a center against which "the region" is seen as eccentric. Bukowski does not juxtapose, either implicitly or explicitly, his fictional Los Angeles against another world that is more central to his imagination, that is in fact "home" for the writer and his characters—"home" in the idealized sense of Maria's Silver Wells in *Play It As It Lays* or in the more attenuated sense of the rural Tennessee community of the narrator in *Windowlight* or in the sense of deliberate rejection as George's native England in Isherwood's *Single Man.* Thus Bukowski's Los Angeles is not wonderful or strange. Its freeways are not for him the locus of extreme despair as they are for Didion's Maria, nor are its beaches the environment of personal emancipation as Venice Beach is for the narrator in *Windowlight.* For Bukowski, Los Angeles is a given; it is the ordinary world that assaults one's freedom; it is the unexotic world of working-class deprivation or the stark marginality of the unemployed, not the territory of cosmic discovery as in *Single Man,* of chic alienation as in Didion's *Play It As It Lays,* or of campy, picturesque deracination as in Gavin Lambert's *The Slide Area* (1968).

Bukowski, consequently, does not exploit the rich metaphoric possibilities of the diverse topography and geography of Southern California. Desert, mountain, ocean, and earthquake are absent from the rigorously human and urban topography of Bukowski's fiction. Los Angeles fiction, written generally by immigrants or visitors, characteristically exploits these metaphoric possibilities. Such a technique implies a perceptual mobility that is absent in Bukowski. It implies the power to move freely and unencumbered from ocean to mountain, from city to desert, a mobility that first manifests itself in the Los Angeles fiction of Raymond Chandler and James Cain. It is such mobility, such expansive personal territoriality that makes crime, deception, mystery, and detection possible in Chandler, and which is the very source of the opportunities of crime and violence in Cain's *The Postman Always Rings Twice* (1937).

It is this expansive territory that becomes the prison of personal alienation and homelessness that Maria, in *Play It As It Lays,* traverses through the greater Los Angeles freeway system, a prison that runs from Hollywood to the Valley, from Oxnard to the Mojave. In Bukowski's fiction such mobility cannot easily be assumed. In the story **"A Rain of Women,"** from his ***Erections, Ejaculations, Exhibitions and General Tales of Ordinary Madness,*** the narrator is stranded while he waits for a desultory mechanic to repair his very used '62 Comet, for which he is still making payments. Bukowski-Chinaski is consistently threatened by immobility and by the loss of physical freedom. (He is also threatened at various times by constipation, employment, boors, hangovers, impotence, and acne.) It is through the bars and rooming houses of central Los Angeles, not through its mythical beaches, freeways, and deserts, that Bukowski-Chinaski most freely and easily moves.

Many of these characteristics are evident in Bukowski's most recent novel ***Ham on Rye*** (1983). The two extreme geographical limits of this bildungsroman are the orange groves of the San Bernardino foothills and the beach at Venice. Both function as illusory paradisal loci in which Henry Chinaski is presented as an intruder. As a child, Chinaski accompanied his immigrant parents on excursions in their Model-T through the San Bernardino foothills where they enjoyed picnicking amid "miles and miles of orange trees always either in blossom or full of oranges." One Sunday, Chinaski's father leads the family into the groves to pick oranges. The owner of the groves discovers them and, brandishing a shotgun, expels them: " 'I'm the law here. Now move'." He forces the Chinaskis to leave behind the oranges they picked and warns them not to return " 'or next time it might not go so easy for you'." This episode defines the territorial and social limits that Chinaski and his family are confined to. The paradisal abundance of Southern California is forbidden them, and Chinaski's father, who loses his job as a milkman during the Depression, becomes an increasingly embittered, frightened, and tyrannical father. Confined to the working-class neighborhood of 21st St. and Crenshaw Ave., he will terrorize Henry with the threat of his strop into mowing the family lawn so that not a blade of grass sticks up to mar its perfection. To this has been reduced the father's American Dream.

The second episode that takes the young Chinaski of ***Ham on Rye*** beyond the limits of central Los Angeles occurs when, as a teenager, he bicycles one Sunday down to the beach at Venice with his friend Jimmy. Afflicted by a terrible case of acne (of which more later), Henry, ashamed of his boils and scars, at first resolves "that the beach belonged to everybody. I had a right. My scars and boils weren't against the law." He races down Washington Blvd. on his bicycle, outdoing the handsome Jimmy as a cyclist, but once at the beach he becomes aware of his strangeness and his state as monstrous outsider. When, from a distance, a group of girls shows an interest in them, Jimmy warns him to turn over on his back when the girls approach so that his boils will not be visible. Later, when the girls invite the boys to join them on their blanket, Henry, because of this physical affliction, cannot go. Abandoned by Jimmy and physically immobilized from exposing himself and his acne, Henry watches the frolics of California adolescence from the estranged point of view of monster-outsider. As Jimmy flaunts his chest and genitals to the girls, Henry closes his eyes and has a vision of "endless mouths and assholes swallowing and shitting. The whole earth was nothing but mouths and assholes swallowing and shitting, and fucking." While Jimmy appears to the girls a Water-God, "the possibility and the promise," Chinaski feels that he is "just a 50-cent turd floating around in the green ocean of life." The Pacific, which in Isherwood's *Single Man* is the scene of George's "stunning baptism of surf" (George becoming "bejeweled" in its phosphorus and foam, losing his personal past and identity, "becoming cleaner, freer, less") is for Henry the locus of extreme isolation where he becomes aware of his monstrous otherness amid the beaches of the young, his misanthropy transforming the ocean into a sewer of life in which he remains an isolated, insoluble feces.

Henry's extreme and disfiguring acne is the central ordeal of his adolescence. Sent to the upper middle-class Chelsey High School by his naively ambitious father, Henry, amid the beautiful, healthy children of affluence, cannot participate in gym classes out of fear of exposing his acne, and instead chooses ROTC, where the woolen uniforms only exacerbate his condition. He must even temporarily quit high school and undergo treatment at L. A. County General Hospital, where his boils are lanced by electric needles.

Bukowski extrapolates Henry's acne into a powerful metaphor for his isolation from the mythic California of the American Dream, which Kevin Starr identifies as "charged with human hope," as "linked imaginatively with the most compelling of American myths, the pursuit of happiness." Because of his incurable acne, Chinaski is never permitted this illusory hope.

When the adolescent Henry looks in the mirror, he is horrified:

> No wonder people stared, no wonder they said unkind things. It was not simply a case of teenage acne. These were inflamed, relentless, large, swollen boils filled with pus. I felt singled out, as if I had been *selected* to be this way.

Henry is a fictional descendent of both Frankenstein's monster and Kafka's Gregor. It is as if all the excrement that Henry retained as a child in grade school, because of his shame of letting others know of his bodily functions, surfaces in his incurable boils. The excrement of his childhood, a metaphor for his repressed anger against his father, expresses itself as the pus of his adolescent boils that isolate him from others. During his treatments, Henry spends his time at home confined to his bedroom, timing the flights of planes overhead. Once, his German grandmother visits his bedroom and prays, holding a crucifix over his boils, that God purge the Devil from his body.

Because of his acne Henry will never be able to look at his society from the point of view of an insider. His acne is not only the literal source of his alienation, but his disfiguring and offensive boils are themselves metaphoric equivalents to Bukowski's own writing, which expresses the offensive, "acned" reality of Los Angeles working and sub-working class life without stylistic ointment or clothing. Bukowski takes us to the skin of Southern California; we see the skin of his society close-up, like tiny Gulliver's unflattering microscopic vision of the skin of the Brobdingnagian maidens. Unlike the wealthy B. Z. in Didion's *Play It As It Lays* (1971), "perpetually tanned, oiled, gleaming," who kills himself in a desert motel, Chinaski, with his ugly skin, survives to tell the truth about the skin of his society.

Disease, it should be pointed out, is a common motif in the Los Angeles novel (e.g., Carmen Sterwood's epilepsy in Chandler's *Big Sleep* [1939], Monroe Stahr's heart disease in Fitzgerald's *Last Tycoon* [1941], and E. Z.'s and Maria's depression, and her child's autism, in *Play It As It Lays*). These texts represent a tradition that opposes the dominant popular myth of Los Angeles as the locus of health and regeneration that one finds restated in recent serious novels like *Single Man* and *Windowlight* that, in turn, deliberately oppose the earlier demythological tradition. But epilepsy, heart disease, and depression are romantic diseases that, in the texts cited above, afflict the wealthy, beautiful, and desirable. These diseases show an affliction that lies beneath an alluring surface. In ***Ham on Rye,*** in contrast, Chinaski's disease is a disease of the surface, of the skin. Beneath Chinaski's ugly surface, however, there develops, because of the disfiguring acne that separates him from others, notable powers of incorruptible skepticism, candor, independence, endurance, and self-assertion.

Throughout the last third of ***Ham on Rye,*** empowered by his affliction, Chinaski asserts himself physically against his oppressors and his mockers. The most dramatic assertion occurs on the parking roof of Mears and Starbuck where, after graduation, he is employed as a stock boy. Here he takes on successfully Jimmy Newhall, the beautiful football star, bound for USC, who insults him in the department store's men's department. Henry, whose acne has taught him how to negotiate defeat and humiliation, has become stronger than those who have been chosen by nature or society.

One of the recurrent motifs in ***Ham on Rye*** is that of the spider and the fly. Henry's adversaries, from his father and the bullies of his childhood to Jimmy Newhall and the English teacher at Los Angeles City College who makes the class recite Gilbert and Sullivan lyrics to improve their diction, are the spiders. The spider web becomes the metaphor for the depressed working-class Los Angeles of Henry's childhood, a region of failed hopes and petty tyranny. Although Henry cannot fully extricate himself from this web, he comes to realize that the fly does not have to accept passively the role of spider's victim. He can fight back:

> And as I was coming down the hill I ran into a giant spider web. I was always doing that. I stood there pulling the sticky web from myself and looking for the spider. Then I saw him: a big fat black son-of-a-bitch. I crushed him. I had learned to hate spiders. When I went to hell I would be eaten by a spider.

Ham on Rye concludes with the outbreak of World War II. Henry, thrown out of his home by his father, who has discovered Henry's shocking first attempts at fiction, has been living in a series of downtown rooming houses. Despite the patriotic blandishments of a friend, Henry refuses to join the Marines. He enters a penny arcade on Main Street and invites a Mexican boy to play the boxing machine with him. The boy's mechanical boxer wins the first match, but Henry, not discouraged by his own boxer's failure, continues to play:

> I put in another dime and blue trunks sprang to his feet. The kid started squeezing his one trigger and the right arm of red trunks pumped and pumped. I let blue trunks stand back a while and contemplate. Then I nodded at the kid. I moved blue trunks in, both arms flailing. I felt I had to win. It seemed very important. I didn't know why it was important and I kept thinking, why do I think this is so important?
>
> And another part of me answered, just because it is.

Ham on Rye concludes soberly (blue trunks goes down again) but affirmatively. Henry Chinaski reaches neither the extremity of despair, like Didion's Maria and E. Z., nor the extremity of regeneration, like Isherwood's George, neither desert nor ocean, only a shooting gallery on Main Street. He resolves at the end of ***Ham on Rye,*** as America enters World War II, to fight his own private war, to resist the society that is appalled by him and his scars. He will continue to appall it and thereby to reveal its own less visible scars. He will fight it by refusing its myths, blandishments, responsibilities, and wars. ***Ham on Rye*** narrates Henry's growth to self-awareness in a Southern California denuded of its regional myths. It is not a special place, but a representative America, an America against whose dominant myths and institutions solitary struggle is seen as the only available and honorable option. (pp. 4-8.)

Ernest Fontana, "Bukowski's 'Ham on Rye' and the Los Angeles Novel," in The Review of Contemporary Fiction, *Vol. 5, No. 3, Fall, 1985, pp. 4-8.*

Jimmie E. Cain, Jr. (essay date Fall 1985)

[*In the following essay, Cain provides a brief overview of Bukowski's novels* Post Office *and* Factotum *and addresses "the salient conflicts and resolutions" in* Women.]

Bukowski's novels—***Post Office, Factotum,*** and ***Women***—coalesce in a trilogy of similar imagery and theme. Obviously autobiographical, they offer a chronology of the author's physical, psychological, and, to a greater degree, aesthetic development. As befits its position in this literary corpus, ***Women*** brings to fruition not only an emerging talent, but also a worldly vision, clearly establishing Bukowski's pessimism and concomitant salvational scheme. Taken as a whole, the novels offer what might be seen as a classical quest motif rendered in contemporary lineaments. As a modern-day Odysseus, Henry Chinaski seeks a knowledge that can make life worthwhile and fulfilling. And, after evading the death-laden shoals of the Sirens' calls in ***Women,*** such knowledge is his. To appreciate fully the salient conflicts and resolutions in ***Women,*** a brief overview of their genesis in ***Post Office*** and ***Factotum*** is necessary.

Though published in an inverted chronology—the events in ***Post Office*** actually follow those in ***Factotum***—the themes in the early novels remain the same. Chinaski, whether a young man just setting out on the high road of life or a middle-aged profligate, suffers from a growing disenchantment with himself and the world around him. He lives in a multitude of environments and works an array of jobs, yet he still finds all of life blighted with a malaise peculiar to his America: a thoroughgoing boredom. Passing through the "Hades" of urban-industrial society, he

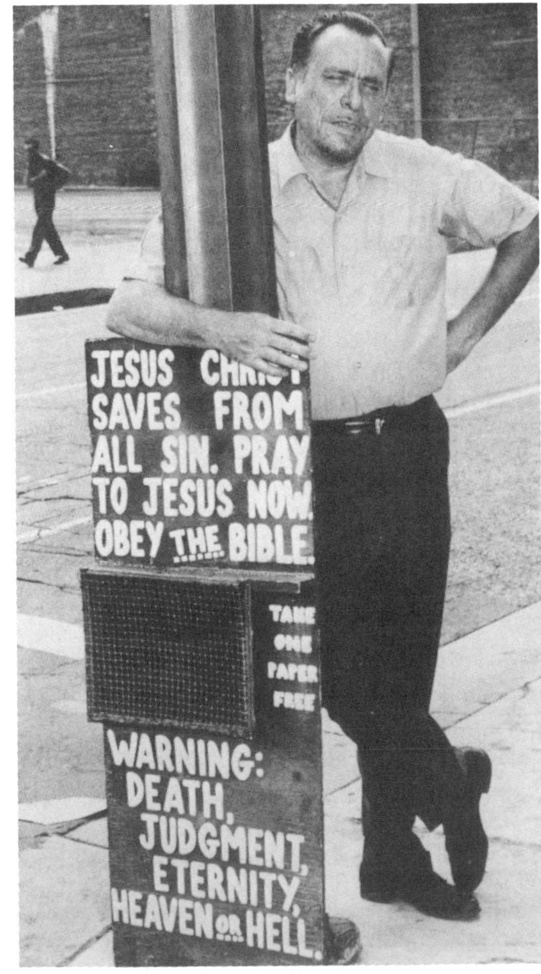

Bukowski visiting Skid Row, Los Angeles, 1971.

comes to recognize that boredom sickens all, driving men to elaborate perversions. The U.S. Postal Service, that cyclopean bureaucratic monster, reduces men to faceless automatons tied to wickedly monotonous and mindless tasks, creating a panoply of sick minds driven to despair by boredom. One aberration, a clerk named Butchner, indulges in hollow taunts and insults, "talking to the ceiling, insane" as Chinaski notices, for distraction. Another postal worker, Janko, seeks refuge in bravado and groundless ostentation, fabricating a web of fantasies detailing sexual and literary accomplishments to give his dull, uneventful life color and panache.

Such perversities abound in the hellish landscape of ***Factotum*** as well. At an art supply house, Chinaski meets Maurice, a janitor who passes himself off as a painter, a French painter at that, although he does not "have much of a French accent." While at the same job, Chinaski encounters another outré worker, Paul, a clerk with a passion for pills and a weight-reducing machine which "moves up and down," allowing him to "fuck" himself. The manager of an auto parts warehouse must recount his and his wife's sexual exploits to Chinaski in florid terms to break the monotony of his occupation. Though the magnitude of perversion is perhaps greater in ***Factotum,*** it derives from the same evils populating ***Post Office.***

As an observer, Chinaski is not immune to the dangers of boredom, however, and in both ***Post Office*** and ***Factotum,*** he succumbs. After eleven years as a mail handler, Henry is but a ghost of his former self:

> It was the stool and the same motion and the same talk. And there I was, dizzy spells and pains in the arms, neck, chest, everywhere. I slept all day resting up for the job. On weekends I had to drink in order to forget it. I had come in weighing 185 pounds. Now I weighed 223 pounds. All you moved was your right arm.

At the end of ***Factotum,*** Henry wanders aimlessly through an empty life, devoid of ambition and even interest in pleasure. The last scene of the novel documents the extent of his desolation:

> Darlene fingered her naked breasts, showing them to us, her eyes filled with the dream, her lips moist and parted. Then suddenly she turned and waved her enormous behind at us. The beads leaped and flashed, went crazy, sparkled. The spotlight shook and danced like the sun. The four man band crackled and banged. Darlene spun around. She tore away the beads. I looked, they looked. We could see her cunt hairs through the flesh-colored gauze.
>
> The band really spanked her ass. And I couldn't get it up.

Seemingly crushed by boredom like the Butchners, Jankos, Maurices, and Pauls, the commonly libidinous Chinaski cannot even find retreat in promiscuity.

Nevertheless, no matter how close to capitulation he may come, Chinaski never throws in the towel, refusing to negate his human integrity. Conversely, he retaliates by becoming something of what David Galloway terms an "absurd hero" [in his *The Absurd Hero in American Fiction*], after recognizing the apparent meaninglessness of his life, confronting the absurdity of his existence, and coming away determined to make of life what he can. Echoing the demands of Camus in *The Myth of Sisyphus* in ***Post Office,*** Chinaski rejects the easy escape of suicide and decrees to find sanctuary from boredom in a life replete with meaningful trivialities:

> I even had the butcher knife against my throat one night in the kitchen and then I thought, easy, old boy, your little girl might want you to take her to the zoo. Ice cream bars, chimpanzees, tigers, green and red birds, and the sun coming down on top of her head, the sun coming down and crawling in the hairs of your arms, easy, old boy.

It is later on in ***Women*** that Chinaski's status as an absurd hero, as a man in search of worth in an apparently worthless and boring world, reaches its fullest potential. In ***Women*** Bukowski reveals his response to the evils of ennui and the illness they breed.

> But among jackals, panthers, and hound-bitches
> Monkeys and vultures, scorpions and serpents,
> The yelping, roaring, growling monsters, rampant
> In the infamous menagerie of our vices,
>
> Is one more vicious, ugly, and perverse!
> Though he makes no great gesture, no loud cry,
> He would gladly turn out earth into debris
> And in a yawn engulf the universe;
>
> Ennui!—his unwilling tears brim over
> As, pulling at his hookah, he dreams of scaffolds.
> You know him, reader, this fastidious scoundrel,
> —Hypocritical reader, my fellow, my brother!
>
> From "Au Lecture" by Baudelaire

Women is the finest example of Bukowski's prose art and dark weltanschauung. His characters, reflecting the artifice of this vision, are stereotypical "packages" rather than well-defined human beings, their inanimate possessions usually communicating more about them than their human qualities. Human emotions suffer a similar devaluation. Love—a function reserved for "guitar players, Catholics and chess freaks"—devolves into sexual gratification, which in turn becomes little more than a party trick. In ***Women*** Bukowski posits boredom as the great illness of modern America, an illness that leads man to such perverse states. Chinaski, through his many amours, finds that boredom taints all human relations to some extent. Nonetheless, he also finds a positive response, a modus vivendi, for this condition.

Women picks up Chinaski's life after ***Post Office.*** After completing a stint with the postal service, he is writing his first novel. In the twenty to thirty years since his wanderings in ***Factotum,*** Chinaski has learned much. Subsequently, the depression that haunted him throughout ***Post Office*** and ***Factotum*** has been replaced by a sense of resignation and an acceptance of the vicissitudes of life:

> When I was young I was depressed all the time. But suicide no longer seemed a possibility in my

> life. At my age there was very little left to kill. It was good to be old, no matter what they said. It was reasonable that a man had to be at least 50 years old before he could write with anything like clarity. The more rivers you crossed, the more you knew about rivers—that is, if you survived the white water and the hidden rocks. It could be a rough cob sometimes.

Chinaski now seems to speak with the voice of wisdom, as a quintessential absurd hero, resisting the easy escape into suicide and mindlessness. He has not yet completed his epic quest, however. Even though his material circumstances improve somewhat—he achieves limited success as a writer and poetry reader—he still exists in a world teeming with bored, disturbed people—professors, publishers, lapsed ingenues, and bartenders in this instance—caught in the debilitating throes of ennui. And, for the third time, Chinaski, however well equipped age and reason have left him, falls prey himself, turning to an indulgence in a welter of random sexual relations for solace.

If anything, Chinaski stands consummately bored at this point, and few things can excite him. For one thing, he finds common pursuits unattractive:

> Nature didn't interest me. I never voted. . . . Outer space bored me. Baseball bored me. History bored me. Zoos bored me.

Even that all-consuming American passion, shopping, leaves him dissatisfied:

> I hated department stores, I hated the clerks, they acted so superior, they seemed to know the secret of life, they had a confidence I didn't possess. My shoes were always broken down and old, I disliked shoe stores too. I never purchased anything until it was completely unusable, and that included automobiles. It wasn't a matter of thrift, I just couldn't bear to be a buyer needing a seller, seller being so handsome and aloof and superior.

But, though caught up in boredom himself, Chinaski can still see that, as was the case in ***Post Office*** and ***Factotum,*** the blighted around him often turn to the bizarre and fantastic for relief. Such behavior produces equally bizarre effects in human relationships, forcing what should be otherwise tranquil, compassionate friends and lovers into demonic actions:

> Human relationships didn't work anyhow. Only the first two weeks had any zing, then the participants lost their interest. Masks dropped away and real people began to appear: cranks, imbeciles, the demented, the vengeful, sadists, killers. Modern society had created its own kind and they feasted on each other. It was a duel to the death—in a cesspool.

People also become "blindly" eclectic, desperately grasping after any fad or device to dispel monotony:

> Nothing was ever in tune. People just blindly grabbed at whatever there was: communism, health foods, zen, surfing, ballet, hypnotism, group encounters, orgies, biking, herbs, Catholicism, weight-lifting, travel, withdrawal, vegetarianism, India, painting. . . . People had to find things to do while waiting to die.

Probably the most deranged of all human relationships is the sexual one. Although the novel opens with Henry's lamenting not having slept with a woman for over four years, by novel's end he has tasted well over twenty women—a protean crew ranging from eighteen to forty-five, blondes to redheads, and hippie vamps to executive nymphomaniacs; often regretfully, most harbor eccentricities that make coitus something less than a romantic fling. Lydia, the first of Henry's many partners, a would-be poet, hippie, sculptor, married and divorced, mother of two, fancies herself an educated practitioner, casually moving through a cornucopia of men. Quite the devotee, she takes great pleasure in reading all the latest sex guides and later discussing her findings with her sister. His experiences with Lydia convince Chinaski that sex for the sake of mere gymnastic diversion corrupts and perverts the act. After Lydia refuses to take a walk with him so that she might rather read *Love and Orgasm: A Revolutionary Guide to Sexual Fulfillment,* Henry reflects on the "tragic" nature of textbook love:

> I was trapped in the mountains and woods with two crazy women. They took all the joy out of fucking by talking about it all the time. I liked to fuck too, but it wasn't my religion. There were too many ridiculous and tragic things about it. People didn't seem to know how to handle it. So they made a toy out of it. A toy that destroyed people.

A no less eccentric woman, another of Henry's encounters, Dee Dee, "jewish, hip, freaky," acts as if she were living in "the early 1960's and Love-In Time." As an avocation, she wanders about prominent Hollywood cemeteries sitting on the graves of such past stars as Rudolph Valentino, Tyrone Power, and Douglas Fairbanks all the while imagining with each stop a different sexual interlude. Also very fond of the "haut monde," Dee Dee knows "all the names: the right publishers . . . the right revolutionaries, anybody, everybody." Sex for Dee Dee is a ticket into the "right" circles of fashionable society, wherein she participates in "swinging," the ultimate perversion of sex in which human emotion disappears and people function as "dead" machines. Chinaski finds sex for the sake of social acceptance as a form of intellectual suicide:

> I detested that type of swinging, the Los Angeles, Hollywood, Bel Air, Malibu, Laguna Beach kind of sex. Strangers when you meet, strangers when you part—a gymnasium of bodies namelessly masturbating each other. People with no morals often considered themselves more free, but mostly they lacked the ability to feel or to love. So they became swingers. The dead fucking the dead. There was no gamble or humor in their game—it was corpse fucking corpse.

Chinaski meets other women with sexual mores akin to those of Lydia and Dee Dee, and for a time Chinaski seems to "swing" himself. He never forgets, however, that for sex to be fulfilling requires true human interaction and warmth. Chinaski really wants to find the one woman with whom he can have such a life. Unfortunately, his experiences in ***Post Office*** and ***Factotum*** have left him uncertain as to whether that woman can be found in his world.

Though capable of experiencing emotion in love, Chinaski avoids women who seem able to reciprocate. Although he appreciates the benefits of a "good" woman, he refuses to place full confidence in one, for he fears he will become merely the "possession" of a woman should he give in to her affections:

> When I came I felt it was in the face of everything decent, white sperm dripping down over the heads and souls of my dead parents. If I had been born a woman I would certainly have been a prostitute. Since I had been born a man, I craved women constantly, the lower the better. And yet women—good women—frightened me because they eventually wanted your soul, and what was left of mine, I wanted to keep. Basically I craved prostitutes, base women, because they were deadly and hard and made no personal demands. Nothing was lost when they left. Yet at the same time I yearned for a gentle, good woman, despite the overwhelming price. Either way I was lost. A strong man would give up both. I wasn't strong. So I continued to struggle with women, with the idea of women.

Having lived a life riddled with the perverse and bizarre manifestations of boredom, Chinaski has obviously not come away unscarred. Though a loner, a rebel against most popular societal conventions, a man used to the rigors of isolation, he finally accepts the fact that he is lonely at heart. At the end of ***Women,*** Chinaski realizes that being alone never feels "right," although it may feel "good" at times. He has at last grown tired of running from one hasty affair to another, and he desires the permanence and stability of a lasting relationship with a "good" woman. He understands that he is a victim of the boredom he has seen afflicting others, concluding that his checkered sexual past results from ennui and not an insatiable appetite. At last, he seeks redemption.

Appropriately, his redemption comes in the form of a "good" woman, Sara. Sara amazes Chinaski because she embodies every quality he associates with such a woman, yet she makes no demands on his time or his "soul." Containing all that makes Chinaski capable of maintaining human integrity and more, she not only avoids the pitfalls of boredom, but she achieves the dimensions of an absurd hero as well. Chinaski recognizes this when she shows him kindness without offering him sex. Her goodness is of the heart, not the genitalia. She is the first woman he meets who wants him for his warmth and humanity, not for his fame and sexual prowess. After meeting Sara, Henry disdains the profferings of a coquette for the first time. His peregrinations have led him to see that too much of anything can be harmful:

> Sara was a good woman. I had to get myself straightened out. The only time a man needed a lot of women was when none of them were any good. A man could lose his identity fucking around too much. Sara deserved much better than I was giving her. It was up to me now.

By accepting the responsibility for constructing a lasting relationship with Sara, Chinaski finds fulfillment and a raison d'être. Sartre's statement [in *Existentialism and Human Emotions*] that "existentialism's first move is to make every man aware of what he is and to make the full responsibility of his existence rest on him" appears very fitting for Chinaski now. By accepting the status of an absurd hero, Chinaski shoulders the "responsibility" not only for his life but for Sara's as well.

Through Sara, Chinaski finally emerges from his quest armed with a knowledge for making life more than just "a duel to the death in a cesspool." He at last shrugs off the influences of boredom and gives up a lonely existence for the happiness of a richly substantial human contract. This contract is not a compromising of ethics on Chinaski's part; instead, it is the realization of a dream. In Sara he finds an equal. Together, they can create a life of integrity wherein a commitment to human interaction replaces the perverse, often machine-contrived fantasies many turn to for escape and distraction in a world plagued by boredom. Sara is the mast pole which gives Chinaski the strength to overcome the sickly sweet "Siren calls" of ennui. (pp. 9-14)

Jimmie E. Cain, Jr., "Women: 'The Siren Calls of Boredom'," in The Review of Contemporary Fiction, *Vol. 5, No. 3, Fall, 1985, pp. 9-14.*

Gerald Locklin (essay date Fall 1985)

[In the essay below, Locklin praises the diversity of Bukowski's poems in War All the Time *and* Horses Don't Bet on People & Neither Do I.]

I felt that Bukowski returned to top form as a poet in ***Dangling in the Tournefortia*** (1981), and I explained why in *American Book Review* [see excerpt above]. These two recent collections [***War All the Time & Horses Don't Bet on People & Neither Do I***] do not represent a falling off; on the contrary they present numerous examples of Bukowski at work in what has always been his strongest mode: the scenic or dramatic narrative (or more simply, the story poem with lots of setting and dialogue), but added to his achievements of the past is a diversity that should confound those who would parody the "typical" Bukowski poem of booze, horses, and sex.

In ***War All the Time*** there are poems of the working class, poems of the aspiring writer, poems of the aging writer, antiwar poems, antinuke poems, poems that move in and out of the bourgeois world, sports poems, television poems, European poems, and elegies for a cat and for the Los Angeles writer, John Fante. Of course there are still track poems, but why shouldn't there be? It's a world Bukowski knows intimately, one he can treat as a microcosm, one where stories offer themselves—it is a world of inherent narrative tensions. And of course there are still poems about women, but they range from the aroused to the satiric and culminate in a moving remembrance of a loved woman dead twenty-eight years. There are still poems of intoxication and withdrawal, but even here there is something new in the investigation of the current cocaine epidemic.

It is not that Bukowski is trying to placate any critics in these poems. It is, I think, that his affluence and fame of recent years have widened the world about which he can write firsthand. He may still prefer Hollywood Park to Hollywood premieres but he has been to the latter now as well. While this book contains some withering attacks on turncoat friends and lovers, his greater security also allows him to laugh at himself and to let bygones be bygones. Many if not most poets do their best work young (E. E. Cummings is a case in point), but it may be that Bukowski, in his mid-sixties, is indeed, as he keeps insisting, just reaching his prime.

I'll draw examples from ***Horses Don't Bet on People*** of the narratives that abound in both volumes. Anyone who has ever owned a home can identify with **"Locks,"** a five-page saga of the tribulations of getting the house locks changed. In **"Fight"** the narrator tries to convince his woman that he was made late by stopping to watch a vicious street fight. Those who would insist that there are not significant differences between men and women, or that there shouldn't be, may not like **"Fight"** or a good deal of Bukowski. But a poem's not catering to a current ideology does not by itself mark it as a bad poem in the long run, or even now. **"Independence Day"** provides an object lesson in dealing with juvenile delinquents. The **"Token Drunk"** negotiates a media party in Marina del Rey.

"There Are So Many Houses and Dark Streets without Help" is an unfortunate title for an otherwise likable poem psychoanalyzing the poet's penchant for getting wildly lost in his car. All his women have the same explanation: "You're just a fool." The title character of **"A Boor"** wins no laurels from waitresses.

Just to make sure no one is left with the impression that Bukowski has gone soft, the final poem, about the predictable advice given by a talk-show psychologist to a cuckolded husband, is entitled **"In My Day We Used to Call It Pussy-Whipped."**

It is, however, the penultimate poem in the volume, **"*Kenyon Review,* After the Sandstorm,"** that quietly assesses Bukowski's place in, and importance to, contemporary American poetry:

> coming off that park bench after that all night
> sandstorm in El Paso
> and walking into the library
> I felt fairly safe even though I had less than
> two dollars
> was alone in the world
> and was 40 pounds underweight.
> it still felt normal and almost pleasant to
> open that copy of the *Kenyon Review*
> 1940
> and marvel at the most brilliant way those
> professors used the language to criticize each
> other for the way they criticized literature.
> I even felt that they were humorous about it,
> but not quite: the bitterness was rancid and
> red steel hot, but at the same time I felt the
> leisurely and safe places that language had
> evolved from: places and cultures centuries
> soft and institutionalized.
>
> I knew I would never be able to write
> in that manner, yet I almost wanted to be
> one of them or any of them: being guarded,
> fierce and witty, having fun
> in that way.
>
> I put the magazine back and walked outside,
> looked south north east west.
>
> each direction was wrong.
> I started to walk along
>
> what I did know was that overeffusive language
> properly used
> could be bright and beautiful.
>
> I also sensed that there might be
> something else.

The astounding thing about this revelatory poem is that Bukowski demonstrates a more objective, fair, and sensitive appraisal of his place in relation to the literary establishment than the rest of us, with our supposed aesthetic distance, have been able to articulate on his behalf. Of course poetry today, as then, abounds with the bright and beautiful, but what is Bukowski's "something else"? It is to an extent a matter of the vernacular (as Professor Julian Smith of Hull, England, is elaborating in a dissertation-in-progress), and it has a lot to do with his freedom, but it is perhaps primarily a matter of his having gone ahead and told stories in free verse while the "serious" poets continued their decades-long debates upon the best ways of returning the narrative and dramatic modes to poetry.

Readers are still surprised to find Bukowski employing the same stories in poems, short stories, and novels. They seem to feel there is a law against this, and maybe such a prohibition is taught in some creative writing classes, but I have yet to see it written down. And those readers who do not really like Bukowski's work, but who bend over backwards to appreciate him, go on praising his occasional attempts to be bright and beautiful, which generally result in his most parodied efforts. It is interesting that there are few such poems in these two volumes: Bukowski has always said that he has no quarrel with critics of his work, that those who have bothered to write about him at all have generally written sympathetically. He seems now to have heeded a valuable message from his parodists and unsuccessful imitators. Or else, since he has written me that these poems represent only about a sixth of his poems composed during this time period, the credit may be due to his editors, John Martin and Marvin Malone. (pp. 34-6)

Even the poem quoted above, while not an obvious narrative in the manner of the classic **"fire station"** or so many of the poems of horses, violence, and women, is certainly a story reminiscent of the most icebergian of Hemingway's. In less than forty lines we find scene, characterization, conflict, irony, meditation, resolution, retrospective. It is a short story of a young writer, down and out, who reads a literary magazine and experiences a quiet epiphany of what he will never be and who he *will* be as a writer in the postmodern world. There is emotional complexity and emotional change. Why is it, although it has but a single character, no dialogue or waiters, and the setting is not a café, that this story/poem reminds me of "A Clean Well-Lighted Place"?

The answer might begin with the observation that not a word is wrong or wasted or misplaced, and that an entire lifetime, world, and literary career are left to our inferring. (p. 36)

Gerald Locklin, "Bukowski's 'War All the Time' and 'Horses Don't Bet on People & Neither Do I'," in The Review of Contemporary Fiction, *Vol. 5, No. 3, Fall, 1985, pp. 34-6.*

Novelist Jory Sherman on Bukowski's myth-making:

Bukowski's hemorrhoids figure prominently in his poetry and prose. They are, or were, very real. He had a painful operation, in fact, and this curtailed his beer-drinking. He wrote truthfully and majestically about the operation ("All the Assholes In The World And Mine") but there is more to the story than the painful protuberances in his anus. The hemorrhoids were a way of instilling another connection in the reader's mind between Buk and Hem, Ernest Hemingway. When Hemingway was in Europe he encouraged the sobriquet, "Ernie Hemorrhoid." The G.I.s there, taking it from Papa's own lips, called him "Ernie Hemorrhoid, the poor man's Pyle." Bukowski knows the stuff of myth-making just as Hem did.

Jory Sherman, in his Bukowski: Friendship, Fame & Bestial Myth, *1981.*

Loss Glazier (essay date Fall 1985)

[*In the essay below, Glazier provides an overview of Bukowski's novel* Post Office.]

When ***Post Office,*** Bukowski's first published novel, came off the press in 1971, an important moment in the history of modern American literature occurred. Bukowski stood like a giant, one foot astride each of two continents: poetry and prose; pornography and belles lettres; suicide and sainthood; Europe and America; the underground press and the brackish water of the literati. A truly historic first novel, ***Post Office*** was as definitive as a line drawn in the dirt.

Bukowski had stepped forward from the maelstrom of prophetic vision, having established himself securely by such visionary poetic works as ***Flower, Fist and Bestial Wail*** (1960), ***Crucifix in a Deathhand*** (1965), and the collection ***The Days Run Away Like Wild Horses over the Hills*** (1969). He was able to turn his hand to fiction with a perspective unequalled in contemporary American letters. He had been through a stripping-down that would've killed any ordinary person. And yet Bukowski, rather than being weakened by each successive defoliation, seemed to get stronger with the knowledge of what was necessary. He approached a level of immediate experience that was almost religious in nature. And when he came out of his motel room with the manuscript of ***Post Office,*** the essential worth of his novel was inescapable, built with a prose style that was sparse, honest, and brilliant in its Epicurean asceticism.

The setting for this visionary work is quite uncontrived. Unlike a generation of previous writers who drew their inspiration from Paris, Italy and the Riviera, Bukowski created his universe from the stuff at hand. Everything that was necessary could be found wherever he found himself: in a motel room in Los Angeles, in a cottage in Texas, sitting in his car, in the jaws of the post office. The post office represents dynamically the duality which is the relentless metronome of daily life. Here we have literacy and communication; letters are flashes of narrative whereby events are caught in brief written images sent from one person to another. Yet on the other hand, the post office is representative of another side of modern life: order, authority, bureaucracy, a methodical and corporate process of dehumanization where each person is supposed to feel enriched by the contribution he is making to the organization's goal. This point of view is established firmly before the start of the narrative in "Code of Ethics":

> Postal employees have, over the years, established a fine tradition of faithful service to the Nation, unsurpassed by other groups. Each employee should take great pride in this tradition of dedicated service. Each of us must strive to make his contribution worthwhile in the continued movement of the Postal Service toward future progress in the public interest.

The assumptions underlying this code form the justification for the dissolution of individuality in society. Here is represented the kind of conditionality and blind obedience that makes the isolation and madness of modern life possible.

The lesson of ***Post Office*** lies in the cleaning up of this mess. The novel provides a clear guide to the necessary first step: realizing that there is nothing to understand. There is no *reason* for it. Those that reason are those that either contribute to the strata that distance us from humanity or that contribute equally to its power through their own act of retreating. The only way of beginning to understand our predicament is to understand that there is *no asking why.*

Bukowski opens ***Post Office*** with a single simple paragraph: "It began as a mistake." Henry Chinaski, Bukowski's alter ego, enters the post office quite by accident, hearing that they would hire anyone. He takes the exam and physical, and goes through the motions, finally becoming a temporary mail carrier. Life is a breeze—for the moment. The novel's action starts when he is transferred to Oakford Station and the tyrannical rule of a supervisor named Jonstone. Immediately Chinaski finds himself under the degradation of a normal, ordered world. And it's clear that this world—of bondage—was made possible only through one utterly ironic condition: man's acceptance of tyranny. "The subs themselves made Jonstone possible by obeying his impossible orders," Chinaski explains. He rebels immediately and is quashed. He persists in his rebellion and continues to be suppressed. And though at one point he is even a millionaire through marriage, the process of ***Post Office*** is one that continually strips Chinaski down; yet each time this occurs, he pulls himself up with purified vision.

Post Office presents man as a curiosity, blind to his responsibility for creating the process of dehumanization through his own submission to it. The inhabitants of Bukowski's universe are constantly under the thumb of this principle. They are people motivated by temper, attachment, people who are spiritually starved yet stuffed with illusions. Suffering by their own hands, these people question their lot. These are the people on Chinaski's route, caught in a self-consuming cycle between disappointment and anger. For example:

> ". . . I know you have a letter for me!"
>
> "What makes you say that?"
>
> "Because my sister phoned and said she was going to write me."
>
> "Lady, I don't have a letter for you."
>
> "I know you have! I know you have! I know it's there!"

Or, more commonly:

> I handed her mail to her.
>
> "BILLS! BILLS! BILLS!" she screamed. "IS THAT ALL YOU CAN BRING ME? THESE BILLS?"

Bukowski's power of straightforward "seeing" is evidenced, in the face of this hysterical loss of human dignity, by his honest reply, " 'Yes, mam, that's all I can bring you.' " Or, again, in a moment of quiet emptiness:

> When Betty came back we didn't sing or laugh, or even argue. We sat drinking in the dark, smoking cigarettes, and when we went to sleep, I didn't put my feet on her body or she on mine like we used to. We slept without touching.
>
> We had both been robbed.

These are people, like Chinaski's millionairess wife, Joyce, who have lost touch with what is real. Chinaski's value as antihero is his resiliency, his ascension from the "death" of blind obedience. He speaks no other language but the real. There is no swaying, no circumnavigating the issues. Bukowski is without sympathy in standing true to the world as it exists in front of him. We witness this when Chinaski, married to Joyce and living in Texas, experiences a rare mood of benevolence and leaves work early to do a little shopping. By the time Joyce gets home that evening, Chinaski has prepared a feast, including a plate of golden, fried-in-butter snails that repulse her immediately. Eventually, however, she tries one, then examines the others on her plate closely. Finally she breaks:

> "They all have tiny *assholes*! It's horrible! Horrible!"
>
> "What's horrible about assholes, baby?"
>
> She held a napkin to her mouth. Got up and ran to the bathroom. She began vomiting. I hollered in from the kitchen:
>
> "WHAT'S WRONG WITH ASSHOLES, BABY? YOU'VE GOT AN ASSHOLE, I'VE GOT AN ASSHOLE! YOU GO TO THE STORE AND BUY A PORTERHOUSE STEAK, THAT HAD AN ASSHOLE! ASSHOLES COVER THE EARTH! IN A WAY TREES HAVE ASSHOLES BUT YOU CAN'T FIND THEM, THEY JUST DROP THEIR LEAVES. YOUR ASSHOLE, MY ASSHOLE, THE WORLD IS FULL OF BILLIONS OF ASSHOLES, THE PRESIDENT HAS AN ASSHOLE, THE CARWASH BOY HAS AN ASSHOLE, THE JUDGE AND THE MURDERER HAVE ASSHOLES."

The line that Bukowski draws in ***Post Office*** is one that encompasses an essential decision. Man stands at an important moment in world history and cannot seem to step forward out of sheer blindness to common, ordinary facts. Man can be seen in the birds that Bukowski sets free in ***Post Office,*** birds that Bukowski could no longer bear to see imprisoned. He takes the cage outside and opens the door, daring the birds to step across the line. There is a dramatic moment of hesitation while they deliberate about whether or not to go. The essential challenge of ***Post Office*** is before them. Their accountability for their own self-determination is placed squarely under their eyes. They fly off. When Joyce returns, she is beside herself:

> "Do you mean to say you let those birds out of the cage? Do you mean to say you really let them out of the cage?"
>
> "Well, all I can say is, they are not locked in the bathroom, they are not in the cupboard."
>
> "They'll starve out there!"
>
> "They can catch worms, eat berries, all that stuff."
>
> "They can't, they can't. They don't know how! They'll die!"
>
> "Let 'em learn or let 'em die."

Chinaski does not simply *express* this philosophy: his life embodies it. Taking your fate into your own hands, despite the outcome, initiates the process of restoring man's humanity.

The marriage to Joyce ends, just as do all of Chinaski's relationships in ***Post Office,*** just as Chinaski's association with the post office will. After a long grueling battle, there will have been enough. It will be time to look at life with clearer eyes. To make a simple statement. There is an almost mystical wisdom expressed each time Chinaski moves on.

> She even helped me pack. Folding my pants neatly into suitcases. Packing in my shorts and razor. When I was ready to leave she started crying again. I bit her on the ear, the right one, then went down the stairway with my stuff. I got into the car and began cruising up and down the streets looking for a For Rent sign.

This scene, on its own, is compelling; yet the philosophical insight comes with Chinaski's observation of his own humanness. Stripped again of everything and looking for a place to live with no previous preparation, he comments, "It didn't seem to be an unusual thing to do." Chinaski survives because he keeps his eyes on the road and refuses to wallow in any kind of self-pitying analysis.

Post Office sums up the entire human dilemma in a few simple choruses. The proof of the truth of Bukowski's vision lies in the continued popularity of ***Post Office*** and all of Bukowski's work, both here and abroad. There is a delicate balance that must be evaluated—between what we endure and what little ground we need to claim for ourselves. Without complex theories or expressions of insurmountable entanglements, Bukowski provides a clean and simple answer in a clear and direct style: the answer is right here. It's as easy as looking in the mirror. (pp. 39-42)

> *Loss Glazier, "Mirror of Ourselves: Notes on Bukowski's 'Post Office'," in* The Review of Contemporary Fiction, *Vol. 5, No. 3, Fall, 1985, pp. 39-42.*

Russell T. Harrison (essay date 1985)

[*In the essay below, Harrison explicates Bukowski's treatment of sexual and social relationships in his poem "Fire Station."*]

Although Charles Bukowski's poem **"Fire Station"** presents sexual relationships at the crudest of levels, the poem is an unusually insightful exploration of the problematic nature of relations between men and women and between the individual and the social world, themes that are central to Bukowski's work. Because the poem presents the vivid particulars of a unique subjective experience in an extremely spare, objective style it allows us to view the unique personal experience as an abstract depiction of human relationships as well. While the poem may seem to bear little relevance to the lives of its probable readers I think we are finally more involved than we might, at first, care to admit and through its dedication the poem hints at what broader meaning may lie in the experience the poem describes, and in the poem itself.

In the poem we see a male narrator and his female companion leave a bar where they have been drinking together, apparently for some time because they are reduced to the narrator's last "43 cents." They plan to return to their room where they have "a couple of wine bottles," to continue drinking. On their way back they pass a fire house. The narrator's companion, who " 'just love(s) / FIRE engines,' " goes into the station "followed" by the narrator. She tries to climb up into one of the fire engines and is aided in doing so by a fireman who "ran up" to her. She and the fireman engage in a good-natured conversation with an obvious double-entendre:

> the other guy was up in the seat with
> her. "you got one of those big THINGS?"
> she asked him. "oh, hahaha!, I mean one of
> those big HELMETS!"
>
> "I've got a big helmet too," he told
> her.

Meanwhile the narrator asks another fireman, " 'you play cards?' I asked *my* / fireman." and succeeds in starting a card game:

> "come on in back," he
> said. "of course, we don't gamble.
> it's against the
> rules."
>
> "I understand," I told
> him.
>
> I had run my 43 cents up to a
> dollar ninety
> when I saw her going upstairs with
> her fireman.
>
> "he's gonna show me their sleeping
> quarters," she told
> me.
>
> "I understand," I told
> her.
>
> When her fireman slid down the pole
> ten minutes later
> I nodded him
> over.
>
> "That'll be 5
> dollars."

Most of the firemen in the fire house go upstairs, seriatim, and give the narrator five dollars when they come down although, "I figured a few had slipped by me / but I was a good / sport." While all this is taking place the narrator continues to win at the card game. After a while ("it was getting dark outside") there is an alarm. The firemen respond and the narrator and Jane leave.

> "let's go back to the
> bar," I told
> her.
>
> "ooh, you got
> money?"
>
> "I found some I didn't know I
> had . . . "

As they sit drinking at the bar Jane, in reference to her visit to the firemen's sleeping quarters, says " 'I sure got a good / sleep!' " to which the narrator replies:

> "sure, baby, you need your
> sleep."
>
> "look at that sailor looking at me!
> he must think I'm a . . . a . . ."
>
> "naw, he don't think that. relax, you've got
> class, real class. sometimes you remind me of an
> opera singer. you know, one of those prima d's.
> your class shows all over
> you. drink
> up."
>
> I ordered 2
> more.
>
> "you know, daddy, you're the only man I
> LOVE! I mean, really . . . LOVE! ya
> know?"

"sure I know. sometimes I think I am a king
in spite of myself."

"yeah. yeah. *that's* what I mean, somethin' like
that."

I had to go to the urinal. when I came back
the sailor was sitting in my
seat. she had her leg up against his and
he was talking.

I walked over and got in a dart game with
Harry the Horse and the corner
newsboy.

In the poem the unemployed narrator and his apparently unemployed companion have spent a good part of the day drinking and socializing in a bar. We are told very little about the status of their relationship but it is fair to assume that it is something more than a casual one because the two are living together. We are told nothing of their history, their characters, or even their physical appearance. For the most part we learn what we do about them through their actions, conversation, and the narrator's thoughts in the course of the afternoon. From the narrator we learn that Jane (I think the dedication justifies our calling her this) is a "nice clean girl" with whom the narrator has a sexual relationship ("I ride it myself"). We are also told that she is "a real woman. nothing but guts / and / ass." While we learn that Jane has a promiscuous side to her we also know that she tells the narrator he is " 'the only man I / LOVE! I mean, really . . . LOVE!' " We know, too, that the narrator feels that she has " 'class, real class.' " Although there is an element of sarcasm in that statement I think it also expresses something the narrator does, in truth, feel.

Thus, what Bukowski presents to us, although with unusual clarity, is the not uncommon relationship between a man and a woman in which the woman is, apparently, seen almost solely in terms of sexual use (strikingly expressed in the sentence, "I ride it myself.") while the man is, for the woman, the object of deeper, if ambivalent, feelings. There is more than a hint, too, that the depth of the woman's feelings is upsetting to the man, as is evidenced by his leaving the bar to go to the urinal when she expresses something of these feelings.

Certainly Jane's actions in the fire house are what most strike the reader, on first reading the poem. Yet, extreme though they be, they have an explicable emotional dynamic underlying them, as well as, undoubtedly, a number of biographical and social causes. The immediate cause of her acting as she does is interpersonal in nature. It is an attempt to force the narrator to show some kind of a human interest in her beyond that minimal interest expressed in drinking with her. She becomes involved with the fireman because the narrator refuses to really engage with her. And the narrator's response to Jane's behavior prompts certain questions.

The narrator apparently realizes that Jane's behavior as they pass the fire house may be a prelude to something out of the ordinary; that her interest in the firehouse may have something to do with the firemen. That he does realize this is hinted at when, before anything actually happens, she is described as starting "to go crazy." What she actually says, undoubtedly and understandably a little uninhibited after an afternoon of drinking, is not really indicative of any kind of irrational or wild behavior: "a FIRE STATION! oh I just love / FIRE engines, they're so red and / all! let's go in." This is enthusiastic, but not "crazy," even in the sub-clinical sense of "a little odd or unusual." The narrator, though, feels justified in using the term, we can only assume, because on the basis of past experience he is aware of what this behavior may be a prelude to. In any event, within a few moments of Jane's becoming intrigued by the fire station the narrator has considered the situation and made a decision. Both the decision itself and the way in which it is presented reflect a passivity which is often present in Bukowski's work and is a part of its underlying appeal, perhaps all the more so in that what is often actually manipulative behavior masks itself under a "tough guy" stoicism.

The narrator describes himself as "following her on in" and her as "already trying to climb into a fire engine." But it is not quite as simple as that. The narrator has paused to think things over. By the time Jane tries to climb up into the fire engine he has had time to take in the situation and its implications. The use of "already" is a subtle piece of rhetoric designed to make the reader think that the narrator has been caught unawares and doesn't realize what is going on. He would like us to believe that before he has even had a chance to think about what is happening Jane is "already" out of control, "crazy." The proof of its rhetorical function is twofold. The earlier use of "crazy" in the proleptic sense that it must be taken to have undercuts the naive stance expressed in "already." If she is going "crazy" then he should not have been caught off-guard in the way that he would like us to believe that he has been. Second, in the context of the poem, is there a function for "already" other than a rhetorical one? I don't think so. Strictly speaking it is not necessary for the bare descriptive presentation Bukowski favors. Indeed, it is one of only three adverbs of time in a poem of one hundred and seventy-five lines. No, that "already" is too loaded. If Jane is "already" involving herself with the firemen then, we might say, the narrator "should have known better already."

At this point, with Jane "pulling her skirt up to her / waist, trying to jackknife up into the / seat," i.e., engaging in obviously provocative behavior, the narrator certainly has something to think about. With his knowledge of Jane it must be clear to him that the situation has become problematic. Two obvious alternatives for the narrator to the increasing probability of an unpleasant scene come to mind. The narrator can try to persuade Jane to leave or, if this fails or looks too hopeless to even attempt, he can leave by himself. He chooses neither of these alternatives. Nor does he choose to act as does Henry Chinaski in Bukowski's novel, ***Factotum,*** when he finds himself in a similar, if less extreme, situation. It is a passage worth quoting both for its relevance to the issue at hand and because it will also be referred to later in this essay.

About midway through that novel the relationship between Chinaski and his lover, Jan, with whom he has been living, has deteriorated significantly. As a result of Chinaski's lessening interest in her Jan would

> argue with me, get me enraged and then run out into the streets, the bars. All she had to do was to sit on a barstool alone and the drinks, the offers would follow. I didn't think that was fair of her, naturally . . . But I always let her go as I sat helpless in my chair and drank my whiskey and tuned in the radio to a bit of classical music. I knew she was out there, and I knew there would be somebody else. Yet I had to let it happen, I had to let events take their course.

One evening, though, "something just broke" in Chinaski and he decided to intervene. He goes out to look for Jan:

> I walked along past the bars and I knew she was in one of them. I made a guess, walked in, and there was Jan sitting at the far end of the bar. She had a green and white silk scarf spread across her lap. She was sitting between a thin man with a large wart on his nose, and another man who was a little humped mound of a thing wearing bifocals and dressed in an old black suit.
>
> Jan saw me coming. She lifted her head and even in the gloom of the bar she seemed to pale. I walked up behind her, standing near her stool. "I tried to make a woman out of you but you'll never be anything but a goddamned whore!" I back-handed her and knocked her off her stool. She fell flat on the floor and screamed. I picked up her drink and finished it. Then I slowly walked toward the exit. When I got there I turned. "Now, if there's anybody here . . . who doesn't *like* what I did . . . just say so."
>
> There was no response. I guess they liked what I just did. I walked back out on Alverado Street.

This is yet another possible reaction to such behavior on Jane's part but I think it is clear why he does not resort to this alternative at the fire house. The fire house, unlike the bar, is not populated by thin men and "little humped mound(s) of thing(s)." Had he struck Jane in the fire house the firemen would *not* have liked what he did and would have done something about it, we can assume.

Now the two alternatives that I proposed as rational are based on a premise that bears examination, the premise that it would be unpleasant for a man to witness his lover going off and engaging in sex with a fire station full of firemen. It would be something he would like to avoid, if possible. Is it correct to make this assumption with respect to the narrator of this poem? Not, I think, without some qualification. I do think that Jane's behavior is genuinely painful to the narrator. Although he does not say this in the poem, it is implied: the sarcastic reference to "*my* fireman" as well as the sarcasm in " 'naw, he don't think that. relax, you've got / class, real class' " etc. and the hostile act of pimping her to the firemen all suggest a discomfort at what is going on and various defenses against that discomfort. Indeed, the poem would lose a good deal of its power to involve at least the male reader if there were not this undertone of the aggrieved male bearing it all with a stiff upper lip that runs through the poem.

But there is gratification as well. It allows the narrator to feel confirmed in his low opinion of women. It also allows him to express his ambivalent feelings towards men. The homoerotic act of sharing his woman with other men expresses a mediated desire for them and, at the same time, by charging them money he is exploiting them as well and also establishing himself (in his own eyes) as their superior. This dichotomy of affection / hostility is mirrored in the card game where a solidarity / distance split may be noted. They play cards together but the players are presented as unequal, with the narrator far superior to the firemen in ability:

> they were bad players really.
> they didn't bother to memorize the
> deck. they didn't know whether the
> high numbers or low numbers were left. and ba-
> sically they hit too high,
> didn't hold low
> enough.

There is another parallel here to the situation that was referred to earlier in ***Factotum.*** In that episode we are told that one of the reasons that Jan went out to the bars was that she was being neglected by Chinaski. The reason for this neglect is not only that he is working and doesn't have as much time for her as when he was unemployed but that he has been very successful at the track. Not ony does he bet (and win) his own money but he and one other worker, take the money of many of their co-workers who cannot go to the track to bet it for them. But Chinaski and his friend do not bet this money. These other workers are such poor horseplayers that he knows that they won't pick the winning horse except on the rarest of occasions. So Chinaski, and his accomplice, pocket this money, paying off only on that rare occasion when one of these less-skilled players does happen to pick the right horse.

There are a number of similarities between this situation and the one presented in "fire station." First we have the Bukowski / Chinaski figure establishing his superiority, as card- or horseplayer, in the one instance to the firemen, in the other to his co-workers. Next we have a situation where he is expressing a preference for male companionship over that of his lover. Finally, we have an interesting correspondence between his victimizing his fellow workers and his victimizing Jane. In both instances he gains money—either directly from his victims (taking their money but not wagering it in ***Factotum***) or indirectly as when he exploits Jane (taking money from the firemen for her sexual services)—without his victims knowing that he is profiting at their expense. If one were to ask oneself what the function of this dynamic might be (acknowledging, of course, that in both instances he cannot reveal what he is doing because then he couldn't do it) one might say that by keeping what he is doing secret he, in some ways, does not really have to acknowledge to himself what he is doing. Of course he knows, but . . .

In general what all three of these actions (the establishment of his superiority over the other men, the preference for male companionship to that of his lover and the duplicity of his victimizing actions) reveal is a refusal to accept any kind of solidarity, equality or mutuality in relationships with others which, in its most extreme form, leads to his treating other people purely as a means to his own profit. This reaches an apex in his treatment of Jane in the poem.

After Jane has engaged in the badinage related in my exposition of the poem, the narrator washes his hands of her and engages some of the other firemen in a card game. If Jane's provocative behavior was an attempt to arouse a show of interest or expression of feeling on the part of her lover, it failed. His response of organizing a card game with the other firemen may even be construed by Jane as encouraging her to go off with "her" fireman although even then, she does not do so immediately but only after the narrator has resolutely confirmed his lack of interest:

> I had run my 43 cents up to a
> dollar ninety
> when I saw her going upstairs with
> *her* fireman.
>
> "he's gonna show me their sleeping
> quarters," she told
> me.
>
> "I understand," I told
> her.

It is not clear whether Jane, at this point, has consciously, or unconsciously for that matter, made a decision to have sex with the fireman. But whether she has or not she is protective enough of the narrator's feelings to put a smooth face on things. The narrator's "I understand" has, of course, more than one meaning as is the case with its use nine lines earlier. On one level it indicates a belief in the face value of the statements while on another it means that the narrator understands that what is really being communicated is, in the earlier instance the exact opposite of the literal message, i.e., that the fireman *do* gamble and, in this instance, that the fireman is going to do more than just *show* Jane their sleeping quarters. The statement is also a feeble attempt on the narrator's part to assert some kind of control over the situation. There is perhaps an implication that Jane is asking his permission (to do what? Go upstairs? None of this, of course is explicit) and that by his response he is allowing what takes place, to take place, that it is his decision and that if he responded differently she would not go upstairs with the fireman. And in fact we don't know that this isn't true. Whether such is really the case remains unknown because it remains untested. But because untested the possibility, especially in the narrator's mind, still exists.

Jane goes upstairs with the fireman and the narrator continues his card-playing with the other firemen. Then:

> when her fireman slid down the pole
> ten minutes later
> I nodded him
> over.
>
> "that'll be 5
> dollars."

Why does the narrator decide to charge the fireman money for having had sex with Jane? This seems to me the most striking action of the poem. While transient economic necessity may have had something to do with the narrator's action I don't think it can be seriously considered as its prime cause. Most immediately two reasons come to mind. First, by charging the fireman money he clears up any doubt he may have had as to what has taken place upstairs. If the fireman gives him the money then Jane has performed some form of sexual service for him. Second, it alters the relationship between him and Jane, in the eyes of the firemen. If he had *not* charged for her services he would have looked quite the fool in their eyes as a man who accepts his lover having sex with a firehouse full of firemen. By charging the firemen money and by saying " 'nice clean girl. I / ride it myself.' " he is attempting to make it appear that they are not lovers but only pimp and prostitute, thus managing to preserve something of his male pride.

However, we must look elsewhere for the deeper meaning of the narrator's action. The sociologist Georg Simmel wrote of prostitution [in his *On Individuality and Social Forms*] that

> Of all human relationships, it is perhaps the most significant case of the mutual reduction of two persons to the status of mere means . . . Certainly the nadir of human dignity is reached when what is most intimate and personal for a woman, that which should be given only on the basis of a genuine individual impulse and only when there is a comparable contribution from the man (even though it may have a different meaning for him), is offered for such thoroughly impersonal, externally objective remuneration.

When the narrator demands money for Jane's sexual services he completes his objectification of her in his own eyes, emphasized in the "it" of the lines just quoted as well as by his characterization of her in purely anatomical-physiological terms as "nothing but guts / and / ass." Jane is not, of course, a prostitute but the narrator feels compelled to make her one. (This is in sharp contrast to Henry Chinaski's view in the similar situation quoted earlier: "I tried to make a woman out of you but you'll never be anything but a goddamned whore!")

It should be noted that prostitutes do not play a large role in Bukowski's work. It may at times seem that they do because of the subjective comments of the Bukowski / Chinaski persona as, for example, when, in ***Factotum,*** Chinaski reflects with respect to himself and Jan:

> I couldn't understand why I didn't get rid of her. She was compulsively unfaithful—she'd go off with anyone she met in a bar, and the lower and dirtier he was the better she liked it. She was continually using our arguments to justify herself. I kept telling myself that all the women in the world weren't whores, just mine.

Relationships that are described at any length, or that last for any length of time are not with prostitutes and, of course, Jane is not here a prostitute. Rather, what attracts the narrator of "fire station" and Henry Chinaski in the novels and stories is making a prostitute (at least in his own eyes) out of a woman who in fact is not one. One reason might explain why this action appeals to such an individual. The low esteem in which such a person holds

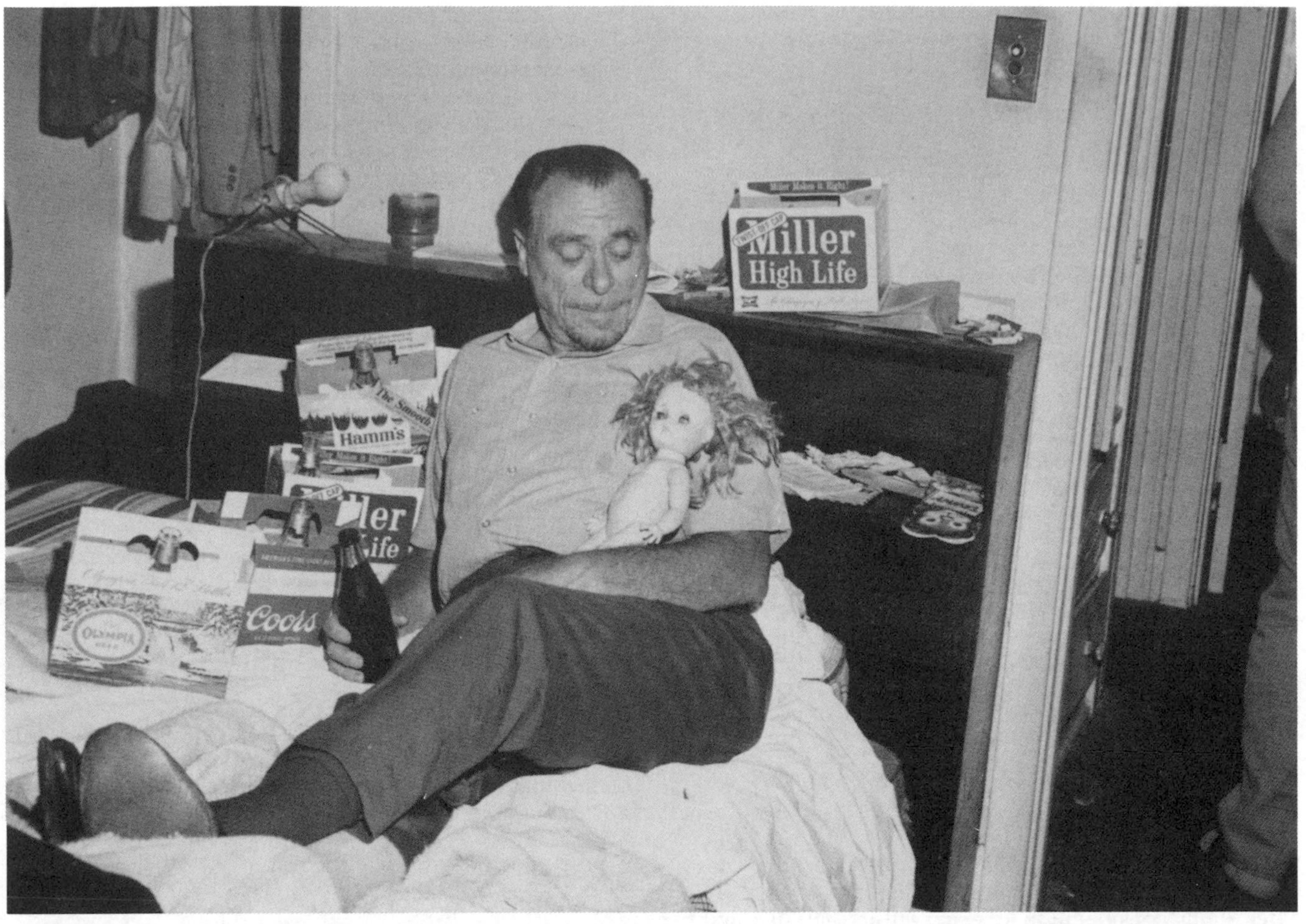

Bukowski relaxing at home, 1969.

women cannot really be confirmed by the fact that some women are prostitutes. This is unsatisfactory for two reasons. First it is a broad statement with little applicability to the immediacy of interpersonal relationships and second, it also means that some women are *not* prostitutes. What better way to confirm the fact that all women, really, are prostitutes than by making all the women with whom one gets involved prostitutes in the way that the narrator of the poem does? One might then ask why such an individual doesn't just patronize prostitutes and leave it at that. This, though, would only be confirming the fact that prostitutes are, in fact, prostitutes. It would not confirm his underlying view that all women are prostitutes.

Within the context of the poem there is another reason for the narrator's actions. It is important for him to be in control of the situation. If Jane were to charge for her services then that would be *her* choice. This would show an independence that the narrator would, I think, view as threatening. If he makes the decision he can still view himself as remaining in control.

I want to return briefly to an aspect of the poem noted earlier. This is the relationship of the narrator to the firemen and the conflict between solidarity and competition. Games are an ideal medium for this conflict in that a good deal of cooperation is necessary before one can have the competition. As mentioned, the narrator has a low opinion of the fireman's skills at Twenty-One but for all the narrator's exploitativeness there is also an atmosphere of camaraderie surrounding the card game. They chat, and the firemen, at least, do not appear at all antagonistic towards him. As in the last lines of the poem, "I walked over and got in a dart game with / Harry the Horse and the corner / newsboy" there is the feeling that the male companionship provides a relief from the emotional tension of the relationship with Jane. At the same time sharing Jane, for money, with the firemen is the perfect mechanism for gratifying that narrator's two-fold desire for friendship (the homoerotic aspect of the transaction) while at the same time objectifying the firemen (as well, of course, as Jane), making nameless consumers of them.

Walter Benjamin, in his essay "The Storyteller" [in *Illuminations*], wrote that:

> Actually, it is half the art of storytelling to keep a story free from explanation as one reproduces it . . . There is nothing that imprints a story more forcefully on one's memory than that chaste compactness which removes it from the realm of psychological analysis. And the more naturally the renunciation of psychological

> shadings is achieved by the storyteller, the greater will be its prospect of a place in the listener's memory . . .

A good part of the power of "fire station" and, indeed, part of its meaning is the author's eschewal of any analysis of the motives behind the character's actions. The uselessness of any such reflection is a basic credo of Bukowski, nowhere so charmingly expressed as in the passage in ***Factotum*** where Henry Chinaski and Jan have twice walked a mile downtown to the Los Angeles *Times* building to get a check that is owed Chinaski for two days' work. After a bureaucratic runaround he gains admission to the office of one of the higher-ups:

> I walked down to 309. The sign said "John Handler." I opened the door. Handler was alone. An officer and a director of the largest and most powerful newspaper in the West. I sat down in the chair across from him.
>
> "Well, John," I said, "they booted my ass, caught me asleep in the ladies' crapper. Me and my old lady have walked down here two days' running only to be told you don't have the check. Now, you know, that's pure crap. *All I want to do is get that check and get drunk. That may not sound noble but it's my choice.* If I don't get that check I'm not sure what I'll do."
>
> Then I gave him a look straight out of *Casablanca.* "Got a smoke?"

"fire station" is an intriguing poem and one of its most puzzling aspects is its dedication: "(For Jane, with love)." After slight consideration it seems clear that Bukowski does not mean this dedication in any way facetiously. If there is any irony it attaches to the word *love* and not to Jane. It is perhaps depressing, when viewed in this light, because what can Bukowski be saying other than this, that the relationship and behavior described in the poem is love. It seems a pessimistic view of life and relationships, in which people exist to exploit and be exploited, manipulate and be manipulated and it is apparently our fate to go from one such situation to another with explanations and analyses only so much wasted verbiage. Benjamin praised the achievement of removing a story from a limiting psychologism, and it is a tenet of Bukowski's writings that such analyses should be omitted. In the terms of Benjamin's essay he is a chronicler of the social microcosm rather than a historian who feels called on to explain the events he relates to us. The form of **"fire station"** aids in presenting this view of life. The laconicism underlines the cut and dried nature of the events. For the most part the lines are short, especially in the middle sections so that the poem moves along quickly imparting to the events it describes a certain inevitability. The short lines, lack of reflection and minimum of description result in one of the central "meanings" of the poem as a whole (aided, I think, by the dedication). This could be called understanding, or acceptance. Understanding not in the cynical sense meant by the narrator each time he says, " 'I understand,' " but in a deeper sense allied to the meaning of the dedication, understanding as acceptance and the foregoing of judgment. When I first read the poem I felt a certain sympathy with the narrator in his role of injured party, victim. Then, on closer examination it appeared that if anyone was victimized it was Jane although she doesn't feel or act victimized because she doesn't know what the narrator has done. While it is perhaps not the case in every instance that for a person to be victimized he must feel victimized I think it holds true here. Jane, after all, has presumably enjoyed, in one way or another, having had sex with the firemen. Although *they* have lost, collectively, a fair amount of money, and are at first somewhat taken aback by being made to pay for Jane's favors, still, *they* don't seem like victims either. After all, they've had an interesting afternoon in the otherwise dull routine of the fire house. Certainly it would be difficult, all in all, to see them being upset at the way the day has gone. They even respond to an alarm and so can feel that they are earning their pay. Perhaps, I thought to myself, it was the *reader* who had been victimized. And there's a certain amount of truth to this. His (hers would be a different story!) emotions and expectations are played with, aroused and then left hanging, unresolved in any simple way. Perhaps he even comes away slightly depressed. Ultimately, it is an ambiguous poem in terms of judgments so judgments are probably best left out of it. There are no victims, no crimes, no recriminations.

What there is, is a reconciliation inherent in the creation of the poem and reinforced by its dedication. It cannot be denied that that is not the most satisfactory of resolutions, nor, though, that it is one. (pp. 67-83)

Russell T. Harrison, "An Analysis of Charles Bukowski's 'Fire Station'," in Concerning Poetry, *Vol. 18, Nos. 1 & 2, 1985, pp. 67-83.*

James E. Nolan and L. John Cieslinski (review date February 1987)

[*In the excerpt below, Nolan and Cieslinski offer a favorable review of Bukowski's poetry collection* Relentless as the Tarantula.]

So many people try to be Bukowski, including Bukowski. Who needs them? The last thing we need is a cheap imitation. Prime Bukowski is the real thing and [in ***Relentless as the Tarantula***] he is relentless—as relentless as the tarantula—relentless as the death and taxes tarantella. The delivery is Whitmanesque but the punch is as staccato as Eliot Ness.

> . . . Somebody's going to
> drive by and
> spray your guts with a
> submachine gun.
>
> **("Relentless as the Tarantula")**

While Bukowski shoots straight from the hip, there is a unique whiff of something else in his gunsmoke. Filtering through these lines is a faint phobia that he might be on the brink of entering the establishment. He tries to recoil; he doesn't want to appear to be a sellout. He needn't worry as he has written himself into his own establishment. However, the irony is, he has no apparent difficulty with the masses becoming him. Charles Bukowski has the startling ability to snatch poetry from the reader. "John Crowe Ransom meets Red Chief."

Then he gets that nagging feeling that the words have abandoned him and there's nothing more for him to say. In **"For the Concerned"** Buke tells us he doesn't want to repeat—doesn't want to say old things. His desire is to move on. Well, what's keeping him? Could it be his readers' desire to hold him back, to keep a poet the same—for their own sake? His imitators may need a concrete target. He shouldn't worry.

Repetition is not a problem to Bukowski and most likely will never be. His keen ability for looking at life straight on keeps him fresh. His style easily accomodates all the phases of life. You don't need just a cock to write poems. You also need a cheap white port and a place to scab up.

But don't be put off by his crust. It's not meant to shut down. No rebuke. It's a brown paper bag bottle to share, the way bums share conversation. His work is so conversational you get through the whole thing before you realize you've read poetry. Prose poetry. Damned strong narrative.

> When I drive the freeways
> I see the soul of the
> humanity of my city and
> it's ugly, ugly, ugly:
> the living have choked
> the
> heart
> away
>
> **("a drive through hell")**

He hits life on the head with only a salty bit of self pity. While he juggles immortality, he pursues an examination of death. The stuff that lives on in "old age," after we're gone. It is still difficult to see our own death approaching, even when we are . . . "Gifted with the shortest journey." Is this some kind of last will and testament? The "Apologia Pro Vita Sua" of the "Carnal Old Man" meeting Cardinal Newman.

Is he a realist or a naturalist? Or does he straddle the line? Some of his poetry makes us a bit uncomfortable. But that gives him great pleasure. His only embarrassment is for other poets. Life goes on.

Don't worry about the Buk! He will type on no matter what—relentlessly—not stopping here.

James E. Nolan and L. John Cieslinski, "Prime Bukowski," in The Small Press Review, *Vol. 19, No. 2, February, 1987, p. 12.*

Molly Haskell (review date 11 June 1989)

[*Haskell is an American critic, nonfiction writer, and dramatist. In the following review, she deems Bukowski's novel* Hollywood *a "classic" depiction of the American film industry.*]

Charles Bukowski, West Coast poet and patron saint of drinking writers, or writing drinkers, author of the screenplay for the movie ***Barfly,*** has written a classic in the take-the-money-and-don't-run category of Hollywood fiction. This is the genre wherein Real Writers who have been seduced into screenwriting (than which nothing is more lowercase) live to tell all shamelessly.

The difference between Mr. Bukowski and other literary avengers is that he is neither a martyr nor a fallen angel. In ***Hollywood,*** he surveys the absurdities of the passing scene with the complicitous eye of a cast member in the theater of the grotesque, and has no delusions that he can fall any lower in life than a short drop off a barstool. Of course, the image of himself as a drunk who sleeps till noon and practices craft, not art, is itself a theatrical feint, the hipster's mask for his softness, the ballet dancer pretending to be a boxer, the writer cunningly demoting himself as someone who hits "the typer."

The basic motif of the novel consists of the endless wrangles and cons that characterize the making of a movie with a tiny budget, a movie that almost nobody wants to make and that almost nobody will pay to see. They couldn't have been any more operatic if the film had been a megastar superproduction like *Cleopatra.*

The lower the stakes, the more frenzied the power struggles . . . and the more often the word "genius" is thrown around. Chinaski, the drinking-gambling-typing persona that runs through Mr. Bukowski's writing, refuses to be impressed by hyped-up art house deities such as Wenner Zergog and Jon-Luc Modard. Need I say, this is fiction disguised thinly enough for even non-cinephiles to see through the pseudonyms.

The clipped phrases and deadpan style recall the hard-boiled affectations of literary drunkards such as Hemingway and Hammett. In Chinaski's presence, Jon-Luc, who has never said more than a sentence at a time, opens up. About him: "Jon-Luc was on a roll. I no longer understood what he was saying. I saw lips moving. He was not unpleasant, he was just there. He needed a shave. And. . . ." A haze of alcohol always descends in time to rescue Chinaski from having to listen too closely to what goes on below the surface of his own or other people's lives. It is also, one comes to realize, a protection from his own acute vision. Anyone who sees life this clearly needs something to cloud his lens.

Among the cast of characters are a couple of producers, Friedman and Fischman, who pay $2,000 for a full-page ad, with photo, to advertise themselves in *Variety,* while signing rubber checks. A canny and sympathetic director named Jon Pinchot (based on Barbet Schroeder, who directed ***Barfly***) writes a letter to the producers, threatening to cut off parts of his body if they renege on their agreement, signs it "love, Jon," then arrives at a contract-signing session with an electric chain saw. He plugs it in and, when the lawyer hesitates over a requested change, he holds the whirring blade over his pinkie finger. (The lawyer accedes.) Stars will surrender a good portion of their customary salary to work on a "serious" picture, but not their temperaments. Francine Bowers (a k a Faye Dunaway, one of the stars of ***Barfly***) demands a shot that will show her fabulous legs; Chinaski writes it in. Jack Bledsoe (a k a Mickey Rourke), playing the young

Chinaski, refuses to read his lines until just before going on camera; Chinaski shrugs his shoulders.

Money evaporates and the members of the Euro-trash "artiste" contingent sell off their vehicular assets (the motorcycles go first), then decamp from Marina del Rey and return to France. Later, when pennies miraculously rain down from the Hollywood heaven, they reappear and move into a ghetto in Venice, Calif.

"THIS IS A WAR ZONE!" says Jon Pinchot on the phone. "The police do not come in here, it's like a separate state with its own rules. I love it! You must visit us!" Bukowski-Chinaski, no stranger to mean streets and marginal neighborhoods himself, is nevertheless shocked by the pure hate emanating from the eyes of two black kids. In one brief, pungent paragraph, he conveys more of the bitter truth of race relations than all the verbiage spouted by sociologists and pundits on both sides of the divide:

> Poor blacks hated. Poor whites hated. It was only when blacks got money and whites got money that they mixed. Some whites loved blacks. Very few, if any, blacks loved whites. They were still getting even. Maybe they never would. In a capitalistic society the losers slaved for the winners and you have to have more losers than winners. What did I think? I knew politics would never solve it and there wasn't enough time left to get lucky.

Bukowski-Chinaski watches the filming of Jack Bledsoe-Mickey Rourke-Chinaski and feels pangs of envy and yearning for his younger self, yet the real hero is this 67-year-old man on the sidelines, whose brain and liver have survived 40 years of strenuous—if intermittent—alcoholism. He talks a tough game, but there's a wide streak of fellow feeling—for sagging, used-up women, for gamblers, for professionals. For the flotsam and jetsam. His wife, Sarah, is more than a supporting player: she gets her share of good lines and, as the one responsible for getting him off meat and hard liquor (thus adding 10 years to his life), comes off as an unlikely combination of drinking companion, drinking conscience, straight talker, muse and nursemaid.

Where women are concerned—and women, for him, are always a concern—***Hollywood*** shows Mr. Bukowski as a more sympathetic figure than in his earlier, no less fiendishly observant ***Post Office,*** a comic horror story about his 12-year stint as a mailman. Beneath the bravura appetite for female flesh that runs through the stories and poems is a fierce struggle: theirs to seize and capture his pure male essence, his to keep it and move on.

There are points of comparison with Norman Mailer, who enters ***Hollywood*** in a cameo role as Victor Norman, another "genius" on the dubious payroll of the confrères Friedman and Fischman, a tough-guy peer whom Chinaski admires as "one of the last defenders of maleness . . . in the U.S." Both Mr. Bukowski and Mr. Mailer are writers whose greatest achievement lies in the intelligence of their reporting, where, ironically, they give of themselves more freely than in their ostensibly more imaginative work. Both are writers who've made a fetish out of their masculinity, but the contrasts may be more striking than the similarities.

At one point, Chinaski is worried about the casting of Bledsoe, wants him to "stop that New York strut." "Jon," he says, "he can't be *New York.* This main character is a California boy. California boys are laid back, in the woodwork. They don't come rushing out, they cool it and figure their next move. Less panic. And under all this, they have the ability to kill. But they don't blow a lot of smoke first." Charles Bukowski might be describing the difference between Norman Mailer and himself.

Molly Haskell, "So Much Genius! So Little Money!" in The New York Times Book Review, *June 11, 1989, p. 11.*

Toby Moore (review date 11-17 August 1989)

[*In the following excerpt, Moore provides a descriptive review of Bukowski's novel* Hollywood.]

Hollywood intrigues writers. They treat it as part centre for commercial film production, part literary convention and, almost incidentally, as a suburb of Los Angeles. Charles Bukowski in ***Hollywood*** concentrates on the first, while C. K. Stead in *Sister Hollywood* studies the second. The physical place of preposterous stucco houses is, as always, taken for granted. Bukowski has created a raw, teasing fiction based on his experience of writing a screenplay for one of the "mini-major" film studios, Cannon.

[Bukowski] eschews all analysis, nearly all of ***Hollywood*** being composed of dialogue. But what emerges is a parable for the disappointment, dottiness, decadence and deceit that somehow end up on screen as an ordered three acts with set-up, confrontation and resolution. His is a thinly disguised account of the making of ***Barfly,*** which starred Mickey Rourke and Faye Dunaway.

The story begins when Bukowski, as Hank Chinaski, is asked by a visionary, struggling director, John Pinchot, to turn one of his own stories about drunken low-life into a screenplay, his first. Pinchot has to devote most of his time to hustling and intriguing in order to make the film. But that's Hollywood, a place where people spend years raising money and then, in a frenetic few weeks, build instant companies through advertisements in the *Hollywood Reporter,* with secretaries, directors of photography, grips and caterers, to create over a few months the ninety-minute dream. Bukowski depicts perfectly a business where your cheque is always in the post: the elation never lasts and rip-offs are standard practice.

Authenticity is important to Bukowski, who leaves unsent no signal to the reader or passing libel lawyers that his is *ciné vérité.* The novel is littered with walk-on parts by such as Francis Ford Lopolla, and often irrelevant swipes. One Tab Jones, a Las Vegas singer who churns and squirms before his female audiences is described in long, priapic detail. Even Norman Mailer, or Victor Norman, as Bukowski has him, is applauded gratuitously as "the last defender of maleness and balls in the US".

But what of screen heroes? "They usually were talentless,

eyeless, soulless, they were walking pieces of dung, but to the public they were god-like, beautiful and revered." The words often jar and Bukowski is better when he lets his dialogue do his griping for him. But this is still a superb snapshot of what filmmaking at the fag-end of the Hollywood dream is all about.

Bukowski would doubtless concur with Stead's fictional studio chief, Marvin Major, who, in a fit of unexpected honesty, explains the film-writer's life: "We treat you like dirt, ruin your best ideas, turn your characters into cardboard and sprinkle sugar over your dialogue—and what do you get from it? A fortune!"

Toby Moore, "Unreal City," in The Times Literary Supplement, *No. 4506, August 11-17, 1989, p. 877.*

Lois E. Nesbitt (review date 25 November 1990)

[*In the following review of* Septuagenarian Stew, *Nesbitt characterizes Bukowski as a writer "capable of surprising insights" yet "unwilling to push his language to produce something extraordinary."*]

Charles Bukowski loves to present himself as a crusty arrogant old man, proud of his years spent as a heavy-drinking bum, living the low life and thumbing his nose at the literary world and bourgeois society in general. In this regard, he shares company with William Burroughs, but while Mr. Burroughs specializes in weirdly vivid imagery and nearly hysterical satire, Mr. Bukowski's prose reflects bemused wonder at life's ongoing and all too familiar atrocities. In ***Septuagenarian Stew,*** his subjects are nearly always the same: drinking and womanizing; hanging out in bars, at the racetrack, in low-rent neighborhoods and low-down apartments; once in a while being recognized as the great writer fallen on hard times. Elsewhere, however, Mr. Bukowski's authorial persona, having come into some money from an indulgent publisher, rather relishes the good life he has so long eschewed. Aside from the rather harrowing story **"Son of Satan,"** in which a group of young toughs nearly succeeds in murdering a friend, most of the stories in this collection never get off the ground. Mr. Bukowski doesn't empathize with others—especially not with women—and the further characters stray from his own likeness, the flatter they become. His loosely constructed poems range from narratives forced into staggered lines to spare meditations leavened by a knowing wit. At best Mr. Bukowski comes across as a benign, somewhat bewildered spirit capable of surprising insights, at worst as a lazy writer unwilling to push his language to produce something extraordinary.

Lois E. Nesbitt, in a review of "Septuagenarian Stew: Stories & Poems," in The New York Times Book Review, *November 25, 1990, p. 19.*

Janis Helbert (review date November 1990)

[*In the following mixed review, Helbert implies that Bukowski's novel* Hollywood *lacks the "edge" of Bukowski's usual anger.*]

"I'm afraid of Hollywood," says Hank Chinaski in Charles Bukowski's latest novel ***Hollywood.***

He ought to be. The momentum of the Hollywood deal-making process contains a nastiness that dwarfs the personality of even the most powerful player. And Bukowski has made a career out of celebrating the small-time nastiness of his alter-ego and by-now-familiar character Chinaski.

Like Bukowski himself, Chinaski is a minor cult figure—a blowhard writer and self-proclaimed alcoholic well-acquainted with L.A.'s skidrow flophouses and their denizens. Bukowski's 1987 film ***Barfly*** was a semi-autobiographical tour of this world. The plot of ***Hollywood*** recounts the making of a movie that sounds virtually identical to ***Barfly.*** Chinaski is the picture's screenwriter.

In ***Hollywood*** Chinaski brags that in the past he's been a "really top-notch fuck-up." But now the "fuck-up" is cutting Hollywood deals and driving a Beemer. "We thought they were shit . . . and now we are," Chinaski's anachronistically compliant wife says as they shmooze at Musso Franks, the legendary Hollywood watering hole.

Selling out is probably the oldest—and therefore the most treacherous—theme in the history of the Hollywood novel. A modicum of success seems to have taken the edge off Bukowski's rage, and rage is generally what propels the best novels on selling out.

The most affecting moments in ***Hollywood*** are those that occur on a small scale. Chinaski runs from a barroom crowd of his biker fans, unable to respond to their need for an encounter with him. He wants to throw his arms around them "like some Dostoevsky," but "the world had somehow gone too far, and spontaneous kindness could never be so easy. It was something we would all have to work for once again" he thinks as he makes his exit.

One thing success hasn't blunted is Bukowski's brutal and unapologetic sexism. Chinaski aligns himself with those who have "no fear of the Feminists (sic). . . . the defenders of maleness and balls in the U.S." Don't look for Bukowski's aging crotch rocket to pop up in anybody's canon of the politically correct.

Janis Helbert, in a review of "Hollywood," in Western American Literature, *Vol. XXV, No. 3, November, 1990, p. 264.*

Stephen Kessler (review date October-November 1991)

[*In the essay below, Kessler defines Bukowski's major characteristics as a writer and provides a positive assessment of* The Roominghouse Madrigals, Hollywood, *and* Septuagenarian Stew.]

Whatever else you can say about Charles Bukowski, there's no denying his endurance. Revered by many as an anti-literary hero, reviled by others as an affront to decency, regarded by still others as an amusing but negligible underground eccentric, Bukowski at seventy continues to document his days and nights with a seemingly unstoppable flow of poems and stories that have firmly established him as a survivor in the international literary landscape. His informal, conversational, nasty yet crafty style as a poet has influenced, for better and worse, two or three generations of younger writers. The prose of his novels has grown clearer and sharper even as the tone has become kindlier. The sheer volume and diversity of his output—thirty-five books in thirty years—make him something of a poor man's answer to Joyce Carol Oates.

But Bukowski is poor no more. Sales of his books in the U.S. and abroad have long since turned him into a comfortable homeowner and BMW driver who commutes to the racetrack with classical music on the car stereo and drinks French wine instead of steering his wreck to dead-end jobs and guzzling cheap booze. And he keeps on, publishing three books in the last three years: ***The Roominghouse Madrigals,*** a selection of early poems previously uncollected or out-of-print; ***Hollywood,*** a novel based on his experiences with director Barbet Schroeder making the movie ***Barfly;*** and ***Septuagenarian Stew,*** an assortment of more recent stories and poems. As if to cap the author's successful arrival at venerability, Random House has just brought out Neeli Cherkovski's *Hank*—"the first biography written with Bukowski's full cooperation," says the flap copy—apparently signaling that New York's literary-industrial complex has finally acknowledged his importance.

We'll see about that. First it's worthwhile to consider just what it is that has earned this writer such a large and devoted readership. Initially emerging in the magazines of the mimeo explosion of the 1960s, Bukowski's poems revealed him as a rough and original voice aligned with none of the prevailing schools or movements, a voice whose dignity and clarity and humor were startlingly unique. His work seemed to show up everywhere, soon attracting wide attention throughout the underground grapevine. His evident ease of expression had been earned over four decades of difficulties that would have killed most people, or at least crushed the poetry out of them. Raised in Los Angeles in the 1920s and 1930s by a brutally abusive father and a meek German-immigrant mother, the young Henry Charles Bukowski, Jr., suffered social ostracism as a child, a hideous case of acne as an adolescent, and chronic alcoholism as an adult. He took various jobs, bummed around, drank continuously, went in and out of jails, trying meanwhile to write short stories and sending them unsuccessfully to magazines. In 1955 he was hospitalized with a bleeding ulcer. One of his doctors told him he was a dead man if he took another drink. When he got out he resumed drinking but he also started writing poetry. The latter somehow seems to have worked as an antidote to the former, and since the age of thirty-five, Bukowski has been steadily doing both.

In 1967 his weekly column "Notes of a Dirty Old Man" began appearing in *Open City,* a Los Angeles underground newspaper of the day, and later in the L.A. *Free Press.* While developing his prose style in the short form of the column, Bukowski was also vastly expanding his audience from the limited network of the little presses to the general if "alternative" readership. Independent publisher John Martin discovered him around the same time, and Martin's Black Sparrow Press began bringing out his books, which continue to be a mainstay of that operation. Profits from sales of Bukowski have helped keep alive one of the most reputable small publishers in the business, enabling Black Sparrow to bring into print the work of many less celebrated writers.

The tale of Bukowski's climb from the gutter to glamour would be almost romantic if not for the crummy details recorded along the way by the author's unflinching eye. Rather than portray himself as a hero in his autobiographical saga, Bukowski bares himself, scars and all, as an unsavory everyman who nevertheless notices a lot of what's going on around him and renders it in language anyone can understand. He is an antipoet obsessed with senselessness and cruelty and decay and death, yet also on the alert for tiny moments of redeeming joy that surface when you least expect them, "the click of miracle," when the sunlight falls on the jockeys' silks just so, or the cat looks at you in a certain way.

Even in ***The Roominghouse Madrigals,*** poems written during his hardest years, there is a lyric impulse in Bukowski's language that reaches through its misery for transcendence:

> sterile faces squeezed out from squalid tubes of
> bodies ream and blind me to any
> compromise.
> I would crawl down into the black volcanic gut
> of a
> chicken and
> hide hide hide.
> listen, I know you think I am bitter and
> maybe insane, well
> that's all right
> but find me a place . . .

In another poem entitled, **"I Don't Need a Bedsheet with Slits for Eyes to Kill You In,"** the poet declares in a vicious echo of Carl Sandburg tinged with shades of Faulkner:

> if the fog comes in like soft cleanser
> and you can see old men looking out at it
> from behind curtains
> these warm old men smoking pipes
> I will tell you stories to make your dreams
> easier;
> but if you mutilate me
> hang me alongside the scarecrow like a
> cheap Christ
> and let some schoolboy hang a sign about my
> throat
> I'm going to walk your streets of night
> with a knife . . .
> and when I decide finally that we will
> meet
> you will not understand
> because you did not want
> to
> and the flowers and the dogs and the
> cities and the children will not
> miss you.

These poems display the rage and agony of the outcast, or more accurately, as Cherkovski notes, the outsider, the self-exiled misfit who has assumed the role of loser with a mixture of resignation, dignity, irony, and defiance. It is the voice of the "lone nut," the ruined individual, the homeless person one can see any day on the streets of virtually every American city. But it is also an existential voice, speaking from beyond alienation, a voice affirming itself through the act of writing and thereby summoning the courage to carry on.

Not that the writer has any inside track on reality; as Bukowski informs us in another poem, writers

> . . . are the most sickening
> of all the louts!
> yellow-toothed, slump-shouldered,
> gutless, flea-bitten and
> obvious . . . in tinker-toy rooms
> with their flabby hearts
> they tell us
> what's wrong with the world—
> as if we didn't know that a cop's club
> can crack the head
> and that war is a dirtier game than
> marriage . . .

He doesn't exclude himself from this judgment, honestly assessing the vanity of trying to change the world with words. The most one can hope for is to talk back at bad luck, make it give a little, ease up on the pressure. At worst such bleak defeatism results in the blubbering bathos of the drunk, but Bukowski's tough-guy posture and comic self-awareness give him the strength to go on building, word by word, a cumulative body of evidence that he's anything but defeated.

In a story called **"Action"** in ***Septuagenarian Stew,*** he scans the patrons at the racetrack:

> Most of the people didn't look too happy. There were many Mexicans and blacks in the crowd, hoping to score, hoping to break their chains. They never would. They were only adding more links to their chains. The whites seemed most pitiful, flabby, with their deadly angry eyes. Most were male. One thing about the white male, though, he was wonderful material for the writer. You could write anything you wanted to write about the white American male and nobody ever protested. Not even the white American male. But if you write anything about any other race or class or gender the critics and the public became furious and your hate mail stacked up, although book sales didn't seem to drop off. When they hated you, they had to read you. They were aching to see what you would say next about their world. While the white American male didn't give a damn what you said about him because he ruled the world—at the moment, anyhow.

There's a complexity of perception at work here that encompasses both identification with these pitiful pale creatures and mockery of their predicament, both a humorous contempt for those who scream racism or sexism whenever they get the chance and an ironic gratitude for those critics' attention. The writer also shows a sly understanding of the tenuousness of the sociopolitical status quo.

Which is not to suggest that Bukowski is a political writer. It doesn't matter to him who rules the world or is run over by it; they're all fair game, nobody's innocent. As Cherkovski points out, he has consistently rejected the notion of the writer as social reformer or activist. Bukowski finds consolation for the common disappointments in a few reliable companions: the horses, classical music, the bottle, and the typewriter, a combination of elements that recur continuously, especially in the more recent work. As might be expected, this somewhat limited sphere of reference tends to dilute through repetition the power of some of his later collections. Still, frequently enough the vision crystallizes in a perfect poem or story. His goal as an artist is clearly not to make a flawless artifact but to document a life in all its contradictory ugliness and grace. Like Robinson Jeffers, another California recluse whom Cherkovski identifies as a forebear, Bukowski is not attempting to please the crowd. His words on Jeffers in ***Stew*** reflect an aspect of his own integrity:

> his voice was dark
> a rock-slab pronouncement
> a voice not distracted by
> the ordinary forces of
> greed, cunning and
> need
>
> he was on a hunt
> listening to life

In these later poems Bukowski's style is leaner, flatter, more linear, more narrative than in the ***Madrigals,*** but the flatness itself has a certain relentless force.

As age and prosperity have caught up with him, Bukowski has sweetened a little—evidently with help from his wife of the last several years, Linda Lee Beighle, who has improved his eating and drinking habits—and his work since the mid-1980s has assumed a warmer tone, dwelling as much on the everyday pleasures of his middle-class life in L.A.'s South Bay suburbs as on the nightmares of his urban past. He is obviously grateful for having survived all those earlier horrors, yet hasn't abandoned the crustiness of his outlook, combing his memory for revealing moments of illumination, relishing the routines of the present and invoking the friendship of the great dead in whose traditions he sees himself: Li Po, Celine, John Fante. In a poem called **"drunk with the Buddha,"** he writes:

> there is this small Buddha
> he
> sits on the desk
> across from me and he
> appears to be
> laughing at
> me.
>
> I attempt to read
> him: it seems as if he was saying:
> our limitations are our
> strengths.
> let
> everything else
> go.

This has been Bukowski's strategy from the beginning, cultivating his limitations and, even with his recent success, resisting the illusions of celebrity, refusing to play the role of the distinguished writer, opting instead for drunken solitary laughter.

And yet it is those famous illusions that are so entertainingly portrayed in the novel ***Hollywood.*** While it lacks the urgency, intensity, and anguish of his earlier novels—***Post Office*** (1971), ***Factotum*** (1975), ***Women*** (1978), and ***Ham on Rye*** (1982), all published by Black Sparrow—***Hollywood*** is an easygoing and bemused account of the author's adventures in the motion-picture business. It should be noted that Bukowski is a local writer in the best sense of the term, rooted in his Los Angeles turf and endlessly unearthing its indigenous reality without ever pretending to speak as a public voice. Throughout his works he has mapped the nervous energy of L.A.'s streets, its automotive obsessions, its architectural pathos, the truly mundane and unglamorous side of its media-warped facade. In ***Women,*** especially, one gets the sense of frenetic desperation that permeates the city. But because he grew up in Los Angeles and knows its people—its postal workers and skid-row winos and down-at-the-heels residents of shabby courts—his portrayal of the city and its inhabitants lacks the bitterness and contempt so often found in the writings of newcomers taking a fantasy-shattering peek into the dream factory.

In ***Hollywood*** Bukowski has a long look at the flashier side of L.A., its producers and directors and actors and other toilers and hustlers in the industry, and exercises a wise restraint in his judgments. After witnessing a tantrum by Jack Bledsoe, the young star of the film he has written, Bukowski's alter-author Henry Chinaski tries to make sense of the actor's behavior:

> I just decided that actors were different than we were. They had their own reasons for things. You know, when you spend many hours, many years pretending to be a person who you aren't, well, that can do something to you. It's hard enough just trying to be yourself. Think of trying very hard to be somebody that you're not. And then being somebody else that you're not. And then somebody else. At first, you know, it could be exciting. But after a while, after being dozens of other people, maybe it would be hard to remember who you were yourself, especially if you had to make up your own lines.

A younger Chinaski/Bukowski might have ripped into the pretense of the star mentality, shredding the veil of arrogance to show the vacancy and vanity that drives such deluded egos. Instead, he gently attempts to analyze the nature of the syndrome. This good-humored perspective on the follies of showbiz gives ***Hollywood*** a lightness of touch absent not only from most of his earlier writing but also from that of most other authors outraged and exasperated by their encounters with the film industry's trappings. Bukowski's no-fault vision of Hollywood is a genial complement to Nathanael West's horrific take in *The Day of the Locust* (1939, 1983) fifty years before.

Beyond being a book about the movies, ***Hollywood*** is, like ***Stew,*** a relaxed and confident account of the coming of age. It is a self-portrait of someone comfortable with his own durability yet constantly conscious of impending death. This sense of inevitable oblivion may be what gives the book its sweetness. The bite is gone, the writing is less exciting as the anguish has subsided, but there's an earned wisdom and self-assurance that show a fairly contented old fart telling his story for the pleasure of it. It is, after all, the only life he's got. (pp. 16-17)

Stephen Kessler, "Bukowski at Seventy: Talking Back," in The Bloomsbury Review, *Vol. 11, No. 7, October-November, 1991, pp. 16-17.*

Jules Smith (review date 18 December 1992)

[*Below, Smith offers a mixed appraisal of Bukowski's* The Last Night of the Earth Poems.]

After five decades of typing and more than forty books, ***The Last Night of the Earth Poems*** finds Charles Bukowski well into the twilight phase of gruff philosophizing, mainly about death and writing ("the words will never / truly come through for any of / us"). Though Bukowski has always exercised the freedom to write as much and whatever he likes, and each of his verse collections since the late 1970s has been bulky, this latest volume is his largest—the size of many a more cautious author's *Collected Poems.* As ever, many of the 160 poems within could be "improved" by judicious cutting, their characteristic proportions of redundancy, repetition and sentimentality more rigorously reduced. But, living out his subject-matters, his funny, relentless, desperate perspectives, Bukowski is simply not that fastidious. The stance remains open and inclusive, lineation a matter of chopped-up units, or "hard-driven" lines; ***The Last Night*** is occupied with the essentials, as he sees them, of writing and drinking and death.

Contemplating dying, his wife finding the body, his constant acts of remembrance are focused, aptly enough, on the Depression era; "all the households were under / siege but I believe that ours / held more terror than the average". He recalls watching Foreign Legion movies, the incessant local rains of those years, in a Los Angeles when there was no smog and "it was a short ride to the orange / groves", and one registers that Bukowski's customary elegizing of life as a continual process of loss has strayed into nostalgia. Hard times are again dusted off anecdotally, half-starving in New Orleans rooming-houses, trying to be a writer, unloading boxcars of frozen fish (**"A good job"**), or failing to sell Christmas trees outside a bar (**"No sale"**). He revisits rapacious landladies, cowed fellow-workers, loose women, his parents and others "long gone along the way".

Bukowski habitually praises those figures—here, Jack London, e.e. cummings, even Aldous Huxley—whose works provided youthful diversion from the bars. Sometimes he counterpoints his tributes with a debunking, man-in-the-street view of the pretensions of high art and artists. **"Them and Us"** imagines Hemingway, Faulkner, Pound, "Wally" Stevens and other Modernist titans out on the front porch of the Bukowski family home, arguing, with dismissive interjections by his parents: " 'they are talking garbage', said my / father, 'they ought to get / jobs' . . . 'and he', my father pointed to me, / 'wants to be like them!' ".

Those pieces not in reminiscent or fictive modes affect an intimacy with readers and a frankness about himself ("I / no longer / read / I / no longer / breed", he informs us) and his current situation as a successful author. The bartender at a fashionable restaurant remembers him when he was in rags, and Bukowski facetiously worries that the acquisition of a word-processor will finish him, "where booze and women and poverty / have not". Bukowski's septuagenarian existence has mellowed down to typing and drinking wine while listening to classical music, the company of his wife and cats, and going to the racetrack, aware that he is running out of days.

This latter realization has been implicit in all his best work, but it also results in a degree of portentousness at times, the wished-for significance of terminal connotations—as in the book's title—falling into banality. Bukowski's world-view remains uncompromisingly negative, even apocalyptic; relishing the potential destruction of Los Angeles by earthquake, pollution, or drought, but cursing the car-jams on the freeways. Contemporary Californians, the people encountered in movie theatres, as racetrack hangers-on or unwelcome telephone callers, are equally scorned. In a riposte to Carl Sandburg, "it is The People, No / then and now".

Bukowski has indeed shown an ungodly durability, an almost heroic perseverance and strength of purpose. A rigorously edited *Selected Poems* would reveal his achievement. Perhaps it is inevitable that a life-centred author ends up by being fixated on death. He may be waiting for extinction, but there is likely to be a great deal more Bukowskiana to come from the Black Sparrow Press. As it did for Hemingway, writing has become Bukowski's greatest vice and greatest pleasure, and only death can stop it.

Jules Smith, "Bad Times Again," in The Times Literary Supplement, *No. 4681, December 18, 1992, p. 19.*

FURTHER READING

Bibliography

Dorbin, Sanford. *A Bibliography of Charles Bukowski.* Los Angeles: Black Sparrow Press, 1969, 93 p.

Partially annotated primary and secondary bibliography through 1968.

Fox, Hugh. *Charles Bukowski: A Critical and Bibliographical Study.* Somerville, Mass.: ABYSS Publications, 1969, 121 p.

Contains a primary bibliography listing Bukowski's stories, poems, reviews, and interviews from 1944 to 1968.

Biography

Cherkovski, Neeli. *Hank: The Life of Charles Bukowski.* New York: Random House, 1991, 335 p.

Detailed biography of Bukowski.

Criticism

Byrne, Jack. "Bukowski's Chinaski: Playing Post Office." *The Review of Contemporary Fiction* 5, No. 3 (Fall 1985): 43-51.

Surveys critical reaction to Bukowski's work, addressing the thin division between the author and his character Chinaski in *Post Office.*

Review of *Crucifix in a Deathhand: New Poems, 1963-1965,* by Charles Bukowski. *The Carleton Miscellany* VI, No. 4 (Fall 1965): 92-3.

Praises Bukowski's "absolute lack of self-pity" and "almost terrifying honesty."

Conroy, Jack. "A Skidrow Poet." *The American Book Collector* XVI, No. 6 (February 1966): 5.

Favorable assessment of Bukowski's collections *Crucifix in a Deathhand* and *Cold Dogs in the Courtyard.*

Glover, David. "A Day at the Races: Gambling and Luck in Bukowski's Fiction." *The Review of Contemporary Fiction* 5, No. 3 (Fall 1985): 32-3.

Contends that in his fiction Bukowski makes use of gambling and the variability of luck to "structure and direct a narrative, creating dilemmas and turning points, shifting the story along by quite literally changing tracks."

Kessler, Stephen. "Notes on a Dirty Old Man." *The Review of Contemporary Fiction* 5, No. 3 (Fall 1985): 60-3.

Detects a "compassionate tenderness" in Bukowski's personality and writing that vindicates distasteful aspects of his work.

Locklin, Gerald. "Setting Free the Buk." *The Review of Contemporary Fiction* 5, No. 3 (Fall 1985): 27-31.

Asserts that Bukowski's uniqueness as a writer stems from his sense of improvisational freedom.

McGonigle, Thomas. "A Bottle Stain." *The Review of Contemporary Fiction* 5, No. 3 (Fall 1985): 37-8.

Applauds Bukowski's willingness to address unconventional subjects and briefly explores Bukowski's short story "The Copulating Mermaid of Venice, Calif.," in which two drunks kidnap and have sex with the corpse of a beautiful woman.

Peterman, Michael. "Yawping across the Border." *Essays on Canadian Writing,* No. 33 (Fall 1986): 181-84.

Mixed appraisal of Bukowski's correspondence with Canadian poet Al Purdy in *The Bukowski/Purdy Letters, 1964-74: A Decade of Dialogue.*

Sherman, Jory. *Bukowski: Friendship, Fame & Bestial Myth.* Augusta, Ga.: Blue Horse Publications, 1981, 38 p.

Incorporates letters from Bukowski to novelist Sherman, a reminiscence of their acquaintance by Sherman, several photographs, and Bukowski's "Notes of a Dirty Old Man: A Story."

Walker, Susan. Review of *The Bukowski/Purdy Letters, 1964-1974,* ed. Seamus Cooney. *Quill and Quire* 50, No. 5 (May 1984): 34-5.

Favorable review of Bukowski's and Purdy's correspondence.

Weinstein, Norman. "*South of No North:* Bukowski in Deadly Ernest." *The Review of Contemporary Fiction* 5, No. 3 (Fall 1985): 52-5.

Discusses the influence of Ernest Hemingway on Bukowski's 1973 short fiction collection.

Additional coverage of Bukowski's life and career is contained in the following sources published by Gale Research: *Contemporary Authors,* Vols. 17-20, rev. ed.; *Contemporary Authors New Revision Series,* Vol. 40; *Contemporary Literary Criticism,* Vols. 2, 5, 9, 41; *Dictionary of Literary Biography,* Vols. 5, 130; and *Major 20th-Century Writers.*

Paul Celan

1920-1970

(Born Paul Antschel) Romanian-born German poet, essayist, and translator.

This entry presents coverage of Celan's works from 1973 through 1991. For further information on the author's career, see *CLC,* Volumes 10, 19, and 53.

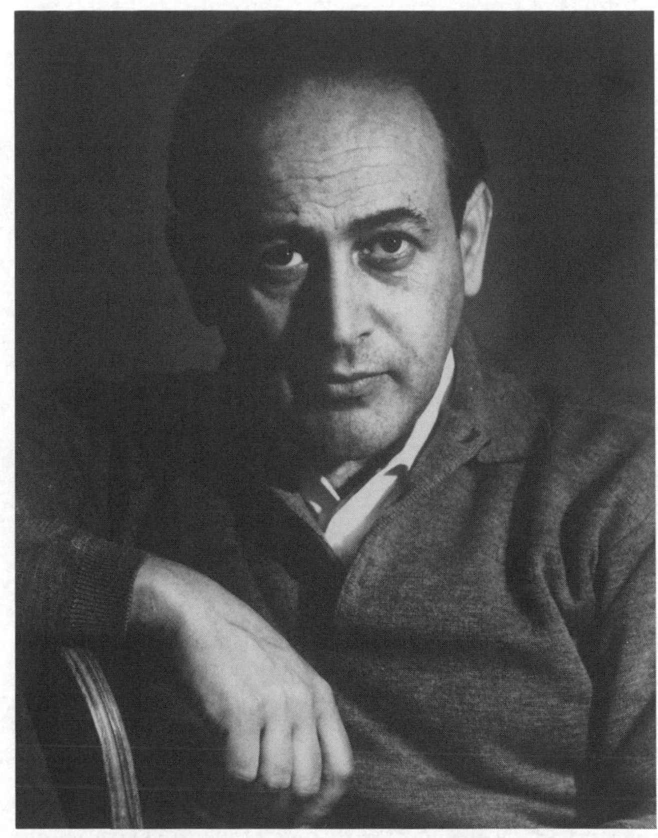

INTRODUCTION

Celan is regarded as among the most important poets to emerge from Europe after World War II and, with Rainer Maria Rilke, is widely considered the finest German lyric poet of the twentieth century. Often described as obscure and hermetic, his inventive poetry reveals the influences of symbolism, expressionism, surrealism, and Hasidic mysticism, and addresses serious historical and theological themes—the most prominent of which is the suffering associated with the Jewish experience of the Nazi Holocaust. Rika Lesser commented: "Celan's language—peculiar, idiosyncratic, transformational, at times almost incomprehensible—seems the only one capable of absorbing and expressing a world changed by the Holocaust. His language and poetry issue from the urgent need to communicate, to speak the truth that lies in deeply ambiguous metaphors."

Celan was born in Czernovitz, the capital of the Romanian province of Bukovina, to German-speaking Jewish parents. As a youth, he became proficient in several languages, including Hebrew and French. After beginning premedical studies in France, Celan returned home prior to the outbreak of World War II and witnessed the Soviet occupation of his hometown. His parents were captured and killed following the German invasion of Czernovitz in 1941, and Celan himself was interned for eighteen months in a Nazi labor camp. The anguish and grief Celan experienced during this period informed his verse throughout his career. In 1944, for example, he wrote "Todesfuge" ("Death Fugue"), a lyric piece which has been lauded by some critics as one of the most powerful holocaust poems ever written. Celan left Czernovitz in 1945 for Bucharest, where he joined a circle of surrealist artists, befriended leading Romanian writers, and worked as a reader and translator for a publishing house. Following a brief period in Vienna, where he associated with a group of avant garde artists, Celan settled in Paris and began studies in German philology and literature. He received his *Licence des Lettres* in 1950, and in 1952 he married the graphic artist Gisèle de Lestrange, with whom he had a son in 1955. In 1959 Celan became a professor of German Language and Literature at L'École Normale Superieure, a position he held until his death. Celan committed suicide in 1970 by drowning himself in the Seine River.

Characterized by such lyric elements as rhythmical repetition and surrealistic imagery, Celan's first two poetry collections, *Der Sand aus den Urnen* and *Mohn und Gedächtnis,* combine paradox, negation, and intricate word association to convey the psychological trauma suffered by survivors of Nazi atrocities. With his next volume, *Von Schwelle zu Schwelle,* Celan became increasingly concerned with the nature of poetic language—a theme which distinguished his poetry throughout his career. In *Sprachgitter,* for example, he employed ruptured syntax, unusual diction, enigmatic imagery, and condensed lines to address the inability of language to genuinely convey profound misery. The persecution and suffering that Jews have endured throughout history is the subject of *Die Niemandsrose,* which presents a negative theology derived from Jewish and Christian mysticism. The longer lines and rhyme in this collection are reminiscent of the comparatively traditional style of his early volume *Mohn und Gedächtnis.* In *Atemwende* Celan turned from Jewish subject matter to focus again on the nature of poetic language. His last three volumes, *Fadensonnen, Lichtzwang,* and *Schneepart,* are progressively cryptic and fragmented, evincing a technique some critics interpreted as reflecting the poet's search for new ways to express the ineffable horrors of the

Holocaust. Many of Celan's poems have been translated and published in such collections as *Selected Poems, Poems of Paul Celan,* and *Last Poems.*

In his prose writings, Celan elaborated upon his aesthetic and poetic theories. For example, *Edgar Jené und der Traum vom Traume,* ostensibly a study of the surrealist paintings of Edgar Jené, develops into an investigation of what Celan termed the "deep sea" of the writer's consciousness, the psychological realm where poetry originates. In the essay "Gespräch im Gebirg" ("Conversation in the Mountains"), Celan engages in an imaginary dialogue with philosopher Theodor Adorno about such topics as language, nature, perception, and God. In "Der Meridian" ("The Meridian"), his acceptance speech for the 1960 Georg Büchner Prize which is constructed as a dialogue with his audience, Celan describes poetry as the process of freeing oneself by searching for a utopia. Celan's translated essays and speeches were published in *Collected Prose.* In addition to his poetry and nonfiction, Celan translated into German the work of such writers as Arthur Rimbaud, Osip Mandelstam, and William Shakespeare.

Celan has been praised by many critics for virtually inventing a new poetic language to describe an unspeakable episode in history. The difficulty of interpreting and translating his cryptic poetry has been the subject of extensive discussion, with many critics concluding that the obscurity of his verse is a necessary product of its mysticism and varied literary, theological, and linguistic allusions. Commenting on *Last Poems,* Reginald Gibbons stated: "[These poems] are not joyful, nor erotic, nor often textured with either the reality of the physical world or that of social relations or politics; they are therefore not very 'accessible.' . . . They offer not a revelation of their meaning but rather a containment of it—as if protecting it." Some critics, however, have disputed the critical emphasis on the esoteric nature of Celan's poetry, arguing that his writings are informed by social and historical reality rather than personal concerns. J. M. Cameron, for example, commented: "From the collection *Die Niemandsrose* to his death in 1970 Celan's poetry becomes more fragmentary and obscure. It is often sharply beautiful, but it has seemed to some critics to have sense only in relation to a private world. . . . [Celan's obscurity] is rather the sign of an attempt to work into his poetry, in his own idiom, material that belongs to the harsh public world. He is not—he protested he was not—a hermetic poet."

PRINCIPAL WORKS

Der Sand aus den Urnen (poetry) 1948
Edgar Jené und der Traum vom Traume (essays) 1948
[*Edgar Jené and the Dream about the Dream* published in *Collected Prose,* 1987]
Mohn und Gedächtnis (poetry) 1952
Von Schwelle zu Schwelle (poetry) 1955
Gedichte: Eine Auswahl (poetry) 1959
Sprachgitter (poetry) 1959
Der meridian: Rede anläßlich der Verleihung des Georg-Büchner-Preises, Darmstadt, am 22. Oktober 1960 (essay) 1961
["The Meridian" published in *Paul Celan: Prose Writings and Selected Poems,* 1977 and *Collected Prose,* 1987]
Die Niemandsrose (poetry) 1963
Gedichte (poetry) 1966
Atemwende (poetry) 1967
Ausgewählte Gedichte: Zwei Reden (poetry) 1968
Fadensonnen (poetry) 1968
Ausgewählte Gedichte (poetry) 1970
Lichtzwang (poetry) 1970
Schneepart (poetry) 1971
Speech-grille, and Selected Poems (poetry) 1971
Nineteen Poems (poetry) 1972
Selected Poems (poetry) 1972
Gedichte: In zwei Bänden. 2 vols. (poetry) 1975
Zeitgehöft: Späte Gedichte aus dem Nachlaß (poetry) 1976
Paul Celan: Prose Writings and Selected Poems (prose and poetry) 1977
Paul Celan: Poems (poetry) 1980; also published as *Poems of Paul Celan* [revised and enlarged edition], 1988
Gesammelte Werke in fünf Bänden. 5 vols. (poetry) 1983
Todesfuge (poetry) 1984
Gedichte: 1938–1944 (poetry) 1985
65 Poems (poetry) 1985
Last Poems (poetry) 1986
Collected Prose (essays and dialogues) 1987
Das Frühwerk (poetry) 1987

CRITICISM

Hugo Huppert (essay date 26 December 1973)

[*In the following essay, which is based on an interview conducted with Celan in 1966 and first published in German in 1973, Celan discusses the "abstract" qualities of his verse and the concept of "concrete poetry." Huppert concludes with comments on Celan's last poems and his suicide.*]

I had known my friend Paul Celan for some twenty years—since Vienna in 1947—when I visited him on December 26, 1966 in his next-to-last Parisian dwelling, 78 Rue de Longchamp. His book of poems ***Breath-Turning (Atemwende)*** had just been published in a deluxe edition together with a selection of crystalloid color illustrations by his wife, Gisèle Lestrange. Perhaps because German-speaking visitors were seldom in his cold and spacious roof-apartment, Celan greeted me with an excited request to read a few of the ethereally de-materialized texts from that book, mouthing silently the words as I read them out loud. "Indescribably abstract," I told him, "imponderably spiritual," and could not hide my inner agitation about certain mental turns in the intermittently gentle and musical passages of this lyric expression. Celan responded, "I am glad that you say 'abstract'; and 'spiritual' is also fitting. Perhaps you are, like myself, no supporter of the 'socialization' of one's inner life. I hope that the information in my verse is spiritual. Formerly, in Vienna, I experimented with psychic mediums of communication. I was playing hide and seek behind the metaphors. Today, after twenty years of conflict between inner and outer worlds, I have banished the word 'like' from my workshop. One of my poems, **'Speech-Grille,'** became the title of an entire collection of poems. Do you know what a 'grille' can be? In that book I used, for a nearly final time, 'like' in the following four lines:

> Were I like you. Were you like me.
> Did we not stand
> under *one* tradewind?
> We are strangers.

That was my farewell to the treacherous 'like.' I stand at another point in time and space than my reader—who can only understand me 'from afar,' cannot get hold of me, can only grasp the grille bars between us:

> Flickering monad eyelid
> oars upwards
> lets a glance go
> (releases a glance)

So goes my text. And this 'glance, released' through bars, this 'distant understanding' is already forgiving, already beneficial: a reconciliation, perhaps a hope. No one is 'like' another; that's why one should try to see the other, even if it's through a grille. This seeing is my 'spiritual' poetry, if you wish."

"And how do you explain your abstract expression?" I asked.

"This follows a similar track. My abstraction is a processed freedom of expression. The rehabilitation of the word. Are you familiar with 'concrete poetry?' It's an international phenomena; but neither concrete nor poetry. A narrow-minded misuse of language. A sin against the word. As long as this mischief is called concrete, I will call myself abstract, even if I very well know that, in a phenomenological sense, I have next to nothing in common with abstract art in the sense of 'l'art pour l'art.' "

While preparing a small tea-snack, Celan confided that his apartment was very difficult to heat, that his wife and little son had gone south to the Mediterranean for the cold weeks. Then he showed me his wife's atelier, filled with various apparatus for the reproduction of steel engravings, etchings and lithographs. "I am very impressed, and influenced, by the intellectual precision of this—what I would call the French—style of engraving," Celan began; "it too is only outwardly abstract; its crystallographic features are formulas made visible—sensual, vital, instructive nonetheless, like Dürer's woodcuts, but also no less deceiving, conflicting and ambivalent than those. Rational control has yielded plenty of room to trial and error here. I am for comprehensibility; but these dissected printing plates, called 'clichés' in French, cannot be typecast. . . . "

"The fine and keen-edged outlines of Madame Lestrange," I added, "seem to be in opposition to your (own) language cipherings, Herr Celan."

"That is a question of special techniques, rules of style and production. I do not work with graving tools, even in the figurative sense of the word. I also no longer play music, as I did in the days of the notorious **"Death Fugue"**—a poem so thrashed about that it's now ripe for anthologies. Now I make an important distinction between music and lyric poetry. I feel closer to drawing today; in the same vein, I use more shadows than Gisèle, I intentionally darken curves for the sake of nuance in truth, faithful to my own kind of spiritual realism. As for my so-called ciphering, I would use another description: ambiguity without masks, exactly corresponding to my sensitivity to overlapping terms and relationships. You probably know about (the appearance of) interference, the affects of coherent waves colliding with each other. You know about the dialectic of progression and reversal—transference to adjacents, to successions, even into opposites. This corresponds, at certain points of pivot and conjunction, to my own use of ambiguities. It also accounts for the computation of every object's edges, its 'polished sections,' the multitude of angles from which it can display itself and be observed, the 'breaks' and 'fractures' which are far more than just mere 'appearances.' I attempt to, at least linguistically, render sections from the spectral analysis of things, to show them in many aspects and permutations simultaneously: their relations, sequences and oppositions. Unfortunately I am unable to observe objects from *all* sides.

"I remain basically sensory in my approach, never pretending to be 'extra-sensory' . . . which would be against my nature, a pose. I refuse to consider the poet as prophet, as 'oracle,' visionary or fortune-teller. In this I hope you see clearly why I consider my so-called abstraction and my actual ambiguity to be moments of realism. As for the inflated 'concrete poetry,' I see it as nothing but charlatanism, senseless imposture. We should not overrate such stammering and stuttering, nor project into it (nonexistent) values. . . . A language that no one *speaks* is anti-poetic. I reject all prophecies."

. . . . .

One and a half years later, a large audience in an overcrowded room in Vienna's Palais Paffy waited through a long delay to learn that Paul Celan had canceled, at the last moment and without apparent explanation, his reading tour of Austria. I was among the people who went home disappointed that evening. That disparaging gesture by the resigned poet of ***The No-man's Rose*** **(*Die Niemandsrose*)** seemed to me a distant alarm signal, the warning of an elevated spirit's imminent destruction. I wrote to him, announced a pending visit and received no answer. He had changed domiciles in Paris. On the next-to-final day of April 1970, he chose to end his life in the waters of the Seine.

> We were
> hands,

we baled the darkness empty, we found
the word that ascended summer:
flower.

Flower—a blind man's word.
Your eye and mine:
they see
to water.

Never had a person's silence prompted a more imponderable muteness inside of me. It was madness, like a narrow mountain pass, with no way out. This poet was not even 50 years old. Once he had told me, "my blood group is O, the same as primitives and monsters. I'm a neither-nor." In late Spring of that year, I read some of his final poems, among them these lines:

Contact-Mines on your left
moons, Saturn.

Sealed against shards
the orbits out there.

Now is the hour
for a righteous
birth.

And:

The self-transfigured
guns
ascend to heaven,

ten
bombers yawn,

a quick-firing flowers,
certain as peace

a handful of rice
expires as your friend.
("For a Brother in Asia")

And then the following indelible words of total darkness:

Laden with reflection, with
the sky-beetles,
inside the mountain.

The death
you still owe me, I
carry it
out.

In December of 1971, during a Nekrassov Festival in Leningrad, a Russian literature researcher and Celan expert said to me, in a sober tone devoid of any mourning: "You must recognize and accept the fact that this poet was an incurable schizophrenic. But what does that mean? Beethoven was also probably schizophrenic in his last years. Apparently Kleist as well. And most certainly Strindberg. Does that say enough?" (pp. 160-62)

Hugo Huppert, "'In the Prayer-Mill's Rattling': A Visit with Paul Celan," edited by Benjamin Hollander, in Acts: A Journal of New Writing, *1988, Nos. 8-9, pp. 156-62.*

Reginald Gibbons (review date Fall 1986)

[Gibbons is an American poet, critic, and translator. Below, he offers a positive assessment of Last Poems.]

Most of the poems in Paul Celan's ***Last Poems*** have been translated into English for the first time, from his last three [collections, ***Fadensonnen, Lichtzwang,*** and ***Schneepart***]. But the greatest service this volume performs is in providing American readers with the facing German, for no translation of Celan is complete without the original poem because of the layered significance of his many plays on words. "Play" is an inappropriate metaphor for Celan's anguished utterances, which seem to have been wrung from him, by his own hand but against his own will. Faced with the impossible simplifications and imprecise interpretations that Celan's poems force on his translators, [Katharine] Washburn and [Margret] Guillemin have done a good job of conveying something of this difficult work. . . . Perhaps going any further with the translations seemed impossible, but it would have been a help to have had at least a few footnotes to the allusions and references in the poems.

Celan was Jewish; he grew up multilingual in Romania; his parents were shot by the S.S. and he survived the laboring to which he was condemned by the Germans, only to leave Romania for Paris when the Russian occupiers replaced the German. As Katharine Washburn writes in her introduction to this collection, "perhaps the most coherent narrative of those [wartime] years lies in his poetry, in the constellation of images around debris, barges, stone, rock, darkness, snow, and minerals." What is astonishing—and at the heart of all his work as a kind of essential riddle with a complex, weighty answer—is that he chose, of all languages, German for his poetry.

Celan—he chose to publish under a name formed as an anagram of his family name, Ancel—translated Mandelstam; he filled his work with the kinds of polysemous resonances that a multilingual poet can summon more easily than one bound to one language. He lived in Paris till he killed himself in 1970.

This is not a volume with which to make one's first acquaintance with Celan's poetry; any reader who does not speak German fluently must look at every available translation of Celan, and Michael Hamburger's ***Celan: Poems*** (1980) is a good place to start. After prior acquaintance with Celan's work, which is to say after a warning about the tortured density of his poems, this book too is fascinating. As Washburn's introduction also points out, these last poems before Celan's suicide in 1970 use his familiar vocabulary of simple words at the heart of his poetry: "eyes," "stone," "star," "leaf," "mouth," "snow" and others.

The instructive thing for American readers might be how intensely charged such words are in Celan's poems. It's one of the American poetic manners, since the 1970's or earlier, to make a kind of would-be mystical use of words like these, and the result has often been—and continues often to be—a tone of wan sensitivity bordering on self-pity. But Celan's poems are much fiercer, as they simultaneously attack the deadening inertia of silence in the face of dread and sorrow, and yet utilize the silence around the poem—around the individual words, it sometimes seems—to make those words seem larger than usual, resonant, echoing, each one a riddle and poem itself. Here are two complete (untitled) poems (most of the poems are brief; the capital letters are Celan's, not the typesetter's, device):

IN DIE NACHT GEGANGEN, helferisch,
ein stern-
durchlässiges Blatt
statt des Mundes:

es bleibt
noch etwas wild zu vertun,
bäumlings.

GONE INTO THE NIGHT, complicit,
a star-
porous leaf
for a mouth:

something remains
for wild wasting,
treeward.

WURFSCHEIBE, mit
Vorgesichten besternt,

wurf dich
aus dir hinaus.

DISCUS,
starred with premonitions,

throw yourself

out of yourself.

These poems are never likely to have many readers in America. They are not joyful, nor erotic, nor often textured with either the reality of the physical world or that of social relations or politics; they are therefore not very "accessible." They are a kind of residue—hard, blackened perhaps, or sometimes ash-white, or as brilliant as gemstones. They offer not a revelation of their meaning but rather a containment of it—as if protecting it. And in some sense such poems do make a protective gesture over the irreducible residue of spirit and memory that can be seen in a refusal to speak, and in an insistence on speaking only enough, only just so, only a certain difficult way—while the language of daily life (including not only casualness of speech but also deceit of all sorts) rushes onward in a tide of noise and printed paper.

But there is no mystification or false depth here; the poems have a convincing authority, perhaps of the kind partly validated by the author's suicide. (Read Theodore Weiss's poem, on someone else, called "The Last Letters.") They are a kind of tonic—a bitter refreshment of language, even in translation. (pp. 172-74)

Reginald Gibbons, in a review of "Last Poems," in TriQuarterly *67, Fall, 1986, pp. 172-76.*

David Young (review date Winter 1987)

[*In the following excerpt, Young questions the value of Celan's poetry but nevertheless concludes that* Last Poems *"deserves a wide readership."*]

Paul Celan, whose last name was an anagram of his given name, Ancel, grew up in Czernowitz, the capital of Rumanian Bukovina, in an Orthodox Jewish family. His parents perished under the Nazis, but he somehow escaped, possibly by switching from a line headed for extermination to one headed for hard labor. The death of his parents and, perhaps, the death of whoever was killed in his place, marked him with a lifelong sense of guilt and melancholy. By the time he killed himself in 1970, by drowning in the Seine, he had produced a body of poetry that continues to intrigue readers and commentators by its dense, elusive, and experimental character. Celan insisted that he was not a hermetic poet, but by most understandings of the term he was precisely that: cryptic, minimalist, ingrown.

Translation of Celan, who placed enormous demands on individual words and syllables, fashioning elaborate puns and exploring the expressive possibilities of homophones, has proved especially challenging. It is a matter of no small interest, therefore, that Katherine Washburn and Margaret Guillemin have produced a bilingual edition that selects generously from his last three volumes. . . . ***Last Poems*** is a handsomely produced and thoughtfully presented selection. Its publication is a welcome event.

I should say here that I have been reading Celan off and on for twenty years without being able to develop the unshakable admiration that many feel for him. I waver between interest and irritation, enthusiasm and dislike. There is something downright old-fashioned and a bit absurd in the insistent minimalism of his poems. Isn't his unwillingness to commit himself to accessibility a somewhat confrontational and tired version of modernism? In any case, it allowed his generation to make a kind of symbol of him, an artist-saint, disabled by the Holocaust, whom they knew better than to emulate too closely. Critics are of course delighted to have poems that require lengthy teasing out and solemn explication, but readers may wonder whether all the fuss is warranted. At the same time, the reader who persists with Celan is sooner or later absorbed by the intensity with which he approaches language. He may be glum and cryptic, but he subjects sounds and syllables to a kind of magnification that produces a special fascination.

I would recommend that an interested reader begin with Katharine Washburn's thoughtful and detailed introduction to ***Last Poems,*** then read the collection straight through, slowly and with as much patience as he or she can muster. Having the German texts on the opposite page is in this case a necessity. Sooner or later they must be engaged too, for in one sense these translations are only glosses on them, so fundamentally do the poems resist translation. Here's a comparatively simple case in point:

DISCUS,
starred with premonitions,
throw yourself
out of yourself.

I would characterize this translation as successful and comparatively accessible. One can read it and go on. But eventually one might want to glance at the original text across the page, even if one does not read German:

WURFSCHEIBE, mit
Vorgesichten besternt,
wirf dich
aus dir hinaus.

It's interesting to see that the word placement is a little different. It's interesting to realize that "discus" in German is not a Greek word but a verb-noun combination ("throwndisc") with a flavor all its own. A little burrowing in a dictionary will show you that *Vorgesichten* is close to our own "foresight." But it is a coinage, so far as I can tell, a word that did not exist until Celan invented it. It carries the suggestion of "future sights" and "faces to come," but just as we can have "forebears" as well as "foresights," so this word looks back and suggests something like "ancestral countenances." We are pretty far from that tame and predictable word, "premonitions."

A little more dictionary work will reveal that the *scheib* of *Wurfscheibe* is a face, the face of a dial or a clock, and the *gesicht* of *Vorgesichten* is a face, a visage or countenance. The wordplays, in other words, are so inextricably tied to the original language that the translator cannot hope to extract and replicate them. He or she can try to produce others and/or provide notes and glosses, but there's no doubt that even this short and attractive little poem about a starred throwing-disc redolent of past and future, receiving instructions to throw itself beyond itself or out of its own grasp (and is it, for example, the night sky? or the poem itself?) is murder to translate.

The Washburn/Guillemin ***Last Poems*** is, then, something of a heroic enterprise, but one that the reader who relies solely on the English will be likely to find frustrating. Second-guessing translators is a favorite sport of reviewers. It's inevitable and it's also often unfair. In this case, it's probably the necessary way to a greater acquaintance with the poems, some of which will reward study, others of which will frustrate it. I myself think Celan's late poems are rather uneven, and that the "finds," poems a reader will want to cherish and return to, are few and far between. Still, time may prove me wrong. In the poems I have looked at most closely, scrutinizing the translators' choices and weighing them against the originals, there is a haunting quality that suggests that all the fuss about this poet may not be unwarranted. I'm not ready to jump on the bandwagon just yet, but I'm thinking it over and keeping the matter open. A case in point:

GROWN WEARY
of each other,
roaming the edge,
come of age,

air
adjoins itself, and
water too,

the card-reader slain
cleaves to
the ace of hearts.

When I have consulted the German and found that *adjoins* does not do justice to its verb (*schaufelt sich zu* suggests that the air is shoveling itself in and out of itself, as water also does) and that the dead card-reader (a woman, by the way) is *behind* the ace of hearts in some way (*hinterm*), I feel I understand the poem better and still find it too minimal and arbitrary. I don't really care for it but I suspect I may come back to it and that I may change my mind. That is why this book is important to me and why it deserves a wide readership, despite the problems of translating Celan and despite questions about the value of his poetry. (pp. 95-7)

David Young, "Recent Poetry in Translation," in The Antioch Review, *Vol. 45, No. 1, Winter, 1987, pp. 90-7.*

Lesley Chamberlain (essay date 1988)

[*Chamberlain is an English journalist, critic, and lecturer in Russian and German languages who has written several books on Eastern Europe. In the following essay, she asserts that Celan's poetry is informed by "extreme negativity" and "personal grief"—emotions that are often expressed through images of nature and death in his poems.*]

Celan's poetry presents difficulties for the English reader at once linguistic, cultural and spiritual. He was marked ineradicably by the deaths of his parents in a Nazi extermination camp and his senses seem to work fitfully in the scores of poems written in tribute. They suddenly fasten on an object, spurt into life, exaggerate its proportions, only to name the place of that object in a world beyond healing. His language throws out words in unpredictable rhythms, becomes obsessed with certain sounds and colours, then denies them. The lyrical heart broken, the troubled senses try by perceiving patterns and analogies to build beyond it. Celan's experience of the wasteland is more personal and more self-destructive than Eliot's, not so much a doubting of culture but a declaration of a seismic fault in the possibility of living.

Celan writes out of a loss of faith in death. To describe what it is to dwell in the human space without this prospect of grace and ultimate companionship is his bleakest vision. Men exist virtually beyond solace, when nothing is loved or hated or possessed in memory which is not devastated into random fragments.

Extreme negativity produces in Celan an hallucinatory after-hope, resembling Sartrean nausea, of a return to nature. Viewing dehumanization as a change of substance, he plays with endless metamorphoses, creating a new mythology out of unnatural death. Shocked feeling becomes aqueous matter and the heart and the head become stones. **'Dark eye in September'** for instance begins (my translation): 'Stone bonnet age. And the locks of pain / flow round the earth's face more luxuriously'. In that poem an eye is alone and arguing when it catches sight of 'the slim itinerant figure of feeling'. Then the poet switches into the second person and the argument is forestalled as both feeling and the ability to see it are destroyed: 'You plunge your sword into the wet of its eye.' Another poem, **'The Stone from the Sea',** speaks of the white heart of 'our' world having rolled away, leaving 'us' to spin the reddish wool of dreams. The heart is a stone from the depths of the sea with 'hair' and a memory of mussels and waves. From these tortured surreal dreams it is as if Celan is recovering his mother's transubstantiated remains from the earth or the seabed, or, as in **'Aspen Tree',** from within the substance of the rain.

The metamorphosed landscape only faintly recalls the familiar earth. Colours once drawn from nature come on the other side of death from the laboratory of chemical analysis and reconstruction. The greens and blues of the forest and the browns and golds of a mother's hair, having lost their emotional meaning, have seemingly been put under a microscope to be verified and classified and their relationship with other natural phenomena established. The eye chronically shocked no longer sees with feeling but inhabits a new realm, in which it is itself a visible object, a hangover from a past emotional life, a bluish thing, related to the rain and the sea. In the ghostly, mournfully erotic **'Chanson of a Lady in the Shade',** two eyes are petrified into a jewel on a ring. 'He wears them like shards of sapphire and lust', the lady sings. In **'Night',** included in the 1959 collection, two petrified human eyes which in life had the physiological capacity to exchange glances now in eternity audibly collide in a moment before dawn. 'Heart-grey puddles' on the flagstones are 'two mouthsfull of silence' in the poem **'Language Mesh'.**

It is a particular combination of history, personal grief and a sense of the crisis of language they have engendered, which allows Celan's poetry to resist comparison in any language. He is at once painter, pained man, and chronicler of grief. As fascinated by colour as by words, he finds both receding from his grasp *in extremis.*

One experience of Celan's which seems essential to understanding his idiom was a unique year of happiness he enjoyed as a medical student in France in 1938, at the age of eighteen.

The medical experience gave him a language in which to analyse the difference between living and dead tissue dispassionately, which helped stabilize, at least on the page, his revolted vision of his parents' asphyxiation. With a pathologist's and a physiologist's vision he set about the metamorphosis of his unhappiness and the device created a bridge between the human body and the human language. He wrote often in terms which related as much to the hurt organism as to the disabled word.

Grief does not interfere with the working of the elements, with plant cycles, or with the properties of oxygen or the functions of the blood. By recalling their certainty Celan can achieve a vision of the first signs of life struggling to start anew, such as we might imagine after the nuclear destruction of the planet, and such as Celan experienced in the years he chose to remain living after the Holocaust.

It is not a generous vision. The rebuilt emotional landscape of his poetry can resemble a microscopic slide. Likewise the position of his poetry in the surrounding silence resembles that of one living cell pinpointed in a blank mass. But the vision is of necessity strange. He declared in a speech in 1960, on being awarded the Büchner prize, that poetry was perhaps 'congenitally dark'.

In several of Celan's poems there is a crossing-over, a point at which the order of the familiar world is reversed into a new, similar but absurd order. In this sense Celan's work seems to be a vast chiasmus. The rhetorical figure establishes an order of words; the other side of a dividing line that order is reversed. This scheme built into Celan's poetry charts the relationship of organic to inorganic, blood to stone, eye to water, humanity to its bodily fate, meaning to senselessness, language to babble, as each phenomenon passes through the point of death into its dehumanized complement.

It is a particular combination of history, personal grief and a sense of the crisis of language they have engendered, which allows Celan's poetry to resist comparison in any language. He is at once painter, pained man, and chronicler of grief.

—Lesley Chamberlain

The idea of the chiasmus helps us understand Celan's simultaneous exploration of the death of the body and the death of language. The dual crisis is contained in the very idea of the *Sprachgitter,* for which the English translation 'language mesh' can only be provisional. The word *Gitter* suggests language is both imprisoned, fenced in behind bars, and that it might through itself create a lattice or a series of crossings-over, of meaning. It suggests both involuntary confinement and voluntary building. The poetry often amplifies this theme, even when the word *Gitter* is absent. **'Crowned Out'** from ***Die Niemandsrose,*** for instance, opens with these lines about weaving the stuff of painful memory:

> Crowned out,
> spewed out into night.
>
> Under what
> stars! So much
> grey-beaten heart-hammer silver. And
> Berenice's head of hair, here too.—I plaited.
> I unplaited,
> I plait, unplait.
> I plait.

By analogy the mesh suggests one of the body's key healing processes, the clotting of the blood. Human tissue heals itself by spinning sticky fibres which enmesh themselves, catching up platelets of hard blood in the spaces. Celan, the ex-medical student, speaks often of wounds and scars and scabs, and scab formation gave him a scheme for all potential healing. In those positive moments Celan seems to have believed that healing was possible.

The closest Celan came to spelling out the philosophy of the absurd the chiasmic scheme implies was in his prose, a scant collection of forced but important utterings, invaluable as accessories to the poems. (Now translated by Rosmarie Waldrop [in] ***Selected Prose.***) A speech after he received the Büchner prize in 1960 picked up the traditional German comparison between man and puppet. Though death made us believe we were puppets of fate there would always be voices to declare the absurdity of the human predicament as a triumph. Poetry, driven to extremes, taking metaphors to the last degree of absurdity, and tending towards silence, belonged among those voices. Going beyond Celan's own immediate references we can compare his outlook with that expressed in Kleist's classic essay 'On the Puppet Theatre' (1811). Kleist wrote of the impetus towards artistic creation out of humanity's disasters, using an image recalling Celan's in the last stanza of **'Aspen Tree'**:

> Failures . . . are inevitable, since we have eaten from the tree of knowledge. Yet Paradise is locked and bolted and the Cherub is behind us; we must make a journey around the world, and see if perhaps somewhere it is open from behind.

His description of art as reconstituted nature also recalls the chiasmus in Celan:

> We see that in the organic world, as reflection becomes weaker and more obscure, grace emerges all the more gloriously and commandingly. Just as the intersection of two lines, on one side of a point, suddenly comes out on the other side after passing through infinity, or the image in a concave mirror, after it has moved away into infinity, suddenly reappears right in front of us; so it happens too that when the mind has as it were passed through something infinite, grace reappears; so that at the same time it is most purely manifest in that human form which either has no consciousness or infinite consciousness, i.e. in the puppet or in the God.

Celan's petrified hearts and the blinded 'slim itinerant figure of feeling', however they are evaluated, belong in this realm of puppets, as does his imagined reconstruction of his parents' deaths.

In *Shoah,* Claude Lanzmann's film about the extermination camps, the German guards referred to their prisoners, even before they fell like rag dolls out of the gas chambers, as *Figuren* (figures, puppets).

Yet Celan insisted for many years on trying to recall nature back from the realm beyond, an impulse which is also well documented in his prose. He spoke in 1958 of the poet 'being in the open air':

> . . . not only my own efforts, but also those of other lyric poets of the younger generation . . . are the efforts of those with stars above their heads, the achievements of men; they are the efforts of those who are also tentless in this previously unrealised sense and thereby most strangely in the open air; the efforts of those who with their existence go and seek out language, sore with exposure to reality and seeking reality.

Celan's negativity thus gathers positive momentum. The Büchner speech expresses a fundamental, metaphysically charged, even erotic desire to communicate: For the poem is not outside time. Certainly it stakes a claim to eternity, it tries to grasp something beyond time, but by passing through it, not over and above it.

The poem can be, since it is a manifestation of language and therefore in essence dialogue, a message in a bottle, sent off in the belief—albeit not always a very strong hope—that it might sometime and somewhere be washed up onto land, perhaps onto land of the heart. In this way poems are on the move: they are aiming to get somewhere. (pp. 32-4)

Lesley Chamberlain, " 'Into Your Narrowest Being': The Poetry of Paul Celan," in P. N. Review, *Vol. 14, No. 6, 1988, pp. 32-4.*

Robert Pinsky (review date 31 July 1989)

[*Pinsky is an American poet and critic. In the following review, he discusses the difficulty of accurately translating Celan's highly inventive poetry and praises the sensitivity of Michael Hamburger's translation in* Poems of Paul Celan.]

In the writing of Paul Celan, even we readers who can hear poetry only dimly in German can sense the greatness of his invention: the cadences of a music tilted against music's complacency; words punished for their plausibility by being reinvented and fused together and broken apart; syntax chopped and stretched to crack and expose its crust of dead rhetoric. Language in general, perhaps German in particular, is associated by Celan not with light but with darkness, ice and snow. In one poem, truth makes its unlikely appearance among mankind in the midst of our "*Metapherngestöber,*" a neologism translated by the English poet Michael Hamburger [in ***Poems of Paul Celan***] as "flurrying metaphors." The term suggests an obliterating, aimless, and smothering proliferation of things that stand for other things, a storm that covers all in its cold, blank drifts.

This idea of language against itself is a 20th-century commonplace, but Celan, a victim of Nazism writing in German, gives it the full emotional pertinence of the century's history. His work and his life of exile, ending in 1970 with his suicide in Paris at the age of 49, seem a defining outgrowth of that history. Celan's late work is justly known as "difficult," but its difficulty has the authority of its material. A Romanian Jew whose parents were murdered in the notorious work camps of Transnistria, Celan chose to write his poems in German, and after the war he chose to live in Paris. Thus, a person of many European cultures and languages, but also of none, Celan was historically situated so as to witness Europe's great spasm of self-destruction, and to re-create that massive unmaking in his poems.

Elliptical, rhythmically hypnotic, each word obdurate and inward as a geode, these poems embody the conviction that the truth of what has been broken and torn must be told only with a jagged grace. German was the language of his parents, Romanian and Hebrew the languages of his schools, French the language of his adult daily life. From English Celan translated poems by Shakespeare, Dickinson, Frost, and from Russian Mandelstam and Blok. The act of translation that most determines his writing is the translation from the world of the living to the world of the dead.

Caught in the language-net (*Sprachgitter,* in the title of one of his volumes) or metaphor-storm, the living can lose all touch with the dead. Celan's imaginative pilgrimage to the world of the slaughtered seems to be couched in a discovered language of destruction:

Augen, Weltblind, im Sterbegeklüft: Ich
 komm,
Hartwuchs im Herzen.
Ich komm.

Mondspiegel Stailwand. Hinab.
(Atemgeflecktes Geleucht. Strichweise
 Blut.
Wölkende Seele, noch einmal gestaltnah.
Zehnfingerschatten—verklammert.)

Augen weltblind.
Augen im Sterbegeklüft,
Augen Augen:

Das Schneebett unter uns beiden, das
 Schneebett.
Kristall um Kristall,
zeittief gegittert, wir fallen,
wir fallen und liegen und fallen.

Und fallen:
Wir waren. Wir sind.
Wir sind ein Fleisch mit der Nacht.
In den Gängen, den Gängen.

("Schneebett")

Comparison of the original and the translation of this one poem can stand both for the virtues of the translator's achievement and for translation's necessary, severe limitations. Michael Hamburger has earned our gratitude for rendering these poems in a reasonably inventive English that has the tact to gesture toward the impossibility of his task. (The present volume [***Poems of Paul Celan***] is a revised and expanded version of Hamburger's ***Paul Celan: Poems,*** which appeared in 1980 and has had a great impact on American poets.) Since Celan's implosions and distortions, his oblique puns and his violent exaggerations of German's compound words, can be neither rendered nor ignored, Hamburger can only indicate them, as if with a gesture.

Such salvaging and rendering from language to language is a specialized case of the difficulty of making poems, the difficulty of creating a presence that is not a version of something else, but an actual emotional reality in language. Frost said that poetry is what is lost in translation; but like translation, poetry itself pursues what has been lost. Both translation and metaphor put one thing in the place of another. George Steiner (Celan's advocate) suggests in *After Babel* the identity of poetic composition and translation. If perfect translation is impossible, translation itself is inevitable, part of the ongoing process of culture moving through time. Everything we say, according to Steiner, is a kind of translation.

There is all the more reason, then, to read Celan's poems in at least two languages at once, and to absorb as best one can their peculiar defiance of translation. Here is Hamburger's version of the first three stanzas of the poem I have quoted:

Eyes, world-blind, in the fissure of dying; I
 come,
callous growth in my heart.
I come.

Moon-mirror rock-face. Down.
(Shine spotted with breath. Blood in
 streaks.
Soul forming clouds, close to the true
 shape once more.
Ten-finger shadow, clamped.)

Eyes world-blind,
eyes in the fissure of dying,
eyes:

("Snow-bed")

The first three terms—*Augen, weltblind, Sterbegeklüft*—launch a journey to the dead, a process embodied by the broken-off substantives of the second stanza. Then, in a good example of the term "untranslatable," *Augen, weltblind, Sterbegeklüft* return again in the third stanza, but transmuted. How can English evoke that syntactical repetition, which brings the poet himself closer to those three terms of death, as in a macabre version of Keats's "already with thee"?

Celan's imaginative pilgrimage to the world of the slaughtered seems to be couched in a discovered language of destruction.

—Robert Pinsky

A translator in the manner of Ezra Pound might try for cognate English terms like "deathcleft" for Hamburger's "in the fissure of dying." But "Hard-waxed" for "*Hartwuchs*" would sound like car polish, while the syllable "*wuchs*" indicates a waxing as in the growth of the moon, the "*Mond*" of "*Mondspiegel Steilwand.*" So in the two collided syllables "*Hartwuchs,*" the hard-spot that has formed on the human heart—a heart-wart—is associated with the hard rock-wall of the reflective moonmirror, with its breath-flecked light that seems to condense again the cloudy souls of the exterminated and long-buried, now nearly formed anew: *gestaltnah*—"gestalt-nigh," to form another impossible English cognate. Somewhere between such inventions or the pseudo-Hopkins "death-cleft" (or "deathchasm"?) and "breath-flecked" (*Atemgeflecktes*) on one side, and Hamburger's discrete solutions on the other side ("shine spotted with breath," "close to the true shape once more") lies the extraordinary, tormented verbal music I can only imagine and half-sense. It is the music of a death embrace, living imagination and irrefutable death clamped together like the jammed syllables of "tenfingershadow—full-clamped."

After that stanza of horrific nouns, the opening words come back as subjective rather than objective: the eyes, world-blind, that are addressed by the poet in the first line become those of the poet, or merged with his, in the third stanza. The epic theme of the Journey to the Underground governs the arc of all Celan's language. Here in the Snow-bed that arc is completed with terrible thoroughness. "I come," the poet tells the dead in the first line, but by the third stanza, with the adjective following the noun, as in English "eyes open"; now he not merely comes but arrives, eyes open and eyes world-blind, his eyes in the staring binary repetition of the line *"Augen Augen"* as purely and merely eyes as the unblinking eyes of the frozen dead. The double noun, each half modifying the other—these eyes are not seeing eyes or brown eyes or blue eyes, but eye eyes: not eyes awake or eyes open or eyes sleeping, but entirely eyes eyes—executes its grim tautological joke. In *"Augen Augen"* one thing does not stand for another: here where *a* equals *a* the metaphor-flurry is still.

And indeed, the rest of the poem is made mainly of binary repetitions:

> The snow-bed under us both, the snow-
> bed,
> Crystal on crystal,
> meshed deep as time, we fall,
> we fall and lie there and fall.
>
> And fall.
> We were. We are.
> We are one flesh with the night.
> In the passages, passages.

The journey to the dead is a great falling and lying down and falling, like the coming apart of sentences and distinctions: eye-eye and crystal on crystal, an interwoven mesh or network of negations, "meshed deep as time," as Hamburger's English has it. But the weave of *"zeittief gegittert"* has a jammed, explosive eloquence, as if we could say something like "timedeep engridded." *"Gegittert"* recalls that the book in which **"Snow-Bed"** appeared was titled after a poem called **"Sprachgitter"**: **"Languagemesh,"** the trapping and supporting grid of crosses that entangles life, the metaphor-flurry as a binding trellis. The force of that net or latticework, connecting everything with the sticky web of words, finds its counterforce and its representation in Celan's laconic repacking of language into painfully overfreighted fragments.

And yet this overpacking is characteristically yoked with the echo of a grammar textbook: *"Wir waren. Wir sind."* We were, we are: the symmetry and relentlessness of a language lesson. The tyrannical entropy of everything boiling down to one thing, eye eyes, crystal on crystal, devolves into the poem's final line: *"In den Gängen, den Gängen."* "In the passages, passages." But also, in German, the ways, the ways of going and the ways of walking, and also the works, as in the movements of watches, so not only the corridors of Night and the passages of Night's flesh, but also Night's gears and its gaits and its wellsprings.

In short, the words of the poem seem to hover in the land of the dead, partly by using traditional aspects of poetic language with a kind of destructive, raging terseness, so that repetitions, figures of sound, and images seem ready to collapse into a furious silence. That is the genius of Celan, and in translation the fury and unmaking recede, while a more ordinary poetry of construction takes the foreground.

At the age of 23, immediately after the war, Celan wrote the **"Todesfuge" ("Deathfugue").** John Felstiner has described the remarkable career of this poem (in TNR, "The Biography of a Poem," April 2, 1984). It became a central part of the German school canon, much anthologized and translated and quoted ("Black milk of daybreak we drink it at sundown . . . "), an essential work in Holocaust literature and—in short—one of those great works that are pressed by the weight of attention toward the shape of a chestnut. The honoring integument of anthology and pedagogy seemed to muffle, nearly to deride, the poem's rejection of poetry's euphony, a rejection that in the poet's work became more stringent and sardonic. (For whatever reason, Celan began refusing permission to reprint the poem in anthologies.) From a great poet of explicit rhetoric, Celan became a great anti-rhetorical poet, with a moral strictness that makes mere "experiment" seem frivolous, and mere literal translation seem tepid. Language undoes itself best, these poems suggest, in the original.

None understands this situation better than Hamburger, a gifted poet and resourceful translator. In the reprinted version of his 1979 introduction, Hamburger speaks of the "process of reception" by which poems by Celan over repeated readings and over many years "became accessible." The magnitude and humility of this work are a great gift to us readers who with Hamburger's guidance pick our way through the German on the facing page.

That halting labor is itself a reflection of the work of Celan's poems, an effort to pick out the truth from among the swirling flurry or network of mere representations, the interstices where *this* is oriented by *that.* In his Jewish family in a now lost region of Romania, German was his mother tongue, and the language in which the order was given to shoot his mother in the head when she became too weak to work. Steiner has said that only Primo Levi and Celan among survivors have found language adequate to that period. Celan's resource appears to be something like a disassembly of language's network of expectation, a commensurate destruction and mastery. In the phrase from **"Todesfuge"** "Death is a master from Germany," the poet's word *Meister* surely conveys some sense not only of "boss" but also of the prowess in art we indicate in English by the Italian borrowing "maestro," and in "masterpiece."

Death is a maestro from Germany, in these austere German poems, and in the **"Todesfuge"**: *süsser,* "play more sweetly," he calls out to the musicians as the forced labor digs the graves. That dramatic scene, in the later poems, becomes transformed into an inward drama. Michael Hamburger helps us perceive that drama, a contest like the more explicit **"Todesfuge,"** of music and torment, labor and despair, the accursed and the articulated, sweetness and breaking. (pp. 36-9)

Robert Pinsky, "The Language Net," in The New Republic, *Vol. 201, No. 5, July 31, 1989, pp. 36-9.*

George Steiner (essay date 28 August 1989)

[*In the following essay, Steiner provides a laudatory assessment of* Poems of Paul Celan, *commenting on Celan's literary and theological influences and his use of experimental language to describe inhumanity, mystery, and sorrow.*]

Between trains, some twenty years ago, I browsed in a Frankfurt bookstore. A volume of poems, slimmer than slim, in a wrapper of austere white, caught my eye. The very first line I read told of a language "north of the future." That line went through me like a quiet flame. A neighboring poem spoke of the recession of words—hopelessly wasted, sullied by the bestiality of our age—into stones. (I learned later that the wife of the poet was a distinguished lithographer.) In that north of the future, when the ash of the death ovens had found peace, had become lit with remembrance, those stones, word-charged, would speak. It was only then, I seem to recall, that I turned back to the title page and the poet's name, Paul Celan. Somehow, it struck me as a pen name, and later I learned that the writer's real name was Paul Antschel. But I knew with certainty that the poems and the voice of Paul Celan (was he alive and, if so, where, and had he published other collections?) would alter my inward existence as only the very greatest art, music, philosophic-metaphysical argument, or poetry can do. . . .

Poems of Paul Celan [presents a wide-ranging selection of Celan's poems] in the German original and with facing-page translations by Michael Hamburger. How am I to proceed? The self-evident impulse is to say, "Go at once and buy this book. Insist that your bookstore order it if it has not yet done so. Borrow it from a friend while you wait for your own copy. Steal it if you must. But, now that Celan is in some measure available in English, let him enter your life. At risk. Knowing that he will change it. Knowing that his poems are like the 'Archaic Torso of Apollo,' which in Rilke's famous poem bids us do precisely that: 'Now change your life.' " And with that this review or any other should end.

But there are obstacles to so plain an imperative. Even the native German-speaker may find himself utterly baffled by many of Celan's lyrics—particularly those from the later phases of his work. Celan's poetry and prose—he published a handful of speeches and a parable, which are transforming the landscape of poetic theory and of the philosophy of language—are among the most resistant in Western literature to ready understanding. In a poem, the difficulties are, as it were, layered. They surround a core of overwhelming directness with successive screens of "alternative codes," as in those multi-layered manuscripts and parchments we call palimpsests. Very often, the initial veil is biographical. Celan's life—as a child during the Holocaust, as an exile in Paris, as a translator from half a dozen languages, as one inebriate with the light-bursts of Jerusalem and of the beloved woman he encountered there—is immensely complex. No one who met him, it seems, failed to sense the sombre radiance, the desolation and apartness of his being. But as yet we know little about him. Celan's discretions and elisions were labyrinthine. He could, under pressure of nervous exhaustion or in brief moments of luminous confiding, lay himself bare to certain friends. But on the whole he detested and strove to frustrate the prying gossip, the inquisitions into the lived source of poetic invention which plague a journalistic culture. There are elements that remain enigmatic about his death—by suicide, in Paris in 1970. In consequence, much that we cannot grasp in Celan's poems may one day be cleared up by the decipherment of their contingent biographical references to and their disguised nominations of this or that place and incident, and by an authorized chronology that would allow us to unravel Celan's playfulness with dates. No edition so far, in German or in any other language, has the information needed.

A second stratum of difficulty is that of technique. Some of Celan's most famous finds—"black milk," the "blood-ray of the moon," filaments of light, of vegetable green, and of nerves which are also hair and the spindrift of dreams—have their stylistic provenance in the world of Rimbaud and of Russian orphic Futurism and of the Surrealist masters. But Celan goes much farther. His best poems make haiku seem wasteful. Their conciseness is such that the only legitimate way of reading them is by Talmudic and Cabalistic methods. This is to say that in Celan minimal units of language—the individual syllable, sometimes the single letter—matter unconditionally. These poems are, indeed, "lithographs"—letters, markers of "black fire," incised in stone. The syntax is compressed into a kind of implosive tension. The modifiers, the pronominal detours, the connectives that have given modern Western discourse its logical fluency, its openness to understanding and to paraphrase, are chiselled away. There is in Celan an anathema on "talk" (here he is at one with the great philosopher Martin Heidegger, one of the few crucial presences in Celan's later life and writings), which is the contrary of "saying":

> Led home into oblivion
> the sociable talk of
> our slow eyes.
>
> Led home, syllable after syllable, shared
> out among the dayblind dice, for which
> the playing hand reaches out, large,
> awakening.
>
> And the too much of my speaking:
> heaped up round the little
> crystal dressed in the style of your silence.

In Michael Hamburger's version, however, "heaped up" fails to suggest the siege of a city and the nomadic note in "*angelagert,*" and "dressed" doesn't catch the resonance of meditation and self-withdrawal of "*Eintracht in Tracht.*"

Add to this the inwoven multi-lingualism of Celan's idiom. Hebrew, Yiddish, Russian, French, and Italianate words, turns of phrase, acoustic transparencies abound in his German. The Psalms, the poetry of Mandelstam, Shakespearean tags (Celan's translations from the Sonnets are rigorous and incomparable) are raw material that enters the fabric of Celan's verse hardly modified. As John Felstiner, of Stanford University, himself a penetrating translator of Celan, is showing, an awareness of the Old Testament and of the prodigal speech arts of Yiddish is indispensable to our hearing of Celan. If we know these sources, difficulties open up for us into something far more exciting—mystery. The withdrawal of our literacy from matters liturgical or theological has eroded the evidential force of that word. I want to use it in a straightforward, workshop manner. "Mystery" in art signifies the capacity of expressive forms for meaning much more than they say. It includes the leap of metaphor in language, of juxtaposition in painting, of harmonies and discord in music from which spring new ways of experiencing our own identity and that of the world. That much is common to all major art and literature. In Paul Celan's case, "mystery" takes on a more specific pressure.

Writing in German after Auschwitz, knowing himself to be of the company of Hölderlin and Rilke—that is to say, one who would be bringing further radiance and life force to the tongue in which his parents and his community (that of East European Judaism) had been condemned to hideous death—Celan sought to break through speech and syntax as we know them, even as the pioneers of abstract and minimalist painting sought to break through the constraints and privileges of representation. Celan plays, in the deepest sense of that term, both with the notion of an Adamic tongue—of words that, in some irretrievable state of grace, spoke the truth because they exactly matched the world—and with the notion of a future idiom whose clarity and whose total refusal of falsehood, of hatred, of inhumanity would tell us of the coming of the messianic hour. The ancient motif of the giving of names by Adam in Eden is constant:

In the seminal
sense
the sea stars you out, inmostly, for ever.

There's an end to the giving of names,
over you I cast my fate.

(Hamburger would be the first to concede that English here is helpless before the oracular thrust of that sea "starring," or before the fractured literalness of *"Im Samen- / sinn,"* in which the "seed," the "seminal," the "semantic," and the entire theme of the origins both of man and of saying are implicit.) No less frequent are intimations of a time after time, in which these poems will move into the light of immediacy.

My tentative counsel is this: the reader of, the listener to, Celan's poetry might look first at those poems (already they have classic status in German) in which the poet indicts God. The cry is as old and as new as the Holocaust: *"Der Herr brach das Brot, / das Brot brach den Herrn"* ("The Lord broke the bread, / the bread broke the Lord"—and observe how Judaic and Christological symbols, of the Jewish blessing and of the sacramental incarnation, are conjoined). The death camps, the ash mounds are the breaking of the covenant between God and man. The God who was *not* at Auschwitz or Belsen inhabits Celan's urgent despair like an animate absence. Hence his celebrated uses of and variations on *Niemand*—"no-one." (The hyphen, though omitted by Hamburger, is vital to any full rendition of the inherent negations, refusals, closures on hope.) To enter Celan's world, one would also do well to learn by heart his famous **"Psalm"**:

Praised be your name, no one.
For your sake
we shall flower.
Towards
you.

A nothing
we were, are, shall
remain, flowering:
the nothing—, the
no one's rose.

With
our pistil soul-bright,
with our stamen heaven-ravaged,
our corolla red
with the crimson word which we sang
over, O over
the thorn.

And here the translation lets us down badly. The terrible flowering of innocent blood is *"Dir / entgegen."* "Towards / you," yes, but, more emphatically, "against you." The death-Psalm is sung *against* the *Niemand*-God, the *Niemandsrose* flowers *against* its Maker. How, asks Celan in poem after poem, can He have created those destined to inhabit the ovens?

Or consider the wholly **untr**anslatable coda to **"Engführung"**—perhaps the most specific of Celan's Shoah poems:

Driven into the
terrain
with
the unmistakable
track:

Grass.
Grass,
written asunder.

Visually and acoustically, the fragmented shards tell of the notorious railroad tracks to the camps. *"Verbracht"* is appallingly more inert, more expressive of nameless, unspeakable waste and oblivion, than "Driven into." *"Gelände"* has resonances at once vaguer and more ominous than "terrain." It hints at the earth banks over the death pits. But it is the final word that marks the greatness of Celan. Walt Whitman knew about "leaves of grass," about the chromatic and symbolic interplay between grass and the leaves of the book. Here the grass is *"auseinandergeschrieben"*: dispersed, dishevelled, as by the death winds ("Shoah" also signifies such a wind)—made barren of sense and of record. And all this is only to scratch the surface. By comparison, Keats' "writ in water" is almost reassuringly literary.

Over and over, Celan put his terrible question: In the "nooneness" of God, who "shall bear witness for the witness"? Celan and Primo Levi, before their elected deaths, came nearest to bringing human language to bear on that which no tongue ought ever to have known or articulated—on that which should, since it is morally and rationally unspeakable, terminate man's primordial contract with the wonder and "wording" (Emerson's term) of the world. That these poems exist is at once a kind of miracle of ultimate need and a kind of grievous indecency. Celan was self-laceratingly possessed of this contradiction, of the intuition that his own genius was active in the denial of the nothingness of speech and metaphor which should have followed on the Holocaust. (Why, indeed, have art and poetry not gone on strike?) But from the deeps of his incensed sorrow came, undeniably, the counterpoint of creative mastery, the conviction that

A tree-
high thought
tunes in to light's pitch: there are
still songs to be sung on the other side
of mankind.

It is to this credo that we owe some of the most inspired lyric and love poetry in this century. And it is by attending to this second, or counter, motion that the reader can accede to the other sphere in Celan's work.

Osip Mandelstam became Celan's secret sharer. Himself done to sordid death by Stalin and Stalinist Jew-hatred, this marvellous writer found in Celan the guardian of his afterlife, the chosen partner in a posthumous dialogue: through Celan's translations, adaptations, allusions he was given a new force of echo. In German, *Mandel* signifies "almond." Vertiginous yet profoundly intimate and playfully loving are the chimes and changes that Celan rings on this equivalence. The Russian companion flowers in the almond tree, in its branches (*Stamm*), in the almond-shaped and tinted eyes of the beloved—itself a simile with Biblical precedent. But there is more: divided Jerusalem had its notorious Mandelbaum Gate, the almond-tree aperture between the two halves of the warring city. Thus the name of the poet, the gate of suffering and of messianic awaiting, and the flowering and eyes of the loved one are intertwined in a sequence of very late poems that are, to put it simply, among the finest witnesses to love and to uncertain but irreducible hope in any literature:

The Poles
are inside us,
insurmountable
when we're awake,
we sleep across, up to the Gate
of Mercy,

I lose you to you, that
is my snowy comfort,

say that Jerusalem *is*,

say it, as though I were this
your whiteness,
as though you
were mine,

as though without us we could be we,

I open your leaves, for ever,

you pray, you bed
us free.

Even a superficial gloss on this poem would need much space. It would point to the resonance in the German *Erbarmen* (the mercy, the compassion, of that gate), which includes both "inheritance" (*Erb*) and the "arms" with which lovers hold each other. It would dwell on the role of snow or almond-blossom whiteness in Jewish mourning and try to elucidate the sheer psychological magic in that "as though without us we could be we," whose laconic and lapidary clarity crystallizes the definition of love. "I open your leaves" is faithful to the erotic of the original but not to the deep, manifold wit: *ich blättre dich auf* means "I leaf you open" in the sense in which we "leaf through" a book (those "leaves of grass" again). It has enormous sexual, psychic, and intellectual connotations. And it is these which literally explode in the closing two lines. Here, too, English is powerless. *"Du betest, du bettest / uns frei"*: even the non-reader of German can make out the word-play on *beten* ("to pray") and *betten* ("to bed")—a verb that Brecht used sardonically in a famous song text. The intercourse of the lovers in messianic, mourning, almond-flowering Jerusalem is at once a prayer and a fusion of "we" into a final "us." Prayer may open the Gate of Mercy as bedding opens the inmost of the beloved. In these two openings, which are one, surges, like the mystery of blossoming itself, the homecoming to the other who is ourself.

What I have cursorily remarked on will have conveyed my sense of Michael Hamburger's translations. No one today has done more to bring to the English-speaking world the greatest of German poetry, that of Hölderlin, of Rilke, of Paul Celan. Himself a poet, Hamburger has been one of the most informed, scrupulously acute, and self-sacrificial of translators, an indispensable courier between languages and cultures. One's gratitude for his Celan versions, for the exceeding labor and faith that have gone into them, is unstinted. But Hamburger would, I believe, be the first to admit that Celan is as yet frequently untranslatable—both into current, everyday German and into other tongues. It will take a long time for our sensibilities to apprehend poetry of these dimensions and this radicality. Like any great pioneering art form—non-objective painting, twelve-tone or atonal music—Celan's poetry will very gradually educate perception. What we can do at present is listen, misunderstand fruitfully, let the as yet hidden clarities in Celan's language and insights be patient within us. *"Hohles Lebensgehöft"* ("Hollow homestead of life": the neologism is no "easier" in German than in English), says Celan. One day, this body of poetry and prose may do something to help fill that hollow, that black hole of our inhuman age. But not quite yet. (pp. 93-6)

George Steiner, "North of the Future," in The New Yorker, *Vol. LXV, No. 28, August 28, 1989, pp. 93-6.*

J. M. Cameron (review date 18 January 1990)

[*Cameron is an English critic, essayist, nonfiction writer, and professor of philosophy. In the following review of* Poems of Paul Celan, *he argues that despite the obscurity of much of his verse, Celan should not be regarded as a hermetic poet but rather as "a public poet, a writer concerned with the great events of the time."*]

The character of Paul Celan's work raises the question how far poetry can be—is—a central human activity in our time. Even when Milton played with the thought of

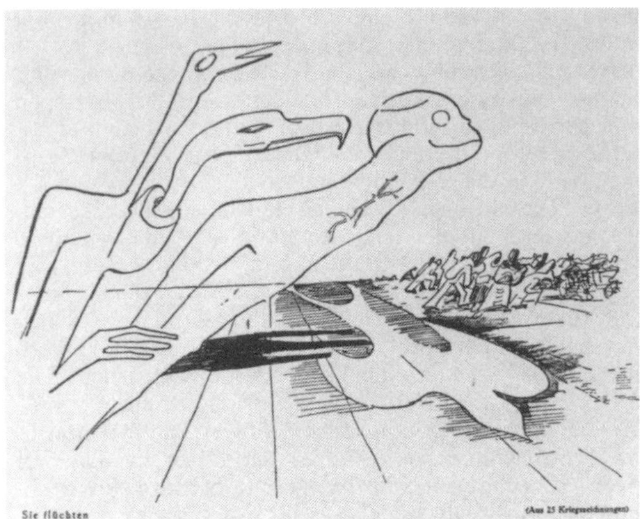

Edgar Jené's lithograph "Sie flüchten," which Celan discussed in his book Edgar Jené und der Traum vom Traume.

writing a poem "doctrinal to a nation," at first having in mind an Arthuriad, such a project, in a lively form, was scarcely possible. Milton had in mind Homer and Virgil. Homer was certainly doctrinal to a nation, a principal source of moral and theological ideas current in Hellenic culture, and this was the ground for Plato's attack upon his poems—they taught false doctrines and offered bad examples. Virgil was not the shaper of a culture but rather the celebrant of a certain moment in the history of the Roman republic. His real triumph was in the Middle Ages, when he is taken to be a prophet, or a magician, and in the early modern period:

> his single words and phrases, his pathetic half-lines, giving utterance, as the voice of Nature herself, to that pain and weariness, yet hope of better things, which is the experience of her children in every time.

What the poet's role may now be is obscure. With the rise of industrial society and the drying up of oral culture we are overcome with doubts over the significance of poetry. We hesitate to make big statements, even though we may be confident that poetry in its manifold shapes is still an important part of our culture, that within the great secular shifts in the outlook on the world the poets are still nibbling at their pens and bringing themselves to write. But we cannot now think of the poets as their publics thought of Byron and Wordsworth. The direct relation Byron and Wordsworth had to their own time seems no longer possible today. Everything that comes within the Modernist movement employs modes of discourse and sequences of images that are oblique; such poetry is on the whole inaccessible to many readers and perhaps to all readers unprovided with some kind of commentary.

This transformation of poetry is linked with stylistic changes in other arts as well. In successive periods poets have felt unable to write "in the old way," just as other artists could no longer paint or compose in the old way, and have cast about for new styles, new voices. The old styles and voices persist, sometimes without great change, as in Philip Larkin's work, more often as elements in a new way of speaking. Milton and Pope are thus present in Wordsworth's *The Prelude.* Sometimes the old voices are used for particular purposes, as when in *Don Juan* Byron uses the voices of Dryden and Pope in a satirical, mocking way. Sometimes, the use of the old is startling. It startles me to find Skelton's voice in Yeats; and this goes with the use of quotation, as in *The Waste Land* and the *Four Quartets;* the effect is arresting just because it starts up against the background of a new kind of discourse. Some wish to argue that more is involved, more than I have so far suggested, in the dislocations of syntax, the fracturing of common uses, the breaking of ordinary semantic connections, that begins with Mallarmé and Rimbaud; and they fly to the terminology of linguistics, and see the received link between signifier and signified as having been broken, sometimes through a felt pressure to diversify the poetry and escape banality and stock responses, sometimes because what the poet has directly in mind is unassimilable to the older poetic modes. This last consideration is, as we shall see, decisive for Paul Celan's work, and especially for his later work.

Much of his poetry, and this is plain in his earlier work, is "about" the great massacre of the Jews in the death camps of the Third Reich. (I prefer, with others, not to use the term "holocaust"; a holocaust is traditionally a burnt offering to the God of Israel, and even those who on account of the massacres wish to repudiate the God of Abraham, Isaac, and Jacob don't—I think—want to use "holocaust" with such savage irony.)

There are in Celan's poetry two other presences: the Russian poet Mandelstam, done to death by Stalin; and—this shakes the mind—the philosopher and Nazi Martin Heidegger, to whose disintegrative pressure on the German language Celan is manifestly indebted, and to whom—or rather to whose house—Celan consecrates a poem.

Little of Celan's poetry, then, can be thought to be self-referential or hermetic. Most of the poetry is obscure, some of it grievously so. But however oblique may be Celan's manner of proceeding, and however much he takes on this manner because he feels the moral force of Theodor Adorno's saying that it is impossible to write poems about—or after—Auschwitz, the obscurity can always in principle be dissipated by a commentary. The poems are "messages," as he himself insisted, like messages in bottles cast into the ocean. Some of the bottles may be lost; if they are not lost it is a matter of chance which person gets hold of a particular message. The message, when it is taken out of the bottle, turns out not to be the polished aphorism of a mandarin but a Delphic pronouncement, portentous, teasing, mysterious, beautiful. (This insight, along with much else, I owe to George Steiner.) The poems are messages, then, but not directed to an elected public and are in a form of discourse that doesn't readily yield up its meaning.

His most famous poem, often translated and much commented on, anthologized, a subject of study in German schoolrooms, is **"Todesfuge," "Death Fugue"** in Michael Hamburger's translation. It is one of the least Delphic, most available, of the poems. The phrases with which it begins transfix us:

> Schwarze Milch der Frühe wir trinken
> sie abends
> wir trinken sie mittags und morgens
> wir trinken sie nachts
> wir trinken und trinken
>
> Black milk of daybreak we drink it
> at sundown
> we drink it at noon in the morning
> we drink it at night
> we drink and we drink it . . .

This is incantatory and provokes a recognizably poetic response in us, and the rest of the poem, painful as it would be if it were a matter of direct reporting, a direct account of the reduction of human beings to ash and smoke, doesn't travel too far from the obscenity of the death camp and the incident that is one of the occasions of the poem. The commandant of the camp impressed gypsy musicians into a band and ordered them to play the tango and other dance measures to accompany the processions of victims to the ovens. Of course, in the end the musicians themselves perished, presumably in silence. Later Celan seems to have distanced himself from this poem, in part because it was used in the immense scholastic discussions of German guilt, in part because he found it too direct in its references to the bitter realities.

In his introduction to the poems Hamburger suggests that we should compare **"Todesfuge"** with the later **"Engführung" ("The Straitening")**; we shall see, he urges, "how daring, cryptic, and spare Celan's manner has become" in the thirteen years since **"Todesfuge."** Without a knowledge of the poet's life, dates, and situation it would be a rare and penetrating reader who would be able to guess at the poem's ultimate reference. It is plain from this late section that the extremes of human horror provide the ground of the poem.

> In der Eulenflucht, beim
> versteinerten Aussatz
> bei
> unsern geflohenen Händen, in
> der jüngsten Verwerfung,
> überm
> Kugelfang an
> der verschutteten Mauer:
>
> At owl's flight, near
> the petrified scabs,
> near
> our fled hands, in
> the latest rejection,
> above
> the rifle-range near
> the buried wall.

In **"Todesfuge"** there is a fair amount of more or less explicit material; here in **"Engführung"** the material is deliberately hidden, as though he is constructing a deep parable and choosing not to provide a key. "He that hath ears to hear, let him hear."

From the collection ***Die Niemandsrose*** (1963) to his death in 1970 Celan's poetry becomes more fragmentary and obscure. It is often sharply beautiful, but it has seemed to some critics to have sense only in relation to a private world. His last years seem to have been unhappy and he had severe paranoid episodes. Paranoid beliefs are rarely quite groundless, and there was something right in his feeling that the world was ranged against him. In particular, quite unjustified charges that he had plagiarized the work of Yvan Goll troubled him severely. One who was not predisposed to have a paranoid vision of the world would have shrugged it off, finding the accusation preposterous. All the same, the dense obscurity is not, at least for the most part, a sign of mental derangement; it is rather the sign of an attempt to work into his poetry, in his own idiom, material that belongs to the harsh public world. He is not—he protested he was not—a hermetic poet.

Despite the difficulties his work offers the reader, Celan is a public poet, a writer concerned with the great events of the time.

—J. M. Cameron

Many themes, alongside the dominant theme of the great massacre, are present in the later poems. There are some exquisite love poems; and there is much that is religious, a wrestling with the deepest and most troubling problems in Judaism and Christianity. He stands within the tradition of Meister Eckhart and the later developments of "negative" theology. He is far removed indeed from the optimistic theodicy of Leibniz and from German liberal theology, Jewish or Christian.

I choose for comment, using Hamburger's translations, some of the more accessible poems. First, **"Tenebrae":**

> We are near, Lord,
> near and at hand.
>
> Handled already, Lord,
> clawed and clawing as though
> the body of each of us were
> your body, Lord.
>
> Pray, Lord,
> pray to us,
> we are near.
>
> Wind-awry we went there,
> went there to bend
> over hollow and ditch.
>
> To be watered we went there, Lord.
> It was blood, it was
> what you shed, Lord.
>
> It gleamed.
>
> It cast your image into our eyes,
> Lord.
> Our eyes and our mouths are so
> open and empty, Lord.
> We have drunk, Lord.

The blood and the image that was in
  the blood, Lord.
Pray, Lord.
We are near.

Almost certainly the title refers to the Holy Week—the week devoted to the contemplation of Christ's Passion—office of Tenebrae (ironically, abandoned in the recent liturgical reform). The Eucharistic imagery is plain; the body and blood of the suffering Christ, and what goes with the savage eating—clawing—of the spiritually famished, are central images in the poem. (The reference is also, I take it, to the Passover meal.) The great inversion—we feel it like a blow—is that the relation between the Lord and those who are participants in the rite (not a ritual act but the actual bloody processes of living and dying in the camps) is the reverse of the traditional relation; the Lord is comforted, reassured that *we* are near; he is asked to pray to *us;* and there is a dreadful ambiguity about "It was blood, it was what you shed, Lord."

A very different poem strikes me as full of charm, soberly beautiful.

Led home into oblivion
the sociable talk of
our slow eyes.

Led home, syllable after syllable,
  shared
out among the dayblind dice, for
  which
the playing hand reaches out, large,
  awakening.

And the too much of my speaking:
heaped up round the little
crystal dressed in the style of your
silence

("Below")

In German the last three lines are:

Und das Zuviel meiner Rede:
angelagert dem kleinen
Kristall in der Tracht deines
  Schweigens.

But it is the poetry of indictment, the expression of what might without absurdity be called God's dereliction that remains with us. A short poem linked to **"Tenebrae"** is:

I heard him,
he was washing the world,
unseen, nightlong,
real.

One and Infinite,
annihilated,
ied.

Light was. Salvation.

("Once")

("annihilated, / ied" is the translator's rendering of *vernichtet, / ichten.*)

The supreme expression of the poetry of indictment is undoubtedly **"Psalm."**

No one moulds us again out of
  earth and clay,
no one conjures our dust.
No one.

Praised be your name, no one.
For your sake
we shall flower.
Towards
you.

A nothing
we were, are, shall
remain, flowering:
the nothing-, the
no one's rose.

With
our pistil soul-bright,
with our stamen heaven-ravaged,
our corolla red
with the crimson word which we
  sang
over, O over
the thorn.

Celan stands within the tradition of Hölderlin and Rilke and it seems the common judgment of competent critics that his achievement is not less than theirs. Despite the difficulties his work offers the reader, he is a public poet, a writer concerned with the great events of the time. He stands in the same relation to the world of the massacres as does the author of *Lear* to the cruelty, poverty, and madness of his time. And just as in *Lear* the horror is not diminished or tempered, so in Celan's work the death camps and what went on within them are not made less terrible. But we have also to say, though the analysis of this isn't clear, that in each case the effect of the poetry is that we do in a mysterious way come to a new understanding of the horror, though not, emphatically not, through our being reconciled to it. On the contrary, it is the poetry that keeps the crust of familiarity from forming.

Michael Hamburger's translation is a great achievement. Any translation is an arduous business; but to translate Celan is uncommonly arduous. It is not the job of the translator to make what is obscure clear but to give us an equivalent obscurity. I once heard a man say that a certain modern translation of Paul Celan's letters made them understandable for the first time. I thought this a dubious compliment and a misconception of what a good translation is for. Celan's being a polyglot, with Romanian, French, Yiddish, Hebrew, English (he himself made a remarkable translation into German of Shakespeare's sonnets) under and sometimes on the surface of the poetry, presents the translator with peculiar difficulties. So far as I can judge, Hamburger has come close to overcoming them. It is a memorable volume and will influence our moral outlook and the practice of poetry for a long time to come. (pp. 3-4)

J. M. Cameron, "Poet of the Great Massacre," in The New York Review of Books, *Vol. XXXVI, Nos. 21 & 22, January 18, 1990, pp. 3-4.*

Peter Filkins (review date 1991)

[*In the following review, Filkins praises Michael Hamburger's translations of Celan's poems in* Poems of Paul Celan *and discusses Celan's quest to develop a new form of language to express himself.*]

One of the strongest merits of Paul Celan's poetry is the way in which his work becomes more immediate and comprehensible as time goes on. Given how difficult and paradoxical so many of the poems are on the surface, this not only says a lot for Celan's talent and knowledge of what language can be and become, it also indicates what a fine job Michael Hamburger has done over the years in translating a poetry daunting in its obscurity, at times frustrating in its sealed despair, but never so oblique that we lose touch with the consciousness at work within it. In fact, it would appear that time, speech, and our own approach to language will eventually catch up to Celan, his vision and voice having been ahead of his time simply through his refusal to confront the unutterable with anything less than a new form of utterance, his own suffering and despair made palpable by the wrenched vocabulary and syntax he used to give life to them in words.

Born in Rumania in 1920, Celan remained throughout his life a poet obsessed with the loss of his parents to the death camps of the Holocaust. His father dead of typhus, his mother shot in the neck, Celan learned of their grisly fate while serving as a road laborer for the state in 1943. Returning to the study of medicine after the war, he eventually escaped to Vienna in 1947, moving to Paris the following year where he lived until his suicide by drowning in 1970 at the age of forty-nine. Celan's first book, published in 1952, brought him immediate fame, especially with the influential Gruppe 47, and along with Ingeborg Bachmann's, his continued to be one of the most prominent voices in postwar German letters. Because his work became increasingly obscure, some of his later volumes were not as well received, but as Hamburger's useful introduction informs us, Celan's own clinical paranoia, coupled with a bogus charge of plagiarism leveled against him, was really what led to his early end. An accomplished translator and renowned polyglot, Celan may have found it more and more difficult to lay hold of the real within the horrific, but never as a writer did he give in to silence.

The despair Celan felt over the loss of his mother in particular permeates his early poems. At times directly referred to in lines like "Oaken door, who lifted you off your hinges? / My gentle mother cannot return" (**"Aspen"**), it's also clear that she is the omnipresent "you" that haunts many of the poems, such as here in **"The Years From You to Me"**:

> Your hair waves once more when I weep. With
>   the blue of your eyes
> you lay the table of love: a bed between summer
>   and autumn.
> We drink what somebody brewed, neither I nor
>   you nor a third:
>
> we lap up some empty and last thing.
> We watch ourselves in the deep sea's mirrors
>   and faster pass food to each other:
> the night is the night, it begins with the morning,
> beside you it lays me down.

As this points out, it is the "night," or at least Celan's confrontation with it, that allows him to return to the mother by conjuring her anew. Hence, despite the sense of deep personal loss, the poem is not really confessional. Instead its source stems more from ambivalence, as well as wonder at the power of memory to reinvent and resurrect that which seems lost for good.

This is also what makes Celan a poet of the mystical. Rather than being interested in capturing the real for what it is or was, he remains more intrigued by the pathos inherent to his own inability to ever quite set down what was, while at the same time finding himself transformed and closer to the unutterable as a result of his failure. Ambivalence, then, becomes as much a credo as it does a final destination. In another early poem, Celan refers directly to such a need when in the first two stanzas of **"Speak, You Also"** he writes:

> Speak, you also,
> speak as the last.
> have your say
>
> speak—
> But keep yes and no unsplit.
> And give your say this meaning:
> give it the shade.

Functioning almost like a manifesto for Celan's later work, the poem goes on to state, "He speaks truly who speaks the shade." Celan, however, is never one given to narrow polemicism, for his concern with speaking "the shade" demands by its very nature a confluence of plurals and dualities. Thus, as if the only way out were through, the poem's last stanza finds Celan moving from the shade to the light:

> But now shrinks the place where you stand:
> Where now, stripped by shade, will you go?
> Upward. Grope your way up.
> Thinner you grow, less knowable, finer.
> Finer: a thread by which
> it wants to be lowered, the star:
> to float farther down, down below
> where it sees itself gleam: in the swell
> of wandering words.

It is precisely Celan's own ambivalence towards "wandering words" and their ability to seize hold of experience that marks his true note as a poet. Deeply influenced by the philosophy of Martin Heidegger (despite his own horror and disgust with Heidegger's Nazi sympathies), Celan found language to be both limitation and sustenance in his effort to capture despair. Because of the ability of German to combine words into new words, Celan had the opportunity to turn language upon its head. The result was that, through the deft use of Yiddish and Hebrew sources as well as the creation of new words that pointed to their own telling roots, the language he created for his poems worked to free him from those who had persecuted his parents and the Jews as a whole. Nothing short of a revolutionary act, the founding of a new tongue meant for Celan the creation of another life, one that could appropriate experience on its own terms, the powers inherent to such a process becoming nothing short of godly.

From 1963 onwards the difficult turns in Celan's speech also mark the spiritual urge of his poems in their effort to name what cannot be named, both in this world and whatever lies beyond. One of his most famous works, **"Psalm,"** points towards his desire for a kind of transcendence fostered by an immersion into human suffering in order to assert the dignity of the victim, as well as the victim's ultimate right of control over his suffering through expression. Stating that "No one moulds us again out of earth and clay, / no one conjures our dust," Celan identifies himself paradoxically with "no one" by raising a song of open protest in the last two stanzas:

A nothing
we were, are, shall
remain, flowering:
the nothing-, the
no one's rose.

With
our pistil soul-bright,
with our stamen heaven-ravaged,
our corolla red
with the crimson word which we sang
over, O over
the thorn.

At a moment like this Hamburger faces his toughest challenge as a translator, for even the apt "no one's rose" hardly does justice to the compression at work in "die Nichts-, die / Niemandsrose" of the German. Nonetheless, as a "Psalm," the translation does convey the power and strangeness of the voice behind it, as well as the sadness involved in the potential for impalement upon "the thorn." Celan's identification with the "we" and the distinguishing "rose" that springs from "nothing" and "no one" is also what opens the poem up to an array of experience, a shibboleth for those who suffered, but one that refuses to limit suffering to the narrow confines of the literal.

As time went on, the inability of language to name the reality of the pain and despair at work in this century became the *idée fixe* of Celan's work. Strangely enough, what rises out of his ambivalence and frustration with speech is both a deep sense of wonder and a growing tenderness towards those with whom he can identify. In short, Celan is not a despairing poet, but rather a poet *of* despair, his own immediate knowledge of what could be salvaged from it evident in an untitled lyric:

To stand in the shadow
of the scar up in the air.

To stand-for-no-one-and-nothing.
Unrecognized,
for you
alone.

With all there is room for in that,
even without
language.

To stand as one with those who had no one to stand by them was for Celan the only means by which he could survive. "To stand in the shadow," however, also required that he name it, as well as construct his own identity in the face of the surrounding darkness. Just how he managed to do so remains as mysterious as it does mystical, for it will be some years before the many obscure sources and references at work in his poems are sorted out by critics, scholars, and translators alike. In the meantime, we do have these poems to help guide us in both poetry and life, our own sense of wonder enlarged by a conscience that could not help but "Think of It" and demand from us the same:

Think of it: your
own hand
has held
this bit of
habitable
earth, suffered up
again
into life.

Think of it:
this came towards me,
name-awake, hand-awake
for ever,
from the unburiable.

(pp. 569-73)

Peter Filkins, "Uttering the Unutterable," in Partisan **Review,** *Vol. LVIII, No. 3, 1991, pp. 569-73.*

Amy Colin (essay date 1991)

[*In the following excerpt from her critical study* Paul Celan: Holograms of Darkness, *Colin analyzes Celan's poetic techniques and the political, historical, and literary influences evident in his early poetry.*]

Paul Celan's early poetry strikes the reader through its multiplicity of themes, ranging from love encounters and linguistic play to Jewish suffering. Similar to the texts of other Bukovinian poets, Celan's poems play with different modes of writing: some allude to *Minnedichtung* and German ballads, others to Rilke's and Trakl's poetry or to Roumanian folklore; biblical images, metaphors from the New Testament, and a nihilistic view of the world often clash in these early verses. While his texts display thematic and stylistic diversity, they share an interest in problems of language.

Though a poet's literary beginning sheds light on his later work and helps others understand his poetic development, there is no *critical* edition of Celan's early poetry. Some of the verses Celan wrote in Czernowitz were published in various literary journals such as *Der Plan* (1948) and in his first collection of poems, ***Der Sand aus den Urnen*** (1948); others appeared as ***Gedichte 1938-1944*** (1985). Yet for a long time many of them existed only in manuscript form, scattered among the private collections of his friends. The recently published complete collection of Celan's early texts—***Das Frühwerk*** (1989)—is no substitute for a critical and annotated edition, because it does not include the different versions of poems and comprehensive commentaries on their sources, history, and genesis.

In contrast to Celan's late, enigmatic work, which often resists interpretation, his early poetry appears so accessible that some critics try to reduce its meaning to preconceived frames of reference, such as biographical or literary allusions. In her book *Antschel Paul—Paul Celan,* Wiedemann-Wolf includes a detailed discussion of the few available studies of Celan's early poetry and shows how critics, including Stiehler and Chalfen take their own psychological or biographical speculations for the poem's ultimate function and sense. Wiedemann-Wolf's book presents a researched overview of various poetic devices and themes in Celan's early texts and analyzes some of these in detail. Most critics have assumed that Celan's ***Von Schwelle zu Schwelle*** (1955) includes his earliest reflections on linguistic problems, but Wiedemann-Wolf's *Bestandsaufnahme* reveals self-reflective elements inherent in such early Holocaust poems as the **"Todesfuge."** Wiedemann-Wolf views Celan's use of diverse literary traditions as a manifestation of his growing concern for poetic language. According to her, Celan's love and flower poems, written prior to the **"Death Fugue,"** anticipate some poetic devices of the later works but do not reflect poetological ideas, for they do not thematize them. Since words such as *Name* and *Wort* rarely appear in these early texts, she argues: "Antschel reflektiert zwar noch kaum explizit die Funktion des dichterischen Wortes . . . " (Antschel hardly reflects upon the function of the poetic word explicitly . . .).

But poetic language is by its very nature self-reflective. In his later poetry Celan succeeds in making words vibrate so as to uncover their literariness. In contrast, his early poems do not yet attain such an innovative mode of writing. Still, as textual analysis shows, his concern with linguistic problems is already apparent in the playful verses and love poems he wrote prior to 1944. Moreover, Celan's poetic ideas disclose themselves not merely in response to literary traditions (as Wiedemann-Wolf assumes) but throughout his early poems, in subtle allusions to the inadequacy of poetic language, as well as in his untiring quest for new means of poetic expression.

The war and the Holocaust did not prevent Celan from continuing his literary endeavors. In the midst of the ongoing deportations, Celan studied Rilke, Apollinaire, Blok, and Esenin, while hiding in the apartments of various friends. He translated some of Shakespeare's sonnets into German at that time, in an attempt to compete with Kraus's and George's renditions. During those months, he also created his first German adaptations of poems by Eluard, Housman, Verlaine, and Yeats. Not only in the ghetto, but also during the months in the Roumanian labor detachment, he continued to write poetry. As for many Bukovinian writers, literature became for Celan the crucial means of intellectual survival. The experiences of the Holocaust, the persecutions of the Bukovinian Jews, and the death of his parents in Transnistria left their imprint upon his early poems.

Like Bukovinian poets of his time, including his mentor Margul-Sperber, Celan believed that poetry created a world unto itself, detached from a reality overshadowed by the war. In April of 1943, while working in the Roumanian labor detachment, Celan composed several neo-Romantic love poems—**"Tulpen," "Rosenschimmer," "Windröschen,"** and **"Von diesen Stauden"**—for his friend Ruth. Celan's note from the labor camp [an unpublished letter to Ruth Kraft dated 16 April 1943], conveys his feeling of joy as well as pride at having succeeded in writing these poems in such somber surroundings: "In einer Landschaft, der auch die allergeringste Blume fehlt, kann ich diese Gedichte schreiben" (I could write these poems in a setting where there is not even a single flower). He likewise expresses confidence and satisfaction with the progress he has made: "meine Gedichte sind reifer geworden und schöner . . . " (my poems have become more mature and more beautiful . . .).

Celan's **"Tulpen"** appeared in the volume ***Gedichte 1938–1944.*** The different version cited here has not been published elsewhere.

Tulpen, ein stummes Gestirn
von Schwermut und süsser Gewalt,
liess ich, dein Herz zu entwirrn:
findet ihr Leben dich bald?

Was in den Kelchen geheim
ein Staubblatt mit Schimmer befiel,
schwört den unsäglichen Reim
für deinen wehen Gespiel.

Sind es die Tulpen heut, sieh,
die herrschen im Dämmergemach,
hegst du ein Dunkles noch wie
einst, als ich Rotdorn dir brach?

Tulips, a silent constellation
of heavy heartedness and sweet violence
I left, to unravel your heart:
Will their life find you soon?

That which overcame a stamen with a shimmer
in the calyxes privately
swears the unspeakable rhyme
for your wounded playmate

Look: is it the tulips today
that reign in the growing dimness of the room,
do you foster a darkness still as
when I cut red hawthorn for you, once?

The artistic structure of Celan's **"Tulpen"** recalls Stefan George's elaborate verse. Similar to them, Celan's three-stanza poem consists of long sentences whose interpolated appositions and relative clauses conceal the connections between subject, object, and verb. Each stanza is one sentence, and the recurrent enjambments heighten the flow of speech. As Celan's statements gradually transform themselves into questions, they enhance the intricacy of the text and suggest the idea of a linguistic unity. Only the poem's dactylic meter and the repetition of close, front, rounded vowels *(u, o)* lend these lines a grave tone, attuning the reader to their themes.

Here, Celan imbues the poem's almost classical form with romantic images of flowers, love, and a feeling of sorrow. As silent constellations of "Schwermut und süsser Gewalt," the tulips suggest a symbolist idea of metaphors as the flowers of language, and assume the speaker's sadness and melancholy. Since their function is to decipher the beloved's heart, they become a means of both cognition and communication. But as the subsequent line reveals, these messengers have not fulfilled their task, and the final question—"findet ihr Leben dich bald?"—implies a doubt about, rather than a belief in, their adequacy.

Through the image of stamens on which a glimmer falls, lines 5 to 6 lend to the strongly erotic image of pollination an impression of secrecy: "Was in den Kelchen geheim." These verses evoke an oath in unutterable rhymes and an unspoken wish for a language beyond words that may mediate between the speaker and his beloved: "schwört den unsäglichen Reim / für deinen wehen Gespiel."

The contrast between tulips and other messengers further develops this motif: "Rotdorn," whose color and thorns may stand for passion and suffering, reminds the speaker of past disharmony. In the published version of the poem, Celan writes: "hegst du ein Dunkel noch, wie / einst, als ich Rotdorn dir brach?" The interpolated comma ("noch, wie") and the substantivization of the adjective "dunkel" to "Dunkel," rather than "Dunkles," interrupt the melody of the line, enacting the moment of disruption. As the poem's concluding verse suggests, Celan questions the metaphors' commensurability with their task. Although tulips have become the speaker's new messengers, the poet—in "hegst du ein Dunkles noch wie / einst, als ich Rotdorn dir brach?"—still doubts whether they will accomplish the decipherment of the beloved's heart and the mediation between the speaker and "You."

Since Celan's romantic and symbolist images point to the inadequacy of metaphor as a cognitive device and as a means of poetic expression, they undo the harmonic unity evoked by the poem's classical form. In light of these connotations, the poet as "wehe(r) Gespiel" may suffer not only because of his unfulfilled love, but also because of his play with tropes, which makes him aware of their insufficiency. The differences between the published and unpublished version are significant. In the unpublished version, Celan uses the image of "silent constellations" for "shining constellations" (*leuchtend Gestirn*), thus emphasizing the linguistic ideas of his poem. As silent and even secret codes, the tulips bring to mind Hugo von Hofmannsthal's *The Lord Chandos Letter (Ein Brief),* which pleads for a language beyond words as the only still-adequate means of expression. The poem's unpublished version also stresses the discrepancy between its classicist form and its romantic images, because—in contrast to the published version—it does not disrupt the flow of speech in the concluding line. Such slight changes in Celan's diction point to his increasing awareness of the fissures inherent in poetic language. They also exhibit Celan's growing ability to play with words as a means of uncovering the incongruities between the poem's form and its themes.

Many of Celan's early love poems, which speak of the "You" as the mother or the sister, evoke a rather peaceful relationship between "You" and "I." In contrast, **"Tulpen"** shows the beloved to be a source of suffering—a destabilizing force. The speaker's unsuccessful attempt to establish a harmonious relationship with his beloved parallels the endeavor to come to terms with language. In fact, the poem suggests that it is the unsettling love for the "You," rather than a response to war and violence, that inspires the poet's quest for another, more adequate poetic idiom.

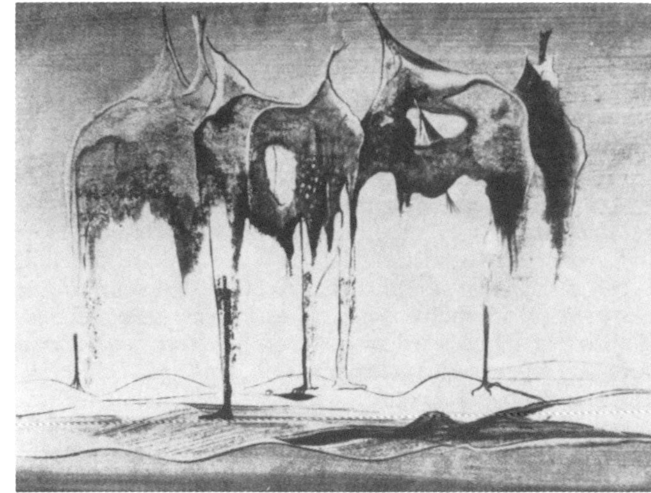

Edgar Jené's "Das rote Meer geht über Land," discussed in Celan's Edgar Jené und der Traum vom Traume.

Celan's doubts about metaphors and the subversive elements inherent in his poem signal a difference between the Bukovinian confidence in words and Celan's own view of poetic language. These doubts show that Celan, unlike his compatriots, remained receptive to the disruptive aspects of romantic poetry, which had deeply influenced avant-garde writings. In contrast to the Bukovinian poets, he was much more interested in the language crisis of such fin de siècle Austrian authors as Hofmannsthal than in Kraus's attempts to revive trite phrases and traditional poetic devices.

Celan's earlier **"Weiß sind die Tulpen"** conveys another difference between his own romantic thought and the ideas of other Bukovinian poets. A version of the poem appeared in ***Gedichte 1938–1944,*** and Ruth Kraft placed it in the period July/August 1941; a second version (marked "23 Mai 1942") is one of the few early poems which Celan dated himself. The text cited here is this latter version.

Weiß sind die Tulpen; neige dich über mich.
Die Nacht tauscht Wind für fächelnde Hände
ein.

Sag:

es werden die Falter schwärmen?

Sag:

mein Mund wird der einzige Kelch sein?
Und du schließt dein Aug vor dem rötlichen
Schimmer—

sag?

Denn diesmal—fühlst du?—läßt dich mein Arm
nicht mehr in die Welt . . .

Weiß sind die Tulpen; neige dich über mich!
"(Liebeslied.)"

White, the tulips; bend over me.

The night trades wind for fluttering hands.

Say:

will the butterflies swarm?

Say:

My mouth is to be the only cup?
And you shut your eye on the reddish shimmer—

Say?

For, this time—do you feel it?—my arm is no longer letting
you into the world . . .

White, the tulips; bend over me!
"(Lovesong.)"

Critics such as Wiedemann-Wolf have already pointed to the remarkable innovative structure of the poem, which—unlike other early texts—no longer uses rhyme and a regular meter, but engages in sound interplay. Through the contrast between one-word and two-line stanzas, Celan integrates the blank space into the poem's form, recalling a stylistic device often used by French Symbolists to illustrate silence. The poem's imagery reflects its formal composition. Celan's **"(Liebeslied.)"** deploys metaphors of love and flowers in a remarkable way: the opening lines create a dreamlike atmosphere where erotic allusions merge with the image of the night exchanging wind for fanning hands. Gradually, almost unnoticeably, the text introduces the speaker's questions to a beloved. But the speaker not only poses questions; he also provides the answers to his persistent "Sag," subverting the idea of a dialogue. As the "I" implies—and even dictates—the answers of his partner and anticipates his beloved's feelings, the text evokes an ultimate unity between these lovers. The line "mein Mund wird der einzige Kelch sein?" associates the speaker's mouth with the calyx of a flower, conveying his wish for truthfulness and a harmonious relation. In "fühlst du?—läßt dich mein Arm nicht mehr in die Welt . . . ," the speaker reveals that "I" and "You" now reside within a realm that belongs to the world no longer.

The differences between the two versions are slight, but significant. In the opening line, Celan had originally written: "Weiß sind die Tulpen: neige dich über mich"; in the later version Celan replaced the colon after "Tulpen" with a semicolon, perhaps he realized that the second part of the line neither explains nor details the initial image, but rather introduces a new metaphor of love. Initially line 6 did not contain a verb, but "wird" (see later version) is, in fact, necessary in order to emphasize the flow of speech. In line 7, the poem replaced the conventional "rosigem Schimmer?" with "rötlichem Schimmer—" which suggests the color of lips, and a dash for a question mark at the end of this line evokes the image of the "I" closely observing his beloved. The first version of this poem had no title. According to Wiedemann-Wolf, the parentheses in the title of the second version—**"(Liebeslied.)"**—signal the stylistic difference between Celan's text and a *Lied* in the German romantic tradition. But the parentheses may also signify that love is not the poem's major theme and that these lines participate only marginally in the tradition referred to in their name.

In the wake of Theodor W. Adorno's theories, some critics might be inclined to interpret poems such as **"(Liebeslied.)"** as a political act: the poet's withdrawal into poetic language is ultimately his protest against violence and war. But Celan's text contains other connotations as well. It recalls the romantic idea that "I" and "You" constitute themselves within language. The image of the speaker discloses itself through his speaking to an "other," and the beloved is created through and exists only within "I's" monologue. The interplay between "I" and "You" thus enables the poem to come into being. Celan's nationalist Bukovinian contemporaries used these concepts from German Romanticism to argue that the national identity of their people manifests itself in their native tongue and folk poetry. In contrast to these poets, Celan subverts the link between poetic language and its referents. As his verse "läßt dich mein Arm nicht mehr in die Welt . . . " implies, "I" and "You" inhabit a poetic sphere that is entirely detached from the "outside world."

Like most other German poets of Jewish descent from the Bukovina, Celan turns poetic language into a home and a refuge for lovers attempting to evade reality. Yet his poem also varies from the German-Jewish tradition of his homeland because of Celan's strong interest in more fundamental linguistic problems and phenomena. Celan's concept of the "You" as an idea inherent in the speech of the "I" even anticipates basic thoughts in **"The Meridian,"** which explicitly treats the interaction between "I," "You," and poetic speech: "Das Gedicht will zu einem Anderen . . . es spricht sich ihm zu. . . . Erst im Raum dieses Gesprächs konstituiert sich das Angesprochene. . . ." (The poem intends another, needs this other, needs an opposite. It goes toward it, bespeaks it . . . Only the space of this conversation can establish what is addressed.) In light of these connotations, the image of the tulips in Celan's love song appears as a symbol for his play with tropes, which come to generate the poem. A comparison of the two versions of this poem reveals not only Celan's stylistic progress but also his growing awareness of the potential implications in the images he uses. Metaphors such as "mein Mund wird der einzige Kelch sein?"—which bring to mind his later enigmatic image "Trink / aus meinem Mund" (Drink / from my mouth) [in **"Das angebrochene Jahr"**]—testify to the innovative dimensions of his early work.

Celan's awareness of rhetorical devices and linguistic questions is also evident in his earlier **"Dein Schimmer,"** written in 1940.

Dein Schimmer, dein Schimmer
naht nimmer, naht nimmer. .

Dein Schweigen, dein Schweigen
trieft von den Zweigen.

Daß Krähen, daß Krähen
staunen und spähen.

Dann eifern die raschen
nach Tränen zu haschen.

Doch viele, doch viele
sterben beim Spiele.

Dein Schimmer, dein Schimmer
naht nimmer, naht nimmer . . .

Your shimmer, your shimmer
never nears, never nears . . .

Your silence, your silence
drips from the branches.

So that crows, that crows
wonder and watch.

The quick ones then hurry
to snatch after tears.

But many, but many
die in the gamble.

Your shimmer, your shimmer
never nears, never nears . . .

The poem strikes the reader through its interplay of sounds, recalling not only the writing of Russian Symbolists, but also children's rhymes and magic spells. As Celan omits or adds a letter, he transforms a combination of repeated sounds into new words: *n* for an *sch* in "Schimmer" generates "nimmer"; a *z* for a *sch* alters "Schweigen" into "Zweigen"; *sp* instead of *kr* in "Krähen," creates the term "spähen"; and an interplay of the two consonants *r* and *h* reveals a phonetic kinship between "raschen" and "haschen." In stanzas 3 and 4, configurations of three phonemes—*sta* and *trä* in "staunen" and "Tränen"—attest to the variety within the repetitions. Since one sound cluster triggers the next, it is their sequence rather than semantic necessity that determines the choice of words and images. By unsettling the apparent thematic linkage, Celan makes language vibrate and free itself from usual semantic structures.

At first glance, the phonetic interplay appears to move beyond meaning, but a closer analysis reveals its direction and sense. The poem opens with absence: "Dein Schimmer . . . naht nimmer" draws on the colloquial German expression "keinen Schimmer haben," pointing to a lack of ideas or clues, and evokes the distance of the "You" from the speaker. In the subsequent verses, absence and negation manifest themselves in silence, which is associated here with raindrops falling off the tree branches ("dein Schweigen / trieft von den Zweigen."). These heterogeneous metaphors converge in a powerful image of death: the raindrops turn into tears snatched by the crows that die while playing with them. The poem ends as it began, assuming a circular structure: "Dein Schimmer, dein Schimmer / naht nimmer, naht nimmer . . . " As in **"(Liebeslied.),"** the *absence présente* of the "You," here a symbol for the missing traditional thematic bond between words, generates an interplay of tropes and images.

"Dein Schimmer" is not Celan's only early poem to play with phonetic and semantic elements to destabilize a familiar verbal coherence and to undermine customary modes of reading. His **"Zauberspruch"** (1940), **"Dämmerung"** (1940), and **"Mein Karren knarrt nicht mehr"** (spring 1941), [all from ***Gedichte 1938-1944***], also engage in similar childlike linguistic experiments. In **"Mein Karren knarrt nicht mehr,"** Celan uncovers potential meanings by expanding "Herbstzeitlose" (meadow-saffron), the name of a flower, into an unusual image: "Die Zeitlose holt / Atem für tausend Herbste. . . . " In the concluding verse of this poem, "Das Herz der Espe / setzt aus" (the heart of the asp / ceases to be), the acoustic play on sibilants, rather than semantic principles, determines the choice of words and thus the creation of an image. These early poems anticipate aspects of Celan's later linguistic experiments in **"Grosses Geburtstagsblaublau mit Reimzeug und Assonanz"** and **"Abzählreime"** (1962) and his use of paronomasia in late, somber poems such as **"Huhediblu,"** where the interplay of phonemes turns words into "wordweeds" and "wordaxes"—"als Beikraut, als Beiwort, als Beilwort" [***Gesammelte Werke***]. In contrast to his later poems on the Holocaust, **"Dein Schimmer"** (like his **"Abzählreime"** from the early sixties), works with the theme of death, not as an expression of a tragic personal experience but as a trope that elucidates a playing with words and their acoustic components. Still, both types of poem exhibit Celan's dissatisfaction with traditional poetic devices and his quest for new means of poetic expression. In this respect, these entirely different poems represent two aspects of the same phenomenon. Celan's verbal experiments in his early and late poetry mark yet another difference between his own work and Bukovinian poetry, which rejected such language games.

When Celan wrote his poems **"Dein Schimmer," "Zauberspruch,"** and **"Dämmerung,"** he had already acquired a comprehensive knowledge of French Surrealism in Tours (1938) and had already read Breton, Eluard, and Aragon. Yet his early texts reveal that, despite his fascination with the avant-garde, he had not yet succeeded in transforming his poetic language according to their linguistic ideas. His early texts, however, signal the direction in which his poetry was to evolve.

In response to the Holocaust and the experience of the war, some of Celan's early poems—such as his **"Ballade von der erloschenen Welt,"** written in Czernowitz around 1942—use linguistic play to undo familiar notions of the transcendent.

Der Sand. Der Sand.
Vor die Zelte, die zahllosen Zelte
trägt der Sand sein Geflüster.
"Ich bin das Meer. Ich bin der Mond.
Lasst mich ein."
"Nacht", murmeln die Zelte.
"Sei Nacht".

Da rücken die Speere heran:
"Wir sind es.
Und das eiserne Blau des Morgens.
Lasst uns die Schwingen alle
durchbohren." . . .

Da regen,
da regen sich bange die Arme der Krieger:
"Uns gaben die gottlosen Engel recht—
und Fremde häufen hier Finsternis?
Wir dringen ein.["]

(Doch was,

doch wer ist im Gezelt?)

Ein atmendes Antlitz
hängt sich hell vor die Zelte:
"Regengrünes Geschick
bin ich.
Und ich bin das Gras.
Ich wehe.
Und ich wehe hinein."

(Doch was,
doch wer ist im Gezelt?)

Versanken sie alle?
Der Sand? die Speere?
Die Arme der Krieger? das atmende Antlitz?

Versanken, versanken sie?

Die stammelnden Seelen der Neger ringsum
tanzten rundum und drangen ein:
die Schatten fanden sie, die Schatten
von Keinem.
Zersprengt ist der Seelenreigen.
("Ballade von der erloschenen Welt")

The sand. The sand.
Before the tents, the tents without number
the sand carries its whisper.
"I am the sea. I am the moon.
Let me in."

"Night," murmur the tents.
"Be night."

The spears approach:
"We are the ones.
And the iron blue of the morning.
Allow us to pierce through all
pinions." . . .

In fear then
the arms of the warriors move, they move:
"The godless angels granted us right—
and strangers heap up darkness here?
We will press in."

(But what,
but who is in the tents?)

A breathing face
hangs bright before the tents:
"I am
raingreen fortune.
And I am the grass.
I drift.
And I drift inside."

(But what,
but who is in the tents?)

Did they all sink?
The sand? the spears?
The warriors' arms? the breathing face?

Did they sink, did they sink?

The stammering souls of the Blacks all around
danced in circles around and pressed in:
the shadows, they found the shadows
of No One.

Exploded, the soul's roundelay.
("Ballad of the World Extinct")

Like **"Dein Schimmer,"** this ballad orchestrates diverse clusters of sounds. One phoneme configuration engages the other, and their interplay determines the acoustic structure of each stanza. In the opening lines, the sibilants *s* and *z* (in "Sand," "Zelte," and "zahllosen") dominate the linguistic interaction; they are counteracted by alliterations of *m* and *n* (lines 6–7) and repetitions of *r* (lines 8–16). The subsequent lines work with prolonged vowels *e* and *i,* while the concluding two stanzas imbue the initial configuration of sibilants with the consonant *r.* This interweaving of sounds lends the text a melody which unsettles the narrative tone of traditional ballads.

Celan's poem, a dramatic scene in which different voices are contrasted with one another, derives its unusual character from the personification of objects, such as the sand, the spears, the tents, and the arms of the warriors. It recalls fables and ballads by the Bukovinian Yiddish writers Manger and Steinbarg, texts in which objects become the protagonists.

In the opening lines, a narrator's voice confronts the reader with the vision of a world devoid of life. Sand covers up the earth; of our entire civilization nothing is left but tents, the shelter of the Bedouins and of the Jews who once wandered through the desert after leaving Egypt. Winds carry the sand's whisper: one with the sea and the moon, the sand forces its way into the tents—tents which call, however, for the night, and thus perhaps for suffering and death. Gradually other voices resonate in the somber scenario: the spears—whose metallic sheen resembles the color of the morning—seek to break through "all wings," perhaps the wings of an angel guarding the entrance to the "inner world." But the arms of the warriors question the right of others to cause evil ("und Fremde häufen hier Finsternis?") and claim that the "godless angels" justify their actions alone. The unusual image of the "gottlose(n) Engel" hints at their deceptive holiness and at God's absence.

In a series of questions that interrupt the narration—"(Doch was, / doch wer ist im Gezelt?)"—the voice of a commentator urges the reader to reflect upon why these forces seek entrance into the tents. But instead of providing answers, the subsequent lines heighten the suspense: they mention yet another entity that seeks to penetrate the tents; this is a breathing face identified here with both nature and fate, "Regengrünes Geschick." In the next line the poem finally signals a denouement: though the indicative in "Wir dringen ein" and "Ich wehe. / Und ich wehe hinein" implies that the forces may have succeeded in intruding into the tents, the final question "Versanken sie alle?" suggests their destruction, anticipating the surprising end: the souls of Black people who perform a round dance, perhaps a *Todesreigen,* intrude into the tents; they discover nothing but "die Schatten / von Keinem," and, as a result, the souls disperse: "Zersprengt ist der Seelenreigen."

Such an ending leaves room for speculation, compelling readers to explore the multiple potential meanings of images such as the tents. In his late texts, Celan often associates tents with the world itself: his commentary ***Edgar Jené and the Dream about the Dream*** (1948) compares the world devastated by the war with a "Blutzelt" (tent of blood), and his ***Bremen Speech*** (1958) characterizes man's *Dasein* as "zeltlos" (unsheltered), meaning here a lack of protection and the absence of "God." Celan's early ballad seems to anticipate these later images by conveying the vision of a world after an exodus, after an atomic war, when there is nothing left of humankind but its shadows.

Yet the poem's self-reflective moments lend these lines another meaning. By juxtaposing the tents with forces residing outside the tents, the text evokes a contrast between an inside and an outside realm. Since the intrusion into the tents is linked to images of the world's extinction, the poem ultimately breaks down the inside/outside polarity that it evokes. Moreover, the enigmatic image "die Schatten / von Keinem," describing the tent's inside, conveys a paradox: the nonexistence of a person, "Keinem," presupposes here the existence of a shadow. To "intrude" into the tents thus ultimately means to discover the paradox inherent in such cognitive models as inside/outside.

Rainer Maria Rilke, in "Am Rande der Nacht," used an interplay of sounds and antithetical images to first evoke and then undo the idea of a synthesis of the poem and the universe, of an "inside" and an "outside." Under the impact of violence and war, Paul Celan takes up Rilke's poetic devices as a means of conveying his disbelief in a transcendent force that may protect human life from destruction. The non-existence of a world's "inside"—whether a divine spirit or an inner sense—becomes a conceptual frame for his poem **"Legende,"** also written around 1942:

> Nach dem rostigen Rätsel der Erde
> komm Bruder forsch mit mir mit hellem Spaten-
> stich.
> Ich fand nichts. Du findest nichts.
> Doch die Erde splittert dabei.
>
> For the rusty riddle of the earth,
> come, brother, search with me with bright spade
> cut.
> I found nothing. You found nothing.
> But the earth splits with our work.

The poem searches for the secrets, and perhaps for a meaning in the world. But the speaker does not find anything; his search ends in nothingness and the destruction of the earth. The "rusting riddle of the earth" is nothing but a myth. Celan's early **"Ballade vom Auszug der drei"**—also written during the war—characterizes the entire universe and eternity as empty: "In die leere Ewigkeit ziehn wir mit schwelenden Fackeln" (Into empty eternity we draw ourselves with flickering torches) say the three fictional characters of the poem, which evokes the total annihilation of their and Celan's homeland. Again, the play with phonemes and use of paronomasia become the poet's means of unsettling universal concepts and beliefs such as the idea of a sheltered human existence.

Celan's early artistic endeavors also consciously relate themselves to his political engagement of that time, an engagement which—as Marlies Janz has shown [in *Vom Engagement absoluter*]—deeply marks his later poetry as well. In fact, Celan's literary aspirations were to a certain extent a direct result of his political activities.

As a high-school student, Celan joined the illegal Communist youth organization in the Bukovina, braving the severe Roumanian reprisals against all Communist activities. Together with his friends, Celan studied Karl Marx, Gustav Landauer, Rosa Luxemburg, Peter Kropotkin, Mikhail Bakunin, Werner Sombart, and even the economist Karl Kautsky; they illegally brought out a leftist pamphlet, *Elevul Roşu* (The Red Student), and distributed it among students and workers. These leaflets included not only Celan's translations into Roumanian of passages from Marxist writings, but also essays by some of his friends on the situation of the working class. . . . (pp. 53-66)

After the show trials and after reading André Gide's *Retouche du "Retour de l'U.R.S.S." (Afterthoughts: A Sequel to "Back from the U.S.S.R.")* (1937), Celan turned away from Soviet Communism, but he remained an attentive observer of political events. Celan's **"Fackelzug,"** probably written during the war, illustrates the relationship between the author's political engagement and his growing awareness of potential connotations inherent in poetic images and rhetorical devices.

> Kamerad, die Fackel heb
> und den Fuß setz stramm.
> Ferne ist nur Drahtgeweb.
> Und die Erde Schlamm.
>
> Kamerad, die Fackel schwing,
> meine Fackel raucht.
> Deine Seele ist ein Ding,
> das jetzt Feuer braucht.
>
> Kamerad, die Fackel senk,—
> und verlösche sie.
> Wie das Leben ist bedenk.
> Und das Sterben wie.
>
> (**"Fackelzug"**)
>
> Comrade, raise the torch
> and stand at attention.
> Distance is but woven wire
> and the earth slime.
>
> Comrade, swing the torch
> my torch is smoking.
> Your soul is a thing
> that now needs fire.
>
> Comrade, lower the torch
> and put it out.
> Consider what life is.
> And what death.
>
> (**"Torch Procession"**)

The poem's regular, accelerated rhythm recalls a military song. Through the iambic meter, alternating rhyme, and parallelisms, Celan enhances both the poem's emphatic tone and its structural symmetry, which appears even in the recurrence of indented lines. In the last stanza, however, the reversals ("Wie das Leben ist, bedenk. / Und das Sterben wie.") counteract the poem's repetitive aspects, signaling a change in the poetic mood.

The title, **"Fackelzug,"** evokes the procession of torches often used in Nazi demonstrations and thus attunes the reader to the subsequent images of violence. Such a traditional Nazi term as "Kamerad" and the military commands "die Fackel heb / und den Fuß setz stramm" reveal that the opening lines are written not only in the style, but also from the perspective, of Nazi war propaganda. The subsequent prosaic observations, devoid of any sorrow or regret, typify the attitude of comrades during World War II. For them the earth is nothing but mud, the horizon a wire netting, and the world a trench. Even the soul is a *thing,* that is, an object to be used or misused according to need and necessity.

But in the second stanza, the speaker contrasts the appeal to start the battle with the image of a burned-down torch, a symbol of the waning of the fighting spirit. In the same emphatic tone as appears in the opening lines, he urges the comrade to lower, to extinguish his torch and thus to put an end to violence. The poem closes compelling a "You" to reflect upon the value of life and the consequences of war: "Wie das Leben ist, bedenk. / Und das Sterben wie."

The poem's employment of idioms of Nazi war propaganda urging comrades first to fight and then to recognize the significance of life and peace, shows that Celan was well aware of the writer's capacity to manipulate language. Celan's **"Fackelzug"** consciously uses the comrades' military language to make them rethink the outcome of their violence. Although the poet was politically active, his text propagates no particular ideological view, but protests violence independent of its political justification. Like other European authors, including Kraus and some of Celan's Bukovinian contemporaries, he attacks the society of his time for misusing poetic language to drive people into war.

The interaction between Celan's political engagement and his artistic creativity also manifests itself in his **"Chanson Juive,"** which was later entitled **"An den Wassern Babels"** and was probably written during the war.

Wieder an dunkelnden Teichen
murmelst du, Weide, gram.
Weh oder wundersam
keinem zu gleichen?

Den deine Kralle zaust,
sucht sich in Sünden.
Wendet sich von deinem Zünden
flammende Faust.

Kehr mit grausem Getös
ein in kauernde Hütten.
Komm unser Blut verschütten.
Den Lehm erlös.

Again at darkening pools
You murmur, willow, grieving.
Wounded or wondrous
Equal to none?

The one whom your claw clutches
seeks himself in sins.
Turns away from your enflaming,
flaming fist.

Come with hideous roar
into cowering huts.
Come spill our blood.
Redeem the clay . . .

("Chanson juive")

Despite the title's explicit allusion to Judaism, **"Chanson Juive"** follows the German stanza tradition of a "Lied." The poem's musicality expresses itself through the alternation of close, front, rounded vowels, and open, back, unrounded vowels *(u, e, ei),* as well as through the sibilants *s* and *z* that accompany the diphthongs *ei* and *au.* As in the texts of Russian Symbolists, the poem's melody is attuned to the imagery: in the opening lines, the willow motif evokes suffering and death, and the image of the darkening pools intensifies the poem's somber tone, which is counteracted only by the play of sounds in "Weh oder wundersam." The stanza emphasizes that the murmur of the willow has been heard before, and inquires into the nature of that which resembles the mourning tree.

In the second stanza, the sibilants *z* and *s* signal violence and aggression. Yet the *f* in "flammende Faust" prolongs the emphatic articulation of the stanza, anticipating the nearly hesitant attitude of the ending line. The willow, characterized by tugging claws, metamorphoses into a figure of punishment that forces self-recognition in a past of sins, "Den deine Kralle zaust, / sucht sich in Sünden." The speakers address themselves to this threatening force, requesting its intrusion into their homes and spilling their blood. In the concluding line, this gruesome death wish becomes an appeal for redemption, "den Lehm erlös."

Similar to **"Chanson Juive,"** the second title of the poem, **"An den Wassern Babels"**—alluding to Psalm 137, **"By the Waters of Babylon"**—also sets the metaphors of violence and aggression in the context of Jewish suffering. As a burning fist and punishing force, the "You" assumes characteristics of the Jewish God, YHWH. The "fire" in "brennnende Faust" is a recurrent biblical metaphor of God (Gen. 19:24, 22:7; Ex. 3:2, 32:20, 40:38). Time and again, the Hebrew Bible characterizes YHWH as entering the "tents" of the Jews (Ex. 40:38, for example), proving His power or punishing their sins. These images also recur in the poem's concluding lines, "Kehr mit grausem Getös / ein in kauernde Hütten. / Komm unser Blut verschütten."

As the second title and the biblical allusions imply, Jewish songs from the time of the Babylonian captivity come to life in Celan's "Lied." The willow's murmur, a symbol of these songs, can be heard in the present time; ultimately, such images reveal that Celan identifies the fate of Jews in the death camps with their persecution in antiquity. The speakers plead for their own destruction, as death appears the only possible escape from their captivity and persecution. Bitter irony resonates in these lines: God offers His chosen people nothing but violence and death. Such an ironic tone underlying the melody of the concluding stanza ultimately questions the Jewish ideas that the poem seems to evoke. It points to Celan's doubt in the Jewish belief that God punishes only those whom he really loves and that past sins brought about the Holocaust.

The differences between the two versions of the poem illustrate Celan's quest for greater linguistic precision. Thus Celan in the later version **"An den Wassern Babels"** writes: "Weh oder wundersam: / Keinem zu gleichen?"

The colon after "wundersam" marks a halt; it emphasizes the poem's rhythm, drawing the reader's attention to the subsequent "Keinem zu gleichen?" Moreover, by capitalizing "Keinem," Celan stresses its significance in this context. In stanza three Celan includes a direct address to both the willow and YHWH—this is the "Du" so characteristic of his later poetry: "Kehr du mit grausem Getös / ein in kauernde Hütten." In addition, the later version ends in an ellipsis implying silence or perhaps "a turning of our breath."

The poem's themes and second title were a source of inspiration for Celan's friend Weißglas, who wrote his "Babylonische Klage" many years after Celan wrote **"Chanson Juive."** Though Celan's poem and Weißglas's text share some thematic affinities, their style and thoughts vary considerably. In contrast to Celan, Weißglas does not disguise his motifs through an intricate interplay of sounds and images, but presents them rather explicitly. Moreover, as the interpretation of Weißglas's verses exposed, the poet internalizes prejudices against his people, while Celan protests Jewish acceptance of anti-Semitism. These substantial differences between the two poems show that Weißglas "learned" as much from Celan as Celan supposedly learned from him.

In contrast to **"Chanson Juive,"** which places Jewish suffering in a broad historical context, Celan's poem **"Dornenkranz"** evokes a tragic and personal experience, the deportation and death of his mother. As a poetic expression of a biographical event, this poem creates a space of interaction between reality, poetry, and poetics:

Lass von dem Purpur.

Die Nacht
hämmert den Herzschlag der Stunde zurecht:
die Zeiger, zwei Speere,
bohrt sie dir brennend ins Aug.

Die Blutspur dunkelt und winkt nicht.

Dein Abend,
der Seen entschleiertes Antlitz,
sank ins spärliche Schilf;
der Engel besiegte Heerschar
löscht ihn mit ihrem Schritt.

Im Wald
schnitzen die Messer der Winde
in die Eschen dein zierliches Bild.
Mit dem Nachtwind birg mich in deinen Armen.
An die eschenen Brüste zünd ich dir Sterne zum Abschied.

Bleibe nicht. Blüh nicht mehr.

Es ging das Schneelicht aus. Allein sind alle Entblössten . . .

Ich ritt in die Nacht; ich kehre nicht um.
(**"Dornenkranz"**)

Let go the purple.

The night
hammers the hour's heartbeat into place
the clock hands, two spear points,
it bores burning into your eyes.

The trace of blood darkens and ceases to sign.

Your evening
unveiled face of the seas
sank into sparse reed;
the angels' heavenly host, conquered,
extinguishes it with its stride.

In the forest
the knives of the winds carve
in the ash trees your delicate image;
take me with the night wind into your arms.
At ashen breasts I light you stars goodbye.

Don't stay. Bloom no more.

The snow-light went out. All the naked are alone . . .

I rode into the night, I will not return.
(**"Crown of Thorns"**)

The poem plays with heterogeneous traditions, combining allusions to the New Testament with expressionist metaphors for violence ("Die Blutspur dunkelt") and romantic motifs with images recalling Rilke's poetry. The "crown of thorns," a metaphor for Christ's suffering, sheds light on the poem's seemingly unrelated opening line: "Lass von dem Purpur." "Purpur" evokes the scarlet cloak—a symbol of power and splendor—in which the Roman soldiers wrapped Christ to mock him (Matt. 27:28). In such a context, line I is an appeal to detach one's self from the world of power and beauty when confronted with death. As the color of the dusk and of blood, "Purpur" anticipates the subsequent description of the night. Like the Roman soldiers with their spears (Matt. 26:47), the night bores its hands into the eyes of the "You," causing eternal darkness (line 5). The verb "dunkeln" fuses the previous night-metaphor with the image of a blood trace ("Blutspur"), the evidence of the crime.

Stanza 3 speaks of the wind carving the image of the "You" into ash trees and of the speaker's wish to be concealed in the arms of the "You." In Germanic myth, the ash tree is the center of the world and symbolizes eternal life, and the carving of an image into such a tree of life appears as a means of preserving the memory of a "You." Yet the Middle High German word *asch,* from which *Esche* derives, denotes not only ash trees but also ashes, the telling residue of destruction. As a species of olive tree, the "ash tree" may stand for the olive garden, where the Roman soldiers captured Christ. The text's hidden connotations recall Rainer Maria Rilke's "Der ÖlbaumGarten," one of Celan's favorite poems, which also speaks of Christ's isolation and loneliness.

Lines 14 to 16 introduce a decisive thematic change. Words such as "Brüste" and "zierlich" as well as the maternal embrace in "birg mich in deinen Armen" suggest that the death and suffering motifs refer to a woman rather than to Christ. Moreover, Celan here fuses the image of the extinguished light, with the idea of barrenness and deprivation, turning them into powerful metaphors for the bodies of murdered Jews that were thrown naked into mass graves.

In the last lines, Celan presents a new theme. The speaker

suddenly exhorts himself not to stay any longer: "Bleib nicht. Blüh nicht mehr." His/her wish to ride into the night and never to return resonates with pain and suffering: "Ich ritt in die Nacht; ich kehre nicht um."

These unusual images referring to Christ, to a woman, and to the speaker himself resist interpretation. Yet in another of Celan's early poems that displays strong similarities to **"Dornenkranz,"** similar metaphors recur:

> Es fällt nun, Mutter, Schnee in der Ukraine:
> des Heilands Kranz aus tausend Körnchen
> Kummer. .
> von meinen Tränen hier erreicht dich keine;
> von frühern Winken nur ein stolzer stummer. .
>
> There falls now, Mother, snow in the Ukraine:
> the Saviour's crown of thousand grains of
> grief . . .
> from my tears here, none will reach you
> from past winks, a proud, a silent one alone. .

'Es fällt nun, Mutter, Schnee in der Ukraine," later entitled **"Winter"** [in ***Gedichte 1938–1944***], associates the falling snow with maternal suffering, death, and with Christ's passion. In the unpublished version, Celan replaced the phrase "Empfang den Kranz" with "Heiland," the synonym for Christ the Savior, thus stressing the relation between the mother's and Christ's fates. These lines work with the same set of motifs as "Dornenkranz"—deprivation, barrenness, redemption: "erlöst das Linde und entblößt das Scharfe?" (the gentle, does it redeem and the cutting, does it strip naked?). In the last lines of **"Winter,"** Celan anchors the speaker's reflections in his wish to follow the mother into a realm of darkness and death: "Was wär es, Mutter: Wachstum oder Wunde— / versänk ich mit im Schneewehn der Ukraine? . . . "

Through the connotations and allusions that invisibly link stanzas and lines and give silence a crucial part in the structure of the poem, **"Dornenkranz"** suggests the identification of the mother's suffering in a death camp with Christ's passion and the speaker's desire to share their fate.

In his painting "Crucifixion" (1943), Chagall used the image of the crucified Jesus as a symbol for the Jews who died in pogroms. Chaim Potok's *My Name is Asher Lev* (1972) works with a similar theme. In this book, the protagonist sees his mother leaning against the crossed window bars in her fearful wait for his return and imagines her crucified: the Orthodox father considers such a thought unforgivable blasphemy. For a German writer or poet of Jewish descent, this comparison is novel and points in Celan's case to his secular education.

Through the fusion of such diverse stylistic devices and motifs, Celan's **"Dornenkranz"** ultimately enacts its title, a "crown (or rather a wreath) of thorns." The wreath metaphor implies linkage and rupture, interweaving and separation. As a linguistic *Geflecht* (wreath, netting), Celan's poem anticipates his later basic concept of poetry as a *Sprachgitter* (speech-grille). Critics have associated Celan's term *Sprachgitter* with a multiplicity of often disparate meanings, ranging from a cloister window with a grating, and a metaphor for a divine realm or for a prison, to a barrier of linguistic expression and a symbol of the impossibility of communication. As Alfred Kelletat has pointed out, the term *Sprachgitter* suggests not only separation but also an inextricable link, because *Gitter* derives from the Indo-European verb *godh,* meaning "unite, bind tightly." In contrast to most scholars, Jean Bollack, in his essay "Paul Celan sur la langue: Le poème *Sprachgitter* et ses interprétations," relates this key term of Celan's poetry to poetic language itself and points out that it evokes the texture of Celan's poem **"Sprachgitter,"** in which a poetic idiom quests for its own space, by "composing, decomposing and recomposing itself . . . , by being trapped within and at the same time transgressing its own contradictions in search of its own space."

Although Celan's **"Sprachgitter"** became a focal point of diverse readings, scholars have not realized the crucial relationship between this poetic concept and Celan's early work. In the sense of "linkage," **"Sprachgitter"** continues **"Dornenkranz"** and other early poems which draw together elements from different literatures and cultural traditions. As a separation of motifs, **"Sprachgitter"** further advances subversive tendencies already apparent in the texts Celan wrote in Czernowitz. Ultimately, Celan's **"Sprachgitter"** enacts a characteristic of his cultural background, the simultaneity of receptivity to and the barriers between multilingual cultural traditions.

"Dornenkranz," with its image of the speaker's ride into the darkness and into a realm of death, anticipates yet another key motif of Celan's later work: the movement of the "I" and the poem toward an "Other." As Celan writes in **"The Meridian,"**

> Das Gedicht . . . ist einsam und unterwegs. Wer es schreibt, bleibt ihm mitgegeben. . . .
>
> Das Gedicht will zu einem Andern, es braucht dieses Andere, es braucht ein Gegenüber. Es sucht es auf, es spricht sich ihm zu.
> Jedes Ding, jeder Mensch ist dem Gedicht, das auf das Andere zuhält, eine Gestalt dieses Anderen.
>
> The poem . . . is lonely and *en route.* Its author stays with it. . . .
> The poem intends another, needs this other, needs an opposite. It goes toward it, bespeaks it.
>
> For the poem, everything and everybody is a figure of this other toward which it is heading.

Though these reflections on the nature of poetic language are much more intricate then Celan's early poetic ideas, **"Dornenkranz,"** along with many early texts written in Czernowitz, laid the foundation for Celan's later poetic development. (pp. 66-74)

Amy Colin, in her Paul Celan: Holograms of Darkness, *Indiana University Press, 1991, 211 p.*

FURTHER READING

Biography

Cassian, Nina. " 'We Will Be Back and Up to Drown at Home': Notes on Paul Celan." *Parnassus: Poetry in Review* 15, No. 1 (1988): 108-29.

Cassian, a former friend and translator of Celan, relates episodes in the poet's life and art.

Chalfen, Israel. *Paul Celan: A Biography of His Youth.* Translated by Maximilian Bleyleben. New York: Persea Books, 1991, 214 p.

Biography of Celan with an introduction by John Felstiner. Felstiner comments: "Chalfen has assembled a firsthand account [of Celan's life] from numerous interviews, memoirs, and other documentary sources."

Criticism

Felstiner, John. " '*Ziv,* That Light': Translation and Tradition in Paul Celan." In *The Craft of Translation,* edited by John Biguenet and Rainer Schulte, pp. 93-116. Chicago: University of Chicago Press, 1989.

Demonstrates the complex process of translation "by reconstructing the multiple linguistic, cultural, and historical forces that went into the creation of Paul Celan's poem 'Nah, im Aortenbogen.' " Originally published in the Spring 1987 issue of *New Literary History.*

Glenn, Jerry. Review of *Gesammelte Werke,* by Paul Celan. *The German Quarterly* 58, No. 4 (Fall 1985): 634-35.

Positive review of *Gesammelte Werke.*

Myers, Saul. "The Way Through the Human-Shaped Snow: Paul Celan's Job." *Studies in Twentieth-Century Literature* 11, No. 2 (Spring 1987): 213-28.

Analyzes Celan's poem "Weggebeizt" in order to show "how Celan's volatile, synthetic German veers close to [specific passages in the *Book of Job*], so close in fact that some of Celan's astonishing neologisms are cryptic translations and glosses of the Hebrew."

Oppenheimer, Paul. "Language Mesh." *American Book Review* 12, No. 1 (March-April 1990): 17, 29.

Positive review of *Poems of Paul Celan.*

Roditi, Edouard. "Paul Celan and the Cult of Personality." *World Literature Today* 66, No. 1 (Winter 1992): 11-20.

Argues that genuine critical understanding of Celan has been obscured by a "cult of personality" surrounding the author.

Rolleston, James. "Double Time, Double Language: Benn, Celan, Enzensberger." In his *Narratives of Ecstasy: Romantic Temporality in Modern German Poetry,* pp. 133-74. Detroit: Wayne State University Press, 1987.

Compares Celan's poetry to the works of Gottfreid Benn and Hans Magnus Enzensberger, focusing on the themes of time and history in their works.

Additional coverage of Celan's life and career is contained in the following sources published by Gale Research: *Contemporary Authors,* Vols. 85-88; *Contemporary Authors New Revision Series,* Vol. 33; *Contemporary Literary Criticism,* Vols. 10, 19, 53; *Dictionary of Literary Biography,* Vol. 69; and *Major 20th-Century Writers.*

John Dos Passos

U.S.A.

The following entry presents criticism on Dos Passos's novels *The 42nd Parallel* (1930), *1919* (1932), and *The Big Money* (1936) collectively published as *U.S.A.* in 1938. For further information on Dos Passos's life and career, see *CLC,* Volumes 1, 4, 8, 11, 15, 25, and 34.

INTRODUCTION

Considered Dos Passos's masterpiece, *U.S.A.* presents a fiercely critical and pessimistic portrait of American society during the first three decades of the twentieth century. The trilogy stands as his most forceful presentation of his central concerns: the failure of the American Dream, the exploitation of the working class, the loss of individual freedom, and America's emphasis on materialism. The novels also represent Dos Passos's most successful experiments in narrative form. Building on the innovative techniques of his earlier works, Dos Passos interspersed the narrative with prose poem passages, excerpts from newspapers and popular songs, and biographical portraits of famous Americans, thus evoking multiple layers of detail and realism. Described as an epic novel as well as an historical study, *U.S.A.* established Dos Passos's reputation as an important literary innovator and as a major chronicler of twentieth-century American life.

Dos Passos began work on *U.S.A.* in 1927. Although it is not clear that he envisioned his new work as a trilogy, he intended from the beginning to craft a long narrative, combining fiction and history, that would examine the entangled lives of several Americans during the first three decades of the twentieth century. Summarizing his concept of fiction in his "Statement of Belief" written in 1928, Dos Passos wrote that "the only excuse for a novelist, aside from the entertainment and vicarious living his books give the people who read them, is as a sort of second-class historian of the age he lives in." With *U.S.A.* Dos Passos refined the technical innovations he introduced in *Manhattan Transfer,* where he juxtaposed prose poems against popular songs and diverse images to create a cinematic collage of New York City society from 1900 to the 1920s. Commenting on Dos Passos's method of composition for *U.S.A.,* Donald Pizer has postulated that Dos Passos worked on each mode as a separate entity, beginning with the biographical and narrative sections, and then alternated segments of the different forms for ironic effect. Early critical reaction to the three novels was overwhelmingly positive. Although a few reviewers faulted them as excessively pessimistic and lacking in warmth and emotion, most commentators lauded the trilogy's innovative style and wide-ranging, satirical portrait of American society.

The style, form, and scale of *U.S.A.* render any type of concise plot summary impossible. In terms of the periods covered, *The 42nd Parallel* deals with events from 1900 to 1917; *1919* focuses on World War I and its immediate aftermath; and *The Big Money* covers the 1920s. Dos Passos relied primarily on the juxtaposition of the four modes—the fictional narratives, Newsreel segments, Camera Eye sections, and biographies—to create irony and convey meaning. Indeed, A. S. Knowles, Jr. has noted that the fictional narratives, in isolation, are "deliberately verbose, tedious, banal, and unselective, meant to give a precise effect of real people thinking, talking, and acting their way through series of experiences to which they can bring only a limited understanding." Dos Passos covers, in varying levels of detail, the lives of over a dozen characters through the narratives. J. Ward Moorehouse—a pompous, opportunistic public relations expert who rises to prominence in the first two novels and then declines to moral bankruptcy in *The Big Money*—emerges as the trilogy's principal character. In the Newsreels, which are excerpts from popular songs as well as actual newspaper headlines and articles, Dos Passos presents mass culture as a cacophony of fads and events. The Camera Eye segments are impressionistic prose poem passages in which Dos Passos describes his feelings and observations at specific moments during his life. The biographies, which many critics consider his best writing in the trilogy, recount the lives of famous Americans—businessmen, entertainers, inventors, philosophers, and politicians—through often-ironic layerings of various details that culminate in final, telling portraits of Dos Passos's subjects.

Critics generally agree that Dos Passos intended *U.S.A.* to encapsulate the essential characteristics of America during the early twentieth century. Indeed, the Newsreels capture the mood of the period, and many commentators note that characters in the fictional narratives represent archetypes rather than unique individuals. J. Ward Moorehouse and Margo Dowling, for instance, are exploiters; Mac McCreary and Janey Williams are exploited; while Mary French and Ben Compton are examples of those who work for a cause beyond personal interest but prove ineffectual. The hollowness of capitalism, the pervasiveness and destructive power of greed, and the betrayal of the ideals and values of the founding fathers emerge as the trilogy's overriding themes. For instance, the biographies portray businessmen such as Andrew Carnegie and J. P. Morgan as villains; the narrative depicts the moral collapse of Moorehouse and Charley Anderson, the owner of an aircraft manufacturing company; and Camera Eye (50), near the conclusion of *The Big Money,* expresses Dos Passos's profound sense of despair over the execution of Nicola Sacco and Bartolomeo Vanzetti—two Italian immigrants who, Dos Passos and many others believed, were wrongly convicted of murder and electrocuted in 1927. Although Dos Passos was associated with the Left in American politics during the 1920s and 1930s and clearly condemned capitalist excesses in *U.S.A.,* contemporary critics emphasize that the trilogy should not be interpreted as a proletarian novel since the book lacks an explicit political message, characterizes the Communist Party as exploitative, and suggests that individuals from the proletariat can be as morally bankrupt as the people who exploit them. In summarizing Dos Passos's themes, Alfred Kazin has argued that in *U.S.A.* "the only defense against the ravages of our century is personal integrity" and that "Dos Passos makes it clear that . . . democracy can survive only through the superior man, the intellectual aristocrat, the poet who may not value what the crowd does."

The style and tone of *U.S.A.* have generated much critical analysis. In assessing Dos Passos's style, many commentators have focused on his ironic juxtaposition of the four modes. Critics assert that although Dos Passos did not invent the styles employed in the different modes, his use of these varying styles in a single work was innovative, and the skill with which he arranged the novels' various parts represents his foremost artistic achievement in *U.S.A.* For example, in *The 42nd Parallel* the narrative account of Mac eating at a train station lunch counter and traveling coach is contrasted with the Camera Eye image of Dos Passos, as a child, traveling in luxury in a private railroad car. The subsequent Newsreel contains an excerpt from a speech by Michigan Governor Hazen Pingree, who warns that inequality will result in revolution. The following Camera Eye segment concludes with Dos Passos's mother discussing, in a trivial manner, the shooting of a working-class Mexican. The story about the Mexican is then interrupted by the phrase "Lover of Mankind," which is the title introducing the biographical sketch of Eugene Debs, a prominent American socialist. Critics have disagreed about the overall tone of *U.S.A.* Commentators who consider the trilogy negative and deterministic emphasize the lack of psychological growth in the characters from the narrative sections, the empty and unhappy endings to these character's lives, and their apparent lack of free-will in the face of social conditions. Providing a contrary interpretation, others argue that the Camera Eye sections reveal the psychological development of an individual whose sense of identity and understanding of the world is increasing. These critics also contend that the biographies depict individuals who do indeed affect history, shaping their lives and those of others. In summarizing the trilogy's critical reception, Robert Rosen has asserted that "diverse political perspectives lurk somewhere behind . . . critical evaluations of *U.S.A.,* but few would disagree with [Alfred] Kazin's praise that Dos Passos 'brings energy to despair.' "

PRINCIPAL WORKS

One Man's Initiation—1917 [abridged edition] (novel) 1920; also published as *First Encounter,* 1945; and *One Man's Initiation—1917* [unabridged edition], 1969
Three Soldiers (novel) 1921
Rosinante to the Road Again (travel essays) 1922
Manhattan Transfer (novel) 1925
**The Moon Is a Gong* (drama) 1925; also published as *The Garbage Man,* 1926
Facing the Chair: Story of the Americanization of Two Foreignborn Workmen (pamphlet) 1927
Orient Express (travel essay) 1927
**Airways, Inc.* (drama) 1928
†*The 42nd Parallel* (novel) 1930
†*1919* (novel) 1932
**Fortune Heights* (drama) [first publication] 1933
†*The Big Money* (novel) 1936
‡*Adventures of a Young Man* (novel) 1939
The Ground We Stand On (history) 1941
‡*Number One* (novel) 1943
‡*The Grand Design* (novel) 1949
The Prospect before Us (nonfiction) 1950
Chosen Country (novel) 1951
The Head and Heart of Thomas Jefferson (biography) 1954
The Theme Is Freedom (essays) 1956
The Men Who Made the Nation (history) 1957
Prospects of a Golden Age (history) 1959
§*U.S.A.* [with Paul Shyre] (drama) 1959
Midcentury (novel) 1961
Mr. Wilson's War (history) 1962
The Best Times: An Informal Memoir (memoirs) 1966
The Shackles of Power: Three Jeffersonian Decades, 1801-1826 (history) 1966

Easter Island: Island of Enigmas (nonfiction) 1971
The Fourteenth Chronicle: Letters and Diaries of John Dos Passos (letters and diaries) 1973
Century's Ebb: The Thirteenth Chronicle (unfinished novel) 1975

*These works were published as *Three Plays: The Garbage Man, Airways, Inc., Fortune Heights* in 1934.

†These works were published as *U.S.A.* in 1938.

‡These works were published as *District of Columbia* in 1952.

§This drama is an adaptation of the trilogy *U.S.A.*

CRITICISM

Edmund Wilson (review date 26 March 1930)

[*Wilson is generally considered twentieth-century America's foremost man of letters. A prolific reviewer, creative writer, and social and literary critic, he is best known for* Axel's Castle *(1931), a seminal study of literary symbolism, and as the author of widely read reviews and essays. In the following excerpt from a review written in March 1930, he praises Dos Passos's character depictions and fusion of intellectual and public concerns in* The 42nd Parallel.]

The 42nd Parallel—which it seems to me Dos Passos's publishers have made a serious mistake in not announcing for what it is: the first section of a large-scale novel—is to deal with the role of the United States in relation to the rest of the world during the early years of the present century; but though it is written from the point of view of an unusually internationally minded American of unusually wide culture, the author has been able to immerse himself in the minds and the lives of his middle-class characters, to identify himself with them, to a degree that must astonish any reader of Dos Passos's other novels. In this respect, ***The 42nd Parallel*** is quite different from ***Manhattan Transfer*** and marks a striking advance beyond it. ***Manhattan Transfer,*** after all, might almost have been written by a very intelligent and very well-documented foreigner: the characters are seen from the outside and do not always seem organically human. But in this new work of fiction, Dos Passos has abandoned the literary baggage that encumbered his exploration of New York. Here one finds no elaborate backdrops and no Joycean prose-poems. For the method of ***The 42nd Parallel,*** Dos Passos has perhaps gone to school to Ring Lardner and Anita Loos; he is, at any rate, the first of our writers—with the possible exception of Mark Twain—who has successfully used colloquial American for a novel of the highest artistic seriousness. This has enabled him to keep us close to the characters as we never were in ***Manhattan Transfer.*** He still has moments of allowing his people to contract into two-dimensional caricatures of qualities or forces he hates; but, in general, we live their lives, we look at the world through their eyes.

These characters of ***The 42nd Parallel*** belong mostly to the white-collar class. Almost all of them begin as obscure and more or less mediocre-appearing people, who, from the ordinary American point of view, are anxious to improve their condition. Neither the gentle spinster stenographer from Washington, the amiable publicity director from Wilmington nor the sharp woman interior decorator from Chicago, has an intimation of any other values than those of the American business office, of the American advertising game, of the American luxury trade, out of which they make their salaries and in terms of which they conceive their ambitions. Only the nephew of the radical Irish printer reacts against the habits of the white-collar class and tends to identify his interests with those of a proletariat. The author introduces separately each one of his five principal characters—we have of each a continuous history from childhood. For this, he has invented a narrative method which enables him to cover a great deal of ground with astonishing rapidity and ease, yet to give us the illusion of finding out all about his people's lives: their friends and the members of their families, their amusements and their periods of stagnation, the places where they work and how much they get, the meals they eat, the beds they sleep in. And without any explicit commentary, each of these sequences of data and incident is made to create a character. Eleanor Stoddard's cold-blooded shrewdness and passionate appetite for refinement or J. Ward Moorehouse's unconscious charlatanry is presented entirely in terms of *things.* And when these commonplace individuals, who have first been presented to the reader independently of one another, are finally brought together, they take on a further significance—we realize that what we have been witnessing is the making of our contemporary society. And as Dos Passos can indicate in masterly fashion the shift from one city to another, so that we understand, without having been overtly told, the difference between the way people behave and feel in Chicago and the way they behave and feel in New York, in Washington, Minneapolis, Pittsburgh or Mexico City; so—also, apparently, without being told—we at last seem to understand the national character of America. The author has sandwiched in, between the sections of the life-histories of his characters, what he labels as "newsreels"—that is, medleys of newspaper-clippings—that give us a picture of the public consciousness running parallel with the private events of the lives that are narrated in detail; as well as a series of brief biographies (very well done) of eminent contemporary Americans, all shown as hampered, stunted or perverted by that same commercial society in which the characters of the novel are submerged. And at the end of this first instalment, with the entrance of the United States into the war and the appearance of the last of the characters, a young garage man from North Dakota, who in his wanderings has fallen in with a rich and drunken cracker from Okeechobee City and been persuaded by him that he ought to go over and get a load of the fun in Europe "before the whole thing goes belly-up"—Dos Passos, in the perfectly aimed final paragraphs, reveals this character suddenly as a symbol for the American people, adventurous and well-intentioned but provincial and immature, voyaging out from its enormous country into a world of which it knows nothing.

This novel, when it has been completed, may well turn out to be the most important that has yet been produced by any American of Dos Passos's generation. Dos Passos seems the only one of the novelists of this generation who is concerned with the large questions of politics and society; and he has succeeded in this book in bridging the gap, which is wider in America than anywhere else and which constitutes a perpetual problem in American literature and thought, between the special concerns of the intellectual and the general pursuits and ideas of the people. The task of the intellectual is not merely to study the common life but to make his thoughts and symbols *seem* relevant to it—that is, to express them in terms of the actual American world without either cheapening them or rendering them vapid. Dos Passos, who has read as much and traveled as widely as Wilder, does not always avoid spinning literature—especially in the first section, which has a flavor of *Huckleberry Finn;* and, in consequence, he is sometimes flimsy. . . . But, though in neither intensity nor skill is Dos Passos superior to Hemingway, ***The 42nd Parallel*** seems to me, from the point of view of its literary originality and its intellectual interest, by far the most remarkable, the most encouraging American novel that I have read since the end of the war. (pp. 447-50)

Edmund Wilson, "Dahlberg, Dos Passos and Wilder," in his The Shores of Light: A Literary Chronicle of the Twenties and Thirties, *Farrar, Straus and Giroux, 1952, pp. 442-50.*

V. S. Pritchett (review date 27 September 1930)

[*Pritchett is a highly esteemed English novelist, short story writer, and critic. Considered one of the modern masters of the short story, he is also one of the world's most respected and well-read literary critics. In the excerpt below, he offers a negative assessment of* The 42nd Parallel.]

The 42nd Parallel is about everything—everything that happens in the America of labour agitators, underdogs, men "on the bum," spurious Big Business men, their wives, mistresses and secretaries. Not only everything that happens in America, for there are interpolated tape-machine extracts from the news of the world. The book is divided mainly between six life stories which converge eventually in the Great War, but there is no emotional unity to it, for once the convergence is vaguely effected, the narratives peter out. The first life story, that of a young printer and labour agitator, who eventually drifts into Mexico; and the last, that of an underdog who gropes blindly through the squalor and violence of the slums to the War, are the best. The Business Men are tedious. Mr. Dos Passos is, like all the modern American realists, a reporter, a community singer, who is obsessed with the idea that he has got to shout the whole history of the United States since 1900 through a megaphone. He has no emotions, only moods: moods of revulsion, satire, lyricism, sensuality. He writes with startling, kaleidoscopic vividness. He has vitality. The opening chapters suggest that, if he abandons mechanical stunts and devices, and leaves American history and biography to look after themselves, he has the makings of a first-class picaresque novelist—American literature's greatest present need. At the moment he is like a man who is trying to run in a dozen directions at once, succeeding thereby merely in standing still and making a noise. Sometimes it is amusing noise and alive; often monotonous. (p. 422)

V. S. Pritchett, "The Age of Speed?" in The Spectator, *Vol. 145, No. 5335, September 27, 1930, pp. 421-22.*

USA looked like a Marxist book to many of its contemporaries, but it is not. It is an American book in the agrarian tradition which sees the defeat of America in the victory of a mechanized society worshipping power and money over a society of simplicity devoted to the needs of human beings and individual felicity.

—John Willard Ward, in his "Lindbergh, Dos Passos and History," in **The Carleton Miscellany,** ***Summer, 1965.***

Malcolm Cowley (review dates 27 April 1932 and 9 September 1936)

[*An American critic, editor, poet, translator, and historian, Cowley has made valuable contributions to contemporary letters with his writings as a literary critic for* The New Republic, *and his chronicles and criticism of modern American literature. In the following excerpt, the first half of which was originally published in* The New Republic *on April 27, 1932, he distinguishes* 1919 *from Dos Passos's other works and praises it as a collectivist novel of American society. In the second half, which first appeared in* The New Republic *on September 9, 1936, he revises some of his earlier opinions, particularly his views on the value and function of the Camera Eye segments.*]

John Dos Passos is in reality two novelists. One of them is a late-Romantic, an individualist, an esthete moving about the world in a portable ivory tower; the other is a collectivist, a radical historian of the class struggle. These two authors have collaborated in all his books, but the first had the larger share in ***Three Soldiers*** and ***Manhattan Transfer.*** The second, in his more convincing fashion, has written most of ***The 42nd Parallel*** and almost all of ***1919.*** The difference between the late-Romantic and the radical Dos Passos is important not only in his own career: it also helps to explain the recent course of American fiction.

The late-Romantic tendency in his novels goes back to his years in college. After graduating from a good preparatory school, Dos Passos entered Harvard in 1912, at the beginning of a period which was later known as that of the Harvard esthetes. I have described this period elsewhere, in reviewing the poems of E. E. Cummings, but I did not discuss the ideas which underlay its picturesque manifestations, its mixture of incense, patchouli and gin, its erudition displayed before barroom mirrors, its dreams in the Cambridge subway of laurel-crowned Thessalian dancers. The esthetes themselves were not philosophers; they did not seek to define their attitude; but most of them would have subscribed to the following propositions:

That the cultivation and expression of his own sensibility are the only justifiable ends for a poet.

That originality is his principal virtue.

That society is hostile, stupid and unmanageable: it is the world of the philistines, from which it is the poet's duty and privilege to remain aloof.

That the poet is always misunderstood by the world. He should, in fact, deliberately make himself misunderstandable, for the greater glory of art.

That he triumphs over the world, at moments, by mystically including it within himself: these are his moments of *ecstasy,* to be provoked by any means in his power—alcohol, drugs, madness or saintliness, venery, suicide.

That art, the undying expression of such moments, exists apart from the world; it is the poet's revenge on society.

That the past has more dignity than the present.

There are a dozen other propositions which might be added to this unwritten manifesto, but the ideas I have listed were those most generally held, and they are sufficient to explain the intellectual atmosphere of the young men who read *The Hill of Dreams,* and argued about St. Thomas in Boston bars, and contributed to *The Harvard Monthly.* The attitude was not confined to one college and one magazine. It was often embodied in *The Dial,* which for some years was almost a postgraduate edition of *The Monthly;* it existed in earlier publications like *The Yellow Book* and *La Revue Blanche;* it has a history, in fact, almost as long as that of the upper middle class under capitalism. For the last half-century it has furnished the intellectual background of poems and essays without number. It would seem to preclude, in its adherents, the objectivity that is generally associated with good fiction; yet the esthetes themselves sometimes wrote novels, as did their predecessors all over the world. Such novels, in fact, are still being published, and favorably criticised: "Mr. Zed has written the absorbing story of a talented musician tortured by the petty atmosphere of the society in which he is forced to live. His wife, whom the author portrays with witty malice, prevents him from breaking away. After an unhappy love affair and the failure of his artistic hopes, he commits suicide. . . . "

Such is the plot forever embroidered in the type of fiction that ought to be known as the art novel. There are two essential characters, two antagonists, the Poet and the World. The Poet—who may also be a painter, a violinist, an inventor, an architect or a Centaur—is generally to be identified with the author of the novel, or at least with the novelist's ideal picture of himself. He tries to assert his individuality in despite of the World, which is stupid, unmanageable and usually victorious. Sometimes the Poet triumphs, but the art novelists seem to realize, as a class, that the sort of hero they describe is likely to be defeated in the sort of society which he must face. This society is rarely presented in accurate terms. So little is it endowed with reality, so great is the author's solicitude for the Poet, that we are surprised to see him vanquished by such a shadowy opponent. It is as if we were watching motion pictures in the darkhouse of his mind. There are dream pictures, nightmare pictures; at last the walls crash in and the Poet disappears without ever knowing what it was all about; he dies by his own hand, leaving behind him the memory of his ecstatic moments and the bitter story of his failure, now published as a revenge on the world of the philistines. (pp. 76-8)

Dos Passos in a sketch by Adolph Dehn.

Dos Passos' early books are neither masterpieces nor are they pure examples of the art novel. The world was always real to him, painfully real; it was never veiled with mysticism and his characters were rarely symbolic. Yet consider the plot of a novel like ***Three Soldiers.*** A talented young musician, during the War, finds that his sensibilities are being outraged, his aspirations crushed, by society as embodied in the American army. He deserts after the Armistice and begins to write a great orchestral poem. When the military police come to arrest him, the sheets of music flutter one by one into the spring breeze; and we are made to feel that the destruction of this symphony, this ecstatic song choked off and dispersed on the wind, is the real tragedy of the War. Some years later, in writing ***Manhattan Transfer,*** Dos Passos seemed to be undertaking a novel of a different type, one which tried to render the color and movement of a whole city; but the book, as it proceeds, becomes the story of Jimmy Herf (the Poet) and Ellen Thatcher (the Poet's wife), and the Poet is once again frustrated by the World: he leaves a Greenwich Village party after a last drink of gin and walks out alone, bareheaded, into the dawn. It is obvious, however, that a new conflict has been superimposed on the old one: the social ideas of the novelist are now at war with his personal emotions, which remain those of *The Dial* and *The Harvard Monthly.* Even in ***1919,*** this second conflict persists, but less acutely; the emotional values themselves are changing, to accord with the ideas; and the book as a whole belongs to a new category.

1919 is distinguished, first of all, by the very size of the project its author has undertaken. A long book in itself, containing 473 pages, it is merely the second chapter, as it were, of a novel which will compare in length with *Ulysses,* perhaps even with *Remembrance of Things Past.* Like the latter, it is a historical novel dealing with the yesterday that still exists in the author's memory. It might almost be called a news novel, since it uses newspaper headlines to suggest the flow of events, and tells the story of its characters in reportorial fashion. But its chief distinction lies in the author's emphasis. He is not recounting the tragedy of bewildered John Smith, the rise of ambitious Mary Jones, the efforts of sensitive Richard Robinson to maintain his ideals against the blundering malice of society. Such episodes recur in this novel, but they are seen in perspective. The real hero of ***The 42nd Parallel*** and ***1919*** is society itself, American society as embodied in forty or fifty representative characters who drift along with it, struggle to change its course, or merely to find a secure footing—perhaps they build a raft of wreckage, grow fat on the refuse floating about them; perhaps they go under in some obscure eddy—while always the current sweeps them onward toward new social horizons. In this sense, Dos Passos has written the first American collective novel.

The principal characters are brought forward one at a time; the story of each is told in bare, straightforward prose. Thus, J. Ward Moorehouse, born in Wilmington, Delaware, begins his business career in a real-estate office. He writes songs, marries and divorces a rich woman, works for a newspaper in Pittsburgh—at the end of fifty-seven pages he is a successful public-relations counselor embarked on a campaign to reconcile labor and capital at the expense of labor. Joe and Janey Williams are the children of a tugboat captain from Washington, D. C.; Janey studies shorthand; Joe plays baseball, enlists in the navy, deserts after a brawl and becomes a merchant seaman. Eleanor Stoddard is a poor Chicago girl who works at Marshall Field's; she learns how to speak French to her customers and order waiters about "with a crisp little refined moneyed voice." All these characters, first introduced in ***The 42nd Parallel,*** reappear in ***1919,*** where they are joined by others: Richard Ellsworth Savage, a Kent School boy who goes to Harvard and writes poetry; Daughter, a warm-hearted flapper from Dallas, Texas; Ben Compton, a spectacled Jew from Brooklyn who becomes a Wobbly. Gradually their careers draw closer together, till finally all of them are caught up in the War.

"This whole goddam war's a gold brick," says Joe Williams. "It ain't on the level, it's crooked from A to Z. No matter how it comes out, fellows like us get the s———y end of the stick, see? Well, what I say is all bets is off . . . every man go to hell in his own way . . . and three strikes is out, see?" Three strikes is out for Joe, when his skull is cracked in a saloon brawl at St. Nazaire, on Armistice night. Daughter is killed in an airplane accident; she provoked it herself in a fit of hysteria after being jilted by Dick Savage—who for his part survives as the shell of a man, all the best of him having died when he decided to join the army and make a career for himself and let his pacifist sentiments go hang. Benny Compton gets ten years in Atlanta prison as a conscientious objector. Everybody in the novel suffers from the War and finds his own way of going to hell—everybody except the people without bowels, the empty people like Eleanor Stoddard and J. Ward Moorehouse, who stuff themselves with the proper sentiments and make the right contacts.

The great events that preceded and followed the Armistice are reflected in the lives of all these people; but Dos Passos has other methods, too, for rendering the sweep of history. In particular he has three technical devices which he uses both to broaden the scope of the novel and to give it a formal unity. The first of these consists of what he calls "Newsreels," a combination of newspaper headlines, stock-market reports, official communiqués and words from popular songs. The Newsreels effectively perform their function in the book, that of giving dates and atmospheres, but in themselves, judged as writing, they are not successful. The second device is a series of nine biographies interspersed through the text. Here are the lives, briefly told, of three middle-class rebels, Jack Reed, Randolph Bourne and Paxton Hibben; of three men of power, Roosevelt, Wilson and J. P. Morgan; and of three proletarian heroes. All these are successful both in themselves and in relation to the novel as a whole; and the passage dealing with the Wobbly martyr, Wesley Everest, is as powerful as anything Dos Passos has ever written.

The "Camera Eye," which is the third device, introduces more complicated standards of judgment. It consists in the memories of another character, presumably the author, who has adventures similar to those of his characters, but describes them in a different style, one which suggests Dos Passos' earlier books. The "Camera Eye" gives us photographs rich in emotional detail:

> Ponte Decimo in Ponte Decimo ambulances were parked in a moonlit square of bleak stone working-people's houses hoarfrost covered everything in the little bar the Successful Story Writer taught us to drink cognac and maraschino half and half
>
> havanuzzerone
>
> it turned out he was not writing what he felt he wanted to be writing What can you tell them at home about the war? it turned out he was not wanting what he wrote he wanted to be feeling cognac and maraschino was no longer young (It

> made us damn sore we greedy for what we felt we wanted tell 'em all they lied see new towns go to Genoa) havanuzzerone? it turned out that he wished he was a naked brown shepherd boy sitting on a hillside playing a flute in the sunlight.

Exactly the same episode, so it happens, is described in Dos Passos' other manner, his prose manner, during the course of a chapter dealing with Dick Savage:

> That night they parked the convoy in the main square of a godforsaken little burg on the outskirts of Genoa. They went with Sheldrake to have a drink in a bar and found themselves drinking with the Saturday Evening Post correspondent, who soon began to get tight and to say how he envied them their good looks and their sanguine youth and idealism. Steve picked him up about everything and argued bitterly that youth was the lousiest time in your life, and that he ought to be goddam glad he was forty years old and able to write about the war instead of fighting in it.

The relative merit of these two passages, as writing, is not an important question. The first is a good enough piece of impressionism, with undertones of E. E. Cummings and Gertrude Stein. The style of the second passage, except for a certain conversational quality, is almost colorless; it happens to be the most effective way of recording a particular series of words and actions; it aspires to no other virtue. The first passage might add something to a book in which, the plot being hackneyed or inconsequential, the emphasis had to be placed on the writing, but ***1919*** is not a novel of that sort. Again, the Camera Eye may justify itself in the next volume of this trilogy—or tetralogy—by assuming a closer relation to the story and binding together the different groups of characters; but in that case, I hope the style of it will change. So far it has been an element of disunity, a survival of the art novel in the midst of a different type of writing, and one in which Dos Passos excels.

He is, indeed, one of the few writers in whose case an equation can accurately and easily be drawn between social beliefs and artistic accomplishments. When he writes individualistically, with backward glances toward Imagism, Vorticism and the Insurrection of the Word, his prose is sentimental and without real distinction. When he writes as a social rebel, he writes not flawlessly by any means, but with conviction, power and a sense of depth, of striking through surfaces to the real forces beneath them. This last book, in which his political ideas have given shape to his emotions, and only the Camera Eye remains as a vestige of his earlier attitude, is not only the best of all his novels; it is, I believe, a landmark in American fiction.

. . . . .

Four years ago in reviewing ***1919,*** the second volume of John Dos Passos' trilogy, I tried to define two types of fiction that have been especially prominent since the War. An *art novel,* I said, was one that dealt with the opposition between a creatively gifted individual and the community surrounding him—in brief, between the Poet and the World. Usually in books of this type the Poet gets all the attention; he is described admiringly, tenderly, and yet we learn that he is nagged and broken and often, in the end, driven to suicide by an implacably stupid World. Dos Passos' earlier novels had applied this formula, but ***The 42nd Parallel*** and ***1919*** belonged to a second category: they were *collective novels,* whose real hero was American society at large, and this fact helped to explain their greater breadth and vigor. I added, however, that certain elements in these later books—and notably the autobiographical passages called the "Camera Eye"—suggested the art novel and therefore seemed out of place.

But after reviewing ***The Big Money*** and rereading the trilogy as a whole, it seems to me that this judgment has to be partly revised. I no longer believe that the art novel is a "bad" type of fiction (though the philosophy behind it is a bad philosophy for our times), nor do I believe that the collective novel is necessarily a "good" type (though it has advantages for writers trying to present our period of crisis). With more and more collective novels published every year, it is beginning to be obvious that the form in itself does not solve the writer's problems. Indeed, it raises new problems and creates new disadvantages. The collective novelist is tempted to overemphasize the blindness and impotence of individuals caught in the rip tides of history. He is obliged to devote less space to each of his characters, to relate their adventures more hastily, with the result that he always seems to be approaching them from the outside. I can see now that the Camera Eye is a device adopted by Dos Passos in order to supply the "inwardness" that is lacking in his general narrative.

I can see too that although the device is borrowed from the art novel—and indeed is a series of interior monologues resembling parts of Joyce's *Ulysses*—it is not in the least alien to the general plan of the trilogy. For the truth is that the art novel and the collective novel as conceived by Dos Passos are not in fundamental opposition: they are like the two sides of a coin. In the art novel, the emphasis is on the individual, in the collective novel it is on society as a whole; but in both we get the impression that society is stupid and all-powerful and fundamentally evil. Individuals ought to oppose it, but if they do so they are doomed. If, on the other hand, they reconcile themselves with society and try to get ahead in it, then they are damned forever, damned to be empty, shrill, destructive insects like Dick Savage and Eleanor Stoddard and J. Ward Moorehouse.

In an earlier novel, ***Manhattan Transfer,*** there is a paragraph that states one of Dos Passos' basic perceptions. Ellen Herf, having divorced the hero, decides to marry a rich politician whom she does not love:

> Through dinner she felt a gradual icy coldness stealing through her like novocaine. She had made up her mind. It seemed as if she had set the photograph of herself in her own place, forever frozen into a single gesture. . . . Everything about her seemed to be growing hard and enameled, the air bluestreaked with cigarette smoke was turning to glass.

She had made up her mind. . . . Sometimes in reading Dos Passos it seems that not the nature of the decision but the mere fact of having reached it is the unforgivable offense. Dick Savage the ambulance driver decided not to be a pacifist, not to escape into neutral Spain, and from that moment he is forever frozen into a single gesture of selfishness and dissipation. Don Stevens the radical newspaper correspondent decides to be a good Communist, to obey party orders, and immediately he is stricken with the same paralysis of the heart. We have come a long way from the strong-willed heroes of the early nineteenth century—the English heroes, sons of Dick Whittington, who admired the world of their day and climbed to the top of it implacably; the French heroes like Julien Sorel and Rastignac and Monte Cristo who despised their world and yet learned how to press its buttons and pull its levers. To Dos Passos the world seems so vicious that any compromise with its standards turns a hero into a villain. The only characters he seems to like instinctively are those who know they are beaten, but still grit their teeth and try to hold on. That is the story of Jimmy Herf in ***Manhattan Transfer***; to some extent it is also the story of Mary French and her father and Joe Askew, almost the only admirable characters in ***The Big Money.*** And the same lesson of dogged, courageous impotence is pointed by the Camera Eye, especially in the admirable passage where the author remembers the execution of Sacco and Vanzetti:

> America our nation has been beaten by strangers who have turned our language inside out who have taken the clean words our fathers spoke and made them slimy and foul
>
> their hired men sit on the judge's bench they sit back with their feet on the tables under the dome of the State House they are ignorant of our beliefs they have the dollars the guns the armed forces the power-plant . . .
>
> all right we are two nations

"The hired men with guns stand ready to shoot," he says in another passage, this one dealing with his visit to the striking miners in Kentucky. "We have only words against POWER SUPERPOWER." And these words that serve as our only weapons against the machine guns and tear gas of the invaders, these words of the vanquished nation are only that America in developing from pioneer democracy into monopoly capitalism has followed a road that leads toward sterility and slavery. Our world is evil, and yet we are powerless to change or direct it. The sensitive individual should cling to his own standards, and yet he is certain to go under. Thus, the final message of Dos Passos' three collective novels is similar to that of his earlier novels dealing with maladjusted artists. Thus, for all the vigor of ***1919*** and ***The Big Money,*** they leave us wondering whether the author hasn't overstated his case. For all their scope and richness, they fail to express one side of contemporary life—the will to struggle ahead, the comradeship in struggle, the consciousness of new men and new forces continually rising. Although we may be for the moment a beaten nation, the fight is not over. (pp. 79-86)

Malcolm Cowley, "John Dos Passos: The Poet and the World," in Dos Passos: A Collection of Critical Essays, *edited by Andrew Hook, Prentice-Hall, Inc., 1974, pp. 76-86.*

Horace Gregory (review date 9 August 1936)

[*Gregory was an American poet and critic. In the following review of* The Big Money, *he discusses the themes, techniques, and characters of* U.S.A., *lauding the trilogy as an impressive contribution to literature.*]

It was perhaps inevitable that the Dos Passos trilogy, the work of some half dozen years, should at last betray concern for the problem of truth. I quote the forty-ninth installment of "The Camera Eye" which appears in ***The Big Money***:

> pencil scrawls in my notebook the scraps of recollection the broken half-phrases the effort to intersect word with word to dovetail clause with clause to rebuild out of mangled memories unshakably (Oh Pontius Pilate) the truth

I suspect that the truth toward which Mr. Dos Passos reaches is of protean structure and not the least considerable of its influences has been the wise and saturnine instruction of Thorstein Veblen's *Theory of the Leisure Class.* Meanwhile we have the cumulative force of three novels, each complete in itself which in time read as one entire work.

It has been characteristic of Mr. Dos Passos never to stand still, never to take for granted those truths and realities accepted by other novelists. That is why ***The Big Money,*** with its rapidly moving scenes of action in New York, Washington, Detroit, Hollywood and Miami seems to reflect an energy which has its source in a fresh point of view. He has chosen the places where big money seems to pour in an unending stream, among politicians, movie magnates, the automotive industries, and real estate speculators. The people in ***The Big Money*** are ex-war aces, movie stars, promoters from Wall Street, social workers, reformers, Communist leaders and United States Senators—and all are influenced by the kind of living that demands the quick reward, the millions that are made today and lost tomorrow. ***The Big Money*** proves again that the popularity of Mr. Dos Passos's novels in Europe is well deserved, for here, as in his earlier work, he has caught the reckless speed at which the big money is made, lost, wasted in America; he, more than any other living American writer, has exposed to public satire those peculiar contradictions of our poverty in the midst of plenty. And in each of the narratives which carry the theme of this novel to its conclusion the reader shares the sensations of speed and concentrated action. Only the most unresponsive reader would fail to appreciate the humor which is the force behind the keen stroke of Mr. Dos Passos's irony.

To those who have read ***The 42d Parallel*** and ***1919*** Mr. Dos Passos's devices of "the camera eye" and "newsreel" are familiar properties of a technic which has been skillfully borrowed from the motion picture. "The camera eye" as he employs it is usually a subjective, soft-focus close-up and the "newsreel" time sequence throughout the progress of thirty-five years, from 1900 to 1935, and contained within these thousand four hundred odd pages. But what was not clear in the earlier sections of the trilogy and which now emerges in ***The Big Money*** is the fact that the entire work may be described as an experiment in *montage* as applied to modern prose. We may assume that the work is a scenario of contemporary American life, and to appreciate its eloquence the trilogy should be read in three successive sittings quite as one might witness three successive performances of a single motion picture. I would almost insist that the three novels be read as fast as one can *see,* for here we are to be concerned with the stream of action in social history; no single character dominates the picture, no single force drives toward a conclusion; it is rather the cumulative forces, characters, episodes that are gathered together under the shifting lens of the camera; images of action are superimposed and from the long rolls of film Mr. Dos Passos (to complete the analogy), like another Griffith, Pabst or Eisenstein, has made a selection of cell units in news, subjective observation, biography and fictional narrative.

It is significant, I believe, that the trilogy opens on board a train going west to Chicago and closes in ***The Big Money*** with a flash of a large passenger plane in transcontinental flight far overhead speeding westward from the Atlantic seaboard to the Golden Gate. The first observation is made from the point of view of a small boy who was to share the poverty of his family in a Chicago slum; the last is seen through the eyes of a young man, jobless, distinctly one of the unemployed, hitchhiking his way to anywhere, still following the forty-second parallel cross country to the Pacific Coast. Between the two we have news of events at home and abroad, short biographies of American heroes, and the life history of more than a dozen characters of which the most important are Mac, J. Ward Moorehouse, Richard Ellsworth Savage, Anne Elizabeth ("Daughter"), Eveline Hutchins, Joe Williams, Ben Compton, Mary French, Margo Dowling and Charley Anderson.

We are introduced to Moorehouse in ***The 42d Parallel,*** the shadow of his success story lengthens in ***1919*** (ex-advertising man public relations counsel, dollar-a-year man, adviser to Woodrow Wilson at the Peace Conference in Paris) and the figure dwindles to a neurotic tangle of nerves and dyspepsia half-dead from overwork in ***The Big Money.*** The blue-eyed charm is gone: the rosy platitudes now roll into heavy, sententious, oily phrases; his assistant, Richard Ellsworth Savage, now does most of his work, high pressure work, with periodic release in violent drinking.

Savage (we remember), once the handsome Harvard poet of ***1919,*** was an ambulance driver during the war (he resented the war, but at its close was made secure by appointment under Moorehouse). We are led to assume that he will inherit the Moorehouse rewards, the well oiled platitudes, the loss of energy.

Moorehouse and Savage are good type specimens of the American success story on the upper middle class level, but I believe the careers of Joe Williams (***1919***) and Charley Anderson (***The 42d Parallel*** and ***The Big Money***) are equally if not more significant. In these two lives we have the ironic recital of a fable in contemporary American ethics: both boys start at the bottom of the social scale. Joe is a sailor, rises to second mate rating, then slips back to able seaman, and never dares to play for large stakes—perhaps his greatest crime is stealing a pair of women's silk stockings—and he is killed in a drunken brawl. Anderson, garage mechanic, enlists for war service, emerges from it an aviator, drifts home to the Middle West, drifts back to New York and enters airplane manufacturing. He then plays for larger stakes, dabbles in Wall Street speculation (the slow corruption of his character is vividly revealed in the succeeding episodes); he betrays his friends and climbs high into the infinities of paper profits; like Williams he is destined to complete his career in violent death, and it is important to remember that Anderson, like Williams, dies without a cent left to his name. Neither Williams nor Anderson escapes the threat of danger always near: from the very start their lives were insecure, and when at last they realize (however dimly, however subconsciously), that danger which surrounds them, they step forward to meet it, fulfilling their social destiny. Like the heroes in Stephen Crane's *War Is Kind,* "These men were born to drill and die"; and it is one of Mr. Dos Passos's great merits that there are no tears wasted over their remains and we soon learn from him that such violence which seems so casual, so accidental, is actually a form of half-willed suicide.

I find Mr. Dos Passos's women less clearly defined than his men; they seem to follow the course of sex adventure with too much repetition, and in that sense they all seem too much alike. I would say that his detailed study of Eveline Hutchins (***1919, The Big Money***) is a shade too logical. We recognize her as the archetype of war heroine who wears short skirts, who possesses the restlessness as well as the kind of half-ironic despair which made her choose colorless, weak Paul Johnson as a father for a baby; but her disintegration throughout the narrative of ***The Big Money*** is all too obvious. Anne Elizabeth (***1919***) with her embarrassing aggressiveness, her helplessness and her death in dramatic suicide, is far more interesting; I suspect that she is an ironic portrait of the "new woman," one of those millions sacrificed to the "new freedom" who were the girls who talked too loud, who believed too literally in the hope of a single standard and lost; it is her honesty which gives her a touch of awkward dignity. In ***The Big Money*** it is Margo Dowling who is most interesting as a typical American phenomenon; she is the shrewd little chorus-girl-dress-model who rises to the rewards of our bi-annual American sweethearts in Hollywood; she is the face behind that smooth close-up reflected from a million silver screens. Mr. Dos Passos's subtlety in recording her conversation saves him from the mere repetition of Anita Loos's earlier success in *Gentlemen Prefer Blondes.* It is Mr. Dos Passos's refusal to caricature Hollywood that makes his portrait of Margo and her associates convincing; they are both comic and terrifying and they are given the semblance of reality through understatement.

Granting that the origins of Mr. Dos Passos's technic may be found in the art of the motion picture, it is not surprising that some of the best passages in ***The Big Money*** should deal with Hollywood directly; and it is significant that Mr. Dos Passos's final commentary on the American success story should leave Wall Street and Hollywood with the few victories to be gained in the making of big money. There can be no doubt about *that* conclusion, that segment of the picture is perfectly clear. But it is also clear that the conclusion is a concrete statement of the ironic generalities contained in Veblen's *Theory of the Leisure Class,* and we must not confuse Mr. Dos Passos's objectives with those of the strictly Marxian critics. Mr. Dos Passos's trilogy is as important to them as Veblen's own work, no more, no less; but they must supply the means by which his work may be applied to fit Marxian theory.

By this route we return at last to Mr. Dos Passos's concern for truth which for the most part remains a split objective: on one side lies esthetic truth; on the other, the truth of social observation. The present work is an attempt to create a synthesis out of untractable material within a new technic (which has already resulted in a number of flattering imitations by younger novelists). In one sense the present trilogy has been a record of Mr. Dos Passos's own learning process, a record of unhasty knowledge in the use of the "newsreel" and biography devices. Contrast the inadequate biographies of ***The 42d Parallel*** with the brilliant sketches of Henry Ford, Frederick Winslow Taylor, Isadora Duncan, Frank Lloyd Wright and Thorstein Veblen in ***The Big Money.*** What was mere time notation in the earlier "newsreels" is a well integrated instrument of commentary in "newsreels" XLVII and LV. In these the potentialities of the device are excellently realized. But for a very few exceptions the problem of the "camera eye" remains unsolved; in these Mr. Dos Passos always seems uncomfortably arty rather than artful—they seem to move contrary to that final truth, that final integration of method and content toward which Mr. Dos Passos is moving. There is still some doubt as to whether the Dos Passos method of recording social history (despite its accuracy in stating the truth of our present defeat in radical activity which is illustrated by the stories of Ben Compton and Mary French) can bring a satisfactory conclusion to the trilogy. There would be little to prevent a fourth volume being written to the refrain of the echo now heard in motion picture theaters: "Time Marches On!" Yet while admitting these flaws in the structure of Mr. Dos Passos's trilogy it is also plain that the work is one of the most impressive contributions made to the literature of our time. The speed at which it travels is a cleansing force, dismissing the "destructive elements" in our civilization as transitory and unreal. Mr. Dos Passos offers no consolations of prophecy. He continues to perceive the realities of the life around him and in that sense he remains one of the most important of our contemporary poets. ***The Big Money*** establishes his position as the most incisive and direct of American satirists. It has been his hope "to rebuild . . . unshakably (Oh Pontius Pilate) the truth" and in that hope discover the truth that makes men free. (pp. 1-2)

Horace Gregory, "Dos Passos Completes His Modern Trilogy," in New York Herald Tribune Books, *August 9, 1936, pp. 1-2.*

Robert James Butler on social dynamics in *U.S.A.*:

U.S.A. endows the American search for pure motion with epic significance. At its worst, Dos Passos' America is falling apart because its movements are not controlled by any humanizing force. At its best, however, his America is surprisingly similar to the fluid world which Emerson and Whitman celebrated. Like Emerson, who claimed "The world is his who can see through its pretensions," Dos Passos observed "I rather divide people into those who see and those who drift." The stories of Mac, J. Ward Moorehouse, Eleanor Stoddard, Charley Anderson, Joe Williams, and others, provide a deterministic vision of lives stripped of human meaning because they drift to no significant purpose. But ***U.S.A.*** is finally centered in "seers"—people who move independently and meaningfully. Vag, Mary French, the persona of the Camera Eye, and the heroes of many of the biographies all reactivate in an admittedly diminished but nevertheless real way the classic American dream of possibility through pure motion. Far from embodying a lifeless despair, therefore, Dos Passos' magnificent trilogy provides us with a complex and tough-minded double vision of modern American life.

Robert James Butler, in his "The American Quest for Pure Movement in Dos Passos' U.S.A.*," in* Twentieth Century Literature, *Spring, 1984.*

Joseph Warren Beach (essay date 1941)

[*Beach was an American critic and educator who specialized in American literature and English literature of the Romantic and Victorian eras. In the following excerpt, he focuses on the principal characters in* U.S.A., *asserting that the essential aim of the trilogy is "the destructive analysis of 'bourgeois' sentiment."*]

Brilliant and serious as was Dos Passos' performance in ***Manhattan Transfer,*** this work was to yield in significance and impressiveness to his later rendering of the same subject in the three volumes of ***U.S.A.—The 42nd Parallel*** (1930), ***1919*** (1932) and ***The Big Money*** (1936). Dos Passos must have felt that he had not done full justice to his theme in confining his view to the city of New York, even though that is the metropolis of our world, the place where all threads cross. He wanted to bring in the big towns of the hinterland, the prairie farms and lumber camps, the seven seas and the Central America which are the arena of our commerce and imperialism, and the wartime France and Italy that were the playground and the graveyard of our crusading youth. He must have felt, again, that in ***Manhattan Transfer*** he had given an inadequate selection of our national types; that he needed to lay more emphasis, both on the industrialist, the promoter, and the financier, and on the obscure men who do the chores. Perhaps he felt that, effective as it was in its way, and even a trifle theatrical, his dot-and-dash system of striking the high points in many lives left something to be desired in the way of sobriety and thoroughness; and he now chose to feature fewer characters and give a fuller and more consecutive account of their lives. In the first two volumes, he confined himself to five leading persons; in ***The Big Money,*** to four. What he gives in each case is a detailed biographical chronicle of the character featured, so that we have a complete case history—parantage, childhood environment, education, occupations, favorite diversions, marital status, down to the circumstances of death, if it occurred within the period of the chronicle—

everything that might be required by a sociologist for whom no detail is without significance and who wants his file complete.

The subjects chosen for this thorough biographical study are the following:

Mac McCreary, son of a Connecticut factory hand. He works as typesetter and as migrant laborer at various points in the Northwest, and becomes an enthusiastic supporter of the IWW; but this last yields to the demands of family life. When he decides that his wife is simply milking him, he goes to Mexico, still interested in the labor movement. He sets up housekeeping with a Mexican girl, and ends up very comfortably as keeper of a radical bookstore.

J. Ward Moorehouse, son of a station agent in Wilmington, Delaware. In school he distinguishes himself as a debater and orator and wins a scholarship at the U. of P. He starts life in a real estate office; he finds that he has a genius for promotion, and bright blue eyes, and that he can put on an engaging look that people like. His two marriages are with wealthy women. When his first marriage goes on the rocks, he feels that he is entitled to some compensation for the loss of time he has suffered. In Pittsburgh he becomes an advertising expert for steel products, conceiving the idea of winning the favor of the public for his company with a long-range educational campaign. He then sets up an office in New York as public relations counselor. He specializes in propaganda showing the identity of interest of capital and labor, and in keeping down subversive influences among miners. When our country enters the War, he offers his services to the government and is promptly sent to Paris as publicity director for the Red Cross. He is prominent in shaping the Versailles Treaty, and is able to serve the interests of large investors in oil. On his return to New York he promotes various enterprises and lobbies in Washington against pure food laws which are disadvantageous to his clients, makers of patent medicines. He is a man of great refinement and distinction of manner. While in France he has love affairs with several Red Cross workers, but he never lets women interfere with business.

Janey Williams, daughter of a retired towboat captain of Georgetown, who takes up stenography, and becomes the efficient secretary of J. Ward Moorehouse, first in his New York office and then in Paris. She leads a very limited life, concerned for comfort and respectability; gradually turns into a peroxide blonde; and watches over her employer with jealous care.

Eleanor Stoddard, daughter of a workman in the Chicago stockyards. She greatly dislikes her father, and her ruling passion is the avoidance of all that is ugly and gross. She works in a lace shop, studies at the Art Institute, has a job at Marshall Field's, and goes into business with a friend as interior decorator in New York, where she does the Moorehouse home. She sees a lot of Moorehouse, but his wife is mistaken in thinking that their friendship is anything more than platonic. She follows him to Paris, where she has an important position in the Red Cross and meets all the most interesting people. She brings back lovely Italian panels from her mission to Rome. She has a discreet affair with Moorehouse in Paris; but in the end she marries a Russian prince and burns candles before an ikon while her guests drink tea from a silver samovar.

Charley Anderson, son of a boarding-house keeper in Fargo, N.D., starts life as an automobile mechanic. He works in various places, enlists in the army, becomes an aviator, and on his return from France takes up the business of making airplanes, for which he has a natural gift. But he catches the Big Money fever and goes in heavily for speculation. His relaxations are women and drink, and he goes in heavily for these. He makes and loses a lot of money and marries a Detroit society girl. He has an affair with Margo Dowling, glamorous actress, at Miami, and loses his life in an automobile accident while taking a drive with a girl he met at a night club.

Richard Ellsworth Savage, of a poor but cultured family of Oak Park, is put through Harvard by a lawyer with literary tastes; is prominent there as poet and college editor, then goes abroad in the volunteer ambulance service. After a jaunt through Europe he is called back home for talking too freely about the War; but through influence he is given a captain's commission; he is attached to several high-ranking officials in France, and buzzes about importantly far behind the lines. He has an affair with a Texas girl, but doesn't think he ought to spoil his career by marrying. He gets acquainted with the Red Cross set; and after the War he goes into Moorehouse's firm, carries on a campaign for Americanism and Bingham Health Products, and lobbies against pure food laws. He is a literary prostitute. His talents and charm are sold to the highest bidder; his life is one long picnic, though without happiness, and tending toward sprees in Harlem.

Besides these, there are Eveline Hutchins, daughter of a Unitarian minister, who becomes an interior decorator, a Red Cross worker in Paris, knows a lot of interesting men, marries a rather stodgy one, and dies of an overdose of

J. W. Moorehouse and Gertrude Staple in an illustration by Reginald Marsh from The 42nd Parallel.

sleeping powders; Joe Williams, Janey's brother, who joins the navy, deserts, serves commerce through the War as seaman and petty officer, is several times torpedoed, once married, and never amounts to much; Daughter, lively Texas girl, who goes abroad on Near East Relief, has a lot of fun, has an affair with Captain Savage in Rome, but instead of bearing his child, ends her life in an airplane crash with a French pilot; Margo Dowling, the glamorous girl who comes of stage people, marries a dope-taking Cuban, has a series of adventures, and lands very much on her feet when Sam Margolies in Hollywood picks her for a star. And then finally there are Benny Compton, the Jewish communist boy, who strives mightily for the cause of labor and is sent to Atlanta for opposing the draft; and Mary French, who works at Hull House, and for labor organizations in Pittsburgh, goes to prison in Boston for protesting the execution of Sacco and Vanzetti, is a friend of various "comrades," and is jilted by Don Stevens on his return from Moscow.

With the exception of Ben Compton and Mary French, we may say that the characters are pretty much all alike in assuming that the world is their oyster. Only they differ in imagination and opportunity. Ward Moorehouse is the chief of the exploiters, those who know how to make the most out of everything—business, advertising, marriage, the War, relief, and the misunderstandings of capital and labor. Eleanor Stoddard and Margo Dowling stand very high in this category: the one so shrewd in her exploitation of art and charity, the other in her exploitation of art and sex. Charley Anderson had everything for him and was going good; but he didn't have the sense to stick to his honest trade of constructing planes. The Big Money got him, and the little pleasures. Mac and Janey and Joe stand for the small people, seeking their own but without imagination and without opportunity. They are of the race that is used and exploited, and get nothing from the game but hard knocks and prison fare and occasional sprees.

No, Mac is not quite so simple. He had leanings toward something more rewarding and less purely selfish. "A man," he said, "has got to work for more than himself and his kids to feel right." "I wanta study an work for things; you know what I mean, not to get to be a goddam slave-driver but for socialism and the revolution an like that, not work an go on a bat an work an go on a bat like those damn yaps on the railroad." Thus he had a glimpse of some ideal objective, of something more than selfish and casual round which to organize his effort. But he found his socialism was not to be reconciled with the demands of his family. And when he had thrown off the yoke and gone to Mexico, he hardly more than drifted with the current. He was a man of good intentions, but he did not have the stuff of heroes and martyrs. As for Ben and Mary, they are the two characters in the story who consistently worked for something more than themselves. But they were so obscure and ineffectual, such wisps and straws in the wind of fate, that they do not greatly affect the tone of the whole exhibit.

So these are the dozen men and women whose private histories are served up in ***U.S.A.*** as typical of Americans living in the first thirty years of the twentieth century. Together they form a valuable file of case histories. But how are they brought into form and pattern, how organized into an artistic whole? Again, as in ***Manhattan Transfer,*** it is not through a central plot or dramatic intrigue. The characters, many of them, come to be associated together in business or in "love," as front-page people are likely to be in so small a world. But their connections are loose and casual; no more is made of these than of many other aspects of their lives; they are not played up in the manner of drama with issue, climax, resolution. The narrative flows along in a steady stream of small events, with a minimum of formal scenes or "constituted occasions." The characters are taken up in rotation, with the smallest apparent regard for the bearings of one on another or upon any "story" in which they are all involved.

Here again, the pattern is largely thematic, and depends on the reference from the private and individual case to matters of general and public import. But here it is not by symbolic chapter-headings and introductory prose poems that Dos Passos suggests the wider reference. He has hit upon a new set of technical devices of startling originality to carry this burden—in which the symbolic and the poetic give way to the literal and the factual, so arranged that the critical attitudes may be supported with the utmost weight of documentation. The first of these devices is called the newsreel. This is a selection from newspaper headlines and articles of a date corresponding to that of action in the private lives which follow; it places the private action in the calendar of history, reminding the reader of what things were of concern to the world at large at the moment when such an individual was dealing with such an item in his obscure life. There is no comment, no reference from public to private; but as the thing repeats itself over and over, there is a growing sense that private and public must be related in the order of things: that the capture of Mafeking or the execution of Ferrer must have its bearing, however remote, upon the career of Mac; that Polish pogroms are of concern to Richard Ellsworth Savage; that the appointment of Daugherty has its long-range significance for Margo Dowling, and the landing of American marines in Nicaragua its importance for Charley Anderson.

Still more, there is the growing sense that the private life is of a piece with the culture complex in which it is embeded, that the spirit of the citizen is deeply colored by the world in which he lives. The topics featured in the newsreel are not chosen at random; they are an exact reproduction of what one reads in the most widely circulated newssheets: disaster, scandal, politics, society, finance, labor. These items are placed more or less helter-skelter in the newsreels as they appear in the newspaper. In the newsreels they are often given in fragments, running into one another and "pied," as they are "pied" in the consciousness of the subway reader, thus making a perfect symbol of the average mentality as it is concerned with public affairs. But gradually the discerning reader will become aware that the choice and arrangement of topics and their very confusion are not so planless and haphazard as one might suppose. Disasters and scandal and society are the screen behind which the serious business of the world is carried on; the dope with which the public mind is put to sleep. And seldom is political news unaccompanied by news of industry and finance and of the organization or suppression of labor. The world in which Joe Williams and Moorehouse represent the opposite poles is a world in which war is closely bound up with the price of steel and sugar, and in which the Treaty of Versailles is followed by the violent putting down of the IWW. The connections are not made in the newsreel any more than they are made by the thoughtless reader; but for the discerning reader they become more and more obvious as the story proceeds. And this is one of the principal means by which Dos Passos gives shape and direction to his work.

Along with the newsreels, and interspersed like them among the records of private lives, are the brief biographies of actual public figures of the time. These are the Representative Men of our country and day; they more or less sum up our national achievement, our official contribution to modern culture. There are twenty-five of these figures: seven from the business world, five from politics, four from applied science and invention, three from the leaders of labor, three from the arts (Isadora Duncan, Rudolph Valentino, Frank Lloyd Wright), two from journalism (the radical John Reed and the liberal Paxton Hibben), and one from social science. The proportion from the several categories indicates the author's general estimate of our cultural effort. Literature does not appear except in the form of journalism, nor pure science at all, unless in the case of Steinmetz. These sketches are for the most part masterpieces of incisive and tendentious writing; they give the author his best chance to show his hand, to indicate his attitudes and bias. The businessmen are most uniformly the object of his irony—Carnegie, the Prince of Peace; Hearst, Poor Little Rich Boy; Insull, Power Superpower. Frederick Winslow Taylor (the American Plan) gives him his chance to suggest the social wastefulness of American efficiency and the speed-up. Minor C. Keith, Emperor of the Caribbean, gives him his text on American imperialism. His political figures are all liberals—spurious and stupid (Bryan), playboy (Theodore Roosevelt), doctrinaire and misguided (Wilson), sincere and forceful but relatively ineffectual (La Follette), and simply heroic (Debs). The one serious thinker in the outfit is Thorstein Veblen, whose analysis of bourgeois mentality and bourgeois economics is (at a guess) the greatest single influence on the work of Dos Passos of anything in print, and whose *Theory of the Leisure Class* offers the most promising clues for the interpretation of ***U.S.A.***

Taken together, these twenty-five figures pretty well sum up Dos Passos' notion of what we have to offer in the way of intellectual and spiritual distinction. They do not demonstrate Carlyle's theory of history as the creation of Great Men. But they do suggest the kind of greatness available for the inspiration of Joe Williams and Charley Anderson, of Eleanor Stoddard and Margo Dowling.

One further device Dos Passos has for broadening the reference of his fictitious chronicle. He has left himself out of the narrative proper; but he knows in his heart that perfect objectivity is not to be had in a human record; that even in physical science account must be taken of the position of the observer in reckoning the speed, mass and direction of moving bodies. In presence of documents like these, the reader may well ask: who is their author and sponsor? what is he like? of what authority and bias? Is he not himself an American citizen of our time—involved, like the others, in our common culture, subject to human limitations of knowledge and spirit, faced with the same complex and bewildering problems? Dos Passos has the current reluctance of writers of fiction to mix in his story with sentimental commentary and moral. But he cannot altogether evade the challenge of these natural questions. He has chosen to insert in the narrative a series of flashes called "The Camera Eye," which by fleeting hint and impression suggest the character of the artist whose work it is, his own involvement in the social structure, the conditions that molded him, and his aims and motives in his work.

In ***The 42nd Parallel,*** we see him as a child in Tidewater Virginia, traveling in Europe, at school in England, his "four years under the ether cone" at Harvard, his presence at protest meetings and cafés in New York on the night of our entrance into the War. In ***1919*** we have glimpses of him in the ambulance service in France and Italy, emptying slop-pails in the medical corps, and finally in Paris, a civilian going to concerts and witnessing riots of working men in protest against the Versailles Treaty. In ***The Big Money,*** we see him making a precarious living as a newspaperman, protesting the execution of Sacco and Vanzetti, and raging against the unjust sentence imposed on striking miners in the South.

We see him as a typical product of bourgeois gentility, soft, refined and fastidious, shrinking from the contact of "muckers." But there is in him some protestant strain which leads him to question the assumptions of his class. He envies the freedom of the mucker, and he doubts the legend that he is a dirty fellow who puts stones in his snowballs. He resents the middlemen who milk the profits from the truck-farmers and keep them starving. He resents the snobbishness and the sterile culture of the university. He resents the sacrifice of our boys to save the bankers' investments. He witnesses the waste and horrors of war, and its exploitation by a host of *embusqués,* who occupy posts of safety and make a picnic of the tragedy. He returns to America disillusioned, unwilling to cut the melons of exploitation; he is trying to determine his own moral identity, seeking in Greenwich Village salons a social faith, a formula of action; he is "peeling the onion of doubt." He sees Italian anarchists killed for upholding the principles of Plymouth Rock. He sees the miners enslaved and the bosses triumphant.

> They have made us foreigners in the land where we were born they are the conquering army that has filtered into the country unnoticed they have taken the hilltops by stealth they levy toll they stand at the minehead they stand at the polls . . . they have clubbed us off the streets they are stronger they are rich they hire and fire the politicians the newspapereditors the old judges the small men with reputations the collegepresidents the wardheelers (listen businessmen collegepresidents judges America will not forget her betrayers).

The wool has been pulled over the eyes of his people. His rôle is to make them see again: "rebuild the ruined words slimy in the mouths of lawyers districtattorneys collegepresidents judges." "How can I make them feel how our fathers our uncles haters of oppression came to this coast how say Don't let them scare you make them feel who are your oppressors America?"

Such is the project, but how is it to be accomplished? In what terms shall he "rebuild the ruined words worn slimy"? What formula of action shall he recommend? It is clear that Dos Passos has been some kind of a socialist, champion of organized labor and the cooperative commonwealth. But it is equally clear how little he trusts the Communist Party or any other party to bring about what must be essentially a moral revolution. Already in ***The Big Money,*** his best man Benny Compton has been expelled from the party, and his best woman Mary French has been shabbily treated by Don Stevens, typical party member. The young man of the Camera Eye is carrying in his pocket a letter from a college boy asking him to explain why radicals, though right in principle, are such stinkers in their private lives.

In ***The Adventures of a Young Man*** (1939) Dos Passos has given a most illuminating account of the predicament of a friend of labor who cannot reconcile himself to the communists' unconcern for the workmen they profess to champion. This book is not to be compared to ***U.S.A.*** in craftsmanship and imaginative power; but it makes, for all that, a precious commentary on the author's *magnum opus.* (pp. 52-63)

[***The Adventures of a Young Man***] is an affecting picture of a man of feeling and independent mind made victim to the heartless officialism of a party machine. And the author's gift for irony finds ample scope, besides, in the parlor and bedroom radicalism of New York bohemian society, from which [Glenn Spotswood, the protagonist,] makes his escape into the life of hardship and danger. The predicament of Glenn was doubtless that of Dos Passos, with this addition, that while Glenn was by nature a man of action—speaker and organizer—Dos Passos is by nature the artist and speculative thinker. He is not at home on the soapbox. His place is the study. And even in the study he has no gift for heartening prophecy and exhortation. He has not the spirit of a proletarian propagandist. The good and honest people he admires—Ben Compton and Mary French—but he cannot invest them with the warm colors of sentiment like Fielding Burke or with heroic glamour like André Malraux. The poor things are so plain and awkward, so homeless and unfavored, that one shivers with discomfort at the thought of them. And for the most part his sense for truth precludes his featuring of characters so well inspired as these. His artistic conscience bids him set down what he has seen. And what he has mostly seen are, on the one hand, boobs and drifters like Janey and Joe, and on the other hand slickers and exploiters like Moorehouse and Savage, with a sample of those, like Charley Anderson, who are boobs and drifters playing the rôle of slickers and exploiters without the staying power required to carry it through.

In the record of these lives the author keeps a curious even tone. One incident follows another without distinction of emphasis, as if they were all on a level of importance or unimportance. The point of view is that of the character concerned, but no one is allowed to build up to a climax of emotion. There is singularly little excitement or depth of feeling. It is as if the author were unwilling for us to get too sympathetic with any of the characters, to become emotionally involved; we are to maintain our distance and objectivity. We are scientists observing the reactions of human beings to stimuli; and at this distance we cannot make out that these organisms are directed by any long-range, any ideal objectives.

It is true that the characters think well of themselves, as is the way with human beings, who cannot see far beyond the limits of their own immediate concerns. Above all, they are persuaded, the more favored characters, of their own "niceness" of sentiment, and totally unaware of their shallowness and confusion of ideas. The crowning exhibits of "bourgeois" mentality are Eleanor Stoddard and J. Ward Moorehouse, in whom an almost complete want of heart and an essentially unsocial and amoral attitude toward the world are compatible with the utmost correctness of sentiment. These two have developed a considerable tenderness for each other. As the time approaches for our entry into the War, from which they are to profit so shrewdly, they have worked themselves up to a high pitch of sentimentality; but they do not distinguish clearly among their feelings nor understand their connection.

> The sight of the French flag excited her always or when a band played Tipperary; and one evening when they were going to see the Yellow Jacket for the third time, she had on a new fur coat that she was wondering how she was going to pay for, and she thought of all the bills at her office and the house on Sutton Place she was remodelling on a speculation and wanted to ask J. W. about a thousand he'd said he'd invested for her and wondered if there'd been any turnover yet. They'd been talking about the air raids and poison gas and the effect of the war news downtown and the Bowmen of Mons and the Maid of Orleans and she said she believed in the supernatural, and J. W. was hinting something about reverses on the Street and his face looked drawn and worried; but they were crossing Times Square through the eight o'clock crowds and the skysigns flashing on and off. . . . When they got to the theatre Eleanor hurried down to the ladies room to see if her eyes had got red. But when she looked in the mirror they weren't red at all and there was a flash of heartfelt feeling in her eyes, so she just freshened up her face and went back to the lobby, where J. W. was waiting for her with the tickets in his hand; her grey eyes were flashing and had tears in them.

This passage will give a notion of the schoolgirl naïveté and intellectual immaturity of a woman of great practical shrewdness, who knows how to make the utmost profit out of every situation. It will give a notion of an insincerity and a confusion of mind which are no bar to success in a world of free-for-all competition, where much is gained by the cultivation of the right forms of sentimentalism.

It will give a notion, too, of Dos Passos' skill in rendering the very logic and syntax of his characters' thought. This is perhaps his greatest gift; it is at any rate the gift of which he makes the most effective use. His method is essentially that of irony—an intellectual jiu-jitsu by which a character is left to throw himself by his own weight. This ironic tone is dominant throughout ***U.S.A.*** And we might have cause to complain if Dos Passos were a socially irresponsible writer like, say, Somerset Maugham, by whom the irony would often seem to be employed for the demolition of individuals, and no philosophical theme is served unless it be a kind of moral nihilism. But the characters of Dos Passos are never merely individuals. They are types of the mentality prevailing in our world of individualistic sentiment and social cynicism. And each one makes his important contribution to the destructive analysis of "bourgeois" sentiment which is Dos Passos' undertaking. This is, as I have suggested, the fictional counterpart of Veblen's theoretic study of the leisure class.

The whole thing is highly credible and diverting. It is most stimulating intellectually. It has for the imagination its architectural grandeur, its bleak magnificence. Its appeal to the emotions is negative. But morally it is most educative. Not so much in a positive way, of inspiration and ideal guidance. But in a negative way, tonic and disciplinary for those who can read its meaning. And it does prepare the way for more positive teaching. If Dos Passos is not himself a prophet of the good life, he is most emphatically the voice of one crying in the wilderness. (pp. 63-6)

Joseph Warren Beach, "John Dos Passos: Theory of the Leisure Class," in American Fiction: 1920-1940, *The Macmillan Company, 1941, pp. 47-66.*

Charles Child Walcutt (essay date 1956)

[*Walcutt is an American educator and critic. In the following excerpt from his* American Literary Naturalism: A Divided Stream, *Walcutt praises Dos Passos's Newsreels, biographies, and Camera Eye segments as stylistic expressions of Naturalism but faults Dos Passos's judgments of American society.*]

[The] technique of ***Manhattan Transfer*** is inconspicuous beside that of the trilogy ***U.S.A.*** (1937), composed of three huge novels, ***The 42nd Parallel*** (1930), ***Nineteen Nineteen*** (1932), and ***The Big Money*** (1936). In these novels Dos Passos has extended his method of projecting the kaleidoscope to the point where he fashions his pattern out of three elaborately contrived elements which interrupt and supplement the central narratives—the Newsreel, the Camera Eye, and the Biography. With this invention he seeks to find styles that are appropriate to the various types of material treated and that in blending give the effect of variousness, energy, and turmoil that we saw in a simpler way in ***Manhattan Transfer.***

The body of the trilogy is devoted to the careers of a dozen representative people through the years from about the turn of this century to the big money days of the twenties. The first novel approaches World War I, the second deals

An excerpt from *U.S.A.*

The Camera Eye (51)

. . . the law stares across the desk out of angry eyes his face reddens in splotches like a gobbler's neck with the strut of the power of submachineguns sawedoffshotguns teargas and vomitinggas the power that can feed you or leave you to starve

sits easy at his desk his back is covered he feels strong behind him he feels the prosecutingattorney the judge an owner himself the political boss the minesuperintendent the board of directors the president of the utility the manipulator of the holdingcompany

he lifts his hand towards the telephone

the deputies crowd in the door

we have only words against

Power Superpower

In eighteen-eighty when Thomas Edison's agent was hooking up the first telephone in London, he put an ad in the paper for a secretary and stenographer. The eager young cockney with sprouting muttonchop whiskers who answered it

had recently lost his job as officeboy. In his spare time he had been learning shorthand and bookkeeping and taking dictation from the editor of the English *Vanity Fair* at night and jotting down the speeches in Parliament for the papers. He came of temperance smallshopkeeper stock; already he was butting his bullethead against the harsh structure of caste that doomed boys of his class to a life of alpaca jackets, penmanship, subordination. To get a job with an American firm was to put a foot on the rung of a ladder that led up into the blue.

He did his best to make himself indispensable; they let him operate the switchboard for the first halfhour when the telephone service was opened. Edison noticed his weekly reports on the electrical situation in England

and sent for him to be his personal secretary.

Samuel Insull landed in America on a raw March day in eightyone. Immediately he was taken out to Menlo Park, shown about the little group of laboratories, saw the strings of electriclightbulbs shining at intervals across the snowy lots, all lit from the world's first central electric station. Edison put him right to work and he wasn't through till midnight. Next morning at six he was on the job; Edison had no use for any nonsense about hours or vacations. Insull worked from that time on until he was seventy without a break; no nonsense about hours or vacations. Electric power turned the ladder into an elevator.

Young Insull made himself indispensable to Edison and took more and more charge of Edison's business deals. He was tireless, ruthless, reliable as the tides, Edison used to say, and fiercely determined to rise.

John Dos Passos, in his The Big Money *from his* U.S.A., *Houghton Mifflin Co., 1960.*

largely with civilian activities during the war, in New York and Paris, the third explores the big money boom after the war. There is no central character in ***U.S.A.*** Each novel deals with about four of the dozen, and there is a slight carry-over from one novel to the next. (pp. 283-84)

These interweaving careers (all the characters know some of the others at one time or another) are given in larger segments than those in ***Manhattan Transfer***; but always with a clinical detachment that makes them seem like figures on a screen compelled by drives the inwardness of which we never know, until finally we come to the conclusion that all their drives are instinctive or compulsive. The total effect is much like the strident chaos of the first novel.

The three devices which interrupt the central narratives and "formalize" the chaos depicted represent the ultimate stylistic expressiveness of the naturalistic movement. The Newsreel introduces a section with bits of headlines, advertisements, feature articles, and phrases of news, interwoven with lines of poetry which presumably represent some of the emotions—usually popular and sentimental—being experienced at the time. (pp. 285-86)

The Biographies—there are twenty-five of them scattered through the three volumes—are condensed records of typical public figures of the time, from the fields of business, politics, technology, labor, and the arts. (p. 286)

The Camera Eye is Dos Passos' subjective and rather poetic commentary on this world. It occurs fifty-one times through the trilogy, revealing the character, interests, and life history of the artist—how he came out of Virginia, went to school abroad and at Harvard, drove an ambulance during the war, was disillusioned by the Versailles Treaty and the rampage of materialism which followed it, and lived as a newspaper reporter and radical through the big money days of the early twenties. He is an oversensitive and fastidious intellectual, recoiling from the grubby masses and yet seeing in them the backbone and heart of the America which the great sweep of his novel shows being corrupted, debauched, and enslaved by the forces of commercial rapacity. He sees America through the lens of a poetic tradition—Whitman, Sandburg, perhaps Hart Crane—which impels him to identify the physical elements of our nation with the dream of greatness and individual realization that it has always embodied for the transcendentalist.

Here the characteristics I have attributed to American idealism when it breaks away from its scientific discipline and control—of unfocused idealism and uncontrolled protest—become increasingly evident in the notions that virtue is in the people, waste is the natural expression of the exploiters, and wealth is in a long-term conspiracy to sabotage labor and destroy our resources. It is perhaps not extravagant to identify the perfectly expressive form of this work with the final division of the great stream of American idealism. The form expresses a chaos; it is a fractured world pictured in a novel fractured into four parts through four styles from four points of view. This division of the subject combines with the range and variety of the materials treated to give the impression that nothing can be done because the problem is too complex to take hold of. It can be watched in the frantic samples that Dos Passos gives us, but we get no sense of comprehensible process that might be analyzed and controlled by the application of scientific method, because it is, finally, a *moral* deterioration that Dos Passos depicts. Thus with the radical writer we come full circle to the conservative position.

The point can be illustrated by samples of the Camera Eye taken from ***The Big Money***: returning from Europe,

> throat tightens when the redstacked steamer churning the faintlyheaving slatecolored swell swerves shaking in a long green-marbled curve past the red lightship.
>
> spine stiffens with the remembered chill of the offshore Atlantic
>
> and the jag of framehouses in the west above the invisible land and spiderweb rollercoasters and the chewinggum towers of Coney and the freighters with their stacks way aft and the blur beyond Sandy Hook

and the vision spreads over the nation, to

> the whine and shriek of the buzzsaw and the tipsy smell of raw lumber and straggling through slagheaps through fireweed through wasted woodlands the shantytowns the shantytowns

He refuses a profitable job because he cannot become part of the exploiting machine, talks with other seekers in Greenwich Village, listens skeptically to orators in Union Square, identifies himself in Whitmanesque fashion with hunters and adventurers in the West, and toward the end makes a pilgrimage to Plymouth to hear about Sacco and Vanzetti.

> pencil scrawls in my notebook the scraps of recollection the broken halfphrases the effort to intersect word with word to dovetail clause with clause to rebuild out of mangled memories unshakably (Oh Pontius Pilate) the truth . . .
>
> . . . how can I make them feel how our fathers our uncles haters of oppression came to this coast how say Don't let them scare you how make them feel who are your oppressors America
>
> rebuild the ruined words worn slimy in the mouths of lawyers districtattorneys collegepresidents judges without the old words the immigrants haters of oppression brought to Plymouth how can you know who are your betrayers America

And the final cry of denunciation:

> they have clubbed us off the streets they are stronger they are rich they hire and fire the politicians the newspapereditors the old judges . . . America will not forget her betrayers . . .
>
> America our nation has been beaten by strangers who have bought the laws and fenced off the meadows and cut down the woods for pulp and turned our pleasant cities into slums and sweated the wealth out of our people . . .
>
> we stand defeated America

The trouble here is that the indictment has been torn loose

from the facts. People are not virtuous because they are poor. If we choose to be sentimental about trees, it was the poor pioneer who cut down and burned the hardwood forests over half a continent, a fearful waste, whereas the big corporations that cut the pulpwood conserve their trees carefully and have over the decades increased their reserves beyond the nation's needs. The prairies were gulched by the poor farming and overgrazing of the pioneers, too, long before they were fenced and restored and protected by the avaricious big money farmers.

Particularly significant of this division and confusion is the fact that most of the central characters are sexually frigid, inhibited, deprived, or frustrated. Margo Dowling is unfeeling; Janey is terrified of sex; Eleanor Stoddard is apparently quite frigid; Daughter is confused and repressed, and her sudden passion for Dick Savage causes her destruction; Mary French is completely inhibited and neurotic. Where the sexual life is presumed to be satisfactory, Dos Passos ignores it, but with the others a substantial preoccupation of the author is to explore the fears, the desolation, and the guilty aimlessness which he relates to the sense of being unloved. This preoccupation gives the book a pervasive dreariness which combines with the fact that people seem always to be smoky, grimy, gritty, and tired to make a desolation that is, ultimately, wholly subjective. It is a literary effect contrived by careful selection of detail and control of language.

It is true that the possessors of great wealth and power have abused both, and yet he has loaded the dice so heavily in favor of the common man that the reader is skeptical when Dos Passos is most earnest. His idealism has lost its hold on fact. The result, as usual, shows the facts (in the stream of materialism) as grim, dark, and uncontrollable, whereas the optimism of spirit is dissipated in fierce but unreliable indignation. The form of this trilogy is a perfect embodiment of this division between nature and spirit: the main blocks of the narrative portray characters groping in a hopeless jungle of sensation and instinct, whereas the Camera Eye cries its somewhat irresponsible protest against the retreat from the American Dream, denouncing the wrong culprit as often as the right one. (pp. 286-89)

Charles Child Walcutt, "Later Trends in Form: Steinbeck, Hemingway, Dos Passos," in his American Literary Naturalism, A Divided Stream, *University of Minnesota Press, 1956, pp. 258-89.*

Dos Passos has revealed the falsity of the unity of action. He has shown that one might describe a collective event by juxtaposing twenty individual and unrelated stories.

—Jean-Paul Sartre, in his "American Novelists in French Eyes," in* The Atlantic Monthly, *August 1946.

Jules Chametzky (essay date February 1960)

[Chametzky is an American educator and critic. In the following essay, he comments on the continued relevance of U.S.A. *and faults the dramatic adaptation of the trilogy for lacking depth.]*

The off-Broadway production of ***U.S.A.,*** "a new dramatic review" written by John Dos Passos and Paul Shyre and based on Dos Passos' novel, has been running in the theatre of New York's Hotel Martinique for several months, so that it seems to have won popular acceptance along with the critical praise that greeted its appearance. I am more than usually interested in this fact, since I recently taught Dos Passos' novel and found that its reception by intelligent students nurtured in the Eisenhower years was an equivocal and conditioned one. To be crude about it, my students responded to the technique of the novel, not to its content; after seeing the dramatization based on it, I wonder if the same—or worse—may not be true of the contemporary theatre audience. "Worse" because it seems to me that in this production the aspect of communion and revelation which the theatrical experience always contains, intensified in this instance by the technically brilliant sense of immediacy evoked, is in the service of a content that is only superficially and momentarily challenging, disturbing, *felt.* The production is, finally, the occasion for a species of audience self-congratulation.

Reflecting upon these conclusions—and, no doubt, in coming to them—I am led back to my recent experience with the novel. I assigned the book in a seminar on "problems" in American literature and language. The "problem" set for the course was recognizably academic—"The Writer and Society"—but, as it developed, the literature we concentrated on—American literature in the 1930's—often made the class crackle with excitement. At times one could almost imagine that a decade or two did not matter: a few mornings a week there was the possibility of recreating a passionate intellectual atmosphere—if not of a cafeteria on 14th Street, then at least of what a college classroom in the era of FDR might have been like. Almost, but not quite. For we were at the end of the 50's, and many of the issues of the 30's were (happily) dead and academic, many of the formerly stirring appeals and heroic postures caused only polite embarrassment, and—most unnerving to a teacher—there was too often only the students' blank incomprehension.

This last was the group's initial response to ***U.S.A.,*** a book that I thought should hit them like a bombshell. After all, had not a college generation seen in the book, as Harry Levin has observed, a "putting together what seemed to be the contradictions of the world we were growing into"? Had not trustees objected, careers been threatened, when ***The Big Money*** was taught at the University of Texas not too long ago? In my class of sophisticated undergraduate and graduate students in the academic year 1959-1960, however, the novel threatened to be a dud. It was Dos Passos himself who, very dramatically, saved the situation. The ice was broken when I played for them a tape-recording of a statement Dos Passos had made in 1956 [on a radio program produced by the Literary Society of the University of Massachusetts] about his methods and purposes in writing ***U.S.A.*** Because it is such an effective statement and of value to anyone interested in the work of Dos Passos as well as to the course of these reflections, I shall here reproduce the full text:

> When I started ***Manhattan Transfer*** thirty or more years ago, my aim was to contrive a highly energized sort of novel. I wanted to find some way of making the narrative carry a very large load. Instead of far away and long ago, I wanted it to be here and now. A good deal of the French and Italian writing that fell into my hands while I was serving in the Ambulance service during the first of the great wars, was headed in the same direction. The Italian futurists, the Frenchmen of the school of Rimbaud, the scraps of verse of the poets who went along with cubism in painting, were trying to do something that stood up off the page. "Simultaneity," they called it.
>
> Of course, I'd been very much affected by the sort of novel Stendhal originated in French with his *Chartreuse de Parme* and Thackeray in English with *Vanity Fair.* I remember reading *Vanity Fair* for the tenth time rather early in my life. After that I lost count. It was the sort of novel in which the story is really a pretext for the presentation of the slice of history the novelist has seen enacted before his own eyes. The personal adventures keep merging with the social chronicle. Historic events, dimly imagined, misunderstood, incompletely envisioned, take the place of the Olympians of the ancient drama. I read James Joyce's *Ulysses* a little later, on my way home from Europe with a bad case of flu, in a tiny inside cabin on one of the big English liners. It got linked in my mind with Sterne's *Tristram Shandy.* Sterne, too, was trying to make his narrative carry a very large load. I had for some time been taken with the meticulous discipline of Defoe's narrative, and Fielding's and Smollett's rollicking satire. But I have to admit that Fielding and Smollett really came to me through old Captain Marryat's sea stories that gave me infinite pleasure when I was a small boy.
>
> I began with using whatever I had learned from all these methods to produce a satirical chronicle of the world I knew. I felt that everything should go in—popular songs, political aspirations and prejudices, ideals, delusions, clippings out of old newspapers. The raw material of this sort of fiction is everything you've seen and heard and felt—your childhood, your education, serving in the army, and travelling in odd places and finding yourself in odd situations. It's those rare moments of suffering and delight when a man's private sensations are amplified and illuminated by a flash of insight that give him the certainty that what he is seeing and feeling is what millions of his fellow-men see and feel in the same situation. This sort of universal experience is the raw material of all the imaginative arts. These flashes of insight, when strong emotions key all the perceptions up to their highest point, are the nuggets of pure gold. They are rare, even in the lives of the greatest poets.
>
> The novelist has to use all the stories people tell about themselves, all the little dramas in other people's lives he gets glimpses of without knowing just what went before or just what will come after, the fragments of talk he overhears on a subway or on a streetcar, the letter he picks up on the street addressed by one unknown character to another, the words on a scrap of paper found in a trashbasket, the occasional vistas of reality that flash from the mechanical diction of newspaper reports—these are the raw materials the chronicles of your own time are made up of. No matter how much leg-work you do, you can't see it all yourself. You're dealing with scraps and fragments. A lot of it has to be second-hand. The fictional imagination depends on being able to reconstruct the whole unseen animal from a tooth and a toenail and a splinter of skull. Of course sometimes you go wrong, like the anthropologists who fell for Piltdown man.
>
> It was that sort of impulse that produced the three ***U.S.A.*** novels. Somewhere along the line I'd been impressed by Eisenstein's contrived documentaries, such as *Potemkin.* "Montage" was the word used in those days to describe the juxtaposition of contrasting scenes in motion pictures. I took to montage to try to make the narrative stand up off the page. In the next set of the ***District of Columbia*** novels, I was trying to fuse the whole thing into a single flow of narrative, with more emphasis on the satirical intent. In ***Chosen Country*** I tried to make the current of the narrative even more dense, in an elegiac mode very different from the continual present-tense of ***Manhattan Transfer*** and ***U.S.A.*** And so it goes.

Here was enough material for discussion during a month of Tuesdays, Thursdays and Saturdays. What happened in my group was this: when they heard Dos Passos, who had been invited to comment on the content *and* technique of ***U.S.A.,*** speak so fully—and almost exclusively—about the technical problems he had faced and the means he had used to solve these problems, they relaxed, their responses thawed, they "understood" Dos Passos and his book. The interrelationship of the juxtaposed narrative, Biographies, Newsreels, Camera Eye now could be charted with a "shock of recognition" and pleasure as each element did its work of commenting upon, paralleling, bridging, foreshadowing, underscoring the others. To these close and agile readers, the class war emerged only as a convenient structural device organizing the various stories of the haves and the have-nots (and, incidentally, earning Dos Passos a demerit for his lack of complexity). The motif of failure was bound up with the formal effort to write "a satirical chronicle." ***U.S.A.*** was primarily significant as the contrivance of "a highly energized sort of novel." The montage technique was brilliantly effective in achieving this end; and insofar as it did, the work was alive, it was not "far away and long ago, . . . [but] here and now." And my heart sank.

For, finally, in this technique of reading, the only ground of response seemed to be the perception of lesser or greater patterning, control, self-containment. Only in this way was ***U.S.A.*** apparently adaptable to the "here and now":

that is, before it could come alive for students today the bitterness of the controlling social vision that filled the book had to be drained.

Now I am not urging the notion that "meaning" exists apart from formal and aesthetic considerations; I *am* disturbed, however, by the absorption in technique alone, as the means and end of a work of art. Meaning and form are inconceivable apart from each other—this is a truism, yet it merits ceaseless repetition. And in ***U.S.A.*** technique is wholly integrated with and at the service of a forceful expression about society. Despite my students' absorption in the mechanics of expression, despite the introductory lyric in the book that tells us U.S.A. is "mostly the speech of the people," despite Dos Passos' avoidance in his broadcast of the ideological content of his novel, ***U.S.A.*** is more than just "a highly energized sort of novel." The book fairly shrieks at us its "message": U.S.A. is jangling headlines; public and private banalities; corruption in speech, thought, action; histories of lives of tragic desperation, betrayal, martyrdom, futility, bitterness. When the stories of failure and defeat at every turn in the novel—Centralia, and Veblen, and Debs, and (most crucially) Sacco-Vanzetti—are to be "saved" from being "dated" by seeing them as pieces in a formal and abstract mosaic rather than as the center of the book, it is a hollow victory. If this *is* the price we have to pay in order to read the book today, then perhaps we would be better off to recognize that ***U.S.A.*** is dated and relegate it to its proper place in some historical limbo. Otherwise, while no one in his right mind would call ***U.S.A.*** a "happy" book, it surely cannot be confronted in the way that it has a right to be: wholly, and as, in Alfred Kazin's judgment, "one of the saddest books ever written by an American."

The play at the Martinique is by no means a sad one, a fact which, as a paying customer, I will admit to be pure gain; yet, from another standpoint, this may represent a loss. The sadness—or bitterness—in the novel had the power to inform and transform; the play—which as the program notes, is only "based" on the novel—strikes an occasional sombre note that promises to penetrate to the heart, but these turn out to be only titillations, and the object has been only entertainment, after all.

Let me say at once that the production is excellent and, I would guess, superior to almost anything on Broadway this season. The virtuosity of the actors, writers, and director in fashioning a smooth-flowing continuous action that embodies a recognizable point-of-view is remarkable. In view of this, one soon abandons the skeptical idea that so panoramic a novel cannot be adapted to the dimensions of an evening's drama. Mr. Shyre proves once again that through a daring use of theatrical resources requiring only mind and talent, very little is outside the province of theatre. Our audiences are ready for almost anything, technically. On the other hand, there is a good deal lost in the transition from the novel (as I read it) to the play. What I should like to suggest is that this loss is due less to the requirements of the dramatic form than to the demands of the "here and now"—in this case, to the real or supposed expectations of the well-dressed, well-cushioned, well-coifed audience that helps the play keep going. The reduction—especially the excision of almost everything "radical" (Debs is kept: the image of the saint deserted by the workers)—may also reflect Dos Passos' own changed social philosophy.

The setting is simple, geared to the work's demand for fluidity. The audience is seated on three sides of a small theatre; the fourth wall is covered with a large yellow backdrop on which is sketched a jagged mural suggesting aspects of the years between 1900 and 1930. Six wire-backed high stools are placed against this wall for the actors—three men and three women. From here the actors step forward to play their various parts in the narratives (the props down front are reduced to essentials: several chairs, a table or two), chant the headlines of the Newsreel portions, or address the audience directly in the Biography and Camera Eye sections. This is no concert reading, such as Mr. Shyre has successfully prepared with the work of O'Casey: the overall result represents a successful synthesis of Living Newspaper techniques, Epic theatre, a variety show, a review. The production is exciting.

Unfortunately, I do not feel that the content of the play and the conception behind it evenly fulfill the high expectations generated by its technical excellence. While the play was in rehearsal [I have been told], Dos Passos reminded the actors that scenes are like icebergs and that they must always be aware of all that does not show. With the exception of some memorable moments, however, I had the uncomfortable feeling that I was seeing an inverted iceberg—almost everything *was* surface—the sense of depth was missing. This was perhaps due to the unrelieved sense of the actors "playing" their parts. The frequency of change in person and situation tended to force the actors into stock mannerisms in order to convey quickly a character and mood, so that the portrayals were too often caricatures. As a way of forcing the audience to achieve an ironic detachment and cool intellectuality towards the characters this is commendable, but the objects of our deliberation must be complex enough to justify the effort. Where the range of irony is limited, where, for example, only a few examples of spurious attitudes and personalities are isolated from the richness and complexity of the novel, the technique wears a little thin. We are repeatedly urged to consider the same absurdities—self-importance, self-infatuation, mindless reliance on cant and jargon, hypocrisy—until, finally, their concrete embodiments are only illustrations, not realities. And when the satirical treatment of these "humors" is not too general, it goes off in search of dead or dying horses.

By heavily underlining the inane aspects of the popular and official culture, the Newsreel portions attempt to locate these absurdities in the society as a whole. But soon the play of voices takes on a pattern: the politicians all begin to sound like Senator Claghorn; the sole radical demonstrator in the play is given a comically whining Brooklyn accent; Gertrude Ederle lumbers down to deliver her headlines in a tough male voice. The actress who plays Gertrude gets a deserved laugh as she bangs the water from her ear, but too much of this sort of thing has the effect, finally, of reducing the whole social scene to a kind of cartoon. The audience laughs, and is comfortably assured that there can be no connection between them and *them.* It's all good clean fun. And nice to be reminded how we've outgrown those dear, dead days of long ago—and the funny clothes, and the funny dances.

The chief burden of the play is carried in the stories of Janey Williams, J. Ward Moorehouse, and Richard Ellsworth Savage. The problem is not that *everyone* in the novel could not be in the play; the problem is, why these three? They each begin as touching or promising people, and each becomes, in one way or another, hollow, corrupt, opportunistic. Although individual corruption is surely an important aspect of the thematic structure in the novel, the play lacks the corrosive effect of a whole society hell-bent on the big money and futility. Of course Moorehouse and Savage occupy positions of power in society and are not merely its victims, so that as products and carriers of our society's illness they could be doubly ominous. But the actors have such fun making fun of these self-evidently absurd characters that the threat to our composure they might represent is minimized. The iceberg does not seem so deep or so treacherous. It seems significant that the people selected for sharp focus are in the public relations game. Moorehouse and Savage are early Madison Avenue—which may be an effective symbol of general emptiness at that, but the rest of us *know* we're not Madison Avenue, so that as an all-inclusive symbol it is bound to fail. The play ends with Dick Savage settling smugly and cynically into his new role as a titan in the field. I suppose that is the "message" for the "here and now"—here is the menace in American life. This is certainly part of the truth—but it is such a *fashionable* thing to attack.

Greater depths are hinted at in the play: the wonderfully comic World War I private soldier—an American Schweik—bombarded on all sides by voices filling the air with platitudes and patriotic slogans, plaintively asking, "Can't anyone tell me how to get back to my outfit?"; the unutterably sad scenes between Joe and Janey Williams amidst the shabby-genteel pretensions of Georgetown; the savage irony in the passages dealing with the selection of an Unknown Soldier. The raw bitterness is occasionally there—the play still says more than most contemporary works—but for the most part it serves as a counterpoint, teasing the imagination.

The emphasis in the Biographies is necessarily selective and interestingly slanted. Five biographies are offered: the Wright Brothers, Debs, Valentino, Henry Ford, Isadora Duncan. Isadora's portrait is last and receives the fullest and most "dramatic" treatment, as if it were intended to be the symbolic center of the play. The note that a society is hostile to its most sensitive people is certainly a serious one and should be sounded clearly and unambiguously, to lodge implacably in our minds and hearts and do its transforming work. But here, too, the effect is muffled: Isadora, after all, was terribly eccentric (and who can say that she was driven to it by our hostility?), and her mode of life too remote to make a full assault upon the audience's sensibilities. Everyone knows we have treated an occasional artist shabbily—but times have changed, and besides, Isadora had her glory.

I think there are Biographies in the book, and stories, that would lie upon us like open wounds, but they were not done. Instead, a narrator reminds us at the close of the play that "U.S.A. is the lives of its people,"—forgetful of all those who did not receive a hearing—and smiles at us. We smile back. The lights go up; the playing is over. (pp. 391-99)

Jules Chametzky, "Reflections on 'U.S.A.' as Novel and Play," in The Massachusetts Review, *Vol. I, No. 2, February, 1960, pp. 391-99.*

George Knox (essay date Spring 1962)

[An American educator and critic, Knox is the coauthor of Dos Passos and the Revolting Playwrights *(1964). In the essay below, he analyzes the function and style of the biographies in* U.S.A.*]*

Late in the fall of 1959, in the off-broadway theater, The Martinique, Dos Passos' ***U.S.A.*** was reincarnated in dramatic performance. Actors in 1920's "costume" read one thread of the trilogy, the J. Ward Moorehouse story, and some of the short biographies, apparently with powerful effect. One is not surprised to hear this, particularly of the short biographies. Dos Passos worked a good deal in the theatre, not only writing plays but designing sets as well, during the twenties. The short biographies interest us particularly here. In ***U.S.A.*** they serve a structural function similar to the color harmonies in such early works as ***One Man's Initiation*** and ***Three Soldiers.*** But color contrast and harmony have given way to personality tones and "voices." The effect of these interstitial lives, or biographical asides, is largely aural. We hear with the authorial-listener, who in ***U.S.A.*** expresses our cultural identity through these representative heroes.

Don Passos, speaking a kind of divine-average language, a synthesis of Flaubert and Sandburg, links the biographies and the fictional lives "tight by the tendrils of phrased words." Epic bard of barbed words, poetic Veblen, he erects ironic memorials to our cultural identity in the saga of ***U.S.A.,*** "riveted into the language: the sharp clear prism of his mind." Amidst the Newsreels, which establish the mass-mind atmosphere, and the Camera Eye, the interior monologue of a sensitive observer, himself a part of the drama, sound the biographies. The newspaper headlines are staccato and cacophonic. The Camera Eye fragments are lyrical, subjective, brooding. The impressionistic portraits are the aural-images most closely tuned to reality, in the sense that they constitute identifiable historical voices. The biographies exemplify, ironically, many of Carlyle's (*Heroes and Hero-Worship*) and Emerson's (*Representative Men*) tenets about the "poetic" nature of biography. Achieving a maximum dramatism, they combine the Carlylean dictum that biography is the true poem and the Emersonian dictum that men have a pictorial or representative quality.

Dos Passos, like his "Luther Burbank," hybridizes forms in an era of form-destroying, the form of art imitating the formlessness of life in the twenties. The three novels are reduced to situations, the plot to scenes, the characters to humors and tones. The historical dramatis personae, or "parts," constitute a setting for the fiction, a harmony-in-contrast, seen and heard as they are through the ironic language.

Hence, a vibrant and charged aural dimension exists as the middle-ground between audience and subject, as well as in the background between author and subject, arrested momentarily in the detrital flow of American legendry. Dos Passos effaces contours, working through indirect exposition, speech fragments, vocabulary tics, odd verbal gestures, representative locutions. The "color" of the characters shades into the tones of the authorial conversation with history, which is unfinished, unending.

> . . . it was the speech that clung to the ears, the link that tingled in the blood; U.S.A. . . . U.S.A. is the letters at the end of an address when you are away from home. But mostly U.S.A. is the speech of the people.

The "young man" who anonymously introduces the three volumes appears in the last sketch in ***The Big Money,*** "Vag." He is a kind of Wolfian-Whitmanesque center-of-consciousness, our lost youth, our innocent wanderer on the road. As we read the introductory sketch we perhaps hear echoes of the voice in Whitman's "The Sleepers":

> I wander all night in my vision,
> Stepping with light feet, swiftly and noiselessly stepping and stopping,
> Bending with open eyes over the shut eyes of sleepers,
> Wandering and confused, lost to myself, ill-assorted, contradictory,
> Pausing, gazing, bending, and stopping.

And now Dos Passos:

> The young man walks by himself, fast but not fast enough, far but not far enough (faces slide out of sight, talk trails into tattered scraps, footsteps tap fainter in alleys); he must catch the last subway, the streetcar, the bus, run up the gangplanks of all the steamboats, register in all the hotels, work in the cities, answer the wantads, learn the trades, take up the jobs, live in all the boardinghouses, sleep in all the beds. One bed is not enough, one life is not enough. At night, head swimming with wants, he walks by himself alone. No job, no woman, no house, no city.

In the biographies, "talk trails into tattered scraps," one of the major devices. The tones are remembered tones, a collage of voices:

> Only the ears busy to catch the speech are not alone; the ears are caught tight, linked tight by the tendrils of phrased words, the turn of a joke, the singsong fade of a story, the gruff fall of a sentence; linking tendrils of speech twine through the city blocks, spread over trucks leaving on their long night runs over roaring highways, whisper down sandy byroads past worn-out farms, joining up cities and fillingstations, roadhouses, steamboats, planes groping along airways; words call out on mountains pastures, drift slow down rivers widening to the sea and the hushed beaches.

Recognizing this pervasive recitative quality in ***U.S.A.,*** we come closer to appreciating the formal propriety of the biographies, a choral background to the voices of the young man of the fictional characters.

All of the portraits are built upon conventional third-person narration, although the use to which Dos Passos puts this convention is sometimes peculiar. The broken quality of the narrative is accentuated in the Cummingsesque irregular line length, unconventional punctuation, and lack of capitalization. Sometimes (as in the sketches of Roosevelt and Bryan) the voice of the subject is indicated in italics. In the portraits of Roosevelt and Bryan we hear passages from their speeches. Sometimes the speaker's voice is implied in indirect discourse which is actually the author speaking. In the portrait of Veblen, we hear a "public" voice which often merges with auctorial voice to reinforce the desired feeling of disapproval or approval. Direct dramatic dialogue occurs occasionally, as in "Paul Bunyan," where Everest talks with the mob who attack and kill him. Again, the subject's voice may be used in ballad fashion, as in refrain. "The Body of an American" offers an excellent example of this: *"And there's a hundred million others like me,"* and "Say feller tell me how I can get back to my outfit," or "Say buddy can't you tell me how I can get back to my outfit?" Finally, "Say soldier for chrissake can't you tell me how I can get back to my outfit?" These entries of subject-voice assume a cumulative force, as in the incremental repetition of lines in the ballad, even though they be separated by one or more paragraphs of other textual material.

Dos Passos uses the incremental repetition technique for several effects. First, he is dealing impressionistically with each person. What is it about that person's life that he wishes to accent? Having selected this factor, he will make it a motif by repeating it. Sometimes such a factor is a statement that person made; or it is the peculiarity of some action. That is, Dos Passos essentializes character through isolating some feature and by repetition making it a "tic." Often we find this in a quoted remark, sometimes in italicized intrusion by the author himself, sometimes in a repeated opinion of the populace. In "Fighting Bob," we find "He was one of 'the little group of willful men expressing no opinion but their own' " repeated crucially at the end:

> a stumpy man with a lined face, one leg stuck out in the aisle and his arms folded and a chewed cigar in the corner of his mouth
> and an undelivered speech on his desk,
> a willful man expressing no opinion but his own.

Thus, Dos Passos accents a person's ruling passion, his dominant mood, his prevailing humor, or the consistency of a public reaction.

Dos Passos does not often intrude overt evaluative statements, although his bias is usually obvious enough through innuendo, tonal intensification, and irony. Often, he asks at the end of the selection some question that needs no answer. It contains the answer and a built-in judgment. The portrait of Minor C. Keith, superimposed on the fictional career of J. Ward Moorehouse and amidst the minor swirl of little people struggling in business, ends this way:

> Why that uneasy look under the eyes, in the picture of Minor C. Keith the pioneer of the fruit-trade, the railroad-builder, in all the pictures the newspapers carried of him when he died?

Endings are particularly important in the portraits. Often the ending is diminuendo, trailing off into anticlimax for ironic effect. Sometimes the whiplash ending achieves its effect through mock concession to opinion hostile to the subject. Again, Dos Passos employs the barbed ending through implied quotation, the echo of a previously repeated direct quotation, from a hostile opponent. A poem-like ending can also embody a final pronouncement, benediction, or malediction. Such is the ending to "The House of Morgan" in ***1919***:

> (Wars and panics on the stock exchange,
> machinegunfire and arson,
> bankruptcies, warloans,
> starvation, lice, cholera and typhus:
> good growing weather for the House of Morgan.)

The distaste for the Morgan financial operations can be contrasted with the neutral-pose which ends "Joe Hill" in ***1919***:

> They put him in a black suit, put a stiff collar around his neck and a bow tie, shipped him to chicago for a bangup funeral, and photographed his handsome stony mask staring into the future.
>
> The first of May they scattered his ashes to the wind.

Or, the ending is an ironic understatement ("The Body of an American"), the dying-fall, or diminuendo for the trailing-off into futility ("The American Plan" and "Tin Lizzie"). We find also the double-ending, as in the portrait of Thorstein Veblen ("The Bitter Drink"), a last request in italics followed by the author's own tribute. Then, there is the ironic anecdote for ending, as in "Art and Isadora." We also find an example of imitative form in the soaring ending to the portrait of the Wright brothers, an ending of positive force.

Most of the portraits utilize parentheses for varied effects. Usually, the parentheses serve for authorial aside, as Dos Passos takes a position of omniscient observer situated above the drama as narrated. In addition to the parentheses enclosing authorial interpolation, he (as in "The Boy Orator of the Platte") inserts repeated extracts from public statements in order to give the portrait depth and to create an illusion of massive force. Group and "class" opinion is echoed in parentheses, echoes which give the portraits a dialectical dramatism, indicating oppositions between the subject portrayed and the society or segment of society in which the subject acted. He makes use of italicized passages to intensify the dramatic impact. For one thing, he injects extracts from speeches ("Meester Veelson," "The Boy Orator," "The Happy Warrior") for accretive, incremental build-up of tone. Sometimes the public statement is found in lower-case fine print and in upper-case italics ("The Body of an American"). The portrait can end with an italicized statement by the subject, in most cases for irony. He may also interject passages from newspapers ("Adagio Dancer"), and other "documentary" materials, such as telegrams and letters, in italics.

Throughout the trilogy we notice some similarities to Carlylean harangue, as in *The French Revolution,* but more modern stylistic analogues suggest themselves, particularly cinematic techniques. ***U.S.A.*** as a whole is constructed in the fashion of a panoramic movie, the Hollywood epic, although no derogation of ***U.S.A.*** is intended in this parallel. The "Newsreel" and "Camera Eye" passages need no detailed explanation to show such correspondence in style. The portraits themselves are perhaps like movie shorts; or, better, documentary film; or "The March of Time" style of exposition. Fluidity of form is primary. Dos Passos tries to establish a sense of background and foreground simultaneously, as when the speeches of Roosevelt, Bryan, Wilson, Wright, *et al.,* intrude in the flow of events. We also get the impression of temporally distinct events concurrently.

The portrait of Paxton Hibben, "A Hoosier Quixote," illustrates some of these features very well. It begins with an extract from the 1928-1929 *Who's Who.* In small italics we get the most fragmentary, neutral, statistical portrayal of a "life," ending with *"A.M. Harvard 1904."* Next, we are projected into a historical context: "Thinking men were worried in the Middle West in the years Hibben was growing up there." And so the narrator fills in the milieu and recreates the cultural background from the barren entries of *Who's Who.* After about eighteen lines we come back to the "actor," Paxton Hibben, as a boy. To move from boyhood to the diplomatic service takes Dos Passos another eighteen lines. There he intrudes another italicized fragment from the *Who's Who* record, carrying him up to the time of retirement. The anticlimactic, cold impersonality of these passages breaks our mood abruptly, whereas the more casual exposition in which they are embedded expands, exhumes, so to speak, the humanity of the subject. We begin to feel through contrast the drama that lies cold in the mere statistics: "3rd sec and 2nd sec American Embassy St. Petersburg and Mexico City 1905-6" is taken up in the next passage thus: "Pushkin for de Musset; St. Petersburg was a young dude's romance . . . "

Once launched into the life, once having given the obituary skeleton some warm flesh, we flashback for kaleidoscopic effect, for crescendo:

> goldencrusted spires under a platinum sky,
> the icegray Neva flowing swift and deep under bridges that jingled with sleighbells;
> riding home from the Islands with the Grand Duke's mistress, the most beautiful most amorous singer of Neapolitan streetsongs;
> Staking a pile of rubies in a tall room glittering with chandeliers, monocles, diamonds dripped on white shoulders;
> white snow, white tableclothes, white sheets, Kakhetian wine, Vodka fresh as newmown hay, Astrakhan caviar, sturgeon, Finnish salmon, Lapland ptarmigan, and the most beautiful women in the world;
>
> but it was 1905, Hibben left the Embassy one

night and saw a flare of red against the trampled snow of the Nevsky
and red flags,
blood frozen in the ruts, blood trinckling down the cartracks;
he saw the machineguns on the balconies of the Winter Palace, and Cossacks charging the unarmed crowds that wanted peace and food and a little freedom,
heard the throaty roar of the Russian Marseillaise; revolt, he walked the streets all night with the revolutionists, got in wrong at the Embassy
and was transferred to Mexico City where there was no revolution yet, only peons and priests and the stillness of the great volcanoes.

And so the sketch progresses, alternating passages of dramatic acceleration, things seen, comments, breaks—in true Carlylean fashion. The contrast between the mere record, in fragmentary intrusions, and the compelling excitement of the narrator's mood builds our own excitement and creates a paradoxical impression of historical urgency and timelessness, something sadly happened and gone. This is film realism, the moment held in closeup while the historical flow moves in the background:

In Paris they were still haggling over the price of blood, squabbling over toy flags, the river frontiers on reliefmaps, the historical destiny of peoples, while behind the scenes the good contractplayers, the Deterdings, the Zahkaroffs, the Stinnesses sat quiet and possessed themselves of the raw materials.
In Moscow there was order,
In Moscow there was work,
In Moscow there was hope;
the *Marseillaise* of 1905, *Onward, Christian Soldiers* of 1912, the sullen passiveness of American Indians, of infantrymen waiting for death at the front was part of the tremendous roar of the Marxian *Internationale.*
Hibben believed in the new world.

Here, stylistic condensation tells, particularly in the stream of consciousness and the flashback, as we flow within the mind of Hibben, unsympathetic as one may be with those lost allegiances, those pathetic moments. Notice, then, an abrupt time transition:

Back in America
somebody got hold of a photograph of Captain Paxton Hibben laying a wreath on Jack Reed's grave; they tried to throw him out of the O.R.C.:
at Princeton at the twentieth reunion of his college class his classmates started to lynch him; they were drunk and perhaps it was just a collegeboy prank twenty years too late but they had a noose around his neck,
lynch the goddam red,
no more place in America for change, no more place for the old gags: social justice, progressivism, revolt against oppression, democracy; put the reds on the skids,
no money for them,
no jobs for them.

Then on the screen flashes the last fragment of the *Who's Who* data Volume 15, 1928-1929:

Mem Authors League of America, Soc of Colonial Wars, Vets Foreign Wars, Am Legion, fellow Royal and Am Geog Socs. Decorated chevalier Order of St. Stanislas (Russian), Officer Order of the Redeemer (Greek), Order of the Sacred Treasure (Japan). Clubs Princeton, Newspaper, Civic (New York)
Author: Constantine and the Greek People 1920, The Famine of Russia 1922, Henry Ward Beecher an American Portrait 1927.
d. 1929.

So ends, ironically in fadeout, the portrait of Paxton Hibben, "A Hoosier Quixote."

Throughout a reading of the ***U.S.A.*** trilogy one feels the power of Dos Passos' dramatic sense, the keen antennae which he kept sensitive to the morality, speech, and physical identity of America. The cultural and individual voices fuse in our consciousness to convey moods of dissonance, danger, strain. Technically, ***U.S.A.*** envelops a powerful narrative continuum, in imagistic but elliptical style, constructed of strata of fact and bias. But it aesthetically creates unity while conveying a sense of disunity and disintegration. Reportorial and detached in one sense, the authorial voice nevertheless reveals a deep personal sincerity, a serious choral commitment.

We feel, as we read the portraits, the need for sympathy and identification. We feel the problems of freedom and authority in a society where sympathy and identification are too often based on false criteria. Where we find the absence of refinement, sympathy, and love we know that these elements are being called for. There is a moral sense binding the diversity and chaos together in an optative mood. We are moved to visions of wholeness by the impressions of discontinuity and inconclusiveness. Through the cacophony and journalistic clangor of discord we imagine harmony and melody.

We understand this dramatic hybrid of poetry and prose by listening. Dos Passos has listened with the ear which registers all that is precise and revealing. In reading these pieces aloud we will appreciate his genius for compressing into image and tone the essence of personality, his capacity for fluming documentary erudition into poetic substance, his skill in marshalling detail and incident for illuminative purpose and dramatic effect. (pp. 109-16)

George Knox, "Voice in the 'U.S.A.' Biographies," in Texas Studies in Literature and Language, *Vol. IV, No. 1, Spring, 1962, pp. 109-16.*

John Lydenberg (essay date 1964)

[*Lydenberg is an American educator and critic. In the essay below, he examines the relationship between the characters in* U.S.A. *and the ideals and values of American society.*]

Because James Baldwin, like Tocqueville a decade or more ago, has now become so fashionable that one cannot decently take a text from him, I shall start with Yevgeny Yevtushenko, in the hope that he has not quite yet reached that point. In one of his poems appear the simple lines:

U.S.A. is less a demonstration of historical determinism and the futility of Man's efforts to free himself from a vast social and economic mechanism which controls his destiny, than it is a bitter indictment of a nation's collective failure to make the machine run the way it ought to.

—Barry Maine, in his "Representative Men in Dos Passos's* The 42nd Parallel,*" in* Clio, *Fall, 1982.

"Let us give back to words / Their original meanings." My other non-Dos Passos text is so classic that it cannot be over-fashionable. In *A Farewell to Arms,* Gino says, "What has been done this summer cannot have been done in vain." And, as you all know, Hemingway has Frederic Henry reply: "I did not say anything. I was always embarrassed by the words sacred, glorious, and sacrifice and the expression in vain. . . . Abstract words such as glory, honor, courage, or hallow were obscene."

These quotations suggest the concern of writers with abstract words representing the ideals and values of their society. Both Yevtushenko and Hemingway say that these words have lost their glory, their true meaning. But they take diametrically opposed attitudes toward the role the words will play in their writings. Representing the party of Hope, Yevtushenko is the social and political idealist, the reformer, the artist who sees his art as a weapon in man's unceasing struggle for a better world. Representing the party of Despair, Hemingway abjures political concerns, makes his separate peace, and develops an art unconcerned with social ideals. Thus they symbolize two extremes: writers at one pole—Yevtushenko's—will utilize the words, will insist on doing so; writers at the other—Hemingway's—will dispense with them altogether, or try to do so, as did Hemingway in most of his early fiction.

Dos Passos falls between the extremes, but instead of presenting us with a golden mean he gives something more like an unstable compound of the two. Hemingway abandons the words because he can see no relation between them and the realities, and creates a world stripped of the values represented by the words. By contrast, reformers—who are equally insistent on the disparity between the ideals and the realities—are unwilling to reject the words and strive, like Yevtushenko, to give back to them their original meanings. Dos Passos can neither abandon nor revivify the words. Like Hemingway he feels that they have been made obscene and he can find no way in his art to redeem them. Yet like any reformer he puts them at the center of his work.

Critics have often held that the protagonist of ***U.S.A.*** is society. I could almost maintain that it is, instead, "the words." Dos Passos seems obsessed by them: he cares about them passionately and cannot abandon them, but at

Reginald Marsh's illustration of the sheriff slugging Ben Compton from 1919.

the same time he is made sick at heart—nay at stomach—by the way they have been spoiled. So he concerns himself with problems of social values, ever returning to the words, "as a dog to his vomit" (to use the inelegant but expressive Biblical phrase). ***U.S.A.*** tastes sour because the words are tainted and indigestible, but neither here nor in his other fiction can Dos Passos spew them forth once and for all as could the Hemingways of our literature.

In two well-known passages, Dos Passos makes explicit his feeling about the words. These—the most eloquent and deeply felt parts of ***U.S.A.***—are the Camera Eyes focused on the execution of Sacco and Vanzetti. In the first, immediately preceding the Mary French section on the last desperate days before the executions, he asks:

> how make them feel who are your oppressors America
>
> rebuild the ruined words worn slimy in the mouths of lawyers districtattorneys collegepresidents judges without the old words the immigrants haters of oppression brought to Plymouth how can you know who are your betrayers America . . . ? (***Big Money***)

In the second, after the execution, he says:

> we the beaten crowd together . . . sit hunched with bowed heads on benches and hear the old words of the haters of oppression made new in sweat and agony tonight
>
> our work is over the scribbled phrases the nights typing releases the smell of the printshop the sharp reek of newprinted leaflets the rush for Western Union stringing words into wires the search for stinging words to make you feel who are your oppressors America
>
> America our nation has been beaten by strangers who have turned our language inside out who have taken the clean words our fathers spoke and made them slimy and foul

Just as Dos Passos makes the Sacco-Vanzetti affair symbolic of his vision of the state of the nation, so, in talking about the "old words," "the clean words our fathers spoke," and "the old American speech," he is alluding to his ideals, to the American dream, and in describing the words now as "ruined," "slimy and foul," and "turned . . . inside out," he is expressing his sense of the betrayal of the dream.

"Mostly U.S.A. is the speech of the people," says Dos Passos to conclude the prose poem he added as preface to the trilogy. Maybe. But ***U.S.A.,*** the novel, in no way carries out that Sandburg-like suggestion of faith in the people and delight in their talk. It contains none of the salty talk, the boastful talk, the folksy talk, the "wise" talk that is the staple of much "realistic" American fiction. Actually, we discover, on re-examination of these novels, that dialogue plays a smaller role than we might have thought it did. What little talk there is is either purely functional, merely a way of getting on with the narrative: "Shall we go to bed?" "Where can I get a drink?" "God I feel lousy this morning." Or it is banal and stereotyped. Whenever his characters express anything resembling ideas they talk only in tired slogans; the words have been drained of meaning, and the characters mouthing them are empty puppets.

Here is one example. I would give many more, had I time, for the real effect is gained only through the continuous repetition of the vaporous phrases. This is from ***1919,*** the novel written during the time Dos Passos was presumably most favorably inclined toward Marxism and the Communists. One might have expected that here if anywhere the words of a communist, Don Stevens in this instance, would carry some conviction. Instead Dos Passos makes them sound mechanical, false, flat, like counterfeit coins. The effect is heightened here, as in many other places, by giving us the words in indirect dialog.

> He said that there wasn't a chinaman's chance that the U.S. would keep out of the war; the Germans were winning, the working class all over Europe was on the edge of revolt, the revolution in Russia was the beginning of the worldwide social revolution and the bankers knew it and Wilson knew it; the only question was whether the industrial workers in the east and the farmers and casual laborers in the middle west and west would stand for war. The entire press was bought and muzzled. The Morgans had to fight or go bankrupt. "It's the greatest conspiracy in history."

This is the way the words sound in passage after passage. The ruined words dribble from the mouths of Dos Passos' hollow men. Within is nothing but clichés, phrases having no meaning for the speaker and conveying none to the listener. *This* is the speech of the people in Dos Passos's ***U.S.A.,*** and it does much to establish the tone of the whole trilogy.

But if the words are often empty and meaningless, they often too have a very real meaning, vicious and perverted. The old words of the American dream have been "turned . . . inside out"; now they are the lies by which the new Americans live. The theme of the transformation of the clean words into lies had been baldly stated in Dos Passos's first novel, ***One Man's Initiation.*** Early in the book, Martin Howe dreams romantically of his mission as the ocean steamer carries him "over there":

> And very faintly, like music heard across the water in the evening, blurred into strange harmonies, his old watchwords echo a little in his mind. Like the red flame of the sunset setting fire to opal sea and sky, the old exaltation, the old flame that would consume to ashes all the lies in the world, the trumpet-blast under which the walls of Jericho would fall down, stirs and broods in the womb of his grey lassitude.

Then as Martin is first going up to the front, he comes to adopt a new conception in which the lies are all-inclusive, his "old watchwords" now no different from the rest of the world's lies. A stranger appears and explains it to him:

> Think, man, think of all the oceans of lies through all the ages that must have been necessary to make this possible! Think of this new particular vintage of lies that has been so industriously pumped out of the press and the pulpit. . . . [The] lies are like a sticky juice overspreading the world, a living, growing flypaper to catch and gum the wings of every human soul.

Finally, Martin talks in much the same way himself: " 'What terrifies me . . . is their power to enslave our minds. . . . America, as you know, is ruled by the press. . . . People seem to so love to be fooled. . . . We are slaves of bought intellect, willing slaves.' " And a French anarchist takes up the theme and makes the moral explicit: " 'Oh, but we are all such dupes. . . . First we must fight the lies. It is the lies that choke us.' "

In ***U.S.A.,*** Dos Passos does not *tell* us about the lies, he makes us feel them. The Newsreels are his most obvious device for showing us the "sticky juice" of lies in which Americans are caught. The opening lines of ***The 42nd Parallel*** are: "It was that emancipated race / That was chargin up the hill; / Up to where them insurrectos / Was afightin fit to kill." The hill is not San Juan but a hill in the Philippines. And that first Newsreel ends with Senator Beveridge's Lucid bluster: "The twentieth century will be American. American thought will dominate it. American progress will give it color and direction. American deeds will make it illustrious. . . . The regeneration of the world, physical as well as moral, has begun, and revolutions never move backwards."

One recognizable pattern keeps recurring in the shifting kaleidoscope of the Newsreels: that is—the official lies disguised as popular truths. We see—and hear—the rhetoric of the American Way drummed into the heads of the American public, by advertisements, newspaper headlines, newspaper stories, politicians' statements, businessmen's statements. In contrast to these standardized verbalizations about happy, prosperous, good America, the Newsreels give continual flashes of Dos Passos's "real" America—of fads and follies, hardships and horrors. More striking even than the contrasts within these collages are those between the shimmering surface of the Newsreels and the sardonic realities of the Portraits, and above all the dreary lives of his fictional characters.

The narratives of these lives take up the greater part of the book, of course, and our reaction to it depends to a great extent on our evaluation of the characters. My suggestion is that it is by their use of "the words" that we judge them. And here, *mirabile dictu,* we come at last to the theme of "determinism."

That ***U.S.A.*** is strongly naturalistic and deterministic is obvious to all. Readers who judge it a major work of fiction do so in part because of its success in portraying characters as helpless individuals caught in a world they have not made and can not control. Less admiring critics are apt to consider its weakness to be the weakness of the characters, sometimes even implying that Dos Passos's failure to create free, responsible heroes was a failure of execution. Whatever their assessment of the novel, all agree that ***U.S.A.*** is starkly deterministic. None of its characters has free will, none determines his fate, all move like automatons.

The chief way in which Dos Passos makes us feel that his characters—or non-characters—are determined is by showing their choices as non-choices. In ***U.S.A.*** Dos Passos's people do not make decisions. Or, if you insist that human beings all make decisions, choose one road over another, I will say instead that he presents his characters to us so that we do not feel their choices to be decisions. They simply are doing so and so, and continue thus until they find themselves, or we find them, doing something else.

Here are two examples. The first, a long one, includes two decisions, one a reversal of the other. Note here—for future reference—what the protagonist, Richard Ellsworth Savage, does with the words, and note also how the indirect dialogue accentuates the feeling of cliché and slogan. Dick is "deciding" what he should do about the war and about his college education.

> In the Easter vacation, after the Armed Ship Bill had passed Dick had a long talk with Mr. Cooper who wanted to get him a job in Washington, because he said a boy of his talent oughtn't to endanger his career by joining the army and already there was talk of conscription. Dick blushed becomingly and said he felt it would be against his conscience to help in the war in any way. They talked a long time without getting anywhere about duty to the state and party leadership and highest expediency. In the end Mr. Cooper made him promise not to take any rash step without consulting him. [Note that Dick has now "decided" that his "principles" forbid him to enter any war work.] Back in Cambridge everybody was drilling and going to lectures on military science. Dick was finishing up the four year course in three years and had to work hard, but nothing in the courses seemed to mean anything any more. He managed to find time to polish up a group of sonnets called Morituri Te Salutant that he sent to a prize competition run by *The Literary Digest.* It won the prize but the editors wrote back that they would prefer a note of hope in the last sestet. Dick put in the note of hope [so go the words!] and sent the hundred dollars to Mother to go to Atlantic City with. He discovered that if he went into war work he could get his degree that spring without taking any exams and went in to Boston one day without saying anything to anybody and signed up in the volunteer ambulance service. [Now he has "decided" that his "principles" no longer prevent him from war work.] ***(1919)***

And here is the sound of a Dos Passos character "deciding" to have an abortion:

> Of course she could have the baby if she wanted to [Don Stevens said] but it would spoil her usefulness in the struggle for several months and he didn't think this was the time for it. It was the first time they'd quarreled. She said he was heartless. He said they had to sacrifice their personal feelings for the workingclass, and stormed out of the house in a temper. In the end she had an abortion but she had to write her mother again for money to pay for it. ***(Big Money)***

These examples of important decisions presented as simply something that the character happened somehow to do are not exceptional; they are typical. I think I can say safely that there are *no* decisions in the three novels that are presented in a significantly different way.

To this extent, then, ***U.S.A.*** is systematically, rigidly, effectively deterministic. But there is a fault in its rigid structure, a softness in its determinism, and—in opposition to both the friendly and unfriendly critics of Dos Passos—I would suggest that a large part of the book's success comes precisely from the author's failure to be as consistently deterministic as he thinks he wants to be. True as it is that we never identify with any of his characters as we do with conventionally free characters, it is equally true that we do not regard them all with the nice objectivity required by the deterministic logic. Some we consider "good" and some "bad," just as though they were in fact responsible human beings making free choices. And these judgments that we make, however illogically, we base largely upon the way in which the different characters treat those crucial abstract words.

Some characters are essentially neutral—or perhaps I should say that we feel them to be truly determined. We look upon Margo Dowling, Eveline Hutchins, Eleanor Stoddard, and Charley Anderson with a coolly detached eye, even though we may feel that in their various ways the women are somewhat bitchy. And although Daughter, and Joe and Janey Williams tend to arouse our sympathies, we view them quite dispassionately. Certainly we do not consider any of these as responsible moral agents. And none of them shows any inclination to be concerned with the words.

In contrast to the neutral characters are Mac, Ben Compton, and Mary French. Dos Passos likes them and makes us like them because they affirm the values which he holds and wishes his readers to accept. Each of them uses the words, tries to uphold the true meaning of the "old words," and fights to rebuild the ruined words. Although their decisions are described in the same way that all other decisions are, we feel that their choices of the words are deliberate, and are acts of freedom for which they take the responsibility. Mac leaves his girl in San Francisco to go to Goldfield as a printer for the Wobblies because he finds that his life is meaningless when he is not using and acting out the words. Later, after his marriage, he escapes again from the bourgeois trap because he can't bear not to be talking with his old comrades about their dream and ideals. Finally, unable to do anything but talk and unable to find a way to make the old words new or effective, he sinks back into the conventional rut of the other unfree characters. Ben Compton insists on talking peace and socialism after the United States has entered the war, freely choosing thereby to be taken by the police and imprisoned. During the war, it seems, the old words may not be used in public until they have been converted into the official lies.

Mary French is generally considered Dos Passos's most sympathetic character in ***U.S.A.*** She is certainly associated with the words throughout, and in her work with the 1919 steel strikers and the Sacco-Vanzetti committee she is actively engaged in the attempt to "renew" the words and make them effective in the fight for justice. But, significantly, she does not employ them much. Not only have they been worn slimy in the mouths of her enemies, but they are continually being perverted by her coworkers and supposed friends, the ostensible renovators of the words. So, in the final section of ***The Big Money,*** we find her collecting clothes for the struck coal miners, doing good, but not a good that goes beyond the mere maintenance of brute existence. Anything of more significance would demand use of the words, and at this point in his writing, the words, to Dos Passos, have been ruined beyond redemption.

And then there are the bad guys, J. Ward Moorehouse and Richard Ellsworth Savage. They are as hollow as any other Dos Passos men, their decisions, like all others, nondecisions. But where Joe and Janey Williams make us sad, these make us mad. We dislike them and blame them, just as though they had really chosen.

Dos Passos makes us feel that a character is responsible for the words he chooses. To explain just *how* Dos Passos does that is not easy, but I think it goes, in part, something like this. We don't blame Dick for drinking too much or for wenching, any more than we blame Charley Anderson or Joe Williams. These activities seem to be instinctive reactions, self-defeating but natural escapes from freedom. Part of the reason we feel Dick and the others determined in their dissipation, and consequently do not blame them, is because the characters blame themselves, regret what they do and feebly resolve not to do it again. Thus when they fall back into their old, familiar ways, we feel that they are doing what they do not want to do, do not will to do. But when we come to another sort of action, the choice of words, no character is shown regretting the abstract words he uses. Thus the character implicitly approves his choice of words, he seems to be acting freely, and we tend to hold him responsible.

To get back to our bad guys, Moorehouse and Savage are the successful exploiters in the trilogy, and on first thought we might assume that that fact would suffice to make them culpable. But they are not the usual exploiters found in proletarian novels: big bad businessmen gouging the workers, manufacturers grinding the faces of the poor. Indeed they don't seem to hurt anyone. They exploit not people but words, or people, impersonally, by means of the words. Their profession is "public relations." (We might look at them as precursors of the Madison Avenue villains of post-World War II fiction, and infinitely superior ones, at that.) Their job is to persuade people to buy a product or to act in a particular way. Their means of persuasion is words. And the words they use are to a great extent "the words," the words of the American dream. They talk cooperation, justice, opportunity, freedom, equality.

Here are two brief quotations from J. Ward Moorehouse. He and Savage are preparing a publicity campaign for old Doc Bingham's patent medicines—now called "proprietary" medicines. (You will remember that Doc was Mac's first employer at the beginning of the trilogy, as owner-manager of "The Truthseeker Literary Distributing Co., Inc.") The first quotation is part of J. W.'s argument to a complaisant senator: "But, senator, . . . it's the principle of the thing. Once government interference in business is established as a precedent it means the end of liberty and private initiative in this country. . . . What this bill purports to do is to take the right of selfmedication from the American people." And in this next one he is talking to his partner Savage about the advertising—no, publicity—campaign: "Of course self-service, independence, individualism is the word I gave the boys in the beginning. This is going to be more than a publicity campaign, it's going to be a campaign for Americanism."

Here at last we have arrived at the source—or at least one major source—of the cancerous evil that swells malignantly through the books. Here we observe the manufacturers of the all-pervasive lies busily at work, here we see the words being deliberately perverted. And we cannot consider the perverters of the words as merely helpless automatons or innocents; they deliberately choose their words and we judge them as villains.

So, in conclusion, Dos Passos finds that the old words of the immigrant haters of oppression, which should have set Americans free, have instead been worn slimy in their mouths. And these words are in effect central actors in ***U.S.A.*** They determine our attitudes toward the characters who use and misuse them, establish the tone of hollow futility that rings throughout the trilogy, and leave in our mouths the bitter after-taste of nausea. The novels that followed, to make the ***District of Columbia*** trilogy, emphasize Dos Passos's sick obsession with these words. In the first, the humanitarian socialist dream comes to us in the clichés and jargon of American communists; in the second, the American dream is conveyed to us through the demagoguery of a vulgar Louisiana dictator; in the third the dream of New Deal reform has been turned into a nightmare by cynical opportunists and time-serving bureaucrats who exploit the old words anew.

No longer able to imagine a way of giving to words their original meanings, after ***U.S.A.,*** Dos Passos could still not abandon them for some more palatable subject. And so he seemed to take the worst part of the worlds of Yevtushenko and Hemingway. But in ***U.S.A.*** he could still write about Mac and Ben Compton and Mary French; he could still feel some hope that the ruined words might be rebuilt;

he could still imagine the dream to be yet a possibility. In ***U.S.A.*** his despair was not yet total and his dual vision of the words brought to these novels a tension, a vitality, and a creative energy he would never be able to muster again. (pp. 97-107)

John Lydenberg, "Dos Passos's 'U.S.A.': The Words of the Hollow Men," in Essays on Determinism in American Literature, *edited by Sydney J. Krause, Kent State University Press, 1964, pp. 97-107.*

Whitman's influence . . . pervades *U.S.A.,* although it is most explicit in *The Big Money* and in the sketch "U.S.A.," which introduces the trilogy. The sketch is somewhat reminiscent of "Song of Myself," which portrays Whitman as going everywhere in the country and identifying himself with every type of individual.

—*Melvin Landsberg, in his* Dos Passos' Path to *U.S.A.:* A Political Biography, 1912-1936, *1972.*

John Dos Passos with Frank Gado (interview date 16 October 1968)

[*Gado is an American educator and critic. In the following excerpt from an interview conducted in October 1968, Dos Passos discusses the writing of* U.S.A., *the Sacco-Vanzetti case, and some of his literary and nonliterary influences.*]

[*Gado*]: *One of the most remarkable features of* **U.S.A.** *is the Biographies. It's a form I think you originated and I don't know of anyone who has been able to copy you successfully. (In fact, for a writer acclaimed as one of the most experimental of our century, you have had incommensurately little influence, technically, on younger writers; I think this is due to your having so fully developed the innovation that its possibilities for others have been exhausted.) You had started advancing toward the multi-centered novel from the beginning. Certain elements of it were in* **One Man's Initiation** *and* **Three Soldiers;** *more were added in* **Manhattan Transfer;** *but it wasn't until* **U.S.A.** *that all the components of the formula found their place. Although there were small hints of the Biography device earlier, it was essentially a new element, and contributed mightily to the overall effect of the trilogy. What impelled you toward the Biography? What aesthetic concept was involved?*

[Dos Passos]: It's rather hard to remember how one happens to hit on these things. The Newsreels were intended to give the clamor, the sound of daily life. In the Biographies, I tried to produce the pictures.

I have always paid a good deal of attention to painting. The period of art I was very much interested in at that time was the thirteenth and fourteenth centuries. Its tableaux with large figures of saints surrounded by a lot of little people just fascinated me. I tried to capture the same effect in words.

That was one of the ideas, but then a lot of things appear in books without the author knowing exactly how they got there. Also, I always had an interest in contrast, in the sort of montage Griffith and Eisenstein used in films. I was trying to put across a complex state of mind, an atmosphere, and I brought in these things partly for contrast and partly for getting a different dimension.

It has always seemed to me that the trilogy was very carefully thought out before it was ever begun. As I believe others have noted, in trying to achieve an amalgam, you were working on four levels: first, the Camera Eye, the personal experience of life in the twentieth century of the author himself; second, the narratives, mirroring the growth of this century, the emergence of this new beast **U.S.A.** *following the Spanish-American War through which we became an imperial power—in fact, if not in name, an empire; third, the Newsreels, the Greek chorus in this heroic, hubristic, tragic drama; fourth, the Biographies, the men who influenced or typified that age. All these various levels kept moving toward a point of union which occurs in the final novel. As in* **Three Soldiers,** *was it your conscious plan to go from stress on the commonly human experiences of youth to the rusting away of machinelike life at the end of the trilogy?*

Yes, I think it was. I started out to do it as one book. Then it became obvious the thing was going to be so long that it would be better to publish it in sections. But I did have a plan about the end particularly. Poe, you know, gives a very good maxim in one of his critical pieces: an author should always know what the end of a story is going to be before he starts the beginning.

Did any of these characters change in your own mind?

Yes. They always do. They change enormously. If the character is going to come to life, he is going to have to take things into his own hands.

Did you intend at any point to have one character or set of characters somehow typify each of the volumes? It seemed to me that Mac was the central character in the first novel, Joe Williams and Dick Savage the twin stars of the middle novel, Charlie Anderson the central character in the last, and J. Ward Moorehouse perhaps the key figure of the whole trilogy.

Yes, that's about right. I think I did have that in mind, although I'm not sure how much I knew when I *started* about who was going to turn out most important in the various novels.

In **1919** *you had a Biography on a man named Jack Reed. I was reading some critical material which discussed the emergence of "parajournalism"—writing which is half newspaper reporting, half personal reactions. It said that Mr. Reed had influenced such reporting. . . .*

Jack Reed was a great character and, in addition, he wrote very well. His book on Mexico was excellent. And although it was not the most accurate, he gave us the most vivid account of the Bolshevik Revolution.

. . . in the newspaper vein . . .

Oh, it was better than that. It was the tops of American reportorial writing, in the same line as Stephen Crane and that fellow from San Francisco—what was his name? He wrote short stories.

Bierce?

Yes, of course, Ambrose Bierce. That was a great period in American journalism. We had awfully good writing in newspapers—which, unfortunately, you can hardly find today. Reporters then had much more freedom and there were a great many more newspapers. If writing according to your own tastes and standards lost you your job on one paper, you'd go on to another. Now we have journalistic monopolies and the business-like attitudes of the management are to some extent reflected in the reporters. The colorful styles, the flamboyance are largely gone.

What influence did the expatriate movement have on your work during that period?

Not very much. I was always opposed to it; I thought the whole idea was nonsense and I didn't spend very much time with any of those people. Hemingway was quite a good friend of mine and much of what I saw of all that was through him, although even he was not that much a part of that scene. Malcolm Cowley, whom I'd known ever since he turned up at Harvard, was more typical. He went on to popularize the expatriate thing, but he always had a genius for getting things wrong—just a little bit wrong, wrong enough to be not quite true. (pp. 42-4)

Did you ever feel impelled to be a poet?

Not exactly, no.

[Allen Ginsberg] listed you along with Whitman as an important influence on his poetry. I think he had in mind the similarity to Whitman in the beginning and end of **U.S.A.** *(the Vagabond part), but he might also have been referring to the relationship between the voice of the poet and the society he is commenting on.*

That's interesting. Some work I've been doing has sent me to my Whitman again; it's been a delight re-reading *Democratic Vistas*—I had forgotten how much insight there was there.

One of the things that strikes you about the great figures of that period is their ethics. At that time, people read the Bible and absorbed a body of tested wisdom about the conduct of life. Even when I was a boy, it was expected that children read the Bible; I remember my father seeing to it that I read chapters regularly. That's missing today and we're the poorer for it. No individual, no society can survive without ethics. I'm always very suspicious of the fellow who claims to have a personal morality; what he means is that he has no morality at all and feels free to do you dirt. (p. 47)

Earlier, you stated that Eisenstein and Griffith influenced **U.S.A.;** *do you see any current relationship between cinema and fiction which might be producing something new?*

I haven't been following recent movies very much. I did see *2001* and was much taken with it. It's a very attractive, poetic piece of work—one of the few poetic things I've seen come out of Hollywood in a long while. It is, of course, reflective of a great mass of science fiction being written. I'm ashamed that I am not as up on science fiction as I might be, because that may be one form of writing where something quite good is being done. Some of Ray Bradbury's things, for instance, are really excellent.

The relationship between Eisenstein and Griffith and your work was one of technique. . . .

Entirely technique. It had nothing whatever to do with content.

Don't you see any connection between Godard, Truffaut, Polanski, and the rest of the cinematic avant-garde and the novel? Between the nouvelle vague and the mixture of comedy and tragedy, of farce and the real you get in writers like Barth and Vonnegut?

I don't think so. There is now probably less interest by writers in cinema because we have become so accustomed to this medium that it is less exciting than when it was very new.

Before our time runs out, might we talk a bit about the Sacco-Vanzetti case? Being of Italian extraction, I've always felt what happened to those two men to be part of my heritage. Because of your intimate ties to that agony, I was wondering whether you have read Francis Russell's Tragedy in Dedham?

Yes. It is very interesting, although I don't agree with it. I was very good friends with Carlo Tresca. . . .

That's why I brought this up. Russell bases his conclusion that Sacco was guilty on two things: the ballistics test he ran at the time of writing his book and Carlo Tresca's off hand statement just before he died that although Vanzetti was innocent, Sacco wasn't.

I wonder about his examination of the evidence because it was so long after the trial; and my report of what Tresca said would be different. As I remember it, Tresca was pointing out that there was no question but that Sacco and Vanzetti were both trying to protect members of the anarchist group. Carlo thought—and he knew more than he told about it—that his group had been involved with a professional criminal gang in some of these hold-ups.

You no longer think that Madeiros was involved in that crime?

It's very hard to tell. He might have been. Tresca's view doesn't necessarily rule out Madeiros. Madeiros's reasons for saying what he did were, I thought, perfectly honest and aboveboard. The way he put things sounded as if he knew what he was talking about.

How much similarity do you perceive between the agitation over Sacco-Vanzetti, which was something of a watershed dividing the "two nations" in America, and current agitation over Viet Nam and the race issue, which is also dividing us into two nations?

To me, the Sacco-Vanzetti agitation was much more understandable. I had great sympathy for the anarchist movement at that time, even though it was obvious the solutions they were suggesting were nonsensical. But it seemed to me that those attitudes served to freshen people's minds. It was also interesting because it was the last expression of the great anarchist movement before it was finally crushed by the Soviet Union. (pp. 50-2)

In reading your novels, one is hit by how often figures appear who are modeled in part on yourself. Very often you are quite unflattering to these people. Why do you expose yourself so? What makes you claw at such obvious personae *as Ro Lancaster and Jed?*

It's part of the search for objectivity. Any novelist gets a great deal of himself into all of his characters, although he usually starts by trying to describe something else and does get a great deal of other people mixed into these characters. Perhaps to say that he ends up describing himself would be an over-simplification. The blood and nerves of the characters have to come from the writer's emotions and frustrations. My system has always been to try to do it objectively. That's why I put the Camera Eye things in ***U.S.A.***; it was a way of draining off the subjective by directly getting in little bits of my own experience.

For you, then, the author's relation to his novel is both that of the puppet master and puppet. You probably don't remember a chat we had seven years ago in which you mentioned the various influences on your work. One you mentioned was Thackeray in Vanity Fair. *I took this to mean that you were intrigued by the tension between the man standing above his theater (like the Camera's Eye) and the characters on his stage (like the narratives.)*

No. What influenced me in Thackeray was that he tried to give a picture of society in *Vanity Fair* through primary and secondary figures. It's a marvelous job.

Judging by that criterion, which of your books would you say are best?

I haven't the faintest idea. It's up to the critics to fight that out.

How do you begin to write a novel?

I get started somehow, and then one word just follows another. I have a fairly definite notion of what I am trying to do. I try to do it, then I rewrite. In the early stages particularly, I find things have to be rewritten a good many times. Then, later, I fall into the style I've created and the writing falls together more easily.

Someone reported, perhaps not accurately, that you were in the habit of filing away newspaper headlines in a drawer until, eventually, a novel suddenly emerged.

I did keep a lot of them. That's how the Newsreel thing started. I kept cutting out little clippings that seemed amusing. I started doing that quite early in my career. In ***Manhattan Transfer,*** I didn't use them directly, but I introduced them to show that I knew more or less what was going on in the world in which my characters lived. It was important to know what these people were reading, seeing, thinking. Then some of these collections of bits started to look so good to me that I put them in intact. Later, I started searching for apt headlines and collecting what would fit the story.

Did you ever make them up?

No. I didn't have to. It was a period in which the newspapers were rather amusing. (pp. 52-3)

John Dos Passos and Frank Gado, in an interview in First Person: Conversations on Writers & Writing, *edited by Frank Gado, Union College Press, 1973, pp. 31-55.*

Barry Maine on the historical element of *U.S.A.*:

U.S.A. holds virtually no place at all in American historiography (despite the fact that it is based on historical research), not only because of its blending of fact and fiction, but because it appears to lack what we expect most from history—historical explanation. Apart from a few isolated passages in the Biographies and Camera Eye, there is no historical commentary to speak of in ***U.S.A.*** But to argue that historical explanation is absent from ***U.S.A.*** because there is no historical commentary is to rule out narrative assertions of causality which are made in forms other than explanatory statements using the word "because." The logic of historical causality is only rarely made explicit in ***U.S.A.***; more often it is communicated through "montage": for Dos Passos deliberately exploited the language, structure, and rhythm of the cinema to write his own experimental history of America from the turn of the century to the Great Crash.

Barry Maine, in his "U.S.A.: *Dos Passos and the Rhetoric of History," in* South Atlantic Review, *January 1985.*

Leo Gurko (essay date 1968)

[*Gurko is a Polish-born American educator and critic. In the following excerpt, he surveys the themes and stylistic devices of* U.S.A. *, notes some of the trilogy's strengths and weaknesses, and distinguishes it from the works of other proletarian novelists.*]

Through the Early Thirties the work of Dos Passos and the work of the proletarian writers ran along the same track. They shared certain attitudes: distrust of big business, hostility to the capitalist system, sympathy for the oppressed worker and the "little man," contempt for money values, and a conviction that the individual, by himself, was helpless in the grip of society. Their novels displayed characters as class types and centered on the conflict between those selfishly devoted to their own interests and those dedicated to advancing the interests of others. Their morality leaned toward the simple ascription of wickedness to the haves and virtue to the have-nots. The principal dilemma of their novels was whether a particular figure would "sell out" to the interests or continue, at great sacrifice, to struggle for the better world.

The differences, however, were equally striking and became, by the end of the decade, overriding. Dos Passos was a pessimist. He had had his love affair with Soviet Russia and become disillusioned even before the depression began. He had begun ***The 42nd Parallel,*** volume one of ***U.S.A.*** (published in 1930), in 1927, and worked on a number of chapters while visiting Russia in the summer of 1928. Stalin's ice age, as he called it, had not yet set in, but the signs of it were already evident. "Writers of the world, unite! You have nothing to lose but your brains!" was the acrid slogan he subscribed to upon returning. He was still attracted to Marxism, but was disturbed by the advancing menace of the dominant Stalinist variety. ***The 42nd Parallel*** was therefore saturated with a sense of hopelessness about the better world. If it came at all, it was not going to come about neatly through a simple uprising of the workers. This mood grew stronger in ***Nineteen-Nineteen,*** volume two of the trilogy, which appeared in 1932, and rose to a climax in volume three, ***The Big Money*** (1936).

The proletarian novelists were younger than Dos Passos. Few of them had had any firsthand view of Bolshevik society. They were almost entirely molded by the depression at home, and they, together with other sections of liberal-left America, were to have their love affair with Soviet Russia in the Thirties, an affair that came to its formal end with the Nazi-Soviet pact late in 1939. Their view of the future, even the immediate future, was the standard Marxist brand of excited optimism and expectancy, nourished by the general optimistic ambience of the New Deal. Where each of Dos Passos' three novels began at a high emotional pitch and gradually declined, the average proletarian novel ended on a rising note. Even some final disaster, generally a lost strike, was seen as preparing the way for a forthcoming breakthrough.

There was also a difference in aesthetic theory. The proletarians looked upon the novel as a tool for social reform. Jamesian preoccupations with fiction as an art form were so much decadent nonsense. Concern with aesthetics as such was empty, frivolous, or irrelevant. The proletarian writers did not as a rule go to the extreme of Zhdanov or Mao Tse-tung and regard the artist as a soldier of the revolution whose energies and thoughts were entirely at the service of the state, but they moved far enough in that direction to regard art for art's sake or D. H. Lawrence's "art for my sake" as degenerate slogans. Dos Passos, even at the height of his social consciousness, never equated art and propaganda, nor did he ever waver in his conviction that *his* writing should express *his* vision of things, not the state's, the party's, or the revolution's. One therefore finds in him an element singularly absent in the proletarians: a joy in style and technique, even in the display of technical fireworks, that is one of the vibrant aspects of ***U.S.A.***

Still a third difference between them was their view of power. To the proletarians power was neither good nor evil; it was simply an instrument to be used for beneficent ends and to be kept away from those who would use it wrongly. Dos Passos regarded it as dangerous in itself. Power was an unavoidable fact of life and could not be eliminated. All the more reason for it to be controlled. The wise society would prevent an excessive concentration in the hands of any group, and would diffuse it instead over as wide a spectrum as possible. No group or class could be trusted with too much. Dos Passos' whole career as a novelist and historian has been devoted to the decentralization of power: to remove it from the hands of Big Business during the first thirty years of the century, from Big Government during the Thirties and Forties, from Big Labor in the Fifties and Sixties, and presumably Big anything else in the future, whether engineers, technocrats, political parties, or potential dictators. Even Dos Passos' involvement with Trotskyism in the Thirties can be read as an assault on Stalin's assumption of absolute power. The proletarian writers, whether they admired Stalin or not, could never accept the idea that unchecked power in the hands of the working class or the oppressed masses could prove corrupting or could lead to anything but a better world.

U.S.A., covering the years 1899-1929, is concerned with the first power group to confront Dos Passos as a writer, the great corporations—what Mr. Dooley called "the interests" and F. D. R. labelled "the economic royalists." But though central to the story, they are subordinate to Dos Passos' larger theme, the life process of the nation to which the title of the trilogy refers. As a work of fiction, ***U.S.A.*** illustrates the qualities of the country it takes as its theme: energy, ceaseless movement, dazzling techniques, admiration of quantity, and an irresistible tendency to subserve individuals to the social process. The trilogy is a metaphor for its subject. Few works have set up so close an intimacy between their form and substance.

At the outset, Uncle Tim, an apostate Irish Catholic printer in Chicago and a Socialist, announces an essential motif.

> "It ain't your fault and it ain't my fault . . . it's the fault of poverty, and poverty's the fault of the system. It's the fault of the system that don't give a man the fruit of his labor. . . . The only man that gets anything out of capitalism is a crook, an' he gets to be a millionaire in short order. . . . But an honest workin' man like John or muself we can work a hundred years and not leave enough to bury us decent with. And who gets the fruit of our labor, the goddam business men, agents, middlemen who never did a productive piece of work in their life. It's the system, John, it's the goddam lousy system."

Not a word here with which the proletarian writers would disagree. A few pages farther on, in the biographical sketch of Eugene Debs, one of the true saints in the author's American galaxy, Dos Passos introduces his counter-theme.

> Where were Gene Debs' brothers in nineteen eighteen when Woodrow Wilson had him locked up in Atlanta for speaking against war,
>
> Where were the locomotive firemen and engineers when they hustled him off to Atlanta Penitentiary?

The abandonment and betrayal of Debs by the workers whom he organized links them morally with the exploiting bosses. They are no better than their exploiters; they are only worse off. To be exploited, to be worse off is a lamentable condition, but it does not of itself bespeak a superior virtue. Dos Passos was bitter at the misery imposed on the proletariat and sympathized with the struggle of the I. W. W. to improve its lot. But he never accepted the idea of the superior proletarian soul. He thus freed himself from an a priori dogma which froze the average proletarian novel into a predetermined moral formula.

_U.S.A._ illustrates the qualities of the country it takes as its theme: energy, ceaseless movement, dazzling techniques, admiration of quantity, and an irresistible tendency to subserve individuals to the social process. The trilogy is a metaphor for its subject.

—Leo Gurko

The first of the fictional characters in the trilogy, Mac, has the most authentic working-class origin. His father is a night watchman in a New Haven factory, and after losing his wife, turns himself and his two children over to Uncle Tim. Mac grows up in Chicago, and at that mid-point in the country begins his picaresque adventures in the lower reaches of the American scene.

The conception and treatment of Mac, at the very start of ***U.S.A.,*** announce the qualities of the whole work. He descends from Tom Jones, revealing the author's debt to the episodic novelists, Defoe, Fielding, and Smollett, of the eighteenth century. Like Tom, Mac is good-natured, well-intentioned, vaguely idealistic, and incurably sensual. Uncle Tim's admonitions about the evils of capitalism serve him as a hand-me-down philosophy of life. He drifts about the country, going from place to place on the spur of the moment. He helps the amiable charlatan, the Reverend Bingham, sell Bibles and pornography to lonely farmers' wives, bums his way across the continent to California, whoring, drinking, and working at odd jobs, meanders over to Goldfield, Nevada, where he joins in the miners' strike, listens to inspirational words from Big Bill Haywood, and prints inflammatory leaflets for the I. W. W., wanders down to San Diego where he marries an ambitious middle-class girl, has two children, feels suffocated by his wife's longing for money, goes to Mexico to join the Zapata revolution only to wind up as the comfortable owner of a left-wing bookshop in Mexico City and in the arms of a pretty Mexican girl named Carmen.

Like Fielding, Dos Passos uses his protagonist to describe the national milieu in dense detail. We learn what life is like in the slums of Chicago, on isolated farms in Michigan, in shabby cafés in Duluth, in Nevada mining towns patrolled by company guards. We are bombarded with information about strikes, trade union struggles, class warfare, and the travails of the poor. Mac's temperament, like Tom Jones', is essentially passive, so that he never interferes with this exposition of the American experience.

Passivity, descending at last to inertia, characterizes Dos Passos' figures. Mac is the supreme example of involuntary movement. The world happens to him, not he to the world. He shares the cheerful, slothful, directionless passivity of his eighteenth-century ancestor. He enjoys eating, drinking, making love, doing things with his hands and body in mindless passage from moment to moment. He may be a radical, but a radical from family upbringing and economic circumstance rather than compelling personal conviction.

At one point he thinks, "A man's got to work for more than himself and the kids to feel right." An admirable sentiment, but in the end he winds up working for himself. On another occasion he remarks, "I wanta study an' work for things; you know what I mean, not to get to be a goddam slavedriver but for socialism and the revolution an' like that, not work an' go on a bat an' work an' go on a bat." But when last seen, he is on a kind of perpetual "bat." He has just enough self-awareness to realize that "I was just on the point of selling out to the sons of bitches." Yet, as time passes, it is a fear that grows dull and flickers out. The tenuous hold of ideology on Mac is what makes him so convincing a portrait of an American "working stiff." He lives in the flesh, in the passing instant, and under the patina of ideology he is the petit bourgeois to the life, edging his way at last into a secure nook, governed by prudence, comfort, and safety. Looking back upon Mac with the hindsight of the whole trilogy, the reader sees that he did not drift into his last retreat after all, that it expressed instead his deepest self.

The central act of Mac's life, and the lives of the other characters in ***U.S.A.,*** is travel. Dos Passos is the great roadmaster of American fiction. His figures rack up more mileage than any since Smollett. They are constantly, incessantly on the go. The railroad train is the common carrier, with J. Ward Moorehouse ensconced in a compartment and Mac riding the rails, passengers making the same journey through space. The two may be only a few feet apart, but that narrow distance suggests the class division between them even as it highlights their intimate juxtaposition. They meet briefly in Mexico, just long enough for Mac and his friend Ben to tag Moorehouse with a derisive epithet.

> "Jez, Ben, that's a smooth bastard," said Mac after J. Ward Moorehouse had gone.
>
> "Mac," said Ben, "that baby's got a slick cream of millions all over him."

Travel has traditional advantages for the novelist. It freshens his story with a running current of new impressions and sensations. It increases and renders more plausible the chances of his characters' meeting, especially if they grow up in widely separated places: Moorehouse and Mac, because of their differences in background, were not likely to have met in their home cities; their encounter in Mexico is more probable. It supplies a built-in mechanism for dissolving personal entanglements.

But for Dos Passos it has two special uses. First, it enables him to suggest the transience of life in America. Rootlessness is the prime aspect of American civilization. No one settles down anywhere or is attached to anything for long. Moorehouse has no visible connection with his father, a station agent in Wilmington, Delaware, nor with either of his two rich wives. He becomes a public-relations man, unattached to any corporation or product, selling his services and his ideas for "pacifying" or "reconciling" labor to the highest bidder, and moving ceaselessly from one city to another. Joe Williams, an able-bodied seaman, is as unattached as Mac and Moorehouse. He goes from one ship and port to another without thinking beyond the day. He marries, but his marriage comes to a quick end. Thousands of small incidents happen to him without making any special impression, and at the end he is still bobbing aimlessly on a tide of small sensations. Meanwhile he logs as vast a distance on sea as Mac does on land. The transience of life is registered in his case, as with all the others, in the simple but continuous act of moving from place to place.

Second is the striking and dramatic equation of travel and the American mania for quantity, the conviction that reality is established by the heaping up of things. The advancing juggernaut of technology creates vast numbers of goods and services, swamping the individual's power to discriminate among them and tending to reduce him to an object haplessly absorbing the kaleidoscope of new objects constantly assembled and paraded before him. To embrace this idea fictionally, Dos Passos creates in the imaginative consciousness of his characters an equivalent of this hectic process. Through his special kind of compulsive travelogue, his people are exposed to an equivalent barrage of sensations and experiences, so numerous and demanding that they finally reduce the wanderers to recording mechanisms and leave the reader with the overwhelming impression of an endless unreeling of detail that soon seems much the same, reaches a saturation point and yet continues to spin without letup and with increasing acceleration. The result is an overpowering monotony, from which everyone, characters and reader alike, emerges numbed and flattened out. It is this pervasive sense of formless monotony which is one of the manifest triumphs of ***U.S.A.,*** for it expresses simultaneously the lives of the characters and the larger life of the country of which theirs is now the demonstrated microcosm.

Space and the spatial dimension of travel are suggested by the title of the first volume. The 42nd parallel stretches across the United States like a magnetic line from coast to coast, drawing the characters into incessant pursuit. With America's entry into the First World War they are drawn, as through an immense suction pump, to New York, the eastern end of the parallel, and follow the soldiers across the Atlantic. Here the second volume, ***Nineteen-Nineteen,*** begins. Most of the figures join the Red Cross, and in Europe resume their peripatetic commutations, this time between Paris and Rome, with side trips to Greece, Switzerland, and Spain. The relatively stationary position of the armies in the front lines only throws into stronger relief the constant roaming-about of Moorehouse, Joe Williams, Eleanor Stoddard, Eveline Hutchins, Richard Savage, and Daughter.

Their experiences produce no psychological growth and create no inner substance. As their external sensations become denser and more rich, the characters grow emptier. Moorehouse had reached his climax as a human being when, as a boy in grade school, he cornered the agate market and made a small fortune renting out marbles to the other pupils; his life subsequently is only a complicated degeneration into an attractive smile and a charming manner. Joe Williams, rought and uneducated but thoroughly masculine and alive, searches in vain for some solid ground to stand upon, whether as husband, ship's officer, or just plain citizen; his life is doomed to be as shifting and unsteady as the sea on which he spends it. Eleanor Stoddard, cut off in childhood from a healthy sensuality by the daily sight of her father coming home bloody from his job in the stockyards, becomes a fashionable interior decorator, trying to make up what was originally destroyed in her by aesthetic bric-à-brac and brittle, meaningless human relationships. Eveline and Daughter are two restless young women whose sexual misfortunes lead them to suicide. And Richard Savage winds up as Moorehouse's assistant, feeling "sour and gone in the middle like a rotten pear." The aimlessness of his career is brilliantly suggested in the moment when he deliberately throws his compass overboard.

After three years, they all trail back to America, and in ***The Big Money*** are caught up in the boom of the Twenties. Moorehouse, Savage, and Eleanor Stoddard continue to prosper and be influential while running downhill emotionally. They are not producers; they do not make things or contribute anything to the economy. They are simply arrangers, and their arrangements symbolize the hollowness of American capitalism as Dos Passos, anguished over its human emptiness, sees it. Of the short biographies that punctuate ***U.S.A.*** perhaps the greatest is that of Thorstein Veblen in ***The Big Money.*** This crotchety student of conspicuous consumption is the sociologist made to order for an America incarnated by J. Ward Moorehouse on the male side and Eleanor Stoddard on the female.

Equally wasteful is the career of Charley Anderson. An itinerant garage mechanic in ***The 42nd Parallel,*** he had fought as an aviator during the war, and perhaps for that reason had not appeared at all in ***Nineteen-Nineteen,*** for that novel, like the others, devotes itself less to the doers than to the wasters, hangers-on, influence peddlers, and parasites. After the war Anderson gets into the airplane industry, is an inventor and developer, and seems on the verge of becoming productive when he is seized by stock market fever, plunges on Wall Street all the way to the great crash, and in private life turns into an alcoholic playboy finally killed in an automobile smash-up. His companion during much of this joyride, Margo Dowling, after a raffish beginning in the nether regions of American poverty and mean living, winds up bizarrely in Hollywood as a movie queen. The movies, like the stock market, are another of the illusion-making substitutes for the real thing—a process of displacement that is, in the author's view, all too characteristic of the American scene.

Meanwhile, on the other side of the class struggle, Mary French and Ben Compton are doing what they can to advance the cause of labor. Their efforts are pathetic and relentlessly futile. Every strike to which Mary French attaches herself fails, every cause into which she throws herself—notably the Sacco-Vanzetti case—loses. Her love affairs are with second-rate men and end in frustration or betrayal. There hangs over all her activities an air of shabby heartbreak. Ben Compton is a dedicated Communist, humorless, fanatical, self-important. Nothing he does seems to help either the working class or the Communist party and, like Debs, he winds up in Atlanta for opposing the war. He has managed to commit the two crimes defined in ***The Big Money.*** The first is public: "Tried to organize the workingclass, that's the worst crime you can commit in this man's country." The second is private: he uses human beings, himself included, as instruments for abstract ends, the same crime being committed by his deadly enemies the capitalists—an ironic similarity that Dos Passos takes pains not to overlook. This also provides the answer to a question posed in a letter to the "I" of the Camera Eye: "Explain why being right the radicals in their private lives are such shits."

The titles of the three volumes suggest, as does the overall name of the trilogy, that Dos Passos is concerned with more than the private destinies of his dozen fictional figures. ***The 42nd Parallel*** introduces the dimension of space; ***Nineteen-Nineteen,*** time; ***The Big Money,*** value, with the adjective "big" referring not simply to the American glorification of money but to its equal glorification of size. The country is far larger than the sum total of its individual characters. To fill the gap and adequately express the larger theme, Dos Passos introduces three other technical devices which, though not strictly new, taken one by one, are new in their assemblage.

The first of these is the Newsreel, a splicing of newspaper headlines interlaced with snatches of popular songs. The typefaces are cunningly arranged to suggest our topsy-turvy judgments of what is important and unimportant at any given time, while the abrupt running of one news item into another suggests the disconnectedness of the historical moment. The Newsreel seizes history in the mass, the events shared in common by everyone, seen by the mass eye through the large end of the telescope. The song hits, with their instant nostalgia and amusing pathos, bring us back at once to the year in question. The device was a magnificent technique for organizing and countering the chaos of history. Dos Passos borrowed it from the German expressionist drama of the Weimar Republic. It flourished later in the plays of Bertolt Brecht, but no more successfully than in ***U.S.A.*** Dos Passos had written two plays of his own in the late Twenties, though he was less interested in the drama as such than in scene designing. It was the theatre-as-spectacle that attracted him. He remembered loving the circus when at Harvard and thinking that "Boris Godunov" was the greatest theatrical work of the age. The Newsreel was in itself a dramatic spectacular, which Dos Passos, as his own impresario, handled with astonishing dexterity.

Juxtaposed with the Newsreel is the Camera Eye. Here the events are seen through the small eye of the telescope. The viewer is as anonymous as the mass viewer of the Newsreel, but though never named he is always the same unique, quivering individual. He has an exquisite capacity for suffering. The grass blades he treads on as a small boy seem to wince with pain. After growing up, he associates himself with the victims of every terrible thing done to human beings, experiencing with them, sometimes vicariously, sometimes in fact, the anguish of existence. He seems flayed; without the barrier of skin, there is nothing to interfere with or muffle the piercing impact of a cruel, tormenting universe. This nameless, faceless, almost abstract sensibility, defenseless and totally susceptible, is rendered in a stream-of-consciousness flow. There are no punctuation marks or capitalization, only blank spaces to indicate breaks in thought. Dos Passos absorbed *Ulysses* and *Mrs. Dalloway,* borrowing from them as freely as he did from the expressionist dramas of Wedekind and Georg Kaiser. The Camera Eye thrusts as deeply inside the human consciousness as the Newsreel penetrates into the external stream of events. The reader is brought into intimate and successive contact with pure emotion and impersonal event.

Finally there is the insertion of the short biographies. The country exists in fact as well as in imagination, and the actual historical personages who make their separate appearances are a link between the facts of the Newsreel and the fictions of the invented characters. The subjects of the sketches are real people, yet Dos Passos gives each his particular imaginative shape in the semi-cadenced prose-poetry of his biographical interludes. There are twenty-six in all, falling neatly into three categories: heroes, villains, and those with heroic possibilities who failed to live up to them or allowed themselves to be used. Typical of the first is Fighting Bob La Follette, of the second Minor C. Keith, of the third Steinmetz. Heroism and villainy are always defined in proletarian terms. Heroic figures like La Follette, Haywood, and Debs struggled to improve the lot of the common man or, like Veblen, tried to understand the processes by which men were exploited. Villainous ones

Vag in an illustration by Reginald Marsh from The Big Money.

like Keith, who founded the United Fruit Company and set up the banana republics of Central America, were the greedy men who squeezed others to enrich themselves. J. P. Morgan was another such. Henry Ford and Andrew Carnegie were in the same class, though the first mitigated his "sins" by genuinely raising the living standards of his workers and the second gave away many of his ill-gotten millions for libraries and peace foundations.

Sometimes the author's anger at the course of history affects his judgment. His scorn of Woodrow Wilson as a mouthpiece for the Morgan interests during the First World War is a gross oversimplification, provoked by Dos Passos' opposition to the war and bitterness toward the President who led the nation into it and jailed Debs for opposing it. Outside the socio-economic sphere, Dos Passos is singularly unsuccessful in pursuing the sources of heroism. His apparent ignorance of architecture, for example, makes his portrait of Frank Lloyd Wright disastrously superficial and empty.

The biographies, whether individually effective or not, represent the author intervening most directly in the book. His slant is most clearly revealed in them. Of all the extra-fictional techniques in ***U.S.A.*** the biographical vignettes link Dos Passos most closely with the proletarian novelists. These authors went to great pains to establish their own judgments inside their fictions and to work their ideological value systems into their texts. As a rule the proletarian writers relentlessly pumped their messages into their work.

Dos Passos allows himself this luxury only in the biographies, while firmly restraining himself everywhere else. His purely doctrinaire outbursts are widely spaced. One occurs in the sketch of Paxton Hibben, the once well-known liberal diplomat and journalist.

> Something was wrong with the American Republic, was it the Gold Standard, Privilege, The Interests, Wall Street?
>
> The rich were getting richer, the poor were getting poorer, small farmers were being squeezed out, workingmen were working twelve hours a day for a bare living; profits were for the rich, the law was for the rich, the cops were for the rich.

Another appears in the portrait of Veblen.

> Nobody could understand why a boy of such attainments wouldn't settle down to the business of the day, which was to buttress property and profits with anything usable in the debris of Christian ethics and eighteenth-century economics that cluttered the minds of the college professors, and to reinforce the sacred, already shaky edifice with the new strong girderwork of science Herbert Spencer was throwing up for the benefit of the bosses.

Such straight, quasi-Marxist statements, baldly injected into the narrative flow, was standard proletarian procedure. But on the whole Dos Passos avoids the overt utterance and allows his trilogy to speak for itself.

The overwhelming impression it leaves is an acute disaffection with life in America during the first thirty years of the century, without, however, proposing any specific blueprint for remedy or reform. Dos Passos does not mark out the path to an ideal world, and even doubts that it is possible. He once described his credo as a writer with uncompromising pessimism: "The basic tragedy my work tries to express remains monotonously the same: man's struggle for life against the strangling institutions he himself creates."

Though this struggle is one-sided, it is at the same time unending, and from it Dos Passos drew the narrative energy that sustains his celebrated work. No aspect of the world around him escaped his interest or failed to arouse his close attention. Whatever he may have thought of it on the moral or philosophical side, he was magnetized by it on the dramatic. The fantastic amount of detail he managed to pack into his story, covering every conceivable genre of experience, flowed from this fascination with the life process in its endless proliferation.

What keeps the lives of his characters from being sociological case studies, pinned down to the last small fact, is this fascination with metamorphosis, movement, and change. Moreover, the movement is emotionalized, and the perpetual changes in fortune are minutely accompanied by the analogous changes in feeling. In the scheme of things, these changes, whether of situation or thought, are necessarily small, perhaps even minuscule, but they are recorded with an enthusiasm, a passionate fervor not exceeded in the great panoramic novels of scene, like *War and Peace,* or of the soul, like *Anna Karenina,* where the author believes in vast changes and they do take place. It is this commitment to the larger field of human experience that underlines the claim of ***U.S.A.*** to being a masterpiece and that frees Dos Passos from the narrower framework of the proletarian school to which he is in some ways allied.

Within this larger field, his energies as a writer are freely released. There is the poet in Dos Passos, and his trilogy is peppered with marvelous moments of sensory evocation. Here is one, a description of Paris during a Zeppelin raid.

> They stood on the porch of the Sacré Coeur and saw the Zeppelins come over. Paris stretched out cold and dead as if all the tiers of roofs and domes were carved out of snow and the shrapnel sparkled frostily overhead and the searchlights were antennae of great insects moving through the milky darkness. At intervals came red snorting flares by the incendiary bombs. Just once they caught sight of two tiny silver cigars overhead. They looked higher than the moon.

There is Dos Passos the image-maker, who can sum up an undergraduate education at Harvard as "four years under the ethercone," refer to Wilson's drive for war against Germany in 1917 as a "crazy steamroller" which six opposition senators tried "to hold back with their bare hands," and metaphorize the mind of one of his characters in a single trenchant statement: "Words, ideas, plans, stockquotations kept unrolling in endless tickertape in his head."

There is Dos Passos the organizer, perhaps his most impressive role. Confronted with a task of colossal magnitude, nothing less than imaginatively rendering and penetrating three decades of American history, he attacks it on all sides with an élan that refuses to shirk or slough off any part of the assignment. Everything must be included, every subject and emotion not simply touched on but explored. "He must run up the gangplanks of all the steamboats," exclaims the young man in the preface, "register in all the hotels, work in the cities, answer the wantads, learn the trades, take up the jobs, live in all the boardinghouses, sleep in all the beds." The refrain of *all* announces the intention and sets the tone.

Aside from his four narrative devices, which keep the multiplicity of the subject within bounds, Dos Passos has a highly developed sense of the concrete, and it is this sense which prevents his many abstractions from remaining simply and remotely abstract. By rooting them in the specific, he makes them quickly intelligible and thereby manageable. Wall Street is an immense and arcane abstraction, like the science of economics in general. Dos Passos' first reference to it is "a column of stockquotations rubbed out and written in by a Western Union boy on a blackboard." The revealing little action of the uniformed boy performing his feverish ritual on a blackboard (with the hungry eyes of anxious speculators upon him) lights up and releases the whole scene. Culture is another of the large abstractions that inevitably turn up. The writer first speaks of it as "a public library full of old newspapers and dog-eared history books with protests scrawled on the margins in pencil." Again a subject that threatens to be too formless for definition is neatly caught in an instantly recognizable scrap of familiar experience that yet contains without distortion the large whole of which it is a small part. This remarkable ability effectively to lodge the universal in the particular is what makes ***U.S.A.*** a true work of the imagination, not what it might easily have been in other hands, history disguised as fiction or an essay posing as a novel.

But for all its skills and ingenuities, for all its author's admirably applied talents, the trilogy is singularly lacking in memorable characters. Mac, Moorehouse, Joe Williams, Charley Anderson are well done but hardly arresting, and in retrospect blur and fade. They exist only within the context of the novel and even there struggle for a secure footing. Though natural and credible, they lack dimensionality and do not generate their own sources of life and power. Dos Passos is no Tolstoy, with his mysterious capacity to convince us that his heroes and heroines are superior creatures. Yet the narrowing of his psychological range is due as much to his theory as to any creative shortcomings. The theory of the individual being strangled by social forces makes it all but impossible to allow him his own independence and latitude. From the start he is doomed to a losing battle. The battle is never wholly lost; it goes on continuously, perpetually. But it is not to be won, nor is the pressure of society to be equably borne. Without hope of victory or even the possibility of a draw, the autonomous existence of the individual is denied; without autonomy, he cannot grow into the fullness of stature, into the richest possibilities of his own nature that alone can make him memorable.

This lack—failure would be too misleading a word—Dos Passos shares with the earlier writers of the naturalist tradition. *Nana, Esther Waters, The Red Badge of Courage, The Octopus* are equally void of distinctive personalities. The external stream of events is more heavily weighted than the internal response. Inevitably Dos Passos addresses his major energies to the social and historical process, to which his characters are slowly subserved. They have a certain freedom of movement as children while still shielded from the full-scale world, after which they proceed to survive rather than grow. Dos Passos whips them into instant shape; they are indeed instant characters, appearing full-blown at the very beginning. By the end of the first paragraph of Eleanor Stoddard's first appearance, the central distortion of her nature is already driven home to us by the terrible dream she has over and over again as a small girl. Nothing that happens to her afterward changes her in any significant way. And so with the others. Dos Passos is as resourceful as ever in finding the right key in which to launch his figures. Thereafter, in terms of inward development, they become peripheral.

Much, though obviously not all, is redeemed by the masterly demonstration of the outside. Yet even this does not hide the irony behind the career of a writer who, though devoted to protecting the individual against the institutions strangling him, should achieve a more vivid portrait of these very institutions than of their human victims. The paradox is shared by the proletarian novelists, who were also dedicated to protecting the exploited people and also emerged from their work with a far less keen perception of these people as individual human beings than of the abstract forces pressing them down.

The triumph of ***U.S.A.*** is primarily a triumph of organization, but of an organization so complex and ordered as in itself to constitute an original vision of its subject. It has the added virtue of being open-ended. The trilogy begins with a young man walking fast through a night crowd and ends thirteen hundred pages later with the sketch called Vag. Here the young man is whirled along on a last, breathlessly accelerated tour of the country. The final image is a quick view of a crowded highway, stretching "a hundred miles down the road." The anonymity of the young man fuses with the size, speed, technological power, and lonesomeness of his journey to suggest in the brilliant microcosm of this ultimate travelogue the heart of the literary enterprise that Dos Passos has managed with such supreme virtuosity. (pp. 46-63)

Leo Gurko, "John Dos Passos' 'U.S.A.': A 1930's Spectacular," in Proletarian Writers of the Thirties, *edited by David Madden, Southern Illinois University Press, 1968, pp. 46-63.*

Alfred Kazin (essay date 1969)

[*A highly respected American literary critic, Kazin is best known for his essay collections* The Inmost Leaf *(1955),* Contemporaries *(1962), and particularly* On Native Grounds *(1942), a study of American prose writing since the era of William Dean Howells. In the essay below, he distinguishes Dos Passos from other "lost generation" writers and interprets* U.S.A. *as a trilogy about average people caught in the historical circumstances of early twentieth-century America.*]

John O'Hara once said that the development of the United States in the first half of the twentieth century is the greatest possible subject for a novelist. He left the implication that anyone lucky enough to have been part of this change, to have made the subject his own, had an advantage over the younger novelists who since 1945 have taken American power for granted and have missed the drama of its emergence.

Whatever else may be said of this proposition, or of the gifted but now "old-fashioned" and resentful novelist who made it, it is a fact that this faith in subject matter as the novelist's secret strength, especially in the "big change" as the greatest of social facts, does characterize the novelists born around the turn of the century—writers otherwise so unlike each other as John O'Hara and John Dos Passos. This faith also distinguishes them from those younger writers like Saul Bellow, Ralph Ellison, Norman Mailer, Flannery O'Connor, who grew up in depression or war, and have never thought the United States to be as unique in world history as Americans used to think it was in 1917. The younger writers have been impressed by America's resemblance to old-world powers, not by the legends of America's special destiny. History, as they see it, sooner or later becomes everywhere the same. And all history is essentially obscure and problematical, in some ways too unreal ever to be fully understood by the individual novelist, who will not feel that *he* can depend on "history" to hold him up, to supply him with material, to infuse him with the vitality that only confidence in one's subject can.

Henry James said that the "novelist succeeds to the sacred office of the historian." The old faith that "history" exists objectively, that it has an ascertainable order, that it is what the novelist most depends on and appeals to, that "history" even supplies the *structure* of the novel—this is what distinguishes the extraordinary invention that is Dos Passos' ***U.S.A.*** from most novels published since 1940. And it is surely because "history" as order—to say nothing of "history" as something to believe in!—comes so hard to younger writers, and readers, that Dos Passos has been a relatively neglected writer in recent years.

It is often assumed that Dos Passos was a "left-wing" novelist in the thirties who, like other novelists of the period, turned conservative and thus changed and lost his creative identity. ***U.S.A.*** is certainly the peak of his career and the three novels that make it up were all published in the thirties—***The 42nd Parallel*** in 1930, ***1919*** in 1932, ***The Big Money*** in 1936. But the trilogy is not simply a "left-wing" novel, and its technical inventiveness and the freshness of its style are typical of the twenties rather than the thirties. In any event, Dos Passos has always been so detached from all group thinking that it is impossible to understand his development as a novelist by identifying him with the radical novelists of the thirties. He began earlier, he has never been a Marxist, and in all periods he has followed his own perky, obstinately independent course. Whatever may be said of Dos Passos' political associations and ideas in recent years, it can be maintained that while some (by no means all) of his values have changed, it is not his values but the loss by many educated people of a belief in "history" that has caused Dos Passos' relative isolation in recent years.

Dos Passos was born in Chicago in 1896, graduated from Harvard in 1916, and served as an ambulance driver in France and Italy before joining the American army. None of the other writers associated with the "lost generation"—not Hemingway or Fitzgerald or Cummings, though they were all close friends—had the passion for history, for retracing history's creative moments, that Dos Passos has shown in his many nonfiction studies of American history as well as in ***U.S.A.*** Alone among his literary cronies, Dos Passos managed to add this idea of history as the great operative force to their enthusiasm for radical technique, the language of Joyce, and "the religion of the word." Dos Passos shared this cult of art, and ***U.S.A.*** grew out of it as much as it did out of his sense of American history as the greatest drama of modern times. But neither Fitzgerald, Cummings nor Hemingway ever had Dos Passos' interest in the average man as a subject for fiction.

Most oddly for someone with his "esthetic" concerns, Dos Passos was sympathetic to the long tradition of American radical dissent, and he has always been hostile to political dogma and orthodoxy. ***The 42nd Parallel*** opens with the story of Mac, a typically rootless Wobbly and "working-class stiff" of the golden age of American socialism before 1917; ***The Big Money*** ends on the struggles of Mary French (and John Dos Passos) to save Sacco and Vanzetti in 1927. To round out his trilogy when it was finally published in a single volume, Dos Passos added, as preface and epilogue, his sketches of a young man, hungry and alone, walking the highways. "Vag," the American vagrant, is Dos Passos' expression of his life-long fascination with the alienated, the outsider, the beaten, the dissenter: the lost and forgotten in American history. Mac, the American Wobbly and drifter at the beginning of ***U.S.A.,*** is as much an expression of what has been sacrificed to American progress as Mary French, the middle-class Communist, is at the end of the book. These solitaries, along with the young man endlessly walking America, frame this enormous chronicle of disillusionment with the American promise much as the saints in a medieval painting frame the agony on the cross. The loner in America interested Dos Passos long before he became interested in the American as protester. And despite Dos Passos' disenchantment since the thirties with the radical-as-ideologist, the Communist-as-policeman (at the end of ***The Big Money*** lonely Mary French identifies herself with a Stalinist orthodoxy to which she will inevitably fall victim), Dos Passos is still fascinated, as witness his books on the Jeffersonian tradition, with the true dissenter, whether he is alone in the White House or on the highway.

It is in his long attraction to figures who somehow illustrate some power for historic perspective (no matter what solitude this may bring) that we can see Dos Passos' particular artistic imperatives. The detachment behind this is very characteristic of those American writers from the upper class, born on the eve of our century—Hemingway, Cummings, Edmund Wilson—whose childhoods were distinctly sheltered and protected, who grew up in stable families where the fathers were ministers (Cummings), lawyers (Wilson), doctors (Hemingway), the mothers the conscious transmitters of the American Puritan tradition in all the old certainty that Americans were more virtuous than other peoples.

To these writers of the "lost generation," brought up in what is now thought of as the last stable period in American history—before America became a world empire—"Mr. Wilson's War," as Dos Passos calls it in [***Mr. Wilson's War,*** 1962] his recent book on this central episode in the life of his generation, came as an explosion of the old isolationism and the old provincial self-righteousness. "Mr. Wilson's War" tied America to Europe in a way that was to be stimulating at the time to Dos Passos, Hemingway and Cummings, but it destroyed their image of America. "Mr. Wilson," the very embodiment of Puritan American high-mindedness and didacticism, managed by "his war" to rob America of its good conscience. From now on the old familiar identification of America with righteousness was a subject for the history books. It was the writers—and some political dissenters—who were the new elect and keepers of the American conscience. "Mr. Wilson's War," from *their* point of view, was a moral cheat and a political catastrophe; as they saw it, it would soon give free rein to the speculators, financiers, and other "rugged individualists" whose unbridled greed was a dangerous American tradition that only men of intellectual principle had ever kept in check. But the writers who went to war (symbolically as ambulance drivers) found in Europe the same detachment from American money-making that they had found in their sheltered childhoods in professional families—plus a passion for the new language of twentieth-century painting and literature. Dos Passos and his friends would yet create something human out of so much destruction.

To these gifts and postures of detachment, natural to creative individualists, Dos Passos brought family circumstances that were certainly distinctive among those members of his social class who also graduated from Choate, Harvard, and the very select Norton-Harjes Volunteer Ambulance Service. The novelist's full name is John Roderigo Dos Passos; his paternal grandfather emigrated to the United States from the Portuguese island of Madeira. The novelist's father, John Randolph Dos Passos, was born in 1844, fought in the Civil War (he was at the Battle of Antietam), and became one of the most famous corporation lawyers of his time, an authority on the law of the stock market (he wrote a famous legal text on the subject). He was a deep-dyed Republican stalwart when this really meant something, in the age of McKinley. He was fifty-two years old when his son was born in Chicago to Lucy Addison Sprigg, who was of an old Maryland and Virginia family. The novelist's complex attitude toward American society may have one source in this complicated heritage. Another source was probably the distant yet flamboyant presence of Dos Passos *père,* who by all accounts was a man of very great abilities and a pillar of Wall Street, but was not a Sunday-school type when it came to women. Both the exotic name and the sexual scandal in the background of Dos Passos' family history possibly explain why the autobiographical "Camera Eye" sections of ***U.S.A.*** dealing with childhood and early youth are deliberately evasive as well as blurred in the style of Joyce's *A Portrait of the Artist as a Young Man.* The impressionistic style which is Dos Passos' general inspiration enables him to field certain family embarrassments. The perhaps deliberate murkiness of these early "Camera Eye" sections is in striking contrast with the later autobiographical chronicle and the bristlingly clear prose of the "biographies" of famous Americans and the narrative sections proper.

Dos Passos was clearly brought up with the immense reserve of the upper classes in America, and readers encountering him are usually amazed by the contrast between the fluent fast prose he writes and the extraordinarily shy, tight, embarrassed self he shows to strangers. It may be that the concentrated sensitivity of his public personality helps to explain the "streamlined" and even gimmicky side of his famous book; the sensibility that conceived ***U.S.A.*** is obviously complicated enough to have produced this complicated division into "Camera Eye," "newsreel," "biography," and narrative sections. This structure is surely, among other things, a way of objectifying one vulnerable individual's experience to the uttermost, of turning even the individual life into a facet of history. The hardness behind ***U.S.A.*** is an idea, not a feeling; it is an esthetic proposition about style in relation to the contemporary world; Dos Passos carries it off brilliantly, but it always remains distinctly *willed.* Malcolm Cowley once pointed out that Dos Passos' college years were those of the "Harvard esthetes." He learned to think of experience as separable into softish dreams and hard realities, of a world coming down on subjectivities of the poet, thus leading him doggedly to train his "camera" on an external world conceived of as a distant *object*—necessarily separable from man's hopes for unity with his surroundings.

The hardness behind *U.S.A.* is an idea, not a feeling; it is an esthetic proposition about style in relation to the contemporary world.

—Alfred Kazin

The creed behind Dos Passos' first novels—***One Man's Initiation*** (1919), ***Three Soldiers*** (1921), ***Manhattan Transfer*** (1925)—was learned at college and at war, supported by his "esthetic" training and his experiences as an ambulance driver and medical corpsman. The modern world is ugly, hopelessly corrupt, and is to be met not by love or social protest, but by "art." For the writers of the "lost generation," "art" was the highest possible resistance to the "swindle" of the social world and the ultimate proof of one's aristocratic individualism in the modern mass world. Art was the *nuova scienza,* the true science of the new period, the only possible new language—it would capture the discontinuities of the modern world and use for itself the violent motions and radical new energies of the post-war period. The new language was to be modeled on painting, sculpture, architecture—the arts that alone could do justice to the transformation of space. Dos Passos first went to Europe to study architecture in Spain, and drawing has been his "second" art; he has illustrated some of his early travel books. He saw Europe even in wartime as the unique treasure house of architecture and painting. His obvious imitation of the impressionistic word-ties of Joyce (and perhaps Cummings as well, another painter among writers) was surely motivated by the plastic sense of composition among those writers, like the Futurists, who admired the new technology, the twentieth-century feeling for speed. Dos Passos is actually one of the few American writers of his generation who has been inspired by the industrial landscape and he sought to duplicate some of its forms in ***U.S.A.*** He has taken from technology the rhythms, images, and above all the headlong energy that would express the complexity of the human environment in the twentieth century.

Dos Passos' first novels no longer have much interest for us today, for they are too moody, self-dramatizingly "sensitive," and marked by the romantic despair that is the individual's conscious sacrifice of his hopes to the world of war, modern plutocracy, the inhuman big city. But with ***The 42nd Parallel*** (which, coming out in 1930, is of course not a book of the thirties but of the individualistic twenties), one is struck above all by the sharp, confident, radical new *tone* with which Dos Passos gets his singularly new kind of narrative under way. The novel opens with the "newsreel" flashing before us the popular songs, headlines, and the national excitement as the twentieth century opens. Behind his "Camera Eye," Dos Passos first remembers himself as a boy with his mother in Europe, escaping a hostile pro-Boer crowd that thinks them English. The first character in the book is "Mac," Fenian O'Hara McCreary from Middletown, Connecticut, who will devote his restless, baffled life to the "movement." The first biography of an important maker and shaper of the new century is of Eugene V. Debs.

The material from the first is that of labor struggles, imperialism, socialism, war—and the personal sense of futility that expresses itself in whoring, violent drinking, and the aimless moving on of Americans that conveys the prodigality of our continent. With Mac, we start at the bottom of the social pyramid, among the Wobblies, "Reds," militant "working-class stiffs" who will be central to the whole long trilogy because "socialism" has been the great twentieth-century issue, even in America; the radicals in the book seal its meanings like a Greek chorus. These radicals, though they fail like everybody else, are a judgment on the profit system whose business is business, whose most dramatic form of intelligence is money making, and whose violent competitiveness always leads to war. But though Dos Passos' sympathies, at least in ***The 42nd Parallel,*** are clearly with radicals who are off the main track, he does not particularly respect them. It is inventors, scientists, intellectuals of the highest creative ability, statesmen of rare moral courage who are his heroes. There are no such figures among the characters of the novel; even among the biographies we see the type only in Steinmetz, General Electric's "Socialist" wizard. For the same reason, the tonic edge of the book, its stylistic dash and irony, its gay inventiveness, are the greatest possible homage to art as a new kind of "practicality" in getting down the facts of human existence in our century.

What Dos Passos created with ***The 42nd Parallel*** was in fact another American invention—an American *thing* peculiar to the opportunity and stress of American life, like the Wright Brothers' airplane, Edison's phonograph, Luther Burbank's hybrids, Thorstein Veblen's social analysis, Frank Lloyd Wright's first office buildings. (All these fellow inventors are celebrated in ***U.S.A.***) ***The 42nd Parallel*** is an artwork. But we soon recognize that Dos Passos' contraption, his new kind of novel, is in fact (reminding us of Frank Lloyd Wright's self-dramatizing Guggenheim Museum) *the greatest character in the book itself.* Our primary pleasure in reading ***The 42nd Parallel*** is in being surprised, delighted, and provoked by the "scheme," by Dos Passos' shifting "strategy." We recognize that the exciting presence in ***The 42nd Parallel*** is the book itself, which is always getting us to anticipate some happy new audacity. A mobile by Alexander Calder or a furious mural design by Jackson Pollock makes us dwell on the specific originality of the artist, the most dramatic thing about the work itself. So ***The 42nd Parallel*** becomes a book about writing ***The 42nd Parallel.*** That is the tradition of the romantic poet, and reading him we are on every side surrounded by Dos Passos himself: his "idea."

The technical interest of ***The 42nd Parallel*** was indeed so great for its time that Jean-Paul Sartre, whose restless search for what is "authentic" to our time makes him a prophetic critic, said in 1938: "Dos Passos has invented only one thing, an art of story-telling. But that is enough. . . . I regard Dos Passos as the greatest writer of our time." Thirty years later, that tribute will surprise even the most loyal admirers of ***U.S.A.,*** for Dos Passos has been more involved in recent years with social and intellectual history than with the art of the novel. Yet he has so absorbed what he invented for ***U.S.A.*** that even his nonfiction books display the flat, clipped, peculiarly rushing style that at his worst is tabloid journalism but at his best a documentary prose with the freshness of free verse. When we look away from his recent books and come back to ***The 42nd Parallel,*** however, we can see the real ingenuity that went into it. Though the trilogy gets better and stronger as it goes along, this first volume shows what a remarkable tool Dos Passos has invented for evoking the simultaneous actualities of existence.

The 42nd Parallel opens in 1900. It follows Mac the "working-class stiff" as he constantly moves about, recites the biographies of Debs, Luther Burbank, Big Bill Haywood, William Jennings Bryan, Minor Keith of the United Fruit Company, and ends with Charley Anderson the garage mechanic from North Dakota going overseas. (Charley will come back in ***The Big Money*** an airplane ace and inventor.) The other main characters are Janey Williams, who will become private secretary to J. Ward Moorehouse, the rising man in the rising public relations industry; Eleanor Stoddard, the interior decorator who will become Moorehouse's prime confidante; Eleanor's friend Eveline Hutchins, who is not as frigid and superior as Eleanor (and tired of too many love affairs and too many parties, will commit suicide at the end of ***The Big Money***).

The important point about J. Ward Moorehouse's racket, public relations, and Eleanor Stoddard's racket, interior decorating, is that both are new, responsive to big corporations and new money, and are synthetic. J. Ward Moorehouse and Eleanor Stoddard are in fact artificial people, always on stage, who correspondingly suffer from a lack of reality and of human affection. But on the other side of the broad American picture, Mac the professional agitator has no more direction in his life; marriage to a thoroughly conventional girl in San Diego becomes intolerable to him, but as he roams his way across the country, finally ending up in Mexico just as the revolution begins, he is at the mercy of every new "comrade" and every new pickup. The only direction in his life seems to be his symbolic presence wherever the "action" is—he is in Goldfield, Nevada, when the miners go on strike under the leadership of Big Bill Haywood, and he is in Mexico because the Mexican Revolution is taking place.

With the same "representative" quality, J. Ward Moorehouse rises in the public relations "game" in order to show its relation to big business and big government, while Eleanor Stoddard's dabbling in the "little theater" movement represents the artiness of the newly "modern" period just before World War I. History in the most tangible sense—what happened—is obviously more important in Dos Passos' scheme than whom things happened to. The matter of the book is always the representative happening and person, the historical moment illustrated in its catchwords, its songs, its influences; above all, in its speech. What Dos Passos wants to capture more than anything else is the echo of what people were actually saying, exactly in the style in which anyone might have said it. The artistic aim of his book, one may say, is to represent the litany, the tone, the issue of the time in the voice of the time, the banality, the cliche that finally brings home to us the voice in the crowd: the voice of mass opinion. The voice that might be anyone's voice brings home to us, as only so powerful a reduction of the many to the one ever can, the vibrating resemblances that make history. In the flush of Wilson's New Freedom, 1913, Jerry Burnham the professional cynic says to Janey Williams—"I think there's a chance we may get back to being a democracy." Mac and his comrades are always talking about "forming the structure of a new society within the shell of the old." Janey Williams' "Popper" notes—"I don't trust girls nowadays with these here ankle-length skirts and all that." Eveline Hutchins, who will find life too dreary, thinks early in the book, "Maybe she'd been wrong from the start to want everything so justright and beautiful." Charley Anderson, leaving the sticks, thinks—"To hell with all that, I want to see some country."

Yet more important than the sayings, which make ***U.S.A.*** a compendium of American quotations, is the way in which Dos Passos the objective narrator gets popular rhythms, repetitions, and stock phrases into his running description of people. Terse and external as his narrative style is, it is cunningly made up of all the different speech styles of the people he is writing about. This is the "poetry" behind the book that makes the "history" in it live. The section on J. Ward Moorehouse begins—

> He was born in Wilmington, Delaware, on the Fourth of July. Poor Mrs. Moorehouse could hear the firecrackers popping and crackling outside the hospital all through her labor pains. And when she came to a little and they brought the baby to her she asked the nurse in a trembling husky whisper if she thought it could have a bad effect on the baby all that noise, prenatal influence you know.

Moorehouse will always be a parody of the American big shot—all "front"; so this representative figure is born on the Fourth of July. Later in the book, when Eleanor Stoddard's "beautiful friendship" with Moorehouse helps to send Mrs. Moorehouse into a decline, we see all that is chic, proud and angry in Eleanor concentrated into this description.

> She got into a taxi and went up to the Pennsylvania Station. It was a premature Spring day. People were walking along the street with their overcoats unbuttoned. The sky was a soft mauve with frail clouds like milkweed floss. In the smell of furs and overcoats and exhausts and bundled-up bodies came an unexpected scent of birchbark. Eleanor sat bolt upright in the back of the taxi driving her sharp nails into the palms of her gray-gloved hands. She hated these treacherous days when winter felt like Spring. They made the lines come out on her face, made everything seem to crumble about her, there seemed to be no firm footing any more.

1919, the second volume of the trilogy, is sharper than ***The 42nd Parallel.*** The obscenity of *the* war, "Mr. Wilson's War," is Dos Passos' theme, and since this war is the most important political event of the century, he rises to his theme with a brilliance that does not conceal the fury behind it. But it is also clear from the greater assurance of the text that Dos Passos has mastered the special stylistic demands of his experiment, that his contraption is running better with practice. So, apart from the book's unforgettably ironic vibrations as a picture of waste, hypocrisy, debauchery, ***1919*** shows, as a good poem does, how much more a writer can accomplish by growing into his style. History now is not merely a happening but a bloody farce, is unspeakably wrong, is a complete abandoning of all the hopes associated with the beginning of the century. This is equally true for fictional characters like Joe Williams, Janey's brother, who will be dropped from one ship to another like a piece of cargo, and will eventually be killed in a barroom brawl on Armistice Day; historic personages like the writer and anti-war rebel Randolph Bourne, who died a pariah in 1918, and Paxton Hibben, "A Hoosier Quixote," who sided with the Russian Revolution when he represented the United States abroad. Wesley Everest, whose life is told as a biography under the title "Paul Bunyan," was a Wobbly leader who was castrated and lynched by a mob of businessmen in Centralia, Washington, in 1919. The fictional characters and the historic figures are equally the casualties of war. Just as Dos Passos' own creations are representative Americans, so the historic figures whom he has selected for his biographies become myths in the collective imagination of American history. One of the most brilliant things about Dos Passos' trilogy is the way in which the fictional and the historic characters come together on the same plane. One character in the book is both "fictional" and "historic": The Unknown Soldier. He is fictional because no one knows who *he* is; yet he was an actual soldier—picked at random from so many other dead soldiers. The symbolic corpse has become for Dos Passos the representative American, and his interment in Arlington Cemetery Dos Passos blazingly records in "The Body of an American," the prose poem that ends ***1919*** and is the most brilliant single piece of writing in the trilogy:

> they took to Châlons-sur-Marne
> and laid it out neat in a pine coffin
> and took it home to God's Country on a battleship
> and buried it in a sarcophagus in the Memorial
> Amphitheater in the Arlington National Cemetery
> and draped the Old Glory over it
> and the bugler played taps
>
> . . . . .
>
> Woodrow Wilson brought a bouquet of poppies.

But on the other side of the representative American picture are those who made a good thing of war, like Theodore Roosevelt, "the happy warrior" who loved war and became Governor of New York by riding up San Juan Hill; J. P. Morgan,

> Wars and panics on the stock exchange,
> machinegun fire and arson,
> bankruptcies, warloans,
> starvation, lice, cholera and typhus:
> good growing weather for the House of Morgan;

"Meester Veelson," who despite his premonitions took the country into war; Richard Ellsworth Savage, who went back on his early idealism and profited from the corruption that war had encouraged.

What invests ***1919*** beyond all else is the contrast of the official and popular idealism with the hysterical hedonism of young gentlemen in the ambulance service. Ed Schuyler keeps saying, "Fellers, this ain't a war. It's a goddam whorehouse." The echoes of speech are now our last ties with the doomed. This monument to a whole generation sacrificed is built up out of those mythic quotations and slogans that make up the book in its shattering mimicry. "In Paris they were still haggling over the price of blood, squabbling over toy flags, the river-frontiers on relief maps"; "tarpaper barracks that stank of carbolic"; "the juggling mudspattered faces of the young French soldiers going up for the attack, drunk and desperate, and yelling *à bas la guerre, mort au vaches, à bas la guerre*"; "an establishment where they could *faire rigazig, une maison propre, convenable, et de haute moralitá*"; "Did Meester Veelson know that in the peasants' wargrimed houses along the Brenta and the Piave they were burning candles in front of his picture cut out of the illustrated papers?"

The Versailles Peace Conference is cut to the style of Dos Passos' generation—"Three old men shuffling the pack, dealing out the cards."

Woodrow Wilson is caught forever when he says in Rome—". . . it is the greatest pride of Americans to have demonstrated the immense love of humanity which they bear in their hearts." But this mimicry is brought to a final pitch of brilliant indignation in the person of the Unknown Soldier, who *is* anybody and everybody. In "The Body of an American" we see that Dos Passos' book is not so much a novel of a few lives as an epic of democracy. Like other famous American books about democracy—*Representative Men, Leaves of Grass, Moby Dick*—its subject is that dearest of all American myths, the average man. But unlike these great romantic texts of what Whitehead called "the century of hope," ***U.S.A.*** does not raise the average man to hero. Dos Passos' subject is indeed democracy, but his belief—especially as he goes into the final volume of his trilogy, ***The Big Money***—is that the force of circumstances that is twentieth-century life is too strong for the average man, who will probably never rise above mass culture, mass superstition, mass slogans.

The only heroes of ***The Big Money*** are in the "biographies"—Thorstein Veblen, who drank the "bitter drink" for analyzing predatory American society to its roots; the Wright Brothers, because

> the fact remains
> that a couple of young bicycle mechanics from
> Dayton, Ohio
> had designed constructed and flown
> for the first time ever a practical airplane

and the super-individualist architect, Frank Lloyd Wright, whom Dos Passos thoroughly admires, though Wright never understood that architecture could serve the people and not the architect alone. The other biographies are of celebrities—Henry Ford, Rudolph Valentino, Isadora Duncan, William Randolph Hearst—whose lives ultimately fell victim to the power of the crowd. The mass, the popular idolatries of the time, have become the enemies of "our storybook democracy." (In the forties John Dos Passos will go back to "storybook democracy" in writing about Thomas Jefferson.) Charley Anderson, the garage mechanic who comes back from war a famous ace, gets so caught up in the dizzying profusion of drink, money and girls that his self-destructive ride through New York, Detroit and Miami resembles the mad gyrations of an airplane out of control. Margo Dowling, the movie actress, is a cold, utterly scheming trollop who in Hollywood turns her Cuban ex-husband into her chauffeur. But even she, like the Richard Ellsworth Savage who is now cynically writing advertising copy for "health foods," is just another victim rather than a villain. Society has gone mad with greed. The only fictional character in ***The Big Money*** who gets our respect is Mary French, the doctor's daughter and earnest social reformer who becomes a fanatical Communist in her rage over Sacco and Vanzetti. The emotions of the Sacco-Vanzetti case provide Dos Passos with his clearest and most powerful "Camera Eye" sections, but Mary French is futilely giving her life to the Communist Party. The chips are down; the only defense against the ravages of our century is personal integrity.

The particular artistic virtue of Dos Passos' book is its clarity, its strong-mindedness, the bold and sharp relief into which it puts all moral issues, all characterizations—indeed, all human destiny. There are no shadows in ***U.S.A.,*** no approximations, no fuzzy outlines. Everything is focused, set off from what is not itself, with that special clarity of presentation which Americans value above all else in the arts of communication. Yet in these last sections of ***The Big Money,*** Dos Passos makes it clear that though the subject of his book all along has been democracy itself, democracy can survive only through the superior man, the intellectual aristocrat, the poet who may not value what the crowd does. This is the political lesson of ***U.S.A.*** and may explain, for young people who come to the trilogy for the first time, why the book did not fertilize other books by Dos Passos equal to it. The philosophy behind ***U.S.A.*** is finally at variance with its natural interest, its subject matter, its greatest strength—the people and the people's speech. Like so many primary books in the American literary tradition, ***U.S.A.*** is a book at war with itself. It breathes American confidence and is always so distinct in its effects as to seem simple. But its sense of America is complex, dark, and troubled. Perhaps this gives it the energy of disenchantment. (pp. v-xviii)

Alfred Kazin, in an introduction to The 42nd Parallel *by John Dos Passos, A Signet Classic, 1969, pp. v-xviii.*

Townsend Ludington (essay date November 1977)

[*An American educator and critic, Ludington edited* The Fourteenth Chronicle: Letters and Diaries of John Dos Passos *(1973) and authored* John Dos Passos: A Twentieth Century Odyssey *(1980). In the essay below, he discusses the ordering of the Camera Eye segments in* U.S.A.]

The Autobiographical Elements in the Camera Eye sections of John Dos Passos' trilogy ***U.S.A.*** are the subject of a well-researched essay ["Autobiographical Elements in the Camera Eye," *American Literature,* November 1976] by James N. Westerhoven. His discussion is valuable because "once an autobiographical framework has been established, the Camera Eye gains in credibility as the impression not of an invented persona, but of the author himself." Understanding that the Camera Eye is impressionistic autobiography, we can accept more readily Dos Passos' assertion [in "An Interview with John Dos Passos," edited by Frank Gado, in *Idol: The Literary Quarterly of Union College,* 1969] that it is his attempt at "draining off the subjective" so as to make the other three devices in the trilogy—the twelve narratives about fictionalized characters, the twenty-seven clipped biographies, and the sixty-eight Newsreels—appear to be objective.

But having demonstrated the autobiographical nature of the Camera Eye, Westerhoven finds no particular reason for Dos Passos having ordered it as he did. Westerhoven points out that in ***U.S.A.*** there are fifty-one Camera Eye sections but that they are not evenly divided among the three volumes of the trilogy. ***The 42nd Parallel*** has twenty seven; ***Nineteen Nineteen,*** fifteen; and ***The Big Money,*** nine—a reduction by almost half in each successive volume. He remarks only that:

> For some reason, Dos Passos used the Camera Eye less as his trilogy progressed. ***The Big Money*** contains only nine Camera Eyes, most of them very general in character, as if the author had decided that his personal memories are not really as important as he had thought originally. Whatever his motives, the authorial presence in the Camera Eye is diminished dramatically. . . .

And in his concluding paragraph, Westerhoven asserts that "What stands out in the last Camera Eye is the despair."

His failure to attach significance to Dos Passos' grouping of the Camera Eye is not unusual. Critics have seldom noted the twenty-seven-fifteen-nine order and to my knowledge have never discussed its significance. Further, they have generally agreed with Westerhoven's assessment that the mood at the end of the work is one of despair. Alfred Kazin, for example, has labeled ***U.S.A.*** "one of the saddest books ever written by an American" and "a history of failure that is irrevocable, and of final despair." It is, he concluded [in *On Native Grounds: An Interpretation of Modern American Prose Literature,* 1956], "a brilliant hecatomb, and one of the coldest and most mechanical of tragic novels."

What Dos Passos attempted to show through the entire group of Camera Eyes was his gradual assimilation into a world beyond the shelter of his self-conscious imagination.

—Townsend Ludington

I do not disagree with assessments like those of Westerhoven and Kazin. Far from it, because Dos Passos' intention in ***U.S.A.,*** as he told Malcolm Cowley after completing ***Nineteen Nineteen,*** was to trace "a certain crystalization (call it monopoly capitalism?) of society that didn't exist in the early part of ***42nd Parallel*** (call it competitive capitalism?)." He could only add, "but as for the note of hope—gosh who knows?" Anything that smacked of monopoly was anathema to his individualistic, even anarchistic, instincts.

In the total organization of the Camera Eye, however, I think there is a note of personal hope even as Dos Passos decries the growth of "Power Superpower," symbolized by the escapades of the financier Samuel Insull, which menaces the narrator and the coal miners portrayed in the final Camera Eye as they struggle together in 1931 to improve the working conditions in Harlan County, Kentucky. What Dos Passos attempted to show through the entire group of Camera Eyes was his gradual assimilation into a world beyond the shelter of his self-conscious imagination. The more he could find his place in that world, the less of a separate, subjective life was there to portray. Thus in the twenty-seven Camera Eyes of ***The 42nd Parallel*** we read the impressions of a child, then of an adolescent, and finally of a young man sailing to France in 1917 for his first encounter with war. Throughout he is still for the most part uninitiated and in his own private world. In the fifteen Camera Eyes of ***Nineteen Nineteen,*** he has moved partway beyond his earlier shelter as he experiences the war, army life, and Paris immediately after the armistice of November, 1918. Then in ***The Big Money*** he has gone even farther beyond his own small world. He struggles with his identity: in Camera Eye (46) he tells of walking the streets, searching "for a set of figures a formula of action an address you don't quite know" as he tries "to do to make there are more lives than walking desperate the streets hurry underdog do make." But that comes to naught, and he can only "lie abed underdog (peeling the onion of doubt) with the book unread in your hand and swing on the seesaw maybe after all maybe topdog make." The next word in the stream-of-consciousness passage is "money." He begins to understand the forces at work in a capitalist society, but still he cannot be satisfied that he has found the necessary answers. Financiers are the oppressors; and yet, he reminds himself, the radicals, while being right, "are in their private lives such shits." In the next Camera Eye, he has progressed not at all, finding himself "(if self is the bellyaching malingerer so often the companion of aimless walks) . . .

> an unidentified stranger
> destination unknown
> hat pulled down over the   has he any?   face"

But by the final Camera Eye, after experiencing the trauma caused by the executions of Sacco and Vanzetti, he has found an identity. No longer is he an "unidentified stranger"; he has become a part of the "we" who are the striking Harlan County miners and the labor organizers, the common men with whom his sympathies have always lain who stand against "Power Superpower." Despite the individual American's failure to defeat monopoly capitalism, Dos Passos has gained a measure of hope because he can identify with this group, and—at least for the moment—he has achieved a personal victory in the face of a larger defeat. Perhaps success is ever thus for the creative writer; certainly it was for Dos Passos. His greatest achievements occurred while he struggled to find himself and when he thought he was one of an outcast group standing defiantly against the Establishment. When later in his life he had at least partly reconciled himself with "the system," he was less driven to write his chronicle novels of protest; and he came in time to write, instead, narrative histories about the roots of the system he had once opposed.

I am not suggesting that, contrary to what critics have asserted, ***U.S.A.*** is an affirmation of life as Dos Passos saw it to be in America. None of the figures in the twelve narrative sections ends well off, unless, like Margo Dowling and Eleanor Stoddard, he or she has become devoid of human warmth. J. Ward Moorehouse, for instance, who more than anyone else is the central figure of the trilogy, suffers a heart attack after collaborating with his protegé, Richard Ellsworth Savage, to bribe a U. S. Senator to protect an important advertising account. Savage, one of the two key figures in ***Nineteen Nineteen,*** is at the end of ***The Big Money*** in line to take over Moorehouse's firm. He celebrates too much, gets drunk, and ends the night being knocked unconscious and robbed by two male prostitutes, who he fears will attempt to blackmail him. Charley Anderson, the central figure of ***The Big Money,*** has died after failing to beat a train through a railroad crossing. Mary French and Ben Compton, dedicated radicals who try to be loyal to the Communists, are manipulated and become disillusioned. She remains working for the party as the narrative about her concludes; he, however, has been expelled. [In a footnote, Ludington adds: "The point about there being central characters in the three 'collective' novels is interesting. While they seem to be novels without heroes, Dos Passos did intend one or two figures to typify each volume, and Moorehouse, to represent the general drift of the trilogy. When during his interview Frank Gado asked Dos Passos if he had intended 'to have one character or set of characters somehow typify each of the volumes,' he replied, 'Yes, that's about right.' "] But in the Camera Eye sequence we see Dos Passos coming of age as a public man, committed to the cause of the average person, if not to the rigid doctrines of the Communist Party. Ultimately he offers at least a tentative note of hope in the subjective Camera Eye, which he consciously set apart from the other three narrative devices that he interwove to create a bleak panorama of American society drifting during the first three decades of the twentieth century toward the Great Depression. (pp. 443-46)

Townsend Ludington, "The Ordering of the Camera Eye in 'U.S.A.'," in American Literature, *Vol. 49, No. 3, November, 1977, pp. 443-46.*

Charles Marz (essay date Summer 1979)

[In the essay below, Marz analyzes the function of the Newsreels in U.S.A.]

> The public world with us has become the private world. . . . The single individual, whether he so wishes or not, has become part of a world which contains also Austria and Czechoslovakia and China and Spain. . . . What happens in his morning paper happens in his blood all day, and Madrid, Nanking, Prague, are names as close to him as the names by which he counts his dearest losses.
>
> Archibald MacLeish

The Newsreels of ***U.S.A.*** operate at several levels of meaning. Most obviously, and perhaps least significantly, they mark time chronologically. The panoramic, historical aspect of ***U.S.A.*** is now a critical given. The Newsreels locate the historical background for the action of the trilogy; they provide its setting; they generate atmosphere; they indicate the passage of time in the world and in the text. It seems also given that the Newsreels may be linked to themes and actions in adjacent narrative, Camera Eye, and biographical passages; they date, comment on, and link the various persons and events in the trilogy. However, even if we could identify the historical source or referent for each of the Newsreel fragments, even if we could "plot" (as "conspiratorial" critics engaged in the "burial" of the text) the chronological progression of the trilogy from Newsreel I to Newsreel LXVIII, we would be no closer to explaining the power of ***U.S.A.,*** no closer to articulating the significance of the Newsreels. The trilogy must be understood dynamically. Its power and meanings come ultimately from vertical, atemporal, simultaneous events, and not from horizontal, biographical, successive actions. They are not generated by the historical exactness but by the random collisions of voices. The voices in the Newsreels collide with one another and with the rest of the text. Those collisions generate grotesque ironies. It is not uncommon in a Newsreel to find celebrations and horrors of America, dream and nightmare, juxtaposed:

> MACHINEGUNS MOW DOWN MOBS IN KNOXVILLE
>
> America I love you

Dos Passos resists as he records the noise of history. Random collisions set off random explosions; the novelist is historian and saboteur.

The Newsreels chronicle the voices of the public sphere; they are the most banal, most impersonal, most mechanical registration of persons and events in the trilogy; they are the "nightmare of history," uncolored and uncontrolled by the private voice of the Camera Eye. Violence is objectively reported; the lies of the public voice reveal themselves in absurd and ironic incongruities: "woman and children blotted out admits he saw floggings and even mutilations but no frightful outrages" (***42P***). Death is reduced to statistical tabulation and the exalted rhetoric of the Great War: "army casualties soar to 64,305 with 318 today; 11,760 have paid the supreme sacrifice in action and 6,193 are severely wounded" (***1919***). It is reported in the same manner and in the same space as a surge in the market. Like the "Great War," the "Big Money" is deflated, exploded by collision, over and over again:

> Apparently some of them had been injured when the explosion occurred and several of them tripped and fell. The hot metal ran over the poor men in a moment.
>
> PRAISE MONOPOLY AS BOON TO ALL (***42P***)
>
> SIX HUNDRED PUT TO DEATH AT ONCE IN
> CANTON
>
> SEE BOOM YEAR AHEAD (***BM***)
>
> MARKET SURE TO RECOVER FROM SLUMP
>
> DECLINE IN CONTRACTS
>
> POLICE TURN MACHINE GUNS ON COLORADO
> MINE STRIKERS KILL 5 WOUND 40 (***BM***)

Violence permeates the world and the text. And in the Newsreels devastations of vastly different magnitudes—though typographically and structurally equivalent—collide:

> For there's *many a man* been *murdered* in *Luzon and Mindanao*
>
> *GAIETY GIRLS MOBBED IN NEW JERSEY* (***42P***)
>
> ARMY WIFE SLASHED BY ADMIRER
>
> THREE HUNDRED THOUSAND RUSSIAN NOBLES
> SLAIN BY BOLSHEVIKI (***1919***)

Our sense of scale is annihilated; experience in the public sphere is reduced to formula, cliché, echo—headline; war and politics to the front page, love to the society page, and death to the obituary column. In a world in which private voices give way to the public noise, all private experience soon becomes public knowledge. The army wife slashed by her admirer and the death of three hundred thousand Russian nobles become equivalent public events. The most private destinies become public, and all men become—if only for a moment—celebrities.

As the noise of the world increases, the Newsreel demands economies of presentation, the brief notation of persons and events; it becomes an automated, dehumanized, faceless form of communication. There is neither the time nor the space in the public sphere for the continuous enactment of coherent, private lives. Narrative and voice contract, atrophy, and disappear. And all that remains in the Newsreels is the residue of voice, the debris of character, action, and experience. ***U.S.A.,*** like ***Manhattan Transfer*** before it, is a novel of physical and spiritual erosion. Dos Passos continues to catalogue the wreckage, the fragmentary form, the broken objects that invade and bury persons and landscapes. The Newsreels are composed of unintelligible and multiple verbal fragments in agitated motion. They surface, collide, and disappear much like the garbage in the Ferryslip section of ***Manhattan Transfer.*** Significance is drained from any single event by typographical uniformity, by the mechanical equivalence of the presentation:

> PARIS SHOCKED AT LAST
>
> TEDDY WIELDS BIG STICK
>
> . . . . .
>
> MOB LYNCHES AFTER PRAYER (***42P***)

Each headline is a verbal snapshot, a mechanical recapitulation of some part of the world. Each snapshot is a short-lived event, incompletely defined at any particular moment, and limited by space-time constraints to verbal accidents or collisions. Persons and events are "shot" and the Newsreels preserve their remains:

> SNAP CAMERA: ENDS LIFE (***42P***)

Susan Sontag has noted that photography makes forgetting the world, escaping history's debris, increasingly difficult. The reader of the Newsreels, like the photographer, must passively receive and suffer the world and its debris. The world prints the image. Transitory meanings are occasionally available in the accidental configurations and collisions of fragments—the grotesque ironies previously mentioned. But the wreckage and the noise increase and it is not enough to simply chronicle the devastation. The collisions of public voices generate that devastation, the noise of history that creates Dos Passos's dilemma—perhaps the central dilemma of his time—how both to chronicle and resist a disintegrating world.

In the Camera Eye passages of ***U.S.A.*** there is a refusal to abdicate personal control; the embattled individual stands at the center of the world, almost to the exclusion of it; there is an intense—though never transcendent or religious—residual individualism. In the Newsreels, however, the person exists nearer the periphery of the world. And the subject, the everpresent "I" and "you" of the Camera Eye, recedes. The public voices of the Newsreels are speakerless. They are voices over which men have no control. Individuals are not subordinated—they simply cease to exist. There are no coherent or continuous interior lives in the Newsreels. The space allotted to persons contracts. And the Newsreels become collages of torn spaces, broken and layered samplers of persons and events. The subjects of actions are often collective, as in Newsreel I: "CAPITAL CITY'S CENTURY CLOSED," "LABOR GREETS NEW CENTURY," "CHURCHES GREET NEW CENTURY," "NATION GREETS CENTURY'S DAWN" (***42P***). Or the subject may be absent: "say circus animals only eat Chicago horsemeat" (***42P***), "holds dead baby forty hours" (***42P***), "LAYS WREATH ON TOMB OF LAFAYETTE" (***1919***), "CLASPS HANDS OF HEROES" (***BM***). Occasional subjects may be public figures, "CARNEGIE TALKS OF HIS EPITAPH" (***42P***), "SACCO AND VANZETTI MUST DIE" (***BM***), "LIEBKNECHT KILLED ON WAY TO PRISON" (***1919***), or anonymous individuals or groups, "INFANT BORN IN MINNEAPOLIS COMES HERE" (***42P***), "COLLEGE HEAD DENIES KISSES" (***42P***), "MOBS PLUNDER CITIES" (***1919***). "ARTIST TAKES GAS IN NEW HAVEN" (***1919***). The Newsreels are spoken by anonymous public voices, spoken by the conspiratorial "they" of Camera Eyes 49 and 50. The world of the Newsreels is a lawless, violent world out of control, a world of personalities or celebrities and not characters, personalities whose lives are only as complete as the information available in the headlines. The speakerless world of the Newsreels is a constantly eroding world, a world without human responsibility or moral content.

The dispassionate, technological voices of the Newsreels speak constant destruction and violence: "Woman of Mystery Tries Suicide in Park Lake" (***BM***), "BODY FOUND LASHED TO BICYCLE" (***BM***), "GANG LEADER SLAIN IN STREET" (***1919***), "BRYAN'S THROAT CUT BY CLARK: AIDS PARKER" (***42P***). They register the nightmare that is history. And in that nightmare the human scale is reduced; things become the locus and power of values:

DETROIT IS FIRST
IN PHARMACEUTICALS
STOVES RANGES FURNACES
ADDING MACHINES
PAINTS AND VARNISHES
MARINE MOTORS
OVERALLS
SODA AND SALT PRODUCTS
SPORTS SHOES
TWIST DRILLS
SHOWCASES
CORSETS
GASOLINE TORCHES
TRUCKS (***BM***)

The individual is "heaped" by the world, slowly buried by its objects and its debris. Philip Fisher has noted [in "Looking Around to See, Who I Am: Dreiser's Territory of the Self," *ELH,* 1977] that "For a man inside the city his self is not inside his body but around him, outside his body." And for a man in the U.S.A. that Dos Passos chronicles, his voice is not inside his body, but around him, outside his body in the verbal objects that engulf him—in the public space.

The Newsreels are ultimately verbal objects—word and world debris. They are the residue of the natural world, divested of their original functions and contexts, wrenched from private and public occasions. In the trilogy they become ahistorical, noncontextual verbal acts, always possible but never actual verbal utterances. They are in many ways like "found poetry" in that their presentation invites a certain critical ingenuity; they are "the representation of a natural utterance in an implicit dramatic context, designed to invite and gratify the drawing of interpretive inferences" [Barbara Herrnstein Smith, "On the Margins of Discourse," *Critical Inquiry,* June 1975]; they exist on the margins of discourse.

The borders between natural and fictive discourse, history and fiction, shift and dissolve in ***U.S.A.*** History is introjected and eroded in the text. And the Newsreels are the location of the debris. They are cemeteries and museums (both burial grounds of objects) of verbal artifacts. They preserve the afterlife of verbal objects—echoes and clichés. In them the world is dematerialized; scale is destroyed as persons and events are uniformly fragmented in space and in time. Those verbal fragments of the world are catalogued and displayed. The voice fragments exhibited become increasingly remote as one moves away from familiar historical events and persons. What may once have been most public, most accessible—most immediately verifiable news—becomes most strange. The information in Newsreel V, for example,

BUGS DRIVE OUT BIOLOGIST

elopers bind and gag; is released by dog

EMEROR NICHOLAS II FACING
REVOLT
OF EMPIRE GRANTS SUBJECTS
LIBERTY

paralysis stops surgeon's knife by the stroke of
a pen the last absolute monarchy of Europe
passes into history miner of Death Valley
and freak advertiser of Santa Fe Road may
die sent to bridewell for stealing plaster
angel

On the banks of the Wabash far away (***42P***) may have

made immediate historical sense to a reader forty years ago; that sense has by now eroded and the information become unfamiliar. We are without access to persons and events reported. Contexts are ignored and without explanations the most intriguing observations remain hermeneutically sealed. The reader is estranged from the text by the insufficiency, the incompleteness of information. An intimate relation with the text is denied. We must scan the text—as we must scan the world—as strangers, in search of recognizable characters and events. And as the text and the world erode we must deal increasingly with their debris—with the bits and pieces of lives and actions—with the fragments of experience.

The meanings of the Newsreels are not located finally in the world of historical actions and consequences. Tracing the former lives of these artifacts is irrelevant. For they do not simply date the action of the trilogy; they do not simply provide atmosphere. They invade the text; they collide with the Camera Eye; scraps of reality, records of things, vestiges of the past set adrift; the wreckage of public voices buries the individual and silences him. Man is gradually replaced by his artifacts, by word and world debris, by the slowly and inevitably triumphant noise of history. (pp. 194-99)

Charles Marz, "Dos Passos's Newsreels: The Noise of History," in Studies in the Novel, *Vol. XI, No. 2, Summer, 1979, pp. 194-200.*

When one rereads *U. S. A.* in the light of later events, it seems to be an absurdly pessimistic novel, but even the bleak prose of the narrative section has the power of deeply held convictions. The book holds together . . . and it expresses what many people besides the author felt in those years when the nation seemed to be careening into the depths.

—Malcolm Cowley, in his*—And I Worked at the Writer's Trade: Chapters of Literary History, 1918-1978, *1978.

Robert C. Rosen (essay date 1981)

[*Rosen is an American educator and critic. In the following excerpt from his* John Dos Passos: Politics and the Writer, *he examines Dos Passos's views on American society, describes the evolution of Dos Passos's social thought, and very briefly summarizes critical opinion on* U.S.A.]

U.S.A. proved to be a more ambitious undertaking than Dos Passos realized when he first began writing it in the months after the execution of Sacco and Vanzetti. Originally conceived as a single book, a "series of reportages in which characters appeared and re-appeared," it grew over a decade into a 1,450-page trilogy whose subject was nothing less than the history of American life in the first thirty years of the twentieth century. Though the consummation of Dos Passos's experiments with literary form, ***U.S.A.*** represents neither a conclusion to the evolution of his political thought, nor a totally coherent analysis of American society. Its contradictions and tensions contribute to the trilogy's great energy and continuing appeal.

In order to make American society as a whole his subject, Dos Passos creates an elaborate structure out of four distinct modes of expression in ***U.S.A.*** (pp. 78-9)

The paths of these structural elements [the narratives, Newsreels, biographies, and Camera Eye sections] often converge. Woodrow Wilson's biography, for example, comes roughly at the point where a major character attends the Versailles Peace Conference and the Newsreel entries are alluding to that same conference. More important is the continuous implicit interaction of these elements. Montage creates meaning. The fictional lives, the historical currents we see in the Newsreels and biographies, and the inner world of the Camera Eye character illuminate one another in complex ways. As in ***Manhattan Transfer,*** the fragmentary form prevents our easy identification with individual characters; the focus is shifted instead to the larger social patterns, and the reader is driven to an active participation in the political analysis. ***Manhattan Transfer*** dramatizes the essential aloneness of its characters at the expense of any real sense of the social nexus that relates their individual alienation to the nature of the city's institutions. ***U.S.A.*** re-creates that social nexus. Alienated and isolated as its major characters may be, they exist in history; the historical developments of the Newsreels and biographies impinge on their everyday lives.

Most of those lives end in defeat, corruption, or premature death. A gulf between virtue and success informs ***U.S.A.*** as it does ***Manhattan Transfer.*** In this fast-paced novel of rootlessness and social mobility, those who rise are often corrupted in the process. Those few who try to act morally—namely, the radicals: Mary French, Ben Compton, and sometimes Mac—meet repeated defeat. All seem to move through their lives too rapidly to comprehend what is happening to them; their experience and their understanding of their own lives are almost as chaotic and confused as the Newsreels' version of public events. Only the reader is allowed to see the larger patterns, the causes as well as the effects.

Existence itself is often degraded in ***U.S.A.,*** characters alienated from themselves and others. Flat characterization depicts lives flattened by society. Joe Williams, for example, is an itinerant seaman, a perpetual outsider, a failure. Dos Passos describes Joe's marriage proposal to Del: "When he kissed her goodnight in the hall, Joe felt awful hot and pressed her up in the corner by the hatrack and tried to get his hand under her skirt but she said not till they were married and he said with his mouth against hers, when would they get married and she said they'd get married as soon as he got his new job." Though narrated in the third person, this is Joe's own language, the "speech" Dos Passos refers to in his description of "straight writing." The very externality of the description—"awful hot" is a diminished token for passion—suggests an impoverished inner life, as does the absence of imagery. As in ***Manhattan Transfer,*** parataxis helps create this externality and dramatizes the hurried, uncontemplative, almost driven lives these characters lead. This "behavioristic" style, as he called it, is not relentless in ***U.S.A.***—some characters are more introspective than others and some passages are almost lyrical—but Dos Passos makes clear from the start that his is a debased world.

Obviously, and sometimes superficially, Dos Passos uses alcohol and sex to dramatize this debasement, to highlight the driven nature of his characters' lives. The frequency with which drunkenness is a symptom as well as the cause of a character's decline prompted Upton Sinclair, in a letter to Dos Passos, to call ***The Big Money*** a "temperance sermon." Sexual encounters—themselves often drunken—are often depicted as sordid and degraded, almost to the point of making ***U.S.A.*** seem puritanical. University of Texas students defending the inclusion of ***The Big Money*** on a reading list against the charge by conservative regents that it was "indecent, vulgar and filthy" could, with some justice, argue that the novel was in fact "deeply moral," for the characters' "sin" almost inevitably resulted in unhappiness.

U.S.A. goes deeper than this and illustrates the kind of systemic evils of American society that Dos Passos wrote about in his nonfiction: poverty, unemployment, political repression, imperialism, and the degrading mechanization of work. We see the destructive effects of "dawg eat dawg" values and the psychological damage done to both rich and poor by great disparities of wealth. Beneath the images of ***U.S.A.*** is what Dos Passos calls "the sabotage of life" by capitalist institutions.

Dos Passos devotes an entire volume of his trilogy, ***1919,*** to the war. He suggests that the United States entered the war solely to fatten the armament industry's profits and to "mak[e] the world safe" for powerful American bankers with loans in Europe. As significant as the causes of the war are its consequences, which Dos Passos knew quite well: a general coarsening of American sensibilities, the stifling of dissent, and an explosion of propaganda and lies. "The war was a blast that blew out all the Diogenes lanterns" (***1919***). The bitterly ironic biography of the Unknown Soldier powerfully evokes the war's cost in lives. Dos Passos presents American involvement in the war as the grotesque expression of twentieth-century American values, a logical and organic unfolding of the destructiveness inherent in the present organization of society. "*War,*" writes Randolph Bourne, "*is the health of the state.*"

The life of Charley Anderson dramatizes what Dos Passos calls "the sabotage of production by business." A talented mechanic with vaguely radical sentiments, Charley joins a friend after the war in starting a successful business manufacturing airplane starter motors. As he moves up into the world of high finance and begins speculating in the stock market, Charley's technical skill degenerates. In a quarrel with his loyal friend and mechanic, Bill Cermak, he defends speed-ups in his factory—it is the pressure of competition, he explains. When the two of them go up for a test flight, the plane fails mechanically, and Cermak is killed. Charley has lost his last contact with his former way of life. The big money has lured him away from his true calling, and his personal life deteriorates. In the figure of Charley Anderson the connection between historical forces and individual lives is actual as well as symbolic.

Several biographies in ***U.S.A.*** expand the historical dimension of Charley's experience and indicate a significant development of Dos Passos's views here beyond the simple anxiety about technology per se expressed in **"A Humble Protest"** and ***Rosinante to the Road Again.*** Dos Passos often judges scientists by their social consciences in ***U.S.A.***: he admires but pities the mathematician Steinmetz who, though a principled socialist, was absorbed and used by General Electric; he disparages Edison, who "cashed in" on his inventions and "never worried about . . . the social system"; and he praises the Wright brothers as simple, hard-working mechanics, though he alludes darkly to the military use of their inventions. But the real direction of contemporary technological development is determined by the work of Frederick Winslow Taylor and Henry Ford. As Dos Passos wrote in a manuscript version of ***The Big Money,*** "the same ingenuity that went into improving the performance of a machine [the automobile] could go into improving the performance of the workmen producing the machine." It is the exigencies of profit that guide the use of scientific management—"the substitution for skilled mechanics of the plain handyman . . . who'd move as he was told / and work by the piece"—and that increase the pace of the assembly line until "every ounce of life was sucked off into production and at night the workmen went home grey shaking husks" (***The Big Money***). The need for and the creation of a worker "who didn't drink or smoke cigarettes or read or think" debases not only work itself but all social life. The 1920s wave of capitalist expansion that carries Charley Anderson to the top drags down others as it corrupts him.

Dos Passos particularly fears the great concentration of power that capitalism creates. A large number of his biographical subjects aid or manage that concentration (Carnegie, Keith, Morgan, Wilson, Hearst, Taylor, Ford, and the scientists, for example) or else, however ineffectively, oppose it (Haywood, Debs, La Follette, Reed, Hibben, Everest, Joe Hill, Veblen). In the world of ***U.S.A.,*** the majority of individuals are powerless; the real centers of power are beyond their reach. This helps explain the shallow lives and moral passivity of most of the novel's major characters. Much as he had once insisted that "organization is death," Dos Passos in his later years would vehemently attack any concentration of power—the Kremlin, labor unions, the New Deal—whatever its origin or consequences. But in ***U.S.A.*** his subject is "a society dominated by monopoly capital."

This domination is not static: it intensifies as history moves forward. Nor is domination total, for characters often possess a great deal of individual freedom and social mobility. Joe Williams may be doomed to a life of transient and unremunerative labor; and Mary French, Ben Compton, and even Mac for a while, may forsake middle-class comforts on principle; but many do climb or connive toward success. Throughout, ***U.S.A.*** bitterly condemns the American Dream: success not only corrupts, but fails to bring satisfaction. Moneyed lives are easier, to be sure, but no more fulfilling than other lives. The exploitation of the many by the few brings genuine happiness to none.

That the rich are not much happier than the poor might seem to undercut Dos Passos's attack on economic injustice. But inequality itself is destructive. It creates dehumanizing ambition, an isolating individualism, and feelings of inferiority among the losers. Janey Williams, for example, cruelly shuns her brother Joe once she moves into middle-class circles; Joe knows his place, and sadly keeps his distance.

The destructive nature of racial injustice gets far less attention than that of class injustice in ***U.S.A.*** There are hints, though. With obvious sarcasm, Dos Passos places the headline "PLAN LEGISLATION TO KEEP COLORED PEOPLE FROM WHITE AREAS" right in the middle of a Newsreel announcing American entry into the war to make the world safe for democracy. He touches on the harm racism can do to whites by suggesting, as one critic points out, a connection between the traumatic racist taunts—"Niggerlover"—that greet young Janey Williams as she plays with a black friend and her later development into a cold and stiff adult. The racism of Dos Passos's white characters—when we do see it—is depicted as part of their very degraded consciousness.

Blacks themselves are almost invisible in ***U.S.A.,*** however. Of the twelve major characters in the trilogy, meant in some sense to be representative of the nation, none are black. Nor are any of the subjects of the twenty-seven biographies black, though A. Philip Randolph—to give but one example—a man whom President Wilson once called "the most dangerous Negro in America," might have fit quite well beside Debs, Bourne, and the other radicals and pacifists. The few black figures that do appear in the novel appear as minor characters, their experiences seen only from another's point of view. Perhaps worst is Richard Savage's night in Harlem bars—itself meant to dramatize his decadence—where the black people he runs into are no more than stereotypes.

At least two critics have read ***U.S.A.*** as a sexist novel: Bianca T. Lalli has written [in *Dos Passos,* 1974] of the "misogyny" of the trilogy, and Eleanor Widmer has suggested [in "The Lost Girls of *U.S.A.*: Dos Passos' 30s Movie," in *The Thirties: Fiction, Poetry, Drama,* 1967] that Dos Passos's major women characters are merely stock female stereotypes. Dos Passos's flat characterization and his effort to focus on social more than individual history inevitably involve some stereotyping of all characters; and unless informed by a feminist impulse, conscious or unconscious, such writing is bound to reflect not only its author's unexamined assumptions but the sexism of the society it depicts. There is no analysis in the novel of the oppression of women as there is of the oppression of the working class. And many important women—birth control advocate Margaret Sanger, for example, whose work certainly had bearing on the lives of the novel's many characters troubled by unwanted pregnancies—are noticeably absent from the gallery of biographies. Only Isadora Duncan appears. But fully half of Dos Passos's twelve main characters—whose perspectives he fully develops—are female, and Mary French earns our sympathy and respect (for her political commitment) above any other character in the trilogy—hardly a misogynist's vision of the world. Nonetheless, the radical social criticism of ***U.S.A.,*** however thoroughgoing, is male as well as white.

Those at the top in ***U.S.A.*** have the power to influence, even manipulate the consciousness of the vast majority. There are reasons why characters like Joe or Janey see themselves and the world the way they do. When, for example, Charley Anderson sees *The Birth of a Nation,* the "battles and the music and the bugles [make him] all jelly inside." He thrills as the Ku Klux Klan charges and feels, for a moment, a great urge to enlist and fight in the war, which he eventually does. William Randolph Hearst, a deliberate manipulator of public opinion, succeeds in "putting his own thoughts / into the skull of the straphanger." In Dos Passos's biography of Rudolph Valentino, whose funeral ignites mass hysteria, we learn of Hollywood's great image-making power; through the rise to stardom of one character, Margo Dowling, we learn of its vulgarity. The public mind that the Newsreels exhibit—much like the mind of Fuselli in ***Three Soldiers***—is largely the product of mass culture, not the creator of a genuinely popular culture. (pp. 80-5)

The effectiveness of . . . propaganda is not total, however. Various characters in ***U.S.A.*** read Marx, Veblen, Edward Bellamy, and Upton Sinclair as well as the Hearst papers. Mary French learns firsthand not to trust the press when, as a reporter in Pittsburgh, she is fired for writing an honest story about striking steelworkers; the editor of this company town newspaper wants an article about extravagant wages, lazy immigrants, and red agitators paid by Russia with stolen jewels. Even casual political conversations can loosen the hold of the prevailing ideology. Dissenters as well as rulers are subjects for biographies; occasional signs of protest, like the Wobbly song "Pie in the Sky," appear in the Newsreels; and the Camera Eye records one individual's long struggle toward genuine understanding of his society.

Still, defeat pervades the trilogy. The truth does not liberate characters like Mary French and Ben Compton; as radical activists they can be as "deadalive" and as unhappy as anyone else. Their triumph is at best a moral one. Some critics have seen an ironclad determinism in this: characters are "billiard balls" in this "closed system of despair." Others describe ***U.S.A.*** as a self-defeating novel of protest: characters are so degraded they seem incapable of full human development in any social order; there is nothing to be saved. As in ***Manhattan Transfer,*** there are naturalistic elements in ***U.S.A.*** Dos Passos strives to show environment shaping character, because he wishes to attack society as a whole. But the twelve major characters possess varying degrees of will. Joe Williams is passive, almost deterministically conceived, but Richard Savage is capable of choice and is the target of Dos Passos's severe moral criticism when he callously abandons pregnant Anne Trent. The tension between naturalism and the intense moral indignation that pervades ***U.S.A.*** gives the novel much of its energy. Its bleak vision of nearly universal defeat demands radical social change.

Dos Passos portrays himself, through the Camera Eye, least deterministically of all. His various experiences—his privileged but lonely childhood and his participation in the war, for example—certainly condition his development. But the almost totally subjective point of view, the internal characterization, focuses our attention on the exercise of his will. His halting development into a radical appears as a series of choices, though in the context of the novel as a whole, his own choice ironically seems to be the only possible, the only moral path for a sensitive individual. None of these choices is easy, however; his eyes "sting from peeling the speculative onion of doubt" (***The Big Money***). In a world as complex as the Newsreels make it seem, and as hopeless as the fictional characters make it seem, action is indeed difficult. When he speaks, "urging action in a crowded hall," he wants to give his audience "the straight dope," but it is triumphal slogans that bring him applause. He is ashamed for not having told the truth: "that we stand on quicksand," that "doubt is the whetstone of understanding." ***U.S.A.*** itself is that more complex truth. Like the hero of ***One Man's Initiation—1917,*** he moves gradually from observer—a mere camera eye—to committed radical. He eventually writes and marches to save Sacco and Vanzetti, although, like those symbols of martyred virtue, he too ends in defeat.

Despite his eventual political commitment, the Camera Eye character (like Dos Passos himself) experiences much uncertainty about his role as a middle-class writer. Everyone is isolated in the atomized world of ***U.S.A.,*** and as an artist he is doubly isolated: the formal separation of the Camera Eye sections from the world of the fictional characters helps dramatize this. From his earliest fearful attraction to "laborers travailleurs greasers" (***The 42nd Parallel***) to his impotent despair at the plight of Harlan County miners—"what can we say to the jailed?" (***The Big Money***)—he feels isolated from the working class whose cause he wants to champion. (pp. 86-7)

Dos Passos also dramatizes his own conflicts and choices through the contrasting lives of Richard Savage and Mary French. Savage's experiences at Harvard and in the war, as well as the radicalism and aesthetic interests of his youth, are very similar to Dos Passos's own. But Savage sells out. He hasn't even the strength of his own weak political convictions and ends up as the right-hand man and probable successor to J. Ward Moorehouse. Mary French, however, grows politically more committed every day. Like Dos Passos, she works madly to save Sacco and Vanzetti and raises money to aid striking miners. Her total devotion to causes and her too close association with the Communist party impoverish her personal life. While Savage cares only about himself, she seems to care only about others. Thus, as Savage's life demonstrates the moral decline inherent in abandoning political ideals, and French's suggests the perils of political commitment, the Camera Eye shows us the path Dos Passos himself struggled to find.

The contrast between the IWW and the Communist party is also central to ***U.S.A.*** Liberals—such as Woodrow Wilson and George Barrow, the "laborfaker"—discredit themselves throughout the trilogy; only explicitly radical groups promise any real hope for change. Through Mac, in ***The 42nd Parallel,*** Dos Passos portrays the IWW—which he long admired—as a loose, exciting, energetic organization. We share their easy, glad comradeship when fellow Wobblies run into each other on the road. "The boys" drink, talk socialism, and fight hard for the rights of "the working stiff." The "cooperative commonwealth" they envision seems appealing and necessary.

The Communists, on the other hand, insist upon hard work, discipline, and ideological conformity in order to bring about the revolution. While the local party member Eddy Spellman may be as happy and friendly as a Wobbly, it is the suspicious, extremely unpleasant Don Stevens who rises in the organization. If Dos Passos romanticizes the Wobblies, he seems to caricature the Communists.

The war divides these two worlds, and the experiences of Ben Compton in ***1919*** help explain the differences. At first, Ben works with the Wobblies and is brutally beaten by sheriff's deputies in Seattle. When the war comes, his unrelenting opposition to it lands him in jail. At every turn he refuses to compromise his principles; as those around him give in to prowar pressures, his almost fanatical behavior comes to seem admirable. He eventually becomes the "wellsharpened instrument" he wanted to be, and joins the party. Only after he is expelled for deviationism does he realize that he and Mary French should have had that child he insisted on postponing until after the revolution.

The contrast between the IWW and the Communist party is an integral part of Dos Passos's vision of a gulf between virtue and success. The appealing Wobblies dissipate their energies in disorganized behavior, as when Mac impulsively goes off to Mexico to "see the revolution" and ends up a bourgeois store-owner. And they are repeatedly crushed by force—the castration of Wesley Everest epitomizes this. The Communists, on the other hand, seem to be building a strong organization, despite the setbacks they suffer. But they are almost dehumanized in the process. The violent course of Revolutionary Russia—suggested by a long, detailed Newsreel account of the execution of the czar and his family, striking as the only single-item Newsreel in the trilogy—casts a shadow over the revolutionary hopes of Ben Compton and others. So the future holds little real promise. We are left at the end with the image of the vagrant, "Vag"—"wants crawl[ing] over his skin like ants"—who hitchhikes hungrily down the road, as a plane filled with self-satisfied, well-fed passengers flies overhead.

Vague nostalgia creeps into the later parts of ***U.S.A.*** The prewar heyday of socialism is over. Radical heroes, except for the embittered Veblen, have disappeared from the biographies. The night Sacco and Vanzetti are executed, the Camera Eye character reaches far back into the American past to invoke the Founding Fathers: "America our nation has been beaten by strangers who have turned our language inside out who have taken the clean words our fathers spoke and made them slimy and foul."

A formerly great land corrupted by nebulous "strangers" somehow alien to the American way of life is not what Dos Passos saw his country as in 1927. ***Facing the Chair*** and his many essays and articles make this clear. The biographies in ***U.S.A.*** of people like Morgan, Wilson, Hearst, and Ford show how quintessentially American are those who helped mold the world in which Sacco and Vanzetti had to die.

U.S.A. chronicles not only the changes America underwent over three decades, but also the evolution of its author's own social thinking. The muted optimism of ***The 42nd Parallel,*** the anger and militance of ***1919,*** and the despair of ***The Big Money***—these contrasts cannot be completely explained by the varying epochs Dos Passos recreates, nor by any plan such as the transition, as he suggested in a 1932 letter to Cowley, from "competitive capitalism" to "monopoly capitalism." Between 1927 and 1936, Dos Passos experienced an intensification of his radicalism with the onset of the depression, and, later, a growing pessimism and disillusionment with the Communist party that led him to search America's past for a viable radical tradition. The trilogy thus is strained with tensions that even its elaborate formal structure cannot entirely hold.

Such tensions, along with the complexity of its form, may help account for the wide spectrum of critical opinion about ***U.S.A.*** American Communist critics in the 1930s looked eagerly to this talented and prestigious writer as a potential supporter, hoping he might give literary expression to their view of the world. Consequently, they often saw too much or too little in ***U.S.A.*** Granville Hicks heaped praise on ***The 42nd Parallel,*** but saw "the characteristic futilitarianism of the age creep[ing] slimily" across its pages. The more militant ***1919*** brought Dos Passos greater tribute: V. F. Calverton placed him in "the mainstream of the proletarian tradition," and Michael Gold saw him growing politically "like corn in the Iowa sun," although Hicks, again, pointed out that Dos Passos had "yet to master the whole body of revolutionary theory." The pessimistic ending of the trilogy no doubt surprised many overly optimistic Communist readers of ***1919,*** for ***The Big Money,*** along with Dos Passos's increasing public criticism of the party itself, brought harsh attack. Gold thundered that ***U.S.A.*** was nothing but a world of "merde," that its author was trapped in "the muck of bourgeois nihilism" and must "hate the human race." Dos Passos, it seems, had been read out of the Communist literary pantheon. (pp. 87-90)

In general, critical discussion of ***U.S.A.*** has focused on its technical devices and on its seeming determinism. Most French critics have delighted in its complex structure; Sartre in 1938 called Dos Passos "the greatest writer of our time." But Marshall McLuhan thought ***U.S.A.*** an "extreme simplification" of what Joyce had achieved and complained that Dos Passos saw "nothing inevitable or meaningful in human suffering." Alfred Kazin praised the narrative style of ***U.S.A.*** highly, but thought the trilogy too tightly sealed in despair, too "symmetrical a series of hell pits," and concluded that Dos Passos's "opposition to capitalism [was] no greater than his suspicion of all societies." Diverse political perspectives lurk somewhere behind all these critical evaluations of ***U.S.A.,*** but few would disagree with Kazin's praise that Dos Passos "brings energy to despair." (p. 91)

Robert C. Rosen, in his John Dos Passos: Politics and the Writer, *University of Nebraska Press, 1981, 191 p.*

Donald Pizer (essay date 1988)

[*Pizer is an American educator and critic. In the following excerpt from his* Dos Passos' U.S.A.: A Critical Study, *he describes the writing and juxtaposing of the four compositional modes used in* U.S.A.]

Each of the modes of ***U.S.A.*** is a distinctive literary form. Put oversimply, the Camera Eye is prose-poem bildungsroman; the biographies are ironic impressionistic pen portraits; the Newsreels, surreal collages; and the narratives, free-indirect-discourse renderings of archetypal lives. Each mode is also characteristic of a major tendency in the literary expression of the 1920s and is thus not strikingly original to Dos Passos. Although Dos Passos was extending the range and the level of execution of these experimental forms, he did not discover them. What is unique in ***U.S.A.*** is thus not the modal devices themselves but their combination in a single work that seeks to exploit the special quality of each to achieve an effect that is at once complex and unified.

Dos Passos himself always stressed in accounts of the genesis of ***U.S.A.*** that his principal creative act in the writing of the trilogy was the placing of the modal segments in relation to each other. His meeting with Sergei Eisenstein in Russia in 1928 confirmed, he later recalled [in ***Best Times: An Informal Memoir,*** 1966], his belief in "the importance of montage" in expressing theme in all serial art. "By that time I was really taken with the idea of montage," he remarked [in an interview with David Sanders in *Writers at Work: The "Paris Review" Interviews, Fourth Series,* 1976]. As he explained to [Frank Gado in an interview in *First Person: Conversations on Writers and Writing,* 1973], "I always had an interest in contrast, in the sort of montage Griffith and Eisenstein used in film. I was trying to put across a complex state of mind, an atmosphere, and I brought in these things [the Newsreels and biographies] partly for contrast and partly for getting a different dimension."

Several commentators early in the critical history of ***U.S.A.*** remarked that the trilogy seemed to have been prepared in a manner similar to a film that relies heavily on montage. Delmore Schwartz noted in ["John Dos Passos and the Whole Truth," *Southern Review,* October 1938], for example, that Dos Passos seems to have "put the book together as a motion-picture director composed his film, by a procedure of cutting, arranging, and interposing parts." But in fact ***U.S.A.*** is far more complex in origin and nature than a film, in that the units that are being cut, arranged, and interposed are strikingly different from each other, while in a film the visual image is the single mode. In other words, by relying on montage in a work that already had a mix of four different literary modes, Dos Passos was raising the stakes, so to speak, beyond those present either in most films or in the fiction of other modernists (Faulkner, for example) who depended on montage. Now a reader would not only be asked to find connections and an ultimate spatial unity in juxtaposed scenes that derive from different plot lines, points of view, and chronologies. He would also be asked to perform the same task in response to modes of expression that were very different from each other both in substance and in manner. And since, as in most writing, the reader's task is also the author's, it is no wonder that Dos Passos recalled his intense preoccupation with this phase of his preparation of the trilogy.

It is possible, with the aid of Dos Passos' surviving notes and manuscripts, to trace with some confidence the way in which he wrote ***U.S.A.*** Although ***The 42nd Parallel*** and ***Nineteen-Nineteen*** are available only in incomplete notes and drafts, ***The Big Money*** is extant in an almost cradle-to-grave genealogy, from early notes to final printer's copy typescript (only proof is lacking). And since the three novels are essentially similar in form, it is reasonable to extrapolate from ***The Big Money*** (with confirming details from the manuscripts of the other two novels) to the trilogy as a whole.

Dos Passos began the preparation of each novel in the trilogy by drawing up lists of the characters he wished to include and of the focus of their activities. An early plan for ***Nineteen-Nineteen,*** entitled "Geography of *Nineteen Nineteen,*" reveals his method. We know that this is an early sketch, drawn to help Dos Passos scheme out the basic plan of the novel, because Richard Savage is here "Donald Savage" (a name not used in any of the surviving manuscript drafts) and because Alsace and Constantinople are not centers of action in the completed work. Another hint as to Dos Passos' method of construction is present in his early notes for ***The Big Money.*** Here, a group of notes that includes a list of "Characters for last volume" (some of whom do not appear in the novel) also contains both a list of biographical figures for possible inclusion and a page in which the two kinds of figures appear together. That Dos Passos' method was to begin each novel by thinking principally of the narrative and biographical figures (and thus of their relationship) is fully confirmed by the initial three draft tables of contents for ***The Big Money,*** which are (except for the first Camera Eye and the first two newsreels) limited to these two modes. These plans also precede full composition of the novel, since several of the biographies cited (Norris of Nebraska, Oil King, Kingfish the First) do not appear in ***The Big Money*** and seem never to have been written.

We know from other manuscript evidence that Dos Passos wrote each of the modes independently of the others. That is, for each unit of modal expression—a biography or Newsreel or Camera Eye or complete narrative—there exists a separate and distinctive body of notes, drafts, and final typescript. Thus, the first full typescript of ***The 42nd Parallel*** (before a missing clean printer's copy was prepared) and the final printer's copy of ***The Big Money*** have crossed out pagination sequences that reveal that each modal unit had an independent pagination before its inclusion in the full typescript of the novel. (An analogy with assembly-line production, in which independently manufactured components are at last brought together, inevitably comes to mind.) But the separate composition of each mode did not mean that Dos Passos suddenly plunged into the montage process at the completion of the writing of the modes. The evidence of his early lists, charts, and tables of contents is that he was thinking from the beginning both of the relationship of narrative figures to each other, including interlacings (as asides to himself in his notes reveal), and of the relationship of narrative to biographical figures. That Dos Passos began the montage process in this fashion is not surprising. The two modes that allowed him the greatest latitude and thus required the greatest initial planning were the narratives and the biographies. For the Camera Eye and the Newsreel he had in a sense both substance and sequence in hand before composition. The events of his own life supplied a core subject matter and a chronology for the Camera Eye, and the major events of each period served a similar purpose for the Newsreels.

Relying both on manuscript evidence and on hypotheses drawn from the nature of the modes, it is possible to sketch a theory of the composition of the novels of ***U.S.A.*** that has considerable significance for the quality of the completed work. A general belief about an era leads Dos Passos to the choice of narrative and biographical figures who exemplify the belief, with these figures conceived of from the first in juxtapositional relationships (an Eleanor and a Moorehouse together in Paris, a Hearst implicitly compared to a Moorehouse). The composition of each of the modes now commences, with each written independently of the others and with the Newsreels probably the last undertaken. The composition process as it proceeds has a twofold character. As Dos Passos wrote a narrative or a Camera Eye, he was composing with confidence and authority within the conventions he had established for that mode. But as he wrotc hc was also both consciously and unconsciously exploring the juxtapositional possibilities of each modal segment, for he was of course aware that a final and overt act of juxtapositional composition would be required when the modal segments were in fact dispersed throughout the novel. Much of the strength of ***U.S.A.*** arises out of this combination of a "purity" of expression within a particular mode—pure in the sense of the observance of firm and consistent modal conventions—and the far more indirect suggestiveness of the modal mix.

The effort and care that Dos Passos brought to the writing of each of the modes are revealed by the extant drafts of the narratives of ***The Big Money.*** For each narrative figure, Dos Passos initially sketched, in broad terms and in only a few pages, the major events of the character's life, with these divided into narrative segments. His next step was to block out in far greater detail the action of a single segment. The final segment of Dick Savage's narrative, for example, is outlined in fifteen numbered incidents. There would then follow a first holograph draft of the entire narrative. (Dos Passos' letters reveal that he conceived of and wrote each narrative as a single "story," and that he gave all his energy to this narrative until it was completed.)

From this holograph a typescript would be prepared, which Dos Passos cut and revised heavily. A second typescript, itself revised, provided the text for integration into the full text of the novel. The seemingly unshaped and artless flow of the narratives, though strikingly different from the mannered symbolism of the Camera Eye, underwent a stone-by-stone preparation similar to that of the prose poems. And what was true of the narratives was also true of the biographies and Newsreels.

Much of the strength of *U.S.A.* arises out of the combination of a "purity" of expression within a particular mode—pure in the sense of the observance of firm and consistent modal conventions—and the far more indirect suggestiveness of the modal mix.

—Donald Pizer

Even before he had completed the writing of the individual modes, Dos Passos was engaged in elaborate planning of the juxtapositional order of the modal segments in the book as a whole. His early division of each narrative into segments, and his attachment of specific biographical figures to specific narrative figures (Taylor to Ike Hall, for example), no doubt supplied him with a rough arrangement for this portion of the novel almost from the beginning of the compositional process. But given the complexity and indeterminacy of the task, he was also led to prepare, at various stages in the composition of the novel, draft tables of contents both to record his ideas and to serve as a basis for revision of these ideas. Between approximately early 1935 and early 1936, he prepared at least seven (that is, seven have survived) draft tables of contents of ***The Big Money.*** The tables are not numbered or dated, but their sequence can be determined by internal evidence. The tables reveal:

1. Although the narratives supplied the base subject matter and structure for the novel, significant changes in narrative content and order did occur in the course of the novel's preparation. Charley, Margo, and Mary are present in the first table in the number of segments for each narrative as in the published work, except for the minor change of an increase in Mary's segments from three to four. The major changes that occur as the novel goes forward are: the complete cutting of the narrative of Ike Hall (an automobile worker who had appeared as a minor figure in Mac's narrative in ***The 42nd Parallel***); the substitution of a Richard Savage for a J. Ward Moorehouse segment at the close of the novel; and a shift in the order of the narrative segments to achieve an even greater early emphasis on Charley Anderson and a later one on Margo and Mary. The Hall material was no doubt cut at a late stage to shorten the novel (even without it ***The Big Money*** is still the longest novel in the trilogy), though Dos Passos had completed most or all of the narrative. (He later published several of its segments separately.) Its loss means that the novel lacks a "pure" working-class figure parallel to Mac in ***The 42nd Parallel*** and Joe Williams in ***Nineteen-Nineteen*** and in contrast to the middle-class or upward-striving figures in ***The Big Money.*** The change from Moorehouse to Savage is not so much a change in subject matter—the stress is still on New York advertising and "artistic" life—as in angle of vision through which to depict this world. And the shift in emphasis in the placing of narrative segments appears to follow from Dos Passos' recognition that Charley's New York and Detroit experiences epitomize the early stages of the 1920s boom, while Margo and Mary's movie and radical activities more fully reflect a later phase.

2. Although the biographies were also a key element in the early planning of the strategy of ***The Big Money,*** they reveal a greater volatility than the narratives. Six of the nine biographies in the completed novel were planned from the beginning (Taylor, Duncan, Ford, Veblen, Hearst, and Frank Lloyd Wright), but in attempting to choose the other three Dos Passos eliminated at various stages George W. Norris, John D. Rockefeller, Huey Long, Coolidge, and Vanzetti before finally selecting the Wright brothers, Valentino, and Insull. Dos Passos' "raw" juxtapositional planning was in terms of the relationship of narrative to biographical figures, as is indicated by the first three draft tables of contents. So, even in the first table, Taylor (the inventor of industrial engineering) is juxtaposed against Anderson and Ike Hall (a user and a victim of the assembly line), Margo is juxtaposed against Duncan, Charley against Ford and Coolidge, Mary against Veblen, and so on. The flexible spine of the novel is thus constructed. But the organizational strategy of the novel, which required that fictional and public archetypes be balanced, usually for ironic effect, lent itself to change in the selection of examples as the compositional process went forward and new possibilities for ironic effect came to mind. And since the biographies were far more adaptable to change than the narratives, it was they that underwent the greatest change in the course of preparation of the novel.

3. Although the first table contains the first Camera Eye and the first Newsreel, the splicing in of these two modes did not in fact begin until the fourth table for the Newsreels and the fifth for the Camera Eye. Three overlapping internal conventions determined the placing of these modal segments. First, and most mechanically, Dos Passos used them as a form of punctuation in the structure of the novel, in that at least one Camera Eye or Newsreel occurs between narrative segments. When a lengthier "pause" in the narrative movement is desired, at the point of introducing a new narrative figure, for example, a group of Newsreels and Camera Eyes will appear between narrative segments. Second, Dos Passos sought to place Camera Eye segments and Newsreels at points where the external events depicted in them coincided roughly, and sometimes precisely (as in the abortive 1919 May Day Paris uprising), with events present in the narratives. And last . . . , he sought to place them at points at which an underlying theme of the Newsreel and especially of the Camera Eye

segments was relevant to a theme in the juxtaposed narrative segment or biography.

4. Dos Passos undertook a reshaping of the final portion of the novel at a late stage of revision, as is revealed by the major differences between the conclusions of the next-to-last and last tables. In the first of these two, the ending was: Mary French, Camera Eye, Huey Long, and Ike Hall. Dos Passos cut the Ike Hall narrative, shifted Savage's segment to a place just before Mary's, added a Newsreel, substituted Insull for Long, and added the Vag epilogue. The revised conclusion was thus: Savage, Newsreel, Camera Eye, Insull, Mary, and Vag. Aside from the Vag addition, which served primarily as an epilogue to the trilogy as a whole, Dos Passos' purpose in revising the conclusion appears to have been to sharpen its irony. The earlier ending was more emphatically downbeat in that Ike Hall and Mary French—a down-and-out workingman and a worn radical dispirited by ideological disputes—were expressions of the mood of the 1930s. A biography of Huey Long, a potential American dictator of the early 1930s, would have contributed further to this mood. With the omission of Hall and the addition of Savage and Insull, the tone becomes more mixed, since the conclusion now contains figures who have seemingly climbed to success. The more openly depression aura of the first ending now gives way to material and themes more characteristic of the trilogy as a whole, in that the ironic depiction of the American success story dominates many of the narratives and biographies. It was perhaps the reintroduction of this theme in the revised conclusion that led Dos Passos to one of his final revisions . . . , the addition of the Vag epilogue. For Vag . . . is in archetypal form a final story of an American who believed in the myth of success.

Dos Passos' use of juxtaposition for thematic effect can be divided into three rough categories: a grouping of a large number of varied modal segments around a major theme or event; a more specific, more closely knit grouping, usually limited to several segments; and a precise thematic link across two segments. The draft tables of contents reveal something about the evolution of each of these effects. The first table, for example, indicates, as is shown by the penciled-in divisions in the left-hand margin, that Dos Passos thought of the material of the novel in relation to large chronological/thematic units, even though these units and their titles do not appear in the finished work. (It will be recalled, however, that ***The 42nd Parallel*** was divided into five parts in the 1930 edition.) "The bright lights," for example, deals with the apex of the mid- and late-1920s boom. Margo, Charley, and Moorehouse are at the height of their success, a success validated by the biographies of Coolidge, Rockefeller, and Hearst, while Mary, Norris, and Veblen represent the unheeded critical voices of the period. This theme, stated here grossly, will of course resonate far more subtly in the finished work. But this later complexity has its origins in Dos Passos' early grouping of a substantial number of narratives and biographies around a large-scale general idea.

Dos Passos' search for tighter, more specific juxtapositional effects (the second and third kinds noted above) is also evident from the beginning in his juggling of narrative/biography relationships to refine thematic implication. This simultaneous effort both to sharpen and to deepen reached a peak with the blending in of the Newsreels and Camera Eye segments. These modes, as I have already noted, have their own internal coherence—the reflection, in chronological order, of major public and private events—and thus were probably written independently of the planning and composition of the narratives and biographies, as is suggested by their absence from the first three draft tables of contents. But once stated, this notion of "independence" must be qualified by the fact that the same creative mind, compartmentalized only to a degree, wrote all the modes. A good many Newsreel segments were therefore no doubt "composed" because of Dos Passos' realization that their events would also be present in the narratives, as with the Florida land boom. And Dos Passos' choice of specific instances of the Camera Eye persona's experience in New York as a radical writer was also no doubt influenced by his awareness of the relationship of these activities to the lives of Charley, Savage, and Mary in the city and to Margo's career as an artist.

The first draft table of contents reveals an obvious example of a planned and specific juxtapositional effect when Charley's arrival in New York to face an uncertain future after heroic war service is followed by the parallel arrival of the Camera Eye persona (Camera Eye 43) and by a Newsreel (XLIV) that also deals with a number of returns from Europe to an unquiet America. Much more often, however, the Camera Eye and Newsreel segments are truly "spliced in," in the sense that their relationship to their adjacent

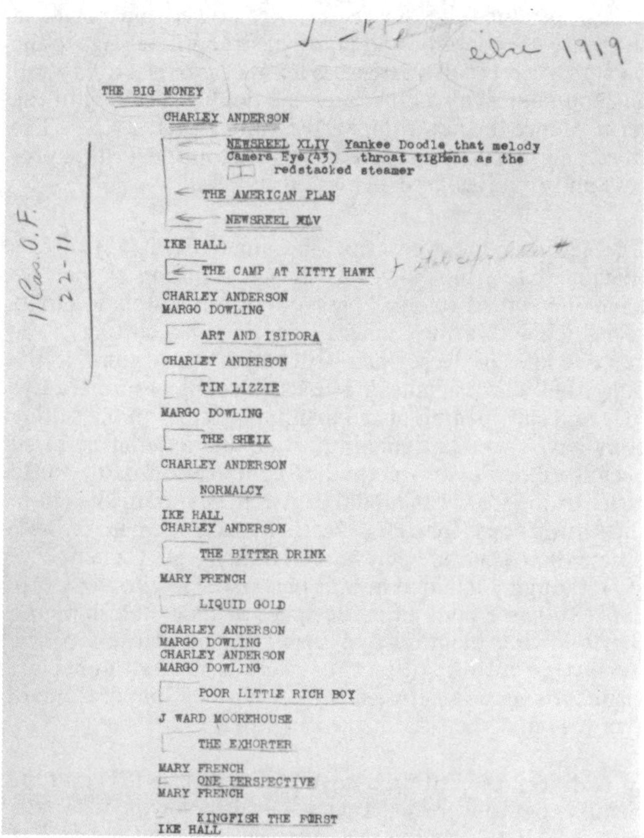
THE BIG MONEY
CHARLEY ANDERSON
NEWSREEL XLIV Yankee Doodle that melody
Camera Eye (43) throat tightens as the
redstacked steamer
THE AMERICAN PLAN
NEWSREEL XLV
IKE HALL
THE CAMP AT KITTY HAWK
CHARLEY ANDERSON
MARGO DOWLING
ART AND ISIDORA
CHARLEY ANDERSON
TIN LIZZIE
MARGO DOWLING
THE SHEIK
CHARLEY ANDERSON
NORMALCY
IKE HALL
CHARLEY ANDERSON
THE BITTER DRINK
MARY FRENCH
LIQUID GOLD
CHARLEY ANDERSON
MARGO DOWLING
CHARLEY ANDERSON
MARGO DOWLING
POOR LITTLE RICH BOY
J WARD MOOREHOUSE
THE EXHORTER
MARY FRENCH
ONE PERSPECTIVE
MARY FRENCH
KINGFISH THE FIRST
IKE HALL

Early draft of a table of contents for The Big Money.

biography and narrative segments is neither planned in advance nor precise. Rather, as in the creation of certain kinds of surreal and abstract paintings, Dos Passos was hoping for an inner resonance that might or might not follow from the mixing of modal segments only loosely connected in external character. In order to gain this effect, however, he needed to experiment, to try out relationships. Hence the seven tables of contents, as Dos Passos sifted the mix that constituted this potential, both to express more cogently already planned juxtapositional themes and to bring to the surface unforeseen juxtapositional inference.

The general nature of Dos Passos' experiments in the creation of thematic implication between modal segments can usefully be illustrated by a return to the "only words against / POWER SUPERPOWER" passage. . . . The process of juxtapositional experimentation that produced the passage is as follows. First, Dos Passos decided to substitute Insull for Huey Long as a final biography in the trilogy. (He had listed Insull as a possible biographical figure in early notes but had not included him in the first six draft contents.) In making this change, he was perhaps attracted by the link between a reference to "the manipulator of the holding company" at the close of the Harlan County Camera Eye and Insull, an infamous holding-company magnate of the 1920s. A second step was the revision of the characteristically ironic title of the Insull biography, "Immigrant Boy Makes Good," to a title that links the Camera Eye and the biography even more tightly, in that "power" is doubly present in both segments. The coal miners produce the raw material of power, but power in the sense of economic and political strength belongs to the owners. And Insull's career, as a director of electricity and gas companies, also illustrates the double meaning of the term. Hence the new title, POWER SUPERPOWER. The third and final step occurred even later in the writing process and requires an explanation in detail.

The setting-copy typescript of Camera Eye (51) reveals that in this version Dos Passos was thinking of the "we have only words against" passage entirely in relation to its relevance within the Camera Eye. Even his cutting of the last two lines of the segment still leaves "their guns" as the object of "words against." The setting copy of Camera Eye (51) and the opening of the Insull biography in the setting copy have two additional important characteristics. First, because Dos Passos' method of composition had been to write in independent modal units, he maintained even in the setting copy, for ease of further rearrangement of these units, their separate physical identities. So Camera Eye (51), though paginated now as part of the setting copy (pp. 616-18), has a body of white space at its conclusion, and the following biography of Insull begins at the top of a fresh page with its title. Thus there is still no immediate visual connection between the concluding line of Camera Eye (51) and the title of the biography.

In addition, the setting copy of Camera Eye (51) and the Insull biography reveal that galley proof would, for the first time, have brought the conclusion of the Camera Eye and the title of the biography into inescapable visual juxtaposition. The presence of galley mark 162 on page 616 and of 163 on page 620 indicates that the segments would have been set in close proximity on galley 162. Not only would Dos Passos have seen this physical juxtaposition at this stage—we know that he carefully read and revised proof for ***The Big Money***—but he would also have realized that the juxtaposition would be maintained in the printed book, since each new segment did not begin on a new printed page, but was run-on from the preceding segment. It was thus while reading galley that Dos Passos must have seen for the first time the possible relationship between the close of Camera Eye (51) and the title of the Insull biography, realized that that relationship would be preserved in the printed book, and took the leap into a precise but immensely suggestive juxtapositional theme by cutting "their guns."

The process by which Dos Passos reached this explicit crossing of modal barriers is characteristic of analogous but less dramatic and less specifically verbal instances throughout the trilogy. Dos Passos' desire to have the conclusion of ***The Big Money*** express a theme close to a major theme in the trilogy as a whole had led him to recast the ending of the novel, including the introduction of a new biography with a stronger relationship to its immediately preceding Camera Eye. Once present, this relationship was further tightened and sharpened by a revision of the title of the biography and a final strategic cutting. In approximate form, this was Dos Passos' method throughout, though the degree of interpenetration between specific adjoining modal units, even after their mutual reflection had been increased by shifting, revision, and cutting, differs considerably from instance to instance. In some sections, a large idea planned from the beginning controls the broad statement of theme in a large number of modal segments. In others, at the opposite extreme, a precise event, symbol, or verbal motif connects two segments. Or there is some mix of these extremes. In addition, the degree of planning versus serendipity differs greatly. In this instance, both are present. The shift to Insull and the change in title were the result of conscious efforts to restructure and to sharpen; the discovery of the "words against / POWER SUPERPOWER" passage was the fortuitious product of the earlier experimental industry. Dos Passos, in short, had no uniform way of producing juxtapositional theme, and he produced juxtapositional theme that varied greatly in openness, depth, and intensity. He had realized that the nature of his enterprise required a combination of planning and of seizing upon opportunities that arose when potentially mutually reflective units were already in place. He took advantage of both methods to produce the immense variety and density of juxtapositional implication that is ***U.S.A.*** (pp. 84-95)

Donald Pizer, in his Dos Passos' 'U.S.A.': A Critical Study, *University Press of Virginia, 1988, 209 p.*

FURTHER READING

Bibliography

Reinhart, Virginia S. "John Dos Passos, 1950-1966: Bibliography." *Twentieth Century Literature* 13, No. 3 (October 1967): 167-78.
Lists books and essays by and about Dos Passos published between 1950 and 1966.

Rohrkemper, John. "Criticism of John Dos Passos: A Selected Checklist." *Modern Fiction Studies* 26, No. 3 (Autumn 1980): 525-38.
Indexes books and essays on Dos Passos's works.

———. *John Dos Passos: A Reference Guide.* Boston: G. K. Hall & Co., 1980, 300 p.
Comprehensive bibliography of writings about Dos Passos and his work, covering the years 1921 through 1979.

Biography

Carr, Virginia Spencer. "The Demise of a Theater and a New Life, 1929," "A Middle-Class Liberal in the Depressed Thirties, 1930-33," "The French Riviera and Spain: A Summer Interlude, 1933," and "Life under the Blue Eagle, 1933-36." In her *Dos Passos: A Life,* pp. 249-63, pp. 265-314, pp. 315-20, pp. 321-56. Garden City, N.Y.: Doubleday & Co., 1984.
Chronicles Dos Passos's life during the writing of *U.S.A.*

Geismar, Maxwell. "John Dos Passos: Conversion of a Hero." In his *Writers in Crisis: The American Novel, 1925-1940,* pp. 89-139. New York: Hill and Wang, 1947.
Biographical and critical overview of Dos Passos's career through 1941.

Landsberg, Melvin. *Dos Passos' Path to "U.S.A.": A Political Biography, 1912-1936.* Boulder: Colorado Associated University Press, 1972, 292 p.
Treats Dos Passos's family background and life up to the completion of the *U.S.A.* trilogy.

Ludington, Townsend. "Arrival at the Political Left, 1926-1928," "Russia and Marriage, 1928-1929," and "Part V: The Great Depression, 1930-1936." In his *John Dos Passos: A Twentieth Century Odyssey,* pp. 250-65, pp. 267-81, pp. 284-359. New York: E. P. Dutton, 1980.
Covers Dos Passos's life during the time he was writing *U.S.A.*

Criticism

Becker, George J. " 'Visions. . . . ' " In his *John Dos Passos,* pp. 57-79. New York: Frederick Ungar Publishing Co., 1974.
Thematic and stylistic overview of *U.S.A.* Becker notes that despite the trilogy's pessimistic tone, "the American dream, battered and corrupted by men of ill will, or little will, still manifests itself."

Belkind, Allen, ed. *Dos Passos, the Critics, and the Writer's Intention.* Carbondale: Southern Illinois University Press, 1971, 288 p.
Collection of critical essays by major critics, several of which deal directly with *U.S.A.*

Bradbury, Malcolm. "The Denuded Place: War and Form in *Parade's End* and *U.S.A.*" In *The First World War in Fiction: A Collection of Critical Essays,* edited by Holger Klein, pp. 193-209. London: The Macmillan Press, 1976.
Compares Dos Passos's and Ford Maddox Ford's historical depictions of the changes World War I occasioned in society, individual psychology, and aesthetics.

Brantley, John D. "*U.S.A.*—The Natural History of a Society." In his *The Fiction of John Dos Passos,* pp. 55-78. The Hague, The Netherlands: Mouton & Co., 1968.
Thematic and stylistic overview of *U.S.A.* Brantley asserts that Dos Passos's principal interest was "in the relation of man as an individual to the 'machines' which are created by the political, economic, and social forces of his time."

Colley, Iain. "America Can Break Your Heart: *USA.*" In his *Dos Passos and the Fiction of Despair,* pp. 66-119. Totowa, N.J.: Rowman and Littlefield, 1978.
Considers *U.S.A.* a "work of defiant pessimism" that is informed not by Marxist philosophy but rather "a view of human existence as ultimately planless."

Foley, Barbara. "From *U.S.A.* to *Ragtime*: Notes on the Forms of Historical Consciousness in Modern Fiction." *American Literature* 50, No. 1 (March 1978): 85-105.
Compares *U.S.A.* and E. L. Doctorow's *Ragtime,* noting that there is a "profound divergence between the two works—a divergence which comments significantly upon the changing strategies by which novelists of the twentieth century have chosen to depict historical materials in their fiction."

Geismar, Maxwell. "John Dos Passos: The *U.S.A.* Trilogy." In his *American Moderns: From Rebellion to Conformity,* pp. 65-76. New York: Hill and Wang, 1958.
Reprints the introductions Geismar wrote for the Pocket Books editions of *The 42nd Parallel, 1919,* and *The Big Money.*

Goldman, Arnold. "Dos Passos and His *U.S.A.*" *New Literary History* I, No. 3 (Spring 1970): 471-83.
Argues that Dos Passos's trilogy is an epic history that "chronicles progressive disenfranchisement from Twentieth Century America, the reverse of an epic justification of a country through its hero and its history."

Hicks, Granville. "John Dos Passos." *The Bookman* LXXV, No. 1 (April 1932): 32-42.
Favorably reviews *1919,* stating that the second novel in the trilogy "does much to strengthen the conviction that John Dos Passos is the most considerable figure in contemporary American literature."

Hook, Andrew, ed. *Dos Passos: A Collection of Critical Essays.* Englewood Cliffs, N.J.: Prentice-Hall, 1974, 186 p.
Contains essays focusing on *U.S.A.* by such well-known critics as Jean-Paul Sartre, Lionel Trilling, and John William Ward.

Kazin, Alfred. "Into the Thirties: All the Lost Generations." In his *On Native Grounds: An Interpretation of Modern American Prose Literature,* pp. 312-59. New York: Reynal & Hitchcock, 1942.
Discusses the works of F. Scott Fitzgerald, Ernest Hemingway, and Dos Passos, noting that "the defeatism of the lost generation has been slowly and subtly transferred by [Dos Passos] from persons to society itself."

Knox, George. "Dos Passos and Painting." *Texas Studies in Literature and Language* VI, No. 1 (Spring 1964): 22-38.
Examines Dos Passos's interest in painting and its influence on his literary works, including *U.S.A.*

Masteller, Richard N. "Caricatures in Crisis: The Satiric Vision of Reginald Marsh and John Dos Passos." *Smithsonian Studies in American Art* 3, No. 2 (Spring 1989): 23-45.

Discusses Dos Passos's and Marsh's use of cultural satire in the prose and graphic art of *U.S.A.* to express "the loss of depth and dimension—the loss of human integrity" that they believed characterized American society.

Millgate, Michael. "John Dos Passos." In his *American Social Fiction: James to Cozzens,* pp. 128-41. New York: Barnes & Noble, 1964.

Asserts that the rationale for Dos Passos's attack on power and corruption in *U.S.A.* "may have been economic and political, but his impetus, however closely identified with the rationale, was moral and emotional."

Modern Fiction Studies, Special Issue: John Dos Passos 26, No. 3 (Autumn 1980): 398-467.

Contains four essays that deal directly with *U.S.A.,* addressing such topics as the Camera Eye, Walt Whitman's influence on the trilogy, and Dos Passos's treatment of time.

Rohrkemper, John. "The Collapse of Faith and the Failure of Language: John Dos Passos and the Spanish Civil War." In *Rewriting the Good Fight: Critical Essays on the Literature of the Spanish Civil War,* edited by Frieda S. Brown, et al., pp. 215-28. East Lansing: Michigan State University Press, 1989.

Cites *U.S.A.* as the height of Dos Passos's creative achievement and attributes his subsequent decline to disillusionment and loss of faith in the constructive powers of language.

Sanders, David, ed. *The Merrill Studies in U.S.A.* Columbus, Ohio: Charles E. Merrill Publishing Co., 1972, 95 p.

Collection of contemporary reviews and excerpts from critical studies dealing with *U.S.A.*

———. "John Dos Passos as Conservative." In *A Question of Quality: Popularity and Value in Modern Creative Writing,* edited by Louis Filler, pp. 115-23. Bowling Green, Ohio: Bowling Green University Popular Press, 1976.

Compares Dos Passos's *U.S.A.* trilogy and his 1961 novel *Midcentury.*

Seed, David. "Media and Newsreels in Dos Passos' *U.S.A.*" *Journal of Narrative Technique* 14, No. 3 (Fall 1984): 182-92.

Examines the function of the Newsreels.

Snell, George. "John Dos Passos: Literary Collectivist." In his *The Shapers of American Fiction: 1798-1947,* pp. 249-63. New York: E. P. Dutton & Co., 1947.

Critical overview of Dos Passos's career in which Snell praises *U.S.A.* as Dos Passos's masterpiece for its technical originality and influence on younger writers of the 1930s.

Trilling, Lionel. "The America of John Dos Passos." *Partisan Review* IV, No. 5 (April 1938): 26-32.

Argues that Dos Passos's primary concern in *U.S.A.* is personal morality.

Vanderwerken, David L. "*U.S.A.*: Dos Passos and the 'Old Words.'" *Twentieth Century Literature* 23, No. 2 (May 1977): 195-228.

Examines Dos Passos's use of the Biography, Camera Eye, Narrative, and Newsreel devices to demonstrate how the "old words"—"the language embodying the idea and the promise of America"—have been betrayed.

Westerhoven, James N. "Autobiographical Elements in the Camera Eye." *American Literature* 48, No. 3 (November 1976): 340-64.

Investigates Dos Passos's use of personal recollections and emotions in the Camera Eye segments of *U.S.A.*

Wrenn, John H. "U. S. A." In his *John Dos Passos,* pp. 154-66. New York: Twayne Publishers, 1961.

Contends that "*U.S.A.* is a great agglomerate tragic history" that Dos Passos constructed from personal memories and his study of American history.

Interview

Sanders, David. "The Art of Fiction XLIV: John Dos Passos." *The Paris Review* 12, No. 46 (Spring 1969): 147-72.

Interview in which Dos Passos discusses the genesis and writing of *U.S.A.*

Additional coverage of Dos Passos's life and career is contained in the following sources published by Gale Research: *Concise Dictionary of American Literary Biography, 1929-1941; Contemporary Authors,* Vols. 1-4, 29-32, rev. eds.; *Contemporary Authors New Revision Series,* Vol. 3; *Contemporary Literary Criticism,* Vols. 1, 4, 8, 11, 15, 25, 34; *Dictionary of Literary Biography,* Vols. 4, 9; *Dictionary of Literary Biography Documentary Series,* Vol. 1; *DISCovering Authors; Major 20th-Century Writers;* and *World Literature Criticism.*

Anna Kavan

1901-1968

(Born Helen Emily Woods; also wrote under the name Helen Ferguson) English novelist and short story writer.

The following entry provides an overview of Kavan's career. For further information see *CLC,* Volumes 5 and 13.

INTRODUCTION

Kavan's novels and short stories are characterized by a lyrical prose style and themes of alienation, victimization, and addiction. Frequently autobiographical, these works reflect her unhappy childhood, her sense of isolation, her failed relationships, and her longtime drug addiction.

Born in Cannes, France, Kavan spent her early years traveling with her parents or staying with relatives in England. She said she was "betrayed" at the age of six when her parents placed her in an American boarding school. Although her family had a home in California, Kavan's parents continued their extensive traveling, and Kavan was often left at school. Her feelings of abandonment and betrayal intensified after her father's suicide in 1915. She spent the following years in Swiss and English boarding schools, where she displayed an aptitude for writing and painting. At the age of nineteen Kavan married Donald Ferguson and moved to Burma. Two years later she left her husband and went to France with their young son. There she met Stuart Edmonds, with whom she lived for several years. Her first novels were published during this time, including *Let Me Alone,* in which she introduced the character of Anna Kavan, a young girl who marries a man she dislikes after her father abandons her. She used her mother as a model for the cruel aunt and based the main character's husband on Donald Ferguson. While she had previously been admitted to mental hospitals for depression and drug addiction, the deterioration of her relationship with Edmonds acted as the catalyst for her most severe breakdown. Following a period of hospitalization, Helen Ferguson began writing as Anna Kavan; *Asylum Piece, and Other Stories,* her first book published under her new pen name, incorporated her experiences as a psychiatric patient. During this time, she broke off most of her former relationships and associated with a limited number of people, including her doctor, K. T. Bluth; her publisher, Peter Owen; and Welsh writer Rhys Davies. Kavan supplemented the income from her books by renovating houses and submitting articles to the *New Yorker, Harper's Bazaar,* and *Horizon.* She continued to battle mental illness and drug addiction for the rest of her life. Kavan died in 1968.

Kavan's early novels tend to follow a conventional narrative structure, while the later works with which she is usually identified are more experimental in an attempt to represent her alienated characters' disturbed perceptions of reality. Kavan frequently portrays characters seeking escape, either physically or mentally, as in "Asylum Piece," where she compares the asylum to a cage and the inmates to birds. *House of Sleep,* a stream-of-consciousness narrative, explores the isolation of a young girl who creates her own fantasy world, and *Ice,* Kavan's best-known work, traces the flight of a young girl pursued by her cruel husband and a former lover. Characterized by a nightmarish atmosphere, the latter book reflects the influence of Alain Robbe-Grillet's theories of the French New Novel in its rejection of the conventions of character, plot, place, and time. *Ice* is often categorized as science fiction because of its vision of a dystopian world. *Julia and the Bazooka, and Other Stories,* a posthumously published collection of short stories, studies the self-destructive behavior of drug addicts and reveals their sense of futility and emptiness in an indifferent world.

PRINCIPAL WORKS

A Charmed Circle [as Helen Ferguson] (novel) 1929
The Dark Sisters [as Helen Ferguson] (novel) 1929
Let Me Alone [as Helen Ferguson] (novel) 1930
A Stranger Still [as Helen Ferguson] (novel) 1935
Goose Cross [as Helen Ferguson] (novel) 1936
Rich Get Rich [as Helen Ferguson] (novel) 1937
Asylum Piece, and Other Stories (short stories) 1940
Change the Name (novel) 1941
I Am Lazarus (short stories) 1945
House of Sleep (novel) 1947; also published as *Sleep Has His House,* 1948
A Scarcity of Love (novel) 1956
Eagles' Nest (novel) 1957
A Bright Green Field, and Other Stories (short stories) 1958
Who Are You? (novel) 1963
Ice (novel) 1967
Julia and the Bazooka, and Other Stories (short stories) 1970
My Soul in China (novella and short stories) 1975
My Madness (novels and short stories) 1990

CRITICISM

Leo Lerman (essay date 10 August 1946)

[*In the following excerpt, Lerman reviews* Asylum Piece *and compares it to Mary Jane Ward's* The Snake Pit, *commenting on its portrayal of the mentally ill.*]

Asylum Piece, as published in America, contains Miss Kavan's first book, her third, and two additional pieces of fictional prose. I hesitate to classify her pieces as stories, for she is less concerned with formal story structure—plot, characterization, time, place, personality—than she is with communicating the integral essence of mental upheaval. Psychasthenia is her theme: its ramifications are her variations. There are thirty-four pieces in this book. Some of them are sustained narratives in themselves, some are fragments—a page or two of interior observation carefully, almost clinically noted. Crackup invents the content and shape of her pieces, dictates the sparse case history lineaments of her prose. Since in crackups there is almost no geography—no concrete names, places, personalities—all these are almost completely lacking in ***Asylum Piece***. In their place is emotion: fear, hatred, passion, love springing fiercely or climbing as pallidly as a tendril never sun-exposed. Emotion is the cipher here, the clue to both victims and anonymous persecutors.

The atmosphere is reminiscent of Kafka. "I am a victim," says the victim. "Someone is my enemy. He is persecuting me. Why?" But Kafka is not concerned with the individual per se, his domain is everyone—people. To him we are all victims. Anna Kavan is concerned with the individual, the specific. That the individual is, perhaps, increasingly distraught, increasingly aware of his individual sicknesses at this time lends her a validity, a universality which is paradoxically inherent and exoteric. She removes the case from the watch and shows us the works ticking madly away inside.

Sometimes ***Asylum Piece*** seems to be an integrated record of a single mental collapse, sometimes this record itself collapses and stages, or states, of other collapses are recorded. The artistic problem here is basic: how successfully has Miss Kavan communicated mental disaster using her own peculiar technique of sitting, diligent pen in hand, within the sick head? This problem of communication is fundamental in any art. Without communication the art remains moribund, unseen, unheard, unread, uncreative—it does not contribute. Miss Kavan is almost inhumanely successful in communicating an interior impression of mental sickness. But her contribution is a fragile one, for although it is intellectual it is essentially subjective. And the subjective when quite divorced from action, when dedicated almost exclusively to emotions, ideas, and experiments in craftsmanship, communicates only to those prepared to decode the message.

Comparisons with Mary Jane Ward's *The Snake Pit* are here inevitable and obviously apposite. ***Asylum Piece*** and *The Snake Pit* are both concerned with the same subject matter: one is set in the victims' heads and one is set in an institution. Both are concerned with the individual, but Mary Jane Ward's book does hold an implicit indictment of society. Everyone is implicated in *The Snake Pit*—all of us. You are implicated in ***Asylum Piece*** only if "it" happens to you—*The Snake Pit* implies that "it" is happening to more of us all the time. The obvious universality of *The Snake Pit,* the author's keen storytelling sense, and the shock value of the subject has made this book a best seller. ***Asylum Piece*** will probably never be a best seller. It tells no story or even stories: telling a story was not the author's problem. Mary Jane Ward is related to Dickens, Anna Kavan to Virginia Woolf. The two books are excellent examples of the variety which modern fictional forms engender. *The Snake Pit* is a traditional novel, a formal novel of action. It tells an exhausting but always exciting tale. ***Asylum Piece*** conveys moods, emotions, and mental situations.

But both are fiction, for the basic problem has been the translation from reality (or what is construed as reality) to a prose form—a fiction form, a feigning of life observed. The volume of a novel's sales does not determine its artistic worth. Each of these books is artistically worthy upon its own level. *The Snake Pit* is a smoothly constructed and written conventional novel about an unconventional subject which daily becomes more conventional; ***Asylum Piece*** is definitely experimental writing, but experimental writing of a very high order. There is no mystery in *The Snake Pit.* Mrs. Ward did not intend any. Everything is there for the reader to see—past, present, future, and suspense. ***Asylum Piece*** is all mystery, and the reader has to read carefully and work very hard to see anything. Doubtless in choosing to present mystery (remember that Mrs. Ward experienced her crackup, Miss Kavan scientifically assists others in theirs), in choosing the interior method, the first person singular method rather than the more formal objective from-the-outside-looking-in approach, Anna Kavan has presented crackup with a more intellectually substantial artistic success. Each is, however, successful, for each seems to have accomplished what she set out to do.

What you get out of ***Asylum Piece*** depends on how hard you are willing to work. It's not Joyce, but it is intentionally difficult to read. Anna Kavan is definitely a most important new writer. Has she anything else to say?

Leo Lerman, "Variations on a Current Theme," in The Saturday Review of Literature, *August 10, 1946, p. 9.*

John Farrelly (essay date 23 September 1946)

[*In the following excerpt, Farrelly discusses the structure of* Asylum Piece.]

It is a particular relief, at a time when the art of fiction seems to have fallen on such evil days, to find a writer who regards it as something more than the mere mixing of staple ingredients, like cooking. In [***Asylum Piece***] one is apt to be most impressed by the skill of Miss Kavan's devices, since the majority are told from the viewpoint of the central character, who is mentally deranged. Intelligibility had to be rescued from chaos, and a language created out of gibbering. The author has constructed a new and parallel world, rather in the manner of parable, which we would call a world of fantasy, but which her uneasy characters inhabit as the natural order. The stories are grouped in three sections which, in their sequence, suggest the cycle of a particular experience: first, the obsession, then the incarceration, and finally an adjustment or conclusion, which is usually despair.

In the early stories, a young woman, as the first-person narrator, illustrates the gradual deterioration of the personality, its dissociation from a human social order, its consequent abandoned loneliness, and the eventual recreation of its own world of fears and sanctions as complex as the world on the other side of the mirror from which it has become detached. These stories all begin reassuringly enough with a perfectly commonplace incident like a luncheon party or the occupation of a new house. But we are wary and observe the character as anxiously as a nurse might watch her patient. Each time the snag occurs. The mind jumps the tracks. The character crosses to the shady side of the street, perhaps, and logic goes awry; a determined cheerfulness gives way to unutterable depression and fatigue. Malevolent conspiracy is evident in what were, a moment before, the happiest omens. The character is now alone, but in a peopled solitude, for she finds herself in relation to a baffling complexus of her own imaginings, which Miss Kavan represents as a Kafka-like bureaucratic authority, omnipotent and inaccessible, a mean Providence whose workings are always mysterious but never adorable.

The subject attempts to come to terms with this power, by conciliating it or by persuasion. But the mind cannot placate what is, after all, its own conscience, and reason is the cracked logic of the maniac, impossible of solution. As the character reads with painful attention the impersonal communications of the Authorities, the mind puzzles the obscurity of its own decrees. Even as it condemns itself, it protests its innocence, harping in self-pity on "all the catastrophes which have fallen on me." It is within this dualism that the stories operate: the mind-character trapped in itself, baffled, resentful, terrified, while every attempt at escape buries it deeper in its isolation.

After this impression of the feverish chaos of their inner world, we see a group of patients in a mental hospital. Inert and ineffectual, they are like sleepers whose restlessness and occasional moanings barely suggest the turmoil of their nightmares. These stories are static. The only instance of progression (which in this context means cure) is that of a young man who has been coaxed by a year's treatment from the wilds of extreme dementia to the state of simple idiocy in which the doctors can anticipate the patient and congratulate themselves.

In the final section, the first person singular returns. It is the original I of the early stories, but by this time she has achieved a kind of control over her situation. After dealing with the Authorities for several years, she is regarded as an expert by her acquaintances, who come to her for advice. She cannot persuade them that there are actually no rules, that the secret is that there is no secret, and like a canny maniac she has learned her way around the maze of the lunatic asylum which by now is everywhere and from which, in spite of apparent freedom, there is no longer even any question of escape.

"It is the personal nature of the experiences which is incommunicable," Miss Kavan says in one of the stories. But the incommunicable is largely the substance of these stories, for the experiences of the insane are personal in the strictest sense of the term. They are isolated from most common experience and inhabit a world of their own creation in which the faces are blank and all situation is merely the aberration of an obscure disease. So that in these fictions a poverty of fact supports a surfeit of reference which often exhausts and exasperates the attention, like the signs of a mute in a language one doesn't understand. Even where this obscurity is avoided, it is difficult to sympathize with a character whose joys and sorrows are regulated by what are, for the supposedly more balanced reader, mere fantasies. The interest is usually sustained and often acute, but it is the impersonal interest, mentioned before, of the nurse for the patient, compounded of anxiety and curiosity and occasional annoyance.

But in the best of these stories, Miss Kavan has created with poetic devices those states of mind between reality and illusion in which contradictories hold each other in a terrified embrace. This is the hell of souls lost within themselves, and she has charted the territory of loneliness they inhabit and has registered the persistent single voice that forms their silence. (pp. 355-56)

John Farrelly, "Souls in Limbo," in The New Republic, *Vol. 115, No. 10, September 23, 1946, pp. 355-56.*

Kavan wrote in a mirror. It imprisoned her. Watching only herself, her men are wraiths, and nearly always treacherous—as perhaps shadows must be.

—Rhys Davies, in his introduction to Anna Kavan's* Julia and the Bazooka, *1975.

John Woodburn (essay date 23 August 1947)

[*In the following excerpt, Woodburn favorably reviews* House of Sleep.]

In her three previous books, and now in [***The House of Sleep***], Anna Kavan has concerned herself with the unbalanced mind, the pathos and terror of the intellect in the tragic act of slipping its tether to reality. It is this tiger of the mind which, like Blake's, burns so brightly, which has fascinated her by its fearsome beauty, and which she has tried to capture in her delicate and discerning prose. This is a brave and unpopular thing for her, or any writer, to attempt, and it is due her to say that she has done it more sensitively, more respectfully, has thrust farther into the wild brilliance and darkness of the world beyond reality than has any writer of her time. To my mind, no contemporary can approach her in the articulation of the esthetics of insanity.

The House of Sleep tells of a girl, nameless and glimpsed, rather than known, whose progressive neurosis caused her, first of necessity and finally in exultant volition, to reject the jagged pattern of daytime living for a borderline world which she enters eagerly at night. As a means of elucidating the difficult and demanding architecture of the book, the author has prepared an explanatory preface:

> The creative impulse is the result of tension; without tension life would not exist. If human life be accepted as the result of tension between the two polarities of night and day, the negative pole, night, must have at least equal importance with the positive day.
>
> At night, under the negative influence, subjected to cosmic radiations of a different kind, human affairs are apt to come to a crisis; at night most human beings die and are born.
>
> ***The House of Sleep*** describes in the nighttime language certain critical stages in the development of one individual human being. No interpretation is needed of the dream tongue we all, as a matter of course, have spoken in sleep and childhood; but for the sake of absolute clearness, a short paragraph at the head of each section indicates the corresponding day situation.

These short, daytime paragraphs are condensed, and dense with association. They trace the path of the reality which the young girl walked in such unhappiness and distaste. Here in luminous, small images, is the essence of her predicament: her fading childhood and the mother who died when the girl was a child; her father, a man of surfaces and brusqueness; the loneliness and separation of her days at school and at the university. They are followed by the passages which report the night-journeys of her freed imagination, high, wandering flights of the richest and most brilliant sort, a bright Cloud Cuckoo Land in which the *id* comes exuberantly to life, with imagination its companion and competitor.

At times, many times, it seems that Anna Kavan is using a private language. The inhibitions of our daytime communication are so strong, we are so conditioned to the unconsciously guarded speech, so much the prisoner of our rational selves, that it is difficult at first to recall the changelings we can become at the borderline of sleep. This is a strange, softly terrifying book. It is difficult not to yield helplessly to its beauty, and it is impossible not to be profoundly disturbed by it. The final and most desperately-defended privacy is that of the secret, inner consciousness, that corridor of the mind through which each of us walks alone; and Anna Kavan invades that privacy brilliantly, humbly, and insistently. She knows a great deal about the tiger of the mind, and it disturbs us to know that she knows.

John Woodburn, "Nocturnal Madness," in The Saturday Review, *New York, Vol. XXX, No. 34, August 23, 1947, p. 15.*

Diana Trilling (essay date 20 September 1947)

[*Trilling is an American critic and essayist. In the following review, she finds Kavan's subjective portrayal of abnormal mental states in* House of Sleep *to be without artistic or intellectual value.*]

The only thing that makes Anna Kavan's ***The House of Sleep*** worth writing about—nothing makes it worth reading—is the point of view it shares with a considerable section of our literary culture, the most "advanced" section, that madness is a normal or even a rather better-than-normal way of life. Although Miss Kavan's book is called a novel, it has no single characteristic of fiction—no narrative, no characters, no insight into or enlargement of our common reality. In fact, it deliberately avoids reality except in so far as it uses words which, however arbitrarily arranged, yet manage to evoke fleeting glimpses of a momentarily recognizable universe. A kaleidoscope of the subjective states of an increasingly disordered mind, recorded half as if from within the sick mind itself and half as if through the eye of an outsider much too closely identified with her subject, ***The House of Sleep*** seems to me to have been published only by virtue of our utter confusion as to what life and literature are all about. I haven't the slightest idea what it means to be told of such a pretentious piece of non-communication that it is a "penetrating insight into the subconscious world of dreams and shadows." To me, insight necessarily proceeds from some kind of organized vision of reality. And the subconscious world of dreams and shadows is interesting only if it adds to our information about the world of consciousness, which Miss Kavan's book does not.

But it is clear that Miss Kavan has a principled disagreement with this position. She explains her own stand in an introduction sufficiently brief to be quoted entire:

> The creative impulse is the result of tension; without tension life would not exist. If human life be accepted as the result of tension between the two polarities of night and day, the negative pole, night, must have at least equal importance with the positive day.
>
> At night, under the negative influence, subjected to cosmic radiations of a different kind, human affairs are apt to come to a crisis; at night most human beings die and are born.
>
> ***The House of Sleep*** describes in the night-time language certain critical stages in the development of one individual human being. No interpretation is needed of this dream tongue we all, as a matter of course, have spoken in sleep and childhood; but for the sake of absolute clearness a short paragraph at the head of each section indicates the corresponding day situation.

Every sentence of this statement invites examination. It is the second sentence, however, that reveals the serious misapprehension under which Miss Kavan has conceived her book. For believing that human life is a tension between the two polarities of reason and non-reason and that nonrationality, instead of being an element in the human composition that normally is and should be under the dominion of reason, asserts an "at least equal" authority with reason, Miss Kavan sets herself firmly against our common social view. She distinctly refuses the usual attitude whereby the whole test of health lies in this delicate matter of degree, the attitude which says that when a person's non-reason approaches even a 50 percent dominion over his reason it means that the person is sick and of only questionable use to society.

As to the sentences that follow this one, they too make rather singular assumptions. When Miss Kavan writes, "at night, under the negative influence," one is moved to ask her why negative; what makes night negative? And when she continues, ". . . subjected to cosmic radiations of a different kind," one wants to know what is meant by a cosmic radiation of *any* kind. In support of Miss Kavan's affirmation that "at night most human beings die and are born," one asks for statistics; and in support of Miss Kavan's assertion that her text is written in the "dream tongue we all, as a matter of course, have spoken in sleep and childhood," one inquires whom Miss Kavan means by "we all." Certainly, even as a matter very much *out* of course, this reviewer was never capable of an infant- or sleep-speech of such fineness as the following: "the blessed genii who walk about in the light gazing with blissful eyes of still, eternal clearness. The perennially clear eye of the Heaven-Born opens to a stare of shockingly bright moonlight. The eye is located at presumptive Godheight so that the terrestrial globe is seen as if from an airplane cruising over it at about three thousand feet." And I pick my passage at random; there are others of an even more exacerbated delicacy.

But, as I say, none of this would be worth stopping over were Miss Kavan's book only an isolated instance of its kind, unrelated to the culture of our time. Actually, the author of ***The House of Sleep*** not only has a distinguished reputation both in her own England and in this country but also speaks for an attitude that is finding a frighteningly wide adherence among our literary advance guard. Almost in the degree that our popular writing has moved more and more into the power realm and tried to mold itself into an instrument to control a world of the most immediate realities, our art literature has moved more and more into the realm of shadow and dreams and tried to substitute for the grimness of reality the poetry of nonrationality. The very people who are in the advance guard of complaint that ours is a schizophrenic society have themselves, it seems, little better than schizophrenia to offer as a cure. (pp. 291-92)

Diana Trilling, in a review of "The House of Sleep," in The Nation, *New York, Vol. 165, No. 12, September 20, 1947, pp. 291-92.*

The Times Literary Supplement (essay date 12 March 1970)

[*In the following review, the critic discusses Kavan's depiction of drug addiction in* Julia and the Bazooka.]

For more than thirty years Anna Kavan, who died in 1968, was a heroin addict. Much of her life, which she tried on many occasions to end, was spent in psychiatric clinics. "Human beings are hateful; I loathe their ugly faces and messy emotions. I'd like to destroy them all . . . they've always rejected me and betrayed me", she wrote, defiantly claiming that with the help of drugs she and her beloved fast car could speed towards isolation, "the mineral beauty of the non-human world" among the cold high mountains where she would be aloof and invulnerable. Her paranoia obtrudes everywhere—even the considerable critical praise she received for ***Asylum Piece*** (1940) and ***Ice*** (1967) or appreciation of her talent for painting and interior decoration could not alter her concept of an inimical world or save her from despair.

It might seem, therefore, that this small, slim book of a dozen or so short pieces [***Julia and the Bazooka***] collected with an introduction by her friend Rhys Davies, would provide merely a depressing curiosity, a too-intimate intrusion into a sad case-history, the kind of tribute about which it is both impertinent and soulless to make literary comments. Yet although these stories may, as the introduction says, provide "some inkling of the reason why a person begins to take drugs", the striking—and perhaps frightening—impression they give is not merely that Anna Kavan was a very good writer but that it was drugs, and her paranoiac state of mind, that made her good. Because of her despair, because of her experience of hallucination and psychedelic vision, because of her willing, even persuasive, acceptance that she was doomed, she seems to have been capable of extraordinary insight and perfect control over the words in which she describes what it is like to be herself. Like Sylvia Plath, she deliberately uses the simplest, most matter-of-fact language about her state of mind:

Anna Kavan with her mother, 1947.

> Darkness thickens, rises, creeps up to my knees. To my waist. Vertebrae collapse, spine sinks into the dark. Hair goes next. Face now. Eyes sucked out of sockets, smooth as oysters sliding down the black drain. Suddenly they're all among the lost things. The dark ingurgitates everything, myself included. It's disturbing all right.

In all the stories there is an X, or a K, or "Oblomov"—a man, various men, who make some feeble gesture of involvement or love, who momentarily appear as possible redeemers in the shape of doctor, night visitor, or sympathetic companion. Yet only the impersonal race-track heroes, who adopted an unhappy adolescent girl as a sort of den-mother, unsentimentally sharing her from car to car, and sharing with her their reckless cynicism and gaiety, gave her the feeling of belonging, of living "a real fairy tale". Even this, the only happy period of her life, was doomed after "the extreme bad luck" of being saved from a fatal crash to spend two years hating the doctors battling for her life. In the title story, Julia, her plastic syringe ("my bazooka") safely in the bag hooked over her arm, lies alone under a dirty blanket, all the bright brave moments of her life flickering in confusion across the scene of her death by a flying bomb. It would not have done for Anna Kavan to give up either her "bazooka" which provided such a premonitory vision, or the bitter, despairing detachment which enabled her to describe the "nothing" that Julia has become: horrifying and poignant as this epitaph may be, it is also, paradoxically, evidence of a talent those doctors were right to save and which all her own efforts failed to destroy.

"Fruits of Despair," in The Times Literary Supplement, *No. 3550, March 12, 1970, p. 275.*

Robert Nye (essay date 14 March 1970)

[Nye is a noted British critic, poet, fiction writer, and playwright. He has asserted that novels should depict life poetically, and often rejects the conventions of realistic fiction in his depictions of the workings of the mind. In the following review, Nye examines drug addiction in Julia and the Bazooka.]

According to Rhys Davies, who has edited and written an introduction to the stories of hers collected under the title ***Julia and the Bazooka,*** [Anna Kavan] was a heroin addict for the last thirty years of her life and a syringe lay in her hand when her body was found. These rather gory and sensational details might not be thought worth mentioning if Mr Davies did not make a point of mentioning them. On reflection, though, he is probably right to begin his account of Anna Kavan's art with some such straightforward acknowledgment of her drug dependence.

I do not know if the use of heroin could be made to account for the febrile and highly coloured brilliance of some of her longer pieces; it seems on the whole more likely that she was a woman of clairvoyant imaginative power who used drugs to cope with the comparative drabness of the world outside her writing. What does emerge from these stories is the boredom and the cold, the inner emptiness and death-wishing deadness of the hardened addict. "Hardened" indeed is in this context merely a descriptive word.

At her best, Anna Kavan was as vulnerable and sensitive as any of the writers of the "great subjective-feminine tradition" to which Lawrence Durrell claimed she belonged. The title story of the present volume—a summing-up of her life, the "bazooka" being her pet name for the syringe—tells how far she felt she had fallen from that tradition, into dullness, monotony, death. "There is no more Julia anywhere. Where she was there is only nothing."

Some of these stories—for example **"The Old Address,"** in which an addict released from hospital comforts herself with the fantasy that her blood, spilled in a road accident, will drown the world she hates—fail to rise above the level of an organised hysteria. Others—e.g., **"Fog," "The Mercedes,"** and **"Experimental"**—are urgent and moving without quite satisfying, as stories, the tensions they postulate. Some half dozen things here, however, are as fine as the best sketches in Anna Kavan's first book, ***Asylum Piece*** (1940), and should not be missed by anyone who cares for contemporary writing. Chief among these I would place **"A Visit,"** a near perfect piece of work with a quality of rightness to its illogic that can only be termed poetic.

Robert Nye, "Death-Wish Life," in The

Guardian Weekly, *Vol. 102, No. 11, March 14, 1970, p. 21.*

The Times Literary Supplement (essay date 5 February 1971)

[*In the following review, the critic offers an analysis of* A Scarcity of Love.]

Anna Kavan's novel, ***A Scarcity of Love,*** is written with alarming intensity. Its fairy-tale touches and allegorical hints, combined with a structure which seems dictated by the progress of obsession rather than the conventions of a plot, suggest extraordinary violence and disorganization of feeling.

The story starts in a castle and ends with a dreamlike suicide in a jungle river, and the characters are seen clearly outlined, like a child's drawings, against frozen mountains, lush tropical gardens, vast mirrored hotels. At the centre of the story is a snow queen woman, who rejects her baby, forces her husband to suicide, and devotes the rest of her life to the worship and preservation of her beauty and the incidental destruction of men, who serve her as acolytes rather than lovers. The baby she abandoned is returned to her as a girl already mutilated by a loveless childhood, and the second half of the novel watches the girl grappling feebly for some possible life, disliked by her mother, spurned by a young husband, until she offers herself gratefully to that river in the jungle.

The landscapes of the book are projections of the girl's fogged, distorted perceptions, and the novel's considerable interest lies in what is a kind of territorial ambiguity, a constantly shifting uncertainty about the reality of the experiences which are so lucidly described and even explained. There is mindless cruelty on the one side, passive suffering on the other; or is this the way the world looks through tormenting paranoia? People, landscape, objects acquire monstrous and menacing properties. The more wraithlike and drained the girl becomes the more solid and bold become her visions of corruption and the characters who embody evil for her.

The battle between mother and daughter is fought wordlessly and without contact, they gesture with the sort of imprecision drowning swimmers might, and it seems difficult to intercept the struggle with either pity or horror. A bewildering aspect of the novel is the way that this scene blots out those other characters which are seen sharply for a moment—the doctor who delivers the baby and falls in love with the mother, the other frozen woman who cares for the baby and abandons it for the doctor—before they melt back, perhaps into a reality denied the girl and her mother.

"Death by Drowning," in The Times Literary Supplement, *No. 3597, February 5, 1971, p. 144.*

The Times Literary Supplement (essay date 14 June 1974)

[*In the following review, the critic suggests that* Let Me Alone *is fascinating despite its flaws.*]

Rhys Davies's introduction to the reissue of Anna Kavan's 1930 novel [***Let Me Alone***] suggests that its heroine's passion for mental and physical isolation, and her horror of marriage, are connected with the tenets of the women's liberation movement. But the Anna of this book would be appalled and terrified by the real beliefs of that group, assuming as they do all sorts of personal responsibility and effort on the part of the woman. Anna's life-style is totally parasitic, absurdly so, and it is only the extraordinary mesmeric quality in Miss Kavan's writing that intercedes for her heroine's self-pity.

After a childhood in the Pyrenees with a depressive father and a governess, Anna is handed over to her rich, feline aunt. At boarding-school she is taken up by the headmistress, Rachel, then transfers her attention to two girls. After some months of lolloping about at home, she is married off to a dry and disagreeable nonentity called Matthew, whom she sees as an escape from her aunt. Recoiling from his demands, she hooks off to see Sidney, only to find her in smock and gaiters, happily breeding dogs with another lady. So Anna returns to Matthew, accompanies him to Borneo, submits to him, then, finding that she is not pregnant as she had feared, suddenly takes a huge resolve to conduct life out of herself only, acknowledging no claims.

One of Anna's few positive remarks is to suggest to Matthew's sister, downtrodden and overworked in their mother's big house in Richmond, that she should go off and do anything rather than remain at home. But Anna has no such advice for herself, and so drifts irritatingly on, helpless, inert, suffering, and inflicting fairly basic wrongs on the husband whom she need never have married in the first place. The steamy but apparently chaste dealings with other women presumably don't count as intrusions on Anna's trembling spirit, for she summons Catherine to Borneo at the end of the novel to extricate her from her colonial and marital ennui.

The wonder is that such vulnerable stuff should be so fascinating to read. The secret seems to lie in a sort of obsessed courage; Anna is treated throughout as a justified philosopher; the reader has to remind himself that Anna's symptoms as represented are those of a person in the profoundest psycho-sexual trouble. Heedless of inconsistencies, risibility, a tendency to sub-Lawrentian repetition of particular words and ideas, Miss Kavan drives straight on, leaving the reader maddened, but still somehow interested.

"Trembling Spirit," in The Times Literary Supplement, *No. 3771, June 14, 1974, p. 644.*

Eliot Fremont-Smith (essay date 7 April 1975)

[*Fremont-Smith is an American critic. In the following review, he praises* Julia and the Bazooka.]

Julia and the Bazooka, and Other Stories [is a collection of] icily precise, intensely felt stories by a writer who achieved recognition only after her death, in 1968, and is still far better known in England than here. In **"World of Heroes"** a woman shields herself from particular choices (one lover over others) by sharing with her "heroes" the voluptuous risks of driving huge, fast sports cars. It's the camaraderie of danger that makes her feel alive, intensifies her perceptions, guards her against nameless mundane treacheries. And when she loses it, she loses all; she shrinks, her visions become constricted, the world reduces, closes in. The story is brief, crisp, as haunting as they come. The title story is in the form of an anguished obituary of an unhappy girl who became a tennis star and drug addict ("bazooka" is her jokey word for syringe) and died in the London blitz. It's like a series of snapshots, remarkably compressed yet revealing everything. All the stories come out of the author's own experience, as Rhys Davies's intelligent introduction makes plain. Death, the pain of shyness, perceptual lust (red flowers, fast cars, heroin), the terrors of strangeness and loneliness, extreme yearning and melancholia—these are the constant themes. The writing is pure ozone.

Eliot Fremont-Smith, "Spotwrites," in The Village Voice, *Vol. XX, No. 14, April 7, 1975, p. 33.*

An excerpt from *Julia and the Bazooka*

I know I've got a death-wish. I've never enjoyed my life, I've never liked people. I love the mountains because they are the negation of life, indestructible, inhuman, untouchable, indifferent, as I want to be. Human beings are hateful; I loathe their ugly faces and messy emotions. I'd like to destroy them all. People have always been horrible to me; they've always rejected me and betrayed me. Not one of them has ever been kind. Not one single person has even attempted to understand me, to see things from my point of view. They've all been against me, ever since I can remember, even when I was six years old. What sort of human beings are these, who can be so inhuman to a child of six? How can I help hating them all? Sometimes they disgust me so much that I feel I can't go on living among them—that I must escape from the loathsome creatures swarming like maggots all over the earth.

Anna Kavan in her Julia and the Bazooka, *Alfred A. Knopf, 1975.*

Janet Byrne (essay date Spring 1982)

[*In the following essay, Byrne examines the unconventional narrative structure of* Ice.]

The development of an apocalyptic strain in Anna Kavan's writing culminates in ***Ice,*** her only science fiction novel. The male narrator, who often is used as a direct expression of Kavan's thoughts and feelings, explains her turn to science fiction: " . . . My surroundings . . . seemed vaguely familiar, and yet distorted, unreal. My ideas were confused. In a peculiar way, the unreality of the outer world appeared to be an extension of my own disturbed state of mind." As the objective, "outer world" became distorted for Kavan, so too her narrator is "aware of an uncertainty of the real, in [his] surroundings and in [himself]. What [he] saw had no solidity, it was all made of mist and nylon, with nothing behind." Kavan's deflection to science fiction was thus a turn away from the familiar and external. She had found a new medium for the interworkings and the moral universe of the unreal.

Kavan's use of science fiction is particularly interesting in light of her previous writings. Throughout her career, Kavan consistently saw the world as peopled by characters who treated each other cruelly or foolishly, or were so lost in their own private hells that they had no relation to each other. As Kavan became increasingly obsessed with these themes, it appears that she needed a new technique to develop them fully, and thus turned from the subjective-feminine tradition in which she had established her reputation to the world of science fiction. The tenets and conventions of the real world were Kavan's bane, and the narrator of ***Ice,*** Kavan's mouthpiece, constantly speaks as though he were Kavan rationalizing her choice of a new genre: "The world had become an arctic prison from which no escape was possible, all its creatures trapped as securely as were the trees, already lifeless inside their deadly resplendent armour." When Peter Owen, her publisher and friend, asked Kavan during the 1960s about her predilection for science fiction, Kavan said simply, "That's the way I see the world now."

The last of her novels to be published while she lived, ***Ice*** is a searing interior monologue broken up by unexpected dream segments and other fragments from another time and place. The story centers on a nameless narrator in frenzied pursuit of a girl he once loved. Their flight takes them through a world ravaged by cascading ice cliffs, the result of a nuclear disaster. The world situation crumbles sickeningly and humans plunge toward annihilation, playing out their collective "death-wish." This rampant confusion and destruction mirror the inner turmoil of the protaganist, providing an appropriate background both for Kavan's concentration on the subjective experience of her characters and for the author's prophetic and highly subjective importunings. The dream sequences which abruptly interrupt the narrative reinforce the eerie, bizarre vision of the novel. They slip in with almost no demarcation or warning and slip back out as easily as brittle, ice-encrusted twigs snap off a tree in winter. The trunk, obdurate and implacable, remains as testimony to the continuing problem. This trunk is the heart of Kavan's sensibility as a writer: a litany of dread and despair, compassionlessness and real or imagined cruelty.

A few pages into ***Ice,*** we see that the nameless narrator is not so much a character in his own right as the manifestation of a divided self. He is part of the girl and part of a third character, the warden—a high ranking, ruthless official who presides over the general ruin with impunity, eating grand meals and bullying the others. The presence of the warden's functionaries, an armed, "sullen-faced" group of "outlandish, even menacing" men in severe uniforms, suggests that a state resembling martial law is in effect. The warlike state, characterized as it is by people acting out the most hideous aspects of human nature, seems to parallel the nightmarish confusion of identity from which the character triptych—narrator, warden, and girl—suffers. The narrator and warden wage a psychological "war" of identity, described here by the narrator:

> In an indescribable way our looks tangled together. I seemed to be looking at my own reflexion. Suddenly I was entangled in utmost confusion, not sure which of us was which. We were like halves of one being, joined in some mysterious symbiosis. I fought to retain my identity, but all my efforts failed to keep us apart. I continually found I was not myself, but him. At one moment I actually seemed to be wearing his clothes. I fled from the room in utter confusion: afterwards did not know what had happened, or if anything had.

Like the narrator, both the girl and the warden are nameless. At times the narrator seems indistinguishable from Kavan herself. For Kavan, the world was fraught with conspiracy, and it is not surprising that in a world of conspiring, abusive people, an insidious connection exists among the narrator, warden, and girl. "The fear she lived with, always near her, close behind the world's normal façade, had become concentrated on him [the warden]. And there was another [the narrator] connected with him, they were in league together, or perhaps they were the same person."

The narrative is complex in sequence as well as in voice. Though there is a time progression in the story, the dream sequences both interrupt the chronological flow of time and deemphasize and distort the weight of the plot, as the dream serials recur increasingly like symptoms of a worsening diseased condition. The arbitrary infiltration of the dreams underscores the narrator's hazy sense of whether the experiences are real or hallucinations. "I could not think. The hallucination of one moment did not fit the reality of the next."

Characteristically, a dream sequence is repeated more than once, and in differing versions. These aberrations of the original scene give a key to the narrator's mindset. The repetition seems therapeutic, too, as though Kavan were purging herself of these nightmares of which she is victim. In chapter one, the narrator drives through a frozen, remote, unspecified area to visit the girl and her husband. It is the second visit he has paid them. The first of repeated hallucinations occurs when the narrator imagines he sees the girl's slight, white, frozen body lying stiff and unearthly along the road, naked. He feels neither compassion nor pity. Throughout the drive such hallucinations recur, while at the same time the narrator dwells on his first visit to the couple. When he arrives this second time, he finds himself the butt of sardonic remarks from the husband. The girl's marriage has deteriorated; the man is coarser, more brutal and wraithlike; she is frailer, more withdrawn. She generally keeps out of sight, and the narrator remains for a short time only. When he leaves, he suffers another hallucination, as the interior of the house itself reaches out in a monstrous way to grab the girl, who has just whispered an entreaty from the doorstep. She seems literally to crack to pieces.

Chapter two begins with a rumor circulating that the girl has fled her husband. The narrator resolves to find her. He again reminisces about the first visit he paid the girl and her husband, and this pivotal scene is then elaborated. Curious, fantastic changes in climate are reported: the narrator tells of being in a room in the couple's house, chilled; but opening a window, he sees that the air outside is mild and that it is brilliantly sunny. Here he stops his recollection to summarize the present chaotic world situation in objective terms—foreign aggressors, government secrecy, the explosion of a nuclear device, clandestine politics—but the dreams have a stronger rhythm and a more convincing ring. The summaries of events in the outer world are perceived through the "mist and nylon" of a dream world; and as such, the contradictory route that the narrator takes to find the girl, combined with the surreal climatic changes, show that the narrator's compulsion to find this ever-vanishing image is an obsession rather than literally the point of a search. "When I considered that imperative need I felt for her, as for a missing part of myself, it appeared less like love than an inexplicable aberration, the sign of some character-flaw I ought to eradicate, instead of letting it dominate me." The narrator approaches a sense of entropy when he finds it more and more difficult to distinguish outer events from the preponderance of dreams. As snow and ice pad the visible world, obliterating his only truly natural referent, symptoms of dissolution consume him.

Not only does the self split indefatigably and uncontrollably like an atom (until it is small enough to be crushed, or diffuse enough to go out of focus and cause one to lose perspective), but the landscape, too, is unrecognizable; and time oozes into an indistinguishable mass. "The past had vanished and become nothing; the future was the inconceivable nothingness of annihilation. All that was left was the ceaselessly shrinking fragment of time called 'now'." As the narrator says, there is "a wider confusion, not of identity only, but also of time and place." Kavan herself spent the last years of her life in London in a house of her own design, shades drawn, shut off from the outside. Again, the narrator explains her retreat: "I . . . felt I had moved out of ordinary life into an area of total strangeness. All this was real, it was really happening, but with a quality of the unreal; it was reality happening in quite a different way."

[In his introduction to the 1970 edition of ***Ice***] Brian Aldiss called ***Ice*** the best science fiction novel of 1967, its year of publication. He seems right in suggesting that the scenery is unreal—"not painted to ape reality." I would take the analysis a step further and call the backdrops not scenery but mental landscapes, for in the final analysis there is no logical explanation for the narrator's varying states. They are represented in ***Ice*** as places, but they parallel Kavan's own vagaries more closely than they follow the plot line. In one, a bloody battle rages; in another, mild weather and euphoria prevail. These mental states are precipitous and come on as unpredictably as moods, just as in Kavan's own "world of reality her social conduct was apt to become erratic, passing too swiftly from the most delicate perception of a guest's mood to hurling a roast fowl across the table at him, then retiring to her bazooka and shortly afterwards [being] discovered on her bed reading a novel and eating chocolates out of a box" [Rhys Davies in *London Magazine* (1970)]. The persistent, plaintive keening of the earlier Kavan—her own personalized accounts in which she distorted reality because it appeared twisted to her—gives way in ***Ice*** to a total abdication of the real world.

Science fiction traditionally has been an outlet for novelists who feel that the world is nearing dissolution. In ***Ice,*** the narrator's deflection into many selves is symptomatic of a universal chaos that Kavan perceived, with the narrator taking his cue from his depersonalized, derealized surroundings. "It could have been any town, in any country. I recognized nothing. Snow covered all landmarks with the same white padding. Buildings were changed into anonymous white cliffs." Kavan's portrayal of the end of the world is ominous, for whereas in previous writings she had escaped into subjectivity, in ***Ice*** subjectivity gives way to anonymity. There is a more sinister tone, as when, for example, the impartiality of killing is stressed. Again, very specific instances of killing as perceived by the narrator are symptomatic of a more general, progressively deadened sensitivity to destruction: "The guards came closer, formed a circle round us. To shade their eyes, prevent recognition, or inspire dread, they wore as part of their uniform black plastic visors which covered the upper part of the face so that they looked masked. . . . They closed in, inhuman in their black masks."

Ultimately the dissolution takes place psychologically rather than in nature. Each of the three selves—narrator, warden, and girl—becomes a more vivid, extreme, self-centered entity. They do not fuse, and none becomes multi-dimensional the way a character in conventional fiction typically does. Rather, they form a color separation of sorts: placed atop one another, they make up a complex pattern of color, an intricate psychological texture, a disturbing, opalescent color exposure. It is a microcosm of the entire population, and it describes in particular the haphazard, unthinking way of life to which everyone has been reduced. As individual characters, Kavan obviously intended for these selves to be one-dimensional. To the frail, terrorized girl—the icemaiden who is a projection of Kavan—the narrator and warden are at times interchangeable, and she feels that she has no identity herself. As Kavan dissociated herself from her own identity in the real world, she created in ***Ice*** a paradox of recognition and derealization, making them synonymous, as perhaps she experienced them personally. "Nobody took the least notice of me," remarks the narrator. "I must have been recognized, but received no sign of recognition from anyone, felt increasingly derealized."

In a June 1980 review, Joyce Carol Oates suggested that Kavan "wrote most convincingly when she wrote in the realistic mode of her own life—her childhood, her marriages, her isolation. . . ." Oates felt that Kafka, to whom many have compared Kavan, had a deleterious effect on Kavan. But it is more likely, I think, that reality itself had a noxious effect on Kavan, stymieing her when she had to live in it, then acting as a catalyst when she wrote. In ***Ice,*** her tenuous connection with reality breaks, splintering like the cliffs and rending the imperfect order in which she and her characters had lived.

In the aftermath of the narrator's steady dissolution—ascribed to "character-flaw"—we see each self staring back in horror at the parts it has left behind, then running from them headlong into a hostile, hated, and hateful environment. The narrator has no positive, intact reference point left in nature, so he disperses into a science fiction nether-world in which "it's impossible to distinguish between the violent and the victims." Kavan found in her own life that judgments were handed down automatically and unfeelingly. ***Ice*** is a prolonged, metaphorical description of the scene of personal dissolution—an accident of birth, in one sense. Blame is being attributed here, possessions sorted out, and parts identified but never reclaimed.

In this sense, Kavan's most expressive single metaphor is a deathly ride in a car that seems not to be driven but instead has assumed a power of its own which it imputes to the paralyzed driver. Kavan hates and loves these huge, sleek automobiles. They appear everywhere in her writing in the most unnatural spots: tearing through forests and jungles, ravaging forest beds while they hurtle their passengers into a last-ditch, heightened, high-pitched paralysis. In cars, Kavan's characters temporarily survive the worst of hallucinations, mow down people and problems, slice through entire battle scenes:

> There was chaos, the guards had no time to interrogate me. I bluffed my way through and drove on. I knew I had not satisfied them, that they suspected something; but I thought they were too busy to worry about me. I was wrong. I had only gone a few miles when searchlights spotlit the car, I heard the roar of supercharged motorcycles behind me. One rider hurtled past, ordering me to stop. Just ahead, he braked hard, stayed straddled in the middle of the road, suicidal, his gun pointed at me, spitting bullets which bounced off like hailstones. I put on speed, hit him squarely, glanced back, saw a black shape fly over the handlebars and another crash down, as the next two machines skidded into the wreck and piled up. The shooting went on for a bit, but no one came after me. I hoped the survivors would stay to clean up the mess and give me time to get right away. The rain stopped, warlike noises died out, I began to relax. Then my headlights caught figures in uniform hurrying off the road, patrol cars blocking it, parked right across. Somebody must have telephoned on ahead. I wondered why they thought me important enough to send out all these people, decided they must already have found the man who should have been driving, and that the importance was his. They started firing. I accelerated, vaguely recalling the warden's story of crashing a frontier barrier, as the car burst through the obstruction like tissue paper. More shots followed harmlessly. Soon all was quiet, I had the road to myself, no further sign of pursuit. When I crossed the border half-an-hour afterwards, I knew I was clear at last.

Anna Kavan on publication of Ice, *1967.*

> *The chase had a bracing effect on me. Single-handed I had defeated the organized force which had been used against me. I was stimulated, as if I had won a fast and exciting game. . . .*
>
> *. . . I was pleased with my achievement, and with myself. I did not think about the killing involved.* If I had acted differently I should never have gotten here. In any case, the hour of death had only been anticipated slightly, every living creature would soon perish. The whole world was turning towards death. (emphasis mine)

Fleeting connections with these heavy mechanized animals give Kavan's characters the sense of real-world power that they normally lack. The brutality of a ride puts the driver back on his axis.

Kavan's intractably pessimistic outlook stayed essentially unaltered throughout her career. But in ***Ice,*** death is imminent and unavoidable, and in every way Kavan's characters have been primed for this type of dissolution: "I had grown used to the feeling that I was going toward execution. It was something in the distance, an idea with which I had become familiar. Now it suddenly sprang at me, stood close at my elbow, no longer an idea." Because they have been primed, they no longer lie in wait, subject to silent mistreatment by clinicians, executioners, a cold unwavering mother, and the other resolute officials who appear in earlier writings. Fleeing from their histories of abuse, they go full speed to destruction. The book's ending shows the narrator speeding off with the girl in a giant, high-powered automobile, with "the weight of the gun in his pocket . . . reassuring." There seems no more fitting way for them to approach onrushing disintegration than swathed in the artificial warmth of this inanimate, mechanical vestige of "the living world we had always known." It is their mnemonic incubator, this car. ***Ice*** was Kavan's novel of cataclysm. It is a departure not only because it is science fiction, but because in writing it Kavan experimented with a less wary, less personalized tone in an effort to convey something larger than personal doom. (pp. 5-11)

> *Janet Byrne, "Moving toward Entropy: Anna Kavan's Science Fiction Mentality," in* Extrapolation, *Vol. 23, No. 1, Spring, 1982, pp. 5-11.*

Sue Roe (essay date 11 May 1990)

> [*In the following essay, Roe looks at the sense of displacement and chaos expressed by Kavan's characters in* My Madness.]

[***My Madness***] provides a welcome opportunity to reconsider the work of a writer who has become something of a cult figure. [Anna Kavan] has acquired a reputation as a fantasist and as a writer of science fiction as well as inviting comparisons with Kafka, but as Brian Aldiss suggests in his introduction to this volume (which includes the "autobiographical" works ***Sleep Has His House*** and ***My Madness*** as well as her extraordinary novel, ***Ice***), none of these classifications or comparisons is altogether apt. Aldiss rightly stresses her originality, and draws attention to the symbolist aspects of her art.

Kavan was a covert heroin addict and a schizophrenic, and her writing nudges the world out of shape, offering insight in unique and unfamiliar forms. Like Kafka, she created characters whose sense of displacement renders others and their systems absurd, but her protagonists express not so much the Kafkaesque plight as the experience of being stranded in the scintillating inertia of an almost autistic world. Their interior narratives are more significant than their speech, and the organic world is perceived by them as being positively invasive rather than simply alien; living can feel like negotiating a chaos of shifting glaciers; one false move and they are likely to be banished from the human game.

Adults in Kavan's world are depicted as striving against the odds, endlessly trying to subvert the rules and invent new codes, and taking comfort from a leopard as readily as from other human beings (perhaps because a leopard, unlike human beings, can reputedly be relied on never to change its spots). The world of Kavan's child is precarious in a different way: exquisitely fragile, it begins in "a prerealist fantasia [which] opens up in an inchoate sort of Marie Laurençin dream of delicate tints. . . . a pearly billowing and a subsiding of fondant chromatics."

"Fondant chromatics" is a useful encapsulation of Kavan's technique. In ***Sleep Has His House*** it juxtaposes the kind of icing-sugar world in which frivolous adults recast childhood with the suggestion of a real child's studied and austere attention to the nuances of every single semitone. What follows is the heart-rending story of a child left alone to amuse itself with a book when what it really needed was someone to teach it how to live. It hardly matters whether or not this is the formative imagery of Kavan's own story: what matters is that there *is* a logic at the heart of her work and a place from which her art may be seen to originate. It is perhaps a metonymic rather than a strictly symbolic logic, based on suggestive contiguities and launching a series of risky flights from a kind of mental tarmac of deprivation and denial.

Kavan's vision constructs a nightmarish struggle to inhabit a world composed of often indecipherable and irreconcilable juxtapositions, shot through with inspiring new variations on the "delicately tinted" original. This selection contains enough of her work to give some sense of what, for her, was at the precarious heart of things and represents an important revival of an artist for whom there was never any question of manipulating it into crudely predictable forms.

Sue Roe, "A Scintillating Inertia," in The Times Literary Supplement, *No. 4545, May 11, 1990, p. 496.*

FURTHER READING

Biography

Callard, David. *The Case of Anna Kavan.* London: Peter Owen Publishers, 1992, 168 p.

Biography that includes a bibliography and photographs.

Davies, Rhys. Introduction to *Julia and the Bazooka, and Other Stories,* by Anna Kavan, pp. vii-xii. New York: Alfred A. Knopf, 1975.

Brief sketch of Davies's friendship with Kavan and the effects of her drug dependence on her career.

Owen, Peter. Introduction to *Asylum Piece, and Other Stories,* by Anna Kavan, pp. vii-x. New York: Michael Kesend Publishing, 1972.

Account of Owen's professional and personal relationship with Kavan.

Criticism

Crosland, Margaret. "Experimenting (2)." In her *Beyond the Lighthouse: English Women Novelists in the Twentieth Century,* pp. 186-92. New York: Taplinger Publishing Co., 1981.

Short overview of Kavan's life and career.

Pochoda, Elizabeth Turner. "Trapped Imagination." *Ms.* IV, No. 3 (September 1975): 42.

Review of *Julia and the Bazooka* in which Pochoda maintains that the extreme subjectivity of Kavan's work is detrimental to its artistic value.

Additional coverage of Kavan's life and career is contained in the following sources published by Gale Research: *Contemporary Authors New Revision Series,* Vol. 16; *Contemporary Literary Criticism,* Vols. 5, 13; and *Major 20th-Century Writers.*

Jakov Lind

1927-

(Born Heinz Landwirth) Austrian-born novelist, short story writer, autobiographer, nonfiction writer, and playwright.

This entry provides an overview of Lind's career. For additional information on Lind's life and works, see *CLC,* Volumes 1, 2, 4, and 27.

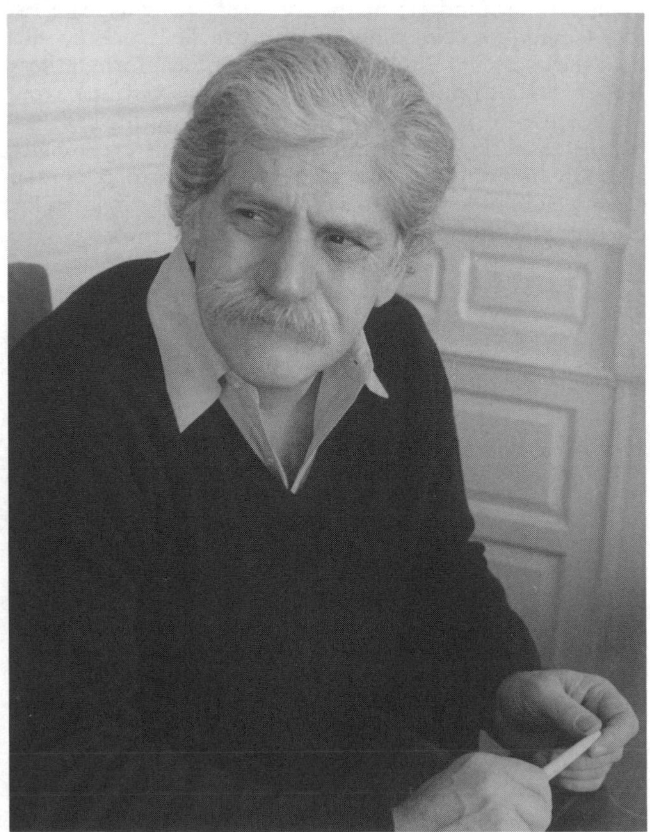

INTRODUCTION

Lind is best known for works in which he chronicles the atrocities committed by Nazi Germany during World War II. Citing Germany's mass extermination of Jews and general indifference to human suffering during the war as proof that humankind is intrinsically amoral, Lind often addresses the theme of human depravity through the use of black humor, allegory, and surrealism. While some critics consider his fiction excessively nihilistic, Lind himself views his work as an "attempt to save and change the world with the greatest possible speed."

Lind was born in Vienna, Austria. After the Nazis occupied his homeland in 1938, he was sent to Holland by a Zionist refugee group to escape persecution. His parents, who remained in Vienna, were eventually taken to a concentration camp and killed. When the Nazis invaded Holland in 1940, Lind fled to Gouda in rural Holland, where he worked on a collective farm. Eventually, however, German laws ordered Jews to leave the provinces and concentrate in Amsterdam. After obtaining a forged identification card on which he was listed as Dutch farmer Jan Gerard Overbeek, Lind traveled to Germany and worked as a deckhand on a barge on the Rhine river. When the war ended in 1945, Lind moved to Israel, where he lived until 1950. Since then he has lived primarily in England and the United States. Fluent in six languages, Lind has written in English since the late 1960s.

In his most renowned works—the short story collection *Eine Seele aus Holz* (*Soul of Wood, and Other Stories*) and the novel *Landschaft in Beton* (*Landscape in Concrete*)—Lind employs satire and grotesque symbolism to allegorically examine acts of barbarism reflecting those which occurred during World War II. *Soul of Wood* focuses on men and women who commit horrendous acts of violence—including mass murder, cannibalism, and incest—without any apparent shame or guilt. In "Hurrah for Freedom," for example, a group of incestuous Lithuanians eat their own illegitimate children; in another story, "Journey into the Night," a man informs the story's narrator that he is going to kill and eat him after he falls asleep. Lind's novel *Landscape in Concrete* addresses the mass hysteria associated with German nationalism in the 1930s and 1940s by focusing on a German soldier who goes insane. Regarding this work, Daniel Stern has stated that "Lind's landscape is as violent, as unstructured, as any modernist would wish. Yet there stands behind the lunatic horror a viewpoint, not summed up, only hinted at in imagery and allegory." While both *Soul of Wood* and *Landscape in Concrete* have been occasionally faulted for unsympathetic characters and fantastic plots, most critics praise their powerful depictions of the atrocities of war and the ambiguities of human nature.

Lind continues to examine the violent nature of modern civilization in his later fiction. *Eine bessere Welt* (*Ergo*), a novel about two men seeking to destroy each other, addresses the inability of some Germans to acknowledge their role in World War II. In *Travels to the Enu: The Story of a Shipwreck,* Lind satirizes postwar Western society through his depiction of a fictitious group of people who engage in meaningless sex, eat excrement, and initiate wars for no apparent reasons. *The Inventor* centers on a man who seeks to build a "Redemption Machine," a computer that would "know how to cope more efficiently than human agencies with the scandals of half the world starving while the other half drowns in unspeakable plenty." Critical reaction to these works is mixed, with some commentators faulting their overt polemicism and others praising Lind's satire, symbolism, and examination of morality and redemption.

Lind's autobiographies, including *Counting My Steps, Numbers,* and *Crossing: The Discovery of Two Islands,* have also received mixed reviews. While some critics maintain that Lind's thematic concerns, surrealistic narrative techniques, and emotionally detached tone do not lend themselves well to the autobiographical form, others recognize that Lind's documentation of his wartime experiences provide insights into his fiction. One critic has stated, for example, that "Lind derives from his experiences a rueful humour and self-aware toughness to cover the sheer weight of loss and misery which bore down upon his identity and the very language he spoke."

PRINCIPAL WORKS

Eine Seele aus Holz (short stories) 1962
[*Soul of Wood, and Other Stories,* 1964]
Landschaft in Beton (novel) 1963
[*Landscape in Concrete,* 1966]
Das Sterben der Silberfüchse (dramas) 1965
[*The Silver Foxes Are Dead, and Other Plays,* 1968)
Eine bessere Welt (novel) 1966
[*Ergo,* 1967]
* *Ergo: A Comedy* (drama) 1968
Counting My Steps: An Autobiography (autobiography) 1969
Numbers: A Further Autobiography (autobiography) 1972
Der Ofen (short stories) 1973
[*The Stove,* 1983]
The Trip to Jerusalem (nonfiction) 1974
Travels to the Enu: The Story of a Shipwreck (novella) 1982
The Inventor (novel) 1987
Crossing: The Discovery of Two Islands (autobiography) 1991

*This drama is an adaptation of the novel *Ergo.*

CRITICISM

Maxwell Geismar (review date 24 January 1965)

[*Geismar was an American educator, editor, and critic who was best known for his studies of the American novel. In the essay below, he praises* Soul of Wood, and Other Stories, *calling Lind the "most notable short-story writer to appear in the last two decades."*]

The best contemporary novelist is probably Günter Grass; or at least *The Tin Drum* is to me *the* contemporary novel. To me, the best contemporary playwright is Rolf Hochhuth of *The Deputy,* and what a work *that* is! Now, to these two names—who make such American figures as Saul Bellow or James Baldwin or Philip Roth look very inadequate indeed—we must add that of Jakov Lind as the most notable short-story writer to appear in the last two decades.

The long title story in [***Soul of Wood, and Other Stories***] is utterly unlike any other short story I have read. Lind was born in Vienna in 1927. Both his parents were victims of Hitler. He now lives in London, where he has published his first novel, ***Landscape in Concrete.*** He comes out of that central European Jewish culture which was in effect obliterated by the Nazi purge; and he records this horror even more directly and intimately, perhaps more poetically, than Grass or Hochhuth. And with what symbolism, what nightmare visions and surrealistic drama—what art!

[***Soul of Wood***] is actually a *novella,* and so complex and intricate that it is hard to convey its quality. A paralytic boy is left by his parents who are cremated in the little Polish town of Oswiecim. That is to say, Anton Barth has been entrusted to the care of Hermann Wohlbrecht, a one-legged Viennese veteran of World War I, who promptly deposits the boy's helpless body on an isolated mountain top, and takes over the Barths' apartment, since after all they are, or have been, Jewish. What else can a man do in the Vienna of 1942?

Or that is to say, Wohlbrecht *tries* to sell this purloined apartment to Hochrieder, the avaricious *Ortsgruppenleiter* (district leader); and for his pains Wohlbrecht finds himself condemned to the Vienna "sanatorium" where—

> Wimper sat in his shirtsleeves and held his syringe aloft like a sceptre. Strapped to their wheel chairs, the patients were rolled past him one by one. . . . Cursing his boss in the most obscene terms, he thrust in the needle with practised hand and pumped fresh country air (as he called it) into the patient's carotid artery.

This hospital, sanatorium, rest home, disposal plant for Jews and other criminals in Nazi-occupied Austria becomes, in this horrifying, brilliant, fantastic account, a microcosm of the whole Nazi system—where the "doctors" are all mad, and the patients are all sane, and condemned. One reads this story, one dwells in this universe of utter evil, as if in a trance—and the worst is yet to come.

Like any poet, Lind keeps balancing off the savagery (and beauty) of nature with the bestiality of civilization; this story is filled with such contrasts and imagery. But no writer could achieve the level of ***Soul of Wood*** more than once or twice in a book, and some of these stories dip below it.

"The Pious Brother" is the story of a former Nazi officer who has become a Jesuit painter and friend of the Princess Ernestine von Trautenstein. The Princess has given six sons to the Führer, "who had buried them one by one in Russia." This story is a gruesome concoction of perverted sex, high theology and Germanic cruelty. A lesser story, **"The Judgment,"** is the account of a mass murderer (this one illegal) and his father. There is another tale of a cannibal in a railroad coach.

At times, Lind seems a Viennese blend of Charles Addams and Roald Dahl—though he is more serious and more talented. Even in **"Hurrah for Freedom,"** the story of Lithuanian refugees who are incestuous nudists and eat their own illegitimate children—they have plenty of fresh vegetables but at that time in history could get no meat—even here, Lind presents the portrait of an Eastern European peasantry which is appalling.

There are some people, he implies, who should not be allowed to be free, and some of them are running the contemporary world, and some of them manage to live in it very happily. And in the final story, called **"Resurrection,"** this new European talent rises to another peak. This tale about two Jews hidden in a closet in Holland, might be from the Theater of the Absurd. Around the central situation Lind weaves another narrative which is hilarious, tragic and beautiful.

I am not writing this review lightly; I have not read a book like this one in some time. (pp. 4, 34)

Maxwell Geismar, "A Universe of Utter Evil," in The New York Times Book Review, *January 24, 1965, pp. 4, 34.*

Roger Klein (review date 21 February 1965)

[*In the following essay, Klein praises Lind's innovative narrative techniques in* Soul of Wood, and Other Stories, *but faults the author for failing to create sympathetic characters.*]

Of all the peoples in Europe haunted by the war, none, quite naturally, are more haunted than the Germans. Twenty years after the Nazi defeat, serious German authors continue to return to the subjects of war, Nazism, guilt, complicity, almost to the exclusion of all others. Indeed, it is not at all rare for a German author to go back, time and time again, to the theme of the Nazi past.

In other countries, this practice might raise doubts about the author's ability to develop. Not in Germany. Every new novel dealing with questions of conscience raised by the war promises to get closer to the truth of this almost incomprehensible period of history. Perhaps the German reading public senses that a great deal remains to be told, that the true feelings have not yet been captured; perhaps the authors feel that they have not yet found the methods, the right characters, the exact situations, which can satisfactorily convey the madness, mystery, pathos of those years.

Authors of other European nationalities—Elie Wiesel, Jorge Semprun, Giorgio Bassani, Andre Schwarz-Bart, Michel del Castillo—have all been content to describe the most incomprehensible experience of the war, the planned annihilation of large groups of people, within the framework of the traditional realistic novel. Obviously they felt that the realistic mode was still supple enough to allow them to overcome the reader's natural reaction to the death camps which Hannah Arendt describes in *The Origins of Totalitarianism:* "the very immensity of the crimes guarantees that the murderers who proclaim their innocence with all manner of lies will be more readily believed than the victims who tell the truth."

In the last ten years, though, the newer German writers have evidently assumed that the totalitarian phenomenon cannot be represented in the old ways. Günter Grass (to mention only the most accomplished of them) has used a wide variety of techniques to create the sense of bewilderment, despair, insanity, of the Nazi experience. He has pushed forward every innovation, depending heavily on distortion, fantasy, the juggling of time sequences and withholding of essential information. When it suits him, he borrows from Kafka, surrealism, the *nouveau roman.* Because of his immense talents, but also because of his daring, he has emerged without question as the leading, most adventurous, yet most serious young writer in Europe today.

Now Jakov Lind, though Vienna-born and Jewish, in his first book of short stories [***Soul of Wood, and Other Stories***] has tried to follow the German lead. His choice of subject indicates that he wants us to sense the horror of the war, though only three of the seven stories deal directly with it. The others involve cannibalism, infanticide, suicide (as do the war stories). They reveal a vivid imagination and great technical skill. Yet they are lacking something essential. What distinguishes Lind from Grass is that Grass still relies on the human personality, however fragmentarily presented, to carry interest and sympathy in his books, whereas in most of Lind's stories the interest is in the extremes of emotion for their own sake. Lind seems to want to see how far their hatred, cruelty or indifference can go; he is not concerned with characters as particular individuals.

In the longest story, which gives its title to the collection, a paralyzed Viennese Jewish boy, Barth, is entrusted to a male nurse by the boy's parents, who are deported. Barth can neither speak, nor close his eyes. In fact, up to the age of five, he never grew, then suddenly his neck developed at five, his shoulders at six, his arms at seven, and so forth. In order to take over the Jewish parents' apartment, the nurse has to get rid of the boy, but since he promised to take good care of him, he can't merely kill him off. He must construct a special crate, smuggle it out of the city, and finally leave the boy to die on a lonely mountainside, and a pursuit, complicated by the arrival of the Russians, follows.

What strikes one in this story, apart from the author's brilliantly inventive twists and turns and the boisterous style reminiscent of [Robert] Schweik, is the almost total dependence on the grotesque. It quite often leads to macabre comedy, but ultimately ends by wearying the reader. After all, in a story so inherently sad, how can one laugh with much pleasure? And how can one take seriously a tale which seems to pile up so many gruesome and improbable details? One admires the writer's skill, but is baffled by his intentions.

Other stories involve two men in a railway carriage, one explaining that as soon as the other falls asleep, he will saw him to pieces and eat him [**"Journey into the Night"**]; a man who comes upon a house where everyone is naked and drinking the blood of their incestuously produced children [**"Hurrah for Freedom"**]; a young Jesuit who commits suicide when he gives a proudly grieving Nazi mother the faked picture of her dead son, dressed up to look like an Orthodox Jew; a mass-murderer who plans to kill his father as he mounts the scaffold steps, but who is murdered by his father instead [**"The Judgment"**]; and [**"Resurrection"**], the only affecting story in the book, about two bickering Jews (one of whom pretends to be Christian) hidden from the Nazis in an Amsterdam home. Here again, by emphasizing the grotesque and the ironic, rather than creating particular characters, Lind often achieves an atmosphere of anonymity and relentless barbarity. Yet without the glimmer of compassion anywhere, the stories become a series of freak shows without any moral impact. They ring hollow and bring us no closer to the truth of the holocaust. (pp. 4, 12)

Roger Klein, "Punching Away at Our Stomachs," in Book Week—New York Herald Tribune, *February 21, 1965, pp. 4, 12.*

Time (review date 19 March 1965)

[*In the following review, the anonymous critic discusses Lind's treatment of evil in* Soul of Wood, and Other Stories.]

[The disturbing fables in ***Soul of Wood, and Other Stories***] might have as their epigraph the theme of Goya's nightmarish etching cycle, the Caprichos: "The sleep of reason produces monsters." With merciless humor, Goya gave the forms of grotesque man-beasts to 18th century hypocrisies. Jakov Lind, writing cheerily of cannibals and cripples in Nazi Germany, imprisons the reader in sweaty dreams of guilt. The guilt is not merely German. Lind's force lies in his ability to suggest that the sleep of reason in this century produced not only monsters but a monstrous complicity—a pact signed and mutually witnessed by murderers, accessories, victims and the world's bystanders.

Lind, the son of Austrian Jews who were deported and killed by the Nazis, mocks German pretensions of decency with slapstick caricature in [***Soul of Wood***]. Wolbricht, the protagonist, prides himself on his honesty. A one-legged veteran of World War I, he is employed by a Jewish couple to care for their paralytic son, Anton. When the parents are ordered off to an extermination camp, he agrees to take care of Anton in return for the lease to their apartment.

After the parents are carted off, does Wolbricht take the easy course and turn Anton over to the authorities? Certainly not: he is honest. At great trouble to himself, he smuggles the boy to the country in a crate and leaves him alone in a mountain cabin with a three-week supply of food. Anton cannot feed himself, of course, being paralytic, but that is not Wolbricht's problem. Thinking well of himself, he returns to the city to sell the apartment lease. But what's this? A bump on his forehead the size of a pigeon's egg. Wolbricht presses the bump in, but pop, it comes out on the back of his head. He presses again. Pop, over one ear. Again. This time on the top of his head. That's better, he can wear his hat over it. No harm done.

In this caricature of conscience, gaily colored symbols jump at the reader like pop-up pictures in a children's book. It must be painful to be a German and read this novella: it is hard enough to read it as a bystander.

"Journey into the Night" is particularly hallucinatory. Two men are taking an overnight train to Paris. One tells the other in a friendly way that he is a cannibal and intends to eat his companion as soon as he falls asleep. Ridiculous, naturally. No, really, the first man is quite serious. He opens a small satchel and brings out a salt shaker and tools for dismembering a body.

"I don't believe a word of it. You can't saw me up."

"I can't eat you as you are. Sawing's the only way."

Half-mad himself by now, half-asleep, the traveler muses: "Here is a madman, he wants to eat me. At least he wants something. What do I want? Not to eat anybody. Is that so noble?"

The traveler blunders free at last, but the cannibal, too, escapes. "He stepped cautiously down the embankment and vanished in the dark. Like a country doctor on his way to deliver a baby." Evil lives, Lind is saying; it lives. (pp. 116, 118)

"A Monstrous Complicity," in Time, *New York, Vol. 85, No. 12, March 19, 1965, pp. 116, 118.*

Howard Green (review date Summer 1965)

[*In the following review of* Soul of Wood, and Other Stories, *Green praises Lind's integration of fantasy and realism, as well as his examination of the brutality underlying civilized existence.*]

The "magic" in ***Soul of Wood*** is an element of fable, extravagant and horrifying, interwoven with reality to elicit an acute sense of nightmare. Death and the perception of dread live on every page; and perhaps most terrifying of all is his power of making "normal experience" seem like the dream from which we must always and finally awaken to find ourselves in the reality of nightmare. And there is no melodrama here, no bombast—on the contrary, a dispassionate and matter-of-fact tone and a sustained play of grotesque and sardonic humor.

In [**"Hurrah for Freedom"**] an Austrian doctor travelling in Sweden spends the night with a Lithuanian family of refugees—pale, bloated, ugly—who live completely naked in their overheated house with its piano and television set and other mechanical comforts . . . and eat their own children. In another, [**"Journey into the Night"**] the narrator is alone in the compartment of a train with a man who tells him that he is going to kill him, cut him up and eat him as soon as he falls asleep. He describes the process of dissection very precisely and meticulously, and the narrator saves himself only by pulling on the emergency cord, at which point the cannibal lets himself out and disappears in the dark, "Like a country doctor on his way to deliver a baby."

From *Soul of Wood* there emerges the warning—never stated, always chillingly implied—that Nazi inhumanity was no aberrant historical explosion, but the manifestation of a brutality which lies just beneath the civilized life we like to think of as normal and which is always liable to erupt. After reading Lind, this is a danger one is never likely to forget.

—Howard Green

I mention these stories, not because they are the best, although they are very good, but because they suggest something about Lind that one may overlook. His parents were deported and killed after Hitler took over Austria, and since three of these stories, including the title story (which is the longest and most impressive) are about the Nazi experience, one might assume that it is the Nazi experience which he is essentially writing about. To a certain extent this is true, of course, but from this extraordinary book there emerges the warning—never stated, always chillingly implied—that Nazi inhumanity was no aberrant historical explosion, but the manifestation of a brutality which lies just beneath the civilized life we like to think of as normal and which is always liable to erupt. After reading Lind, this is a danger one is never likely to forget. (p. 289)

Howard Green, "The Countess' Hat," in The Hudson Review, *Vol. XVIII, No. 2, Summer, 1965, pp. 278-89.*

Christopher Lehmann-Haupt (review date 20 June 1966)

[*Lehmann-Haupt is a prominent American critic who has served as chief daily book reviewer for the* New York Times *since 1969. In the following review of* Landscape in Concrete, *he praises Lind's use of irony and the grotesque, but faults his characterizations for being "disconnected from humanity."*]

Gauthier Bachmann, the focal character of Jakov Lind's second book and first novel, ***Landscape in Concrete,*** is everybody's German soldier, a commodious receptacle for all the outrage, disgust and loathing inspired by Germany's conduct in World War II. Bachmann is a large, good-natured *Wehrmacht* sergeant earnestly seeking his duty near the end of the war—a lobotomized Till Eulenspiegel in fatigues. He is descended from a long line of goldsmiths and silversmiths—a craftsman. He has the deepest appreciation of art, music and literature. He admires fine technology. Nature's splendors move him easily to tears. He's deeply religious. He's clean and hygienic. In sum, he's a prototype, *"Homo bachmannus,"* "above consideration of nationality. He lives in wartime and when peace comes, he doesn't die. He can be used for anything, there's nothing he's not capable of. The salt of the earth."

Jakov Lind's hallucinatory tale provides Sergeant Bachmann with an ample setting to display himself. After helping to machine-gun 2,000 Russians to death on the Eastern front (Bachmann's most vivid impression of this experience is how beautifully they sang while digging their own graves), he has lost his regiment and been discharged for mental instability. At the opening of the book he is searching for a unit to fight with and prove his manhood.

His odyssey takes him first to Ardennes, France, where he captures, turns in and executes a pathetic deserter, in the hope of ingratiating himself with the unit commander, a homosexual whose lover the jealous deserter has poisoned. The gambit fails; Bachmann is transferred to Norway. There, as the tool of a mad Norwegian quisling who appeals to Bachmann's sense of pride, he blandly slaughters a family of four, all the while wrapt in wonder at the beauty and craftsmanship of a teapot. Back in Germany he joins his mammoth girl friend Helga. After a tavern brawl which involves them in a legal interrogation in which Helga becomes the object of the judge's masochistic sexual fantasies, Bachmann washes himself preparatory to making love to Helga (". . . forward march, to bed"). The act is consummated by Helga's vivid and frightening homosexual dream.

Finally, having mindlessly violated every human decency, Bachmann is declared sane. He abandons Helga in a nightmare version of paradise to march off "toward the East, toward the war, to search for his regiment once more."

Mr. Lind has worked out this grotesque tale with nearly perfect cerebral irony. Bitter beyond tears, almost cheerfully macabre, it is a cartoon with animation by George Grasz. Yet for some disturbing reason, reading the book is like watching a movie without hearing its soundtrack. One recognizes the meaning, but the effect is muffled; it touches no nerve endings.

The fault is partly the language. For an American audience there is a dated quality to expressions like "sawing the wood" (sleeping), "bean" (head), "wild and woolly" and similar archaisms that bounce up throughout the text. Perhaps such expressions are accurate translations of German equivalents, and perhaps the German blends with the satirical texture of the story. Either literary German is more resistant than English to idiomatic mutation or the translation is plain bad. In any case, in English the idioms of ***Landscape in Concrete*** are out of phase, and satire of such weight needs the support of piercingly sharp language.

But more significantly, the characters and plot of Mr. Lind's novel are so appallingly grotesque, so disconnected from humanity, that the reader must retain intense private rage and fresh memory of the 20-year-old nightmare to be directly engaged by the emotion generated by the book.

And we have been reminded most eloquently—by Günter Grass, Heinrich Böll, Uwe Johnson, Hans Hellmut Kirst and Jakov Lind himself, in his collection of short stories, ***Soul of Wood***—that to be alive in Germany 20 years ago was not exactly a source of strength and joy. Jakov Lind's novel approaches quaintness. That's probably the most frightening thing about it.

Christopher Lehmann-Haupt, "A Plague Revisited," in The New York Times, *June 20, 1966, p. 31.*

Daniel Stern (review date 25 June 1966)

[*Stern is an American novelist whose works include* The Suicide Academy *(1968) and* An Urban Affair *(1980). In the review below, he praises Lind for transcending nihilism and presenting man as a "meaning-seeking animal" in* Landscape in Concrete.]

There is a notion abroad that history has gotten away from us; that our lives are beyond control; that there are no points of reference which mean anything any more. This nihilistic nonsense, which was not true when Swift wrote his infuriated *Modest Proposal,* was no more true when Joseph Heller wrote *Catch-22.* The idea has, however, bred a host of whining or abstractly cool writers who say, in effect, "Don't expect us to create something with meaning or value when everything is upside down and no one can be sure he believes in anything any more—or, worse, that the man next to him could believe anything *he* might possibly believe in."

In France Robbe-Grillet and Sarraute are attempting to substitute pure experience for the Balzacian novel of moral psychology. In America Hubert Selby, Jr., presents a world of empty violence with absolute detachment and a careful avoidance of point of view (which is itself, of course, a strong point of view). The only choice left us, the implication is clear, is between the boy-scout moralities of Herman Wouk and the amoral, a-literary stance of William Burroughs.

The latest voice to give the lie to this position is that of the Austrian Jakov Lind. And let us thank whatever gods preside over literature for him. Because Lind writes like a devil (and don't forget that Lucifer was an angel), and he deals with the contemporary nightmare at its most desperate. As in ***Soul of Wood,*** his first book of short stories, Lind's actual material in his novel ***Landscape in Concrete*** is the Third Reich near the end of World War II. But the overtones are far-reaching. Lind's landscape is as violent, as unstructured as any modernist would wish. Yet there stands behind the lunatic horror a viewpoint, not summed up, only hinted at in imagery and allegory. It lends to Lind's picture of the abyss the stature of prophecy.

The madness commences at once as we meet, on the first page, Sergeant Gauthier Bachmann, who was separated from his regiment after it was almost wiped out in the mud at Voroshenko. He has been told that he is to be discharged due to combat fatigue, or the German version of it. He knows better than the Board of Officers. Discharged? Ridiculous. As Bachmann says to the Lieutenant who tells him to go home and forget about fighting: "No, I'm not sick any more than millions of my comrades who are fighting for their country right now. If I'm sick, so is all Germany, all Europe, the whole world . . . I'm ready to die, to die, yes, to make the supreme sacrifice! IS THAT MADNESS?"

Thus having proved his sanity to his own satisfaction, Bachmann presses forward in the search for his lost regiment. ***Landscape in Concrete*** is the picaresque tale of his adventures along the way. Funny, bloody, and more than a little crazy, they form an explosive journey that is continuously fascinating.

Bachmann's insistence on serving, on killing, is as single-minded as that of the hero of *Catch-22* on making his separate peace. It has already brought him into the orbit of Schnotz, a soldier who poisoned his company cook because of homosexual jealousy. In his zeal to serve, Bachmann is tricked into executing Schnotz a few hours before the poisoner's pardon comes through.

Pushing on, Bachmann arrives in Norway, where he meets Hjalmar Halftan and is immediately embroiled in the latter's private vendetta with the family of a young man who, he feels, has threatened him. There ensues a blood bath, described with such detachment that every paragraph is like a slap in the face, in the course of which Bachmann shoots a couple and their cook and disembowels their son.

Just before this Bachmann has admired a beautiful silver tea set by the artisan Carl Erzman. (In civilian life Bachmann was a silversmith, one of a long line of craftsmen.) He concentrates half on the slaughter and half on the tea set; when he finally leaves the corpse-strewn scene he is tempted to steal the teapot. But no—"good upbringing is stronger than greed." There is a hint of even deeper truth in the reaction of the murdered couple's daughter to the sight of her parents' bodies: "That's what I've always longed for, said Gudrun, her smile was like a mask over her lips, I've dreamed of it often. And now it's come true." Even Halftan is shocked at this. And Bachmann thinks, "Here we sit, the two of us, Halftan and I, we've turned to stone animals . . . "

Halftan later kills the cold-blooded daughter and then himself. But even here he is in search of some mad vision that will place himself, his murders, God, everything in some kind of meaningful order.

This horrendous episode brings Bachmann to his senses, temporarily. He returns to seek his old girl friend, Helga, with marriage and civilian life on his mind. But numerous difficulties intervene, among them Police Chief Muschel. In this section the emphasis shifts abruptly from death to sex. Here the range of experience is equally varied; the sexual life, too, has been deranged by the times. The long-drawn-out scene in which Muschel interrogates Bachmann and Helga while entertaining a delicate and exquisitely imaginative sexual fantasy about Helga is brilliant comedy. A real though pallid sexual encounter between Helga and Bachmann is transformed in her mind into a burning Lesbian dream.

One of the extraordinary dimensions Lind brings to our understanding of the German nightmare is the element of fantasy. We have learned the hard lesson that very real dead bodies may be the result of unreal but driving inner fantasies. In tapping them and in relating them to human experience, although in the extreme, Lind is connecting us all to the violent horror in which our century's drama has taken place. Our idealistic ambitions and our passions have led us into hell, Lind seems to be suggesting. And by presenting ambition at its most extreme, as well as the wildest fantasies of murder and sexuality, in the cold light of realistic action, Lind is speaking directly to his reader: *hypocrite lecteur, mon semblable, mon frère.*

To this end Jakov Lind's style serves him as an extraordinarily flexible instrument. The wildest flights of poetry are followed by passages of plain prose, like a dash of cold water in the face. Bachmann is no mere fanatic. He is subject to wild fits of grief at the way things are. He is full of philosophical maxims for good behavior upon which he reflects between murders. He recognizes horrible onslaughts against other human beings in all their desperation, and moments later sees them as ordinary occurrences, all in a day's living. One remembers the replies of concentration camp guards when they were being interrogated about their ghastly duties. They too rode a pendulum between blood and banality. In our time midnight often arrives at noon.

Landscape in Concrete is a mad, brilliant book that calls to mind Emily Dickinson's phrase "zero in the bone." In presenting one of the most piercing pictures of the nihilism of this century, Lind has gone beyond nihilism. (It is no accident, by the way, that his hero is fond of quoting Nietzsche.) God is deaf (or dead) in Lind's world, and Man is in imminent danger of turning into stone. But his man is a meaning-seeking animal. And in his own wild way he has not stopped seeking. Destined by his family tradition to create beautiful things out of precious metal, he destroys instead. Yet the other possibility is always there, and it makes this not merely a startling and shivery book but a valuable one. (pp. 25-6)

Daniel Stern, "A Contemporary Nightmare," in The Saturday Review, *New York, Vol. XLIX, No. 26, June 25, 1966, pp. 25-6.*

Ross Wetzsteon (review date 3 July 1966)

[*Wetzsteon is an American critic. In the following review of* Landscape in Concrete, *he praises Lind for "translating into art the simultaneously incomprehensible and omnipresent terrors of our age."*]

Reason is a parody of sanity. Priding ourselves on our rationality, we behave monstrously. Obeying the logic of self-preservation, we approach race suicide. In his insistence that the experience of our century is not insane but "reasonable," Jakov Lind is one of the handful of writers who can even begin to utter, if only in grunts, the first syllables of the unspeakable.

The key to understanding Lind's fiction (his highly praised collection of short stories, ***Soul of Wood,*** and now his first novel [***Landscape in Concrete***]), is to realize that despite its setting in war-time Germany, despite its subject matter of madness and mass murder and even cannibalism, it deals not with excess but with normality. For to Lind, an Austrian Jew who survived the war years on forged papers, the horrors of the 20th century are not a grotesque aberration but merely a small distortion here, a slight exaggeration there, a few subtle changes in emphasis—so that inhumanity is not the reverse image of humanity but its recognizable caricature.

Lind's discovery, in short, is that in attempting to comprehend the incomprehensible, we've tried too hard. The world seems upside down, so we stand on our heads; experience seems irrational, so we hold a mirror up to madness. But seeking the source of the cataclysm of contemporary history only in these extremes is like trying to hold the end of a yawn, stretching your mouth wider and wider, forcing open your jaws, contracting your throat, reaching, reaching—and finally locking your jaw. In our search for anti-Christs, we find only Eichmanns. In pursuit of the nature of evil, we discover only banality. And most ironic of all, our attempt at understanding ends in the acceptance of insanity.

Instead of trying to rediscover the norms our experience seems to contradict, Lind accepts that experience itself as the norm. Instead of trying to go beyond, he goes back. Back to the irreducible human acts of murder and urination, to prayer and execution and "taking the wool out of our bellybuttons." Back to the flat declarative sentence: "When you lose your way in the Ardennes," the novel begins, "you're lost"—as if to ask, how much can one really say? And finally back to Eden, for the novel ends in a second Paradise, after the holocaust, a monstrous Adam and Eve wandering in a garden of hot ashes and charred wood and asking if even rebirth could redeem man from bestiality.

Lind's naturalistic allegory, a unique and powerful blend of journalism and fairy tale, relates the grotesquely reasonable adventures of Gauthier Bachmann, a 300-pound Wehrmacht sergeant. Discharged as mentally unfit after taking part in a disastrous battle on the Russian front, Bachmann tries to regain his rationality by finding the remnants of his regiment—an odyssey in search of not Ithaca but Troy. Having seen thousands of his fellow soldiers sink dead into the mud, as if killed by the earth and not by men, he wants to restore rationality in nature as well: ". . . all those weeds, and the grass growing wherever it feels like it. Everything scattered all over the place. One big chaos. It's got to be put in order. Somebody ought to pick it all up, sort it out carefully. . . . When it is all put under the concrete and the sun shines fiercely on it, nobody'll know any more what's underneath."

Essentially three separate stories, a triptych of terror, Bachmann's search for reason takes him from firing squads in the Ardennes to decapitation in Norway to a slapstick *Götterdämmerung* in Germany, the thousand-year Reich burlesqued in bar brawls and belches and bad dreams in Brünnhilde's bed—and in the end to the echoless "extinguished landscape" where finally "everything fitted strangely together."

At first, Lind's characteristic device seems to be irony. But irony implies a norm to be reversed and Lind allows us none. Or rather, when every situation (and nearly every sentence) is ironic, the ironic situations themselves become the norm. One passes beyond irony into chaos—or reality. For example, Bachmann accidentally kills a fellow soldier rather than an "enemy"—but don't we always kill our own? He is told that "most of the duties a war imposes on us . . . are revolting, let's face it, insane, and yet the soldier who performs them has to be fully responsible"—an irony that is built into reality and becomes a norm of "rational" behavior. Even though his novel contains no concentration camps, no combat scenes, no Jews, and certainly no "Nazis," Lind succeeds in translating into art the simultaneously incomprehensible and omnipresent terrors of our age—by focusing on a well-meaning character, his attempts at decency, his gestures of rationality.

War novels have often focused on gestures of sanity—desertion, for instance, as an act both of disillusionment and hope. For if society has betrayed its ideals, the self still has value: Frederic Henry deserts to make a separate peace, Yossarian to save his skin. But for every act of sanity there are millions of acts of rationality. Far from deserting, Bachmann is trying to *find* his regiment. Alone he is "a manure pile that breathes." But back in action he becomes "a rational Bachmann," a sharpshooter rejoining the men who sight each other along the barrels of their rifles and pull their triggers.

Ross Wetzsteon, "Normal Murder," in Book Week—New York Herald Tribune, *July 3, 1966, p. 3.*

Lind on the Holocaust:

"How could it happen?" people ask me now, meaning the *Shoah,* the Holocaust.

The answer is simple: It could happen because we couldn't and wouldn't even dare to sit on a bench in the park when it said on it (in big black gothic letters) *Fuer Juden Verboten* ("Forbidden For Jews").

We also couldn't do anything against Nuremberg laws that forced people in mixed marriages to divorce, ordered non-Jewish servants to leave their Jewish employers, forbade Jewish doctors to attend to "Aryan" patients (except for Goering who secretly kept on his Jewish physician). It was these slow and gradual, seemingly unimportant anti-Jewish measures aimed at dividing the population as much as intimidating their will to resist that gradually, (as in Kafka's legend of the Metamorphosis) turned men into cockroaches which you may then kill without moral qualms and apparently with impunity.

Jakov Lind, in his essay "Danube Blues," Contemporary Authors Autobiography Series, *Vol. 4, 1986.*

Irving Halperin (review date 17 October 1966)

[*Halperin is an American educator and critic who has written works on the Holocaust. In the review below, he judges Lind's emotionally detached tone in* Landscape in Concrete *to be repellent.*]

Although Jakov Lind has written only two books, ***Soul of Wood,*** a collection of short stories published two years ago, and his current novel, ***Landscape in Concrete,*** he has already acquired a considerable reputation. Within the critical view which holds that the sufferings and horrors of World War II should not—and perhaps cannot—be rendered by direct emotional involvement, but rather obliquely, dryly and, above all, coolly, Lind has been widely praised for his style, fantasy and lunatic humor.

Certainly these qualities are conspicuous throughout ***Landscape in Concrete.*** The protagonist, Gauthier Bachmann, a *Wehrmacht* sergeant in the last days of the Second World War, goes on a macabre odyssey in search of his regiment from which he was separated on the Russian front. Army doctors have discharged Bachmann after finding him mentally unfit, but this ruling does not deter him from wanting to rejoin his regiment and to fight for the honor and glory of the fatherland. The novel charts a series of adventures which befall Bachmann along the route of his search. In France, he is tricked into shooting a homosexual *Wehrmacht* cook who deserted his unit. In Narvik, Norway, on orders from a vindictive quisling, he shoots four members of a prominent local family. Returning to Germany, he is declared sane by another board of army doctors. As the story closes, Bachmann is still determined to find his regiment.

Nazi Germany was indeed a place of organized madness, which men like Wohlbrecht in ***Soul of Wood*** and Bachmann in ***Landscape in Concrete*** epitomize. Lind's wit is lethal in pointing up the compulsions of Germans for order, duty, solid burgher comfort, hygienic cleanliness, fate and "universal cosmic unity." But if the characters and their situation are true to the demented world of the Third Reich, the trouble is that the reader never gets beyond the frozen atmosphere of Lind's landscape: "As far as the eye could see a desert of ashes under a lead-gray sky. The stillness was palpable, as colorless and bare as the walls of a monk's cell. Nothing moved in the deathly silence, nothing crawled, rustled, or murmured." This same gelid condition is especially present in Lind's grotesques. They feel neither anger nor hate nor concern for one another. Mainly they keep cool. Bachmann describes how "without batting an eyelash" he killed four people: "No, I didn't lose control of myself, I wasn't upset, I kept cool. That's the main thing." All this is in keeping with Lind's intention to underscore the inhuman in Hitler's Germany. But the unrelieved, chilling lifelessness of the novel's characters ultimately repels the reader.

Certainly a sufficient detachment between the writer and his work is necessary to fiction, but there is an excess of distance in ***Landscape in Concrete.*** In a story concerned with the atrocities of Hitler's bloodletting, what is wanted is the kind of wounded outrage against totalitarian barbarism which characterizes Picasso's painting, "Guernica." Surely it is no disservice to art to approach work with the kind of anger and hate powerfully and *directly* rendered by other writers on this subject. A study of the differences involved is instructive. In *The Last of the Just,* Ernie Levy, having been assaulted and humiliated by Hitler Youth hooligans, in turn destroys scores of insects:

> The swallowtail landed on a violet. Ernie Levy enveloped the flower and the insect in his still moist handkerchief, and slipping a hand beneath it, he snatched at both things together, the butterfly and the violet, and then kneaded them between his already sticky palms. After the swallowtail came a dragonfly, a giant cricket, a beetle, a small butterfly with pearly-blue wings, other butterflies, other dragonflies, other grasshoppers. Ernie Levy ran through the meadow, arms spread wide, flapping his hands, gummy with vermin. . . .

Tadeusz Borowski's short story, "This Way for the Gas," also openly expresses anger and hate. A concentration camp prisoner is assigned to a special work detail to strip fellow prisoners of their food, valuable belongings and money, and turn the loot over to the Nazis. Despising himself for submitting to this assignment in order to save his own skin, he pathologically hates the victims he betrays:

> I am furious, furious, unreasonably furious at these people—that I must be here because of them. I don't feel any pity for them. I'm not sorry that they're going to the gas. Damn them all! I could throw myself at them with my fists.

By contrast, whatever hate for the murderous robots of Nazi Germany lies behind the writing of ***Landscape in Concrete,*** such emotion is insulated from the reader by the icily manipulated performance of grotesque caricatures. The novel becomes a sick-joke cartoon strip on a human disaster. In the end, Lind's novel does not bring us closer to the truth of the recent past. Moreover, coolness of presentation begets coolness of effect. The third and fourth lines of Lind's book may be read as a comment upon his method: "A landscape without faces is like air nobody breathes. A landscape in itself is nothing." (pp. 393-94)

Irving Halperin, "The Cool of Jakov Lind," in The Nation, *New York, Vol. 203, No. 12, October 17, 1966, pp. 393-94.*

Judith Sklar (review date 28 October 1966)

[*In the following review, Sklar praises Lind's "talent, invention, and savagery" in* Landscape in Concrete, *but faults the dullness of his protagonist.*]

When Jakov Lind created Anton Barth and Hermann Wohlbrecht in his superb novella, ***Soul of Wood,*** he created a great comic team. The two of them are grotesques, but they are also characters, live personalities with quirks and attitudes. We want to know what happens to them, and we read to find out.

Lind's first novel, ***Landscape in Concrete,*** is a totally different matter. It concerns German Sergeant Gauthier Bachmann, the only member of the 8th Hessian Infantry Regiment to survive the battle of Voroshenko. He has (understandably) suffered a nervous breakdown, and when the novel begins he is on sick leave pending discharge. But Bachmann's conception of his own state of mind is considerably different from the army's—"I'm not sick any more than millions of my comrades who are fighting for their country right now. If I'm sick, so is all Germany, all Europe, the whole world"—and he calmly sets out to find his regiment.

This is a brilliant notion, a classic statement of the madness of war, in which only "sane" men are licensed to shoot one another. And if Lind were able to sustain this inversion, in all its irony, horror, and bitterness, ***Landscape in Concrete*** would be a brilliant book. But he cannot, and it is because of the very nature of his main character.

From the first page of the novel, Lind describes Gauthier Bachmann in terms of the inanimate: he is "heavy and shapeless, like the blanket of clouds that covered the fields." In civilian life his specialty is metals: he is a gold- and silversmith. He cannot tolerate dirt or disorder, and he is comfortable only when things are precisely black or precisely white. "Dead things didn't bother him . . . they didn't remind him of anything living. If you could only get through the couple of minutes between life and death." Nature confuses him because it is chaotic: "Somebody ought to pick it all up, sort it out carefully, cut it down to size when necessary, and pack it all neatly in big boxes and little boxes."

Bachmann, in short, is not a man; he is a machine. He can be programmed to do anything. Burning villages, killing two thousand Russian prisoners in one afternoon is "all routine, nothing unusual"; murdering a family "without batting an eyelash" is "good and necessary." In fact it is proof of his manhood, confirmation of his humanity, because the most essential part of himself, his brute force, is being realized. In peace he is an ordinary respectable citizen; in war he "comes to himself"—he is a horse, pure strength, unconditionally available to the programmer. He says, "As a horse I could amount to something—as a man I am a manure pile that breathes." The choice is obvious: though he is momentarily converted to peace, at the end of the book he marches off toward the East, toward the war, to search for his regiment once more.

This rote behavior, this force without brain, makes Bachmann a very good symbol but a very dull character. Both the structure and the impact of the book rest completely on his automatic personality, and he cannot carry them. He has no complexity, no variation in his constitution, and it is all too easy to tire of his endless philosophizing and his mindless brutality. One hopes for some insight, some independent act, some passionate cruelty; but he witnesses only the monotonous, mechanical execution of orders. The net effect is the total neutralization of Bachmann's atrocities. One becomes anesthetized, like Bachmann. As he says when he kills the two thousand Russians, "it is more boring than horrible." This in itself is a horrifying vision, if only one could be compelled to continue reading. But instead one ceases to care, to be interested at all.

The most persuasive and exciting elements of ***Landscape in Concrete*** are the minor ones. Lind has drawn a grand succession of characters to accompany Bachmann: the weasel Schnotz who poisoned a Belgian cook out of homosexual jealousy; the Norwegian schoolmaster Halftan with a "talent for malice" who decapitates a young man, sells the head to his family, and kills them all; the lecherous police chief Muschel who pays no attention in interrogations because he is mentally stripping a six-foot woman.

In them all the humor-horror that is so evident in ***Soul of Wood*** is brilliantly equalled, for they, at least, are passionate. The theme of sexual deviation that runs beneath it all is ultimately much more interesting than the major theme. Germany is "a nation of queers," "governed by perverts." Bachmann, who looks "too virile," is always proving his manhood; yet he is "seduced like a child," "used," and "abused," and he is impotent with Helga, his girlfriend. Helga is actually a Lesbian; Muschel the police chief is a masochist who imagines welts on his back with relish. Everything is its opposite, inverted, unexpected, interesting, like the book's initial idea.

These things almost compensate for Bachmann's failure, but not quite. One keeps thinking, "What a brilliant idea, and what a disappointment." When someone has as much talent, invention, and savagery as Lind, and when he turns them on such important material, it is a disappointment indeed. (pp. 112-14)

Judith Sklar, in a review of "Landscape in Concrete," in Commonweal, *Vol. LXXXV, No. 4 October 28, 1966, pp. 112-14.*

Peter Wolfe (review date Winter 1966)

[*Wolfe is an American educator and critic who has written works on such authors as Iris Murdoch, Graham Greene, and John Fowles. In the review below, he discusses Lind's use of humor and irony to explore complex philosophical issues in* Landscape in Concrete.]

"When you lose your way in the Ardennes, you're lost. . . . A landscape without faces is like air nobody breathes. A landscape in itself is nothing." So begin the strange, tragi-comic fortunes of Sergeant Gauthier Bachmann, a three-hundred-pound lover and killer of humankind. The year is 1944 and Bachmann has been separated for some weeks from his regiment. A lost, misplaced soul whose loneliness is driving him mad, he has many familiars in recent literary portraiture.

But ***Landscape in Concrete*** is not just another existential novel about an anti-hero. (Let's admit that *most* literary works can be cut to the pattern of existentialism and run up the existential flagpole.) Lind teases us, distracts us, and mixes solemnity with raucous laughter. A comparison with American black humor is almost apt; like that of Kafka, Grass, and Böll, his keen sense of the macabre expresses itself in a peculiarly German sort of comedy—often called *Galgenhumor* or gallows humor. His omission of chapter numbers and quotation marks to set off dialogue chimes well with his attempt to rectify ordinary explanations of the way things work. Using discontinuity and reversal to describe how grievously our century has lost its way, Lind challenges all normal expectations: a German police officer entertains highly graphic sexual fantasies while he magisterially presides at a legal trial; stormtroopers convert a theological seminary into a barracks, which later becomes the setting for a homosexual murder; characters battle fiercely over trivialities but grin or yawn indifferently in the face of terror. Blending the casual and the horrid, Lind's canny verbal irony also demolishes conventional categories of logic and morals:

> Piptol is terrific. No cackling and howling like with arsenic. . . . Arsenic is all wrong. It sticks to your fingers, three weeks later you still have to keep washing your hands. Or cyanide. Cyanide is stupid. If you get a whiff of it, you conk out yourself. And it's much too quick. No, Piptol's the stuff. Piptol is O.K. Your eyes crawl out of their sockets like snails and they can't get back in. . . . Your tongue gets stiff and hard as shoe leather, black leather, and your nostrils contract so tight you couldn't stick a needle in . . . your ears hang down like dry leaves, and your hands . . . turn into claws . . . and then, very, very, slowly you suffocate. That's piptol, friend.

Bachmann, a former gold- and silversmith who must now work with baser metals, mirrors his torn environment. Cowardly, selfish, and treacherous, a murderous blond conqueror proudly serving Hitler and Fatherland, he merits all our scorn. Yet we prize him while we shrink from him; we recoil from him, weep over him, and laugh at him. His comic lostness in a lost world makes him supremely important. While he is not modern enough to succeed in today's society, his failure stands to his credit. He has religious scruples; he washes himself obsessively; he wants to find himself by finding others, namely, the members of his lost regiment. If his fellows took him seriously, he could convert his tarnished family tradition of guild craftsmanship into workable ideals. But he is ignored, duped, and, finally, turned away by the army.

As his name suggests, Bachmann is as outdated as the humane spirit of medieval handicrafts. Yet he endures. And he knows that being alive is coterminous with avoiding the stone-state, even if being alive means sickness, violence, and pain: concrete hardens, chips, crumbles, but only living flesh can bleed. Thus, while he prefers the companionable South to the icy blankness of the North, his hasty choice of friends and his inability to phrase his thoughts consecutively usually bear bitter harvest. The book's heavily symbolic ending is characteristically ambiguous. Bachmann rescues a young boy from an air-raid and then escapes the bombed city with his sweetheart, a sixteen-year-old prostitute, the stench of explosives and concrete shards numbing his already addled mind. Enriched by symbol, fantasy, and irony, ***Landscape in Concrete*** is more of a vision or an evocation than a direct statement. Its world is baffling and complex: the simple moral values of earlier generations help Bachmann avoid the cynical opportunism of deserting the army or acting as a political informer. A second look, however, shows that these same values have grown hopelessly obsolete and that Bachmann is causing needless pain by stupidly clinging to them. Capable of unspeakable crimes, he deserves the severe punishment he receives. Life staggers on at a tremendous cost in human suffering. But Lind makes us marvel that it can continue at all. (pp. 371-72)

Peter Wolfe, "End of the World Gestapo Style," in Prairie Schooner, *Vol. XL, No. 4, Winter, 1966, pp. 371-72.*

Edward M. Potoker (review date 21 October 1967)

[*Potoker is an American educator and critic who has written about post-World War II German fiction. In the review below, he briefly surveys Lind's career and provides a mixed assessment of* Ergo.]

Born in Vienna in 1927, Jakov Lind was transported to Holland on a children's refugee train in December 1938. His parents, who could not leave, were murdered. For two years Lind enjoyed relative security among the tolerant, democratic Dutch. Then the Nazis invaded Holland, and the Jews were rounded up and shipped "to Poland." They did not realize what this meant until they arrived at the gates of Auschwitz, Sobibor, and Treblinka. Lind survived, after spending two years in Germany with forged papers that identified him as one Jan Overbeek, a citizen of the Netherlands. These episodes are crucial to an understanding of his fiction, since they explain his preoccupation with "collective guilt"—a concept which appears at times to conceal a sense of personal guilt.

After such experiences, one is bound to have strange tales to tell. Lind began relating them in ***Soul of Wood,*** a brilliant, macabre collection of short stories, which appropriately begins with the line "Those who had no papers entitling them to live lined up to die." Predictably, these stories, often reminiscent of Gogol, Kafka, Beckett, and Grass, were filled with savagery; but the atmosphere of grotesquerie did not mitigate the author's ugly fascination with cannibalism. Accusing all civilized men, particularly blond ones, Lind specifically attacked the institutionalized insanity of the Third Reich.

In ***Landscape in Concrete,*** his not wholly successful first novel, Lind gave us Gauthier Bachmann, a typical German soldier, "a manure pile that breathes." *Homo Bachmannus,* as Lind defines the species, is above considerations of nationality. "He lives in wartime and when peace comes, he doesn't die. He can be used for anything; there's nothing he's not capable of. The salt of the earth." Madness, mayhem, and mass murder, Lind insists, are not to be equated with excess but with normality: he is dealing with the ordinary, even pedestrian events of our time.

Ergo, his second novel, is set in the 1960s. (In the original German the title is, ironically, *A Better World.*) Here the Nazis are treated as a generalized metaphor for contemporary "humanity," and the author's hatred goes beyond the bounds of artistic control, emerging as an indictment of Western man.

Only a filament of plot and a small clump of shadowy characters hold ***Ergo*** together. Roman Wacholder, his son Aslan, Leo Schön-Waldhaus, and Ossias Würz are the principal *dramatis personae.* They reside in Vienna, "which calls itself the teat of the occident and has suckled nothing but madness." They feel that no one is to blame for the war: "people who deserve a Hitler get a Hitler, and people who don't deserve a Hitler don't get a Hitler. Hitler can't help it." Wacholder, who has a semi-detachable, eighteen-inch penis weighing five pounds, wants to kill Würz, whose fate is "dirt" but whose philosophy is "neat and clean, the heritage of many generations of Protestant pastors and artisans." At first Wacholder tries to get somebody from the water department to help him blow "nerve foam" through Würz's plumbing. "You open up the pipe someplace, you'd know the best place, and I pour in two three bottles of my medicine, and when this joker opens the faucet, he gets it *whish swish* in the face. He'd die laughing. Wouldn't that be a lark?" This idea has to be abandoned, for the water department is uncooperative.

Next, Wacholder enlists the support of his boarder, Leo Schön-Waldhaus, who advises that Würz be done away with by reason rather than violence. "We take away his being by maintaining that he doesn't exist. . . . You won't even have to touch him." Leo quickly summons a conclave of Viennese citizens for the purpose of "removing existence" from Ossias Würz, "a mortal enemy of our society." There is, however, a catch. A vote must be taken, and it must be unanimous. If a single individual recognizes Würz's existence, the whole plan falls through. Aslan, who tries to be reasonable, secedes from the conclave. "The whole lot of you can stand on your heads, I know what's true and what's not true. Würz exists and so he's there and that's that." As a kind of reward, Aslan has his leg chopped off with an ax.

It is impossible to do justice to the "plot" of ***Ergo,*** just as it is impossible, in any brief space, to explicate and clarify its elaborately interrelated layers of symbol and allegory for Lind often equates insanity with reason, piles paradox upon paradox, and is not above pulling the reader's leg. In rejecting nonsense Lind purposely, sometimes purposefully, creates it. Sharply clear, nevertheless, is the author's hatred of Austria and his condemnation of its long history of anti-Semitism.

> A few mountains, a little water and a little night music. That's my country. The country of men without character. In this country a man's ashamed to have character. . . . A country that shipped off its own citizens as if they were rabbits for Christmas and has the gall to complain about it now is no country at all. I can't stand it here any more. . . . Why not come right out and say people are evil period and the crummiest of the lot are the Austrians.

It is equally clear that Austria is a metaphor for the history and fate of Western man. "Today persecution is infrequent because tomorrow everybody's going to be slaughtered. Today you only have a right to say Austrian if you mean the whites in the east and west in other words if you think that nothing has really changed and that's what you do think." The act of creation offers no escape: "We'll never be rid of Austria even if we write in Greenlandic like some of my fellow writers. That only makes the problem more unintelligible. Estheticism won't rid us of guilt. Behind an iceberg of hypersensitivity there's nothing but insensibility."

Ralph Manheim, an exceptionally able translator, has done everything he could with the extremely difficult German prose. There is much experimental writing, reminiscent of James Joyce; experimental typography, which seems merely quaint in English; interpolated letters and short stories, and complicated parodies of German and Austrian writers.

Ergo is a gloomy, mysterious book with flashes of genius and terror. It will be highly acclaimed and strongly censured. It is also an embarrassing book because, in his attempt to distill literature from horror, Lind occasionally shows that he is deficient in the discipline needed to make hatred, obscenity, and blasphemy functional. (pp. 35-6)

Edward M. Potoker, "A Distillation of Horror," in The Saturday Review, *New York, Vol. L, No. 42, October 21, 1967, pp. 35-6.*

Stanley Reynolds (review 3 November 1967)

[*In the review below, Reynolds praises Lind's examination of post-World War II Germany*].

Jakov Lind is an Austrian Jew who at 11 years of age had to go on the run in Europe from the Nazis. ***Ergo*** is about post-war Austrian and German war guilt and you cannot expect him to write about this like Margaret Drabble writing about the problems of pregnancy. He is obscure but unlike many other modern novelists he is not being obscure to make a small and insignificant talent seem like a big and significant one. His is the literary style that has come out of Auschwitz and Dachau, it was foretold in the visions of Kafka, and bears some resemblance to the later work of Beckett, but his style is the only style that a sane man, or at least a man with a background like Lind's, can use with a subject like this. We have all seen too many newsreels and read too many newspaper articles to be affected by neo-realistic novels about Germany's war guilt, and we have been bombarded too often with psychology to make a psychological novel about war guilt effective. So Lind's novel is inevitable, as logical as the weird logic and mad dialectics his characters use. Like most memorable nightmares ***Ergo*** has a simple plot. Wacholder is a grubby monster riddled with guilt and encumbered with an 18-inch penis, who lives in a ramshackled building surrounded by tramps whom he allows to live rent free. Wacholder hates Wurz, his former friend who lives in a hermetically sealed, germ-free house in the same city. Wacholder tries to get at Wurz with poison pen letters, with a lunatic plan to put something called nerve foam (once he has invented it) in Wurz's water pipes, and with a final scheme to legislate Wurz out of existence by getting enough people to agree that Wurz never existed. In the middle of this action we have the reminiscences of the main characters: Wacholder remembers how he killed a whore in Chicago with his enormous penis and how he fled back to Nazi Germany to find it almost beautiful with red and black flags everywhere and bands playing almost as in the Kaiser's time and Wurz recalls the days when he worked for 'the gas company'.

Ralph Manheim's translation has a smooth rhythm, something we are told most modern translations from the German miss, so the novel has a unity of tone that is usually only found in poetry. This is a poetic novel with a style as recognisable as Hemingway's *The Old Man and the Sea* or Genet's *Our Lady of the Flowers.* It is also a very funny novel. Like Beckett, Lind can bring on a music hall turn just at the right moment to lighten the action. There is an hilarious 'turn' where Wacholder and a newspaper seller called One Eared Wondra in the Other World talk at comic cross purposes. Yet even here Lind has his eyes on the message: what One Eared Wondra is saying is really a satire on the guilt felt for killing the Jews and on the phoniness of the supposed post-war egalitarian society. The novel, we are told, was a literary event in Germany last year, and naturally one cannot expect it to have the same effect on the British reader. Nevertheless, aside from aesthetic pleasures, it should give any reader a clearer picture of the tremendous and tortuous soul searching of the post-war Germans. Only the shallowest and most insular of English-thinking minds would attempt to pass Lind off as yet another heavy-handed Teuton. (pp. 593-94)

Ergo should give any reader a clearer picture of the tremendous and tortuous soul searching of the post-war Germans. Only the shallowest and most insular of English-thinking minds would attempt to pass Lind off as yet another heavy-handed Teuton.

—Stanley Reynolds

Stanley Reynolds, "Guilt," in New Statesman, *Vol. 74, No. 1912, November 3, 1967, pp. 593-94.*

Curt Leviant (27 November 1967)

[*Leviant is an American editor, translator, and critic. In the review below, he praises Lind's use of irony in* Ergo, *but faults the novel's lack of "inner logic."*]

Jakov Lind, whose two previous books, ***Soul of Wood*** and ***Landscape in Concrete,*** have established him as one of Europe's most original and talented writers, has in his works taken a central 20th-century experience, perhaps the most cataclysmic in history, and treated it with uniqueness and originality. Since no straightforward account of the holocaust can match the brutal reality, artistic interpretation of these facts must make a symbolic, imaginative leap. This Lind does, and there is nothing phony or arty about his symbolic constructions.

Lind's vision objectifies the emotional impact of the holocaust tragedy and its metaphysical hangover into purely literary terms: bizarre caricature *à la* George Grosz, and a Kafkaesque comic-within-the-grim. Characters are usually deformed or oversized, jokes on normality, the physical condition metaphoric of the spiritual state—wooden-legged Wolbracht in ***Soul of Wood,*** behemoth Bachmann in ***Landscape in Concrete,*** and in ***Ergo,*** Wacholder with his gigantic member.

Although the physical setting of ***Ergo*** is rather ambiguous—a vague Vienna of the imagination—its moral landscape is quite precise: the sane-insane nexus of Germany-Austria, a spiritual locale by now well delineated in Lind's fiction. ***Ergo's*** major scenes take place in two households whose inhabitants are exaggerated only several degrees beyond probability. Würz, a man incapable of love or hate, lives in an insulated, sanitized home with his wife Rita and her two sons, Arnold and Arnulf, stylish and morally perverse young dudes. Würz never leaves his superclean abode, equating his mini-world of neatness and order with freedom. His rooms are numbered; nature—stuffed animals, pinned butterflies—is carefully placed under glass, and the prime enemy is dust, against which are launched search, destroy and burn missions. But even dust doesn't burn clean, and the family's equilibrium is upset by smoke from the gas stove.

"We do our best," Würz cries, "After every incineration we take a hot bath. Plenty of soapsuds, plenty of water. . . . "

"Incineration" and "gas," words with a host of associations, are the key to the allegory: in the Würz home moral defilement has prompted the fetish of cleanliness. Guilt can be brushed, washed, scrubbed and painted (at one point Würz paints himself completely white, hair and all); yet, like the blood on Lady Macbeth's hands, it cannot be removed.

The other household, a ramshackle sty stuffed with 30 tons of government-owned paper, is the physical opposite but moral equivalent of Würz's place. As Würz seeks to extirpate dirt, Wacholder attempts in vain to get rid of the endless reams, which represent guilt in another guise. Wacholder, Leo Waldhaus and Aslan, the three proprietors, are sterile pseudo-intellectuals whose scribbling bears only the fruits of narcissism. Aslan is up to page 5 of *The Better World,* a novel he is secretly writing (Lind ironically uses this phrase as his original title in German—*Eine bessere Welt*); and Waldhaus, reminiscent of the intellectual buffoons of [Jonathan] Swift's satires, contributes to knowledge *The Placental Theory of Existence,* which postulates a set of theorems centered about the primacy of the afterbirth, and is dedicated to the elevation of nonsense.

Wacholder's zealous goal is to lure Würz from his lair through the use of a nerve shower—"a gush of words, gibberish, something outlandish and foreign, some kind of Hungarian." Since this scheme is impractical, Wacholder utilizes a host of epistolary tricks (increasingly incoherent letters) to assault Würz's psyche and make him return to "normal" life. (In Lind's world, every madman ascribes normality only to himself and insanity to all others.)

Here, antagonisms exist not only between households but within them, too. Würz's two degenerate stepsons plot against him, and Wacholder continually bickers with his two cronies. Although Wacholder actually did nothing, he proudly claims to be a very dangerous Nazi because he "wanted what happened to happen." To which Leo Waldhaus replies: "If they started locking everybody up who wanted what happened to happen, they'd have to surround the whole country with barbed wire. No wall would be high enough."

After Leo calls Wacholder and others complete idiots, Wacholder makes a little speech into which intrude the author's satiric sensibilities:

> I won't let you insult my people. We're a very old people, Leo, perhaps the oldest there is. We existed when nothing else existed, we had an emperor when nobody else wanted an emperor, and we had a republic when nobody else wanted a republic, we had Nazis when there were no Nazis and we had no Nazis when there were Nazis everywhere else. We had a liberation when everybody else was still occupied, and we got rid of our occupation because we turned neutral, when nowadays hardly anybody is neutral.

Würz, personification of perennial German order, is clean and efficient as clockwork, a cover for familial corruption and omnipresent guilt. With Wacholder we have intellectual puffery, disorder and filth: the paper that symbolizes German bureaucracy; and the gobbledygook of language that hides meaning yet puts teeth on intent. The two sets of characters, then, are not enemies, but interlocking jigsaws of one schizophrenic personality. Wacholder admits that Würz is half his mutilated soul, that an umbilical cord binds them. "Some pleasant kind of lunacy is always attractive. If I didn't have this life mission of liberating Würz, believe me I'd sometimes be tempted. Actually . . . I might like to change places with him."

Lind's previous works have kineticized allegory and parable, story and flights of fancy. Despite the occasionally surreal landscape there was a forward thrust, a central core, to the fictions. In ***Ergo,*** Lind expands the directions of his imaginative world, but the inventions are not thoroughly assimilated. ***Ergo*** has loose ends, action switches inexplicably in swift cinematic fashion, a surrealist graph rising out of control. Brilliant individual scenes coruscate throughout the book (Wacholder coupling with Frau Doktor Böckling, the Valkyrie-like state minister: Arnold's confessed perversions of the Würz family); yet as a whole ***Ergo*** is curiously static, lacking an emotional—though not necessarily a cerebral—totality and inner logic. I suspect the fault lies in the conception. Hitherto Lind has let symbol grow organically out of story; in ***Ergo*** he has apparently reversed his usual process and fashioned story out of symbol. (No doubt the light of ***Ergo***'s stage version will unfuzz some of the novel's murky corners.) Nevertheless, Lind's imagination, wit and symbolic architectonics are once more present in generous supply, and despite the novel's lopsided emotional effect, the reader's intellect is challenged to unravel meaning. (pp. 567-68)

Curt Leviant, "A Story Out of a Symbol," in The Nation, *New York, Vol. 205, No. 18, November 27, 1967, pp. 567-68.*

Geoffrey Wolfe (review date 6 October 1969)

[Below, Wolfe discusses how Lind's autobiography

Counting My Steps *provides insight into the author's fiction.*]

Lind loves mysteries, paradoxes and conundrums, often to excess. ***Landscape in Concrete*** is about a German soldier's odyssey through the ruins at the end of World War II, and it varies scenes of photographic detail with moments of encroaching insanity, and is enhanced by the jumps from careful reenactment to metaphysics. "Evil has its good sides too." Such puzzles belong in the novel. ***Ergo*** I found to be a preposterous bit of self-indulgence, a pastiche of [Samuel] Beckett and [William] Burroughs, a make-shift modern idea kit. It seems to hold its own exercise in contempt: " . . . only the writing of nonsense is worthwhile, since, as everyone knows, sense can have no sense." And: "I never hate what I hate. I neither hate what I love nor love what I hate. On the other hand, I don't hate what I hate either, and I'm not capable of loving what I love." More: "Literature ought to be abolished once and for all."

Now the antecedents for ***Ergo*** are clear to see. ***Counting My Steps*** shows that Lind's obsessions with identity tricks, his distrust of all consoling certainties, are born not of his reading but of his experiences. When he writes in this book that "to be schizophrenic is to be normal; unreality is reality," he means just that. To escape the Germans he assumed a variety of roles while he was an adolescent, when it is difficult at best to hammer out a single persona. He survived on his wits, by twists and dodges and lies. He spoke a variety of tongues, came to loathe German. His beliefs shifted chaotically: socialism, anti-Semitism, faith in superhuman powers, Zionism, belief in his invisibility—all these claimed his allegiance at one time or another. But since the war, Lind has been unencumbered: "No love and no hatred and no language."

And yet for all the terrors he endured, he tells us he has never seen a dead man. So his imagination is still hospitable to any visions of death that care to fill it. To get to the dead center of his fear he went to Germany, the only place, he reckoned, where he would be safe: "I was afraid to go anywhere but to the very heart of the monster. Inside the lion's mouth I would not have to fear the animal's teeth and claws."

It is lonely inside the lion's mouth, and dangerous. Lind writes his books in there, taking the big chances, daring the big dares. If he doesn't always get away with what he tries, someday he will. Now he has a new language and a new country. But: "To be is to be hated, I think." To believe that should be to exhaust the will. He still calls reading and writing "a kind of perfect insanity." He cannot mean it. He should stop writing it. It is a kind of bravado unworthy of him, and of all of us to whom what he writes matters. (pp. 127-28)

Geoffrey Wolfe, "Inside the Monster," in Newsweek, *Vol. LXXIV, No. 14, October 6, 1969, pp. 127-28.*

Christopher Lehmann-Haupt (review date 8 October 1969)

[*In the following review of* Counting My Steps, *Lehmann-Haupt relates Lind's life to his fiction.*]

Jakov Lind's fiction has always hit me like a local anesthetic—a needle in the spine. The deeper things get, the less one feels. His characters cry out and inflate empty word balloons. Their blood is raspberry juice and their bones are Dresden china. Their catastrophes freeze the reader and leave him guiltily unconcerned, strangely preoccupied with the surface of Mr. Lind's art. I had always thought that either he was badly translated or that the subjects of his short stories (collected in ***Soul of Wood***) and his novels (***Landscape in Concrete*** and ***Ergo***) were beyond the conventions of fiction—that the worst excesses of the 20th-century German character had drifted out of reach of irony and imagination. But now his autobiography, ***Counting My Steps,*** sheds new light on the matter.

It isn't what Mr. Lind writes about that is numbing, or we the readers that are numbed. It is Mr. Lind himself—his subliminal cues—that we have been responding to. ***Counting My Steps*** explains why that is and how it came to be.

Consider first the raw material of his life, apart from the form of his account of it. He was born in Vienna on Feb. 20, 1927, the son of middle-class Jewish parents—an unsuccessful businessman from Poland and a cultured, "saintly" woman from "good stock." He was sent to Catholic school and made to hear of Paradise and Hell, while he was assured at home that Jews were superior. When the Nazis marched into Austria, he was packed off to Amsterdam and placed in a Dutch home.

After the Germans invaded the Netherlands, he hid in attics and avoided deportation until finally he decided to run in the other direction. Disguising himself as one Jan Gerrit Overbeek ("My nose is straight, as straight as Hitler's"), he hired himself out as a deckhand on a German barge and sailed for Germany, "the very heart of the monster." There he survived, ducking bombs and avoiding detection, until the war was over.

Afterward, he changed his name to Jakov Chaklan, lied his way to Palestine, was reunited with the remains of his family ("We probably lost only 84 uncles, aunts, and cousins in the last war. That's all."), worked on a kibbutz and served in the army. Today, he lives in London with his wife and two children.

Enough to wear calluses onto the toughest soul, and certainly it affected Mr. Lind. But not by numbing him. In fact, these biographical details—this potentially hackneyed story—hardly matters in ***Counting My Steps;*** one finds these details lying in obscure corners of the narrative. Much more prominent is his spiritual development.

From earliest childhood Lind was fascinated by nothingness. (He dreamed of climbing to the attic window to see the "nothing" that his mother told him lay beyond a neighboring fence.) All the same, he searched long and hard for somethingness, and each of the three sections of his autobiography corresponds to phases of his search. "School for Metaphysics" takes him from God to Zionism

("When the Germans marched into Austria one Friday morning . . . God lost his last chance to be recognized by me."). "School for Politics" takes him into a world of sex, survival and hatred for the Jews. ("I hated their names, their faces, their manner of speech, their humor, and their nervous diligence. They were a rotten lot and one should get rid of them.")

And the final section, "School for Alchemy," takes him back to the beginning—to his fascination with nothingness ("Things are not what they are, and they are not what they are supposed to be, and they are not what they can be, and they are never what they were. Things are not.") and with words ("Things that have no name, nameless things, lie on my chest, and I'm not dead yet."). He discovers himself as a writer. ("I found images yet undeveloped. . . . I grasped the essence of my own reality as a mixture of inner and outer experiences.")

Yet ***Counting My Steps*** is no more an agonized account of the progress of the esthete's soul than it is the standard melodrama of the Jew who escaped the fate of the Six Million. It is simply an expression of Lind's character as it was shaped by the external and interior events that are embedded in his narrative.

And Jakov Lind is a droll, comic, tough, earthy, independent-minded, delightful man. As he tells it, he understood the absurd from his earliest Vienna schooldays, when "Ferdinand Hartl, fat, dark, pink-cheeked, unfolded a clean handkerchief to make sure that there were no rabbits inside," and taught his class how to blow the nose systematically ("I thought that this is not required learning for a Jewish child . . . "). And nothing had changed when he contracted gonorrhea during the war and had to explain to hospital attendants his being circumcised. ***Counting My Steps*** is most of all a comedy.

So it explains the problem I've had with Lind's fiction. It wasn't the translations: ***Counting My Steps*** was written in English, and while the language is far superior to that of his translated fiction, the effect is similar. What interferes with the horrors his fiction depicts is his sense of reality. He is too much himself, and his sense of the absurd is too profound for the fiction he has tried to write so far.

Christopher Lehmann-Haupt, "Portrait of the Comedian in Spite of Himself," in The New York Times, *October 8, 1969, p. 45.*

Richard M. Elman (review date 2 November 1969)

[*Elman is an American novelist, short story writer, poet, and critic who has written novels about the Holocaust. In the review below, he characterizes* Counting My Steps *as "moving reading that is excruciatingly swift and alum bitter."*]

"On the handle of Balzac's walking stick," wrote Kafka, in an obscurely aphoristic mood, "I shatter all obstacles. On that of my own, all obstacles shatter me."

Quite the opposite was the case with Jakov Lind, as ***Counting My Steps,*** his autobiography, tellingly reveals, though Lind was born into pretty nearly the same lower-middle-class, *echt Deutsch* Jewish culture, and at a far worse moment in history than Kafka. It was the era of the so-called Thousand Year Reich through which he managed to survive for 12 years. To do so (and immigrate finally to Palestine at war's end) Lind had to come to hate passive victimized Jews like a German, and hate his German victimizers like a Jew. He donned a variety of disguises: a young Zionist, a Dutch laborer, a farmworker, a sailor boy with quisling leanings, an anti-Semite, a Palestinian D.P. In short, Lind—as the saying goes—really freaked out.

His original identity as a Viennese Jew from an impoverished but respectable family with certain smug pretensions to betterness was so entirely hateful to him that it was relatively easy for him to turn schizoid in the face of that past and what the present and future held out. Lind changed identities, became a survival expert. Still only in his early adolescence at the time of *Anschluss,* he came of age away from home and family, a schizoid Nietzschean, but also a Socialist, who ended the war in the very heartland of battered Germany as the confidential factotum of sorts to a fairly high-ranking Nazi metallurgist. Lind had watched the others being gathered up in Vienna, Amsterdam, the Hague, Rotterdam, and he decided he did not want to go along with them. He donned the Nazi youth emblem and, fortunately, survived to tell the tale.

Lind's story of his daily struggle to live as one thing or another, always convinced of his right to survive at such a desperate time, is ironic, exact in its portraits of wartime venality, apathy, ignorance and greed, and also extremely funny with a laugh that is often like a sobbing in the chest. His recall is often impressionistic or even surreal, but just as often specific, precise, detailed and devastatingly political with the proportions exactly fitted to the mind of its adolescent raisonneur. His aim is to show, in part, that one grows in the midst of a rubble pile so long as one is careful to dodge the various crushing footsteps of one's enemies; but in the process, enemies and friends are given a thorough going-over.

In a phrase he summons up his ne'er-do-well salesman father and his band of cafe-sitting acquaintances as "hippies in galoshes." He unleashes as one brilliant set piece the comic monologue of his first teacher Hartle on the uses and abuses of the pocket hanky, and then deftly counterpoints this with the fiendish daily catechisms he had to undergo from his intellectually precocious Jewish playmates in Vienna about the various works of Tolstoy, Werfel, Mann, etc.

His professors at *gymnasium,* who "talked me out of my daydreams" are remembered by name, face and crotchet. Against his mother's shame-faced gluey platitudes that he must try to "feel God" is poked his first attempts at masturbation, for two packs of Wings cigarettes in a Dutch foster home. It is characteristic of Lind's demonic demythologizing, I think, that in one lengthy passage Nazi racial epithets for Jews are intermixed in comic staccato with Jewish lower-middle-class social epithets for just about everybody else. In short, in less than 100 pages, prewar Vienna is summoned up with a clear ironic wit and a vivid—though occasionally wooden and stilted—prose, which only helps to make all the more clear that what was human was not necessarily glamorous and what was historic was always inhuman.

Lind does almost as well with his adventures as an immigrant with forged papers in wartime Holland, where he was sent by a Zionist refugee group to escape *Anschluss*, and where he later managed to evade the Nazi roundups of June, 1943, though his narrative becomes somewhat abrupt and cursory when the war ends and he is forced, for lack of anything better to do, to immigrate to Palestine. Part of the problem is, I think, that Lind—for all the terror of it—found his forays in the land of his enemies to be a great adventure whereas going, among the dispossessed Jews, to Palestine, a new homeland, was rather like being sent back to Vienna again, only with sand and palm trees added.

In Holland and Germany he had come to know women, strong drink and Nietzsche. He narrowly escaped being bombed. He learned to contain his loneliness and to satisfy his needs. Like Huck Finn before him, many of Lind's most crucial experiences in coming of age transpired on a river, in this case the Rhine—surely an equal of the Mississippi in mythological possibilities—and among disreputable characters whom his proper Viennese family would have never tolerated. He had a job, a monthly salary, reasonably adequate food, watched Nazi movies, sat in cafes and wondered to himself all the while if he was who he thought he was, and if so why didn't anybody else know. It was the best of times for Lind. At least, he had never really known any that were better.

The whole tale makes moving reading that is excruciatingly swift and alum bitter. This is not simply a series of war anecdotes that Lind is seeking to relate. To make the horror of the Final Solution credible, he banalizes daily existence amid that horror, shows how he had to reduce himself, at times, to that horror so that he might survive it. "I think wrecked baby prams with wheels," he exclaims early on; and later when the war is over, lets fall with the accuracy of a guillotine blade: "They didn't hang them and they didn't shoot them, they wouldn't have known whom to start with."

Lind is the author of ***Soul of Wood, Landscape in Concrete, Ergo*** and other works, including some plays, and in nearly all his short fiction, including this so-called autobiography, there is a figure who constantly emerges: He is sometimes German and sometimes anonymously European or even Jewish. Male or female, he or she can be fat or skinny, moving up the social ladder to some unspecified goal, or having hopelessly fallen off to grumble bitterly. Always this figure is irrational, callous and cruel. Indifferent because so crazy and crazy to be so indifferent, or for being so.

He is Man himself, the beast inside that suet suit of skin and hair and bones and blood and nervous tics and wind. The Humanist ideal reduced to mere humanity, to his fists and his anus, his mouth and his anger. No matter how high up he is thought to be, he will always feel cheated; no matter how humble, persecuted. He is the "fear" that "roots in self-humiliation" to which Lind refers in his preface, autobiographically.

From out of the ash heaps that are being refurbished in Europe, Asia, here, the Middle East, during, after the war and even now, he leers at us, proof that not only the six million were destroyed, but that the holocaust is ongoing, that apocalypse is now and that that which can no longer be pretended is that which even anti-Semites once claimed to uphold—the concept of Man's essential difference from the other beasts. This was destroyed not only in the abstract, but in the young person of Lind himself who, as he reveals in this most eloquent piece of autobiographical writing, had to reduce himself to a ferret to live among his fellow ferrets who were all, it seems, good Germans. (pp. 5, 54)

Richard M. Elman, in a review of "Counting My Steps," in The New York Times Book Review, *November 2, 1969, pp. 5, 54.*

Times Literary Supplement (review date 21 May 1970)

[*In the following review of* Counting My Steps, *the anonymous critic discusses Lind's experiences during the Holocaust.*]

The European turmoil of 1939-45 must contain many personal histories similar to that of Jakov Lind; but very few men will have been so uniquely placed to observe the dissolution of an entire central European culture. And it is difficult to believe that anyone will write a more subtly entertaining and mordantly discerning account of it than Lind does in this autobiographical essay [***Counting My Steps***]. The task of writing an autobiography of deprivation and suffering must always offer, understandably enough, the temptation of personal dramatization in revealing the bitter plight of the individual caught up in a tragic destiny. Instead, Lind derives from his experiences a rueful humour and self-aware toughness to cover the sheer weight of loss and misery which bore down upon his identity and the very language he spoke. At the end, these horrors left him committed permanently to that tendency to a dissatisfied wandering which his mixed and colourful ancestry bred in him. But he is as quirky, resilient, and solidly human as ever.

Born the obstinate, introspective son of a Polish-Viennese-Jewish businessman and a Russian-Jewish cattle-dealer's daughter, Lind went to school in Vienna among the contemptuous goyim and under a maniacally rigid Nazi teacher (a beautifully comic portrait). These early passages of ***Counting My Steps*** have some of those amplifying hindsights which make the childhoods of so many literary men, in retrospect, a fascinating, agonized coming-to-terms with words and experience. But what the young Jakov also saw (with only a little help from the older one) was his curiously special position as the member of a class of "better people". As a cosmopolitan, first-generation, Jewish intellectual he was higher than the bourgeois Viennese *and* the ordinary Jews: an aspiring Ubermensch who also ranked in that class Einstein, Freud, Herzl, Hesse and Dostoevsky.

This attitude (which facilitated a convincing pretense of anti-Semitism) and a stubborn native wit, enabled him both to despise and to escape from the labour-camp parties of Jews transported from Holland, where he settled as a child refugee after the Anschluss. He now took on a Dutch identity and the Dutch language: worked as a gardener; and escaped (when things bccamc too hot for able-bodied adolescents) to work in Germany itself on a cargo barge. Discharged from a German hospital after a dose of gonorrhoea, he fell—again with astonishing luck and a magical ability to survive—into the employ of a German Air Ministry agent working on new weapons with the aid of a cyclotron. As an early immigrant into Israel after the war, he was still emotionally unsatisfied, and it is clear that the wandering will go on: "back to face the rats of this plague-stricken continent again".

What survives in Lind, despite the constant changes of scene and identity, the loss of idealism, love, hatred—and "worst of all, language"—is the indestructible desire to write. His poems go on in his head, his prose is entered in unsent letters and torn-up diaries. In the midst of confusion and terror, he is pared down to an irreducible minimum: a being who perpetuates himself by acts of minimal artistic creation. Truthfully, he includes in ***Counting My Steps*** some of his most bewildered and fragmentary notebook writings of the time. Set among the frank and factual accounts of "muddling through" the European holocaust, they are an oddly touching testimony to the will of this professional survivor to escape martyrdom. Many books have been and will be written to carry more of the bestiality and pathos of these years. None is more likely to affirm in so beautifully and movingly individual a way the capacity of European civilization to transcend them.

"Through the Holocaust," in The Times Literary Supplement, *No. 3560, May 21, 1970, p. 559.*

Savkar Altinel (review date 29 May 1987)

[*In the review below, Altinel, while faulting Lind's "self-indulgently inventive" narrative in* The Inventor, *praises the author for suggesting that "any clear-cut solution to humanity's problems can only be a fiction and that fiction itself, or art, is the only real refuge."*]

Emmanuel Borovsky, the inventor of the battery-operated fountain-pen, the electric scissors and the radio hat, is a worried man. An alligator farm he had bought in the Cayman Islands has turned out to be a worthless investment, leaving him without the capital to develop his latest and most ambitious invention, the Redemption Machine, a super-computer which, by taking the decisions for the disposal of the planet's resources out of human hands, will at last make social justice a reality.

In an effort to find financial assistance, Emmanuel embarks on a journey that takes him to Reykjavik, Berlin, Amsterdam, New York and Jerusalem, and brings him into contact with several members of the new diaspora made up of refugees from the Holocaust, who are described in a series of letters to his brother Boris, a London doctor. One of those Emmanuel meets is a banker who wants to breed kosher pigs so that Christian, Jew and Muslim can at last share the same table and a new age of peace and harmony can begin; another believes himself to be the reincarnation of Sabbtai Zvi, the seventeenth-century Turkish Jew who proclaimed himself the Messiah, and is determined to show that everyone in recent history was secretly Jewish, including Moshe Zung, better known as Mao Tse-tung; a third comes from Tiflis, is quite possibly a KGB agent, and has a plan for putting a giant Star of David into orbit.

Meanwhile, as Boris's letters in reply indicate, not all is well at home. The doctor's fifth wife, Oksana, an Eskimo from Siberia, has said to him, "You are focking happy, basta!" and, rather than argue with a woman brought up to rip bears limb from limb and bite steak out of live bison, he has decided to agree. In fact, however, he is going mad.

[***The Inventor***], Jakov Lind's second novel written in English (the first was ***Travels to the Enu,*** 1982) contains a remark which hostile readers might wish to see as a comment on the book itself. "Strong stuff ", Boris writes to his brother at one point, "[but] I have no idea what you are trying to tell me with this tale." This, though, would be unfair. Although self-advertisingly and self-indulgently inventive, the novel is not merely an exercise in cleverness, and what this prolific author is trying to say is almost painfully clear. Lind obviously believes that the grandiose schemes of his eccentric characters have little chance of success, but still retains a certain admiration for the Jewish messianic tradition they spring from and knows that, barring a return to the lost innocence of Eden (the reward which the happy but improbable ending in a way bestows on Emmanuel), such attempts will continue to be made. It is suggested both that any clear-cut solution to humanity's problems can only be a fiction and that fiction itself, or art, is the only real refuge. In one way or another, all men have to invent their salvation, even though, as Emmanuel's favourite passage in Job has it, "The righteous and the wicked are equal before God, who holds all mankind in contempt and laughs at the trial of the innocent."

Savkar Altinel, "Plans for Redemption," in The Times Literary Supplement, *No. 4391, May 29, 1987, p. 588.*

Linda Taylor (review date 9 July 1987)

[*Below, Taylor offers a positive assessment of* The Inventor.]

[In ***The Inventor***] Jakov Lind's characters, Emmanuel and Boris Borovsky (Jewish ex-Poles living in England) are in search of liberation. The novel comprises a sequence of letters written by the brothers to each other, in which Lind explores their relative freedoms. Emmanuel, 'the inventor', roams the world looking for financial supporters for his latest hobby-horse, the Redemption Machine: a pragmatic supercomputer which would 'know how to cope more efficiently than human agencies with the scandals of half the world starving while the other half drowns in unspeakable plenty'. On the way, Emmanuel meets Elim Ffinger, a self-styled Messiah who winds up in a mental hospital in Jerusalem, where he invites Emmanuel to be his guest—'Playing chess with the "Messiah" in the heart of Jerusalem, the spiritual capital of the Western world, is a fate I can endure.' Emmanuel feels it is up to the Jews (he's their representative) to redeem the world because of their famous crime and consequent guilt, but it looks like this Messiah may have out-manoeuvred him.

***The Inventor* is a marvellously inventive joke about mankind; a dialogue with the self in which the grass is both always greener and to be advised against at all costs. Jakov Lind creates this dilemma with panache and wild good humour.**

—Linda Taylor

Boris, on the other hand, believes himself to be most free when he is embroiled with his bear-fighting Eskimo wife, Oksana. He is, in fact (as Emmanuel points out), her slave, and also ends up in a mental home. The paralleling of the mental homes points up the nature of the fraternal letter-writers. Emmanuel and Boris are aspects of a corporate identity: their fates are finally reversed when Emmanuel chooses domestic bliss with the antipodean alternative to Oksana (a big woman called Australia), and when Boris, divorced, is liberated into taking an interest in saving the world.

The Inventor is a marvellously inventive joke about mankind; a dialogue with the self in which the grass is both always greener and to be advised against at all costs. Jakov Lind creates this dilemma with panache and wild good humour.

Linda Taylor, "In Search of Liberation," in The Listener, *Vol. 118, No. 3019, July 9, 1987, p. 31.*

Publishers Weekly (review date 1 July 1988)

[*Below, the critic provides a brief description of* The Inventor.]

This epistemological romp [***The Inventor***] between the Borovsky brothers—Emmanuel writing from every compass point on the globe, Boris from staid London—revolves around Manny's super-computer, a machine for the redemption of the world. But he's broke, having sunk several fortunes in such technological doo-dads as a pair of electric scissors and a radio hat, and he touches his rich doctor-brother for a loan. He needs, as he says, investors who believe in him, not necessarily in his machine, and although Boris sends him a couple of thousand pounds, Manny seeks out other Jewish visionaries from Reykjavik to Jerusalem. They're an astounding bunch, wallowing in wealth: a new messiah or Divine Will; a bisexual fop who simply wants to live forever, fornicating; a banker who dreams of developing kosher pigs, edible by both Jews and Muslims; and a maker of ladders who plans to put a Star of David in orbit. In the meantime, Boris is having his own problems with his fifth wife, Oksana, a Jewish Eskimo, who exhausts him sexually in her fervor for a child and eventually settles for a dog. This animal literally drives Boris mad; he shoots it and is forthwith taken to a sanitarium. In a rather abrupt ending, Manny engineers his brother's release and, by dint of a whopping sum, his freedom from Oksana. He himself returns to the Cayman Islands, to cultivate his garden with a native woman, who also dreams of a new messiah, this time black. This slim, pithy text by the author of ***Travels to the Enu*** cleverly depicts a madcap world that, the author seems to suggest, may be the true state of the universe.

A review of "The Inventor," in Publishers Weekly, *Vol. 234, No. 1, July 1, 1988, p. 65.*

Gary Houston (review date 7 August 1988)

[*In the review below, Houston provides a positive assessment of* The Inventor.]

This skinny novel about Jewish messianism and universal madness [***The Inventor***] is very funny and very fecund. It mulls over love, guilt, impotence, money, justice, schizophrenia and Zionism, all in an absurdist vein that once enabled Austria's Jakov Lind to share the post-war spotlight with Günter Grass.

But Lind eventually found German grammatically cumbersome, moved to London and has since been mining English literature for new ways to express old torments. ***The Inventor*** also uses the epistolary form, which is as old as the modern English novel itself. But Lind's debt ends there.

The tale is told in letters between Emmaunel and Boris Borovsky, brothers and Polish-Jewish emigres. Manny is the inventor, though to Boris he's a *luftmensch* (dreamer); past concoctions include a radio hat and motorized shoes. Boris, a well-propertied London M.D., husbands a half-Eskimo, half-Jewish virago named Oksana, who in Siberia learned to rip bears apart.

Boris' determination to stop Oksana from keeping a dog as a child-surrogate launches his odyssey to serious craziness, but not before his brother has undertaken an odyssey of his own. Manny conceives the Redemption Machine, a super computer "electric Messiah" that will replace the UN as a justice-meting authority, and his search for investors takes him to Reykjavik, Berlin, Amsterdam, New York, Zurich and Jerusalem.

Several nutty non-investors are met—including the New York couple whose counter-notion is a Star of David hitched to a satellite, in order that the world may know of Jewish superiority without the Jews having to assert it.

But none is nuttier than an Antwerp chameleon named Elim Ffinger, a.k.a. Sam Butterfeld, a professed reincarnation of Sabbatai Zvi, the 17th Century Turkish Jew who claimed to be the Messiah.

Ffinger—who practices cabalistic magic with digits "long and bony and probably triple-jointed, like the fingers of an ape"—avers that every gentile is a Jew, just as surely as "the universal invades the particular," and that he is the Redeemer who will make this manifest to Israel's friends and foes.

Manny hates Elim, he assures Boris, but he considers a human Messiah to be better than an electric one. Or is Manny really Elim (they look alike) and his letters untrue? Or are Manny and Boris one, and the correspondence one man's fantasy?

Lind's use of false identity to elude the SS taught him self-invention for survival's sake. Perhaps he is saying that only invention redeems us, as it does writers like himself.

Gary Houston, "At Times Fantasy is the Mother of Invention," in Chicago Tribune, *August 7, 1988, p. 6.*

Paul West (review date 3 December 1989)

[*West is an English-born American novelist, critic, poet, short story writer, and essayist. In the review below, he compares Lind's works to those of Günter Grass and calls* Counting My Steps *a "blueprint for, the motive behind, his fictions."*]

It may be that a man who is tired of Günter Grass is tired of life; equally, it may mean that he has discovered Jakov Lind. Many people have read right through Grass's *The Tin Drum* (the cumulative pull of its angry farcicality being hard to resist), and Grass has just about had his due, from the attentions of *Life* magazine to a visiting appointment at Columbia University—a fat man with a fat purse filled by the proceeds from at least one fat book. Lind, on the other hand, has a smaller reputation, both is and writes leaner, managing in his two novels, ***Landscape in Concrete*** and ***Ergo,*** and in his book of short stories, ***Soul of Wood,*** to strip hallucinated indignation down to the very bone.

Both writers address themselves to the atrocities and the aftermath of Nazism, but whereas Grass the German looks back, say, to Grimmelshausen, Goethe and Brecht, Lind the Austrian Jew looks back to more fastidious, altogether more enigmatic writers such as Kafka, Hesse and Rilke. The one overwhelms, the other undercuts; the one is a military band playing marches grossly out of tune whereas the other is a soloist playing discordant gas-chamber music. What they have in common is the grotesque, and Grass's version is the easier to come to terms with: he repeats himself, and the reader has time and room to accustom himself to Grass's verbal gait, whereas Lind—so concise and unebullient and spare—offers no room at all to practice in: you have to win from every sentence whatever purchase it offers on the narrative, and even then may get stranded. Grass, affable impresario, seems always present, guaranteeing continuity, supplying hints; Lind, on the other hand, remains out of sight behind his monsters, leaving us to shudder and stumble, and fathom them as best we may.

So it is useful now to have Lind's autobiography, a book that shows how and why the compressed, inscrutable expressionism of his fiction began. "Counting my steps from one tree to the next," he writes, "the forest of infinite madness is, at least, terminated by a real space and a real time." And that curiously abstract metaphor refers, of course, to much more than his own experience of Europe during World War II, his being sent as a boy from Vienna to Holland by parents who then left for Palestine. It refers to matters beyond the fantastic adolescence he had as "Jan Overbeek," posing as a Gentile and even as a Nazi, and then sailing on a barge from Holland into Germany itself ("the lion's mouth"), where he incongruously got a job in the Air Ministry, and finally, as "Jakov Chaklan," wangling his way to Palestine and there beginning to write books.

In one sense, the tree-stepping metaphor, like the autobiography itself, isn't autobiographical at all: It implies a dispassionate estimate of what life can be and usually is for everyone everywhere—*bio* in the wide sense just as much as *auto* in the narrow. Of course Lind writes about Lind and Lind's aliases, revealing all the pain of being a drop-out Jew who went one stage further and schooled himself not only to hate the Jews themselves ("I have to hate because I love life") but even to drop his hatred of the Germans (the only recourse of such a hatred being to declare itself, which is suicidal). And there we have it, not so much the career of a born survivor as a sample of how life drives all men into stances of semi-impersonality and has driven Lind himself, for example, to create such a figure as Bachmann, the ghoulish Nazi sergeant who in ***Landscape in Concrete*** marches across Europe, yearning always for orders to obey, he too "counting [his] steps from one tree to the next," never having to think.

Always, in spite of his evident delight in eccentricity, Lind sees the race in the individual rather than the individual in the race: quirks, foibles, personal uniqueness strike him as decorations on the basic human *matériel.* He has, in fact, what many German writers have—a sense of life as process, chemical and mechanical and electrical, which heeds identities not at all and induces men to minimize the self in the Oriental way or to bottle it up by joining a group.

In the long run this caustic, reluctant-feeling self-interpretation restores us to the almost inhuman inclusiveness of Lind's novels and stories: a concrete inscape where wooden but not quite soulless ogres keep busy lest they go mad. History for Lind is the brain seeking to confirm its own presence in time. "That's why," he says, "the search for man's origin will continue until he feels no need for identity." Man, not Self, and types rather than individuals (*Anna Karenina,* he says, taught him that "every lonely woman on a forlorn railway platform is ready to throw herself under a train"). It's not often that we see near-schizophrenia providing a man with a world-view, but here it does.

There is trauma in these pages—an aftermath to horror, a deep sense of identity's fragility, and a longing for the mindlessness that goes with stereotypes—all recollected in tranquility. But I feel the trauma was what Lind's temperament required; and it's likely that, given a wholly different life, he would have come up with the same general view: "There is a plague called man," as the epigraph to ***Landscape in Concrete*** puts it. It's the over-view of a Jewish Dante with an unappeasable hunger and a knack of converting rage into vengeful caricatures of sub- and super-men. The inhumanity of man, Lind realizes, echoes and fulfills the inhumanity of Nature; and this baneful book makes and implies that point time and again.

Jakov Lind is now settled and thriving in London, which is an unlikely roost for one of Europe's most individualistic and black-minded surrealists. I wonder how many of the English literati relish his version "of a stream of life engulfing the earth—it looked like millions of naked humans being vomited up from a crater . . . just like the opening of Dante's Hell." *That,* among the striped ties, the soccer pools, and the incinerated mutton! To me, anyway, Lind is worth a thousand Lucky Jims, and this now phantasmagorical, now prosaic, account of how his mind got the way it is is appallingly instructive: It's the blueprint for, the motive behind, his fictions—those *machines infernales* which, seemingly built only to shock and offend, can now be read as horrific rebounds from a childhood defiled at source. (pp. 3-4)

Paul West, "Gas-Chamber Music," in Book World, *December 3, 1989, pp. 3-4.*

FURTHER READING

Criticism

Hofman, Michael. "Praying for an End." *The London Review of Books* 14, No. 2 (30 January 1992): 12.

Reviews *Crossing: The Discovery of Two Islands,* the third installment of Lind's autobiography in which Lind discusses why he immigrated to England and how he became a writer.

Karpowitz, Stephen. "Conscience and Cannibals: An Essay on Two Exemplary Tales—*Soul of Wood* and *The Pawnbroker.*" *The Psychoanalytic Review* 64, No. 1 (Spring 1977): 41-62.

Comparative study of Edward Wallant's novel *The Pawnbroker* and Lind's *Soul of Wood, and Other Stories.*

Lively, Adam. "Defence of the Unarmed Man." *Books,* No. 2 (May 1987): 6.

Feature article on Lind's life and career.

Meyer, David. "Tired Terror." *The North American Review* 250, No. 2 (May 1965): 60.

Faults the stories in *Soul of Wood* for being "dull and tired."

Thompson, John. "Stories about Terrible Things." *Commentary* 44, No. 6 (December 1967): 77-80.

Questions the validity of Lind's depiction of torture and death in *Ergo.*

"Pie-Eaters, Scroungers, Assassins &c." *The Times Literary Supplement,* No. 3,473 (19 September 1968): 1052.

Short review of Lind's drama collection *The Silver Foxes Are Dead* in which the critic states that readers of the works are "more aware of the extravagant savagery than of the humour to which the blurb lays claim."

"The High Way Home." *The Times Literary Supplement,* No. 3,775 (12 July 1974): 745.

Discusses Lind's portrayal of Israel in his *Trip to Jerusalem.*

Tucker, Martin. Review of *Ergo,* by Jakov Lind. *Commonweal* LXXXVII, No. 16 (26 January 1968): 508.

Compares Lind's *Ergo* to Ishmael Reed's *The Free-Lance Pallbearers,* stating that both authors rely too much on "the in-joke" and are a part of "a growing army of writers who 'grotest' too much."

Additional coverage of Lind's life and career is contained in the following sources published by Gale Research: *Contemporary Authors,* Vols. 9-12 (rev. ed.); *Contemporary Authors Autobiography Series,* Vol. 4; *Contemporary Authors New Revision Series,* Vol. 7; and *Contemporary Literary Criticism,* Vols. 1, 2, 4, 27.

Anne Morrow Lindbergh

1906-

(Born Anne Spencer Morrow) American novelist, essayist, diarist, and poet.

The following entry provides an overview of Lindbergh's career.

INTRODUCTION

Anne Morrow Lindbergh is best known as the author of the essay collection *Gift from the Sea* and for the publication of five volumes of her diaries. Also recognized as the wife of the pioneering aviator Charles Lindbergh, her perceptive records of the dramatic events of her life and of a woman's role in society garnered public attention and critical acclaim.

Lindbergh was born into what Jane Howard described as "what may have been the closest-knit nuclear family in modern history." Her father, Dwight Morrow, was at various times a partner to banker J. P. Morgan, an ambassador, and a U.S. senator. Her mother, Elizabeth Cutter Morrow, was a poet, a trustee of Smith College, and a crusader for equal education for women. The Morrows' wealth and status ensured that their children were well-educated and well-traveled at an early age. Lindbergh attended Mrs. Chapin's School in New York, and then followed in her mother's footsteps by going to Smith College. After a composition professor encouraged her talent for writing, Lindbergh contributed to college publications and published a poem in *Scribner's Magazine.* She met Charles Lindbergh in 1928 at a family Christmas party in Mexico, and married him in 1929. Anne learned the skills necessary to serve as Charles' co-pilot, navigator, and radio operator, and the couple spent most of the early days of their marriage exploring the world through air travel including a 1931 survey flight to the Orient via the Arctic circle.

While Lindbergh had been in the public eye as an ambassador's daughter and as the wife of a well-known aviator, the 1932 kidnapping of her and Charles' first child, Charles A. Lindbergh III, generated even greater media coverage. The Lindberghs were besieged by reporters, photographers, and state troopers, and over 12,000 people, including Al Capone, offered their assistance. The baby's body was found on May 12, 1932 in a ditch not far from their home. Following the death of their child, Charles encouraged Lindbergh to write her first book, *North to the Orient,* an account of their 1931 survey flight. To regain some measure of privacy after the 1935 trial of the alleged kidnapper, Bruno Hauptmann, the couple and their second child moved to England and resided in Europe until the outbreak of World War II. Lindbergh detailed her opposition to the war in *The Wave of the Future,* a controversial book that contributed to the Lindberghs' erroneous reputation as Nazi sympathizers. She published sporadically from 1944—1966, during which time she wrote her most significant work, *Gift from the Sea,* and a volume of poetry, *The Unicorn and Other Poems.* Although John Ciardi's scathing review of *The Unicorn and Other Poems* in the January 12, 1957 issue of *The Saturday Review* generated an extensive debate, the book was commercially successful, as were the diaries. Widowed in 1974, Lindbergh resides in Connecticut and Hawaii.

In her diaries, novels, and essays, Lindbergh sensitively portrays her struggle to maintain her identity in marriage, to balance the demands of a family and a literary career, and to cope with living a private life subjected to public scrutiny. The diaries, encompassing her college years through the post-World War II years, and *Gift from the Sea* especially reflect these conflicts. She asks in *The Flower and the Nettle: Diaries and Letters of Anne Morrow Lindbergh, 1936-1939,* for example, if it is "possible for a woman to be a woman and yet produce something tangible besides children, something that stands up in a man's world." Although writing served as the lens through which she viewed the world and by which she placed events into perspective, as a wife and mother she questioned how much time she should devote to her craft. *Gift from the Sea* similarly discusses women's roles, with a focus on marriage. Using different kinds of seashells to symbolize the stages of marriage, she recommends periods of solitude devoted to creativity to rejuvenate the spirit, resulting in the ideal relationship: "the meeting of two fully developed people as persons." Elizabeth Gray Vining commented that *Gift from the Sea* "is like a shell, itself, in its small and perfect form, the delicate spiraling of its thought, the poetry of its color, and its rhythm from the sea, which tells of light and life and love and the security that lies at the heart of intermittency."

Despite the fact that Lindbergh is noted for her explorations of the self in relation to society, for her treatment of the diary as a serious literary form, for her historical documentation, and for her feminist themes, her works have received relatively little critical attention. Due in part to the fact that Anne Lindbergh was frequently overshadowed by her famous husband, this critical neglect is also a result of the unique genres with which she worked. Such works as *North to the Orient* and her diaries, for example, do not fit into typical literary categories, and *Gift from the Sea,* a variation on the literary essay, is commonly classified as "inspirational reading." David Kirk Vaughan commented that Lindbergh "is not really to be thought of as a poet or novelist. She is a philosopher at heart. Her philosophic message is the importance of developing a clear perception of self, of others, and of one's surroundings."

PRINCIPAL WORKS

North to the Orient (nonfiction) 1935
Listen! The Wind (nonfiction) 1938
The Wave of the Future (nonfiction) 1940
The Steep Ascent (novella) 1944
Gift from the Sea (essays) 1955
The Unicorn, and Other Poems, 1935-1955 (poetry) 1956
Dearly Beloved (novel) 1962
Selections from "Gift from the Sea" (essays) 1967
Earth Shine (nonfiction) 1969
Bring Me a Unicorn: Diaries and Letters of Anne Morrow Lindbergh, 1922-1928 (diaries) 1972
Hour of Gold, Hour of Lead: Diaries and Letters of Anne Morrow Lindbergh, 1929-1932 (diaries) 1973
Locked Rooms and Open Doors: Diaries and Letters of Anne Morrow Lindbergh, 1933-1935 (diaries) 1974
The Flower and the Nettle: Diaries and Letters of Anne Morrow Lindbergh, 1936-1939 (diaries) 1976
War Within and Without: Diaries and Letters of Anne Morrow Lindbergh, 1939-1944 (diaries) 1980

CRITICISM

Antoine de Saint-Exupéry (essay date 1939)

[Saint-Exupéry was a French novelist, essayist, and aviator, best-known for his story Le Petit Prince. *In the following excerpt from his preface to the French translation of* Listen! The Wind, *originally published in 1939, he discusses Lindbergh's successful use of the mechanics of flight as a metaphor for psychological and spiritual themes.]*

Anne Lindbergh's [***Listen! The Wind***] seems to me something quite different from a forthright account of her flying adventures. This is why it is beautiful. Now, it is true that in her book the author has mustered only concrete facts, technical observations and reflections—in a word, the raw materials of her profession. But this is not the point. What could it matter to me to learn that this takeoff was difficult or that that wait-over was long, or that in the course of the flight Anne Lindbergh was bored or in high spirits. All this is only the *gangue.* The question is: What did she extract from it? What face did she put on these experiences? Is the essence of a work of art created as the structure is built that will capture it? No. The snare and the thing snared are not of the same essence. Consider the builder of cathedrals. He has used stones, and out of stones he has built silence.

A true book is like a net, and words are the mesh. The nature of the mesh matters relatively little. What matters is the live catch the fisherman draws up from the depths of the sea, the flashings of silver that we see gleam within the net. What has Anne Lindbergh brought back from her inner universe? What is the flavor of her book?

This is difficult to say, for to convey its flavor one must write and speak of many things. Nevertheless . . . I sense a faint anguish suffusing these pages. It takes different forms, but it circulates tirelessly through the book like a silent blood stream.

It is my observation that every profoundly coherent creative work can almost always be reduced to an elementary common denominator. I remember a film in which, without the director's being aware of it, the real hero was heaviness. Everything in this film weighed heavily. Atavism weighed upon a degenerate emperor; heavy winter furs weighed on his shoulders; crushing responsibilities weighed on his prime minister. Even the doors in the film were heavy. And in the last scene you saw the conqueror, burdened by his heavy victory, slowly climb a shadowy stairway toward the light. Now, this common denominator of heaviness was not a preconceived effect. The author had not planned it. But the fact that it was there and could be detected was the sign of the film's subterranean continuity.

I remember also the gist, not the exact words, of a strange remark Flaubert made about his *Madame Bovary:* "I was trying, first of all, to express the particular shade of yellow you find in the crack of a wall where cockroaches hatch."

Reduced thus to a rudimentary formula, what Anne Lindbergh has expressed is an unease that is caused by a tendency to be late. How hard it is to move forward in step with an inner rhythm when one must struggle against the inertia of the physical world. Everything is always so nearly on the verge of grinding to a halt. One must be most vigilant if one is to preserve life and motion in a universe that is threatening to break down. . . .

Lindbergh is out in a small boat in a Porto Praia bay, checking water currents. From the crest of a hill, his wife watches him labor like a tiny insect mired in a huge, sticky trap. She walks on, and every time she turns to the sea, it seems to her that her husband has made no headway. The insect flutters its wings in vain. How difficult to cross a bay; if one were to slow down just a little, one would never reach the sea. . . .

For several days they have been prisoners of this island where time has no meaning, where time does not move. Here men live and die in the same place; in a whole lifetime they will have conceived one idea, only one and always the same, until the day comes when even that simply stops.

"I am *chef* here," their host tells them a dozen times over, until the repetition becomes as meaningless as a distant echo. But for them time must be set in motion again. They must rejoin the continent, reenter the stream, return to where men are worked hard, where they can change and be alive. Anne Lindbergh is afraid not of death but of eternity.

Eternity is so near! It is so easy never to cross the bay, never to escape from an island, never to get the plane off the ground at Bathurst. They are both, she and Lindbergh, a little late. . . . Only a little late. . . . Hardly late at all. . . . But let the delay be one moment too long, and no one in the world waits for you.

We have all known the little girl who can't run as fast as the others. The others are playing up ahead. "Wait for me! Wait for me!" But she has fallen behind, and they are going to get tired of waiting and they are going to leave her behind, forget her, and she will be all alone in the world. How should one reassure her? This kind of anguish is incurable. For if she takes part in their game now, and then has to leave, and is slow about leaving, she will wear out their patience. They're murmuring among themselves already, they're already looking at her askance. . . . They are going to leave her alone again, all alone.

It is an extraordinary revelation to see this kind of inner anxiety in a couple whom the whole world has applauded. When a telegram from Bathurst informs them that they are welcome to land there, lo and behold, they are infinitely grateful. Later, at Bathurst, they are unable to take off as planned, and they are embarrassed by what seems to them an imposition. It is not a question of false modesty on their part; it is their sense of mortal danger. A small delay, and everything is lost.

Such anguish is fertile. It is this inner compunction—and nothing will ever cure it—that makes them start out two hours before dawn, outpioneer even the pioneers, cross oceans that hold other men in check.

This is a far cry from the fast-paced action of the stereotyped adventure story. In her book, Anne Lindbergh is secretly leaning on something as impossible to formulate, as elemental and universal as a myth. Yet, through all the technical data and observations, she is able to make us acutely aware of the problem of the human condition. She is not writing *about* the airplane but *via* the airplane. Her professional imagery serves as her vehicle for conveying to us something at once concealed and essential.

Lindbergh has not been able to get his plane airborne at Bathurst. It is overloaded. For such a pilot, however, a sea breeze would be enough to enable him to take off. But the wind has fallen. Once again, the travelers struggle vainly in the sticky trap. Then they decide to sacrifice: the less essential food, accessories, and spare parts are jettisoned. Again and again they attempt a takeoff, and each time they fail they decide on fresh sacrifices. Little by little, the floor of their room is littered with precious objects that they weigh out ounce by ounce and regretfully cast aside.

The professional setback is actually relatively minor, yet Anne Lindbergh expresses it with gripping veracity. Furthermore, she never mistakes the pathos of the airplane. This is not found in sun-gilded clouds at sunset. Sun-gilded clouds are rubbish. It is to be found in the use of a screwdriver—when, for example, you are working on an empty socket that gapes like a broken tooth among the orderly array of dials on an instrument panel. Make no mistake, however. Mrs. Lindbergh has been able to make the lay reader as well as the working pilot share their dejection because she has moved beyond a purely professional disappointment to a more general pathos. She has rediscovered the old myth of sacrifice whereby salvation is achieved. We were already familiar with other forms of it—the trees that must be pruned if they are to bear fruit; the men who within the prison walls of a monastery discover the full breadth of the spirit and who pass from renunciation to renunciation until they achieve plenitude.

But the help of the gods is needed, too. Anne Lindbergh has rediscovered Fatality. To prune the heart of man is not enough to save him; he must also be touched by grace. To prune the tree is not enough for it to bud; spring must also have a hand in the matter. To lighten the load is not enough for the plane to take off; a gust of wind from the sea is needed.

Quite effortlessly, Anne Lindbergh has restored Iphigenia to life. She writes on a sufficiently high level for her struggle against time to assume the significance of a struggle against death, for the lack of a breeze at Bathurst to confront us almost imperceptibly with the problem of destiny—and to make us feel how the hydroplane, which on the water is nothing but a heavy, cumbersome machine, changes substance and becomes a pure, pulsing blood stream when the grace of the sea wind has touched it. (pp. 171-77)

Antoine de Saint-Exupéry, "A Fertile Anguish," in his A Sense of Life, *translated by Adrienne Foulke, Funk & Wagnalls Company, Inc., 1965, pp. 167-78.*

An excerpt from *Listen! The Wind*

The lights flashed on in the front cockpit, outlining my husband's head and shoulders. Then off again quickly. He was looking at the chart. We turned low over the shadowy land. I reached up and wrenched back the sliding cockpit cover, shutting out the noise and wind. The papers in my lap stopped fluttering wildly. I took out my large pad. Still taut from excitement, I wrote down by moonlight, "Took off Bathurst 2:00 GMT." Looking at the sentence scrawled unevenly across the top of the big sheet of blank paper, I said sternly to myself, "Well, you needn't get so excited—After all, we've got the whole flight ahead of us. Heaven knows if we'll get there." But I could not help feeling that the worst was over, now we were off, that after this all would be easy.

It was just as well, however, to be pulled down to practical affairs. There was no time now for fear or exaltation, for speculation or doubt. The windless bay, the docks, the lights, the palm trees, had dropped off behind us. I was concerned with them no longer. Neither was the great dark world outside my cockpit cover any business of mine. The moon, the stars, the wind, the formless stretch of land we were crossing, the vast ocean we were headed toward—all these I must shut out. For me they did not exist. All that existed now was this small cockpit, pulled over me like the shell of a snail.

Anne Morrow Lindbergh in her Listen! The Wind, *Harcourt, Brace & Company, 1938.*

John Chamberlain (essay date 1972)

[*Chamberlain is an American essayist and critic, noted for his writings on social and economic subjects. In the following essay, he discusses* Bring Me a Unicorn: Diaries and Letters of Anne Morrow Lindbergh, 1922-1928.]

Along about page 36 of Anne Morrow Lindbergh's diary-cum-letters of 1922-28 [***Bring Me a Unicorn: Diaries and Letters of Anne Morrow Lindbergh, 1922-1928***] I scribbled the initials H. D. (for Hilda Doolittle, the Imagist poet) in the margin. The influence seemed to be predominant in the fresh diary prose about the foam reaching inward as the tide rose at Mont-Saint-Michel. One hundred and thirty pages later the diarist, then a senior at Smith, makes her own jotting: "H. D.—exquisite."

So this was Anne Morrow as a child of a rather precious literary culture. Images are never enough. Anne Morrow was gifted but caught within the conventions; the daughter of a Morgan partner, she was expected to be "seen but not heard" while the great of Dwight Morrow's world—M. Monnet, General Pershing, Governor Montagu Norman of the Bank of England—talked about finance or post-Versailles politics. Within the bounds of her family—two sisters, a brother and the formidably able father and mother—she lived an intense life, jealous at times of her older sister Elisabeth but unwilling to admit it, more open in her letters to her mother than she was in any face-to-face relationship. The words evidently came easily when she was not trying to force them into form for a college book review or essay. Her sensitivity to nature, to the fluctuation of winds and weather, was both a source of delight and of pain; her eye for color was that of a painter.

She had a moment of rebellion: She wanted to go to Vassar, but as a child of duty, she followed the family tradition to Smith, where she was frightened by examinations she never seemed to have time to finish. Her professors couldn't account for her occasional failures, not realizing that they were dealing with a perfectionist who couldn't be hurried. She always knew more about her subject than she could tell in an hour.

The perfectionist could write—she surprised herself by making the literary monthly and winning a couple of prizes—but there wasn't much in the way of experience to write about. She lived within a walled garden. The college boy friends, listed charitably in the diaries as "Y" and "B" and dubbed "middling" and "mediocre," gave her nothing. She was terribly torn up by the suicide of a friend at Smith, but she couldn't comprehend it. Freud, Marx, Eugene O'Neill, had not yet hit Northampton. Miss Kirstein, her writing teacher, helped her with composition, but her pre-Miss Kirstein letters show that she didn't really need courses in the mechanics of writing. What she needed to do was to get out of the culture of the upper-class Smith girl of the mid-Twenties, to be jolted into an awareness of another world. She says as much in her open-eyed introduction.

The jolt came in the form of the Hero of the Twenties, Charles Lindbergh, who dropped in out of the sky at the U.S. embassy in Mexico City not long after Dwight Morrow had been appointed ambassador by Coolidge. Suddenly Anne Morrow's diary-cum-letters narrative becomes a most compelling love story in spite of herself. The overtones are pure Booth Tarkington, recalling our age of innocence. She can't believe that Colonel Lindbergh would actually prefer her company to that of sister Elisabeth or sister Constance. She can't make Lindbergh out: the Norse god gives way to the hands-in-pockets little boy, he can't contrive any small talk, he has deplorable taste in poetry (Robert Service), he is from a technological world that has never held any interest for her. But in the air, where he can hit Le Bourget Field on the nose, he has incomparable grace.

This is the meeting of C. P. Snow's "two cultures," and, with Anne Morrow's first air flight and Charles Lindbergh's awareness that she has some of the "spirituality" which even then he talked about (he was never just an aerial chauffeur), the two cultures began to merge. She learned to fly and to operate the radio, and to live in a world of ceaseless technological change. His growth was more complex, as a comparison of *We,* written in the Twenties, and his *The Spirit of St. Louis,* which came a quarter-century later, indicates. In the end the philosopher buried the technician.

In her unblinking honesty Anne Lindbergh talks in her introduction about spending her girlhood behind brambled hedges; she was the "sheltered Emelye" of Chaucer's "Knight's Tale." Where, then, did she gain the character that was to see her through tragedy, and the fortitude to stand against the crowd when public passions were running high? It could not have been from a literary education that, surprisingly, does not seem to have included Dreiser, Sherwood Anderson or even Floyd Dell or Scott Fitzgerald. She knew nothing of the muckrakers, nothing of the likes of Lenin. The truth would seem to be that the normal culture of her girlhood operated independently of a literary culture that brings H. D. and James Stephens and Rupert Brooke (the only tough Titan she mentions is Thomas Hardy) into her adolescent pages. The Morrows were Presbyterian to the marrow, they believed in duty, in putting one's back and one's whole heart into anything they thought worth doing. The Puritan in Anne Lindbergh did not come from her reading; it came from an inculcation at the hearthside. It gets only tangential mention in her diary and letters. Nevertheless, the slight mention is there—and the case for the non-permissive society is at least implicitly made.

Anne Lindbergh now knows the inadequacy of youthful travel bounded by Henry James' *A Little Tour in France.* But, unwilling to tamper with the record, she insists on presenting an adolescent on the adolescent's own terms. Of that adolescent she says "I can laugh at her . . . but I don't want to betray her." She hasn't, and we are the richer for her forbearance. (pp. 528, 530)

John Chamberlain, "Old Fashioned Girl," in National Review, *Vol. XXIV, May 12, 1972, pp. 528, 530.*

David Kirk Vaughan on the value of the diaries and letters of Anne Morrow Lindbergh:

Lindbergh's published diaries and letters may well prove to be the most enduring of her written works. They reveal the creative processes of a talented and perceptive writer; they provide an insight into the life of her husband, one of the most unusual and controversial fliers of the twentieth century; they describe numerous important historical events; they contain accurate portraits of several major personages of the period; and they chronicle twenty-five of the most important years of the century. The woman who wrote these diary entries and letters was struggling to give shape to the events and ideas that surrounded her. They were, as Lindbergh herself acknowledged, a "crucible" through which she passed the daily experiences of her life in order to determine as best she could their meaning and impact. The appeal of these volumes is in their repeated verbal assessment, in the changes that occur as the ideas and opinions are constantly reviewed and examined. Because Lindbergh is constantly questioning her responses and her motives, these writings reflect the vitality of her continuous process of self-definition.

David Kirk Vaughan in his Anne Morrow Lindbergh, *1988.*

Alfred Kazin (essay date 1973)

[*A highly respected American literary critic, Kazin is best known for his essay collections* The Inmost Leaf *(1955),* Contemporaries *(1962), and particularly for* On Native Grounds *(1942), a study of American prose writing since the era of William Dean Howells. In the following excerpt, he offers a favorable review of* Hour of Gold, Hour of Lead, *discussing "the occasion of hysterical mass interest" associated with the kidnapping of the Lindberghs' son.*]

"There's absolutely no space limit on this story," a city editor told his reporters when the Lindbergh baby was kidnapped on March 1, 1932. "Only a war would be of equal interest." Charles Lindbergh had come to feel after his famous flight to Paris in 1927 as the "lone eagle" that he was at the mercy of the public. After his marriage in 1929 to the intensely shy, very literary, 22-year-old Anne Morrow, daughter of a Morgan partner who was United States Ambassador to Mexico, the Lindberghs were always in the news as they flew back and forth across the country to survey and plan transcontinental routes for commercial aviation. They were regularly on the front page when they made their pioneering flights to Latin America and the Orient.

Then, after the birth of Charles Augustus Lindbergh, Jr., their life became such a continuing public record and total public exposure that this brilliant, stunningly "American"-looking, already legendary young couple had good reason to bewail some of their fame even before May 12, 1932. That was the day their 20-month-old baby was found dead in a ditch not far from their Hopewell, N.J., home, killed by a blow on the head.

Both the Lindberghs have always been intensely private persons, with an austere, restrained, glowingly creative sense of life. Their laconic self-confidence (old American style) hardly prepared them for the hideous absurdity (contemporary American style) of their public anxiety and laceration. Both had a fear of crowds and a certain predictable scorn for the popular mind even before their natural sensitiveness was intensified, after the kidnapping, by armies of reporters, photographers, marauders, publicity seekers, vandals who drove by the house just long enough to kill a dog, shakedown artists of every kind who tried to cash in on the case. One young Englishwoman in the Lindberghs' employ, Violet Sharpe, committed suicide in order to escape the endless interrogation by frantic police.

Yet the Lindberghs have themselves constantly publicized the "Lindbergh story." Both natural and gifted writers, they have between them published more than a dozen books. Anne Morrow Lindbergh has all her life been an indefatigable and even obsessive recorder of her daily experiences and emotions; her marriage plunged her into an endless adventure to which her delicate style has proved fully equal. She is a lyricist of action. So it is not altogether strange—after the books she has written on her flights with her husband, on the "wave of the future" that owes so much to *his* sense of himself as an American prophet-leader—to have this record in the second volume of her own letters and diaries, of the horror that she and all her family went through after that March night in 1932, when she went into the baby's room and found him missing.

***Hour of Gold, Hour of Lead* [*Diaries and Letters of Anne Morrow Lindbergh 1929-1932*]** is a totally expressive, often unbearable record of an extreme personal anguish that followed the greatest possible happiness. It also suggests a bitterness that was all the deeper for Mrs. Lindbergh's well-bred inability to express it. To millions around the world—reading of the Lindberghs flying everywhere in their own Lockheed Sirius seaplane, looking at photographs of the "perfect"-looking couple ("the lone eagle and his mate") landing in Siberia, China, Japan—the Lindberghs seemed to enjoy the greatest possible good fortune that a young couple could have. What the Nixon family today tries to reflect, the standard American look, the young Lindberghs manifested excitingly, romantically, satisfactorily—especially when they posed with the Hoovers in the White House Garden, Lindbergh so slim and straight, Mrs. Lindbergh so demure.

The Lindberghs seemed to have *everything* except privacy. Suddenly this openness to the outside world engulfed them in the abduction of their little boy, the excruciation of having to make exactly the right decision in dealing with the many psychotically self-deluded as well as viciously dishonest people offering themselves as contacts to the supposed kidnappers.

As Mrs. Lindbergh does not say here, many police experts felt that the New Jersey State Police, a quasi-military force, should not have been in exclusive charge of the case. But she does intimate the inevitable sense of guilt that she and her husband felt about their fame, about the security arrangements they had made at the Hopewell house. Many forced and mistaken judgments were made under the extreme pressure of the weeks between March and May when their home was always siege to photographers and reporters, occupied by troopers, and when thousands of letters and messages poured in on them. In the first five weeks 12,000 people wrote of their personal dreams about the case!

The kidnapping of the Lindbergh baby was the occasion of hysterical mass interest in every detail, whipped up by tabloids that had extras ready at every hour announcing the safe return of the baby. In Madison Square Garden, Mrs. Lindbergh reports to her mother-in-law, "they stopped a big boxing match or hockey game and asked everyone to stand for three minutes and pray for the safe return of the baby—and that whole great square full of people stood quiet (just as they did for C's flight)." There were innumerable well wishers (like the many people who dreamed just where the baby could be found), many of whom could not be kept from contributing their unconscious joy-in-the-misery-of-the-famous. There was a whole hierarchy of crooks (including Al Capone) and would-be crooks who tried to be "helpful."

"We have come to an understanding with two of the biggest men of the underworld," Anne Lindbergh writes to her mother-in-law—

> men who have tremendous power with all gangs, even though they are not in touch with them and are not responsible for their actions. We do not know where the baby is or who has him, but everyone is convinced it was the work of professionals and therefore can be reached through professionals, and they seem to be convinced that the baby is safe and well cared for. It may take a good time to get him back because they naturally are *not* going to run any risks of being caught and the police and press will *have* to quiet down—the headlines *must* go before they will move.

All this is described in Anne Lindbergh's letters to her mother, her two sisters, her mother-in-law. Mrs. Lindbergh is a markedly "straight" person, with a great gift for communicating directly her joy, pain, and above all her consuming love for her family. Her "straightness" is at such variance with the hysteria of the time—the many-sided corruption within the case and surrounding the case—that the contrast between the Lindbergh character and the Lindbergh case is painful and ominous in its interest. A whole simplistic "American" idea of life died with the Lindbergh baby. One question this book does not answer is how much it died for the Lindberghs themselves. (pp. 1, 10)

[Charles] Lindbergh is a pivotal figure in American history, not just "the last hero," a symbol, but a great force. This book catches him, in his wife's dutiful, lovingly attentive eyes, in all the splendor of his early fame and as the courageous, resourceful, subtly forbidding man he became under the laceration of his son's murder. Anne Morrow Lindbergh said about the killing—"If this is true, I'll never believe anything again." Lindbergh said, "It is like war." Rarely has a personal tragedy had such public reverberations and consequences. But as Mrs. Lindbergh says in her introduction, though masses of people in the world have lived through horrors unexpected in 1932—"the holocausts of war, of civilian bombing, of concentration camps, of torture, of gas chambers, of mass executions, of Hiroshima and Nagasaki, of lynchings and civil rights murders . . . suffering—no matter how multiplied—is always individual." There are actually writers today who, like so many politicians, generals and lightning calculators in the social sciences, do not understand this. (p. 10)

Alfred Kazin, "Hour of Gold, Hour of Lead," in The New York Times Book Review, *March 4, 1973, pp. 1, 10.*

Catharine R. Stimpson (essay date 1974)

[*Stimpson is an American writer and critic. In the following review, she offers a positive assessment of* Locked Rooms and Open Doors.]

Sincerity is the sinew of Anne Morrow Lindbergh's third volume of diaries and letters, [***Locked Rooms and Open Doors: Diaries and Letters of Anne Morrow Lindbergh, 1933-1935***]. She is, she says in her introduction, now over 60 years old. She claims a "last chance" to bear accurate witness to her past.

Part of a later generation, I must work to grasp a sense of the charisma that Anne Morrow Lindbergh and her husband Charles radiated in that past. To their honor, they refused to massage their wild celebrity. The diary mentions neither press agents nor business managers. The pictures of the Lindberghs are appealing: a handsome, brave, ardent, self-sufficient couple, free spirits too devoted to each other to be lonely. Yet if the diary, prose and photographs shows how attractive the Lindberghs were, it fails to tell why they provoked such frantic awe.

Such an omission is deliberate. Anne Morrow Lindbergh's purpose is not to explore our mass compulsion to create and then to touch that special category of being—the famous—but to record the strains of being one of its members. She notes the tensions, and pleasures, of public and domestic events. In 1933 she and Lindbergh, in a single-engine seaplane, each allotted only 18 pounds of personal equipment, spend nearly six months flying around the Atlantic to map transoceanic air routes. (The leg from Africa to South America was to become the subject of her 1938 book ***Listen! The Wind.***) Though she misses her "treasure," a second son, she and Lindbergh, in their small plane, find a welcome freedom and privacy.

In 1934 she mourns the early death of her older sister. In 1935 she publishes her narrative ***North to the Orient.*** In the same year, the family must endure the trial of Bruno Hauptmann, found guilty of the 1932 kidnap-murder of their first son. The diary's last entry is Dec. 31, 1935. The Lindberghs, in a less cheerful trip across the Atlantic, this time by boat, dock in England. Their hope is to live in peaceful exile from America. The gallant adventurers have become harassed fugitives from the reputation their adventuring has brought.

Unifying the happenings of Anne Morrow Lindbergh's life is the effort to create a stable sense of self, a serene "I." Her confessions are more reticent and less gamey than those of, say, Vita Sackville-West, but they document an unexpected anguish and anxiety. ***Locked Rooms and Open Doors*** is an autobiography of being imprisoned in bad dreams, great demands, self-doubt, and painful fatigue. From 1933 to 1935 "The Terror" often enveloped her. Sometimes, she physically feared death, as she flew with Lindbergh as radio operator, navigator and co-pilot. At other times the terror was psychic. Often an insomniac, she would remember, as if it were a garish mental tic, the death of her first child, or, as if she were regressing to a state of adolescent panic, she would believe herself to be a duckling as useless as it was ugly.

Her love for Lindbergh steadied her. A muffled conflict of the diary is that of her love and desire for Lindbergh's happiness, of her sense of children as the nurturing core of life, of her wish to write and of her feminism, which she calls proving to the world that a woman can do anything a man can. Lindbergh tends to dominate the conflict. He is "life and the whole purpose of life." She berates herself for momentary losses of faith in him. She praises his control, courage, intellectual clarity and emotional sweetness. She tells some charming, homely anecdotes: Lindbergh visiting Minnesota relatives, or making the seats of their plane into a bed for a night spent anchored in a river separating Spain and Portugal, or disguising himself to have a night out with Anne. Despite the evocations of joy, Lindbergh remains opaque, a heroic mask.

Other parts of the diary also call for amplitude. Many entries are terse: the brevity of a hard-working aviator or of a shy woman who fears that self-revelation may be a dangerous self-indulgence. Among the scenes that suffer from abbreviation is the account of a visit by the Charles Lindberghs to the George Putnams. The two wives—Anne Morrow Lindbergh and the great flyer Amelia Earhart—ask each other if they have read Virginia Woolf's essays about the condition of women, *A Room of One's Own.* The answers? Unrecorded. An incidental interest of the diary is its evidence of the influence of the literature of Virginia Woolf. For Anne Morrow Lindbergh and some of the favored, intelligent, earnest, often perplexed people whom she knew, Woolf crystallized their sense of the tenuous structures of being.

The sensibility that most vividly animates ***Locked Rooms and Open Doors*** is moral, psychological and esthetic. Anne Morrow Lindbergh looks to art for a consoling sense of form; to writing for proof of consciousness. Though she worries about a coming European war, she ignores most large political and social questions. She mentions Franklin D. Roosevelt only three times, and the Depression once. Then, briefly, in retrospect, she admits that her family's affluence made her feel timid and anachronistic. She lived on the sharp edge of history, as observer, actor, and symbol; but the energy for analysis of the great forces of the present seems to have been blunted or deflected. Perhaps to ask her to have done more than she did do is simply to make another one of those noisy claims upon the famous. (pp. 28, 30)

Catharine R. Stimpson, "Locked Rooms and Open Doors," in The New York Times Book Review, *March 24, 1974, pp. 28, 30.*

Elizabeth Johnston Lipscomb (essay date 1977)

[*Lipscomb is an American critic. In the following essay, she analyzes* The Flower and the Nettle [Diaries and Letter of Anna Morrow Lindbergh, 1936-1939]*as both a public and private document.*]

In the diaries and letters that make up ***The Flower and the Nettle [Diaries and Letters of Anne Morrow Lindbergh, 1936-1939]***, Anne Morrow Lindbergh weaves together the varied strands of her life from 1936 to 1939, recording and reflecting on her experiences as wife, mother, writer, housekeeper, co-pilot, world traveler, society matron, and even artist's model. Her position as wife of the world's best-known pilot, daughter of American ambassador and senator Dwight Morrow, and established writer in her own right, made her a welcome guest at embassies, palaces, and airport hangars throughout Europe and Asia. A part of the fascination of this book is the glimpses she gives of the people she met: King George VI and Queen Elizabeth, the Duke and Duchess of Windsor, Lady Astor, George Bernard Shaw, Russian officers and French artisans, American diplomats and English gardeners. Yet many readers will find the real richness of the work elsewhere, in the author's vivid descriptions of the many facets of her life and in her musings on the meaning of this existence that seemed at times so fragmentary.

In January, 1936, Charles and Anne Lindbergh moved to Europe with their three-year-old son Jon in an effort to escape the press harassment, public curiosity, and threats of violence that still plagued them four years after the kidnaping and murder of their first son. They spent two and a half years in Kent, England, where they lived at Long Barn, the country home of British statesman Harold Nicolson (the biographer of Dwight Morrow) and his wife, novelist Vita Sackville-West. In the summer of 1938 the Lindberghs purchased and moved to Illiec, a tiny island off the northern coast of Brittany, near the home of Dr. Alexis Carrel, who was collaborating with Lindbergh on a scientific study of tissue culture. The last months of 1939 found them in a Paris apartment near the Bois de Boulogne.

As Anne Lindbergh writes in her introduction, these were years of great personal happiness for her and her family, highlighted by the birth of a third son, Land, on Coronation Day in May, 1937. However, the "flower" of domestic contentment was accompanied by a "nettle," the threat of war that grew more ominous from week to week. The diaries are thus public as well as private documents, providing insights into the attitudes of influential Americans and Europeans during a critical period in history.

In both the introduction and her letters and diaries Anne Lindbergh defends her husband and herself against charges that they were Nazi sympathizers. They were, she admits from the perspective of the 1970s, "naïve" in their pacifism and in their desire to believe what the Germans professed their goals and motives to be. Visiting Germany in 1936, 1937, and 1938 at the request of United States intelligence officers, the Lindberghs were impressed by the enthusiasm and vigor of the young people, the apparent prosperity of the workers, and the rapid technological progress. Yet even at the time they recognized the darker side of the Nazi regime in the ubiquity of uniformed soldiers, the regimentation of German life, and the brutality they observed. Lindbergh repeatedly warned the English and French governments that the German Air Force was dangerously stronger than theirs, and he certainly recognized the possibility, even the probability, that his warnings would be used against him. Both Lindberghs were appalled by the anti-Semitism of the Nazis, and they abandoned their plans to spend the winter of 1938 -1939 in Berlin after the bloody pogrom of November, 1938.

Although the political observations of the book have considerable historical interest, its real vitality comes from the character of the author. Through the flowing, unobtrusive prose of her diaries and her letters to close friends and relatives, she shows her intense awareness of her natural surroundings, her sensitivity to the people around her, her self-doubt, her courage, her humor, her acute judgment of others, and, above all, her dedication to her responsibility to her family, her work, and herself. She reveals herself page by page through her accounts of the wide variety of activities that make up her life: conversing with young Jon about lions, school, or dead stumps; arranging flowers as a gesture of welcome for guests; writing and rewriting ***Listen! The Wind,*** her account of her flight across the South Atlantic; rearranging furniture at Long Barn; trying to appease the children's nurse, who could not tolerate the primitive living conditions on Illiec; sitting impatiently through dozens of sessions with French sculptor Despiau as he modeled her head; chatting with the Duke and Duchess of Windsor about the problems of living constantly under the eye of the press.

The author communicates clearly the pain of the intrinsically shy, private person forced by circumstance to become a public figure. Each social occasion—tea with the Nicolsons, a weekend with Lord and Lady Astor at Cliveden, a ball at Buckingham Palace—swept her with new waves of insecurity. Over and over she expresses surprise at finding herself welcome or at having some titled dinner partner indicate that he enjoys her conversation. Paradoxically, this woman who looked upon a dinner party as an ordeal, could easily summon up the courage to set out, six months pregnant, to fly alone with her husband in a small plane from England to India. She emerged from a narrow brush with death in heavy cloud cover over Italy not shaken and stunned, but newly appreciative of the land to which they had returned: "Miraculously warm it seemed, soft air, good to breathe, good to walk and be alive."

Running as a constant theme through Anne Lindbergh's life and work, most notably in her 1955 bestseller ***Gift from the Sea,*** is her need to mold the contradictions and conflicting responsibilities of her existence into some kind of whole. Why, she asks herself, should she continue to struggle with her writing, when it would be far easier to devote her energies entirely to her family and her home? She answers her question in a letter to her sister Constance in 1936: "I have finally come around this year to realizing that for me the twisted-thread kind of life is and must be my special talent. But in order to do it well I must also somewhat specialize. I must write . . . because the 'thread' will not be strong without the strand." On another occasion she reflects, "Living is a more important art than any other one . . . writing is only important in that it gives me the balance required to live life as an art."

Anne Lindbergh recognizes the limitations inherent in this view of woman's role. One who makes her work but one strand of a thread cannot, she feels, "equal a man in technical ability in technical lines." She does not in any way deny that women are capable of having successful careers, but she does suggest that to do so they must adopt a "concentration," "ruthlessness," and "narrowness" that exclude many of the elements she values in her own life. She sees her position, and that of women like her, as

> something wheel-like, with the essence of you at the center, reaching out on all sides in various directions. Of course there must be a concentrated core, a hub at the center that is specialized, in order to hold all those diverse spokes together. And each person must find her own specialized core. But she must never fool herself into thinking that the core is the whole. It is just there so that the wheel can go round—to keep the whole going.

"Keeping the whole going" could be a formidable task, even with several servants to help. The reader marvels as this self-effacing young woman, who so often expresses her doubts about her competence, moves husband, children, secretary, nurse, and dog to a large, dilapidated old stone house on an island, accessible only by boat at high tide and by foot at low, and equipped with neither heat, electricity, nor running water. Forty years after the fact the author observes wryly, "the 'simple' life that many men extol . . . is extremely complicated for women." Living in an elegant Paris apartment was not always a great deal easier; there she found her energies dissipated in trying to settle quarrels between her butler, cook, and housekeeper.

Three things seem to have sustained Anne Lindbergh through a period filled with stress and challenge: nature, family, and friends. She often turned to the out-of-doors for calm and reassurance, walking in the snow on a visit to her mother's home in New Jersey, sitting on the steps overlooking the garden at Long Barn, or hunting crabs and cockles around Illiec.

Her strongest sense of purpose and worth, however, seems to have come out of her love for her family. At the heart of her life are the affection, admiration, and trust she feels for her husband. She calls marriage "the most interesting, difficult, and important thing in life," and she views the relationship as a living entity that requires constant nourishment. It was this belief that compelled her to leave her children and her work to accompany Lindbergh on his missions to Germany, Russia, and the Far East, feeling that if she refused to be a part of important times in her husband's life, "some flow or growth would stop."

Second only to her marriage as a "source of strength and repose" are her children. Away from them for several weeks on a trip to the United States, she muses, "When I am dissatisfied with how other things are going, with my progress in something else, with my mind, eyes, reading, writing, I turn to them as to a rock. It seems strange because I feel as though they were more necessary to me than I to them."

Yet even family relationships as close as these do not fulfill all her needs. One also needs friends, she writes, to keep alive "the straight stick inside of you that was there before you got married and goes on existing somehow irrespective of marriage." This self, she adds, "gets rather soft and vinelike without outside contacts." Her gift for creating lasting friendships—with her mother and sister as well as with those outside her family—is evident throughout the book. In both her correspondence and her accounts of her meetings with others she communicates her willingness to share her own deepest feelings and her ability to listen receptively. She was not, however, uncritically accepting of everyone she met. She could be quite caustic in her comments about new acquaintances, particularly those in the upper reaches of society, and she found the English as a whole cold and unapproachable, noting with regret as she prepared to leave Long Barn, that although she had come to love the place dearly in her two years there, she had made no new friends.

The Flower and the Nettle will appeal to many as a full, engrossing account of political and social life in western Europe in the years just before the war. Others will be attracted to the book by the same qualities that have drawn readers to ***Gift from the Sea*** for two decades—the author's perception of the forces constantly threatening to break her life and ours into fragments and her ability to share those insights that have helped her to remain whole in the face of conflicting demands and pressures. Both men and women may find meaning for themselves in this record of one woman's attempt to "live life as an art." (pp. 294-97)

Elizabeth Johnston Lipscomb, "The Flower and the Nettle: Diaries and Letters of Anne Morrow Lindbergh, 1936-1939," in Magill's Literary Annual, 1977, *pp. 294-98.*

David Kirk Vaughan (essay date 1988)

[*In the following excerpt from his critical study* Anne Morrow Lindbergh, *Vaughan describes the content and style of, as well as the response to, the highly controversial work* The Wave of the Future.]

Probably none of Anne Morrow Lindbergh's books has been the subject of more argument, criticism, and misunderstanding than her third book, ***The Wave of the Future.*** This small forty-one-page book produced a tremendously animated public response; evidence of one aspect of the book's influence can be seen today in repeated uses of the phrase "wave of the future," often used in connection with the development of some new product or technological breakthrough. But most people who use the phrase are probably not aware of its origin. Written primarily as Lindbergh's attempt to clarify in her own mind her rationale for American noninvolvement in the war on the European continent, ***The Wave of the Future*** became a focal point of the debate over neutrality versus direct involvement in the months before the Japanese attack on Pearl Harbor. Its antiwar, noninvolvement sentiment evolved, in part, from her response to her husband's isolationist speeches in the early months of World War II. But it also owed its genesis to the philosophical views of her father, Dwight Morrow, primarily his middle-of-the-road, practical approach to solving international disputes. Although Lindbergh later expressed regret for some of the views presented in the book, ***The Wave of the Future*** nevertheless remains a significant literary achievement because it was written during an important moment in American history, and because it represents an essential expression of the rational outlook that pervades her writing.

In spite of the work's stronger appeal to emotion than to fact, Lindbergh articulated in a calm and persuasive manner thoughts that were on the minds of many Americans in late 1940, by arguing that the conflict in Europe was more than a simplistic confrontation of the forces of Good and Evil. In addition to a quiet and reasoned style, she incorporated natural elements as symbols, including the sea and features of the American landscape. In ***The Wave of the Future*** Lindbergh worked toward a goal that was probably impossible to attain, but she achieved an impressive level of success.

The Wave of the Future is the central, keystone document in a three-part statement of Lindbergh's fears of and reactions to the early events of World War II. Her initial views of the war in Europe appeared in an article entitled **"Prayer for Peace,"** published in the *Reader's Digest* in January 1940. ***The Wave of the Future*** was published in October of that year. Her third statement, **"Reaffirma-**

tion," a response to critics of ***The Wave of the Future,*** appeared in the *Atlantic Monthly* in June 1941. The three works are integrally linked; to consider ***The Wave of the Future*** in an appropriate context it is necessary to consider the three essays as a whole and to review the events in the Lindberghs' lives and world conditions that preceded the writing of these three sequential works.

Charles Lindbergh's knowledge of German aircraft production capacities gained during his and his wife's three-and-a-half year stay in Europe made him fearful of German technological superiority, and he despaired of a peaceful outcome of the European political situation. Anne, who accompanied him on many of his trips, came to share these views from her own observations and from discussions with her husband and the people they met on their travels. Within five months after their return to the United States, Germany invaded Poland, and the war they had been dreading began. From the fall of 1939 until the attack on Pearl Harbor in December 1941, Charles was involved in nonintervention activities, giving thirteen addresses across the country and becoming allied with the America First Committee.

In April he resigned his commission in the Air Corps, a move prompted by his desire not to bring adverse publicity upon his friends in the military service, and by his repeated attacks on President Roosevelt's foreign policy. On 11 September in a speech at Des Moines, Iowa, he addressed some of his remarks toward American Jews, suggesting that they were pressuring the administration into involvement in the war to serve their own interests. These remarks brought a great outcry against him, so intense that even some of his hard-line conservative friends on the America First Committee began to distance themselves from him.

Anne shared her husband's concern over German war preparedness, but was not by nature an isolationist in her views as was her husband. Her educational and literary inclinations led her toward a more universal perspective. While she was willing to believe that the United States was largely unprepared for involvement in the war, she was less enthusiastic about nonintervention. As a result of her wide reading and the many personal contacts the Lindberghs had made during their stay in Europe, she was reluctant to speak out for the kind of position that her husband had taken, a position that appeared to counsel turning a deaf American ear to the plight of their European friends. Thus torn between two opposing stands—one in favor of nonintervention, the other of sympathy and support for England and France—she began to work out a philosophical position that she hoped would accommodate both views. Her trilogy conveying her concern over world affairs—the three works mentioned above, with ***The Wave of the Future*** as the cornerstone—was the result. (pp. 52-4)

In late May 1940 Lindbergh wrote a long letter to her former teacher of creative writing at Smith College, Mina Curtiss. After discussing the challenges and difficulties of writing, she reflected on the world condition: "The wave that is sweeping over Europe will, it seems to me, surely sweep over us too. I don't mean necessarily war or Nazi domination. But, rather, something else which is trying to push up through the crust of the world's habits and has thus far only found its expression in such horrible and abortive forms as communism, nazism, and war."

Four months later this comment was given greater articulation in ***The Wave of the Future,*** a work that disturbed the already troubled minds of Americans. ***The Wave of the Future*** is an expanded version of the thought Lindbergh shared with her former teacher; but it became one of the most widely discussed books to appear during the course of the war.

According to her diary, Lindbergh wrote ***The Wave of the Future*** in a ten-day period, from 16 to 25 August 1940. This was not her normal mode of writing, which was to work and rework her material over an extended period of time. A diary entry [included in ***War Within and Without***] dated 16 August, when the aerial Battle of Britain was at its most crucial stage, suggests the reason for the rapidity with which she worked: "I work on an article [***The Wave of the Future***] all morning. I do not 'write' it exactly, I am so full of it (the whole winter's travail of thought, anguish, doubt, arguments, defense—and affirmation). It flows out of me, unmindful of how it is 'written.' " As her earlier comments to Mina Curtiss indicate, the ideas of ***The Wave of the Future*** had in fact been formulating themselves in her mind for many months.

The essay begins on the same note of philosophical questioning that characterized **"A Prayer for Peace."** She emphasizes that her essay is to be thought of as a "confession of faith" (the subtitle of the book), and she suggests that a faith "is not seen, but felt; not proved, but believed; not a program, but a dream."

Addressing the key question of whether involvement with the Allied cause is as clear-cut a case of good against evil as the pro-Ally forces argue, she suggests that such a perspective may be too simplistic in its outlook, and that while the aggressions of the German forces may be "sins," there are "other sins, such as blindness, selfishness, irresponsibility, smugness, lethargy, and resistance to change—sins which we 'Democracies,' all of us, are guilty of."

Lindbergh returns to an idea that appeared also in **"A Prayer for Peace,"** as she argues that the democracies could be accused of not acting in good faith toward the German people after World War I, and that if support instead of penalties had been extended to Germany there might have been "no Naziism and no war." Borrowing an image from Yeats's "The Second Coming," she suggests that something important and ultimately valuable is "trying to come to birth" even though its first appearance may take an unpleasant shape. She characterizes the nationalist, expansionist movements at work in Germany, Italy, and Russia as parts of a "vast revolution," whose forces and effects represent something larger than the struggle between the agents of good and evil. The leaders of these countries, she says, have discovered how to use the new social and economic forces that have surged up in the world. These forces may have been misused, but the leaders of Germany, Italy, and Russia "have sensed the changes and they have exploited them. They have felt the wave of the future and they have leapt upon it. The evils we deplore in these systems are not in themselves the future; they are scum on the wave of the future." She urges her readers to take a larger, "planetary" view of the world's troubles, and to avoid moving toward pro- or anti-war positions in reaction to the "gigantic specter of fear" which exists in America.

Although Lindbergh later expressed regret for some of the views presented in the book, *The Wave of the Future* nevertheless remains a significant literary achievement because it was written during an important moment in American history, and because it represents an essential expression of the rational outlook that pervades her writing.

—David Kirk Vaughan

Asking her readers to consider the dangerous conditions that helped to produce the war as a threat as serious as that of military invasion, Lindbergh returns to her metaphor of the sea to suggest the hopelessness of struggling against the forces of change at work in the world: "The wave of the future is coming and there is no fighting it." She recommends reconsideration of personal and national value systems instead of marshaling for war. She challenges her readers to consider the merits of adapting to change, for, she says, "only in growth, reform, and change, paradoxically enough, is true security to be found." She expresses the hope that change can occur without "such terrible bloodshed" as is occurring in Europe.

She closes by urging her readers to accept the "tremendous challenge" of bringing this dream of change "to birth in a warlike world," for, she concludes, "like all acts of creation it will take labor, patience, pain—and an infinite faith in the future." Her comparison of her dream of change to the process of birth was more than a literary device; shortly after ***The Wave of the Future*** was published she gave birth to her fourth child—her first daughter.

Public reaction to ***The Wave of the Future*** was mixed and intense. Those who disagreed with its message often misread or misinterpreted certain key passages in the text, primarily those in which the expression "the wave of the future" appeared. In the essay Lindbergh specifically identifies the wave of the future with the widespread force of revolution at work in the world, not with the individual national movements, such as fascism, Nazism, and communism; these, she makes repeatedly clear, are the "scum" on the surface of the wave. But a common reaction was to argue that Lindbergh had identified Nazism and fascism as the "wave of the future," and that she was urging submission to their programs of expansion. This misreading of her essay appeared in numerous forms in the months following its publication; even E. B. White's thoughtful and generally insightful review in *Harper's Magazine* in February 1941 illustrated this tendency.

In a diary entry for 8 April 1941 [from ***War Within and Without***] Lindbergh notes that she has been reading over her "old notes, including my 'answer' to my critics. Wish now I had published it—and the thought disturbs my morning." Because this is her first mention of any "reply" to critics of ***The Wave of the Future,*** we can assume that she must have been mulling over her reaction to critics for a number of months. A diary entry for 27 October 1940 recorded the comfort she received from a sympathetic letter from the poet W. H. Auden, who wrote to her that "the hardest solitude to bear" is "the knowledge that everything one writes goes out helpless into the world to be turned to evil as well as good." On 14 April 1941 she noted that her husband thought she should publish her reply; two weeks later it was in the hands of the *Atlantic Monthly* editors. It appeared in the June issue of the magazine under the title **"Reaffirmation."**

The tone of **"Reaffirmation"** is stronger, more confident, than that of the previous essays. Gone is Lindbergh's need to apologize for speaking out on the issue of world peace. Her aim now is not to lay the foundation of a new philosophy, but to clarify her previously expressed argument. She begins by reminding her readers that ***The Wave of the Future*** was written not as a political pamphlet but as an expression of her personal philosophy, and that some commonly voiced objections to the essay need to be answered. The most troublesome aspect expressed by her critics is their almost universal misreading of her metaphorical use of the image of the *wave;* the wave, she says, was intended to represent the force of change. But in the minds of many readers, she continues, it has become a "protean symbol which has been used to mean whatever the critic desires." She denies that she ever associated it with the Nazi, fascist, or communist movements: "To me, the Wave of the Future is none of these things. It is, as I see it, a movement of adjustment to a highly scientific, mechanized, and material era of civilization, with all its attendant complications, and as such it seems to me inevitable." She repeats her description of the evils of fascism and Nazism as the "scum" on the surface of the wave, and she argues that her intent was not to suggest giving way before the wave but to prepare for it and to guide its forces in the best way possible.

In this clarification, and in the comments that follow, Lindbergh emphasizes the impact of *science* and *mechanization* much more heavily than she had in the earlier two essays. The causes of the current worldwide upheaval, she now says, are due as much to the effects of science and mechanization as to post-World War I economic conditions: "The causes, it seems to me, go back to actions of our own in the last century, to the impact of science on the delicately balanced life of man." In this section Lindbergh demonstrates for the first time her concern about the problem of appropriate social accommodation of technological developments. She restates her idea that the present period is "revolutionary," adding that she believes that this revolution is "in its essence good" because "the effort to adjust to a mechanized world is a necessary one."

Lindbergh restates at some length her belief that America should avoid involvement in the war in Europe because America is in a state of "internal and external unpreparedness." Her stronger nonintervention message in **"Reaffirmation"** may be partly the result of her husband's intensive speech-making activities at the time.

Lindbergh closes by returning to her assessment of the causes of the current world revolution, in which she sees the advances of science and the emphasis on material things as important factors:

> The revolution that will have to take place over the world before it can again begin its march forward seems to me not alone the conquest of machine by man, but much more deeply the conquest of spirit over matter. The material world has outstripped us, and we must try to make up our lost ground.

She concludes by suggesting that "we have in our heritage and in our temperament both the man of action and the dreamer; both the practical man and the visionary, the technician and the mystic," qualities that she hopes will enable America to "give her greatest possible contribution to civilization."

In her 1940 and 1941 essays Lindbergh was fighting a losing battle against the American mood and world events.

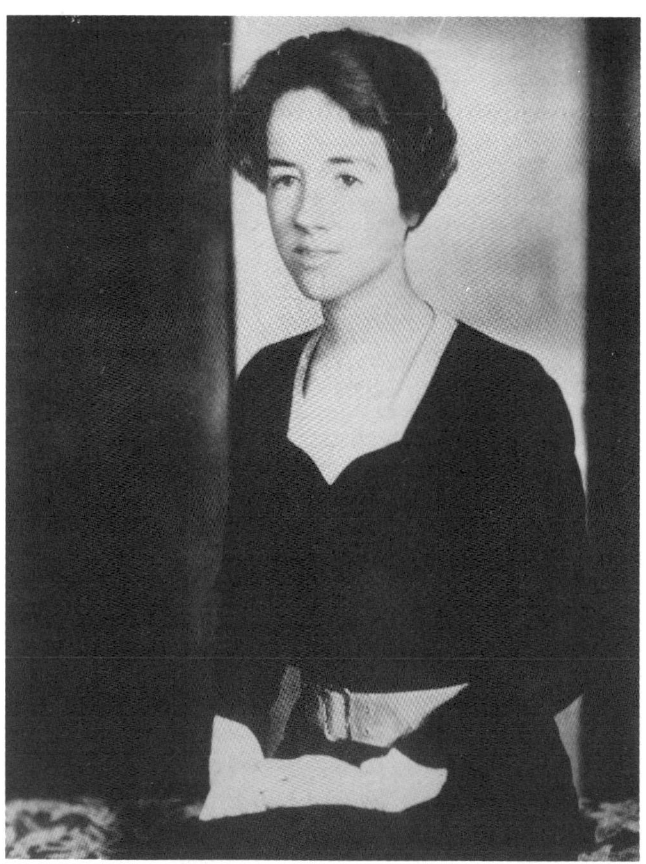

Anne Spencer Morrow in 1928.

But these noninterventionist writings, and ***The Wave of the Future*** in particular, are significant in terms of what they represented to the American public at large and what they tell us about Lindbergh as a writer. ***The Wave of the Future***—and to a lesser extent the two essays that precede and follow it—is significant because it reflects American confusion and concern over events in Europe. It attempts to articulate the conflicting feelings of revenge and guilt in regard to initial German aggression. It draws attention to the real need to avoid hasty and unthinking movement toward entering a war that America was, in 1939 and 1940, at least, ill prepared to wage. And it represents a significant rhetorical achievement in that it is able to present successfully a philosophically complex argument to an audience who received those arguments sympathetically (for the most part), even if it did not always agree with the viewpoints presented. ***The Wave of the Future*** both participates in and symbolizes a central intellectual issue at a crucial time in American history.

As a result of writing these essays, Lindbergh increased her commitment to social and political issues, strengthened her tendencies to describe personal growth, added dimensions of religious and spiritual elements to her writing, and confirmed her preference for images and metaphors of nature—especially of the wind and the sea. Even though she later abjured some of the ideas in and motivations for ***The Wave of the Future,*** it is in many ways the pivotal work of her creative career, generated in the crucible of personal commitment and public clamor. (pp. 56-61)

David Kirk Vaughan, in his Anne Morrow Lindbergh, *Twayne Publishers, 1988, 138 p.*

Elsie F. Mayer (essay date 1988)

[*In the following excerpt from her critical study* My Window on the World: The Works of Anne Morrow Lindbergh, *Mayer discusses the significance of* Gift from the Sea.]

On 27 March 1955, one week after Elizabeth Vining's review of Lindbergh's ***Gift from the Sea*** in the *New York Times,* the book appeared on the best-seller list, where it remained for eighty consecutive weeks. For fifty-one of the eighty weeks it occupied first place before it was nudged from the list by another of Lindbergh's works, ***The Unicorn and Other Poems.*** During the first year of publication ***Gift from the Sea*** sold approximately 320,000 copies. In 1975 Pantheon Books published a twentieth-anniversary edition. Total sales of both editions, including hardcover and paperback, exceed 6,000,000 copies and continue to rise.

How can one account for the success of ***Gift from the Sea,*** a series of personal philosophic reflections made by a middle-aged woman vacationing on an island off the Florida coast? One answer may be that its author was the wife of a great national hero. Lindbergh's readers, who had been thrilled by ***North to the Orient*** and ***Listen! The Wind,*** were curious to see what else she was capable of writing. Yet curiosity as a cause of the book's success is inconclusive since the Lindberghs' popularity had plummeted to its nadir as a result of their objection to American involvement in World War II.

The success of ***Gift from the Sea*** can also be attributed to the beauty of its language. Sara Hay, one of its reviewers, notes [in *The Saturday Review*]:

> Anne Morrow Lindbergh has the poet's capacity for investing the thing seen with its subjective raiment, of choosing the valid external symbol of an idea or an emotion. She has, as well, a quick responsiveness to the natural world about her, and a way of transmitting that awareness to the reader.

Hay accurately identifies a strength of the work, the discovery in nature of the appropriate symbols to embody human experience. Lindbergh nurtured this talent through frequent reflections on nature, long a practice of hers, and through keeping a dairy—confessional in tone and descriptive in substance. In ***Gift from the Sea*** the rhythm of the sea, contrasting with the rhythm of modern living, illustrates the need to recapture the former if one expects to explore the depth of one's being. The effectiveness of individual tropes to depict the different stages of human relationships and to differentiate women's and men's lives is clearly evident.

But poetic language alone only partially explains the merits of a book that continues to be widely praised. A principal cause of its sustained appeal rests on its thematic import. The essays focus on three kinds of love: passionate *(eros),* maternal *(storge),* and mutual *(philia).* Throughout, the essayist not only explores the relationships associated with these forms of love but also seeks greater self-knowledge. In the main, these are universals which have continuously engaged the human mind and heart. With delicacy Lindbergh clothes these universals in modern dress, enhancing their relevance for her audience. So successful are her efforts that to read ***Gift from the Sea*** is to experience a moment of calm in which one identifies with the subject as a whole.

Assuming that most other women were content with their lives, Lindbergh notes in the opening comments of the work that initially the essays constituting ***Gift from the Sea*** were intended to be private. Her goal was to define "my own particular pattern of living, my own individual balance of life, work, and human relationships." In time, however, she discovered her life was not unique. Many women and men were searching for solutions to the problems surfacing in the essays. Beyond appearance were the attempts to shape more creative lives, to satisfy individual needs, and to develop more sensitive relationships. When discussion with her contemporaries revealed the similarity of their thinking, she decided to share the essays with others. Hence, what began as private reflections became a collection of significant truths worthy of publication. In assuming the role of spokeswoman for others, Lindbergh resembles Montaigne, who was attracted to the idea that he was a representative human being throughout his essays. Moreover, what Roy Pascal observes about the autobiographer can also be said of Lindbergh in ***Gift from the Sea.*** A single personality can sum up a whole social trend, a generation, or a class.

The explicit ideas of ***Gift from the Sea,*** woman's need for solitude and creativity and the complexity of human relationships, were rooted in Lindbergh's thoughts long before they appeared in the famous work. A sensitivity to people's needs and a penchant for reflection and introspection are apparent in her life. Beginning in the early diaries and letters, and continuing thereafter, she often reflects on the characteristics of people around her as a prelude to examining her own self-consciousness and fears. She believes in the interdependence of people and nature. Nature, to which she keenly responds, is impregnated with meaning for the observer who seeks it.

Especially relevant to ***Gift from the Sea*** is her stance on marriage. Early in the diaries she criticizes the romantic view of human relationships including marriage: "the falsity of the romantic pattern in life." Love she perceives to be a "motivating power" for good; it is "a force" that inspires a person to give to others. Marriage founded on anything other than this kind of love she rejects as spurious: " 'Love [in marriage] does not consist in looking at one another but in looking together in the same direction.' " This common vision she has experienced with Charles. The images scattered throughout the diaries emphasize the realistic character of marriage over the romantic. For example, the images describing the middle years of marriage, symbolized by the oyster shell in ***Gift from the Sea,*** are adumbrated in the diary by sea images rugged and harsh: "*That* is marriage, . . . those old twisted hemp ropes that hold the boats, gray and salt-drenched, and not beautiful at all, but tough and holding." Amidst passages dealing with the middle years of her marriage, there is a glimpse of Lindbergh's ideal, later formulated in the essay "Argonauta." In contrast to the "pre-marriage intensity" she had experienced earlier, her reunion with Charles after he returned from a trip to Detroit in 1942 is described in glowing terms of the ideal fulfilled [in ***War Within and Without***]:

> the casual give and take, the wonderful blending of silence and communication, sharing and solitariness, being bored and being stimulated, disputes and agreements, the everyday and extraordinary, the near and the far—that wonderful blending that makes for the incredible richness, variety, harmoniousness, and toughness of marriage.

Noteworthy in this passage is the balance between opposites and the harmony that Lindbergh perceives to be essential in the ideal marriage.

Despite her objection to the romantic view of marriage, she respects marriage for the opportunity it offers for human growth and happiness. Denying the possibility of the perfect marriage in the early reflections on the subject, she nevertheless believes marriage capable of transforming women and men into better human beings. "It is like your face, or your body. . . . It's given to you to make something out of." Circumstances provided in marriage play a special role in the maturing process. For instance, the public indictment of Charles and herself because of their objection to the country's involvement in World War II strengthened not only their awareness of the mercurial nature of public opinion but also the personal bond between them as husband and wife.

If evidence for Lindbergh's attitude towards marriage abounds in the diaries, so also does her advocacy of solitude and friendship. As a young wife and writer she objects to her lack of solitude. She wonders why greater distance between women and men cannot be managed and why mutual respect for individual endeavors cannot be maintained. Is solitude compatible with marriage? This is a persistent question, whose answer is postponed until it is addressed in ***Gift from the Sea.*** Like solitude, friendship is viewed as essential to a balanced life. Although Lindbergh acknowledges that old friendships often dissolve after marriage, she admits the continued need for friends if marriage is to be whole and complete. Loneliness, which sometimes invades marriage, can be alleviated by friendships. Without them a "kind of scurvy of the mind sets in. . . . Your husband and your marriage may be *life* itself but you haven't got the spark to live that life without something from the outside." Lindbergh's insistence on the need for friendships to nurture marriage loosens the soil for the eventual unearthing of the significant truth in ***Gift from the Sea;*** in the latter work she illustrates how the relationship between married women and men changes.

The need for solitude intertwines with the need for creativity. The connection is explored first in the diaries and letters before surfacing in ***Gift from the Sea.*** The conflict between Lindbergh's personal need for creativity and the demands of marriage and motherhood appears intermittently. Her comments illustrate her attempts to understand and balance the two. In one particularly revealing passage [from ***The Flower and the Nettle***] she distinguishes between men's activities, symbolized by a straight line, and women's activities, symbolized by a circle. The straight line represents a concentration of energy directed towards the achievement of a single goal; the circle a dispensing of energy over several goals. Clearly, the dispensing of energy and the number of goals differ for women and men. Men's success notwithstanding, Lindbergh maintains that women must not change in order to conform to the male pattern; instead, they must work towards fulfillment of their own potential:

> I don't think women should try to be straight lines. I think they should be circles. . . . I think they should be rounded and receptive and . . . aware and open to many currents and calls and—yes—even distractions. . . . And the women who compete in men's fields sacrifice these peculiarly feminine aptitudes in order to get "straight-line" results.

In effect, Lindbergh insists that women must reaffirm the female pattern. To do otherwise would deprive them of a source of strength and fulfillment.

The satisfaction this stance affords, however, is temporary; the struggle for a satisfactory answer to an apparent conundrum persists. In her diary dated 3 April 1941, the struggle reappears: "The problem of the woman and her 'work' is still so unsolved. It eats at me perpetually." In the same entry she is consoled by the eventual success that perseverance promises: "Can you write a book and have children at the same time? Yes, if you're content to do it very, *very* slowly." As late as 1942, however, Lindbergh, taking her cue from George Sand, whom she believes chose life over art, endorses the position that women's creative endeavors remain secondary in their lives. Not until ***Gift from the Sea,*** in which she sees more clearly the role creativity plays in women's self-fulfillment, does she alter her position and elevate creativity to a human need for women as well as men.

In ***Gift from the Sea*** Lindbergh recasts her diffused and often problematic ideas on women and marriage. Here these ideas are given their clearest expression. The work demonstrates her predilection for literary shapeliness. The predominant pattern of the essays includes a description of the environment or a sea shell, followed by a philosophic reflection evoked by either, and, finally, a resolution. Specifically, the reflection usually focuses on a personal problem. The autobiographical nature of the essays adds to their interest and emotive impact, but the explicitness with which the problem and solution are depicted in ***Gift from the Sea*** displaces the gradual discovery of truth, characteristically present in the intimate style of the personal essay.

The structure of the work is chronological, its mode experiential. In eight essays, six of which are symbolized by seashells, Lindbergh reflects on the nature and role of American women. Each essay treats a topic independently but is thematically connected to the others. Moreover, after the first, each essay builds on its forerunner, leading to a conclusion that resembles a climax in fiction. Together the essays resemble a mosaic whose interrelated facets reflect a single entity, whole and intricate.

In the opening chapter, "The Beach," Lindbergh notes that the planned activities for her seashore vacation, reading and writing, have failed. She soon faces the simple truth that in the presence of the sea "one is forced against one's mind, against all tidy resolutions, back into the primeval rhythms of the seashore." One enters nature's rhythms: rollers on the beach, swaying pines, and flying herons. One becomes part of a scene "erased by today's tides of all yesterday's scribblings." All the while one listens to the sea, one must exercise patience and faith, for "the sea does not reward those who are too anxious, too greedy, or too impatient." It reveals its treasures, cosmic and intuitive truths, intermittently; they can be neither forced nor willed. When the mind eventually awakens from the stupor imposed by the sea, it awakens to new insights "not in a city sense—no—but beachwise."

Emerging early in the following essay, "The Channelled Whelk," is the first truth rendered by a seashell. This shell, abandoned first by a whelk and later a hermit crab, reminds Lindbergh of her withdrawal from home. The shell, simple, bare, and beautiful, contrasts with her suburban life, "blurred with moss, knobby with barnacles." Its spiral curve culminating in a point evokes thoughts of her goal: to acquire "a singleness of eye, a purity of intention, a central core to my life." One mode of achieving this goal suggested by the shell is "simplification of life" but immediately thereafter appear obstacles to its achievement, domestic minutiae and social involvement that collectively consume the time of modern women. These constitute a "life of multiplicity," which lead "not to unification but to fragmentation."

There follows a major metaphor of the work, a wheel whose hub represents women's inner core and whose spokes radiating towards the circumference women's many activities. Women experience tension because their preoccupation with the peripheral activities (the spokes) distances them from their inner self (the hub). Hence, the ideal of "the inner inviolable core, the single eye," represented by the channelled whelk, is, indeed remote. The query this essay raises is how to cultivate one's inner strength when circumstances threaten "to crack the hub of the wheel." The channelled whelk offers one answer and the beach another. The shell suggests controlling life's distractions, the beach reducing one's possessions. The result, as life on the island proves, is serenity and beauty. Unfortunately, reality interrupts this moment of revelation, reminding Lindbergh that the beach experience is temporary. She concludes that if transported home, the channelled whelk can remind her of the need to simplify her life. Meanwhile, on the island the channelled whelk has set in motion an inner journey.

The following essay, symbolized by the moon shell, which stares with a "mysterious single eye," establishes the isolation of the island ringed by waves. Reflection on this fact brings to the foreground a basic truth of human existence: the "solitariness" of each individual. Despite this truth, however, modern society eschews solitude. What was originally nurtured as necessary for dreams is now extrapolated from life by filling solitary moments with trivia. Lindbergh insists that solitude be restored to one's life because it offers opportunities for spiritual renewal. Her solitude on the beach has proven its worth; it has drawn her closer to nature and ironically to the people in her life. While allowing her to experience contact with her inner core, the solitude provided by the island has strengthened her awareness of the interdependence of all human beings. Exhilarated by this insight, she feels her spirit overflowing to embrace others.

The moon shell offers another lesson. Traditionally, women have given themselves often to the point of depleting their inner resources. The paradox of women's lives is that they desire to give of themselves yet resent giving "in small pieces." In Lindbergh's term they resent giving themselves "purposelessly." As a consequence, women hunger, not knowing for what they hunger. To restore "*purposeful* giving" to women's lives and to alleviate their spiritual hunger, they must find again the true essence of themselves, "that firm strand which will be the indispensable center of a whole web of human relationships." In order to experience this restoration, solitude, not ever increasing activity is necessary. Women suffer from "*Zerrissenheit*—torn-to-pieces-hood," and only the activity that allows them to be "inwardly attentive" can lead to more self-fulfilling lives. Cultivation of the inner life undervalued in modern society must be rediscovered. The moon shell emphasizes the role solitude plays in this venture.

The double-sunrise shell, perused by Lindbergh after the moon shell, is a delicate bivalve representing human relationships, in particular the early stages of marriage. The double-sunrise shell is "pure, simple and unencumbered," resembling life on the island. But like life on the island the first stage of marriage is short-lived and yields to a more complicated stage when partners accept the sex roles imposed on them by social custom. Men become immersed in work, women in home and family. Unfortunately, with this second stage comes a loss: men in personal relationships and women in "creative identity." Although the desire for the first stage of marriage may persist, it can only be experienced temporarily, for "no permanent pure-relationship exists." Relationships change, expand, and build "new forms." For Lindbergh the double-sunrise shell is significant because it so clearly encases the essence of the first stage of marriage: "two flawless halves bound together with a single hinge, meeting each other at every point, the dawn of a new day spreading on each face." Its delicacy may enchant the reader momentarily, but its beauty changes with the passage of time. The double-sunrise shell reinforces the truth that the enthusiasm experienced in the first stage of marriage, although beautiful, is fleeting and will eventually vanish.

While the double-sunrise shell represents the early self-contained relationship between women and men in marriage, the middle years with their multitudinous responsibilities is represented by the oyster shell. For Lindbergh the oyster shell reflects women's lives during these years: "untidy, spread out in all directions, heavily encrusted with accumulations." The bonds of marriage are nevertheless strengthened during this period as husband and wife are drawn into an intricate web of shared loyalties and experiences. There is, moreover, the common struggle "to achieve a place in the world." Unfortunately, this struggle, usually for the sake of the children, demands a price in inner growth. To compensate for this deprivation, one must weigh carefully the value of the activities undertaken so that the loss of these years may not be irretrievable. Although these years are replete with activities, they need not be without merit. If the activities are worthwhile, the years can be fruitful. Despite its ugliness, Lindbergh is fond of the oyster shell because of its adaptability and its tenacity. More importantly, it points to future possibilities for shedding the past and acknowledging personal limitations. It offers for reflection the new opportunities for growth that enter life in middle age along with the newly acquired freedom necessary to cultivate "the neglected side of one's self."

Although Lindbergh's ideas thus far radiate insight and hope for the future, they pale against her brilliant vision of the ideal human relationship, drawn in the essay entitled "Argonauta." From the outset of this essay the reader expects to witness the extraordinary, for the qualities of the argonauta bespeak unusual beauty: "transparent, delicately fluted like a Greek column." Lindbergh notes the truth issuing from the double-sunrise and oyster shells, as valuable as they are, have been left behind; the argonauta, "lovely shell, lovely image," belongs to a unique collection. Through the argonauta she has entered "the chartless seas of the imagination," source of her ideal. Does the possibility of a new relationship in middle age exist? By leaving its shell for the open sea after depositing her young, the argonauta answers affirmatively. The newly acquired freedom of middle age can effectuate the ideal, here specified as "the meeting of two whole fully developed people as persons." The essay illustrates how this ideal, gradually realized by Lindbergh, originated with Rilke, whose ideas she ponders. Rilke imagines the ideal marriage consisting of " 'two solitudes [that] protect and touch and greet each other.' " In Lindbergh's view, equality and maturity will enable two people to develop into unique individuals. Her realistic eye leads her, nonetheless, to acknowledge that the ideal marriage belongs to the distant future since the process of human growth is evolutionary and slow.

In the final pages of this essay, Lindbergh dramatizes an ideal relationship, "a glimpse of the argonauta," in the form of two sisters sharing a single day on the island. Acknowledging such a relationship differs from that between women and men, she claims her portrayal reveals "the essence of relationships" generally. To justify further her choice of two women as an exemplum of the ideal, she adds, "The light shed by any good relationship illuminates all relationships." When morning arrives, the sisters fall in tune with the rhythm of the wind and waves. The day progresses from work and study in the morning to relaxation on the beach in the afternoon and conversation before a final walk on the beach in the evening. Throughout the day there is solitude for work and time for sharing experience; all the while their emotions correspond to the sea's rhythm. Above all, a balance exists, combining intellectual, physical, and social activities. Lindbergh's inquiry into the cause of the day's perfection draws the response—freedom, that "limitless feeling" of space and time as well as the variety of activities performed with "unforced rhythm."

Following this passage the ideal relationship is further symbolized by two dancers in harmony with each other. The dance, when executed by the same set of rules for both partners, brings forth "the joy of creation . . . and the joy of living in the moment." One learns the harmony of the dance through love. When both partners love unconditionally, they participate in a common rhythm. From this particular rhythm comes an awareness of universal rhythm, the divine order in creation, symbolized by the pattern of the argonauta's life from parenthood to independence. Should not, Lindbergh asks, two persons be able "to swing from the intimate and the particular and the functional out into the abstract and universal" as suggested by the argonauta?

At this point the metaphor of a swinging pendulum reveals persistent obstacles in the movement towards the ideal. Borrowing from St. Exupéry, Lindbergh decries belief in the permanency of human feelings when "the only continuity possible, in life as in love, is in growth, in fluidity—in freedom." The "veritable life" of the emotions changes just as the pendulum swings from one point to another. Although humans crave security in their relationships, the only security rests in the relationship of the present moment. This truth and the inevitability of the "intermittency" of all human emotions stand as important insights emerging from Lindbergh's reflections. Each cycle of life, regardless of its imperfections, she discovers, must be credited with its own contribution just as the ebb, although less dramatic than the incoming tide, possesses its unique beauty.

As Lindbergh prepares to leave the island, she selects shells from among the many in her collection to carry home. The need for selectivity generates a new reflection in which life on the island is contrasted with life in modern society. Unlike the island, her suburban home suffers from excess. It is crowded with activity, people, and possessions. On the island there is time to explore and appreciate nature, not so at home. Silence, balanced activity, simplicity—all contrast with life at home. Her retreat to the island has not only dramatized this awareness but also introduced a new set of values, "island-precepts," by which she hopes to guide her life hereafter:

> Simplicity of living, as much as possible, to retain a true awareness of life. Balance of physical, intellectual, and spiritual life. Work without pressure. Space for significance and beauty. Time for solitude and sharing. Closeness to nature to strengthen understanding and faith in the intermittency of life.

Anne Morrow Lindbergh in 1985 with a statue of her husband by sculptor Paul Granlund.

The few shells selected for her perusal at home will hopefully remind her of these truths.

In the last essay, "The Beach at My Back," Lindbergh expresses her concern over the ever-increasing number of global problems facing Americans at the time. Although their circle of responsibilities has widened, their response to them remains limited. They have not yet learned to cope with the problems that have emerged after World War II. At the outset of the reflection, women's penchant for nurturing individuals seems to Lindbergh ineffective for alleviating the suffering of the masses. But before the end of the essay, she asserts otherwise. The solution is for each person to meet the present needs: "the here, the now, the individual and his relationships." That women have tended to these in the past places them in a position to contribute to the world's need for healing the wounds inflicted by war. Together women and men can begin to solve social problems by attention to the "neglected realities" in themselves. In short, improving society begins with improving individuals. To assure herself that such improvement is possible, she repeats the message of the sea: "Patience—Faith—Openness . . . Simplicity—Solitude—Intermittency."

Towards the end of ***Gift from the Sea*** Lindbergh comments: "Island living has been a lens through which to examine my own life in the North." Specifically, "life in the North" means the life as spouse and mother in an American suburb following World War II. Within this context the work becomes a challenge to the current mores of Lindbergh's day. Since the problems addressed in the essays were indigenous to the period, they were easily identified by her contemporaries. In particular, her call for change, ardent and urgent, demonstrates her disagreement with the popularly held attitudes about the nature and role of women.

To begin with, during the early postwar years the life of the suburban woman was held aloft as the model for women to emulate. In the main, her function was to serve; her world consisted of home, community, church, and in a few instances local politics. Every woman was said to be ruled by the "female principle"; its ideal embodied in the word "nurture." Lindbergh, although ostensibly conforming to the model, questions its validity. As ***Gift from the Sea*** demonstrates, a life bound exclusively by outward activities inhibits inner growth. Moreover, the conflict between unfulfilling activity and the personal desire for inner growth creates anxiety. Together the essays emphasize that the multiple roles assumed by modern women, contrary to popular belief, have created in them a spiritual vacuum.

If women were dissatisfied, the commonly accepted cause was the denial of their femininity. Since a woman's basic need was to be a wife, mother, and homemaker, the denial or suppression of this need invites dissatisfaction and in extreme cases neurosis. But Lindbergh suggests that impairment of personal growth, not the denial of socially assigned sex roles, is the principal cause of discontent, a truth revealed to her by the double-sunrise shell. In the essay focusing on the latter, she argues that women and men must find a way of compensating for their neglected side: women for the lack of creativity, men for the lack of nurturing. The implication for both sexes is clear. Without filling the void created by inattention to their neglected side, they cannot develop the whole self; and without this development there is discontent. Lindbergh seeks to transcend sex roles in the search for psychological harmony.

Lindbergh accepts the value of current studies delineating the physiological and sexual needs and habits of women if the limitations of such studies are acknowledged. Presumably the reference in ***Gift from the Sea*** to "mechanistic studies of her [woman] as a female animal" is to Alfred C. Kinsey's *Sexual Behavior in the Human Female,* subject of much discussion when published in 1953. Among its many observations on female sexuality, Kinsey notes that marriage should fulfill women's and men's aspirations as long as both can be sexually satisfied. Lindbergh, albeit subtly, points out the limitations of sex in the development of the inner self. Self-fulfillment is imperative, but she insists that a woman will discover "the true center of being a whole woman" through solitude and creativity. Moreover, as women cultivate the inner life through solitude, they must strive for self-sufficiency and eschew competition. Theirs is a pioneering endeavor challenging "tradition, convention and dogma," perpetrators of the present status of women. Lindbergh repudiates a purely biological foundation for marriage because it ignores women's spiritual nature. In effect, she rejects the concept of the idealized marriage of the 1940s and 1950s in which it was sufficient for women to assert their identity through their roles as wife and mother. Instead, Lindbergh calls for a recognition of women as individuals independent of their relationships.

Contrary to the popular adulation of the family, ***Gift from the Sea*** demonstrates its limitations for the individual striving for self-fulfillment. It is true that the busy years symbolized by the oyster shell offer some opportunities for personal growth, but these opportunities are limited. When grown children leave home to pursue their interests, a change in the family structure occurs, and parents are left facing an unknown future. Alarming is the absence of a talisman to guide middle-aged adults emerging from the oyster shell years, for society prefers to ignore them in favor of attending to youth. Lindbergh's reflection illustrates the shortsightedness of those who view the family as sacrosanct. A position that accentuates the value of familial relationships tends to underestimate the importance of other relationships. Those who idealize the family must eventually acknowledge its limited contribution to total human development.

A popular idea associated with marriage throughout the postwar years was embodied in the term "togetherness." The term stressed that a man's and a woman's place was in the home, "the true center of life." That the idea remained unchallenged testifies to the wholeheartedness with which it was endorsed. Lindbergh's rejection of the continuity of human emotions in favor of intermittency, however, places her at odds with this idea. For her, "togetherness" is restrictive. Her retreat to the island for private reflection and the cry for solitude testify to the fundamental independence of human beings. "Togetherness" is unrealistic because relationships change: "All living relationships are in process of change, of expansion and must perpetually be building themselves new forms." Lindbergh recognizes better than her contemporaries that exclusiveness stifles inner growth; and because "togetherness" promotes exclusiveness, it can be detrimental to marriage.

During this same period a paradoxical phenomenon surfaced concerning wives and mothers. As the drudgery of women's work decreased because of newly introduced household appliances, glorification of the suburban housewife increased. Betty Friedan observes that the popularizers of modern women deified their domestic functions, presupposing that history reached a glorious conclusion in the model of the modern housewife-mother. Before Friedan, Lindbergh cautions against the effects of technology on women's lives, for when used to decrease domestic chores, technology ironically increases them. Fewer chores do not free women from drudgery; instead they create a temporary vacuum, quickly filled by additional chores. Women are thus reduced to "a collection of functions." And, as Lindbergh insists, excessive activity creates a spiritual vacuum, which eventually entraps women in *Zerrissenheit.* While her barbs against the popular postwar image of the emancipated woman are delicately drawn, they are, nonetheless, barbs.

Gift from the Sea establishes that many women of the period found the role of wife-mother unfulfilling, an idea subsequently proven by the copious case studies found in Friedan's *The Feminine Mystique.* Lindbergh's solution to women's dissatisfaction illustrates her deviation from the popular position. Endorsing the current custom, she agrees that generally women should seek to fulfill themselves through marriage. But her concept of the ideal marriage with its freedom for both women and men necessitates that they be perceived differently. Whereas the public saw a woman in an "auxiliary status to her man," Lindbergh stresses the equality of wife and husband striving to become two wholly mature persons. Their fulfillment derives not from their functions, one subordinate to the other as the public maintained, but from their inner growth as human beings of equal worth.

Lindbergh's advocacy of fulfillment-through-marriage assumes broader significance in "The Beach at My Back." As identified here, the global problems facing society are tension, conflict, and suffering. For individuals these problems occupy the circumference of life's circle; at the center lies "the here, the now, and the individual." The connection between social and personal problems is securely grounded in the metaphor. The popular means of combating these problems was to accept the family as a haven against them: "the happy family huddling together against the visceral terror of modern times." Instead of escaping these problems, as the popular image suggests, Lindbergh faces them intelligently. As already noted, her solution rests on the belief that individuals can solve global problems by first solving personal problems. Thus, marriage and the family should provide not an escape from global problems but a means of solving them. Reflecting a socially sensitive consciousness, her ideas here reveal fresh insight at a time when the fear released by the atomic bomb paralyzed the national mind.

The simplification of life, solitude, creative activity, the recognition of intermittency as a quality of human emotion—all rendering Lindbergh more "beach-wise"—constitute essentials necessary for happiness on the deepest level of our being. If her advocacy of marriage as a salutary relationship for women bears some resemblance to the view of her contemporaries, clearly the potentiality of marriage to effect self-fulfillment is greater than they could imagine. In her solutions to the problems of married women she strikes out like a free spirit down an infrequently traveled path, rendering popular solutions superficial. Like its predecessor, ***The Wave of the Future, Gift from the Sea*** proves Lindbergh to be not only keenly aware of the social problems surrounding her but also independent in her pursuit of their solutions.

In the afterword to the twentieth-anniversary edition of ***Gift from the Sea,*** puzzled by continued interest in the book, Lindbergh asks the question: "Why should ***Gift from the Sea,*** after all we have undergone in these tumultuous twenty years have any validity for a new generation of women?" A response to her question can be found in Elizabeth Vining's review of the first edition. While most critics were eager to praise Lindbergh's poetic style and sensitive understanding of nature, Vining emphasized her ideas:

> Though it [***Gift from the Sea***] deals with the essential needs, gifts, obligations and aspirations of woman as distinct from those of man, it is in no sense merely what is sometimes slightingly called a woman's book. A sensitive, tensile, original mind probes delicately into questions of balance and relationship in the world today, and the result is a book for human beings . . . in search of maturity, whether man or woman.

Implicit in Vining's remarks are the universal themes: the search for identity, the complex nature of relationships, and the human craving for self-fulfillment. These themes, often overshadowed by Lindbergh's strikingly precise symbols, nevertheless explain the book's continuous appeal and ensure its worth.

Vining enforces the seriousness of ***Gift from the Sea*** by distinguishing it from the pejorative category, "a woman's book"; her recognition of the author's concern with "maturity" prepares the way for an interpretation of the book as an inward journey. Driven by personal need, Lindbergh, who undertakes the journey, explores the meaning of "femaleness." In this respect the book belongs to the literature of self-discovery, defined by Elaine Showalter as "a turning inward freed from some of the dependency of opposition, a search for identity." Lindbergh's exploration of the self combines sincerity, memory, anxiety, choice, and vision formed in the unconscious and raised to reality in the essays. The exploration itself is ensconced in the archetypal pattern of departure, journey, and return. There is Lindbergh's need to withdraw temporarily from the social conventions that shape her life in order to understand them. Having temporarily abandoned her familiar surroundings, she experiences insights capable of transforming her life. She returns home, confident of her ability to endow the circumstances of life with meaning. The choice of an island for her retreat reveals Lindbergh conforming to a time-honored tradition, for the island, like the desert and the mountains, has long served human beings as a place appropriate for reflection. Like poets and prophets she feels bound by the restraints of life and withdraws to a remote place in order to escape them. Through her reflections she discovers the means of transcending these restraints and thus succeeds in coming to terms with life.

Throughout the essays Lindbergh's behavior reveals the changes occurring within her. In the early essay, "Channelled Whelk," she describes her life as "blurred with moss, knobby with barnacles, its shape is hardly recognizable any more." Her reflection evokes the desire for inner peace, "a singleness of eye, a purity of intention, a central core to my life." Dissatisfied with her life at this point, she hovers at the edge of self-effacement. Before the time of departure arrives, however, her persistent questioning yields valued insights along with a plan for their implementation. Strengthened by them, she experiences a restoration of self-esteem. With enthusiasm she expresses hope that she can change her life. Hers is not a hope based on presumption, but rather on faith in the integrity of her vision.

Inherent in Lindbergh's thought is the acknowledgment that women and men must accept certain conditions as indigenous to life. Her rendering of the ideal marriage, for instance, with its balance and harmony, presupposes acceptance of equality as the prerogative of both sexes. The new freedom in marriage, symbolized by the argonauta, ushers in the ideal: "the meeting of two whole fully developed people as persons." Influenced by Rilke, Lindbergh anticipates the day when domination and submission in marriage will yield to a relationship allowing "space and freedom for growth, and in which each partner would be the means of releasing the other." It is evident that Lindbergh views the inferior status of women as unnatural and culturally derived. But the inferiority of women can be corrected; by acknowledging their mutual needs women and men can effect the independence and egalitarianism characteristic of the ideal marriage.

Throughout ***Gift from the Sea*** Lindbergh represents the self longing for fulfillment of her aspirations. In her view women and men will experience self-fulfillment when they come spiritually of age by developing the "neglected side" of their personality. The reward will be "a world to oneself." With this state comes a greater separation between two persons even in as intimate a relationship as marriage. Terrifying? Not for Lindbergh, who accepts Rilke's observation that by nature the distance between two persons is infinite. Clearly, Lindbergh's ideal for the individual person is androgynous. Except for biological differences the bifurcation between male and female is artificial. The self-fulfilled person of whom she dreams, neither purely female nor male, will experience a balance among all the faculties. The *animus* and *anima,* components which Jung claims inhere in every human personality, will be brought into conscious harmony. This harmony will continue to be postponed, however, as long as women and men limit themselves to the roles imposed on them by social custom.

With a realistic eye Lindbergh admits that the argonauta stage of marriage and the fulfillment of the self require many changes in both the individual and society. Hers is a vision that recognizes the interconnection between ontogenesis and phylogenesis. Its foundation rests on the concept that cultivation of the self precipitates individual change, which in turn precipitates social change. This interconnection, informing Lindbergh's thinking, enriches the texture of her ideas.

Lindbergh's sincerity is evident in her acknowledgment of the natural process of life. With her customary modesty she notes her solutions to problems are not definitive; the search for solutions is unceasing. Tomorrow will undoubtedly bring other problems, other solutions, just as the ebb and flow of the sea continues. Without intellectual pretensions, she courageously bares the vulnerability of modern women in the form of her own psyche. Collectively, the essays demonstrate what they advocate: a simplified life, rhythm and balance, and a measure of self-fulfillment that comes with solitude and creativity.

Admittedly, the verities in the work are not always revelatory, but the fusion of substance and form is extraordinary. Hence, it remains her most significant work. (pp. 64-82)

Elsie F. Mayer, in her My Window on the World: The Works of Anne Morrow Lindbergh, *Archon Books, 1988, 151 p.*

David Kirk Vaughan on Lindbergh's postscript to *Gift from the Sea:*

Lindbergh did acknowledge, in a postscript to *Gift from the Sea* added twenty years after its initial publication, "*Gift from the Sea* Reopened," that she had misspoken in two aspects of her discussion. The first was her assumption that "women's coming of age had been largely won by the Feminists of my mother's generation," and she admitted that many victories in the area of women's rights remained to be won. The second aspect involved the omission of a final stage in the progress of a woman's life, the period that occurs after the children have left the home. Lindbergh referred to this stage as the time of "the abandoned shell," a period she had not reached when *Gift from the Sea* was first published. This stage is characterized by solitude, the commodity she wished for more of in earlier stages: "when a mother is left, the lone hub of a wheel, with no other lives revolving about her, she faces a total re-orientation. It takes time to re-find the center of gravity."

David Kirk Vaughan in his Anne Morrow Lindbergh, *1988.*

Elsie F. Mayer (essay date 1988)

[In the following assay, the "Afterword" to her critical study My Window on the World, *Mayer discusses Lindbergh's treatment of personal and social issues in her*

works, concluding that "her forte lies in writing nonfiction: the diary and the essay."]

Lindbergh's works are autobiographical disclosures. In the nonfiction the disclosures convey her ideas and experiences directly to the audience. Although she attempts to detach herself from her subject in the poetry and fiction, the veil that hangs over them is transparent; like the nonfiction the source is autobiographical. Binding the works together is an absorption with the self, which identifies her as a twentieth-century writer whose roots lie in English romanticism. That outer events can stimulate exploration of the inner life she discovered early when writing ***North to the Orient*** and ***Listen! The Wind.*** She applied the same principle to ***The Steep Ascent,*** in which adventure serves as a means to explore the protagonist's psyche. Unlike those whose exploration of the self is narrowed to the individual, Lindbergh, like Wordsworth in *The Prelude,* strives to understand not only the individual self but also the self in relation to the universe. As a diarist dedicated to the genre, she seeks to understand the mysterious forces moving beneath the surface of life. Throughout, both the search and the discoveries ring true because they capture a segment of reality.

Lindbergh's works demonstrate how romanticism is integrated into the modern consciousness. That the nineteenth-century poets assimilated elements of romanticism is evident in such influence as Shelley on Browning and Wordsworth on Arnold. Lindbergh helps extend the influence into the twentieth century. Like Wordsworth she views the self as a microcosm of reality, whose development is important not only for herself personally but also for the truth it reveals about life as a whole. If she approaches this truth hesitantly, it is because she reflects an age for which truth has become tentative. Her exploration of the self occurs amidst the fear of modern warfare and the changing role of women in society.

Past influence is seldom exclusive; it is grafted to other influences, especially in one whose social consciousness is as finely tuned as Lindbergh's. Basic to her sense of life is the belief in human perfectibility arrived at through gradual evolution. This belief she shares not only with Wordsworth but also with Pierre Teilhard de Chardin, a contemporary whose ideas she admires. She believes that humans change unceasingly, and their response to change determines their selfhood. Her works expose the anxiety and stagnation that can result from resistance to change. In contrast, the acceptance of change ushers into life possibilities for creativity and greater maturity.

Lindbergh, for whom nurturing the inner life is important, has created a body of work in which the responses are subjective and the central image is the solitary pilgrim journeying through familiar and unfamiliar environments. Her solitariness, however, never prevents her from addressing the problems of modern society. In ***Gift from the Sea,*** her most celebrated work, and ***Dearly Beloved,*** a technical tour de force, her themes are feminist. Although her feminism is overshadowed by the distinctive style of these works, it is, nonetheless, central to them. With laser-like precision she identifies the inadequacies of marriage, especially as they impact on women. In the role of Everywoman she articulates women's concerns about marriage which contradict the socially accepted ideal. When Americans debated their involvement in World War II, she expressed her objection to war in ***The Wave of the Future*** even though she knew she risked public condemnation. Realizing the potential danger of technology, she was among the first to call for safeguards to control the atomic bomb. In **"The Heron and the Astronaut"** her concern focuses on protecting a fragile environment against the threats of an ever-flourishing technology. Viewed chronologically, her works reveal her concern over the serious problems of the age.

Lindbergh responds to these problems in her own voice. Not only is she the artist identifying the social cankers that inhibit human growth, but she is also the visionary offering solutions. As she matures, her voice grows less didactic, her vision less airborne, and her tone less exuberant. Nevertheless, she continues to ask the pertinent questions of life and to explore solutions to problems.

***The Wave of the Future* notwithstanding, Lindbergh's forte lies in writing nonfiction: the diary and the essay. As a whole, her works reinforce the idea that literature—even the most personal—is rooted in a social base. They demonstrate how the artist combines this social base and art without sacrificing integrity.**

—Elsie F. Mayer

Lindbergh's works vary in their merit. Her major works comprise the diaries and ***Gift from the Sea.*** The diaries are worthy of attention for the limit to which she extends the genre. In her hand the diary is more than a record of events or personal musings to be shaped into poetry or fiction sometimes hence. It is biographical writing capable of capturing the nuances of a human personality. She explores the flexibility the diary offers in recording her growth and change. Her diaries give credence to the theory that the diary preserves experience in the purest sense because of its amorphousness. If one is faithful to the diary, it requires no reordering or recasting of experience, unlike biography or autobiography. As Lindbergh demonstrates, language is the only constraint facing the diarist.

Gift from the Sea belongs to those literary works whose effects continuously satisfy their readers. It resembles Shelley's description of a great poem: "a fountain forever overflowing with the waters of wisdom and delight." Its insight into human relationships and its imaginative prose speak not only to Lindbergh's contemporaries but also to succeeding generations. Each group has discovered in it the truth relevant for its own age and circumstances without exhausting its meaning.

Less significant than the diaries and ***Gift from the Sea*** are the poetry, the novels, and the travel books. For Lindbergh the lyric is a means of exploring different states of consciousness. In her successful attempts, imagery and feeling coalesce to form a simple harmony. In general, her lyrics lack the depth and breadth of feeling associated with the greatest lyrics. Nevertheless, her understanding of the genre is evident in the manner the inwardness of feeling, central to the lyric, emerges.

Although vastly different in style, Lindbergh's novel, ***The Steep Ascent,*** resembles Joseph Conrad's *Heart of Darkness.* Both novels share a common archetype, the search for self-knowledge. In the beginning, the protagonists, naïve but curious, experience adventure in unfamiliar surroundings. As they progress towards their destination, they are beleaguered by dangers so grave that their lives are threatened. In the end their reward for persevering is greater than expected and proves worth the price paid in fear and anxiety. In ***Dearly Beloved,*** Lindbergh, like Jane Austen in *Pride and Prejudice,* attempts to define the good marriage. Like Austen she clothes her definition in contemporary dress. What strikes Lindbergh's readers is an awareness that these ideas have been expressed more effectively in the diaries and ***Gift from the Sea*** than in the novels. Had Lindbergh not written the diaries and ***Gift from the Sea,*** the novels might attract more attention.

For an age grown accustomed to satellites and space laboratories in orbit, ***North to the Orient*** and ***Listen! The Wind*** strike the modern reader as quaint. The technology which was sophisticated in the 1930s is deemed primitive today. These books are not, however, without historical significance, for they illustrate how simple and immutable are the truths of human existence in contrast to technology which feeds on obsolescence and complexity.

Also noteworthy is their literary quality. Lindbergh blurs the distinction between genres in these books. The presence of a reflective narrator expressing her thoughts draws upon the personal essay, and the narrative with its dramatic events draws upon fiction. The result is a variation of the conventional travel literature with its emphasis on place. What makes the travel books less effective than a work like ***Gift from the Sea*** is their matter-of-factness. In the travel books the manifestation of truth and experience remains literal. Their local and actual elements are unassimilated by the imagination as they are in ***Gift from the Sea.***

As an artist Lindbergh possesses the ability to enhance the ordinary by unearthing its intrinsic meaning. She favors the experiences of darkness—danger, personal loss, death, and disillusionment—from which she attempts to extract some light. ***The Wave of the Future*** notwithstanding, her forte lies in writing nonfiction: the diary and the essay. As a whole, her works reinforce the idea that literature—even the most personal—is rooted in a social base. They demonstrate how the artist combines this social base and art without sacrificing integrity. To her readers Lindbergh offers a valuable study of their relationship. (pp. 127-30)

Elsie F. Mayer, in her My Window on the World: The Works of Anne Morrow Lindbergh, *Archon Books, 1988, 151 p.*

FURTHER READING

Ciardi, John. "A Close Look at the Unicorn." *Saturday Review* XL, No. 2 (12 January 1957): 54-7.

A scathing review of *The Unicorn, and Other Poems,* in which Ciardi displays his contempt for Lindbergh's book, calling it "inept," "slovenly," "illiterate," and "akin to Original Sin." The controversial review prompted an enormous response from readers.

———. "The Reviewer's Duty to Damn." *The Saturday Review* XL, No. 7 (16 February 1957): 24-5, 54-5.

Ciardi defends his negative assessment of *The Unicorn and Other Poems* in a response to the "avalanche" of letters he received after the publication of his January 12 review in *The Saturday Review.*

Cousins, Norman. "John Ciardi and the Readers." *The Saturday Review* XL, No. 7 (16 February 1957): 22-3.

Cousins, the Editor of *The Saturday Review,* responds to the controversy surrounding Ciardi's review of *The Unicorn, and Other Poems,* which produced the "biggest storm of reader protest in the thirty-three-year history" of the magazine.

Culligan, Glendy. Review of *Bring Me A Unicorn: Diaries and Letters of Anne Morrow Lindbergh, 1922-1926. Saturday Review* LV, No. 10 (4 March 1972): 72-5.

Favorable review in which Culligan praises the artistry and spontaneity of *Bring Me A Unicorn.*

Edman, Irwin. "The Poetry of Appeasement." *The New York Herald Tribune* 17, No. 8 (20 October 1940): 2.

Review of *The Wave of the Future* in which Edman commends Lindbergh's delicate prose style, but questions her opposition to the war and faults the book's ambiguity.

Mann, Klauss. "Two Confessions." *Decision: A Review of Free Culture* 1, No. 1 (January 1941): 54-8.

An unfavorable review of *The Wave of the Future* in which the critic faults the book for inconsistencies and suggests that Lindbergh is a Nazi sympathizer.

Peterson, Virginia. "Memories of Married Life." *The New York Times Book Review* (10 June 1962): 6, 23.

Comments on Lindbergh's second novel, *Dearly Beloved.*

Richart, Bette. "Since Sappho." *The Commonweal* LXIV, No. 23 (7 September 1956): 568-70.

Richart expresses disappointment with *The Unicorn, and Other Poems,* which she describes as "a product of a polite tradition of women writing for women."

Sherman, Beatrice. "Anne Morrow Lindbergh Writes Her First Novel." *The New York Times Book Review* (19 March 1944): 3.

Remarks on the charm and simplicity of Lindbergh's *The Steep Ascent,* an autobiographical novel.

Vining, Elizabeth Gray. "Islands All—In A Common Sea." *The New York Times Book Review* LX, No. 12 (20 March 1955): 1.

Favorable review of *Gift from the Sea.*

White, E. B. "The Wave of the Future." In his *One Man's Meat,* pp. 203-10. New York: Harper & Brothers Publishers, 1944.

Comments on the ambiguity of *The Wave of the Future.*

Additional coverage of Lindbergh's life and career is contained in the following sources published by Gale Research: *Contemporary Authors,* Vols. 17-20, rev. ed.; *Contemporary Authors New Revision Series,* Vol. 16; *Major 20th-Century Writers;* and *Something about the Author,* Vol. 33.

Malcolm X

1925-1965

(Born Malcolm Little; changed name to Malcolm X; later adopted religious name El-Hajj Malik El-Shabazz) American autobiographer, orator, and speechwriter.

The following entry provides an overview of Malcolm X's career.

INTRODUCTION

An influential African-American leader, Malcolm X rose to prominence in the mid-1950s as the outspoken national minister of the Nation of Islam under Elijah Muhammad. He opposed the mainstream civil rights movement, publicly calling for black separatism and rejecting nonviolence and integration as effective means of combatting racism. In the 1960s, however, Malcolm repudiated Muhammad and the Nation of Islam and embraced conventional Islam. He documented his various experiences in *The Autobiography of Malcolm X,* a work prepared with the help of American writer Alex Haley. Published after his assassination, the *Autobiography* has been called a "compelling and irreplaceable book" comparable to the autobiographies of Benjamin Franklin and Frederick Douglass.

Born Malcolm Little in Omaha, Nebraska, Malcolm was exposed to white racism and the black separatist movement at an early age. His father, Earl Little, was a Baptist minister and a follower of Jamaican-born black nationalist Marcus Garvey. When the Littles lived in Nebraska, the Ku Klux Klan tried to prevent the Reverend Little from conveying Garvey's teachings. The Littles consequently left Nebraska, eventually settling in Mason, Michigan, where they found the racial climate no better. In 1929 members of the Black Legion, a white supremacist group, reputedly burned down the Littles' home and later murdered Malcolm's father. His death, officially labeled suicide, left Louise Little to care for the children. Unable to cope with the financial and emotional demands of single parenthood, she was placed in a mental institution, and the children were sent to separate foster homes. Despite the traumas of his early youth, Malcolm was among the best students in his class. Popular with his white classmates, he was elected president of his seventh-grade class. However, when he told an English teacher that he wanted to become a lawyer, the teacher suggested carpentry instead, urging Malcolm "to be realistic about being a nigger."

Malcolm soon became angry toward his white teachers and friends, whom he believed viewed him not as their equal, but as their "mascot." His interest in academic study waning, he quit school after completing the eighth grade. Living in Boston, New York City, and later Detroit, he held several low-paying jobs. To fit into his new urban environment, Malcolm altered his outward appearance, treating his hair with corrosive chemicals to straighten it and frequently wearing a zoot suit. As "Detroit Red," a name derived from his fair complexion and red hair, he made his living as a hustler, pimp, and drug dealer. Malcolm was arrested in early 1946 and charged with robbery. Not yet twenty-one, he was sentenced to ten years in prison; the exceptionally long term is thought to reflect the judge's revulsion at Malcolm's liaisons with white women. Malcolm was restless in prison. "I would pace for hours like a caged leopard, viciously cursing aloud to myself," he noted. "Eventually the men in the cellblock had a name for me: 'Satan.' " Another convict, Bimbi, introduced him to the prison's extensive library, and Malcolm became an avid reader. When his siblings revealed to him that they had become followers of Elijah Muhammad—the leader of the Nation of Islam, popularly known as the Black Muslims—Malcolm pored over Muhammad's teachings and initiated a daily correspondence with the man. Upon his release from prison in 1952, Malcolm became a follower of Muhammad. He took the name "Malcolm X" to signify the loss of his true African name and to reject the "slave name" of Little.

Elijah Muhammad preached a' doctrine of black pride based on the contention that whites are evil. W. D. Fard, Muhammad's teacher, had held that a black scientist, Yacub, genetically engineered the white race out of the original black race in order to test the strength of the latter. Although the whites will rule for six millennia, the Black Muslims believe, the end of that reign is quickly approaching. I. F. Stone commented on Muhammad's teachings: "The tendency is to dismiss Elijah Muhammad's weird doctrine as another example of the superstitions, old and new, that thrive in the Negro ghetto. It is not really any more absurd than the Virgin Birth or the Sacrifice of Isaac. The rational absurdity does not detract from the psychic therapy." In 1953 Malcolm was appointed assistant minister of Detroit's Temple Number One of the Nation of Islam. He believed that every black person would gravitate to Muhammad's teachings, for "when he thinks about his own life, he is going to see where, to him personally, the white man sure has acted like a devil." Malcolm rose swiftly in the ranks of the Black Muslims, becoming Muhammad's national representative and, in 1954, the head of a major mosque in Harlem. There he became known as an articulate spokesperson for the radical black perspective. Peter Goldman recalled: "Offstage and off-camera, he was a man of enormous charm, priestly in his bearing and his private life, warm and witty in company, gallant toward white people even in the days when he considered them universally and irremediably evil. But given a platform and a microphone, he became a pitiless scold." In addition to denouncing integration, nonviolence, and Dr. Martin Luther King, Jr., Malcolm "identified whites as the enemy of blacks and cheered at tornadoes, hurricanes, earthquakes, airplane crashes, even the Kennedy assassination—anything that might cause them anguish or pain." Malcolm termed the killing of John F. Kennedy a case of "chickens coming home to roost"—a statement that severely damaged Malcolm's career. He later explained that he meant only that "the hate in white men . . . finally had struck down the President," but he was immediately censured by Muhammad. Muhammad ordered him to refrain from public comment for ninety days, and Malcolm complied.

Malcolm's remark about the Kennedy assassination gave Muhammad an opportunity to expel his national minister from the movement's hierarchy, for Malcolm had been in conflict with the leader of the Nation of Islam for some time. Malcolm had privately condemned Muhammad's materialism—his expensive cars and business suits and lavishly furnished estate—and was shocked by allegations that Muhammad had seduced several women and sired their children. Feeling estranged from Muhammad, Malcolm canceled the original dedication to his autobiography-in-progress, in which he had written that Muhammad "found me here in the muck and mire of the filthiest civilization and society on this earth . . . and made me the man that I am today." Only at the urging of Alex Haley did Malcolm agree not to make his autobiography into a polemic against his former mentor. Proceeding to break officially with the Nation of Islam, he made a pilgrimage to Mecca, taking the religious name El-Hajj Malik El-Shabazz. In Mecca he underwent a transformation in his beliefs. He explained in his autobiography: "Since I learned the truth in Mecca, my dearest friends have come to include all kinds—some Christians, Jews, Buddhists, Hindus, agnostics, and even atheists! I have friends who are called capitalists, Socialists, and Communists! Some of my friends are moderates, conservatives, extremists—some are even Uncle Toms! My friends today are black, brown, red, yellow, and white!" On a diplomatic trip to Africa, Malcolm began the work of uniting blacks across the world, later establishing the Organization of Afro-American Unity in the United States. However, Malcolm now believed that the Nation of Islam saw him as a threat. "Now I'm out," he said. "And there's the fear [that] if my image isn't shattered, the Muslims in the movement will leave." Indeed, Elijah Muhammad wrote in his periodical *Muhammad Speaks* that Malcolm was "worthy of death." On February 21, 1965, he was assassinated while addressing an audience of four hundred in the Audubon Ballroom in Harlem. Three men associated with the Nation of Islam—Talmadge Thayer, Norman 3X Butler, and Thomas 15X Johnson—were apprehended and eventually convicted of the crime.

The Autobiography of Malcolm X was published posthumously to widespread critical acclaim. Although some critics questioned Haley's influence over the work's production, commentators generally agreed that the story is Malcolm's own. Of the work's importance, Charles H. Nichols asserted in 1985: "*The Autobiography of Malcolm X* is probably the most influential book read by this generation of Afro-Americans. For not only is the account of Malcolm Little an absorbing and heart-shattering encounter with the realities of poverty, crime and racism. It is a fantastic success story. Paradoxically, the book, designed to be an indictment of American and European bigotry and exploitation, is a triumphant affirmation of the possibilities of the human spirit." In the decades since its initial publication, the *Autobiography* has prompted diverse critical readings, including analyses of its properties as a political and rhetorical text, as a conversion narrative reflecting Malcolm's search for identity, and as a work that both affirms and challenges the tradition of American autobiography.

Several of Malcolm's speeches have also been published, including *Malcolm X Speaks,* but his autobiography remains by far his most noted contribution to literature. As Malcolm X has increasingly been recognized as a leading figure in the African-American struggle for recognition and equality, *The Autobiography of Malcolm X* has grown in stature. Truman Nelson concluded: "Viewed in its complete historical context, this is indeed a great book. Its dead-level honesty, its passion, its exalted purpose, even its manifold unsolved ambiguities will make it stand as a monument to the most painful of truths: that this country, this people, this Western world has practiced unspeakable cruelty against a race, an individual, who might have made its fraudulent humanism a reality."

PRINCIPAL WORKS

The Autobiography of Malcolm X [with Alex Haley] (autobiography) 1965

Malcolm X Speaks: Selected Speeches and Statements (speeches) 1965
Malcolm X on Afro-American History (speeches) 1967
The Speeches of Malcolm X at Harvard (speeches) 1968
Malcolm X and the Negro Revolution: The Speeches of Malcolm X (speeches) 1969
Malcolm X Talks to Young People (speeches) 1969
Two Speeches by Malcolm X (speeches) 1969
By Any Means Necessary: Speeches, Interviews, and a Letter by Malcolm X (speeches, interviews, and a letter) 1970
The End of White World Supremacy: Four Speeches (speeches) 1971
Malcolm X: The Last Speeches (speeches) 1989

CRITICISM

Truman Nelson (review date 8 November 1965)

[*An American novelist and nonfiction writer, Nelson has contributed introductions to modern editions of W. E. B. Du Bois's* The Souls of Black Folk *(1905) and* The Gift of Black Folk *(1924). Nelson commented in an interview with* Contemporary Authors: *"My position is that man can, through knowledge and awareness brought on by communicative art, understand and perhaps control the physical and political facts of his existence, rather than submitting to them with a defeated whimper." In the following review of* The Autobiography of Malcolm X, *Nelson praises the book's "honesty, its passion, its exalted purpose, even its manifold unsolved ambiguities" in addressing the injustice of American racism.*]

[***The Autobiography of Malcolm X***] is the story of a man struck down on his way to becoming a revolutionary and a liberator of his people. It is the real American tragedy: a fall from great heights of promise, not from inner weakness or self-betrayal, but because assassins stood up in plain sight, like a firing squad, and put thirteen shotgun slugs into his chest and bullets in his legs and thighs as he lay dying.

Malcolm had known the white man's violence from infancy. Five of his father's six brothers died by violence; one was lynched, another killed by white police. His father, very strong, very black, a gun-carrying Baptist minister and a Garveyite organizer, was killed by having his head bashed in and he then was laid on a car track to be cut in half. The white insurance company called it suicide. When Malcolm, his father's seventh child, died in Harlem on February 21, 1965, he was accused by the white press of having "initiated violence."

His mother was nearly white, looked white, but she could not keep a job when any of her black children showed up, or her small-town employers found out whose widow she was. Keeping food on the table and some dignity around it for a family of eight was an insoluble problem in the 1930s. It drove her into insanity. The family was broken up, and Malcolm began a delinquent's progress through the ghettos of Boston and New York, with conked red hair, a sky-blue zoot suit and orange knob-toed shoes, all so grotesque on his 6-foot-5 gangling frame that he would stop traffic crossing the street. He became a hustler, a pimp, a narcotics addict and peddler, a petty thief and armed robber.

The stupendous transformation came while he was serving a ten-year sentence for armed robbery in Massachusetts. He had become the prototype of the hustler, by his own definition: "The hustler out there in the ghetto jungle has less respect for the white power structure than any other Negro in America. He is internally restrained by nothing. To survive he is out there constantly preying on others, probing for any human weakness like a ferret . . . forever frustrated, restless and anxious for some *action.* Whatever he undertakes, he commits himself to it fully, absolutely."

A man who calls himself Elijah Muhammad knew how to get through to the Malcolms, the hustlers, the wretched of the earth. He is the leader of an indigenous Muslim group. He has a touch of genius. He knows, like Luther before him, how to look in the mud for the fallen and redeem them. He wrote to every Negro he knew of in prison, sent each a little money and a lot of message. His contact with Malcolm brought that unregenerate hustler to an instantaneous conversion equal to those described in the pages of William James's *Varieties of Religious Experience.* James would have understood Mr. Muhammad better than his critics: James always argued that the significance of a belief should not be judged by its source, but its fruits. Regardless of Elijah Muhammad's historical and theological eccentricities—all religions have their absurdities—he has transformed many of the worst of men into some of the best.

Malcolm began to write to Mr. Muhammad every day. He had to study so he would have something to say to him. He had to study because he had virtually forgotten how to write. In the prison library there happened to be a rare collection of old anti-slavery tracts. Malcolm there honed his new revolutionary edge on the abrasive rhetoric of the great abolitionists, on Garrison and Phillips whose volcanic eruptions on the shame and guilt of the slaveholder, and a nation that suffered them to live, have never been equaled. This became his basic vocabulary of assault.

When he was released he had impacted in him two explosive elements; the "blessed assurance" of the converted man; and a place in a community which was believed to be destined to redeem an oppressed people. In three magnificent chapters titled "Saved," "Savior" and "Minister Malcolm X," the making of a new Malcolm is revealed. (The reader must put aside any prejudice he may have about a book "as told to" someone. You can hear and feel Malcolm in this book; it is a superb job of transcription. The tapes seem to run onto the paper with the clacking efficiency of a wire-service machine.) Malcolm was saved because Mr. Muhammad convinced him that no Negro has to fear the intellectual power of any man who tries to defend or justify what has been done to the black man by the white man in this country: saved because he was taught that he had sinned and fallen in a world he had not made, and had no power to shape or correct in any way whatsoever.

So Malcolm went from the anonymous brutality of prison life to his brother's Muslim household in Detroit, with its beautiful disciplines and dignities: where the father is the first to rise in the morning and prepare the way for the family to live out their day in cleanliness, order and love, and with passionate loyalty toward one another. He began to function in the Detroit ghetto as a missionary. His message was simple but overpowering: "The Honorable Elijah Muhammad teaches us that since Western society is deteriorating, it has become overrun with immorality and God is going to judge it, and destroy it. And the only way the black people, caught up in this society, can be saved is not to integrate into a corruption, but to separate from it, to a land of their own where we can reform ourselves, lift up our moral standards and try to be godly."

Mr. Muhammad was reviving *revolutionary separatism,* which he believes to be the only way a persecuted minority can liberate themselves. Along with it, Mr. Muhammad had to write his new testament. A people who have had their history stolen from them usually embrace an apocryphal one until they are strong enough to wrest the truth from its suppressors. And to achieve this strength they have to be made to believe, somehow, that they are "the chosen people of God." The more one questions Mr. Muhammad's "history," the more one is forced to admit Malcolm's genius in defending it and building on it a movement of such regenerating dynamism.

Fishing for men in the ghettos of Detroit, Boston, New York, Philadelphia and elsewhere, Malcolm changed a little store-front cult into a powerful religion with more than a hundred places of worship spread over the fifty states. Mr. Muhammad was the Messenger; he gave him the WORD, but Malcolm was pre-eminently the Missionary. He knew the streets as a hustler does, how to work the shifting, indeterminate fringes of public Black Nationalist or civil rights gatherings. He caught the people coming out, with unanswered questions, demands, yearnings from the Christian churches. The Muslims grew from 400 to 40,000.

Their suddenly visible strength attracted the white mass media, looking for new sensations to merchandise. A nation-wide TV program called *The Hate That Hate Produced* started a reaction that began to portray the Muslims as a potential source of violence, the shock troops of black racism. Malcolm, rushing to their defense, became disastrously diverted from the necessary organizing of his own people. He became a victim of the great American "image" psychosis. He began to "hustle" again, but this time among the whites. He thought he was "explaining and defending the Honorable Elijah Muhammad," but he was only playing the oppressor's game, on battlefields they were choosing. With his consciousnesss that their history, their humanities, their constitutions and churches were all part of an ideology of lies, easily exposed when examined in practice, he won Pyrrhic victories before microphones, TV cameras and forums, but this had very little to do with building a liberation force among his own people. The expanding nation of Islam, the only genuine movement of, by and for the black people since the deportation of Marcus Garvey, came to a halt. The Muslim ministers, including Mr. Muhammad, were too busy explaining themselves to people who didn't give a damn about them, but only wanted to assess how deeply they should be feared.

Doubts began to creep into Malcolm's own mind. He heard that Mr. Muhammad was beginning to disapprove of his many public appearances before whites. He thought it was jealousy. The outside pressure upon the Muslim movement, the mixed adulation and horror, began to disintegrate it. For his statement on Kennedy's assassination, Malcolm was silenced, then expelled. Again there were the white reporters at his elbow, urging him, daring him to talk, explain, justify! Malcolm never lost his real power of presence and personality; but, expelled from the Muslims, he lost his base. Mr. Muhammad taunted him brilliantly: "Who is Malcolm leading? Who is he teaching? He has no truth. I am not going to let the crackpots destroy the good things Allah sent to you and me."

Malcom became convinced that the Muslims were going to kill him. He felt he had to raise a counter force strong enough to protect himself. He tried to recruit in Harlem among this potential of a million followers. But again he was drawn off into a tragic diversion: a pilgrimage to Mecca to prove that he, not Elijah Muhammad, was the real Muslim. This had no relevance to the streets of Harlem. There, they thought he was running away. Malcolm was not aware of the disintegration that had taken place in him after his god had cast him out. He was so dynamic that fragments of him seemed more powerful than the whole. In fact, he was like some exploding piece of fireworks, with its fiery particles dying in the sky.

He was talking integration now, under the banner of the True Islam. Whites again took up his time with interminable discussions of religious and ethical abstractions. And always he felt stalked by killers hired by his chosen father on earth and his own beloved brothers and sisters.

The complexities of his situation were unbearable. He would have had to leave Muhammad anyway; he had outgrown him. He had internationalized himself. Always he traveled, back and forth across the continent, abroad for eighteen weeks again, and then back to Harlem for some pathetic efforts at organizing by a handful of his faithful. And to write this marvelous book that is not a book but a man, a tragic, agonizing, palpable man.

He ended it in a chapter called "1965." It is unresolved. He is admitting he needs much more time to reflect, to clarify . . . if he could only study, rest a while from this interminable explaining, this mania for justification. He knew he had not gathered an adequate protective force. Almost the last sentence of the book is: " . . . societies often have killed the people who have helped change them."

But the great revelation comes in the Epilogue by his perceptive and enormously skillful amanuensis, Alex Haley. Malcolm was invited to speak in France by a group of African students. He had been talking, in late '64, of the great power of the black and yellow races when seen internationally. I heard him in Harlem, on a platform with Babu, the Zanzibar revolutionary, say the problem is now simply the oppressed against the oppressor. He had begun to renew himself, and his regenerated purpose began to take form, a political form. He was talking now like a member of a revolutionary majority. When he arrived in France, the government banned him as "an undesirable person." He was wrathful and puzzled when he came back to New York.

On Saturday, February 20, he made a most significant phone call to Alex Haley. "I'm going to tell you something, brother. The more I think about what is happening lately, I'm not at all sure it's the Muslims. I know what they can do and what they can't do, and they can't do some of the stuff that's happening to me lately. The more I think of what happened to me in France, I think I'm going to quit saying it's the Muslims. . . . I'm glad that I've been the first to establish official ties between Afro-Americans and our blood brothers in Africa." Then he hung up.

Twenty-four hours later, in the dressing room of the Audubon Ballroom, he said he was going to announce that he had been too hasty in accusing the Muslims because, "things are happening that are bigger than they can do . . . in fact, I'm going to ease some of this tension by telling the black man not to fight himself . . . that it's all part of the white man's big maneuver, to keep us fighting against ourselves." But before he could get this noble resolve on the record, the executioners rose in the first row and the sentence was carried out.

Viewed in its complete historical context, this is indeed a great book. Its dead-level honesty, its passion, its exalted purpose, even its manifold unsolved ambiguities will make it stand as a monument to the most painful of truths: that this country, this people, this Western world has practiced unspeakable cruelty against a race, an individual, who might have made its fraudulent humanism a reality. (pp. 336-38)

Truman Nelson, "Delinquent's Progress," in The Nation, *New York, Vol. 201, No. 15, November 8, 1965, pp. 336-38.*

I. F. Stone (review date 11 November 1965)

[*In the following review, Stone provides a favorable appraisal of Malcolm's life and thought as recorded in* The Autobiography of Malcolm X *and* Malcolm X Speaks.]

[As ***The Autobiography of Malcolm X*** and ***Malcolm X Speaks*** reveal], Malcolm X was born into Black Nationalism. His father was a follower of Marcus Garvey, the West Indian who launched a "Back to Africa" movement in the Twenties. Malcolm's first clash with white men took place when his mother was pregnant with him; a mob of Klansmen in Omaha, Nebraska, waving shotguns and rifles, warned her one night to move out of town because her husband was spreading trouble among the "good" Negroes with Garvey's teachings. One of his earliest memories was of seeing their home burned down in Lansing, Michigan, in 1929, because the Black Legion, a white Fascist organization, considered his father an "uppity" Negro. The body of his father, a tall, powerful black man from Georgia, soon afterwards was found literally cut to pieces in one of those mysterious accidents that often veil a racial killing.

His mother was a West Indian who looked like a white woman. Her unknown father was white. She slowly went to pieces mentally under the burden of raising eight children. When the family was broken up, Malcolm was sent to a detention home, from which he attended a white school. He must have been a bright and attractive lad, for he was at the top of his class and was elected class president in the seventh grade. Many years later, in a speech on the Black Revolution which is included in the collection, ***Malcolm X Speaks,*** he was able to boast bitterly, "I grew up with white people. I was integrated before they even invented the word." The reason for the bitterness was an incident that changed his life. His English teacher told him he ought to begin thinking about his career. Malcolm said he would like to be a lawyer. His teacher suggested carpentry instead. "We all here like you, you know that," the teacher said, "but you've got to be realistic about being a nigger."

Malcolm X left Lansing deeply alienated and in the slums of Boston and New York he became a "hustler," selling numbers, women, and dope. "All of us," he says in his ***Autobiography*** of his friends in the human jungle, "who might have probed space or cured cancer or built industries, were instead black victims of the white man's American social system." Insofar as he was concerned, this was no exaggeration. He was an extraordinary man. Had he been wholly white, instead of irretrievably "Negro" by American standards, he might easily have become a leader of the bar. In the underworld he went from marijuana to cocaine. To meet the cost he took up burglary. He was arrested with a white mistress who had become his look-out woman. In February, 1946, not quite twenty-one, he was sentenced to ten years in prison in Massachusetts. The heavy sentence reflected the revulsion created in the judge by the discovery that Malcolm had made a white woman his "love slave." In prison, he went on nutmeg, reefers, Nembutal, and benzedrine in a desperate effort to replace the drugs. He was a vicious prisoner, often in solitary. The other prisoners nicknamed him "Satan." But the prison had an unusually well stocked library to which he was introduced by a fellow prisoner, an old-time burglar named Bimbi. Through him, Malcolm first encountered Thoreau. Prison became his university; there also he was converted to the Nation of Islam, the sect the press calls Black Muslims.

The important word here is conversion. To understand Malcolm's experience, one must go to the literature of conversion. "Were we writing the history of the mind from the purely natural history point of view," William James concludes in his *Varieties of Religious Experience,* "we would still have to write down man's liability to sudden and complete conversion as one of his most curious peculiarities." The convert's sense of being born anew, the sudden change from despair to elation, bears an obvious resemblance to the manic-depressive cycle, except that the change in the personality is often permanent. But those who experience it must first—to borrow Gospel language—be brought low. James quotes the theological maxim, "Man's extremity is God's opportunity." It is only out of the depths that men on occasion experience this phenomenon of renewal. The success of the Black Muslims in converting and rehabilitating criminals and dope addicts like Malcolm X recalls the mighty phrases James quotes from Luther. "God," he preached, "is the God . . . of those that are brought even to nothing . . . and his nature is . . . to save the very desperate and damned." Malcolm had been brought to nothing, he was one of those very desperate and damned when he was "saved" by Elijah Muhammad, the self-proclaimed Messenger of Allah to the lost Black Nation of that imaginary Islam he preaches.

The tendency is to dismiss Elijah Muhammad's weird doctrine as another example of the superstitions, old and new, that thrive in the Negro ghetto. It is not really any more absurd than the Virgin Birth or the Sacrifice of Isaac. The rational absurdity does not detract from the psychic therapy. Indeed the therapy may lie in the absurdity. Converts to any creed talk of the joy in complete surrender; a rape of the mind occurs. "*Credo quia absurdum,*" Tertullian, the first really cultivated apologist for Christianity, is said to have exulted, "I believe because it *is* absurd." Tertullian was himself a convert. Black Nationalists may even claim him as an African, for his home was Carthage.

There is a special reason for the efficacy of the Black Muslims in reaching the Negro damned. The sickness of the Negro in America is that he has been made to feel a nigger; the genocide is psychic. The Negro must rid himself of this feeling if he is to stand erect again. He can do so in two ways. He can change the outer world of white supremacy, or he can change his inner world by "conversion." The teachings of the Black Muslims may be fantastic but they are superbly suited to the task of shaking off the feeling of nigger-ness. Elijah Muhammad teaches that the original man was black, that Caucasians are "white devils" created almost 6,000 years ago by a black genius named Yakub. He bleached a number of blacks by a process of mutation into pale-faced blue-eyed devils in order to test the mettle of the Black Nation. This inferior breed has ruled by deviltry but their time will soon be up, at the end of the sixth millenium, which may be by 1970 or thereabouts. To explain the white man as a devil is, as Malcolm X says in the ***Autobiography,*** to strike "a nerve center in the American black man" for "when he thinks about his own life, he is going to see where, to him personally, the white man sure has acted like a devil." To see the white man this way is, in Gospel imagery, to cast out the devil. With him go his values, as he has impressed them on the Black Man, above all the inner feeling of being a nigger. To lose that feeling is to be fully emancipated. For the poor Negro no drug could be a stronger opiate than this black religion.

With rejection of the white man's values goes rejection of the white man's God. "We're worshipping a Jesus," Malcolm protested in one of his sermons after he became a Black Muslim Minister, "who doesn't even *look* like us." The white man, he declared, "has brainwashed us black people to fasten our gaze upon a blond-haired, blue-eyed Jesus." This Black Muslim doctrine may seem a blasphemous joke until one makes the effort to imagine how whites would feel if taught to worship a black God with thick African lips. Men prefer to create a God in their own image. "The Ethiopians," one of the pre-Socratic Greek philosophers observed a half millenium before Christ, "assert that their gods are snub-nosed and black" while the "Nordic" Thracians said theirs were "blue-eyed and red-haired." When Marcus Garvey, the first apostle of Pan-Africanism, toured Africa, urging expulsion of the white man, he called for a Negro religion with a Negro Christ. Just as Malcolm Little, in accordance with Black Muslim practice, rejected his "slave name" and became Malcolm X, so Malcolm X, son of a Baptist preacher, rejected Christianity as a slave religion. His teacher, Elijah Muhammad, did not have to read Nietszche to discover that Christianity was admirably suited to make Rome's slaves submissive. In our ante-bellum South the value of Christian teaching in making slaves tractable was widely recognized even by slaveholders themselves agnostic. The Negro converted to Christianity was cut off from the disturbing memory of his own gods and of his lost freedom, and reconciled to his lot in the white man's chains. Here again the primitivistic fantasies of the Black Muslims unerringly focus on a crucial point. It is in the Christian mission that what Malcolm X called the "brainwashing" of the blacks began.

Racism and nationalism are poisons. Sometimes a poison may be prescribed as a medicine, and Negroes have found in racism a way to restore their self-respect. But black racism is still racism, with all its primitive irrationality and danger. There are passages in the ***Autobiography*** in which Malcolm, recounting some of his Black Muslim sermons, sounds like a Southern white supremacist in reverse, vibrating with anger and sexual obsession over the horrors of race pollution. There is the same preoccupation with rape, the same revulsion about mixed breeds. "Why," he cried out, "the white man's raping of the black race's woman began right on those slave ships!" A psychoanalyst might see in his fury the feeling of rejection by the race of his white grandfather. A biologist might see in the achievements of this tall sandy-complexioned Negro—his friends called him "Red"—an example of the possibilities of successful racial mixture. But Malcolm's feelings on the subject were as outraged as those of a Daughter of the Confederacy. He returned revulsion for revulsion and hate for hate. He named his first child, a daughter, Attilah, and explained that he named her for the Hun who sacked Rome.

But hidden under the surface of the Black Nationalist creed to which he was won there lay a peculiar anti-Negroism. The true nationalist loves his people and their peculiarities; he wants to preserve them; he is filled with filial piety. But there is in Elijah Muhammad's Black Muslim creed none of the love for the Negro one finds in

W. E. B. du Bois, or of that yearning for the ancestral Africa which obsessed Garvey. Elijah Muhammad—who himself looks more Chinese than Negro—teaches his people that they are Asians, not Africans; that their original tongue is Arabic. He turns his people into middle-class Americans. Their clothes are conservative, almost Ivy League. Their religious services eschew that rich antiphony between preacher and congregation which one finds in Negro churches. The Nigerian, E. U. Essien-Udom, whose *Black Nationalism* is the best book on the Black Muslims, was struck by their middle-class attitudes and coldness to Africa and African ways. In Black Muslim homes, when jazz was played, he writes that he was "often tempted to tap his feet to the tune of jazz" but was inhibited because his Black Muslim hosts "listened to it without ostensible response to the rhythm." In their own way the Black Muslims are as much in flight from Negritude as was Booker T. Washington. Indeed Elijah Muhammad's stress on Negro private business and his hostility to trade unionism in his own dealings with Negroes are very much in the Booker T. Washington pattern. The virtues of bourgeois America are what Elijah Muhammad seeks to recreate in his separate Black Nation. This is the banal reality which lies behind all his hocus-pocus about the Koran, and here lie the roots of his split with Malcolm X.

For Elijah Muhammad practices separation not only from American life but from the American Negro community, and from its concrete struggles for racial justice. Malcolm X was drawn more and more to engagement in that struggle. In the midst of describing in the ***Autobiography*** his happy and successful years as a Black Muslim organizer, Malcolm X says:

> If I harbored any personal disappointment, whatsoever, it was that privately I was convinced that our Nation of Islam could be an even greater force in the American black man's overall struggle—if we engaged in more *action.* By that I mean I thought privately that we should have amended or relaxed, our general non-engagement policy. I felt that, wherever black people committed themselves, in the Little Rocks and Birminghams and other places, militantly disciplined Muslims should also be there—for all the world to see, and respect and discuss. It could be heard increasingly in the Negro communities: "Those Muslims *talk* tough, but they never *do* anything, unless somebody bothers Muslims." [Italics in original.]

This alone was bound to divide the prophet and disciple. But there were also personal factors. Elijah Muhammad won Malcolm's devotion by his kindness in corresponding with the young convict when Malcolm was still in prison. But Malcolm's intellectual horizons were already far wider than those of the rather narrow, ill-educated, and suspicious Messenger of Allah. In the prison library Malcolm X was finding substantiation for the Black Muslim creed in *Paradise Lost* and in Herodotus; this passionate curiosity and voracious reading were bound to make him outgrow Elijah's dream-book theology. On the one side envy and on the other disillusion were to drive the two men apart. The crowds drawn by Malcolm and his very organizing success made Elijah Muhammad and his family jealous. On the other hand, Malcolm, who had kept the sect's vows of chastity, was shocked when former secretaries of Elijah Muhammad filed paternity suits against the prophet. Malcolm had nothing but a small salary and the house the sect had provided for him. Elijah Muhammad's cars (two Cadillacs and a Lincoln Continental), his $200 pin-striped banker-style suits, his elegantly furnished 18-room house in one of the better sections of Chicago's Hyde Park, began to make a sour impression on Malcolm. The hierarchy lives well in practically all religions, and their worldly affluence fosters schism. Malcolm was too big, too smart, too able, to fit into the confines of this little sect and remain submissive to its family oligarchy. He began to open up a larger world, and this endangered Elijah Muhammad's hold on the little band of unsophisticated faithful he had recruited.

Muhammad Speaks, the weekly organ of the Black Muslims, had begun to play down Malcolm's activities. The break came over Malcolm's comment on Kennedy's assassination. Within hours after the President's killing, Elijah Muhammad sent out a directive ordering the cult's ministers to make no comment on the murder. Malcolm, speaking at Manhattan Center a few days afterward, was asked in the question period what he thought of the assassination. He answered it was a case of "the chickens coming home to roost." Malcolm explains in the ***Autobiography,*** "I said that the hate in white men had not stopped with the killing of defenseless black people but . . . finally had struck down the President." He complains that "some of the world's most important personages were saying in various ways, and in far stronger ways than I did, that America's climate of hate had been responsible for the President's death. But when Malcolm X said the same thing it was ominous." Elijah Muhammad called him in. "That was a very bad statement," he said. "The country loved this man." He ordered Malcolm silenced for ninety days so that the Black Muslims could be "disassociated from the blunder." Malcolm agreed and submitted. But three days later he heard that a Mosque official was suggesting his own assassination. Soon after, another Black Muslim told him of a plan to wire his car so that it would explode when he turned the ignition key. Malcolm decided to build a Muslim Mosque of his own, and open its doors to black men of all faiths for common action. To prepare himself he decided to make the pilgrimage to Mecca.

This visit to Mecca was a turning-point for Malcolm. His warm reception in the Arabic world, the sight of white men in equal fraternity with black and brown, marked a second conversion in his life. "For the past week," Malcolm wrote home, "I have been utterly speechless and spellbound by the graciousness I see displayed all around me by people *of all colors.*" The italics were his. The man who made the seven circuits around the Ka'ba and drank the waters of Zem-Zem emerged from his pilgrimage no longer a racist or a Black Muslim. He took the title of El Hajj earned by his visit to Mecca and called himself henceforth El-Hajj Malik El-Shabazz. He turned Muslim in the true sense of the word. How indelibly he also remained an American go-getter is deliciously reflected in a passage of the ***Autobiography*** where he says that while in Mecca:

> I saw that Islam's conversions around the world could double and triple if the colorfulness and the true spiritualness of the Hajj pilgrimage were properly advertised and communicated to the outside world. I saw that the Arabs are poor at understanding the psychology of non-Arabs and the importance of public relations. The Arabs said "Inshah Allah" ("God willing")—then they waited for converts, but I knew that with improved public relations methods the new converts turning to Allah could be turned into millions.

He had become a Hajj but remained in some ways a Babbitt, the salesman, archtype of our American society. A creed was something to *sell.* Allah, the Merciful, needed better merchandising.

Malcolm returned from abroad May 21, 1964. Several attempts were made on his life. On February 21, 1965, he was killed by gunmen when he got up to speak at a meeting in New York's Audubon Ballroom. He was not quite forty when he died. The most revealing tribute paid him was the complaint by Elijah Muhammad after Malcolm was killed. "He came back preaching that we should not hate the enemy . . . He was a star who went astray." What nobler way to go astray? In Africa and in America there was almost unanimous recognition that the Negro race had lost a gifted son; only the then head of the U. S. Information Agency, Carl Rowan, immortalized himself with a monumental Uncle Tomism. "All this about an ex-convict, ex-dope peddler who became a racial fanatic," was Rowan's obtuse and ugly comment; it ranks with his discovery, as USIA Director, of what he called the public's "right *not* to know."

From tape-recorded conversations, a Negro writer, Alex Haley, put together the ***Autobiography;*** he did his job with sensitivity and with devotion. Here one may read, in the agony of this brilliant Negro's self-creation, the agony of an entire people in their search for identity. But more fully to understand this remarkable man, one must turn to ***Malcolm X Speaks,*** which supplements the ***Autobiography.*** All but one of the speeches were made in those last eight tumultuous months of his life after his break with the Black Muslims when he was seeking a new path. In the pages one can begin to understand his power as a speaker and to see, more clearly than in the ***Autobiography,*** the political legacy he left his people in its struggle for full emancipation.

Over and over again in simple imagery, savagely uncompromising, he drove home the real truth about the Negro's position in America. It may not be pleasant but it must be faced, "Those Hunkies that just got off the boat," he said in one of his favorite comparisons, "they're already Americans. Polacks are already Americans; the Italian refugees are already Americans. Everything that comes out of Europe, every blue-eyed thing, is already an American. And as long as you and I have been over here, we aren't Americans yet. They don't have to pass civil rights legislation to make a Polack an American." In a favorite metaphor, he said "I'm not going to sit at your table and watch you eat, with nothing on my plate, and call myself a diner. Sitting at the table doesn't make you a diner, unless you eat some of what's on the plate. Being here in America doesn't make you an American. Being born here in America doesn't make you an American." He often said, "Don't be shocked when I say that I was in prison. You're still in prison. That's what America means—prison." Who can deny that this is true for the black man? No matter how high he rises, he never loses consciousness of the invisible bars which hem him in. "We didn't land on Plymouth Rock," Malcolm was fond of saying. "It landed on us."

He counselled violence but he defended this as an answer to white violence. "If they make the Klan non-violent," he said over and over again, "I'll be non-violent." In another speech he said, "If violence is wrong in America, violence is wrong abroad. If it is wrong to be violent defending black women and black children and black babies and black men, then it is wrong for America to draft us and make us violent abroad in defense of her." He taunted his people in the same speech that "as long as the white man sent you to Korea, you bled . . . You bleed for white people, but when it comes to seeing your own churches being bombed and little black girls murdered, you haven't any blood." In a speech he made about the brutal beating of Fannie Lou Hamer of Mississippi, he said of the white man, "if he only understands the language of a rifle, get a rifle. If he only understands the language of a rope, get a rope. But don't waste time talking the wrong language to a man if you really want to communicate with him." In preaching Pan-Africanism, he reached down into the aching roots of Negro self-hatred as few men have ever done. "You can't hate Africa and not hate yourself," he said in one speech. "This is what the white man knows. So they make you and me hate our African identity . . . We hated our heads, we hated the shape of our nose, we wanted one of those long dove-like noses, you know; we hated the color of our skin, hated the blood of Africa that was in our veins. And in hating our features and our skin and our blood, we had to end up hating ourselves." No man has better expressed his people's trapped anguish.

Malcolm's most important message to his people is muted in the ***Autobiography,*** perhaps because Alex Haley, its writer, is politically conventional, but it comes out sharply in ***Malcolm X Speaks*** which was edited and published by a group of Trotzkyists. This was the idea that while the Negro is a minority in this country, he is part of a majority if he thinks of common action with the rest of the world's colored peoples. "The first thing the American power structure doesn't want any Negroes to start," he says in the ***Autobiography,*** "is thinking internationally." In a speech at Ibadan University in Nigeria, he relates in the ***Autobiography,*** he urged the Africans to bring the American Negro's plight before the United Nations: "I said that just as the American Jew is in political, cultural, and economic harmony with world Jewry, I was convinced that it was time for all Afro-Americans to join the world's Pan-Africanists." Malcolm persuaded the Organization of African Unity at its Cairo conference to pass a resolution saying that discrimination against Negroes in the United States was "a matter of deep concern" to the Africans, and *The New York Times* in August 1964 reported that the State and Justice Departments had begun "to take an interest in Malcolm's campaign because it might create 'a touchy problem' for the U.S. if raised at the UN." In the UN debate over U. S. intervention to save white lives in the Congo, African delegates at the UN for the first time accused the U.S. of being indifferent to similar atrocities against blacks in Mississippi. This is what Malcolm wanted when he spoke of putting the Negro struggle in a world context.

An Italian writer, Vittorio Lanternari, published a remarkable book five years ago, which appeared here in 1963 as *The Religions of the Oppressed: A Study of Modern Messianic Cults.* It suggests that wherever white men have driven out or subdued colored men, whether in the case of the American Indians, or in Africa, or with the Maoris in New Zealand, as with the Tai-Pings in China and the Cao Dai in Vietnam or among the uprooted blacks and harried Indians in the Caribbean and Latin America, Messianic cults have arisen, rejecting white men's values and seeking the restoration of shattered cultural identities as the first step toward political freedom. He did not include in his survey the cults which thrive in our Negro ghettoes though they are of the same character. One striking common bond among all these sects of the oppressed has been their effort to free their people from drinking the white man's "firewater" or (in China) smoking his opium. To see the Black Muslims and Malcolm's life in this perspective is to begin to understand the psychic havoc wrought around the world by white imperialism in the centuries since America was discovered and Afro-Asia opened up to white penetration. There are few places on earth where whites have not grown rich robbing the colored races. It was Malcolm's great contribution to help make us all aware of this.

His assassination was a loss to the country as well as to his race. These two books will have a permanent place in the literature of the Afro-American struggle. It is tantalizing to speculate on what he might have become had he lived. What makes his life so moving a story was his capacity to learn and grow. New disillusions, and a richer view of the human condition, lay ahead for the man who could say, as he did in one of his last speeches, when discussing the first Bandung conference, "Once they excluded the white man, they found they could get together." Since then India and Pakistan, Singapore and Malaysia, the rebellion against the Arabs in Zanzibar and the splits in Black Africa itself have demonstrated that fratricide does not end with the eviction of the white devil. Various Left sects, Maoist and Trotzkyist and Communist, sought to recruit him, but he was trying to build a movement of his own. He was shopping around for new political ideas. He was also becoming active in the South instead of merely talking about a Dixie Mau-Mau from the relative safety of Harlem. I believe there was in him a readiness painfully to find and face new truths which might have made him one of the great Negroes, and Americans, of our time. (pp. 3-5)

I. F. Stone, "The Pilgrimage of Malcolm X," in The New York Review of Books, *Vol. 5, No. 7, November 11, 1965, pp. 3-5.*

Alex Haley (essay date 1965)

[*Haley, who assisted Malcolm in writing* The Autobiography of Malcolm X, *is an American journalist and novelist best known for his multigenerational epic* Roots: The Saga of an American Family *(1976). In the following excerpt from his epilogue to Malcolm's* Autobiography, *Haley recounts his experiences with Malcolm and provides a historical overview of the final years of Malcolm's life.*]

During nineteen fifty-nine, when the public was becoming aware of the Muslims after the New York telecast "The Hate That Hate Produced," I was in San Francisco, about to retire after twenty years in the U.S. Coast Guard. A friend returned from a visit to her Detroit home and told me of a startling "black man's" religion, "The Nation of Islam," to which, to her surprise, her entire family was converted. I listened with incredulity to how a "mad scientist Mr. Yacub" had genetically "grafted" the white race from an original black people. The organization's leader was described as "The Honorable Elijah Muhammad" and a "Minister Malcolm X" was apparently chief of staff.

When I entered a civilian writing career in New York City, I collected, around Harlem, a good deal of provocative material and then proposed an article about the cult to the *Reader's Digest.* Visiting the Muslim restaurant in Harlem, I asked how I could meet Minister Malcolm X, who was pointed out talking in a telephone booth right behind me. Soon he came out, a gangling, tall, reddish-brownskinned fellow, at that time thirty-five years old; when my purpose was made known, he bristled, his eyes skewering me from behind the horn-rimmed glasses. "You're another one of the white man's tools sent to spy!" he accused me sharply. I said I had a legitimate writing assignment and showed him my letter from the magazine stating that an objective article was wanted, one that would balance what the Muslims said of themselves and what their attackers said about them. Malcolm X snorted that no white man's promise was worth the paper it was on; he would need time to decide if he would cooperate or not. (pp. 383-84)

Finally, Minister Malcolm X told me that he would not take personal responsibility. He said that I should talk about an article with Mr. Muhammad personally. I expressed willingness, an appointment was made, and I flew to Chicago. The slightly built, shy-acting, soft-voiced Mr. Muhammad invited me to dinner with his immediate family in his mansion. I was aware that I was being carefully sized up while he talked primarily of F.B.I. and Internal Revenue Service close surveillance of his organization, and of a rumored forthcoming Congressional probe. "But I have no fear of any of them; I have all that I need—the truth," Mr. Muhammad said. The subject of my writing an article somehow never got raised, but Malcolm X proved far more cooperative when I returned. (p. 384)

My article entitled "Mr. Muhammad Speaks" appeared in early 1960, and it was the first featured magazine notice of the phenomenon. A letter quickly came from Mr. Muhammad appreciating that the article kept my promise to be objective, and Malcolm X telephoned similar compliments. About this time, Dr. C. Eric Lincoln's book *The Black Muslims in America* was published and the Black Muslims became a subject of growing interest. During 1961 and 1962, the *Saturday Evening Post* teamed me with a white writer, Al Balk, to do an article; next I did a personal interview of Malcolm X for *Playboy* magazine, which had promised to print verbatim whatever response he made to my questions. During that interview of several days' duration, Malcolm X repeatedly exclaimed, after particularly blistering anti-Christian or anti-white statements: "You know that devil's not going to print that!" He was very much taken aback when *Playboy* kept its word.

Malcom X began to warm up to me somewhat. He was most aware of the national periodicals' power, and he had come to regard me, if still suspiciously, as one avenue of access. Occasionally now he began to telephone me advising me of some radio, television, or personal speaking appearance he was about to make, or he would invite me to attend some Black Muslim bazaar or other public affair.

I was in this stage of relationship with the Malcolm X who often described himself on the air as "the angriest black man in America" when in early 1963 my agent brought me together with a publisher whom the *Playboy* interview had given the idea of the autobiography of Malcolm X. I was asked if I felt I could get the now nationally known firebrand to consent to telling the intimate details of his entire life. I said I didn't know, but I would ask him. The editor asked me if I could sketch the likely highlights of such a book, and as I commenced talking, I realized how little I knew about the man personally, despite all my interviews. I said that the question had made me aware of how careful Malcolm X had always been to play himself down and to play up his leader Elijah Muhammad. (pp. 384-85)

Malcolm X gave me a startled look when I asked him if he would tell his life story for publication. It was one of the few times I have ever seen him uncertain. "It will have to give a book a lot of thought," he finally said. Two days later, he telephoned me to meet him again at the Black Muslim restaurant. He said, "I'll agree. I think my life story may help people to appreciate better how Mr. Muhammad salvages black people. But I don't want my motives for this misinterpreted by anybody—the Nation of Islam must get every penny that might come to me." Of course, Mr. Muhammad's agreement would be necessary, and I would have to ask Mr. Muhammad myself.

So I flew again to see Mr. Muhammad, but this time to Phoenix, Arizona, where the Nation of Islam had bought him the house in the hot, dry climate that relieved his severe bronchial condition. He and I talked alone this time. He told me how his organization had come far with largely uneducated Muslims and that truly giant strides for the black man could be made if his organization were aided by some of the talents which were available in the black race. He said, "And one of our worst needs is writers"—but he did not press me to answer. He suddenly began coughing, and rapidly grew worse and worse until I rose from my seat and went to him, alarmed, but he waved me away, gasping that he would be all right. Between gasps, he told me he felt that "Allah approves" the book. He said, "Malcolm is one of my most outstanding ministers." (p. 386)

Back East, Malcolm X carefully read and then signed the publication contract, and he withdrew from his wallet a piece of paper filled with his sprawling longhand. "This is this book's dedication," he said. I read: "This book I dedicate to The Honorable Elijah Muhammad, who found me here in America in the muck and mire of the filthiest civilization and society on this earth, and pulled me out, cleaned me up, and stood me on my feet, and made me the man that I am today." (pp. 366-87)

We got off to a very poor start. To use a word he liked, I think both of us were a bit "spooky." Sitting right there and staring at me was the fiery Malcolm X who could be as acid toward Negroes who angered him as he was against whites in general. On television, in press conferences, and at Muslim rallies, I had heard him bitterly attack other Negro writers as "Uncle Toms," "yard Negroes," "black men in white clothes." And there I sat staring at him, proposing to spend a year plumbing his innermost secrets when he had developed a near phobia for secrecy during his years of crime and his years in the Muslim hierarchy. My twenty years in military service and my Christian religious persuasion didn't help, either; he often jeered publicly at these affiliations for Negroes. And although he now would indirectly urge me to write for national magazines about the Muslims, he had told me several times, in various ways, that "you blacks with professional abilities of any kind will one of these days wake up and find out that you must unite under the leadership of The Honorable Elijah Muhammad for your own salvation." Malcolm X was also convinced that the F.B.I. had "bugged" my studio; he probably suspected that it may even have been done with my cooperation. For the first several weeks, he never entered the room where we worked without exclaiming, "Testing, testing—one, two, three. . . . " (pp. 387-88)

For perhaps a month I was afraid we weren't going to get any book. Malcolm X was still stiffly addressing me as "Sir" and my notebook contained almost nothing but Black Muslim philosophy, praise of Mr. Muhammad, and the "evils" of "the white devil." He would bristle when I tried to urge him that the proposed book was *his* life. I was thinking that I might have to advise the publisher that I simply couldn't seem to get through to my subject when the first note of hope occurred. I had noticed that while Malcolm X was talking, he often simultaneously scribbled with his red-ink ball-point pen on any handy paper. Sometimes it was the margin of a newspaper he brought in, sometimes it was on index cards that he carried in the back of a small, red-backed appointment book. I began leaving two white paper napkins by him every time I served him more coffee, and the ruse worked when he sometimes scribbled on the napkins, which I retrieved when he left. Some examples are these:

> Here lies a YM, killed by a BM, fighting for the WM, who killed all the RM. (Decoding that wasn't difficult, knowing Malcolm X. "YM" was for yellow man, "BM" for black man,

> "WM" for white man, and "RM" was for red man.)
>
> Nothing ever happened without cause. Cause BM condition WM won't face. WM obsessed with hiding his guilt.
>
> (pp. 388-89)

It was through a clue from one of the scribblings that finally I cast a bait that Malcolm X took. "Woman who cries all the time is only because she knows she can get away with it," he had scribbled. I somehow raised the subject of women. Suddenly, between sips of coffee and further scribbling and doodling, he vented his criticisms and skepticisms of women. "You never can fully trust any woman," he said. "I've got the only one I ever met whom I would trust seventy-five per cent. I've told her that," he said. "I've told her like I tell you I've seen too many men destroyed by their wives, or their women."

"I don't *completely* trust anyone," he went on, "not even myself. I have seen too many men destroy themselves. Other people I trust from not at all to highly, like The Honorable Elijah Muhammad." Malcolm X looked squarely at me. "You I trust about twenty-five percent." (p. 389)

[One night] Malcolm X arrived nearly out on his feet from fatigue. For two hours, he paced the floor delivering a tirade against Negro leaders who were attacking Elijah Muhammad and himself. I don't know what gave me the inspiration to say once when he paused for breath, "I wonder if you'd tell me something about your mother?"

Abruptly he quit pacing, and the look he shot at me made me sense that somehow the chance question had hit him. When I look back at it now, I believe I must have caught him so physically weak that his defenses were vulnerable.

Slowly, Malcolm X began to talk, now walking in a tight circle. "She was always standing over the stove, trying to stretch whatever we had to eat. We stayed so hungry that we were dizzy. I remember the color of dresses she used to wear—they were a kind of faded-out gray. . . . " And he kept on talking until dawn, so tired that the big feet would often almost stumble in their pacing. From this stream-of-consciousness reminiscing I finally got out of him the foundation for this book's beginning chapters, "Nightmare" and "Mascot." After that night, he never again hesitated to tell me even the most intimate details of his personal life, over the next two years. His talking about his mother triggered something. (pp. 390-91)

At intervals, Malcolm X would make a great point of stressing to me, "Now, I don't want anything in this book to make it sound that I think I'm somebody important." I would assure him that I would try not to, and that in any event he would be checking the manuscript page by page, and ultimately the galley proofs. At other times, he would end an attack upon the white man and, watching me take the notes, exclaim, "That devil's not going to print that, I don't care what he says!" I would point out that the publishers had made a binding contract and had paid a sizable sum in advance. Malcolm X would say, "You trust them, and I don't. You studied what he wanted you to learn about him in schools, I studied him in the streets and in prison, where you see the truth." (p. 392)

When something had angered Malcolm X during the day, his face would be flushed redder when he visited me, and he generally would spend much of the session lashing out bitterly. When some Muslims were shot by Los Angeles policemen, one of them being killed, Malcolm X, upon his return from a trip he made there, was fairly apoplectic for a week. It had been in this mood that he had made, in Los Angeles, the statement which caused him to be heavily censured by members of both races. "I've just heard some good news!"—referring to a plane crash at Orly Field in Paris in which thirty-odd white Americans, mostly from Atlanta, Georgia, had been killed instantly. (Malcolm X never publicly recanted this statement, to my knowledge, but much later he said to me simply, "That's one of the things I wish I had never said.")

Anytime the name of the present Federal Judge Thurgood Marshall was raised, Malcolm X still practically spat fire in memory of what the judge had said years before when he was the N.A.A.C.P. chief attorney: "The Muslims are run by a bunch of thugs organized from prisons and jails and financed, I am sure, by some Arab group." The only time that I have ever heard Malcolm X use what might be construed as a curse word, it was a "hell" used in response to a statement that Dr. Martin Luther King made that Malcolm X's talk brought "misery upon Negroes." Malcolm X exploded to me, "How in the hell can my talk do this? It's always a Negro responsible, not what the white man does!" The "extremist" or "demagogue" accusation invariably would burn Malcolm X. "Yes, I'm an extremist. The black race here in North America is in extremely bad condition. You show me a black man who isn't an extremist and I'll show you one who needs psychiatric attention!"

Once when he said, "Aristotle shocked people. Charles Darwin outraged people. Aldous Huxley scandalized millions!" Malcolm X immediately followed the statement with "Don't print that, people would think I'm trying to link myself with them." Another time, when something provoked him to exclaim, "These Uncle Toms make me think about how the Prophet Jesus was criticized in his own country!" Malcolm X promptly got up and silently took my notebook, tore out that page and crumpled it and put it into his pocket, and he was considerably subdued during the remainder of that session. (pp. 394-95)

Malcolm X and I reached the point, ultimately, where we shared a mutual camaraderie that, although it was never verbally expressed, was a warm one. He was for me unquestionably one of the most engaging personalities I had ever met, and for his part, I gathered, I was someone he had learned he could express himself to, with candor, without the likelihood of hearing it repeated, and like any person who lived amid tension, he enjoyed being around someone, another man, with whom he could psychically relax. When I made trips now, he always asked me to telephone him when I would be returning to New York, and generally, if he could squeeze it into his schedule, he met me at the airport. I would see him coming along with his long, gangling strides, and wearing the wide, toothy, good-natured grin, and as he drove me into New York City he would bring me up to date on things of interest that had happened since I left. I remember one incident within the airport that showed me how Malcolm X never lost his racial perspective. Waiting for my baggage, we witnessed a touching family reunion scene as part of which several cherubic little children romped and played, exclaiming in another language. "By tomorrow night, they'll know how to say their first English word—*nigger,*" observed Malcolm X.

When Malcolm X made long trips, such as to San Francisco or Los Angeles, I did not go along, but frequently, usually very late at night, he would telephone me, and ask how the book was coming along, and he might set up the time for our next interview upon his return. One call that I never will forget came at close to four A.M., waking me; he must have just gotten up in Los Angeles. His voice said, "Alex Haley?" I said, sleepily, "Yes? Oh, *hey,* Malcolm!" His voice said, "I trust you seventy per cent"—and then he hung up. I lay a short time thinking about him and I went back to sleep feeling warmed by that call, as I still am warmed to remember it. Neither of us ever mentioned it. (pp. 399-400)

[Some time later] I read with astonishment that Malcolm X had been suspended by Elijah Muhammad—the stated reason being the "chickens coming home to roost" remark that Malcolm X recently had made as a comment upon the assassination of President Kennedy.

Malcolm X did telephone, after about an hour, and I met him at the Black Muslims' newspaper office in Harlem, a couple of blocks further up Lenox Avenue from their mosque and restaurant. He was seated behind his light-brown metal desk and his brown hat lay before him on the green blotter. He wore a dark suit with a vest, a white shirt, the inevitable leaping-sailfish clip held his narrow tie, and the big feet in the shined black shoes pushed the swivel chair pendulously back and forth as he talked into the telephone.

"I'm always hurt over any act of disobedience on my part concerning Mr. Muhammad. . . . Yes, sir—anything The Honorable Elijah Muhammad does is all right with me. I believe absolutely in his wisdom and authority." The telephone would ring again instantly every time he put it down. "Mr. Peter Goldman! I haven't heard your voice in a good while! Well, sir, I just should have kept my big mouth shut." To the *New York Times:* "Sir? Yes—he suspended me from making public appearances for the time being, which I fully understand. I say the same thing to you that I have told others, I'm in complete submission to Mr. Muhammad's judgment, because I have always found his judgment to be based on sound thinking." To C.B.S.: "I think that anybody who is in a position to discipline others should first learn to accept discipline himself."

He brought it off, the image of contriteness, the best he could—throughout the harshly trying next several weeks. But the back of his neck was reddish every time I saw him. He did not yet put into words his obvious fury at the public humiliation. We did very little interviewing now; he was so busy on telephones elsewhere, but it did not matter too much because by now I had the bulk of the needed life story material in hand. When he did find some time to visit me, he was very preoccupied, and I could *feel* him rankling with anger and with inactivity, but he tried hard to hide it. (pp. 405-06)

I had now moved upstate to finish my work on the book, and we talked on the telephone every three or four days. He said things suggesting that he might never be returned to his former Black Muslim post, and he now began to say things quietly critical of Elijah Muhammad. *Playboy* magazine asked me to do an interview for them with the new champion [and recent Muslim convert] Cassius Clay, and when I confidently asked Malcolm X to arrange for me the needed introduction to Clay, Malcolm X hesitantly said, "I think you had better ask somebody else to do that." I was highly surprised at the reply, but I had learned never to press him for information. And then, very soon after, I received a letter. "Dear Alex Haley: A quick note. Would you prepare a properly worded letter that would enable me to change the reading of the contract so that all remaining proceeds now would go to the Muslim Mosque, Inc., or in the case of my death then to go directly to my wife, Mrs. Betty X Little? The sooner this letter or contract is changed, the more easily I will rest." Under the

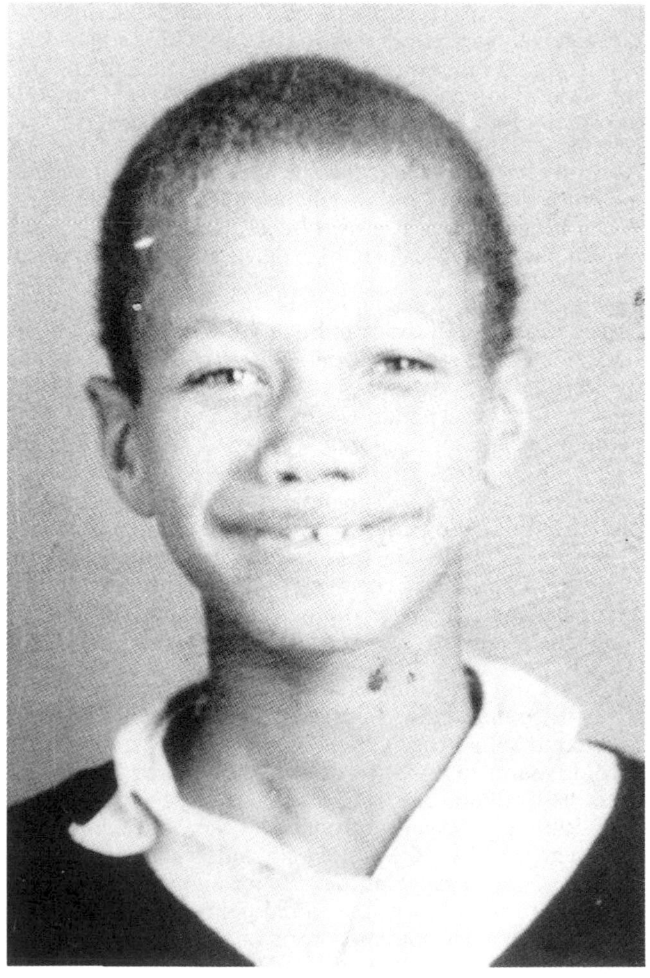

Malcolm Little as a boy.

signature of Malcolm X, there was a P.S.: "How is it possible to write one's autobiography in a world so fast-changing as this?"

Soon, I read in the various newspapers that rumors were being heard of threats on Malcolm X's life. Then there was an article in the *Amsterdam News:* The caption was "Malcolm X Tells Of Death Threat," and the story reported that he had said that former close associates of his in the New York mosque had sent out "a special squad" to "try to kill me in cold blood. Thanks to Allah, I learned of the plot from the very same brothers who had been sent out to murder me. These brothers had heard me represent and defend Mr. Muhammad for too long for them to swallow the lies about me without first asking me some questions for their own clarification."

I telephoned Malcolm X, and expressed my personal concern for him. His voice sounded weary. He said that his "uppermost interest" was that any money which might come due him in the future would go directly to his new organization, or to his wife, as the letter he had signed and mailed had specified. He told me, "I know I've got to get a will made for myself, I never did because I never have had anything to will to anybody, but if I don't have one and something happened to me, there could be a mess." I expressed concern for him, and he told me that he had a loaded rifle in his home, and "I can take care of myself."

The "Muslim Mosque, Inc." to which Malcolm X had referred was a new organization which he had formed, which at that time consisted of perhaps forty or fifty Muslims who had left the leadership of Elijah Muhammad. (pp. 408-09)

Elijah Muhammad at his headquarters in Chicago grew "emotionally affected" whenever the name of Malcolm X had to be raised in his presence, one of the Muslims in Clay's entourage told me. Mr. Muhammad reportedly had said, "Brother Malcolm got to be a *big* man. I made him big. I was about to make him a *great* man." The faithful Black Muslims predicted that soon Malcolm X would be turned upon by the defectors from Mosque Number 7 who had joined him: "They will feel betrayed." Said others, "A great chastisement of Allah will fall upon a hypocrite." Mr. Muhammad reportedly had said at another time, "Malcolm is destroying himself," and that he had no wish whatever to see Malcolm X die, that he "would rather see him live and suffer his treachery."

The general feeling among Harlemites, non-Muslims, with whom I talked was that Malcolm X had been powerful and influential enough a minister that eventually he would split the mosque membership into two hostile camps, and that in New York City at least, Elijah Muhammad's unquestioned rule would be ended.

Malcolm X returned. He said that he had been in Boston and Philadelphia. He spent ample time with me, now during the day, in Room 1936 in the Hotel Americana. His old total ease was no longer with him. As if it was the most natural thing in the world to do, at sudden intervals he would stride to the door; pulling it open, he would look up and down the corridor, then shut the door again. "If I'm alive when this book comes out, it will be a miracle," he said by way of explanation. "I'm not saying it distressingly—" He leaned forward and touched the buff gold bedspread. "I'm saying it like I say that's a bedspread."

For the first time he talked with me in some detail about what had happened. He said that his statement about President Kennedy's assassination was not why he had been ousted from the Muslims. "It wasn't the reason at all. Nobody said anything when I made stronger statements before." The real reason, he said, was "jealousy in Chicago, and I had objected to the immorality of the man who professed to be more moral than anybody."

Malcolm X said that he had increased the Nation of Islam membership from about 400 when he had joined to around 40,000. "I don't think there were more than 400 in the country when I joined, I really don't. They were mostly older people, and many of them couldn't even pronounce Mr. Muhammad's name, and he stayed mostly in the background."

Malcolm X worked hard not to show it, but he was upset. "There is nothing more frightful than ignorance in action. Goethe," he scribbled one day. (pp. 409-11)

And at another time there in the hotel room he came the nearest to tears that I ever saw him, and also the only time I ever heard him use, for his race, one word. He had been talking about how hard he had worked building up the Muslim organization in the early days when he was first moved to New York City, when abruptly he exclaimed hoarsely, "We had the *best* organization the black man's ever had—*niggers* ruined it!" (p. 411)

I had become worried that Malcolm X, bitter, would want to go back through the chapters in which he had told of his Black Muslim days and re-edit them in some way. The day before I left New York City to return upstate, I raised my concern to Malcolm X. "I have thought about that," he said. "There are a lot of things I could say that passed through my mind at times even then, things I saw and heard, but I threw them out of my mind. I'm going to let it stand the way I've told it. I want the book to be the way it was."

Then—March 26, 1964—a note came from Malcolm X: "There is a chance that I may make a quick trip to several very important countries in Africa, including a pilgrimage to the Muslim Holy Cities of Mecca and Medina, beginning about April 13th. Keep this to yourself."

While abroad, Malcolm X wrote letters and postcards to almost everyone he knew well. His letters now were signed "El-Hajj Malik El-Shabazz." (p. 412)

[Following his return from Mecca, as] I resumed writing upstate, periodic notes came from Malcolm X. "I hope the book is proceeding rapidly, for events concerning my life happen so swiftly, much of what has already been written can easily be outdated from month to month. In life, nothing is permanent; not even life itself (smile). So I would advise you to rush it on out as fast as possible." Another note, special delivery, had a tone of irritation with me: he had received from the publisher a letter which indicated that he had received a $2500 check when the book contract was signed, "and therefore I will be expected to pay *personal* income tax on this. As you know, it was my repeated specification that this entire transaction was to be made at that time directly with and to the Mosque. In fact, I have never seen that check to this very day."

The matter was straightened out, and I sent Malcolm X some rough chapters to read. I was appalled when they were soon returned, red-inked in many places where he had told of his almost father-and-son relationship with Elijah Muhammad. Telephoning Malcolm X, I reminded him of his previous decision, and I stressed that if those chapters contained such telegraphing to readers of what would lie ahead, then the book would automatically be robbed of some of its building suspense and drama. Malcolm X said, gruffly, "Whose book is this?" I told him "yours, of course," and that I only made the objection in my position as a writer. He said that he would have to think about it. I was heart-sick at the prospect that he might want to re-edit the entire book into a polemic against Elijah Muhammad. But late that night, Malcolm X telephoned. "I'm sorry. You're right. I was upset about something. Forget what I wanted changed, let what you already had stand." I never again gave him chapters to review unless I was with him. Several times I would covertly watch him frown and wince as he read, but he never again asked for any change in what he had originally said. And the only thing that he ever indicated that he wished had been different in his life came when he was reading the chapter "Laura." He said, "That was a smart girl, a *good* girl. She tried her best to make something out of me, and look what I started her into—dope and prostitution. I wrecked that girl." (pp. 413-14)

The manuscript copy which Malcolm X was given to review was in better shape now, and he pored through page by page, intently, and now and then his head would raise with some comment. "You know," he said once, "why I have been able to have some effect is because I make a study of the weaknesses of this country and because the more the white man yelps, the more I know I have struck a nerve." Another time, he put down upon the bed the manuscript he was reading, and he got up from his chair and walked back and forth, stroking his chin, then he looked at me. "You know this place here in this chapter where I told you how I put the pistol up to my head and kept pulling the trigger and scared them so when I was starting the burglary ring—well," he paused, "I don't know if I ought to tell you this or not, but I want to tell the truth." He eyed me, speculatively. "I palmed the bullet." We laughed together. I said, "Okay, give that page here, I'll fix it." Then he considered, "No, leave it that way. Too many people would be so quick to say that's what I'm doing today, bluffing." (pp. 415-16)

Before long, Malcolm X called a press conference, and announced, "My new Organization of Afro-American Unity is a non-religious and non-sectarian group organized to unite Afro-Americans for a constructive program toward attainment of human rights." The new OAAU's tone appeared to be one of militant black nationalism. He said to the questions of various reporters in subsequent interviews that the OAAU would seek to convert the Negro population from non-violence to active self-defense against white supremacists across America. On the subject of politics he offered an enigma, "Whether you use bullets or ballots, you've got to aim well; don't strike at the puppet, strike at the puppeteer." Did he envision any special area of activity? "I'm going to join in the fight wherever Negroes ask for my help." What about alliance with other Negro organizations? He said that he would consider forming some united front with certain selected Negro leaders. He conceded under questioning that the N.A.A.C.P. was "doing some good." Could any whites join his OAAU? "If John Brown were alive, maybe him." And he answered his critics with such statements as that he would send "armed guerrillas" into Mississippi. "I am dead serious. We will send them not only to Mississippi, but to any place where black people's lives are threatened by white bigots. As far as I am concerned, Mississippi is anywhere south of the Canadian border." At another time, when Evelyn Cunningham of the *Pittsburgh Courier* asked Malcolm X in a kidding way, "Say something startling for my column," he told her, "Anyone who wants to follow me and my movement has got to be ready to go to jail, to the hospital, and to the cemetery before he can be truly free." Evelyn Cunningham, printing the item, commented, "He smiled and chuckled, but he was in dead earnest." (pp. 416-17)

One morning in mid-summer 1964, Malcolm X telephoned me and said that he would be leaving "within the next two or three days" for a planned six weeks abroad. I heard from him first in Cairo, about as the predicted "long, hot summer" began in earnest, with riots and other uprisings of Negroes occurring in suburban Philadelphia, in Rochester, in Brooklyn, in Harlem, and other cities. The *New York Times* reported that a meeting of Negro intellectuals had agreed that Dr. Martin Luther King could secure the allegiance of the middle and upper classes of Negroes, but Malcolm X alone could secure the allegiance of Negroes at the bottom. "The Negroes respect Dr. King and Malcolm X because they sense in these men absolute integrity and know they will never sell them out. Malcolm X cannot be corrupted and the Negroes know this and therefore respect him. They also know that he comes from the lower depths, as they do, and regard him as one of their own. Malcolm X is going to play a formidable role, because the racial struggle has now shifted to the urban North . . . if Dr. King is convinced that he has sacrificed ten years of brilliant leadership, he will be forced to revise his concepts. There is only one direction in which he can move, and that is in the direction of Malcolm X." I sent a clipping of that story to Malcolm X in Cairo. (pp. 417-18)

[Following his return], Malcolm X wanted to "huddle" with me to fill me in on details from his trip that he wanted in the book. He said that he was giving me only the highlights, because he felt that his carefully kept diary might be turned into another book. We had intensive sessions in my hotel room, where he read what he selected from the diary, and I took notes. "What I want to stress is that I was trying to internationalize our problem," he said to me, "to make the Africans feel their *kinship* with us Afro-Americans. I made them *think* about it, that they are our blood brothers, and we all came from the same foreparents. That's why the Africans loved me, the same way the Asians loved me because I was religious."

Within a few days, he had no more time to see me. He would call and apologize; he was beset by a host of problems, some of which he mentioned, and some of which I heard from other people. Most immediately, there was discontent within his organization, the OAAU. His having stayed away almost three times as long as he had said he would be gone had sorely tested the morale of even his key members, and there was a general feeling that his interest was insufficient to expect his followers' interest to stay high. I heard from one member that "a growing disillusion" could be sensed throughout the organization.

In Harlem at large, in the bars and restaurants, on the street corners and stoops, there could be heard more blunt criticism of Malcolm X than ever before in his career. There were, variously expressed, two primary complaints. One was that actually Malcolm X only talked, but other civil-rights organizations were *doing.* "All he's *ever* done was talk, CORE and SNCC and some of them people of Dr. King's are out getting beat over the head." The second major complaint was that Malcolm X was himself too confused to be seriously followed any longer. "He doesn't know *what* he believes in. No sooner do you hear one thing than he's switched to something else." The two complaints were not helping the old firebrand Malcolm X image any, nor were they generating the local public interest that was badly needed by his small, young OAAU.

A court had made it clear that Malcolm X and his family would have to vacate the Elmhurst house for its return to the adjudged legal owners, Elijah Muhammad's Nation of Islam. And other immediate problems which Malcolm X faced included finances. Among his other expenses, a wife and four daughters had to be supported, along with at least one full-time OAAU official. Upon his return from Africa, our agent for the book had delivered to me for Malcolm X a check for a sizable sum; soon afterward Malcolm X told me, laughing wryly, "It's *evaporated.* I don't know where!" (pp. 419-20)

Malcolm X for some reason suddenly began to deliver a spate of attacks against Elijah Muhammad, making more bitter accusations of "religious fakery" and "immorality" than he ever had. Very possibly, Malcolm X had grown increasingly incensed by the imminence of the court's deadline for him to have to move his wife and four little daughters from the comfortable home in which they had lived for years in Elmhurst. And Sister Betty was again pregnant. "A home is really the only thing I've ever provided Betty since we've been married," he had told me, discussing the court's order, "and they want to take that away. Man, I can't keep on putting her through changes, all she's put up with—man, I've *got* to love this woman!"

A rash of death threats were anonymously telephoned to the police, to various newspapers, to the OAAU office, and to the family's home in Elmhurst. When he went to court again, fighting to keep the house, he was guarded by a phalanx of eight OAAU men, twenty uniformed policemen, and twelve plain-clothes detectives. The court's decision was that the order to vacate would not be altered. (p. 421)

Malcolm X steadily accused the Black Muslims as the source of the various attacks and threats. "There is no group in the United States more able to carry out this threat than the Black Muslims," he said. "I know, because I taught them myself." Asked why he had attacked the Black Muslims and Elijah Muhammad when things had seemed to be cooled down, he said, "I would not have revealed any of this if they had left me alone." He let himself be photographed in his home holding an automatic carbine rifle with a full double clip of ammunition that he said he kept ready for action against any possible assassination efforts. "I have taught my wife to use it, and instructed her to fire on anyone, white, black, or yellow, who tries to force his way inside."

I went to New York City in December for Malcolm X's reading of final additions to the manuscript, to include the latest developments. He was further than I had ever seen him from his old assured self, it seemed to me. He kept saying that the press was making light of his statements about the threats on his life. "They act like I'm jiving!" He brought up again the *Saturday Evening Post* editorial. "You can't trust the publishing people, I don't care what they tell you." The agent for the book sent to my hotel a contract dealing with foreign publication rights which needed Malcolm X's and my signature. I signed it as he observed and handed the pen to him. He looked suspiciously at the contract, and said, "I had better show this thing to my lawyer," and put the contract in his inside coat pocket. Driving in Harlem about an hour later, he suddenly stopped the car across the street from the 135th Street Y.M.C.A. Building. Withdrawing the contract, he signed it, and thrust it to me. "I'll trust you," he said, and drove on. (pp. 422-23)

[Early in 1965, Malcolm X was] served with a court order of eviction from the Elmhurst home. He telephoned me upstate. His voice was strained. He told me that he had filed an appeal to the court order, that on the next day he was going to Alabama, and thence to England and France for scheduled speeches, and soon after returning he would go to Jackson, Mississippi, to address the Mississippi Freedom Democratic Party, on February 19. Then he said—the first time he had ever voiced to me such an admission—"Haley, my nerves are shot, my brain's tired." He said that upon his return from Mississippi, he would like to come and spend two or three days in the town where I was, and read the book's manuscript again. "You say it's a quiet town. Just a couple of days of peace and quiet, that's what I need." I said that he knew he was welcome, but there was no need for him to tax himself reading through the long book again, as it had only a few very minor editing changes since he had only recently read it. "I just want to read it one more time," he said, "because I don't expect to read it in finished form." So we made a tentative agreement that the day after his projected return from Mississippi, he would fly upstate to visit for a weekend with me. The projected date was the Saturday and Sunday of February 20-21. (p. 426)

[Malcolm X was asleep with his family in New York City

on Saturday, February 13th] when at about a quarter of three the following Sunday morning, a terrifying blast awakened them. Sister Betty would tell me later that Malcolm X, barking commands and snatching up screaming, frightened children, got the family safely out of the back door into the yard. Someone had thrown flaming Molotov cocktail gasoline bombs through the front picture window. It took the fire department an hour to extinguish the flames. Half the house was destroyed. Malcolm X had no fire insurance.

Pregnant, distraught Sister Betty and the four little daughters went to the home of close friends. Malcolm X steeled himself to catch a plane as scheduled that morning to speak in Detroit. He wore an open-necked sweater shirt under his suit. Immediately afterward, he flew back to New York. Monday morning, amid a flurry of emergency re-housing plans for his family, Malcolm X was outraged when he learned that Elijah Muhammad's New York Mosque Number 7 Minister James X had told the press that Malcolm X himself had fire-bombed the home "to get publicity."

Monday night, Malcolm X spoke to an audience in the familiar Audubon Ballroom. If he had possessed the steel nerves not to become rattled in public before, now he was: "I've reached the end of my rope!" he shouted to the audience of five hundred. "I wouldn't care for myself if they would not harm my family!" He declared flatly, "My house was bombed by the *Muslims!*" And he hinted at revenge. "There are hunters; there are also those who hunt the hunters!"

Tuesday, February 16th, Malcolm X telephoned me. He spoke very briefly, saying that the complications following the bombing of his home had thrown his plans so awry that he would be unable to visit me upstate on the weekend as he had said he would. He said he had also had to cancel his planned trip to Jackson, Mississippi, which he was going to try and make later. He said he had to hurry to an appointment, and hung up. I would read later where also on that day, he told a close associate, "I have been marked for death in the next five days. I have the names of five Black Muslims who have been chosen to kill me. I will announce them at the meeting." And Malcolm X told a friend that he was going to apply to the Police Department for a permit to carry a pistol. "I don't know whether they will let me have one or not, as I served time in prison." (pp. 427-28)

The blackboard in the OAAU office counseled members and visitors that "Bro. Malcolm Speaks Thurs. Feb. 18, WINS Station, 10:30 P.M." Earlier Thursday, Malcolm X discussed locating another home with a real estate dealer. On Friday, he had an appointment with Gordon Parks, the *Life* magazine photographer-author whom he had long admired and respected. "He appeared calm and somewhat resplendent with his goatee and astrakhan hat," Parks would report later in *Life.* "Much of the old hostility and bitterness seemed to have left him, but the fire and confidence were still there." Malcolm X, speaking of the old Mosque Number 7 days, said, "That was a bad scene, brother. The sickness and madness of those days—I'm glad to be free of them. It's a time for martyrs now. And if I'm to be one, it will be in the cause of brotherhood. That's the only thing that can save this country. I've learned it the hard way—but I've learned it. . . . "

Parks asked Malcolm X if it was really true that killers were after him. "It's as true as we are standing here," Malcolm X said, "They've tried it twice in the last two weeks." Parks asked him about police protection, and Malcolm X laughed, "Brother, nobody can protect you from a Muslim but a Muslim—or someone trained in Muslim tactics. I know. I invented many of those tactics."

Recalling the incident of the young white college girl who had come to the Black Muslim restaurant and asked "What can I *do?*" and he told her "Nothing," and she left in tears, Malcolm X told Gordon Parks, "Well, I've lived to regret that incident. In many parts of the African continent I saw white students helping black people. Something like this kills a lot of argument. I did many things as a Muslim that I'm sorry for now. I was a zombie then—like all Muslims—I was hypnotized, pointed in a certain direction and told to march. Well, I guess a man's entitled to make a fool of himself if he's ready to pay the cost. It cost me twelve years." (pp. 428-29)

The Audubon Ballroom, between Broadway and St. Nicholas Avenue, on the south side of West 166th Street, is a two-story building frequently rented for dances, organization functions, and other affairs. A dark, slender, pretty young lady, occupationally a receptionist and avocationally a hardworking OAAU assistant to Malcolm X, has since told me that she arrived early, about 1:30 P.M., having some preliminary work to do. Entering, she saw that the usual 400 wooden chairs had been set up, with aisles on either side, but no center aisle; the young lady (she wishes to be nameless) noticed that several people were already seated in the front rows, but she gave it no thought since some always came early, liking to get seats up close to the stage, to savor to the fullest the dramatic orator Malcolm X. On the stage, behind the speaker's stand were eight straight brown chairs arranged in a row and behind him was the stage's painted backdrop, a mural of a restful country scene. The young lady's responsibilities for this day had included making arrangements and subsequent confirmations with the scheduled co-speaker, the Reverend Milton Galamison, the militant Brooklyn Presbyterian who in 1964 had led the two one-day Negro boycotts in New York City public schools, protesting "racial imbalance." She had similarly made arrangements with some other prominent Negroes who were due to appeal to the audience for their maximum possible contributions to aid the work of Malcolm X and his organization.

The people who entered the ballroom were not searched at the door. In recent weeks, Malcolm X had become irritable about this, saying "It makes people uncomfortable" and that it reminded him of Elijah Muhammad. "If I can't be safe among my own kind, where can I be?" he had once said testily. For this day, also, he had ordered the press—as such—barred, white or black. He was angry at what he interpreted as "slanted" press treatment recently; he felt especially that the newspapers had not taken seriously his statements of the personal danger he was in. (pp. 431-32)

Malcolm X entered the ballroom at shortly before two o'clock, trudging heavily instead of with his usual lithe strides, his young lady assistant has told me. By this time several other of his assistants were filtering in and out of the small anteroom alongside the stage. He sat down sideways on a chair, his long legs folded around its bottom, and he leaned one elbow on a kind of counter before a rather rickety make-up mirror that entertainers used when dances were held in the ballroom. He wore a dark suit, white shirt and narrow dark tie. He said to a little group of his assistants that he wasn't going to talk about his personal troubles, "I don't want that to be the reason for anyone to come to hear me." He stood up and paced about the little room. He said he was going to state that he had been hasty to accuse the Black Muslims of bombing his home. "Things have happened since that are bigger than what they can do. I know what they can do. Things have gone beyond that." (p. 433)

[Following a brief introduction, Malcolm X greeted the group he was to address at the Audubon Ballroom.] About eight rows of seats from the front, then, a disturbance occurred. In a sudden scuffling, a man's voice was raised angrily, "Take your hand out of my pocket!" The entire audience was swiveling to look. "Hold it! Hold it! Don't get excited," Malcolm X said crisply, "Let's cool it, brothers—"

With his own attention distracted, it is possible that he never saw the gunmen. One woman who was seated near the front says, "The commotion back there diverted me just for an instant, then I turned back to look at Malcolm X just in time to see at least three men in the front row stand and take aim and start firing simultaneously. It looked like a firing squad." Numerous persons later said they saw two men rushing toward the stage, one with a shotgun, the other with two revolvers. Said U.P.I. reporter Stanley Scott: "Shots rang out. Men, women and children ran for cover. They stretched out on the floor and ducked under tables." Radio Station WMCA reporter Hugh Simpson said, "Then I heard this muffled sound, I saw Malcolm hit with his hands still raised, then he fell back over the chairs behind him. Everybody was shouting. I saw one man firing a gun from under his coat behind me as I hit it [the floor], too. He was firing like he was in some Western, running backward toward the door and firing at the same time."

The young lady who was in the backstage anteroom told me, "It sounded like an army had taken over. Somehow, I knew. I wouldn't go and look. I wanted to remember him as he was."

Malcolm X's hand flew to his chest as the first of sixteen shotgun pellets or revolver slugs hit him. Then the other hand flew up. The middle finger of the left hand was bullet-shattered, and blood gushed from his goatee. He clutched his chest. His big body suddenly fell back stiffly, knocking over two chairs; his head struck the stage floor with a thud.

In the bedlam of shouting, screaming, running people, some ran toward the stage. Among them Sister Betty scrambled up from where she had thrown her body over her children, who were shrieking; she ran crying hysterically, "My husband! They're killing my husband!" An unidentified photographer snapped shots of Malcolm X prone on the stage floor with people bent over him snatching apart his bloody shirt, loosening his tie, trying to give him mouth-to-mouth artificial respiration, first a woman, then a man. Said the woman, who identified herself only as a registered nurse, "I don't know how I got up on the stage, but I threw myself down on who I thought was Malcolm—but it wasn't. I was willing to die for the man, I would have taken the bullets myself; then I saw Malcolm, and the firing had stopped, and I tried to give him artificial respiration." Then Sister Betty came through the people, herself a nurse, and people recognizing her moved back; she fell on her knees looking down on his bare, bullet-pocked chest, sobbing, "They killed him!"

Patrolman Thomas Hoy, 22, was stationed outside the Audubon Ballroom entrance. "I heard the shooting and the place exploded." He rushed inside, he saw Malcolm X lying on the stage, and then some people chasing a man. Patrolman Hoy "grabbed the suspect."

Louis Michaux, the owner of the Nationalist Memorial Bookstore at 125th Street and Seventh Avenue in Harlem, said "I was arriving late at the meeting where Malcolm X had invited me, I met a large number of people rushing out."

Sergeant Alvin Aronoff and Patrolman Louis Angelos happened to be cruising by in their radio car when they heard shots. "When we got there," said Aronoff, "the crowds were pushing out and screaming 'Malcolm's been shot!' and 'Get 'im, get 'im, don't let him go!' " The two policemen grabbed by the arms a Negro who was being kicked as he tried to escape. Firing a warning shot into the air, the policemen pushed the man into their police car, not wanting the angry crowd to close in, and drove him quickly to the police station.

Someone had run up to the Columbia-Presbyterian Hospital's Vanderbilt Clinic emergency entrance at 167th Street and grabbed a poles-and-canvas stretcher and brought it back to the Audubon Ballroom stage. Malcolm X was put on the stretcher and an unidentified photographer got a macabre picture of him, with his mouth open and his teeth bared, as men rushed him up to the hospital clinic emergency entrance. A hospital spokesman said later that it was about 3:15 P.M. when Malcolm X reached a third-floor operating room. He was "either dead, or in a death-appearing state," said the spokesman.

A team of surgeons cut through his chest to attempt to massage the heart. The effort was abandoned at 3:30 P.M.

Reporters who had descended upon the hospital office fired questions at the spokesman, who kept saying brusquely, "I don't know." Then he took the elevator upstairs to the emergency operating room. A small crowd of friends and Sister Betty had also pushed into the hospital office when the hospital spokesman returned. Collecting himself, he made an announcement: "The gentleman you know as Malcolm X is dead. He died from gunshot wounds. He was apparently dead before he got here. He was shot in the chest several times, and once in the cheek."

The group filed out of the hospital office. The Negro men were visibly fighting their emotions; one kept smashing his fist into the other cupped palm. Among the women, many were openly crying.

Moments after the news flashed throughout Harlem (and throughout the entire world), a crowd began to gather outside the Hotel Theresa where Malcolm X's OAAU had its headquarters. They learned over transistor radios that the man whom the two policemen had taken from the murder scene initially identified himself as Thomas Hagan, 22 (he was later identified as Talmadge Hayer), in whose right trousers pocket the policemen had found a .45 caliber cartridge clip containing four unused cartridges, and then at Jewish Memorial Hospital doctors had reported that Hayer had been shot in the left thigh, his forehead was bruised and his body was beaten. "If we hadn't gotten him away, they would have kicked him to death," Sergeant Aronoff had said, and Hayer had been taken to the Bellevue Hospital Prison Ward. (pp. 434-37)

A number of questions have been raised. The "suspect" arrested by Patrolman Hoy as he was being chased from the meeting has, at present writing, not been identified publicly. Deputy Police Commissioner Walter Arm's statement that Malcolm X refused police protection conflicts directly with the statements of many of his associates that during the week preceding his assassination Malcolm X complained repeatedly that the police would not take his requests for protection seriously. Finally, although police sources said that a special detail of twenty men had been assigned to the meeting and that it had even been attended by agents of the Bureau of Special Services, these men were nowhere in evidence during or after the assassination, and Talmadge Hayer, rescued from the crowd and arrested as a suspect immediately after the assassination, was picked up by two patrolmen in a squad car cruising by. (pp. 438-39)

[Following Malcolm X's funeral], prominent Negro figures were being quoted by the various press media. The famed psychologist Dr. Kenneth B. Clark told *Jet* magazine, "I had a deep respect for this man. I believe that he was sincerely groping to find a place in the fight for Civil Rights, on a level where he would be respected and understood fully. I looked forward to his growth along those lines. It doesn't matter so much about his past. It is tragic that he was cut down at the point when he seemed on the verge of achieving the position of respectability he sought." A *New York Times* correspondent in a London press conference quoted the author and dramatist James Baldwin, who thought the death of Malcolm X was "a major setback for the Negro movement." Pointing at white reporters, Baldwin accused, "You did it . . . whoever did it was formed in the crucible of the Western world, of the American Republic!" European "rape" of Africa began racial problems and was therefore the beginning of the end for Malcolm X, Baldwin said. (p. 443)

"For the Negroes in America, the death of Malcolm X is the most portentous event since the deportation of Marcus Garvey in the 1920's," said Dr. C. Eric Lincoln, author of *The Black Muslims in America,* who talked to the press at Brown University in Providence, R.I., where he was a visiting professor and research fellow. "I doubt there are 'international implications' in the slaying. The answer is closer to home. The answer is in the local struggle among contending rivals for leadership of the black masses, which are potentially the most volatile sub-group in America." Said Roy Wilkins, Executive Secretary of the National Association for the Advancement of Colored People, "Master spell-binder that he was, Malcolm X in death cast a spell more far-flung and more disturbing than any he cast in life." (p. 444)

Far from Harlem, in lands where Malcolm X had traveled, the press had given the murder a coverage that had highly irritated the Director of the United States Information Agency, Carl T. Rowan, himself a Negro. In Washington, addressing the American Foreign Service Association, Rowan said that when he first heard of the murder, he knew it would be grossly misconstrued in some countries where people were unaware what Malcolm X represented, and he said the USIA had worked hard to inform the African press of the facts about Malcolm X and his preachments, but still there had been "a host of African reaction based on misinformation and misrepresentation."

Said USIA Director Rowan, "Mind you, here was a Negro who preached segregation and race hatred, killed by another Negro, presumably from another organization that preaches segregation and race hatred, and neither of them representative of more than a tiny minority of the Negro population of America—" Rowan held up some foreign newspapers. "All this about an ex-convict, ex-dope peddler who became a racial fanatic," continued Rowan. "I can only conclude that we Americans know less about what goes on in the minds of other peoples than we thought, or the need to inform is even greater than we in USIA thought it to be." (pp. 446-47)

Friday morning New York City press headlines concerning Malcolm X's slaying were devoted to the police department's apprehension of a second slaying suspect. He was a stocky, round-faced, twenty-six-year-old karate expert named Norman 3X Butler, allegedly a Black Muslim, and a week later, this was followed by the arrest of Thomas 15X Johnson, also allegedly a Black Muslim. Both men had been earlier indicted in the January, 1965, shooting of Benjamin Brown, a New York City Correction Officer and a Black Muslim defector. Both men were indicted, along with Hayer, for the murder of Malcolm X on March 10.

With the news announcement of Butler's arrest, and his at least tentative identification as a member of Elijah Muhammad's organization, tension reached a new high among all who had any role in the feud. The Black Muslim National Convention was scheduled to begin that Friday in Chicago, to last for three days. (p. 448)

[At the meeting, Elijah Muhammad] said in his speech: "For a long time, Malcolm stood here where I stand. In those days, Malcolm was safe, Malcolm was loved. God, Himself, protected Malcolm. . . . For more than a year, Malcolm was given his freedom. He went everywhere—Asia, Europe, Africa, even to Mecca, trying to make enemies for me. He came back preaching that we should not hate the enemy. . . . He came here a few weeks ago to blast away his hate and mud-slinging; everything he could think of to disgrace me. . . . We didn't want to kill Malcolm and didn't try to kill him. They know I didn't harm Malcolm. They know I loved him. His foolish teaching brought him to his own end. . . . "

Both physically and emotionally worked up, often Elijah Muhammad would begin coughing. "Take it easy! Take your time!" his audience pleaded with him. "He had no right to reject me!" Elijah Muhammad declared. "He was a star, who went astray! . . . They knew I didn't harm Malcolm, but he tried to make war against me." He said that Malcolm X would have been given "the most glorious of burials" if he had stayed with the Black Muslims and had died a natural death; "instead, we stand beside the grave of a hypocrite! . . . *Malcolm!* Who was he leading? Who was he teaching? He has no truth! We didn't want to kill Malcolm! His foolish teaching would bring him to his own end! I am not going to let the crackpots destroy the good things Allah sent to you and me!"

Elijah Muhammad drove his frail energy to speak for about an hour and a half. He challenged any would-be assassins: "If you seek to snuff out the life of Elijah Muhammad, you are inviting your own doom! The Holy Quran tells us not to pick a fight but to defend ourselves. We will fight!" It was midafternoon when Elijah Muhammad turned back to his seat with some three thousand Black Muslim men, women, and children shouting "Yes, *sir!* . . . So sweet! . . . All praise to Muhammad!" (pp. 450-51)

[At the Unity Funeral Home in Harlem], I got into the quietly moving line, thinking about the Malcolm X with whom I had worked closely for about two years. Blue-uniformed policemen stood at intervals watching us shuffle along within the wooden gray-painted police barricades. Just across the street several men were looking at the line from behind a large side window of the "Lone Star Barber Shop, Eddie Johns, Prop., William Ashe, Mgr." Among the policemen were a few press representatives talking to each other to pass the time. Then we were inside the softly lit, hushed, cool, large chapel. Standing at either end of the long, handsome bronze coffin were two big, dark policemen, mostly looking straight ahead, but moving their lips when some viewer tarried. Within minutes I had reached the coffin. Under the glass lid, I glimpsed the delicate white shrouding over the chest and up like a hood about the face on which I tried to concentrate for as long as I could. All that I could think was that it was he, all right—Malcolm X. "Move on"—the policeman's voice was soft. Malcolm looked to me—just waxy and *dead.* The policeman's hand was gesturing at his waist level. I thought, "*Well—good-bye.*" I moved on. (pp. 451-52)

After signing the contract for this book, Malcolm X looked at me hard. "A writer is what I want, not an interpreter." I tried to be a dispassionate chronicler. But he was the most electric personality I have ever met, and I still can't quite conceive him dead. It still feels to me as if he has just gone into some next chapter, to be written by historians. (p. 456)

Alex Haley, in an epilogue to The Autobiography of Malcolm X *by Malcolm X and Alex Haley, 1965. Reprint by Balantine Books, 1973, pp. 383-456.*

Robert Penn Warren (essay date December 1966)

[*Author of the acclaimed novel* All the King's Men *(1946), Warren is recognized as one of the most distinguished men of letters in twentieth-century American literature. In the following essay, he profiles Malcolm X and speculates as to his future had he lived.*]

James Farmer, lately the National Director of the Committee of Racial Equality, has called Malcolm X a "very simple man." Elijah Poole, better known to the Black Muslims as Muhammad and, indeed, as Allah, called him a "star gone astray." An editorial writer of the *Saturday Evening Post* put it: "If Malcolm X were not a Negro, his autobiography would be little more than a journal of abnormal psychology, the story of a burglar, dope pusher, addict and jailbird—with a family history of insanity—who acquires messianic delusions and sets forth to preach an upside-down religion of 'brotherly' hatred." Carl Rowan, a Negro, lately the director of the United States Information Service, substantially agreed with that editorial writer when he said, in an interview after Malcolm's assassination, that he was "an ex-convict, ex-dope peddler who became a racial fanatic." Another editorial writer, that of the *Daily Times* of Lagos, Nigeria, called him a martyr.

Malcolm X may have been, in varying perspectives, all these things. But he was also something else. He was a latter-day example of an old-fashioned type of American celebrated in grammar school readers, commencement addresses, and speeches at Rotary Club lunches—the man who "makes it," the man who, from humble origins and with meager education, converts, by will, intelligence, and sterling character, his liabilities into assets. Malcolm X was of that breed of Americans, autodidacts and home-made successes, that has included Benjamin Franklin, Abraham Lincoln, P. T. Barnum, Thomas A. Edison, Booker T. Washington, Mark Twain, Henry Ford, and the Wright brothers. Malcolm X would look back on his beginnings and, in innocent joy, marvel at the distance he had come.

But in Malcolm X the old Horatio Alger story is crossed, as has often been the case, with another typical American story, America has been prodigally fruitful of hot-gospellers and prophets—from Dr. Graham and his bread, Amelia Bloomer and her bloomers, Emerson and the Oversoul, and Brigham Young, on to F.D.R. and the current Graham, Billy. Furthermore, to round out his American story and ensure his fame, Malcolm X, like John Brown, Abraham Lincoln, Joseph Smith (the founder of Mormonism), and John Fitzgerald Kennedy, along with a host of lesser prophets, crowned his mission with martyrdom. Malcolm X fulfills, it would seem, all the requirements—success against odds, the role of prophet, and martyrdom—for inclusion in the American pantheon. . . .

[***The Autobiography of Malcolm X***] is "told" to Alex Haley, a Negro, a retired twenty-year man of the Coast Guard turned journalist. From 1963 up to the assassination, Haley saw Malcolm for almost daily sessions when Malcolm was in New York, and sometimes accompanied him on his trips. Haley's account of this period, of how he slowly gained Malcolm's confidence and how Malcolm himself discovered the need to tell his story, is extremely interesting and, though presented as an Epilogue, is an integral part of the book; but the main narrative has the advantage of Malcolm's tone, his characteristic movement of mind, and his wit, for Haley has succeeded admirably in capturing these qualities, as can be checked by the recollection of Malcolm's TV appearances and conversation and by his taped speeches (***Malcolm X Speaks: Selected Speeches and Statements***).

The ***Autobiography*** and the speeches are an extraordinary record of an extraordinary man. They are, among other things, a record that may show a white man (or some Negroes, for Malcolm would say that many Negroes do not know the nature of their own experience) what it means to be a Negro in America, in this century, or at least what it so dramatically meant to one man of unusual intelligence and powerful personality. Being a Negro meant being "black"—even if black was no more than a metaphor for Malcolm, who was himself "marigny," a dull yellowish skin, pale enough to freckle, pale eyes, hair reddish-coppery. He had been "Detroit Red" in his hustling days.

To be black, metaphorically or literally, meant, according to Malcolm, to wear a badge of shame which was so mystically and deeply accepted that all the practical injustices the white world might visit upon the black would seem only a kind of inverted justice, necessary in the very nature of things, the working out of a curse. The black man had no history, no country, no identity; he was alienated in time and place; he lived in "self-hate," and being unable to accept "self," he therefore was willing to accept, supine or with random violence, his fate. This was the diagnosis of his own plight, as Malcolm learned it from the "Nation of Islam."

As for the cure, what he found was the doctrine of the Black Muslims. This involved a history of creation and a metaphysic which made the black man central and dominant, and a secular history of kingly achievement in Africa. The divine and secular histories provided a justification for the acceptance of the black "self." In addition, the doctrine provided an understanding of the iniquity of the white man which would account for the black man's present lot and would, at the same time, mobilize an unquenchable hate against him. Total withdrawal from the white man and all his works was the path to virtue, until the day of Armageddon when he would be destroyed. Meanwhile, until the Chosen People had been relieved of the white man's presence, the black man was presented with a practical program of life: thrift, education, cleanliness, diet (no pork, for example, pork being a "nigger" food), abstemiousness (no alcohol or tobacco), manners and courtesy, puritanical morality and reverence for the home and Muslim womanhood—a general program of "wake up, clean up, and stand up." In fact, on the practical side, in spite of the hatred of the white man and contempt for his culture, the Black Muslim doctrine smuggled into the life of the Negro slum the very virtues which had made white middle-class America what it was—i.e., successful.

After Malcolm's death Dr. Kenneth B. Clark, the Negro psychologist and the author of an important book called *Dark Ghetto,* said that he had been "cut down at the point when he seemed on the verge of achieving the position of respectability he sought." In the midst of the gospel of violence and the repudiation of the white world, even in the Black Muslim phase, there appears now and then the note of yearning. In the ***Autobiography*** we find, for instance, this passage: "I was the invited speaker at the Harvard Law School Forum. I happened to glance through a window. Abruptly, I realized that I was looking in the direction of the apartment house that was my old burglary group's hideout. . . . And there I stood, the invited speaker, at Harvard."

Malcolm, still in prison, gave up pork and tobacco, and undertook a program of reading in the good library there available. He read in Plato, Aristotle, Schopenhauer, Kant, Nietzsche, and the "Oriental philosophers." He read and reread the Bible, and could match quotations with a Harvard Seminary student who conducted a class for prisoners. He studied *The Loom of Language,* by Frederick Bodmer, and memorized Grimm's *Law.* He read Durant's *Story of Civilization,* H. G. Wells' *Outline of History,* Herodotus, Fannie Kimball, *Uncle Tom's Cabin,* Gandhi, Gregor Mendel, pamphlets of the "Abolitionist Anti-Slavery Society of New England," and J. A. Rogers' *Sex and Race.* He was trying to find the black man's place—and his own—in history, trying, in other words, to document the doctrine of the Black Muslims. He wrote regularly to Muhammad to tell what he had found. While he was still in prison Malcolm also had a vision. He had written an appeal to Muhammad to reinstate his brother Reginald, suspended as a Muslim for "improper relations" with the secretary of the New York Temple. That night he spent in desperate prayer. The next night he woke up and saw a man sitting, there in the cell, in a chair by him. "He had on a dark suit, I remember. I could see him as plainly as I see anyone I look at. He wasn't black, and he wasn't white. He was light-brown-skinned, an Asiatic cast of countenance, and he had oily black hair. . . . I had no idea whatsoever who he was. He just sat there. Then suddenly as he had come, he was gone." The color of the man in the vision is an interesting fact. So is his immobility and silence.

When Malcolm Little came out of prison, he was Malcolm X, the "X," according to the practice of the Black Muslims, standing for the true name lost long ago in Africa to take the place of the false white name that had been forced on him. He had been reborn, and he now entered upon his mission. Soon he was an accredited minister of Muhammad, the official defender of the faith and the intellectual spokesman of the movement. His success, and especially the fact that he was invited to colleges, where Muhammad would never be invited, led to jealousy and, as Malcolm reports, contributed to his "silencing" as soon as a good justification appeared.

Malcolm X was not the only man drawn from the lower depths to be reborn in the Nation of Islam. It is generally admitted that the record of rehabilitation by the Black Muslims of dope-addicts, alcoholics, prostitutes, and criminals makes any other method seem a waste of time. They have, it would seem, found the nerve center that, once touched, can radically change both the values and the way of life for a number of Negroes in America; and it is important here to use the phrase "Negroes in America" with special emphasis, and no other location, for those redeemed by the Black Muslims are those who have been only in, but not of, America, those without country, history, or identity. The Black Muslims have found, then, a principle that, if not of universal validity (or, in one perspective, isn't it? for white as well as for black?), at least involves a truth of considerable psychological importance. That truth is, indeed, shrouded in metaphysical mumbo-jumbo, political and economic absurdity, and some murderous delusions, but even these elements have a noteworthy symbolic relation to the central truth. It is reported that Martin Luther King, after seeing Malcolm X on TV, remarked: "When he starts talking about all that's been done to us, I get a twinge of hate, of identification with him. But hate is not the only effect." A man as intelligent, as cultivated, and as experienced as James Farmer has testified in his recent book *Freedom When?* that the Black Muslims and Malcolm X have had a very important impact on his own thinking and in helping to change his basic views of the Negro Revolution, especially on the question of "blackness" and on the nature of integration and the Negro's role in an open society.

If this is the case, then the story of Malcolm X assumes an added dimension. It shows the reader the world in which that truth can operate; that is, it shows the kind of alienation to which this truth is applicable. It shows, also, the human quality of the operation, a man in the process of trying to understand his plight, and to find salvation, by that truth. But there is another aspect to the ***Autobiography.*** Malcolm X was a man in motion, he was a seeker, and that motion led, in the end, away from orthodox Black Muslim doctrine. The doctrine had been, he said, a straitjacket. He was now in the process of stripping away, perhaps unconsciously, the mumbo-jumbo, the absurdities, and the murderous delusions. He was trying, as it were, to locate the truth that had saved him, and divest it of the irrelevancies. In the end, he might have come to regard the religion that, after his break with the Black Muslims, he had found in Mecca as an irrelevancy, too. Certainly, just before his death he could say that his "philosophy" was still changing. Perhaps what Mecca gave him, for the time being at least, was the respectability, the authority, of the established thing. But he might have finally found that authority in himself, for he could speak as a man whose very existence was witness to what he said. Something of that purely personal authority comes through in these books.

Malcolm X had, in his last phase, lost the mystique of blackness so important to the Black Muslims; he had seen the blue-eyed and fair-haired pilgrims in Mecca. He was no longer a separatist in the absolute sense of the Black Muslims. He had become enough of an integrationist to say: "I believe in recognizing every human being as a human being . . . and when you are dealing with humanity as a family, there's no question of integration or intermarriage. It's just one human being marrying another human being or one human being living around with another human being." And just before his death he had made a down-payment on a house, in Long Island, in a largely Jewish neighborhood. He no longer saw the white man as the "white devil"—metaphysically evil; and he was ready, grudgingly, not optimistically, and with a note of threat, to grant that there was in America a chance, a last chance, for a "bloodless revolution." He was ready to work with other Negro organizations, even those which he had most derided, to try to find common ground and solutions at a practical level.

Certain ideas were, however, carried over from the Black Muslim days. The question of "identity" remained, and the question of race pride and personal self-respect divested of chauvinism, and with this the notion of "wake up, clean up, and stand up," the notion of self-reliance, self-improvement, self-discipline. If he could say such things, which smacked of the discredited philosophy of Booker T. Washington, and which few other Civil Rights leaders would dare to utter, it was because he did so in the context of his intransigence vis-a-vis the white world and his radical indictment of white society. Even in the last phase, even if he believed in "recognizing every human being as a human being," and no longer took the white man to be metaphysically evil, his indictment of white society was still radical; unless that society could really be regenerated, the chance for the "bloodless revolution" was gone.

This radical indictment leads to what may be the greatest significance of Malcolm X, his symbolic role. He was the black man who looked the white man in the eye and forgave nothing. If the white man had turned away, in shame or indifference, from the awful "forgiveness" of a Martin Luther King, he still had to face the unforgivingness, with its shattering effect on his accustomed view of himself and with the terrifying discovery, as Malcolm's rage brought his own rage forth, of the ultimate of which he himself would, under pressure, be capable. To put it another way, Malcolm X let the white man see what, from a certain perspective, he, his history, and his culture looked like. It was possible to say that that perspective was not the only one, that it did not give the whole truth about the white man, his history, and his culture, but it was not possible to say that the perspective did not carry a truth, a truth that was not less, but more, true for being seen from the angle of "Small's Paradise" in Harlem or of the bedroom to which "Detroit Red," the "steerer," brought the "Ivy League fathers" to be ministered to by the big black girl, whose body had been greased to make it look "shinier and blacker" and whose Amazonian hand held a small plaited whip. . . .

What would have been Malcolm's role had he lived? Perhaps, as some Negro leaders said shortly before his death, he had no real organization, and did not have the talent to create one. Perhaps his being in motion was only, as some held, a result of confusion of mind, a groping that could not be trusted to bring results. Perhaps, as James Farmer had put it, Malcolm, for all his talk, was not an activist; he had managed all along to be out of harm's way whenever harm was brewing, and he was afraid of the time when he "would have to chirp or get off the perch."

But perhaps the new phase of the Negro Revolution, with the violence of the great city slums, might have given him his great chance. He might have, at last, found himself in action. He might have found himself committed to blind violence, but on the other hand he might have had the power to control and canalize action and do something to reduce the danger of the Revolution's degenerating into random revolt. For, in spite of all the gospel of intransigence, Malcolm had always had a governing idea of a constructive role for the Negro, some notion of a society. After all, he had personal force, as no one who ever spent as little as ten minutes with him would have doubted: charisma, to use the fashionable word, and that to a degree possessed by no other leader except Martin Luther King. And he had one great asset which Martin Luther King does not have: he was from the lower depths and possessed the authority of one who had both suffered and conquered the depths.

Whatever the future might have held for him had he lived, his actual role was an important one, and in one sense the importance lay in his being rather than his doing. He was a man of passion, depth, and scale—and his personal story is a moving one. There is the long struggle. There is the sense of desperation and tightening entrapment as, in the last days, Malcolm recognized the dilemma developing in his situation. The "so-called moderate" Civil Rights leaders, he said, dodged him as "too militant," and the "so-called militants" dodged him as "too moderate." Haley reports that he once exclaimed "They won't let me turn the corner! I'm caught in a trap!" For there is a trap in the story, a real and lethal one. There is the gang of Black Muslims covering his every move in the Statler Hilton at Los Angeles, the mysterious Negro men who tried to get his room number at the Hilton in New York City, and the sinister telephone call to his room in the hotel the morning of his death. There is the bombing of his house, and his despairing anger when the event was widely taken as a publicity stunt. There is his remark to Haley, as he asked to read the manuscript of his book for a last, unnecessary time: "I just want to read it one more time, because I don't expect to read it in finished form"—wanting, as it were, to get a last sense of the shape of his own life as he felt the trap closing. There is, as with a final accent of pathos, the letter by his six-year-old daughter Attilah (named for the Scourge of God), written just after his death: "Dear Daddy, I love you so. O dear, O dear, I wish you wasn't dead." But entrapment and pathos was not all. He had been bred to danger. When he stepped on the platform that Sunday afternoon, in the face of odds which he had more shrewdly estimated than anybody else, he had nerve, confidence, style. He made his last gesture.

As one reads the ***Autobiography,*** one feels that, whatever the historical importance of Malcolm Little, his story has permanence, that it has something of tragic intensity and meaning. One feels that it is an American story bound to be remembered, to lurk in the background of popular consciousness, to reappear some day in a novel, on the stage, or on the screen. No—the right medium might be the ballad. Malcolm was a figure out of the anonymous depth of the folk, and even now, in a slum bedroom or in the shadowy corner of some bar, fingers may be tentatively picking the box, and lips fumbling to frame the words that will mean, long after our present problems are resolved and forgotten, the final fame, and the final significance. (pp. 161-71)

Robert Penn Warren, "Malcolm X: Mission and Meaning," in The Yale Review, *Vol. LVI, No. 2, December, 1966, pp. 161-71.*

Carol Ohmann (essay date Summer 1970)

[*Ohmann was an American educator and critic. In the following study, which helped to initiate critical efforts to place* The Autobiography of Malcolm X *within the American autobiographical tradition, she compares Malcolm's rhetorical strategy to that of Benjamin Franklin in* The Autobiography of Benjamin Franklin.]

There is nothing in Benjamin Franklin's *Autobiography* to match the moment when Malcolm X for the first time straightens his hair, or, as he tells it in his ***Autobiography,*** "lay[s] on his first conk," his scalp burning under a homemade mixture whose operative ingredient is Red Devil lye. Franklin went to Philadelphia and success by way merely of New York, Perth Amboy, Burlington and Cooper's Creek; Malcolm X's road to his achievements took him, far more perilously, from a detention home in Mason, Michigan, through the ghettoes of Roxbury, Massachusetts and of Harlem, where he hustled women, marijuana, numbers bets and whiskey, and through Charlestown Prison, to which he was eventually sentenced for burglary. ***The Autobiography of Malcolm X*** testifies to a side of the American experience that has been traditionally obscured; in his own seventh-grade textbook Malcolm X, born Malcolm Little, found that the portion devoted to the history of the Negro in America was "exactly one paragraph long." He was a few years later astonished to find among Boston's historic monuments a statue of a Negro, Crispus Attucks, the first man to fall in the Boston Massacre. He had not thought, for so his astonishment signified, that there were *any* such memorials.

The Autobiography of Malcolm X testifies to the black experience in America. More precisely, it testifies to the personal cost of the black experience in America. The first chapter records the death of Malcolm's father, the victim apparently of whites who resented his propagandizing for Marcus Garvey's back-to-Africa movement; in the "Epilogue," Alex Haley describes the assassination of Malcolm X, shot by three black gunmen on February 21, 1965 as he began to speak in a Harlem ballroom in favor of his Organization of Afro-American Unity. The continuity of experience from first to last in the ***Autobiography*** is inescapable. The lives of father and son alike were fundamentally shaped to their violent ends by the fact that they were born black in America and tried to combat the inferiority to which their color condemned them.

And yet, at the same time that the ***Autobiography*** unforgettably tells those of us who do not know it about the black experience, and helps to explain it to those who know it and have yet to understand it—at the same time, the ***Autobiography*** is in many ways a traditionally American work. The evidence of the book itself insists on both its differences from and its similarities to the general American experience. At a time when one hears so often simply that Black is Different (I have just put down a college newspaper in which a black faculty member assures me that as a white I cannot possibly appreciate the aesthetic quality of a certain black drama), it seems to me useful to note some of the ways in which Malcolm X's story, as he told it over a period of two years to Alex Haley, reflects American culture. Despite the fact that Benjamin Franklin could not have bought a bottle of Red Devil lye, and would have had no need or wish to, his *Autobiography* and ***The Autobiography of Malcolm X*** resemble each other in the conceptions of the self they convey, in the categories by which they apprehend men and events, in the standards by which they judge them, and in the ways, looking backward as autobiographers do, they pattern or structure the raw materials of their own lives. Roughly, what Benjamin Franklin wanted and got for himself and his fellow citizens, Malcolm X also wanted for himself and his people—until in the last year of his life he changed his mind. To put this in a practical academic way, ***The Autobiography of Malcolm X*** belongs not only in an Afro-American course but in a course in American literature or American autobiography. Both Benjamin Franklin and Malcolm X testify to certain strengths and certain weaknesses in our national ethos, strengths and weaknesses that have characterized us very nearly from, if not from, the beginning.

Franklin and Malcolm X both pause at early points in their autobiographies to allow us to see them as very young men. Franklin as he arrives at the age of 17 in Philadelphia; Malcolm X as he arrives at 15 in the ghetto of Roxbury, Massachusetts. In the well-known passage from Franklin:

> I was in my Working Dress, my best Cloaths being to come round by Sea. I was dirty from my Journey: my pockets were stuff'd out with Shirts and Stockings. . . . [At a baker's I bought for three pennies] three great Puffy Rolls. I was surpriz'd at the Quantity, but took it, and having no room in my Pockets, walk'd off, with a Roll under each Arm, and eating the other. Thus I went up Market Street as far as fourth Street, passing by the Door of Mr. Read, my future Wife's Father, when she standing at the Door saw me, and thought I made as I certainly did a most awkward ridiculous Appearance.

And the parallel description of Malcolm X reads:

> I looked like Li'l Abner. Mason, Michigan was written all over me. My kinky, reddish hair was cut hick style, and I didn't even use grease in it. My green suit's coat sleeves stopped above my wrists, the pants legs showed three inches of socks. Just a shade lighter green than the suit was my narrow-collared, three-quarter length Lansing department store topcoat.

As Malcolm X's friend Shorty put it later, "Cat's legs was so long and his pants so short his knees showed—an' his head looked like a briar patch!"

In each case, the descriptions suggest structural principles that order the respective autobiographies. Both books tell, despite the episodic unfolding to which their genre and the particularly versatile achievements of their respective authors dispose them, stories of men who move from inexperience to sophistication, from ignorance to enlightenment, from obscurity to worldly prominence. Both books offer spectacular contrasts between then and now, between Benjamin with a roll under each arm and Mr. Franklin beginning to write the story of his life at Twyford, near Winchester, the country house of the Bishop of St. Asaph; between Malcolm Little showing three inches of socks and Malcolm X dictating his autobiography late in the evenings after days of public speaking and debate, media appearances and appointments with African diplomats. The rising curve to success which governs the two books suggests already that Franklin and Malcolm X are both interested in external rather than subjective events; they are both concerned with objectively measurable achievements and how they may be obtained. This disposition shows itself habitually, not only when they speak of their own accomplishments but in the remarks they make more casually or more briefly of other persons who figure in their autobiographies.

In the first part of his *Autobiography* for example, Franklin describes a religious recluse whom he happened to meet because they lodged in the same building in London. The recluse, a Roman Catholic, was natively English and had gone as a young woman to join a convent on the Continent. The foreign establishment she found uncongenial; so she returned to England living independently in a garret a life of conventual rigor, retaining of her inherited fortune only £12 a year for herself. When Franklin visited her, he was as usual observant. He noticed her manner of meeting him ("chearful and polite") and her possessions: a mattress, a table, a stool, a book and a crucifix, a picture of St. Veronica. The vignette concludes with the remark, "She look'd pale, but was never sick, and I give it as another Instance on how small an Income Life and Health may be supported." Franklin was not—the observation is, of course, an old one—very much interested in the inner life. His curiosity in this instance stops remarkably short of speculating, even of asking: what did she think? what did she feel? When Franklin does make psychological observations, he more often than not makes them because they have been useful to him and may be so to his readers. He remarks, for example, on the utility of allowing for other men's pride. He has learned to curb his own delight in overriding his antagonists in argument; where he used to contradict or assert positively, he now suggests or diffidently wonders if it might not be the case that Philadelphia needs its streets paved, swept and illuminated, a system of police patrol and another of fire protection, a library, an academy, a hospital.

Neither is Malcolm X very much inclined to describe the inner life, to explore it or to analyze it, whether his own or anyone else's. Early in his ***Autobiography,*** he makes a revealing remark about the mental illness for which his mother was confined to a Michigan state institution for over twenty-five years: "It was so much worse than if it had been a physical sickness, for which a cause might be known, medicine given, a cure effected." The statement goes so far as to display a distrust of the inner life, even an antipathy to it, because it is intangible and mysterious; because it does not yield up its secrets the way the physical universe does, and hence frustrates the effort to control it. Revealingly, also, the ***Autobiography*** states (the italics are mine): "You can't name a thing the white man can't *make.* You can hardly name a scientific problem he can't *solve.*" Or again, when Malcolm X deplores the waste of black brains and black talent in America, he expresses the deprivations of his people in these terms: "All of us . . . might have probed space, or cured cancer, or built industries." The black man who is found behind bars in any one of our prisons might have been "a lawyer, a doctor, a scientist."

Franklin would have sympathized with the values held implicit in all these lines. Both Franklin and Malcolm X admire men who make conquest of the external or material world; who learn its principles and use them to practical ends, who *solve* problems and *make* things. Each accordingly cherishes an idea of the self wherein the faculties that permit making and solving are primarily valued. The self is, as it were, separate or discrete; it is the rational subject that perceives the rest of the world as object, to be understood and then manipulated or managed. And the self receives its final definition not in terms that denote the qualitative nature of its inner life but in terms that record its measurable accomplishments, as printer, legislator, statesman, as lawyer, doctor, scientist.

Franklin left his home and Malcolm X his detention home for precisely the same reason: they both found their opportunities for achievement limited. Franklin records how he suffered under the tyranny of his brother James, to whom he was bound as printer's apprentice and who did not scruple to thrash him on occasion. He mentions also that he had gained in Boston a reputation likely to be practically inconvenient, a reputation as an impertinent thinker, one who criticized the government of the colony and put hard questions to the conventionally devout. For Malcolm X, the realization that determined his departure came when his English teacher asked him what he planned to do after school. He hadn't really thought about it, at least not consciously, but he answered that he would like to be a lawyer. The teacher urged him to be realistic; even though he was one of the best students in his class, law was not for a Negro a sensible goal. The teacher suggested that he set his mind on carpentry instead, since he was good with his hands in shop. The advice, delivered quite matter-of-factly, was shockingly disheartening, and yet it was, Malcolm had to acknowledge, realistic. Already, he had noticed that, in the Michigan towns he knew, the Negroes who were successful were really only "successful." They were domestic servants and janitors; at best, they were waiters at the country club and shoeshine boys at the state capitol.

In both autobiographies, the early self-portraits are followed by later ones; after leaving home and adventuring a while in worlds of larger opportunity, both Franklin and Malcolm X, one by boat and the other by train, went back to visit wearing, literally, the signs of the success they had won, except that in the case of Malcolm X it was still only "success," although he did not yet know it. Home again, they both acted in much the same manner. Handsomely dressed in a new suit, Franklin entered his brother's printing shop, carrying in his pockets a watch and nearly five pounds in silver. When one of his brother's journeymen asked him what kind of money they used in Philadelphia, he displayed his silver coins. Unasked, he then displayed his watch. Then he gave the journeymen a piece of eight to buy drinks with.

Malcolm X impressed old friends in Michigan with his straightened hair, his gray sharkskin zoot suit, his yellow knob-toed shoes, his slang, his extraordinarily agile lindy-hopping—all acquirements from the hipster world of the eastern ghettoes. His appearance, the ***Autobiography*** claims, caused at least one local traffic accident. And he did not have to be pressed to sign autographs after a dance in a Negro high school.

The disposition in both men is the same—to wear home the visible signs of their sophistication and their worldly advancement. But the two portraits viewed side by side, Franklin in his gentleman's tailored suit and Malcolm X in his sharkskin zoot bought off a rack in the Roxbury ghetto, reveal a difference owing to more than the lapse of two hundred years. The zoot betokened, really, a "success"; its owner still lived according to the dispensation he had left Michigan to escape. Green suit and topcoat and sharkskin zoot, he would realize years later, were equally shoddy and graceless, equally significant of his continued exclusion from the order of men who could really make anything and solve almost any problem.

Indeed, from the moment Malcolm X left Michigan until his conversion several years later to the faith of the Black Muslims, his life runs in ironic parallel to Franklin's, and his ***Autobiography*** relates disconcertingly to the early American classic, as the narratives, say, of Samuel Beckett's Watt or Molloy relate to those of the heroes of true romance, by a process of parodic inversion. Ambition, ability, a sharp eye for opportunity, and industry are all there and working, but circumstances invariably intrude between them and their wished-for effects. So the recorded quest for achievement spirals downward from defeat to defeat, and comes to rest for Malcolm X, not in a Beckettian ditch or asylum, but in Charlestown Prison.

When Malcolm X first came East, he recognized at once the obvious Roxbury equivalent of the sham success of the Michigan towns he knew. Not only was Roxbury divided into black and white; the black community itself was split into the Hill and the ghetto. The Negroes on the Hill, Malcolm X observed, might have been studied as models of dress and deportment. Properly attired, refined in manner, they were wont to say that they worked " 'in government,' 'in finance' or 'in law'." What they meant, in truth, was that they were janitors, messengers and shoeshine boys in buildings where *white men* worked in government, in finance and in law.In contrast to the Hill, Malcolm X chose the life of the black ghetto, which seemed to him authentic and self-aware. A friend named Freddie prepped him to shine shoes in the men's room at the Roseland State Ballroom, where the great jazz bands played, both Negro and white. Shining shoes was almost incidental to purveying reefers, liquor, contraceptives, accommodating phone numbers; everything in life is a hustle, Freddie said, and Malcolm X learned the ways of his new world attentively and avidly. As shoeshine boy, and later as soda jerk, bus boy, sandwich man on the railroad, waiter, pimp, messenger in the numbers racket and pot peddler, he worked hard. The ***Autobiography*** presents us more than once with assurance of his rational assessment of opportunity, his mastery of technical know-how, his economic prowess. Of his Harlem traffic in marijuana, he remarks: "I kept turning over my profit, increasing my supplies, and I sold reefers like a wild man. I scarcely slept. . . . Every day, I cleared at least fifty or sixty dollars." Later, forced back to Roxbury because he had enemies in Harlem, he formed a burglary ring because "burglary, properly executed, though it had its dangers, offered the maximum chances of success with the minimum risk."

In the long view backward which prison was to provide, Malcolm X came to see that, in Roxbury and Harlem both, all his successes as hipster and hustler had once again been only "success." With his conk and with his white woman, whom he escorted around Boston and New York as a status symbol, his life was just as false, just as self-deceived as that of any Hill janitor who claimed he worked in finance because he scrubbed the floors of an investment firm. Like the janitor, Malcolm X looked toward the white world for his own authentication. He valued himself, really, insofar as he could imitate or establish connection with the white world. In Harlem, according to his later assessment, he entered a world of black "servants and psychologists" who catered to white pleasures directly or indirectly. It was not simply that, while Malcolm X made $500 selling ersatz whiskey in brand bottles, his employer made $10,000. It was not simply that the big money from drugs, liquor, women and gambling did not linger in Harlem, at least not in black pockets and bank accounts. Worse, as pimp and numbers man and the like, Malcolm X came into an acutely ironic and humiliating relationship with the privileged men who made the things and solved the problems he had originally wanted to make and solve; he pandered to the vices they indulged in, in their off-hours.

When he speaks in his ***Autobiography*** of his prison conversion, Malcolm X is quite emphatic about this point: the faith of the Nation of Islam instantly gave coherence to the variegated experiences of his life. The Black Muslim faith gave him a cosmology to which he could consent, to which he had long since consented inwardly. To him, the white man *was* the devil who had bereft him of the paradise he was born to possess. And which, it is safe to add, he had been with no more than "success" struggling all his life to regain.

Paradise and the way back to it, moreover, appeared in the Muslim cosmology in a guise that was in part familiar,

Malcolm X during his teenage years as "Big Red."

that was, in fact, consonant with Malcolm's first ambitions. The movement before Malcolm X encountered it had already set its members on the road to moral perfectibility and worldly reward. Muslims were already intent on following a list of virtues analogous to Franklin's famous list: cleanliness, temperance, chastity, frugality, industry, resolution. Moral discipline was to bring its rewards in no distant heaven but here, now. As its final goal, the Nation of Islam envisioned the American black man elevated to power in a separatist state, whether back in Africa or in the United States. In the words of ***The Autobiography of Malcolm X,*** "the true knowledge of ourselves would lift up the black man from the bottom of the white man's society and place the black man where he had begun, at the top of civilization."

His conversion to the Nation of Islam, Malcolm X records in his ***Autobiography,*** transformed his life. Certainly, in many impressive ways the statement proves true. After his conversion, Malcolm submitted himself to a regime stricter even than prison required. He was already separated from women and alcohol; he now voluntarily gave up prison-made substitutes for the cocaine and marijuana on which he had been used to depend; he gave up cigarettes as well, and he followed Muslim dietary prescriptions. He directed, moreover, all his energies toward a strenuous program of self-education that would fit him to further the Nation of Islam.

Even so, it can be argued that the change Malcolm X underwent at this time did not entail a complete or radical revision of his conception of himself or of his values, although it did lead him to make a thorough reassessment of the world he lived in. He did realize that he had lived a parody of success, that he had played the roles of servant and pandering psychologist; he saw how meager his opportunities as a black man had been and must be as long as the condition of his people in America remained what it was. But he confirmed at the same time his belief in his original goals (to be a lawyer or the equivalent; to make things and solve problems). For the time being, in what may be called the first of his conversions, for there was to be a second later, Malcolm X took with him into his new faith essentially the same idea of self and essentially the same modes of evaluating experience with which he had left Mason, Michigan. The kind of success which he had originally wanted for himself he now wanted for the larger entity with which he identified himself and in which he now submerged his personal ambition, the black race in America.

The essential continuity between his old self and his new one, between his values before and after his conversion to the Nation of Islam, appears in the account he gives of his self-education in prison. His self-education had its first impetus, just before his conversion, from a convict named Bimbi, whose knowledge and whose skill with words represented power. Bimbi commanded respect by virtue of what he said, so that Malcolm X felt "envy of his stock of knowledge." In his days in Roxbury and Harlem, Malcolm X had often had to acquire a "stake" in order to venture on a new hustle. In prison, he viewed a stock of knowledge as much the same as a stake, a sort of capital that could be laid out to advantage, yielding a return in prestige and power. He tried at first to emulate Bimbi by reading books. He found, though, that in every sentence he read he met one or more words that he didn't know; so he took away even from the books he finished very little in the way of understanding. Then deliberately, painstakingly, he proceeded according to the system of which he has left this description:

> I saw that the best thing I could do was get hold of a dictionary—to study, to learn some words. I was lucky enough to reason also that I should try to improve my penmanship. It was sad. I couldn't even write in a straight line. It was both ideas together that moved me to request a dictionary along with some tablets and pencils from the Norfolk Prison Colony School.
>
> I spent two days just riffling uncertainly through the dictionary's pages. I'd never realized so many words existed! I didn't know *which* words I needed to learn. Finally, just to start some kind of action, I began copying.
>
> In my slow, painstaking, ragged handwriting, I copied into my tablet everything printed on that first page, down to the punctuation marks.
>
> I believe it took me a day. Then, aloud, I read back, to myself, everything I'd written on the tablet. Over and over, aloud, to myself, I read my own handwriting.
>
> I woke up the next morning, thinking about those words—immensely proud to realize that not only had I written so much at one time, but I'd written words that I never knew were in the world. Moreover, with a little effort, I also could remember what many of these words meant. I reviewed the words whose meanings I didn't remember. . . .
>
> I was so fascinated that I went on—I copied the dictionary's next page. And the same experience came when I studied that. With every succeeding page, I also learned of people and places and events from history. Actually the dictionary is like a miniature encyclopedia. Finally the dictionary's A section had filled a whole tablet—and I went on into the B's. That was the way I started copying what eventually became the entire dictionary.

Significantly, the whole account Malcolm X gives of his conversion to the Nation of Islam dwells very little on the subjective nature of the experience. It concentrates, as in the passage above, on measurable achievements, on feats of learning, performed early and late, at the expense of sleep and in neglect of meals, day by day, month by month, year by year; his account of his conversion is a tally of words learned, letters penned in an increasingly competent hand, grammar rules recaptured, correspondence courses completed, debates entered and won, and books read; books of history, economics, sociology, anthropology, anything that might shed light on the history of the black man in America and illumine his way to independent power. Like Franklin's before him, Malcolm's drive to learn was intense, consuming and effective; and it was directed to decidedly practical ends. It fit him to contend intellectually with men who had enjoyed every formal educational advantage and to hold his own, as Franklin had, dining with kings, or with the 20th century equivalent of kings.

Out of prison, Malcolm X revised one of Poor Richard's most famous maxims: "I felt that Allah would be more inclined to help those who helped themselves," he said in reference to a debate over Black Muslim methods of recruitment. As Elijah Muhammad's ablest assistant, he was ceaselessly energetic, inventive in regard to tactics, and persuasive. His thrust was toward the immediate acquisition of power, especially of economic power that would impress the outside world at the same time that it assured the Muslims of their strength and importance. His attitudes are revealed in the following remarks he makes about the years when he led the drive that increased Muslim membership from approximately 400 to 40,000: "Our mass rallies, from their very beginning, were astounding successes"; "as many as 150, 200 and even as many as 300 big, chartered buses rolled the highways to wherever Mr. Muhammad was going to speak." Elijah Muhammad himself traveled in his "personal jet plane." "Nearly all bills and far from all one-dollar bills, either, filled the waxed buckets" which were passed at the rallies. The Islamic Center, which was planned for construction in Chicago, would include "a beautiful mosque, school, library, and hospital, and a museum documenting the black man's glorious history." Even the last statement primarily quantifies the visible achievement the Center would represent rather than dwelling on any of the various purposes it might serve; the Center would include such is the emphasis of the sentence a mosque *and* a school *and* a library *and* a hospital *and* a museum.

As George Breitman convincingly argues in *The Last Year of Malcolm X,* whatever personal motives may have contributed to the rupture between Elijah Muhammad and Malcolm X, Malcolm's expulsion from the Nation of Islam in early 1964 was primarily caused by a fundamental disagreement in policy. Muhammad was inclined to await Allah's intervention in the course of human events, whereas Malcolm X was increasingly determined to anticipate Allah, whatever risks activism might entail. Malcolm X wanted, in fact, to establish connections between Islam and other black power groups; and, as the speeches he made in the last year of his life indicate, he had added to his initial interest in economic power an increasing concern with the potentialities of political power. In brief, he asked the black man to assume a competitive and combative stance along all the lines of effective power, economic, political, and in a local sense, military as well. He asked for black ownership of factories and stores; black candidates for civic, state and federal offices; black guns ready to answer wherever white guns fired first; violence as a response to violence, if white police went on using dogs, fire hoses, tear gas against civil rights demonstrators. He sought, finally, to enlarge the scene of confrontation by enlisting the emergent African nations in the struggle for black equality in America. During his second trip abroad, in 1964, he tried to persuade African diplomats to bring the case of the American Negro before the United Nations, as an egregious instance of the abrogation not of civil, but of human rights.

In his program for Black Nationalism, Malcolm X logically extended to the stage of public events the concept of the self he projected in much of his ***Autobiography*** (though not in all of it, as I shall be concerned to note in a moment). In the public program, the private self is still bent on conquest of the external or material world, save that it is joined now with other selves, whose interests are the same, in a common strategy of competition or combat. Black men confront the white establishment and attempt to get from it the equal opportunities the establishment has always denied them. Ideally, they will record their victories in terms of measurable accomplishments, in terms of technical and professional attainments, in terms of the acquisition of economic and political and armed power.

The program is not humanistic. Neither is the conception of the self that underlies it. Both impose severe limitations on the development of the individual sensibility and on the kinds of relationships the individual can sustain with other human beings. Even if the individual gains ground in the struggle for power, he remains locked in a calculating and militant stance, saving his advantage or pressing it further in a world composed, for him, merely of allies and opponents. Now, to turn back to Franklin at this point, such is the view of self and society that his *Autobiography* primarily transmits. It was reflective of our culture when he wrote it. Just how far, after its publication, it shaped succeeding generations of Americans remains problematic, but there is no doubt that it tripped off sympathetic responses through the 19th and into the 20th centuries.

It can be said, it is true, that in his *Autobiography* Franklin does not do justice to himself. And it is time to acknowledge that this essay has not even done justice to the *Autobiography.* For it has given so far no nod in the direction of personal qualities expressed in the *Autobiography* that lie beyond its celebration of opportunistic individualism or, in its later phases, of opportunistic citizenship or statesmanship. Consider, for example, the summation Franklin makes of his relationship with his wife: "She prov'd a good and faithful Helpmate, assisted me much by attending the Shop, we throve together, and have ever mutually endeavour'd to make each other happy." Franklin evaluates his wife as the biases generally prevalent in the *Autobiography* have led us to expect; although he does stress their mutuality, he evaluates his wife primarily in terms of her economic role: she is a *helpmate, useful* in tending his printer's shop; he and she have *prospered.* Then the last part of the sentence suddenly admits the possibility of another mode of evaluating a human relationship. Franklin and his wife have always tried to make each other happy. The syntax implies, not that happiness proceeds from success, but that it is an additional matter, something apart from the business of thriving.

Many other passages in the *Autobiography* might be called on to witness that Franklin had a capacious sensibility; that he was, say, loving and tolerant and humorous; that he could experience a simple delight in human nature for what it is. And yet it is the case that these genial traits exist apart from his programs. They do not figure on his list of thirteen moral virtues, and they have no direct bearing on the worldly success which he is in the *Autobiography* mainly concerned to describe. His genial traits simply appear from time to time (like the Cheshire cat, smiling) in a plain, unemphatic relationship of addition to temperance, silence, order, resolution, frugality, industry and the like. Not surprisingly, it was Franklin's programs rather than his sympathetic or ironic asides that posterity mainly apprehended reading the *Autobiography,* whether they admired it and placed it generation after generation on high school reading lists or whether they lodged complaints against it, like Melville, Hawthorne, Charles Francis Adams and, loudest of all, Lawrence.

Like Franklin's, Malcolm's ***Autobiography*** also shows personal qualities that are not allowed for in his public program. In the pages of ***The Autobiography of Malcolm X,*** in fact, two sets of values compete, and two conceptions of the self; side by side with the would-be lawyer, hustler and black nationalist, another self, or another dimension of the self, struggles toward expression.

The nature of the struggle may be glimpsed in the opening pages of the ***Autobiography,*** as Malcolm X speaks of some of his earliest memories. He retains, he says, two images of his father as a public man. In one image, his father is a Baptist preacher, leading a congregation given to express in singing, shouting and gesture their religious feelings. His father in the other image is an organizer for Garvey's Universal Negro Improvement Association. Taken by his father to U.N.I.A. meetings, the boy Malcolm noticed how different these assemblies were from the congregation in church, even though in part the same Negroes attended both. At the U.N.I.A. meetings, his father and the rest were "more intelligent and down to earth." The meetings ended with his father repeating the slogan, "Up, you mighty race, you can accomplish what you will!"

The passage implicitly acknowledges two modes of living, two ways of being, one expressive of the heart, the other, of the mind; and to the boy Malcolm, they exist in tension with each other. The emotional way of life is associated with a traditional folk image of the American Negro, letting himself loudly go in the worship of God, forgetting this world in rapturous anticipation of the next. The boy Malcolm in this passage prefers the alternate way of being; he prefers what intelligence can plan and what will can accomplish, and the cultivation of the mind rather than the heart he associates with a counter-image of the Negro, an image wherein the Negro in competition with, in emulation of, the white man would create his own state.

The same tension between the emotional and the rational dimensions of the self appears later in the ***Autobiography*** in an account of Small's Paradise, one of Harlem's most famous restaurants, where Malcolm X worked for a time as a waiter. Of Small's regular clientele, he remarks, "Many times since, I have thought about it, and what it really meant. In one sense, we were huddled there, banded together in seeking security and warmth and comfort from each other, and we didn't know it. All of us—who might have probed space, or cured cancer, or built industries were, instead, black victims of the white man's American social system." Here again, the emotional life, represented now by the camaraderie of Small's, exists apart from the life of reason and of will, which in this case is directly associated with the white power structure. The warm fellowship of Small's is good, but, the passage implies, it is second-best; it is enjoyed in compensation for exclusion from the power structure.

In a third revealing passage of the ***Autobiography,*** Malcolm X speaks of dancing to the jazz bands at Roseland. White dancers, as he saw them at Roseland, were inferior to black ones. They danced as though they were deliberately performing a series of lessons they had memorized, whereas the blacks created their steps, dancing spontaneously. Of his own dancing, Malcolm X remarks, "It was as though somebody had clicked on a light. My long-suppressed African instincts broke through, and loose." Once again, the mode of being that permits emotional expression, that allows the release of instinct or of impulse, is specifically identified as black and, beyond that, as African, and in this passage Malcolm X clearly prefers it to the deliberativeness which, for him, characterizes the white world.

The three passages do not appear in the ***Autobiography*** in a sequence that signifies an orderly shift in attitude from rejection to acceptance of black modes of life which provide in one way or another for the expression of the emotional, instinctive dimension of the self. Malcolm X knew Roseland before he saw Small's; so the account of the dancing appears between that of the two images of his father and of the warm, but compensatory, fellowship of Small's. Taken together, the passages do suggest divisions within the self of the autobiographer. Briefly, if he rivals the white power structure, he leaves behind the modes of feeling his heritage has made available to him; but if he gives play to the emotional dimension of himself, he *remains* behind, in his father's congregation, in Small's, on the Roseland dance floor, excluded from the prerogatives of power. The divisions within the self in ***The Autobiography of Malcolm X*** are sharper than any that appear in Franklin's record of his life. Indeed, at this point the two autobiographies begin to part company altogether. They are alike in predominantly projecting an idea of a rational self bent on understanding the world and manipulating it. Alike, also, in logically extending that idea of the self into various programs of public action. They are alike, finally, in giving evidence of personal qualities that lie outside the limited concept of the rational, publicly effective self, and that do not receive, or even defy, incorporation into the programs. However, while the divisions of the self are sharper in Malcolm X than in Franklin, the pressure toward the resolution of those divisions is correspondingly greater in ***The Autobiography of Malcolm X.*** Hearing the evangelist Whitefield, Franklin could not resist emptying his pocket into the collection plate, but during subsequent sermons he remained unmoved, calculating the geographical reach of the speaker's voice and precisely assessing the niceties of his delivery, "every Accent, every Emphasis, every Modulation of Voice." Malcolm X had, finally, no such detachment, no such prudence.

Malcolm X was *converted* to the Nation of Islam. Even though his account of his conversion concentrates mainly on his self-education, on his measurable achievements, the very notion of conversion pays tribute to the vitality of the inner life and of the emotional dimension of the self. The headings of certain chapters in the ***Autobiography*** form an elaboration upon the experience of conversion: Hustler, Trapped, Caught, Satan, Saved, Savior, Minister Malcolm X, Black Muslim, Icarus, Out, Mecca, El-Hajj Malik El-Shabazz. The chapter headings suggest a religious rather than a secular way of ordering the experiences of a lifetime. While ***The Autobiography of Malcolm X*** is in many striking ways analogous to Franklin's *Autobiography,* our prototypical American story of secular success, it may also be compared to our, still earlier, Puritan examinations into the nature of the inner life, examinations which include, indeed stress, the life of the heart. Hustler, Trapped, Caught, Satan, Saved, Savior, Minister Malcolm X. The paradigmatic curve suggested here is that of the sinner repentant, touched by grace, submissive to God, and saved, like Thomas Shepard, like cotton Mather, like Jonathan Edwards and like John Bunyan before them, and Saint Augustine before him.

The religious paradigm and the secular one both inform the account Malcolm X gives of his conversion to the Nation of Islam, and at moments they come into open collision. Thus, of the time when he formed his burglary ring, the secular Malcolm X says in self-congratulation: "I wasn't rushing off half-cocked. I had learned from some of the pros, and from my own experience, how important it was to be careful and plan." In the religious ordering of his experience he gives another view of the same period of his life. It is the time when he nears the nadir of his spiritual state; it is the time approaching his conversion, when he is most sinful, increasingly addicted to drugs, dependent on a woman for money, idle, profane, blasphemous. It is the dark night of the soul, before God tenders his grace.

Still, the list of suggestive chapter headings continues beyond Malcolm X's association with the Nation of Islam: Icarus, Out, Mecca, El Hajj Malik El-Shabazz. At first, it is true, the language here simply fails. The ***Autobiography*** has already exhausted the conventional terms of religious reference to the experience of conversion; so it proffers, inappropriately, Icarus and, blandly, Out. But the list intends to signal a second conversion and it ends firmly denoting the completion of a pilgrimage and the assumption of a new identity.

In many ways, Malcolm X's responses to his first trip abroad, when he made the pilgrimage to Mecca and visited a number of African nations, are disappointing, if understandable. Abroad, instead of facing again the hostility or suspicion he knew at home both before and after his celebrity, he was met with friendship, and he is mainly concerned to render his wonder, his delight and his gratitude for his welcome. He tends, moreover, to reckon up the courtesies extended by his Arabian and African hosts in measurable terms; a private car, a chauffeur, a guide, a hotel suite, an excellent dinner, a reception at a club and the like. He plainly enjoys his prestige and its perquisites and his secular self accompanies him right to the Holy City itself. On his pilgrimage to Mecca, he comments:

> It was the largest Hajj in history, I was later told. Kasem Gulek, of the Turkish Parliament, beaming with pride, informed me that from Turkey alone over six hundred buses—over fifty thousand Muslims—had made the pilgrimage. I told him that I dreamed to see the day when shiploads and planeloads of American Muslims would come to Mecca for the Hajj. . . . I saw that Islam's conversions around the world could double and triple if the colorfulness and the true spiritualness of the Hajj pilgrimage were properly advertised and communicated to the outside world. I saw that the Arabs are poor at understanding the psychology of non-Arabs and the importance of public relations. The Arabs said *"insha Allah"* ("God willing")—then they waited for converts. Even by this means, Islam was on the march, but I knew that with improved public relations methods the number of new converts turning to Allah could be turned into millions.

This passage is a choice one, epitomizing as it does so many of Malcolm's responses to his pilgrimage; both Edward Margolies and I. F. Stone have quoted from it, the one to illustrate what he calls the "booster quality" of Malcolm X [*Native Sons: A Critical Study of Twentieth-Century Negro American Authors,* 1968], and the other, to remark: "He had become a Hajj but remained in some ways a Babbitt, the salesman, archtype of our American society. A creed was something to *sell.* Allah, the Merciful, needed better merchandising" [I. F. Stone, *New York Review of Books,* 11 November 1965].

And yet, Malcolm X was also reacting to his journey in less material and less opportunistic ways. Beside the sounding brass of his boosterism, of his Babbitry, other responses bespeak a growing sense of connection with the entire human community, black and white. Certainly, he was disposed to feel this by the cordial reception he received in Cairo, in Jedda, in Mecca. Arabs who were white men were being kind to *him.* His fellow Muslims, moreover, were of all colors, traveling peacefully together to Mecca, each one clad as he himself was in two white towels and a pair of sandals. Malcolm X was experiencing, he had been experiencing ever since he left Kennedy International Airport, a feeling of liberation from the American racial situation. Although he never forgot that situation and never missed a chance to lecture on it, he was, within, unlocked from his habitual stance of competition and combat.

"My whole life," he remarks toward the end of the ***Autobiography,*** "had been a chronology of—*changes.*" The inward change he began to undergo when he first left America completed itself one night when he lay on the ground at Muzdalifa among other pilgrims, who were sleeping. The situation as it is described in the ***Autobiography*** is unusual in many ways. Malcolm X was, of course, far from home, dressed in pilgrim simplicity, on holy ground. More than that, he was at rest, whereas the ***Autobiography*** as a whole presents a man in hurried, even frenzied motion ("I sold reefers like a wild man . . ."; " . . . I would guess I wrote a million words"). This moment of rest he associated with others, with lying on his back on a certain hill outside Lansing when he was a boy of only eight or nine, daydreaming; with lying on his prison bunk seeing in his mind's eye himself addressing "large crowds." The phases of his life recurred in memory; they fit together now in unity, in harmony, and he experienced a new mode of being, entire and fulfilled. He had, indeed, reached the end of a pilgrimage. "In my thirty-nine years on this earth," he would remark later in summary of his feelings, "the Holy City of Mecca had been the first time I had ever stood before the Creator of All and felt like a complete human being."

Coincident with his new sense of himself, was a new sense of his fellow pilgrims:

> . . . the Muslim world's customs no longer seemed strange to me. My hands now readily plucked up food from a common dish shared with brother Muslims; I was drinking without hesitation from the same glass as others; I was washing from the same little pitcher of water; and sleeping with eight or ten others on a mat in the open. I remember one night at Muzdalifa [the same night when he passed his life in review] with nothing but the sky overhead I lay awake amid sleeping Muslim brothers and I learned that pilgrims from every land—every color, and class, and rank; high officials and the beggar alike—all snored in the same language.

The pilgrims are described in a way that is unusual in the ***Autobiography.*** They are, so to speak, physically there; Malcolm X is directly aware of their substantial presence, and of his own likeness to them. The pilgrims are neither black nor white, allies nor enemies. They are liberated—the perceiver has been able to liberate them—from such categories. They have lost their race, their wealth, their status in the common possession of their palpable, homely and vulnerable humanity; they eat, drink, sleep, snore. "I've had enough of someone else's propaganda," Malcolm X wrote home. "I'm for truth, no matter who tells it. I'm for justice, no matter who it is for or against. I'm a human being first and foremost, and as such I'm for whoever and whatever benefits humanity *as a whole.*"

Recording the experiences of Muzdalifa and Mecca, ***The Autobiography of Malcolm X*** does separate itself from Franklin's *Autobiography;* here, the late account finds no equivalent, whether straight or ironic, in the earlier one. At Muzdalifa and Mecca, an impulse sent from heart to mind, from private self to public, effected a personal integration. The power to feel intensely, the power to feel connection with other human beings, the power to express that feeling, all were freed from the limits previously set on them by black/white divisions and hostilities. The emotional dimension of the self joined the rational dimension and gave it cause to reconceive the nature of the individual and of his relationship to the world. In the reconception, every man is subject rather than object, to be cherished rather than managed or manipulated, and true brotherhood excludes no one.

It is worth turning back to remark that the point of departure for this second stage of Malcolm X's response to his reassessment of his world, for what this essay has called his second conversion, was a stance of competition or opportunism essentially like that revealed in Franklin's *Autobiography.* Fundamentally similar limitations of sensibility appear in both autobiographies; they are limitations that confine the development of the self, restrict the possibilities of human relationships and, extended into programs, institutionalize such confinement and such restrictions. The ethos in the work from the earliest days of the republic is re-created, until the days and nights at Muzdalifa and Mecca, in the account of a life lived in our contemporary towns and ghettoes. The fact argues for considerable cultural continuity, across time and across the black/white line. It offers a particular instance, moreover, of a kind of relationship that not uncommonly obtains between subject and object, between the privileged and the underprivileged, between, for the terms are appropriate in speaking of the black experience in America, the oppressor and the oppressed. That is to say, in a most personal way the oppressed may model himself in the very image of his oppressor. What his oppressor is, he aspires to be ("I kept turning over my profit, increasing my supplies. . . . "; "burglary . . . offered the maximum chances of success with the minimum risk . . . "); so he may unwittingly perpetuate the ethos he opposes, though he would himself no longer suffer the role of object. The similarity between the autobiographies of Franklin and Malcolm X points finally, then, to common areas of experience and suggests that, black and white, we share a common problem: to render human or humane the ideas by which we have traditionally shaped ourselves and our programs or institutions.

Experiencing his own personal integration at Muzdalifa and Mecca and transcending there, as he so admirably did, the ambition merely to imitate or rival the white power structure, Malcolm X had yet to translate his, now, deeply humanistic conviction of universal brotherhood into practical action. Such translation must be difficult always. Malcolm X had, in the event, little time even to attempt it. After his pilgrimage and his subsequent journey to Africa, he formed his Organization of Afro-American Unity, in June 1964. He visited Africa again, from July to November of the same year. He was shot on February 21, 1965 at the age of 39, before he had formulated a program for his Organization. It may well be, as George Breitman has argued, that in the last year of his life he was disposed to embrace, or actually did embrace, a socialist solution of America's problems of racial and class discrimination. A number of statements he made in the last year of his life offer support for that conclusion. But there is no doubt whatever that, socialist or not, after his first trip abroad, he changed in his attitudes toward the ultimate objectives of Black Nationalism. He still preached the need for black power, just as sharply and uncompromisingly as he had before. Now, however, he saw this combative stance as provisional. It would be necessary as long as the black race in America felt inferior, lacked incentive and purpose, remained disadvantaged. Beyond the stage of combat, though, he envisioned another; he wanted his Organization of Afro-American Unity to be "an all-black organization whose ultimate objective was to help create a society in which there could exist honest white-black brotherhood." In his last speeches, also, he alludes a number of times to men who possess "sincerity"; from the context of these allusions, it seems clear that by "sincere" men he means those of whatever race who have experienced, who have felt, the conviction of universal brotherhood that came to him on his pilgrimage.

It may well be that many readers of ***The Autobiography of Malcolm X*** will continue to focus, like Ossie Davis, like Eldridge Cleaver, on the dominant image it projects; that of militant black manhood. But the final chapters show a later portrait for readers who approach it in the frame of mind Petrarch imagined when he set down on the first page of his autobiography the words, "Perchance you will want to know what manner of man I was. . . . "(pp. 129-49)

Carol Ohmann, " 'The Autobiography of Malcolm X': A Revolutionary Use of the Franklin Tradition," in American Quarterly, *Vol. XXII, No. 2, Summer, 1970, pp. 129-49.*

Warner Berthoff (essay date Winter 1971)

[*In the following excerpt, Berthoff declares* The Autobiography of Malcolm X *"a contemporary classic."*]

No one can read very much of Malcolm's writing, more precisely listen to the voice transcribed in ***The Autobiogra-***

phy of Malcolm X (dictated to the journalist Alex Haley) or the printed versions of his public speeches, without forming the sense of an extraordinary human being: fiercely intelligent, shrewdly and humanely responsive to the life around him despite every reason in the world to have gone blind with suspicion and hate, a rarely gifted leader and inspirer of other men. The form of autobiographical narration adds something further; he comes through to us as the forceful agent of a life-history that was heroic in the event and has the shape of the heroic in the telling, a protagonist who (in Francis R. Hart's fine description) has himself created and now recreates "human value and vitality in each new world or underworld he has entered" [*New Literary History,* Spring 1970].

The power of Malcolm's book is that it speaks directly out of the totality of that life-history *and* the ingratiating openness of his own mind and recollection to it. It seems to me a book that . . . does not require any softening or suspension of critical judgment. In the first place it is written, or spoken, in a quick, pungent, concrete style, again the plain style of popular idiom, improved and made efficient by the same sort of natural sharpness and concentration of attention that gives life and color to the best of Mark Twain's recollective writing, or Franklin's, or Bunyan's. In the run of the narrative the liveliness of observation and recollection, the "histrionic exuberance" (Professor Hart again), are continuously persuasive—and incidentally confirm as elements of a true style Alex Haley's assurance that the book is indeed Malcolm's own and not a clever piece of mimicry or pastiche. The casually vivid rendering of other persons is worth remarking, a test some quite competent novelists would have trouble passing. People who were especially important to Malcolm—his strong-minded half-sister Ella; the motherly white woman who ran the detention home he was sent to at 13, who was always kind to him and would call his people "niggers" to his face without a flicker of uneasiness; Shorty from Boston, who set him up in business; West Indian Archie, who "called him out"; or the tough convict Bimbi in Charlestown prison, strange little man of unexpected thoughts and arguments, who broke through the wall of rage and hate Malcolm was closing around himself—all these figures are precisely defined, according to their place in the story. The grasp of the narrative extends in fact to whole sociologies of behavior. The Harlem chapters in general, with their explanation of hustling in all its major forms—numbers, drugs, prostitution, protection, petty inghetto thievery—offer one of the best accounts in our literature of the cultural underside of the American business system, and of the bitter psychology that binds its victims to it; Malcolm came to see very clearly how the habituations bred by ghetto poverty operate to destroy individual efforts to break out of it, and he could use that insight with force and point in his preaching. Most generally it is just this blending of his own life-story with the full collective history of his milieu and the laws of behavior controlling it that gives Malcolm's testimony its strength and large authority—and sets it apart, I think, from the many more or less skillfully designed essays in autobiography we have had recently from writers like Frank Conroy, Claude Brown, Norman Podhoretz, Willie Morris, Paul Cowan, David McReynolds, to mention only a few; sets it apart also from the great run of novels about contemporary city life.

But it is Malcolm himself, and his own active consciousness of the myth of his life's progress, that most fills and quickens the book, making it something more than simply a valuable document. His past life is vividly present to him as he speaks; he gives it the form, in recollection, of a dramatic adventure in which he himself is felt as the precipitating agent and moving force. It is not unreasonable that he should see himself as someone who has a special power to make things happen, to work changes on the world around him (and to change within himself); and thus finally as one whose rise to authority is in some sense in the natural order of things, the working out of some deep structure of fortune. That is my way of putting it; Malcolm himself, as a Muslim, of course uses other words.

The force of this continuously active process of self-conception and self-projection is fundamental to the book's power of truth. It gives vitality and momentum to the early parts of the story, the picture of Malcolm's salad days as a Roxbury and Harlem sharpie, with conked hair and "knob-toed, orange-colored 'kick-up' shoes," the wildest Lindy-hopper and quickest hustler of all, delighting always in his impact on others—as in the interlude of his first trip back to Lansing, Michigan, to wow the yokels with his Harlem flashiness—finding satisfaction, too, in the names, the folk-identities, that attach to him at each new stage: "Homeboy," "Harlem Red" or "Detroit Red," "Satan" in the storming defiance of his first imprisonment. Most decisively, this force of self-conception is what brings alive the drama of his conversion, and his reemergence within the Nation of Islam as a leader and teacher of his people. For Malcolm's autobiography is consciously shaped as the story of an "education," and in so describing it I am not merely making the appropriate allusion to Henry Adams or the *Bildungsroman* tradition; "education" is Malcolm's own word for what is taking place.

Above all, the book is the story of a conversion and its consequences. We can identify in it various classic features of conversion-narrative. A full detailing of the crimes and follies of his early life makes more astonishing the change of changes that follows ("The very enormity of my previous life's guilt prepared me to accept the truth"). In the central light of this new truth, particular events take on symbolic dimensions; they stand as the exemplary trials and challenges which the redeemed soul must pass through and by which it knows the meaning, feels the reality, of its experience. That meaning and reality, to repeat, are not merely personal. The outlines of grander historical patterns are invoked and give their backing to the story—the whole long history and tragedy of the black race in America; then, at the crisis, the radically clarifying mythology of the Black Muslim movement (a mythology which, to any one willing to consider it objectively, has the character of a full-blown poetic mythology; a source, once you place yourself inside it, of comprehensive and intrinsically rational explanations for the life-experience it refers to, that of the mass of black people in a historically racist society).

And always there is Malcolm's own fascination with what has happened to him, and what objectively it means. As if establishing a leitmotif, the climaxes of his story repeatedly focus on this extraordinary power to change and be changed that he has grown conscious of within himself and that presents itself to him as the distinctive rule of his life. Malcolm speaks with a just pride of his quickness to learn, to "pick up" how things are done in the world; of his readiness, even when it humiliates him, to accept schooling from those in possession of some special competence or wisdom; of a "personal chemistry" of openmindedness and quick realism that requires him to find out the full vital truth of his own experience and that keeps it available to consciousness from that time forward. His curiosity about life is unquenchable ("You can hardly mention anything I'm not curious about"). He has a driving need to understand everything that happens to him or around him and to gain a measure of intelligent control over it; it is a passion with him to get his own purchase on reality.

It thus makes *narrative* sense, of a kind only the best of novelists are in command of, that he should discover his calling in life as a teacher and converter. Malcolm has his own theories for nearly everything that interests him—theories of language and etymology (he has an autodidact's sense of word-magic, dating from the time in prison when studying a dictionary, page by page, in a folklorish fury of self-improvement, began quite literally to give him an extravagant new intuition of power and freedom, as of one suddenly finding a key to his enemy's most treasured secrets); theories about how Socrates' wisdom came from initiation into the mysteries of black Egypt and about the persecuted black philosopher Spinoza and the black poet Homer (cognate with Omar and Moor) and about who really wrote Shakespeare and translated the English Bible and why. Of course we can laugh at a lot of this from the pewboxes of a more orderly education, but I find myself impressed even in these odd instances with the unfailing rationality of the uses to which Malcolm put his thought, the intelligence even here of what really matters to him—which is the meaning of his life as a black man in the United States and the enormous responsibilities of a position of authority and leadership in which he can count on no help from the official, institutionalized culture but what he wrenches out for himself.

But it is, again, the prodigy of his own conversion that gives him the most direct confirmation of his beliefs; the awareness of himself as a man capable of these transforming changes that gives him confidence in his testimony's importance, that lets him say, "Anything I do today, I regard as urgent." The ***Autobiography*** was written to serve at once a religious and a political cause, the cause of the religion of Islam and the cause of black freedom, and it is filled with the letter of Malcolm's teaching. In the later chapters especially, more and more of the text is portioned out to explanations of essential doctrine and to social and political commentary and analysis. But here, too, it is a personal authority that comes through to us and makes the difference. I should like to try to characterize this authority a little further. I first read Malcolm's autobiography when I happened also to be reading through the Pauline epistles in the New Testament; the chance result was a sharp consciousness of fundamental resemblances. Resemblances, I mean, to the voice and manner of the Paul who not only is teaching his people the law of the new faith (to which he himself is a late comer, and by hard ways) but who suffuses his teaching with all the turbulence of his own history and masterful personality. Two recent students of Paul's letters, Charles Buck and Greer Taylor, have commented on the singularity of this element in Paul: "a presumption of personal authority on the part of the writer which is quite unlike that of any other New Testament author." Malcolm, too, writes as the leader of a new, precariously established faith, which he is concerned to stabilize against destructive inner dissensions yet without losing any of the priceless communal fervor and dedication that have been released by it. So at every point he brings to bear the full weight of his own reputation and active experience, including his earlier follies and excesses—precisely as Paul does in, for example, the astonishing final chapters of Second Corinthians, full as they are of the liveliest and most immediate self-reference. The tangible genius of both Paul and Malcolm as writers is to bring the authority of living personality, and of self-mastery, into the arena of what is understood to be an argument of the utmost consequence; a matter of life and death for those who commit themselves to it.

Malcolm's concerns are of course civil and political as well as sectarian. In his last years he had become, and knew it, a national leader as important as Dr. King; a leader moreover who, as the atmosphere of the Washington March of August 1963 gave way to the ghetto riots of the next summer, was trusted inside Harlem and its counterparts as the established black leadership no longer was. And the last academic point I want to make about the literary character of Malcolm's book is that in this regard, too, as a political statement, its form is recognizably "classic." The model it quite naturally conforms to is that of the Political Testament, the work in which some ruler or statesman sets down for the particular benefit of his people a summary of his own experience and wisdom and indicates the principles which are to guide those who succeed him. The historian Felix Gilbert has called attention to this rather special literary tradition in his study of the background of Washington's Farewell Address. It is necessarily, in the number of its members, a limited tradition; besides Washington's address Professor Gilbert mentions examples attributed to Richelieu, Colbert, the Dutch republican Jan de Witt, Robert Walpole, Peter the Great, and Frederick the Great, who wrote at least two of them. My argument is not that Malcolm was in any way guided by this grand precedent, merely that in serving all his book's purposes he substantially recreated it—which is of course what the work of literature we call "classic" does within the occasion it answers to. (pp. 316-21)

Warner Berthoff, "Witness and Testament: Two Contemporary Classics," in New Literary History, *Vol. II, No. 2, Winter, 1971, pp. 311-27.*

Barrett John Mandel (essay date March 1972)

[*In the essay below, Mandel interprets* The Autobiography of Malcolm X *as a didactic account of a conversion experience.*]

The ***Autobiography of Malcolm X*** is a richly didactic work—didactic in the best sense of the word. As a man who spent the greater part of his life in learning how to be a *human* being, always working toward the goal of humanizing those around him. Malcolm X has written his autobiography in the hagiographical spirit of one who has found hope and even peace and now wishes to help others find them. (p. 269)

Like St. Augustine, John Bunyan, Jonathan Edwards, and Vavasor Powell, Malcolm has written a spiritual conversion autobiography. The ***Autobiography*** is that of a sinner who becomes a saint, and the saint, like his Christian parallels, is a preacher. One notices the parallels especially to John Bunyan, who as he became a "saint"—the word was commonly used for puritan bretheren in the seventeenth century and was still used by the Plymouth Bretheren in the nineteenth century—became increasingly repugnant to the established authorities, who went to great lengths to stop his preaching.

Malcolm, trapped in a Manichean world of Evil and Good, is pulled from pole to pole in his slow ascent to self-knowledge. And there are many other parallels to familiar conversion literature. The treatment of sex can serve as an important example. Malcolm tells of his youth spent among pimps and whores. Like the young St. Augustine, Malcolm at first found the good life to be one of fleshly pursuits; his narrative skill goes a long way toward recreating the attractiveness of the early temptations. It is only as the rhythm of his life starts to carry him toward self-regeneration in Islam that he recognizes the need of self-imposed abstinence: "I had always been very careful to stay completely clear of any personal closeness with any of the Muslim sisters. My total commitment to Islam demanded having no other interests, especially, I felt, no women." In ***The Autobiography of Malcolm X,*** St. Augustine's *Confessions,* Bunyan's *Grace Abounding,* one finds lusty men repressing their physical desires and channeling their energy into their social and spiritual obligations. Sex is vitally, but negatively, important in most spiritual autobiographies; the author's life is to some degree molded by his self-conscious avoidance of sexual intercourse. One's life becomes the phallus.

In an autobiography whose rhetorical end is to reach out and serve as a pattern of moral regeneration, it becomes acceptable, paradoxically, for an author to leave the actual facts and fictionalize when such verbal manipulation can serve the larger moral ends of the work. Malcolm embroiders the facts when he feels that art can create a higher kind of truth than that to which mere "reality" can aspire.

> Talking to them [his criminal accomplices] laying down the plans, I had deliberately sat on a bed away from them. All of a sudden, I pulled out my gun, shook out all five bullets, and then let them see me put back only one bullet. I twirled the cylinder, and put the muzzle to my head.
>
> "Now, I'm going to see how much guts all of you have" I said.
>
> I grinned at them. All of their mouths had flapped open. I pulled the trigger—we all heard it *click.*
>
> "I'm going to do it again, now."
>
> They begged me to stop. I could see in Shorty's and Rudy's eyes some idea of rushing me.
>
> We all heard the hammer *click* on another empty cylinder.
>
> The women were in hysterics. Rudy and Shorty were begging, "*Man . . . Red . . . cut it out, man! . . . Freeze!*" I pulled the trigger once more.
>
> "I'm doing this, showing you I'm not afraid to die," I told them. "Never cross a man not afraid to die . . . now, let's get to work!"

The importance of this episode in Malcolm's life is that it helps to create the character—the aesthetic illusion—of the man who later will be capable of suffering for his beliefs and worthy of leadership in a trying period.

Anyone who has read the ***Autobiography*** knows the impact of this episode in context. But the event narrated so convincingly in Chapter Nine is only partially true to the facts of Malcolm's life. Malcolm has left out relevant, crucial details, and has produced, therefore, a fiction—the same sort of distortion of data common in *exempla* and medieval hagiography. In the Epilogue to the book; Alex Haley, the writer to whom the "autobiography" was dictated, reports Malcolm's attitude toward this dramatic episode upon reading it several months after he had dictated it. Haley's whole paragraph is important:

> The manuscript copy which Malcolm X was given to review was in better shape now, and he pored through page by page intently, and now and then his head would raise with some comment. "You know," he said once, "why I have been able to have some effect is because I make a study of the weaknesses of this country and because the more the white man yelps, the more I know I have struck a nerve." Another time, he put down upon the bed the manuscript he was reading, and he got up from his chair and walked back and forth, stroking his chin, then he looked at me. "You know this place here in this chapter where I told you how I put the pistol up to my head and kept pulling the trigger and scared them so when I was starting the burglary ring—well," he paused, "I don't know if I ought to tell you this or not, but I want to tell the truth." He eyed me, speculatively. "I palmed the bullet." We laughed together. I said, "Okay, give that page here, I'll fix it." Then he considered, "No, leave it that way. Too many people would be so quick to say that's what I'm doing today, bluffing."

There are two especially interesting words in this passage: "bluff " and "effect." Malcolm's actual life was not a bluff; the bullets which killed him were no bluff. But in some significant ways, his autobiography is a bluff. His comment to Haley and the episode in Chapter Nine allow us to catch a glimpse of Malcolm at his literary task. He is caught fashioning a character or a "type" which does not mirror the whole truth of his real life, but which generates its own kind of convincing, fictional truth. The reason for Malcolm's "creative" rendering of the facts is that he wished to have a particular *effect* on his readers—both black and white—and to do this, he sensed that he would have to create a particular illusion. As a writer who knew that he had to capture not the daily habits and chronological routines of his life, but its essense or meaning. Malcolm X has entered the ranks of the great artist-autobiographers—Gibbon, Wordsworth, Gosse. Like all great autobiographers, Malcolm X knew that one's memories take on importance as they are shaped by one's perspective on them and by one's *Weltanschauung* in general.

In real life Malcolm was one emerging Negro leader among several. The book reviewer of *Newsweek* put Malcolm into perspective by speaking of his wasted gifts. (What, one wonders, should Malcolm have done with his "gifts" in order not to have wasted them.) Indeed, during his lifetime, as Haley points out, Malcolm had considerably less appeal for the majority of Negroes than either Roy Wilkins or Martin Luther King (whose death Malcolm predicted). Whites feared and hated him as a peripheral maniac, acrimonious and aggressive.

But Malcolm designed his autobiography in order to *effect* his readers. Malcolm's artistic task is to convert his reader from the fiction of him as a threat to society, operating on the fringes of the black world, to the fiction (or suggestion) of him as a central figure of major stature and integrity. The book's artistry reduces the significance of the other black leaders by placing Malcolm's own ego at the center of the literary action. The world one discovers in his pages is not the world of *Newsweek* or CBS Television ("fictions" in their own right) in which Malcolm appeared as a bitter fanatic, but a world which *needs* the dynamic, not to say the titanic, moral honesty, modesty, and dedication of this man, a one-time hustler turned puritan turned culture-hero. Because Malcolm's sensibility is at the center of the work, the reader sees and understands the world through Malcolm's eyes. Instead of a perspective on Malcolm characterized by the vulgar gaping of a frightened white world, the perspective is Malcolm's, as he scrutinizes, judges, and, finally opens his arms to the black and white world. The reader is inevitably caught up—effected—by the rhetoric of inclusion.

> Since I learned the *truth* in Mecca, my dearest friends have come to include *all* kinds—some Christians, Jews, Buddhists, Hindus, agnostics, and even atheists! I have friends who are called capitalists, Socialists, and Communists! Some of my friends are moderates, conservatives, extremists—some are even Uncle Toms! My friends today are black, brown, red, yellow, and *white!*

We do not see the unexplained data of a life. What we see is the special perspective which is the result of the narrator's continual sifting. He tells us what to see and how to see it. Regardless of how one has been accustomed to judging Malcolm in real life, the book's brilliant rhetoric creates the illusion of a man who suffers, learns, and loves. This is a man whose language is hard and uneuphemistic: "To come right down to it, if I take the kind of things in which I believe, then add to that the kind of temperament that I have, plus the one hundred per cent dedication I have to whatever I believe in—these are ingredients which make it just about impossible for me to die of old age." This kind of language, more striking and unsettling, even, than the brilliant descriptions of his hustling days, is written to do a job, to have an effect. The job Malcolm feels his autobiography must do necessitates that he project himself in the role of "hero" or "natural leader."

Malcolm's seemingly immodest presentation of himself as a culture-hero and his departure from verifiable fact, are justified by the works didacticism—a word which should be understood in its fullest sense. Malcolm is not depicting a human life for the sake of the portrayal itself; he is trying to be of use or service in the community. It was not enough that he actually had a following in Harlem and elsewhere. He needed to extend his appeal to a larger more suspicious audience of middle-class blacks and whites. The aim of his autobiography is to galvanize all sorts of people into action. One must put the book down chastened, subdued, ennobled, and converted. The book is a modern saint's life and wants to make saints of its readers. Malcolm's drive is to convert his reader—the black man to self-respect, the white man to human decency. This consuming moral drive finds the sculpture in the marble. As author, Malcolm creates a narrator, whose task it is to tell the story of a huge man singled out for a huge task by God himself. The narrator is a preacher—and where he does not convert, he, at least, confronts his reader:

> Where the really sincere white people have got to do their "proving" of themselves is not among the black *victims,* but out on the battle lines of where America's racism really *is*—and that's in their own home communities; America's racism is among their own fellow whites. That's where the sincere whites who really mean to accomplish something have got to work.

Because the book is an allegedly true story of a real man and the issues pressingly contemporary, the reader is steadily made to feel that he is part of the author-preacher's congregation. Malcolm may not have every reader's sympathy, but he does have every man's attention.

Malcolm's conversion is essentially true to the familiar regeneration pattern. Life before the moment of transcendent illumination is bestial. "When you become an animal," he says of his own pre-conversion days, "a vulture, in the ghetto, as I had become, you enter a world of animals and vultures. It becomes truly the survival of only the fittest." You think you are living by a code, and you think that life is hanging together tolerably. Only in retrospect does the sinner know that he has been "going through the hardest thing," struggling toward an ability "to accept that which is already within you, and around you." ("But what good was all this to me," St Augustine cries in *The Confessions,* "holding, as I did, that you, Lord God and Truth, were a vast luminous body and that I was a sort of piece broken off from this body? What an extraor dinary perversity I showed! Yet this was what I was then.")

Malcolm undergoes a false conversion—also typical of spiritual autobiographers. How does one tell the difference between the true God and beguiling, cunning Satan? Through his false conversion to the Muslim faith of Elijah Muhammad ("I found Allah and the religion of Islam and it completely transformed my life"), he made possible his final illumination at Mecca in 1964 and also his ultimate martyrdom. Malcolm's worst sin was not knowing the true God soon enough. This mistake started the train of events which destroyed him.

Malcolm's hajj to Mecca was a pilgrim's progress. Saudi Arabia treated him regally. "Never would I have even thought of dreaming that I would ever be a recipient of such honors—honors that in America would be bestowed upon a king—not a Negro. All praise is due to Allah, the Lord of all the Worlds." To the rest of society, this second, real conversion seemed like instability and immature emotionalism. *Newsweek* found in Malcolm's renunciation of Elijah Muhammad and in his affirmation of True Islam a "maze of contradictory words." When Malcolm could be simplistically characterized as a Black Muslim (an expression he rejected), he could be dealt with by the white world, but as he grew in complexity and depth, he became less accessible to reductive minds and, consequently, a target for their resentful attacks. To Malcolm this painful reappraisal of his life and views was a great awakening; it was a sudden expansion of his intellect, conscience, and social sensibility. He was now in possession of what he felt to be the full truth and able to accommodate whatever spiritual value there had been in the creed of Mr. Muhammad, while rejecting the narrow, hate-producing mythology.

The autobiography does not end in the moment of spiritual illumination at Mecca, a fitting end for a novel, but not for a conversion autobiography. No Rex Warner has written *The Converts* on the theme of Malcolm X yet, ending the book, as Warner does his on Augustine in the moment of religious intensity which transforms the subject's life. Anxiety characterizes the last pages of most conversion autobiographies. William Cowper's *Memoir* traces his sincere religious regeneration but ends the account by the record of fears of "back-sliding" and "many a lifeless and unhallowed hour" since the conversion. The last pages of Malcolm's autobiography are characterized by the ambivalent tension generated by the devotee's desire to keep his faith pure and intense in the face of terrible earthly catastrophes and temptations. It is Malcolm, after all, who has been converted, not society. To be alive in New York and to be El-Hajj Malik El-Shabazz is to experience unendurable assaults on one's fledgling convictions. The struggle of spirituality is never over, the struggle is Now.

There are two Malcolm X's in this book: the protagonist (the young man who struggles from darkness to light, from cynicism and despair to hope and integrity) and the older, wiser man—the narrator—who tells the story. The autobiography is greatly enriched by the fact that the narrator is engaged in his *own* struggle, though it is no longer the same kind of struggle that characterized his past. Not only does he have the struggle to fight off bitterness and "backsliding." He also has the artist's struggle inherent in attempting to preach the truth which is upon him, responding with modesty to a call which demands that he immodestly present himself and his life as a model worthy of emulation. If Malcolm as narrator (soon in reality to be engulfed by the very destructive power described with such gothic fear in the last pages of the book) creates a protagonist somewhat too fictionally heroic and invincible, it is because he is responding to the call of a Force larger than himself. This Force magnifies Malcolm by singling him out to preach, but, of course, the same call to the foot of Allah's throne humbles the spokesman. "What," cries John Bunyan, "shall I be proud because I am a sounding Brass? is it so much to be a Fiddle"? Malcolm ends his book: "And if I can die having brought any light, having exposed any meaningful truth that will help destroy the racist cancer . . . then, all of the credit is due to Allah. Only the mistakes have been mine." The narrator continually interjects the modest tone of the true believer: "I believe, today, that it was written, it was meant for Reginald [his brother] to be used for one purpose only: as a bait, as a minnow to reach into the ocean of blackness where I was, to save me." Malcolm is the chief of sinners to whom grace has been abounding: in a fallen world this paradox produces a modest culture-hero.

To the degree that Malcolm's spiritual growth and commitment seem enviable (that is, worth imitating), the autobiography is an important twentieth-century document. It clearly has lasting value for sociologists, cultural historians, psychologists, theologians, and literary critics. Besides revealing the emotional structure of one of the most compelling radicals of the century, the book will continue to be read for its brilliant depiction of the struggle up from the back alleys and brothels of the black ghetto by one of the major directors of the social revolution currently under way.

Principally, however, ***The Autobiography of Malcolm X*** is a great work of didactic literature with a wide audience which its narrative and emotional appeal are doing their share to mold and direct. The impact of the work on most readers is intense, immediate, and enduring.

The character portrayal at each stage is compellingly vivid. Malcolm's ability to capture the scene and sound of the city and its lingo is that of the novelist. But just as we are caught up in the rhythms of his dissipation, he reminds us, however indirectly, of his slow and painful self-mastery.

> Shorty would take me to groovy, frantic, scenes in different chicks' and cats' pads, where with the lights and juke down mellow, everybody blew gage and juiced back and jumped. I met chicks who were fine as May wine, and cats who were hip to all happenings.
>
> That paragraph is deliberate, of course; it's just to display a bit more of the slang that was used by everyone I respected as "hip" in those days. And in no time at all, I was talking the slang like a lifelong hipster.

The gap in time, space, and sensibility suggested by the

differences between these two paragraphs is that yawning abyss which only the agonizing process of real education can fill.

Malcolm's autobiography exists as a personal testimony to the fact that it is yet possible, even in the face of very great social and psychological opposition, for a man to learn how to be human. Malcolm's literary aim is to put that seemingly easy goal within the reach of many people. Conversion is possible; the message is loud and clear. (pp. 270-74)

Barrett John Mandel, "The Didactic Achievement of Malcolm X's Autobiography," in Afro-American Studies, *Vol. 2, No. 4, March, 1972, pp. 269-74.*

David P. Demarest, Jr. (essay date December 1972)

[*In the following essay, Demarest refutes prevailing critical perceptions of* The Autobiography of Malcolm X *as a work of didacticism (see, for example, Mandel's essay dated March 1972), maintaining that the white reader of Malcolm's book "feels that he has been converted by something larger than and different from the ideas Malcolm specifically espouses—by something beyond didacticism."*]

For many black readers, one ventures, ***The Autobiography of Malcolm X*** will be a didactic experience. After all, Malcolm's words are often clearly intended for a black audience, and more often than not he is preaching and scolding blacks to assert control over their own lives. Moreover, for most blacks Malcolm's reputation will have preceded any reading of the book, and they will be predisposed to see him as symbol of an idea, to admire him for his reputation of standing up to whitey and telling it loud and clear like it is—and challenging other blacks to stand with him. As Ossie Davis puts it in his postscript:

> . . . Malcolm kept snatching our lies away. He kept shouting the painful truths we whites and blacks did not want to hear from all the housetops. And he wouldn't stop for love nor money.

For blacks, ***The Autobiography*** will simply confirm and augment the general reputation to which Ossie Davis pays homage—a reputation that has grown ever more vivid in the black world since Malcolm's death. ***The Autobiography*** will also reiterate many ideas that have been made familiar by black militants. For black readers, Malcolm's fame will not rest on personal knowledge of a book.

Whites—if they are to get beyond the fading memory of an often harsh TV image—must read ***The Autobiography.*** And unless they are indelibly biased or lack literary imagination, they will become admirers of both Malcolm and the book. Here, then, is a problem for the white critic. What makes ***The Autobiography*** so effective with white readers? In part, the appeal must involve ideology, though of a far more generalized sort than the advice applicable to the black community. Certainly ***The Autobiography*** attracts white readers who feel that they too are exploited by the "system." But the white reader experiences ***The Autobiography*** as a *literary* work, and if he is converted to admiration of Malcolm, it is not simply because of ideology. He feels that he has been converted by something larger than and different from the ideas Malcolm specifically espouses—by something beyond didacticism.

Clearly ***The Autobiography***'s literary effectiveness is enhanced by some of its didactic aspects—its carefully symmetrical structure, for instance. Beginning at the beginning, Malcolm narrates his childhood and his teenage life of crime. Finally in prison, feeling that he has become Satan incarnate, he undergoes his first conversion, to Elijah Muhammad's religion. The chapter titled "Saved" is right at mid-point in the book—pages 169 through 190 in a total that runs to 382. After chronicling his activities in the Nation of Islam and his gradual estrangement from Elijah, Malcolm ends with his trip to Mecca and Africa and his conversion to a larger, more inter-racial faith. Such a schematic pattern might be expected of a didactic autobiographer who sees his life as moral exemplum and who seeks converts through advertisement of the road to wisdom that has been opened to him. Undeniably, ***The Autobiography*** gains a good deal of strength from the balanced clarity of this overall structure.

Further, this conversion pattern lends strength to the book—at least for the white reader—because it evokes the tradition of spiritual autobiographies and wayfarings that runs deep through Christian literature. The stay in prison, as metaphor for man's fallible nature or unregenerate state, recalls Boethius and, more closely, *Grace Abounding to the Chief of Sinners.* Less literally, the prison episode suggests the adventures of another wayfarer, Robinson Crusoe, whose island imprisonment served, like Malcolm's legal detention, as stimulus to self-effort, self-education and conversion. Malcolm's procedure of learning language by copying the dictionary word by word and then studying the words of Elijah Muhammad is specifically reminiscent of the self-help faith of Robinson Crusoe's bibliolatry; it also recalls the scheduled self-improvements of the young Benjamin Franklin. Echoes of *Pilgrim's Progress* are found in the clean-living zeal, the puritanical quality of the Black Muslims emphasized by Malcolm. Literarily, *Pilgrim's Progress* is evoked by the journey to Mecca, the holy city, but it is also there in the early description of Harlem, which Malcolm presents as an entrapping Vanity Fair. When Malcolm calls the roll of the street names of the hustlers he knew, an allegorized world springs to life—The Four Horsemen (black cops who worked Sugar Hill); Cadillac Drake ("the world's most unlikely pimp"); Sammy the Pimp; Alabama Peach (a white prostitute who worked for Sammy); Dollarbill (another pimp who liked to flash his "Kansas City roll"); Fewclothes (a pickpocket); Jumpsteady (a burglar). Like Bunyan's, Malcolm's world is alive with identifying tags of meaning: every name signals a story—some adjustment to the hellish pressures of Harlem.

Such echoes of traditional Christian literature surely enrich ***The Autobiography*** for the white reader: through them he is able to connect more intimately to Malcolm. But in important ways, ***The Autobiography*** does *not* fit the tradition of conversion autobiography. The white reader finds himself appreciating the book both because it invokes a familiar pattern and because it goes beyond that pattern.

The style of ***The Autobiography*** is an instance of both didactic patterning and variation.

> The world's most unlikely pimp was "Cadillac" Drake. He was shiny baldheaded, built like a football; he used to call his huge belly "the chippies' playground." Cadillac had a string of about a dozen of the stringiest, scrawniest, black and white street prostitutes in Harlem. Afternoons around the bar, the old-timers who knew Cadillac well enough would tease him about how women who looked like his made enough to feed themselves, let alone him. He'd roar with laughter right along with us; I can hear him now, "Bad-looking women work harder."

This paragraph—chosen almost at random—is perfectly typical of the style attributed to Malcolm by ***The Autobiography.*** It illustrates the simple and, above all, concrete vocabulary, and it shows the unelaborate sentence pattern that underlines the clarity and directness of Malcolm's voice. Also typical is the moralizing structure of the paragraph. The first sentence, neatly and explicitly, is the topic sentence; the last sentence lets Cadillac draw the moral. But the moralizing has a complex effect because its end is comic, and the reader warms to Malcolm as he senses a moralizer who can laugh at the conventions of moral-drawing.

Almost all the chapters, as well as the smaller episodes, end with exhortation and advice. Malcolm comments, for instance, about his decision to leave Michigan and go to Boston: "All praise is due to Allah that I went to Boston when I did. If I hadn't, I'd probably still be a brainwashed black Christian." After his first "conking" he concludes:

> I'm speaking from personal experience when I say of any black man who conks today, or any white-wigged black woman, that if they give the brains in their heads just half as much attention as they do their hair, they would be a thousand times better off.

Most of such moralizing is aimed at blacks—whether about conking, hustling, the numbers rackets, or about religious and political attitudes. But Malcolm calls for something larger than such specifics—self-awareness, self-criticism, and, often, the concomitant ability to laugh at oneself. Thus Malcolm can describe his zoot-suited elegance as a teenager and a visit back home to Michigan this way:

> . . . I'd go through that Grand Central Station rush-hour crowd, and many white people simply stopped in their tracks to watch me pass. The drape and the cut of a zoot suit showed to the best advantage if you were tall—and I was over six feet. My conk was fire-red. I was really a clown, but my ignorance made me think I was "sharp." My knob-toed, orange-colored "kick-up" shoes were nothing but Florsheims, the ghetto's Cadillac of shoes in those days. . . . My conk and whole costume were so wild that I might have been taken as a man from Mars. I caused a minor automobile collision; one driver stopped to gape at me, and the driver behind bumped into him. My appearance staggered the older boys I had once envied; I'd stick out my hand, saying "Skin me, daddy-o!"

The specific advice here is directed at blacks; whites respond to something beyond didacticism—to Malcolm's comic self-awareness.

One might expect that a preacher (as Malcolm was) who wrote his autobiography in order to persuade and convert his readers would maintain a tone of voice that supported his didactic maxims. Everything should serve the purpose of conversion. Malcolm's voice—as in the examples above—is far more flexible. From his post-conversion perspective, Malcolm must look back at Small's bar in Harlem as a meeting place of ill-spent, misdirected lives, and he must lecture his black brothers to extricate themselves. But in his descriptions the world of the rackets and the hustlers—like his teenage zoot-suiting—comes brilliantly, even lovingly, to life. Malcolm relives it all in retrospect, not for a moment falling into the moralizer's trap of turning what he condemns into clay pigeons. A fine example of his ability to avoid the rigidities of didacticism is his description of dancing:

> If you've ever lindy-hopped, you'll know what I'm talking about. With most girls, you kind of work opposite them, circling, side-stepping, leading. Whichever arm you lead with is half-bent out there, your hands are giving that little push, that little push, touching her waist, her shoulders, her arms. She's in, out, turning, whirling, wherever you guide her. With poor partners, you feel their weight. They're slow and heavy. But with really good partners, all you need is just the push-pull suggestion. They guide effortlessly, even off the floor and into the air, and your little solo maneuver is done on the floor before they land, when they join you, whirling, right in step.

It is still an instructor's voice talking, but coming from a religious convert who is bent, overall, on showing his dancehall experiences as the corrupt follies of ignorant youth, the teacher's voice is startlingly vivid with remembered pleasure. Malcolm's relish for the verve of some of his early life may technically point him toward contradiction with some of his preachments. But more significantly, in violating the demands of a strict, narrow logic, Malcolm's attitude reveals a more complex, even a more tolerant personality than one might expect.

It is unrealistic to talk long about ***The Autobiography***'s undogmatic tone without speculating on how the book's double authorship (Malcolm-to-Alex Haley) may have been a determinant. One is tempted to feel that had the book been entirely Malcolm's, or had he lived and possibly forced certain revisions, the book would have revealed less of Malcolm than it now does. At least it probably would have been more dogmatic, cut more rigidly to the pattern of Malcolm's latest position. That Malcolm—the one that might have emerged from a book entirely controlled by Malcolm—would have revealed one true side of the real man, but it might have suppressed the qualities of openness and growth that Haley, as outside observer, could appreciate. As it stands, ***The Autobiography*** may avoid the problems of both the autobiographer's lack of objectivity and the biographer's limited knowledge.

Haley's comments in the Epilogue make it clear that Malcolm felt drawn by the spiritual autobiographer's temptation to adjust events to fit updated moral positions. Malcolm's personal feud with the Black Muslims in the last year of his life and his attempt to define for himself a more international position might well have led him to revise ***The Autobiography*** into a running attack on Elijah Muhammad. Alex Haley recounts how Malcolm's shifted attitude affected his literary judgment:

> . . . I sent Malcolm X some rough chapters to read. I was appalled when they were soon returned, red-inked in many places where he had told of his almost father-and-son relationship with Elijah Muhammad. Telephoning Malcolm X, I reminded him of his previous decision, and I stressed that if those chapters contained telegraphing to the readers of what would lie ahead, then the book would automatically be robbed of some of its building suspense and drama. Malcolm X said, gruffly, "Whose book is this?" I told him "Yours, of course," and that I only made the suggestion in my position as a writer. He said that he would have to think about it. I was heart-sick at the prospect that he might want to re-edit the entire book into a polemic against Elijah Muhammad. But late that night, Malcolm X telephoned. "I'm sorry. You're right. I was upset about something. Forget what I wanted changed, let what you already had stand." I never again gave him chapters to read unless I was with him.

In such fashion, the double authorship of ***The Autobiography*** checked Malcolm's tendencies to make the book too overtly polemic.

It is again a matter of speculation how differently Malcolm, left to his own devices, might have been tempted to treat the doctrinal tenets of the Nation of Islam that ***The Autobiography*** explains during and after the prison conversion. Either extreme might be expected in the didactic self-advertisement of the spiritual autobiography—either the unqualified affirmation of the new convert to the Nation of Islam, or a retrospective critical commentary—if not contempt—from the final convert to another creed. But Malcolm—perhaps checked by Haley—goes to neither extreme. A tone of qualified assent, for example, is given to the Muslim tenet that the white man is the devil. In his introductory comments, M. S. Handler states that what was "most disconcerting in our talk was Malcolm's belief in Elijah Muhammad's history of the origins of man, and in a genetic theory devised to prove the superiority of black over white—a theory stunning to me in its absurdity." But it is hard to know whether Malcolm accepted this theory literally. In the context of the autobiography, the theory is not fanatically supported—or attacked—but is presented rather as a useful metaphor, true in its expression of black superiority. The story is introduced at key points by "Elijah Muhammad teaches," and Malcolm expresses his initial incredulity at the story's details. What emerges in the tone of Malcolm's account is the belief in and retrospective regard for the truth of intention in Elijah's mythology—not that it need be literally true, but that it calculated truly the radical revision of race perspective needed to cope with the American problem. And what further emerges in Malcolm's tone is his refusal to be caught simplistically in dogma, his openness to revisions of his own.

The specific slogan that the white man is the devil is also handled with more qualification that one might expect. Malcolm records his first hesitations of belief, remembering how his consent balked at Hymie, the Jewish bootlegger he'd once worked for. And then after his conversion, he explains the rationale and effect of the slogan.

> I always had to be careful. I never knew when some brainwashed black imp, some dyed-in-the-wool Uncle Tom, would nod at me and then go running to tell the white man. When one was ripe—and I could tell—then away from the rest, I'd drop it on him, what Mr. Muhammad taught: "The white man is the devil." That would shock many of them—until they started thinking about it. . . .
>
> You tell that to any Negro. Except for those relatively few "integration"-mad so-called "intellectuals," and those black men who are otherwise fat, happy, and deaf, dumb, and blinded, with their crumbs from the white man's rich table, you have struck a nerve center in the American black man. He may take a day to react, a month, a year; he may never respond, openly; but of one thing you can be sure—when he thinks about his own life, he is going to see where to him, personally, the white man sure has acted like a devil.

The frankness with which Malcolm explains this slogan as a rhetorical device and apt metaphor again underscores his undogmatic sophistication. (A story told by Haley in the Epilogue suggests that even before his break with Elijah, Malcolm would not be trapped in belief in the literal truth of Elijah's doctrine: "The first time I ever heard Malcolm X speak of Handler, whom he had recently met, he began, 'I was talking with this devil—' and abruptly he cut himself off in obvious embarrassment. 'It's a reporter named Handler, from the *Times*—' he resumed.")

Just as such details enforce a picture of Malcolm as a man who will appeal to white readers in his refusal to be a narrow and fanatic preacher, so too the book's symmetrical structure finally emphasizes personal growth and intellectual receptivity more than it does doctrine. The structure of the double conversion of course itself emphasizes the expanding, dynamic quality of Malcolm's personality. And further emphasis is given to this effect by the fact that the second conversion is not to another narrow and sectarian creed but to a worldwide religious and political perspective.

But again the pattern of ***The Autobiography*** varies from what one might expect—a climatic summation of true values arrived at in the end. The apparent climax to Malcolm's book is in the two penultimate chapters, the journeys to Mecca and Africa as symbolic capstones to the twin religious and political thrusts of Malcolm's career.

The last chapter, titled "1965," tends to be anticlimactic, to eddy into fragments—as though Malcolm does not quite know how or where to move next. Such, indeed, is the note sounded at the chapter's start: "I must be honest. Negroes—Afro-Americans—showed no inclination to rush to the United Nations and demand justice for themselves here in America." Haley's epilogue, which is integral to completing the chronology of Malcolm's life, emphasizes the false starts, the indecisions, the groping of Malcolm's last days. In one sense, the ending of ***The Autobiography*** is thus weak. The book does not end—as a didactic spiritual autobiographer might like it to and insist that it did—at the symbolic high-point. But again this variation from neat structure, if momentarily a letdown, actually has a positive effect—at least for the reader interested in the general human theme of the book. The ending enforces the questing nature of Malcolm's personality, making it seem too big to be summed up. Malcolm's growth has not stopped with Mecca and Africa but seems instead to be beginning anew on another expanding cycle.

The motto of Malcolm's book—if one insists on the didactic, extractable maxim—might be this comment in the last chapter: "I would just like to *study.* I mean ranging study, because I have a wide-open mind." It is this quality—expressed in so many ways in the artistry of ***The Autobiography***—that will convert the white reader to admiration: Malcolm comes through as a man who was above all bent on discovering and expanding himself to his fullest limits. The book has all sorts of didactic advice and moral and political insight that may often be more applicable to blacks than to whites (though many whites will be sympathetic). But, above all, the book will appeal to whites because of its literary achievement of showing the fullness of Malcolm as a man. And doubtless it is just that quality of Malcolm's personality that, at base, makes Malcolm the hero of blacks of our era. Putting Malcolm in the perspective of the racial struggle as a black who advised, "Get up off your knees and fight your own battles," Ossie Davis sums up, "—whatever else he was or was not—*Malcolm was a man.*" (pp. 179-87)

> *David P. Demarest, Jr., " 'The Autobiography of Malcolm X': Beyond Didacticism," in* CLA Journal, *Vol. XVI, No. 2, December, 1972, pp. 179-87.*

Stephen Butterfield (essay date 1974)

[*Butterfield is an American educator and critic. In the following excerpt from his* Black Autobiography in America, *he examines rhetorical strategies in* The Autobiography of Malcolm X.]

It is one thing to be "inside history," and another to live history inside the self, to pump blood and oxygen through its facts across the placenta of your personal concerns. The past is the womb that contains us; the future is the history we contain in the seeds of our individuality, the embryo that we must bring to birth with our actions. Full consciousness of both is necessary if the truer and better self is to awaken, and another world be born. The language of modern black autobiography is a heroic effort to make the individual a meeting place for the past and future. When the meeting succeeds, the result, expressed concisely by the subtitle of Lester's *Search for the New Land,* is "history as subjective experience."

The long shadow of the slave narrative still falls across this meeting place. Whenever the terrain resembles the wilderness of slavery, the achievements of the narrative are on hand like special equipment for wilderness travel, which the writer may take out and refurbish according to his needs. The ***Autobiography of Malcolm X*** uses approximately the same form. The progression of events is familiar: the gradual realization of the limitations imposed on the narrator by the white world, the accumulated resentment and hostility toward white condescension and racism, the desire for economic independence, the flight to a Northern city, the discovery of a system of ideas that gives him a vision of the road to freedom, and the active participation in organizations that fight for the interests of black people. The slave narrative tradition adopts a particular stance toward this pattern in which the author's life is treated as an object lesson, and his role in the book is to use himself as the text of a sermon; he is a minister or teacher, demonstrating how the moral and political obstacles he faced can be overcome by others in the same circumstance. "I have given to this book so much of whatever time I have because I feel, and I hope, that if I honestly and fully tell my life's account, read objectively it might prove to be a testimony of some social value."

In keeping with his objective, Malcolm X tells his story as though it were a moral parable. Each separate incident has a message for the reader; the first part of the paragraph, commonly, presents the incident, and the second part draws the lesson:

> He had on a big Army overcoat. He took that off, and I kept laughing and said he still had on too many. I was able to keep that cracker stripping off clothes until he stood there drunk with nothing on from his pants up, and the whole car was laughing at him, and some other soldiers got him out of the way. I went on. I never would forget that—that I couldn't have whipped that white man as badly with a club as I had with my mind.
>
> I heard the usual hustler fates of so many others. Bullets, knives, prison, dope, diseases, insanity, alcoholism. I imagine it was about in that order. . . . I was thankful to Allah that I had become a Muslim and escaped their fate.

There are dozens of examples of how Malcolm's role as a "messenger of Allah" informs the structure and direction of the book. . . . Malcolm's message is as unsparing of himself as of white society. As an adolescent, he had seduced and abandoned a girl named Laura, who later became a "wreck of a woman," a drunkard, prostitute, and lesbian; Malcolm blamed himself for this, offering only the excuse that "like so many of my black brothers today, I was just deaf, dumb, and blind." But the chief object of the message is the white man, because he is the one who needs it most: "It was right there in prison that I made up my mind to devote the rest of my life to telling the white man about himself—or die."

The Christian religious rhetoric of the slave narrative is echoed sometimes in Malcolm's Muslim imagery: Mr. Muhammad is a "little humble lamb of a man," whose teachings cut back and forth like a "two-edged sword" from his mouth "to free the black man's mind from the white man." (pp. 256-58)

Malcolm X seems to adjust his colloquialisms according to which stage of his life he is relating. In the early part of the ***Autobiography,*** ghetto slang is used to create a gestalt of his career as a hustler and to display his moral authority as a regenerated sinner offering leadership to others like him:

> Shorty would take me to groovy, frantic scenes in different chicks' and cats' pads, where with the lights and juke down mellow, everybody blew gage and juiced back and jumped. I met chicks who were fine as May wine, and cats who were hip to all happenings.
>
> That paragraph is deliberate, of course; it's just to display a bit more of the slang that was used by everyone I respected as "hip" in those days.

Later the language shifts to Muslim rhetoric, shaped by Malcolm's personal eloquence and magnetism.

As they had in the slave narratives, the political speech, the sermon, and the oration animate the contemporary styles—old spirits drawn to the new voices by the urgency of the occasion.

> It's a crime, the lie that has been told to generations of black men and white men both. Little innocent black children, born of parents who believed that their race had no history. Little black children seeing, before they could talk, that their parents considered themselves inferior. Innocent black children growing up, living out their lives, dying of old age—and all of their lives ashamed of being black. But the truth is pouring out of the bag now.
>
> *Think* of it—think of that black slave man filled with fear and dread, hearing the screams of his wife, his mother, his daughter being *taken*—in the barn, the kitchen, in the bushes! *Think* of it, my dear brothers and sisters! *Think* of hearing wives, mothers, daughters, being *raped!* And you were too filled with *fear* of the rapist to do anything about it! And his vicious, animal attacks' offspring, this white man named things like "mulatto" and "quadroon" and "octoroon" and all those other things that he called us—you and me—when he is not calling us "nigger!"
>
> The Honorable Elijah Muhammad teaches us that since Western society is deteriorating, it has become overrun with immorality, and God is going to judge it, and destroy it. And the only way the black people caught up in this society can be saved is not to *integrate* into this corrupt society, but to *separate* from it, to a land of our *own,* where we can reform ourselves, lift up our moral standards, and try to be godly. The Western world's most learned diplomats have failed to solve this grave race problem. Her learned legal experts have failed. Her sociologists have failed. Her civil leaders have failed. Her fraternal leaders have failed. Since all of these have *failed* to solve this race problem, it is time for us to sit down and *reason*! I am certain that we will be forced to agree that it takes *God Himself* to solve this grave racial dilemma.

The first passage, taken from Malcolm's text, differs very little in tone and style from the second two, which are quoted from his speeches. In keeping with his objective to make the truth pour out of the bag, the main effort of passages one and two is to re-create for his listeners the visible impact of the indignities they have been made to suffer. Referring to Thomas Merton, a Trappist monk and social critic, [Eldridge] Cleaver wrote [in his *Soul on Ice*] that he had only to read Merton's essay on the racist oppression of Harlem "to become once more a rigid flame of indignation." The intention of Malcolm X's rhetoric is to produce that reaction in the audience; to flush the racism of the whites out to the surface, and steel the determination of the blacks to resist. [According to Cleaver in his *Post-Prison Writings and Speeches*], "Malcolm talked shit, and talking shit is the iron in a young nigger's blood. Malcolm mastered language and used it as a sword to slash his way through the veil of lies that for four hundred years gave the white man the power of the word."

The methods of Malcolm's language were also used by Ward, Thompson, and Douglass. In the sequence of clauses beginning "little innocent black children," the three sentences elaborate on each of the three adjectives

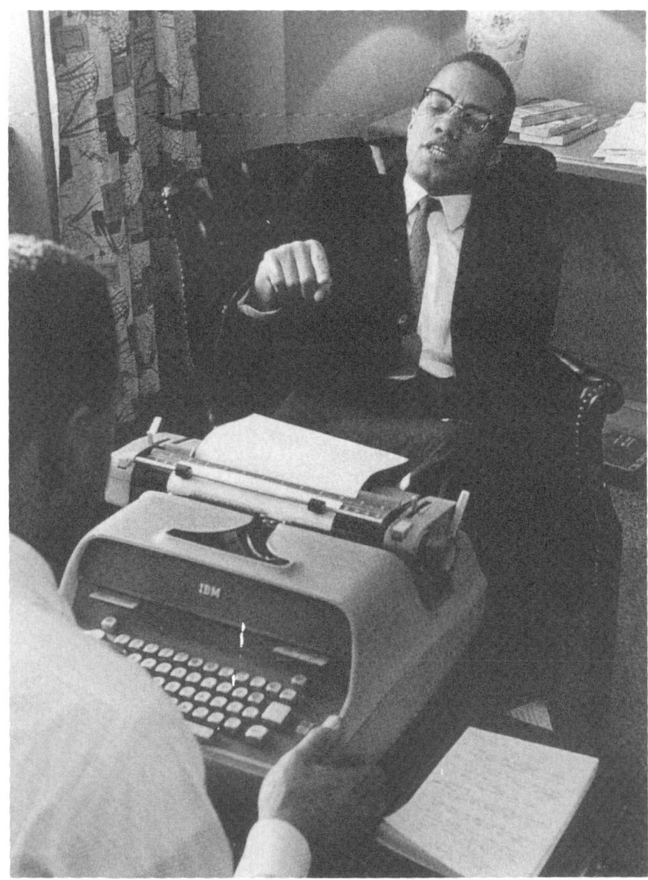

Malcolm X at the time of his Playboy *interview with Alex Haley.*

modifying "children." In the first sentence, the indignity centers around being black: it is because they are black that their history has been concealed. In the second, the indignity is centered around being little, because they are too young to protect themselves from the belief of their parents that they are inferior. In the third, the locus of the bitterness is the word "innocent," which connotes both ignorance and guiltlessness: all their lives the children, through no fault of their own, are ignorant of the truth that could free them. The parallelism enables the clauses to resonate backward and forward. The word "black" is repeated each time, stressing the reason for all the indignities—racism.

Passages two and three achieve emphasis by suggesting in print the tone of the spoken voice. In the third, the repeated italicized words, "think," "taken," "raped," "fear," "nigger," contain the main idea of the speech. The parallel clauses proceed by elaborating and extending that idea, adding extra detail with each repetition and providing variety within a set rhythmic pattern. The stressed words in the fourth example do the same thing: "integrate," "separate," "own," "failed," "reason," "God Himself" are the anchors of the paragraph. Besides emphasizing the main idea, they also carry the tone of the voice, modulating between reason and anger, urgent talk and shouting. Short, parallel repetitive sentences again elaborate the central theme; "The Western world's most learned diplomats have failed. . . . Her learned legal experts have failed. Her sociologists have failed. Her civil leaders have failed. Her fraternal leaders have failed. Since all of these have *failed* to solve this race problem. . . . " The advantage of parallel structures and repetition in an oral speech, besides holding the attention of the audience and insuring that they respond to the point, is that the speaker need not be at a loss for words. Extemporaneous speech and extemporaneous music (blues and jazz, for example) both have in common the technique of variation on a single basic pattern. Instead of having to lapse into silence while he gropes for a new pattern, the speaker or musician can extend, invert, or punctuate the old one, increasing or decreasing its tempo and volume. The word "failed" is the basic pattern in the preceding series; in the first five sentences, the subjects would be stressed, and the voice would drop slightly on the verb, thus highlighting the list of personages. In the final sentence, the voice would rise, putting stress on the verb as the conclusion of the list.

Malcolm's rhetoric is thus fairly typical of black expression. We have noted the resemblance between the syntax of Langston Hughes and the black music that he admired and imitated. Dick Gregory's recording, "The Light Side, The Dark Side," carries along certain refrains, such as "you youngsters got a big job," "we tired of these white insults," that his jokes and anecdotes illuminate. This excerpt from a Stokely Carmichael speech exemplifies the technique of refrain and repetition varied by the voice:

> Now you've got to be crystal clear on how you think and where you move. You've got to explain to people. I didn't go to Mississippi to fight anybody to sit next to them. I was fighting to get them off my back. That's what my fight is. That's what my fight is. I don't fight anybody to sit next to him. I don't want to sit next to them. I just want them to get the barriers out of my way. Because I don't want to sit next to Jim Clark, Eastland, Johnson, Humphrey, or none of the others. I just want them to get off my back. Get off my back.
>
> [*Blackamerican Literature,* ed. Ruth Miller]

In Malcolm X, the modulations of his speaking voice also impel his writing voice. The tone is the same; "isn't" and "victims" are italicized; the key idea is repeated within parallel and inverted forms.

Cleaver's writing bears the mark of the same oral tradition:

> In America everything is owned. Everything is held as private property. Someone has a brand on everything. There is nothing left over. Until recently, the blacks themselves were counted as part of somebody's private property, along with the chickens and goats. The blacks have not forgotten this, principally because they are still treated as if they are part of someone's inventory of assets—or perhaps, in this day of rage against the costs of welfare, blacks are listed among the nation's liabilities. On any account, however, blacks are in no position to respect or help maintain the institution of private property. What they want is to figure out a way to get some of that property for themselves, to divert it to their own needs. This is what it is all about, and this is the real brutality involved. This is the source of all brutality. [Cleaver, *Soul on Ice*]

(pp. 264-68)

The indignation of Malcolm X has a strong moral and intellectual slant; he chooses the pejorative word "crime," for example, to describe the children's ignorance of black history; he emphasizes the white man's sexual degeneracy, recalling the scenes from slavery that inspire the most vivid moral and psychological horror; the chief focus of his criticism is the white man's *historical* treatment of black people, which must be evoked vicariously through the images of rape, whereas the focus of the Panthers is more likely to be the immediate experience of police brutality and suppression. Malcolm's tone is highly serious and didactic, even prophetic, when he speaks of the doom God has planned for white civilization; he assumes the role of a Jeremiah. In listing the various experts of the West who have failed to solve the racist problem, he is addressing himself as a leader to a world community of leaders, condemning their ignorance and offering advice to correct their mistakes. His attitude toward the "sincere" whites is similar; he is a teacher with a lesson, demanding that his pupils change before it is too late. His voice is individualized by the stress patterns, which give the impression of inspired fervor, as of a minister with a message.

The focus of Cleaver's attack is not moral, but political and economic (the difference being a question of emphasis). The source of brutality is to be found in the institution of private property. He justifies assaults on property on the grounds that blacks have always been excluded from this institution; and, by implication, he identifies with the black so-called "criminal" who would walk into a bank with a gun and clean out the vault. Like Proudhon, he believes that property is theft. Malcolm X, on the other hand, tended to assume that the "racist problem," as he correctly designated it, stems in the first instance from white moral corruption and ignorance, and that the propertyless condition of blacks was a moral question. Cleaver's tone balances between anger and humor. The anger is serious, but the tone mocks and parodies the idea of property as a social value by repeating it in different contexts. He pauses to explore the satiric possibilities in the metaphor of inventory and cost. Each of the short sentences at the beginning, by repeating the idea of ownership, asks the reader to meditate on its ironies. What kind of order can be expected of a society where "someone has a brand on everything?" If there is "nothing left over," how and where are black people going to get "some of that property for themselves" except by taking it? The high moral plane of Malcolm's voice called attention to how far behind he had left his old pre-Muslim identity: he was in effect looking both ways—at his "brainwashed brothers and sisters" and at the guilty leaders of white society, both of whom he was urging to change. (pp. 270-71)

> *Stephen Butterfield, "History as Subjective Experience," in his* Black Autobiography in America, *University of Massachusetts Press, 1974, pp. 256-83.*

Paul John Eakin (essay date Summer 1976)

[*In the following essay, Eakin argues that* The Autobiography of Malcolm X *challenges traditional notions of the genre to which it ostensibly belongs.*]

When a complex and controversial figure writes a book that has achieved the distinction and popularity of ***The Autobiography of Malcolm X,*** it is inevitable that efforts will be made to place him and his work in the perspective of a literary tradition. Barrett John Mandel, for example, has identified in Malcolm X's story the paradigm of the traditional conversion narrative. His reading of Malcolm X's autobiography, and it is a characteristic one, assumes that the narrative expresses a completed self [see excerpt dated March 1972]. Further, Ross Miller has suggested that such an assumption is central to the expectations we bring to the reading of any autobiography: "The pose of the autobiographer as an experienced man is particularly effective because we expect to hear from someone who has a completed sense of his own life and is therefore in a position to tell what he has discovered" [see Further Reading]. Even Warner Berthoff, who has admirably defined Malcolm X's "extraordinary power to change and be changed" as "the distinctive rule of his life," seems to have been drawn to this sense of the completed self when he attempts to locate the ***Autobiography*** in a special and limited literary tradition, that of the political testament in which "some ruler or statesman sets down for the particular benefit of his people a summary of his own experience and wisdom" [see excerpt dated Winter 1971]. The rhetorical posture of Malcolm X in the last chapter would seem to confirm Berthoff's reading and to fulfill Miller's autobiographical expectations, for it is indeed that of the elder statesman summing up a completed life, a life that has, as it were, already ended:

> Anyway, now, each day I live as if I am already dead, and I tell you what I would like for you to do. When I *am* dead—I say it that way because from the things I *know,* I do not expect to live long enough to read this book in its finished form—I want you to just watch and see if I'm not right in what I say: that the white man, in his press, is going to identify me with "hate."

If Malcolm X's anticipation of his imminent death confers on this final phase of autobiographical retrospection a posthumous authority, it is nevertheless an authority that he exercises here to defend himself against the fiction of the completed self that his interpreters—both black and white, in the event—were to use against him. Each of his identities turned out to be provisional, and even this voice from the grave was the utterance not of an ultimate identity but merely of the last one in the series of roles that Malcolm X had variously assumed, lived out, and discarded.

Alex Haley's "Epilogue" to the ***Autobiography*** reveals the fictive nature of this final testamentary stance which Berthoff regards as definitive. Here Haley, Malcolm X's collaborator in the ***Autobiography*** reports that the apparent uncertainty and confusion of Malcolm X's views were widely discussed in Harlem during the last months of Malcolm X's life, while Malcolm X himself, four days before his death, said in an interview, "I'm man enough to tell you that I can't put my finger on exactly what my philosophy is now, but I'm flexible." Moreover, the account of the composition of the ***Autobiography*** given by Haley in the "Epilogue" makes it clear that the fiction of the autobiographer as a man with "a completed sense of his own life" is especially misleading in the case of Malcolm X, for even Haley and the book that was taking shape in his hands were out of phase with the reality of Malcolm X's life and identity. Thus Haley acknowledges that he "never dreamed" of Malcolm X's break with Elijah Muhammad "until the actual rift became public," although the break overturned the design that had guided Malcolm X's dictations of his life story to Haley up to that point. The disparity between the traditional autobiographical fiction of the completed self and the biographical fact of Malcolm X's ceaselessly evolving identity may lead us, as it did Malcolm X himself, to enlarge our understanding of the limits and the possibilities of autobiography.

. . . . .

The original dedication of the ***Autobiography,*** which Malcolm X gave to Haley before the dictations had even begun, places the work squarely in one of the most ancient traditions of the genre, that of the exemplary life:

> This book I dedicate to the Honorable Elijah Muhammad, who found me here in America in the muck and mire of the filthiest civilization and society on this earth, and pulled me out, cleaned me up, and stood me on my feet, and made me the man that I am today.

This dedication (later cancelled) motivates more than half of the ***Autobiography*** in its final version. This book would be the story of a conversion, and Malcolm X's statement recapitulates in capsule form the essential pattern of such narratives: in the moment of conversion a new identity is discovered; further, this turning point sharply defines a two-part, before-after time scheme for the narrative; the movement of the self from "lost" to "found" constitutes the plot; and, finally, the very nature of the experience supplies an evangelical motive for autobiography.

What concerns us here, however, is not the much-studied features of conversion and the ease with which they may be translated into the formal elements of autobiographical narrative, but rather the natural and seemingly inevitable inference that the individual first discovers the shape of his life and then writes the life on the basis of this discovery. Some version of this temporal fiction, of course, lies behind most autobiography, and I would emphasize it as a corollary to Miller's definition of the completed self: the notion that living one's life precedes writing about it, that the life is in some sense complete and that the autobiographical process takes place afterward, somehow outside the realm of lapsing time in which the life proper necessarily unfolds. The evangelical bias of conversion narrative is especially interesting in this regard, for it supplies a predisposition for such an autobiographer to accept this supporting fiction as fact, since he believes that conversion works a definitive transition from shifting false beliefs to a fixed vision of the one truth. It is, accordingly, when a new discovery about the shape of one's life takes place during the writing of one's story that an autobiographer may be forced to recognize the presence and nature of the fictions on which his narrative is based. The experience of Malcolm X in his final period did foster such a recognition, and this knowledge and its consequences for autobiographical narrative may instruct us in the complex relation that necessarily obtains between living a life and writing about it. However, before we consider the ***Autobiography*** from the vantage point of the man who was becoming "El-Hajj Malik El-Shabazz" (Chapter 18), let us look at the ***Autobiography*** as it was originally conceived by the man whose first conversion in prison had transformed him from "Satan" (Chapter 10) to "Minister Malcolm X" (Chapter 13). This is, of course, the way we do look at the ***Autobiography*** when we begin to read it for the first time, especially if we are relatively unfamiliar with the life of Malcolm X.

The Malcolm X of these years was firmly in command of the shape of his life, tracing his sense of this shape to the pivotal and structuring illumination of conversion itself. At this point his understanding of the design of his experience, especially his baffled fascination with the radical discontinuity between the old Adam and the new, closely parallels the state of St. Augustine, Jonathan Edwards, and many another sinner touched by gracious affections, so much so that the student of spiritual autobiography is likely to feel himself at home on familiar ground:

> For evil to bend its knees, admitting its guilt, to implore the forgiveness of God, is the hardest thing in the world. . . . When finally I was able to make myself stay down—I didn't know what to say to Allah. . . . I still marvel at how swiftly my previous life's thinking pattern slid away from me, like snow off a roof. It is as though someone else I knew of had lived by hustling and crime. I would be startled to catch myself thinking in a remote way of my earlier self as another person.

If we consider Malcolm X's account of his life up to the time of his break with Elijah Muhammad (in Chapter 16, appropriately entitled "Out"), what we have in fact is a story that falls rather neatly into two sections roughly equal in length, devoted respectively to his former life as a sinner (Chapters 3-9) and to his present life as one of Elijah Muhammad's ministers (Chapters 10-15). This two-part structure is punctuated by two decisive experiences: his repudiation of the white world of his youth in Mason, Michigan, and his conversion to Islam in prison at Norfolk, Massachusetts.

Malcolm X describes the "first major turning point of my life" at the end of the second chapter, his realization that in white society he was not free "to become whatever *I* wanted to be." The shock to the eighth-grade boy was profound, for despite his traumatic childhood memories of the destruction of his family by white society, Malcolm X had embraced the white success ethic by the time he was in junior high school: "I was trying so hard . . . to be white." What follows, in Chapters 3 through 9, is Malcolm X's account of his life as a ghetto hustler, his first "career," just as his role as a Black Muslim minister was to be his second. If Allah preserved him from the fate of an Alger hero or a Booker T. Washington, from a career as a "successful" shoeshine boy or a self-serving member of the "black bourgeoisie," he was nevertheless destined to enact a kind of inverse parody of the white man's rise to success as he sank deeper and deeper into a life of crime. This is the portion of the ***Autobiography*** that has been singled out for its vividness by the commentators, with the result that the conversion experience and its aftermath in Chapters 10 through 15 have been somewhat eclipsed. It would be possible, of course, to see in the popularity of this section nothing more than the universal appeal of any evocation of low life and evil ways. In addition, this preference may reflect an instinctive attraction to a more personal mode of autobiography with plenty of concrete self-revelation instead of the more formal testimony of an exemplary life. Certainly Alex Haley responded strongly to this narrative, and so did Malcolm X, though he tried to restrain himself:

> Then it was during recalling the early Harlem days that Malcolm X really got carried away. One night, suddenly, wildly, he jumped up from his chair and, incredibly, the fearsome black demagogue was scatsinging and popping his fingers, "re-bop-de-bop-blap-blam-" and then grabbing a vertical pipe with one hand (as the girl partner) he went jubilantly lindy-hopping around, his coattail and the long legs and the big feet flying as they had in those Harlem days. And then almost as suddenly, Malcolm X caught himself and sat back down, and for the rest of that session he was decidedly grumpy.

Haley captures here the characteristic drama of the autobiographical act that the juxtaposition of the self as it is and as it was inevitably generates. Malcolm X's commitment to his public role as "the fearsome black demagogue" conflicts with his evident pleasure in recapturing an earlier and distinctly personal identity, the historical conked and zooted lindy champ of the Roseland Ballroom in Roxbury, the hustling hipster of Small's Paradise in Harlem.

If the ***Autobiography*** had ended with the fourteenth or fifteenth chapter, what we would have, I suggest, is a narrative which could be defined as an extremely conventional example of autobiographical form distinguished chiefly by the immediacy and power of its imaginative recreation of the past. It is true that this much of the ***Autobiography*** would usefully illustrate the survival of the classic pattern of conversion narrative in the contemporary literature of spiritual autobiography, but this interest would necessarily be a limited one given Malcolm X's reticence about the drama of the experience of conversion itself. For Malcolm X the fact of conversion is decisive, life-shaping, identity-altering, but unlike the most celebrated spiritual autobiographers of the past he chooses not to dramatize the experience itself or to explore its psychological dynamics.

. . . . .

It seems probable that when Malcolm X began his dictations to Haley in 1963 he anticipated that his narrative would end with an account of his transformation into the national spokesman of Elijah Muhammad's Nation of Islam (the material covered in Chapters 14 and 15 of Haley's text). This was not destined to be the end of the story, however, for the pace of Malcolm X's history, always lively, became tumultuous in 1963 and steadily accelerated until his assassination in 1965. In this last period Malcolm X was to experience two events that destroyed the very premises of the autobiography he had set out to write. The most well-known convert to the Black Muslim religion was first to break with Elijah Muhammad (Chapter 16, "Out") and then to make a pilgrimage to Mecca (Chapter 17), where he underwent a second conversion to what he now regarded as the true religion of Islam. The revelation that Elijah Muhammad was a false prophet shattered the world of Malcolm X and the shape of the life he had been living for twelve years:

> I was like someone who for twelve years had had an inseparable, beautiful marraige—and then suddenly one morning at breakfast the marraige partner had thrust across the table some divorce papers.
>
> I felt as though something in *nature* had failed, like the sun or the stars. It was that incredible a phenomenon to me—something too stupendous to conceive.

The autobiographical fiction of the completed self was exploded for good, although Malcolm X, with a remarkable fidelity to the truth of his past, was to preserve the fragments in the earlier chapters of the ***Autobiography,*** as we have seen.

The illumination at Mecca made Malcolm X feel "like a complete human being" for the first time "in my thirty-nine years on this earth," and he assumed a new name to symbolize this new sense of identity, El-Hajj Malik El-Shabazz. In the final chapters of the book (18 and 19) we see Malcolm X in the process of discarding the "old 'hate' and 'violence' image" of the militant preacher of Elijah Muhammad's Nation of Islam, but before he created a design for the life of this new self he was brutally gunned down on February 21, 1965. In fact, it is not at all certain that Malcolm X would have arrived at any single, definitive formulation for the shape of his life even if he had continued to live. In the final pages of the last chapter he observes:

> No man is given but so much time to accomplish whatever is his life's work. My life in particular never has stayed fixed in one position for very long. You have seen how throughout my life, I have often known unexpected drastic changes.

With these words Malcolm X articulates a truth already latent but ungrasped in the autobiographical narrative he originally set out to write in his evangelical zeal: his life was not now and never had been a life of the simpler pattern of the traditional conversion story.

Because this complex vision of his existence is clearly not that of the early sections of the ***Autobiography,*** Alex Haley and Malcolm X were forced to confront the consequences of this discontinuity in perspective for the narrative, already a year old. It was Haley who raised the issue when he learned, belatedly, of the rift between Malcolm X and Elijah Muhammad, for he had become worried that an embittered Malcolm X might want to rewrite the book from his new perspective, and this at a time when Haley regarded their collaboration as virtually complete ("by now I had the bulk of the needed life story material in hand"). Malcolm X's initial response settled the matter temporarily: "I want the book to be the way it was." Haley's concern, however, was justified, for a few months later, following Malcolm X's journey to Mecca, Haley was "appalled" to find that Malcolm X had "red-inked" many of the places in the manuscript "where he had told of his almost father-and-son relationship with Elijah Muhammad." Haley describes this crisis of the autobiographical act as follows:

> Telephoning Malcolm X, I reminded him of his previous decision, and I stressed that if those chapters contained such telegraphing to readers of what would lie ahead, then the book would automatically be robbed of some of its building suspense and drama. Malcolm X said gruffly, "Whose book is this?" I told him "yours, of course," and that I only made the objection in my position as a writer. He said that he would have to think about it. I was heartsick at the prospect that he might want to re-edit the entire book into a polemic against Elijah Muhammad. But late that night, Malcolm X telephoned. "I'm sorry. You're right. I was upset about something. Forget what I wanted changed, let what you already had stand." I never again gave him chapters to review unless I was with him. Several times I would covertly watch him frown and wince as he read, but he never again asked for any change in what he had originally said.

Malcolm X's refusal to change the narrative reflects, finally, his acceptance of change as the fundamental law of existence, and yet, curiously, by the very fidelity of this refusal he secures for the remembered past, and for the acts of memory devoted to it, such measure of permanence as the forms of art afford.

The exchange between the two men poses the perplexing issue of perspective in autobiography with an instructive clarity: to which of an autobiographer's selves should he or even can he be true? What are the strategies by which he may maintain a dual or plural allegiance without compromise to his present vision of the truth? In fact, the restraint of the "telegraphing" does leave the climax intact, and yet Malcolm X's decision not to revise the preceding narrative does not produce the kind of obvious discontinuity in authorial perspective that we might expect as a result. Haley's part in this is considerable, for his contribution to the ultimate shape of the ***Autobiography*** was more extensive and fundamental than his narrowly literary concerns here with foreshadowing and suspense might seem to suggest. Despite his tactful protest that he was only a "writer," Haley himself had been instrumental in the playing out of the autobiographical drama between one Malcolm X, whose faith in Elijah Muhammad had supplied him with his initial rationale for an autobiography, and another, whose repudiation of Elijah Muhammad made the ***Autobiography*** the extraordinary human document it eventually became. If the outcome of this drama was formalized in Malcolm X's expulsion from the Nation of Islam, it was already in the wind by the time the dictations began in earnest in 1963. Alex Haley was one to read between the lines.

Haley recalls in the "Epilogue" that at the very outset of the project he had been in fundamental disagreement with Malcolm X about the narrative he would help him write. He reports that Malcolm X wanted the focus to be on Elijah Muhammad and the Nation of Islam: "He would bristle when I tried to urge him that the proposed book was *his* life." At this early stage of the collaboration Haley portrays two Malcolms: a loyal public Malcolm X describing a religious movement in which he casts himself in a distinctly subordinate and self-effacing role, and a subversive private Malcolm X scribbling a trenchant counter-commentary in telegraphic red-ink ball point on any available scrap of paper. Determined to feature this second Malcolm X in the autobiography, Haley lured this suppressed identity out into the open by leaving white paper napkins next to Malcolm X's coffee cup to tap his closed communications with himself. Haley carefully retrieved this autobiographical fall-out, and taking his cue from one of these napkin revelations, interestingly about women, Haley "cast a bait" with a question about Malcolm X's mother. Haley reports that with this textbook display of Freudian savvy he was able to land the narrative he was seeking:

> From this stream-of-consciousness reminiscing I finally got out of him the foundation for this book's beginning chapters, "Nightmare" and "Mascot." After that night, he never again hesitated to tell me even the most intimate details of his personal life, over the next two years. His talking about his mother triggered something.

From the very earliest phase of the dictations, then, the autobiography began to take on a much more personal and private coloration than Malcolm X originally intended. What Elijah Muhammad accomplished, autobiographically speaking, when he "silenced" Malcolm X, was to legitimatize the private utterance of the napkins which had already found its way into the mainstream of a narrative initially conceived as an orthodox work of evangelical piety. After his separation from the Nation of Islam, Malcolm X comments that he began "to think for myself," "after twelve years of never thinking for as much as five minutes about myself." Haley reports two napkin messages of this period that signal the consequences of Malcolm X's new sense of himself and his power for the nearly-completed ***Autobiography:***

> He scribbled one night, "You have not converted a man because you have silenced him. John Viscount Morley." And the same night, almost illegibly, "I was going downhill until he picked me up, but the more I think of it, we picked each other up."

Not only was Malcolm X rejecting the simple clarity of the original conversion narrative he had set out to tell, but he was no longer disposed to sacrifice to the greater glory of Elijah Muhammad his own agency in the working out of his life story.

. . . . .

In the final chapters of the ***Autobiography*** and in the "Epilogue," as Malcolm X moves toward a new view of his story as a life of changes, he expresses an impressive, highly self-conscious awareness of the problems of autobiographical narrative, and specifically of the complex relationship between living a life and writing an autobiography. All of his experience in the last packed months, weeks, and days of his life worked to destroy his earlier confident belief in the completed self, the completed life, and hence in the complete life story. Thus he writes to Haley in what is possibly his final statement about the ***Autobiography:*** "I just want to read it one more time because I don't expect to read it in finished form." As Malcolm X saw it at the last, all autobiographies are by nature incomplete and they can not, accordingly, have a definite shape. As a life changes, so any sense of the shape of a life must change; the autobiographical process evolves because it is part of the life, and the identity of the autobiographical "I" changes and shifts. Pursuing the logic of such speculations, Malcolm X even wonders whether any autobiography can keep abreast of the unfolding of personal history: "How is it possible to write one's autobiography in a world so fast-changing as this?" And so he observes to Haley, "I hope the book is proceeding rapidly, for events concerning my life happen so swiftly, much of what has already been written can easily be outdated from month to month. In life, nothing is permanent; not even life itself."

At the end, then, Malcolm X came to reject the traditional autobiographical fiction that the life comes first, and then the writing of the life; that the life is in some sense complete and that the autobiographical process simply records the final achieved shape. This fiction is based upon a suspension of time, as though the "life," the subject, could sit still long enough for the autobiographical "I," the photographer, to snap its picture. In fact, as Malcolm X was to learn, the "life" itself will not hold still; it changes, shifts position. And as for the autobiographical act, it requires much more than an instant of time to take the picture, to write the story. As the act of composition extends in time, so it enters the life-stream, and the fictive separation between life and life story, which is so convenient—even necessary—to the writing of autobiography, dissolves.

Malcolm X's final knowledge of the incompleteness of the self is what gives the last pages of the ***Autobiography*** together with the "Epilogue" their remarkable power: the vision of a man whose swiftly unfolding career has outstripped the possibilities of the traditional autobiography he had meant to write. It is not in the least surprising that Malcolm X's sobering insights into the limitations of autobiography are accompanied by an increasingly insistent desire to disengage himself from the ambitions of the autobiographical process. Thus he speaks of the ***Autobiography*** to Haley time and again as though, having disabused himself of any illusion that the narrative could keep pace with his life, he had consigned the book to its fate, casting it adrift as hopelessly obsolete. Paradoxically, nowhere does the book succeed, persuade, more than in its confession of failure as autobiography. This is the fascination of *The Education of Henry Adams,* and Malcolm X, like Adams, leaves behind him the husks of played-out autobiographical paradigms. The indomitable reality of the self transcends and exhausts the received shapes for a life that are transmitted by the culture, and yet the very process of discarding in itself works to structure an apparently shapeless experience. Despite—or because of—the intractability of life to form, the fiction of the completed self, which lies at the core of the autobiographical enterprise, cannot be readily dispatched. From its ashes, phoenix-like, it reconstitutes itself in a new guise. Malcolm X's work, and Adams' as well, generate a sense that the uncompromising commitment to the truth of one's own nature, which requires the elimination of false identities and careers one by one, will yield at the last the pure ore of a final and irreducible selfhood. This is the ultimate autobiographical dream. (pp. 230-42)

Paul John Eakin, "Malcolm X and the Limits of Autobiography," in Criticism, *Vol. XVIII, No. 3, Summer, 1976, pp. 230-42.*

G. Thomas Couser (essay date 1979)

[*Couser is an American educator and critic. The following excerpt is taken from his* American Autobiography: The Prophetic Mode, *in which Couser includes* The Autobiography of Malcolm X, *among other works, in an examination of "what was distinctly American about our classic, or major, autobiographies." Couser commented in an interview with* Contemporary Authors: *"The most striking feature about these books is their tendency to venture prophetic interpretations of American history. The shape of the author's life is often compared to the course of American history, either actual or ideal; as a result, the tradition becomes a dialogue on what it means to be American."*]

It was probably inevitable that [***The Autobiography of Malcolm X***] would display the characteristics of the prophetic mode, for, as his biographer [Peter Goldman has noted in *The Death and Life of Malcolm X*], Malcolm's essential role was not that of an original thinker or even a strategist but that of a "revolutionary of the spirit"—a prophet. His awareness of his prophetic role in life is obvious in the narrative, and evidence in his collaborator's epilogue suggests that he was aware that tact and delicacy were required for the successful treatment of that role in autobiography. He strove to resist the temptation to attribute too much importance to himself and to write an exemplary and didactic narrative in which his own experience of family instability, poverty, unemployment, and discrimination would stand for the plight of all American blacks.

Ironically, however, the power and the complexity of the narrative result from the frustration of Malcolm's original intentions. This irony and the evolving form of the autobiography are best understood in the context of his predicament as an autobiographer. When the book was begun in 1963, Malcolm was still a member and faithful minister of the Nation of Islam; the original dedication was to Elijah Muhammad, and the proceeds were to go to the Black Muslims. Malcolm saw himself more as a prophet or propagandist than as an autobiographer. Instead of exploring the inconsistencies in the Black Muslim ideology, Malcolm wished simply to convey its powerful message. The autobiography was conceived, then, wholly within an orthodox framework. Just as he frequently prefaced remarks in his speeches with a conventional formula attributing his ideas to "the Honorable Elijah Muhammad," Malcolm chose, as an autobiographer, to ascribe the coherence and significance of his life to Elijah or Allah. His conception of his role as a passive agent of God encouraged him to cast his autobiography in the form of a spiritual autobiography with the emphasis on his conversion and his ministry. Thus, his collaborator, Alex Haley, reported [in his "Epilogue" to the ***Autobiography***] that in the early stages his notebook "contained nothing but Black Muslim philosophy, praise of Mr. Muhammad, and the 'evils' of 'the white devil.' He would bristle when I tried to urge him that the proposed book was *his* life." At this point, Malcolm seems to have been reluctant to consider his personal identity as separate or separable from the corporate identity provided by the Nation. Had this conception of his identity and role been realized, the autobiography would have been a one-dimensional polemic. Paradoxically, as events frustrated Malcolm's original prophetic impulse, the book became not only a multidimensional self-portrait but more compelling prophecy.

Two significant developments complicated the process of writing and thus enriched the book. First, Haley, impatient with Malcolm's singlemindedness, probed his almost compulsive misogyny until he touched its source—Malcolm's pity and anger toward his mother, who had broken down under the strain of managing her family alone. This breakthrough released Malcolm into preconversion life, not only his nightmarish childhood but also his career as a ghetto hustler. In doing so, it freed him from the confining role of the didactic autobiographer. While the retrospective interpretation of these years is that of the doctrinaire ideologue, the nostalgic treatment of some episodes belies this. For even as the sober Black

Muslim minister narrated his escape from a misguided youth, the private Malcolm recaptured some of the sensations and emotions of those years. Notably, he delighted in recalling the music, re-creating the language, and reliving the uninhibited dancing he enjoyed in his early days as a hustler. As spontaneous memory competed with detailed analysis, the pleasure in the retelling conflicted with the didactic interpretation. Thus, with Haley's prompting, the self-styled prophet became a reminiscent autobiographer, and the autobiography was individualized and deepened.

A second complication stemmed from Malcolm's growing disenchantment with Elijah Muhammad and his sudden excommunication from the Nation. Although this development actually paralleled and reinforced the first, Haley did not welcome it, for it changed Malcolm's perspective on events already recorded and thus threatened to invalidate the form the narrative had taken. For Malcolm, of course, it did more than that; it threatened his sanity by depriving him of the source of his sense of identity. Ultimately, however, this unexpected dislocation, which complicated Malcolm's life and autobiography simultaneously, forced him out of conventional autobiographical forms and toward a new prophetic vision. The stature of the book, finally, derives from the fact that its composition coincided with a crisis that demanded a radical reexamination of his ideas and a redefinition of himself.

The finished narrative divides Malcolm's life into four fairly distinct periods: his childhood and adolescence (chapters 1 and 2), his hustler phase (chapters 3 to 10), his career as a Black Muslim (chapters 11 to 15), and his life after excommunication (chapters 16 to 19). The first section is characterized by a strong didacticism, which locates the origins of his later activities and uses his experience to expose American racism; for example, he describes his family's condition when they were wards of the state as "legal modern slavery." The second section combines nostalgic reminiscence and titillating confession with an initiation narrative (as Malcolm gives up his naive assimilationist ambitions and enters the underworld of the black community) and a parodic success story (as he gains status and power in his new environment). However, the framework that orders and controls the narrative, even in this evocative section, is that of the didactic conversion narrative. This becomes clear in the middle of the book—at its structural and thematic center—when Malcolm X, in prison, is converted to the Nation of Islam. His exposure to the Black Muslim myth of black supremacy came at an opportune moment when his mind was prepared for illumination and his soul for salvation. The new ideology explained and excused Malcolm Little's troubled life and provided him with a new sense of himself: "I still marvel at how swiftly my previous life's thinking pattern slid away from me, like snow off a roof. . . . I would be startled to catch myself thinking of my earlier self as another person." This conversion also gave a new impetus and a new focus to a self-education already begun in the prison library. Investigating history in search of a communal past and probing the dictionary in quest of a new voice and language appropriate to a new vision, Malcolm unwittingly prepared himself for his role as a Black Muslim minister and prophet. In fact, even before his release from prison and his formal acceptance into the faith, he began to proselytize among his fellow inmates.

Malcolm notes ironically that the most liberating experience of his life thus far had occurred in prison. Yet he is less successful at communicating the sense of this experience than he had been at re-creating his previous life. The narrative of Malcolm's previous life certainly makes his conversion credible, and there is no doubt of its sincerity and significance. But the reader is given no sense of the experience which suggests that it consisted of more than an intellectual and emotional commitment to an ideology which offered him a redeeming self-image and a useful mythology. Nor does Malcolm acknowledge at this point the possibility that his experience of liberation had made him, in a sense, a prisoner of a racist ideology. Instead of indicating the provisional nature of his conversion, he lets it stand as a crucial, if imperfectly communicated experience.

Upon leaving prison in 1952, Malcolm immediately purchased new glasses, a suitcase, and a watch—symbols of his new vision, his new vocation, and his new time-consciousness. As part of his initiation into the Nation, he also acquired an "X" in place of his last name—to signify both the things he was no more (a Christian, for example) and the unknown quantity he now represented to the white man. Malcolm X then became a Black Muslim minister—a faithful servant of and eventually the spokesman for Elijah Muhammad. Because of his responsible position and his positive and stable self-image, this section lacks the exciting incidents and rapid role changes of the previous section. Rather, it becomes a mixture of clerical memoir and political testament as Malcolm seeks to recount his achievements as a Muslim organizer and to communicate the essence of Muslim ideology. This section, then, records not personal growth but the growth of the Nation, not self-education but the enlightenment of the black masses.

The narrative does recount another Franklinian rise to prominence and power—now within an administrative hierarchy rather than the fluid and treacherous society of the underworld. But Malcolm's didacticism, previously limited to the commentary upon events, now becomes the *content* of the narrative as he sets forth the prophetic myth of the Black Muslims. As a result, in this section the exposition of doctrine not only supplements but also displaces narrative. There is much precedent for this in Thoreau, Adams, Sullivan, and Wright, and the tendency derives naturally from a prophetic impulse. Yet this section, which most closely corresponds to Malcolm's original intentions, is the least compelling part of the book; the narrative's polemical extreme does not provide its climax.

Nor does this section deliver what it promises. Although Malcolm claims to have acquired a radically new vision of himself and of history, the narrative fails to demonstrate this. As Carol Ohmann has observed, he continued to be more interested in objectively measurable achievements than in subjective experience [*American Quarterly* 22, No. 2, 1970]. Just as his ideology, like a mirror image of white racism, reverses some elements while others remain the same, Malcolm remains interested in power over others, for different reasons. Similarly, his vision of society is still that of a jungle, although individual competition has been replaced by racial struggle. Thus, although his goals and his cosmology are new, his consciousness does not seem essentially different, and his prophetic vision, however revolutionary, is secondhand and somewhat simplistic. Furthermore, while Malcolm has clearly grown as a *man,* he seems to have retreated, as a *narrator,* from a complex, ambivalent viewpoint to a monocular, orthodox one.

The final chapter of this section, "Icarus," concludes with a pledge of loyalty to the movement that had rescued, defined, and ordained him: "I silently vowed to Allah that I would never forget that the wings I wore had been put on by the religion of Islam. That fact I have never forgotten . . . not for one second." Yet Malcolm found that his role as the dynamic organizer of new temples and as spokesman for the movement to the world inevitably drew attention to himself and away from the reclusive leader of the Nation. Inevitably, too, his mind became impatient with the orthodoxy, and engaged by the paradoxes, of Black Muslim ideology. Soon he was accused of personal ambition and insubordination—in effect, of forgetting that he was a humble servant of Elijah Muhammad.

More than a clash of personalities, the friction between Malcolm X and Muhammad was a manifestation of power politics within the Nation: Malcolm's aggressive efforts as an organizer and proselytizer threatened Muhammad's control of the movement even as they expanded his power base. But the friction also stemmed from Malcolm's growing tendency to distinguish between Allah and Elijah and to assert his right to interpret Allah's will for himself. To put it another way, he was beginning to resolve the inconsistencies in Black Muslim ideology in his own way.

Thus certain tensions, suppressed in the early part of the narrative, begin to surface: those between the Black Muslims' disciplined bourgeois morality and their revolutionary rhetoric; between their policy of nonengagement in politics or protest and their militant posture; between the claim that the Nation was a brotherhood and the fact of its strict hierarchical organization; between the religious and secular aspects of the movement; and finally, between the indictment of American racism and the adoption of a mythology of reverse racism. Malcolm's personal tendency was to secularize the ideology and move toward a more activist stance than that endorsed by Muhammad. By degrees, he diverged from an almost Calvinistic dependence on God to deliver his people and began to assume a more Arminian position that held black people responsible for achieving their own liberation. (In this respect, his development recalls Franklin's secularization of Puritan and Quaker myths and Douglass's movement from a providential framework of interpretation to an acknowledgment of his own initiative in his "conversion.") Although he stopped short of recommending violence or revolution, he posed a threat both to the authority of Muhammad and to the vested interests of the Nation.

The chapter entitled "Out" records Malcolm's silencing and his excommunication from the church that had saved him. The narrative takes on yet another conventional form—that of the apologia—as Malcolm attempts to defend himself against the Nation's portrayal of him as a heretic and traitor. His brief against this accusation consists of the argument that he was more faithful to the Nation's true ideals than were its other established leaders, that if he erred it was only through an excess of zeal: "If I harbored any personal disappointment whatsoever, it was that privately I was convinced that our Nation of Islam could be an even greater force in the American black man's overall struggle—if we engaged in more *action.*" Although this apologia is sincere, it is not entirely convincing, for the narrative has revealed in him an eagerness, a determination, a willfulness, and a degree of personal initiative that would threaten such an autocracy as that of the Nation. The reader can understand his ouster without sympathizing with it; it is easier to side with Malcolm than it is to accept his careful self-defense.

More important than the real reasons for his expulsion from the Nation was its effect on Malcolm's life. He confesses that it was a traumatic experience for him: "I felt as though something in *nature* had failed, like the sun or the stars." Deprived of all communal support from the institution that had offered him a new identity and provided his entire frame of reference for over a decade, Malcolm had to refashion his thought and his self-conception simultaneously: " . . . after twelve years of never thinking for as much as five minutes about myself, I became able finally to muster the nerve and the strength to start facing the facts, to think for myself." The expulsion did not negate his conversion: he could still cling to his faith in Allah. Yet it instantly deprived him of the institutional and ideological security of the Nation. Carrying on his work meant generating new organizations and new programs and revising his ideology even as he attempted to redefine himself. In effect, he had to re-create both the authority and the content of his prophecy.

The rest of the narrative is dominated by his attempt to reconcile the sometimes divergent secular and religious aspects of his thought. This tension is obvious in his need to create two institutions in order to further his goals. On the one hand, he founded the Muslim Mosque, Inc., which he hoped would attract some converts from the Nation of Islam and provide a broader religious base for economic, political, and social programs. On the other hand, the Organization of Afro-American Unity was to have its base in a more secular sense of international racial brotherhood. Both were intended to free him from the restrictions of Black Muslim orthodoxy on his thought and action. Yet the OAAU represents a new dimension in his thought, an international perspective on the race problem, while the Muslim Mosque reveals his desire to maintain some continuity with his past.

The establishment of the Muslim Mosque may also be seen as part of an attempt to maintain a claim to religious legitimacy, for his excommunication had threatened to deprive him of his prophetic stature. His new inquiry into orthodox Moslem religion and his eventual pilgrimage to Mecca also helped reestablish this sense of himself, but the new conversion he experienced on his pilgrimage further complicated his predicament. Among pilgrims of many races at Mecca, Malcolm X experienced a novel kind of color-blind tolerance and underwent at least a partial liberation from the Black Muslims' narrow race-consciousness to a more universal, more humanistic set of values: "Everything about the pilgrimage atmosphere accented the Oneness of Man under One God." In part, this conversion may be accounted for by the special treatment afforded him when he was recognized as a celebrity among the pilgrims and by the much-needed feeling of acceptance into a community; in part, by his consciousness that he needed to build a wider base of support in the United States. But at its core was a spontaneous awakening to a point of view that judged men not by their color but by their deeds.

This pilgrimage seems to have afforded him a rare but necessary moment of respite, tranquility, integration, and growth, and this conversion, more than his first one, was a truly liberating experience. Like John Woolman, he found that extending his geographical horizons extended his moral ones as well. Yet like his first conversion, this one is passed over rather quickly and superficially; we are told about rather than allowed to share in the change that occurred. Again, the spiritual or emotional dimension of his experience is sacrificed to the business of translating it into power. Once he is converted, as El-Hajj Malik El-Shabazz, he devotes himself to working out the ramifications of this potent new ideology for the resolution of racial problems. His "American-style thinking" is concerned with the application of public relations methods to the promotion of his new faith. Thus, although his pilgrimage did provide him with a momentary release from the opportunistic ethos which had dominated his experience, his new spiritual energy was soon diverted into secular channels, as though the sources of his new consciousness were not as worthy of attention as were programs designed to give it political expression.

Whatever tranquility and new assurance Malcolm experienced while on his pilgrimage and during his triumphal tour of Africa was challenged immediately upon his return to America, where he was beset by the everyday pressures of the life of a protest leader. The last chapter of the book portrays a prophet overwhelmed by the need to develop new organizations and tactics while still trying to assimilate his new vision. During this period of his life, the paradoxes of his predicament tended to become irresolvable contradictions. Even as he sought to establish his personal authority, he recognized that his new movement should have a more democratic organization than the Nation of Islam. In addition, his new sense of human brotherhood tended to evaporate amidst rumors that his life was in danger. Yet his fundamental problem was one of translating a less racist ideology into programs that would more effectively combat white racism, for his sense of the ideal unity of man did not alter his knowledge of the actual oppression of American blacks. In order to achieve broad-based support, he needed media coverage, but the media had stereotyped him as a militant racist and were not equipped to register his more subtle new ideology.

Malcolm's predicament as an autobiographer was also difficult, for his excommunication had invalidated the viewpoint that had governed most of the narrative. Nor did his second conversion yield a simple formula according to which the narrative could be continued or revised. Alex Haley discouraged Malcolm from revising the autobiography to make it an anti-Muhammad polemic in response to his own ouster; such a revision would sacrifice suspense and drama, he argued. After some hesitation, Malcolm accepted this viewpoint, arguing that a revision would, in a way, falsify his experience of his career as a Black Muslim; but he did insert material that criticized Muhammad and telegraphed the split. Deprived of his didactic narrative formula, Malcolm came to see the impossibility of writing an autobiography that would be a true equivalent of continual growth; events steadily outran the viewpoints they generated. He expressed his frustration in a note to Haley: "How is it possible to write one's autobiography in a world so fast-changing as this?"

Like *The Education of Henry Adams*, ***The Autobiography of Malcolm X*** is weighted in favor of the later years; the chapter "Out" comes about three-quarters of the way through, so that nearly a quarter of the book is dedicated to the last years of his life. Thus, in spite of the impossibility of his task, Malcolm continued, and he succeeded in conveying a sense of the desperation and hope of his final year. Increasingly, he sensed that his time was limited, but he did not abandon the autobiography to save languishing projects. Rather, as the threats against him escalated, he devoted more of his energy and dwindling time to his book, which he hoped would carry on his prophetic mission. One strong motive for continuing was to ensure that the book would include his second conversion and thus prevent his exploitation as a symbol of race hatred after his death. This intention was only partly realized, for Malcolm never fully assimilated his new vision, and the effect of the last chapter is one of groping, stumbling growth—of a man attempting to find adequate expression for a vision he found at once liberating and frustrating.

The indecision of this final period and the incompleteness of the autobiography have made it possible for members of various groups to claim, on the basis of partial evidence, that Malcolm was becoming one of them. It is truer to state that in his last years he was simply absorbed in the process of *becoming;* in spite of the dramatic changes that had already characterized his life, the text suggests that in his final phase the most profound transformation of all was under way. Thus, the book's power as prophetic autobiography lies not in its blunt exposition of Black Muslim ideology but in its bold portrayal of a prophet deprived of both his stature and his vision; its value as prophecy is not in the vision it contains but in the one it moves toward and prophesies.

As I have noted, the book displays features of many conventional autobiographical forms—success story, reminiscence, apology, and conversion narrative. But just as Malcolm X's identity could not be long confined to a single social role—even that of the Black Muslim minister whose ideology seemed to freeze his previous roles in a teleological progression—so his autobiography finally outruns the forms he retrospectively imposed upon his experience.

The narrative was finally completed, as well as cut off, by Malcolm's death, for the final stretch of the narrative, which seems so formless, is definitively shaped by an event which had not happened. The knowledge that his future was going to be taken from him, as his past had been, impelled Malcolm's efforts to make his life whole in autobiography. As he refused, in his last year, to be defined by others, so he avoided conventional formulas in bringing his life up to date.

Finally, his impending death becomes the crucial event of the book. His assassination gives the narrative symmetry, for its end recalls its beginning. Just as the dual role of his father as Baptist minister and Garveyite organizer is reflected in Malcolm's attempt to reconcile the religious and secular aspects of his thought at the end of his life, so the death of his father anticipates Malcolm's fate. Now, however, the perpetrators of the violence are not white bigots but, apparently, Black Muslims unwilling to tolerate a heretic and competitor. Malcolm's anticipation of his imminent death in the final pages recalls his days as a hustler, but his courage is now based on faith rather than drugs. Living each day resigned to death and struggling to complete a book he does not expect to read in finished form, he recalls the attributes of the traditional spiritual autobiographer. In his book, as in his life, his devotion was to the defeat of racism, and if he failed to destroy "the racist cancer . . . in the body of America," he did at least achieve an exemplary victory over it in his own soul. The price of that victory was his life, for Malcolm was destroyed by men who thought he had betrayed them, when in fact he had prophesied their liberation. (pp. 165-75)

G. Thomas Couser, "Three Contemporaries: Malcolm X, Norman Mailer, and Robert Pirsig," in his American Autobiography: The Prophetic Mode, *Amherst: The University of Massachusetts Press, 1979, pp. 164-96.*

Gordon O. Taylor (essay date Summer 1981)

[*Taylor is an American educator and critic. In the following excerpt from a discussion of the autobiographies of Malcolm X, Richard Wright, and James Baldwin, Taylor places* The Autobiography of Malcolm X *within a black American autobiographical tradition, asserting that the works of these authors share "the urge to articulate, as if for the first time, a sensibility at once determined and precluded by history."*]

"The problem of the twentieth century is the problem of the color-line," says [W.E.B.] Du Bois, "1900" to him as critical a symbolic juncture as Henry Adams would soon claim, for different reasons, in his [*Education of Henry Adams*]. The problem shared with Du Bois by Wright, Baldwin, Malcolm X, and others is that of voicing black self-consciousness so as to create it, or to re-create it in the context of twentieth-century America. At the common core of *Black Boy, Notes of a Native Son,* and ***The Autobiography of Malcolm X,*** in addition to [Du Bois's] *The Souls of Black Folk*—granting crucial differences among them—is the urge to articulate, as if for the first time, a sensibility at once determined and precluded by history. The same urge is felt in, and is itself a subject of, such novels as James Weldon Johnson's *The Autobiography of an Ex-Coloured Man* and Ralph Ellison's *Invisible Man.* Never fully possessed of what Baldwin calls the "white centuries" of European culture, dispossessed as well of the African past, the Afro-American protagonists in these works, whether fictional or autobiographical personae, project themselves in terms of both being and nothingness. They imagine their lives as both shaped and negated by historical pressures rooted in race—lives in at least one respect over before begun. Yet they also envision their individualities as unformed, and therefore open to unbounded possibility residing in personal energies compressed and awaiting release. (pp. 341-42)

"How is it possible to write one's autobiography in a world so fast-changing as this?" asks Malcolm X, in a letter quoted by Alex Haley in his epilogue to ***The Autobiography of Malcolm X*** (1965). The question is one asked implicitly by Henry Adams from first page to last of [*The Education of Henry Adams*], the outer world as ostensible subject having long since given way to demands of the inner, the autobiographical act compelled by the changes within and without which seem to prevent it. Change is for Malcolm X a matter of escalating tension between the idea of black life in America, as fixed in the design imposed by slavery, and a contrary notion, inseparable from the first, of possibilities achievable through black resistance to that design. This is essentially the double-consciousness Du Bois projects in *The Souls of Black Folk,* which gave Malcolm his first "glimpse into the black people's history before they came to this country." Under pressure of double-consciousness reminiscent of Wright, between narrowing lines of historical force, Malcolm's voice accelerates toward the end he foresees, creating in the process a self who survives before in fact destroyed. Considered in relation to the literary patterns surveyed above—of interplay between the written and the unwritten record, of the urge to articulate black self out of silence—the fact that the book was spoken to Haley is of secondary importance. ***The Autobiography of Malcolm X*** is what it has been called (here in Peter Goldman's words) by many, "a great American life, a compelling and irreplaceable book." The life violently ended (but no more violently, Malcolm argued before the fact, than the inner lives of black Americans continue to be lived) is now begun on a pilgrimage of text, which Haley makes clear is in its essence Malcolm's. The issue is finally one of readership as much as authorship, as Du Bois suggested in his plea to God the Reader that his book be truly heard. As Ellison's narrator says in *Invisible Man* (the words welling in the silence after "There's Many a Thousand Gone" is sung), "A whole unrecorded history is spoken then, . . . listen to what is said."

The story is told as Baldwin said it must be, compulsively, in symbols and signs, in hieroglyphics such as the cryptic notations Malcolm made on paper napkins Haley learned to leave near him during interviews. Malcolm X speaks from beyond his conversion to "the Lost-Found Nation of Islam here in this wilderness of North America," beyond also his break with Elijah Muhammad, a change in a "life of changes" moving him toward a core of constant self. He speaks at times from a sense of being "already dead," premonitions of assassination blending with the "whispered" rather than the documented truth of his father's lynching, with the historical fatality of his race's enslavement. Violence, as he puts it, "runs in my family." Such "posthumous[illegible]s" of voice, recalling moments of similar sensibility in Baldwin, Wright, and Du Bois, is no less emotionally convincing for being a rhetorical pose. The making of the book is on one level a political act, like Malcolm's reenactment of his father's involvement in Marcus Garvey's "back to Africa" movement in his own commitment to the Muslim doctrine of separation from white America. The personal progressively absorbs the political statement, however. He presents himself throughout as embodying the historical situation of "the black man in North America" (the equivalent but also the revision of "the Negro in America," the phrase in which Baldwin asserted his representative role), and the psychological tension collectively experienced by blacks.

Although the ***Autobiography*** contains no indication that he knew *Native Son,* in several passages Malcolm *is* Bigger, holding within him the same prophecy of our future. He accepts (without limiting himself to) the role of "America's most dangerous and threatening black man, . . . the one who has been kept sealed up by the Northerner in the black ghetto." This type, like the conditions which create it, "needs no fuse; . . . it spontaneously combusts from within." Malcolm makes of himself the archetypal "black prisoner," in whose ineradicable "memory of the bars" is also remembrance of the "first landing of the first slave ship." Such memory, from which historical identity has been erased, is itself the historical identity here reclaimed.

In prison, however, Malcolm also first felt free. "Transformed" by conversion, he also was liberated into the "new world" of books. The acts of reading and writing coalesced, as they had for Wright, into a means of self-verification against the cultural record from which he felt absent. He developed this more in terms of the spoken than the written word, his discovery of oratorical power simultaneous with the Muslims' discovery of its uses (as with narrator and Brotherhood in *Invisible Man*). But he emphasizes in the ***Autobiography*** his release through reading, and a consequent control of self in writing. After "lights out," the lamp's faint glow inversely suggesting the 1,369 bulbs blazing in Ellison's narrator's room, Malcolm feigns sleep as the guard passes, then re-enters the "area of that light-glow" to read on. As he listens to Elijah Muhammad "make a parable of me" while introducing him to the Muslims after he leaves prison, he is already launched on an effort to recompose himself in words.

Thus the fixity of each image of imprisonment is countered, though not negated, by a sense of fluid potentiality. Anger remains a creative force—"I *believe* in anger," Malcolm proclaims. He also comes to believe, however, in a different power of emergence from the past. The mental "wings" bestowed by conversion to Islam are those he rhetorically spreads as an angel of black vengeance against the white devil. They are also the wings on which the Muslims accuse him of flying too near the sun of Elijah's Muhammad's supremacy within the sect. But Malcolm X experiences the growth of other wings, within the chrysalis of personal history, to be spread in imaginative self-reincarnation.

His names, shed like snakeskin, convey the metamorphosis—Malcolm Little, "Homebody," "Detroit Red," "Satan," Malcolm X, El-Hajj Malik El-Shabazz. Whole phases of inner experience slide away "like snow off a roof," each previous phase "back there, without any remaining effect." During a pilgrimage to Mecca, carrying him past Black Muslim brotherhood to the true fulfillment of his Muslim life, he recalls a vision which takes him back in time as easily as the flow of time (with which he is obsessed) has taken him forward through his narrative. Lying awake among sleeping pilgrims,

> my mind took me back to personal memories I would have thought were gone forever . . . as far back, even, as when I was just a little boy, eight or nine years old. Out behind our house . . . there was an old, grassy "Hector's Hill," we called it—which may still be there. I remembered there in the Holy World how I used to lie on top of Hector's Hill, and look up at the sky, at the clouds moving over me, and day-dreaming all kinds of things. And then . . . I remembered how years later, when I was in prison, I used to lie on my cell bunk—this would be especially when I was in solitary. . . .

His dreamings of the future are unencumbered by the past; in solitary reflection he can feel his immersion in—more than his racial removal from—the world. In Mecca, but in memory as well, he feels for the first time "like a complete human being." Prison at the time of his conversion was in Concord. He notes a link between Thoreau and himself forged in political resistance, suggesting in the process that one exists in the act of literary self-creation too. Hector's Hill, from which in the telling he reads again in moving clouds the symbols and signs of human possibility, is for a moment the imaginative place from which Thoreau would "fish in the sky, whose bottom is pebbly with stars."

In idiom also Malcolm slides easily through time and space, metamorphically slipping into the breaks of colloquial speech as Ellison's narrator [in *Invisible Man*] slips into the breaks in Louis Armstrong's music, descended ("What did I do/ To be so black/ And blue?") from the sorrow songs. He naturalizes the hustler's language into the narrative (after flaunting it at the outset, a verbal equivalent of the zoot suit he wears while inducting his Gentle Reader into the Harlem underworld). He then moves past it, as he moves beyond that phase of experience, but a fund of street intelligence remains, stenciled in his mind like the memory of the bars. As he says when he realizes that his discredit among the Muslims is being subtly arranged, "I hadn't hustled in the streets for years for nothing. I knew when I was being set up."

"What if history was a gambler," wonders the narrator in *Invisible Man.* "What if history was not a reasonable citizen, but a madman full of paranoid guile," life thus a matter of "running and dodging the forces of history instead of making a dominating stand." Malcolm presents hustling as a way of life rooted in a sense similar to Ellison's, paranoid guile the only sane response. "Internally restrained by nothing," the hustler is also in Malcolm's terms a "gambler," a Rinehartian being to whom anything is possible, inhabiting a world in which anything can happen. In the act of narration Malcolm's voice runs and dodges, talk from those days spilling into the present, from one form of the dangerous and reverberating silence of which Baldwin spoke. At the heart of the hustler's life is what Wright saw in his earliest stories, a "yawning void," an autobiographical vacuum with "no plot, . . . nothing save atmosphere, and longing and death." In the hustler's inability to "appraise" his own activity, lest in such distraction he fall prey to another, is the analogue to Baldwin's sense of being prohibited by external pressure from examining his own experience, a similar loss of experience the result.

Rescued from this death-in-life by the religion he encountered in prison, Malcolm found the Muslim precept "The white man is the devil" an echo, in his role as "the black prisoner," of the general experience of the black man in North America. Hence his susceptibility to conversion, and his insistence on the emotional truth (long after rejecting the historical absurdity) of the Muslim creation myth of "Mr. Yacub." Of a "tale" told in the ghetto, about a black woman's revenge against the whites who lynched her husband, Wright wrote in *Black Boy:*

> I did not know if the story was factually true or not, but it was emotionally true because I had already grown to feel that there existed men against whom I was powerless, men who could violate my life at will. . . . The story of the woman's deception gave form and meaning to confused defensive feelings that had long been sleeping in me.

Baldwin reports in *Notes of a Native Son* a "rumor" of a black soldier's being shot in the back by a white policeman in Harlem's Hotel Braddock, and dying while protecting a Negro woman from the officer. Baldwin's correction of the facts—the soldier was neither shot in the back nor dead, and the woman did not necessarily need protection—is secondary to the force with which the rumor swept the streets. An "instantaneous and revealing invention," it gave form and meaning to confused feelings in those who heard it: "They preferred the invention because [it] expressed and corroborated their hates and fears so perfectly." In this sense, for "that black convict" (as Malcolm calls himself) at the time of conversion, as for Malcolm having passed through self-narration beyond such faith, "The teachings ring true—to every Negro."

Malcolm also mentions the incident in the Hotel Braddock, but makes no interpretive comment, relating the "flash" of the rumor of the shooting without inquiring into its factuality. For him factuality is in that flash, out of which a riot spontaneously combusts. This is an instance of the ***Autobiography***'s lack of "literary" development of its material. The sequence is perfectly aligned, however, with the sense of reality governing this phase of Malcolm's life. "A writer is what I want, not an interpreter," Haley says Malcolm told him when the publishing contract was signed. Or, as Ellison's narrator puts it, "This is not prophecy, but description." In such description, nonetheless, is a cumulative prophecy, igniting as inevitably in Malcolm's mind as the riot explodes in Harlem.

Whatever the mix of Malcolm X's motives—outrage at a leader's lapses from Muslim morality, perhaps the pride of a "Satan" who would rule—in breaking and in turn being cut off from the Muslims, he finds himself, in his final year, again on his own. "Thinking for myself," running and dodging through the psychological debris of the failure for him of Muslim historical design, he is exhilarated by freedom yet desperate for the new community he has set out in his mind to create in this wilderness of North America. He experiences the return—it had never really left him—of the old double-consciousness. THEM, hieroglyphically inscribed by Malcolm on one of Haley's napkins and meaning The Honorable Elijah Muhammad, becomes a Pynchonesque suggestion of the justifications in reality for resumption of paranoid guile, like WASTE in *The Crying of Lot 49.*

As Malcolm begins to see in former friends the faces of those who will end his life, he feels (like Ellison's narrator and in Ellison's words) that in the Brotherhood "was the only historically meaningful life that I could live. If I left it, I'd be nowhere," that place of internal emptiness so often arrived at in the works discussed above. Then he begins to feel (in his own words as we learn from Haley's epilogue, but also like Ellison's narrator for whom in the novel's epilogue invisibility has become a form of strategic flexibility) that while "I can't put my finger on exactly what my philosophy is now, . . . I'm flexible." The statement, made in an interview not printed until after his death, reflects his having gone (in Ellison's sense) underground. It also reflects his posthumous determination, reemergent in text, on lower narrative frequencies to keep on speaking for us all. This is where Malcolm X—his voice turning inward in a tightening gyre like the same tight circles he often walked while talking to Haley—makes his dominating stand.

When Malcolm lost faith in Elijah Muhammad, he felt "as though something in *nature* had failed, like the sun, or the stars." Elijah Muhammad, interpreting to the Muslim faithful Malcolm's fall from grace, said "He was a star, who went astray." Malcolm is yet another of Du Bois' falling stars, dying throughout history. But he is also in his book—in which he steps into self-fulfilling imagination rather than into Rinehart's mastery of chaos—the embodiment of Du Bois and of other black American autobiographers of this century. His parents' seventh child, he is also Du Bois' "seventh son, born with a veil, and gifted with second-sight in this American world," the gift of insight being the curse of double-consciousness. When Eldridge Cleaver says, "Black history began with Malcolm X," he ignores a history begun long before Du Bois yet testifies truly to the seminal as well as the culminating power of the record of Malcolm's personal journey up from slavery.

In the last lines of his *Narrative of the Life of Frederick Douglass, An American Slave, Written by Himself* (1845), Douglass states:

> The truth was, I felt myself a slave, and the idea of speaking to white people weighed me down. I spoke but a few moments, when I felt a degree

> of freedom, and said what I desired with considerable ease. From that time until now, I have been engaged in pleading the cause of my brethren—with what success, and with what devotion, I leave those acquainted with my labors to decide.

Malcolm's voice encompasses without overriding the voices of those who have spoken "from that time until now." In tones reminiscent of Douglass he says:

> I have given to this book so much of whatever time I have because I feel, and I hope, that if I honestly and fully tell my life's account, read objectively it might prove to be a testimony of some social value.

He dares humbly as well as in anger and pride "to dream to myself" back now on Hector's Hill as well as nearing death—"that one day, history may even say that my voice . . . helped to save America from a grave, possibly even a fatal catastrophe." With what success remains unknown, to be revealed in cities of words as yet unbuilt in the wilderness of North America, in signs yet to appear on the open pages beneath Wright's pencil at the end of *American Hunger.* With what devotion, however, is amply answered in ***The Autobiography of Malcolm X.***

Malcolm's fallen star merges with the morning star of Thoreau, his "two-edged sword" of Islamic truth with the scimitar in *Walden,* "the sun glimmer[ing] on both its surfaces," its edge "dividing you through the heart," as in *Invisible Man* the narrator hears the shattering stroke of his heart in "There's Many a Thousand Gone." In his parable of unfinished self, Malcolm X moves time-haunted toward the perfect work into which time does not enter, an autobiographical act in which the tale Du Bois called "twice told but seldom written" becomes one in which (in a sense other than, yet comprehending that of the Islamic prophecy Malcolm invokes) "everything is written." (pp. 354-60)

Gordon O. Taylor, "Voices from the Veil: Black American Autobiography," in The Georgia Review, *Vol. XXXV, No. 2, Summer, 1981, pp. 341-61.*

James Craig Holte (essay date Summer 1982)

[*In the following excerpt, Holte cites* The Autobiography of Malcolm X, *among other American works of self-disclosure, in an assessment of the contrast between conventional modes of expression in American autobiography and innovative approaches that result from ethnic experience.*]

The American literary tradition is not a mere catalogue of related but isolated masterpieces; it is an almost obsessive inquiry into what it means to be an American. Every generation asks this question and comes up with its own answers, but the way in which the answers are discovered is influenced by the literary tradition as well as the individual concerns of each generation of writers. For perceptions are influenced by conventions; we discover what we set out to seek. For some, the tradition of frontier millenial evangelicalism imbues every act and confrontation with moral significance, while for others every event is part of the class struggle or an unconscious mythic pattern. To be aware of the conventions which influence us is to be aware of the nature and structure of our perceptions and our literature. In answering the question of what it means to be an American, our writers, in a relatively fluid society, put little emphasis on class and manners as indices of worth. As Cooper, Hawthorne, James, and others have noted, this society had very little cultural tradition. Thus, writers had to look to themselves for their literary resources and to their own lives as the primary source of value and meaning. Thus, the American question is a question of self, and the autobiography is a central part of the American literary tradition.

To understand how our writers have responded to this question, what it means to be an American, one must look at some of the conventions of the autobiography. From the earliest settlers to the writings of Constantine Panunzio, Malcolm X, and Piri Thomas there exist both a continuity of convention and concerns as well as radical differences in the contexts in which the literature was created. (p. 25)

The option of melting into the middle class was never available for Blacks in the United States. The melting pot was an image for whites only. Cultural pluralism would seem to suggest a pattern for interracial relationships, but most Americans have refused to face the full racial, social, and cultural implication of total pluralism, especially the effects of that pluralism on the Anglo national character, if indeed there is such a thing as a single national character in the United States. From the vantage point of the outsider, Malcolm X used his conversion narrative not only to describe his development but also to speak to the crucial cultural conflicts of his time.

The Autobiography of Malcolm X (1964) is clearly a conversion narrative which raises the issue which confronted so many American autobiographers—what is an American. G. Thomas Causer, in *American Autobiography: The Prophetic Mode,* places Malcolm's narrative within the tradition of American letters by drawing a number of useful parallels to earlier writers. Like Quaker and Puritan writers, Malcolm X created a narrative in which the first half shows him as a member of a persecuted minority while the second half depicts him as both member of and spokesman for a religious and political community which literally offered him a new life. Again, like Puritan writers, he saw his conversion as the crucial event in his life even as he viewed history as teleological. The conversion experience itself led him to a sense of the brotherhood of man, and although there are great differences between the ideologue of progress and the Black Nationalist prophet, like Franklin's *Autobiography,* Malcolm's narrative is a kind of success story which draws a parallel between the development of a sense of self to the liberation of a colonized people. Although the setting and material seem far from Puritan conversion narratives, the structure of the text is classically American. Malcolm's book opens with an account of his family and early life leading to a moment of crisis and illumination. This is followed by a dramatic conversion, which in turn leads to study, preparation, and then the assumption of the role of the prophet and speaker for the community. It would seem an archetypal conversion, but the power and complexity of the text arise from Malcolm's frustrated original intentions and his continuing development and movement away from the Nation of Islam. It is, in a sense, both a conversion and an analysis of the conversion.

As Causer has noted, the book was begun in 1963 when Malcolm was still a member and minister of the Nation of Islam, and the original dedication was to Elijah Muhammed, with all proceeds to go to the Black Muslims. At this stage of the project he saw himself as a propagandist rather than an autobiographer, and the work was to be completely orthodox. As Alex Haley later said of Malcolm's notebook, "it contained nothing but Black Muslim philosophy, praise of Mr. Muhammad, and the evils of the 'white devil.' He would bristle when I tried to urge him that the proposed book was *his* life." Haley's arguments with Malcolm about the didactic nature of the work and Malcolm's own unhappiness with the movement and his excommunication from the Nation of Islam forced Malcolm out of the role of propagandist and compelled him to re-examine his life, and the product of the crisis and reexamination is ***The Autobiography of Malcolm X,*** a book that uses the conventional forms of the conversion narrative but goes beyond the limitations of that mode.

The conventions of the conversion narrative demand a contrast built around the conversion itself, and Malcolm's narrative employs this structure. The first section presents his childhood and adolescence. Here he establishes the roots of his later activities and uses his personal experiences to expose American racism. The tensions are set up on the first page of the first chapter, "Nightmare," where Ku Klux Klan riders are juxtaposed with Marcus Garvey's United Negro Improvement Association. The first action is of Klan riders threatening his mother in Omaha. The second section builds from the first, showing Malcolm in his role as a "hustler." Here the narrative becomes an initiation story as Malcolm moves away from attempted assimilation into the underground world of the Black community. Here he gains status and some degree of success, but the direction of the narrative is controlled by the idea of conversion. In the middle of the text, the structural and thematic center, Malcolm, in prison, is converted to the Nation of Islam, and the conversion makes him a new man. Conversion has to do with casting off and taking on, and Malcolm used the convention of breaking of habits, a device employed by many writers of conversion narratives, in the description of his conversion.

> Quitting cigarettes wasn't going to be difficult. I had been conditioned by days in solitary without cigarettes. Whatever this chance was, I wasn't going to fluff it. After I had read that letter [from his brother introducing him to the Nation of Islam], I finished the pack I then had open. I haven't smoked another cigarette to this day, since 1948.
>
> It was about three or four days later when pork was served for the noon meal.
>
> I wasn't even thinking about pork when I took my seat at the long table. Sit-grab-gobble-stand-file out; that was the Emily Post in prison eating. When the meat platter was passed to me, I didn't even know what the meat was; usually you couldn't tell, anyway—but it was suddenly as though don't eat any more pork flashed on a screen before me. . . .
>
> Later I would learn, when I had read and studied Islam a good deal, that, unconsciously, my first pre-Islamic submission had been manifested. I had experienced, for the first time, the Muslim teaching, "If you will take one step toward Allah—Allah will take two steps toward you."

All of the traditional conventions of conversion are here: the descent into the depths of sin, confusion, despair and prison; the flashing of an idea on a screen, much like Jonathan Edwards' sweet infusion of saving grace; and an outer transformation matching an inner conversion. The use of external change to mirror inward transformation continues, as Malcolm describes his purchase of new clothes, new glasses, and a watch as he leaves prison. He has, of course, also taken on a new name to match his awareness of himself as a new man.

What follows also is part of the conversion convention, a description of the convert as spokesman for the community, defending the faithful from attack and supporting them and their faith. Again, like earlier conversion narratives, ***The Autobiography of Malcolm X*** depicts the oppressed community's conflict with the larger unconverted community. After conversion, the works and acts appear.

The final section of the narrative treats Malcolm's life after excommunication, and in this section a reexamination of the conversion takes place. Again, Malcolm is in a state of confusion and crisis: "I felt as though something in nature had failed, like the sun or the stars." The expulsion denied him the support of the community, and his role as spokesman for that community, and while he did not abandon his conversion, he began to see in it a new light, especially after his pilgrimage to Mecca. Like his earlier conversion, a second, or an affirmation of the first, takes place in Mecca. And again, the result is a renewed political activity.

Actual events transformed the original intended direction of the narrative. The simple, single-minded vision of conversion to the Nation of Islam is replaced by a more complex self-examination. Conversion, as Malcolm ultimately came to see it, was an ongoing process, not a static experience, and his narrative faithfully demonstrates this complexity. The final sections show the autobiographer in the state of transformation, the state of becoming, moving away from a complete separatist view to a more complex one which refused to hold, for example, that all whites were "devils." As Causer maintains, "the book's power as prophetic autobiography lies not in its blunt exposition of Black Muslim ideology but in its bold portrayal of a prophet deprived of both his stature and his vision; its value as prophecy is not in the vision it contains but in the one it moves toward and prophesies." Malcolm X sees the answer to the question of what an American is as a very complex one, and his evolving definition of self, through two conversions, suggests possible answers rather than providing a simplistic one. (pp. 39-42)

James Craig Holte, "The Representative Voice: Autobiography and the Ethnic Experience," in MELUS, *Vol. 9, No. 2, Summer, 1982, pp. 25-46.*

A Reminiscence of Malcolm X by Alex Haley:

Usually two nights a week, sometimes three, Malcolm would park his blue Oldsmobile somewhere near my Greenwich Village apartment. It was probably bugged by the FBI, and always Malcolm would snap, "One, two, three—testing!" when he first came in. Next he'd telephone his wife, Betty Shabazz, tell her where he was and jot down messages she gave him. Then, rather than take a seat, for the first half hour, at least, he preferred pacing the room like some caged tiger, talking nonstop about the Nation of Islam and its leader in Chicago, Elijah Muhammad. Whenever I'd gently remind him that the subject of the book was him, Malcolm's hackles would rise. One wintry midnight, however, in sheer frustration I blurted, "Mr. Malcolm, could you tell me something about your mother?" He turned, his pacing slowed, and I'll never forget the look on his face—even his voice sounded different. "It's funny you ask me that. . . . I can remember her dresses; they were all faded out and gray. I remember how she bent over the stove, trying to stretch what little we had. . . . "

It was near dawn when Malcolm left for home, having spilled from his memory most of what I'd later use in the first chapter of *The Autobiography of Malcolm X,* appropriately titled "Nightmare." It tells the story of the small boy, Malcolm Little, one of eight children watching their mother's struggles to keep the family intact after the brutal, racially motivated murder of their father, a militantly outspoken Baptist minister and supporter of Marcus Garvey. After that session Malcolm never hesitated to relate any aspect of his later life in the most detail his memory could muster. And I find myself now experiencing a diversity of emotions as I recall random memories of that truly singular and very special human being.

Alex Haley, in Essence, *November 1983.*

Shirley K. Rose (essay date Spring 1987)

[In the following excerpt, Rose suggests that Malcolm's perpetuation of "the dominant culture's myth that literacy is the path to autonomy" in The Autobiography of Malcolm X *served as a means for him to find "both the community in which he could participate and an autonomous identity as a man."]*

In the process of selecting episodes from memory and shaping them for telling and retelling, autobiographers make coherent their incoherent experience. At the same time, these writers reveal the shared cultural values and assumptions which allow them to shape that experience for themselves and their readers. One's experience is defined by sociocultural factors; it is further defined in the act of writing a narrative and the subsequent act of reading it (whether the reader is oneself or another). For writing is a powerful act. By writing one constructs one's reality. In examining their pasts, autobiographers re-affirm their power to determine their futures. (p. 3)

As Arnold Rampersad has pointed out [in *Yale Review* 73, 1982], Alex Haley's role in the composition of the ***Autobiography of Malcolm X*** complicates this issue of autobiography as creation of self. Haley was trained as a writer in the context of white-dominated institutions. In his attempt to aid in the re-creation of a black life, he may have been an "intellectual [agent] of the very power that inflicted misery on [his] subject." Such a claim does not, however, invalidate the use of this work to exemplify autobiography as construction of cross-cultural identity, for such an act of construction requires the writer to make use of the materials of both cultures. He must employ the cultural myths of the readers he wishes to reach. Malcolm X, with Alex Haley, has employed the dominant culture's myth that literacy is a path to autonomy, and in doing so he has asserted his autonomy.

A continuous, chronologically arranged narrative, ***The Autobiography of Malcolm X*** begins with the author's rememberances of his father's violent death and ends with his prediction that he too would be murdered, thus reflecting in its organization the author's sense of the continuity of history and his own role in it.

The chronological organization allows readers to trace Malcolm X's development as a literate person from school child to internationally famous human rights activist. Each stage of his development can be marked by the name by which he was called or assumed for himself and later used to title each chapter of his narrative. Each change of name corresponds to a change of geographical place, representing the changing versions of reality in which and by which he explains the identities he creates for himself. While the changes of names are indications of changes in his developing sense of autonomy, the changes of place reflect the change of cultural groups in which he sought to participate. Together, these changes are represented in the narrative structure as a *pilgrimage,* a metaphor which becomes explicit near the end of his story, when he travels to Mecca. The difficulties he encounters on his quest for the sacred goal of autonomy are caused by his attempts to participate in the wrong communities—communities which limit who and what he can be.

The author first discusses learning to read and write in his account of his experiences at Mason Junior High School while he was living in a foster home. At this time, however, the actual acquisition of literacy skills is secondary to his socialization to the values of a literate society. Malcolm Little, the only black student in the class, was so popular among his classmates that he was asked to join numerous extracurricular organizations. But the acceptance he enjoyed was an acceptance based on his difference from his classmates, not on his equality with them.

Though he knew that as a black boy he was not a part of the white mainstream society, he believed in and accepted its myth that literacy and education gave one access to power, privilege, and autonomy. However, when he re-

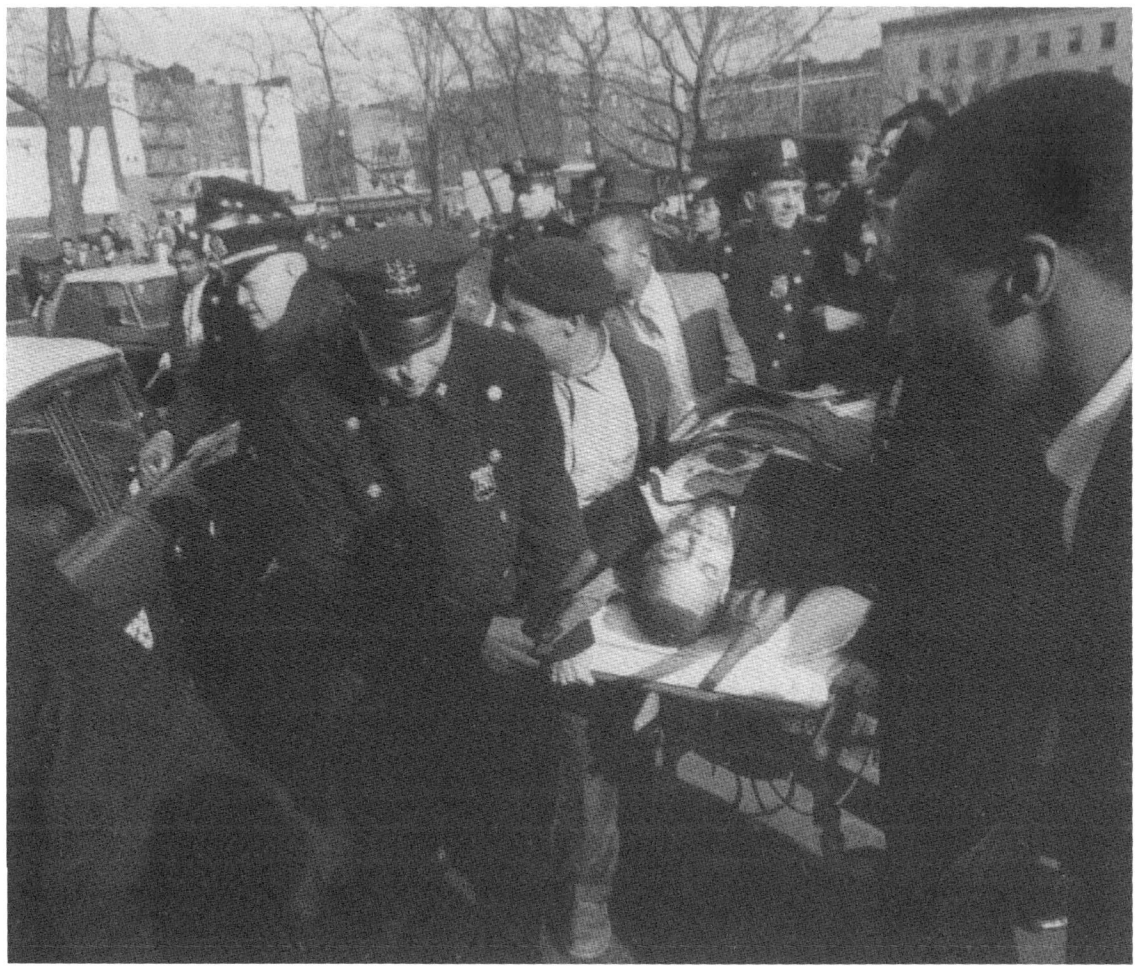

Malcolm X's death.

vealed his belief that the cultural myth could be extended to include him, that his literacy would give him power too, he learned that those who were part of the mainstream culture did not believe their reality included Malcolm Little.

The author chooses a telling incident to convey this lesson to his reader: When Mr. Ostrowski, his English teacher, asked Malcolm Little what he planned to do after he finished school and received the reply that he would like to be a lawyer, this teacher advised Malcolm to "be realistic . . . a lawyer—that's no realistic goal for a nigger." He suggested that instead Malcolm, the smartest student in his class, consider being a carpenter. Malcolm's response, to withdraw from his classmates, friends, and foster parents, was merely a manifestation of his recognition that the rewards which they expected for themselves were to be withheld from him.

The new identity which Malcolm assumed for himself when he left Michigan to live with his older half-sister, Ella, was that of a "Homeboy," the name given to him by his first friend in Boston. The author notes that this marked his real introduction to and immersion in black culture and the beginning of his street education, his socialization into a culture that would allow his participation. "Every day I listened raptly to customers who felt like talking, and it all added to my education. . . . I was thus schooled well." His teachers were hustlers and criminals. The subjects were "the numbers, pimping, con games of many kinds, peddling dope, and thievery of all sorts, including armed robbery."

He pursued his new alternative education with all the intelligence and energy he was discouraged from devoting to an academic education. By his own account, his immersion in his street education led to success on the street. "Detroit Red" carried on a variety of hustles and other illegal activity until he was eventually imprisoned for robbery.

Once in prison he resumed, or rather began again, his acquisition of conventional literacy. His description of his "homemade education" during his seven years of imprisonment represents the myth of literacy as a path to autonomy. When his experience as a junior high school student had shown Malcolm X that this myth was not intended to be a part of the reality of a black person, he had substituted for it the success myth of the black ghetto. Later, as an inmate in the prison's white society had created for those who would not live by its laws, he responded by embracing the myth of literacy for autonomy and employing it against the cultural group from which he had learned it.

This myth also provides the plot for his account of his time in the Charlestown Prison, where "Satan" was first incarcerated. Here he began to read again in an effort to emulate a fellow inmate who was able to "command total respect . . . with his words." He began correspondence courses in the mechanics of English grammar and in Latin. Though he was aware of the usefulness of literacy skills, he was frustrated by his inability to read with comprehension. He says, "Pretty soon, I would have quit even these motions, unless I had received the motivation that I did."

He was motivated by a need for literacy skills in order to carry on a correspondence with his brothers and sisters as well as with the Black Muslim prophet Elijah Muhammad. Through this correspondence he found a way to fight against white society for his human rights. The correspondence began with that first one-page letter which he wrote at least twenty-five times, trying to make it legible and understandable. He describes his skills at this time: "I practically couldn't read my handwriting myself; it shames even to remember it. My spelling and my grammar were as bad, if not worse."

He did not let the frustration stop him, but instead practiced the literacy skills repeatedly until, eventually, he was not only writing a letter a day to Elijah Mohammad and a letter a day to one or another of his brothers and sisters, but was also writing to the people he had known on the streets in Harlem. His sense that this practice of literacy was changing him, that he was becoming a literate person, is reflected in his remark that the hustlers to whom he wrote were "too uneducated to write a letter . . . privately, they would get someone else to read a letter if they received one."

His awareness of himself as literate led to a growing confidence that he could use his literacy to bring about further changes in his life. The unique program of study he describes—copying from the dictionary "to study, to learn some words . . . to improve my penmanship"—was totally self-motivated and it was effective. He could "for the first time pick up a book and read and now begin to understand what the book was saying." To describe the effect of this new awareness of his literacy, he uses such expressions as "a new world that opened" and claims "I had never been so truly free in my life."

Though the author notes that "an inmate was smiled upon if he demonstrated an unusually intense interest in books," he insists that this self-imposed adult literacy program was not carried out to please or impress prison officials and parole boards. His description of his "really serious reading" after hours during 'lights out' makes it clear that he viewed his effort to acquire literacy as an act of defiance against not just the prison regulations, but the entire social system which had made him into a prisoner.

He tells us that he read everything from Will Durant's *Story of Civilization* to Mendel's *Findings in Genetics* in order to find information or facts he could use to back up his denunciation of white supremacy. Of the ultimate effect of his self-directed education in the evils that white people had perpetrated upon black people, he says:

> I have often reflected upon the new vistas that reading opened to me. I knew right there in prison that reading had changed forever the course of my life. As I see it today, the ability to read awoke inside me some long dormant craving to be mentally alive. I certainly wasn't seeking any degree, the way a college confers a status symbol upon its students. My homemade education gave me, with every additional book that I read, a little bit more sensitivity to the deafness, dumbness, and blindness that was afflicting the black race in America . . . You will never catch me with a free fifteen minutes in which I'm not studying something I feel might be able to help the black man.

The author presents his reading and writing as more than acts in defiance of or rebellion against a white-dominated system of justice; his practice of literacy redirected the "course of [his] life" and redefined his purpose: to awaken other blacks to an awareness of the self-hatred white domination had taught them.

The same intelligence and energy that he directed into this educational purpose was in the last months of his life directed into his search for the true religion of Islam. Assuming a new name, El-Hajj Malik El-Shabazz assumed a new identity in a new version of reality as a result of his pilgrimage to Mecca. This reality, or myth, explained life not in terms of black versus white, but in terms of the "brotherhood of all men" regardless of race and nationality.

The goal of his lifelong quest for autonomy as a Black man was achieved when he became a participant in a community in which his race did not matter. One of his first acts upon achieving this goal and receiving this new vision was to write letters—to his wife, to his sister Ella, to Elijah Muhammad's son Wallace, and an open letter to his assistants in his newly formed organization, "with a note appended, asking that [his] letter be duplicated and distributed to the press." Beginning with a letter to an audience of one and ending with a letter to an unnumbered public audience, Malcolm X's acquisition of literacy had been a pilgrimage to find both the community in which he could participate and an autonomous identity as a man. (pp. 4-8)

Shirley K. Rose, "Metaphors and Myths of Cross-Cultural Literacy: Autobiographical Narratives by Maxine Hong Kingston, Richard Rodriguez, and Malcolm X," in MELUS, *Vol. 14, No. 1, Spring, 1987, pp. 3-15.*

Joe Wood (review date 27 November 1989)

[*In the following review, Wood provides a mixed assessment of* Malcolm X: The Last Speeches.]

Do we measure activists' lives by the breadth of their hopes or their earnestness in trying to make them real? Or do we measure activists by where they actually end up, failures and disillusionments included? And how do we figure someone like Malcolm X?

In Malcolm's case, myth has long since taken the place of research in the imagination of Americans, black and white. Malcolm's myth, widely circulated in [***The Autobiography of Malcolm X***], makes him a very current African-American figure: the resistant seminationalist, a hero for the "lost and (now I'm) found" strain of gritty American individualism. In the popular view, Malcolm represents the real black thing; one's reaction to Malcolm's myth, then, becomes a measure of one's understanding of, or sympathy with, the "strong side" of black experience—the side that is ready to embrace other Americans without forfeiting any self-respect. Unfortunately, this neat package [***Malcolm X: The Last Speeches***] smoothes over significant details about Malcolm's life.

In March 1964, Malcolm X left the Nation of Islam, the organization that had both nurtured him into responsible adulthood and shaken America's political consciousness. The break was real. During the last eleven months of his life, Malcolm made an eye-opening pilgrimage to Africa and the Middle East, and he publicly renounced Elijah Muhammad's theology as unorthodox and racist. He also began pondering conceptual alternatives to the movement's black nationalism, eventually deciding to activate a human rights campaign in America, and to place new emphasis on brotherhood, internationalism, anti-imperialism and, most important, progressive action.

But never did he cease being, as is said in the vernacular, hard. After establishing the orthodox Muslim Mosque Inc., Malcolm formed the ecumenical Organization of Afro-American Unity (O.A.A.U.), and he gave it the slogan "By Any Means Necessary." He never failed to remind audiences that while he didn't advocate violence, he did believe in the right to self-protection, particularly in a country as racially inequitable as the United States. And while white liberals and black (dare I say it) integrationists like to stress his embrace of brotherhood, even a cursory examination of his speeches reveals that Malcolm never changed his mind about what the chief enemy was: white American racism.

In 1965 Pathfinder Press published ***Malcolm X Speaks,*** a collection of speeches, interviews and correspondence that, with one exception, are from the last year of his life. The editing of both that book and ***Malcolm X: The Last Speeches*** emphasizes Malcolm's political evolution; its obvious intent is to reinforce the notion that Malcolm was loosening up, becoming more intellectually honest and, most significant, more willing to embrace white revolutionaries and traditional leftisms.

Malcolm X: The Last Speeches actually offers readers glimpses of more than that. The book's first two examples are standard Black Muslim fare, delivered in 1963 to predominantly white audiences at Michigan State University and the University of California at Berkeley. In the book's pair of radio interviews (December 1964), Malcolm distances himself from speeches like these, contending that he was only "parroting" Elijah Muhammad's propaganda. But as parrot propagandists go, Malcolm performed brilliantly, making points he would later alter but never abandon:

> [The] new type [of black man] rejects the white man's Christian religion. He recognizes the real enemy. That Uncle Tom can't see his enemy. He thinks his friend is his enemy and his enemy is his friend. And he usually ends up loving his enemy, turning his other cheek to his enemy. But this new type, he doesn't turn the other cheek to anybody. He doesn't believe in any kind of peaceful suffering. He believes in obeying the law. He believes in respecting people. He believes in doing unto others as he would have done to himself. But at the same time, if anybody attacks him, he believes in retaliating if it costs him his life. And it is good for white people to know this. Because if white people get the impression that Negroes all endorse this old turn-the-other-cheek cowardly philosophy of Dr. Martin Luther King, then whites are going to make the mistake of putting their hands on some black man, thinking that he's going to turn the other cheek, and he'll end up losing his hand and losing his life in the try. [*Commotion and laughter*]

Malcolm is giving voice to this "new" type of black man; he is tapping into a rather traditional African-American will to self-determination and proclaiming his strength in terms anybody can understand and respect. In such talk one can witness the genesis of Malcolm's slogan, By Any Means Necessary, and observe the reason for his appeal to black *and* white audiences.

Yet behind Malcolm X's incredible ability to pick metaphors from the air, and behind his clarity and brutal earnestness, lurked a basic deception: Malcolm didn't believe a lot of what he was saying. In 1960, for instance, Elijah directed Malcolm to conduct secret talks with the Ku Klux Klan about the possibility of carving a black nation out of South Carolina. These negotiations made Malcolm uncomfortable—cutting deals with the blue-eyed devils simply did not sit well. But like any disciplined revolutionary, Malcolm felt he couldn't break ranks and did so only after internal politics and personal disillusionment forced him out.

In the last year of his life, Malcolm offered piecemeal explanations for his abrupt departure. Among these were what he described as the movement's willful lethargy and its racist unorthodoxy; these concerns surface with passionate cogency in the book's only gem, a speech Malcolm made the night after his house was firebombed (allegedly by members of Elijah's movement). Delivered on February 15, 1965, at Harlem's Audubon Ballroom—the site of his assassination less than a week later—these remarks show the profundity of his disappointment with the movement:

> And there has been a conspiracy across the country on the part of many factions of the press to suppress news that would open the eyes of the Muslims who are following Elijah Muhammad. They continue to make him look like he's a prophet somewhere who is getting some messages direct from God and is untouchable and

> things of that sort. I'm telling you the truth. But they do know that if something were to happen and all these brothers, their eyes were to come open, they would be right out here in every one of these civil rights organizations making these Uncle Tom Negro leaders stand up and fight like men instead of running around here nonviolently acting like women.
>
> So they hope Elijah Muhammad remains as he is for a long time because they know that any organization that he heads, it will not do anything in the struggle that the black man is confronted with in this country. Proof of which, look how violent they can get. They were violent, they've been violent from coast to coast. Muslims, in the Muslim movement, have been involved in cold, calculated violence. And not at one time have they been involved in any violence against the Ku Klux Klan. They're capable. They're qualified. They're equipped. They know how to do it. But they'll never do it—only to another brother. [*Applause*]

What throbs at bottom here is a very painful distress: Malcolm is rejecting, and has been rejected by, his spiritual/political father. Elijah's movement made Malcolm, forming him even as he helped form the Nation. Like any good lieutenant, Malcolm served with his eyes open. He'd heard the rumors about Elijah's character, had sat across the table from the Klan and had also concealed any doubts that had occurred to him. For his faith Malcolm was given the truth, which hurt.

By the time he made that speech, Malcolm had traveled through newly postcolonial Africa, and thereby broadened and sharpened his thinking. His essential "Black Muslim" outrage, however, remained, only with complications. The problems clearly did not come from his broader understanding of internationalism or anticapitalism or brotherhood. Malcolm never had much time to investigate these ideas thoroughly, nor did he ever abandon the sexism attendant on his notions of black manhood, nor did he fool himself about the privileges whites enjoy in this country. Rather, Malcolm's new perspective was made more complicated by his realization that he hadn't known his friends from his enemies, just like the Uncle Tom house Negroes he harped on in his Black Muslim speeches. Where in his old scheme, after all, does one place Elijah? The awful and unavoidable truth is that he must be classed alongside other useful revolutionaries turned sorry despots, men seduced by the jeweled trappings of institutional power.

What emerges, then, as Malcolm's most significant final-year revelation is not his admission of the possibility of white good, but his encounter with the disillusioning reality of "new" Negro corruption. ***The Last Speeches*** records Malcolm's most significant postrevolutionary change: his realization that he could not be *sure.* Readers will be reminded that the gun Malcolm holds in that famous photograph was being readied not for enemies who were white, but former comrades who were black. (pp. 650-52)

Joe Wood, "His Final Days," in The Nation, *New York, Vol. 249, No. 18, November 27, 1989, pp. 650-52.*

Shelby Steele (essay date 21 December 1992)

[*In the excerpt below, Steele assesses the significance of Malcolm X for contemporary America following the release of Spike Lee's film biography* Malcolm X *(1992).*]

When asked recently what he thought of Malcolm X, Thurgood Marshall is reported to have said, "All he did was talk." And yet there is a kind of talk that constitutes action, a catalytic speech that changes things as irrevocably as do events or great movements. Malcolm X was an event, and his talk transformed American culture as surely, if not as thoroughly, as the civil rights movement, which might not have found the moderation necessary for its success had Malcolm not planted in the American consciousness so uncompromised a vision of the underdog's rage.

Malcolm staked out this territory against his great contemporary and foil, Martin Luther King Jr. Sneering at King's turn-the-other-cheek Christianity, he told blacks, "Don't ask God to have mercy on him [the white man]; ask God to judge him. Ask God to do onto him what he did onto you. Ask God that he suffer as you suffered." To use the old Christian categories, Malcolm was the Old Testament to King's New Testament. Against the moral nobility of the civil rights movement, he wanted whites to know that he was not different from them; that he, too, would kill or die for freedom. "The price of freedom is death," he often said.

Like all true revolutionaries, Malcolm had an intimate relationship with his own death. By being less afraid of it than other men, he took on power. And this was not so much a death wish as it was the refusal of a compromised life. These seemed to be his terms, and for many blacks like myself who came of age during his era, there was nothing to do but love him, since he, foolishly or not, seemed to love us more than we loved ourselves.

It is always context that makes a revolutionary figure like Malcolm X a hero or a destroyer. Even when he first emerged in the late '50s and early '60s, the real debate was not so much about him (he was clear enough) as about whether or not the context of black oppression was severe enough to justify him. And now that Malcolm has explosively re-emerged on the American scene, those old questions about context are with us once again.

Spike Lee has brought Malcolm's autobiography to the screen in one of the most thoroughly hyped films in American history. Malcolm's life is available in airport bookstalls. Compact discs and videotapes of his "blue-eyed devil" speeches can be picked up at Tower Records. His "X" is ubiquitous to the point of gracing automobile air fresheners. Twenty-seven years after his death, in sum, he is more visible to Americans than he was during his life. Of course Americans will commercialize anything; but that is a slightly redundant point. The really pressing matter is what this says about the context of race relations in America today. How can a new generation of blacks—

after pervasive civil rights legislation, Great Society programs, school busing, open housing, and more than two decades of affirmative action—be drawn to a figure of such seething racial alienation?

The life of Malcolm X touched so many human archetypes that his story itself seems to supersede any racial context, which is to say that it meshes with virtually every context. Malcolm X is a story. And so he meets people, particularly young people, in a deeply personal way. To assess whether or not he is a good story for these times, I think we have to consider first the nature of his appeal.

Let me say—without, I hope, too many violins—that when I was growing up in the 1950s, I was very often the victim of old-fashioned racism and discrimination. These experiences were very much like the literal experience of being burned. Not only did they hurt, they also caused me to doubt myself in some fundamental way. There was shame in these experiences as well, the suspicion that by some measure of human worth I deserved them. This, of course, is precisely what they were designed to make me feel. So right away there was an odd necessity to fight and to struggle for both personal and racial dignity.

Those were the experiences that enabled me to hear Malcolm. The very soul of his legend was the heroic struggle that he was waging against racial doubt and shame. After a tortuous childhood and an early life of crime that left him shattered, he reconstructed himself—against the injuries of racial oppression—by embracing an ideology of black nationalism. Black nationalism offered something very important to Malcolm, and this quickly became his magnificently articulated offering to other blacks. What it offered was a perfectly cathartic distribution of love and hate. Blacks were innocent victims, whites were evil oppressors, and blacks had to distribute their love and hate accordingly. But if one focuses on the called-for hatred of whites, the point of Malcolm's redistribution of emotion will be missed. If Malcolm was screaming his hatred of whites, his deeper purpose was to grant blacks a license to give themselves what they needed most: self-love.

This license to love and to hate in a way that soothed my unconscious doubts was nothing less than compelling by the time I reached college. Late at night in the dorm, my black friends and I would turn off the lights for effect and listen to his album of speeches, ***The Ballot or the Bullet,*** over and over again. He couldn't have all that anger and all that hate unless he really loved black people, and, therefore, us. And so he massaged the injured part of ourselves with an utterly self-gratifying and unconditional love.

With Martin Luther King, by contrast, there were conditions. King asked blacks—despised and unloved—to spread their meager stock of love to all people, even to those who despised us. What a lot to ask, and of a victim. With King, we were once again in second place, loving others before ourselves. But Malcolm told us to love ourselves first and to project all of our hurt into a hatred of the "blue-eyed devil" who had hurt us in the first place.

In Malcolm's deployment of love and hate there was an intrinsic logic of dignity that was very different from King's. For King, racial dignity was established by enlarging the self into a love of others. For Malcolm, dignity came from constriction, from shrinking to the enemy's size, and showing him not that you could be higher than he was, but that you could go as low. If King rose up, Malcolm dropped down. And here is where he used the hatred side of his formula to lay down his two essential principles of black dignity: the dehumanization of the white man and the threat of violence.

What made those principles essential to the dignity of blacks for Malcolm was that they followed a tit-for-tat logic—the logic by which, in his mind, any collective established its dignity against another collective. And both these principles could be powerfully articulated by Malcolm because they were precisely the same principles by which whites had oppressed blacks for centuries. Malcolm dehumanized whites by playing back, in white-face, the stereotypes that blacks had endured. He made them animals—if they like their meat rare, "that's the dog in 'em." In the iconography of his Black Muslim period, whites were heathen, violent, drooling beasts who lynched and raped. But he often let his humor get the best of him in this, and most blacks took it with a grain of salt.

What made Malcolm one of the most controversial Americans of this century was the second principle in his logic of dignity: the threat of violence. "If we have a funeral in Harlem, make sure they have one downtown, too." "If he puts his hand on you, send him to the cemetery." Tit-for-tat logic taken to its logical conclusion. In fact, Malcolm's focus on violence against whites was essentially rhetorical. Like today's black street gangs, his Black Muslims were far more likely to kill each other than go after whites. Yet no one has ever played the white hysteria over black violence better than Malcolm.

He played this card very effectively to achieve two things. The first was to breach the horrible invisibility that blacks have endured in America. White racism has always been sustained by the white refusal or reluctance to see blacks, to think about them as people, to grant them the kind of place in the imagination that one would grant, say, to the English or even the Russians. Blacks might be servile or troublesome, but never worthy of serious, competitive consideration. Against this Malcolm sent a concrete message: we are human enough to want to kill you for what you have done to us. How does it feel to have people you never paid much attention to want to kill you? (This was the terror Richard Wright captured so powerfully in *Native Son:* your humble chauffeur may kill your daughter. And that novel, too, got attention.) Violence was a means to black visibility for Malcolm, and later for many other militants.

Today this idea of violence as black visibility means that part of Malcolm's renewed popularity comes from his power as an attention-getting figure. If today's "X" is an assertion of self-love, it is also a demand to be seen. This points to the second purpose of Malcolm's violent rhetoric: to restore dignity to blacks in an almost Hegelian sense. Those unwilling to kill and to die for dignity would forever be a slave class. Here he used whites as the model. They would go to war to meet any threat, even when it was far removed. Many times he told his black audiences that whites would not respect them unless they used "any means necessary" to seize freedom. For a minority outnumbered 10-to-1, this was not rational. But it was a point that needed to be made in the name of dignity. It was something that many blacks needed to feel about themselves, that there was a line that no one could cross.

Yet this logic of dignity only partly explains Malcolm's return as an icon in our own day. I believe that the larger reason for his perdurability and popularity is one that is almost never mentioned: that Malcolm X was a deeply conservative man. In times when the collective identity is besieged and confused, groups usually turn to their conservatives, not to their liberals; to their extreme partisans, not to their open-minded representatives. The last twenty-five years have seen huge class and cultural differences open up in black America. The current bromide is that we are not a monolith, and this is profoundly true. We now have a black governor and a black woman senator and millions of black college graduates and so on, but also hundreds of thousands of young blacks in prison. Black identity no longer has a centrifugal force in a racial sense. And in the accompanying confusion we look to the most conservative identity figure.

Malcolm was conservative through and through. As a black nationalist, he was a hard-line militarist who believed in the principle of self-mastery through force. His language and thinking in this regard were oddly in line with Henry Kissinger's description of the world as a brutal place in which safety and a balance of power is maintained through realpolitik. He was Reaganesque in his insistence on negotiating with whites from a position of strength—meaning the threat of violence. And his commitment (until the last year of his life) to racial purity and separatism would have made him the natural ally of David Duke.

In his personal life, moreover, Malcolm scrupulously followed all the Islamic strictures against alcohol, tobacco, drugs, fornication, and adultery, and his attitude toward women was decidedly patriarchal: as a Black Muslim minister he counseled that women could never be completely trusted because of their vanity, and he forbade dancing in his mosque. In his speeches he reserved a special contempt for white liberals, and he once praised Barry Goldwater as a racial realist. Believing entirely in black self-help, he had no use for government programs to uplift blacks, and sneered at the 1964 Civil Rights Bill as nothing more than white expedience.

Malcolm X was one of the most unabashed and unqualified conservatives of his time. And yet today he is forgiven his sexism by black feminists, his political conservatism by black and white liberals, his Islamic faith by black Christians, his violent rhetoric by non-violent veterans of the civil rights struggle, his anti-Semitism by blacks and whites who are repulsed by it, his separatism by blacks who live integrated lives, and even the apparent fabrication of events in his childhood by those who would bring his story to the screen. Malcolm enjoys one of the best Teflon-coatings of all time.

I think one of the reasons for this is that he was such an extreme conservative, that is, such an extreme partisan of his group. All we really ask of such people is that they love the group more than anything else, even themselves. If this is evident, all else is secondary. In fact, we demand conservatism from such people, because it is a testament of their love. Malcolm sneered at government programs because he believed so much in black people: they could do it on their own. He gave up all his vices to intensify his love. He was a father figure who distributed love and hate in our favor. Reagan did something like this when he called the Soviet Union an "evil empire," and he, too, was rewarded with Teflon.

The point is that all groups take their extreme partisans more figuratively than literally. Their offer of unconditional love bribes us into loving them back rather unconditionally, so that our will to be literal with them weakens. We will not see other important black leaders of the 1960s—James Farmer, Whitney Young, Andrew Young, Medgar Evers (a genuine martyr), Roy Wilkins, John Lewis—gracing the T-shirts of young blacks who are today benefiting more from their efforts than from Malcolm's. They were too literal, too much of the actual world, for iconography, for the needs of an unsure psyche. But Malcolm, the hater and the lover, the father figure of romantic blackness, is the perfect icon.

It helps, too, that he is dead, and therefore unable to be literal in our own time. We can't know, for example, if he would now be supporting affirmative action as the reparation that is due to blacks, or condemning it as more white patronization and black dependency. In a way, the revival of Malcolm X is one of the best arguments I know of for the validity of the deconstructionist view of things: Malcolm is now a text. Today we *read* Malcolm. And this—dare I say—is one quality he shares with Christ, who also died young and became a text. He was also an Odyssean figure who journeyed toward self-knowledge. He was a priest and a heretic. For many whites he was a devil and for many blacks a martyr. Even those of my generation who grew up with him really came to know him through the autobiography that he wrote with Alex Haley. Even in his time, then, he was a text, and it is reasonable to wonder if he would have the prominence he has today without that book. (pp. 27-30)

Shelby Steele, "And Big. Malcolm Little," in The New Republic, *Vol. 207, No. 26, December 21, 1992, pp. 27-31.*

FURTHER READING

Bibliography

Davis, Lenwood G. *Malcolm X: A Selected Bibliography.* Westport, Conn.: Greenwood Press, 1984, 146 p.

Book-length bibliography of works about Malcolm X.

Johnson, Timothy V. *Malcolm X: A Comprehensive Annotat-*

ed Bibliography. New York: Garland Publishing, Inc., 1986, 192 p.

Bibliography of works by and about Malcolm X; includes a subject index, citations from African newspapers, and citations from Malcolm's own writing and speeches.

Biography

Breitman, George. *The Last Year of Malcolm X: The Evolution of a Revolutionary.* New York: Pathfinder, 1967, 169 p.

Described as an outgrowth of *Malcolm X Speaks,* which the author helped prepare for publication, this work details Malcolm's activities during the final year of his life.

Breitman, George; Porter, Herman; and Smith, Baxter. *The Assassination of Malcolm X.* Rev. ed. New York: Pathfinder, 1991, 196 p.

Uncovers new evidence regarding Malcolm's death to demonstrate "that the official government version of how the assassination occurred is not credible. The evidence points to government complicity in the murder."

Cone, James H. *Martin & Malcolm & America: A Dream or a Nightmare.* Maryknoll, N.Y.: Orbis Books, 1991, 358 p.

Examines the relationship between Malcolm X and Martin Luther King, Jr., as well as "their meanings for America."

Goldman, Peter. *The Death and Life of Malcolm X.* Rev. ed. Urbana: University of Illinois Press, 1979, 470 p.

Described in the preface as a "white book about Malcolm X," this revised work is among the most substantial biographies by an admirer who interviewed Malcolm between 1962 and 1964.

Perry, Bruce. *Malcolm: The Life of a Man Who Changed Black America.* Barrytown, N.Y.: Station Hill Press, 1991, 568 p.

Comprehensive biography of Malcolm X, focusing on the more personal aspects of the leader's life.

Criticism

Abbot, H. Porter. "Organic Form in the Autobiography of a Convert: The Example of Malcolm X." *CLA Journal* XXIII, No. 2 (December 1979): 125-46.

Compares the lives of Malcolm X and St. Augustine in terms of their mothers, their religious conversions, and the structure of their autobiographies.

Abbott, Philip. "Hustling: Benjamin Franklin, Malcolm X, Abbie Hoffman." In his *States of Perfect Freedom: Autobiography and American Political Thought,* pp. 27-57. Amherst: University of Massachusetts Press, 1987.

Examines the autobiographies of the three political figures and explores their image as "hustlers."

Benson, Thomas W. "Rhetoric and Autobiography: The Case of Malcolm X." *The Quarterly Journal of Speech* 60, No. 1 (February 1974): 1-13.

Argues that *The Autobiography of Malcolm X* "achieves a unique synthesis of selfhood and rhetorical instrumentality."

Boulware, Marcus H. "Minister Malcolm: Orator Profundo." *Negro History Bulletin* 30, No. 7 (November 1967): 12-14

Profile of Malcolm X focusing on his skills as an orator.

Clarke, John Henrik. *Malcolm X: The Man and His Times.* Toronto: The MacMillan Company, 1969, 360 p.

Collects speeches by and interviews with Malcolm X, as well as analytical and commemorative essays, and personal reminiscences of Malcolm.

Groppe, John D. "From Chaos to Cosmos: The Role of Trust in *The Autobiography of Malcolm X.*" *Soundings* LXVI, No. 4 (Winter 1983): 437-49.

Argues that *The Autobiography of Malcolm X* is "the story of the loss, and then the regaining, of the capacity to trust," which ensures Malcolm's "pilgimage from self to cosmos."

Haley, Alex. "The Playboy Interview: Candid Conversations with Cuba's Revolutionary Leader, Comedy's Wackiest Improvisor and the Founding Father of Black Power." *Playboy* 36, No. 1 (January 1989): 135, 296.

Reprints Haley's May 1963 interview with Malcolm X, in which he discusses his origins and involvement with Muslim leader Elijah Muhammad.

Hoyt, Charles Alva. "The Five Faces of Malcolm X." *Negro Amercan Literature Forum* 4, No. 4 (Winter 1970): 107-12.

Divides Malcolm X's life into five stages and five identities: Malcolm Little, Detroit Red, Satan, Malcolm X, and El-Hajj Malik El-Shabazz. Hoyt concludes that Malcolm "*earned* his way to the top; not inherited it, or bought it or fallen into it, as almost every other American political leader seems to have done, but earned it by the pain of his own experience, his growth from mascot to hustler to criminal to controversialist to philosopher."

Leigh, David J. "Malcolm X and the Black Muslim Search for Ultimate Reality." *Ultimate Reality and Meaning* 13, No. 1 (March 1990): 33-49.

Traces Malcolm's search for "ultimate reality" by providing a chronology of his life, "a study of the spiral pilgrimage form" of the *Autobiography,* a summary of Malcolm's changing beliefs, and "several reflections on the social and metaphysical implications of his growth as a religious leader and thinker."

Miller, Ross. "Autobiography as Fact and Fiction: Franklin, Adams, Malcolm X." *The Centennial Review* XVI, No. 3 (Summer 1972): 221-32.

Reconstructs a "coherent American literary tradition" from autobiographies by Benjamin Franklin, Henry Adams, and Malcolm X, demonstrating the mixture of fact and fiction in their works.

Nichols, Charles H. "The Slave Narrators and the Picaresque Mode: Archetypes for Modern Black Personae." In *The Slave's Narrative,* edited by Charles T. Davis and Henry Louis Gates, Jr., pp. 283-98. New York: Oxford University Press, 1985.

Analyzes the influence of slave narratives on modern black autobiographies, including *The Autobiography of Malcolm X.*

Rampersad, Arnold. "Biography, Autobiography, and Afro-American Culture." *Yale Review* 73, No. 1 (October 1983): 1-16.

Briefly cites Malcolm's *Autobiography* as one of three examples, along with Claude Brown's *Manchild in a Promised Land* and Maya Angelou's *I Know Why the Caged Bird Sings,* of "the distinct force of black autobiography, which stamped its influence over virtually every important literary statement of the era of civil rights and the 'black power' years."

Rustin, Bayard. "Making His Mark: A Strong Diagnosis of America's Racial Sickness in One Negro's Odyssey." *Book Week—New York Herald Tribune* (14 November 1965: 1, 8, 10, 12, 16-17.

Review of *The Autobiography of Malcolm X* in which the critic surveys the life of Malcolm X and his role as a leader in the black community.

Stone, Albert E. "Collaboration in Contemporary American Autobiography." *Revue Française d'Études Américaines,* No. 14 (May 1982): 151-65.

Briefly explores the collaboration between Malcolm X and Alex Haley on *The Autobiography of Malcolm X.*

Terry, Eugene. "Black Autobiography: Discernible Forms." *Okike* 19 (September 1981): 6-10.

Investigates a trend in autobiographies by Malcolm X, W. E. B. Du Bois, and Frederick Douglas in which the subject "is first unaware of his life as it differs from the lives of others," then becomes aware and despairs, and ultimately experiences some conversion. Ultimately, the autobiographies "claim the authors' humanity through an ultimate insistence on brotherhood with the humanity of others."

Additional coverage of Malcolm X's life and career is contained in the following sources published by Gale Research: *Black Literature Criticism,* Vol. 2; *Black Writers;* Contemporary Authors, Vols. 111 [obituary], 125; *DISCovering Authors;* and *Major 20th-Century Writers.*

Bobbie Ann Mason

1940-

American short story writer, novelist, and critic.

This entry provides an overview of Mason's career through 1993. For further information on Mason's life and works, see *CLC,* Volumes 28 and 43.

INTRODUCTION

Set primarily in rural western Kentucky, Mason's fiction depicts a rapidly changing South in which individuals who once lived and worked on farms and shared deep-rooted family traditions are now employed by national retail stores, live in subdivisions, and experience the modern world largely through television, popular music, shopping malls, and fast-food restaurants. Unable to reconcile their present lives with the past, Mason's characters have been viewed as grotesques who are experiencing, in Anne Tyler's words, "the sense of bewilderment and anxious hopefulness that people feel when suddenly confronted with change." Mason employs a plain, laconic prose style and often highlights mundane but evocative details to illustrate the impact of mass culture.

Mason grew up on a farm in Paducah, Kentucky, where many of her stories are set. A withdrawn child, she spent much of her youth reading books and listening to popular music on the radio. After attending the University of Kentucky, Mason relocated to New York, where she worked as a writer for the fan magazines *Movie Life* and *TV Star Parade.* While pursuing an advanced degree at the University of Connecticut, Mason began writing short stories, which she submitted for publication to the *New Yorker* magazine. *New Yorker* fiction editor Roger Angell, while offering encouraging comments, rejected nineteen of Mason's submissions before finally accepting one of her stories in 1980; this twentieth story, "Offerings," is included in *Shiloh, and Other Stories.*

Mason has earned critical respect for her compelling and unsentimental depictions of rural, working-class people attempting to adjust to an increasingly modernized South. Her collections of short fiction, *Shiloh, and Other Stories* and *Love Life,* are marked by present-tense narration, often inconclusive endings, and characters who are torn between the security of their familiar lives and the desire for change and independence. Several of Mason's protagonists are alienated from their heritage and have sought refuge in television evangelism, call-in radio mysticism, or aerobic dancing. Her fiction describes not only the commercial, material aspects of her characters' lives, but also examines the threatening changes in social mores that characterize modern life. Most critics attribute Mason's success to her vivid evocation of Southern dialect and the physical and social geography of the region.

In her longer works, Mason further explores the themes and subjects introduced in her short stories. Her first novel, *In Country,* concerns the experiences of Samantha, a seventeen-year-old Kentucky girl whose father was killed in the Vietnam War and whose mother abandoned her as a child. Living with her uncle, an emotionally unstable and physically handicapped Vietnam veteran, Samantha tries to come to terms with the war and the cultural context in which it occurred. However, her attempts to uncover a heritage deeper than the commercialized culture around her are met with reticence and misunderstanding. In *Spence + Lila,* Mason utilizes spare, occasionally lyrical language to tell the story of a long-married couple forced to consider mortality and dissolution when confronted with breast cancer. Most commentators applaud the novel's understated narrative, but some critics find Mason's plain, lean dialogue prevents the development of fully realized characters. In *Feather Crowns,* a historical novel set in 1900, Christie Wheeler gives birth to quintuplets, and the event brings fame and change to her town and family. Critics praise Mason's eye for detail and description, applauding in particular her effective evocation of turn-of-the-century Kentucky and her subtle, often humorous dialogue.

Although some reviewers have faulted Mason's fictional works for employing the same unvarying narrative voice and for lacking definite resolutions, most agree that her works portray contemporary Southern life with accuracy, humor, and poignancy. Summarizing her significance, Roz Kaveney asserts that Mason "illuminates ordinary lives with a quiet, clear diction, and celebrates not only the almost unchanging human values which her characters embody, but also the passing details of fashion and social evolution which their personalities refract."

PRINCIPAL WORKS

Nabokov's Garden: A Guide to "Ada" (criticism) 1974
Shiloh, and Other Stories (short stories) 1982
In Country (novel) 1985
Spence + Lila (novel) 1988
Love Life (short stories) 1989
Feather Crowns (novel) 1993

CRITICISM

Robert H. Brinkmeyer, Jr. (essay date Spring 1987)

[*In the following essay, Brinkmeyer explores Mason's place in contemporary Southern literature and examines the important role that a sense of history plays in her fiction.*]

In the opening chapter of his intriguing study of contemporary Southern literature, *Another Generation: Southern Fiction Since World War II,* Lewis A. Lawson locates a cluster of significant themes and outlooks in the fiction of the Southern renascence and then discusses how these themes and attitudes have been superseded by a new set in the fiction of the contemporary South. Writers of the renascence (those writing roughly between 1920 and 1945), says Lawson, viewed humans as free moral agents, responsible both for their own actions and for those of their ancestors. These writers also had little sympathy for theories espousing social or psychological determinism, and did not see themselves or their fellow Southerners as suffering from, in Lawson's words, "the nameless anxiety concomitant with urban, industrialized existence, the anxiety that drained off vitality and love of life, the anxiety that compelled people to live frantically, yet fruitlessly." While depicting Southerners as being essentially free from modern *angst,* the writers of the renascence nonetheless were keenly aware of the inroads that the modernist experience was making in the South, and thus much of their literature focussed on the disintegration of the old ways, particularly the traditions of family and community. To understand better this increasingly fluid and unstable world, these writers turned to the past for vision and perspective. Writes Lawson: "The past existed not merely for its own sake, but because it provided the metaphors through which the present could be described and understood. Shared history could provide ready reference points for private experience."

There is little shared history in contemporary Southern literature, argues Lawson. The Old Order (a society based on myth and tradition) has given way to the New (a society based on science and marketplace—the land of cotton has become the Sun Belt), and contemporary Southern writers must struggle with these new circumstances. Their view of humanity shifts dramatically from that of their forerunners; rather than free moral agents, Southern writers now see themselves and their neighbors as, in Lawson's words, "product[s] of present social complexities, not of past philosophic simplicities." With their focus moving from the disintegration of society and its valued traditions to the disintegration of the self, contemporary writers frequently explore the individual whose interior life is in shambles and who is adrift in a meaningless world. History has little to offer these individuals; the struggle to survive has less to do with one's historical roots (history is no longer a vital force in a world without traditions) than it does with effort to overcome feelings of loneliness and abstraction. Most contemporary Southern writers, Lawson suggests, work from such an outlook; their visions vary, he adds, according to the different alternatives that they suggest for survival.

Lawson's observations here bear particular relevance to the work of one of the South's best contemporary writers, Bobbie Ann Mason. Mason is especially intriguing because her as of yet relatively short fictional career embodies a move from what I will call Lawson's contemporary mode to a richer and more complex mode that bears a number of striking resemblances to the fiction of the Southern renascence. It is just possible that Mason is charting a new direction for Southern fiction, a rebirth of sorts adapting patterns from the past to enrich and comprehend the disorder of contemporary experience.

Almost all of Mason's short stories, most of which have been collected into her volume, ***Shiloh and Other Stories*** (1982), embody what Lawson sees as the prevailing mode of contemporary Southern fiction. These works explore the confusions and isolation of the individual in a world gone awry, focussing most often on people from small towns in western Kentucky struggling to adapt to contemporary life. Gone from the world of these stories is a Southern society of tradition and community, a society that Allen Tate in his 1945 essay "The New Provincialism" calls regional, one where a person's consciousness is shaped and guided by a communal wisdom passed down through the generations. Mason's world fulfills Tate's prophecy of the rise of the provincial society cut off from tradition whose denizens live in a continuous present and grapple less with problems of right and wrong than with matters of technological progress and utility. Living without a sense of history and an historical perspective, the provincial person, says Tate, "assumes that the present moment is unique" and so "without benefit of the fund of traditional wisdom approaches the simplest problems of life as if nobody had ever heard of them before." So too do most of Mason's characters: rather than looking to their elders or to their ancestors, they turn for guidance to the spokespeople of contemporary culture, the Phil Donahues and the Erma Bombecks. Trends instead of traditions hold sway.

Compared with Southerners who generations earlier lived in traditional small-town communities unvexed by the problems of modernity, Mason's characters possess much more individual freedom. Their places in society, unlike those of their forebears, are no longer so rigidly defined. But this freedom comes with a cost. Her characters frequently suffer from severe insecurity; many wallow in feelings of aimlessness and confusion. To compensate for the absence of a moral vision that could give their lives direction and commitment, they look to self-fulfillment as the ultimate ideal. One judges others (and treats them accordingly) not by the integrity of their actions but by the role they play in helping—or hindering—one's quest for self. In such a world, cherished bonds and commitments dissolve seemingly on characters' momentary whims. Priorities seem askew. Perhaps the most succinct statement of this bleak state of affairs comes in Mason's story, **"Lying Doggo,"** when a man pondering the impending death of his dog says, " 'The only people I ever cared about who died were rock heroes.' "

Mason's stories are filled with broken relationships—between people and their friends, husbands and wives, parents and children, people and their extended families—that together embody the collapse of family and community. In this respect her work stands in stark counterpoint to that of Eudora Welty. Both writers frequently portray scenes of family gatherings, but while Welty's reunions usually underscore the power of family bonds to overcome—at least momentarily—the forces of confusion and misfortune, Mason's illustrate the undermining, if not the utter collapse, of the family unit. Rather than standing apart from the cultural chaos—as Welty's families usually do, so that they embody a sense of order and coherence—Mason's families are as much a part of the cultural confusion as the strips of franchise restaurants and K-Marts where they eat and shop.

"Drawing Names," a story about a family's joyless reunion at Christmas, clearly embodies Mason's vision of the demise of the family. The story focusses on Carly Sisson, a young woman who along with her three sisters and their families and boyfriend, has returned to her parent's farm for Christmas. Despite the nature of the holiday, there is little joy at the gathering; the parents and daughters have come together more from a sense of obligation to continue the tradition of Christmas reunions than from any desire to share in love or to reaffirm familial bonds and identities. The family has clearly grown apart and, as the story makes clear, the bonds cannot be reconstructed merely by bringing the family together at a holiday gathering. The dichotomy between the way things used to be and the way they are now is particularly troublesome to the father. " 'Use to, the menfolks would eat first, and the children separate. The womenfolks would eat last, in the kitchen,' " he says at one point, thinking back over the reunions of the past. One of his daughters snaps back: " 'Times are different now, Pappy. We're just as good as the men.' "

Times indeed have changed, and in Mason's world of flux where people live essentially separate lives, cut off from the traditions of family and community, the family reunion becomes finally a sham, an exercise by actors feigning happiness as they try to persevere through a long, stifling day. Significantly, the center of the reunion is not the family dinner (where with everyone together tensions surface most painfully) but the television, a mindless escape where the most pressing concern is who will win the Blue-Gray game. This is Christmas, contemporary style.

While far from optimistic, Mason's vision in her short stories is not entirely bleak. In a number of stories, characters at the end seem to be moving toward a higher level of awareness of their situation. With this new understanding, these characters, one gathers, are in much more control of their lives, even if they are not entirely happy or have few options on which to act. At the conclusion of **"Drawing Names,"** for instance, Carolyn, who has been stunned by her boyfriend's jilting and by a sister's announcement that she and her husband are separating, nonetheless is able to draw sustenance and insight from the joy she witnesses between her sister Laura Jean and her boyfriend Jim. Laura Jean and Jim seem determined not to let the family's problems and tensions undermine their happiness, and it is their strength and resiliency that Carolyn celebrates at the end when she raises her cup—"Cheers," she says—to Jim. While it is not clear whether Carolyn will be able to go forth and forge her own life of happiness, at least she now has a good idea of what she needs to do.

In a sense, Carolyn's growth emerges from her coming to terms with her history as represented by her family. Unlike her father, who is so obsessed with the past that he denies any value in the present, Carolyn now understands that she must free herself from the past and strike anew without history's cumbersome baggage. As appealing as this idea sounds, however, this is not Mason's ultimate vision of humanity's quest for meaning, and I think she means us to see that Carolyn still has a good way to go to reach fulfillment. Denying one's history and striving for happiness based solely on one's relationship with another person is for Mason as fanciful as Carolyn's daydream of sailing away into the snowscape with Laura Jean and Jim (what passes through her mind right before she toasts Jim at the end). Turning away from one's past means losing perspective and structure, and a single relationship with another cannot entirely make up for what is lost: relationships alone are extremely fragile and are limiting in that they fail to provide a transcendent framework of order. Carolyn herself is divorced and her sister Iris is separating from her husband, and there is little evidence to suggest that other relationships that must become the sole means of happiness and understanding will in the end fare much differently.

This lesson is what Carolyn must learn, and indeed what all Mason's characters must realize, to reach fulfillment. Most of Mason's characters do not get as far along as Carolyn; they remain instead sunk in the tedium and dreariness of their lives. They suffer from the modern *angst* Lewis Lawson speaks of in his discussion of contemporary writers, and they make little effort to transcend it. One of the most disturbing aspects of their lives and one which severely undercuts any effort to forge a meaningful existence is that they do not possess a compelling sense of history. The past is no longer vital, as it was for Southerners of the early twentieth century who struggled to comprehend the modern experience from a perspective of community and shared history. Having grown up in an age given to suburbs and shopping malls, Mason's characters (along with characters in much of contemporary Southern fiction) fail to develop a consciousness rooted in history and irony that would add a richness to their vision and would allow them to understand better elemental matters of meaning and existence.

One of the clearest statements of the contemporary loss of historical vision that was once so significant to the Southern mind comes in Mason's story **"Shiloh."** In the literature of the Southern renascence Civil War battlefields and Confederate graveyards are usually extremely significant, often initiating profound meditations and interior probings (one thinks most readily of Allen Tate's "Ode to the Confederate Dead" where the poet struggles to define his modern identity in light of his Southern heritage). But in **"Shiloh"** the battlefield of that name means for Leroy and Norma Jean Moffitt, a couple whose marriage is falling apart, little more than a large park, its historical significance confined (except during one extraordinary moment) largely to the plaques that dot the countryside. As Norma Jean drives aimlessly about the park, Leroy ponders the landscape's immensity but has trouble seeing it as a battlefield—he had expected it to look like a golf course. Norma Jean's sudden admission that she wants out of the marriage, however, stuns Leroy into instinctively searching out the larger significance of the battlefield. He stands by the park's cemetery, trying to grasp the import of his wife's words, but finds himself instead thinking about the dead soldiers that lie before him:

> Leroy takes a lungful of smoke and closes his eyes as Norma Jean's words sink in. He tries to focus on the fact that thirty-five hundred soldiers died on the grounds around him. He can only think of that war as a board game with plastic soldiers. Leroy almost smiles, as he compares the Confederates' daring attack on the Union camps and Virgil Mathis's raid on the bowling alley. General Grant, drunk and furious, shoved the Southerners back to Corinth, where Mabel and Jet Beasely were married years later, when Mabel was still thin and good-looking. The next day, Mabel and Jet visited the battleground, and then Norma Jean was born, and then she married Leroy and they had a baby, which they lost, and now Leroy and Norma Jean are here at the same battleground. Leroy knows he is leaving out a lot. He is leaving out the insides of history. History was always just names and dates to him. It occurs to him that building a house out of logs [what he has promised Norma Jean to do] is similarly empty—too simple. And the real inner workings of a marriage, like most of history, have escaped him.

Leroy's instinctive turning to the graveyard and the past it embodies brings him a larger perspective not only on his failed marriage but also on the continuity of generations and the complexity of history. Yet Leroy does not seem to be a changed man in the sense that he will after this moment of crisis continue to probe history and to open himself up to what he finds. His has been a momentary enlightenment, discovered by accident. The story concludes with Leroy running blindly back to Norma Jean—to a failed marriage and to a woman who has no place in her heart or her life for him. As he himself had admitted a few moments earlier, "the real inner workings of a marriage, like most of history, have escaped him," and they still do.

For Leroy and most of Mason's other characters, history, except during moments of extraordinary crisis, is not a shaping force, alive and vital. Certainly the Civil War experience no longer defines Mason's Southerners. While several other characters—Kay in **"Offerings"** and Nancy in **"Nancy Culpepper"** for instance—gain a larger perspective of their lives by investigating the relevance of their Southern roots, none appears rewarded with a fullness of vision that will carry them forward to further growth. While Mason often establishes in her stories a tension between a traditional past and a modernist present, very similar to the paradigm found in much of the literature of the Southern renascence, she does so only to show how this tension no longer carries any significant weight and authority. The present order is so overwhelming and so pervasive in the modern consciousness that the ways of the distant past pose little challenge to it; only in moments of crisis or in unusual situations does the tension surface, and then it usually leads merely to momentary, not ongoing insight.

Despite the failure of a historical perspective rooted in Old South tradition and community to challenge and probe the contemporary consciousness, Mason nonetheless does not abandon the significance of posing a historical vision against that of the present to spur healthy dialectical interchange and growth. Rather she alters the forces of tension. As she suggests in **"New-Wave Format,"** those characters destined for growth turn their eyes not to the far-off past of North-South strife but to an era of upheaval closer to home—the late 1960s and early 1970s, a period of counterculture experiment and anti-war protest. By pondering these charged times of strife and conflict when the foundations of American society were challenged and defamed, Mason seems to be suggesting, people can find a counterpoint to the status quo that will challenge them to grope for deeper understandings of self and society. Though he probably could not verbalize it in the way I just have, it is nonetheless this knowledge toward which Edwin Creech, a 43 year-old bus driver for mentally retarded adults in **"New-Wave Format,"** gropes. Creech has lived a life of wandering and non-commitment, moving "from job to job as casually as he did with women," but at the time of the story he is undergoing a profound shift in perspective. Where he had once seen himself as an upstart adventurer, "now he believes he has gone through life rather blindly, without much pain or sense of loss." Now involved with a pretty 20 year-old woman named Sabrina, Edwin has become much more interested in evaluating his life.

Music plays a crucial role in his excursions into self and history. For some finally unaccountable reason, he finds himself playing rock music from the 1960s—Janis Joplin, the Doors, the Rolling Stones, and others—on the bus's sound system. Listening to the music and watching his passengers respond happily to it, Edwin thinks about the significance of their lives and his own. For the first time, Edwin begins to sort out the pieces of his scattered past and to shape from them a larger vision of knowledge:

> It makes Edwin sad to think how history passes [his retarded passengers] by, but sometimes he feels the same way about his own life. As he drives along, playing these old songs, he thinks about what his life was like back then. During his first marriage, he worked in a gas station, saving for a down payment on a house. Lois Ann fed him on a TV tray while he watched the war. It was like a drama series. After Lois Ann, and then his travels out West, there was Carolyn and another down payment on another house and more of the war. Carolyn had a regular schedule—pork chops on Mondays, chicken on Tuesdays. Thursday's menu had completely escaped his memory. He feels terrible, remembering his wives by his food, and remembering the war as a TV series. His life has been a delayed reaction. He feels as if he's about Sabrina's age. He plays music he did not understand fifteen years ago, music that now seems full of possibility: the Grateful Dead, the Jefferson Airplane, groups with vision. Edwin feels that he is growing and changing for the first time in years.

Ultimately through his inner investigations Edwin achieves a vision of self and history that promises fulfillment. He is not in a position to chart a new direction for his life, one that will no longer consist of aimless drifting, cold disregard for others, and empty marriages. To the surprise of Sabrina, who does not know what to make of Edwin's deepening spirit, Edwin tells her: " 'I feel like I've had a developmental disability and it suddenly went away. Something like if Freddie Johnson [one of the retarded adults] learned to read. That's how I feel.' "

Thinking back on the 1960s, or indeed on any period that seriously challenges one's present life, is not for Mason a foolproof means of growth. Certainly there are a number of characters in her stories who are acutely aware of the significant changes that their lives have undergone but who nonetheless are anguished and unhappy. These people, who often focus their attention for fulfillment entirely on the present moment, have cultivated a detachment from the past so that whatever meaning it potentially carries is reduced merely either to nostalgia or intellectual curiosity. In both cases, history becomes a set of experiences that bears little relevance to one's present life. Such detachment is what plagues Jack Cleveland in **"Lying Doggo"** until the very end of the story when he opens himself up to the wisdom of the past (from his days of counterculture experiment with his wife) and celebrates a quickening of knowledge and spirit. Jack's growth is similar to Edwin Creech's: both have been renewed by their acceptance into their lives of a vital sense of history. Both, furthermore, draw upon the events of the 1960s and 1970s, a period drastically different from the time in which they now live; and both discover that this searing dichotomy between past and present offers perspective and dialectical challenge.

Mason's most significant and forceful statement of personal growth through the challenge of history comes in her recent novel, ***In Country*** (1985). Again we find a character, Samantha ("Sam") Hughes, who focuses her attention on the 1960s and early 1970s in an effort to define herself and her heritage. Unlike Edwin Creech and Jack Cleveland, however, Sam explores the meanings of that era's most disturbing spectacle: the Vietnam War. Though Sam's birth dates from the Vietnam period (she is almost eighteen at the time of the novel), her quest for discovery is anything but an abstract pursuit: her father, Dwayne Hughes, was killed in the war and her uncle Emmett, with whom she now lives, is a Vietnam veteran who suffers not only from severe psychological trauma but also from symptoms associated with exposure to Agent Orange.

Sam's intense interest in the Vietnam War begins after she hears her high school's commencement speaker, a Methodist minister, talk on the significance of self-sacrifice in our nation's efforts to maintain its strong world power. The minister's words strike a disturbing chord within Sam, and she begins to think about Vietnam and the myriad sacrifices people suffered during the conflict. During the summer following graduation she finds her interest in Vietnam growing increasingly obsessive. Not only does she read books on the war, but she searches out Vietnam veterans to discover what the battle experience was like. She also probes into her family's experience, reading her father's wartime diary, prodding the reclusive Emmett about his feelings and experiences, asking her mother and grandparents about her father and about how they felt when they received word of his death. Sam's pestering of him and others about the war prompts Emmett to observe: " 'Sam's got Nam on the brain.' "

Emmett's words here epitomize both Sam's obsession and the lack of encouragement she encounters from almost everyone in town in her effort to understand the war. Most of the Vietnam veterans she knows would rather not talk about their experiences except to other veterans. For them, Sam's probings are meddlesome and even silly; as they tell her, there is no way for her truly to understand what life was like in the Vietnam jungles—a person had to be there. Her family members are also generally not enthusiastic about her questions since they stir up painful memories. Her mother, Irene, for instance, who has remarried and moved away to Lexington, has little patience with Sam's questions. She is doing her best to create a new life and to distance herself from her past. At one point after telling her about her father, she says to Sam: " 'But I can't live in the past. It was all such a stupid waste. There's nothing to remember.' "

Sam also gets little support for her quest from people in town. As her friend Tom, a Vietnam veteran, points out, the Hopewell population's only interest in the past lies in " 'old-timey days. Antiques and Civil War stuff.' " History for them is merely a saccharine nostalgia, wistful imaginings of days long past. Sam herself wonders if "Hopewell was just now catching up to the Civil War. When would people start putting M-16s and pictures of missiles on their living room walls?" Sam knows the answer to her question—not for a long time, if ever—for, Sylvester Stallone notwithstanding, the experience of the Vietnam War, at home or abroad, is not ripe for nostalgia. " 'Nobody gives a shit,' " Tom tells Sam, after advising her to stop searching out people about the war. " 'They've got it twisted around in their heads what it was about, so that they can live with it and not have to think about it.' " He adds that the townsfolk by and large treated the Vietnam veterans all right when they came home because the anti-war movement was never very strong in Hopewell. " 'But that means,' " he continues, " 'they've got a notion in their heads of who we are, and that image just don't fit all of us. Around here, nobody wants to rock the boat.' "

Despite this widespread resistance, Sam presses forward in her pursuit of history, and it is not long before she begins to show signs of growth and development. Unlike her boyfriend Lonnie and her friend Dawn who focus all their efforts and attention on making do locally (it is clear that the boundaries of their lives, intellectually if not actually, will always be Hopewell), Sam ponders larger matters—the nature of war, honor, national purpose. Not surprisingly, Sam begins to grow away from her old friends and to be attracted to a new set, mostly Vietnam veterans.

Sam's growth, however, is anything but instantaneous. Many of her initial reactions to what she discovers during her quest are of the knee-jerk variety—overly emotional and unthought-out. After reading her father's battlefield diary, for instance, she concludes that the Vietnam War was merely an expression of American machismo. " 'The least little threat,' " she tells Emmett, " 'and America's got to put on its cowboy boots and stomp around and show somebody a thing or two.' " Of course she is partly right, but for Sam to understand the terrible complexity of the war—and more generally of the dark side of human experience—she must open herself more freely and with more detachment to the richness of experience. Her singlemindedness at times not only impedes her growth of vision but also leads her both to ignore and to misinterpret the legitimate needs and concerns of others, particularly those who are not Vietnam veterans or people struggling with similar problems. Sam all too often shows little sympathy and understanding, even of those close to her, including her mother and Emmett. At one point, for instance, she wrongly concludes that Emmett is haunted by the war only because he got hooked on an unbreakable habit of killing, and that his sickness represents something peculiar to all men (not women): "Men wanted to kill. That's what men did, she thought. It was their basic profession." Such thinking leads her to spurn for the moment all the men who are important in her life. "To hell with all of them," she thinks, "—Lonnie, her dad, her uncle, her grandfathers, Lorenzo Jones."

Yet with time and reflection, Sam matures and her vision widens to take in a larger range of experience. In the final scene of the novel, when she, Emmett, and one of her grandmothers visit the Vietnam War Memorial in Washington, D.C., she has a moment of insight that opens the way to new realms of growth and understanding. At the Memorial she sees not only her father's name cut in the stone, but also that of a soldier whose name is hers—SAM A. HUGHES. She touches her name and is filled with a sense of the immense sweep of the war and it pervasive influence on our nation's people. "How odd it feels," she thinks, after running her fingers over her name, "as though all the names in America have been used to decorate this wall."

From a simplistic and emotional understanding of the Vietnam War and human evil, Sam here at the end possesses a deeper knowledge of the dark complexities that shadow all human experience. Moreover, she understands that facing up to these complexities—rather than giving into them in despair—is the nature of growth and regeneration. At one point earlier in the novel, when thinking of the horrors of the Vietnam conflict, Sam calls to mind the soundtrack of *Apocalypse Now* with the Doors singing " 'This is the end . . . the children are insane.' " At the cemetery, however, Sam realizes that these horrors are not the end but actually the beginning, for only by confronting the past, including its atrocities, can a person achieve a perspective on the present that leads to vision. From the struggle to comprehend the dark depths of the Vietnam experience—the sending off of young men to fight an unjust war, the committing of countless atrocities on civilians by soldiers on both sides, the poisoning of a nation's land and people by a deadly defoliant—emerge finally wholeness and vision. The novel ends not only with Sam's regeneration but also with that of her grandmother and Emmett. " 'Coming up on this wall of a sudden and seeing how black it was, it was so awful,' " her grandmother tells Sam, "but then I came down in it and saw that white carnation blooming out of that crack and it gave me hope. It made me know he's watching over us." Emmett undergoes a more profound, almost phoenix-like rebirth. As he sits cross-legged before the wall, searching out the names of those with whom he fought, " 'his face bursts into a smile like flames.' " In finally confronting the terrors of his past, Emmett is ready to forge a new life, something he has been resisting since his return from Vietnam.

This final scene is significant not only as a strong and fitting conclusion to a fine novel but also as a revealing statement on the state of contemporary Southern fiction. The significance of the conclusion of ***In Country***—and indeed of the novel as a whole—to Southern writing becomes most evident, I believe, when it is looked at alongside Allen Tate's "Ode to the Confederate Dead," a poem written almost 60 years before by another Kentuckian. The two works share some striking similarities in terms of theme and message; in essence, at the end of ***In Country*** Mason transposes a crucial paradigm of the Southern literary renascence—that to understand the present, including oneself, one explores the past—into a contemporary setting. In doing so, Mason maintains the integrity of the paradigm but alters its thrust and direction.

For both Tate and Mason, understanding the past is crucial to achieving perspective and growth. Both "Ode to the

Confederate Dead" and the ending of ***In Country*** portray a character standing at a graveyard memorial, struggling to come to terms with himself/herself and with society at large by meditating upon history. For both characters vision can come not by simply mouthing platitudes of allegiance or praise for heroism, but by grappling with the complexities and dilemmas of their inheritance. Trying to will oneself back into history by blindly worshipping the past is finally a fruitless endeavor because that identification can never be complete. Tate's efforts in the poem to call forth the battlefield emotions of the Confederate war dead fail time and again, as do Sam's struggles to experience for herself life in the Vietnam jungles, as seen most clearly when she camps out at Cawood's Pond. Despite these failures, however, through their efforts to comprehend the past both the poet and Sam become guardians of their traditions, ultimately vitalizing the past and in turn being vitalized by it.

Though they share this paradigm of growth and development, Tate and Mason differ in the specific ends to which they put it. Where Tate draws from an explicitly Southern past to define his role as a modern Southern artist, Mason's efforts at definition are less regional. Her focus is less on the Southern experience than on the American, and so for her a Southerner's quest for self-definition means coming to terms with America and not the South, except as an expression of the national experience. This focus leads her back to the era of the Vietnam War, a period that tested the American way of life from within and without.

To point out Mason's larger scope is of course not to assert that she is a better writer than Tate, but merely to suggest that she, like many other contemporary Southern writers, is moving away from seeing the South as a region distinctively set apart from the rest of the nation. Certainly she acknowledges that regional differences still exist, but these differences appear almost inconsequential when placed in the larger context of national concerns. While a commonplace, it is nonetheless true that in our world of easy mobility and instantaneous communication, the barriers between regions are breaking down as never before. For Mason and many other Southern writers, understanding one's "Southerness" is almost (not quite) the equivalent of understanding one's "Americanness."

What better expression of this shift in focus than the conclusion of ***In Country,*** where a Southerner *leaves* the South to ponder history and society at the Vietnam War Memorial in Washington, D.C., our nation's capitol. The tension that Tate sees—and, more generally, his generation—between Southern tradition and modern relativism becomes with Mason the tension between a facile American optimism that overlooks the dark sides of history and the knowledge of defeat and despair in the Vietnam War experience. This distinctly Southern insistence on keeping hold of history, on probing rather than forgetting, on immersing oneself in the experience of defeat so to rise transfigured above it, is perhaps the most telling message that Mason and several other Southern contemporary writers are offering us, writers and readers alike. This profound probing of the darker sides of our national experience, as performed so powerfully in Mason's ***In Country,*** may in time lead us into the next Southern—and American—renascence. (pp. 20-32)

Robert H. Brinkmeyer, Jr., "Finding One's History: Bobbie Ann Mason and Contemporary Southern Literature," in The Southern Literary Journal, *Vol. XIX, No. 2, Spring, 1987, pp. 20-33.*

Michael Dorris (review date 26 June 1988)

[*Dorris is an American poet, novelist, educator, and cultural anthropologist. In the following review, he outlines the plot and characters of* Spence + Lila.]

Bobbie Ann Mason writes in the plain, direct prose of Western Kentucky, a language whose poetry resides in terse idiom, in the shorthand of communally shared assumptions. The characters she has created in previous books—***Shiloh and Other Stories,*** her award-winning debut collection, and ***In Country,*** her fine 1985 novel—are distinguished by their unflinching realism. They shop at K-Mart, eat Colonel Sanders fried chicken, and watch network TV beamed from Paducah. They live in a region equidistant from Louisville, Nashville and St. Louis, a lush, traditionally agricultural land bordered by TVA lakes and the Ohio and Mississippi rivers, a territory in transition whose tobacco and cotton fields are being replaced by retirement trailers parks and condos.

These are steady, church-going men and women, people who deny the existence of high drama in their lives and, when they need advice, seek it in the pages of slick magazines. Their pleasures are simple: "Even after they were married, they looked forward to going out for hamburgers almost as much as they looked forward to making love." Their exoticisms are tame by urban standards: a new hairdo, a senior citizens tour to Hawaii or the Badlands, a child who has moved north and become inscrutable. But eventually in each of their lives, moments and events occur—the unaccountable tragedies of mortality—which cannot be understated or ignored, and at these times a kind of lonely despair, an aching, tongue-tied quest for deeper meaning, consumes them.

Spence + Lila is the chronicle of one such incident. Lila Culpepper, tough farm wife of Spence, mother of three grown children, pillar of the community, a woman who has always enjoyed doing jigsaw puzzles because "the snap of two pieces going together was like knowing something for sure," has grown fatigued on a family visit to Disney World and returned home to discover in her large right breast a lima bean-sized knot of cancer.

She and Spence had once "felt as though they would live forever. They could never imagine one of them without the other," but before she or anyone else can realize what's happening, Lila is in the hospital and has had a modified radical mastectomy. It is only while she waits for a second operation, the removal of plaque from the clogged arteries of her throat, that there is time for reflection, for anticipating death, for taking stock.

The three children—Nancy the eldest, who lives in Boston

with her photographer husband and spike-haired teenage son; Cat, trying to resume her life after a failed marriage; and Lee, sitting watch at Lila's bed—and Spence travel daily from farm to town. In their worry, the family learns the new vocabulary of disease and attempts to make it ordinary and therefore comprehensible by integrating it into the folk wisdom of their accustomed world. They talk in dread of "cobalt," as if the cure and not the ailment is the enemy, and attribute illness to a lifetime of bacon grease. They jokingly normalize a prosthesis by tossing it like a football among themselves. They seek the accustomed comfort and irritation of kin and church, and tentatively re-examine shared memories. Restricted by conventions that forbid the expression of emotions—"Lila married into a family that never knew what to say. Spence is all bottled up and Lee and Nancy are just like him"—they seek each other as though in the dark, trusting that by voicing a little they will communicate a great deal.

And somehow they succeed. Through the accumulation of tiny, almost imperceptible signs, affection is demonstrated, bonds are reaffirmed, inventory is taken and found sufficient. By the time the crisis has passed, the foundation of the family has been renewed by the ordeal. There is a sense of freshness, a replenishment of resources, a purification every bit as risky but ultimately as therapeutic as Lila's carotid cleansing. Spense and Lila, a couple who have "spent a lifetime growing things together," emerge invigorated, ready in their shared strength for whatever surprises await them.

Mason writes about her characters with respect and occasional lyricism. Enhanced by LaNelle Mason's gentle, evocative drawings, ***Spence + Lila*** is a quiet triumph, a paean to long marriage, and another fine installment in Harper & Row's new "short novel" series.

Michael Dorris, "Bonds of Love," in Chicago Tribune—Books, *June 26, 1988, p. 6.*

Frank Conroy (review date 26 June 1988)

[*Conroy is an American editor, critic, and author of a highly praised autobiography,* Stop-time *(1967). In the following review, he discusses the strengths and weaknesses of Mason's narrative technique in her novel* Spence + Lila.]

Bobbie Ann Mason's work has attracted a great deal of attention, and rightly so. In ***Shiloh and Other Stories*** and her novel, ***In Country,*** she has shown a deft touch for the craft of narrative fiction and has charmed many readers with her ability to write dialogue, particularly the dialogue of country folk. Her new short novel, ***Spence + Lila,*** displays some of her strengths quite well, but also suggests she may have gone about as far as she can go with her favored techniques. One wishes she had risked a bit more in this book, taking us under the surface of things instead of lingering there so lovingly and relentlessly.

Spence and Lila Culpepper, farm folk in late middle age, married almost all their lives, face a crisis as Lila's breast cancer and narrowed arteries are dealt with in a modern local hospital. Their three grown children—daughters Cat and Nancy and son Lee—are in nervous attendance. Spence's memories, as he moves back and forth from the farm to the hospital room, and Lila's memories, as she daydreams or dozes through the days, provide a gloss of the history of the family. Spence and Lila emerge as simple people who have lived close to the land and possess only the most limited vocabulary with which to examine their mostly unexamined lives. The children are sketched with as few lines as possible (as they might be in a short story)—Cat, vaguely feminist, who lives in Boston; Nancy the bookworm; Lee, who left the farm for a factory job and mortgage slavery. They seem to be here to make the point that Spence and Lila are loved by their family.

Miss Mason weaves various themes into the unhurried narrative with characteristic skill. A few vignettes of Spence passing shells below decks in World War II, seasick and wondering what's going on; Lila's solo ventures into the world on guided tours, seeing the Pacific and so on; the neighbor Bill growing marijuana along with his corn; celebrations of the fertility of the earth; images of ecological pollution; references to rock-and-roll; the continual contrast of high-tech medicine and down-home earthiness—it all reads very easily.

One wishes Mason had risked a bit more in *Spence + Lila,* taking us under the surface of things instead of lingering there so lovingly and relentlessly.

—Frank Conroy

So what's wrong? Why does one feel increasingly uneasy as this smooth, artful writing flows by page after page? Perhaps out of the suspicion that the author has reduced the central characters down to manageable form to fit them into the book, rather than risking the attempt to deal with fully complex characters who might represent more of a threat to the neatness of the narrative. Are simple country people really as simple as Spence and Lila suggest? (I must confess to a prejudice here. I don't think there are any simple people. Not down on the farm, not in the city, not anywhere. Some people may appear to be so, but that is the surface. We are all extraordinarily complex, it seems to me, albeit in different ways.)

Miss Mason is very good at eliciting the special poignancy of people who don't really understand what is happening to them. For instance, Lila being taken up to the operating room: "As the leprechauns wheel her away, she sees Spence gazing after her helplessly. She has forgotten to tell Nancy and Cat something, something important she meant to say about Spence. His face disappears and she is in an elevator, with music playing, the kind of music they play in heaven."

But this kind of thing degenerates into sentimentality unless it is balanced with believable and surprising moments when people do understand what is happening to them. If we feel the hand of the author preventing the characters from understanding, keeping them down, as it were, we are prevented from fully sympathizing with them.

Spence + Lila is a love story, and if there is a shallowness to this man and this woman, then there are limits as to how much their love means to us. What happens in the novel is that we wind up watching Bobbie Ann Mason being moved by a love story. She seems to know something about these people that isn't there in the text; she knows, in any event, more than us, and even though we trust her, we feel to some extent abandoned. We feel uneasy, forced to peer around the author to catch quick glimpses of her characters.

Despite all this, there are real strengths displayed in this novel. A particular kind of warmth presses through from time to time. Miss Mason's superb ear for dialogue is evident. Toward the end, Spence begins to emerge from the caricature of the taciturn farmer, and there is a brilliant section describing a ride he takes in a crop-duster over his own land that alone makes the book worth reading. ***Spence + Lila*** does not seem to me to be a setback for the author, rather it simply marks time. It may well be preparing the way for more powerful work to come.

Frank Conroy, "The Family at Her Bedside," in The New York Times Book Review, *June 26, 1988, p. 7.*

On Mason's characters:

Some critics have objected that the people Mason writes about are too shallow, too limited to be subjects of fiction—that they spend most of their time at shopping malls. Robert Dunn, writing on the subject in *The New York Times Book Review,* used words such as "disengaged" and "aimless" and "bland and undefined," and "undirected."

"The characters I write about, a lot of times, they seem to me like they're locked away somewhere," Mason responds. "They might not read books, even though their library's right there in town.

"The characters in my world don't have the guidance or perspective to know that there might be this *other* view of television or malls. They're in that world and they like television fine, thank you. And they love the malls, and I don't judge them for it. When they go to the shopping mall, and many of them go just to window shop, they're looking at deliverance from a hard way of life."

She is sitting up now, leaning forward. Obviously, this is something she feels strongly about, something that forms an essential part of her experience.

"I feel that my characters are on the threshold of possibility," she says. "Their lives are being changed, and they're very excited by it. They're getting a chance maybe for the first time in their lives to get somewhere and to prove something and to do something. Many of my characters are caught up in the myth of progress; from their point of view it means liberation, the promise of a better life."

Mervyn Rothstein, in The New York Times Magazine, *May 15, 1988.*

G. O. Morphew (essay date Spring 1989)

[In the following essay, Morphew examines the "downhome feminism" of the main characters in several of Mason's short stories.]

Much has been written about the loss of identity experienced by the characters of Bobbie Ann Mason's short stories; the people of ***Shiloh and Other Stories*** in particular seem to be confused by the onslaught of pop culture, the media, and other forces of social change. The males, perhaps, seem the more affected, and more ineffectual in their attempts to seize or to create some new center for their lives. The women, at least most of them, react to their frustration and discontent more forcefully; they are or become downhome feminists, and the degree of their feminist responses within their culture is largely determined by education, by economic empowerment, and by age, or by some combination of the three.

Almost all of Mason's characters come *from* the rural poor. This is not to say they *are* poor, either in a strict financial or cultural sense. The older characters, survivors of the deprivations of the Great Depression, have jobs that afford them a comfortable if not luxurious lifestyle; some, like Bill, the retired farmer of **"The Ocean,"** can even afford a "big camper cruiser," which he proudly captains around the backwaters of America even if it is a far cry from the destroyer he served on as a youth during World War II.

The culture of Western Kentucky, although unsophisticated in comparison to the big cities of the East, where so many of the more ambitious characters go, has a solidity, a sophistication even, of its own. In **"Nancy Culpepper,"** the main character, a woman who had fled the unpromising life of her Kentucky youth only to return years later, hears her mother say, "We'll never go anywhere. We've got our dress tail on a bedpost." Puzzled, Nancy asks her mother the meaning of the expression. Her mother gives it, adding, "I guess you think we're just ignorant . . . The way we talk." Nancy responds, "No, I don't." And she doesn't, because this folksy saying is exactly one of the little things that richly differentiate her culture, a culture she once dismissed as backward but now the source of an irresistible longing. (She has used the impending move of her grandmother into a nursing home to justify her visiting her relatives, but she is aware this is really an excuse to test her vague desire to move back to Kentucky.)

It is important to see that the downhome feminists of these stories do not want what their city cousins want: equal legal and political rights, equal access to careers, equal pay, government support of child care, and so on. Mason's women simply want breathing space in their relationships with their men. Sometimes only divorce, always initiated by the women, will provide the degree of change these women seek but sometimes their assertiveness merely aims for a change of pace—casual adultery, for example.

The culture of Mason's Western Kentucky is focused on the lower class, defined by a general lack of higher education, by consumer taste, and, increasingly, by choice of leisure activity. Mason's characters have enough discretionary income to buy such big-ticket items as campers and organs, and enough time to take continuing education classes, or, in the case of Shelby, the preacher in **"The Retreat,"** even the flexibility to follow an avocation which does not support him and his family (he is an electrician during the week).

It is Shelby's unhappily married wife, Georgeann, who most suffers from the strictures of her culture and her lack of choice in life. At first she had admired Shelby's commitment to God's calling. Soon, however, the obligations of a country preacher's wife become oppressive: she plays the piano at church services, she types and mimeographs the church bulletins; she prepares the grape juice for communion; she attends weddings and funerals; she goes on the annual summer retreat that so energizes and rejuvenates her husband.

Georgeann especially hates the retreat; it brings her dissatisfaction with her marriage to a head. The retreat is a zeitgeist of time and place, a sort of EST with a fundamentalist twist, replete with trendy workshops and psychobabble. Shelby attends a workshop entitled "The Changing Role of the Country Preacher"; Georgeann goes to a discussion on Christian marriage, where she hears the term "marriage enhancement" a lot, but the only thing she wants of the eleven women gathered at the workshop is to ask them a question:

> "What do you do if the man you're married to—this is just a hypothetical question—say he's the cream of creation and all, and he's sweet as can be, but he turns out to be the wrong one for you? What do you do if you're just simply mismatched?"

Georgeann's question is met with silence—"Everyone looks at her"—a predictable response since seven of the eleven women are ministers' wives. However, religion is not a dominating presence in Georgeann's inner life—nor does it play much of a role in the lives of any of Mason's central female characters. For them, religion is just in the landscape, like the corn fields that surround the Kentucky farm houses.

What *does* influence Georgeann's response to her unhappy situation is her mother's attitude toward marriage: "Although her mother still believes Georgeann married unwisely, she now promotes the sanctity of the union." Like most of the mothers of Mason's female protagonists, Georgeann's mother is a formidable personality, and she evokes strong emotions in her daughter: ". . . Georgeann gets very sad whenever she realizes how her mother threats her marriage like a joke. It isn't fair." The mother, like all the women of her era in this culture, is bound more tightly to the rural conviction that a husband is forever, for better or for worse.

Georgeann is simply not willing to accept the sanctity of an unhappy marriage and her attitude is typical of similarly situated young women in several of the other stories; the difference is that they leave, whereas Georgeann cannot. For one thing, she has little education—she "had wanted to go to college, but they were never able to afford her to go." Nor does she have a job outside the work she does for Shelby. Unlike many of the other unhappy young women in these stories, Georgeann even lacks friends—this is especially emphasized by her sad and unfulfilling encounter with the women at the marriage workshop. For Georgeann, there is no sisterhood in Christendom—or anywhere else.

Throughout the story Georgeann watches over an ailing chicken, a symbol of Georgeann's condition. She, too, is sick, or "disoriented," because of her unhappy marriage, and when she kills the chicken at the end of the story she therefore disposes of her own will, weak though it may be. With no support, emotional or financial, Georgeann has nowhere else to go and she will stay in her unhappy marriage. That is the meaning of the last line, which comes just after she has killed the chicken: ". . . Georgeann feels nothing, only that she had done her duty." Georgeann has become a compliant, dutiful wife, one her mother and husband will now recognize and admire.

Like Georgeann, Norma Jean, the main female character of **"Shiloh,"** is unhappily married. She, too, is restless, or, as she says, ". . . I have this crazy feeling I missed something." The constant presence of her husband, Leroy, a trucker "finally settling down with the woman he loves" because of an accident, is more than Norma Jean can stand. She also must cope with a domineering mother, Mabel, who spends a lot of time with Norma Jean: "When she visits, she inspects the closets and then the plants, informing Norma Jean when a plant is droopy or yellow." Even though Norma Jean is thirty-four, she still hides her smoking habit from Mabel, until one day Mabel barges in and catches her—as Norma Jean says, "She don't know the meaning of the word 'knock.' "

Because she is so dominated by her mother, Norma Jean skirmishes as much with Mabel as with Leroy in her struggle to free herself from a marriage she no longer wants. The struggle is long and difficult because the tradition of the sanctity of marriage in this culture is old and strong. Norma Jean confronts her mother directly as the story develops. At one point Mabel rebukes Norma Jean for saying "for Christ's sake" and Norma Jean retaliates with, "You ain't seen nothing yet." Mabel, sure that Norma Jean will settle down if she will just go on a "second honeymoon," provokes even stronger language during the same conversation: "When are you going to *shut up* about Shiloh, Mama?"

Norma Jean has not used direct confrontation with Leroy; instead, she has sought to create emotional distance by taking up a series of activities that pointedly do not include Leroy. First, she tries bodybuilding, then jogging, then night school. Once, Norma Jean hands Leroy a list, "Things you could do," she says but the alliance of Leroy and Mabel is too strong for her to make her move at home.

Mason's timely usage of military language heightens the marital strife in **"Shiloh."** In response to Norma Jean's list, Leroy discusses his latest project, the log house he wants to build for them. Norma Jean ignores him as she does her exercises, "marching through the kitchen . . . doing goose steps." Also, there is the origin of Norma Jean's name: " . . . from the Normans. They were invaders." This she tells Leroy on their way to Shiloh. Norma Jean's acceptance of her mother's suggestion that she and Leroy go to Shiloh is itself a brilliant tactical move: she has split her enemies. By himself, Leroy is no match for Norma Jean, and, like the Union army of the original battle of Shiloh, she is the aggressor, the invader, and she wins her own battle when she announces she is leaving Leroy.

Certainly Norma Jean has a stronger personality than Georgeann and Mason must allow for this, or else Mason would simply write the same story with the same characters again and again. Still, Norma Jean can support herself—she is a sales clerk at a Rexall drugstore—whereas Georgeann has never worked outside the home. Norma Jean has also had some exposure to higher education through an "adult-education course in composition" and her first paper garners a B, yet another confidence builder. Finally, Norma Jean has had fifteen years of living by herself while Leroy was on the road and this solitude has developed a cherished independence in her, or, as she puts it, "In some ways, a woman prefers a man who wanders."

There are other unhappily married young women in the stories whose problems and solutions are similar to Norma Jean's. In **"Old Things,"** Linda, also in her early thirties, moves in temporarily with her mother, Cleo, to sort out her marital problems. Cleo doesn't miss an opportunity to tell Linda to go back to her husband. Linda doesn't have reconciliation in mind. She says, "I don't feel like hanging around the same house with somebody that can go for three hours without saying a word."

Because she is of a different generation, Linda is more susceptible to the liberalizing influence of the culture at large. While Cleo may listen to the same talk shows on TV that her daughter does—*Tomorrow* and *Today,* for example—she doesn't really accept their pop psychology, their easy solutions to problems:

> "People can't just have everything they want, all the time," Cleo says.
> "I'm not mad at you, Mama. But people don't have to do what they don't want to as much now as they used to."
> "I should know that," Cleo says. "It's all over television. You make me feel awful."
> "I don't mean to. It's for your own good."

Linda's sense of independence is also bolstered by the fact that she works outside the home; her income as a checkout clerk at the local K-mart may not be large but, if need be, she can provide minimal economic security for herself and two children. In contrast, Cleo, like all the wives of her generation, has looked to her husband as the provider of material necessities. Her dependent attitude, closely akin to her sense of economic insecurity, is revealed in several ways. When her granddaughter, Tammy, protests that the family is eating chicken too often for dinner, Cleo says, "Chicken was ninety-nine cents a pound. . . . You better be glad you're where there's food on the table, kid."

After Cleo's husband had died, she gave away his suits and sold the rest of his things. She also sold the farm, knowing her husband would never forgive her for doing that. At one point, in urging Linda to go back to Bob, she says, "You'll be wondering how to buy them kids fine things. You'll be off on your own, girl." For Cleo, a good husband povides material comfort; for Linda, having provided some of the material necessities herself, a good husband provides something else, although, like Norma Jean, she may not have fixed in her mind what, exactly, she wants from a man.

In fact, Linda may not want a husband at all. Her friend, Shirley, is an example of a young woman functioning on her own. She is a natural ally, one sympathetic to Linda's emergent feminist consciousness; that is precisely what is wrong with Shirley, according to Cleo:

> Cleo is afraid Linda's friend Shirley is a bad influence. Shirley had to get married and didn't finish school. Now she is divorced. She even let her husband have her kids, while she went gallivanting around. Cleo cannot imagine a mother giving her kids away.

Shirley is the supportive friend that is missing in Georgeann's life; she is the equivalent of Norma Jean's solitude in that both the friend and the solitude enhance self-confidence and encourage a more aggressive assertion of self.

Sandra, the main character in **"Offerings,"** is yet another unhappily married young woman. Her husband, Jerry, has moved to Louisville, where he works in a K-mart, and, in his leisure time, watches "go-go dancers in smoky bars." Sandra does not want to watch go-go girls; nor does she want to be a good wife in the old sense. Speaking about her husband to her mother, she says, "He'd better not waltz back in here. I'm through waiting on him."

Sandra prefers to live by herself on a farm. She does not have a job but her solitude, like Norma Jean's, nurtures self-confidence. Also, she can provide some basic necessities for herself: she grows vegetables; she keeps ducks, she manages the household by herself even if the woodpile is low and she hasn't yet "found time to insulate the attic and to fix the leak in the basement."

In addition to the rigors of living on a farm by herself, Sandra must also bear the pressure of her family's expectations of marriage. Her mother insists that Sandra's visiting grandmother not be told of Sandra's separation and Sandra grudgingly agrees to be a part of a lie: Sandra's grandmother is told that Sandra's husband isn't around the house much these days because he works the nightshift and overtime as well. (The nature of the lie itself is indicative of the older women's definition of a good husband: extra hours on the job is one of the few acceptable excuses for a husband's absence from the home.)

Sandra is altogether satisfied with her independence and the last two lines of the story affirm this attitude:

> The night is peaceful, and Sandra thinks of the thousands of large golden garden spiders hidden in the field. In the early morning the dew shines on their trampolines, and she can imagine

> bouncing with an excited spring from web to web, all the way up the hill to the woods.

The most educated women in the book follow a decidely different path in their relationship with their men. Their problems are not as dramatic as their lesser-educated counterparts and their solutions are more ambivalent. Nancy Culpepper was married in 1967 in Massachusetts, where she had gone for graduate school. Her husband, Jack, a Yankee, set up his photography business near Philadelphia after the wedding. Nancy's marriage has produced both a son and relative happiness yet she can't shake a longing for her Kentucky roots, which, to her consternation, were on her mind even during her wedding night. After the ceremony Jack takes Nancy outside to look for the northern lights. She searches the sky diligently but she "kept thinking of her parents at home, probably watching *Gunsmoke.*" The *Joy of Cooking,* a wedding gift, makes her wonder what her parents are eating at that very moment. Clumsily, she dances with Jack to a Beatles album. There are no stopping places in the songs and this upsets her: "She was crying. 'Songs used to have stopping places in between.' "

When Nancy learns that she had an ancestor also named Nancy Culpepper, she begins to go by her maiden name. A few years later she insists on visiting Kentucky to help her parents with her invalid grandmother and to look for some lost pictures belonging to her grandmother. Nancy hopes some of the pictures will be of her namesake. This is the catalyst Nancy has been waiting for because lately she had "been vaguely wanting to move to Kentucky." Thus her feminist search for identity is curiously, even atavistically linked to a search for roots. She is willing to put a strain on her immediate family in conducting this search: both her husband and her son resent her staying away so long. During a telephone conversation Jack says, "We're your family too." And her son hangs up without saying goodbye, much to Nancy's distress; moreover, neither husband nor son wants to move to Kentucky.

At the end of the story, the grandmother's photo album is found but the grandmother and Nancy's mother disagree on which person in a group picture is the original Nancy Culpepper. The confusion surrounding the identity of the original Nancy perfectly reflects the confusion of identity of the contemporary Nancy. The ending, with Nancy staring both at the woman her grandmother had thought was Nancy's ancestor and at the woman's husband, emphasizes the ambivalence of Nancy's situation:

> This young woman would be glad to dance to "Lucy in the Sky with Diamonds" on her wedding day, Nancy thinks. The man seems bewildered, as if he did not know what to expect, marrying a woman who has her eyes fixed on something so far away.

At that moment Nancy's own husband is far away and he is as uncertain as the reader about Nancy's next move.

The main character of **"Residents and Transients,"** the first-person narrator, has many things in common with Nancy Culpepper. She, too, left Kentucky for "higher learning," which in her case took eight years. She also came back to Kentucky on a family matter, specifically because her parents were in poor health. Even after her parents are recovered and moved to Florida and even though she admits she feels like an outsider, the narrator has stayed on because, like Nancy, she felt the tug of her roots. Or, as she puts it, . . . I have stayed here, wondering why I ever went away." And she has a Yankee husband, whom she met when he was transferred by his company into the area.

This woman's story is that she is bored in the absence of her husband, who has been transferred again, to Louisville. He is looking for a house there, while she remains on the farm to oversee the auction of household goods for her parents when the farm is sold. She has taken a lover, her dentist, Larry. That she has been unfaithful to her husband sets her apart from Norma Jean and the others. Although she is somewhat surprised at her behavior, she has the air of a big-city sophisticate, a woman who does what she wants, including what some men have done all along: have a satisfying affair and a satisfying marriage at the same time. The key to her attitude is revealed in a lecture she delivers to Larry about cats:

> "In the wild, there are two kinds of cat populations," I tell him when he finishes his move. "Residents and transients. Some stay put, in their fixed home ranges, and others are on the move. They don't have real homes. Everybody always thought that the ones who establish the territories are the most successful—like the capitalists who get ahold of Park Place." . . . "They are the strongest, while the transients are the bums, the losers."
>
> "The thing is—this is what the scientists are wondering about now—it may be that the transients are the superior ones after all, with the greatest curiosity and most intelligence. They can't decide."

The narrator decides that she misses her husband and that she is going to join him in Louisville. However, one gathers she would be just as happy without him. The risks she takes while having her fling—going out to dinner with Larry where she may be recognized, even allowing Larry to answer her phone—illustrate confidence, a sense of her *own* superiority. Her identifying with the transient cats is made explicit in the last five lines of the story:

> I see a cat's flaming eyes coming up the lane to the house. One eye is green and one is red, like a traffic light. It is Brenda, my odd-eyed cat. Her blue eye shines red and her yellow eye shines green. In a moment I realize that I am waiting for the light to change.

She is a transient and transients are just as likely to leave mates as they are to leave territories.

Bobbie Ann Mason has an uncanny ability to capture the state of mind of the women of rural Western Kentucky in the 1970's. As that culture becomes more homogenized, more integrated with the general American culture, these women will lose their special identity and their special problems. They will become more like Nancy Culpepper and the narrator of **"Residents and Transients"** as they become better educated and more economically independent. They will have more complex relationships with their men and families; their lives will be more refined, more introspective—and the trade-off in vigor and earthiness may leave them far less interesting. (pp. 41-9)

G. O. Morphew, "Downhome Feminists in 'Shiloh and Other Stories,' " in The Southern Literary Journal, *Vol. XXI, No. 2, Spring, 1989, pp. 41-9.*

David Y. Todd (review date May-June 1989)

[*In the following review of* Love Life, *Todd addresses the ways in which Mason's protagonists desire, and occasionally achieve, independence.*]

In this collection of fifteen stories [***Love Life***], Bobbie Ann Mason portrays western Kentucky men and women trying to get along with each other as they make their way through shopping malls and multiple cable TV channels. Most of the characters are divorced and tend to move cautiously; though alert to possibilities, they search for appropriate values in a world of accelerating changes.

Mason's first story collection, ***Shiloh and Other Stories,*** won the PEN/Hemingway award, and the film adaptation of her novel, ***In Country,*** is due to be released this fall. In ***Love Life,*** as in those works, Mason shows the influence of our increasingly homogeneous culture on the suburban working class of her native Kentucky.

Love Life, however, is more unified than ***Shiloh*** in the consistency of its focus. The stories all depict courtship, marriage, or divorce; most focus on women exploring the new freedom of a recent divorce or separation. Many of the characters first married shortly after high school—he getting a job at a plant, she staying at home or waiting tables. Adulthood thus begins in a state of entrapment, and we watch as alliances strain and break.

But we watch through the rather plain, thin surface of Mason's prose. Writing in short, literal sentences, often in third person, present tense, she stays close to her characters' views. Her language, fitting itself to their range of thought, reveals how they engage with the world. Mason's refusal to leave their perspective helps sustain the sense of their struggle. But in keeping to their level, she often fails to express the deeper insights that could bring her characters even more to life.

Because Mason's people so rarely incline toward prolonged introspection or analysis, they find it a struggle to communicate beneath the calm surfaces of their lives. Inhibition seems endemic to their culture. In **"State Champions,"** one of the few first-person sketches of the collection, a young girl finds she is inept at consoling a friend whose sister has just died.

> I didn't know what to say. I couldn't say anything, for we weren't raised to say things that were heartfelt and gracious . . . We didn't wish people happy birthday. We didn't even address each other by name . . . We didn't say we were sorry . . . "Love" was a dirty word.

As they mature, this repression traps Mason's men and women in a vicious cycle. The men grow chronically chauvinistic; the women struggle between desire for a mate and a need for a wholeness which the men don't allow. In **"Hunktown,"** a divorced woman bitterly regrets that she expressed her outrage at her husband's excessive demands by getting a tubal ligation. Hearing of this, a friend of hers thinks, "It seemed like a dreadful secret. Debbie had had her tubes tied rather than tell her husband in plain English to treat her better." Yet that same friend chafed silently at her own husband's decision to quit his job to play country music; she later found she was "angry that that was the way women were, that they looked on approvingly while some man went out and either did something big or made a fool of himself."

Most of Mason's women advance beyond such passivity. One young wife, feeling that "there wasn't space deep down in her to move around in," leaves her husband, even though she isn't sure what to do next. Mason concludes: "[her] parents had stayed together like two dogs locked together in passion, except it wasn't passion. But she and Joe didn't have to do that. Times had changed."

If the stories have a hero, it is the divorcee who, rather than seeking quick refuge with another man, frees herself to find a job and to socialize with other women. Mason offers a glimpse of that healthful independence in the quiet, elegant story, **"Bumblebees."** Two middle-aged women, both school teachers—one divorced, one widowed—have bought an old farmhouse, planted fruit trees, and started a garden. The daughter of one, home from college, spends the summer with them. Alternately healing and, on occasion, annoying one another, they talk through their loves and losses as they tend the garden and fix up the house. The story is rendered with an affection for pastoral detail, and the tranquility of the narrative strengthens the image of their self-reliance.

Mason allows that the women of her culture need not always shun men to find happiness. An enlightened male does appear in the well-crafted **"Coyotes"**—perhaps the collection's only rendering of a man and woman who honestly try to relate as equals.

Cobb, who works for the soil-conservation service, and Lynnette, an employee at a twenty-four hour photoprocessor, appear to revel in the pleasure of their offbeat, mutual candor, though at first they both have "an off-limits area, a place they [are] afraid to reveal." As the story develops, however, those limits diminish. At the end, Lynnette reveals a painful family tragedy to Cobb. He responds beautifully: "Every day I get to know you better. This is just the beginning."

It would be nice if Mason could present more of such relationships. But to do that would be false to the people she is writing about. ***Love Life*** tells, without elaboration or embroidery, what their lives are like right now. (pp. 3, 20)

David Y. Todd, in a review of "Love Life," in The Bloomsbury Review, *Vol. 9, No. 3, May-June, 1989, pp. 3, 20.*

Nicci Gerrard (review date 8 December 1989)

[*In the following review, Gerrard discusses linguistic and stylistic elements of* Love Life *and* Spence + Lila.]

Simplicity is a hard art and brevity an underrated virtue.

Bobby Ann Mason's simplicity is not the cool clever minimalism of her urban contemporaries, nor the "dirty realism" that has recently so fired the dissatisfied American imagination. She tells her stories of small-town America in western Kentucky, where folk shop at K Marts and grub their living from the soil, not as an outsider but as a novelist engrossed in the daily hardships and triumphs of an inarticulate people. As Spence, in the short, naively illustrated ***Spence and Lila,*** knows, "using the right simple words at the right time requires courage enough".

The simple writing of simple love stories is perhaps the hardest art of all. But with fumbling dialogue and spare descriptions, Bobby Ann Mason manages to steer a course between sentimentality and condescension: life in her novel and short stories is no rural idyll of plain-speaking and right-living.

Spence and Lila of the novel's title have spent a long and happy married life together. Now they, and their daughters Cat and Nancy, have to confront Lila's cancer and possible death. That's the story line; it has no sub-plot nor neat conclusion. Its chapters are snatches of conversation or random daily tasks; its words are rarely longer than two syllables (except for "chemotherapy", "mastectomy" and "methotrexate"). Nevertheless it is an extraordinarily successful evocation of unspoken love, old age and optimism in the face of tragedy.

The short stories in ***Love Life,*** too, hang together by a single image or figure: in the title story, an ageing, sloppy, happy woman, Opal, dances to rock 'n' roll and sips peppermint liqueur in private; in **"Midnight Magic"** the main character, Steve, drives past an apparently dead body and rings the emergency services, but never finishes the conversation. Sometimes the vignettes seem hardly stories at all—more like tantalising wisps of tales heard in transit.

What Bobby Ann Mason conveys so well, however, is the closeness of her characters to the land. In the poignant unending to ***Spence and Lila,*** Lila is back in her beloved garden, among the vegetables. She beautifully resembles the earth she stands on: the sweat on her forehead a smooth, moist layer; her face rosy, all the "furrows and marks thrusting upwards with her smile the way the okra on the stalk reach upward with the sun"; the scar on her neck like a gully, "washed out but filling in now".

And her face is alight with the glory of the pumpkin.

Nicci Gerrard, "Love among the Pumpkins," in New Statesman & Society, *Vol. 2, No. 79, December 8, 1989, p. 34.*

On Mason's interest in popular culture:

Mason's fascination with rock music clearly transcends merely musical enjoyment—though of course there's clearly much of that too—and might be best understood as a crucial element in her larger interest in and sympathy for popular culture. Despite having a Ph.D. in English literature and a book on Nabokov, Mason recoils from what she sees as the hypocrisy and elitism of "high culture." Her feelings are clearly embodied in her fiction—a fiction of what might best be called "ordinary folks," working-class people and their concerns. "They're the people I'm drawn to," she told Wendy Smith [in *Publishers Weekly,* 1985], and she went on to say that early in her career she consciously chose to write about these people in large part because she "was so sick of reading about the alienated hero of refined sensibility." "It's important to me," she told Smith, speaking of her ties with her characters, "and I can relate to their problems more easily than I can to more middle-class concerns. I think the lives of people like this have just as much depth and sensitivity as anyone else's."

Robert H. Brinkmeyer, Jr., in his "Never Stop Rocking: Bobbie Ann Mason and Rock-and-Roll," Mississippi Quarterly, *Winter 1988-89.*

Richard Giannone (essay date Fall 1990)

[*Giannone is an American educator and critic. In the following essay, he analyzes the roles of mystery and self-awareness in Mason's short stories "Shiloh," "The Retreat," and "Third Monday," which he argues "exemplify Mason's subject and vision."*]

These are at once dispiriting times and revelatory days for the women and men of western Kentucky who people the stories of Bobbie Ann Mason. The heroine of **"Third Monday,"** Ruby Jane MacPherson, expresses the moral mood when she says with dark and knowing nonchalance that "The twentieth century's taking all the mysteries out of life." The secrets that Ruby believes are being eliminated do not concern esoteric phenomena set high above the earth or God's dealings with humankind through inscrutable laws. Rather, Ruby has in mind the obscurities concealed within everyday living that we forbear through disregard but must take into account when recognition of them is forced on us by the swift scientific or cultural advancements of our era. Whereas ignorance of separation, illness, and death allows for hope, the unveiling of submerged realities can instill dread. The contingencies in Mason's story vary in nature and import with the characters' plight, but throughout her writing the mysteries are something personal, sharply felt by the body if incomprehensible to the mind, and intensely alive. And though the disclosures upset all the peace that the characters have been trusting for years, the crisis opens them up to a new unknown, an untried inner resource that might take them beyond dashed equanimity.

With Ruby it is the appearance of a lump in her breast that subverts a previously unalloyed confidence in her body, a young, lovely body that without warning betrays her by harboring a furtive energy beyond her control. Once begun, the shattering gains technological speed. Mammography flattens Ruby's curvaceous breast into X-ray lines "on Xerox paper." A diagnosis of malignancy leads to a radical mastectomy; chemotherapy and radiation may ensue. The cumulative threat of modern medicine is to eradicate Ruby's inmost definition of herself—the feeling of female wholeness that she takes for granted as the basis of her relation with herself, her lover, and her rural Kentucky world. Her shapeliness manifests her integrity. Mystery for Ruby is her irreducible humanness. Her recent awareness that it can be unaccountably imperiled underlies Ruby's disquiet about the demystifying tenor of our century.

Ruby finds a sympathetic audience in Linda, a friend to whom she makes the comment. Both women have need for a gratifying surprise. Linda is thirty-seven, pregnant, unmarried, and resolved not to marry the out-of-towner who fathered her baby. Amniocentesis determines the child's sex and informs Linda that her daughter's chromosomal balance is normal. Given the risks of pregnancy at Linda's age and the hardship awaiting her as a working single parent, the disclosures of genetic screening are reassuring enough for Linda to name her unborn daughter Holly. But medical science also deprives this expectant mother of felt wonder by reducing the awesomeness of childbirth to physiological anticlimax. Glad as Linda is that her baby will be a healthy girl, she still feels cheated of experiencing the inviolate life-giving power of her body. "But in a way," Linda submits to her friends, knowing about Holly before Holly arrives is "like knowing ahead of time what you're going to get for Christmas."

Linda and Ruby define the predicament pervading Bobbie Ann Mason's stories. Her rural characters are caught between an incomprehensible other-worldly force and the actual loss sustained by their this-worldly anguish. Their suffering cuts two ways. All are mystified by contemporary life at the same time that they are robbed of the mysteries of their lives. Mason's Kentuckians grapple with their bewilderment to find the source of their lives, the joyous mystery of being alive, the Christmas gift of marvel that Linda seeks and tries to preserve by naming Holly for the holiday excitement she does not want to lose. Such fundamental desires are the mysteries that our vexing age discounts, and they are the mysteries that Bobbie Ann Mason in her stories sets out to recover. She does so by relying on the appeal in the very physical distress besetting her characters to raise their moral imagination to the possibility of fuller life.

Mason's writing commanded attention when ***Shiloh and Other Stories,*** her first collection, appeared in 1982. In the span of a few years that critical interest has deepened. One contributor to *Since Flannery O'Connor: Essays on the Contemporary American Short Story* (1987) aligns Mason's portrayal of emotional and bodily disfigurement with the tradition of Southern grotesque, and goes so far as to identify Mason as heiress to O'Connor's legacy. If O'Connor's theological handling of physical deformity and her eschatological extension of mystery prove to exceed Mason's deliberate cultural focus, as I think they will, their shared involvement with rural Southernness will certainly provide a source of consideration. In fact, one reader already has initiated the discussion by proposing that Mason charts "a new direction for the Southern renascence" in her adaption of history to understand the disarray of contemporary experience.

The power of Mason's writing does lie in her insight into our historical and cultural dislocations, but she is more than an astute chronicler of how we live now. She is alive to the distant, unseen dimension of life. One way into her art is to see how her characters, who are lost amid the Burger Chefs, K-Marts, and television talk shows that level western Kentucky into the nondescript American landscape, find their spiritual portion in the turmoil. Since inaugural criticism is most useful when anchored in particulars, this essay offers an introduction to Mason's distinguishing strength through readings of three stories **"Shiloh," "The Retreat,"** and **"Third Monday."** These are arguably the best of the sixteen comprising ***Shiloh and Other Stories.*** Mason herself gives prominence to **"Shiloh"** by designating it the title story, and assigns **"Third Monday"** the privilege of bringing the sequence to a close. **"The Retreat"** puts into relief the importance of gender in coping with trauma. Together the stories exemplify Mason's subject and vision.

The larger themes in the stories arise from the breakdown in intimacy. A spouse or lover tries to shatter the bonds tied by love and strained by a medical problem. Whether the struggle in one partner is for release or in another for reconciliation, the outcome is a painful awareness of aloneness that occasions a new response, a momentary self-communication about the heart's desire for freedom.

"Shiloh" begins with Norma Jean Moffitt developing her pectorals with three-pound dumbbells as a warm-up for a twenty-pound barbell. She wants to gain the strength in her muscles that will prime her spirit. Accordingly, she also has a workout for her mind. While spare daytime hours go to firming up the contour of her chest, evenings are devoted to outlining paragraphs for her classes at Paducah Community College. Norma Jean has the idea of female independence in search of a body to flesh it out and of a mental fitness to assert it. Although the reader may smile at Wonder Woman's attempt to shape her inner life by means of cultural formulas, Mason respects the struggle for autonomy, and through the events of the story gauges its effect on Norma Jean's marriage to Leroy.

Leroy Moffitt, thirty-four, is a truckdriver. **"Shiloh"** is his story. Four months before the story begins, his tractor-trailer jackknifed in Missouri, leaving him with a mangled leg fastened by a steel pin. The world of Leroy the king is racked by crisis. His driving days are over. His rig sits in the backyard; Leroy sits on the couch smoking marijuana—two huge birds roosting at home. Miniature instruments of power, such as a model B-17 and a truck, replace the machine he cannot operate. Toys not only allow vicarious control over the engine that crippled him; they also serve as a holding action against thoughts about a more obscure mechanism that he feels keeps him disabled. Handicrafts bring out the trucker's delicate side as he becomes adroit at string art, macrame, and needlepoint. As male traits mark Norma Jean's move toward independence, female qualities underscore Leroy's effort to regain power. The feminine side of Leroy becomes so pronounced that his mother-in-law, Mabel Beasley, mocks him.

Mason, however, does not set the idea of femininity against the idea of masculinity. Rather, her treatment of gender points up her concern for totality. Norma Jean's body-building and Leroy's model-building derive from the same basic need to complete oneself. She needs male strength to transform her life, and he needs female insight to change his life. The new androgynous tone in their relationship suggests that the way to rebuild their marriage is by experiencing the other's vulnerability and by developing the other's complementary skill. Mystery lies in the totality of humanness that both seek by virtue of their painful sense of partiality.

Leroy welcomes a fresh start. Now that he is disabled, he realizes "that in all the years he was on the road he never took time to examine anything." He loves Norma Jean, believes that his marriage has a future, and wants intimacy. This bruiser is not afraid of tenderness. When Norma Jean becomes edgy about his idleness, Leroy does not cover exposure with anger. Nor does he impose his sexual desire on her. He accepts the cool morning place in bed that Norma Jean leaves after disappearing to sell cosmetics at Rexall's. During the lonely years on the highway, Leroy would tell hitchhikers his life story; now, at home and alone in his marriage, he wants to express himself to Norma Jean, "as if he had just met her."

Two plans unfold for Leroy and Norma Jean to reacquaint themselves. Both fail. The first is Leroy's idea to build a log house, "a real home," to lay a foundation for a new life. The dream house gives the grown man a way out of confinement. His maternal instinct for a hearth kindles a feeling of being physically strong and emotionally open. Lincoln logs will provide a refuge from danger and drabness; simplicity will promote healing. The mail-order blueprints covering the table, however, limn a pie in the sky. This twentieth-century idea of how the nineteenth century ought to have been in rural Kentucky cannot bring the security Leroy wants. For one thing, Norma Jean has a contemporary notion of how she wants to live her life; but more ruinous are the structural weaknesses in his conception of the log house. The blueprint is for a shell. Emotions, not Leroy's imaginary timber, build closeness.

The second plan is Mabel Beasley's. Her latest interference in the marriage of Norma Jean and Leroy is to propose a second honeymoon in Shiloh. Shiloh for these Southerners has nothing to do with the Civil War; it is Mabel's cure-all for marital ills. Not surprisingly, the Sunday trip to southwestern Tennessee does not work magic in Norma Jean and Leroy. The national park at Pittsburg Landing to the weary couple is just another place that takes a long drive to reach. The setting bores them. Natural changes over 120 years, enhanced by diligent park attendants, have altered the battleground of one of the bloodiest slaughters on American soil into a neat, immense subdivision. Time and grooming alone do not deprive Shiloh of meaning. Dispossession lies in Leroy and Norma Jean. The act of the mind that brings the past to bear on the present is not part of the Moffitts' post-Vietnam sensibility. Leroy expects a golf course and thinks of the dead soldiers whose markers surround him as "a board game with plastic soldiers." Dissociation cramps Leroy's response to historical catastrophe as well as to marital crisis: he turns suffering into an idea and reacts to the abstraction. He needs a blueprint to deal with the woman he loves. As for Norma Jean, at Shiloh she remains emotionally elsewhere, perhaps lost in the unnamed "book about another century" that absorbed her the evening Leroy badgered her to visit Shiloh.

Since the mind holds no refuge from pain, Leroy and Norma Jean can no more avoid the anguish of separation than the Confederate and Union troops before them could escape each other's gunfire. The second honeymooners enact their private battle. "I want to leave you," Norma Jean declares. Shocked, Leroy slumps on the grass, his stoned mind useless in grasping the blow he receives. Finally, he comes back, "No, you don't," and the fight unfolds like a lyric for country blues awaiting Elvis or Chuck Berry to back up the pain with melody. Norma Jean, in the end, can and will be cruel to a heart that's true, and Leroy has neither the power to stop her nor the words to express his hurting impotence.

But Mason's hero does have the capacity to intuit the pattern of human affairs. Jet Beasley and Mabel married and honeymooned in Shiloh, then Norma Jean was born, and then Jet died. Then Leroy and Norma Jean married, had a baby named Randy, and Randy died of crib death, and now Norma Jean is pulling away. Leroy perceives that love involves separation, a loss having nothing to do with right or wrong. In Mason's world dispersion just happens. By recalling the cycle of engagement and death in the Confederate and Union forces and in his family, Leroy comes to realize that he "is leaving out the insides of history" just as "the real workings of a marriage" escape him. Without the felt life of history, both his and that of others, Leroy remains caught in a discrete, hollow shell of time. To dramatize the trap of being separated from a temporal context, Mason tells Leroy's story in the vivid present and suspends his plight in irresolution.

Leroy's attempt to love and live apart from the inner workings of love is, like his marijuana smoking, a way of avoiding pain. The outcome is self-absorption, the recognition of which points to a possible release. Earlier in the story, Leroy observes goldfinches flying by the window feeder: "They close their wings, then fall, then spread their wings to catch and lift themselves." And so with Leroy Moffitt. After the crash in Missouri, his energy bounces up with the plan to build a log house, a hope razed by Norma Jean's anger. At the end, her announcement that she wants to leave him brings Leroy still lower. Still, battered but not diminished, Leroy "gets up" from the ground to retrieve Norma Jean at the river where she turns toward him, waving her arms. It is unclear whether she is exercising her chest muscles to flex her power or she is beckoning Leroy. The ambiguity of her gesture does not matter to Leroy. What counts is his getting up and going to her. The goldfinch impulse spreads its wings in Leroy to lift him anew. That life-furthering power that is in the air and in the goldfinch and in Norma Jean's desire for freedom also draws Leroy's disordered affections up into its current. **"Shiloh"** brings Leroy from accidental collapse to inexplicable ascent.

"The Retreat" depicts a marriage that would seem immune to the disruption vexing Leroy and Norma Jean. Georgeann and Shelby Pickett are married ten years, have two children, and rarely quarrel. Sacrifice to high purpose binds their partnership. Shelby works weekdays as an electrician to support his calling to be a preacher at the Grace United Methodist Church, a dying rural congregation in western Kentucky. Georgeann helps out by typing weekly bulletins, playing the piano at the worship, and performing other tasks expected of a minister's wife. She serves so that he can serve the ministry. The Picketts' life, in fine, goes by the book, just as Leroy wanted his marriage to run. But Georgeann is unhappy. Unable to pinpoint the trouble, she complains of vague rules that "come out of nowhere." Spite is the woman's only defense against the shadowy menace. One Sunday she reacts to an altercation with Shelby by putting on jeans to clean the henhouse. The picture of a preacher's wife carting manure to the garden on the Lord's Day gratifies her need to flout the rules hemming her in. When she finds a sick hen, she belatedly battles Shelby's patronizing indifference to her feelings by repeating his scorn to the droopy hen. Although symbolic rebuke brings Georgeann no satisfaction, Mason respects the petty ill will of a woman trying to break through the cultural pressures the heroine does not grasp.

All Georgeann gets from shoveling manure is dermatosis on her stomach. When the irritations turn out not to be benign chicken mites, as she assumes, but body lice, Georgeann enjoys researching the disease and announcing to Shelby, "I've got lice." If viewed apart from her suppressed anger, Georgeann's fascination with parasites would be morbid; but as a form of protest, pathology makes sense. Attention to a medical problem takes precedence over the countless priorities set by Shelby that rule her life. There is a certain soundness in her being frank about a disease that disgusts others. Georgeann's irrational joy in physical ailment and therapy is her way of reclaiming her body as alive and personal from a husband whose emotions are shaped by rules and from a culture whose values disparage the physical.

Shelby is not the enemy. Georgeann means it when she says that "he's sweet as can be." His benevolence, unfortunately, embodies a rigid dependence on mind that Georgeann is growing away from. With Shelby, reaching out for goodness evaporates into gnostic yearning. He supplies euphemism for plain action, as when the children take long baths as a precaution against lice and he speaks of "a ritual cleansing, something like baptism." Ten years of such fervor give a disembodied aura to his and Georgeann's intimacy.

The flashpoint for Georgeann's distress is the annual retreat at Kentucky Lake that delighted her for years and now upsets her. Here we see the essential opponent. The retreat in **"The Retreat"** is a flight from the physical that reinforces an individual identity by cultural catchphrases. The retreatants wear badges calling them "BACK TO BASICS," but the values espoused at the retreat bear little relation to the air, water, and soil of Kentucky Lake. Business meetings and televised tapes set the decorum for spiritual renewal. Spontaneity yields to program, and feeling submits to ideology. Activity means workshops. The church, in short, brings the city to the country. Shelby wears a clean suit and hastens from session to session gleaning notes on a yellow pad that tabulates "fifty ideas for new sermons." One would expect Scripture to provide Christians with vital topics for preaching; but instead of approaching life through the Book, the church substitutes books for life. Organized groups establish a community in the mind to offset the isolation everyone feels in the heart.

The peril of such a substitution arises at a group discussing Christian marriage, which Georgeann attends. The underlying assumption here is that life abstracted relieves the terror of life lived. The woman conducting the workshop reduces marriage to seven categories of intimacy through which the women share hints for "marriage enhancements." Soon, cerebration usurps sexuality. A fat woman speaks for the debasement of both sexes that such scorn for flesh engenders: "God made man so that he can't resist a woman's adoration. She should treat him as a priceless treasure, for man is the highest form of creation." This dewy-eyed talk goes unchallenged until a tall woman complains that phoniness so fills the world that we are led to "think that the First Lady doesn't have smelly feet." She speaks for Mason. As religion in **"The Retreat"** encourages an apostasy of the physical, Mason puts in a word for smelly feet and itchy skin. The story argues, moreover, that in an age that dissociates spirit from matter, the body holds open the unknown, the stuff of mystery.

Just how our century can take the mystery out of the body comes to us on the last evening of the retreat, when Georgeann tries to conquer her free-floating sadness. She removes her badge and plays the electronic video games that earlier she saw excited a boy playing them. The machine enthralls her too. Attacking multicolored aliens on the screen liberates Georgeann by giving her momentary control over definite adversaries. The thrill of self-possession also disposes her to the handsome trucker who offers to buy her a beer. Georgeann is hardly a pickup; still, sexual attention reassures her of a physical attractiveness ignored by Shelby. Nothing comes of the encounter. Chasing aliens on the screen blocks all desire in her except for release from a tightening stranglehold. By the time Shelby finds Georgeann, she is depleted by the games. Given the force of her feeling to act decisively, it comes as a surprise that she perceives herself to be a weakling, one of the old invalids requiring Shelby's pastoral cheer. She is not made helpless by age or physical frailty but by infirmity of consciousness, guidance, and resolve resulting from the paralyzing synthetic amusements enchanting her. For Georgeann to fit her spiritual conflicts on a tiny screen shows the compression of which she is capable. Mechanical displacement, however, depersonalizes Georgeann by splitting her body from her mind. Video games blot out "everything but who you are," she tells Shelby with a euphoria discredited by her confusion. What she becomes is a spook. "Your mind leaves your body." Because electronic self-possession is insubstantial, it creates a despairing aloneness.

When the Picketts return to their small brick home, they find a letter reassigning Shelby to a church sixty miles away. Although the house imprisons and change suits her desire for new life, Georgeann refuses to move. "I'm not going with you." The declaration shocks Shelby, and he pulls away from Georgeann's strength and independence. Disdain is his first defense, making her the child before his authority. "What got into you lately, girl?" Before declared pain, his as well as hers, Shelby can only propose evasion. "We can go to a counselor." Shelby does not know how to stand by Georgeann. She realizes that he will write a sermon on the subject for her benefit when he says, "We're going to have to pray over this." His habit of giving abstract value to personal issues drives Shelby to seek solution in the order of reality where it is absent.

Clinging to roles that oppress them conveys the humanness of Mason's characters. Georgeann simultaneously states her intention to be alone and relies on domestic routine to be herself. Before picking up the children, she inspects the chickens. The sick hen still lives and still disturbs her. First, Georgeann takes the eggs to the kitchen; then she gets an ax and decapitates the sick hen. Killing the hen is what Shelby would do to prevent the spread of disease. The precaution is required. Without pausing to reflect, she acts; and in the end she feels that "she has done her duty." These, the last words of **"The Retreat,"** indicate not that Georgeann has cottoned to rules coming "out of nowhere," but that the pressure of organic existence forces certain action. There is the inexplicable confinement she feels at home that compels her to strike out for freedom at the lake and then to pull back once home, and there is the love between her and Shelby that exists without understanding, a love they must live out. Mystery arises in the confluence of physical urgency and the bafflement it stirs. Not the least puzzling quality of this mystery is the way in which the need to be free brings self-restriction.

This paradox takes reverse form in **"Third Monday,"** which brings ***Shiloh and Other Stories*** to a close by showing that an awareness of limits brings freedom. The story takes up Ruby Jane MacPherson's life between dates at the fairgrounds on the third Monday of each month when she meets her lover Buddy Landon, a dealer along the flea market circuit. During this interval the Third Monday world of love collapses, and a concealed bond with others quietly emerges. The pattern is set in the opening scene in which the bowling team of Garrison Life Insurance gives a shower for Linda's unborn daughter, Holly, and showers Ruby with reassurance after her radical mastectomy. If our century takes "all the mysteries out of life," as Ruby observes to Linda, then the sympathy of the women puts some promise of surprise back into their lives. With one another the women can be vulnerable and strong in ways that endanger or embarrass them among men. Each has a secret related to the condition Ruby's mother calls "female trouble" that all are trained to hide from males—a miscarriage, severe cramps, and adverse effects of birth control pills. In sharing them, the women lighten the common plight of solitary pain.

Ruby's trouble is the most acute. In the recovery room, she awakens from a nightmare, thinking the pain in her chest comes from a large bird with a hooked beak feeding at her breast. A phantom nurse suckles a feathered monster. "The mound of bandages mystified her." The dread continues into the day. Torn and patched, deprived of her body's mysterious wholeness, bewildered by the need to surrender control of her body to impersonal forces, Ruby must endure the pain of anticipating rejection by the man she loves. A magazine article instills self-loathing with its warning that "he will be disgusted and treat her as though she had been raped, his property violated." Waiting for the results of post-operative tests expands Ruby's terror. Will she be "baptized in a vat of chemicals" like a dog dunked in flea dip? Will they radiate her? Even if her cancer can be treated, there may be no help for the ultimate isolation it imposes. Will Buddy still want to take her home to Tennessee?

By coping with these obscurities, Ruby gains certain recognitions. With Norma Jean, Leroy, and Georgeann, Ruby in physical pain learns that her body has a life of its own. She cannot will her body to be free of malignancy or will it back as it was. For years, she has wisely refused to measure her unmarried independence against conventional images of being a full woman, and now a new wisdom born of loss tells Ruby that she cannot compare her body's shape with magazine versions of a woman's body. Her body after surgery has its own wholeness, demanding a respect for the force of life in it as it is. Breast cancer naturally makes Ruby approach Buddy and the future with doubts and a sense of limits. At the same time, acceptance of limits marks the beginning of overcoming both surgery and apprehension.

The virtue of Ruby's openness becomes clearer when contrasted with Buddy's approach to trouble. His hurt comes from loneliness and the feeble ego defenses used to alleviate pain. He seeks intimacy with Ruby at the same time he fears the vulnerability of being known. Where love would bring closeness, seduction guarantees distance; and so Buddy takes the stance of footloose charmer. Withdrawal protects him, as it does Leroy Moffitt; and the idealized form of a simple dwelling made by their own hands will shelter them. Since Buddy's fear of intimacy is acute, his detachment is extreme. He wants nothing, neither dog nor woman, neither his previous wives nor his present lover. "I don't want anything to remind me of *any*thing," he says while lying next to Ruby in the dark of a motel room. Buddy's physique and good looks are instruments of pride. The cocky swagger he uses to mask his fear of women also endears him to Ruby, who finds freedom in his distance. At the first Third Monday, she hears the far-off yelp of Buddy's beagles and calls his attention to his dogs' crying. "They love me," he responds. "Stick around and you'll love me too."

Ruby does stick around, and does come to love Buddy. The relationship makes her feel less an oddball as a single woman and more a part of the mainstream. Buddy's pickup truck in her driveway pleases Ruby as a display of a man in her life. Despite this nod to conventionality, Ruby is no credulous sentimentalist looking for a romantic lead. Experience with local "ignorant" men who do not accept her as the woman she is forces Ruby to confront her restricted chance for love long before cancer interrupts her life. Wariness over the years disposes her to self-understanding. When, at a bowling match, Betty Lewis advises Ruby to stand firm the moment Buddy learns of her mastectomy and to insist that he love her for herself, Ruby says, "But people always love each other for the wrong reason!" Need is reason enough. In searching for love that does not compromise her integrity, Ruby learns that we live imperfectly and love imperfectly. However circumscribed and irrational, love bridges the gap between Buddy and her and joins Ruby to the world. Third Monday has the unaccountable effect of fulfilling her need to feel, and to feel with others. Ruby welcomes its mystery.

This power to transform is awesome and for Ruby arises from the source at which she experiences deprivation—her body. The entire volume of stories resonates to this motif. **"Shiloh"** opens the collection with Norma Jean lifting three-pound dumbbells, and near the end of **"Third Monday"** Ruby raises her right arm to restore vitality to the muscles cut by breast surgery. Mason gives a strong emotional quality to this repeated movement. In strengthening the heroines' bodies, the activity makes them alive again after feeling caught. The prospect of reaching "higher and higher" elates Ruby, "as though there were something tangible above her to reach for." There is something. Stretching her arms mobilizes Ruby for the future. Erect and nonsubmissive, her raised arms point upward to the unknown source of energy.

The last two scenes of **"Third Monday"** show that there is always the need to reach beyond confinement and that the exigency is felt by everyone. Still weak from surgery, Ruby goes to the fairgrounds on Third Monday to meet Buddy, who is absent. But Gladys, the old black woman who befriended the couple, is there. Too shy to ask Gladys directly about Buddy, Ruby asks about the mushmelon seeds that Gladys boasts have been in her family over a hundred years. "Is that all the way back to slave times?" "Honey," Gladys laughs, "we's in slave times, if you ask me. Slave times ain't never gone out of style, if you know what I mean." Ruby feels what Gladys means upon hearing that Buddy was put in jail in Missouri for selling a stolen television. The story's ending dramatizes the captivity that is our human finitude as Ruby sits in the clinic waiting room, anticipating her checkup. Claustrophobic fear of aggressive therapy stirs in Ruby a panic over being immersed in a vat of chemicals. Her daymare enlarges to imagine Buddy thrashing around a hard bunk in jail. But because immurement jars with Ruby's image of a fancy-free Buddy, she envisions different scenes in which he returns and they depart for the Rockies, a cinematic finale deepened by Ruby's acknowledgment of its improbability. Romantic or indulgent, reaching for intimacy and freedom sustains the heroine. She, a person with cancer, forges an attitude of waiting with hope, not knowing what it is and, more profoundly, not wanting to know what she waits for.

Mason recommends Ruby's humorous imagination by shifting focus at the end to a chubby man sitting next to Ruby in the clinic. The man stops humming to grin as he announces out of the blue that the joyous little girl across the room is his baby. The woman caring for the man explains to Ruby that he loves children and is waiting for his annual brain test. After an unintelligible mutter, he hugs a magazine, another of his babies, and rocks his offspring in his arms. In the end, Ruby has moved from one astonishment to another. She begins the story celebrating Linda's unborn girl and ends watching the man cradling his invented young in his arms. **"Third Monday"** concludes Ruby's venture and the book by describing the man: "His broad smile curves like the crescent phase of the moon."

The various adventurers into the unknown peopling ***Shiloh and Other Stories*** unite in the mentally impaired man. Through him Mason suggests that mystery is found in human weakness, precisely in the pitible helplessness of human life. That the pudgy man's playful grin before life's certain ridiculousness resembles a crescent moon expresses Mason's meaning. The moon presides over formation and breakdown. Change attends its periodic phases so that the moon has no fixed identity. Waxing or waning, crescent beams the becoming of new life—the baby held in the afflicted man's arms and the new life to come with Holly's birth. The same current operates in the lunar pattern of Ruby Jane MacPherson's story. Between monthly meetings with Buddy, Ruby's body suffers change, but crisis propels her toward the expectant unknown. Bobbie Ann Mason leaves Ruby and the other protagonists in transition from entrapment to a new reaching out for release from the slave quarters of isolation and infirmity. A secret attraction persists at a hidden level of their psyche to the unknown and the new personal form. Mystery implies creativity. Despite every contrary experience, Mason's characters look for change and freedom at the heart of reality. The essence of their life in western Kentucky is not its geographical remoteness or cultural strictures but its interior discoveries of the mystery that their lives add up to something beyond themselves. (pp. 553-64)

Richard Giannone, "Bobbie Ann Mason and the Recovery of Mystery," in Studies in Short Fiction, *Vol. 27, No. 4, Fall, 1990, pp. 553-66.*

Bobbie Ann Mason with Bonnie Lyons and Bill Oliver (interview date Winter 1991)

[In the following interview, Mason discusses the main themes and kinds of characters in her fiction, and she also comments on her working methods and style of writing.]

[Lyons and Oliver]: *In an earlier interview, when asked about your taking up fiction writing fairly late in life, you started out by saying that your experience set up a number of roadblocks to the imagination but ended by wondering whether, in an environment that totally encouraged creativity, "there would be any incentive whatsoever to resist, to bust out, any build-up of energy." Do you think there is an ideal balance between repression and encouragement? Did you need to encounter a certain amount of resistance?*

[Mason]: I've often wondered what I would have done with my life if I had gotten a lot of advantages from the very beginning. I did start writing when I was eleven, but along the way I was stymied quite a lot. I don't know if it's necessary for everybody to have something to resist against for creative energy to build up. It just seems to be the way it happens at times. I think about Nabokov who, to hear him describe it, had an ideal childhood. He had every advantage. He was pampered and indulged. I wonder what it would have been like for him if he hadn't been exiled and if his father hadn't been assassinated. We know that those experiences are the formation of his fiction and that's what his sensibility acts upon. I wonder if he had stayed in that comfortable place where he was the most important person in the world, if he would have anything interesting to tell us. I don't know.

I sense that you have a rebellious strain, that some part of you is impelled to act against whatever people say you ought to be doing or ought to be writing.

You've hit it, haven't you? Because I was going to be that way about half of your questions. Actually I was going to try not to be that way because the last interview I did turned out to be perverse and not as polite as it should have been. I don't know, it is a very quiet rebellion. I'm not outspoken or politically verbal. I don't get upset very easily. I'm a stoic person. I don't get angry. I sit quietly in the corner and say "no."

Isn't your writing a way of saying "no" in certain respects?

I'm glad you see that.

You write about people, places, and subjects that others might tend to dismiss as not very "literary." Do you see yourself as reclaiming materials that otherwise would be lost or ignored?

Yes, it's somewhat natural for me to feel that way. I have my material, what's been allotted to me. And along with that comes a Southern defensive posture and a desire to reclaim a measure of pride and identity for my people.

There's a passage in **In Country** *in which a dilapidated barn is described. It's said to be like an artifact from dinosaur times. Are you something of an archaeologist trying to recapture pieces of the past?*

There are ways of doing that. I don't like to think of myself as romanticizing the quaint old days. I think characters like Spence and Lila know all about how hard the past could be. I just had a conversation with my mother this morning. I was asking her when she was growing up in the country in a large household if she had her own spending money. She said no, never, she never had any money. Once she went to the local fair at the school and didn't take anything with her to eat and nobody gave her a nickel to buy a coke or anything and she said the smell of the hamburgers and hot dogs just about starved her to death that day. She married my father when she was seventeen and when they were courting he would take her out to buy hamburgers and cokes. I remember in my own childhood what an incredible experience a hamburger and coke was. I think, by the way, that's why McDonald's is so popular. People have that residual memory of those days in their families, in American history. All those fast foods are basically farm foods—grease and starch. The past is very appealing to a lot of Americans. They see it as something to hold on to, something more cohesive than this fragmented, chaotic life that we mostly live now. But I find the chaos very exciting. People are getting free of a lot of that baggage of the past and I think that's good. I think that people aren't always capable of dealing with change, and yet the possibility of dealing with it is there. I think that's what I was trying to say in the end of **"Memphis"** [*Love Life*] when Beverly is looking to her future and sees she has choices her parents didn't have. That seems to me an important moment.

Your characters are often enamored of trends and fads. Do you share with them an enthusiasm for what's new?

I'm probably more critical of pop culture than most of them, although they're getting more sophisticated all the time and less interested in a lot of garbage. I think I have a sympathetic understanding of why they're watching soap operas or reading the tabloids or whatever they do.

You don't seem to share the impulse of some writers to attack television, to lament the fact that it has replaced reading. In your most recent novel, television brings a harmony into the home of Spence and Lila.

Television has brought a lot of outside information and pleasure into people's lives. And whether it's good or bad the fact is that some of my characters feel something for the television programs they watch, feel an affection for the characters in the shows, admire their talent. Now those are real emotions, and we all see things on TV that mean something to us. So I accept that. It used to be that people in a town didn't go out at night, they stayed at home and watched the prime-time line-up. They had their favorite shows. They watched "M*A*S*H" on Saturday nights. Maybe they looked forward to it all day. They had it sort of notched in their skulls that that's what they were going to do. "M*A*S*H" was a very popular program; the final episode was watched by more people than had ever watched any such program before. I think that was culturally significant. The big change now is cable television. There is so much to watch that it all seems empty. I think people have caught on to that. Now they watch movies on their VCR or they go out because there are a lot of things happening since the seventies brought us groups to join. People just seem to be going out more. They're doing more things. They're more athletic, for example.

Is it greater prosperity?

I think so.

In Country *obviously has a lot of references to "M*A*S*H." Many of your stories have references to pop culture. Do you ever wonder if twenty-five years from now people will need footnotes?*

No, I don't worry about it.

You have said, "I feel I'm luckier than some of my characters because I've escaped the circumstances that trapped them. It's an insecure feeling so in a way I feel close to them." Could you talk about the insecure feeling?

I feel less threatened now, but I think for a long time I was afraid I might have to get a job in a factory or as an all-night clerk in a motel.

When you left Kentucky, how much of your leaving did you feel was geographical and how much did you feel was cultural or class?

Class. Which is bound up with the South and the North, because the South felt so inferior to the North. Southerners react to that sense of inferiority in two ways. One is to stand up fiercely for the South and sing "Dixie" all the time. The other is to reject it and say that the North is the authority and try to learn their ways and get rid of our accents.

Have you made a conscious effort to change your accent?

When I went away to school and later to New York to work I made a real conscious effort to lose it, and I virtually did for a long time. Then I realized that was ridiculous, and I tried to regain the natural way of talking.

Recently you've moved back to Kentucky from Pennsylvania. Has coming back had any effects on your writing? Is it any different to write from Kentucky, about Kentucky?

I don't know yet. Here's what I imagine, what I think is going to happen: living away for many years, living in the North, I always wrote about Kentucky. Coming back, I think I'm probably going to write about leaving. I'm probably going to send my characters out exploring.

Do you think they'll go north to Pennsylvania?

They might. I never wrote about Pennsylvania. I just wasn't motivated. I think the distance gives you a kind of perspective.

So now you think there might be some Pennsylvania stories?

Well, only if that's one of the places my characters happen to go. You see, my characters roughly evolve from what's going on in my family. It's not that the fiction is autobiographical, but the family's my source, my anchor, my way of finding out what's going on with people and connecting with the region. In the last few years my family has gotten incredibly scattered. For almost all the time that I was away I was the only one who *was* away, and therefore it was my responsibility to come back, to come home at Christmas, to come home for vacation. Now just in the last few years one sister has moved first to Virginia and then to Florida. Her children have grown up and moved to Virginia and Texas, and one of them has moved from Florida back here and works at the Holiday Inn. And another sister has gotten married and moved to California and is currently in Australia. So it's hard to keep up with them. I find it very disorienting.

Could we discuss a moment the kinds of characters you write about? You said in another context that you see a shift in American writing away from the alienated hero toward characters who are trying to make their way higher into society, into a better position, because they've been down near the bottom. Do you see your own writing in this light? Do you see yourself as departing from classical American fiction with its heroes who typically reject society?

I think I did deliberately want to depart from the classics of American fiction in the beginning. Back in graduate school I thought I would like to do that. I tried to do it. I wrote a novel (it was never published) about a twelve-year-old girl, a sort of female Huck Finn. When I was in graduate school I had a wonderful teacher who said all American literature was about the American dream and the American hero who was alienated from American society. He said—this was back in the sixties—in the future, you're going to see a shift, where the hero instead of trying to get *out* of society is trying to get *in*. And of course already that has happened. Much of our fiction now is about marginal people—black literature, Jewish literature, people living on the edge—rather than people who have been in the center and are trying to get out. I have always remembered that my professor said the hero was going to come back in. I didn't know what to make of that, but I thought about it when I started writing about characters who had never been in the center, who had never had that advantage of being able to criticize society enough to leave it, like the hippies were able to do in the sixties.

I think a lot of people wouldn't want to read my work because they might find it too close to their lives. They're not interested in reading something that familiar; it would make them uncomfortable.

—Bobbie Ann Mason

You once observed that the literary hero of the past typically possesses a "superior sensibility." He is, in effect, an artist, at least emotionally. Your characters may feel things deeply, but they hardly ever strike us as being artistic. They often have trouble expressing themselves. Is there a special challenge in writing about inarticulate people?

A character like Spence knows plenty of big words, but he doesn't want to use them.

Why doesn't he want to use them?

I don't agree that he can't express himself. I don't think my characters are inarticulate. They do have a vital language, and when they do talk it is quite vigorous. But they are inhibited in their relationships and they don't want to call on verbal ways of communicating. They can talk as well as I can. Certainly as well as I can in an interview. Their reticence is deep-rooted and it goes back generations and grows out of their class and their culture. They don't often know what to say, but that doesn't mean they don't know words. They don't know how to approach the subject or to find the courage to say what they could say, or maybe they don't want to say it because they are stubborn. At the end of **"State Champions"** [***Love Life***] there is a passage about how country children aren't taught manners, and so they don't say "happy birthday" or "thank you" or things like that. Manners are embarrassing. Verbal communication is very sophisticated and often empty.

Saying "thank you" is something you are taught to do to be civilized. For some of my characters, saying "I love you" is a very negative thing, because the meaning is unquestionable and to say it is to commit yourself to a great emotional thing. It is one of those things you don't say. My people don't want to be that revealing about themselves. I said their language is blunt and saying "I love you" would be a very blunt thing to say, but I'm not sure they want to say that. It would be too embarrassing.

It sounds like your characters have two motives for not speaking up. One is a fear of revealing themselves, and the other is pride, a feeling that to say the words is to cheapen the emotion.

Yes, and I think that to a character like Spence, a man of country speech, many words might seem comically inappropriate. To use a multisyllabic word that is not usually part of his vocabulary, even though he knows it, would seem like a pretension, and he does not want to put on airs.

You've said, "I feel if I can make characters know far fewer words than I know then I won't be scared of them and I'll be in charge." You were joking, but is there perhaps some truth in the comment? You don't often write about characters who have anywhere near your education. Is it partly a control issue?

Oh, I think that's probably it. I think probably I don't have the confidence to write about a lot of things. I would find it hard to write about somebody who has a lot of knowledge about something I don't understand, hard to grasp that person's way of expressing himself.

Most of your audience is, like you, more educated than your characters. Do you picture a particular audience when you write?

No, and I find it odd that I'm writing for an audience that is particularly well educated. I'm sorry the general public can't read what I write. I think that they are capable of it, but they don't have access to it. People don't know that they can go to the library and read. I think they feel a class inhibition. There are plenty of things that people who haven't graduated from high school are capable of reading, but their jobs and their worlds prevent them from taking an interest in it. A factory worker is not going to go to the opera. It's just unthinkable. That's not his world, he wouldn't be comfortable. People are taught that things outside their class are inappropriate, and I think that's unfortunate because there are a lot of things that could be of interest to them. I don't think I write fiction that's for a select group.

What sort of reactions have you gotten from people around here [Mason's hometown of Mayfield, Kentucky] about the way you portray them?

I haven't heard reactions. I'm not sure a lot of people around here read my work. I should qualify that. I think a lot of people wouldn't *want* to read my work because they might find it too close to their lives. They're not interested in reading something that familiar; it would make them uncomfortable. More have probably read ***In Country,*** which sold very widely once it was learned the movie was being made. I think most people are much more interested in the movie.

What do you think it is in your work that would make people uncomfortable?

Well, it's not television. It's not fantasy. It's realistic. I think a lot of people just look for escape, Danielle Steele novels, for instance.

You've said, "Letting the imagination loose is a way of getting at stuff that's underneath." Could you give us an example of a particular work where you did that, a breakthrough, when you felt like you got at something underneath?

I think I meant that in a more general way. I feel that writer's block is a common state of mind and almost constant for many writers. The act of writing is a battle to get at what's underneath, to break down the barriers to expression. I think writing is a matter of opening up channels to your experience. I feel like mine is pretty far down there, so the act of digging it out is hard.

Why do you think it's so far down there?

It's cultural repression and lack of encouragement. I think my experience of going North caused me to repress my own sense of identity and to lose what confidence I had in my own intelligence. I don't even know what I know.

Is there a particular story where you really feel like you got into a vein?

No, I was thinking in general about letting loose and getting into an inspired state where you can feel like you're getting something.

What is that inspired state like?

It's like you're not conscious of your body and you're kind of flying along in a state of excitement with high energy and a good feeling. Working up to that stage is kind of hard because I have all these physical sensations that prevent it. If I can't get started I realize I'm hungry so then I eat, and then I'm sleepy and I drink coffee, then I feel bad. It's kind of a daily battle. If you can transcend all that, you feel good.

How long do these periods of inspiration last?

If I control the coffee and the food just right and get a high energy level, then it could go on for a few hours. And on the best days, really the best times I've ever had, I can write a whole draft of a twenty-page story. That's good.

That's terrific. How often does that happen?

It used to happen a lot more often. There's a kind of innocence that goes into it, letting a story fly around like that. Once you do it often enough you get more self-conscious about it and then your vision of what's possible gets more complicated and you place a lot more expectations on yourself. Then it's harder to get that innocent flow, because you start criticizing everything. So I think the writing ability has improved, though the vision of what's possible has become more complicated and so the writing's harder.

How do you handle the bad days, when the writing's not going well?

I play at it, and then I give up.

It doesn't affect the rest of your life if you have a bad day writing?

I'm not very emotional about it. I don't think about writing when I'm not sitting at the typewriter.

You've been called a minimalist, a dirty realist, a K-Mart realist, and so forth. Obviously these labels are more interesting to critics than to writers. But do any of the labels seem more appropriate than the others? And would you yourself distinguish the brand of realism you write? You once called it "hard realism."

I guess I used that description not so much as a label as a way of saying my writing is plain or matter-of-fact. I don't know about labels. But I got a kick out of that dirty realist tag. John Barth had one, too, that amused me—a blue-collar hyper-realist super-minimalist, something like that.

Do you think that's accurate?

I don't think any label is ever totally accurate.

What about the description of your writing as minimalist?

I'm not sure what's meant by minimalism. I'm not sure if it means something that is just so spare that there is hardly anything there, or if it describes something that is deliberately pared down with great artistic effect, or if it's just a misnomer for what happens in any good short story, which is economy.

Your comments in previous interviews have emphasized style as important to you. You said once, "My favorite writers are those that have a unique style." What do you think your style is like?

I try to approximate language that's very blunt and Anglo-Saxon. Instead of saying "a decorative vase of assorted blooms from the garden," I might say "a jug of flowers." "A jug of big red flowers." A lot of it is not just the meaning but the sound of the words and the rhythm of the words and the way they come out of a way of talking. It's also a certain attitude toward the world. Imagine a person who would say "jug" instead of "vase." Style comes out of a way of hearing people talk.

Is your style an approximation of the sounds you have in your head from when you were a child and from the way people around here speak?

It's not literally the way they speak. It's something you fashion. It has to do with a kind of projection from inside.

One of the complaints about minimalists is that they take too narrow and personal a view, they don't give us a broad context. In stories like ***"Detroit Skyline, 1949"*** *and* ***"The Ocean,"*** *however, you obviously do provide a historical context. Is this part of your purpose? Do you want us to view your characters as in some sense representative?*

It just happens. It just turns out that way. I don't know that I typically set out to establish a larger social context for my work. But I did with ***In Country.*** My editor told me, when I started writing the novel, that the novel in general has a lot broader substance than a short story. Meaning a social context, I think. It has deeper issues. I think I bore that in mind when I was working on it.

You write almost exclusively in the present tense. Did that just happen or did you experiment with it?

Actually, I don't think I've written in the present tense in a few years. All the stories in ***Shiloh*** and most of the stories in ***Love Life*** are in the present tense. But the ones in the back of ***Love Life*** are more recent, and they're in past tense. This signaled a change for me. It wasn't a calculated effect. I just wrote in the present tense because it seemed right at the time. I think it was a fashion; it was perfectly appropriate to the times and that's why a lot of people found themselves using it. It obviously came from television, you know. It's very expressive in a way. But I got bored with it. I started seeing it everywhere and it just made me feel like doing something different.

Did you discover the present tense on your own, or did you read another writer using it and think you'd like to try that?

Everybody was writing in the present tense. I wouldn't say I copied it but I wouldn't say I originated it either. It was in the air.

Does writing in the present tense prevent your characters from having a sense of the past or an ability to step out of their immediate experience?

I think mainly it has to do with the author's authority. If the author is writing in present tense then you get the impression he doesn't know any more than you do about what's happening. You're going along with the author. If the author starts in the past tense, if he says, "Once upon a time," then you assume he has sorted events out, he has a perspective on them, has judged them in some sense. I think the uncertainty of the present tense said a lot about what we were making of the late twentieth century, or were unable to make of it.

But now your stories are primarily in the past tense?

One effect of using past tense is that you go along a lot faster. For example, here in the present tense, the phone is ringing. The waitress wants to answer the phone. She picks up the phone. "Hello," she says. You could get bogged down for days . . . and you can't skip large chunks of time. You can't say she answers the phone today and then say it is three weeks later. How did that consciousness skip all that time? Who's doing the plotting? Who's behind the camera?

Ann Beattie once said that writing in present tense helped her to imagine everything happening.

Yes, that sense of immediacy is very valuable. And also, there's that habit people have, when they tell a story: "So I go . . . then, he goes. . . . " The present tense is a natural storytelling mode. You turn it on and you go.

There are at least a couple of stories in **Love Life** *where you do unusual things with point of view. Unusual for short stories, that is.*

You mean like two different points of view?

There's the shifting third-person point of view in the title story **"Love Life."** *And the first- and third-person points of view in* **"Marita,"** *which is even more unusual.*

Also, in **"Marita,"** I shift between present and past tense.

What was behind that, or do you remember?

No, I don't remember. I'm sure it just developed. I can't imagine that I sat down and said, now I'm going to experiment with point of view and tense. It was a revelation for me to have hit upon the alternating points of view in **"Love Life"** because I'd never tried such a thing before. It seemed to make a breakthrough, force some shift. That story was written before ***Spence + Lila,*** in which I did the same thing.

What about the two different points of view and the shifts between past and present tense in **"Marita"**?

It felt very interesting writing it that way. I tend to write by piecing things together, and it may very well be that I looked at different fragments and then just somehow put them together.

That story is about an abortion, a critical decision. Are the different points of view and tenses perhaps supposed to emphasize the gap between the mother's feelings and the daughter's?

The daughter is the one experiencing it in the present and the one who's feeling it, so the first person, present tense seems to work more for that, but the mother has more critical distance, and third person, past tense seems to fit for her. That's the way I feel about it anyway.

You published a book on Nabokov [**Nabokov's Garden: A Guide to "Ada,"** *1974*] *and have talked about having a strange affinity with Nabokov's sensibility. How would you describe his sensibility?*

I think his extraordinary childhood allowed him to indulge a child's way of seeing that's up close and particular. What I admire about Nabokov's work are his details and his seizing on the tiniest things. He thought these were the essense of reality, things you wouldn't notice necessarily. Nabokov said that the literal meaning is so much more important than what people find underlying it. He was much more interested in the pattern of the butterfly wing than in anything about symbolism or life on the wing or whatever butterflies are supposed to represent.

Do you think that's true of your work?

Obviously, my writing is nothing like his, but details and images can radiate and shimmer and evoke emotions. Whereas, if you talk about a story as showing a contrast between, say, the old and the new ways of life or as being about the New South, well, either that's very obvious or it is something I never even thought of. I have difficulty with abstractions, with questions about themes. I think that when you teach literature that's what you're dealing with a lot of times, because students want to know what it means. There was an article about **"Shiloh,"** which reduced it all to these generalizations, and I felt like it was all very efficiently abstracted, so why did I go to all the trouble to write it as a story? Maybe most students are at an age where qualities and textures don't make much sense. When Nabokov taught modern European literature he typically gave his students exams with factual questions, like what was the color of Madame Bovary's dress, what color were Anna Karenina's eyes. He said he wanted them to read the work so thoroughly that they would remember even those details. I think that's a good approach. Writing is like making a quilt. You spend weeks and weeks doing all these intricate stitches and intricate patterns and colors. And then you finish it and somebody says, "Oh, this is about the Civil War." A total surprise! Abstractions have their place, of course, even for writers. I just kind of make up these terms that I use when I'm looking at my fiction critically to see if it's working. Things like balance and tone and emotional center and emotional direction, continuity, weight. Then somewhere along the way I'll discover what it's about or where the center is. But rarely am I able to reduce it to its meaning.

Something else you said about Nabokov was that you like the way he celebrates life.

He was the most positive writer; everything was just full of joy for him and he wanted to be intensely alive every second.

In Lolita *isn't the world ugly and unfinished and accidental? Doesn't it require the artist's vision to redeem it?*

Well, that may be true in the fiction. Some people think of Nabokov as a very aristocratic, snobbish sort of writer who looks down on anything crude and unformed and limited. I guess I'm influenced by what I read about him as a person and get that confused with his work. But I can see in his work the joy he took in the artistry and so I want to apply what I read about him as a person. By his own statements, the only things that he truly rejected and truly hated were deliberate cruelty and totalitarianism. I don't think he looked down on people. His whole background was very democratic and liberal, and I don't think he dismissed the human race. I think his critics also confuse the life with the work.

Do you think you also celebrate life in your fiction?

Oh, well, yeah, I'd like to think that. I can't believe anybody actually celebrates life every second. But I think I essentially have a positive view of things. I think Nabokov had a comic vision and I think that means celebratory.

Any theories about why **Shiloh** *was such a success?*

All I know is that people did tell me it struck a chord, and very often it was people who were transplanted from small towns and rural backgrounds. It seemed to ring a bell and remind people of something they've tried to get away from. As I have.

Is **"Detroit Skyline, 1949"** *autobiographical?*

It's not autobiographical; it's inspired by one little memory and two or three details, the memory being that I went on a trip to Michigan with my mother when I was nine and saw my first television set. I remember the buses were on strike and we couldn't go into downtown Detroit. And that's just about all I remember. I wanted to write about somebody encountering television for the first time. I was thinking about what that meant. Anyway, I got hold of the *Detroit Free Press* for that period and I found the bus strike and I also found the Red Scare, which got me real interested. So I collected a lot of information from the newspapers.

What differences do you see between the two collections of stories [**Shiloh** *and* **Love Life**]*?*

I think the characters' world changed a good bit between the two. I think life was changing so fast that they got more sophisticated, they've gotten more mobile, and I'd like to think that the stories have gotten more complex. I think my characters' lives were a lot simpler in the first collection.

Do you think the changes in tense and point of view in the second collection are related to the stories' greater complexity?

I'd like to think that.

When you take individual stories and put them in a collection, do you just compile what you think are your best stories at the time, or do you try to shape them into a unified whole?

I try not to put two stories that are very much alike right next to each other. In ***Love Life,*** I began with a story about an old person and ended it with old people, and I think I had the more recent stories in the past tense toward the end because I felt that moved things in a forward direction. **"Bumblebees"** was the central story that it all radiated from. I had a complicated scheme that I can't quite remember now. It was very organic. Maybe you can figure that out.

I really liked the story ***"Midnight Magic"*** *in the second collection. One of the amazing things about it is that even though its protagonist is unintelligent and insensitive, we end up liking him, caring about him.*

That story was inspired by a guy I saw sitting in a car eating chocolate-covered doughnuts and drinking chocolate milk. He looked like he had a hangover and felt horrible. He looked like a really mean person and I wondered about him, so I started writing a story. While I was writing it I couldn't make the person I had seen follow through in my imagination. The real person looked like he could be a rapist and really mean. But I couldn't write him that way. I made him a whole lot nicer than I thought he would be, and I kept thinking he was too nice. I had to explore, and I don't know why he came out the way he did other than, as I said, I kept trying to tone him down. I think we've all seen thousands of people who don't have any sense of responsibility but they want to be liked, they want to do right. They want to be in love and they want to make people happy. They just can't bring themselves to put forth the effort. They're just totally out of control.

In your stories religion is not very often a source of strength and solace for your characters, which seems a little surprising since they live in the Bible Belt. Can you comment on why that is?

It's just a failing on my part. I haven't written much about religion, just like I haven't really written about any black characters. Religion is just not a part of many of my characters' lives. I've tried just to refer to it in passing, to make it a normal part of their lives in some cases. But I don't feel confident about approaching religion. I think it's a tricky subject. I do try to think about religion, and I'm real interested in the evangelists and what effects they've had on people. I even went to Heritage U.S.A. to look around for inspiration for a story. I just haven't been able to write it.

Why is religion a tricky subject? Is it the difficulty of capturing the religious sensibility itself, or is it the fear of seeming to belittle or make fun of people's beliefs?

I think that it's hard to do seriously and delicately, and I don't know how to do it from the inside. One of these days I'll work on it.

Could you talk a little bit about how **In Country** *evolved, what your first thoughts were?*

Well, I don't usually start out being inspired by a whole set of characters that just appear in my mind. Usually I discover the characters through writing and through exploring what they're doing. But in this case I had Sam and Lonnie and Emmett and Irene and the baby there just all of a sudden. The story was inspired by some kids I saw on the street corner selling flowers. I thought how odd they would look doing that in Mayfield, Kentucky. They would be regarded as oddballs. So I started writing about a couple of kids selling flowers. That was a time when unemployment was high, and the kids I was writing about had just graduated from high school, and so I had them try to be entrepreneurs. So I wrote a story about Sam and Lonnie and her crazy uncle, Emmett, and her mother being away. I couldn't make it work as a story, but I liked the characters so much I thought I'd just keep going and write a novella. I wrote about eighty pages and I had Emmett get cancer and die. I thought, this is crazy, I don't know what this is about. Then somewhere along the line I thought of Emmett being a Vietnam vet—I thought, *that's* why he's so weird. And so I went with that for a while, but it was such a stereotype I didn't know what to do with it. By that time I was talking with my editor and told him that I wanted to write a novel about these people and about this guy as a Vietnam vet, and he convinced me I should face the Vietnam issue squarely. Before that point, I realized that Sam's father was killed in Vietnam. That just came to me out of the blue. Then I realized that *that* would take a whole novel by itself. So I had discovered the focus for the novel. Sam's quest for a father was a classic theme, and it was the first time that particular story could be written about Vietnam, because it was just about that year [1984] that kids of Vietnam soldiers would start coming of age. One thing led to another and I started on the novel and I stuck with it because I liked the characters.

Emmett is a great character. Where did he come from?

I think I originally wanted to write about his being out of work, dropping out, and I was interested in the idea of why a guy wouldn't work just because he made a moral choice not to work. I think I heard about somebody like that once. But he wasn't based on anybody in particular.

Why would you be interested in someone who refused to work?

Well, I didn't want to work, not at any conventional job. That was my problem after college. It wasn't laziness. It's not laziness with Emmett. He just doesn't think there's anything worth doing in a conventional job. That was true for a lot of Vietnam veterans.

Recently you said that you had more sympathy for the men in the stories, that women seemed to be breaking through, finding new opportunities, and the men seemed to have lost their way.

That goes back to **"Shiloh."** I didn't have any worries about Norma Jean, but Leroy was quite bewildered by all the change.

Do you think there is a little of that same bewilderment in Emmett? He and the other men in the novel seem to have lost their way. They've lost the old definitions of manhood.

They went over there to do a man's job in the war and they felt ineffectual. A lot of them anyway. When they came home there was nothing they could do that could compare with fighting a war. I think it had an emasculating effect on a lot of men, making them feel ineffectual in anything they tried to do. Some of them decided then that nothing was worth doing.

When I teach ***"Shiloh"*** *many of the women students assume it's Norma Jean's story and cheer her on for trying to take control and move out of her confining background. They overlook Leroy and don't recognize that it's his story, told from his point of view. Is that common?*

Not uncommon. And you can imagine my surprise when I hear that some students think Norma Jean is going to jump because she's standing on the edge of a cliff at the end of the story. That's so weird. Maybe *Leroy* would jump but not Norma Jean. She's a survivor.

"Naming" and "writing" seem to be central motifs in **In Country.** *At the end of the novel when Sam finds her father's name and then her own on the Vietnam Memorial a whole symbolic pattern is completed. The narrator's words—"Writing. Something for future archaeologists to puzzle over, clues to a language"—fit both the Vietnam Memorial and the book itself. Any comments on this idea?*

I often have characters puzzling over words, because I do myself.

I thought Sam's journey through words, from books about Vietnam to her father's letters and journals, reached a climax at the Memorial. It brings together a whole pattern.

Cements it all together? Oh, that's nice. I don't know that I remember doing that consciously.

Doesn't the experience of naming for the characters parallel the novel's naming of experience for the reader?

Oh, that's nice. But as a writer I go at these things in such a different way. For example, you might think I called her Sam so she could find her name on the wall, but she was Sam long before I had the Vietnam focus. And I wrote most of the novel *before* I went to the Vietnam Memorial. When I went to the Memorial I found my own name where Sam turns out to find hers. Fiction is shaped very consciously, but what goes into it is so haphazard. Sometimes you see the patterns as you write and other times you're surprised. To tell the truth, I don't remember if I saw that writing pattern at the time.

Let me ask you about another pattern. **Spence + Lila** *celebrates Lila as a mother-earth figure. At the end of the novel, when Spence goes up in the plane and sees the farm as shaped like a woman's body, doesn't that bring together the whole pattern of Lila and—*

The land? Yes, I considered that pattern consciously. And going back to that other pattern, while I was writing ***In Country,*** the words *sounded* right to me and went together coherently. And then you point out to me *why* and I realize that it's successful and that's because it *sounded* right.

You've talked about how you started writing **In Country.** *What got you started on* **Spence + Lila?**

At eleven o'clock one morning I was looking at this notebook I had been keeping when my mother was in the hospital having a mastectomy. I had taken a lot of notes. I started writing them out and after five minutes I realized. "I'm writing a novel." I had all this material and I could see the whole book.

How did you conceive of the story? What held it together?

I think it was Lila's attitude, her story.

Isn't there more physical affection, both maternal and sexual, in **Spence + Lila** *than in any of your other work?*

It was just the most natural thing to write. I knew their language, I knew how they spoke. It seemed to write itself. It wasn't like piecing together ***In Country***; I had to *discover* that one.

It seems that heroic stature is being claimed for Spence and Lila, even though to the casual observer this farming couple would probably not seem very significant. On what basis are you willing to claim that importance for them?

They're very much based on my parents. But looking at the story, I would say they both face death with courage, they're both successful at having a good, long-standing relationship to their world and to each other, they're welded to each other, they have strong purpose, and they know what their work is. They're capable of great love and sacrifice. They know where they are and what needs to be done. Therefore they're strong models of moral integrity.

Why do you pronounce the title "Spence plus Lila"?

I saw it as a love story, with the title written in a notebook or carved in a school desk, with the words enclosed in a heart.

There's a moving passage in which Spence is looking over his fields and thinks, "This is it. This is all there is in the world—it contains everything there is to know or possess, yet everywhere people are knocking their brains out trying to find something different, something better. . . . Everyone always wants a way out of something like this, but what he has here is the main thing there is." Since this is what you keep returning to in your own writing—this place, these people—would it be accurate to say that Spence's view here is your own?

Yes, I think Spence is very wise and what he says is absolutely true. Somebody asked me recently what about Kentucky inspires me and to name two places that always inspire me. Here's number one: walking through Spence's fields, the fields of my childhood. That always inspires me, always evokes memories. I see myself as a child picking blackberries or going to round up the cows with a collie dog. So I make the connection. And the second place that inspires me is the mall in Paducah, because there I can go and see all my characters. And I can imagine their journey from those fields to the mall.

What do you feel about that journey?

I understand it, I understand the emotional travel. I think of my own mother talking about starving for a hamburger at the fair when she was young. And the mall is just a big version of that fair. This mall attracts people from miles around. Some don't come to buy, just to look.

In that same passage, with Spence pondering his fields, we have this: "the way things grow and die, the way the sun comes up and goes down every day. These are the facts of life. They are so simple they are almost impossible to grasp." Does this describe your own subject as a writer?

Yes, it might do. That's the way I feel about experience. Some of the most profound things are also the most obvious, and they're the hardest to write about. They're clichés.

Both novels, but especially **Spence + Lila,** *have celebratory endings. I wonder if that's your resistance to the part of our culture that suggests that only the tragic or nihilistic is true or serious.*

I don't think it comes out of any sort of perversity or reaction. It's more natural than that. I did come from Spence's fields and I respect that. I think it's temperamental; I think people have different world views.

Just as you bring new kinds of characters to our attention, aren't you also validating certain positive feelings that aren't very prominent in contemporary writing?

I think my stories tend to end at a moment of illumination, and I think that in itself is hopeful. For example, Leroy in **"Shiloh"** recognizes that his life has got to change. His situation is difficult, but he now knows he can't just deny it or ignore it, and I think that knowledge is hopeful. I see the excitement of possibility for a lot of my characters at the end of their stories. At the end of **"Love Life"** and **"Wish"** and **"Memphis,"** for example, I'm really thrilled at what the characters can remember and can conceive in their imaginations. (pp. 450-70)

Bobbie Ann Mason, Bonnie Lyons, and Bill Oliver, in an interview in Contemporary Literature, *Vol. 32, No. 4, Winter, 1991, pp. 449-70.*

Martha Sheridan (review date 26 September 1993)

[*In the following review, Sheridan outlines the plot of* Feather Crowns *and highlights the moral issues broached in the novel.*]

The people of turn-of-the-century Kentucky must have been as Bobbie Mason describes them: proud, hardworking and more than a little confused by the events that forever changed life on the farm.

Advances in communication, increased speed of travel, growth of urban areas—all altered America and its people.

For ***Feather Crowns,*** Ms. Mason clearly has done her history homework. And like her earlier works, including ***In Country*** and ***Shiloh and Other Stories,*** this novel explores the layers beneath outwardly unremarkable lives.

The tale unwinds slowly at first, reflecting the pace of farm life. Activity is dictated by the seasons; work is hard and almost constant. Affiliation with family is a blessing, but the claustrophobic closeness can become a curse.

During a seasonal break from the almost constant work, Christie Wheeler, a pregnant young farm wife, hears warnings of an apocalyptic earthquake during a revival meeting. Her pregnancy is marked by tremors and chaos inside her body. The symptoms become so severe that she wonders whether she is carrying a devil-child.

Instead, Christie gives birth to quintuplets, and the family is thrown into chaos. Newspapers print the story of the amazing birth; strangers come all the way from Memphis to descend on the farm for a glimpse of the tiny babies.

Christie and her husband's family struggle to feed all the children. Christie cannot nurse all the babies on her own, and everyone is puzzled by modern nursing bottles that the pharmacy donates.

As mother and babies battle for survival, people begin to see ways to capitalize on the births as an oddity. A nearby town turns the quints into a claim to fame.

The family is under siege from a curious public. At one point, a complete stranger enters through the window. The train unexpectedly stops near the farm one afternoon, and a mob descends on the little house. Christie and the other farm women are stunned. It is almost impossible to guard Christie's privacy and make sure no one steals a baby.

After the first onrush of people, Christie's husband, James, allows his uncle to charge admission. James owes Uncle Wad $1,000, and Wad makes it clear he expects his nephew to earn that money any way he can.

Their front room is filled with strangers who pay 10 cents to get into the house. They hold the babies, comment on the room's shabbiness and exclaim over the evidence of the father's manhood. Christie's home is transformed into a circus sideshow; her feelings and emotions are rarely considered.

The author allows readers to share Christie's hope that the quintuplets will survive. Although some people advise the Wheelers to keep only the strongest babies, Christie never allows herself to seriously consider that advice. Later, when the babies weaken, she wonders whether she made the right choice.

The book gets its title from the crowns of feathers found in the infants' pillow; some believe such feathers are a sign of impending death.

Feather Crowns has useful messages for modern men and women. Its lessons include the high cost of hiding feelings and lying about emotions to make other people comfortable.

The novel's closing section, a monologue in which Christie tries to make sense of her long life, is set in 1963. The passage is among many sweet rewards for choosing yet another creditable product of Ms. Mason's imagination. (pp. 8J-9J)

Martha Sheridan, "Mason's 'Feather Crowns' Depicts a Farm Family Under Siege," in The Dallas Morning News, *September 26, 1993, pp. 8J-9J.*

Mason has a reputation as a regional writer, but what she is really writing about is the numerous Americans whose dreams and goals have been uplifted and distorted by popular culture.

—*Meredith Sue Willis, in the* Washington Post Book World, *March 26, 1989.*

Jill McCorkle (review date 26 September 1993)

[*McCorkle is an American novelist and short story writer. In the following review, she praises Mason's characterizations, her treatment of intimate relationships, and her attention to evocative details in the novel* Feather Crowns.]

"Christianna Wheeler, big as a washtub and confined to bed all winter with the heaviness of her unusual pregnancy, heard the midnight train whistling up from Memphis. James was out there somewhere. . . . He was riding his Uncle Wad's saddle horse, Dark-Fire."

So begins ***Feather Crowns,*** Bobbie Ann Mason's wonderful new novel, in a passage that sets the smalltown stage of her heroine's life. It is 1900 in Hopewell, Ky., and with the new century have come prophecies of a world-ending earthquake. People are flocking to revivals in preparation for Judgment Day, searching for signs from God. In February of the new year, Christie (the wife of James Wheeler and already the mother of three) delivers quintuplets, a sensational occurrence that brings short-lived fame to Hopewell and changes her life forever.

The passing train, a reminder of the rest of the world, is constant throughout the novel, its whistle the familiar sound Christie listens to night after night. She and James affectionately refer to their lovemaking as "plowing," and her early eagerness for the act, coupled with an erotic dream about a preacher, haunts her entire pregnancy with fears of some terrible punishment for her sin. However, once the babies arrive she finds "the pain gone, the horror evaporated, no devils left inside." She sees the babies as a sign, but has no idea what the message might be.

Christie and James are instant celebrities. The train begins making daily stops in Hopewell, bringing strangers from all over the country to peer at these miracle babies. The travelers arrive in great throngs: reporters, gift-bearers, lost souls who consider a sighting of the Wheeler quints to be something that might change their lives. Ultimately the Wheelers make their own ill-fated pilgrimage, taking the train on a Southern tour, a journey that begins as something they perceive to be a scholarly endeavor—a "Discourse on the Phenomenon of the Quintuplets"—but quickly nosedives into the grotesque underside of carnivals and freak shows.

Surrounding Christie during the birth and the years that follow is a richly rendered cast of characters, from the various Wheeler relatives to the caretakers of the famous Dionne quints, whom Christie travels to Toronto to see some 37 years later. But most memorable are Mittens Dowdy, a black woman who comes to help nurse the babies, and Amanda Wheeler, Christie's best friend and the very young wife of James's Uncle Wad. Through Mittens, Christie is introduced to a whole culture thus far unknown in her isolated existence, one that resurfaces when she witnesses racial prejudice in the South. The relationship between these two women is beautifully drawn, especially in the lovely scenes in which they take turns nursing the babies. Mittens's husband waits outside the house for her, but she refuses to glance out because "it would be bad luck to look at him through glass."

Superstitions abound in this household, and there is no one better versed in them than Amanda, who thrives on signs, including the nestlike clumps of feathers, the "crowns" of the title, which signify death when found in a person's pillow. Amanda is a prisoner in her marriage and lives vicariously through Christie's fame. At the camp meeting where Christie spies the young preacher who later enters her dreams, Amanda confesses her own sexual desires, confirming Christie's suspicions about her. Amanda is the character not yet settled, not yet satisfied, grasping at any sign or symbol.

Bobbie Ann Mason's attention to the microscopic detail of everyday life is, as always, riveting. Whereas in the contemporary stories that are collected in ***Shiloh and Other Stories*** and ***Love Life*** she gives us such modern staples as Phil Donahue, Diet Pepsi and Bruce Springsteen, her turn-of-the-century setting offers clabber and Colonel Happy Tucker's Lovebird Liniment—the kind of details that quickly bring a scene into a particular time and place. Along with the authentically colorful, often humorous dialogue, there are wonderful descriptions of churning and nursing and chopping dark-fire tobacco. And always there are subtle reminders of life's fragility, our uncertainty about what lies ahead.

Thematically, ***Feather Crowns*** is a rich extension of Ms.

Mason's other works. Her novels ***Spence + Lila*** and ***In Country*** explore social changes and the inescapable power of memory; in them, the constant wondering about what might have been takes on the same weight as what was and is. This new novel has a similar effect, and perhaps is most reminiscent of Ms. Mason's story **"Shiloh,"** in which a young couple are trying to hold their marriage together in the aftermath of the loss of a child; at one point in the story, the husband thinks: "Nobody knows anything. The answers are always changing." Repeatedly, Christie Wheeler expresses the same thought: "People had to make something out of the unusual. . . . It had to mean something." And, on another occasion, "There's so much in the world that nobody understands." It is difficult to portray the effects of the unknown, our abstract speculation, and yet this novel quietly succeeds. Near the end, Christie thinks that it is "impossible to tell a life story," wondering, "Where would you start?" With ***Feather Crowns,*** Bobbie Ann Mason shows that it is more than possible; the life of Christianna Wheeler and her babies is memorable and complete.

Jill McCorkle, "Her Sensational Babies," in The New York Times Book Review, *September 26, 1993, p. 7.*

FURTHER READING

Criticism

Blais, Ellen A. "Gender Issues in Bobbie Ann Mason's *In Country.*" *South Atlantic Review* 56, No. 2 (May 1991): 107-18.

Surveys Mason's treatment of gender in her novel, concluding that the "resolution sees the whole human being beyond the separating categories of gender."

Brinkmeyer, Robert H. "Never Stop Rocking: Bobbie Ann Mason and Rock-and-Roll." *Mississippi Quarterly* XLII, No. 1 (Winter 1988-89): 5-17.

Examines the role of rock music in Mason's fiction.

Clute, John. "Raw with Newness." *The Listener* 123, No. 3146 (4 January 1990): 28.

Positive reviews of *Spence + Lila* and *Love Life.* Clute describes these novels as "true descendants of [Raymond] Carver's work; they are triumphant books, intensely contemporary, unblinking."

Durham, Marilyn. "Narrative Stategies in Recent Vietnam War Fiction." In *America Rediscovered: Critical Essays on Literature and Film of the Vietnam War,* edited by Owen W. Gilman, Jr. and Lorrie Smith, pp. 100-08. New York: Garland Publishing, 1990.

Contends that when *In Country* "ends with Sam's visit to the Vietnam War memorial in Washington, we feel that each step on the road to this climactic encounter has been earned by both Sam and reader."

Graff, E. J. "Lives of Quiet Desperation." *The Women's Review of Books* VI, No. 12 (September 1989): 26-7.

Assesses the limitations of Mason's character portrayals in *Love Life.*

Henning, Barbara. "Minimalism and the American Dream: 'Shiloh' by Bobbie Ann Mason and 'Preservation' by Raymond Carver." *Modern Fiction Studies* 35, No. 4 (Winter 1989): 689-98.

Analyzes the minimalist style of the two stories.

Jersild, Devon. "The World of Bobbie Ann Mason." *The Kenyon Review* XI, No. 3 (Summer 1989): 163-69.

Notes the "depressive quality" of Mason's fiction, asserting that her "authorial restraint mirrors her characters' distance from emotion and produces a certain numbing effect."

Kaveney, Roz. "So Much to Accept." *The Times Literary Supplement,* No. 4521 (24 November 1989): 1313.

Positive reviews of *Spence + Lila* and *Love Life,* observing that Mason "illuminates lives with a quiet, clear diction, and celebrates not only the almost unchanging human values which her characters embody, but also the passing details of fashion and social evolution which their personalities refract."

Krist, Gary. Review of *Spence + Lila,* by Bobbie Ann Mason. *The Hudson Review* XLII, No. 1 (Spring 1989): 125-32.

Finds this book distinguished from most other cancer tales by "Mason's extraordinary sympathy for her characters and her ability to perform that Carver-like magic of investing surface detail with large doses of emotion and significance."

Rothstein, Mervyn. "Homegrown Fiction." *The New York Times Magazine* 137 (15 May 1988): 50, 98-9, 101, 108.

Profile of Mason and her work.

Ryan, Barbara T. "Decentered Authority in Bobbie Ann Mason's *In Country.*" *Critique* XXXI, No. 3 (Spring 1990): 199-212.

Claims that "Sam Hughes's search for her father is a symbolic representation of modern man's desire for the Logos-origin of meaning and authoritative discourse."

Stokes, Geoffrey. "Les Fleurs du Mall." *The Village Voice Literary Supplement,* No. 74 (May 1989): 13-4.

Biographical and critical overview of Mason and her work.

Willis, Meredith Sue. "Stories with a Sense of Place." *The Washington Post Book World* XIX, No. 13 (26 March 1989): 11.

Positive review of *Love Life,* contending that although Mason has a reputation as a regional writer, "what she is really writing about is the numerous Americans whose dreams and goals have been uplifted and distorted by popular culture."

Interviews

Smith, Michael. "Bobbie Ann Mason, Artist and Rebel." *The Kentucky Review* VIII, No. 3 (Autumn 1988): 56-63.

Mason describes her background and addresses the role of music in her fiction.

Wilhelm, Albert E. "An Interview with Bobbie Ann Mason." *The Southern Quarterly* XXVI, No. 2 (Winter 1988): 27-38.

Mason discusses the influence of her Southern background and contemporary pop culture on her work.

Additional coverage of Mason's life and career is contained in the following sources published by Gale Research: *Authors and Artists for Young Adults,* Vol. 5; *Contemporary Authors,* Vols. 53-56; *Contemporary Authors New Revision Series,* Vols. 11, 31; *Contemporary Literary Criticism,* Vols. 28, 43; *Dictionary of Literary Biography Yearbook 1987; Major 20th-Century Writers;* and *Short Story Criticism,* Vol. 4.

T.M. McNally

1961-

American short story writer and novelist.

The following entry provides an overview of McNally's career through 1993.

INTRODUCTION

The winner of the 1990 Flannery O'Connor Award for Short Fiction, McNally is known for writings focusing on the emotional consequences of loss and disappointment. His prizewinning collection, *Low Flying Aircraft,* concerns sensitive individuals who are separated from loved ones by death, insanity, pride, and familial conflicts. Incorporating interconnected vignettes in which characters from one story reappear in later ones, *Low Flying Aircraft* has been praised by Joanna M. Burkhardt for "reflecting the tragedies of everyday life." McNally's critically acclaimed *Until Your Heart Stops* similarly focuses on loneliness and sorrow. Set in Scottsdale, Arizona, the novel examines the events surrounding a local teenager's suicide, relating the reactions and struggles of his friends and teachers. Writing in the present tense, McNally alternately shifts the focus of his narrative from one character to another and presents events antichronologically, thereby creating a multilayered web of subjective realities. Incorporating tales of betrayal, violence, obsession, and abuse, *Until Your Heart Stops* has been lauded as a portrait of adolescent angst, adult fears concerning intimacy, and society's search for redemption, innocence, and meaning in a morally ambiguous world. Sam Schumann observed: "[*Until Your Heart Stops*] is a book about how decent but flawed human beings deal with loss, and its perspective on this universal situation is not an easy or a saccharine one. The wounds these characters suffer do not ever completely heal, and sometimes they break forth in violent new pain. This is not an easy novel to read, either in its ideas or its construction, but its philosophy seems serious and valid, and its craftsmanship appropriate and impressive."

PRINCIPAL WORKS

Low Flying Aircraft (short stories) 1991
Until Your Heart Stops (novel) 1993

CRITICISM

Bill Mahin (review date 17 February 1992)

[*In the review below, Mahin provides a mixed assessment of* Low Flying Aircraft.]

Reading T. M. McNally's ***Low Flying Aircraft,*** one of two winners of this year's Flannery O'Connor Award for Short Fiction, is intriguing, occasionally irritating and ultimately rewarding.

Each of the brief, ostensibly simple stories—profiles would be a more accurate term—features one of a group of characters who are connected by family, lovers or childhood friendship. Introduced in one segment, they reappear at different points in their lives in other stories and contexts. Betsy's boyfriend, Eric, in **"Jet Stream: Betsy, 1980,"** shows up 10 pieces later as Sarah's abusive lover in **"Breathing Is Key: Sarah, 1985."** Anna, who is featured in **"Gun Law at Vermillion: Anna, 1988,"** also appears as a successful writer of an advice column for single women in the opening chapter, where she acts primarily as a foil to Orion, whom she harbors briefly, as does Ruth later.

Ruth was Betsy's childhood friend. The two used to sneak onto runways at night, positioning themselves under landing planes, or, as the title says, low-flying aircraft. Holding onto the runway lights, Betsy says, "we feel the pull and heat and feel our legs rise, straight out behind us, hovering like the plane while our bodies get swept up in the afterwash."

Few of the characters seem to have been born on the wrong side of affluence. Orion, undergoing an extended breakdown after 13 months photographing in Nicaragua, having been hired by a church group to "document the situation, do some good," at one point calls his mother and asks her to send several thousand dollars. "This cheered her up, she said she'd wire five."

Despite, or perhaps because of, this background of privilege, these characters are universally lost. They exist—some apparently do well—but they are soulless, empty at their core. Their motives vague, they wait for something with meaning to become manifest. "We spend our lives looking for signs," Helen says, "for this, brief moments of direction."

McNally's treatment of his shallow characters is on occasion flip and insufficient. In one instance, a character describes the breakup of a relationship: "It was as if we had reached a fork in our lives, a fork with only two tines—a tuning fork which when struck would resound with a shattering pitch when struck against something hard." A lovely metaphor, certainly, but one that requires additional information.

It is, in addition, difficult to keep track of the myriad interlocking relationships, which is key to the success of the work. When these strands blur, depth is lost and the episodes begin to read like plots for a yuppie sitcom.

Countering that, however, is the exceptional writing in ***Low Flying Aircraft.*** This is how McNally describes the passage of real and hospital time: "A nurse breaks my I. V. He breaks it at the top of my wrist digging for a vein and the Mexican restaurant [across the street] decides to go Italian and install fountains, two with water."

We're presented with a raft of characters in ***Low Flying Aircraft,*** men and women who are adrift and, though frequently intelligent and sensitive, without motivator or direction. One of McNally's significant accomplishments is that we wind up caring about such characters, often deeply. The occasional sense of needing to know more, either about single characters or their links to the others, is a minor flaw in this remarkable portrait gallery.

Bill Mahin, "A Storyteller's Gallery of Unforgettable Portraits," in Chicago Tribune, *February 17, 1992, p. P3.*

Judith Paterson (review date 20 September 1992)

[Paterson is an American educator and critic. In the following review, she identifies loss as the common theme of the stories in Low Flying Aircraft.*]*

I grew up in the kind of cultural and family confusion that drives children to read like the Victorians—looking for answers to the big questions of survival, morality and happiness. Still reading that way, I am struck by how many writers of recent fiction, especially the young ones, especially the good ones, seem to be haunted by questions of loss. How, they keep asking, does one go on loving and attaching meaning to life in the face of all the relentless losing that begins with the snipped umbilical cord and ends only with the passing of all that comes after? Often the answer is so ambiguous that the Victorians would have had nothing to do with it.

Such is the case in T. M. NcNally's ***Low Flying Aircraft,*** a revolving door of linked narratives in which sorrow spins off sorrow and grief doubles back on grief in a complex design that becomes in the end a meditation on the meaning of loss. In stark, imagistic prose—part Ernest Hemingway and part Wallace Stevens—Mr. McNally, who has taught creative writing at Murray State University in Kentucky, links events randomly and geometrically, the way life links them.

The catastrophe that starts everything in motion occurs in the spring of 1976, when two drunken adolescents set out on an escapade that ends in a freak accident that leaves Helen Jowalski's brother, Peter, dead and Orion McClenahan's brother, Cass, emotionally shattered. This changes forever the lives of their siblings. All this is hinted in the first story, **"Peru,"** which brings Orion—an abstinent alcoholic, sometime cocaine abuser and suddenly successful news photographer—back from Nicaragua, where he had gone to escape his own aimlessness, his vapid, affluent parents and his hapless brother. The book's 14 interlocking stories flash backward and forward over an equal number of years, building plot with images, ironies, repetitions and digressions as well as narrative.

Cass turns up in a New England prep school in 1981, five years after the death of Peter Jowalski, indulging in a wild afternoon of guns, drugs and booze with a workman named Michael, whose wife, Sarah, has just walked out on him. As it turns out, she, like almost everyone else in this collection, is so damaged by past sorrows that she finds it difficult to love anyone. Of the dozens of people in the book, only Sarah, a relatively minor character, will finally start to let go of the past in the interest of love.

Meanwhile, two high school students—Betsy, who will become a musician, and Ruth, whose uncle will torture and sexually abuse her—are saying goodbye to each other and to life as they have known it in Arizona. Betsy leaves behind a sardonic boyfriend and a worthless, though harmless and apparently lovable, stepfather. Ruth is fleeing the death of her lover, who has just killed himself because he didn't go to Vietnam while his twin brother went and never came back.

Indeed, ***Low Flying Aircraft,*** a winner of the Flannery O'Connor Award for Short Fiction, contains enough lost mothers (cancer, madness, ambition, vagary) and lost brothers (disaffection, addiction, suicide, war) to break the heart of America, and enough swimming pools in the background to drown or baptize us all—which is, of course, the point. In the foreground a creative and well-educated coterie of young sufferers drifts across America, touching down in Phoenix and Chicago to pass around the pain. Some fare worse than others, and often their lives look far more settled than they are.

Ruth goes from Arizona to California, where she "kept herself void and uncertain . . . waiting for something she wasn't sure of." Her life, and Betsy's, will eventually intersect with those of Orion and Helen. And Ruth will visit on Orion the same kind of emotional and physical torment her uncle had inflicted on her.

In stark, imagistic prose—part Ernest Hemingway and part Wallace Stevens—Mr. McNally links events randomly and geometrically, the way life links them.

—Judith Paterson

Helen, whose brother's death lies at the center of all their lives, gets pregnant to convince herself that she is "participating in the making of a sensible, meaningful world." The baby dies, and the book ends with the strange tangle of relations at the heart of these stories revealed with rare clarity, though not resolved. Helen, alone again, fleeing a painful visit with a former lover, finds herself wondering "if all this meant something I was going to understand but didn't want to."

As one of her lovers puts it, "Our posture is all a result of our past and the way it made us grow: the way a tree in a forest will twist itself into a knot reaching for the sun." Though the people in ***Low Flying Aircraft*** suffer almost unmitigated disappointment when they reach for the sun, they keep reaching; and that, I believe, is the only solution Mr. McNally offers to the problem of loss. He has written a demanding book that requires—and deserves—more than one reading. Life, he seems to be saying, is too complicated to understand, and almost too complicated to live or write about—but not quite.

Judith Paterson, "A Coterie of Sufferers," in The New York Times Book Review, *September 20, 1992, p. 34.*

Richard Eder (review date 31 January 1993)

[An American critic and journalist, Eder received the Pulitzer Prize for criticism in 1987. In the following review, he examines McNally's depictions of adolescents coping with loss in Until Your Heart Stops.*]*

It is a warm October evening in Scottsdale, Ariz. Outside the high school gym, a few students and teachers are waiting for rides. Walker, a polite boy with big feet, walks past two friends, Edith and Howie, and the swimming coach, Jenna Williams. He sits down 20 feet away, opens a bundle he is carrying and pulls out a pistol. Howie starts slowly toward him.

"No. I'm sorry," Walker says; and then, as Jenna and Howie remonstrate: "Don't look. I'm sorry. Just don't look, then." He kills himself with a bullet through the eye.

Walker's suicide and the currents that lead to it, eddy around it and flow out from it are the material of T. M. McNally's powerfully and finely delineated novel, ***Until Your Heart Stops.*** Its theme goes beyond these things to cast a cold light on the disarray of adults who were young in the '60s, and on the moral and existential wilderness bequeathed to their children, now approaching adulthood themselves.

McNally, a first novelist, handles his theme with a certain degree of awkward rhetoric and a story which, in the events that follow Walker's death, leans too strongly on dire melodrama. The book has several shining strengths; mainly, in the formidably compassionate way in which it evokes the shifting states of mind of Walker, Edith, Howie and a fourth friend, Joe.

The author has an inspired vision of the latency of adolescent character and perception. He uses a technique that is both complex and thrilling to give a sense—as with a photograph developing before our eyes—of the movement between what each of his young people knows and what they are coming to know. His work is less inspired, or perhaps less original, with the adults—Jenna and Ray, the wrestling coach—who are the two other main characters.

For the four adolescents, all victims in one way or another of what McNally sees as the Saturn complex of our times—the older generation's freedoms and indulgences have consumed its progeny—everything is simultaneous. They are not yet able to arrange in linear and hierarchical patterns the data around them. They experience their wilderness without paths.

And so, in the first section, we see Joe going about his day. He works out rigorously for his demanding coach, Ray. He does assignments for a demanding and brilliant writing teacher. He thinks of Edith, his girlfriend. In his father's frequent absences on business, he takes care of his younger brother, Spencer, healing slowly after being hit by a car.

Only casually do we get notice of the chasms in Joe's active and generous-spirited existence. Walker, we learn—long before the event is described—has killed himself. Walker had spent time in a sanitarium after a breakdown. Walker's mother had committed suicide a year earlier. And Joe's mother ran off to Portugal and they have not talked for two years.

With Edith, the book's most touchingly memorable character, the big terrors of past and present are similarly squirreled away in an adolescent's system of power surges and protective cut-outs. She has been near-blind from birth; operations have given her a borderline state of legal blindness and the privilege of using contact lenses three times a week. She insists on taking driver's ed, gets perfect written scores, and only bashes an occasional fender in practice. (Spencer, in a wheelchair, is determined to ski.)

Bit by bit we get the submerged pain. Her family has moved to Arizona to make a new start. Her father has promised to stop doing "those things," and her mother has agreed to stay and love him. "Those things" are various male lovers. And when Edith is driven home in shock after witnessing Walker's suicide, her mother is still at work and there are furtive noises and male voices from the Jacuzzi. Before the book ends, Edith will be living in frozen silence with her father while her mother, staying at a motel, looks for a new home.

Walker's, Joe's and Edith's wounds from parental betrayal are woven in a back-and-forth chronological pattern into the terrible events of the present. The scene of a school assembly to discuss the suicide comes before the suicide scene itself. It makes a rich, ironic and terribly moving palimpsest. There are the teachers, sitting frozen on the platform. There is the principal, who has adopted the newly fashionable disciplinary approach—he expels relentlessly—and wears an aloha shirt to show he's a nice guy. "When people wear the right clothes they think they'll fit in even if the clothes don't fit," Edith reflects.

She will walk out when the principal unctuously refers to the "tragedy." Tragedy, her writing teacher had said, requires choice. One of the glowing things in this book is the young people's need to believe what they are taught. The principal's word is a verbal betrayal of both the much-betrayed Walker and the values his teachers expound.

McNally luminously portrays his adolescents trying to move from day to day on their surfaces and to survive their depths. There is passage after passage of stunning exactness. Spencer, hit by the car, is knocked into a front yard, his head inches from the nozzle of the watering system. When the ambulance arrives, the car's driver stands in shock beside him, wearing one shoe. He had put his other shoe on the nozzle to keep the unconscious boy from getting wet.

There is an unforgettable scene in which Joe, Edith and Howie visit Walker in the sanitarium. McNally renders the patient's brilliant exuberance with sudden trailings-off and repetitions. A similar breakdown comes when Walker's bereaved father cordially receives a visitor and then goes briefly, modestly berserk.

The portraits of Jenna and Ray are skillful in many ways but considerably less effective. Children of the '60s, they represent too recognizably complementary types. She is a former radical and free spirit. He is working-class, an Army veteran and a conservative. Both are boundlessly good people who try to help their anguished adolescent charges and to work out their relationship with each other. Both are too damaged—he is alcoholic, she is spacey—to succeed.

When McNally is showing his adolescents in action, he is, until near the end, almost flawless. Less successful are the poetically voiced but fuzzy passages at the start of each chapter which attempt to give a higher shape to the details that follow. At this stage anyway, the author speaks more beautifully through his characters than directly. Which is no small praise, in fact.

The bloody ending—a second suicide and attempted murder—seems misjudged. It is logically plausible as an expression of the continuing chain of damage but it is dramatically overloaded. McNally is a master of character and scene, but his sense of plot is a little forced. Joe, Edith, Walker and Howie are thoroughbreds on a racecourse that distorts their gait. (pp. 3, 11)

Richard Eder, "They Didn't See It Coming," in Los Angeles Times Book Review, *January 31, 1993, pp. 3, 11.*

Greg Johnson (review date 7 February 1993)

[*Johnson is an American poet, novelist, and critic. In the review below, he praises McNally's characterizations in* Until Your Heart Stops.]

T.M. McNally, winner of the Flannery O'Connor Award for his first volume of short fiction, has now produced a first novel that suggests he is a writer of remarkable sensitivity and range.

Set in Scottsdale, Ariz., ***Until Your Heart Stops*** illuminates the interior lives of four people drawn together by a teenager's suicide. Joe Jazinski and Edith McCaw attend Gold Dust High and were acquaintances of Walker Miller, the dead boy; Jenna Williams and Ray Morrison, teachers at the school, are also affected by the tragedy, Jenna because Walker had suffered a desperate infatuation for her, Ray because he's also (and also unhappily) in love with Jenna. Alternating the narrative viewpoint among these four characters, McNally poignantly evokes their quiet but painful struggles with love and longing.

Joe Jazinski, nicknamed "Jazz," is both the most likable character and the one most convincingly portrayed. A star wrestler, he idealizes his girlfriend Edith—"the most beautiful girl he has ever seen"—while trying to cope (at times, comically) with an ever-burgeoning sex drive. Essentially decent and level-headed, Joe possesses a gentle, romantic soul encased in a powerful young body that is ruled by raging hormones.

Edith, an intelligent girl afflicted with poor eyesight, does well in all classes except Driver's Ed, where she routinely destroys cocker spaniels during her video driving tests: "Yesterday, she blazed through a school zone doing 115 mph . . . she's also always turning into a factory or a tree, depending upon which scenario the kids happen to be following."

Like Joe, Edith must confront her developing sexuality, as in the fleeting moment when she experiences a romantic attraction for a female friend:

> Edith wondered what it might be like to kiss her. She wondered if she'd go to hell if she kissed her, the way Walker Miller was going to have to go to hell because he'd committed suicide without saving anybody else's life. According to the catechism, you could only go to heaven for killing yourself if you saved somebody else's life in the process, like the martyrs, or a guy who falls on top of a hand grenade to save a baby who will grow up to write plays about how bad war really is.

If that scene exemplifies McNally's ability to convey the humor and the pathos of his characters' personal struggles, he is somewhat less persuasive in portraying his adult characters—although Ray's middle-aged bafflement, and his resulting bouts of alcoholism, cast a forbidding shadow across the teenage lovers.

In one of the novel's most powerful scenes, Ray steps fully clothed into the gymnasium showers to confront Joe, who has just "accidentally" broken an opponent's arm during a wrestling match. Here, as elsewhere in this novel, McNally is wonderfully attuned to the psychological burdens of his male characters, their ongoing negotiations between anger and fear, violence and restraint.

Like many first novels, ***Until Your Heart Stops*** is uneven. McNally's present-tense narrative often evokes the raw immediacy of his characters' travails, but at times it deteriorates into the kind of minimalist dullness that has prevailed all too often in recent fiction, as in this description of a high school dance:

> Still nobody is dancing. It's still too early for people to start dancing. People only start dancing once they know the dance is almost over, once they've missed out all the time they could be dancing. . . .

At another extreme, each chapter begins with an abstract, pseudo-poetic pronouncement ("The heart is big as a fist. And shame is the greater part of gravity.") that is evidently meant to place the characters' experiences in a broader context. The author would have been wise to let the scenes carry their own weight.

Fortunately, McNally tends most often toward the measured, careful analysis of character that is one of his most notable gifts. Here, for instance, is how he conveys Ray's immense sadness at the loss of his youth:

> When Ray was a kid he read books and played football and thought about girls. He could distract himself by thinking about things he didn't yet seem to know enough about. But now, when distractions seem increasingly fewer, and less imbued with meaning, life often seems at times to him an illness—drawn-out, complicated and, finally, terminal.

Graced by such prose, by an artfully constructed narrative that builds toward a surprising, unexpectedly violent climax and, especially, by its subtle and humane characterizations, ***Until Your Heart Stops*** is a promising first novel by a writer able to chart the complex motions of the heart.

Greg Johnson, "Teenage Love and Death in Sunny Arizona," in Chicago Tribune—Books, *February 7, 1993, p. 7.*

Eileen Pollack (review date 11 February 1993)

[*Pollack is an American short story writer, journalist, and author of children's books. In the following review, she examines the theme of salvation in* Until Your Heart Stops.]

A troubled young man shoots himself on the lawn of his high school. His teachers and friends try to figure out who's to blame for his suicide and try to keep the plague of violence and death from claiming other victims. This could be the plot for an episode of "Beverly Hills, 90210"

An excerpt from *Until Your Heart Stops*

"This is all about Walker," Carol says.

"What?" Edith says.

"The assembly. They don't want us to think he did the right thing. They want us to think it was a tragedy."

"Tragedy involves choice," Edith says. It's something Mr. Rolf always says. She says, "It was stupid. It was stupid and now everybody knows it."

"He was an asshole!" says the boy sitting next to Edith. "A real dick!"

When Mr. Buckner taps on the microphone, a group of guys yell, "It's working!"

"What?" says Mr. Buckner, meaning he knows exactly who they are.

Even if Mr. Buckner does try to be friendly, he expels people all the time; his voice is suddenly louder than the gym. Sitting in chairs behind the lectern are a woman, Ms. Williams; Mrs. Henderson, the nurse, who's wearing white clothes; and Ms. Owens, who is young enough to look like Edith. Ms. Owens wears jeans and does college placement advising, and Mr. Buckner never wears a suit. He wears light green pants and an aloha shirt because he used to live in the Bahamas. Also, he wants to show he's friendly. When people wear the right clothes, they think they'll fit in, even if the clothes don't fit. Edith thinks everything about this is entirely wrong. She thinks she is going to be sick.

"You guys have something to say?" Mr. Buckner says.

The assembly waits, and now Mr. Buckner is clearing his throat, sounding sad, and explaining, talking about lots of things, indirectly, like parents, explaining . . . *that recently a tragedy has struck the lives of all* . . . and now Edith is standing, trying to make her way down the bleachers, because tragedy involves choice, and because she doesn't want to be here and have to listen to all this. She should have never worn this skirt, the guys in front are turning now, she's moving down the steps, gingerly, careful to land on each step and knowing that at any moment she could be falling down the rest, down all the steps into the middle of the gym. Once on the floor, the pretty wooden floor with blue lines, she begins to walk along the edges of the gym, in front of the bleachers, hugging her books, and now she stops. She stops and looks at where Mr. Buckner is supposed to be standing in front of a microphone: from this distance, she knows he knows who she is. Even if his voice has stopped, he knows who she is . . . *Edith McCaw, the girl who saw everything* . . . and now when she begins to run, running toward the light which will eventually read EXIT, she knows that she is crying. She is crying, and scared, and all she can hear are the sounds of her feet, and her voice, crying, and lifting her across the still, wooden floor.

T. M. McNally, in his Until Your Heart Stops, *Villard Books, 1993.*

or a Brat-Packer's tale of nihilistic sex and self-loathing among overprivileged cokeheads. In the hands of T. M. McNally, it's a means to explore one of the questions that concern us most deeply: Can anyone save anyone else, and, if so, how? ***Until Your Heart Stops,*** McNally's first novel (his collection of stories, ***Low Flying Aircraft,*** won the prestigious Flannery O'Connor Award for Short Fiction) may not be great literature, but it surely comes closer than many first novels do.

Centered on the suicide of 17-year-old Walker Miller, ***Until Your Heart Stops*** is told from the alternating points of view of the people closest to the boy: his friend Joe Jazinski, a wrestler tough enough to splinter an opponent's elbow—on purpose—and smart enough to be headed to Harvard or Yale; Edith, his girlfriend, a swimmer and scholar, though she's legally blind; Jenna Williams, Edith's swim coach and history teacher, a well-meaning woman who long ago posed nude for a men's magazine and has therefore become an object of obsession for Walker and his friends; Ray Morrison, Joe's wrestling coach, Edith's driver's ed teacher and Jenna's sometime lover, a man who can be either violent or gentle depending on what he's been drinking that night.

Each of these characters has been abandoned by a parent, sometimes by both. Only Howie Bently, Joe and Walker's best friend, has two live-in parents, and Howie can't wait to run away and join the Navy and abandon the people who are trying their best to keep him from harm.

If your family can vanish, if your closest friend can blow his head apart right in front of you, if you can find within yourself the potential for violence as well as for love, then whom can you trust? Maybe Joe's father is right when he says, *"In the end you're all you've ever got."* But McNally seems to side more with Jenna, who thinks that even if love will break your heart every time, "it's the only thing that can fix it, after."

McNally is optimistic enough to grant that people can be consoled for their losses not only by their lovers, but also by their friends, neighbors and teachers, even by their fellow inmates at a mental institution or by someone else's mother. Jenna tries to protect nearly everyone around her—Walker, Joe, Howie, Edith and Ray, even her neighbor, a gay black man named Bill. In turn, Bill watches over Jenna: "To confuse would-be intruders, they keep a spare key over each other's porch light." In McNally's world, a sense of safety, of connection, comes only if you're willing to trust someone else with the key to your apartment, with your love, with your life.

True, the coincidences that link the book's characters are sometimes too neat and forced to seem natural. The basic plot is shopworn. The chapter titles and some of the narrator's rhetorical flourishes are pretentious. Now and then a sentence fails to make sense ("Joe has been reading books about body repair, though his father wants him to be a broker, not a lawyer"). A brain-damaged girl who pops up everywhere with her tape recorder seems a symbol for something, but we're never sure what.

Yet the richness of McNally's characterizations and the momentum of his prose—its *adrenalin,* to use one of Edith's words—keep us reading so intently we note these flaws and move on as McNally slips deftly from one mind to the next. He is equally adept at describing what it feels like to be one of the wrestlers working out with the team, or a schoolgirl buying her first box of condoms. He treats his characters with dignity, whether they're young enough to be in high school or old enough to be in a retirement home, crazy or sane.

For all that its characters are deeply in pain, this isn't a novel that reeks of despair; its author has painted just the right shades of darkness and light to be faithful to life. Jenna's efforts to save the people she loves are just as likely to help as to hurt them. After a car knocks Joe's little brother off his bicycle, the driver who caused the accident stands in front of a sprinkler trying to deflect water from the boy, then takes off his shoe and slides it over the sprinkler head. "When the ambulance arrived, the man was wearing only one shoe and his pants were soaked."

In this city in the Arizona desert, water is everywhere—sputtering from sprinklers, gleaming in swimming pools, even spraying from the hose in the produce section of the supermarket. But the water comes from elsewhere, as do the inhabitants of the city itself. To survive in the desert a person must depend on water piped in from less arid climes and on neighbors who've arrived there not long before. Each of us, muses Edith, is 90 percent water, a fragile-skinned balloon waiting to be burst by a bullet or knife or shard of broken glass. With no hand to hold us, no faith to give us weight, we might simply float off. But even as McNally makes us cringe at how vulnerable we are, he also gives us hope that sometimes, through love, we can keep each other anchored and at least partly safe.

Eileen Pollack, "On Love and Salvation," in The Washington Post, *February 11, 1993, p. D4.*

Matthew Stadler (review date 14 February 1993)

[*Stadler is an American novelist, editor, and critic. In the review below, he provides a thematic analysis of* Until Your Heart Stops.]

In his harrowing first novel, ***Until Your Heart Stops,*** T. M. McNally has etched a circuit of linked tragedies across the chipped granite lawns of Paradise Valley, Ariz. Bordered by barren hills in "a territory fraught with geological transition and painfully clean air," this sprawling Phoenix suburb is Mr. McNally's Land of Canaan. Fate, recumbent in the menacing sky, is the prime mover. It powers the tale's relentless forward motion just as surely as God reduced Sodom to dust.

As in Canaan, loss in Paradise Valley is both instructive and total. Cataclysms occur as if on a great stage. Suicides, beatings, maimings and shootings erupt in public places (usually the local high school) before audiences who bear witness to these acts. At center stage is Walker Miller, "a polite boy with big feet," who blows his head off with a gun on the school's front lawn. The book's myriad other tragedies radiate around this hub, joined to Walker's final deadly gesture as causes, effects and just plain coincidences.

In Paradise Valley, bad things happen to seemingly good people. Joe Jazinski is a champion wrestler bound for Harvard, nervously plotting sex with his near-blind girlfriend, Edith. Joe's 9-year-old brother, Spencer, is fascinated by rockets—and by the wheelchair he must use while recovering from a car accident. Jenna Williams, an attractive young teacher (and Edith's swimming coach), has a familiar history of self-destructive loves and youthful indiscretions. Her sometime boyfriend, Ray, has a drinking problem, but he's a well-loved teacher and coach of the successful wrestling team. They are not villains—no one in Paradise Valley is. Yet they are not innocent. Each choice they make brings them a step closer to inevitable and violent loss. Mr. McNally uses their haphazard, persistent complicity to raise a deep and disturbing question: bad things happen, yes, but can there ever really be a "good" person?

Joe, Edith, Jenna and Ray are not good or bad so much as they are fallen. Fate has taken them. There is no state of grace to save them from it. Fate propels them all toward tragedy because pain, in this world, is the sole remaining instrument of revelation. "Accidents are only meaningful if you're young," thinks Joe, watching Spencer deal with his injuries. But everyone here is young. Through stubbornness, weakness and a universal failure of memory, Paradise Valley remains a land of moral infants. Pain is the only language they understand.

Like an Old Testament God, Mr. McNally uses the crucible of violence to refine his subjects, and to bring them to some wisdom. In suburban Arizona, "among all the advocates of a new and excessively impassioned age," he has found his Sodom and Gomorrah—a culture so rife with hubris and the pleasures of the flesh as to be blind to the infinite frailty of human life. No one is singled out for blame in this fallen land, but the New Age worshipers of harmony and health are given especially withering treatment. Walker's mother commits suicide by slicing open her thighs in the Jacuzzi.

Air-conditioned, poolside life in Mr. McNally's menacing desert is more than simply a denial of the real weather and geology: it is a denial of all the greater powers around us. These powers are glimpsed by children, especially Walker and his fellow patients in the adolescent ward of the Superstition Mountain Care Facility. They see them mostly in the sky, with its "hot white light."

Edith observes that

> the sky is bigger than anything she thinks she will ever get to know. It's big enough to get lost in, and she imagines the sounds of her mother's voice, rising up into the sky the way water fills a pool. The way wine will fill your mouth. The way anger, once it passes into the blood, will cause the heart to swell until it bursts.

Told with the eerie impatience and evanescence of the present tense, Mr. McNally's account shuttles backward and forward across time, tracing the connections between tragedies by fits and starts. Memories and speculations are marbled in among the facts, creating a surface of consciousness that encompasses a whole history in its thin, hasty, eternal present. The effect is to make Paradise Valley less a place with a delineated past and more a kind of permanent constellation of violence and anger, forever verging on eruption.

While this maneuver leaves the narrative locked in an unending high-speed skid, it also eventually reveals something to the trapped passengers. Gradually, the machinery of this world becomes evident to those who must live in it: "There is something bigger in the air than chronology. Something random and coincidental and terrifyingly real, something in need of embrace nonetheless." This kind of biblical revelation—in which knowledge brings salvation, but never a solution—is the best, [***Until Your Heart Stops***] seems to suggest, that we can do.

Matthew Stadler, "Gomorrah, Ariz." in The New York Times Book Review, *February 14, 1993, p. 19.*

T. M. McNally with Jeff Chapman, *CLC* (interview date 22 February 1994)

[In the following interview, McNally discusses the major

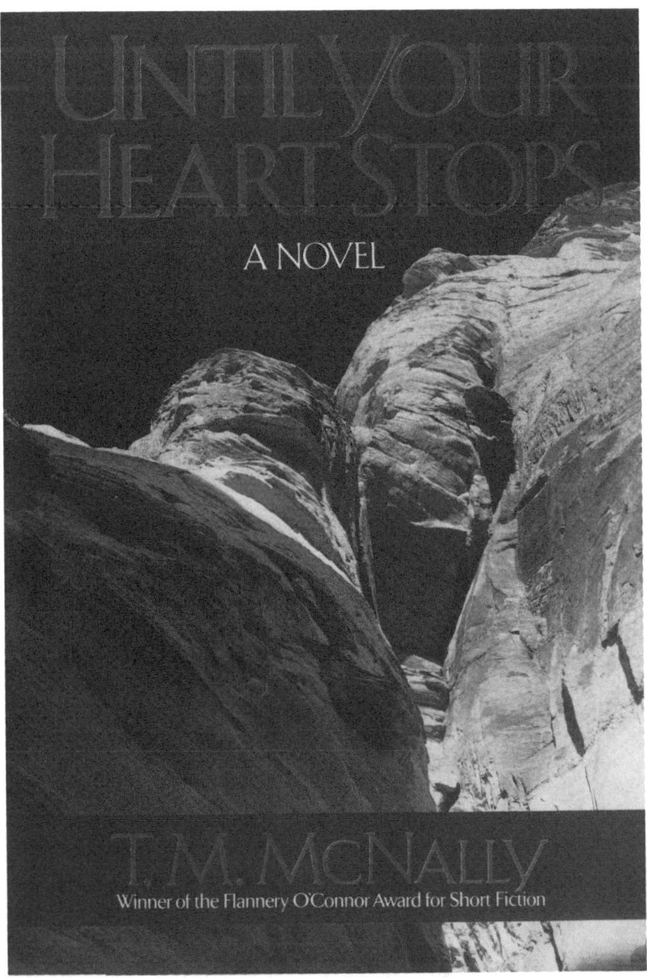

Dust jacket for T.M. McNally's Until Your Heart Stops.

concepts that define his approach to fiction, his literary influences, and his place in contemporary literature.]

[Chapman]: *Did you conduct background research for* **Low Flying Aircraft** *and* **Until Your Heart Stops***?*

[McNally]: No, most of the subjects I'm either familiar with or became familiar with by writing about them. I did do some research on the issue of teenage suicide and how its effects are scattered.

Are your personal experiences incorporated in your work?

Yes, in everything I write. Everything is personal experience. As a friend of mine says: "Everything is real whether it happened or not." So I would say yes and at the same time I would say no. For example, I have never been divorced, but I have written about divorce. Is that based on personal experience? Yes.

Have you known anyone that's committed suicide?

Yes.

Are the characters in your works symbolic, or do you try to create fully-developed people?

I'm not interested in symbols. I'm interested in creating a world. If you can do that, then objects which have meaning become invested with meaning because of the people you write about and their relationships to those objects. So I'm not interested in symbols at all. I'm interested in creating a world which carries its own weight and determines its own meaning towards and for the people therein. Moreover, I also like to avoid that word "character," which smacks of contrivance and falsehood. I want to create lives, like a God, and I want to mold those lives from the stuff of whatever earth they might happen to be living on. Is a stone symbolic? It is if you throw it often.

The reason I asked about symbolism is that both Edith and Spencer from **Until Your Heart Stops** *are in some sense handicapped in that Edith is nearly blind and Spencer is in a wheelchair.*

Edith is blind because she is nearly blind. That's the first reason. Now, do I exploit its metaphoric possibilities? "Love is blind," and the awakening of one's vision? Certainly that becomes involved in the text, but the actual reason why she is blind in the book is because she is almost blind. And the reason why Spencer has a big cast on his leg and walks around with a limp is because he was hit by a car. The things that happen to my people in my books don't happen because I want to invest them with some kind of political association. I'm not trying to create some kind of message that little children are often run over by big adults. Of course that happens, but I don't need to say that.

Numerous critics have commented on the narrative complexity of **Until Your Heart Stops.** *What were you hoping to accomplish through the novel's narrative structure?*

I think a story creates a life, and a novel creates a world. So if I'm writing a book with a lot of people in it, I want that world to be representative of all those different lives. What I mean is your world is different from my world which is different from my wife's world, but if we all write a story and then we all put those stories together, we get a big, more complex and finally knowledgeable, perhaps even sensible, world. So one thing I'm very interested in is the way in which our own personal lives and realities are shaped and influenced by people we know and often do not know. Our lives take shape by things we are not even aware of but which are still nonetheless present. In ***Heart,*** for instance, one thing I'm doing is exploring the ways in which Edith is influenced by what's going on in Ray Morrison's life, even though she is entirely unaware of what's going on in his life. Everything thus becomes interconnected and contained within the world created by the novel. That accounts, I think, for some of its narrative complexity.

In his review of **Until Your Heart Stops,** *Richard Eder has argued that the novel "[casts] a cold light on the disarray of adults who were young in the '60s, and on the moral and existential wilderness bequeathed to their children." Do you agree with this assessment?*

Yes, I do. I wouldn't put it in those words and certainly when I was working on the book I wouldn't have thought that way, but I do think that that relationship of the '60s to the '90s exists and that the '90s is a result of the '60s which is a result of the '40s, etcetera. I think "existential wilderness" may well have become the post-modern landscape. If you are what you do, then you have to figure out what it is you should do, but what happens when you don't know what you should do? So the post-modern adventure becomes one of psychological and interior exploration. We no longer chase cows or rope horses. Instead we try to figure out what we're supposed to do next. And certainly the people I write about are trying not only to do what they want to do, but also the *right* thing, which is something else they must figure out. Of course these are issues that you don't figure out in an afternoon. It takes your entire life to understand them and decide how to act or who to love or who not to love, etcetera. Many of my stories involve people who have been led by way of their histories to the brink of such decision.

Could you describe your writing process?

Long, slow, marked on occasion by dips, fits, bursts. ***Until Your Heart Stops,*** for instance, was written over a period of three years with eight months of absolute silence in between.

So you don't have a rigorous schedule like some writers do?

My schedule is that I have to write every day. When I don't, I feel miserable. So I try to tell myself it's okay when I'm not writing every day by saying that even if I'm not writing that I'm still writing. So I'm always working, even if I'm not working. Silence is far more useful than a lot of bad typing.

As you write, do you have a particular audience in mind or an ideal reader?

I guess my first audience is myself. If I don't discover something in the process then no one else is going to discover anything. There's that line—no surprise for the reader, then no surprise for the writer, or vice versa. The other thing is that when I read something, I want to be told something I don't know. By that I don't mean a fact but a truth. If that can't be done, tell me a truth that I know but have forgotten, remind me of it. So in my work I'm concerned about discovering something through the writing process. You could say I write what I want to read. So my primary audience is myself and associated with that is the reading public—those of like-minds.

What are your primary aims or goals as a writer?

To discover God. For me writing is the pursuit of the unknown; it's the entrance into mystery. I don't want to sound like I'm New Age here, but it's a struggle to come to terms with truth, or several truths, and to determine one's own authority in the world. You could say I'm trying to understand, on a very simple level, my place in this world and at the same time the world in general.

What are your strengths as a writer?

No answer. I know what they are in private, and I also know what my weaknesses are. My weaknesses are often not represented by the people whose work I admire, so I read their work to try and learn something so that my weaknesses are no longer weaknesses.

Who are your primary literary influences, and why?

There are certain novels which have moved me deeply over the past ten years. Books which instruct the heart, the mind, as well as the body. They instruct us all. I also turn to poetry and music. I was raised as a musician and so I often turn to music as some kind of source. Do I read as much contemporary fiction as I should? No, certainly not as much as I used to.

Since you have written both short stories and a novel, which form do you prefer?

Both. When I'm writing stories I hate the story form and when I'm writing a novel I hate the novel. They're different dogs. When I write a story, I have to know everything about that life so I'm creating an entire world for each story. In a way stories are therefore kind of dissatisfying merely because that world is gone through so quickly. That can be a release though if the story isn't particularly good. Right now I've just finished a new book of stories and I'm working on a new novel. Will I go back and forth all the time? I don't know. I may start writing haiku. I don't know. Brevity is the soul of wit.

Do you see a relationship in terms of your development as an artist or thematic concerns between **Low Flying Aircraft** *and* **Until Your Heart Stops***?*

I think ***Low Flying Aircraft*** is concerned with a kind of reality of things, and ***Until Your Heart Stops*** seems to be more concerned with the relationship of that reality to the spirit.

Both your short story collection and your novel are structured around a death. Could you comment on that?

I'm just a dark soul. I don't know. I wouldn't say death, I would say loss. As Robert Hass has said, "All the new thinking is about loss." If life is a process of losing everything from your birth certificate to your mind, then life also becomes a process of trying to fill in those gaps. I think that attempt to fill in gaps, those holes or empty spaces, drives the processes by which I work. "For nothing can be sole or whole that has not been torn or rent"—Yeats.

A more practical answer to that question might be that I want to test people. I want to see what they're made of, what their mettle is. I'm not interested in why terrible things happen to people. I'm not interested in why, for instance, my best friend nuked himself or my father died or my dog died. What I'm interested in is how we survive those kind of losses. My whole operating thesis is that life is hard and that therein lies the glory.

When you're developing an idea for a new novel or story do you begin with a theme?

No, the last thing I want to think about is theme. There is an expression of some sententious statement, like "other people can be mean." I'm not concerned about theme at all. My work often starts from an image or from a phrase, from a voice in my head. But actually what those things are echoing is some kind of tone or mood. I think I write mostly from tone or mood because that's what creates everything else, for me anyway. I know other people write differently.

Your ideas sound similar to those of the French poet Paul Valéry who said that the conception of his poems began with a rhythm.

Yes, rhythm is a part of that mood, which drives the heart. You know how when you turn on the radio while you're driving in your car and all of a sudden you're in this entire misty, moody world? Well that's it. That's what I write from, and it's not always misty, moody. Sometimes it can be unbearably clear.

How do you perceive yourself in relation to the larger picture of contemporary literature?

I'm trying to do what everybody else is trying to do, the best he or she can. We're all trying to find our place.

Are you trying to fit into some type of tradition?

There's naturalism and then there's realism and then there's minimalism. Minimalism seems to me just an attempt to be efficient. I think of myself as a realist but not in the way that people coming from a naturalistic tradition might think of realism. I'm interested in a kind of psychological realism, and if the spirit is real—that is the soul, the heart, the mystery, and everything we simply do not know—then that has to become a part of the re-creation of the real world. Metaphor, of course, inevitably becomes the guiding spirit of that world. In literature, metaphor is God incarnate. Metaphor becomes the stuff of the real world—a rock, a song—transformed into Idea, and then back again. Because only language can perform miracles. Only language can turn water into wine—Homer's wine-dark sea. And when we partake of that language, of metaphor, we enter knowingly into the presence of God. For me, Realism is no longer just the gritty detail of a decaying society. I just don't think that's enough. I want more.

FURTHER READING

Criticism

Gordon, Neil. "Living in Tragedy's Wake." *San Francisco Examiner & Chronicle* (29 March 1992).

Praises McNally's use of language in *Low Flying Aircraft* as disciplined, honest, and skillful and finds that "each story adds a new level of meaning to the ones that came before, and vice-versa."

McAulay, Sara. Review of *Low Flying Aircraft. Studies in Short Fiction* 29, No. 2 (Spring 1992): 221-22.

Mixed assessment of *Low Flying Aircraft.*

Czesław Miłosz

1911-

(Has also written under the pseudonym J. Syruc) Polish poet, essayist, novelist, and translator.

The following entry presents critical essays published between 1986 and 1992. For further discussion of Miłosz's career and works, see *CLC,* Volumes 5, 11, 22, 31, and 56.

INTRODUCTION

The recipient of the 1980 Nobel Prize in Literature, Miłosz is widely considered Poland's greatest contemporary poet, although he has lived in exile from his native land since 1951. Miłosz's writings are concerned with humanistic and Christian themes, the problem of good and evil, political philosophy, history, metaphysical speculations, and personal and national identity. Jonathan Galassi noted: "[Miłosz's] entire effort is directed toward a confrontation with experience—and not with personal experience alone, but with history in all its paradoxical horror and wonder. . . . His own work provides dramatic evidence that in spite of the monumental inhumanities of our century, it is still possible for an artist to picture the world as a place where good and evil are significant ideas, and indeed active forces."

Born in Lithuania in 1911, Miłosz spent much of his childhood in Czarist Russia, where his father worked as a civil engineer. After World War I the family returned to their hometown, which had become part of the new Polish state, and Miłosz attended local Catholic schools. He published his first collection of poems, *Poemat o czasie zastygłym,* at the age of twenty-one. While attending the University of Vilnius in Lithuania during the 1930s, Miłosz won respect for his poetry and became associated with a literary group called the Catastrophists, who prophesied the subversion of cultural values and a cataclysmic global war. Miłosz lived in Nazi-occupied Warsaw during World War II, working as a writer, editor, and translator for Polish Resistance forces. After the war, he served as cultural attaché in Paris for the postwar communist regime in Poland. Disgusted by the hypocrisy and authoritarianism of the government, however, Miłosz defected to the West in 1951. He was subsequently declared a nonperson by the Polish government and his writings were banned in that country for the next 30 years. He lived in Paris until 1960, when he accepted a teaching position at the University of California, Berkeley, and established permanent residence in the San Francisco area. After he was awarded the Nobel Prize, Miłosz received his first officially sanctioned publication in Poland since 1936. In 1981 he visited that country for the first time since his exile and was hailed as a symbol of the resurgence of freedom in Poland.

Critics frequently emphasize Miłosz's important contributions to the development of contemporary Polish poetry, citing his application of modernist and classical verse forms, his lyricism, and his command of synecdoche and irony. His first three volumes, *Poemat o czasie zastyglym, Trzy zimy,* and *Wiersze* include pastoral lyrics, meditations on the poetical process, and commentary on social problems. In the early 1940s, when the predictions of Miłosz and the other Catastrophists were realized by the events of World War II, Miłosz began writing anti-Nazi poetry, which was published clandestinely. Critics have praised Miłosz's restrained approach in these poems to communicating the horror and anguish of the time. Miłosz commented in his nonfiction work *The History of Polish Literature:* "When a poet is overwhelmed by strong emotions, his form tends to become more simple and more direct." Most critics agree that Miłosz's talents matured with *Ocalenie,* a volume that contains several of his most famous poems, including "The World" and "Voices of Poor People." In his next two volumes, *Swiatlo dzienne* and *Trak tat poetycki,* Miłosz blended lyrical, classical, and modernist forms to create poems that are alternately discursive, visionary, and somber. Miłosz's later poetry in such volumes as *The Separate Notebooks* and *The Rising of the Sun* sometimes verges on rhythmical prose and contains many classical elements, including a respect for balance and form and an economical style. In most of his work, Miłosz has avoided the experimentation with language that characterizes much modern poetry, concentrating more on the clear expression of his ideas. Much of Miłosz's work is strongly emotional and conveys a transcendent spirituality. Critics have commented on the influence of his Roman Catholic background and his fascination with good and evil in both his poetry and his prose.

Miłosz's personal experiences, his interest in history and politics, and his aesthetic theories are delineated in his prose works. For example, his essay collection *Zniewolony umysel* (*The Captive Mind*) studies the effects of totalitarianism on creativity, while *Rodzinna Europa* (*Native Realm: A Search for Self-Definition*) is a lyrical recreation of the landscape and culture of Miłosz's youth. In the nonfiction work *Ziemia Ulro* (*The Land of Ulro*) Miłosz laments the modern emphasis on science and rationality that has divorced human beings from spiritual and cultural pursuits by evoking a symbolic wasteland that appears in several of William Blake's mythological poems. His recent essay collection *Beginning with My Streets: Essays and Recollections*—an amalgam of literary criticism, philosophical meditations, and narrative essays—has been praised for its insightful probing of contemporary life, art, and politics. Miłosz's two novels also combine explorations of twentieth-century world events with autobiographical elements. *Zdobycie wladzy* (*The Seizure of Power*) examines the fortunes of intellectuals and artists within a communist state. Blending journalistic and poetic prose, this work elucidates the relationship between art and ideology and offers vivid descriptions of the Russian occupation of Warsaw following World War II. In *Dolina Issy* (*The Issa Valley*) Miłosz evokes the lush river valley where he was raised to explore a young man's evolving artistic sensibility. The mythical structure of this work explores such dualities as innocence and evil, regeneration and death, idyllic visions and grim realities.

In the United States Miłosz is known not only for his work written in Polish, but also for his English translations of his own poems and those of other prominent Polish poets. Many critics cite the profound awareness of history that informs his poetry, a quality sometimes considered lacking in American verse. Despite the broad range of historical and political themes in his poetry, Miłosz is regarded primarily as a metaphysical poet because of his pervasive concern with the nature of existence and identity. Affirming Miłosz's universal relevance, Joseph Brodsky has written: "I have no hesitation whatsoever in stating that Czesław Miłosz is one of the greatest poets of our time, perhaps the greatest."

PRINCIPAL WORKS

Poemat o czasie zastyglym (poetry) 1933
Trzy zimy (poetry) 1936
Wiersze [under pseudonym J. Syruc] (poetry) 1940
Ocalenie (poetry) 1945
Swiatlo dzienne (poetry) 1953
Zniewolony umysl (essays) 1953
[*The Captive Mind,* 1953]
Dolina Issy (novel) 1955
[*The Issa Valley,* 1981]
Zdobycie wladzy (novel) 1955
[*The Seizure of Power,* 1955; also published as *The Usurpers,* 1955]
Trak tat poetycki (poetry) 1957
Kontynenty (poetry) 1958
Rodzinna Europa (essays) 1959
[*Native Realm: A Search for Self-Definition,* 1968]
Czlowiek wsród skorpionów: Studium o Stanslawie Brzozowskim (history) 1962
Krol popiel i inne wiersze (poetry) 1962
Gucio zaczarowany (poetry) 1965
Lied vom Weltende (poetry) 1967
The History of Polish Literature (nonfiction) 1969; revised edition, 1983
Miasto bez imienia (poetry) 1969
Widzenia nad Zatoka San Francisco (essays) 1969
[*Visions from San Francisco Bay,* 1982]
Wiersze (poetry) 1969
Prywatne obowiazki (essays) 1972
Selected Poems (poetry) 1973
Gdzie wschodzi slonce i kedy zapada (poetry) 1974
Utwory poetyckie (poetry) 1976
Emperor of the Earth: Modes of Eccentric Vision (nonfiction) 1977
Ziemia Ulro (nonfiction) 1977
[*The Land of Ulro,* 1984]
Bells in Winter (poetry) 1978
Dziela zbiorowe (nonfiction) 1980
Ogrod nauk (nonfiction) 1980
Nobel Lecture (lecture) 1981
Hymn O Perle (poetry) 1982
The Witness of Poetry (lectures) 1983
Niobjeta ziemia (aphorisms, letters, poetry, and prose) 1984
[*Unattainable Earth,* 1986]
The Separate Notebooks (poetry) 1984
The Rising of the Sun (poetry) 1985
The Collected Poems, 1931-1987 (poetry) 1987
Rok myśliwego (diary) 1990
Provinces (poetry) 1991
Beginning with My Streets: Essays and Recollections (essays) 1992

CRITICISM

Anne Husted Burleigh (review date Spring 1986)

[*Burleigh is an American nonfiction writer. In the following review, she examines Miłosz's discussion of*

Christian theology and modern society in his nonfiction work The Land of Ulro.]

Only the boldest writer would flatly preface his work, "Dear reader, this book was not intended for you, and I feel you should be forewarned before you enter its bizarre tangle." But the poet and essayist Czeslaw Milosz does exactly that as he introduces his reader to ***The Land of Ulro.*** In this book, which by his own admission is both exotic and eccentric, Milosz faces the anguish of being a spiritual exile in an alien twentieth century. He intends here to give free rein to his meditations, declaring that "a writer can afford to produce in his lifetime one maverick work." The result is a rambling book dense with obscure allusions and commentaries on literary works that may be unknown to the American reader. Nonetheless, if we give Milosz the freedom to lead us where he will, we come face to face with the most audacious and courageous confrontation of our twentieth-century negation of moral and spiritual value. (p. 162)

The Ulro of the book's title comes from the poetry of William Blake:

> They rage like wild beasts in the forests of affliction;
> In the dreams of Ulro they repent of their human kindness.

As one of the strongest influences upon Milosz himself, Blake is a key figure in this book. Milosz takes Blake's name Ulro to signify "that realm of spiritual pain such as is borne and must be borne by the crippled man." Ulro is the wasteland of the spiritual wanderer, the alien place that can never be home. It is the realm we have inherited from the scientific mind of the seventeenth, eighteenth, and nineteenth centuries and made absolute in this century. It is the realm of relative value in which nothing can be acclaimed as true, in which good cannot be distinguished from evil, in which there can be no hierarchy of value but only an equality of all value. Ulro demands that religious value, the parent of all other value, cannot be reflected in the secular. Sacred and secular must be absolutely disengaged. Truth can have no spiritual anchor; its justification can lie only in the secular arena. Truth can be only what consensus says it is. The heresy in the land of Ulro is to say that one idea is better than another. Pluralism, consequently, is the tyrant.

In the land of Ulro the religious or philosophical man must keep his thoughts to himself. Religion is a private affair and must never spill over into public life. That there might be a higher reality than man himself, that there might be an end in life beyond this world, that man might have a reference point beyond himself can never be acknowledged.

The only acceptable truth in Ulro is scientific truth that can be demonstrated. This scientific truth, which may be accurate in its own limited knowledge of man as a being in nature, is made to stand for the whole truth about man and his world. It is made to serve a purpose it was not meant to serve. Because man as an object of science is made to stand for the whole man, then the truths of religion, philosophy, art, and poetry cannot be legitimate, for they are subjects upon which not only the reason but also the imagination works. They are invisible, part of the inner life of man. They are not accessible to scientific proof, and hence in Ulro they do not exist. For the poet and the artist, for whom in Milosz's view creativity is synonymous with religious imagination, this enforced severance of the sacred and the secular is excruciating. If the poet or philosopher is to keep his sanity and his integrity, he must go underground. He must think and work in secret, and his works must be aimed at a small group of the initiated. If his ideas, which by their very nature refer to a higher reality than man and the state, become public, then it is also the very nature of the pluralistic society to try to destroy them. In its disregard of truth, in its skepticism, in its refusal to acknowledge a hierarchy of value, the twentieth-century Western democracy is as antithetical to truth as is the totalitarian state. In both cases there is no public recognition of truth. The apparent difference between these two kinds of society may be a matter only of the degree of violence with which contempt for the spiritual and the philosophical is carried out. Surely a democracy which allows its most innocent members to be killed is a society as confused about what is true as is a totalitarian state.

For William Blake the demon of Ulro was Urizen, or reason, that is, reason that had degenerated to a fixation on abstraction; reason that wanted to reduce the world to its own terms so as to control it. "Urizen," says Milosz, "in effect is the god of reduction who reduces everything to quantitative terms." For Blake, as for Swedenborg, Goethe, Dostoevsky, and others who opposed reducing man to a superfluous number in a mechanistic universe, the villains were Bacon, Locke, and Newton.

"Man's conception of the universe," Milosz writes, "has been wrought by three discoveries: (1) Copernicus's refutation of the geocentric theory; (2) Newton's absolutizing of space and time, whereby the universe became a void expanded to infinity; and (3) Einstein's relativizing of space and time, or the primacy of motion. The first two were seen as a diminishment of man and hostile to his purpose; hence the resistance of the poets." The third discovery, on the other hand, may prove to be a liberation. Milosz is hopeful on this point; he recalls being struck when he once met Einstein at Princeton that here was "a holy man of science." And it may be a further note of hope that the most recent advances in physics have brought physics almost to the edge of theology.

But, at any rate, the march of "so-called objective truth" during the seventeenth and eighteenth centuries demanded a negation of three primary points of Christian doctrine; it required denial of original sin, rejection of the Incarnation, and secularization of Christian eschatology. If man is naturally reasonable and good, then original sin is impossible. If miraculous happenings are out of place in a mechanistic universe, then the Incarnation is something that is not really true but exists only as a symbol and myth. The whole character of language and thus of Word is changed. And the Christian idea of fulfillment of the Kingdom of God in the end-time became, at the hands of Enlightenment philosophers, a secular philosophy of unlimited progress in this world, in which man, as his own purpose for being, is god.

Poets and philosophers who fought the Newtonian outlook—Swedenborg, Blake, Goethe, Dostoevsky—set up opposites to the scientific world view, contraries that were alive with imagination but that sometimes were highly unorthodox. To counteract the idea of a reasonable, good man they proclaimed a detestable, miserable man. To foil the deistic idea of God the Father turned into a meaningless abstraction and a God the Son as a mere ethical teacher, they shrank or eliminated God the Father. Without a father, Christ is no longer the Word made flesh, the Son who has come from the Father and who is consubstantial with Him. Christ the man is now the "perfect fulfillment of the Godhead." In him there comes together all that can be said of God. He is the "Human Form Divine." This is a confusing, misty concept of Christ that is full of difficulties. Christ began to look like the strange Adam Kadmon, "the primordial, pre-cosmic man of the Cabala." This picture of the God-man had ties to the ancient Gnostic and Manichaean idea of the primordial war within the godhead as the explanation for good and evil in the world. Swedenborg's Christ, born of a virgin, was a man of sinful flesh who, through resisting temptation, became divinized.

To combat the scientific world view in which man was god, his own redeemer and *telos,* the mystic poets and philosophers knew they had to turn as far as they could from the useless doctrine of God the clockmaker, the deistic God who had wound up the universe and had left it to tick away according to its laws. Horrified at this kind of deterministic world, which they considered immoral and antihuman, these poets tossed out the possibility of a clockmaker god. Instead they made Christ the entire image of the divine. No longer could Christ say that he had come from the Father, that everything he was doing on earth was in obedience to the Father's will.

Dostoevsky, of whom Milosz paints one of the most fascinating portraits in the book, felt the desperation inherent in stripping the Father from the Son. Dostoevsky had inherited only Christ without his Father. Thus his Christ was a God who had taken on all the sufferings of mankind, yet had no power to save the world. This is a world in which evil is nearly overwhelming. Thus Ivan Karamazov can create the "Legend of the Grand Inquisitor," in which a terrible burden is on man. God is absent and Christ does not intervene. The moral man cannot stand the cruelty of a world from which God has withdrawn and yet man still has his freedom. For that reason the Grand Inquisitor, sympathetic toward mankind's pitiable plight, chooses a "benign" enslavement over a free but godless world. Ivan's dilemma was exactly that of Dostoevsky himself, and Milosz thinks that Dostoevsky's religious thought is anything but a relic of the past, that it ought in fact to be treated as a distillation of the controversy of the seventeenth and eighteenth centuries.

The Newtonian world view had also negated the third point of Christian doctrine—Christian eschatology. Dostoevsky answered this attack with a passionate faith "in the Christian Russian peasantry as the only hope for mankind." So concerned was he for the future of Christianity that, according to Milosz, he ran into "heresy, that of the Russian Christ," for "while he resisted all other temptations to make things easier for himself, he could not resist the messianic-nationalistic temptation."

Here we come to a crucial point. The idea we have of God and the idea we have of creation determine our metaphysics. And here lies an irony. Both the Newtonian who accepts only the laws of nature as truth and the poet who makes Christ the "Human Form Divine" have done two things that, however roundabout and apparently opposing their paths, will most likely lead them to the same conclusion. First, they have effectively removed God. A clockmaker God is not worthy of anyone's notice. Nor is Swedenborg's Christ any better in the long run. A Christ whose Father does not exist, or is merely an "inferior demiurge," loses his divinity and becomes only man. Thus, in either a Newtonian or a Blake-Swedenborg world view, God cannot logically exist. Only man exists. For that reason only man can be god. Furthermore, both world views do a second thing—they eliminate freedom. Newtonian determinism rules out a real exercise of will. But the Blake-Swedenborg view does that as well. With God absent man cannot bear his freedom. Freedom must have a reason. If its goal is not God, then it becomes a terrifying abyss that man runs away from, even if he runs into slavery.

"Dostoevsky," says Milosz, "was convinced that all of Western civilization would choose a belief in *man* as redeemer and, consequently, finish in slavery."

Milosz perceives the profound connection of our view of God and creation to our metaphysics when he writes, "Once we cease to view creation as the work of a good God, we are left with few alternatives. Either we remain underground and chew our nails, or we become a Grand Inquisitor to better organize society."

He is much concerned in ***The Land of Ulro*** with the people and sources that have influenced him in his spiritual progression and his work. His Catholicism comes first; it has been his source from childhood—"a childhood of carols, Month of Mary devotions, vespers—and of the Protestant Bible, the only one then available." In addition to the names of Blake, Goethe, Swedenborg, and Dostoevsky he gives high credit to his distant older cousin Oscar Milosz, a poet who emigrated to Paris but who kept his Polish roots, and to the Polish Romantics, particularly Adam Mickiewicz, and finally to Simone Weil.

Milosz lists three motifs on which his lecturing and research have centered. The first is "*unde malum*—wherefrom evil, or the old, all-embracing question of whether the world was the work of some malicious demiurge." Haunted by this question, Milosz delved into church history and the history of doctrines; he eventually taught a course on Manichaeanism. His second motif is nineteenth-century intellectual history, a study through which he has constantly asked himself, "Where did men such as Dostoevsky and Nietzsche come from? Why did they turn out to be so prophetic?" That study led him back to the intellectual sources in the Enlightenment and in Romanticism and spurred him to teach a course on Dostoevsky. Finally, he has always studied and taught Polish literature.

Though his book is not a systematic development of an intellectual theme, there are certain key concepts woven through it. Some concepts Milosz even calls laws. Chief among these is that a human nature actually exists. Man is not an illusion or a negation but a real being. Hence there are qualities of being that are properly human and activities and pursuits that are properly those of man.

Then there is the law of hierarchy. Some things and ideas are better than others. "Wherever we have to do with the human mind and heart," says Milosz, "equality is a fiction; inequality, the general rule." This law of hierarchy is similar to what Oscar Milosz called the "law of analogy" in which the higher can be reflected in the lower.

Furthermore, there is the law of travesty and parody. An idea or an inspiration, no matter how noble, becomes watered down and devalued the more it is worked over by inferior minds; in other words, "everything of substance is undermined, hollowed out by the termites of inferiority." Says Milosz,

> A priest nurtured on the Freudian-Marxian-Chardinian dregs will be a priest in name only; a teacher, though able to read and write, an illiterate and a corruptor; a politician, an outlaw; artists and poets, the helpers of circus managers who stage spectacles with real blood and live copulation, exactly as in those Roman circus-theaters described by Tertullian.

There is the "law of triumphant banality" in which, "weathered by time, the transitory and the spurious fade into gray banality." Fortunately there is another law, Milosz believes, by which "works less abundant in being are put to death . . . by works of greater abundance," works "more abundant in *being*." This law Milosz calls that of "magical intervention through unseen communion."

In addition to these laws two other themes, less formally identified, run through this book. One is the idea of place, rootedness, a spiritual homeland, which, not surprisingly, Milosz has partially identified with his Polish homeland. But place for Czeslaw Milosz, as for his cousin Oscar Milosz, is far more than a geographic location. It is the place to which all things relate, to which all things move. Milosz points out that "among some Jewish cabalists one of the names for God is Place."

A second theme, referred to over and over—and perhaps the strongest thread of the book—is the pull of opposites, God and the devil, good and bad, man and nature, the passionate attraction of life and the equally powerful hatred of it. Milosz, though not a traditional sort of Manichaean, is fascinated by, even drawn to Manichaeanism. He thinks "a certain measure of it is both necessary and unavoidable." He is ever aware of the dangerous juxtaposition of good and evil.

"If the present book has a dominant theme," he says, "it is this 'morbidity' intrinsic to man, this balancing of the human weight on the very edge of the scale so that one pinch dropped on the other is enough to tip it."

Milosz is pessimistic, so much so at times that the reader wants to rebel, yet also senses the rightness of the author's position. Milosz, a Catholic still, directs some of his most withering barbs to the Christian church of the last two decades. The sixties, he contends,

> was a time when theologians, Catholics included, casting themselves as clowns, gleefully proclaimed that Christianity, hitherto in opposition to the world, was now both with and in the world. Meanwhile, their audience, beholders of a spectacle more pathetic than funny, took this to mean that Christians wished to be "the same as others," that is to give up their Christianity. Sophistry, perfected by generations of superior minds, for the sake of self-annihilation has been pursued with such vengeance as to fill even unbelievers with unease.

Milosz is visited by the demon of evil in the world to an extent so troubling that he wonders whether he himself *wills* belief in the absence of any real belief. The evil, the lies of Ulro hound him. He can fight Ulro, but he cannot escape it. What makes Ulro so difficult to overcome is that "a given civilization, or civilization in general, endures in its bodies of thought, forming crystal-like structures obedient to an internal logic." If we accept one thing as true, then we logically accept another proposition as following from it. The crystal-like structure of modernity is a tolerance of all creeds and ideas "provided they be sufficiently loose, syncretic. Thus does the average mind surrender to a noncommittal, a-religious and a-philosophical trance, unconsciously assimilating a certain fund of the cultural inheritance."

The tragedy of living in a decaying society is that people are affected in ways of which they are not consciously aware. The ideal of the best society is lost to them. Being ill, they do not remember what health is. They are like carpenters building a house without a blueprint. Yet civilization obviously does endure, even if only in small pockets. That it does, Milosz claims, "is due to those minute particles of virtue residing in specific individuals, who affect the whole through a complex process whereby each particle, or grain, is multiplied by others."

Despite his pessimism, Milosz has hope. He hopes to be, with others, such a particle of virtue. His strategy is this: to introduce an unorthodox tradition of writers and ideas into the intellectual climate, hoping that these writers, rich in imagination, can supply new blood. (The writers he has in mind include the ones he cites in this book.) Milosz thinks that Christian theology has never recovered from the blow it received in the eighteenth century, "while an unorthodox, even heretical religiosity has enjoyed a great vitality by appealing to the imagination." With Catholicism withdrawing into its fortress and Protestantism in fast retreat from one position after another,

> such minds as Swedenborg, Blake, Mickiewicz, Towianski, and Dostoevsky were stationing themselves beyond the front erected by the theologians. Mickiewicz . . . invoked not St. Thomas Aquinas or St. Augustine but those prophets standing outside the Church—Boehme, Swedenborg, and Saint-Martin.

Milosz contends that the language of theology is dead to the modern mind. He argues that Thomism, "the most closed and rationally compelling of theological systems . . . defies the imagination—that is, it defies that translation into images without which no reading can be efficacious." He thinks that "the inhabitants of Ulro can profit little" from Aquinas but that they do search for something to fill the void. Consequently, they have filled the void "with a syncretic mush, with a religious offal indiscriminately and nonsensically selected. . . . " "I suppose," says Milosz,

> that in the present literary enterprise I am guided, partially at least, by a perverse ambition: can I, by citing an unorthodox tradition, say something about matters I regard as urgent, in a language at once intellectually lucid and evocative, so as to leave an impress on the mind and in that way help to break down the gates of Ulro?

The answer from this reviewer is that, sadly, no, he cannot. This book is brilliant, profound, disturbing, difficult, and altogether compelling. But in this "perverse ambition" it is disappointing. It is extremely hard to envision how the literary exotics of this book, all drawn, like Milosz, to a kind of Manichaeanism, could provide the content or impetus for a solid spiritual revival. Though it is true that they are vibrant with religious imagination, and though it is true that they concern themselves with the right questions, it is also true that they often give the wrong answers. We have suffered through nearly three centuries of faulty logic and wrong answers. Perhaps it is time to look for a revival of another kind of tradition, something that has not been examined, except by a few; indeed, its re-entry into the intellectual picture might be seen by the modern mind as altogether new, imaginative, and exciting. That tradition is the orthodox classical-medieval synthesis. Regardless of Milosz's reservations about Aquinas's inaccessibility to the modern mind, it still seems more likely that a revival of the classical-medieval tradition, re-examined in light of Einstein's theories, might prove more hopeful for Western civilization than veering off on a Blake-Swedenborg course.

There is one figure who is surprisingly missing from this book: Pope John Paul II. Yet this prelate, who with his Polish intellectual and literary background would surely have something in common with Milosz, has been said to be able better than anyone else in our age to cast the thought of the classical-medieval tradition in words that appeal not only to the minds but also to the imaginations of his listeners. If anyone can break down the walls of Ulro, John Paul II may be a better man for the task than Swedenborg. (pp. 162-67)

Anne Husted Burleigh, "In The Land of Ulro," in Modern Age, *Vol. 30, No. 2, Spring, 1986, pp. 162-67.*

Leopold Labedz (essay date December 1986)

[In the essay that follows, Labedz provides an overview of the political and philosophical tenets in Miłosz's poetry and prose.]

Czeslaw Milosz's poetry, essays, and novels have been translated into many languages, but for a Nobel laureate his literary audience is not very wide. This is not, it seems, only because (as Paul Valéry said) "poetry is the thing which is lost in translation. . . . " Milosz pointed out the deeper reason in his Nobel Prize lecture. He said that a newcomer from Eastern Europe, "wherever he finds himself, notices that he is separated from his new environment by the store of his experience. . . . " There is, inevitably, a gap between Milosz's vision, images and reflections, his references and allusions, and their reception by readers with a quite different "store of experience".

In ***The Land of Ulro*** Milosz asked the question:

> How to accept that what is obvious to us may not be so for others? How many ways, on how many levels, do we discover the inaccessibility of another mind? And this makes for unease: if behind the words uttered in conversation lies another perception, another wisdom, then the words, although the same, must connote something different.

In his pessimism on intercommunication—which may be realistic on a mass level, but which his own books can only undermine—Milosz is saying in effect that every national experience is an island unto itself and cannot be approached from outside:

> I do not believe in the possibility of communing outside a shared language, a shared history. . . . One of the most serious and frustrating dilemmas resulting from prolonged residence abroad is having to repress the constantly intruding thought: How would this sound in English? How constructed by a foreign reader? I cannot stand writing in a foreign language.

In this, and in many other respects, he is obviously the opposite of Joseph Conrad (except, perhaps, in their perception of Russia, as can be seen from a comparison of *Under Western Eyes* and of Conrad's essay "Autocracy and War" with the chapter on the subject in ***Native Realm***). Unlike Conrad, Milosz decided that:

> . . . if I am to nourish the hope of writing with a free hand, with gaiety, and not under pressure, then I must proceed by keeping only a few Polish readers in mind. . . . I belong to the estate of Polish literature and to no other.

It is, of course, possible for a writer of Milosz's intellectual breadth to bridge the gap to some extent, to be understood not only by his compatriots. Indeed, while remaining rooted in his particular experience, Milosz tries after all to give it a universal significance. And in this respect it is not just his influential political book of 1953, ***The Captive Mind,*** which is of relevance.

The role of memory in Milosz's writings cannot be overstressed. In his words, "For me memory is mother of all the Muses." He remains "an exile", as have so many fine European writers ever since Dante; but for him memory is not just a question of nostalgia—even though, as he has remarked, the number of "Florences" has grown enormously since Dante's time.

> The exile of a poet is today a function of a relatively recent discovery: today those in power may also control the language, not only through censorship, but by changing the meaning of words.

This Orwellian connection between the manipulation of language and the nature of the totalitarian state was the subject of ***The Captive Mind*** (1953), and it powerfully supplemented *1984;* for, after all, it was a non-fictional report on a really *lived* experience. Milosz recollects that "The Marxists . . . had attracted me as a young man because I sensed in them something vital and bracing." He says that for him "the Russian Revolution was personified not by Lenin, but by Vladimir Mayakovsky." With his strong Manichean predisposition, he felt an affinity with the Communists, who "were bolstered by a variant of a belief in the fundamental and hidden rationality of the historical process. . . . " Eventually, however, he obviously found that Mayakovsky (who committed suicide before Milosz exhibited enthusiasm for him) had played, after all, a less important role than Lenin in shaping Communist reality. As a writer Milosz had discovered the "socialist-realist" compulsion to pretend that this reality is not what it is.

Like so many other disappointed intellectuals, Milosz realised that the most important defence against the Communist denial of "the right to reality" is memory, both for the poet and for the people: they all need to retain their identity. Hence, the primary task of a writer is to preserve memory as the first line of resistance against the enforced falsification of words, images, and ideas. Whatever his subject, and whatever his mood, authenticity is his first duty. His individual awareness inevitably clashes with the fraudulent "truth" forced upon him by the state. The pressure is strong, and the temptation to submit great. Milosz analysed the mechanism of the intellectual rationalisation of such submission in ***The Captive Mind*** in a way that made it comprehensible to a Western audience at a time when very few people in the West were aware of such phenomena in any detail. He pointed out that totalitarianism is not just the sombre drama of horror and purges, that it has more humdrum but no less far-reaching consequences:

> Terror is not, as Western intellectuals imagine, monumental; it is abject, it has a furtive glance, it destroys the fabric of human society and changes the relationships of millions of individuals into channels of blackmail. . . .

Apart from his insight into Stalinised Poland, the other themes of Milosz's poetic memory are his youth in Wilno, the multi-ethnic town in pre-War north-eastern Poland, and his wartime experiences under the Nazi occupation in Warsaw. With the exception of some of his lyrical poems and literary essays, all his writings, in one way or another, echo these three themes. As with all his generation, the basic trauma which divides his memory is the clash between the innocence (and "normality") of his youth before the Second World War and the ensuing horrors during and after it.

As a student, Milosz belonged to a left-wing group opposing the ruling régime in pre-War Poland. As a young poet, he sensed the approaching disaster (he belonged to a poetic school described as "the Catastrophists"). Under the Nazis the reality surpassed anything he may have vaguely feared in his "anti-fascist" imagination. His experiences of the Hitler occupation in Poland were shattering:

> For a study of human madness, the history of the Vistula basin, during the time it bore the curious name of *'Government General',* makes excellent material. Yet the enormity of the crimes committed here paralyses the imagination, and this, no doubt, is why the massacres in the small Czech town of Lidice and in the small French town of Oradour are given more notice in the annals of Nazi-dominated Europe than the region where there were hundreds of Lidices and Oradours. . . .

Milosz gave poetic testimony to one of these horrors in a poem entitled **"Campo dei Fiori",** written at the time of the liquidation by the Germans of the Warsaw Ghetto in 1943. Its last stanza conveys his awe-stricken dread:

> Those dying here, the lonely
> forgotten by the world,
> their tongue becomes for us
> the language of an ancient planet.
> Until when all is legend,
> and many years have passed,
> on a new Campo dei Fiori
> rage will kindle at a poet's word.

Milosz knows only too well that certain experiences cannot be adequately transmitted through words in any language:

> Had I been given the choice, perhaps, I would have blown the country to bits, so that the grass would no longer grow over the ashes of Treblinka and Maidanek and Auschwitz, so that the notes of a harmonica played under a gnarled pine tree would no longer float over the nightmarish pits and dunes on the city outskirts. Because there is a kind of pity that is unbearable. And so one blows it all up, at least in one's mind, that is, one is possessed by one single desire: not to look. . . .

After the War, Milosz joined the Communist régime, less out of ideological enthusiasm for "the New Faith" than from a belief that the victory of the Soviet juggernaut was "historically inevitable". To justify this he accepted a type of philosophical rationalisation elaborated by his friend, the philosopher Tadeusz Kronski—"Tiger", whom he described in his essays as sharing the mental affliction which came to be called "being bitten by Hegel", a Polish counterpart to Schopenhauer's remark that "Whoever becomes infected by *'Hegelei und Schlaiermacherei'* will never be cured."

Tiger, who died in 1958, was his intellectual guru, and Milosz describes him with great warmth. At the same time, the retrospective apologia for Tiger helps Milosz to defend himself from accusations of simple opportunism:

> Words cannot describe the fascination with someone's personality or an intellectual friendship. . . . When Tiger spoke of 'Christians', it was understood he meant Communists. The allegory was justified in so far as the idea of the in-

> evitable progress or of a hidden force behind the scenes—implacable toward all who disobeyed the Teacher's commands—took its origins from Christianity: without Christianity, after all, there would have been no Hegel or Marx. The sacred merely underwent secularization, the immanent replaced the transcendent.
>
> In any case, should not the wise man have drawn conclusions from the inevitable?

Rationalisations know no limits in history. Reflecting on the decline of the Roman Empire, the Greek poet C. P. Cavafy wrote about Roman citizens "waiting for the barbarians", and he concluded his poem with the line: "The barbarians were a kind of solution." Milosz also found for himself a kind of solution.

> In the teaching of 'Ketman' practised by Mohammedan heretics in Persia (it was not unlike the Jesuit *reservatio mentalis*), a distinction was made between the goal toward which we fervently and passionately strive and the veils by which the prudent screen it from view. . . . Wear a mask, throw them off the scent—you will be forgiven if you preserve the love of Good within you.

But although Milosz realised that "there is no immanent divinity that guarantees the moral glory of what is irreversible", he still insists:

> I was right in rejecting the light from the East, but the Communists were also right. Thanks to the Red Army, they soon seized power [in Poland] and then I had to serve them. Whoever claims that force cannot suffice as an argument overlooks the character of politics, where winner takes all. . . . From the dreams of 19th-century Socialists about a perfect society, nothing had really been salvaged. Instead, the foreground was dominated by the Hegelian conviction that certain phases will be victorious over others: that things are as they are, and we are not responsible.

Milosz did not try to make a virtue out of "historical necessity", but, as is his wont, he tried to avoid making a choice: he would not, as he loftily says, "lapse into the comfort of moral intransigency", nor did he "attach himself solely to the present by writing for the Party." His attitude was reminiscent of Joyce's maxim: "Silence, exile and cunning." As the present was both unpleasant and inevitable, the Hegelian snake-bite became for Tiger and Milosz an ideological rationale for moral as well as political impotence. Milosz reflects, however, that:

> . . . the problem with choosing madness (a refusal to recognise necessity) and servility (an acknowledgement of our complete powerlessness) is that one act of obedience can be the start of a downward slide.

He adds that his (imagined) "freedom of manoeuvre remained intact only as long as I lived abroad behind the screen of diplomatic service." But he felt that he was "threatened with sliding because we are drawn into compromise almost without our being aware of it. . . . "

It is, to be sure, a moot point when the "sliding" begins. But although Hegel idealised the Prussian state, and the Russian writer Belinsky "made use of Hegel during a certain period of his life to deify Czardom", Milosz still thought that "History's course is not something to be discarded easily." He referred to his religious instructor, a Catholic priest at his school, as Naphta. But his guru now was Tiger, who perhaps fitted Mann's description even better. According to Milosz, Tiger "had persuaded himself that in the last analysis his deceit served the truth." Milosz continued to cultivate his "dialectical" garden:

> Immobility or resistance to historical changes that time brings with it in the name of unchangeable moral commandments and a stable structure of the universe is deserving of respect. However, those who armour themselves in this way risk punishment, because sooner or later the Spirit of History will appear, 'His face large as ten moons, a chain of freshly cut heads around his neck. . . .' I refused simply to slip out of the antinomy between the divine and the historical that was poisoning my life.

Other "antinomies" were also present. As a Communist diplomat he had to confront constantly the hypocrisy of living on two levels of reality. His private thoughts clashed sharply with his official duties, as he recalls in ***Native Realm:***

> At many a reception in Washington or in Paris, where enthusiastic ladies would approach a Red with a delicious shiver . . . I felt that I was only half present. . . .

He ironically describes "those lady enthusiasts at our receptions at the Embassy, admirers of progress in the East, hens pleading for a few kernels of lying propaganda. . . . One of them gravely asked us how we intend to solve the Negro problem in our country." But at the time—the time when Orwell and Koestler were trying to dispel the illusions of the Western intelligentsia—this was not Milosz's concern.

> I munched *hors d'oeuvres* while exchanging polite clichés with a crowd of progressive writers at various receptions, but I did not attempt to break down the wall that stood between me and them. Their warmed-over Jacobin ideas did not coincide with any reality; they were social diversions. It was not my place to enlighten them or to betray what I thought of them.

But he was very unhappy about it:

> Standing with my glass of vodka at receptions in the Soviet Embassy, I watched how Leftist luminaires of French literature and art minced around a [Soviet] diplomat, seizing upon his every word, nodding approval—polite little boys in front of their teacher. The magic unguent of power must have rubbed off upon me too, a new arrival from the East, with my broad nonWestern face, but I was ashamed of it.

After his service as a cultural attaché in the Polish Embassies in France and the USA, Milosz had eventually had enough of self-deception. In 1951 he "chose freedom". He expounded the reasons for his decision at a press conference chaired by Ignazio Silone (organised in Paris by the Congress for Cultural Freedom), and in an article, **"No"**, published in the Polish émigré magazine *Kultura.* There he stated that a writer in the People's Democracies "has to renounce the truth completely" even though "he witnesses every day human tragedies in comparison with which the tragedies of antiquity pale into insignificance."

His decision and his explanations provoked furious attacks on him in the Polish official press (including one by the poet Antoni Slonimski, who later renounced his own opportunism and became the literary patron of the dissident opposition). Polish émigrés in the West were divided. Some criticised Milosz for "belated discovery of the obvious" after supporting the Communist régime for years, and particularly for becoming its official representative; others welcomed him and demanded tolerance for a writer who had undergone "an honest disillusionment".

Milosz was clearly very wounded by these attacks and polemics (especially from émigrés) about his motives, and replied to them with acerbity. They eventually died down. He became accepted by the Poles, both inside the country and abroad, as a leading contemporary Polish poet. During the period of *Solidarity* he was officially rehabilitated, belatedly published, and even personally fêted during his visit to Poland in 1981. The workers from the Gdansk shipyard put a quotation from a Milosz poem on the monument they built for their murdered colleagues. He became, again, a target of censorship under General Jaruzelski. The Serbian Academy of Arts and Sciences, which made Milosz (in 1986) "a corresponding member abroad", was sharply attacked in the Polish press, and Yugoslav journals were criticised for praising that reprehensible (but still unforgotten) book, ***The Captive Mind.***

Milosz is an intellectual poet; also a metaphysical poet, and one of passion. Each of these elements inevitably clashes with the others, and this becomes a source of a creative tension and of certain problems for his philosophy. Poetry seems to help him clarify his feelings, but philosophy only tends to obfuscate them. While his emotions are always rather obvious, his philosophical attitudes are more often than not equivocal. He almost made the cultivation of *ambivalence* into a programmatic philosophical premise; nothing seems more painful to him than the intellectual necessity of *choice.* This is revealed in the description of his early attitudes both to Marxism and to religion. He indicates that he found it impossible to make up his mind about them:

> Marxists dismissed their opponents by treating them en masse as 'idealists'. Although such an indictment embraced too many elements to be philosophically correct, it did contain a particle of truth. I was stretched, therefore, between two poles: the contemplation of a motionless point and the command to participate actively in history; in other words, between transcendence and becoming. I did not manage to bring these elements into unity, but I did not want to give either of them up.

The roots of the dichotomy go back to his school education where the Catholic priest and the Latin teacher presented him with opposite philosophical positions:

> The mere presence of such a Naphta and such a Settembrini gave us an option. My rebellion against the priest weighted the scale in favour of the Latinist. But my religious crisis was not a final thing; it did not end in a clear 'yes' or 'no'. . . .

In his writings Milosz refers very often to the wisdom of various Biblical sayings. But "Let your communication be, Yea, yea; Nay, nay . . . " is not one of them. He is well aware of this psychological trait. Commenting on his intellectual and political evolution, he wrote:

> The official anti-Communism of the West was false, as is every frozen thought, but many a time its representatives closed their eyes to what they did not wish to see in my works. In that Tower of Babel, language was confounded because the levels of consciousness were different. I had to consent in advance to defeat, which is dangerous, because then we are tempted to exult in our inner readiness to accept the cross. . . . Many of my contemporaries may regard such thrashing about as the neurotic unhinging of a modern Hamlet. Their jobs and their amusements prevent them from seeing what is really at stake. I was not a philosopher. Events themselves threw me into my century's towering philosophical pressures, into the vortex of its hardest and most essential questions. Perhaps these exceeded my grasp, but they mobilised all my energies.

Milosz thinks that in his work "the song of innocence and the song of experience share a common theme." Perhaps. But one cannot help listening to the songs, noting how often he has changed his tune. In the poetic programme of his youth he exclaimed that "one does not wear short pants forever"; in Communist Poland he considered his poetry "a kind of higher politics, an unpolitical politics"; and now he says that "in poetry, I wanted to save my childhood." It is easier to see here the fortuitous continuity of a poet than the serene wisdom of a philosopher.

He is particularly fascinated by the mystical and religious poets and writers: Blake and Swedenborg; Shestov and Dostoevsky; the French poet Oscar Milosz (his cousin) and Simone Weil. He has also been particularly affected by his reading of the Bible, and has even learned Hebrew in order to make a new translation of the Book of Job and the Psalms into Polish.

The religious, if not mystical, motifs are particularly developed in his ***Land of Ulro;*** the autobiographical background is described in his novel ***The Issa Valley*** (1955). In a recent interview for *La Stampa* (5 July 1986) Milosz explained:

> The Lithuania of my youth is for me very much alive because the forests, the valleys and the rivers which I saw in my childhood possess for me a strong evocative force. But, as happened with Proust, childhood also for me became separated from time. If I talk in my writings about Lithuania, it is not out of nostalgia for the past, the nostalgia of an exile, but for artistic purposes, for

> writer's reasons. Already this landscape has become for me mixed in my memory with the landscapes of other countries I have seen since; California, and elsewhere. Thus my poems are both "Lithuanian" and "Californian" at the same time. . . .

He has also declared, "A poet carries his land within him. I never left Poland."

Facing the problem of national identity presents Milosz with one of his crucifying choices. He often refers to his mixed ethnic background. His mother was of Lithuanian ancestry, and in describing her he says that she was responsible for "the tangle of contradictions I see in myself."

> Another trait of hers was patriotism, but not toward the nation or the state—she responded rather coolly to that brand. Instead, she taught me a patriotism of "home", i.e., of my native province.

This is undoubtedly one of the reasons why Milosz is so attached to the realm of his youth. It also accounts for his local "patriotism".

Another person who strongly influenced him was his cousin Oscar Milosz, who faced a similar problem. He opted for Lithuania, and represented its interests at a Paris Peace Conference in 1919. Czeslaw Milosz has described his native Wilno with its ethnically mixed environment in an anthropological symposium, in an essay which could serve as a model for a *verstehende* approach in cultural anthropology, and also reflects his ethnic dilemmas.

> Today, if I call this city the capital of the Lithuanian Soviet Republic, Vilnius, I give a hint of my Lithuanian identify. If I call it Wilno, I present myself to the Lithuanians as probably a Pole or a Russian. Behind the double names lie the complex historical events of several centuries.

In all his other writings Milosz uses the word "Wilno". But this is hardly a reflection of Polish nationalism: he has made quite clear his hatred of the Polish "nationalist party", and particularly of the xenophobic "radical nationalists".

> My allergy to everything that smacks of the "national" and an almost physical disgust for people who transmit such [xenophobic] signals have weighed heavily upon my destiny.

The national strife over Wilno-Vilnius evoked in Milosz some melancholy thoughts:

> The Poles maintained that Wilno should belong to Poland, the Lithuanians that Vilnius has always been and would be a part of Lithuania. Perhaps those sardines fighting each other in the mouth of a whale are not untypical of the relations between humans when they search for self-assertion through ethnic values magnified into absolutes.

A number of Milosz's philosophical reflections and literary essays can be read in ***Emperor of the Earth: Modes of Eccentric Vision*** (1977). His poetry, translated into English by himself and others, has been published in several volumes; and his autobiographical self-definition against the East European background and that of Western civilisation is most vividly expressed in his ***Native Realm*** and in ***The Land of Ulro.*** This short list of his works in English gives perhaps an idea of his range. Some of his writings in Polish are not yet available in translation, but what has appeared in English provides, I think, the Western reader with enough material to appreciate Milosz's stature as a writer and a witness for the times. He has touchingly summarised his life and work in ***The Land of Ulro:***

> In a cruel and mean century, "catastrophism" entertained dreams of an idyllic earth where "the hay smells of the dream", where tree, man, animal are joined in praise of the Garden's beauty. By recalling that the boy and the poet "catastrophist" and the old professor at Berkeley are the same man, I am merely observing the guiding principle of this book, a book both childish and adult, both ethereal and earthbound. Reader, be tolerant of me.

For all his philosophical and political peregrinations, East and West, one cannot but be impressed by Milosz's intact poetic and literary sensibility. From his "store of experience" he has vividly conveyed the meaning of contemporary tragedies and personal dilemmas.

At 75 Milosz remains as intensely puzzled by the world as when he was a child. In his novel ***The Issa Valley,*** he wrote that his birthplace "has the distinction of being inhabited by an unusually large number of devils", and he concluded that "there is no denying the cunning of the demons":

> How ingenious of them to undermine the confidence of Thomas [his childhood *alter ego* in the novel] in his own internal voice, to rob him of his peace of mind by appealing to his scrupulosity. No longer could he implore God for illumination; genuflecting, he would always have the feeling he was kneeling before himself. Thomas wanted to confide in the Real, not in a cloud that, nourised by what is inside us, hangs overhead.

"Tiger" (who bestowed on Milosz "the glorious title of dialectician") argued that "evil is a test of what is *real.*" This is evidently a question which does not at all bother the poet, but to which the philosopher cannot get the answer from the dialectician. That is, perhaps, why Milosz is such an elusive personality and such an open book. (pp. 72-7)

Leopold Labedz, "Appreciating Milosz," in Encounter, *Vol. LXVII, No. 5, December, 1986, pp. 72-7.*

Czesław Miłosz with Paul W. Rea (interview date 27 October 1987)

[In the following interview conducted on 27 October 1987 at the University of Northern Colorado, Miłosz discusses Central European politics and culture, life experiences that have informed his writing, and his role as an artist.]

[Rea]: In 1918, the great Czech scholar and statesman Thomas Mazaryk published The New Europe, *and indeed during the period between the world wars it appeared that*

An excerpt from *The Captive Mind*

The multi-colored setting of Western life is subject to the law of osmosis. The average citizen of the West has no idea that a painter in a garret, a little-known musician, or a writer of "unintelligible" verse is a magician who shapes all those things in life which he prizes. Government officials give little thought to such matters for they consider them a waste of time. Since it is not a planned economy, the Western state cannot come to the aid of people working in the various arts. They go on, each pursuing his own chimera, sometimes dying of hunger; while nearby, wealthy men, not knowing what to do with their money, spend it on the latest whims of their benighted souls. . . .

Fear of the indifference with which the economic system of the West treats its artists and scholars is widespread among Eastern intellectuals. They say it is better to deal with an intelligent devil than with a good-natured idiot. An intelligent devil understands their mutual interests and lets them live by a pen, a chisel, or a brush, caring for his clients and making his demands. A good-hearted idiot does not understand these interests, gives nothing and asks nothing—which in practice amounts to polite cruelty.

Czesław Miłosz, in his The Captive Mind, *Vintage Books, 1953.*

Central Europe, including Poland and Lithuania, might evolve a regional identity. Not long ago you commented that "Central Europe is an act of faith, a project." What did you mean by this?

[Miłosz]: If you look at the real world, the world of borders and partitions and regional conflicts, then there is little reason to speak of "Central Europe." Once Europe was divided into so-called Eastern and Western Europe it became even harder to convince anyone that "Central Europe" was more than a figment of someone's imagination. But I am attracted by what is frankly a utopian project, and I am supported in my faith by what I see as a largely common heritage, a whole range of unifying historical experiences, a common architecture in the major cities, and common religions, and cultural traditions. I can't define the geographical borders of our Central Europe, but clearly architecture might be one way of helping to define them. By that standard, Dubrovnik would surely belong. But so also would the city of Vilno, where I studied, and also Riga and other capitals of Baltic states which represent rather different architectural traditions, not Baroque or Renaissance but Gothic. The architectural standard obviously requires considerable flexibility if it is to be applied.

I'm probably on safer ground when I say that there is a certain feeling we have, when Poles, Czechs, Yugoslavs, Hungarians and Lithuanians gather, that we share some common heritage. And if we are, all of us, drawn to some utopian idea of a Central Europe, well, you know how such ideas require a good deal of faith if they are to be sustained. Very often something which begins as a mere dream of intellectuals comes to pass and, in my opinion, it is better to follow such a dream than to follow the nationalistic dreams favored by most 19th century intellectuals.

The idea of "Central Europe" obviously has much to do with cultural and artistic values. It presupposes a powerful faith in the centrality of living literatures, and you have suggested that the "most striking feature" of Central European literatures is their "awareness of history." What roles do you see as crucial for Central European literatures to play, culturally, politically and psychologically?

Historical awareness is something deeply rooted in those countries and that awareness can work in several ways. It can work to increase the nationalism of each particular nation, or it can work to create a sense of the deep affinities felt by Poles and various Czechs, Croats, and others. It is a fact that countries which suffered very much, as our nations have suffered, usually have a strong historical memory. One sees that in Jewish literature, beginning with the books of the Bible, there is much preoccupation with suffering, much sense of a tragic collective experience, and much sharpening of historical memory and of a faith that can be redemptive.

I always wonder how it happened that in America the feeling of tragedy that must surely have been felt during the Civil War somehow disappeared from memory. Possibly the dramatic changes that occurred after the war, the rapid spread of the industrial revolution, hastened the disappearance of that awareness.

Is there a relationship between your incisive study of political collaboration in **The Captive Mind** *and, say, Klaus Mann's* Mephisto, *or the new Hungarian work by Haraszti* (The Velvet Prison)?

It seems to me that the principles involved in the works you mention are common to many regimes and many situations. In this respect those, like the hero of *Mephisto,* who went to work for the regime in Nazi Germany, and those who went to work for one or another communist system had certain things in common. But the similarities are finally very superficial. There has been an enormous ideological fascination with ideas stemming from the philosophy of Hegel, even a drunkenness which has carried over to ideas associated first with Marx, then with Lenin and even Stalin. People were never bitten with the various fascist systems in the way they were bitten by the Hegelian philosophy of history and all that has followed from it. (pp. 185-87)

Recently the Jaruzelski government in Poland allowed the publication of Res Publica *and other long-suppressed journals. What does such relaxation of censorship really mean for Polish writers, many of whom have had to circulate manuscripts in* samizdat?

Well, you have in Poland a situation of "no win" for the government and "no win" for the opposition. Basically, the publication which receives the official blessing of the government is considered suspect by the public. With *Res Publica,* it was not the initiative of the government but a group of people, mostly young and very energetic, very intelligent, who said, in effect, "let us see what can be done. If they limit the intervention to censorship, occasionally taking out one article or another, we can live with that. If they try to impose upon us official views, then we can quit, stop publishing." So they are putting out *Res Publica,* and it is regarded as an independent and honest publication. Among the other items which are allowed are works published by the Catholic Press. The Catholic Press, of course, is not controlled by the government, though there is negative censorship, in that some articles, occasional sentences are cut by censors. In Poland such publications can still be considered "independent." And of course, in spite of the changes that have occurred, a number of publications continue to appear "unofficially."

Is American media coverage of Eastern Europe anywhere near accurate, or would Americans sometimes be better advised to put their trust in novels or in the films of popular artists like Andrzej Wajda?

Of course I have been observing the coverage of Eastern Europe in the American press, especially *The New York Times,* for many years, and that coverage has certainly improved noticeably. From the years of Solidarity to the present, the American press can boast a very good record in its treatment of Polish matters particularly. On the other hand, I see signs of exaggerated optimism connected with the International Monetary Fund, the vitality of the business community and so on. Here the American press has taken the promises of the government too literally.

In his Varia, *or diary, Witold Gombrowicz writes: "I feel that any artist who respects himself ought to be, and in every sense of the term, an emigre." Do you agree with this?*

If a given country is very sick, as my country has been, then there are special reasons why a writer would wish to emigrate. In such a situation, the writer may find that it is impossible to deal with the anxiety all are bound to feel. But it seems to me that in other situations the artist will have other choices, though in the twentieth century exile seems almost to be the universal condition of the writer. It's not hard to visualize a situation in which the writer might be much more integrated into his community, but this is certainly not the rule in our century.

What is it about the twentieth century that has shifted the conditions of the artist and writer?

If you compare today's writers with, say, the writers in the thirteenth century you see that for the earlier writer there was a common faith uniting him with his people. Literature and art in the twentieth century move in their own realm, and often have more to do with that realm than anything else. That's a realm which is different from the realm experienced by ordinary mortals. Maybe that's very sad, but it is so. At the same time—and here I will contradict or correct myself a little—in a country like Poland, a writer publishing in more or less independent publications may be said to be a voice of the people. And that is true, though often we observe also the writer's resistance to the role imposed upon him by the dissident or underground society.

In **The Separate Notebooks** *you wrote poignantly of the loss "of a homeland, wandering one's whole life among foreign tribes." Obviously historical upheaval and uprootedness are major themes in both your life and your work. But everything considered, do you believe that exile helped or hindered you as a writer and poet?*

My position is always that exile, or emigration, should be regarded as a poison, but if it doesn't kill you it can make you stronger. I have accepted that condition and I try to put the fact and the problem of exile to good use.

Do you find yourself interested in contemporary English language poetry, in poets like Robert Lowell, Seamus Heaney, Geoffrey Hill, Derek Walcott, or Robert Hass?

Yes. I try to follow those writers, some of whom are my friends. However, I feel we come from different sources, speak in different voices. I try to understand their sources as I try to understand my own.

How can readers of a poet like Adam Zagajewski, reading him in English translation, account for the tremendous power his work seems to have? Should we attribute the effect to his translators, to his subject matter, or possibly to some quality in the Polish original that lends itself to English translation?

Well, I am very glad to hear that Zagajewski in English reads so well. Zagajewski's poetry is a poetry in which a great deal is distilled. That distillation is based upon precisely the kinds of historical experiences I have mentioned. I have been observing in recent Polish poetry an attempt quite consciously to use historical experiences. Sometimes in Zagajewski a line which, it appears, has nothing to do with the history of the twentieth century and is full of echoes and references of the past, will reveal an important part of the poet's experience. Probably you have read a poem of Zagajewski's called "Going to Lvov." Lvov is the city where he was born, a city which belonged to Poland and now, of course, belongs to the Soviet Union. Zagajewski sort of reconstructs that city, in his imagination, from nothing—from some scraps of his own family history and so on. Memory here is not a personal memory, however much the elements may seem personal.

Somewhat like what we find in some of your works.

Yes, yes.

You have perhaps seen recent discussions of the lamentable state of higher education in the U.S.—for example the recent books by Allan Bloom and E. D. Hirsch. Do you agree that American universities are promoting a sort of collective amnesia, turning out semiliterate students with little or no feeling for the great works of Western tradition?

I must say that complaints about the deplorable education of the young have been a permanent feature of western societies for centuries. And this we should take into account when we think about recent complaints. But undoubtedly I did see, in many years of teaching at an American university, signs of a basic defect in the teaching of history at the high school level. I could not help noticing that, compared not only with my students, but also with my colleagues, I received a much more thorough training in history during my high school years. History was taught not only in history classes, which anyway gave us nothing interesting, just the bare facts, but in most of the other classes where we studied the Greeks, the Romans, and the culture of medieval Europe. To study Latin meant also to study the history of Latin/Roman institutions, Latin literature, and so on. All that was history. Then we had to study French, which meant again the history of France, of French writers, and so on. And then Polish literature, of course, was very strongly connected with historical events. Above everything, there was required a study of the history of the Roman Catholic church, with all of its heresies, popes, scholastic philosophical debates and so on. In my opinion, the problem of preparing students well should be taken up in high school with colleges as the natural beneficiaries.

In **The Witness of Poetry,** *citing your cousin Oscar Milosz, you spoke of the obligation of the poet, which for him meant giving shape to aspirations of "the great soul of the people." Along the same line, Milan Kundera has remarked that "Poles have always taken literature to be something which must serve the nation." Since winning the Nobel prize, you have no doubt attracted a wider reading audience than ever before. Has this in any way altered your assumptions about your role as a writer—or the writing you have done since that time?*

My own adventures have been quite extraordinary. After all, it's extraordinary to be considered in your own country a non-person, and then after thirty years to return and be given a reception at the royal palace in Warsaw by the Minister of Culture. When my works were suddenly published in editions of one hundred fifty thousand copies and sold out in one or two days, I knew there were factors quite independent of the work, as such. I received the Nobel Prize just as the Solidarity movement emerged in Poland, and though the Swedish Academy could not have known when it chose me that the giving of the Prize would coincide exactly with Solidarity, I inevitably became a symbol, and the right to publish my poetry would then become a symbol of the relaxation of censorship in Poland. But even apart from the special circumstances of my case, I should say that I agree with the sentiment of my cousin, Oscar Milosz. Poets *should* express, and do express, the great soul of the people, and in spite of the many complications poets in our century have confronted. I myself am rather a hermetic poet, but I consider that poetry can express the great soul of the people not only by being accessible. We can say, after all, that Herman Melville expressed in *Moby Dick* the great soul of the people, though *Moby Dick* when it appeared was not understood. So the relationship between a poet and the soul of the people may be quite complex and may take a long time to be worked out. Do you agree?

I certainly do, particularly when exile further complicates things.

Yes.

Have you ever felt that you bear a special responsibility as a "world class writer"?

Yes and no. Of course I receive an infinite number of invitations to take part in various panels, to appear with other Nobel laureates and to make pronouncements of the kind that are especially prized by the leaders of certain countries. But usually people who are competent in one branch of human knowledge, for instance medicine, are willing to make pronouncements on everything, even on affairs with which they are completely unfamiliar, and so I am wary. I am not very eager to play such a role. On the other hand, I know I can make a serious contribution on something in which I am prepared, and so I am sometimes willing.

My position obviously affords me not only duties but opportunities. When I had to write my speech for the Swedish Academy I was terrified. It seemed to me that it was a practically impossible task. But I had to do it, and I felt I had to say something which was on my heart and speak not only of my own personal problems but the problems of other peoples and countries. Thus in that speech I spoke of the fate of the Baltic countries which were incorporated by force into the Soviet Union. And I spoke also of two friends of mine, poets, who shared the fate of some fifteen thousand Polish officers interned after the pact between Hitler and Stalin and murdered by the order of Stalin.

That was a very powerful address, indeed.

So you see that there are some situations where you feel that you are responsible, that you cannot shirk your responsibility. But, at the same time, you try to preserve your privacy and to rely upon your right not to make pronouncements and speeches.

Much of your poetry exhibits a strong feeling for the natural world; have you ever considered yourself in relation to the tradition of Slavic nature writing?

When I was a school boy I wanted to be a naturalist, and my attitude towards nature is very important for my writing. But this attitude is very different from what you find in the American writer. In the American writer there is a kind of a religion of nature, based upon the writer's sense of the beauty and innocence of nature, and a conviction about the positive wisdom of nature. My attitude towards nature has more to do with anger because I fear that nature is extremely cruel, or at least indifferent. These qualities are constantly on my mind, so that for me, if there is innocence in nature, it is the result of an indifference to our values.

That is something you and Camus would have agreed on.

Yes. (pp. 187-93)

It's a truism that poetry can't be translated, and yet you have done some very successful translations of your own work, written originally in Polish. Can you speak a little about this?

Some poetry translates relatively well; some poetry is untranslatable. When I read, for instance, Russian poets, I see there is not very much of the original left in the translation, and this in spite of the fact that the Russians don't use any more rhyme and meter than the Polish poets. In broad terms you have here an interesting question of nonparallel development of different languages. The nature of the language dictates the nature of the poetry. Many years ago, I remember that I had a conversation with the Nobel prize-winning French poet St. Jean Perse (or Alexis Legèr), who said: "French poetry has been so strongly formed by Classicism, by the meter of the Alexandrine, that my generation tried to liberate French poetry from that corset of meter. And that revolution in French poetry of the twentieth century, Modernism, is largely an attempt to do just that." "But," he said, "poets from other countries imitated French poetry without realizing that it was our own internal game." And as a matter of fact, he's right, because if you take French poetry of the 16th century, such as Ronsard, then take a poem by Baudelaire, and put them together and then make a test, asking from what epoch is each, sometimes it is impossible to tell the difference . . .

Every language dictates its tonality. There are languages of strong accents; the Russian language is one of strong and moving accentuation, tending toward iambic meter. And Polish and Czech are languages of weak and stable accents, similar in this respect to Italian, curiously enough, though they are Slavic languages. So I've never translated poetry from Russian, though I know Russian well, because I consider it bad for my ear. For us, Russian poetry is like Edgar Allen Poe—"The Bells," "The Raven"—and, thus very different from Polish versification.

There were several systems of versification, beginning with purely polysyllabic verse modeled on Latin poems of the Middle Ages. Poetry in Latin of the Middle Ages lost the accentuation of the original Latin, and was purely syllabic. And that was the first model for Polish syllabic verse. Then there was the next system of versification, the syllabo-tonic, mixing feet and number of syllables. And still later came other forms. Most Polish poetry today is without meter and without rhyme, based on breathing units. So something may be parallel to what happened in American poetry under the influence of Williams.

Can you comment on the simplicity of your language and yet its ability to convey complex ideas?

That has been my true ambition throughout. My early poetry was very dense and difficult. Of late, my friends offered me for my birthday this year a very strange book—namely a facsimile of my first volume of poems, with an essay dedicated to every poem. That's very dense poetry, and, I should say, poetry as dictated by my subconscious. It was mostly metrical, rhymed. But a certain evolution took place over time, not only my personal evolution but that of Polish poetry. And I should say that crucial to that change of style were the years when Poland was under the Nazi occupation. Then you saw something like a snake changing its skin—it was a painful process, under the impact of painful experiences. Only around 1943, after several years of living in that horror, did I start to discover a new poetry, very condensed and concise, abandoning rhyme, though at the same time I wrote a cycle of poems entitled **"The World,"** written in primers' rhymes, like poems for children. At that time, I was not really familiar with William Blake, and I didn't realize that Blake had attempted something similar; namely, he wrote "Songs of Innocence" and "Songs of Experience." "Songs of Innocence" is a representation of the world as it should be, as opposed to the "Songs of Experience." So my poem **"The World,"** composed of 22 short poems, is an attempt to describe the world as it should be, seen by children, as opposed to the world of horror I knew. It's just what I should call bucolic poetry. The question of translating such poetry is very complex, because you have to imitate the original naiveté of the original. My translators, Bob Hass and Robert Pinsky, try to do their best, but now, for the edition of my collected poems, I decided that those translations are too far from the naiveté of the original, and so I have to sit down to translate them myself. (pp. 193-95)

Czesław Miłosz and Paul W. Rea, in an interview in Salmagundi, *Vol. 80, Fall, 1988, pp. 185-95.*

Judith A. Dompkowski (essay date Winter 1988)

[*In the following essay, Dompkowski interprets* The Issa Valley *as a highly symbolic and autobiographical account of Miłosz's artistic development.*]

Czesław Miłosz's ***Dolina Issy*** (1955; ***The Issa Valley,*** 1981) cannot easily be classified by genre. It is at once, as critic Lillian Vallee sees it, "a seemingly autobiographical novel" and also poetry, a book which could have "established Miłosz's position as a poet had [he] written no poetry at all" [Lillian Vallee, *WLT;* Summer 1978]. Miłosz himself is ambivalent about the nature of the work. During an interview in March 1982, a year after the first English translation of ***Issa*** appeared, Miłosz spoke of the book's autobiographical qualities. However, a few months later he claimed that it was instead "many things."

The book poses a series of questions which enable us to see it as at least one of these "many things": namely, an intellectual chronicle in which Miłosz presents himself to us through Thomas Surkont; a nascent artist. For example, why did Miłosz choose to focus on Thomas's interior life up to his fourteenth year, an emphasis which does not lend itself to an active plot? Why would the book have a highly episodic structure unless Miłosz wanted to highlight it as a chronicle, albeit one presented by a third-person narrator? Why is the narrator himself problematic, creating a strong sense that he and Thomas—and possibly he, Thomas, and Miłosz—are one? Is it simply coincidence that the book is a microcosm of the development of Miłosz's career in Poland, ending with an event which parallels Miłosz's departure from that country: Thomas's leaving the valley at the end of the book for unknown lands? Is the fact that Miłosz wrote the book in France in 1955, during the early years of his exile, of any relevance?

Howard Clark Kee has examined how a geographic and historical shift, the kind involved in exile, can affect a writer's choice of mode: "The changes that occur in literature are geared to artistic creativity and to basic shifts in 'the way men think and react to life, both as a group and as individuals. When the outlook changes in respect to historical experiences, the writer and the genre change as well.' " The "changes" which Miłosz employs are not simply the shift from one form to another, but the weaving of three: the novel, poetry, and the intellectual chronicle. However, the supreme question remains why he attempted a feat of such scope. Has he a need to explore, for himself and the reader as well, whether the isolation demanded of an artist is heroic, antiheroic, or a paradoxical combination of the two?

Miłosz promotes Thomas's growth as an artist through the opposition of tensions between the male and female elements in the book. These occur between the male and female characters and symbolically between the creative energies latent in each. The feminine can be defined as Thomas's desire "to be," to enter the natural world he admires, thus expanding himself through the imagination; the masculine is the actual physical drive to accomplish this end. These tensions are not as neatly polarized as they might seem, however. They exist within the realm of the feminine and the masculine individually, and between Thomas's consciousness and subconsciousness as well. The union of these energies is essential, because woman is, as Lawrence Hyde comments on this process of the creation of an artist, "more attuned to [the] realm of being than is the extroverted male." Hyde continues: "The key to liberation and creativeness lies in a true reconciliation between the extroverted and the introverted modes of consciousness."

Thomas confronts the feminine in his mother and in the surrogate figures he adopts during her long absences: the Issa Valley itself, Grandmothers Misia and Dilbin, and Magdalena—all representative of fertile, creative energies, and all unconventional female types. The masculine model, in the absence of his natural father, is the virile Romuald. Thomas cannot fulfill his creative, feminine role until he proves himself unfit for the one chosen for him by convention: to be a hunter like Romuald. Though Thomas consciously states that he wants to emulate a hero, he subconsciously needs to prove himself a failure in order to enter the world of his choice: one of detachment and contemplation.

Thomas's mother Tekla comes to their village of Gine only "for several months out of the year, and then only rarely; most of the time she had to accompany her husband on his travels, at first in search of work, later because of the war. For Thomas she was almost too beautiful to be real, and he gulped with love at the sight of her. His father was practically a stranger to him, and he was constantly surrounded by women." The passage strongly invites a Freudian reading, but it also shows the extent to which women and feminine qualities will influence the shaping of Thomas's sensibilities.

Still, Thomas's love for his mother is not without ambivalence. In his child's eyes his mother's long absences are abandonments. When Tekla does return, one part of Thomas questions the other, "But I do love her, don't I?" This comment is important not only because it foreshadows his ambivalence about other things as he grows up, but more so because it prefigures his desire for otherness or duality, his wish to be within and without objects in order to heighten his artistic perceptions.

One of the first surrogates to whom Thomas turns in his loneliness is the Issa Valley itself, a world of nature which Thomas loves, but also one he must later war against. The text describes the valley in language suggesting its archetypal femininity and the seclusion it offers from the world. It is lush creation which will beget further creativity: "The Issa is a deep, black river . . . which winds through meadows and between gentle slopes noted for their fecundity. The Valley is blessed with an abundance of black earth—a rarity for us—with the lushness of its orchards, and possibly with its remoteness from the world, something that has never seemed to bother its inhabitants."

The valley is itself dualistic, however. The Polish word for valley, *dolina,* suggests both creation and destruction, for it means "the concave, the feminine principle of birth and renewal, the glory of paradise and the law of annihilation" [according to Vallee]. In these respects the valley is associated with its namesake, Isis, the Egyptian goddess of motherhood and fertility; yet Isis too, who loved the good and is the agent of creation, "allowed [disorderly] Typhon to exist . . . because it was not possible for a complete world to exist if the fiery element left it" [Howard Clark Kee, *Miracle in the Early Christian World: A Study in Socio-Historical Method.*]

The allusion to Isis in the valley's name implies more than fertility, however. Her worship in Egyptian, Greek, and Roman religions is interestingly associated with literature, writing, and heightened rhetorical skills. In one tale from the myths of these religions, when Osiris stepped down as ruler, he wanted Isis to have the benefit of Hermes' presence, since Hermes, as Kee tells us, "should be given credit for inventing the alphabet and language . . . and for developing the principles of interpretation." She is also the goddess whom one ancient writer, Lucius Apuleius, sought for "a New Being," a search much akin to Thomas's. Thus it seems that Thomas is born into a perfect setting, but he still must conquer a symbolic Typhon and prove himself before he can gain what the valley has to offer him.

Thomas first encounters what may be called creative fury in Magdalena, who embodies isolation and attempted freedom, destruction and creation. Thomas feels that he and Magdalena are kindred spirits: they are both outsiders, but for different reasons. Thomas has no companions, although the reasons for his friendlessness are his own conscious and subconscious choices. Magdalena has had a series of blatant rejections. She is jilted by her fiancé and scorned by the villagers, who see her, at twenty-five, as an unlikely marriage prospect. Magdalena chooses a path which ironically puts her above the women who scorn her, yet one which makes them scorn her all the more: she has an affair with the village priest. However, he abandons her too, bringing her to complete the process of her alienation by committing a violent suicide.

Despite the seeming cowardice of her act, her ridding herself of the world, Magdalena acquires an ironically inverted heroic stature. She who is a full-blown version of all that her name implies (she is even buried in a scarlet dress) is interred on 15 August, the Catholic feast of the Virgin's Assumption into heaven. In addition, she becomes immortalized in local tales as a mirror image of a pagan virgin priestess who also chose a violent death rather than surrender to the Teutonic Knights. As the priestess stalks the ruins near the scene of her death, so does Magdalena's ghost supposedly haunt the places in Gine where she was happy, thus adding to the supernatural flavor of her tale.

The rebellion of these women, whether read as self-assertive and thus heroic or as self-destructive and thus cowardly, captures Thomas's imagination. Magdalena especially is no longer a creature of terror, a ghost. Rather, after Thomas's lengthy dream about her, she is his "friend," who connects him with "the other side of existence." Thomas is aware of the immortality she has gained through the stories people tell of her, but he is more drawn to what she presents in the nightmare as a visual representation of the otherness of which he has subconsciously aware: Magdalena was in a corrupting state, yet "at the same time she was close to him, looking exactly as she had that day he had seen her wade into the water." Thomas becomes part of a similar dualistic process. He lay "under the surface of reality," and "even as he was taking part in the annihilation, he perceived that the person below was the same as the one above."

The dream scene confirms several artistic tendencies latent in Thomas at this time: his awareness that in death is recovery, and in destruction, renewal; the demand of a creative ego for more than mortal men observe; and the paradoxical and seemingly heroic notion that man must liberate himself from the world in order both to understand and to preserve it in writing. After the dream experience, Thomas retains a "delicious headiness, the remembrance of lands whose existence he had never dreamed possible," as the memory of his encounter with the outcast spirit lingers in both his consciousness and subconsciousness.

The dream of Magdalena confirms suspicions Thomas has about himself and enhances later experiences with his two grandmothers, Misia and Dilbin. Misia Surkont's "streak of self-willed independence" feeds Thomas's growing admiration of her rebelliousness, which he views as heroic. Her refusal to follow convention gives her a freedom which Thomas envies but never seems able to acquire for himself. Her gestures, to a lesser extent than Magdalena's, were always "carried out in defiance of accepted customs," yet her "tantrums were only on the surface; inwardly, protected by her aloofness, she must have enjoyed herself richly. Thomas was of the suspicion she was made of some durable substance, that inside her ticked some self-winding machine, completely oblivious to the world outside. And what pretexts she could invent to curl up inside herself." Thomas recognizes this as Misia's great egoism, ironically the egoism of an artist, which helped her to survive, to be, as Magdalena persisted in being even after death. Thomas realizes eventually that he is like her, as "he, too, loved to savor his own smell, to curl up and exult in his being *him.*" Ironically, Thomas could do this more effectively by extending himself into other things.

The narrator describes Thomas's attempts to be like Misia, to break the world of convention and enter the world of the imagination beginning at a very young age. In a charming passage he tells us that "Thomas loved to immerse his gaze in [the peonies], straining his whole body to enter their rose-colored palace, as the sun filtered through their petal walls and little bugs wallowed in the yellow pollen—once, when he sniffed too hard, a bug ran up his nose." The tone of the passages in which these desired changes occur grows increasingly darker as Thomas grows older, as he realizes his need to be more, and to be more apart from the world as he knows it. First he wishes to be like the altar boys, who "once a week . . . could be other than what they were." Later, after his experience with Dominic, a friend he subconsciously chooses because he is a reflection of Thomas's own dark nature, Thomas wants to retreat not so much from Dominic as from himself, to a kingdom of plants, one "far removed from reality," for "plants were not mean or vicious, did not wound or exclude"—a chosen but necessary act of escape.

Thomas blames his grandmother Dilbin's "timidity" and scrupulosity for his own weakness, which he was sure undermined his internal voice and peace of mind. However, it is not a genetic imbalance but rather Thomas's choice of weakness that causes him both to hesitate and to move. Ironically, this quest for movement and for change in perspective becomes an element of Miłosz's own needs as an artist, the notion of moving "rhythmically from a smaller to a greater context and the reverse, and [marking] what is revealed in the changes in proportion" [according to Vallee]. It is Thomas's experience with Romuald the hunter, though, which will propel the young man with greatest urgency to the place he wishes to be.

Thus Thomas seeks, gingerly at first, the inwardness of an artist and has an awareness of the need to retreat into a solitariness which he sees as both heroic and unheroic. Romuald is, then, the male principle to be employed to this end, but with some ironic inversion. He represents a power chosen in order to be resisted, and in the resistance a new form of power is created.

Thomas relishes the thought of having an invisible body which can float in and out of things, even things in nature, yet his life on the Issa demands more realistic activities: namely, that he hunt. His involvement with Romuald simultaneously involves him in the world of nature and the hunt and takes him away from it in a way that would be understandable if not acceptable to those around him. As a coward, he could ensure his isolation. Early in his hunting lessons Thomas "experienced a letdown he was not eager to acknowledge. But one had to be manly, to stifle any squeamishness, if one was to earn the title of hunter and naturalist." He moves away from the notion of the hunt with the rationalization that, rather than destroy these living creatures, he wants a "communion" with them. He does not admit that Misia's egoism is at work and that he really wants more: a power over the birds, for example. Rather than shoot a duck, admittedly a "manly" act, Thomas does not raise his gun, and the duck never knows that its life "had been spared by a man."

This kind of valor, if you will, could not continue. Romuald teaches the hunt as a grand ritual into which Thomas must be swept with full regalia, and in so choosing, Thomas severs his relationship with the world of nature as he always knew it. In killing a squirrel, he appears heroic to Romuald's world but unheroic to himself. Still, his unheroic act was necessary for him to move to a higher plane, one he wanted to achieve all along. He is now initiated into the solitariness of the artist, into the solitary activity of shaping books, much like the bird book he made when was younger, for "to name a bird, to cage it in letters, was tantamount to owning it forever"—a process akin to his creation of a "paper kingdom," a domain of maps over which he ruled, a childlike, godlike figure.

Hence, Thomas's failure as a hunter thrust him into "lonely, solitary contemplation." Holy Communion heightened the feeling of separation, for he found when he fasted, he experienced both punishment and the joy of the imagination: "The weaker the body, the more he got outside it, elevating himself—condensed, specklike—to a point just above his head." Made imaginatively smaller, Thomas could enter the towns of a maple tree, but "only figuratively, of course. For there were no towns inside, only in the imagination, though a maple was a colossus that, no less than the one looking on, contained the possibility of endless permutation." There remain no towns for Thomas, however, no place, that is, where he could feel restful and certain. Doubting Thomas that he is, he tries to hunt a second time, only to leave his Berdan against a tree and walk away, having traded gun for pen.

Nevertheless, the otherness for which Thomas—or Miłosz—wished serves ironically as a trap; for what is ecstasy is also punishment, what seems cowardly is also heroic. Perhaps the book, couched in the seeming innocence of childhood, is Miłosz's way of reexamining the paradoxes within which he has become enmeshed, his way of trying to understand a role he was shaped for. Perhaps in the process he will fulfill the words of another artist, T. S. Eliot, whose meditations from the "Four Quarters" may offer the understanding of a kindred soul: "We shall not cease from our exploration / And the end of all our exploring / Will be to arrive where we started / To know the place for the first time." (pp. 34-7)

Judith A. Dompkowski, "Czesław Miłosz' 'Issa Valley': Child as Nascent Artist—Hero or Antihero?" in World Literature Today, *Vol. 62, No. 1, Winter, 1988, pp. 34-7.*

A. Alvarez (review date 2 June 1988)

[*An English-born American educator, critic, poet, and novelist, Alvarez is the author of* Under Pressure: The Writer in Society, Eastern Europe, and the U.S.A. *(1965). In the following review, to which Miłosz voiced his objection in the July 21, 1988 issue of* New York Review of Books *(see excerpt following), he examines* The Collected Poems, 1931-1987 *and designates Miłosz a "witness" to the historical events of the century.*]

Four years ago Milan Kundera published in these columns an essay called "The Tragedy of Central Europe" [26 April 1984]. The tragedy in question was not so much war and occupation, the massacres, destruction, and humiliation at the hands of ignorant invaders; it was, instead, the loss of what Central Europe once embodied: European culture. Central Europe, for Kundera, was not just a collection of small and vulnerable nations with difficult languages and tragic histories; it was the intellectual and artistic center for the whole of Western civilization and the last stronghold of the intelligentsia, a place where essays counted for more than journalism, and books had more influence than television.

Long before Kundera wrote his article Czeslaw Milosz had described a typical day in the life of Central European man. On August 1, 1944, the day the Warsaw uprising unexpectedly began, Milosz and his wife were caught in heavy gunfire while on their way to a friend's apartment to discuss—what else?—poetry in translation. Face down for hours in a potato field, with machine-gun bullets zipping over his head, Milosz refused to let go of the book he was carrying. After all, it was not his to throw away—it belonged to the library of Warsaw University—and anyway, he needed it—assuming the bullets didn't get him. The book was *The Collected Poems of T. S. Eliot* in the Faber & Faber edition. All in all, it was a very Polish situation: bullets and modernism, the polyglot in the potato field, ashes and diamonds.

Milosz has all the other characteristics of Central European man. He was born in Lithuania, a country that has vanished utterly into the Soviet maw, the bulk of its people transported by Stalin to somewhere beyond the Urals. Like his great Lithuanian predecessor Adam Mickiewicz, Milosz writes in Polish and is fluent in several languages. He has also suffered a typically Central European fate—exile. Half his long life has been spent teaching in Berkeley. In other words, he is a man whose only true home is in books, in language; he carries his country around in his head.

The one language Milosz might be expected to speak is German. He claims, however, to understand only two phrases, *Hände hoch!* and *Alle männer vrraus!,* mementos of the five years he spent in Warsaw during the Nazi occupation. His fellow Polish poets, Zbigniew Herbert and Tadeusz Rozewicz, also got their education during the war; whence the starkness of their poetry—Rozewicz's minimalism, Herbert's austere, ironic morality. But they were both teenagers when the Germans marched in and the terrible years of Hans Frank's Government-General were their high school. Milosz, however, was born in 1911 and had published two books of poetry before 1939, so his style was formed in less savage times and what was lost—"a world gone up in smoke" he called it in a poem written in 1941—concerned him as much as what was being done.

What the war taught him as a poet had to do, above all, with priorities:

> I could reduce all that happened to me then to a few things. Lying in the field near a highway bombarded by airplanes, I riveted my eyes on a stone and two blades of grass in front of me. Listening to the whistle of a bomb, I suddenly understood the value of matter: that stone and those two blades of grass formed a whole kingdom, an infinity of forms, shades, textures, lights. They were the universe. I had always refused to accept the division into macro- and micro-cosmos; I preferred to contemplate a piece of bark or a bird's wing rather than sunsets or sunrises. But now I saw into the depths of matter with exceptional intensity.

That is from Milosz's brilliant and understated autobiography, ***Native Realm.*** The experience of total war taught him the supreme value not of art but of life itself, of being, of brute survival in a wholly destructive element.

In ***The Captive Mind,*** his somber denunciation of the sovietization of Eastern Europe, he described a similar experience, transposed into the third person, and drew the necessary aesthetic conclusions:

> The work of human thought *should* withstand the test of brutal, naked reality. If it cannot, it is worthless. . . . A man is lying under machine-gun fire on a street in an embattled city. He looks at the pavement and sees a very amusing sight: the cobblestones are standing upright like the quills of a porcupine. The bullets hitting against their edges displace and tilt them. Such moments in the consciousness of a man *judge* all poets and philosophers. Let us suppose, too, that a certain poet was the hero of literary cafés, and wherever he went was regarded with curiosity and awe. Yet his poems, recalled in such a moment, suddenly seem diseased and highbrow. The vision of the cobblestones is unquestionably real, and poetry based on an equally *naked* experience could survive triumphantly that judgment day of man's illusions. In the intellectuals who lived through the atrocities of war in Eastern Europe there took place what one might call the *elimination of emotional luxuries.* Psychoanalytic novels incite them to laughter. They consider the literature of erotic complications, still popular in the West, as trash. Imitation abstract painting bores them. They are hungry—but they want bread, not hors d'oeuvres.

Before the war Milosz's sense of impending doom had earned him the title of "catastrophist." In the face of a catastrophe greater than he could ever have imagined his own early prose appeared to him paltry and self-indulgent. So did his youthful literary ambitions. He peddled a pamphlet of his verse—printed by an underground press and sewn together by his wife-to-be—in the same spirit and for the same motive as he peddled black-market cigarettes and blood sausage: because he was penniless. Poetry had become, in every sense, a means of survival, a matter of life and death.

The poems he wrote during the war and published in 1945 as ***Rescue*** are a kind of atonement for his earlier frivolity and a reparation made to those who did not survive. The two prose passages I have quoted are glosses, in their different ways, on **"Dedication,"** the famous poem that ended the 1945 volume:

> You whom I could not save
> Listen to me.
> Try to understand this simple speech as I would
> be ashamed of another.
> I swear, there is in me no wizardry of words.
> I speak to you with silence like a cloud or a tree.
>
> What strengthened me, for you was lethal.
> You mixed up farewell to an epoch with the beginning of a new one,
> Inspiration of hatred with lyrical beauty,
> Blind force with accomplished shape.
>
> Here is the valley of shallow Polish rivers. And
> an immense bridge
> Going into white fog. Here is a broken city,
> And the wind throws the scream of gulls on your
> grave
> When I am talking with you.
>
> What is poetry which does not save
> Nations or people?
> A connivance with official lies,
> A song of drunkards whose throats will be cut
> in a moment,
> Readings for sophomore girls.
> That I wanted good poetry without knowing it,
> That I discovered, late, its salutary aim,
> In this and only this I find salvation.
>
> They used to pour millet on graves or poppy
> seeds
> To feed the dead who would come disguised as
> birds.
> I put this book here for you, who once lived
> So that you should visit us no more.

The war released Milosz into an adult world where rhetoric, dogma, and ambition seemed so much childishness. This adult world, however, did not exclude childhood. At the heart of ***Rescue,*** among poems about ruined Warsaw and the destruction of the ghetto, about grief, deprivation, and random death, is a beautiful sequence called, ironically perhaps, **"The World."** The poems are short, calm, so simple as to seem almost translucent, and their subject is the lost world of Milosz's childhood in the deep Lithuanian countryside (the same world that he later wrote about—less convincingly, I think—in his autobiographical novel, ***The Issa Valley***). In their restrained and tender way, they bring "news / From a world that is bright, beautiful, warm, and free," and they make Milosz's subsequent exile seem inevitable. They confirmed him as a poet whose continuing theme, however stern and "naked" the reality he dealt with, was always that of loss.

In Central Europe the war did not end when what Richard Eberhart called "the fury of aerial bombardment" was over. The Stalinist repression that followed merely translated the problem of survival into different terms: moral instead of physical, personal truth in the face of state-imposed hypocrisy. The kind of poetry imagined by Milosz and those like him—poetry that occupies the moral high ground yet is proof against ridicule and impervious to pretension—became more urgently necessary and correspondingly less easy to publish. "A new, humorless generation is now arising, / It takes in deadly earnest all we received with laughter," Milosz wrote in 1946, when he was a Polish diplomat in New York. Five years later, having decided that historical inevitability and the good of the cause were no longer excuses he was willing to tolerate, he went into exile, first in France, where ***The Captive Mind*** was vilified by Sartre's captive left, then in California. It was not an easy decision. "I was afraid to become an exile," he wrote, "afraid to condemn myself to the sterility and the vacuum that are proper to every emigration." For the poet, whose work partly depends on nuances and allusions that only his countrymen can pick up, the vacuum of exile is inevitably more absolute than for the prose writer:

Novels and essays serve but will not last.
One clear stanza can take more weight
Than a whole wagon of elaborate prose.

But not in translation. Although Milosz supervises the English versions of his work and has been well served by his collaborators, his poems have a richness and sinuous flow that make you believe that a good deal has been lost in translation.

The vacuum of exile exists in many forms, the two foremost being the loss of audience and the loss of subject matter. Eventually, Milosz's poems did filter back into Poland, but not officially until long after he had defected, so for years his effective audience was reduced to bickering and malicious café clubs of fellow exiles. But for a poet whose subject matter was loss, who already considered himself to be in exile, like Adam, from some lost Eden of Lithuanian childhood, physical exile merely strengthened him in his themes and preoccupations. As a result, "the sterility of exile" has never been Milosz's problem. ***The Collected Poems*** runs to more than five hundred pages and his serious, wondering, adult tone of voice never lapses into affection or self-consciousness.

Perhaps this is because Milosz has always been a poet of place, a marvelous describer of everything from details—"the tiny propellers of a hummingbird"—to atmosphere. It is ironic that he should have written so vividly *in Polish* about California:

With their chins high, girls come back from the
  tennis courts.
The spray rainbows over the sloping lawns.
With short jerks a robin runs up, stands motion-
  less.
The eucalyptus tree trunks glow in the light.
The oaks perfect the shadow of May leaves.
Only this is worthy of praise. Only this: the day.

His long years in the perennial Californian spring, however, have not softened his vision of the world or of his business in it. "Ill at ease in the tyranny, ill at ease in the republic," he says of himself, and from that unease is born his steady concentration on the essentials of the poet's task when everything superfluous has been removed: "gradually, what could not be taken away / is taken. People, countrysides. / And the heart does not die when one thinks it should." All that is left is language. "You were my native land; I lacked any other," he writes in a poem on **"My Faithful Mother Tongue."** And the poem ends, "what is needed in misfortune is a little order and beauty." This need for the beauty and order of poetry as an alternative to the disorder of homelessness has been Milosz's constant theme. At the end of ***Unattainable Earth,*** published in 1986 and his last book before the ***Collected Poems,*** there is a poignant poem on the **"Poet at Seventy."** It is followed by a kind of prose footnote that encapsulates his whole life's effort:

To find my home in one sentence, concise, as if hammered in metal. Not to enchant anybody. Not to earn a lasting name in posterity. An unnamed need for order, for rhythm, for form, which three words are opposed to chaos and nothingness.

Milosz's pursuit of order and beauty has been curiously disinterested. Someone once said that 90 percent of the *Oxford Book of English Verse* is about God or death or women. Not so in Milosz's poetry. He is a Catholic and the Church figures in his verse, but less for God's sake than because its rituals recall his early upbringing. As for women: in his whole ***Collected Poems*** I found only a single love poem—an exceptionally beautiful one called **"After Paradise."** That leaves death, and the truth is that the people who appear in his poems are mostly ghosts from the past. Milosz is a poet of memory, a witness; his real heroes are the dead to whom his poems make reparation. Perhaps exile makes it hard to forget the past and part of its burden for the poet is the need to bring the imagination to bear on people and places that no longer exist. But, as he explains in a marvelous late poem called **"Preparation,"** living emotions keep getting in the way:

Still one more year of preparation.
Tomorrow at the latest I'll start working on a
  great book
In which my century will appear as it really was.
The sun will rise over the righteous and the
  wicked.
Springs and autumns will unerringly return,
In a wet thicket a thrush will build his nest lined
  with clay
And foxes will learn their foxy natures.

And that will be the subject, with addenda.
  Thus: armies
Running across frozen plains, shouting a curse
In a many-voiced chorus; the cannon of a tank
Growing immense at the corner of a street; the
  ride at dusk
Into a camp with watchtowers and barbed wire.

No, it won't happen tomorrow. In five or ten
  years.
I still think too much about the mothers
And ask what is man born of woman.
He curls himself up and protects his head
While he is kicked by heavy boots; on fire and
  running,
He burns with bright flame; a bulldozer sweeps
  him into a clay pit.
Her child. Embracing a teddy bear. Conceived
  in ecstasy.

I haven't learned yet to speak as I should, calmly.

Like other major witnesses of this century—Primo Levi, Zbigniew Herbert—Milosz is a moralist: his work does not pronounce or make judgments; it simply takes as its criterion human decency—disinterested, modest, and not willingly misled:

poems should be written rarely and reluctantly,
under unbearable duress and only with the hope
that good spirits, not evil ones, choose us for
  their instrument.

(pp. 21-2)

A. Alvarez, "Witness," in The New York Review of Books, *Vol. 35, No. 9, June 2, 1988, pp. 21-2.*

Miłosz comments on his reputation as a historical poet in a reply to Alvarez:

Granted, some horrible events of mass genocide and of deportations took place in my part of Europe and not in England or America. This adds an aura of nightmare to the vagueness that has always characterized the presence of Central and Eastern European countries in the Western imagination. Yet those events occurred many decades ago and facts, through direct testimonies, statistical data, innumerable books are available to whoever wishes to acquaint himself with the history of our century. I brought, unfortunately, my share to the body of knowledge on the subject, by writing, in prose, *The Captive Mind* and *Native Realm*. I say unfortunately, because the effectiveness of such books in dispelling mythologies is doubtful; moreover, they distort the image of their author in the minds of readers and of literary critics, by presenting him as more obsessed with historical events than he is. My struggle as a writer in exile has consisted in liberating my neck from those dead albatrosses; in fact for a long time my name was connected with my books in prose available in translation, while the poetry that I have been publishing since 1931, only slowly made its way to the reading public abroad thanks to its English versions. I am grateful to America and proud of being now one of its poets, reaching young audiences who treat me primarily as a poet. You can imagine my surprise, therefore, when I saw Mr. Alvarez copiously quoting from my old prose books [in his June 2, 1988 review in *The New York Review of Books*] instead of dealing with my poetic *oeuvre* sufficiently exemplified by *Collected Poems*.

Czesław Miłosz, in his letter to the editor, New York Review of Books, *21 July 1988.*

Hank Lazer (essay date Summer 1988)

[*In the essay below, Lazer discusses the dialectical and historical aspects of Miłosz's poetry and his relevance to contemporary American poetry.*]

Tiger, the professor of philosophy who figures prominently in Miłosz's life and in the latter stages of ***Native Realm,*** was right in his assessment. Miłosz is a dialectician, a dialectical thinker if we understand by that term a process of thought capable of self-opposition and a method of thinking that seeks higher orders of thought through self-opposition. In Miłosz's poem **"Tidings,"** which begins by asking a gigantic question, "Of earthly civilization, what shall we say?", this thinking through self-opposition is carefully developed. Miłosz begins with an aesthetic version of civilization's glory: "That it was a system of colored spheres cast in smoked glass, / Where a luminescent liquid thread kept winding and unwinding." But a few lines later he offers an opposing vision: behind "an array of sunburst palaces" there "walked a monstrosity without a face." Miłosz must tell us the deadly, ritualistic side of history that he has witnessed: "That every day lots were cast, and that whoever drew low / Was marched there as sacrifice: old men, children, young boys and young girls."

In **"Tidings,"** as in much of his recent poetry, it is the vision of a delicate earthly beauty that most fully receives his attention:

> Or we may say otherwise: that we lived in a golden fleece,
> In a rainbow net, in a cloud cocoon
> Suspended from the branch of a galactic tree.
> And our net was woven from the stuff of signs,
> Hieroglyphs for the eye and ear, amorous rings.
> A sound reverberated inward, sculpturing our time,
> The flicker, flutter, twitter of our language.
>
> For from what could we weave the boundary
> Between within and without, light and abyss,
> If not from ourselves, our own warm breath,
> And lipstick and gauze and muslin,
> From the heartbeat whose silence makes the world die?

Having proposed such a vision, Miłosz undoes it with his ending: "Or perhaps we'll say nothing of earthly civilization. / For nobody really knows what it was." Except for the fact that the last line places earthly civilization in the past tense, it would seem that in **"Tidings"** the process of opposed thought does not yield to a higher order. These two stanzas, however, do more than offer a contented vision of earth and its civilization. The passage is about speech as much as it is about vision. The aesthetic beauty seen in earthly civilization, the "array of sunburst palaces" and the "golden fleece," is shown to be an artifice of language. Any version of civilization that the poet will present to us comes from "our net." Woven from signs, hieroglyphs, vision, and sound, that net is language. Heidegger suggests that this net defines us, "For man is man only because he is granted the promise of language, because he is needful to language, that he may speak it," and he determines that language *is* our location: "We are, then, within language and with language before all else." In Miłosz's poem our existence within language is acknowledged, and the net of language becomes our means for offering versions of earthly civilization. Since his other versions occupy far fewer lines, we may also infer that language itself *is* the essential measure of our civilization. Most importantly, Miłosz locates language's source in our own breath and heartbeat, and language's silence with our own mortality.

Throughout his work, Miłosz refuses to settle into a unified system of thought. His poems and his thinking are constructed from balanced antipodes that allow for existence. The poems are as basic as the atom itself, held together by virtue of intense negative and positive charges that are attracted to each other. In **"Tidings,"** for example, Miłosz gives us opposed versions of history: a golden fleece as well as a monstrous sacrifice, mythic achievement and deadly ritual. The poem itself consists of an answer to its opening question as well as a conclusion which undercuts that answer. Man is seen as a borderline figure, the boundary line between within and without, light and abyss, heartbeat and silence. It is the passion and power of that heartbeat that endure in his poetry.

A careful consideration of Miłosz's dialectical thought can demonstrate the potential importance of his work to contemporary American poetry. Currently we stand in danger of losing the ability to think in and through poetry. Miłosz's **"On Pasternak Soberly"** presents a pertinent analysis:

> . . . for us a lyrical stream, a poetic idiom liberated from the chaos of discourse was not enough, the poet should also be a *thinking* creature; yet in our efforts to build a poem as an "act of mind" we encountered an obstacle: speculative thought is vile and cunning, it eats up the internal resources of a poet from inside. In any case, if modern poetry had been moving away from traditional meter and rhyme, it was not because of fads and fashions but in the hope of elaborating a new style which would restore an equilibrium between emotional and intellectual elements.

American poetry stands at the crossroads Miłosz has written about. Our poetry, in its rebellion against Eliot and modernist tradition, or more accurately, against the leaden academic verse written in the forties and fifties in homage to Eliot and the English metaphysical poets, has done what it can to explore the deep image and thus fashion an American brand of surrealism. American poets have learned to detest that "intellectual" poetry which, Miłosz rightly observes, "eats up the internal resources of a poet from the inside." Our syntax has been simplified and clarified. We have consciously made our poetry more accessible, more tangible, but along the way we may have forgotten how to think.

Miłosz's poetry and prose could be critical to the development of American poetry because he writes with the clarity we admire, yet he is able to think. If our poetry is to do more than register wonder or record with imaginative freshness the impressions of daily events, it must give serious consideration to Czesław Miłosz and what his work represents. In discussing Pasternak's strengths and failings, he achieves a formulation crucial to our current poetry. Miłosz argues that "if we assume that those periods where poetry is amputated, forbidden thought, reduced to imagery and musicality, are not the most healthy, then Pasternak's was a Pyrrhic victory. When a poet can preserve his freedom only if he is deemed a harmless fool, a *yurodivy* holy because bereft of reason, his society is sick." Whatever the nature of our society's sickness, it is poetry's clinging to a lyricism "forbidden thought, reduced to imagery and musicality" which is so pernicious and enervating. This dangerous divorce from thought in our poetry, shyness in the face of hard thinking, requires immediate attention.

Too often, our poetry reflects a unified, self-assured, even smug consciousness, a moment of wonder, discovery, ecstasy, or despair. There is little intellectual tension in our work. Basic assumptions—nature is symbolic of the realm of spirit, didacticism is bad, abstraction is bad, show instead of tell—go unchallenged. Poets talk about taking risks and then get more personal and reveal "private" experiences. Or our poems risk moments of incoherence and nonrepresentational language. Instead, we should consider taking poetry seriously, with head and heart. That is what Miłosz has done. He is to be praised, as Jan Blonski does in "Poetry and Knowledge," for "the overt identification of poetry with knowledge, the erasing of boundaries between the lyric, the essay and the treatise."

Miłosz provides a special lesson in his understanding of what it means to be a poet. Though in a different way, his example is every bit as important as Rilke's and Neruda's. For Miłosz, the war was the single major catastrophe that produced his new judgments of poetry. As he writes about the Eastern European intellectual,

> He has been deceived so often that he does not want cheap consolation which will eventually prove all the more depressing. The War left him suspicious and highly skilled in unmasking sham and pretense. He has rejected a great many books that he liked before the War, as well as a great many trends in painting or music, because they have not stood the test of experience. The work of human thought *should* withstand the test of brutal, naked reality. If it cannot, it is worthless. Probably only those things are worth while which can preserve their validity in the eyes of a man threatened with instant death.

American poets need not seek out a similar catastrophe for the sake of art. Still, it would be wise to keep in mind Miłosz's caution "how like a smooth slope any form of art is, and of the amount of effort the artist must expend in order to keep from sliding back to where the footing is easier."

For Miłosz, self-opposed thinking, rigorous self-questioning, and resistance to any unified scheme of thought assure the difficult footing necessary for great art. In ***The Captive Mind,*** one such example of heroic, self-opposed thought is Professor Pavlov:

> Professor Pavlov, who originated the theory of conditioned reflexes, was a deeply religious man. Moscow caused him no trouble over this because he was an eminent scientist and because he was old. The creator of the theory of conditioned reflexes—the very theory that constitutes one of the strongest arguments against the existence of some sort of constant called "human nature"! The defenders of religion maintain that this "human nature" cannot change completely; that gods and churches have existed over thousands of years and in all kinds of civilization, and that one can expect this to be true of the future as well. What went on in Professor Pavlov's head if two systems of concepts, one scientific and one religious, existed simultaneously there?

What went on in Pavlov is like what goes on in Miłosz, for Miłosz's mind is that of a doubter who nevertheless believes. When Emerson tells us "a foolish consistency is the hobgoblin of little minds" and when Whitman exclaims, "Do I contradict myself? / Very well then I contradict myself," we pat ourselves on the back, assuming that we can leave consistent, rigorous thought to retentive academics and critics. We are missing the point. Contradiction, as Miłosz expresses it through the life of Pavlov and the example of his own writing, implies two well-developed directions of thought and feeling. True contradiction, especially as it entails dialectical thought and self-contradiction, is painful. To live with contradiction is *not* to escape the responsibilities of thought and reason in favor of feeling and intuition. If our poetry is to have intellectual weight and drama, and it must, we do not need programs, manifestoes, or creeds. We *do* need to start thinking uncomfortable thoughts again; we should engage in a radical questioning of our own writing.

Miłosz's prose, particularly in ***The Captive Mind,*** illustrates well the process of an artist's interrogation of his own motives:

> My poetry has always been a means of checking on myself. Through it I could ascertain the limit beyond which falseness of style testifies to the falseness of the artist's position; and I have tried not to cross this line. The war years taught me that a man should not take a pen in his hands merely to communicate to others his own despair and defeat. This is too cheap a commodity; it takes too little effort to produce it for a man to pride himself on having done so. . . . Whoever has not dwelt in the midst of horror and dread cannot know how strongly a witness and participant protests against himself, against his own neglect and egoism.

His concept of stylistic development requires more than a search for the merely new; it involves recurrent self-suspicion. When he offers a characterization of poetry, it is apparent that his perpetual questioning does not lead to cynicism:

> Poetry is a constant self-negation; it imitates Heraclitean fluidity. And only poetry is optimistic in the twentieth century, through its sensual avidity, its premonitions of change, its prophecies with many meanings. Even if we leave no immortal works behind us, the discipline itself is worthy of praise.

Miłosz presents a late 20th-century negative capability, one whose modernity lies in its unsentimental disillusionment with history and in the sophistication of its psychological insights. His image of the poet as always keeping a sharp eye out on his own self-deceptions, as well as on those of civilization, contrasts sharply with the self-congratulatory introspection and provinciality of many contemporary American poets.

Miłosz commands admiration for his inclusiveness, heroism, and admission of limitations. He thinks with a rigor that disavows any absolute. "All of us yearn naïvely," he explains, "for a certain point on the earth where the highest wisdom accessible to humanity at a given moment dwells, and it is hard to admit that such a point does not exist, that we have to rely upon ourselves." But such an admission does not lead him to the kind of narcissistic, trivial poeticizing that we too often write when we give up that "outmoded" quest for knowledge. In one of the most concise statements of his goals as a poet, Miłosz says: "I endeavored to speak a language deliberately stripped of post-Romantic ornament, and to disentangle my own enigma and ultimately that of my generation." During the past two decades, American poets have attempted the first half of Miłosz's task. But this has been mainly, if not exclusively, a stylistic modification. The rest requires that we begin to think.

In Miłosz's poetry, several specific lessons stand out. The ending of **"Encounter,"** particularly the last line, teaches how important it is to avoid the easy footing of self-indulgence:

> We were riding through frozen fields in a wagon
> at dawn.
> A red wing rose in the darkness.
>
> And suddenly a hare ran across the road.
> One of us pointed to it with his hand.
>
> That was not long ago. Today neither of them
> is alive,
> Not the hare, nor the man who made the gesture.
>
> O my love, where are they, where are they going
> The flash of hand, streak of movement, rustle of
> pebble.
> I ask not out of sorrow, but in wonder.

Temporally and emotionally, the poem provides a perfect example of a dialectical movement. Flat, compressed observation in the past tense gives way to a consideration of mortality in the present. The fact of mortality destroys the flat tone of the poem and for two lines, "O my love, where are they, where are they going / The flash of hand, streak of movement, rustle of pebble," the poet's voice becomes emphatically elegiac. The last line of the poem gathers in the flatness of the opening and the pain of the two immediately preceding lines and provides the poem with a new emotional order. The modification of emotion in the last line takes negativity up into a speculation fueled, but not held down, by sorrow. Without this shift, which is arrived at by the poem's tightly controlled dialectical movement, the poem would be an easy exercise in bitterness over the effects of time.

Of equal importance, there is a mutability of personal identity in Miłosz's poetry that could be instructive. "A Short Recess," the fourth canto of **"From the Rising of the Sun,"** begins:

> Life was impossible, but it was endured.
> Whose life? Mine, but what does that mean?
>
> During recess, biting into a sandwich wrapped
> in paper
> I stand under the wall in chubby meditation.
>
> And I would have been someone I have never
> been.
> And I would have obtained what I have never
> obtained.
> Jackdaws beyond the window would have been
> remembered
> By another I, not the one in whose words I am
> thinking now.

The "I" in Miłosz's poetry is at once personal and universal. His "I" is similar to Eliot's in its intended universality, but the relativism of Miłosz's "I" does not, as in the early Eliot, stem from the poet's sense of his own personal defects and a desire to shield or protect the "real" self. Miłosz's speaker is a particular witness to human history. His relationship to history is personal: "unless we can relate it [history] to ourselves personally, history will always be more or less of an abstraction, and its content the clash of impersonal forces and ideas." But, in his typically self-opposed fashion, as in **"A Short Recess,"** Miłosz acknowledges the unimportance of the specific, actual "I." The purpose of his universalized "I" is to allow an encounter with history to take place in the poem.

Miłosz's encounter with history is slightly different from that of the modernist poets. Unlike Pound and Eliot, who, at least in part, sought a coherent version of history, a way of making man at home in history redeemed by vision, Miłosz's encounter is primarily a questioning one. As **"Tidings"** demonstrates, there is no single version of history; instead, there is a succession of versions, each beginning with the word "or." The poem also makes clear that history and its telling is inextricably bound to the mystery of language. A similar relativism can be seen in **"From the Rising of the Sun,"** which, significantly, begins with the instruments and act of writing:

> Whatever I hold in my hand, a stylus, reed, quill
> or a ballpoint,
> Wherever I may be, on the tiles of an atrium, in
> a cloister cell, in a hall before the portrait of
> a king,
> I attend to matters I have been charged with in
> the provinces,
> And I begin, though nobody can explain why
> and wherefore.

To study history is to study language as well: "It rolls along, it flies by, our speech." The modernist hope for a coherent version of history gets voiced by the Chorus: "When will that shore appear from which at last we see / How all this came to pass and for what reason?"

For Miłosz, there is no such shore. The modernist quest to consolidate history, to claim what is essential, sacred, and eternal, is treated by him with considerable suspicion. In discussing the *Cantos* and Pound's famous definition of an epic as a poem including history, Hugh Kenner writes, "a poem *including* history will contain not only elements and recurrences but a perceiving and uniting mind that can hope one day for a transfiguring vision of order it only glimpses now." Miłosz's encounter with history does not resolve itself into a quest for order and the sacred word. As the ending of **"From the Rising of the Sun"** suggests, such an order, a vision of the eternal forms, may be possible only at the end of time. Within time, as the Rogue River episode in the second canto of **"From the Rising of the Sun"** demonstrates, the original name is not retrievable:

> The name was given to the river by French trap-
> pers
> When one of them stumbled into an Indian am-
> bush.
> From that time on they called it La Rivière des
> Coquins,
> The River of Scoundrels, or Rogue, in transla-
> tion.
> I sat by its loud and foamy current
> Tossing in pebbles and thinking that the name
> Of that flower in the Indian language will never
> be known,
> No more than the native name of their river.
> A word should be contained in every single thing
> But it is not. So what then of my vocation?

The poet must reconsider the goal of his vocation because he discovers that the original names, which would recreate the poetic ideal of a precise correspondence between name and thing, are lost. The substitute name and subsequent translations no longer bear an exact relationship to the thing named.

For Miłosz, the core of history, what Kenner calls "a transfiguring vision of order," is not finally discoverable. The poet does not master history: "And if they say that all I heard was the rushing of a Heraclitean river / That will be enough, for the mere listening to it wore me down." The teacher's speech in **"Over Cities"** best states the nature of Miłosz's encounter with history:

> "Yes, it is undeniable that extraordinary fates befell our species, precisely those from which Maximus the Confessor wanted to protect us, suspecting as he did the devilish temptation in the truth of reason. Yet while we hear everyone advising us to understand clearly causes and effects, let us beware of those perfectly logical though somewhat too eager arguments. Certainly, it is distressing not to know where this force that carries us away comes from or where it leads. But let us observe restraint and limit ourselves to statements which in our intention will be statements and nothing else. Let us formulate it thus: yes, the Universal is devouring the Particular, our figures are heavy with Chinese and Assyrian rings, civilizations are as short-lived as weeks of our lives, places which not long ago were celebrated as homelands under oak trees are now no more than states on a map, and each day we ourselves lose letter after letter from our names which still distinguish us from each other."

History's presence in the poem prevents the complete erasure of identity; memory helps to sustain the particular, even if the act of memory is statement rather than explanation. Miłosz involves history in his poems because he feels we *are* carried and led by it, though we cannot discover how and why. So he attempts statements, and he cites protective warnings. Even in his limited statements, Miłosz's poems show "Life was impossible, but it was endured." The encounter with history must also be included in poetry because the study of history and the study of language, though ultimately incomplete studies, are inseparable.

In contemporary American poetry, the backlash against Eliot's theory of impersonality has been so severe that, until quite recently, only the most limited and idiosyncratic historical meditations have been possible. Miłosz correctly identifies a peculiarly American failing as "a loss of the sense of history and, therefore, of a sense of the tragic which is only born of historical experience." It is this historical dimension that may be the most valuable lesson for us in Miłosz's writing. His sense of history extends beyond, or encompasses more than, personal or national events. History for him entails both memory and the substance of speech itself. As he explained in his Nobel Lecture, "Memory thus is our force; it protects us against a speech entwining upon itself like the ivy when it does not find a support on a tree or a wall." It would belabor the obvious for me to comment on "speech entwining upon itself" in relation to our own recent poetry.

In "From Experience to Discourse: American Poetry and Poetics in the Seventies," Charles Altieri posits a dichotomy between a romantic poetry of experience and a model of the poem as intelligent, subtle discourse. Altieri sees two divergent notions of poetry emerging: one branch is the poetry of perception, the image, emotional intensity, and vision; the other branch is the poetry of discourse, tone, statement, and cognition. Miłosz's poetry, though leaning toward the latter concept, successfully bridges this polarity. Poems such as **"Tidings"** and **"From the Rising of the Sun"** contain and assimilate the distinctions that Altieri raises, for Miłosz engages in both vision, subject to skepticism and self-opposition, and discourse, where tone and judgment come into play. Both functions—vision and discourse—are essential to his poems and his poetics.

To a great degree, Miłosz's importance as a poet rests upon the dialectical method that is at the heart of his work. Opposition and self-questioning in **"To Robinson Jeffers"** lead to an understanding of the poet's role. The poem begins with the author "complaining" about the naïveté of Slavic poetry; its vision and imagination would be of no use to Robinson Jeffers:

> If you have not read the Slavic poets
> so much the better. There's nothing there
> for a Scotch-Irish wanderer to seek. They lived
> in a childhood
> prolonged from age to age. For them, the sun
> was a farmer's ruddy face, the moon peeped
> through a cloud
> and the Milky Way gladdened them like a birch-
> lined road.

Such poetry of the image, with its sun like a farmer's ruddy face and its moon peeping through a cloud, is a vapid lyricism that would not appeal to the cold, serious Jeffers. This image-based poetry, much like the worst of contemporary American neosurrealism, is seen as excessive, romantic, and naïve, especially from the imagined viewpoint of a thinker like Jeffers, or from Miłosz's own perspective.

In the poem, he uses Jeffers as a means for defining his own position. The fundamental question that the poet asks Jeffers is "What have I to do with you?" As might be expected, the answer can be found in opposition. Miłosz contradicts Jeffers' view, affirming his own "naïve" Slavic inheritance. He rebukes Jeffers: "And yet you did not know what I know. The earth teaches / More than does the nakedness of elements." His conclusion is emphatic:

> Better to carve suns and moons on the joints of
> crosses
> as was done in my district. To birches and firs
> give feminine names. To implore protection
> against the mute and treacherous might
> than to proclaim, as you did, an inhuman thing.

It is the poet's dialectical method which yields such a conclusion, and thus his affirmation of Slavic folk tradition is quite different from an unquestioned or naïve faith in nature.

Self-contradiction and self-opposition are the cornerstones of Miłosz's work. His fidelity is to the diversity of being, not to a single encompassing thought, and thus Miłosz is a radically different 20th-century poet from Rilke or Trakl. With these latter two poets in mind, Heidegger offers the following test:

> Every great poet creates his poetry out of one single poetic statement only. The measure of his greatness is the extent to which he becomes so committed to that singleness that he is able to keep his poetic Saying wholly within it.

Rather than a single poetic statement, Miłosz's poetry is committed to dialectical thought. His differences, especially from Rilke, stem from Miłosz's denials. He refuses to wear the Rilkean cape of holiness. Nor will he allow himself to indulge in the poet-as-priest posture. Every bit as profound and universal as Rilke, he eschews Rilke's espousal of the poet's fragility and passivity. Though Miłosz devotes himself to the poet's lifelong work, Rilke's motto of *toujours travailler,* he will not allow himself the persona of mystic nor the grandeur of the Orphic poet.

Yet a poet cannot create an important body of work exclusively out of the act of denial. What then are the tasks Miłosz sets for himself? In **"Temptation,"** he obliquely suggests his task: "for if not I, then someone else / Would be walking here, trying to understand his age." That attempt "to understand his age" is one of a great poet's tasks, one our own recent poetry would like to dodge. Part of the poet's vocation, as he describes it in **"Diary of a Naturalist,"** involves an obligation that he both acknowledges and dreads: "But I will be called to the blackboard, and who can guess when, in what years." The poet is one who is called to write down what he knows. For Miłosz, the exercise at the blackboard is complicated by the many varieties of knowing that his poetry includes. When the poet is called to the blackboard, as he is in every poem that he writes, he must try to express what he knows at that moment. What Miłosz hopes to write down is the craving of all artists: "Artists crave being, a communion with the divine promise inside creation." In **"The Year,"** he comes close to formulating such a communion. He won't tell what it is, only what it could be:

> At the very border of inhabited time the same
> lessons were being learned, how to walk on
> two legs and to pronounce the signs traced in
> the always childish book of our species.
> I would have related, had I known how, every-
> thing which a single memory can gather for
> the praise of men.
> O sun, o stars, I was saying, holy, holy, holy, is
> our being beneath heaven and the day and our
> endless communion.

Naturally, for Miłosz, such a statement of faith involves denial: of personal importance, personal superiority, and final achievement. As he states at the end of **"With Trumpets and Zithers"**:

> I was getting rid of my faith so as not to be better
> than men and women who are certain only of
> their unknowing.
> And on the roads of my terrestrial homeland
> turning round with the music of the spheres

I thought that all I could do would be done better one day.

His statements of faith, the affirmation of our holy being, are only achieved, as he tells us in **"Dedication,"** by a fortunate ignorance:

That I wanted good poetry without knowing it,
That I discovered, late, its salutary aim,
In this and only this I find salvation.

In **"To Robinson Jeffers,"** his conclusion about the poet's role is unequivocal: it is better "To implore protection / against the mute and treacherous might / than to proclaim, as you did, an inhuman thing." Such certainty comes from the act of opposition and application of dialectical thinking. Elsewhere, without a worthy opponent, or faced with the seemingly more nebulous task of self-opposition, Miłosz uses his own humility and his awareness of limitations in a way that may at first dissuade us of his importance. But within the framework of his insistent relativity, no other posture than the failure to arrive at ultimate conclusions is possible. For him, there is no "Datta. Dayadhvam. Damyata. Shantih shantih shantih."

Miłosz's task is one of opposition and attention. As stated in **"Tidings,"** he attends to "A sound reverberated inward, sculpturing our time." To understand his particular action of attention, the differences between Rilke and Miłosz are again instructive. Though both attend to that inward sculpturing and, in Miłosz's words, "the divine promise inside creation," Rilke's poetry, especially in *Sonnets to Orpheus,* ultimately establishes a myth of change, transformation, and thus of hope. The inward sculpturing that Miłosz listens to has more the ring of fact and is less consciously devoted to a beyond. Rather than suggest, as Rilke does, what we *will* be, Miłosz's consideration of a divine promise, as seen in **"On Angels,"** returns us to our *current* condition.

In **"On Angels,"** his thinking is tersely dialectical. He is at once able to rein in romantic excess, the figure of the angel, and reempower that romantic conception by grounding it in earthly, human experience:

All was taken from you: white dresses,
wings, even existence.
Yet I believe you,
messengers.

The way such noble beings are reinvested with their powers is through an epistemological consideration:

They say somebody has invented you
but to me this does not sound convincing
for humans invented themselves as well.

The angels are not seen as "untrue," but as necessary inventions, as necessary as our invention of ourselves and other supreme fictions. Such inventions properly lie at the center of the inward sculpturing that the poet (and the angels) attend to:

There, where the world is turned inside out,
a heavy fabric embroidered with stars and
beasts,
you stroll, inspecting the trustworthy seams.

Especially as it is expressed in dialectical thought, self-questioning, and an encounter with history, the rigor of that attention is the primary lesson that Miłosz's writing holds for contemporary American poets. (pp. 449-65)

Hank Lazer, "Poetry and Thought: The Example of Czesław Miłosz," in The Virginia Quarterly Review, *Vol. 64, No. 3, Summer, 1988, pp. 449-65.*

Stanislaw Baranczak (review date Summer 1989)

[*In the following review of* The Collected Poems, 1931-1987, *Baranczak considers Miłosz's evolution as a poet and maintains that metaphysical themes are his central concern.*]

As I write this review, a minor but highly unusual controversy involving its subject is raging on the pages of *The New York Review of Books.* At first glance, what is happening seems to be pretty common: in a letter to the editor, an author is taking exception to the opinions of a reviewer of his book. Neither this nor the fact that the author and the reviewer are Czeslaw Milosz and the well-known British critic A. Alvarez would by itself raise any eyebrows. What makes the situation exceptional and a little strange is that the author is by no means protesting against any harsh treatment from the reviewer. On the contrary, Alvarez's long and detailed review of Milosz's ***The Collected Poems 1931-1987*** [see excerpt dated 2 June 1988] was nothing but warmly appreciative and even enthusiastic. Milosz does not complain of not having been praised enough; rather—and there's the rub—he complains of having been praised for the wrong reasons. In his opinion Alvarez's review, entitled "Witness," helps trap his work within the worn-out and outdated concept of East European poetry as primarily a moralistic reaction to the pressures suffered at the hands of History and Society. A longer quote is necessary here:

History. Society. If a literary critic is fascinated with them, that's his choice; if, however, he is insensitive to another dimension, he risks to curtail his right to reflect on literature. Perhaps some Western writers are longing for subjects provided by spasms of historical violent change, but I can assure Mr. Alvarez that we, i.e., natives of hazy Eastern regions, perceive History as a curse and prefer to restore to literature its autonomy, dignity, and independence from social pressures. . . . [T]he voice of a poet should be purer and more distinct than the noise (or confused music) of History. You may guess my uneasiness when I saw the long evolution of my poetic craft encapsuled by Mr. Alvarez in the word 'witness,' which for him is perhaps a praise, but for me is not.

Milosz has been known for the contrariness with which he often demolishes critical stereotypes about himself and his work, but the fierceness of his resistance to the "witness" formula may puzzle us a little. Has he himself not written a book called ***The Witness of Poetry***? And yet, whoever has closely followed the latest, truly breathtaking stages of Milosz's soaring career realizes that he has a point here.

The key word in his polemic is "evolution." His poetry has indeed come a long way from the 1930s, the wartime, and the years of Stalinism, and today it cannot possibly be defined solely in political or moralistic terms borrowed from his ***Native Realm*** or ***The Captive Mind.*** To quote Milosz's letter once more:

> Poetry should not freeze, magnetized by the sight of evil perpetrated in our lifetime. My objection to Mr. Alvarez's method of literary criticism is that he seems to be impervious to the dynamics at the very core of any art: after all, a poet repeatedly says farewell to his old selves and makes himself ready for renewals.

At a closer look, Milosz's seemingly curious protest against being praised for the wrong reasons is, then, perfectly understandable as the self-defense of an artist pushed into a compartment which he has already outgrown. It becomes more and more justifiable as we leaf through the book in question. A few years ago, Alvarez or any other Western critic could still claim the validity of the "witness" label by pointing out that this was exactly what Milosz himself propounded in his essayistic books made available in English, from older works such as ***Native Realm*** up to the 1981-82 Charles Eliot Norton lectures, and what also transpired in the majority of his translated poems. After the publication of ***The Land of Ulro*** in 1984 and ***Unattainable Earth*** in 1986, however, such claims no longer hold water. These two books have finally revealed to the English-speaking audience what the Polish reader had grown accustomed to since at least the mid-1970s: they revealed Milosz's true identity as first and foremost—let us use this imprecise term for the sake of brevity—a metaphysical poet. And a careful reading of the five hundred pages of ***The Collected Poems*** backs this presumption with a great deal of supportive evidence.

For ***The Collected Poems,*** formally the fifth book of verse Milosz has published in English, is actually the first book that can finally give the English-speaking reader a fairly accurate idea of what his poetry really is, both in the sense of the largeness of its thematic and stylistic range and the uniqueness of his more than half-century-long creative evolution. This has been achieved in three ways at once. First, a significant number of important poems from earlier periods, previously unknown in English, have now been translated (mostly by Milosz himself in collaboration with Robert Hass) specially for the purpose of incorporation in the present edition: this group includes several poems that to the Polish reader seem indispensable for any attempt at grasping the essence of Milosz's work, such as the prewar **"The Gates of the Arsenal"** and **"Dawns,"** the immediately postwar **"Song on Porcelain"** and **"A Nation,"** the 1957 **"Treatise on Poetry"** (here represented, to be sure, only by three brief fragments), the 1962 **"I Sleep a Lot,"** the 1968 **"Higher Arguments in Favor of Discipline . . . ,"** etc.

Second, the very latest, astonishingly profound and brilliant phase of Milosz's career, known to the Polish reader through his recent volume ***Kroniki,*** has also been well covered here by ending the book with a fair number of hitherto untranslated new poems, including such crucially important larger sequences as the cycle **"La Belle Epoque"** and the **"Six Lectures in Verse"** (these two belonging, in this reviewer's opinion, to the highest achievements of Milosz's art).

Third, odd as it may sound, this is actually the first book of Milosz's poems in English that presents his output in a strict chronological order and indicates the original books that the poems came from. As we remember, with the exception of ***Unattainable Earth,*** which was a translation of Milosz's single Polish volume published in 1984, his previously published ***Selected Poems, Bells in Winter,*** and ***The Separate Notebooks*** made a deliberate point of mixing old and new poems, thus blurring the outlines of the poet's evolution. This has often resulted in the English-speaking critics' confusion, as openly admitted by, for example, Donald Davie's in his recent book *Czeslaw Milosz and the Insufficiency of Lyric.*

To realize to what extent ***The Collected Poems*** may be successful in elucidating, complementing, and otherwise straightening out the image of the poet's work, it is enough to look at the numbers. The book contains more than 180 separate poems ranging from two-liners to extremely large and complex wholes, such as the sixty-page-long poem **"From the Rising of the Sun"** (here published, by the way, for the first time in its entirety). Out of these 180, as many as 49 appear for the first time in this edition, 29 of them being the recently translated older poems (written before ***Unattainable Earth***) and 20 the new poems (written in 1985-87). Not all of Milosz's previous collections of poems in English have been completely superseded by the present edition: ***Unattainable Earth,*** for instance, is still worth reading as a separate book, since its peculiar structure of a modern *silva rerum* consists in including a number of prose fragments, notes, letters, verses of other poets, etc., which are omitted in ***The Collected Poems.*** By and large, however, the book under review is as close as a selective translation could possibly be to achieving the ideal goal of making Milosz's poetic oeuvre available to the English-speaking reader in all its variety, inner complexity, and historically evolving shape.

In order to understand why this goal was not achieved earlier, one has to take into account that the Western recognition of Milosz as a poet had been slowed down, ironically, by his early international success as a novelist and essayist. In contrast to his homeland, he was known in the West for many years as the author of ***The Captive Mind*** rather than any poem, which was due both to political and technical considerations, i.e., the immediate thematic appeal of his prose and the relative difficulty in adequately translating his poetry into any foreign language. Moreover, in the first two decades of his émigré phase he was little concerned with translating his own poetry: instead, he used to spend a great deal of time and energy on introducing other Polish poets to the English-speaking audience. (As he himself likes to remember, before the Nobel prize he was known in American literary circles as a translator of Zbigniew Herbert rather than a poet in his own right.) The first American translators with whom he began to work on his poems seriously were his Berkeley students: for some of those, like Richard Lourie, Louis Iribarne, and Lillian Vallee, this was the beginning of their careers as highly successful translators of Polish literature. Lillian Vallee went on to collaborate with Milosz on the translation of his ***Bells in Winter*** (his previous collection, ***Selected Poems,*** had been a mixed bag of translations done by various hands).

Since 1980 Milosz's work on translation of his own poetry has greatly intensified, thanks both to the increased demand and the efficiency of his new collaborators. A new translating team which has taken shape in the 1980s consists of Milosz himself and two first-rate American poets, Robert Hass and Robert Pinsky; at various times Hass and Pinsky, who do not know Polish, also worked in a "trio" with Renata Gorczynski, or Milosz relied on collaboration with another Berkeley poet, Leonard Nathan. The results of this collective work have more often than not been splendid. Hass and Pinsky, in particular, never hesitate to tackle the most demanding exigencies of rhyme and meter (although, interestingly, Milosz thought it better to include in ***The Collected Poems*** not their rhymed version of the long poem **"The World,"** published earlier in ***The Separate Notebooks,*** but rather a "less ambitious but literal" version done by himself). The English versions of the **"Song on Porcelain"** (Milosz-Pinsky), **"Treatise on Poetry"** (Milosz-Hass), **"Lauda"** (Milosz-Nathan-Hass), **"Rivers"** (Gorczynski-Hass), or **"Six Lectures in Verse"** (Milosz-Nathan), to cite but a few of the most impressive examples, give a whole new meaning to the words "poetic translation," particularly in this country, where translating a poem so often means turning its living flesh into processed meat of some bland prose divided into lines.

Alongside the inclusion of numerous previously unknown poems, the generally high level of translation contributes significantly to the fact that ***The Collected Poems*** finally gives the English-speaking audience the chance to grasp both Milosz's complexity and consistent evolution. To repeat, he emerges from this volume as a primarily metaphysical poet or, to be more exact, a poet whose existential and metaphysical concerns have always been dominant in his works, even when accompanied by moralistic obligations or temporarily overshadowed by a sense of necessity to focus on the ominous course of modern history. From **"Dawns,"** written when he was twenty-one, to the most recent **"Six Lectures in Verse,"** his paramount theme is the universal essence of the human conditions its complex entanglement in various unresolvable conflicts at once—in paradoxes of history and society, yes, but also in paradoxes of time and space, nature and divinity, good and evil, experience and communication, existence and cognition.

Scrutinized in its evolution, Milosz's poetry certainly appears to have gone through many more or less radical changes. In particular, his earliest period, represented by his 1933 debut, ***A Poem on Frozen Time,*** and the years between the end of the war and his emigration (the poetic harvest of which was collected in ***Daylight*** in 1953) strike the observer as two phases during which his poetry frequently deviated from its central obsessions, steering towards direct social and political concerns, and sometimes reaching the point of being overtly didactic. Regardless of these thematic variations, however, the philosophical outlook of his poetry taken as a whole turns out to be a highly consistent system. It is a system based, as it were, on three fundamental premises—a metaphysical, an ethical, and an aesthetic one. The first premise may be construed as follows: In spite of the fallibility of our cognition, external reality does exist objectively, and its very being is a constant reason for our admiration of the world. The second premise: In spite of all relativistic theories and nihilistic ideologies, the borderline between good and evil also does exist objectively, and the existence of evil is a constant reason for our abomination with the world. And the third premise: The task of poetry is precisely to bring into relief this irresolvable paradox and to find the means of expression that would be able to cover the infinite distance between admiration and abomination, between metaphysical rapture and ethical repulsion.

The publication of **"Treatise on Poetry"** more than thirty years ago ushered in Milosz's most accomplished phase, which has stretched up to now. During this phase, all the specific strains of his continuous evolution notwithstanding, his work has been characterized by the ultimate fusion of its metaphysical, ethical, and aesthetic concerns. On the one hand, his poetry continues to be a euphoric hymn to the beauty of objectively existing things, of everything that *is* (cf. **"Esse," "An Hour," and** many other poems). Many of such poems can be defined as epiphanies—sudden illuminations which reveal a sacred truth of Being hidden behind the external appearance of an object, landscape, or human face. In poems like those, the ecstatic tone is not merely a matter of the speaker's emotional state of rapture; rather, it is motivated by his actual discovery of the "holiness of being" which makes the poem a confession of religious faith. As an aesthetic consequence, this utter respect for the "holiness of being" has a tremendous impact on Milosz's concept of poetic language, which strives for extreme concreteness in naming things and reflects, by means of dramatic polyphony, the bewildering richness of various "voices" with which the world speaks.

On the other hand, this ecstatic admiration of the world comes into conflict with Milosz's sober awareness that reality—not only the reality of History but also the reality of nature—is tainted by the irremovable presence of evil. The Manichean roots of such a vision have been pointed out by many critics and by Milosz himself: evil is for him the ineffaceable shadow of all that exists, including, perhaps above all, the poet's own ego (see, among other examples, the poems **"Temptation"** and **"Account"**). If "Earth" seems "unattainable" to him, it is not merely in the sense that the essence of its being cannot be grasped by our imperfect senses and intellect or reproduced by our imperfect language. Earth is also unattainable in that the coexistence of a good God and the indelible fact of unwarranted suffering is something beyond our comprehension. Whatever can be said about the human predicament on this Earth must end up with the conclusion that an individual existence is not rationally justified; rather, it is doomed to senselessness.

Yet Milosz at the same time never loses sight of the fact that, just as God has agreed to take on a human shape in order to share suffering with the Creation, human beings are able at least to "tame" their "affliction" and thus to imbue their apparently senseless existence with some kind of divine sense. And again, numerous aesthetic consequences spring from his conviction that one means of "taming affliction" is through poetry, through "searching for the Real" and trying to give the Real its true name—which is, in fact, the only defense of Being against Nothingness and Good against Evil accessible to the poet.

In the final analysis, the appearance of ***The Collected Poems*** does not, of course, invalidate the popular interpretation of Milosz's poetry as "witness" to his epoch and to the political, social, and moral dilemmas brought by the course of modern history. This function has been performed by his work more than once, and it has been performed magnificently, as many specific examples from **"Campo dei Fiori"** up to **"The Titanic"** would easily prove. Yet it is essential for the critic and the reader to be constantly aware that concerns of this sort do not exist in Milosz's poetry in isolation. On the one hand, they form just an extension of a much more general, all-encompassing, superbly rich and consistent system of thoughts and ideas; on the other, they cannot be assessed properly without taking into account other—aesthetic—extensions of this system, revealed in Milosz's constant quest for "a more spacious form," a more flexible and versatile diction, style, poetics, and genre. By gathering at last under one cover a wide, representative, chronologically ordered, and excellently translated selection from all the phases of the poet's career, ***The Collected Poems*** has the potential to bring Milosz's poetry—and perhaps, as a further consequence, Polish poetry in general as well—much more attention than heretofore. If we consider that the past few months have seen the publication of perhaps the three single most important works of modern Polish literature ever translated into English—Witold Gombrowicz's *Diary,* Aleksander Wat's *My Century,* and Milosz's collection—we have every reason to hope that for American and Polish literatures 1988 marks, as Humphrey Bogart says in the final words of *Casablanca,* "the beginning of a beautiful friendship." (pp. 23-4)

Stanislaw Baranczak, "Between Repulsion and Rapture," in The Threepenny Review, *Vol. 38, Summer, 1989, pp. 23-4.*

Baron Wormser (review date 1989)

[*Wormser is an American poet and critic. In the following review, he discusses major themes and characteristics of Miłosz's poetry as represented in* The Collected Poems, 1931-1987.]

That a man who was born in Lithuania, lived through World War II in Poland, sojourned in France, and wound up in Berkeley, California, should be one of the crucial Western poets of the second half of the twentieth century is one of those strange allegories of which life and art are both fond. That such a life has been a hell and a source of joy for the poet is, of course, not beside the point. Czeslaw Milosz's poetry is imbued with passion in the Christian sense of suffering and in the secular sense of intensity. That bewitching, incarnational way in which art speaks for eras, in which distilled poems leave behind the glosses of film reels and transcripts and archives and pierce the targets of indifference, forgetfulness, and evasion is magnificently evident in the pages that comprise the collected translations of Milosz's poetry into English. ***The Collected Poems*** contains the magic of imagination. No idea or theory or generalization can subdue such a book.

It must be stressed at the outset that ***The Collected Poems 1931-1987*** is a partial accounting of Milosz's poetry. A good deal of very important work is simply not here. In the case, for example, of the long poem from the 1950s, **"Treatise on Poetry,"** only the preface and excerpts from two sections are to be found. It would thus be rash to attempt to sketch any diagrams of the poet's career based upon what is gathered in this book. Given Milosz's habit of laying poems down and then picking them up again years later, and given his proclaimed contradictoriness, such diagrams are foolhardy anyway. The poems constitute a various dialogue between the world and the soul. The path the author's life took was hardly one of his own choosing. Although his career has traversed decades and continents, Milosz in many ways never wanted to go anywhere. The prosperities of post-WWII intellectualism have not been sirens to one who "had to learn to live like a pariah, in self-exile from the 'respectable society' of Western intellectuals, because I dared to offend their most hallowed assumptions, which I took to be a compilation of historical, geographical, and political ignorance." [Prose quotations in this review are from ***The Land of Ulro, The Witness of Poetry,*** or *Conversations With Czeslaw Milosz.*]

Best then to proceed intuitively with such a book, recalling those avenues that seem most prominent and remembering that one is dealing with translations rather than the real thing. This is not to disparage translation—we are all greatly indebted to the efforts of Milosz's translators over the years—but to note that a translation bears the same relationship to the original text as rumor does to truth. That is to say, one feels an impetus, a gist, a persuasiveness, but one lacks the texture that is identical with any sort of firm verity. All the fine shivers and gaits and burrs and curves and pliancies of a poet's language are lost. The purport, however, of the poems has not been lost. The English reader does not know Milosz's poems in the properly sensuous way that one reads poems in one's own language, but the reader does have a definite sense as to what Milosz has been feeling and thinking in his poem-making. That sense, as it bears witness to a ceaseless and powerful confrontation with the ponderables of existence, is not to be lightly dismissed.

Trees:

This may seem to be a curious place to begin. Milosz is famous, after all, as a philosophical sort of poet rather than a Druid. Yet if one were to draw up a heraldic shield for Milosz, surely a tree would be emblazoned on it. In part this fondness stems, no doubt, from the poet's "rural, provincial" childhood in Lithuania, a land of substantial forests. Yet there is more involved than early memories. The tree is an imaginative touchstone, at once a thing of majesty, as when he writes in **"Elegy for Y. Z."** of "the splendor of autumn dogwoods and maples" or in **"The**

View" of "precious oaks," and the biblical tree of life that appears in the poem **"Into the Tree,"** where

> The tree, says good Swedenborg, is a close relative of man.
> Its boughs like arms join in an embrace.
> The trees in truth are our parents,
> We sprang from the oak, or perhaps, as the Greeks maintain, from the ash.
>
> Our lips and tongue savor the fruit of the tree.
> A woman's breast is called apple or pomegranate.
> We love the womb as the tree loves the dark womb of the earth.
> Thus, what is most desirable resides in a single tree,
> And wisdom tries to touch its coarse-grained bark.

Deracinated people have made much of primitivism in this century, but Milosz is hardly an anthropological thrill-seeker. What we find in his poetry is an imagination that is literally thousands of years old, Christian and pagan, sensuous and ruminative, full of pain and companionship. Reading Milosz is much like reading Dante. Touch any word or phrase, and some spring of meaning jets up. The spiritual, natural, philosophical, personal, and often the biblical are all intertwined. What is remarkable, what makes Milosz a great poet, is that he embraces all the meanings he invokes. Thus the assertion that trees are our parents elicits a profound feeling that has touched many people on this planet over millennia. Similarly the story of the tree of knowledge to which the poem alludes is not an outdated myth. The vaunted historicism of modern times is but one more guise of conceit and wishfulness and cannot save us from the tasks of being human. The uncomfortable truth is that the partaking (to say nothing of absentminded worshipping) of knowledge means also the endangering of the angel of imagination and faith. What more dangerous legend is there than the one that denies it is a legend, that dismisses the miraculous in the name of the probable?

Yet the imagination remains alive. At the poem's end "a child opens its eyes and sees a tree for the first time. / And people seem to us like walking trees." The child is not a romantic avatar but simply the freshness of spirit. The biblical epigraph from Mark, "And he looked up and said, 'I see men as trees, walking' " attests to the simultaneity of imaginative insight. There is no superannuation to the imagination nor is there any growing up. The sweet and the harsh lessons are immemorial.

It is important to insist on the degree to which Milosz stands, as he has put it, "on the side of Imagination, of Urthona, of anima." It would be easy to patronize the poet who when acknowledging the coldness of Robinson Jeffers's romanticism writes:

> Better to carve suns and moons on the joints of crosses
> as was done in my district. To birches and firs
> give feminine names. To implore protection
> against the mute and treacherous might
> than to proclaim, as you did, an inhuman thing.
> (from **"To Robinson Jeffers"**)

The reader who considers such evocations to be one more case of quaint and inapplicable folk-longing is overlooking the ferocious price humankind has paid recently for renouncing the humilities and hierarchies of imagination. If there is a grotesque legend of modern times, it is surely that of objective knowledge. As Milosz has written, "The tree of knowledge of good and evil, or the tree of contradictions, is the tree of scientific cognition, based on the principle of consistency. Whoever tastes of the tree is immediately beset by a series of paired negations, casting the mind into the role of an arbiter, which in the moral realm is synonymous with the triumph of arrogance." Poetry attempts to oppose this condition, as in the "Preface" to **"Treatise on Poetry":** "Hearing it, you should be able to see / Apple trees, a river, the bend of a road, / As if in a flash of summer lightning." That a tree should be the first thing to come to mind is as natural as the way children use a tree as their base when they play tag, or as adults nap beneath a tree's shade. It is not *as if* trees were our relatives; the sympathies are instinctively real and healing.

Questions:

Metaphor, the putative genius of poetry, exemplifies its forward thrust—this is like that. The many questions with which Milosz's poems are filled come as a surprise. Poems begin with questions, end with questions. One poem's title is a question. Some poems have whole chains of questions. It is disconcerting. In his attempt to allow for the complexity of the relations between the individual and the circumstances of time, Milosz uses many rhetorical means: letters, incantations, hymns, appeals, studies, journals, ballads, albums, invocations, memoirs, fantasies, dithyrambs, elegies, lectures, conversations, leave-takings. The questions, however, are always there.

The key to this penchant lies in the fragilities of the twentieth century. As Milosz has succinctly noted, "What surrounds us, here and now, is not guaranteed. It could just as well not exist—and so man constructs poetry out of the remnants found in ruins." Countries, people, houses—everything may disappear—and has. What a person is left with is not certainty but confusion. How could all this happen? The poet is at sea: He paddles, floats, bobs, treads water, heroically swims, but there is no beckoning shore. Those shores that have beckoned to such poets of the century as Mayakovsky and Pound were false. It is better to learn to live with doubt than strain for securities this century cannot provide. Milosz's view could not be clearer: " . . . the twentieth century is a purgatory in which the imagination must manage without the relief that satisfies one of the essential needs of the human heart, the need for protection."

The great majority of Milosz's poems are thus not lyric assertions (Milosz has admitted his distaste for simply making statements), but dialogues, encounters. The poet keeps bumping into such intractable realities as suffering, viciousness, egotism, forgetfulness. These are not abstractions but qualities that the poet recognizes in his own refractory life. There are so many piercing, shadowy questions beginning with "how to resist nothingness?"—and yet, how many millions have died in the name of unimpeachable certainties? What Milosz remembers and what this century has too often forgotten is that man is first and last a question. For all our habituation and bravado, what we are doing here is unclear, and there is no difference between the questions that reverberate throughout the Bible and our own questions. We remain on earth and we look toward heaven.

Our peculiar "decadence" (to use Milosz's word) lies in the belief that we do not need to ask any further questions. Everything has been decided by "the laws of physics, biology, psychology, sociology, and so on. . . . " Yet what happens when we look at something that cannot be reduced to fact, like Christ's resurrection? "Christ has risen," Milosz writes at the beginning of "Lecture V" of his **"Six Lectures in Verse."** The poem goes on to describe how present-day Christians muddle along, exchanging presents and looking at "The Book" that admittedly is "contrary to common sense." It is a world where "philosophers / Don't even dare ask: 'What is truth?' " The only answer the individual can give to such an apparent impossibility as Christ's resurrection is that " 'I don't know.' " There the poem ends.

The denizens of the late twentieth century, irresolute and submissive, are more concerned with dieting than their souls, but Milosz is a poet, not a preacher. On the other side of his doubt is amazement. His questions stem in part from a sense of the incredible vitality of life. As he puts it in a section of **"The Separate Notebooks":**

> And why all this ardor if death is so close?
> Do you expect to hear and see and feel there?
> But you know the earth is like no other place:
> What continents, what oceans, what a show it is!
> In the hall of pain, what abundance on the table

There is no attempt to make things appear sweeter than they are. Nature does not ask for our worship. Amplitude is not selective. Without, however, the knack of being amazed, we become slaves and ideologues. Milosz does not forget that life is surprising—sometimes grotesquely, sometimes joyfully. Credulity toward immensity is healthy; what happens one moment may not happen the next. The Christian question "Has he risen?" may stem from doubt, but the answer lies in the admission of wonder.

"Exteriorization":

The word comes from Aleksander Wat's book, *My Century.* Wat, a friend of Milosz's, endured a number of prisons and camps in Poland and Russia during the thirties and forties. The hells and purgatories through which Wat went opened his eyes very clearly to the chief wound totalitarianism could inflict: "the killing of the inner man," a process he dubbed "exteriorization." In this process the individual became a unit, a purely external creature who had no inner resources, beliefs, or doubts. In other words, the individual existed for the state—not for the good of the state, just for the state, period. If, as Milosz has noted, "all thinking since the beginning of the nineteenth century secularizes historical religion," then Stalinism was the logical outcome of a millennarian secularism: absolutism in the destined name of the people. Any means could be justified for such an end.

A number of Milosz's poems attempt to come to terms with this ghastly irony. Perhaps **"Bypassing Rue Descartes"** will be seen by other centuries as an example of how one "cruel and mean century" fell to such chilling depths. The poem's setting is Paris, "the capital of the world," where provincials flocked to become enlightened. These provincials "had left the cloudy provinces behind" and "entered the universal, dazzled and desiring." Milosz was once just such a young man. The wisdom of this century—ideology—was, however, a poison:

> Soon enough, many from Jassy and Koloshvar,
> or Saigon or Marrakesh
> Would be killed because they wanted to abolish
> the customs of their homes.
>
> Soon enough, their peers were seizing power
> In order to kill in the name of the universal,
> beautiful ideas

That "beautiful" is an awful, painful word. Meanwhile, the city went its way, which is to say it embodied the sensuality that survives the lunacy of human abstractions. The city's life of fornicating and drinking and eating continued "indifferent as it was to honor and shame and greatness and glory, / Because that had been done already. . . . " The poet who returns to the city is a chastened man, one who has looked into the heart of human ambition and seen death and the pathos of generations. The tragedy (and bloody farce) of time is the curse of uniqueness, each modern era proclaiming its specialness and disavowing reverence. In fact, "the time of human generations is not like the time of the earth." The pride that rejected the time-honored customs of the provinces, where "choral prayers [were] recited by master and household together," did not believe that genius could so easily become ashes.

The onus of the willfulness that calls itself genius (or impetuous theory or dialectical knowledge or mere whim) is sin. Thus the author remembers at the end of the poem how he once killed a water snake, a precious creature whose murder broke a folk taboo. "And what I have met with in life was the just punishment / Which reaches, sooner or later, the breaker of a taboo." Milosz has never tried to exempt himself from the malignancies of our time, nor has he tried to repudiate his failings. The full horror and fever of time is felt in his poetry because the wantonness of circumstantiality is not avoided. Our ability to turn the particular into the general, to rationalize everything, is always present. For Milosz, we are born into a fallen world where we feast on delusion. Modes of redemption exist, but they are difficult to hold on to. Sin is a fact to which our knowledge abundantly attests. As he phrases it in the poem **"To Raja Rao,"** "Original Sin / . . . is nothing but the first / victory of the ego."

Perhaps someday the hells of Milosz's era will be catalogued. Such a catalogue must consult "Lecture II" of the **"Six Lectures in Verse."** There Milosz presents a vision of a confident Aryan beauty who trusts supremely in the world that has nurtured her, a woman "from a home scented with cigars, well-being, order." Opposing this vision is Christ. The end of the poem bears repeating:

> Jesus has to face
> Flowery teapots, coffee, philosophizing,
> Landscapes with deer, the sound of the clock on
>   the town hall.
> Nobody will be convinced by him, black-eyed,
> A hooked nose, the dirty clothes
> Of a convict or slave, one of those drifters
> The State justly catches and disposes of.
> Now, when I know so much, I have to forgive
> My own transgressions, not unlike theirs:
> I wanted to equal others, behave just like them.
> To shut my ears, not to hear the calls of proph-
>   ets.
> That's why I understand her. A snug home, a
>   garden,
> And from the depths of Hell, a fugue of Bach.

There are numerous terrifying moments in Milosz's poetry, but this passage seems to me one of the most frightening. As it looks honestly at the genius of order and notes felicitous touches, it refuses the anodynes of self-righteousness and empathetic posturing. That we think we know what we are doing as we drink coffee and philosophize, that we applaud the character of outward appearances—if these are reckoned faults, then we are all at fault. This is an uncomfortable conclusion, for no groups are exempted on the basis of their superior knowledge. The unpleasant truth may be that our social strengths stem from a certain hideous weakness, a spiritual conceit and inertia, which grease the oblivious wheels of modern times. The most elevated human creations may be easily besmirched because the hand of social habit is automatic (rather than cyclically renewed). We are eager to comply with this automatism ("the sound of the clock on the town hall"), we celebrate it by proclaiming its infallible lawfulness, and then we are surprised when whole societies comply with orderly deviltry. The forgiveness Milosz extends to himself is very sobering. Who, after all, wants to acknowledge that our temporal security is, as it closes our eyes, our gravest danger?

Powers, Angels, Spirits:

If the darkness of suffering is almost always tangible in Milosz's poetry, so, it must be remembered, is light. Not only the light of nature—wonderful, to be sure, and loved by the poet—but also the light of the other worldly, the light that is both shy and nimble, that succors and eludes us. Although we tend to associate religiosity with doctrine, the heart of spiritual feeling is not so much doctrine (which is often codified anxiety) as it is the apprehension of certain presences and signs that articulate nonhuman energies. Precisely because these energies are other-than-human, they are captivating. We intuit, at once, our own smallness and the depths of being.

To attempt to typecast Milosz's spirituality would be unwise. It is naïve and sophisticated, palpable and cerebral. What matters most is that his sense of the spirit world is real, rooted as it is in the folkways of an epoch and a place that were at home with all manner of spiritual communication. This foundation was refined and strengthened through his contact with his cousin Oskar Milosz, a poet with pronounced mystical interests. He was thus led "into a realm that was, on the one hand, absolutely alien to Polish Catholicism and, on the other, opposed to the entire left intelligentsia for whom, in general, religion did not exist." Perhaps precisely because Milosz's sense of spirituality has gone its own way (neither visionary nor systematic, for instance), its integrity is all the more impressive. To relish the invisible in this century takes a marked degree of both obstinacy and liveliness.

A distinctly spiritual poem such as **"On Angels"** is distinguished by a marvelous freshness and honesty. Again, perhaps because spirituality has fallen into such a state of neglect, it has been possible in this century for some who are truly interested to experience the spiritual in a remarkably candid fashion. In Milosz's offhand and pungent way, the poem treats at once the history of recent spirituality and the unusual subject at hand: angels. The scene is set almost peremptorily:

> All was taken away from you: white dresses,
> wings, even existence.
> Yet I believe you,
> messengers.

The considerable trick is to make these pure creatures sensually credible. This Milosz does beautifully:

> Short is your stay here:
> now and then at a matinal hour, if the sky is
>   clear,
> in a melody repeated by a bird,
> or in the smell of apples at the close of day
> when the light makes the orchards magic.

The occasions still exist. The modern, empirical dogmas that hold that such creatures cannot exist, that humans have invented them, count for very little. Milosz notes that "humans invented themselves as well." Such self-inventions are the work of the inexhaustible ego, and, as the history of humanity richly testifies, tend to immure people in cramped and often blinded identities. For his part, the poet has heard the voices of angels "many a time when asleep" and believes he has understood the gist of their "unearthly tongue":

> day draws near
> another one
> do what you can.

It is simple. We may invoke Blake's sense of salvation that Milosz has defined as "the eternal *now* and not some tomorrow beyond the sunset of life," but the angelic sense is what counts most. The poem is sweet, alert, poised, and unembarrassed.

Our relations with the spirit world are various because spirits are various. We understand them as we are able (which is often not much), and they exist as part of a great continuum. Those spirits that, for instance, possess poets should not be shunted aside as less interesting because they are less holy. Nor is it the poet's fault if he or she is a medium. The situation is in many ways a frightening one for the poet. In **"The Wormwood Star"** Milosz writes that "he hears voices but he does not understand the screams, prayers, blasphemies, hymns which chose him for their medium." We remember that even such an accomplished and assured poet as Auden admitted that after finishing one poem he was never sure whether he would write another. The modern belief in inner creativity seems an attempt to deny the seemingly inferior and uncertain position of the artist. The liberation of the individual has also meant a liberation from the apparent bondage of spiritual possession. Unfortunately our insistence on control runs counter to the unaccountable whys of inspiration. For (from the poem **"Lauda"**) "it is not the skill of the hand / That writes poetry, but water, trees, / And the sky which is dear to us even though it's dark."

Milosz is suspicious of the Protestant-derived notion that the poet's ability to interpret life (as the individual interprets the Bible) gives the poet an exceptional key to life. Milosz's poet is likely to be riven or harrowed: The world keeps erupting. The poet attempts to shape what is powerful and unruly and also acknowledge that some degree of humility and caution may be advisable. **"Ars Poetica?"** investigates this:

> In the very essence of poetry there is something
> indecent:
> a thing is brought forth which we didn't know
> we had in us,
> so we blink our eyes, as if a tiger had sprung out
> and stood in the light, lashing its tail.
>
> That's why poetry is rightly said to be dictated
> by a daimonion,
> though it's an exaggeration to maintain that he
> must be an angel.
> It's hard to guess where that pride of poets
> comes from,
> when so often they're put to shame by the disclo-
> sure of their frailty.

The obedience that is asked of us mortals is—to put it mildly—trying, but we might do well to heed one who has written (in **"Powers"**), "though of weak faith, I believe in forces and powers / Who crowd every inch of the air." Our by now rote Darwinism makes us assume that we are the sums of creation, but human consciousness seems more like a fulcrum than a peak. And there is in any case a sky above each peak. Milosz imagines the powers trying to understand how it is that each of us dies: " 'Why?' / And the powers flow, whir among the tombstones, / 'Who ordered them to die, who needs it?' " This ability to picture the other side of being "in which whatever exists must exist forever" is particularly precious in a time when we keep looking into ourselves for that which we deny is around us. Being, as Milosz portrays it, is an interplay of many different energies. To understand these energies fully is not only impossible but beside the point. What is much more important is hospitality, the wry warmth that feels at home with the multiplicity of being.

Milosz / Not-Milosz:

Witold Gombrowicz elucidated the situation very nicely when he wrote about Milosz that "I am Milosz. I do not wish to be Milosz, being Milosz I must be Milosz. I kill Milosz in myself so that being Milosz, I am Milosz all the more." To assume an identity is to generate expectations; however, the proper concern of an author is not to fulfill expectations but to write. To embrace a persona is to suffocate oneself for the benefit of others. One could fill this page with antinomies ("an ecstatic pessimist," for example) that indicate the range of Milosz's feelings, but that would be irrelevant. Milosz resides in his poetry in much the way Dante resides in *La Commedia.* He is at once a particular man with definite virtues and vices, and any man who is alive. Though implicated in his own coils, he is able to put himself into some sort of perspective. His career is not to acquire but rather to pursue "the Real."

It is tempting simply to call Milosz a wise fellow and let it go at that. There is enough to mull over in ***The Collected Poems*** for a couple of lifetimes. Yet wisdom would not mean in this case a particular set of epigrammatic thoughts, but rather a readiness of mind, an admission of the fluidity of life, a willingness to be honest—not for the sake of honesty as an abstract virtue—but because if one is not honest, life loses its savor. As befits an honest man, Milosz consistently resists the impulse to exaggerate. He refuses the sentimentality which would have us believe that good feelings are an end in themselves. The gauntlet of history is not so easily wished away.

There is something very determined about a man who does not throw in his lot with the creeds of his time, who resists the blandishments of ideas. Milosz has, of course, recognized this about himself. In **"Father Ch., Many Years Later,"** he writes at poem's end:

> I could not understand from whence came my
> stubbornness
>
> And my belief that the pulse of impatient blood
> Fulfills the designs of a silent God

Each term in these lines is of particular importance. "The pulse of impatient blood" testifies to the poet's natural will, the temerity of vitality. Yet there is an element of belief present that is not demanded but that the poet strongly feels, for our blood and our breath bind us to the universal movement that permeates all things. Oskar Milosz noted that "rhythm is the highest earthly expression of what is called thought," and Czeslaw Milosz has written that "I spent my life composing rhythmic spells" (**"Incantation"**). This article of pagan belief may yet fulfill "the designs of a silent God." After all, this God once spoke to men and He may speak again. This hiatus may last for millennia, or it may end tomorrow. His silence may be part of His designs, and the poet's obstinate careering may be in tune with a faith that must precede God-given faith. Or it may not.

Milosz's lack of interest in exonerating himself, his willingness to attempt to be truthful about the states of his soul, gives him a unique ability to appreciate the multiplicity of life. He who swims with the current and he who swims against the current are present in one human being. The only axe the poet has to grind, so to speak, is the one that cleaves each of us—life itself in all its beguiling, bewildering profusion. We see the poet "on the shore of the Pacific . . . translating the Apocalypse from Greek into Polish," and we see the poet "unable to imagine myself among the disciples of Jesus," busy "choosing among bright fabrics sold by merchants from overseas." We see a man who likes this world very much and who often finds it (and himself) hideous, a man who is willing to get along and who refuses alibis, a man who goes on (in "Lecture VI" of the **"Six Lectures in Verse"**) "consoling myself also. / Not very much consoled."

People:

At the heart of Milosz's poetry is the man himself, but he is hardly the only person present. The catastrophes of time have made Milosz acutely aware of the importance of recognition, particularly to one who has loved and known and been fascinated and repelled by many people. There is a great warmth in Milosz's poetry, a sociability akin to someone like Rabelais or Fielding, and there is no small degree of fierceness. What makes many of the people one encounters in Milosz's poetry unforgettable lies both in the offhandedly direct way Milosz presents them and in the feeling one gets of how history enshrouds them. Even if they are unaware of the dynamo of modern historical consciousness, it is still there. Perhaps it is all the more cruelly there because, as he puts it in "Lecture I" of **"Six Lectures in Verse,"** "Those who are unaware / Deserve to be punished: they wanted only to live."

One thus meets Lisabeth, "the old servant woman," who brought in logs for the stove in Milosz's room in Wilno when he was a university student in the early 1930s. Wilno was a city of bells:

> And then the pealing of bells. At Saint John's
> And the Bernardines', at Saint Casimir's
> And the Cathedral, at the Missionaries'
> And Saint George's, at the Dominicans'
> And Saint Nicholas's, at Saint Jacob's.
> Many many bells. As if the hands pulling the
> ropes
> Were building a huge edifice over the city.
>
> So that Lisabeth wrapped up in her cape could
> go to morning Mass.
>
> I have thought for a long time about Lisabeth's
> life.

Lisabeth's life is both singular and plural; her days are informed by centuries. It is of itself—one sees her walking along a wintry street to Mass in her "funny, pointed" shoes—and it is connected to palpable orders and domains. It is also connected, though unaware, to all that destroyed such a world. For, in another section of **"From the Rising of the Sun,"** Milosz writes of "my clear-eyed companions" who were "engaged in weighty discussions on killing for the common good." Lisabeth was not living in some artist's dream, but she was living in some ideologue's dream that was soon to become grimly real. It is like a scale: on one side is Lisabeth's unremarkable life and on the other the ideological demiurge of revolution. Which weighs more depends on the sort of measurements one uses.

In truth, to the poet there is only one set of measurements, and that is the worth of a human life—not as the incarnation of historical forces, but as a mere life. The most moving instance of this belief is set forth in "Lecture IV" of **"Six Lectures in Verse."** There one learns of

> . . . Miss Jadwiga,
> A little hunchback, librarian by profession,
> Who perished in the shelter of an apartment
> house
> That was considered safe but toppled down
> And no one was able to dig through the slabs of
> wall,
> Though knocking and voices were heard for
> many days.

The voice of the world, of Ulro, says, "What of it? Another death in a century of millions of highly unnatural deaths, of mass deaths," as if individuals did not die singly but as a part of some collective body. What of it, indeed?

> So a name is lost for ages, forever,
> No one will ever know about her last hours,
> Time carries her in layers of the Pliocene.
> The true enemy of man is generalization.
> The true enemy of man, so-called History,
> Attracts and terrifies with its plural number.
> Don't believe it. Cunning and treacherous,
> History is not, as Marx told us, anti-nature,
> And if a goddess, a goddess of blind fate.
> The little skeleton of Miss Jadwiga, the spot
> Where her heart was pulsating. This only
> I set against necessity, law, theory.

The poem does not issue from civic-mindedness, or protest, or a belief in the poignant poetic powers of memorialization. The poem attests to the strongest force we know—reality. That is why we try to ignore the real: It is frightening because it is so strong. Our conceits and ideas seem to protect us, but they are matches that may suddenly burst into flames. The resultant fire is quite genuine. As Milosz has written, "The twentieth century has given us a most simple touchstone for reality: physical pain." "Knocking and voices were heard for many days," and one forgets Miss Jadwiga at one's own expense.

The vastness, coldness, and fickleness of history may seem overpowering. Yet human warmth is not to be forgotten or taken lightly. Many of Milosz's poems about people attest to the sheer pungence of personality. In the moving **"Elegy for Y.Z."** Milosz writes,

> Fleshly, woundable, pitiable, ironic,
> You went with men casually, out of unconcern,
> And smoked as if you were courting cancer.

Y.Z. is not a general victim of history but a particular survivor. The list of adjectives portrays a person who is a bundle of disparate yet definite feelings. The question Milosz indirectly asks is, "Who is this person?" The answer lies not so much in the telling anecdotes a life accumulates as in the attitudes that indicate emotions. For what is humanly precious is all that, counter to the edifices of history, does not add up. No arithmetic can approach what we call a "soul." The end of the elegy gets to the heart of the matter:

> I would like everyone to know they are the
> king's children
> And to be sure of their immortal souls,
> I.e., to believe that what is most their own is imperishable
> And persists like the things they touch,
> Now seen by me beyond time's border:

Her comb, her tube of cream, and her lipstick
On an extramundane table.

The Past:

The bond between the present and the past may be likened to the bond between the head and the rest of the body. They form (save for the guillotine) one corporeal identity, but the head is very clever, very important, whereas the rest of the body seems merely to exist, a vast enterprise that works on through days and nights and, one day or night, obscurely or spectacularly fails. The present moment is indeed a very important place to be. We are literally nowhere if we are not in it, but it can be a monster, too, and it can forget that without the foundation of the past, the present is threadbare, pitiably empty. The emotions that the past fosters—particularly loyalty, reverence, and piety—are virtues that may give meaning to an existence otherwise intolerably confined by the manias of the present moment. The review of the past may also adduce a healthy skepticism—a tonic for those blinded by the current fashion. The head needs to be reminded incessantly that the body, too, is very important.

Milosz's poetry is a vast, probing reminder of the value of the past. The poet has said it plainly enough, that "history is extremely real." And yet since history has by definition lost the aura of the present moment's attention, it is easy to forget and may seem, in fact, to be extremely unreal. For someone from Milosz's part of the world, the burden of time has been severe: People, cities, countries, all have disappeared. What the poet insists on is that something was there, that below the head there is something more than a void. It would not be hard to feel, in the light of this century's dire and deadening experiences, that there was only a void, and that the attempt to people and vivify such a void was little more than a harmless pastime. In opposition to the cruelties of glibness, oblivion, and the totalitarian reworking of the past, Milosz has propounded the tangible dignity, "the granularity of historical time." He has made no epic claims for this enterprise; it has been his unhappy fate. He has not so much been a witness as a quizzical defender of that which can no longer speak in the name of meaning. To refashion some pretense of wholeness would be a sentimental lie. There are only many bits and pieces, such as the following passage of prose from **"The Wormwood Star"** section of ***The Separate Notebooks*** (the notebook is perhaps the truest of the episodic forms Milosz has created, as it allows duration to become the seeming arbiter of form):

> He hears voices but he does not understand the screams, prayers, blasphemies, hymns which chose him for their medium. He would like to know who he was, but he does not know. He would like to be one, but he is a self-contradictory multitude which gives him some joy, but more shame. He remembers tents of the Red Cross on the shore of a lake at a place called Wyshki. He remembers water scooped out of the boat, big gray waves and a bulblike Orthodox church which seems to emerge from them. He thinks of that year, 1916, and of his beautiful cousin Ela in the uniform of an army nurse, of her riding through hundreds of versts along the front with a handsome officer, whom she has just married. Mama, covered with a shawl, is sitting by the fireplace at dusk with Mr. Niekrasz whom she knows from her student days at Riga, and his epaulets glitter. He had disturbed their conversation, but now he sits quietly and looks intently at the bluish flames, for she has told him that if he looks long enough he will see a funny little man with a pipe in there, riding around.

War, childhood, places, things, people, and imagination—all the epic substance of life is quietly there. Yet for all the solidity of such a passage (and there are many others in Milosz's poetry), the summoning of the past is a very precarious venture. The poet is confronted at each turn not only with the arbitrariness of imagination and memory, but also with the need to acknowledge fact, the insistence that such-and-such was done or not done by so-and-so and that probity is something more than imaginative inspiration. The semblance of honor toward the dead that the poet provides must be dipped in the caustic of time. How, without being an obsessive bore, can the poet ignore human forgetfulness and indifference? Milosz acknowledges this in "The Accuser" section of **"From the Rising of the Sun"**:

> You say a name, but it's not known to anyone.
>
> Either because that man died or because
> He was a celebrity on the banks of another river.
>
> Chiaromonte
> Miomandre
> Petöfi
> Mickiewicz
>
> Young generations are not interested in what happened
> Somewhere else, long ago.

This is bitter but true. Milosz has been tempered not only by his own suffering but by his allegiance to history, and such an allegiance is humbling. What does he or anyone know of the past, of others? Somewhat later in **"The Wormwood Star,"** this dilemma is addressed:

> Northern sunset, beyond the lake a song of harvesters.
> They move about, tiny, binding the last sheaves.
> Who has the right to imagine how they return to the village,
> And sit down by the fire and cook and cut their bread?
> Or how their fathers lived in huts without chimneys,
> When every roof would smoke as if on fire?

Before such prosaic mysteries one must try to be plainspoken—painful as such plain speaking may be. In the emblematic poem **"Return to Kraków in 1880,"** the author imagines himself returning "from the big capitals, / To a town in a narrow valley under the cathedral hill / With royal tombs." All that is occuring in this town is mere provincial life, the stuff of vanity, suffering, playfulness. The poem ends concisely:

> In a basement a cobbler looks up from his bench,
> A hunchback passes by with his inner lament,
> Then a fashionable lady, a fat image of the deadly sins.

So the Earth endures, in every petty matter
And in the lives of men, irreversible.
And it seems a relief. To win? To lose?
What for, if the world will forget us anyway.

It would be false, however, to lower a curtain after such a poem, as if that were all there was to history. We should remember that there is a certain eschatological glimmer in Milosz's eye. He has never preached the virtues of existential resignation. As he has put it in conversation, "Our hope lies in assimilating that germ of the historical and then leaving it for the metaphysical, to seek the ontological dimension after passing through the purgatory of historical thought, of historicism." To ignore that we live and die in the circumstantial clutches of time is mere wishful thinking. To dwell absolutely on that dilemma and believe that we can master time is the willfulness of historicist ideology. A brief look into the New Testament or Book of Job would remind us that man is not the master of anything. His time is much too short for that, but his time is, in important ways, very real. Inside fluidity lies being.

"The Golden House," Apokatastasis:

If I had to pick one passage as representative of Milosz's poetry (admittedly an impossible project), I would choose this one from the "Spirit of History" section of **"Treatise on Poetry"**:

The survivors were running through fields, escaping
From themselves, knowing that for a hundred years
They wouldn't return. Before them spread
Quicksands where a tree changes into nothing,
Into an anti-tree, where no borderline
Separates a shape from a shape, and where, amidst thunder,
The golden house, the word *is,* collapses
And the word *becomes* ascends to power

The peculiar power of Milosz's poetry derives not only from his great feeling for the sanities and labors and excesses of being, but also from his personal awareness of the powerful lure of becoming. The sort of contemplative dynamism that characterizes Milosz's poetry—the wedding of sharp conceptual thinking to the various details of confused human lives—makes for a style that is, at once, humble and fearless. Many of the techniques and attitudes of modernism—fragmentation, *ex nihilo* pithiness, forthright sensuality, wariness—are put to outstanding use by the erstwhile catastrophist. Dynamism may be a nightmare, but it is, as millions of people in this century would attest, an invigorating nightmare. We recall that for a time Milosz served that "People's Poland" that was going to oppose the cruelties of capitalism. If his heart was never fully committed to such an enterprise, his mind was willing enough. He was one who was "easily enticed by the newest idea" (**"Father Ch., Many Years Later"**). Yet Milosz is the same man who has admitted that "ontological contemplation is my very essence, the thing to which I feel closest." Such contemplation is important in our epoch, for what, after all, is the sickness of modernity but the elevation of becoming at the expense of being? The particularly tormented history of this century gives the lie, however, to the pose of disinterestedness, of connoisseurship, of tourism. Contemplation does not bequeath immunity. As Milosz has written, "The poetic act changes with the amount of background reality embraced by the poet's consciousness." The fullest poetic act is the most impure in the sense that it acknowledges multiplicity but retains its faith in truth-telling. Thus, in Milosz's poetry things are at once still and not still. Matter decays, elegies importune, but our stupid and energetic dance with being goes on. The beginning of the recent poem **"In a Buggy at Dusk"** is one of Milosz's deftest portrayals of the entangling web that is being and time:

To ride in a buggy at dusk. Well-worn ruts.
The road goes past a farm in a dell by a lake.
The roofs nestling together, raw linen spread on the meadow.
Nets drying, smoke rising from the chimney.

What silence. Who are they? Are they among the saved or damned,
Sitting down to supper under pictures of the saints?
And Thomas Aquinas writes about them in his cell,
Nonstop, as punishment no doubt, he was too angelic.
Perhaps I write as punishment, too? I wanted to bow
To the Light, to Majesty, only that, no more.
And here are mere people, their customs, their houses,
A defenseless family, a year on the calendar.

Where does all this being go? Anyone who strongly feels the imprint of existence must ask him or herself such a question. Milosz's learnings are expressed in the "Bells of Winter" section of **"From the Rising of the Sun."** The passage I quote here follows our introduction to Milosz's room on "Literary Lane" in Wilno and the servant woman, Lisabeth:

There is, it would seem, no reason
For I have departed to a land more distant
Than one that can be reached by roads leading through woods and mountains)
To bring that room back here.

Yet I belong to those who believe in *apokatastasis.*
That word promises reverse movement,
Not the one that was set in *katastasis*
And appears in the Acts 3, 21.

It means: restoration. So believed: St. Gregory of Nyssa,
Johannes Scotus Erigena, Ruysbroeck, and William Blake.

For me, therefore, everything has a double existence.
Both in time and when time shall be no more.

Milosz has noted that such a notion is "not a formal belief of mine, because those are heretical ideas. Rather, its meaning is that of a restoration of all moments in a purified form. It's hard to pin down the meaning here, but I wouldn't *want* to be overly precise, either." This is a feeling that many of us have had, a feeling for which there exists, in this case, a formal term and a train of variously unorthodox believers. If time, for instance, is not a dimension but something more like a surface, then what has an outside must have an inside. Or it is as if there is only one moment that contains all moments. This is not exactly what Milosz has proposed, but perhaps the particular doctrine is not so much the issue as the feeling of awe at the fullness of being, a feeling that is terrible and inspiring. To say that nothing is lost in the embrace of eternity may seem glib. So much care invests each moment. . . .

Buddhism?:

Is the famous poet a crypto-Buddhist? Of course not, but there are moments in Milosz's poetry that could be transferred into a totally different spiritual perspective without a wrinkle or a twist, just as if they naturally belonged there. This testifies not so much to the fact that Milosz has lived in California for a long time as that there is a river of perception that is spiritual, that flows through us, and that predates the often Babel-like atmosphere of creeds. Consider, for instance, a poem such as **"A Poetic State,"** where "I was impatient and easily irritated by time lost on trifles among which I ranked cleaning and cooking. Now, attentively, I cut onions, squeeze lemons, and prepare various kinds of sauces." This seems somewhat whimsical, but the ability to live simply in time according to the moment is not a small thing. The poet witnesses that it is possible to do something in life besides strain. The stillness of being can be embodied by humans—even as they go about their little motions. The poet does not tell us how this alteration occurred. Perhaps it is a matter of perspective, as when, in the first paragraph of the poem, the poet speaks of being "given a reversed telescope instead of eyes." There are many paths to reaching such a perspective, but if we happen to proceed far enough along, it may be we all come to a similar promontory.

Reputation:

Milosz has wished at times that he had been born in an age in which it was possible to be a truly great poet. This word "great" may seem a tiresome, idle, and hopelessly subjective anachronism—or it may be the tonic for the most searching appraisal of poetry, one that asks for both passion and sanity and that very few poets can satisfy. It has been Milosz's misfortune to behold a world in ruins, to finger remnants and shards, to look worldliness in its self-serving face, and to feel the hollowness of ideological enthusiasm. His fate, however, has not been a misfortune for poetry. If the robust confidence of a Shakespeare (or the more tortured confidence of a Dickens or Tolstoy) has been denied him, the shrewdness that only doubt can bring forth has flourished. Certainly the travails of the twentieth century are as epic a subject as any. The great difficulty lies in the path of approach. There is no way to limn directly the shattering enormity of modern, ideological times. Rather, life must be approached at angles. The greatest vice is not faith but credulity, yet as the sharp eye pounces it must refuse to abandon human dignity to the appetites of dissection. As Milosz has said on the subject of irony, "I would prefer to write without irony. Except that it's very difficult to speak directly of things, and so you try to catch them in a more roundabout way. Ideally, you would meet your subject head on." The facts of the situation are expressed in the brief poem **"A Task":**

> In fear and trembling, I think I would fulfill my
> life
> Only if I brought myself to make a public confes-
> sion
> Revealing a sham, my own and of my epoch:
> We were permitted to shriek in the tongue of
> dwarfs and demons
> But pure and generous words were forbidden
> Under so stiff a penalty that whoever dared to
> pronounce one
> Considered himself as a lost man.

Ours have not been ideal circumstances for poetry that seeks to be "pure and generous," arising as it does from the instinct of praise. It would be as idle to complain as it would be to pretend that this age was a ripe one. We can say honestly that Milosz is as great as we deserve. It is an uplifting thought. (pp. 67-89)

Baron Wormser, "Grave Combats," in Parnassus: Poetry in Review, *Vol. 15, No. 2, 1989, pp. 67-89.*

Miłosz on the importance of detail in his work:

It is not for me to write the history of European culture; others will take this task upon themselves. For me, the problem is highly personal, because in my poems and prose my support has been the remembered detail. Not an "impression" and not an "experience"; these are so multilayered and so difficult to translate into language that various methods have been discovered in the attempt to grasp them: speech that imitates the "stream of consciousness" even to the point of eliminating punctuation marks, of becoming verbal magma, mere babbling. The remembered detail, for example, the grain of the wood of a door handle polished by the touch of many hands deserved, in my opinion, to be separated from the chaos of impressions and experiences, to be cleansed in some way, so that all that remained would be the eye disinterestedly contemplating the given object. I know how easy it is to find fault with my insistence on making distinctions; all one would have to do is introduce a couple of concepts from a handbook of psychology, but I have no interest in them, since making distinctions at least brings us closer to the essential line of division and practice confirms it.

Czesław Miłosz, in "The Sand in The Hourglass," in his Beginning with My Streets, *Farrar Straus Giroux, 1991.*

George Gömöri (review date Autumn 1991)

[*Gömöri is a Hungarian-born English poet, translator, and educator. In the review below, he appraises* The Hunter's Year.]

Rok myśliwego (The Hunter's Year) is a diary which was kept by the Polish émigré poet and writer and 1980 Nobel Prize winner Czesław Miłosz from August 1987 to August 1988. As the author was in his late seventies at the time, the diary is not only a record of day-to-day activities and speaking engagements throughout the United States and Europe but also a book of reminiscences. He committed these to paper partly in his house in Berkeley overlooking the Bay and partly during long flights while crisscrossing America. Although some of Miłosz's everyday activities are perhaps quite worthy of recording, what makes ***Rok myśliwego*** fascinating is the frequent descent into the well of memory, providing interesting information on many of the author's contemporaries as well as filling out empty spaces in his own biography.

It is probably impossible to write critical reminiscences without embarking upon trials of self-definition. After taking part in a papal conference on Europe organized at Castel Gandolfo, Miłosz writes at some length about John Paul II, including a passage focusing on the pope's "Polishness." He finds the pope too "innocent" for his taste, too much influenced by Norwid's philosophy and thus too ethnocentric. There is a certain logic in Miłosz's discourse, yet I think the link between Norwid's views and the pope's rhetoric is rather tenuous. At any rate, the passage serves a purpose, for it leads to the following confession: "If I want to be honest . . . I have a common language only with the demonized Pole, with such a Pole who has gone through Marxism, atheism, or maybe some kind of a deviation, whether in a national form within his family, or of a sexual kind." Miłosz's own "deviation" from the model of the "upright Catholic Pole" is, by the way, manifold: he was born in multilingual Lithuania, and a branch of his family opted for independent Lithuania (e.g., Oscar Lubicz Miłosz); he was a Leftist in his youth who broke with the postwar communist regime only after several years of diplomatic service; and of course, his Christianity had always contained a Manichean streak. These pecularities, however, never could shock conservative Poles to the same extent as the postures of the late Witold Gombrowicz. As a matter of fact, Miłosz is aware of this last fact and at one point expresses his aversion to much of Gombrowicz's work: "I don't envy [his plays and novels]; I wouldn't like to be their author. But do they trouble me? Yes . . . And my unease stems from the fact that if I accept Gombrowicz as a modern writer, then I must regard myself as an oldfashioned one." In some respects he is right; but then there could be more than one definition of both *contemporaneity* and *modernity.*

In ***Rok myśliwego*** Miłosz gives a frank account of his fascination with Iwaszkiewicz's work and speaks perceptively about such friends and fellow writers as Jeanne Hersch, Aleksander Wat, and Kazimierz Pruszyński. The pages devoted to Józef Mackiewicz, another writer from prewar "Polish" Vilna (Vilnius), are particularly interesting. Miłosz points out the passionate conviction which fueled Mackiewicz's talent as well as his fundamentally self-destructive attitude toward Polish society and public opinion. As for Gałczyński, Miłosz adds a few welcome touches to the picture he had sketched in ***The Captive Mind,*** but he also sows the seeds of a legend: namely, that Gałczyński (according to the sculptor Karny, who made the poet's death mask) committed suicide. Warsaw in 1953 was a much smaller and more rumor-mad city than it is today, yet neither then nor later were there any rumors about Gałczyński's alleged suicide; consequently, it is hard to believe this to be true. In 1953 Gałczyński (whom I myself met on several occasions) was full of vitality, and there was no obvious reason why he would have tried to take his own life.

"One has to bless the gift that one is intellectually active," writes Miłosz toward the end of ***Rok myśliwego.*** Indeed, he has reason to feel satisfied: he has written much poetry in the 1980s, and his prose is sprightly and alert. Although his doubts about the influence a writer *really* exerts on readers are not unfounded, he has become well known on both sides of the Atlantic. ***Rok myśliwego*** is further proof of his continuing vigor as a writer and a critic.

George Gömöri, in a review of "Rok myśliwego," in World Literature Today, *Vol. 65, No. 4, Autumn, 1991, p. 735.*

Donald Davie (review date 16 March 1992)

[*An English poet, critic, educator, and translator, Davie is well respected for both his creative and his critical contributions to literature. During the 1950s Davie was associated with the Movement, a group of poets including Philip Larkin, Kingsley Amis, and Thom Gunn, whose verse emphasized formal structures, restrained language, traditional syntax, and the moral and social implications of poetic content. In the following review of Miłosz's poetry collection* Provinces, *his essay collection* Beginning with My Streets, *and Leonard Nathan and Arthur Quinn's critical study* The Poet's Work: An Introduction to Czesław Miłosz, *Davie focuses on Miłosz's rejection of American lyrical poetry and his concern with metaphysical themes.*]

In his latest gathering of essays, ***Beginning with My Streets***—more a medley than a collection, with a deceptive air of being "thrown together"—Czeslaw Milosz includes an interview from 1988 in which he intimates, mildly enough, his dissatisfaction with the poetry of today, in many languages. His charge against contemporary poetry is that it has been impoverished from within by closing off too many doors in a search for "purity in lyricism." This accusation has been leveled before by Milosz, but never emphatically, because being emphatic is seldom his style. All the same, it is the clue to his achievement; he is one modern poet who has no interest in being a lyrical poet, who thinks indeed that exertions to that end are morally and politically often dubious.

Rather than the lyrical "I," emoting out of its own subjectivity (as Robert Lowell did, or Sylvia Plath), Milosz favors, and in his own poems puts into play, not one voice but several: voices that cross over, contradict one another, dissolve just when we think we have learned to trust them. This can be seen in poems short enough to look like lyrics. For instance, **"Should, Should Not":**

A man should not love the moon.
An axe should not lose weight in his hand.
His garden should smell of rotting apples
And grow a fair amount of nettles.
A man when he talks should not use words
that are dear to him

Or split open a seed to find out what is inside it.

He should not drop a crumb of bread, or spit in the fire
(So at least I was taught in Lithuania).
When he steps on marble stairs,
He may, that boor, try to chip them with his boot
As a reminder that the stairs will not last forever.

Leonard Nathan and Arthur Quinn valuably place this in a series specifically addressed in the first place to Milosz's Berkeley students in the 1960s, when he saw the frivolity of the Parisian intelligentsia monstrously combined with the solemn habits of the Californian mentality: the worst of both worlds. Milosz himself has identified the marble stairs as those of "the Berkeley library." Accordingly, the poem is a series of admonitions. But each new admonition differs, grammatically and in versification, from the one before it. Thus any one admonition may be in isolation challenged. For instance, "a man . . . should not use words that are dear to him": what, *never*? That remonstration is allowed for. More crucial, the person whose boot tries to chip the marble stairs is called "a boor," but is not his endeavor underwritten by what his teachers of the 1960s or even today may rightly impress on him or her as a duty: the questioning of the marmorealized "canon"? A vast amount of work is done by the simple monosyllable "may," breaking into a sequence of "should" and "should not." Does "may" mean "is likely to," or "is permitted to"?

Recognizing these ambiguities, Nathan and Quinn advise us that this poem's "celebration of the acceptance of limitations" is "ironic." On the one hand, this opens up the possibility that the shifts of perspective are just rhetorically determined, on the assumption that no one would have attended to the poet-professor laying down the law over and over. On the other hand, it opens up the more dismaying perspective that the poet doesn't know where he stands on these issues, and is content to leave the matter suspended.

It is instructive, and I think conclusive, to see how Milosz responded when another interviewer offered to him the term "ironic" in relation to this poem. Milosz ducked the question, but conceded that the poem is spoken through a mask: "Yes, it's a mask. What can you do with a strange guy who doesn't understand himself?" And then he happily endorsed something said to him by an admirer of his translations from Scripture: "An instrument, not a human being but a device." The voice that speaks the poem is not that of a human being, whose lyrical "I" might declare itself in love with lunar purity (and sterility), but instead a device, perhaps divine, for which admonitions and prohibitions from Lithuanian folklore are no less binding than others arrived at on other grounds. It is not just the expatriate poet-professor who admonishes his misguided students, but a being more mysterious, drawing its authority from more occult sources. The poet in propria persona, the lyrical "I," is merely "a strange guy who doesn't understand himself," and so he must be discounted.

Normally one would not bear down in this way on a poem translated from a foreign tongue. There is always the possibility that substituting "may" for "should" is the result merely of a translator's inattention. But once Milosz's ***Collected Poems*** appeared in English in 1988, his poetry became a very abnormal phenomenon indeed, perhaps unprecedented. He has busied himself so constantly with the translation of his poems into English, assembling and training and collaborating with an exceptionally gifted team of translators, that we do not hear from him, or from his Polish-speaking admirers, the familiar wail of "how much is lost in translation." Undoubtedly much is lost; but Milosz's position seems to be that he will stand as stoutly by a poem of his in its American-English version as in its original Polish version.

He is even prepared to regard himself as an American poet. It is hard to see how a lyrical poet could take this position, however gifted and devoted his translators. On the contrary, it is the proudest boast made by or on behalf of the lyricist—Keats or Hart Crane, Lermontov or Mandelstam—that he is "untranslatable." Milosz makes no such boast. But this humility should not deceive us; Milosz is on his own admission a haughty man, not at all ingratiating toward the American public. What looks like humility derives not from the sort of person he is, but from the sort of poetry he writes—which is not a lyrical poetry.

Because most American readers have been led to believe that lyrical poetry is the only poetry there is, or the only poetry that can earn respect in modern times, there is a gulf that they have to bridge before they can encounter Milosz's poetry on its own terms. Nathan and Quinn's study is excellent and long overdue. (Nathan has for many years been Milosz's translator, collaborator, and, we may suppose, confidant.) Still, to my mind they concede too much to the assumption that a poet's poems, collected, bear witness to an agon: to an individual going his own way, against the socially or ideologically determined consensus.

This is one way of looking at Milosz's poetic achievement; but it is not the only way, nor is it the way that the poet invites. For instance, the long and forbidding and formally reckless poem in seven sections, **"From the Rising of the Sun"** (1973-74), can be addressed, as they address it, in terms of ecstasy and pessimism, as an expression of ecstatic pessimism. But if we cut the poem free from the moods of its creator, we can see that it is concerned with, and structured about, the historically verifiable facts of what the Roman Catholic Church has declared orthodox and heterodox. There is much drama, for Milosz is greatly drawn to some of the heresies, which he finds borne out by his own experience: for instance, Socinianism, which in the seventeenth century was the form that Protestantism took in Transylvania and northern Poland, produced martyrs whose nonconforming witness Milosz admires as heroic. More readers will think they understand ecstasy and pessimism than are at home with "Socinian" or "Manichaean." But it is these latter words that are exact and definable.

This is not at all to say that Milosz's poetry is "impersonal," as Eliot's aspired to be. Milosz continually draws or drives us back to circumstances peculiar to him, in particular to the Lithuanian / Polish crossroads where he was born and nurtured, which has given him, so he powerfully persuades us, an outlook on the intellectual and factual history of the present century such as we cannot get from any other source. In the same way, by repeatedly harking back, he plainly discerns in his own track through life a development, an Odyssey or a Pilgrim's Progress. If we can't discern that track as he wants us to, part of the reason is that we remain bewildered about the simple chronology, because of the waywardness with which his poetry has been bit by bit disclosed to us in English. It is a bewilderment that the ***Collected Poems*** alleviates but cannot altogether dispel. What does seem clear is that when Milosz looks back, he judges his actions and the actions of his contemporaries against a standard more ancient and more exacting than we are used to—against, for instance, the scale of the Seven Deadly Sins.

Milosz is very sensitive to the allegation that his constant harkings back convict him of nostalgia. Against this charge he can call on the rather powerful precedent of Proust. Milosz will not much relish this association; though two of his books are customarily described as novels, he is very sniffy about the novel as a genre, making a momentous exception for Dostoyevsky. However that may be, I find the Proustian presence helpful especially with ***The Separate Notebooks,*** which were separately published alone in English in 1984 and are also confusingly part of an erstwhile unheard-of collection called ***Hymn of the Pearl*** (1982). "Where is the truth of unremembered things?" is a question at the heart of ***The Separate Notebooks;*** and it is surely a question that Proust prompts if he doesn't explicitly pose it.

This explains, I think, why, in the latest pieces added to ***Collected Poems,*** there appears a seven-part quite straightforward and entertaining sequence, **"La Belle Epoque."** Milosz was born just early enough to experience Proust's world of "women in corsets and tournures, of whom one says either 'ladies' or 'cocottes,' the catechism, the list of sins before confession, music lessons, French verbs." The point is not to mourn the passing of that world, but to wonder at how substantial it seemed, as much in a coach of the Trans-Siberian Railway as on a Paris boulevard. The last thing that Milosz wants is to transcend historical time, to "soar above" it. Like an epic poet, he wants on the contrary to be mired in history in all its particularity—and in geography, too. The effect of such evocations is to locate the speaker of the poems in a segment of historical time as well as in a geographical space. And yet all these particulars are mustered to answer a question that must be called metaphysical.

Certain things he remembers or can reconstruct, others have gone out of mind. And "where is the truth of unremembered things?" Where else but in the mind of God? That is, no doubt, the right answer. But it is not an answer that satisfies Milosz, and we should think the worse of him if it did. For though he is a Christian poet—there's that scandalous cat out of the bag!—he can hardly give offense to unbelievers or to adherents of other faiths. Although he can usually persuade himself that the orthodox Christian answer to tormenting questions is the best on offer, he never deludes himself into thinking that having the answer removes the torment. Who remembers the unremembered dead? The question torments him as much when he's been given an answer as before.

And so, though it is true that in recent years Milosz has written Christian poems unprecedentedly serene and exhilarating, the nature of that serenity must be understood. It is not the serenity of a man who at last has all the answers, but of a man who acknowledges that some tormenting questions are unanswerable. The orthodox answers may be humbly acceded to, but the hurt remains nonetheless. Healing the hurt may be within the capacity of the priest, but the poet cannot and should not pretend to heal it. The priestly and the poetic vocations are distinct; and it is part of the case against the lyrical poets that too often they, or their admirers, blur the one office into the other. It is the business of the learned poet (and Milosz is certainly that) to know the answers on offer, now and in the past, and to discriminate among them; but it is not his duty or his privilege to administer comfort, beyond saying: "Yes, I've wondered about that myself."

There arises, for those few who perhaps pedantically care, the question of how far and in what way Milosz's poetry is related to "modernism" or "the modern movement," to what Amy Clampitt lately . . . called "the fault line that opened in 1912, and has been no more than precariously spanned from that day to this." Though he was only 1 year old in 1912, Milosz recognizes that fault line, and locates himself in relation to it. He is certainly not of those who believe that modernism in poetry was an aberration that he may equably ignore. (His Christianity did not give him that cop-out: Eliot and Claudel, not to speak of Mandelstam and Pasternak, were modernist poets who professed themselves to be Christians.)

What is astringent and refreshing about Milosz's attitude to poetic modernism is that, as an Eastern European moving in and into a society that idolized Paris, he recognized how modernism, the Anglo-American version as much as the Polish version, took its bearings from France, and from a France culturally exhausted, in decline. Not for him the Francophilia that too often predetermined the judgments of Eliot and Pound. He is sure that Baudelaire is a very great poet, but not on the grounds to which Eliot appealed. Thus Milosz will endorse the modernist endeavor in poetry, will even enlist in the enterprise, but with a special sardonic awareness of how tainted its origins were. For him, it is modernism that has reintroduced into poetry the use of multiple voices, as against the single voice of the lyricist.

This explains why, when he looked at the American poetry that he had pitched himself into in 1960, he lit upon the unfashionable figure of Robinson Jeffers. Milosz was searching in American poetry not for a confirmation of truths that he had brought with him from Europe, but for a radical alternative—one that, as it turned out, he could not accept, but for which he was deeply grateful because it posed the alternatives in the starkest terms. Those alternatives were, at bottom, Nature or Culture. Milosz, inescapably European, opted in the end for culture; that is to say, for history. But he honored Jeffers's insistence that whereas Nature might seem at times to be comforting, in truth it was merciless—as Milosz already knew from his hunting in the Lithuanian forests. Whatever Warsaw or Paris or New York might hint, Milosz's attachment to Jeffers's poetry was not a matter of one provincialism calling to another. What was at issue between the Polish poet and the California poet was something on which programmatic "modernism" hardly impinged. Optimism and hope are diffident. Milosz can hope, where Jeffers can't. But he's at one with the Californian in scorning optimism, because nature plainly is pessimist. And of course Jeffers wasn't a lyrical poet, any more than Milosz.

To readers with short memories, it may seem that Milosz is now invulnerable, a consecrated icon carrying himself around—with unflagging energy, astonishing at 80—to artistic occasions here and abroad. But Milosz's international honors shouldn't obscure the true image of him as an intransigent loner. His late-come laurels aren't anything he can rest upon. For he is much resented. Some of the resentments—the Polish ones, for instance—I sense but cannot with confidence explain. He has made enemies; though his style is mostly suave, he does not suffer fools gladly, and his judgments are unsparing, even peremptory.

One Anglo-American class or coterie is particularly resentful. These are the literary warriors of the cold war, who made Milosz's ***The Captive Mind*** (1953) one of their founding texts. With the end of the cold war, these warriors find themselves out of a job, and it particularly irks them that Milosz isn't thrown on the scrap heap as they are, since ***The Captive Mind*** turns out to have been only an episode—heartfelt and never disowned—in a career that was focused on metaphysical, not political, issues; on the human condition at all times, not just in the second half of the twentieth century; on love and death, not chiefly or exclusively on political liberty.

This is what was at issue in Milosz's protest to *The New York Review of Books* about A. Alvarez's review of the ***Collected Poems***—not that the review was grudging, it was laudatory, but in Milosz's view his poems were being applauded for the wrong reason:

> Perhaps some Western writers are longing for subjects provided by spasms of historical violent change, but I can assure Mr. Alvarez that we, i.e., natives of hazy Eastern regions, perceive History as a curse and prefer to restore to literature its autonomy, dignity, and independence from social pressures. . . . The voice of a poet should be purer and more distinct than the noise (or confused music) of History.

And so, considering art in its relation to the polis, we need to look, in his new collection of poems, at **"The Thistle, the Nettle,"** which has for an epigraph something from the poet's kinsman, the Lithuanian poet in French, Oscar de Milosz:

> The thistle, the nettle, the burdock, the belladonna
> Have a future. Theirs are wastelands
> And rusty railroad tracks, the sky, silence.
>
> Who shall I be for men many generations later?
> When, after the clamor of tongues, the award goes to silence?
>
> I was to be redeemed by the gift of arranging words
> But must be prepared for an earth without grammar,
> For the thistle, the nettle, the burdock, the belladonna,
> And a small wind above them, a sleepy cloud, silence.

I do not know whether to thank Milosz, or his collaborator Robert Hass, for the exquisite cadence of that last line. Is it too much to hope that after Auschwitz (which is certainly in Milosz's mind) the end may indeed be in pitiful and appalled silence, not in arguments for and against? Poetry can articulate that silence. Argument cannot, nor priestcraft either. (pp. 34-7)

Donald Davie, "A Clamor of Tongues," in The New Republic, *Vol. 206, No. 11, March 16, 1992, pp. 34-7.*

Sally Laird (review date 22 November 1992)

[*In the following appreciative review, Laird assesses* Beginning with My Streets.

The essays contained in ***Beginning With My Streets,*** says Milosz in his Preface, 'may be considered a travel guide to a certain literary sensibility nourished by "another", less known Europe'. The description is characteristically impersonal, self-distancing. With a modesty that borders occasionally on pomposity, the Nobel prizewinner offers us not just his thoughts, but his mind itself as an object of scrutiny—a case-study for the pathologists of the twentieth century, of whom Milosz has been among the most searching.

If nowadays we can pretend to some familiarity with the mind of 'the other Europe' and its wounds, that is in large part due to Milosz and his endeavour, begun some 40 years ago in ***The Captive Mind,*** to acquaint the West with the reality of totalitarianism and to fight amnesia and indifference. Here, in essays dating mainly from the 1970s, Milosz shows undiminished contempt for the failure of Western *'belles-lettres'* to come to grips with reality, and his observations can leave us wincing. Are Tintin, Maigret and Frodo Baggins really the only heroes worth a name in modern Western literature?

But the prevailing tone is solemn, not spiteful. Totalitarianism, Milosz argues, left everyone speechless: what words could be found to name what had happened, especially when language itself had been usurped by ideology? 'How much reality is poetry able to bear?' Under such circumstances, the defencelessness of literature could not be condemned. What deserves punishment is the failure to recognise the threat or search for tactics to combat it.

These essays—a mixture of 'chatty narratives' in the Polish tradition, philosophical meditation, literary criticism and portraits of friends and writers—are an account of Milosz's own search for an art that could, without false innocence, maintain a 'cool and fastidious distance', yet preserve its vigour and will for truth. Such a feat, Milosz found, was possible only when distance was lent by time, not indifference, and poetic recollection—of every detail, 'beginning with my street'—became a sacred rite.

In his essay on 'Saligia' (the Russian acronym for the seven deadly sins), poet and engaged historian combine to reflect on the meaning of the sins, first in the mind of a Vilnius schoolboy, then in the context of a century that had given new meanings to envy, pride and anger.

The sins which occupied the highest terraces in Dante—covetousness, gluttony and lust—were those, Milosz argues, that derived from an excess of love: a 'centrifugal' will to possess, trained on the rich prodigal world outside, not on the self. That such a love is possible, even in our benighted century, is affirmed in Milosz's tributes to writers who never erred by 'mistaking their life for the world': the Polish emigré Stanislaw Vincenz, whose view of 'permanent, archetypal things' remained unobscured by the tribulations of his time; the seventeenth-century poet Thomas Traherne, able to find 'Paradise on Earth', despite the travails of his century; the poet Aleksander Wat, celebrating, from the prison of his physical sufferings, the 'young day, young times, young world'.

Included in the collection is Milosz's obituary of Zygmunt Hertz, the ebullient editor of the emigré Paris journal *Kultura.* Just as the image of the photographer may by chance be captured in the backdrop of his photograph—mirror, shadow or window—so we catch a suddenly human glimpse of Milosz, 'Czesiu', reproached and cherished friend of the dead man. The essay works as a two-way tribute. Somehow it is reassuring to find that in Milosz's severe world, where we're too often reminded of our failings, there's room in the pantheon for a fat, jolly man with a generous laugh, a liking for gossip, a permanent readiness to feast.

Sally Laird, "Poetic Pathology of Our Century," in Observer, *November 22, 1992, p. 64.*

FURTHER READING

Airaudi, Jesse T. "Eliot, Miłosz, and the Enduring Modernist Protest." *Twentieth Century Literature* 34, No. 4 (Winter 1988): 453-67.

Argues that Miłosz belongs to the Modernist tradition because like T.S. Eliot, his work shares a "sense of catastrophe and the need to remember," and both poets "offer schemes for transforming society through imaginative synthesis."

Czarnecka, Ewa, and Fiut, Aleksander. *Conversations with Czesław Miłosz.* Translated by Richard Lourie. San Diego: Harcourt Brace Jovanovich, 1987, 332 p.

Collects interviews with Miłosz.

Gardels, Nathan. "The Withering Away of Society." *New Perspectives Quarterly* 5, No. 3 (Fall 1988): 55-8.

Interview in which Miłosz discusses his work and the implications of contemporary politics for artists.

Grosholz, Emily. "Miłosz and the Moral Authority of Poetry." *The Hudson Review* XXXIX, No. 2 (Summer 1986): 251-70.

Examines the capacity of Miłosz's poetry to influence individual morality.

Możejko, Edward, ed. *Between Anxiety and Hope: The Poetry and Writing of Czesław Miłosz.* Alberta: University of Alberta Press, 1988, 190 p.

Collection of critical essays about Miłosz and his work.

Nathan, Leonard, and Quinn, Arthur. *The Poet's Work: An Introduction to Czesław Miłosz.* Cambridge, Mass.: Harvard University Press, 1991, 178 p.

Comprehensive discussion of Miłosz's themes.

Additional coverage of Miłosz's life and career is contained in the following sources published by Gale Research: *Contemporary Authors,* Vols. 81-84; *Contemporary Authors New Revision Series,* Vol. 23; *Contemporary Literary Criticism,* Vols. 5, 11, 22, 31, 56; and *Major 20th-Century Writers.*

Paul Monette

1945-

American memoirist, novelist, and poet.

The following entry provides an overview of Monette's career through 1992.

INTRODUCTION

A prominent figure in the genre of gay and lesbian literature, Monette is best known for his autobiographical writings, particularly *Borrowed Time: An AIDS Memoir* and *Becoming A Man: Half a Life Story.* His works focus on contemporary issues within the gay community: AIDS, its impact on relationships, and the political and social controversies surrounding homosexuality. Likening the AIDS epidemic to the genocide of a generation of gay men, Monette has commented that writing about AIDS is "the only thing a gay writer can honestly do right now."

Monette was born in Lawrence, Massachusetts, and raised in Andover. He received a scholarship to Phillips Academy, a prep school in Andover, and following graduation attended Yale University. Monette has described growing up in the 1950s and 1960s as traumatic, noting that the conservative middle class blatantly discriminated against homosexuals and subsequently led him to deny his sexuality. After graduating from Yale, Monette taught English at two prep schools, being disciplined at one for having a relationship with a male student. He spent two years in therapy, during which he came to terms with his homosexuality. Several months after coming out in the early 1970s, he met comparative literature scholar and law student Roger Horwitz, the man who was to become his longtime companion, in Boston. In 1975 Monette's first collection of poetry, *The Carpenter at the Asylum,* was published, and two years later Monette and Horwitz moved to Los Angeles, where Horwitz began a law practice and Monette a career as a novelist and screenwriter. In 1985 Horwitz was diagnosed with AIDS and Monette temporarily gave up writing in order to care for him. Three weeks after Horwitz's death in 1986, Monette began writing *Love Alone: Eighteen Elegies for Rog* and *Borrowed Time* to commemorate their relationship and honor Horwitz's memory. In December 1991, Monette was diagnosed with AIDS.

Monette's earliest novels, set in the Los Angeles gay community, are noted for representing homosexual love as conventional and for addressing the misconception that the relationships of gay men are shallow, their lifestyles hedonistic, and their sexual behavior promiscuous. His first novel, *Taking Care of Mrs. Carroll,* which Monette described as a "baroque scam with some gay sex in it," focuses on a homosexual couple and an actress who conspire to inherit a deceased woman's wealth. *The Gold Diggers* similarly concerns a gay couple and a female friend who become embroiled in an art theft. These first two novels were criticized for their fantastic plots, but were praised for their convincing characters. Monette's 1983 novel, *Lightfall,* a mystery involving a religious cult, was similarly faulted for its contrived plot.

Focusing on the universal themes of love, intimacy, loss, and grief, Monette's subsequent works are highly autobiographical. *Love Alone,* a collection of eighteen elegies for Horwitz, memorializes their love and the tragic end of their twelve-year relationship. Whether Monette is screaming "down an empty road" or taking umbrage with the federal government for its cavalier attitude toward the AIDS crisis, the poems encompass the psychological spectrum of sorrow, memory, despair, and rage. *Borrowed Time,* which was nominated for a National Book Critics Circle Award in 1988 for best biography or autobiography, portrays Horwitz's battle with AIDS and the people and institutions involved. Incorporating notes from his journals, Monette provides a detailed account of Horwitz's mental and physical deterioration: pneumocystis, blindness, incontinence, the threat of dementia, and eventually meningitis. While *Borrowed Time* has been praised for eschewing public condemnation of homosexuals for the spread of AIDS, it has been criticized for failing to overtly address the immediate political issues surrounding the disease, particularly funding for indigent care, discrimination against persons with AIDS, and the promotion of AIDS research as a national priority. Mark Edmundson comments that *Borrowed Time* "rarely concerns itself directly with the larger political issues that [Randy Shilts's *And the Band Played On*] engages," but that it succeeds in increasing public awareness about the epidemic and its devastating impact on the gay community. While *Borrowed Time* concentrates on themes of love and loss, *Becoming a Man: Half a Life Story,* which won a National Book Award for nonfiction in 1992, is Monette's account of growing up gay in the 1950s and 1960s and coming out during the 1970s. The title refers to the second half of Monette's life, the half in which he feels he truly lived. Describing the first twenty-five years of his life as a time of confusion, asexuality, and denial, Monette claims that coming out initiated feelings of self-liberation and self-affirmation despite the discrimination he encountered in mainstream society. Noting that Monette frequently casts himself as a victim of homophobia, Wendy Martin has perceived in *Becoming a Man* the "familiar model of polarization—the oppressed and the oppressors—that has characterized American reform movements."

Monette's most recent novels, *Afterlife* and *Halfway Home,* continue to examine the AIDS crisis and its effect on interpersonal relationships. *Afterlife* documents the friendship that develops between three HIV-positive AIDS widowers. Often described as a fictionalized continuation of *Borrowed Time,* the novel is considered an honest portrait of gay male behavior that speaks to both homosexual and heterosexual audiences. *Halfway Home* concerns a young man dying of AIDS who is reunited with his older brother from whom he has been estranged for several years. As the siblings recall painful childhood memories of rage, abuse, and incest, an ironic role reversal occurs in which the protagonist ends up caring for the emotional needs of the older brother. Critics have observed that *Afterlife* and *Halfway Home* are remarkable for their universal relevance and sensitive portrayal of the stages of death and mourning: denial, anger, acceptance, and forgiveness.

PRINCIPAL WORKS

The Carpenter at the Asylum (poetry) 1975
Taking Care of Mrs. Carroll (novel) 1978
The Gold Diggers (novel) 1979
Nosferatu: The Vampyre [adaptor; from the screenplay by Werner Herzog] (novel) 1979
The Long Shot (novel) 1981
No Witnesses (poetry) 1981
Lightfall (novel) 1982
Scarface [adaptor; from the screenplay by Oliver Stone] (novel) 1983
Borrowed Time: An AIDS Memoir (memoirs) 1988
Love Alone: Eighteen Elegies for Rog (poetry) 1988
Afterlife (novel) 1990
Halfway Home (novel) 1991
Becoming a Man: Half a Life Story (memoirs) 1992

CRITICISM

Alfred Corn (review date September 1976)

[*An award-winning American poet, Corn is also a critic, editor, and lecturer. In the following excerpt, he provides a stylistic and thematic analysis of* The Carpenter at the Asylum.]

The carpenter in the title poem of Paul Monette's first book [***The Carpenter at the Asylum***] represents The Poet—one understood as *homo faber;* an inmate, "certifiable" like the others, but with the difference that he builds. At least Monette so conceives him in one poem. More often his narrator speaks in the manner not of the Carpenter, but of the Walrus in Lewis Carroll's poem, who lulls his audience into dreamy compliance with talk "Of shoes—and ships—and sealing-wax— / Of cabbages and kings— / And why the sea is boiling hot— / And whether pigs have wings." Monette is altogether prepared to accommodate in his poems as much of the world as will go, even if that should prove to be everything. Seasons, museums, laundry, Monette invites a phenomenal sundry to congregate in these poems, not with formal or narrative logic but by simple assemblage, resolute metonymy. The *homo* to speak of here is not *faber* so much as *ludens.* All twenty-five poems are written in the present tense, with a kind of sportive, Thurberesque *élan,* the discourse of a runner in good condition and with excellent wind.

> Come spread out your jigsaw souvenirs,
> the cliff walks in linen shoes at Brighton,
> the calling boatman by your hill window
> in Amalfi. We steer clear of uplands,
>
> our hunger is different. Just now I
> hear the smart knocks and bells throng
> in the beachboard towns. The ocean is
> a clumsy maze at the borders of white,
>
> light sea cities. . . .
>
> **"Hansel to Gretel"**

Each poem is composed in stanzas of a fixed number, from three to eight lines long (no seven-liners, however). This template of pattern is there, I think, largely *pro forma,* for the eye alone. Most of the lines bear four stresses, but the characteristic appears to be accidental, not used in expressive variation. It's as though this minimal, stanzaic shaping is all Monette considers fair to impose on—what to call it?—reality. Beyond that he leaves the world to its own centrifugal tendencies. One could without great distortion read the whole book as a single work, the division of it into separately titled poems so often seeming a purely "fiscal" matter, not made according to any schedule of genre or calendar of recurrence.

One irony attached to the epitaph Keats composed for himself, "Here lies one whose name was writ in water", comes from its having been carved on his tombstone. Another is that, of course, his name will always be remembered, along with all his great poems on flux and transcience. Monette shares with Keats a fascination with the flux of things; he sees poetic fictions themselves, so long at least as they cling to some notion of "truth", as evanescent, provisional "fixes" on a fluid reality. He states the idea memorably:

> . . . This tells
> us nothing of our delays, which dreams
> petrify, which ones trace their figure
> like a brief handprint in wet weather.
>
> **"The Girl in the Field"**

Here, as in other poems, Monette prefers an elegant ambiguity of syntax and reference to lapidary sententiousness. The reader is asked to participate in the creation of meaning because the poems themselves try to catch the world on something like a brink, still innocent of significance, not having yet put on a mask, fallen into meaning, and become "hypocritical". The poems offer not the fruit of knowledge or experience but their flowering, not Ithaca but the journey toward it:

> . . . Keep watch
> for the singular passage. Be casual. Out
>
> of sight of land and about to surrender,
> you arrive without warning at a languid
> shoreline and smile as if nothing at all
> had ended. . . .
>
> **"Contexts"**

By dint of their perseverance toward "singular passages", the poems dazzle; preferring virtuoso effects to plot, they give the kind of pleasure associated with, say, Monet's *Waterlilies,* or the music of Liszt. Monette has many poetic gifts, and he writes with a wonderful lack of strain. This very facility of course may become an obstacle, and the question now is whether in subsequent books he will acquire some kind of strengthening difficulty—formal, narrative, or substantive, for example—which might act as a sieve for his phenomenal embarrassment of riches. (pp. 355-56)

Alfred Corn, "Asylum," in Poetry, *Vol. CXXVIII, No. 6, September, 1976, pp. 355-58.*

Alfred Corn (review date 4 March 1979)

[*In the following review, Corn classifies* The Gold Diggers *as a "prose romance" and praises Monette's use of characterization and setting.*]

Paul Monette is the rule-breaking sort of novelist. Readers noticed that temperament in his first novel, ***Taking Care of Mrs. Carroll,*** and will find it in this second, along with the psychological subtlety and stylistic elaboration that seem to be his special talents. The first rule he breaks prescribes that novels must be "realistic," plausible, and even autobiographical—at least when they're not cast in a fantasy genre like sci-fi. Monette stands between the two extremes: he writes a naturalistic prose romance.

Drawing his setting from the world we inhabit and his characters from the stock of recognizable contemporary personality, he scrambles expectations by introducing untoward and sometimes fantastic happenings into the plot. This kind of prose romance, historically, counts a few master pieces—*Moby-Dick, The Marble Faun, The Trial*—but many more failures or near-failures. *The Picture of Dorian Gray,* for example, despite local incandescences, doesn't finally come off: Wilde loses focus halfway along, and the lurid dénouement could be summed up by recasting something Wilde himself said about Dickens: "Only a man with a heart of stone could fail to laugh at the end of *Dorian Gray.*"

The Gold Diggers has as many flaws as Wilde's prose romance, but in fact most of these go hand in hand with the rare and improbable pleasures offered by the book. The story unfolds in Los Angeles, or rather L.A., as all the characters have it. But this is an L.A. out of movieland or, the same thing, dreamland: an imaginative wizard behind a silver screen keeps the plot always on the boil, arranging for coincidences of the wildest kind, conjuring up sex, violence, cash, and beautiful things—landscapes, houses, silks, jewels, paintings, bronzes, chests—to keep readers enthralled. It's a book filled with what the Industry calls "production values."

What distinguishes ***The Gold Diggers*** from the kind of book you buy in one airport lobby and discard in the next is, first, its believable, in-the-round characters. The linchpin, clearly, is Rita—smart, humane, no longer an ingenue but, as they say, "attractive." She chucks New York, along with a number of other passionate, destructive affairs, and catches up with her friend Peter out on the Coast, where he's become a superstar interior designer. Peter descends, romantically, from displaced Russian nobility, but otherwise there's no nonsense about him. He lives with Nick, handsome and stalwart in a familiar western way. How the destinies of these three reasonable and feeling people (plus a hustler with the heart of a rattlesnake) intertwine among themselves and with a cache of stolen art treasures belongs to the narrative practices of prose romance mentioned before.

More original are these pages' unerring presentation of the way people—at least some of them—talk and think nowadays. For example, Rita's reaction when introduced to Nick: "He didn't look gay in the least, she thought, mentally slapping her hand." Graceful and funny observations like this abound; and much of the freshness comes from the book's taking for granted that people of the same sex are attracted to each other and fall in love. Here, too, Paul Monette breaks the rule that would have the world of the sexual ten percent clouded with guilt, the threat of exposure, and self-destructive behavior. The dilemmas in this novel have nothing to do with either self-recrimination or "coming out as gay." All their heterosexual friends and clients know Nick and Peter are a couple, and, if anything, take a mildly proprietary stance toward the relationship. (Whether this counts as one of the dreamlike ingredients of ***The Gold Diggers*** Angelenos must debate among themselves.)

The real coming out of the closet in the book has to do with the hedonism and "enlightened" materialism of the '70s. L.A. was always a little more of a money town than other American cities. But it's obvious that the new wave cares only about money as a stepping-stone to the real thing—pretty clothes, a fabulous house filled with things, ambrosial food and drink, and beautiful sex partners. Or does this oversimplify matters? Possibly the new sensuousness is only a screen covering a greater pleasure: the sense that the consumer has outdistanced his competition, by knowing what to consume, and then managing to get it. Competition, the harmonic of self-doubt, may be the final American and Puritan passion.

If so, ***The Gold Diggers*** has plenty of data to offer on the question, and L.A. was the logical place to begin research. At the end of the western road civilization has taken, this locale has given Paul Monette a cast of self-improvising Americans who perform in the oldest romantic drama, one asking again whether any earthly moment, however fair, could stay, and stay dissatisfaction. (pp. 1, 4)

Alfred Corn, "Laid Back in L.A.," in Book World—The Washington Post, *March 4, 1979, pp. 1, 4.*

Lola D. Gillebaard (review date 27 March 1983)

[In the following review, Gillebaard offers a negative assessment of Lightfall.*]*

[Paul Monette's ***Lightfall***] made little sense to me during a first reading, so I read it twice. The second time around, it made no sense at all. Critic Robert Kirsch used to say a book can be considered a success if the author accomplishes what he set out to do. If Paul Monette succeeded, his purpose remains his own secret.

The plot doesn't thicken, it veers. Connecticut psychiatrist and mother Iris Ammons is possessed by an unyielding force to go to the isolated village of Pitt's Landing, Calif. On the same day, Michael Roman, Reverend of the Revelation Cult, kills his three closest associates, abandons his hideout and commands his disciples worldwide to join him in the same village.

There, ritual begins. Liturgy rambles as the discontinuous plot continues. Under the strange potency of a full solar eclipse—the lightfall—Michael and Iris love, hate, charm and kill, driving the villagers to leap into the sea.

Animals hover, children chant and the teeth gnash. The reader knows who and what, but never why. Characters are not motivated but driven, controlled by an unknown hypnotic power. They destroy the village piece by piece and enter a nether world of violence, drugs, illicit sex and murder.

Though Monette has a poet's way with words, to whom will this book appeal? The mystery is too thin and slow to appeal to mystery buffs. The characters are too one-dimensional to appeal to escapist tastes.

As Michael himself says about his religious cult, "All they needed was a little mumbo jumbo and a wafer." That's what Monette offers, without the wafer.

Lola D. Gillebaard, "Mystery Darkened by a Full Solar Eclipse," in Los Angeles Times Book Review, *March 27, 1983, p. 13.*

Gregory Woods (review date 21 October 1988)

[An Egyptian-born critic, poet, fiction writer, and lecturer who resides in England, Woods often writes about homosexuality and homoeroticism. In the following review, he offers a positive assessment of Borrowed Time.*]*

In March 1985, after a period of intermittent ill-health, Roger Horwitz was diagnosed as having AIDS. He died in October 1986. ***Borrowed Time*** is his lover's memoir of the calamity they shared. The story involves a gruelling physical descent from weakness and weight loss, via initial tests and rumours, through recurrent lung infection (PCP), blindness, incontinence, the threat of dementia, to death itself.

Their emotional struggle involves coping not only with illness itself, but also with myth, the insensitivity of medics, the deaths of friends, the need to keep the disease secret at a time of media panic, thoughts of suicide, and so on. With the experience of coming out as homosexual behind them, they now find they have to come out again, first to themselves and then to others, as being HIV positive, and then as having developed AIDS. Monette is particularly sensitive to the feelings of Horwitz's parents: having once accepted only slowly the fact that he was gay, they now have to find the courage not to think of his sexuality as mere doom.

Monette is aware of his and his lover's relatively favoured situation. "In this enterprise we were fortunate to have privileges: we knew the right people and had enough money." Indeed, one of the book's consistent horrors is the extent to which they had to rely on such privilege. After barely surviving the toxicity of the drug Suramin, Horwitz became the first patient west of the Mississippi to be put on AZT, this as a consequence of rumours from the east, behind-scenes persuasion, and a healthy bank-balance. Jockeying for drugs becomes a central part of the nightmare: since the US Government has turned drug research over to private industry, the nature of one's treatment is determined by the market. The grotesque result is seen in Monette's account of smuggling missions to buy drugs in Mexico.

The book is written in rather restless, obsessively metaphorical prose. This is obtrusive at first, but the subject soon muscles in with its own momentum. Since both men kept diaries, the account is detailed; and Monette has dutifully checked his own impressions against the memories of relatives and friends. This was his way of negotiating grief and the continuing threat to his own health. Other projects helped, too. During the final weeks of Horwitz's life, Monette anchored himself to "normality" by writing the novelisation of an Arnold Schwarzenegger movie.

To write about AIDS is largely a question of bearing witness. (This clearly evokes a parallel with Holocaust memoirs.) As Monette says, "We cannot all go down to defeat and darkness, we have to say we have been here." The fact that gay men have a voice with which to do so is one of the great triumphs of the Gay Movement in the western democracies. The Seventies gave us, not our vulnerability to AIDS, but the strength to fight it. This is where one must locate the real threat of gagging measures like Clause 28: for we have learnt from our own history that (as the current slogan has it) Silence = Death.

Monette has served Roger Horwitz as well after death as he did before. (He has also published a collection of elegies to his memory.) Homophobes who do not want their minds changed had better steer clear: ***Borrowed Time*** is a massive affirmation of *true* love. It is also an incitement to action. As Monette says, in referring to the courage of Winnie Mandela: "They take your life away whether you fight or not, so you might as well fight." A less robust survivor, succumbing to despair, could have said you might as well *not.*

Gregory Woods, "Last Rites," in New Statesman & Society, *Vol. 1, No. 20, October 21, 1988, p. 36.*

William Goldstein (essay date 2 December 1988)

[*In the following excerpt, based on a conversation between Monette and Goldstein, Monette discusses* Borrowed Time, *his relationship with Roger Horwitz, and his aims as a gay writer.*]

[After touring the country to promote his book ***Borrowed Time,***] Paul Monette realized he had become a sort of "sero-positive poster child" for many who saw him on television or heard him on the radio—the only living representation of a "calamity" that many people, he says, are still only "dimly aware of. I often asked people, 'Is anyone you know or love sick?' and they would shake their head no. Inside I'd be thinking, 'just wait a little while.' "

Monette has tested positive for the AIDS virus but does not have the disease (some reviews of ***Borrowed Time*** indicated he did). "When I talk to any audience," he says, "I realize that the 10% of the audience that's gay is connecting, in one way or another, but that I make no headway at all against people who hate and fear me. I feel myself hoping that I'm connecting to whatever percentage of an audience that's the mothers and fathers and sisters and brothers and friends of gay people, because I can tell how much people long to understand about this situation."

Monette did not write ***Borrowed Time,*** an anguished remembrance of the death of his lover, Roger Horwitz, from AIDS, for the present. "I meant the first sentence of the book when I wrote it: 'I'm not sure I'll live to finish this.' I'm glad I did, I'm glad I'm here. I want to stay here for a while. But I just didn't plan it. . . . If in fact this book sells a lot of copies, great," he says. . . . "But the impulse to write the book was very much to leave a record for the future, rather than the present. I felt every day I was writing this book that I was writing it for people 20 or 50 years from now. Because they will understand that gay people went through a holocaust. I use this word advisedly, I don't mean to appropriate it from the Jewish people, but it is a holocaust. Though the genocide is passive on the part of the Reagan administration, it is no less willful for being passive."

Monette is careful, when speaking of politics, to differentiate his book from Randy Shilts's *And the Band Played On.* Television producers reluctant to book him complained, he says, that there were too many books on AIDS, that they had covered "the Shilts." Monette says: "A lot of people talked to me about that book—a book I immensely admire—and I began to think about what the differences are. Reading *And the Band Played On* is like watching the Titanic move toward the ice—it's just this incredible juggernaut of political energy heading toward catastrophe. I am trying more to give a picture of what things are like from within the borders of the war. . . .

"I wanted to write something," Monette continues, "that would break hearts because it would show how much gay people loved each other; to give my people the record of who we were, so if anyone would try to foist off on them in the future—and I don't doubt they will try to—that it was all about a bunch of people screwing their brains out—that there would be a picture of some of the loving instead."

A nationwide book tour, with appearances on *Good Morning America* and National Public Radio, and a total sale of more than 25,000 copies indicate that ***Borrowed Time*** has found an audience in the present. "It turns out from some of my mail, even from people who are sick or diagnosed," Monette says, "that the book does seem to crystallize some of the anger and pain. I realized while writing that in addition to leaving a record, the book was a chance to join the debate."

With *Borrowed Time* I wanted to write something that would break hearts because it would show how much gay people loved each other; to give my people the record of who we were, so if anyone would try to foist off on them in the future that it was all about a bunch of people screwing their brains out, there would be a picture of some of the loving instead.

—Paul Monette

Writing was, for Monette, a form of "mourning and catharsis. I now see that the year I spent writing about Roger after he died, first the poems [***Love Alone: 18 Elegies for Rog***] and then ***Borrowed Time,*** was very much a way of staying in the white heat of the fight. Our fight had kept him alive, and since keeping him alive was all I'd wanted to do for two years, doing the writing did the same thing. I may have only begun the really bewildering grieving process after I was finished. People ask, 'Was it a hard book to write?' Well, most of it wasn't. It was just so necessary that it didn't matter."

Two of Monette's earlier novels, ***Taking Care of Mrs. Carroll*** and ***The Long Shot,*** have been reissued this year. . . . He is now working on a new novel, *War Widows,* which is about the effect of AIDS on the gay community. One editor who saw Monette's proposal for ***Borrowed Time*** rejected the book, but suggested Monette turn it into fiction. *War Widows* is not, Monette says, a fictionalized version of ***Borrowed Time***—but writing about AIDS, Monette believes, is about the only thing a gay writer can honestly do right now. "I was told by several publishers when I sent out the proposal for ***Borrowed Time*** that they weren't interested because there would be a lot of books like it. But there aren't. The level of suffering is just not reported [in the press]. The world has not adequately understood the death of a generation of gay men."

Monette says: "I don't expect people to understand me as a writer. Somebody said to me, 'What do you think Roger Horwitz would most want to be remembered for?' And I said, 'Well, I know that I'd like to be remembered most for being Roger's friend, and I think that if you asked him he would say the same thing about me.' It's all very well and good to be all the other things we are, but what Roger and I achieved in this life was this relationship. And nothing else made any difference at all. Writing makes a lot of difference to me now. I'm very, very glad I have my writing, and I'm very glad I had my skills as a writer in order to try to tell this story. I feel a kind of comfort that people who read this book understand how wonderful Roger was. That does help." (pp. 19-20)

William Goldstein, "Paul Monette Reflects on AIDS and His Own 'Borrowed Time'," in Publishers Weekly, *Vol. 234, No. 23, December 2, 1988, pp. 19-20.*

Mark Edmundson (review date 2 March 1989)

[*In the following excerpt, Edmundson laments the lack of political commentary on AIDS funding and research in* Borrowed Time, *but praises the volume's elegiac prose style and universal relevance.*]

Borrowed Time is Paul Monette's elegy for his lover, Roger Horwitz, who died of illnesses stemming from AIDS on 22 October 1986, and though the book contains its complement of anger and fear, it is chiefly a labour of grief. Monette pursues a pair of related objectives. He struggles, first, to record every critical moment of his lover's illness and of the life they shared before Roger became ill. The human wish behind this activity is paradoxical, both to preserve and to distance the past. And, like every elegy, ***Borrowed Time*** is about the search for a language that is adequate to the particular loss.

When Monette and Horwitz met in Boston in 1974, important changes were taking place in gay life in America. Both men were born in the Forties, and grew up in a culture that was virulently homophobic: America seemed unwilling to accept men who deviated more than a little from the box-shouldered heterosexual norm. Perhaps the events of the Sixties made society more receptive to human difference, though it's hard to imagine many members of the 'counter-culture' subscribing, for example, to the gay shibboleth that we're all perpetually dressed in drag. (That is, we use clothes and manner to fabricate a conventional gender identity that's inconsistent with the shifting, unconventional nature of our individual desires.) What did matter was the political power gays acquired in cities like New York and San Francisco. By 1977, the Castro district of San Francisco had chosen Harvey Milk for the City Board of Supervisors, making him the country's first openly gay elected official. When a State Senator named John Briggs introduced an amendment that would have prevented gays from teaching in the California public schools, a grass-roots movement, led by Milk, rose and defeated the Bill by a two-to-one majority. Gay power was at its high-water mark. It was around that time that Monette and Horwitz moved west, to Los Angeles, where gays had won a measure of respect—if never quite benevolent acceptance—for themselves. The two men succeeded professionally: Roger opened up a private law practice; Paul sold his novels and wrote screenplays for the major studios. In the midst of numerous distractions and threats, they kept their relationship intact.

In February of 1985, Roger got sick. He had flu that wouldn't disappear—fevers, congestion, sweats. The gay community in Los Angeles was far behind San Francisco and New York in what it knew about AIDS, and most of the available evidence met, as Monette frequently says, with vigorous forms of denial. Gays in America, as in England, have had the responsibility of educating themselves: though various official sources continually remind us that AIDS is 'the gay disease', no government education programmes for young people have been aimed at the gay audience in either country. It is said that brochures about AIDS had to be smuggled into England from America in diplomatic pouches, so that they would not be confiscated as pornography. (p. 22)

In ***Borrowed Time*** Monette habitually describes the AIDS crisis in terms of a war, with those who have AIDS and their lovers and friends cast as a group of determined and continually depleted guerrilla fighters. Two influential dramas, Larry Kramer's *The Normal Heart* and William Hoffman's *As Is,* compared people with AIDS to the Jews suffering Nazi persecution. This comparison has the virtue of rather brutally illuminating the moral condition of those who watch the catastrophe with detachment. Yet the metaphors of combat and persecution seem to me finally to be inadequate. They personify the adversary too much, as though the virus might have motives, might feel pain or fear. Such figurations imply that 'fighting' the disease is a matter of the patient's power of will, which could in turn induce unjust guilt for his 'failure' to hold his own. AIDS is so threatening in part because there probably are no acceptable anthropomorphic images which could dramatise the danger, and thus turn humanity's obligatory encounter with the syndrome into a heroic narrative of some sort.

One constituency that has had no trouble in representing

AIDS to its own satisfaction is the extreme right wing, and particularly the religious Right. Pat Buchanan, an editorial writer who enjoyed high favour in the Reagan White House, achieved some notoriety from his assertion that the 'homosexuals' were now reaping the reward for spilling their seed on barren ground. Moral Majority leader Jerry Falwell, who delivered the benediction for the session of the 1984 Republican Convention at which Reagan was re-nominated, said on one occasion that 'when you violate moral, health and hygiene laws, you reap the whirlwind. You cannot shake your fist in God's face and get by with it.' The seed-spilling/unnatural act topos has been fully developed by the nation's televangelists, a couple of whom, as recent scandals have revealed, had seed-spillings of their own to explain. Some Medieval theologians thought that one of the pleasures of paradise would be that of looking down at the damned writhing in eternal torment; and in the Age of Reason, a Sunday afternoon on the balcony of the local lunatic asylum occasionally qualified as good entertainment. The homophobic zealots can refer back to a long tradition of sanctified sadism. But it is unlikely that even the more devoted could read about the sufferings Monette chronicles in ***Borrowed Time*** with unbroken approval for the acts of their vengeful god.

Almost every infection the Immune Deficiency precipitates is itself treatable, so that Roger is incapacitated many times, only to recover to the point where he can once again go out for a walk, have dinner with friends, see a movie or a play. But then a new infection arrives, and his body, depleted from past sickness, is worn further down. The cruel rhythms of AIDS derange much of our received wisdom about death from protracted illness. Usually a degenerative sickness, despite the sufferings it imposes, allows a person to take gradual leave of the world, and lets his friends and family prepare for the loss. But AIDS continually makes partial restitution. Thus it compounds the sorrow of people who have learned from childhood that a sane and dignified death follows the patterns of closure they encounter in well-wrought poems or musical compositions, with their serenely contoured and allusive trailings-off into silence.

Despite all that is unprecedented about the AIDS affliction, Monette and Horwitz still manage to summon large energies to fight it. They're continually struggling: researching possible new cures; trading information with friends; pressing every doctor they know for fresh data; hustling to get into treatment programmes. Roger improves, but then a fresh infection comes on, or the side-effects from AZT (azidothymidine), the one drug that does palpably slow the progress of AIDS, send him into a relapse. There is—Kafka's epigram is brutally apt—no end of hope: Roger recovers almost completely from a case of pneumonia; he returns to his law office; he hears reports from a friend whose condition has stabilised: but every hope eventually comes to nothing. Part of Monette's achievement in ***Borrowed Time*** lies in his making each moment in his lover's illness a distinct one. He remembers exactly the joy they felt on the day that Roger recovered 30 per cent of his vision, or on the afternoon late in the illness when they could take a quiet swim together. And of course every loss is just as emphatically scored on the text. But the book is as affecting as it is partly because each event isn't cast in the sombre tones of Roger's eventual death. One experiences, though at a remove, what Monette did—vast suffering, but also isolated moments of grace and happiness.

Some assumptions about gay life would be undermined if ***Borrowed Time*** got the wide reading it deserves. The standard mythology that pictures gays as pouty, shallow and self-obsessed doesn't come close to applying here. Two things happen to most of the gay men in the book: they contract AIDS and suffer horribly from it, or they devote themselves to a friend or to friends with the syndrome. They visit, give presents, cook and clean, change dripping sheets, move bedpans, administer injections, extend comfort where they can, share sorrow when comfort would be obscene.

Monette's portraits of friends and acquaintances seem candid, but there's another side of the story about which he's puzzlingly reticent. Part of what's frightening about AIDS is the expense involved in treating it. The hospital care required can, in America, which has no national health insurance, wipe out an average life's savings in a few months. But Monette is never entirely forthright about where he and Roger find the money for treatment. Occasionally Paul does express gratitude for being upper-middle-class and having the right connections to get Roger sophisticated care. But he never pushes that perception to the point where he can reflect on the overall social and economic issues (and injustices) that are involved. Downplaying financial matters puts emphasis on the book's 'human drama': it makes the story seem more 'universal' and 'spiritual', and less determined by a particular social and economic context. This 'spiritualising technique' is in one sense good for the book: it makes it easier for middle-class, heterosexual readers to respond to a story about gays. What's lost in the process is the opportunity for political reflection.

Monette's depictions of the members of the medical community are frequently as affecting as his portraits of the friends who go to such lengths to help. There are a few iced-over medical technocrats and some freshly groomed interns from the heights of the Ivy League who don't want to get too close. But one thinks also of the nurse who rather casually tells a group of her colleagues that medical care now means dealing with AIDS patients, and that anyone who can't handle that should find a new job. There's also Roger's doctor Dennis Cope, to whom the book is dedicated. Cope seems to be one of those rare physicians with both technical expertise and a capacious heart. He's capable of some acute diagnostic work, but also of crying out in grief when Roger calls and tells him that he's lost his sight.

Yet the American medical establishment at large comes in for far less credit than do individuals like Cope. Randy Shilts's comprehensive account of the AIDS crisis, *And the band played on,* persuasively argues that the Government, the mass media and the national medical community were slow to respond to the situation, and for the simple reason that it was gays, drug addicts and prostitutes—marginal social types—who were suffering. AIDS only counted as newsworthy in the early Eighties, when the story involved risks to heterosexuals. When seven people died in 1982 from taking cyanide-laced capsules of Tylenol, a common aspirin substitute, there was an explosion of media interest. The *New York Times* published a story a day on the 'Tylenol scare' for a full month. Government agencies worked in swift concert, changing regulations, clearing the shelves of potentially contaminated drugs, chasing down the perpetrators. At the same point in time, 260 Americans had died of AIDS. The *Times* wrote three stories on the epidemic in all of 1982: this when some doctors were predicting that AIDS would wipe out tens of thousands. Speaking in front of the White House, Arthur Bennett, a person with AIDS, said: 'I think in the beginning of this whole syndrome, that they, over there, and a lot of other people said: "Let the faggots die. They're expendable." I wonder if it would have been 1500 Boy Scouts, what would have been done.'

Borrowed Time rarely concerns itself directly with the larger political issues that Shilts's history engages. Monette's book is in many ways a private meditation, a pained remembrance that the reader overhears. And yet it does have a public effect, which is to make very particular and graphic the loss entailed in the addition of one number more to the rising sum. Of all the array of persons one meets in ***Borrowed Time***—the cast must exceed a hundred—one surely admires Horwitz most. His perseverance and stoical resolve throughout the ordeal are astonishing; it is frequently he who has to prop up Monette. At one point we find Roger—and the image is, I think, the most representative in the book—late in his illness, pulling himself out of bed and fastening on a tie, so that he can deliver on a promise and do free legal work for the Homeless Women's Shelter.

But the subtler evidence of the dimensions of the loss perhaps derives from Monette, who seems to have been changed through the writing of the book. The prose in the first half of ***Borrowed Time*** is frequently embarrassing: people suffer 'stabs' of pain, they 'bristle' with anger, 'bristle' with pride. Monette can be glib and silly: 'If laughter was therapeutic, there were days we could have cured the common cold.' Self-indulgent: 'Narcissus and I are not unacquainted.' And over-dramatic: 'You fight tough, you fight dirty, but you can not fight dirtier than it.' But as the book evolves, Monette comes closer and closer to a language that's adequate to his grief. Here he describes his feelings on changing the dressing over Roger's afflicted eye:

> Finally something to do. And when you do this part you come to see there's something nearly sacred—a word I can't get the God out of, I know—about being a wound dresser. To be that intimate with flesh and blood, so close to the body's ache to heal, you learn how little to take for granted, defying death in the bargain. You are an instrument and your engine is concentration. There's not a lot of room for ego when you're swabbing the open wound of an eye.

The stance here is humbler, more impersonal, and more honestly vulnerable to mystery, than it was earlier in the book. Only the grandiloquent 'defying death in the bargain' remains as a residue. Freud describes the work of mourning as the unfathomable process by which we both separate ourselves from, and change so as to resemble, the one that we have lost. At moments in its last hundred or so pages, ***Borrowed Time*** reaches the state to which every elegy aspires: it compels the reader to imagine that it's been co-authored. (pp. 22-3)

Mark Edmundson, "Taking Leave," in London Review of Books, *Vol. 11, No. 5, March 2, 1989, pp. 22-3.*

Gregory Kolovakos (review date 1989)

[Kolovakos is an American translator, critic, and educator. In the following review, he offers a highly laudatory assessment of Borrowed Time *and* Love Alone.*]*

"exactly half the phenomenal world is gone"
—Paul Monette, **"Half Life"**

Growing up in the desolate suburbs of Buffalo in the 1950s and 1960s, there was no escaping the unrelenting reality of prejudice and bigotry of an economically dying northeastern city. Too much of suburban life centered on school athletic competitions, going to drive-ins on Sheridan Drive, frequenting the new shopping malls, criticizing what was perceived as different. The adults who raised us were frightened of anything deviating from their own experience; we children plotted our escapes and in the late sixties many of us left, to return only for funerals years later.

One of my most tenacious memories is of standing by my mother's side (I was age five), squinting into the sun, as she talked with our neighbor, Mrs. Mackey, over the fence dividing our two backyards. It was this woman whom I adored—large, warm, generous with attention the way my mother was not. A policeman walked up the Mackeys' asphalt driveway that afternoon, handed her a note, and stood waiting for a response. He did not wait long; she began to howl in pain, and continued her sobbing at the kitchen table all that afternoon (now surrounded by other neighboring housewives) and all the next day. Nothing by way of explanation was said to me, but somehow, very deeply and quite unconsciously, I understood there had been a death in the family. And in fact twenty years later, when this scene surfaced in a discussion with my mother, I learned that there had been a death of sorts in the Mackey family. Their son, Billy, overweight, pale, always awkward, had been arrested earlier that day for some sort of homosexual solicitation. This was 1956 and the arrival of such news in an Irish Catholic family in Kenmore was worse than a diagnosis of cancer.

The howling of that wounded woman echoes across this essay.

Life in Kenmore was in some ways quite comfortable. Large houses, great shade trees overhanging the streets in the older sections of the village, schools that were a model for the state. Saturday mornings I headed the eight blocks or so to the public library, stopping off in both directions at my grandmother's house for the pastries she baked every weekend. More than anything else in my first sixteen years, it was those trips to the library—carrying more volumes of fiction and drama and history than my thin arms could manage—that showed me there were other worlds out there, fictive and poetic visions that transcended the daily grayness of upstate New York.

Literature, you see, was *my* utopia, a place of escape. It was about other lives, other cultures, it was views of the world that differed so radically from what in that insular suburb we were taught to ignore, to not see.

. . . . .

"Why is this happening I don't know"
("Current Status 1/22/87")

I have not met Paul Monette. A resident of Los Angeles, he is a poet, novelist, screenwriter. I am, as we say in the trade, in arts administration, a New Yorker, a translator of Latin American writers, a teacher in spare moments. But like the Venn diagrams we learned in elementary school, Paul Monette and I have a few intersecting points: We both sought refuge in large cities hundreds or thousands of miles from our hometowns; we both passed years at Yale (although not concurrently); we both knew that we were different from others in the communities in which we were brought up, different at least from the images they held up to identify themselves.

We share, according to my reading of Paul Monette's [***Borrowed Time: An AIDS Memoir*** and ***Love Alone: Eighteen Elegies for Rog***], varied experiences of sexual coming of age and experimentation. But far more importantly we share, in 1988, a virus in our bloodstream that has diminished our ability to fight infections. We have what is politely called an acquired immune deficiency syndrome.

We have one other characteristic in common: our anger. We are angry about the men and women who have died during this epidemic; we are angry about the hypocrisy unleashed by this virus (or these viruses), both within and outside the gay community; we are angry that people we have loved are dead or have disappeared back to their parents' homes to end miserable, punished lives, their deaths only to be concealed by smart family doctors across the heartlands and in the cities of America. Those families certainly don't want to be connected to this virus in any way, even if their own children are dying the miserable deaths it occasions.

All this conceit in recounting fragments of my life is to establish a context for what follows. None of us growing up in the Kenmores of this country was ever quite prepared for the devastation that AIDS is causing among our generation. Daily the papers carry obituaries of people we have worked with; daily the names of past boyfriends and friends go through my head and I don't even know if those men are alive today.

Certainly nothing in my early years of reading about worlds beyond the concrete reality I lived in ever prepared me for writing as immediate and as strong as is in Paul Monette's two books, ***Love Alone*** and ***Borrowed Time: An AIDS Memoir.*** While these passionate books are about two specific men, two friends, coming to terms with the epidemic that we began to read and talk about in the early eighties, I cannot read either book without recognizing the same experiences, without crying for all the men and women who are *our* disappeared.

To review ***Borrowed Time: An AIDS Memoir*** is, in part, to review the life of Roger Horwitz, Paul Monette's "beloved friend." And to what purpose should any of us pretend to review a life? Roger Horwitz is dead, dead at an age far too young. But then many of us in this country are dying at a young age, deaths that make as little sense. Tens of thousands of this same generation died as senselessly, condemned by their government to serve in a war in Southeast Asia. But to review ***Borrowed Time*** is also to deal in the words of Horwitz's survivor, Paul Monette, and his attempt with this book to come to terms with what has happened.

To set forth the biographical data, which hardly matter: Having met in 1973 in Boston, Paul and Roger moved to L.A. in 1977, where Roger eventually opened his own law practice and Paul became a full-time writer. This was "the time before the sickness," and their lives were very comfortable ones, with trips abroad and across the United States, the right dinners, the right fundraisers, the right cars. It was on a Sunday morning in 1982, as the two men were driving to Palm Springs, that Roger Horwitz read an essay in a gay newsmagazine that raised the rumors of some sort of "gay cancer." These memoirs trace the growing intrusion of what would be identified as a virus (HIV)—and of the so-called opportunistic diseases that it allows to attack the body—into the lives of Paul Monette and Roger Horwitz.

However predictable the story may be—the distant thunder of names coming down with Kaposi's sarcoma and PCP and related illnesses, "the grossest misdiagnosis," the lightning striking their close friends early on (an Uruguayan friend, César, is the first of their friends to fight the battle, but there is a roll call here of boyfriends, professional acquaintances, gym buddies who also begin to fall ill)—there were no early indications that something was beginning to go wrong with Roger's body. In March of 1985, according to the Centers for Disease Control, there had been only four-thousand AIDS-related deaths in the United States (Larry Kramer is right in arguing that the numbers are double, triple, what the government would have us believe. We can both list dozens of acquaintances whose death certificates list more "acceptable" causes of decease.) It was in this month that Roger Horwitz received the news that he had pneumocystis, that he would have to start on Bactrim at UCLA Medical Center. This "inquisition in the gay community" had entered their comfortable home. And while it was not limited to the gay world, this disease made certain that "no event was simply itself anymore."

The names spiral upward as friends, colleagues, lovers are euphemistically "diagnosed," as new medicines and new illnesses multiply. Monette becomes angrier as Horwitz becomes gentler, more stoic about a body that is breaking down. The parents, the friends, the relatives must be dealt with, and none of this is ever very easy. The disease becomes a lightning rod for all sorts of bigotry and self-loathing within and outside the gay community. Stories of new drugs and new protocols come in to their answering machine—their network is truly international—and Roger is the first patient west of the Mississippi to be put on AZT. The tragedy is that the ending of the story is never in question: bronchoscopies, pneumonias, hospitalizations, a blindness against which Horwitz and his lover struggle with a Miltonian ferocity, and the death of a good, gentle human being, of meningitis.

The overwhelming force of ***Borrowed Time,*** as strong as hurricane winds against the California coast, lies in its accumulation of the details surrounding the inescapable conclusion. But I caution readers that this memoir does not pretend to represent a decade's decline or the loss of a generation. It is the story of Roger Horwitz's death and Paul Monette's grief. Period. Perhaps there are chroniclers of the dying on Manhattan's Lower East Side or in New York's parks, though I'm not aware of such brave writers; certainly those dying men and women do not have access to the medical care, health insurance, and drugs that we comfortable white males have found for ourselves. Perhaps, too, Monette's anger would increase exponentially if he were to look at the lives of some of the more disenfranchised people with AIDS. "How was it the world went on like this?" Monette asks. It does go on, all the time, in families where cancers, alcoholism, strokes have entered to disrupt forever the daily ordinariness of life. And while Monette believes that "we were about to join a community of the stricken who would not lie down and die," I can name too many men and women who have given up at the first diagnosis of PCP or KS, who have resigned their jobs to wait for death's arrival.

Borrowed Time is Paul Monette's keening against the virus that caused his lover's death. Beneath all the material comfort of their California lives, behind all the literary allusions of these paragraphs is a passion rarely expressed in gay literature. The book has taken on large themes—of loyalty and suffering, of love that is illegal in this country, of death itself—and succeeds in making the reader a part of this story, the story of a handful of men and women overwhelmed by, and lost to, this epidemic. Monette cares not a bit for the politeness expected of us; like the terrifying scalpel blade slowly eased into Horwitz's lung in one of his many bronchoscopies, Monette's prose biopsies the social cancers that this virus has allowed to develop in our society.

. . . . .

pain is not a flower pain is a root
and its work is underground where the moldering
proceeds the bones of all our joy winded
and rained and nothing grows . . .
(from **"Gardenias"**)

In some ways, ***Borrowed Time*** is to ***Love Alone*** what Richard Ellmann's *Joyce* is to *Ulysses.* It is this slim volume of poems, breathless, run-on, hurrying to beat out death itself, it is these eighteen elegies for Roger Horwitz that I would have you read and re-read. They are hymns to Horwitz, they are unabashedly proud poems about love, they are the most forceful attempt to change what has happened to so many of us.

The elegy as poetic form has come into English free of its classical meter, and its flexibility is perfectly suited to Monette's meditations on love, politics, and the death of his lover and his circle of friends. Rilke's *Duino Elegies,* themselves dealing with the artistic impulse and death, resonate behind Monette's poems, but most of all these elegies recall García Lorca's haunting "Lament for Ignacio Sánchez Mejías." Both Lorca and Monette are writing about the deaths of men in their prime and the feelings of those who can only watch with terror as death gores them. If ***Borrowed Time*** is notable for its ability to capture the dailiness of the disease (the pills, the appointments, the mishaps, the crises), the language of these elegies is pared down to a concentrated expression of pain and loss. Verse following verse with few punctuation marks to give the reader a road sign, these poems demand to be read as Paul Monette's own cosmic graffiti, his scrawled signature to say that we—he and Roger and César and all of us—were here. Each of these elegies is similar to the late-blooming gardenias Monette found growing at the back of their home on Kings Road, blooms that he brought each day to his blind and soon-to-be-dead lover.

why not worry worry is like prayer is like
God if you have none they all forget there's
the other side too twelve years and not once
to fret WHO WILL EVER LOVE ME that was
the heaven at the back of time but we had it
here now black on black I wander frantic
never done with worrying but it's mine it's
a cure that's not in the books are you easy
my stolen pal what do you need is it
sleep like sleep you want a pillow a cool
drink oh my one safe place there must be
something just say what it is and it's yours
(from **"The Worrying"**)

Monette is wrong later on in **"Half Life"** when he says he has loved life too much. But the poet's world in this poem is cleaved in two, is schizophrenic in its love and hate, life and death, in what he once had and in what he has today. But he can find no reconciliation in this bifurcated world, in the way that Julio Cortázar would reconcile hemispheres and universes.

Confronted by friends who advise him that it's "time to turn the page," Monette rages back, "BUT THIS *IS* MY PAGE IT CANNOT BE TURNED." Read the anger in poems like **"The Very Same"** or **"Manifesto."** They are extraordinary backhanded slaps to those who would blame the infected for their problems. ". . . doubtless the work of Mrs. Hay / baghwan of the leper set Pooh-bear in hand / purveying love-is-you with an anchorlady's / do and Diane Arbus eyes straight-faced told / a reporter people in train wrecks bring it on / themselves . . ." (**"Manifesto"**). By seizing control of what is written about *our* lives, and by rejecting the easy answers of the medical establishment, Monette has produced his own revolutionary poetic and political manifesto.

my friend and I we laughed for years on end
and the dark fell anyway and all our people
sicken and have no rage the Feds are lying

about the numbers the money goes for toilet
seats in bombers the State of the Union
is pious as Pius washing his hands of Hitler
Jews are not a Catholic charity when is
enough enough I had a self myself
once but he died when do we leave the mirror
and lie down in front of the tanks
(from **"Manifesto"**)

And while it is his anger for which I so admire Monette, it is the despair in **"Three Rings"** or **"Dreaming of You"** that breaks the heart.

. . . robbed of you as I am promising
shortcuts whispering of a Northwest Passage
I nearly lost my mind last week screaming
too late down an empty road but there you are
we're full of the same agony you for an hour
I for the rest the nameless dark hasn't
spared us a pang my love but give us this
if ever either of us lands we are one
cry one dream tight as a black gold ring
(from **"Three Rings"**)

It was Rog who "saw us through," Monette writes in **"Your Sightless Days,"** who was there for a sobbing Paul Monette with the reassurance that *"I'm still here."*

the day has taken you with it and all
there is now is burning dark the only green
is up by the grave and this little thing
of telling the hill I'm here oh I'm here
(from **"Here"**)

These poems reconcile distances by juxtaposing here and there, present and absent, remembered pleasure and pain branded so deeply into the heart. They see us through, the way Roger Horwitz saw his beloved friend through. And perhaps Monette hasn't "the ghost of a lease on a better / world" (**"Readiness"**), but he understands a certain human solidarity. The act of writing here posits readers who will grasp this unspeakable pain, who will, in their understanding, help the poet through his grief. Monette has "heard each melancholy wail," he has in these eighteen poems sent syllables howling out against the madness.

. . . . .

. . . a month before you went
you cried *What happened to our happy life*
staring blind out over the garden Rog
it's here it's here I know because I am
the ghost who haunts us I am the last window
(from **"The House on Kings Road"**)

The poems and the plays and the novels I took out of the Kenmore Public Library were never like these works by Paul Monette. His two books—especially ***Love Alone,*** to which I keep running back to ponder a verse here and there, to re-read when I am most frightened—talk in some extraordinary way about *my* dying days, too. I place the commas, I take the breaths from verse to verse; these elegies are road signs for me in the years that remain.

Just as Mrs. Mackey's terrible howl upon learning of her son's homosexual encounter in 1956 echoes through my life, so too can I hear, far stronger, far prouder, Paul Monette's wail across all these miles. They mingle, these cries, because they represent repression and liberation, fear and acceptance, bigotry and love. Thirty years stretch between that childhood incident and Roger Horwitz's death—a trajectory that, despite this killing virus, has meant the possibility of loving and living our own lives. For all the overwhelming pain and grief in these poems, in these books, the love of two men—Roger Horwitz and Paul Monette—is triumphant. I am sorry that Roger Horwitz is dead; I am thankful that Paul Monette took a doctor's advice and chose to write about the epidemic.

At thirty-seven I review two books that intersect with my life's story, and I use the review as a means of taking stock of what I've done. Many people have died at an earlier age than mine; most, however, manage to live out their creative years. But like Monette—this is the lesson he and a few close friends have taught me—I shall never cease to rage against bigots, wherever they are. The Buckleys who would tattoo our posteriors and the Dannemeyers who would have us packed off to camps, the Helmses and Falwells who read in this virus some sort of divine intervention against those who are different from them are using language in powerful ways. But these public figures are no worse than the woman who leaned across the dinner table at the Lotos Club last night and, gently making contact with my forearm, asked "Don't you think that just maybe God was pointing his finger at all of you and saying, 'Enough of this sexual liberation'?" A cure will come for the disease, the plague will recede into history, but the bigotry will remain. Many of us, millions of us, will survive this disease, and it is for them that we struggle. Many of us have learned that our silence has always equalled our death.

It is *all* borrowed time, and so—like those wonderful books that made me who I am and that, each Saturday, had to be returned to the Kenmore Public Library—the time we have borrowed must also be returned. With these two books, Paul Monette ensures that he has given back far more than he ever borrowed. (pp. 331-39)

Gregory Kolovakos, "The World Cleaved in Two," in Parnassus: Poetry in Review, *Vol. 15, No. 1, 1989, pp. 331-39.*

[In his writings Monette] uses the epidemic—with its utterly tangible terms of risk and responsibility—to break through our culture's refusal to acknowledge that, for gay people, gay love is as good as it gets.

—Richard Goldstein, in his "Till Death Do Us Part," in* The Village Voice Literary Supplement, *June 1988.

Susan Brownmiller (review date 11 February 1990)

[*A nonfiction writer, critic, novelist, lecturer, and avid feminist, Brownmiller is best known for her bestseller,* Against Our Will: Men, Women, and Rape *(1975). In the mixed review below, she discusses the emotional impact of* Afterlife, *its popularity with audiences, and its contrived plot.*]

Paul Monette writes about love, loss and yearning better than anyone else in America today; and heterosexual readers must confront the irony of this. Monette is a gay man, HIV positive, whose subject is male love in the age of AIDS.

Published in 1987, Monette's ***Borrowed Time*** was a nonfiction elegy to the life and death of his lover, Roger Horwitz, that accomplished what mortality statistics and daily news reports could not. Monette's artful rendering of his and Roger's heroic efforts to stay among the living transcended gender distinctions and left readers wrenched and wrung dry in a centrifuge of universal emotions.

Afterlife is a novel that picks up the pieces after ***Borrowed Time.*** Call it flat-out fiction based on a grim reality Monette would rather not have known. Call it deceptively popular writing that packs a revolutionary wallop.

Steven, who has lost Victor, is an AIDS widower in Los Angeles, one of a circle of emotionally shellshocked men who share their gayness and HIV status, a brotherhood of outsiders ill at ease with, and wary of, the heterosexual world. They count their T-cells, go to support groups, convene for a Thanksgiving dinner and witness yet another death of their own.

Sex is crucial to male identity in Steven's bereft crowd, but "safe" sex is less of a problem than learning to let down traditional male defenses. These are men who can unzip their pants and get into a fantasy quicker than Rumpelstiltskin; they are not used to kissing. The few women permitted to enter their circle hover in the background like Florence Nightingales on a provisional pass. They cook, clean and tend to the dying, submerging their own emotional needs to those of the grieving men.

Steven lets his travel agency go down the tubes while he searches for renewal in the Hollywood Hills with Mark, a handsome television executive not entirely out of the closet. Mark runs from intimacy, preferring a disengaged life of brief encounters. Their slow dance toward commitment is played against the paths chosen by two of their friends.

Dell, a Mexican-American gardener, is driven by rage to become an AIDS terrorist, wreaking havoc on the Los Angeles water supply and an anti-gay evangelical church. Sonny, the golden stud in cashmere and a gray Mercedes, finds solace at the sight of the first purple welt of Kaposi's sarcoma by dreaming that he prospered as an Egyptian pharaoh in another age.

Afterlife is a hard look at gay male behavior within the context of a commercially plotted novel that is flawed in one respect: The story line seems contrived, and the ends tie up too predictably to honor the author's best intentions.

A screenwriter and poet when he is not writing fiction, Monette has an enviable knack for putting a fresh spin on a simile; he upends conventional metaphors with undisguised relish to make an unsuspecting reader gasp at a wry, hidden truth. He is also, in spite of his subject matter, a very funny fellow who knows the value of comic relief.

Apart from the judiciously rationed wit, this fictional report from a hellish nightmare makes few concessions to "hets"—as Steven calls those who are not of his sexual persuasion. Monette does not intend for hets to sleep with ease. Toward that end, he succeeds very well.

It is, however, worth pondering what is lost in the way of dignity by taking a story that lies so close to home and rendering it within the conventions of popular fiction. If Monette's goal was to make gay sexuality and the tragedy of AIDS accessible to the general reader, he has reached it. But ***Afterlife*** will not please the intellectual crowd. If comparisons to Erich Segal are made, they will not be out of order.

Among gay novelists who write on gay themes, John Rechy and Edmund White staked out sex early in their careers, and David Leavitt put a lock on family relations. But Paul Monette pursues the human heart—the most difficult road of all because it lies perilously close to June-Moon-Spoon, despite the graphic sexual descriptions. I applaud him for taking the risks.

Susan Brownmiller, "Paul Monette: A Gay Novelist in Pursuit of the Human Heart," in Chicago Tribune, *February 11, 1990, p. 3.*

Judith Viorst (review date 4 March 1990)

[*Viorst is an American poet, journalist, editor, nonfiction writer, and author of children's books. In the review below, she applauds Monette's use of compassion and humor in* Afterlife, *concluding that the novel succeeds in reaching beyond an exclusively gay audience.*]

In ***Borrowed Time*** (1988), a gallant and wrenching account of his lover's doomed struggle with AIDS, Paul Monette writes that "part of what allowed people to keep the disease at a distance was believing it couldn't touch anyone they cared about." But maintaining that distance grows harder and harder as this friend's child, that friend's brother, a neighbor, a co-worker fall victim to this non-negotiable plague. In ***Borrowed Time,*** Mr. Monette tears down the boundary between Us and Them, searing everyone—straight or gay, male or female—with his anguished story of love and loss.

Afterlife continues, through fiction, where the nonfiction ***Borrowed Time*** leaves off, intertwining the tales of three AIDS "widowers" trying to make some sort of life for themselves following the nightmare deaths of their partners. How to keep going after such loss, and how to deal with the grief and rage and terror, are the compelling themes Mr. Monette addresses with compassion and black humor.

The three men meet in Los Angeles, at Cedars-Sinai Hospital, where—in rooms 904 and 916 and 921—their lovers lie dying. An unlikely trio, Steven Shaw and Sonny Cevathas and Dell Espinoza forge a powerful bond by "outdoing one another with unspeakable details" during the deathwatch. By the time the dying are dead, the survivors "knew one another better than anyone. Or at least how they cried and took their coffee."

For one year after the deaths, the men have been getting together every Saturday night, but now the widowers' club is breaking up. It's time to move on, but their wounds run very deep, and the healing process hasn't gone too well.

Steven is emotionally dislocated and sexually numb, "lost . . . unanchored and alone." He has gained 25 pounds on Mud Pies and Oreos. He can't face returning to work at his travel agency. And he still remains so shattered by the loss of his longtime lover that he can't even risk making friends with a stray dog.

Dell has transformed his grief into rage against anyone and anything that displays a lack of concern—or worse—about AIDS. Up from Mexico, Dell has thrived in L.A. with his gift for making green things grow. But now he is being consumed with the wish to destroy.

Sonny, waiting on tables and keeping in shape at the Body Works, is trying to fill up his emptiness with New Age slogans and compulsive sex. But despite his pride in his Greek-god good looks and his willingness to try almost anyone once, he is seeking something deeper, more . . . metaphysical. He's into crystals, Zodiac signs and reincarnation, searching for an "old soul" who will recognize him in his present guise. But mostly he's into convincing himself—with increasing desperation—that no, he will never get sick, he will never get AIDS.

Will Steven break through his isolation and find a companion in Mark, a television executive who has his own problems with tenderness and intimacy? Has Dell become an AIDS-awareness terrorist, and how far will his terrorism go? Can Sonny, the virus in his blood, continue to maintain his massive denial? The questions are somewhat soap-opera-ish, and the answers somewhat predictable, but that won't stop you from wanting to read on.

The stories of Steven and Dell and Sonny unfold against a Los Angeles of Zen salads and canyons and show-business deals and the turreted mini-chateaus of the rich and famous. In this sun-blessed land, however, reports from the battlefield—losing reports—continue to arrive with grim regularity. And the men who carry the virus can see, in those who have already been struck down, the chilling reflection of their own bleak fate.

"They all knew somebody sick was coming, more or less, but no one was ready for this. The moment was so frozen, five heads turning as they came in the room, that Steven swore he could see the split between the men and the women. Dell and Sonny and Andy, who all had the virus, stared at the enfeebled figure in the movable chair with a kind of disbelieving horror, to see as if in a dark mirror the place where they were bound."

But although the AIDS dying and dead are insistent presences in this book, Mr. Monette can make us laugh as well as weep. And his wide array of characters includes a number of darkly comic snapshots: of the platinum-blond evangelist, Mother Evangeline (who had "allowed as how

An excerpt from *Borrowed Time: An AIDS Memoir*

Roger nodded passively, too sick from all the tests to argue, gearing up for another siege of medication. When I tried to raise the issue that we seemed to have a magic-bullet problem here, and maybe it was time to go after Compound S, Sheldon changed the subject to my birthday dinner, only ten days away. Since the doctors were saying Roger would probably be home by then, there was no reason not to proceed on schedule. It was such a seductive idea, to think we could still breeze in in tuxes and put the calamity on hold. I thought of Bruce at the Oscars in March, nominated for *The Natural,* a moment of tonic gaudiness between the first lesion and the pneumocystis. And here we were, agreeing again to the lie of normalcy and holding out for veal chops.

As to the burden of the secret, it wasn't Roger's parents I was worried about right now. I felt dread enough of hitting my parents with the news, assaulted as they were by the complications of my mother's emphysema. Indeed, we had all we could do, in the wake of the nightmare, to preserve our own dignity about being gay. I don't think we knew what to do yet with our parents' hard-won acceptance, the sense they'd had to overcome that being gay was a kind of doom. So the secret wasn't all Sheldon's idea, even now. We'd protect the parents as long as we could.

But I simply couldn't go on smiling at our friends and coasting along as if nothing were wrong. I couldn't face Alfred in the mornings, or all the calls that were pouring in about the party. I phoned Richard Ide in Washington; he was there for a term's sabbatical and bunking with a mutual friend. I had to banter inanely in order to get to Richard, who in turn was required to speak in coded monosyllables. It just couldn't continue this way or we'd go mad—though now was hardly the time to discuss it. Roger wasn't up to talking to anyone new, and especially kept his distance from the fuss of easy sympathy. I recall how we both looked grimly around at the flowers that had welcomed him home from the *last* hospitalization. "What is this," said Rog, with wry dismay, "a funeral?"

But if he didn't need reinforcements, I plainly did. I was berserk, and it was coming out as anger. One afternoon in the underground garage beneath the city of pain, the Jaguar locked in gear again. I came racing up to use the phone in Roger's room, ranting as I dialed and then screaming at the dealer in a sort of free fall of rage. It was a reaction that would soon become a reflex, at every little thing that went wrong in the world of errands and customer service. Pure displacement: I was angry at Roger for being sick.

And it wasn't even being safely funneled off, since Roger had to lie there weak and fevered and listen to the Jaguar rant. "Please, I can't handle all this upheaval," he begged me.

I only wish the yelling had calmed me down, but it didn't. A day or two later he had a call from Tony Smith in Boston, and managed to rise above the fever and nausea to have a quiet talk with his friend. Somehow it made me jealous. *I* couldn't talk to anyone that way now, not in a state of emergency. I don't know what it was I did just then—nagged him to get off the phone, started wailing or getting frantic—but he hung up and turned and shrieked at me. "You can't take it! You just can't take it, can you?"

Paul Monette, in his Borrowed Time: An AIDS Memoir, *Harcourt Brace Jovanovich, 1988.*

Jesus would never have cured a man with AIDS, despite his record on leprosy"). Of the coke-snorting superstar Lou Ciotta ("Untold thousands of hopeful actors looked as good . . . but this one happened to have won the lottery. Happily he was also a moron, so he never lost sleep wondering if he deserved it"). Of the "American Gothic mom and dad" who, learning that their son was gay and had AIDS, "had advised him to go to church and disinvited him for Christmas, saying they were keeping it small this year."

Despite its comic flourishes, this is a tough, painful book about gay sex and love, pursued in the valley of the shadow of AIDS. And its unrelenting descriptions of the ravages of the disease, along with its sexual details and "talking dirty," are surely going to make some readers uncomfortable. But here, as in his memoir, Mr. Monette wants to go beyond Gay Lit and invite us all in. He succeeds with a book that reminds us that we—that all of us—will meet with many losses, that we must learn to comfort one another and that when time starts running out—as it will for everyone—we need to find some joy in the time that remains.

Judith Viorst, "The AIDS Widowers' Club," in The New York Times Book Review, *March 4, 1990, p. 7.*

Aram Saroyan (review date 25 March 1990)

[*A poet, novelist and biographer, Saroyan is the son of American playwright William Saroyan. Here, he offers a highly favorable assessment of* Afterlife.]

Steven Shaw, who owns a travel agency, Dell Espinoza, who has a landscaping business, and Sonny Cevathas, a hustler with New Age leanings, all are likely to die of the same disease they have just seen take the lives of their lovers.

Afterlife by Paul Monette, who wrote the memoir ***Borrowed Time*** about the death of his own lover, is an affecting novel of gay mid-life in the epoch of AIDS. Monette's prose has an engrossing, loose fluency as he tracks his three AIDS "widowers," each trying to come to terms with his loss and get on with what life is left to him. The three frequently converge at Steven's house in the Hollywood Hills along with flames and female friends and coworkers for the support they aren't likely to find in their actual families.

The central figure is Steven, who has gained 30 pounds since the death of his lover, Victor, and no longer is interested in sex. Although he is a pivotal figure in the book's plot, Dell, a Mexican immigrant outraged by a local televangelist on a vendetta against gays, is sketched only with the broadest strokes. Sonny, too, barely comes to life, a narcissistic cartoon. Monette wisely spends most of his time on Steven, a character whose generous sympathy for the others never obscures his own aches and foibles.

Slowly coming back to life, Steven discovers himself drawn to Mark Inman, a former TV star who now is the personal manager of Lou Ciotta, a macho coke freak who rules the Wednesday night TV lineup the way Cosby rules Thursday. Inman lives a double life: nominally straight in his official persona, escorting starlets to the Emmy Awards; promiscuously gay and uncommitted in his off-hours. Then he discovers he too has AIDS, and when his boss rattles impatiently, awaiting a million-dollar check to buy a racehorse on a whim, Inman insults him and walks off his job.

Reconsidering his position, he brings Steven along on a rapprochement visit to the palatial Hollywood estate of the Ciottas. In a wonderful scene, the TV star's street-smart wife, Angela, takes Steven for a tour of the house while her husband and his erstwhile manager confer. Lou has tried to be cool about Mark's sudden coming out, but Angela, who has disrobed in her enormous walk-in closet so she can try out her evening dress on Steven, seems genuinely at ease.

> "You're so good for Mark," she said with vivid good cheer. "I never seen him so relaxed."
>
> "Really, it's not what you think. We're more like . . . brothers or something."
>
> She faced him again, naked except for the black panties. "Don't tell me about love," she offered. "I'm Italian. It's the national sport."
>
> "Oh, I love him all right. Whatever that means." Steven tried to sound breezy—tried too hard. "But gay men are very weird about sex. They can't do it with people they like."

The issue here, in essence the fear of intimacy, isn't unfamiliar to the terms of straight relationships, and it's one measure of ***Afterlife*** that its story—aside from the particulars of erotic play, about which Monette is helpfully both specific and more or less routine—has so broad a resonance.

In perhaps the book's most telling and moving scene, Mark, knowing his days are numbered but showing no external signs yet, visits his father, a jaunty widower named Rob, in his Florida condo in a retirement complex, and lets go with his double-whammy: He's gay, and he's tested positive for the AIDS virus. The old man, who has fallen in love again with a nice lady named Roz, bears the news with surprising grace, and then asks Mark about his new friend.

> "It won't work, Dad. I'm not attracted to him."
>
> Rob made an impatient waving motion, determined not to let the kid off the hook. "How old is he? He's your age?" Mark nodded curtly. "Good, good," said Rob, as if the numbers were very important here. "And he's got this virus too?"
>
> "Uh-huh. He buried his lover last year."

"Well, then, he knows," retorted the father, his ruddy face beaming with satisfaction.

"Knows what?" Mark bit the question off, not quite sure what he was angry at.

"That's all there is, son. Someone to love. You ask anybody here." And he gestured grandly out over the Pitch'n'Putt, but also included the mid-rise condos banked on every side, full of seniors in lonely efficiencies. "They've either been married forty years, and they're holding on to what little time they got left, or they're widowed and only half-alive. The lucky ones are like Roz and me, we get another chance. We know it's not for long. Two years, three years—just like you say. But it's all there is, so you'll take even a little."

AIDS paradoxically has telescoped the generations: The old widower is quite sure that the information he's passing along to his son already is known by his son's friend Steven, a young widower.

Knowing they have the virus that has claimed the lives of their lovers, the protagonists of ***Afterlife*** move variously toward some kind of absolute value. Sonny takes his cues from a New Age guru whom Angela recommends. Dell becomes a gay radical urban guerrilla. And Steven claims with Mark the victory of letting their seasoned, humane awareness of one another lead them all the way into love.

Their lessons in life accelerated, just as their mortal cycle has been shortened by this new Black Plague, they are able to achieve the only real happy ending around. Their story makes ***Afterlife*** a radiant book. (pp. 1, 14)

Aram Saroyan, "Accelerated Emotions in the Era of AIDS," in Los Angeles Times Book Review, *March 25, 1990, pp. 1, 14.*

Writing became the best way to save my life. For some, the tragedy [of AIDS] has been so immense that they couldn't write. But literature is what transforms us. Do books save lives? At best, they can. The truth may be too late, but it's better than no truth at all.

—Paul Monette, in an interview, in* Publishers Weekly, *29 June 1992.

David Kaufman (review date 1 July 1991)

[*Kaufman is a theater critic and a frequent contributor to* The New York Times Book Review. *In the following excerpt, he favorably assesses* Halfway Home, *praising it as "part of a literary movement that testifies that nothing less than a new definition of the American family is in order."*]

The very ambition to categorize so-called gay literature may be something of a self-defeating proposition: By reflecting the larger world, certainly the better examples of the "genre" transcend any categorical limitations we might infer. To insist otherwise would be to reject the assimilation captured so well in a number of new novels, and to hazard stereotypes that they deny.

This emerges as an inescapable message now that the world of commercial publishing is embracing a range of gay male novelists who refuse to depict the world according to an outmoded dualistic convention of "gay" and "straight" (as if it ever really were that) but rather as a more varied whole, the better to describe the ways in which people lead their lives, regardless of sexual orientation. In this light, what tends to be most remarkable about the fiction of David Leavitt, Paul Monette and even newer comers such as John Weir and Michael Cunningham is how unremarkable their gay characters are. These authors demonstrate that, to pervert the cliché, fiction has always been straighter than truth. (The primary exception in mainstream publishing was to allow for gay coming-of-age novels. But in comparison with the concerns of the new generation, consider how quickly even so fine an example as Edmund White's *A Boy's Own Story* has acquired an Uncle Tomish aura.)

Whether relieved by gallows humor or in relentlessly somber prose, AIDS is of course also a ubiquitous presence in today's fiction, where it has arrived with the same vehemence it has in our lives. . . . By now it is a truism that, along with playwrights, novelists are keeping pace with the evolution of the virus and its social ramifications in ways that Hollywood and television have been avoiding like the proverbial plague it is.

The less obvious but more intriguing point is that the twin *leitmotifs* of assimilation and AIDS are related: The real common denominator, whether the virus is treated explicitly or not, is a coming to terms with lost possibilities, a better understanding of the life that was or might have been, in order to get the most out of the one that remains. This is true not only of so-called AIDS novels such as Weir's *The Irreversible Decline of Eddie Socket,* Monette's ***Afterlife*** and ***Halfway Home,*** and David B. Feinberg's *Eighty-Sixed* but also of Ken Siman's *Pizza Face,* set in the 1970s, before AIDS was recognized, and novels such as Cunningham's *A Home at the End of the World,* which treats AIDS peripherally. Deliberately or not, Cunningham's novel and ***Halfway Home*** are part of a literary movement that testifies that nothing less than a new definition of the American family is in order, one that is more dynamic and capacious, more cognizant of the extended possibilities that have already permeated the society. (p. 21)

Probably more than any other writer, Monette has demonstrated just how conventional or mainstream gay relationships can be—even in the midst of the AIDS epidemic.

Published [in 1990], ***Afterlife,*** Monette's previous novel, was also specifically AIDS-related. It seemed naturally to follow ***Borrowed Time,*** his deeply moving nonfiction account of his lover's protracted death from AIDS. But if the three central figures or "widowers" in ***Afterlife*** are primarily concerned with getting beyond their grief over their respective lovers' deaths, ***Halfway Home*** invests far more in confronting the secrets buried in one's youth and upbringing. As with Cunningham, we're offered a sharp contrast between the all-American nuclear family and the more extended kind that, for many, has replaced it.

For Tom Shaheen, the thirtysomething narrator whose days are numbered in ***Halfway Home,*** the end of the journey requires a painful number of backward steps before he can move forward. At the beginning of the novel, Tom observes, "Generally I don't waste a minute . . . figuring how short my time is. I've been at this thing for a year and a half, three if you count all the fevers and rashes. I operate on the casual assumption that I've still got a couple of years, give or take a galloping lymphoma. Day to day I'm not a dying man, honestly." He also recognizes that his own truncated circumstances have a beneficial effect on those around him: "I've found that since my illness I can cut right to the chase with my friends, demanding that they jettison the bullshit from their lives. I am like the toller of the bell: my very presence seizes them with how little time is left."

During the course of the story, which spans a few weeks and is set outside Los Angeles, Tom is visited by his despised older brother, Brian, whom he hasn't seen in nine years. For the first time, he meets his homophobic sister-in-law as well as his young nephew, in whom he sees himself as a child. The presence of Brian's family prompts Tom to re-evaluate his own miserable childhood in Connecticut, entailing an abusive alcoholic father and sordid sex scenes with his brother.

In contrast to the parallel lines drawn between these two unhealthy family situations, Tom is protected and nourished in the present by Mona, who still operates the performance art club they co-founded some years ago, and by Gray, the older man with whom he falls in love as the novel progresses. Referring to Mona and Gray in the midst of one of the many crises Monette whips up, Tom tells himself, "I felt a sharp and guilty pang of relief that the two of them were here. As if I had somehow outwitted the deepest pain by having this family instead, and not those far-off blood strangers who'd just been obliterated."

After Brian and his wife and son arrive at Tom's to escape a "billion-dollar ripoff of federal housing funds" in which Brian is implicated back East, Tom muses,

> We couldn't really talk about the future, because for them there wasn't any yet, and as for me, forget it. They all seemed to be feeling hopelessly misunderstood by each other, bruised into silence. In the days of our old family, even before I could talk, I gave up the idea of being understood. Perhaps these three just had nothing else to say, with their house and former lives in smithereens. I wondered if an outsider, wandering in right now, would even know they were a family. Because if it was Mona and Gray and Foo and me, anyone would know.

Given Monette's slick pop-fiction style and enough melodramatic twists to betray aspirations for a movie-of-the-week sale, the fact that there's also depth and breadth to ***Halfway Home*** might be overlooked. While there is still too much reliance on plot, as some reviewers found in previous novels by Monette, such a drawback is compensated for not only by hip expression but also by an economy of theme. A tendency in ***Afterlife*** to veer in too many directions at once is surmounted in ***Halfway Home.*** As realized in the final pages, Tom's touching reconciliation with Brian is like a magnet that draws all other elements of the narrative into a culminating perspective on families, from the ones that chose us to the ones we choose. (pp. 22, 24)

David Kaufman, "All in the Family," in The Nation, *New York, Vol. 253, No. 1, July 1, 1991, pp. 21-2, 24-5.*

Michael Lassell (essay date 2 June 1992)

[*In the following essay, Lassell provides a brief overview of Monette's writing career and discusses the impact of AIDS on his life and works.*]

The word *fluid* is so often applied by literary critics with nothing in particular to say that the term is a cliché even when aptly applied, as to the writings of Paul Monette. Not that his prose isn't mellifluous; it is elegant, eloquent, even mercurial, flowing at its best on a narrative drive as compelling and subtle as a tide.

But of all writers' works, Monette's books seem best symbolized by liquids. Even those early haute homo novels like ***Taking Care of Mrs. Carroll*** and ***The Gold Diggers***—some of which were attacked, even in the gay press, as glib—might be described as Baccarat stemware half-filled with chilled Cristal or as kidney-shaped pools of frozen strawberry daiquiris. But giddy wish-fulfillment fantasies would soon be torpedoed in icy waters, and a more powerful writing would emerge to record the disaster.

The shift in the Monette career came as a result of the illness and death of his longtime lover Roger Horwitz, his own battle with HIV infection, and his increasing horror at the insanity of the national context in which queer lives are led—and lost. The books of the last five years, and whatever may come after, are clearly the cream of the Monette legacy: ***Borrowed Time,*** the plague memoir, as bottomless and murky with untidy emotion as an unchartered swamp; ***Love Alone,*** a series of 18 elegies for the lost beloved that reads like a jet of blood forced through the first hairline rift in a soon-to-burst dam; then two novels, ***Afterlife,*** a geyser of mounting and often untempered rage, and ***Halfway Home,*** a well of brackish family feeling.

And now there is ***Becoming a Man,*** a deep, clear lake of recollection as tranquil on its surface as it is intensely passionate in the subterranean rills that feed it. Subtitled *Half a Life Story,* it is an autobiography saturated with ironies. The title itself refers to what would clearly be a cheeky mid-career look back in self-anger were it not that Monette, at 46, is likely well past his halfway point. His T-cell count was 100 when he wrote the book; it's 20 now. The poet, novelist, memoirist, screenwriter, and activist received his AIDS diagnosis on Dec. 13, 1991, while writing out his Christmas cards.

Acknowledging that AIDS fueled his creative juices, Monette is acidly sanguine: "I'd rather be writing glib novels than going through the holocaust."

The spine of ***Becoming a Man*** is simple: It's a coming-out story, in essence, although it is better called a "having-come-out story." The life in retrospect is so well-examined that it not only illuminates the adult, who is a presence in our community as well as one of its best writers, but stands as a talisman for the millions of queer lives it so clearly parallels. A cautionary tale of the half life one lives inside closet walls, it is the story of a writer who acquired the means of expression before life gave him the courage to apply it to the man he truly is. Tellingly, Monette "becomes a man" by jettisoning half-truths—and downright lies—about masculinity and homosexuality. In short, by claiming himself. "You do see a self being born," Monette allows, "even if it can't do gay right."

These days Monette is clearly "doing gay" right, although "doing queer" is closer to it. "My writing is inextricably bound up with my being gay," says the writer, who in April received a Visibility Award (which, he assures, is not about eyesight) from the Gay and Lesbian Alliance Against Defamation (GLAAD), a media watchdog group. "That's why I wanted to write," he says of his sexual identity. "That's what I wanted to explore. I know that ***Becoming a Man*** goes over the years in which I was paralyzed, but thank God I'm gay. I wouldn't be much of a writer otherwise."

That ***Becoming a Man*** seemed to "write itself" does not mean it was not difficult. "When I had written 50 or 100 pages of this book," Monette recalls, "I felt so stoked, I thought, *Everybody should do this.* But by the time I got to page 150, I thought, *Nobody should do this. We should all keep this stuff pushed down.* Because we all remember the ten or 20 grisly moments of our lives when we failed ourselves or didn't take the leap out of the closet, when you start to write about them, all kinds of other things, just as awful, start to come up."

Surprisingly, ***Becoming a Man*** betrays almost no panic, no hysteria. It does not appear to have been written in the shadow of an executioner's noose. "That may be one of the good kinds of denial," Monette says thoughtfully. "I do mention AIDS at the beginning, when I'm shrieking at the politicians and the cardinals, and at the end, but I had written so much about it in the previous four books, I didn't feel I had to here."

But, Monette points out, even if the book is not overtly informed by a sense of limited time, he would not have mustered the presumption to write an autobiography at such a young age were it not for the illness ticking in his bloodstream (his own metaphor). Just how much longer Monette may be writing is, of course, an open question. "I'm plugged in enough with the best medications that I may have a good couple of years," he says. "And I'm as optimistic as the most optimistic New Ager. Because who knows what they'll come up with in two years. But I've never been as sick as I was at Christmastime. You just have to have immense awe about what this condition is and that it twists everybody in a different way."

But the writer keeps writing. There's not another novel in the works, but there are some new poems (for his current lover, Winston Wilde) and a couple of AIDS-related television scripts in preparation.

And he keeps on loving. "I'm glad to say I can rise to my best self still and suck out the figs of life, but it's a *great* challenge," he explains. "And then there's the fear. The fear is a lonely business.

"I remember saying to Stephen [Kolzak, a lover prior to Wilde] a few months before he died that I can be as angry as I am at this pig-shit country and all the things that are done to us . . . and yet I'm happy," he adds. "I was happy with Stephen, and now I'm happy with Winston. I don't want to put out the message that the *only* way to live happily is to live in love, but that's how it's been for me, and it all starts with coming out." (pp. 34-5)

Michael Lassell, "Paul Monette: The Long Road to 'Becoming a Man,'" in The Advocate, *June 2, 1992, pp. 34-5.*

Maurice Berger (review date 30 June 1992)

[*In the following review, Berger offers praise for* Becoming a Man.]

The world of the closet is painful and claustrophobic, a dark space where any hint of who we really are spells danger, even annihilation. This tomb, this chamber of self-hatred, is almost impossible to describe. No one has recreated it better, perhaps, than Paul Monette in ***Becoming a Man.*** This is the second of the novelist and poet's memoirs; the first, ***Borrowed Time: An AIDS Memoir,*** chronicled the death of his longtime companion, Roger Horwitz. Tracing the first, tortured half of his life, from his lonely, middle-class youth in a puritan New England town to his education at homophobic Andover and Yale in the late 1950s and '60s, and finally to his coming out in the '70s, Monette weaves a profound tale, wrenching as it is life-affirming, poetic as it is uncompromisingly real.

Monette warns his gay brothers and sisters to come fully out of the closet, to face the light and be vigilant about our fragile, often nonexistent, rights. His vivid yet strangely minimal account of his past life is constantly interrupted by the cooler voice of hindsight. Drawing parallels between himself and Bobby, his congenitally disabled brother, for example, Monette writes: "Thus in my own crippled way I had no choice but to keep on looking in the wrong place for the thing I'd never seen: two men in love and laughing. . . . Everything told me it couldn't exist, especially the media code of invisibility, where queers were spoken of only in the context of molesting Boy Scouts."

Being in the closet has a kind of regularity to it: the experiences may be different but the feelings are the same. It's an uncomfortable, self-deluding, self-hating realm and Monette's exile was no different: the careless and offhanded taunts of "homo"; the unrequited love for his straight college roommate, a boozing, nearly insane architect; the seething resentment that followed other such numerous false starts; the crippling guilt and sexual paralysis that engulfed him after his deflowering by an American sailor he met while vacationing in England; the sense of freakishness; the perfunctory, unsatisfying sex with women; and finally, the joyous consummation of love and sex together—that epiphanic moment when Paul's will to flee the closet matches another man's capacity to love him. All the while, Monette's straight (and gay) oppressors are never let off the hook as he angrily questions the demons both within and outside of himself: "Why do they hate us? Why do they fear us? Why do they want us invisible?"

Equally sophisticated is Monette's awareness of the complexities of growing up in Cold War America and the vagaries of privilege. When a scheming dean at Andover attempts to railroad an insecure Paul away from his rightful place at Harvard or Yale (Monette suspects to substitute one of those "second-string hockey Apollos who hadn't quite made the Ivy team"), we are relieved that Paul cuts his French class in order to fill out his Yale acceptance form before the dean "or anyone else could sell [him] down the river."

As a gay man, I hope that my straight brothers will also read this book. Monette understands that the journey from boy to man is a dangerous one for all men, fraught with wicked traps and devastating turns. His writing rehearses the stifling trajectory of masculine rites of passage: the unwritten rule that our games be violent and not sweet; the smothering of juvenile emotion, sensuality, and passion; the adolescent bullying; the macho fear of intimacy with other men; the empty struggle to achieve someone else's notion of what it means to be a man. The best lesson of this exceptional autobiography is that we as men can transcend repression. Indeed, after decades of ambivalence, Monette has come to love the young man he describes—the awkward, frustrated kid from Andover and Yale who thought no man would ever love him.

Maurice Berger, "Outward Bound," in The Village Voice, *Vol. XXXVII, No. 26, June 30, 1992, p. 68.*

I learned who I was by writing. . . . Writing really is a matter of going into a deep space in yourself to find a tale to tell, a space that knows more about yourself than you do. What can come out will be your truth.

—Paul Monette, in an interview, in* The Washington Post, *13 July 1991.

Wendy Martin (review date 26 July 1992)

[*Martin is an educator and editor. In the following review, she favorably assesses* Becoming a Man *and classifies the book as a narrative map of Monette's journey to self-acceptance.*]

Paul Monette, the author of ***Borrowed Time: An AIDS Memoir*** (1988), an eloquent account of the death of his lover, is "46 now and dying by inches." Although the elegiac memory of his lovers and friends who have been lost to the plague frames his autobiography, Mr. Monette concentrates on life, not death, in ***Becoming a Man: Half a Life Story.*** Fiercely committed to bequeathing a map of his psychic terrain, to spare others the pain of his solitary journey, his fine memoir is affirmative and ultimately celebratory.

Mr. Monette's journey from "internal exile" to self-acceptance begins with his working-class upbringing in Andover, Mass., the proper New England town of his boyhood in the late 1940's and 50's, and continues through his years at Phillips Academy, where he was a scholarship student among the "athlete gods" and "black-tie kids from the cotillions." Aware of his interest in men but unable to "incorporate sex into life," he tells us he was proud of his secretiveness, of "the dark little corner" to which he confined "the Olympian frieze of my fantasies."

With what he calls a "stifling assumption of privilege" he won scholarships to Harvard, Yale and Brown, the only places he applied to. He went on to Yale, and won a summer traveling fellowship after his junior year to go to England and read Tennyson's letters. Author of his class poem, he then got a graduate fellowship teaching English and, crucial to the era, a draft deferment.

After that came years of teaching at minor New England prep schools. At the first school, characterized by "Darwinian savagery," students told him how they had "hounded the man I replaced into early retirement." But the boys saw Mr. Monette as "one of their own, counterculturally speaking, a long-haired older brother who could dance to their kind of music [and] too smart to be kissed off as another old homo."

He describes a year-long affair there with a student named Greg, living "in thrall" to Greg's "unpredictable needs" until "I had become the thing the heteros secretly believe about everyone gay—a predator, a recruiter, an indoctrinator of boys into acts of darkness. Sullying my mission as teacher and guide." Eventually, Greg turned on Mr. Monette, but his revenge backfired and Greg was expelled.

Humiliated, shamed and still a closeted homosexual, in the mid-60's he maintained determined liaisons in Boston and Cambridge with women who "bearded" him—that is, accompanied him to affirm his masculinity in the straight world—but did not diminish his desire for men. After suffering what he felt was a nervous breakdown, he began psychotherapy (with a young, "relentlessly straight" male therapist), which ultimately confirmed his preference. What appears to be a picaresque series of adventures actually became a pilgrimage to confirm his love of men and finally of one man.

Mr. Monette's resolution of his sexual conflict and confusion was a public commitment to homosexuality. A self-acknowledged "love junkie" with a fine classical education, he casts the tale as a conversion narrative in the tradition of the lives of the saints, complete with its moment of revelation and rebirth: "Once I came out, the world was all windows. Suddenly night became day and I could love like anyone else. . . . I became a new man."

In secular terms, he tells the story of a romantic determinist, or a determined romantic, who indeed finds a mate and enduring love, thereby redeeming his suffering, concluding: "If the slightest thing had happened any differently in my checkered life, I wouldn't have been there to meet Roger. . . . That much fate I believe in, the tortuous journey that brings you to love, all the twists and near misses. Somehow it all has a purpose, once you're finally real."

When Mr. Monette casts himself in the role of victim, his memoir slips from romantic declaration to self-pity. At times, feeling helpless about homophobia, Mr. Monette pits straight against gay by using the familiar model of polarization—the oppressed and the oppressors—that has characterized American protest and reform movements (feminists against patriarchs, blacks against whites, working class against ruling class). Frequently, his rage at the straight world echoes the angry rhetorical diatribes of, say, black power in the 60's or the radical feminists of the 70's: "We laugh together then and dance in the giddy circle of freedom. . . . And every time we dance, our enemies writhe like the Witch in Oz, melting, melting—the Nazi Popes and all their brocaded minions, the rat-brain politicians, the wacko fundamentalists and their Book of Lies."

Using his own life and experiences as framework, Mr. Monette often pauses, asking probing and provocative questions about "the terrors and dysfunctions, the self-battering and self-hatred" that he experienced in "the struggles of intimacy." In these sections he is also lively and often witty.

Through anecdote and polemical passages he sets out his education, telling how, as a schoolboy, he learned to read the underground signs of homosexual culture browsing through magazines like *Tomorrow's Man.* Later, he learned how to discern the codes of the camp worlds of the theater and interior decoration, and finally how to appreciate the often fiercely tribal life of urban gay men in the 1960's.

Paul Monette describes the guilt, fear and anger that hound the man who loves men in a culture that condemns homosexuals as deviants and unnatural. But in the end he decides that his "journey through the minefields of the bedroom gave . . . abundant proof that the fear of connection and openness crossed all borders—men and women, gay and straight." (pp. 5-6)

Wendy Martin, "Suddenly Night Became Day," in The New York Times Book Review, *July 26, 1992, pp. 5-6.*

Joseph Cady (essay date 1993)

[Cady is an educator and critic who specializes in the medical humanities and gay and lesbian literature. In the following excerpt, which evolved from a series of lectures presented at annual meetings of the Modern Language Association and the Society for Health and Human Values, Cady characterizes AIDS writings as either "immersive" or "counterimmersive." Offering a stylistic analysis of Love Alone, *he argues that Monette's writing is immersive because it attempts "to jolt his audience out of its denial of AIDS and to urge on it a sense of emergency that he and his community already know too well."]*

The profound denial that has dominated worldwide cultural reaction to AIDS has spurred two distinct responses in the growing body of literature about the epidemic. One, which I call "immersive" AIDS writing, is frankly, though not exclusively, concerned with that denial and confronts it squarely in an effort to undo it. Though immersive AIDS writings go to various lengths in that attempt, central to all of them are prolonged moments when the reader is thrust into a direct imaginative confrontation with the special horrors of AIDS and is required to deal with them with no relief or buffer provided by the writer. The other, which I call "counterimmersive" AIDS writing, also recognizes the dreadfulness of the disease, as all AIDS literature must at least minimally do to be worthy of the name, and also indicates the problem of denial in the larger society. But, in context, its stance toward that denial seems ultimately deferential. Counterimmersive AIDS writing typically focuses on characters or speakers who are in various degrees of denial about AIDS themselves, and it customarily treats its readers the way its characters handle their disturbing contact with AIDS, protecting them from too jarring a confrontation with the subject through a variety of distancing devices. A quantity of counterimmersive AIDS writings might cumulatively have some discomfiting effect, but individual counterimmersive texts characteristically do nothing to dislodge whatever impulse their audience may have to deny the disease. (pp. 244-45)

Paul Monette's writing offers a classic example of immersive AIDS writing. A poet, novelist, and screenwriter who has lived in Los Angeles since 1977, Monette lost his lover of twelve years, Roger Horwitz, to AIDS in October 1986. Two years afterward Monette published two companion volumes about Roger's illness and death and the personal and social havoc of AIDS: ***Love Alone: Eighteen Elegies for Rog,*** a set of long poems narrated by Paul and often directly addressed to Rog, and ***Borrowed Time: An AIDS Memoir,*** a finalist for the National Book Critics' Circle award for the best work of general nonfiction of that year. Since then he has also published two novels in which AIDS is a major concern: ***Afterlife*** (1990), about three Los Angeles "AIDS widowers" who met while their lovers lay dying in the same hospital, and ***Halfway Home*** (1991), about a gay man with AIDS and his heterosexual brother who had earlier rejected him.

In ***Love Alone*** [1988] the experience of AIDS is one of near-total "wreckage" (to adapt a term from **"Three Rings,"** the eleventh poem in the book, in which Monette compares the effect of the disease to "a car wreck"). This devastation is of course partly medical—Rog and other people with AIDS have been struck by a physically horrendous disease that is also, at this early stage in the epidemic, seemingly inexplicable and uncontrollable (Rog was diagnosed in March 1985). However, for Rog, Paul, and other gay men this havoc is multiplied by the special cultural situation of homosexuals mentioned above. AIDS is unthinkable enough simply because of its fearsome physical effects. But it has become doubly so at this early point in the crisis because it seems only to be afflicting the already untouchable and unspeakable homosexual population. The results are a compounded cultural denial of the disease and a near-total isolation for the affected gay male community, which has been left to suffer AIDS almost entirely alone and left almost entirely to its own resources to seek treatment for it.

From the very first in ***Love Alone,*** Monette indicates his concern with this denial—he states in the preface that he wants the poems "to allow no escape." His primary target in the book is what might be called the denying reader, whom he seeks to shock and unsettle out of his or her insensibility to AIDS. (There is of course a paradox to this feature of immersive AIDS writing, for, strictly speaking, a denying reader might avoid AIDS literature in the first place; in real terms, it is perhaps best to think of this reader as someone who has come in contact with the subject for some reason but is still unwilling to confront its painful features and implications.) In this aspect of ***Love Alone,*** Monette effectively follows Kafka's maxim that "A book should serve as the ax for the frozen sea within us" and Tillie Olsen's outlook in her collection *Tell Me A Riddle,* "Better immersion than to live untouched." Monette has a second audience in mind in ***Love Alone*** as well, another feature typical of immersive AIDS writing. This is the population of all people affected by AIDS, but especially his doubly beset community of fellow gay men, reeling from the compound assault of AIDS and their long-standing oppression as essentially untouchable anyway. In one tradition of classic plague literature, Monette wants ***Love Alone*** also to be a work of confirmation, witness, and encouragement for this suffering audience, heartening readers affected by AIDS with evidence that their experience is shared and will not go undocumented.

Love Alone's immersion of its audience in the catastrophe of AIDS is accomplished in part simply by its special content, by the ways in which Monette directly and repeatedly records the medical, social, and human perils of the disease. For example, the book features harrowing specifics about AIDS and its treatment, from a portrayal of Rog's growing blindness in the third poem, **"Your Sightless Days"** ("*How are you* jerks would ask *Read Job* you'd say"), to attacks in the twelfth and fourteenth poems, **"Current Status 1/22/87"** and **"Manifesto,"** on the medical establishment and on what might be called the "New Age AIDS healing establishment" personified by Louise Hay and her followers. Monette sees both as sharing a similar icy abstractness and detachment, the "nerdy white-coat . . . / . . . test-givers" of **"Current Status"** and "Lady Hay" of **"Manifesto,"** whom he describes as proclaiming that "all sickness is self- / induced . . . / every sucker in the ICU's to blame."

Most notably, ***Love Alone*** is dominated by explicit, intense, and unembarrassed statements of painful personal feeling, which, in both their frequency and intimacy, are perhaps the book's most powerful literal representations of the devastation of AIDS. For example, in the ninth poem, **"The Very Same,"** Monette compares all the poems to "blood-cries," and he repeatedly speaks in the language of extremity in depicting the ruin AIDS has wrought on his world, unrestrainedly presenting himself as "sobbing," "howling," "shrieking," "roaring," "burning," "aching," and "screaming" at his loss of Rog: "at this year's close I sobbed / and sobbed for us all" (**"New Year's at Lawrence's Grave"**), "the sundering with its howl that never ends" (**"Half Life"**), "I . . . / . . . shriek your name" (**"Three Rings"**), "the smallest thing will trigger it . . . / . . . roar me back burning" (**"The Losing Side"**), "me . . . / aching to find [you]" (**"The Losing Side"**), "I wake with the scream / in my blood it never never goes. . . / . . . my life has suffered an irreversible stroke" (**"Dreaming of You"**).

These vivid, aggressive, and blunt features of ***Love Alone***'s content are powerfully confronting in themselves. But the quality that makes ***Love Alone*** the fullest and finest example so far of immersive AIDS writing is each poem's seemingly chaotic form, in which Monette consciously disrupts all traditional notions of focus, sequence, tone, and structure. All the poems in ***Love Alone*** are long and impossible to present fully here. Let me take some moments from **"Three Rings,"** already mentioned above, as examples of Monette's disruptive approach throughout the book. The title of this five-page-long poem refers to a ring Rog's father gave him and to two mourning rings Paul buys after Rog's death, one of which he eventually buries at Rog's grave. The first passage consists of the opening lines. The second presents Paul in Taos, where he has bought the mourning rings, jade and gold for himself and a Zuni jet and silver for Rog's grave. In the third Paul is back in Los Angeles, at the cemetery, where he had begun to moan spontaneously as he buried the ring; now he realizes he was echoing Rog's dying sound, which had been a call to him in Rog's last minutes. In the fourth passage, the final lines, Paul has orbited himself into space in answer to Rog's call and nears a tenuous meeting with him (in what may be a metaphor for a reunion he foresees after his own death or simply a moment of imagined transcendence and unity that has chiefly emotional value for him).

before I left you I slipped off the ring
the nurse had taped to your finger so it
wouldn't get lost the last day you think I'd
forget I forget nothing was there the day
Dad gave it to you Chestnut St a continent
ago there when you said in the bathtub ten
years later sobbed really *If something happens*

. . . . .

fingers after the lid's shut all the same
it fit me perfect and what's a Visa for
if not to go a little mad think of
the cabfare one is saving staying home
for the rest of time so the Zuni went into
my pocket I flexed the Jade hand clever
as a showgirl baubled by a sheik of course
I knew right along it wouldn't touch the pain
it was just a game but one hungers so
for ritual that's portable you can't walk out
with tapers burning not to the 7-Eleven you
want

. . . . .

saw it all in a blaze YOU WERE CALLING
ME
my sailor brother oh I didn't know Death
had reached your lips muscles gone words dispersed
still you moaned my name so ancient wild and
lonely it took ten weeks to reach me now
I hear each melancholy wail a roar like
fallen lions holding on by your fingertips
till I arrived for how many drowning hours
to say *Goodbye I love you* all in my name
all by the howl that knows that after love
is nowhere who the fuck cares if we reassemble
as vermilion birds and fields of violets now

. . . . .

no wonder I'm always packing till the moan
became my weather and compass my heart had
no place to go it followed the law and stayed
put but how did they think they could hold us
to one ground we met on a journey that is
why the world though stopped like a car wreck
keeps
doubling back robbed of you as I am promising
shortcuts whispering of a Northwest Passage
I nearly lost my mind last week screaming
too late down an empty road but there you are
we're full of the same agony you for an hour
I for the rest the nameless dark hasn't
spared us a pang my love but give us this
if ever either of us lands we are one
cry one dream tight as a black gold ring

Here, as in all of ***Love Alone,*** Monette matches his harrowing content with a harrowing style by upsetting every conventional expectation of order an audience might bring to the text. Though each poem has a predominant situation and/or concern, Monette typically adds a variety of other content as well, abruptly shifting reference and focus and jumping back and forth in time. Here Chestnut St, sheiks, 7-Elevens, and the Northwest Passage are evoked in the same long breath as emaciation, death moans, howls, and losing one's mind; the settings shift from Los Angeles to Cambridge to Taos back to Los Angeles, and from hospital to graveyard to outer space; and we lunge from present to immediate past to distant past to present to future. The tone of each poem varies in a parallel way. Here, for example, in the course of one work it shifts from toughness ("I forget nothing") to camp humor ("what's a Visa for," "clever / as a showgirl") to heartfelt pathos ("oh I didn't know Death / had reached your lips") to fierce anger ("who the fuck cares") to piercing despair ("I nearly lost my mind last week screaming") to unashamed lovingness and fervent desire ("my love," "we are one / cry one dream"). The same spirit of apparent derangement also governs each poem's structure, which Monette strips of all customary stabilizing markers. As evident here, no poem contains stanza breaks; each moves from first word to last in one single long block. Each poem, moreover, lacks punctuation and extra spacing between sentences, and, except in the cases of proper names and the occasional phrase set in italics or complete uppercase for emphasis, no capitals are used at all. Similarly, the overwhelming majority of lines are run-on rather than end-stopped.

At the stage of the AIDS epidemic recorded in ***Love Alone,*** Rog, Paul, and their affected gay male community are in a state of unrelieved and compound shock. Shattered by the physical horrors of AIDS alone, they are further maddened by society's complete abandonment of them to the disease and by the lonely struggle thus forced upon them. To use his language in **"Three Rings,"** in ***Love Alone*** Monette incarnates this total "wrecking" of his world in a thoroughly "wrecked" form, designed to subject his readers to an immersive "wrecking" in turn—i.e., by throwing them into a completely fractured, unmarked, and destabilizing text and requiring them to make what sense of it they can entirely on their own, he tries to force upon his readers an imaginative version of the shock and isolation that he, Rog, and other affected gay men have had to face. Embodying his devastating content, where the horrors of AIDS are relentlessly thrust in the reader's face, in an equally devastating style, where secure ground is relentlessly taken out from under the reader's feet, Monette hopes to jolt his audience out of its denial of AIDS and to urge on it a sense of emergency that he and his community already know too well.

So great is that denial in the larger culture, Monette implies, that his effort to undo it in ***Love Alone*** must even circumscribe his other, compassionate concern in the book. As mentioned, immersive AIDS writing tends to have two assumed audiences—the denying reader I just discussed, and the audience harrowed by AIDS whom it wants to assure and hearten. For Monette in ***Love Alone*** this second readership is chiefly his fellow gay men, partly because at the time they seemed to be the only group devastated by AIDS, and partly because as traditionally untouchable and unspeakable they will see their suffering go largely unheeded unless one of their own bears witness for them. The strain between Monette's two commitments in ***Love Alone***—to that suffering audience and to his attack on denial—is most pointed in the book's profoundly moving last poem, **"Brother of the Mount of Olives,"** which depicts a spontaneous visit Paul and Rog made to a Benedictine monastery on Mount Olivet while on a 1983 vacation, before AIDS had, to their knowledge, entered their personal lives and indeed before it seemed to have much relevance to them at all.

Throughout ***Love Alone*** Monette is understandably conscious of the malice directed at the gay community even before AIDS, as indicated by his emphasis on gay oppression in many of the poems and by his implicit attack on homosexual stereotype in the book as a whole—e.g., his prominent mentions of Mormons who "for chrissakes want us dead" (**"Black Xmas"**) and of the "cool indifferent genocide" of "the Feds" (**"Manifesto"**), and his defiant emphasis on love in the title of the book, which challenges the popular image of gay men as obsessed with genital sex only and doomed to loveless and lonely lives. In **"Brother of the Mount of Olives"** Monette offers a carefully constructed series of achieved emotional connections designed to offset the potentially corrosive effects of such hatred and defamation, especially to counteract the isolation that can easily befall gay men under oppression and whose threat is compounded now by the onslaught of AIDS. The first of these occurs between Paul and Rog and the old monk who shows them through the monastery, "our particular brother John" of the title. From his delighted and utter attention to them, especially his constant touching ("grips us by the biceps," "clutching my hand"), they conclude that John too, must be gay—"I'm certain now / that he likes touching us that we are a world / inside him whether he knows or not . . . / . . . a blind and ancient hunger not unspeakable / unsayable. Their next surprise connection is forged with gay history, for they discover among the cloister's frescoes a portrait of a "bare-clad Jesus [with] love-glazed eyes" by the homosexual Italian Renaissance painter nicknamed Il Sodoma. This exhilarating discovery raises the even more sustaining possibility that most of the monks may be gay—"JUST WHAT KIND OF MEN ARE WE TALKING ABOUT / are we the heirs of them or they our secret / fathers and how many of our kind lie beneath / the cypress alley crowning the hill."

Each of these moments seems clearly meant to assure Monette's beleaguered gay male readers that they are not the ephemeral, solitary, and eccentric figures depicted by oppression. Here, in contrast, homosexual identity is something profound ("a world / inside him"), universal ("our kind"), and perennial (an "ancient hunger"). Through the first half of the poem, these points are conveyed by connections Paul and Rog achieve with outside figures or with increasingly broad external frameworks (an individual monk, perhaps an entire monastery, gay history as a whole). In the next incident, the culminating event of the visit, Monette shifts to an intimate emphasis. Brother John takes a "sudden noon photograph" of Paul and Rog with their own camera, a photograph that Monette later celebrates as their "wedding portrait," in which they are "joined / . . . [in] a ritual not in the book," and that, in an inescapable indication of its significance to him, he reproduces on the cover of the collection. Focusing now on a solid, joyful, and close homosexuality in the present, with this "wedding" Monette gives his audience "joinings" on every level of the poem and across several dimensions of experience. Besieged by AIDS, his gay male readers can still have historical, public, and private occasions to take heart.

With the rest of **"Brother of the Mount of Olives,"** however, Monette restricts these points, while not negating them. The moments of achieved connection just described are in fact framed by representations of loss and discord in the poem as a whole. While still the central event of the poem, Paul and Rog's visit to the monastery is actually described in retrospect. **"Brother of the Mount of Olives"** starts not with it, but with a bereft Paul in the present, desperately "combing the attic for anything extra / missed or missing evidence of us" and in that way discovering the roll of undeveloped film that yields the "wedding" photograph. Furthermore, the poem ends by returning to a still-suffering and near-disconsolate Paul in the present, where endurance "doesn't get easier," where even an "intrusion / of promise" from the natural world is "dark," and where the happy "evidence" of his and Rog's monastery "wedding" feels "all but lost":

> it doesn't get easier Rog
> even now the night jasmine is pouring
> its white delirium in the dark and I
> will not have it if you can't I shut all
> windows . . . oh help be somewhere near
> so I can endure this dark intrusion
> of promise where is the walled place where we
> can walk untouched or must I be content
> with a wedding I almost didn't witness
> the evidence all but lost no oath no ring

Monette thus sustains ***Love Alone***'s overall note of wreckage even in the book's most "solidifying" poem. While not renouncing his desire to hearten his audience of suffering comrades—his other chief purpose in the poems—Monette implies that under current conditions immersiveness must take precedence. Though support and joy can (and indeed must) be found amid the ruins of AIDS, he seems to say, we are still so wracked by the physical and emotional suffering of the disease, and still so resisted by a majority audience that would deny the urgency of the epidemic, that our foremost duty now in our speech about AIDS is to wrack that audience in turn by relentlessly immersing it in the disease's devastation. The same point and outcome were of course implied in the general style of **"Brother of the Mount of Olives,"** since even the stirring moments of connection in the center of the poem are conveyed in the same seemingly chaotic form as the rest of the collection. (pp. 245-53)

Joseph Cady, "Immersive and Counterimmersive Writing about AIDS: The Achievement of Paul Monette's 'Love Alone,'" in Writing AIDS: Gay Literature, Language, and Analysis, *edited by Timothy F. Murphy and Suzanne Poirier, Columbia University Press, 1993, pp. 244-64.*

FURTHER READING

Criticism

Goldstein, Richard. "Till Death Do Us Part." *The Village Voice Literary Supplement,* No. 66 (June 1988): 11-12.

Comparative review of Monette's *Borrowed Time* and *Love Alone,* George Whitmore's *Someone Was Here,* Robert Ferro's *Second Son,* and Edmund White and Adam-Mars Jones's *The Darker Proof: Stories from a Crisis.* Goldstein identifies narrative approaches, stylistic devices, and thematic concerns that are common to these works and to the genre of AIDS literature.

Lipson, Eden Ross. "An American Romantic." *The New York Times Book Review* XCV, No. 7 (4 March 1990): 7.

Short feature article in which Monette comments about the themes of love, sex, and romance in his works.

Sheppard, R. Z. "Journals of the Plague Years." *Time* 132, No. 3 (18 July 1988): 68, 70.

Mixed review of *Borrowed Time* in which Sheppard claims that "[only] in the deathbed pages does Monette get sufficiently out of himself to write clearly and well."

The critic also profiles AIDS literature by Andrew Holleran and Alice Hoffman.

Watkins, J. F. "Passages of Misery." *The Times Literary Supplement,* No. 4465 (28 October 1988): 1209.

Characterizes *Borrowed Time* as an "elegiac memoir" and praises Monette's use of literary allusions in the volume.

Weinraub, Judith. "Love in the Time of AIDS." *The Washington Post* 114, No. 220 (13 July 1991): C1, C5.

Feature article in which Monette discusses his childhood, his sexual orientation, the experiences that motivated him to write about AIDS, and his HIV-positive status.

Additional coverage of Monette's life and career is contained in the following source published by Gale Research: *Contemporary Authors,* Vol. 139.

Thornton Wilder

1897-1975

(Full name Thornton Niven Wilder) American dramatist, novelist, essayist, and screenwriter.

The following entry presents an overview of Wilder's career. For further discussion of Wilder's works see *CLC* Volumes 1, 5, 6, 10, 15, 35.

INTRODUCTION

The recipient of Pulitzer Prizes for both drama and fiction, Wilder is widely known as the author of such life-affirming and distinctly American works as the play *Our Town.* He is also recognized for the expansive and diverse nature of his writings, wherein he explored erudite themes informed by his travels and extensive education, as well as the simple and ordinary aspects of American daily life. As a dramatist Wilder is considered simultaneously a traditionalist and an innovator who used highly experimental staging techniques to promote values associated with Christian morality, community, family, and the appreciation of life's simple pleasures.

Wilder was born in Madison, Wisconsin. Travel was an important part of his childhood as his family resided alternately in the United States and in China, where his father served as American Consul General. He completed high school in Berkeley, California, attended Oberlin College for two years, and then completed his bachelor's degree at Yale University, where he published his first full-length play, *The Trumpet Shall Sound,* in the Yale *Literary Magazine.* After graduation, Wilder traveled to Rome, where he spent a year studying archaeology. This experience strongly influenced his interest in the human condition in relation to the passage of time—a theme that pervades many of his works. After returning to the United States, Wilder taught French at the Lawrenceville School in New Jersey for four years, and then attended Princeton University, receiving his master's degree in French in 1926. In the same year, he completed his first novel, *The Cabala.* His literary reputation was established, however, with his second novel, *The Bridge of San Luis Rey,* for which he won a Pulitzer Prize. In 1928 Wilder began a tour of Europe with his sister Isabel in order to study stage production techniques in various countries. After returning to America, he taught at the University of Chicago during the 1930s and lectured throughout the United States, becoming well-known as a charismatic public speaker. His landmark play *Our Town* was initially produced in 1938, but received poor reviews until—at Wilder's suggestion—the props and scenery were removed to reflect his goal of capturing "not verisimilitude but reality." The play was subsequently praised for its simplicity and won a Pulitzer Prize. Wilder received his third Pulitzer prize for his play *The Skin of Our Teeth,* which was produced while he was serving in the Air Force during World War II. By the 1950s, Wilder was solidly established as a major figure in American literature. His novel *The Eighth Day,* for which he won a National Book Award, is considered the most significant achievement of his later years. He died in 1975.

Critics have emphasized Wilder's focus on historical and moral themes in his novels. Set in Rome, his first novel, *The Cabala,* depicts a young American student's introduction to a mysterious social group called "the Cabala." The work has been interpreted as both an analysis of the decadent European nobility and an allegory of Christianity, paganism, and modern civilization. Wilder's second novel, *The Bridge of San Luis Rey,* is set in eighteenth-century Peru and portrays a priest's quest to discover a theological meaning for the accidental death of five people when a bridge collapses. Also situated in an exotic setting and presenting a moral theme is *The Woman of Andros,* which contrasts pagan motifs associated with ancient Greek culture with references to the advent of Christianity. Although *The Woman of Andros* was initially well-received, it became the center of controversy when Michael Gold, a noted Marxist writer, criticized Wilder for publishing "escapist" literature rather than addressing the unpleasant social realities of the Great Depression. Wilder responded with *Heaven's My Destination,* a lighthearted picaresque novel set in the Depression which parodies facets of American life such as fundamentalist evangelism. Wilder later returned to historical themes with *The Ides of March,* a novel consisting of four books of documents, proclamations, and letters that relates the events leading to the assassination of Julius Caesar. Considered by some critics to be Wilder's most accomplished work, *The Eighth Day* portrays a man who lives as a fugitive after being falsely convicted of murder.

Wilder's plays focus on broad themes concerning the human condition and frequently use innovative staging techniques. The plays collected in *The Long Christmas Dinner, and Other Plays,* for example, reflect the influence of the experimental, nonrealistic theater Wilder viewed in Europe. *Pullman Car Hiawatha* and *The Happy Journey to Trenton and Camden* both feature a stage manager who speaks to the audience about the play; virtually bereft of scenery, the stagings employ chairs as the only props. Like Wilder's later play *Our Town, Pullman Car Hiawatha* presents formulaic characters that symbolize an individual's place in the universe rather than an individual's unique qualities. Prefiguring *Our Town, The Long Christmas Dinner* treats life as a brief interlude before death. While the play spans ninety years, the action focuses on a single Christmas feast in which characters enter and exit through two doors representing birth and death, with their time onstage symbolizing their entire lives.

In his preface to a 1957 edition of *Our Town,* his most famous play, Wilder commented: "[*Our Town*] is an attempt to find a value above all price for the smallest events of daily life." The work focuses on life in Grover's Corners, a small New Hampshire town, and is presented in three acts entitled "Daily Life," "Love and Marriage," and "Death." The play features an omniscient Stage Manager who narrates the drama, jokes with the audience, and implicitly connects the people of Grover's Corners with the whole universe. In "Death," a deceased woman named Emily Webb is granted the opportunity to relive her twelfth birthday. She returns to earth and is overcome with emotion at every mundane detail of the day. Time is also a prominent motif in *The Skin of Our Teeth.* In this play, stage time is manipulated to portray simultaneously events from various time periods. For example, in Act I a 1940s family from Excelsior, New Jersey, faces the perils of the Ice Age, and in Act II an Atlantic City beauty pageant is held amidst preparations for the Great Flood. Wilder employed staging techniques that were considered quite unusual at the time of the play's first performance—characters step in and out of their roles to share their "true feelings" with the audience, and the stage crew rehearses to fill in for actors and actresses who have supposedly fallen ill.

Wilder's achievement of critical acclaim and popular success is often attributed to his ability to address both scholarly themes and simple, folksy subjects. While drama critics have lauded his innovative staging techniques, crediting him with reviving American drama of the 1930s, Wilder's popular appeal is typically associated with his optimism and affirmation of traditional American morality and values. *Our Town,* for example, continues to be one of the most frequently performed dramas of the American theater. Although some reviewers have complained that his works are either too simplistic or excessively academic, most have praised the diversity and scope of his oeuvre and his independence from the dictates of popular literary trends. As Louis Broussard has asserted: "That Wilder should regard the problems of our age as insignificant within the scope of all time and space labels him a unique optimist among the writers of this century. In such company as O'Neill, Eliot, Anouilh, and many other post-war pessimists, Wilder emerges as a lone dissenter."

PRINCIPAL WORKS

The Cabala (novel) 1926
The Trumpet Shall Sound (drama) 1926
The Bridge of San Luis Rey (novel) 1927
The Angel That Troubled the Waters, and Other Plays (dramas) 1928
The Woman of Andros (novel) 1930
**The Happy Journey to Trenton and Camden* (drama) 1931
**The Long Christmas Dinner* (drama) 1931
**Such Things Only Happen in Books* (drama) 1931
**Love, and How to Cure It* (drama) 1932
**The Queens of France* (drama) 1932
We Live Again [with Maxwell Anderson, Leonard Praskins, and Preston Sturges] (screenplay) 1934
Heaven's My Destination (novel) 1935
The Merchant of Yonkers: A Farce in Four Acts (drama) 1938; also produced as *The Matchmaker* [revised version], 1954
Our Town (drama) 1938
Our Town [with Frank Craven and Harry Chandlee] (screenplay) 1940
The Skin of Our Teeth (drama) 1942
Shadow of a Doubt [with Sally Benson and Alma Reville] (screenplay) 1943
The Ides of March (novel) 1948
A Life in the Sun (drama) 1955; also produced as *The Alcestiad,* 1962
Bernice (drama) 1957
The Wreck of the 5:25 (drama) 1957
Plays for Bleecker Street (drama) 1962
**Pullman Car Hiawatha* (drama) 1964
The Eighth Day (novel) 1967
Theophilus North (novel) 1973
American Characteristics, and Other Essays (essays) 1979

*These plays were published in the collection *The Long Christmas Dinner, and Other Plays,* 1931.

CRITICISM

Clifton P. Fadiman (review date 14 December 1927)

[*Fadiman became a prominent American critic during the 1930s with his insightful and frequently caustic book reviews for the* Nation *and the* New Yorker *magazines. In the following review of* The Bridge of San Luis Rey, *he praises the graceful quality of Wilder's writing.*]

There exists a certain minor prose quality which, in its purest form, seems to have eluded the most eminent of our present-day fiction writers: I mean grace. Grace, unlike other literary virtues, such as sincerity or strength, is a thing learned. Perhaps it is always the product of a continuous tradition, of a devotion to the masters. In America the absence of a homogeneous fictional tradition may partially account for the fact that our most widely advertised stylists are deficient in this very quality of grace. The elements of grace are almost moral: purity and modesty and quiet. Mr. Cabell, Miss Wylie, and all those other practitioners whom good sense (or snobbishness) has caused to revolt against the school-boy vulgarity of our standard literary idiom, have none the less failed to capture these elements. That is because pure grace is incompatible with mannerism or whimsicality; it is the serene steering of a middle course between the Odyssean rocks of artificiality and ruggedness. In our own time it is almost unexampled. Possibly our pioneer prejudices have laid too much emphasis on what is called a masculine style. Perhaps we have no one to learn from in our own tradition. Then there is another deterrent: the realistic ukase which bids our writers transform themselves into dictaphones for the recording of "sinewy native American speech." Finally there is the fear that so delicate a note as pure grace may be lost amid the blatant and monotonous trumpetings of our contemporary American prose.

Mr. Wilder's very beautiful book [***The Bridge of San Luis Rey***], then, possesses an extrinsic as well as an intrinsic value. Intrinsically it is a remarkably confident evocation of the secret springs of half a dozen men, women, and children. But in addition it proves to us that an American, if he be willing to exercise rigorous selection, understatement, and a measured observance of the prose styles of the masters, can create a novel instinct with a pure grace.

To achieve this unique limpidity of style and feeling Mr. Wilder has taken careful thought and made many careful avoidances. The first thing he does is to obviate the possibility of there arising in the reader's mind any vulgar or hackneyed associations. This is effected by a removal of the scene of his novel to an eighteenth-century Peru just barely touched with a gentle unreality. No land of the imagination, this Lima of 1714, for that trick would be too obvious; merely a modest device for arousing in us that sense of purification which is lent by historical remoteness. Then, as grace is not associated with large effects or the complication implicit in a numerous dramatis personae, he reduces his characters to a scant seven or eight—the five who perish when the bridge of San Luis Rey falls, the Perichole whose passions and perversities link delicately the fortunes of those five, and two or three more static personalities to balance the dynamic action of the protagonists. But this mere numerical simplicity is not enough, for grace is achieved through a certain unity, even monotony. It is not generally effected by the depiction of too many emotions. Consequently Mr. Wilder simplifies his feeling-pattern. Though his characters are projected completely and organically, they are for the most part motivated by the single passion of love. There is no schematism here, for this passion expresses itself in almost every conceivable form (except romantic affection) from the almost religious idolatry of little Pepita to the inverse effects of love frustration in the Perichole.

A locale free from impure associations, a parsimonious list of characters, a simplified and coherent emotional material—there is still another device employed by Mr. Wilder to convey a sense of purity. There is a moment in which the love-careers of his five characters reach a psychic turning-point; at that moment they fall from the bridge. Accident? Divine intention? The ruminative and Jesuitical Brother Juniper thinks the latter, but Mr. Wilder does not say. His art knows that to indicate the metaphysical implication underlying his tale is to deepen the sense of mystery. To stress it is to destroy the quality of grace he has so surely built up. He assembles materials so apt for the purpose that he might very well be tempted to furbish up his story and present it as a profound philosophical novel, thus gaining the plaudits of the columnists. But his pen is tipped with the pure gold of an exquisite tact—another word for grace. Just as the simple reticences of his individual sentences offer exactly the correct amount of stimulation to the reader's sensibility, so is his basic conception clothed with a beautiful restraint, lending to his work that gracious and stately modesty we meet with in the old fables of La Fontaine.

Mr. Wilder is not yet an important novelist; but it may be that he decreases the significance of his work by a self-imposed series of limitations. His projects are not ambitious; he refuses to set a complicated or turbulent human scene. Yet there are a sureness, an ease, and an emotional power in this book that indicate more inclusive and far-ranging abilities. There are few young Americans writing today whose development will be watched by the discerning critic with greater hope and confidence.

Clifton P. Fadiman, "The Quality of Grace," in The Nation, *New York, Vol. CXXV, No. 3258, December 14, 1927, p. 687.*

R. P. Blackmur (review date July 1930)

[*Blackmur was a leading American critic who combined social commentary with the close textual analysis of New Criticism. In the following review, he finds* The Woman of Andros *lacking in integrity and originality.*]

Mr. Wilder deals with the "notation of the heart," but he is a literary man for all that. The inspiration behind his three pieces of fiction, and the course of their writing as we have it, does not result so much from direct notation as it does from other literature and from certain general notions which predicate rather than control experience. He is the kind of writer in whom the comment is more important than the thing presented for comment; and his comment itself is of that kind which illuminates the reader more than it does the subject. Poverty and riches are in this method. There is poverty of growing character and there is riches in static characterization. There is riches in textural excellence, poverty in vascular structure. If we ignore what Mr. Wilder does not provide we may be satisfied with the perfection which he exhibits. Some will go further and be deceived, and consider his sermons on the Christian soul to be novels of the thinking heart.

And with this, his last book, deception is rendered easier by the great improvement his style has undergone. ***The Cabala*** was what is called brilliant writing; it was stocked with wise-cracks, and its extraneity was its essence. ***The Bridge of San Luis Rey*** was less obviously brilliant, less extraneous to itself in its minute particulars, and its wise-cracks were more often honest epigrams. Both these books were written in segments, and were held together in their guise as novels by the loose concepts suggested in their titles and by the considerations introduced in their opening and closing chapters. Their form, their body, was nothing of which Henry James could have approved. Their subject matter might be described in the *Poetics* but could not be found in the books themselves. In ***The Woman of Andros*** there is more of a proper theme—the presentation of a certain limit of consciousness—a limit between the boundaries of doubt and faith; and that theme is pretty consistently given the colour of dramatic continuity. The impedimenta of brilliance and epigram have almost disappeared, and we are given instead certain beautiful sayings, sayings which have at their best an air of being distinguished poetic proverbs. Comment generally is simpler, more intensified. The narrative is naturally more convincing, the persons more vivid, the idiom of conversation denser than in the earlier books. A hurried reading, such as the brevity of the book and its spread typography suggest, gives the impression of a sound and beautiful novel.

A second reading reverses the sense of the impression, while somehow keeping its strength. The book remains interesting, and it remains beautiful writing. But it no longer seems to be much of a novel. Although the persons in the book—Chrysis and her sister, and Pamphilus and his father—retain their individuality and what is more important preserve the integrity of their feelings, the book itself is not integral, not individual. It appears to depend for the validity of its final impression upon something not properly part of the book at all, upon something part of the author's mind which has not been digested into the book. There was an ulterior motive in Mr. Wilder's mind which he was not able to merge with the motives of his characters. It is such a motive as the motive of parable, almost that of allegory—either, in its own domain, most proper, but neither fitting the denouement of a tragedy, for in tragedy nothing materially relevant may be left abstract from the lives of the characters.

The nature of Mr. Wilder's failure may be indicated in two ways—by reference to his literary method, and by mention of his prevailing religious preoccupation in relation to his novels.

It does not matter much how loosely or closely Mr. Wilder follows the *Andria* of Terence or the letters of Madame de Sevigné. It does matter a great deal whether what he borrows becomes his own, or whether, on the contrary, it sets up a conflict with what he has in mind. In ***The Woman of Andros*** (and similarly in ***The Bridge of San Luis Rey***) there is a conflict; he has borrowed too much to suit his own purposes: there are outcroppings of the sources which interfere with the story being told. Admittedly, this sort of criticism cannot be proved; it can only be felt that some other context would have been better suited to the development of Mr. Wilder's intention. But there is another matter, on much the same level as the use of purely literary sources, and that is the problem of Mr. Wilder's borrowings from himself. Examination of such should penetrate the marrow of his style. On page eighty-four of ***The Woman of Andros*** begins the following passage:

> It astonished her to find someone laconic in a chattering world and with quiet hands in a gesturing civilization. He was blackened and cured by all weathers. He stood in the squares of the various ports of call, his feet apart as though they were forever planted on a shifting deck. He seemed to be too large for daily life; his very eyes were strange—unaccustomed to the shorter range, too used to seizing the appearances of a constellation between a cloud and a cloud, and the outlines of a headland in rain. . . . He was passing the time and filling the hours in anticipation of release from a life that had lost its savor with the death of his daughter.

In ***The Bridge of San Luis Rey,*** there are some sentences which begin on page 128:

> He was blackened and cured by all weathers. He stood in the Square with feet apart as though they were planted on a shifting deck. His eyes were strange, unaccustomed to the shorter range, too used to seizing the appearances of a constellation between a cloud and a cloud, and the outlines of a cape in rain. His reticence was sufficiently explained for most of us by his voyages.

There follows a letter dealing with the death of this man's daughter, ending, "You will laugh at me, but I think he goes about the hemispheres to pass the time between now and his old age."

It is common to castigate writers as much for this kind of pillage as any other, except when the earlier work has been discarded and the resurrection represents a saving. But it may be in Mr. Wilder's case such a castigation would be an injustice. His repetition is merely a natural event in his literary method. It indicates the quality, extent, and value of his inspiration; and it shows us pretty well how he apprehends experience. He is content to reproduce, with an increment of elegance, an old gesture, when his real business lay in the creation of character; and we may take it that he was not only content but positively willing—so sure was he of its effect. Suppose, even, the gesture to be as effective in one instance as in another (which it ought not to be), there remains the question of the value of this kind of gesture in any circumstance. It sounds well, it has a good rhythm, it arouses a sympathetic set of vague feelings and responses: it gives the mind something easy to play with. But it does nowhere near the work of the opening sentences, for example, of *Lord Jim.*

> He was an inch, perhaps two, under six feet, powerfully built, and he advanced straight at you with a slight stoop of the shoulders, head forward, and a fixed from-under stare which made you think of a charging bull. Etc.

It is not suggested that Mr. Wilder should write in the style of Conrad; comparison has been introduced instead of argument merely to show how essentially vague, how conventional, is this important aspect of Mr. Wilder's writing. He does not locate himself, or his people, physically. He is engaged in the business of setting up states of mind, not in establishing experience. Having himself had the experience, he takes it as granted that the reader will be satisfied without it. . . . The point is, that it may be fairly stated that all the important images in ***The Woman of Andros*** are of this general character. The book is not written; it is written about, and it is very true to say that the reader will find in it only what he brings to it—a circumstance which may very well be true of all "literary" books.

The other reason for Mr. Wilder's failure to write a wholly successful novel—namely, the relation of his religious preoccupation to the body of his novel—has been discussed by Edmund Wilson in *The New Republic* for March 26, 1930. In brief, the point is that Mr. Wilder repeats at the end of his book certain sentences with which he began it, to the effect that Christianity was imminent but not yet. On a second reading it becomes increasingly clear that the life and death of Chrysis the hetaira and of her sister Glycerium were the best and noblest that could be had without knowledge of Christian love and salvation. Such judgment, from the point of view of the novel, is obviously *ex post facto,* and cannot directly concern the characters in the book. It is much as if Mr. Wilder should ask us to judge the tragedies of Aeschylus in the light of Christian piety, or the tragedy of *Tess of the D'Urbervilles* with relation to the polity of Confucius. Yet Mr. Wilder has so written his book that it is impossible to understand many of its passages and certainly impossible to seize its total significance without some such judgment. It is not that Mr. Wilder's Christian bias is to be complained of, but that he has inserted into the book something so real in itself that it cannot be ignored, and yet such that it cannot be real in terms of the book. The result is that he has thinned the book just where he intended to strengthen it—in its central meaning. (pp. 586-89)

R. P. Blackmur, "Thornton Wilder," in The Hound & Horn, *Vol. III, No. 4, July, 1930, pp. 586-89.*

Michael Gold (review date 22 October 1930)

[*Gold was a Jewish-American novelist, short story writer, dramatist, and essayist best known for his autobiographical novel* Jews Without Money, *a poignant account of life in the slums of early twentieth-century New York which puts forth Gold's communist ideals. In the following review, he castigates Wilder for failing to address American social problems associated with the Great Depression of the 1930s in* The Woman of Andros *and his earlier works. This article sparked heated discussion concerning the social responsibility of artists, with many commentators rejecting Gold's utilitarian view of literature.*]

"Here's a group of people losing sleep over a host of notions that the rest of the world has outgrown several centuries ago: one duchess's right to enter a door before another; the word order in a dogma of the Church; the divine right of Kings, especially of Bourbons."

In these words Thornton Wilder describes the people in his first book, ***The Cabala.*** They are some eccentric old aristocrats in Rome, seen through the eyes of a typical American art "pansy" who is there as a student.

Marcantonio is the sixteen-year-old son of one of the group; he is burned out with sex and idleness, and sexualizes with his sister, and then commits suicide. Another character is a beautiful, mad Princess, who hates her dull Italian husband, falls in love with many Nordics and is regularly rejected by them. Others are a moldy old aristocrat woman who "believes," and a moldy old Cardinal who doesn't, and some other fine worm-eaten authentic specimens of the rare old Italian antique.

Wilder views these people with tender irony. He makes no claim as to their usefulness to the world that feeds them; yet he hints that their palace mustiness is a most important fact in the world of today. He writes with a brooding seriousness of them as if all the gods were watching their little lavender tragedies. The style is a diluted Henry James.

Wilder's second novel was ***The Bridge of San Luis Rey.*** This famous and vastly popular yarn made a bold leap backwards in time. Mr. Wilder, by then, had evidently completed his appraisal of our own age. The scene is laid in Lima, Peru; the time is Friday noon, July 20, 1714. In this volume Wilder perfected the style which is now probably permanent with him; the diluted and veritable Anatole France.

Among the characters of San Luis Rey are: (1) A sweet old duchess who loves her grown daughter to madness, but is not loved in return; (2) A beautiful unfortunate genius of an actress who after much sexualizing turns nun; (3) Her tutor, a jolly old rogue, but a true worshipper of literature; (4) Two strange brothers who love each other with a passion and delicacy that again brings the homosexual bouquet into a Wilder book, and a few other minor sufferers.

Some of the characters in this novel die in the fall of a Bridge. Our author points out the spiritual lessons imbedded in this Accident; viz: that God is Love.

The third novel is the recent ***The Woman of Andros.*** This marks a still further masterly retreat into time and space. The scene is one of the lesser Greek islands, the hour somewhere in B. C.

The fable: a group of young Greeks spend their evenings in alternate sexual bouts and lofty Attic conversations with the last of the Aspasias. One young man falls in love with her sister, who is "pure." His father objects. Fortunately, the Aspasia dies. The father relents. But then the sister dies, too. Wistful futility and sweet soft sadness of Life. Hints of the coming of Christ: "and in the East the stars shone tranquilly down upon the land that was soon to be called Holy and that even then was preparing its precious burden." (Palestine.)

Then Mr. Wilder has published some pretty, tinkling, little three-minute playlets. These are on the most erudite and esoteric themes one could ever imagine; all about Angels, and Mozart, and King Louis, and Fairies, and a Girl of the Renaissance, and a whimsical old Actress (1780) and her old Lover; Childe Harold to the Dark Tower Came; Prosperina and the Devil; The Flight into Egypt; a Venetian Prince and a Mermaid; Shelley, Judgment Day, Centaurs, God, The Woman in the Chlamys, Christ; Brigomeide, Leviathan, Ibsen; every waxwork in Wells's Outline, in fact, except Buffalo Bill.

And this, to date, is the garden cultivated by Mr. Thornton Wilder. It is a museum, it is not a world. In this devitalized air move the wan ghosts he has called up, each in "romantic" costume. It is an historic junkshop over which our author presides.

Here one will not find the heroic archæology of a Walter Scott or Eugene Sue. Those men had social passions, and used the past as a weapon to affect the present and future, Scott was the poet of feudalism. The past was a glorious myth he created to influence the bourgeois anti-feudal present. Eugene Sue was the poet of the proletariat. On every page of history he traced the bitter, neglected facts of the working-class martyrdom. He wove these into an epic melodrama to strengthen the heart and hand of the revolutionary workers, to inspire them with a proud consciousness of their historic mission.

That is how the past should be used; as a rich manure, as a springboard, as a battle cry, as a deepening, clarifying and sublimation of the struggles in the too-immediate present. But Mr. Wilder is the poet of the genteel bourgeoisie. They fear any such disturbing lessons out of the past. Their goal is comfort and status quo. Hence, the vapidity of these little readings in history.

Mr. Wilder, in a foreword to his book of little plays, tells himself and us the object of his esthetic striving:

"I hope," he says, "through many mistakes, to discover that spirit that is not unequal to the elevation of the great religious themes, yet which does not fall into a repellent didacticism. Didacticism is an attempt at the coercion of another's free mind, even though one knows that in these matters beyond logic, beauty is the only persuasion. Here the schoolmaster enters again. He sees all that is fairest in the Christian tradition made repugnant to the new generations by reason of the diction in which it is expressed. . . . So that the revival of religion is almost a matter of rhetoric. The work is difficult, perhaps impossible (perhaps all religions die out with the exhaustion of the language), but it at least reminds us that Our Lord asked us in His work to be not only gentle as doves, but as wise as serpents."

Mr. Wilder is the poet of the genteel bourgeoisie.

—Michael Gold

Mr. Wilder wishes to restore, he says, through Beauty and Rhetoric, the Spirit of Religion in American Literature. One can respect any writer in America who sets himself a goal higher than the usual racketeering. But what is this religious spirit Mr. Wilder aims to restore? Is it the crude self-torture of the Holy Rollers, or the brimstone howls and fears of the Baptists, or even the mad, titanic sincerities and delusions of a Tolstoy or Dostoievsky?

No, it is that newly fashionable literary religion that centers around Jesus Christ, the First British Gentleman. It is a pastel, pastiche, dilettante religion, without the true neurotic blood and fire, a daydream of homosexual figures in graceful gowns moving archaically among the lilies. It is Anglo-Catholicism, that last refuge of the American literary snob.

This genteel spirit of the new parlor-Christianity pervades every phrase of Mr. Wilder's rhetoric. What gentle theatrical sighs! what lovely, well composed deaths and martyrdoms! what languishings and flutterings of God's sinning doves! what little jewels of Sunday-school wisdom, distributed modestly here and there through the softly flowing narrative like delicate pearls, diamonds and rubies on the costume of a meek, wronged Princess gracefully drowning herself for love, (if my image is clear).

Wilder has concocted a synthesis of all the chambermaid literature, Sunday-school tracts and boulevard piety there ever were. He has added a dash of the prep-school teacher's erudition, then embalmed all this in the speciously glamorous style of the late Anatole France. He talks much of art, of himself as Artist, of style. He is a very conscious craftsman. But his is the most irritating and pretentious style pattern I have read in years. It has the slick, smug finality of the lesser Latins; that shallow clarity and tight little good taste that remind one of nothing so much as the conversation and practice of a veteran cocotte.

Mr. Wilder strains to be spiritual; but who could reveal any real agonies and exaltations of spirit in this neat, tailor-made rhetoric? It is a great lie. It is Death. Its serenity is that of the corpse. Prick it, and it will bleed violet ink and *apéritif.* It is false to the great stormy music of Anglo-Saxon speech. Shakespeare is crude and disorderly beside Mr. Wilder. Neither Milton, Fielding, Burns, Blake, Byron, Chaucer nor Hardy could ever receive a passing mark in Mr. Wilder's classroom of style.

And this is the style with which to express America? Is this the speech of a pioneer continent? Will this discreet French drawing-room hold all the blood, horror and hope of the world's new empire? Is this the language of the intoxicated Emerson? Or the clean, rugged Thoreau, or vast Whitman? Where are the modern streets of New York,

Chicago and New Orleans in these little novels? Where are the cotton mills, and the murder of Ella May and her songs? Where are the child slaves of the beet fields? Where are the stockbroker suicides, the labor racketeers or passion and death of the coal miners? Where are Babbitt, Jimmy Higgins and Anita Loos's Blonde? Is Mr. Wilder a Swede or a Greek, or is he an American? No stranger would know from these books he has written.

But is it right to demand this "nativism" of him? Yes, for Mr. Wilder has offered himself as a spiritual teacher;/ therefore one may say: Father, what are your lessons? How will your teaching help the "spirit" trapped in American capitalism? But Wilder takes refuge in the rootless cosmopolitanism which marks every *emigré* trying to flee the problems of his community. Internationalism is a totally different spirit. It begins at home. Mr. Wilder speaks much of the "human heart" and its eternal problems. It is with these, he would have us believe, that he concerns himself; and they are the same in any time and geography, he says. Another banal evasion. For the human heart, as he probes it in Greece, Peru, Italy and other remote places, is only the "heart" of a small futile group with whom few Americans have the faintest kinship.

For to repeat, Mr. Wilder remains the poet of a small sophisticated class that has recently arisen in America—our genteel bourgeoisie. His style is their style; it is the new fashion. Their women have taken to wearing his Greek chlamys and faintly indulge themselves in his smart Victorian pieties. Their men are at ease in his Paris and Rome.

America won the War. The world's wealth flowed into it like a red Mississippi. The newest and greatest of all leisure classes was created. Luxury-hotels, golf, old furniture and Vanity Fair sophistication were some of their expressions.

Thorstein Veblen foretold all this in 1899, in an epoch-making book that every American critic ought to study like a Bible. In "The Theory of the Leisure Class" he painted the hopeless course of most American culture for the next three decades. The grim, ironic prophet has been justified. Thornton Wilder is the perfect flower of the new prosperity. He has all the virtues Veblen said this leisure class would demand; the air of good breeding, the decorum, priestliness, glossy high finish as against intrinsic qualities, conspicuous inutility, caste feeling, love of the archaic, etc. . . .

All this is needed to help the parvenu class forget its lowly origins in American industrialism. It yields them a short cut to the aristocratic emotions. It disguises the barbaric sources of their income, the billions wrung from American workers and foreign peasants and coolies. It lets them feel spiritually worthy of that income.

Babbitt made them ashamed of being crude American climbers. Mr. Wilder, "gentle as the dove and wise as the serpent," is a more constructive teacher. Taking them patiently by the hand, he leads them into castles, palaces and far-off Greek islands, where they may study the human heart when it is nourished by blue blood. This Emily Post of culture will never reproach them; or remind them of Pittsburgh or the breadlines. He is always in perfect taste; he is the personal friend of Gene Tunney.

"For there is a land of the living and a land of the dead, and the bridge is love, the only survival, the only meaning." And nobody works in a Ford plant, and nobody starves looking for work, and there is nothing but Love in God's ancient Peru, Italy, Greece, if not in God's capitalist America 1930!

Let Mr. Wilder write a book about modern America. We predict it will reveal all his fundamental silliness and superficiality, now hidden under a Greek chlamys. (pp. 266-67)

Michael Gold, "Wilder: Prophet of the Genteel Christ," in The New Republic, *Vol. LXIV, No. 829, October 22, 1930, pp. 266-67.*

Edmund Wilson (review date 16 January 1935)

[*Wilson is considered one of twentieth-century America's foremost men of letters. He is particularly noted for his seminal study of literary symbolism,* Axel's Castle *(1931), and for numerous reviews and essays in which he introduced the best works of modern literature to the reading public. In the following review, he judges* Heaven's My Destination *Wilder's best novel to date and comments on the author's use of humor and religious themes.*]

Several years ago, Thornton Wilder was the center of a controversy on Marxism and literature. He was challenged by Michael Gold [in *The New Republic,* October 22, 1930] and others to come away from his first-century Greek islands and his imaginary eighteenth-century Perus and turn his attention to the United States. Mr. Wilder has here taken up the challenge; and though, in the course of the polemical battle, he was sometimes unfairly treated, the polemics have been justified if they inspired, as they are said to have done, this new book.

Heaven's My Destination seems to me much Mr. Wilder's best novel. It is as brilliant and sharp as ***The Woman of Andros,*** which seems to me his weakest novel, was comparatively mawkish and pale. In fact, the effect on Mr. Wilder of taking his opponents' advice—if that is what happened—has been so vividly to bring him to life that they are likely to experience a shock. In the first place, he has applied to the smoking-cars, the summer camps and the boarding-houses of the Middle West the gift of social observation which he exercised in ***The Cabala*** on an aristocratic international society, but which in his intervening books has been left more or less unemployed; and Oklahoma City, Kansas City and Ozarksville become much more entertaining places than even his Roman drawing-rooms. Besides this, he has created in his central character, George Brush, the religious textbook salesman, a more complete and living person than in any of his other books. Furthermore, the pathetic Proustian cadences have vanished from Mr. Wilder's style; his sentimentality is nowhere in evidence. The tone is always comic or matter of fact—with the result that Mr. Wilder's vision of an imperfect and suffering humanity comes through a great deal more tellingly than in his earlier books. And—what makes

Heaven's My Destination unique in its Middle Western field—he has handled his Sinclair Lewis material with his characteristic elegance of form and felicity of detail, his peculiar characteristic Mozartian combination of lightness and grace with seriousness. (The Keats and Mozart affinities of Mr. Wilder were what his opponents in the Gold-Wilder controversy tended to leave out of consideration; but he is probably the only contemporary American whom it is possible to mention in connection with such names—the only one, I mean, who is really good and who has anything in common with them.)

Mr. Wilder's hero, George Brush, though professionally a textbook salesman, is by vocation a saint. "Of all the forms of genius," Mr. Wilder quotes on the title-page from ***The Woman of Andros,*** "goodness has the longest awkward age." When we first encounter George Brush, he is attempting to save souls in the smoking-car and annoying hotel managers by writing Bible texts on the blotters. He comes from a farm in Michigan, he has graduated from Shiloh Baptist College, and he has been converted by a child evangelist, full of morphine. But he has thought out his own principles of righteousness and he appears as many kinds of a crank. He feels that he can never become a minister because he once fornicated with a farmer's daughter at a farm where he was spending the night. He has been looking for her ever since to marry her. He is always getting arrested as a result of his unconventional behavior in his attempts to live up to his principles. He insists upon riding in a Jim Crow car because he believes in the equality of the races; draws all his money out of the bank and tries to give the bank the interest because he believes in "voluntary poverty"; and unnecessarily presents a hold-up man with some money in order to "show him that he's really a beggar at heart." In the course of his twenty-fourth year, the period covered by the story, he makes himself absurd and obnoxious in an extraordinary variety of ways. He encounters in his traveling-salesman's adventures many types of human beings: the conscientious and desperate man, the cynical and desperate man (the story takes place during the depression), the intelligent man caught in a routine, the brilliant man made harsh by intellectual pride, the professional prostitute and the professional minister of the Gospel, the criminal and the police. They reason with George Brush, remonstrate with him, play jokes on him, insult him, rob him, beat him up, jail him; but in a sense they are all powerless against him, because he is a genuinely virtuous man sustained by the conviction of the correctness of his intentions. And although his program for edifying people is almost completely wrong, he manages to do them good in ways which he has never contemplated simply by being what he is: a man who takes his obligations to the rest of humanity so seriously that questions of his own interest do not exist for him.

At last he succeeds in finding the girl he has slept with one night and whom he feels he is bound by duty to marry. She is more or less unattractive and doesn't in the least want to marry him. But he finally induces her to do so and she is extremely unhappy with him. He has to go out on the road again, and she lets him know that she wants to leave him. (This is the only part of the story which seems to me incomplete and a little unconvincing. Why was Roberta, when George Brush turned up again, so bitterly opposed to having anything to do with him? Why, when they were married, did he not proceed with his program of producing the six children which he considered essential to an American home?)

He loses his faith on the road and falls ill. He is crushed by the idea that his life has been a failure, that everything he has done has been stupid and that everybody has come to hate him.

But now a strangely important incident occurs. There has been in Kansas City a Polish priest named Father Pasziewski. We have heard almost nothing about him except that he has been at death's door with gallstones, that he has then recovered and gone on with his work, that he is "an awful disappointed man" because the boys and girls of his parish to whom he has devoted himself as "the Knights of St. Ludowick" and "Mary's Flowers" have turned into dance-hall girls and gangsters. He and George Brush have never met, but each has always inquired about the other: each has recognized the other's vocation. George Brush has been deeply moved by the news that Father Pasziewski was praying for him on Fridays. Now Father Pasziewski has died, and he has given his silver spoons away to his friends, and he has sent George Brush one. George recovers and goes on getting into trouble.

Mr. Wilder has told this story with great skill and made it on the surface extremely funny. A scarcely suspected gift of humor is another resource of Mr. Wilder's that has suddenly emerged in this book. But his real theme is George Brush's development, his education in the course of his adventures. And the remarkable feat he performs is to make us end by respecting and liking him.

I do not see any reason why the radical reviewers who have been urging Thornton Wilder to write about his native land should find ***Heaven's My Destination*** unacceptable. Mr. Wilder, through Father Pasziewski, ties George Brush up with the Church. But the act of divine intervention—I suppose that Mr. Wilder intends it as such—the arrival of the silver spoon, is not in itself, like the well timed collapse of the Bridge of San Luis Rey, implausible to the non-believer. And in the meantime Mr. Wilder has given us something more even than an excellent picture of an American variety of religious experience. George Brush is, as I have said, the type of saint, and he is therefore a universal character. The saint is a very special kind of person, but he turns up in other fields besides the religious one. The radical movement, too, has its saints, and they are people fundamentally akin to George Brush. Upton Sinclair in his early phases resembled him in some ways quite closely and committed some of the same kind of absurdities.

The radical's real objection to ***Heaven's My Destination*** is that Mr. Wilder never allows Brush to encounter a radical. What about the next generation of Father Pasziewskis? I happen to know the child of a family of Polish priests who, taking with him the best features of the family tradition, has become an energetic Communist. And what about George Brush in ten years? We leave him at twenty-four: what is to be the rest of his education? He has apparently already discarded the Fundamentalism which he affirmed at twenty-three. We are apparently intended to understand that he has finally investigated Darwin and no longer accepts the Garden of Eden. But what is to prevent him from going further along these lines? What is to prevent him, with his terrible logic, from turning into a Roger Baldwin? What is to prevent him, with his pacifist principles, from discovering, as did A. J. Muste, that other religious pacifist, with whom, also, George Brush has something in common, that the causes of war are involved with the social-economic system—and turning into a labor organizer?

From the tenor of Mr. Wilder's other work, I assume that when George Brush gets well and goes on trying to live up to his principles, he has recovered his faith in God. But this is actually left rather ambiguous, and perhaps Mr. Wilder ought to be challenged again to make it clear just what George Brush's beliefs are when he goes out on the road again. (pp. 282-83)

Edmund Wilson, "Mr. Wilder in the Middle West," in The New Republic, *Vol. LXXXI, No. 1050, January 16, 1935, pp. 282-83.*

Harlan Hatcher (essay date 1935)

[*Hatcher is an American critic who has written extensively on American literature. In the following excerpt from his study* Creating the Modern American Novel *(1935), he provides an overview of the early years of Wilder's career and emphasizes the versatility and duality of Wilder's writings.*]

[Thornton Wilder] has shown little interest in the contemporary scene, or in the problems that have concerned the War generation of which he is by the calendar a member. His experiences have been varied. Wisconsin born in 1897, six months before William Faulkner, he spent some eight years in China (1906-1914), attended Oberlin, served in the coast artillery, graduated from Yale and from Princeton, studied for two years in Rome and taught French at Lawrenceville. He is a poet and a musician. Neither the native endowment nor the training was likely to constrain the author to a great realistic prose.

His first novel, ***The Cabala*** (1926), was a flight from the contemporary American scene and its problems to a specialized milieu in Rome that was able to include the present day and the death of John Keats in the same time setting. It was episodic in form and was told in the first person. The effect it produced upon a certain public can best be seen in the immoderate words of Herbert Gorman in his preface to the Modern Library edition in 1929. "Now when we look back on the event we may see that ***The Cabala*** appeared at the proper moment as an unconscious disciplinary warning to those younger writers who were running amok." Herbert Gorman was presumably talking as a responsible person. And yet, as a matter of simple fact, ***The Cabala*** dealt with a group of degenerate people familiar to the fiction of the day, and its chief episode was the suicide of a young pervert after an incestuous scene. The "disciplinary warning" was not, evidently, against unpleasant substance but against a too robust frankness in presenting it. The materials of Thornton Wilder have not really been essentially different from those handled by the least restrained realists: a drunken old woman trying to dominate her daughter, an actress of easy virtue, an unfortunate monk, a courtezan, an illegitimate child fathered by a respectable Greek boy and the young Roman of ***The Cabala.*** The difference lies in the atmosphere of classic restraint which the author creates about them, and in the graceful inoffensiveness of the words in which these potentially disturbing matters are couched. In this respect the work of Thornton Wilder was another of the signs of a shift in mood toward the end of the twenties. For it is undeniable that the poetic method of writing transmutes the ill favor of a naked realism into softer and less disturbing patterns.

The Bridge of San Luis Rey (1927), after a short period of neglect, achieved enormous popularity in 1928. Its theme was intriguing because, with all the advance in science through the years, people still knock on wood, observe omens, and in various ways pay tribute to the uncertainty of chance. It raised again the question of Job and a million others: Do events befall by accident or by design? And it isolated the problem with the specific instance of a bridge in Peru breaking and destroying five persons in the year 1714. A naturalist would have answered with no hesitation that it was not by design and suggest an inspector of bridges. To a Christian mind the implications of the question could not even arise. The author quite wisely did not answer yes or no, but perhaps. And he suggested that, accident or design, Love was nurtured by it and the accident (if it were an accident) tended toward some beneficent end.

The thesis was happily not too insistent, and the highly compressed stories of the people involved told in a carefully cadenced style lived on their own merits. They were unified into an artistic whole by the mechanical device of the bridge, and by Brother Juniper's investigation not into the laws of stress and strain in grapevine bridges, but into the lives and souls of those who perished. The resulting stories are beautifully told. They are short, the whole book being less than a third the length of an ordinary novel, yet it gives the effect of a longer work because of the clean economy of the art and the evocative power of its poetic compression. And the short form makes possible a sustained mood. Most of the qualities which distinguished the book were those which the realistic writers had neglected or ignored.

For the setting of ***The Woman of Andros*** (1930) Thornton Wilder chose the romantic isles of ancient Greece. The novel was somewhat disappointing because it was an academic piece, it was self-conscious, and the reader was seldom permitted to forget that this was fine writing. It is a danger to poetic prose. The interest in "beauty" had become sentimental, and the robust sense of life in ***The Bridge of San Luis Rey*** was gone. In the climactic passage, when, after a long day of fasting and silence, Pamphilus is led, through the influence of the memory of Chrysis, to affirm the beauty of life in its dark places, a kind of nobility enters. But it is pale and a little bloodless. The distinction of the novel lay in the perfection of certain scattered passages. "You were happy with her once; do not doubt that the conviction at the heart of your happiness was as real as the conviction at the heart of your sorrow."

It was doubtless inevitable that the praise of critics like William Lyon Phelps for novels of this kind should be extravagant and excessive, and that it should in turn provoke irrelevant rebuttals from those who thought a modern artist should criticize the contemporary scene. Neither seemed to have any great effect upon Thornton Wilder. He followed the dictates of his own genius in his own way. He lectured widely. He was interested in the theater. He translated and adapted a drama for the New York stage, and he wrote a number of one-act plays in many moods as literary exercises in compressed expression. Then, after an interval of four years, he returned to the novel, and in January, 1935, published ***Heaven's My Destination.***

It is a bizarre fantasia showing few traces of the three earlier novels. It is made of the same stuff that went into some of the one-act plays in ***The Long Christmas Dinner*** (1931), particularly ***Pullman Car Hiawatha*** and ***Queens of France.*** The grotesque and potentially comic elements that were peripheral in ***The Cabala*** and ***The Bridge of San Luis Rey*** are central in ***Heaven's My Destination.*** The style is bald, realistic, outspoken, less studied and not cadenced. Instead of poise and high seriousness there is hilarious farce and a tone of mockery. It is a comic and satirical version of Channing Pollock's *The Fool,* with liberal suggestions of *Candide* and *Don Quixote,* and even a nod toward *Elmer Gantry,* but it is still Thornton Wilder. It is diverting, it is provocative, it is irritating. For its hero, George Brush, aged twenty-three, is both superlatively wise and dumb beyond credulity. He is a logical man in a contradictory world, and his logic has its ground in a few elementary propositions that are common to the religious disciplines of the world. He believes in salvation and conversion, in a militant gospel of purity, in pacifism, in voluntary poverty, in chastity, and in honesty. He tries to convert his fellow traveling salesmen, he does not smoke, drink, swear, or distinguish the subtle difference between Ma Crofut's house of beautiful girls where the policeman is welcome and the fine American home of which he dreams. He gives away his surplus money, denounces savings banks as enemies to faith, practices *ahimsa* on a robber, and purifies himself by fasting and exercise. And he takes his job as book salesman seriously and does not pad his expense account. Naturally everybody in the story thinks him crazy, is infuriated by him, and denounces him as "the damdest prig I ever saw."

The farcical humor arises from the simple device of placing so naïve and well-principled a young man in situations of whose nature he is blunderingly unaware. On one or two occasions the book seems to grow serious, as in the very excellent speech on criminology before the mirthful caricature of a judge, and in the sane moment when the hero says of himself: "I made the mistake all my life of thinking that you could get better and better until you were perfect." But these interludes are quickly broken by ironic spoofing, and by the sudden transitions into fantastic invention from boldly realistic descriptions of a book salesman and his travels in the Southwest towns. It is full of energy and go, it disturbs several hundred thousands of the tender minded readers of ***The Bridge of San Luis Rey,*** and it leaves to a later time the answer to the inevitable question: Which of the two opposed elements in his versatile endowment will Thornton Wilder choose to cultivate? For he has, at least temporarily, abandoned the form of poetic realism in which he distinguished himself. (pp. 252-56)

Harlan Hatcher, "Poetic Versus Hard-Boiled Realism," in his Creating the Modern American Novel, *Farrar & Rinehart, Incorporated, 1935, pp. 247-61.*

Brooks Atkinson (review date 13 February 1938)

[*As drama critic for the* New York Times *from 1925 to 1960, Atkinson was among the most influential reviewers in America. In the following notice, which originally appeared in the* New York Times *on 13 February, 1938, and was later included in his collection* Broadway Scrapbook *(1947), Atkinson praises Wilder's treatment of the simple aspects of life in* Our Town *and comments on the play's form and stage techniques.*]

Thornton Wilder's ***Our Town*** is set in Southern New Hampshire near Mount Monadnock. But the New England aspect of his play goes deeper than that. His detached and speculative point of view conveys the New England rhythm. From Cotton Mather through the Concord cosmologists, Longfellow and Lowell to Edwin Arlington Robinson and Robert Frost, the New Englander has tuned himself to the infinite. Perhaps it is the age of the culture of the Puritan heritage, perhaps it is the somber loveliness of the landscape or the barbaric extremes of climate through the turn of the year—whatever the reason, the New Englander is aware of something mightier than his personal experience. The long point of view, which Mr. Priestley discovered in *Time and the Conways,* comes naturally to him. In Santayana, who served a term of collegiate office in New England, it is refined into brooding poetry with classical models, but he puts it into words when he says: "The art of life is to keep step with the celestial orchestra that beats the measure of our career and gives the cue for our exits and entrances." What matters most is not the isolated experience of the day but the whole pattern of life from the ancient past into the depths of the future.

That is the genius of Mr. Wilder's very notable play. By casually dispensing with most of the formalities of the realistic theatre he has given the local doings of Grover's Corners a cosy niche in the universe. He is looking on affectionately from a distance and what he sees is a terribly poignant chapter in living and dying. Although he enfolds the play in the great amplitude of the universe in many ways, he puts the most cogent statement of it on the lips of a wondering child who is gazing at the moonlight one Spring evening; she impulsively recalls the dryly humorous address that some wag has scribbled on the envelope of a letter to a Grover's Corners girl: "June Crofut, the Crofut Farm, Grover's Corners, Sultan County, New Hampshire, United States of America, Continent of North

America, Western Hemisphere, the Earth, the Solar System, the Universe, the Mind of God." "What do you know!" her adolescent brother exclaims incredulously, wondering what all that can possibly mean. But the theatregoer knows that Mr. Wilder simply means to offer Grover's Corners in evidence as a gentle way of life.

From the long point of view the ordinary things in life become infinitely pathetic. Day by day we are buoyed up by the normal bustle of our families, neighbors and friends. But the long point of view is a lonely one and the little living that people do on this spinning planet is tragically unimportant. It has been repeated so many times in so many places without plan or deliberation, and there are centuries of it ahead. Some of the simplest episodes in ***Our Town*** are therefore touching beyond all reason. The scene in which Dr. Gibbs patiently reproves his son for neglecting to chop firewood for his mother becomes tenderly emotional because, in its homely statement, it is a portrait of thoughtlessness and understanding. The shy, faltering scene between George and Emily when for the first time they realize they love each other is, in spite of its romantic material, overwhelmingly compassionate because of what it represents in the immutable ways of men and women. Mr. Wilder's scheme of playwriting distinguishes between what is mortal and what is immortal in the chronicle of normal living. There go all of us, not "but for the grace of God," but "by the grace of God." This is the record of the simplest things we have all been through. Grover's Corners is ***Our Town***—the days and deaths of the brotherhood of man.

Now that ***Our Town*** has been seen, the extraordinary form in which it is written seems to be the least important thing about it. As most theatregoers know by this time, it is produced without scenery, with the curtain always up. There is nothing on the stage except a few chairs and tables and two commonplace trellises to suggest doorways. Frank Craven, stage manager and commentator, opens the performance by setting the stage and then acting as a sort of village host by describing the play, introducing scenes and concluding them, summoning people to the stage to give vital statistics about the town and occasionally playing bits in the performance. On paper this doubtless sounds like a stunt, and almost becomes one when Mr. Craven proceeds to set the stage for a second time in the second act; the mechanical repetition results in audience self-consciousness. But Mr. Wilder's scheme, which probably derives from the Chinese and Greek theatres, is the logical way of achieving the abstraction he is after. It makes for complete theatre and intellectual candor. He is after not the fact but the essence of the fact; and a production stripped of all the realistic impedimenta of the theatre is essential to his theme. (pp. 85-7)

The people of Grover's Corners are not highly cultivated, but they have the New England instinct for knowing where they are and what matters most. "No, ma'am, there isn't much culture," the local editor replies to an inquiring member of the audience, "but maybe this is the place to tell you that we've got a lot of pleasures of a kind here: we like the sun coming up over the mountain in the morning, and we all notice a good deal about the birds. We pay a lot of attention to them. And we watch the change of the seasons: yes, everybody knows about them." Being familiar with New England, Mr. Wilder loves it, and ***Our Town*** probes close to the inner truth and cuts to the quick. Having something beautiful to say, Mr. Wilder has found the most vivid way to express it in the theatre. (p. 88)

Brooks Atkinson, "Our Town," in his Broadway Scrapbook, *Theatre Arts, Inc., 1947, pp. 85-8.*

Mary McCarthy (review date January-February 1943)

[*McCarthy was an American critic, novelist, and short story writer noted for her knowledge of the American theater and her opinionated assessments of popular dramatists. In the following notice, originally published in the* Partisan Review *in 1943, she finds* The Skin of Our Teeth *simple and unchallenging and asserts that it is essentially a work of conventional historical drama.*]

Thornton Wilder's latest play, ***The Skin of Our Teeth,*** is a spoof on history. For all its air of experimentalism, its debt to Joyce, as yet unacknowledged, its debt to Olson and Johnson, paid in full, it belongs to a tradition familiar and dear to the Anglo-Saxon heart. That is the tradition of *The Road to Rome, Caesar and Cleopatra, Hamlet* in modern dress, *Julius Caesar* in uniforms. Its mainspring is the anachronistic joke, a joke both provincial and self-assertive, a joke which insists that the Roman in his toga is simply a bourgeois citizen wearing a sheet, and that Neanderthal man with his bear-skin and his club is at heart an insurance salesman at a fancy-dress ball. The joke has a double fascination which it exerts on the middle-class public and the middle-class playwright alike. In the first place, it is conservative: it affirms the eternity of capitalism, which it identifies with "human nature," and it consoles us for the flatness of the present by extending that flatness over the past, so that whatever our sufferings, we shall at least not be racked by envy, that most dangerous of human passions. In the second place, it is sacrilegious, for it denies time and history, and this, to the modern ear, is the moral equivalent of hubris, of ancestor-desecration, of the sin against the Holy Ghost. Hence it is that such works as ***The Skin of Our Teeth*** almost invariably have an appearance of daring: the shock value of *The Private Life of Helen of Troy,* say, did not derive from its rather mild sexual impropriety. Moreover, art and culture generally find themselves within easy range of the blasphemer (and this is only logical, since culture is an historical phenomenon); you get Mark Twain or Mr. Wilder's third act where the philosophers appear as half-audible quotations from their works, quotations which can only be introduced after a great deal of apologetic discussion: "I don't suppose it means anything," says the stage-manager. "It's just a kind of poetic effect." Mr. Wilder, being a professor, wants to have it both ways: he wants to sponsor the philosophers, but at the same time he does not want the audience to think that he is an ass.

The plot and structure of ***The Skin of Our Teeth*** must by this time be in the public domain. Everybody knows that the play deals with three great crises in human history, the

Wilder's nostalgia, which found a pure and lyrical expression in *Our Town,* . . . has made its way more furtively into *The Skin of Our Teeth* and lurks there as an impediment both to action and to thought. . . .

—Mary McCarthy

return of the Ice Age, the Flood, the War, any war at all or this war in particular. It is Mr. Wilder's fancy that all these events happened to a man named George Antrobus of 216 Cedar Street, Excelsior, New Jersey, father of two, President of the Ancient Order of Mammals, inventor, soldier and occasional philanderer. Man, then, enlightened ape, is seen as the eternal husband, whose destiny is an endless commuter's trip between the Home and the Office, the poles of the human sphere. The trip may not be broken on pain of flood, ice, fascism; a stopover with the Other Woman will result in a disaster of millennial proportions. "Oh, oh, oh! Six o'clock and the master not home yet," says the maid, opening the play. In other words, if George misses the five-fifteen, Chaos is come again. This is the moral of the piece. Man, says Mr. Wilder, from time to time gets puffed up with pride and prosperity, he grows envious, covetous, lecherous, forgets his conjugal duties, goes whoring after women; portents of disaster appear, but he is too blind to see them; in the end, with the help of the little woman, who has never taken any stock in either pleasure or wisdom, he escapes by the skin of his teeth. *Sicut erat in principio*. . . .

It is a curious view of life. It displays elements of Christian morality. Christ, however, was never so simple, but on the contrary allowed always for paradox (the woman taken in adultery, the story of Martha and Mary, "Consider the lilies of the field") and indeed regarded the family as an obstacle to salvation. No, it is not the Christian view, but a kind of bowdlerized version of it, such as might have been imparted to a class of taxpayer's children by a New England Sunday School teacher forty years ago. And here we find again Mr. Wilder's perennial nostalgia, a nostalgia not for the past but for an eternal childhood, for the bedrock of middle-class family life, for *"the old Sunday evenings at home with the tinkling piano our guide."* It is a nostalgia which found a pure and lyrical expression in ***Our Town,*** but which has made its way more furtively into ***The Skin of Our Teeth*** and lurks there as an impediment both to action and to thought, for at the end of each act the play hits the suburban family group, stumbles over it, and comes to a halt; the repetition is inevitable, but not dramatic: the only conflict is the conflict between the submerged idea and the form. The play in general suffers from a certain embarrassment and uneasiness, as if its author were ashamed of the seriousness with which he adheres to his theme. Surely Miss Bankhead's asides to the audience and the whole conceit that the end of the world is only a play that some actors are putting on serve no other purpose than to relieve the author's sense of awkwardness. "I don't understand a word of this play," Miss Bankhead complains again and again, but actually there is not a word in the play which Miss Bankhead cannot and does not perfectly comprehend. All this aspect of the play is, to put it frankly, fraudulent, an illusionist's trick; an elaborate system of mystification has been, as it were, installed in the theatre in order to persuade the audience that it is witnessing a complex and difficult play, while what is really being shown on the stage is of a childish and almost painful naiveté. To some extent, the illusion is successful: middlebrow members of the audience are, as usual, readily induced to disregard the evidence of their own ears and consider the play either monstrously profound or monstrously bewildering. Simpler people, however, who have never heard of Aristotle, see nothing difficult about it. They accept the performance as a sort of lark, which at best it is, a bright children's pantomime, full of boldly costumed figures out of Bible history. As the daily drama critics have said, over and over, with all the relish of Lucifer admitting a new registrant into hell, Mr. Wilder has become a *real* man of the theatre. (pp. 53-6)

Wilder in the role of Mr. Antrobus in The Skin of Our Teeth.

Mary McCarthy, "The Skin of Our Teeth," in her Sights and Spectacles: 1937-1956. *Farrar, Straus and Cudahy, 1956, pp. 53-6.*

Orville Prescott (review date 18 February 1948)

[*Prescott was the daily literary critic for the* New York Times *from 1942 to 1966. In the following review, he discusses Wilder's innovative structuring of* The Ides of March.]

Thornton Wilder, whether he is writing fiction or drama, can be counted upon to brood about the meaning of life and the destiny of man, and to experiment with literary form. When he sprang to sudden fame in 1927 with ***The Bridge of San Luis Rey,*** one of the reasons for the impression made by that essentially slight, although beautiful, book was the very perfection of its structure, the neat way in which the threads of its pattern all were woven together to meet upon a collapsing bridge. That book won a Pulitzer Prize.

Mr. Wilder's two plays, which also won Pulitzer Prizes, ***Our Town*** and ***The Skin of Our Teeth,*** aroused nearly as much attention because of the way they said things, the absence of props and scenery in the first and the mayhem committed upon time and history in the second.

In his new novel, his first in fourteen years, ***The Ides of March,*** Mr. Wilder has contrived still another original and intricate way of presenting his material.

Basically this is a historical novel about Julius Caesar during the last months before his assassination in the Roman Senate. But since it was written by Mr. Wilder it bears no resemblance whatever to the debased variety of popular entertainment offered by much of the contemporary historical fiction. Mr. Wilder calls his book "a fantasia on certain events and persons of the last days of the Roman republic." That is as good a description as any, for ***The Ides of March*** is certainly not a novel in the conventional sense and the liberties it takes with history exceed those usually granted to fiction. A lot of members of the Book-of-the-Month Club, whose March selection it is, are going to be extremely confused about Roman history after reading ***The Ides of March.***

The device Mr. Wilder has chosen is to present a collection of imaginary documents, excerpts from letters and journals. He has arranged them in four parts. Those in each successive part begin earlier in time and continue later than those in its predecessor.

This fantastic complication of chronology does much to obliterate the little narrative pace ***The Ides of March*** might have had in the first place. But since simple story-telling was not Mr. Wilder's principal intention, the advantage of grouping together in each section discussions of the same theme is probably all to the good.

Many of the principal characters whose writings are quoted were actually long dead in 45 B. C. Many of the circumstances of Caesar's life are completely imaginary. This is fiction! But it is so persuasively real, so convincing, that one recognizes a brilliant tour de force. Caesar's letters seem like those of a very great man, a man of contemplation as well as of action, an individual who has indulged every animal appetite without becoming brutalized, a questioning spirit who has outgrown all personal ambition. Cicero's letters are as vain and pompous as they should be. Catullus' are the very quintessence of a young poetic genius driven to distraction by his hopeless love for a debauched woman.

The Caesar of Mr. Wilder's imagination is an interesting combination of a glittering personality, ruthless intelligence and philosophical detachment. He considered most of the Roman religion superstitious nonsense, but could not quite bring himself to abolish it. He employed a secret police to ferret out the intimate secrets of his subjects and so knew all about the conspiracy that killed him, but he could not be bothered to take precautions. He brooded long on abstract matters, religion, fate, poetry, freedom, asking all the intelligent questions that have haunted doubting minds for several millennia, but he reached no particularly impressive conclusions.

So, although ***The Ides of March*** is, to a certain extent, a philosophical novel as well as a historical one, its philosophy is an attitude of mind rather than a system of doctrine. Mr. Wilder himself evidently believes that great minds always have considered the same great questions and that they haven't yet found the answers.

In the end it is Caesar's personality, not his ideas, that is the dominant impression made by ***The Ides of March.*** After Caesar there are three other characters who are given enough space so that their personalities, too, are sharply drawn: Catullus; Clodia, the proud, clever, beautiful woman bent on self-destruction and consumed by hate, and Cleopatra, willful, capricious, ambitious, ruthless, fascinating and treacherous.

The Ides of March is an extraordinarily finished performance. Each document is an integral part of the whole and each document seems as if it could only have been written by the author ascribed to it. But, expert and original as ***The Ides of March*** is, it is an intellectually interesting stunt, not a work of fiction that can stir the emotions. Like a Roman portrait bust, it is cold, precise, artful and quite lacking in the divine fire that glows about a major work of art.

Orville Prescott, in a review of "The Ides of March," in The New York Times, *February 18, 1948, p. 25.*

Thornton Wilder with R. H. Goldstone (interview date Winter 1957)

[*Goldstone is an American critic whose studies include* Contexts of the Drama *(1968),* Mentor Masterworks of Modern Drama *(1969), and* Thornton Wilder: An Intimate Portrait *(1975). In the following interview, Wilder discusses his public image, his writing habits, and his artistic development.*]

A national newsmagazine not very long ago in its weekly cover story limned Thornton Wilder as an amiable, eccentric itinerant schoolmaster who wrote occasional novels and plays which won prizes and enjoyed enormous but somewhat unaccountable success.

Wilder himself has said: "I'm almost sixty and look it. I'm the kind of man whom timid old ladies stop on the street to ask about the nearest subway station: newsvendors in university towns call me 'professor', and hotel clerks, 'doctor'."

Many of those who have viewed him in the classroom, on the speaker's rostrum, on shipboard, or at gatherings have been reminded of Theodore Roosevelt who was at the top of his form when Wilder was an adolescent and whom Wilder resembles in his driving energy, his enthusiasms, and his unbounded gregariousness.

It is unlikely that more than a few of his countless friends have seen Wilder in repose. Only then do you realize that he wears a mask. The mask is no figure of speech. It is his eyeglasses.

As do most glasses, they partially conceal his eyes. The glasses also distort his eyes so that they appear larger: friendly, benevolent, alive with curiosity and interest. Deliberately or not, he rarely removes his glasses in the presence of others. When he does remove them, unmasks himself so to speak, the sight of his eyes is a shock.

Unobscured, the eyes—cold light blue—reveal an intense severity and an almost forbidding intelligence. They do not call out a cheerful "Kinder! Kinder! . . ."; rather, they specify: "I am listening to what you are saying. Be serious. Be precise."

Seeing Wilder unmasked is a sobering and tonic experience. For his eyes dissipate the atmosphere of indiscriminate amiability and humbug that collects around celebrated and gifted men; the eyes remind that you are confronted by one of the toughest and most complicated minds in contemporary America. They are the eyes of a man whose novels have enjoyed the attention and aroused the sensibilities, for thirty years now, of the whole gamut of the reading public in America and Europe. (In Germany he is generally addressed as *Verehrter Dichter.*) His plays have so appreciably affected American theater tradition that few serious dramatists have ignored the fact of their existence.

Why the mask? Ultimately, that must remain Thornton Wilder's secret, as it remains the secret of every artist. A part of the explanation, however, may lie in the fact, as this interview will suggest, that not the least of his virtues is his admirable tact, his consideration for the feelings of others. . . .

. . . . .

[Goldstone]: *Sir, do you mind if we begin with a few irrelevant—and possibly impertinent—questions, just for a warm-up?*

[Wilder]: Perfectly all right. Ask whatever comes into your head.

One of our really eminent critics, in writing about you recently, suggested that among the critics you had made no enemies. Is that a healthy situation for a serious writer?

(After laughing somewhat ironically) The important thing is that you make sure that neither the favorable nor the unfavorable critics move into your head and take part in the composition of your next work.

One of your most celebrated colleagues said recently that about all a writer really needs is a place to work, tobacco, some food and good whiskey. Could you explain to the non-drinkers among us how liquor helps things along?

Many writers have told me that they have built up mnemonic devices to start them off on each day's writing task. Hemingway once told me he sharpened twenty pencils; Willa Cather that she read a passage from the Bible (not from piety, she was quick to add, but to get in touch with fine prose; she also regretted that she had formed this habit, for the prose-rhythms of 1611 were not those she was in search of). My spring-board has always been long walks. I drink a great deal, but I do not associate it with writing.

Although military service is a proud tradition among contemporary American writers, I wonder if you would care to comment on the circumstance that you volunteered in 1942, despite the fact that you were a veteran of the first world war. That is to say, do you believe that a seasoned and mature artist is justified in abandoning what he is particularly fitted to do for patriotic motives?

I guess everyone speaks for himself in such things. I felt very strongly about it. I was already a rather old man, was fit only for staffwork, but I certainly did it with conviction. I have always felt that both enlistments were valuable for a number of reasons.

One of the dangers of the American artist is that he finds himself almost exclusively thrown in with persons more or less in the arts. He lives among them; eats among them; quarrels with them; marries them. I have long felt that portraits of the non-artist in American literature reflect a pattern, because the artists don't really frequent. He portrays the man in the street as he remembers him from childhood, or he copies him out of other books. So one of the benefits of military service, *one* of them, is being thrown into daily contact with non-artists, a thing young American writers should consciously seek—his acquaintance should include also those who have read only *Treasure Island* and have forgotten that. Since 1800 many central figures in narratives have been, like their authors, artists or quasi-artists. Can you name three heroes in earlier literature who partook of the artistic temperament?

Did the young Thornton Wilder resemble George Brush [of ***Heaven's My Destination***] *and in what ways?*

Very much so. I came from a very strict Calvinistic father, was brought up partly among the missionaries of China, and went to that splendid college at Oberlin at a time when the classrooms and student life carried a good deal of that pious didacticism which would now be called narrow Protestantism. And that book ***(Heaven's My Destination)*** is, at is were, an effort to come to terms with those influences.

The comic spirit is given to us in order that we may analyze, weigh, and clarify things in us which nettle us, or which we are outgrowing, or trying to reshape. That is a very autobiographical book.

Why have you generally avoided contemporary settings in your work?

I think you would find that the work is a gradual drawing near to the America I know. I began with the purely fantastic twentieth century Rome (I did not frequent such circles there); then, Peru; then, Hellenistic Greece. I began, first with ***Heaven's My Destination,*** to approach the American scene. Already, in the one act plays, I had become aware of how difficult it is to invest one's contemporary world with the same kind of imaginative life one has extended to those removed in time and place. But I always feel that the progression is there and visible; I can be seen collecting the practice, the experience, and courage to present my own times.

What is your feeling about "authenticity"? For example, you had never been in Peru when you wrote **The Bridge of San Luis Rey.**

The chief answer to that is that the journey of the imagination to a remote place is child's play compared to a journey into another time. I've been often in New York, but it's just as preposterous to write about the New York of 1812 as to write about the Incas.

You have often been cited as a "stylist". As a writer who is obviously concerned with tone and exactness of expression, do you find that the writing of fiction is a painful and exhausting process, or do you write easily, quickly and joyously?

Once you catch the idea for an extended narration—drama or novel—and if that idea is firmly within you, then the writing brings you perhaps not so much pleasure as a deep absorption . . . (Mr. Wilder reflected here for a moment and then continued). You see, my waste-paper basket is filled with works that went a quarter-through and which turned out to be one of those things which failed to engross the whole of me . . . And then for a while, there's a very agonizing period of time in which I try to explore whether that work I've rejected cannot be reoriented in such a way as to absorb me. The decision to abandon it is hard.

Do you do much rewriting?

I forget which of the great sonneteers said: "One line in the fourteen comes from the ceiling; the others have to be adjusted around it." Well, likewise there are passages in every novel whose first writing is pretty much the last. But it's the joint and cement, between those spontaneous passages, that take a great deal of re-writing.

I don't know exactly how to put the next question, because I realize you have a lot of theories about narration, about how a thing should be told—theories all related to the decline of the novel, and so on. But I wonder if you would say something about the problem of giving a "history" or a summary of your life in relation to your development as a writer.

Let's try. The problem of telling you about my past life as a writer is like that of imaginative narration itself, it lies in the effort to employ the past tense in such a way that it does not rob those events of their character of having transpired in freedom. A great deal of writing and talking about the past is unacceptable. It freezes the historical in a determinism. Today's writer smugly passes his last judgment and confers on existing attitudes the lifeless aspect of plaster-cast statues in a museum. They recount the past as though the characters knew what was going to happen next.

Well, to begin—do you feel that you were born in a place and at a time, and to a family—all of which combined favorably to shape you for what you were to do?

Comparisons of one's lot with others teaches us nothing and enfeebles the will. Many born in an environment of poverty, disease and stupidity, in an age of chaos, have put us in their debt. By the standards of many people, and by my own, these dispositions were favorable;—but what are our judgments in such matters? Everyone is born with an array of handicaps—even Mozart, even Sophocles—and acquires new ones. In a famous passage, Shakespeare ruefully complains that he was not endowed with another writer's "scope"! We are all equally distant from the sun, but we all have a share in it. The most valuable thing I inherited was a temperament that does not revolt against Necessity and that is constantly renewed in Hope. (I am alluding to Goethe's great poem about the problem of each man's "lot"—the *Orphische Worte.*)

Did you have a happy childhood?

I think I did, but I also think that that's a thing about which people tend to deceive themselves. Gertrude Stein once said "Communists are people who fancied that they had an unhappy childhood." (I think she meant that the kind of person who can persuade himself that the world would be completely happy if everyone denied himself a vast number of free decisions, is the same kind of person who could persuade himself that in early life he had been thwarted and denied all free decision.) I think of myself as having been—right up to and through my college years—a sort of sleepwalker. I was not a dreamer, but a muser and a self-amuser. I have never been without a whole repertory of absorbing hobbies, curiosities, inquiries, interests. Hence, my head has always seemed to me to be like a brightly lighted room, full of the most delightful objects, or perhaps I should say, filled with tables on which are set up the most engrossing games. I have never been a collector, but the resource that I am describing must be much like that of a collector busying himself with his coins or minerals. Yet, collectors are apt to be "avid" and competitive, while I have no ambition and no competitive sense. Gertrude also said, with her wonderful yes-saying laugh: "Oh, I wish I were a miser; being a miser must be so occupying." I have never been unoccupied. That's as near as I can get to a statement about the happiness or unhappiness of my childhood. Yet: I am convinced that except in a few extraordinary cases, one form or another of an unhappy childhood is essential to the formation of exceptional gifts. Perhaps I should have been a better man if I had had an unequivocally unhappy childhood.

Can you see—or analyze, perhaps—tendencies in your early years which led you into writing?

I thought we were supposed to talk about the art of the novel. Is it all right to go on talking about myself this way?

I feel that it's all to the point.

We often hear the phrase, "a winning child". Winning children (who appear so guileless) are children who have discovered how effective charm and modesty and a delicately calculated spontaneity are in winning what they want. All children, emerging from the egocentric monster-hood of infancy ("Gimme! Gimme!" cries the Nero in the bassinet), are out to win their way—from their parents, playmates, from "life", from all that is bewildering and inexplicable in themselves. They are also out to win some expression of themselves as individuals. Some are early marked to attempt it by assertion, by slam-bang methods; others by a watchful docility; others by guile. The future author is one who discovers that language, the exploration and manipulation of the resources of language, will serve him in winning through to his way. This does not necessarily mean that he is highly articulate in persuading or cajoling or outsmarting his parents and companions, for this type of child is not usually of the "community" type—he is at one remove from the persons around him. (The future scientist is at eight removes.) Language for him is the instrument for digesting experience, for explaining himself to himself. Many great writers have been extraordinarily awkward in daily exchange, but the greatest give the impression that their style was nursed by the closest attention to colloquial speech. Let me digress for a moment: probably you won't want to use it. For a long time I tried to explain to myself the spell of Madame de Sévigné; she is not devastatingly witty nor wise. She is simply at one with French syntax. Phrase, sentence and paragraph breathe this effortless at-homeness with how one sees, feels, and says a thing in the French language. What attentive ears little Marie de Rabutin-Chantal must have had! Greater writers than she had such an adjustment to colloquial speech—Montaigne, La Fontaine, Voltaire—but they had things to say: didactic matter; she had merely to exhibit the genius in the language.

I have learned to watch the relation to language on the part of young ones,—those community-directed toward persuation, edification, instruction; and those engaged ("merely" engaged) in fixing some image of experience; and those others for whom language is nothing more than a practical convenience ("Oh, Mr. Wilder, tell me how I can get a wider vocabulary?").

Well now, inasmuch as you have gone from story-telling to playwrighting, would you say the same tendencies which produced the novelist, produced the dramatist?

I think so, but in stating them I find myself involved in a paradox. A dramatist is one who believes that the pure event, an action involving human beings, is more arresting than any comment that can be made upon it. On the stage it is always *now;* the personages are standing on that razor-edge, between the past and the future, which is the essential character of conscious being; the words are arising to their lips in immediate spontaneity. A novel is what *took place;* no self-effacement on the part of the narrator can hide the fact that we hear his voice recounting, recalling events that are past and over, and which he has selected—from uncountable others—to lay before us from his presiding intelligence. Even the most objective novels are cradled in the authors' emotions and the authors' assumptions about life and mind and the passions. Now the paradox lies not so much in the fact that you and I know that the dramatist equally has selected what he exhibits and what the characters will say—such an operation is inherent in any work of art—but that all the greatest dramatists, except the very greatest *one,* have precisely employed the stage to convey a moral or religious point of view concerning the action. The theater is supremely fitted to say: "Behold! These things are . . . " Yet most dramatists employ it to say: "This moral truth can be learned from beholding this action."

The Greek tragic poets wrote for edification, admonition, and even for our political education. The comic tradition in the theater carries the intention of exposing folly and curbing excess. Only in Shakespeare are we free of hearing axes ground.

How do you get around this difficulty?

By what may be an impertinence on my part. By believing that the moralizing intention resided in the authors as a convention of their times—usually, a social convention so deeply buried in the author's mode of thinking that it seemed to him to be inseparable from creation. I reverse a popular judgment: we say that Shaw wrote diverting plays to sugarcoat the pill of a social message. Of these other dramatists, I say they injected a didactic intention in order to justify to themselves and to their audiences the exhibition of pure experience.

Is your implication then that drama should be art for art's sake?

Experience for experience's sake—rather than for moral improvement's sake. When we say that Vermeer's "Girl Making Lace" is a work of art for art's sake, we are not saying anything contemptuous about it. I regard the theater as the greatest of all art-forms, the most immediate way in which a human being can share with another the sense of what it is to be a human being. This supremacy of the theater derives from the fact that it is always "now" on the stage. It is enough that generations have been riveted by the sight of Clytemnestra luring Agamemnon to the fatal bath, and Oedipus searching out the truth which will ruin him; those circumambient tags about "don't get prideful" and "don't call anybody happy until he's dead" are incidental concomitants.

Is it your contention that there is no place in the theater for didactic intentions?

The theater is so vast and fascinating a realm that there is room in it for preachers and moralists and pamphleteers. As to the highest function of the theater I rest my case with Shakespeare—*Twelfth Night* as well as *Macbeth.*

If you will forgive me, I'm afraid I've lost track of something we were talking about a while back—we were talking about the tendencies in your childhood which went into the formation of a dramatist.

The point that I've been leading up to is that a dramatist is one who from his earliest years has found that sheer gazing at the shocks and countershocks among people is quite sufficiently engrossing without having to encase it in comment. It's a form of tact. It's a lack of presumption. That's why so many earnest people have been so exasperated by Shakespeare: they cannot isolate the passages wherein we hear him speaking in his own voice. Somewhere Shaw says that one page of Bunyan "who plants his standard on the forefront of . . . I-forget-what . . . is worth a hundred by such shifting opalescent men."

Are we to infer from what you say that the drama ought to have no social function?

Oh yes,—there are at least two. First, the presentation of *what is,* under the direction of those great hands, is important enough. We live in *what is,* but we find a thousand ways not to face it. Great theater strengthens our faculty to face it.

Secondly, to be present at any work of man-made order, and harmony, and intellectual power—Vermeer's "Lace-Maker" or a Haydn quartet or *Twelfth Night*—is to be confirmed and strengthened in our potentialities as man.

I wonder if you don't hammer your point pretty hard because actually you have a considerable element of the didactic in you.

Yes, of course. I've spent a large part of my life trying to sit on it, to keep it down. The pages and pages I've had to tear up. I think the struggle with it may have brought a certain kind of objectivity into my work. I've become accustomed to readers taking widely different views of the intentions in my books and plays. A good example is George Brush, whom we were talking about before. George, the hero of a novel of mine which I wrote when I was nearly forty, is an earnest, humorless, moralizing, preachifying, interfering product of the "Bible belt" evangelism. I received many letters from writers of the George Brush mentality angrily denouncing me for making fun of sacred things, and a letter from the Mother Superior of a convent in Ohio saying that she regarded the book as an allegory of the stages in the spiritual life.

Many thank me for the "comfort" they found in the last act of ***Our Town;*** others tell me that it is a desolating picture of our limitation to "realize" life—almost too sad to endure.

Many assured me that ***The Bridge of San Luis Rey*** was a satisfying demonstration that all the accidents of life were overseen and harmonized in providence; and a society of atheists in New York wrote me that it was the most artful exposure of shallow optimisms since *Candide* and asked me to address them.

A very intelligent woman to whom I offered the dedication of ***The Skin of Our Teeth*** refused it, saying that the play was so defeatist. ("Man goes stumbling, bumbling down the ages.") ***The Happy Journey to Trenton and Camden*** received its first performance, an admirable one, at The University of Chicago. Edna St. Vincent Millay happened to be in the audience. At the close of the play she congratulated me at having so well pictured that "detestable bossy kind of mother."

Most writers firmly guide their readers to "what they should think" about the characters and events. If an author refrains from intruding his point of view, readers will be nettled, but will project into the text their own assumptions and turns of mind. If the work has vitality, it will, however slightly, alter those assumptions.

So that you have not *eliminated all didactic intentions from your work after all?*

I suspect that all writers have some didactic intention. That starts the motor. Or let us say: many of the things we eat are cooked over a gas stove, but there is no taste of gas in the food.

Bravo!—In one of your Harvard lectures you spoke of—I don't remember the exact words—a prevailing hiatus between the highbrow and lowbrow reader. Do you think a work could appear at this time which would satisfy both the discriminating reader and the larger public?

What we call a great age in literature is an age in which that is completely possible: that the whole total Athenian audience took part in the flowering of Greek tragedy and Greek comedy. And so in the age of the great Spaniards. So in the age of Elizabeth. We certainly are not, in any sense, in the flowering of a golden age now; and one of the unfortunate things about the situation is this great gulf. And it would be a very wonderful thing if we see more and more works which close that gulf between the highbrows and lowbrows.

Someone has said—one of your dramatist colleagues, I believe, I can't remember which one—that a writer only deals with one or two ideas throughout his work. Would you say your work reflects those one or two ideas?

Yes, I think so. I only have become aware of it myself recently. Those ideas seem to have prompted my work before I realized it. Now, at my age, I am amused by the circumstance that what is now conscious with me, was for a long time latent. One of those ideas is this: an unresting preoccupation with the surprise of the gulf between each tiny occasion of the daily life and the vast stretches of time and place in which every individual plays his role.

By that I mean the absurdity of any single person's claim to the importance of his saying: "I love!" . . . "I suffer!", when one thinks of the background of the billions who have lived and died, who are living and dying, and presumably will live and die.

This was particularly developed in me by the almost accidental chance that having graduated from Yale in 1920, I was sent abroad to study archaeology at the American Academy in Rome. We even took field trips in those days and in a small way took part in diggings. When one has swung a pickaxe which will reveal the curve of a street four-thousand years covered over which was once an active, much traveled highway, you are never quite the same again. You look at Times Square as a place about which you imagine some day scholars saying: "There appears to have been some kind of public center here."

This preoccupation came out in my work before I realized it. Even ***Our Town,*** which I now see is filled with it, was not so consciously directed by me at the time. At first glance, the play appears to be practically a genre study of the picture of a village in New Hampshire. On second glance, it appears to be a meditation about the difficulty of, as the play says, "realizing life while you live it." But buried back in the text, from the very commencement of the play, is a constant repetition of the words: "hundreds", "thousands", "millions". It's as though the audience—no one has ever mentioned this to me, though—is looking at that town at ever greater distances through a telescope.

I'd like to cite some examples of this. Soon after the play begins the Stage Manager calls upon the professor from the geology department of the state university who says how many million years old the ground is they're on. And the Stage Manager talks about putting some objects and reading matter into the cornerstone of a new bank and covering it with a preservative so that it can be read a thousand years from now. Or as minister presiding at the wedding, the Stage Manager muses to himself about the marriages that have ever taken place—"millions of 'em, millions of 'em . . . Who set out to live two by two . . . " Finally among the seated dead, one of the dead says: "My son was a sailor and used to sit on the porch. And he says the light from that star took millions of years to arrive."

There is still more of this. So that when finally the heartbreak of Emily's unsuccessful return to life again occurs, it is against the background of the almost frightening range of these things.

Then ***The Skin of Our Teeth,*** which takes five thousand years to go by, is really a way of trying to make sense out of the *multiplicity* of the human race and its affections.

So that I see myself making an effort to find the dignity in the trivial of our daily life, against those preposterous stretches which see to rob it of any such dignity; and the validity of each individual's emotion.

I feel that there is another important theme running through your work which has to deal with the nature of love. For example, there are a number of aphorisms in **The Bridge of San Luis Rey** *which are often quoted and which related to that theme. Do your views on the nature of love change in your later works?*

My ideas have not greatly changed; but those aphorisms in ***The Bridge*** represent only one side of them and are limited by their application to what is passing in that novel. In ***The Ides of March,*** my ideas are more illustrated than stated.

Love started out as a concomitant of reproduction; it is what makes new life and then shelters it. It is therefore an affirmation about existence and a belief in value. Tens of thousands of years have gone by; more complicated forms of society and of consciousness have arisen. Love acquired a wide variety of secondary expressions. It got mixed up with a power conflict between male and female; it got cut off from its primary intention and took its place among the refinements of psychic life and in the cult of pleasure; it expanded beyond the relations of the couple and the family and reappeared as philanthropy; it attached itself to man's ideas about the order of the universe and was attributed to the gods and God.

I always see beneath it, nevertheless, the urge that strives toward justifying life, harmonizing it,—the source of energy on which life must draw in order to better itself. In ***The Ides of March*** I illustrate its educative power (Caesar toward Cleopatra and his wife; the actress toward Marc Antonio) and its power to "crystallize" idealization in the lover (Catullus's infatuation for the destructive "drowning" Clodia—he divines in her the great qualities she once possessed). This attitude has so much the character of self-evidence for me that I am unable to weigh or even "hear" any objections to it. I don't know whether I am uttering an accepted platitudc or a bit of naïve nonsense.

Your absorbing interest in James Joyce and Gertrude Stein is pretty well known. I wonder if there are any other literary figures who are of particular interest to you.

In present day life?

Well, past or present.

I am always, as I said earlier, in the middle of a whole succession of very stormy admirations up and down literature. Every now and then, I lose one; very sad. Among contemporaries, I am deeply indebted to Ezra Pound and Mr. Eliot. In the past, I have these last few years worked a good deal with Lope de Vega, not in the sense of appraisal of his total work but almost as a curious and very absorbing game—the pure technical business of dating his enormous output of plays . . . I could go on forever about these successive enthusiasms.

Do you believe that a serious young writer can write for television or the movies without endangering his gifts?

Television and Hollywood are a part of show business. If that young writer is to be a dramatist, I believe that he's tackling one of the most difficult of all métiers—far harder than the novel. All excellence is equally difficult, but considered as sheer métier, I would always advise any young writer for the theater to do everything—to adapt plays, to translate plays, to hang around theaters, to paint scenery, to become an actor, if possible. Writing for TV or radio or the movies is all part of it. There's a bottomless pit in the acquisition of how to tell an imagined story to listeners and viewers.

If that young writer has the problem of earning a livelihood, are teaching English, or advertising, or journalism suitable vocations?

I think all are unfavorable to the writer. If by day you handle the English language either in the conventional forms which are journalism or advertising, or in the analysis which is teaching English in school or college, you will have a double, a quadruple difficulty in finding *your* English language at night and on Sundays. It is proverbial that every newspaper reporter has a half-finished novel in his bureau drawer. Reporting—which can be admirable in itself—is poles apart from shaping concepts into imagined actions and requires a totally different ordering of mind and language. When I had to earn my living for many years, I taught French. I should have taught mathematics. By teaching math or biology or physics, you come refreshed to writing.

Mr. Wilder, why do you write?

I think I write in order to discover on my shelf a new book which I would enjoy reading, or to see a new play that would engross me.

Do your books and plays fulfill this expectation?

No.

They disappoint you?

No, I do not repudiate them. I am merely answering your question—they do not fulfill *that* expectation. An author, unfortunately, can never experience the sensation of reading his own work as though it were a book he had never read. Yet with each new work that expectation is prompting me. That is why the first months of work on a new project are so delightful: you see the book already bound, or the play already produced, and you have the illusion that you will read or see it as though it were a work by another that will give you pleasure.

Then all those other motivations to which other writers have confessed play no part in your impulse to write—sharing what experience has taught you, or justifying your life by making a thing which you hope to be good?

Yes, I suppose they are present also, but I like to keep them below the level of consciousness. Not because they would seem pretentious, but because they might enter into the work as strain. Unfortunately, good things are not made by the resolve to make a good thing, but by the application to develop fitly the one specific idea or project which presents itself to you. I am always uncomfortable when in "studio" conversation, I hear young artists talking about "truth" and "humanity" and "what is art?", and most happy when I hear them talking about pigments or the timbre of the flute in its lower range or the spelling of dialects or James's "center of consciousness".

Is there some final statement you would wish to make about the novel?

I'm afraid that I have made no contribution toward the intention of this series of conversations on the art of the novel. I think of myself as a fabulist, not a critic. I realize that every writer is necessarily a critic,—that is, each sentence is a skeleton accompanied by enormous activity of rejection; and each selection is governed by general principles concerning truth, force, beauty and so on. But, as I have just suggested, I believe that the practice of writing consists in more and more relegating all that schematic operation to the subconscious. The critic that is in every fabulist is like the iceberg—nine-tenths of him is underwater. Yeats warned against probing into how and why one writes; he called it "muddying the spring". He quoted Browning's lines:

> "Where the apple reddens do not pry
> Lest we lose our Eden, you and I."

I have long kept a journal to which I consign meditations about the "omniscience of the novelist" and thoughts about how time can be expressed in narration, and so on. But I never re-read those entries. They are like the brief canters that a man would take on his horse during the days preceding a race. They inform the buried critic that I know he's there, that I hope he's constantly at work clarifying his system of principles, helping me when I'm not aware of it, and intimating that I hope he will not intrude on the day of the race.

Gertrude Stein once said laughingly that writing is merely "telling what you know". Well, that telling is as difficult an exercise in technique as it is in honesty; but it should emerge as immediately, as spontaneously, as *undeliberately* as possible. (pp. 37-57)

Thornton Wilder and R. H. Goldstone, in an interview in The Paris Review, *No. 15, Winter, 1957, pp. 37-57.*

Malcolm Cowley (review date 2 April 1967)

[*Cowley is an American critic, poet, translator, and historian who is noted in particular for his critical studies of modern American literature. Below, he provides a positive assessment of* The Eighth Day, *emphasizing Wilder's originality.*]

In the early summer of 1902 John Barrington Ashley of Coaltown, a small mining center in southern Illinois, was tried for the murder of Breckenridge Lansing, also of Coaltown. He was found guilty and sentenced to death. Five days later, at one in the morning of Thursday, July 22, he escaped from his guards on the train that was carrying him to his execution.

That is the beginning of Thornton Wilder's sixth and longest novel [***The Eighth Day***], the first he has published in nearly 20 years. Although the words are printed here without quotation marks, they are the author's words, not mine. In taking notes for this review I tried to paraphrase several of his statements, including those in his opening paragraph, but I found in each case that the paraphrase was longer than the original. Wilder has a way of choosing the necessary facts and of stating them in the simplest and briefest fashion. The facts may be prosaic, but his statements are as hard to change as a finished line of poetry.

Where the reviewer can't paraphrase, at least he can delete and summarize: John Ashley, though tracked to South America, was not recaptured. Five years after his escape, another man confessed to the murder, but Ashley never reappeared. Meanwhile two of his four children had launched themselves, and the youngest was preparing to launch herself, on careers that would make them international figures. They would soon become—I must start quoting again—"the object of that particularly clamorous form of celebrity that surrounds those who are both ridiculed and admired, adored and hated. . . . So it was that as early as 1910 and 1911 people began to study the records of the Ashley Case and to ask questions—frivolous or thoughtful questions—about John and Beata Ashley and their children, about Coaltown, about those old teasers Heredity and Environment, about gifts and talents, and destiny and chance."

Those questions as they relate to the Ashley Case are the theme of ***The Eighth Day.*** Wilder tells us about the adventures of John Ashley in Chile, where he dodges the "rat catchers"; about young Sophie Ashley and how she saves the rest of the household at the cost of her sanity; about the swift rise of Roger Ashley in Chicago journalism; and then about the earlier background of the Ashleys and of Eustacia Lansing, wife of the murdered man. In the course of these rapidly moving stories he introduces dozens of characters from all levels of society, including the saintly and the picaresque. He moves backward and forward in time as if all the stories were threads in a historical tapestry. At the end of the novel Roger Ashley visits a saintly old man and finds him "gazing intently at the homemade rug at his feet."

> Roger's eyes followed his. It had been woven long ago, but a complex mazelike design in brown and black could still be distinguished.
>
> "Mr. Ashley, kindly lift that rug and turn it over."
>
> Roger did so. No figure could be traced on the reverse. It presented a mass of knots and of frayed and dangling threads. With a gesture of the hand the Deacon directed Roger to replace it.
>
> "You are a newspaperman in Chicago. Your sister is a singer there. Your mother conducts a boardinghouse in Coaltown. Your father is in some distant country. Those are the threads and knots of human life. You cannot see the design."

Silence. There are no final answers to the questions. There are only the illuminations we have found by the way, with the author's comments on human destinies, and the pleasure of reading—I almost said "of hearing," since Wilder writes for the ear—a skillfully told and well invented story.

The Eighth Day reminds one distantly of Wilder's most popular novel, ***The Bridge of San Luis Rey*** (1927), which also was concerned with chance and destiny. I can find in it no resemblance to any other novel of the past 100 years. Most of the others imitate reality, or offer us dreams to be substituted for reality, but Wilder has neither of these aims. Instead of imitating or evading, he *illustrates,* and he thus goes back to an older tradition in fiction. What ***The Eighth Day*** most resembles, though on a wider scale, is the *contes philosophiques* of Voltaire, each of which was written to illustrate a principle; its style is like that of *Candide, or Optimism,* though its substance is closer to that of *Zadig, or Destiny.* John Ashley is indeed a sort of Zadig, in both his ingenuity and his misfortunes. Though he never rises to high rank, as Zadig finally rises, his broken career paves the way for the glorious careers of his children.

In writing *Zadig* Voltaire had in mind *The Arabian Nights,* and Wilder also goes back to that still earlier tradition. One is tempted to picture him as a long-robed storyteller in some oriental marketplace. He does not reproduce the life around him in his tales, rather he invents and combines the sort of happenings that will attract a circle of listeners. If the happenings are amazing or touched with the miraculous, why, so much the better; they will be illustrations of the religious faith to which he adheres. Sufism, Taoism, Brahmanism, Zen, all have their cycles of stories. Wilder's faith would be hard to define, but it seems to include both Eastern and Western elements, combined in almost the same proportion that one finds in Thoreau, whom he greatly admires, and Emerson. On that side he goes back to an earlier American day, but he is more sophisticated than any of the Transcendentalists. Though some of the happenings he invents are close to being impossible, he uses his wide experience of the world to adorn them with realistic details and thus to make them plausible.

He is, in other words, an extremely complicated writer under his mask of simplicity. More and more I feel that his work has not received the close attention it deserves—from the critics, that is; the academics and the public have always been generous. Wilder has been awarded half-a-dozen gold medals, including that of the National Institute, and ten or more honorary degrees. Three of his plays have been enormously successful, and two of them won Pulitzer Prizes (besides his first Pulitzer for ***San Luis Rey***). ***Our Town*** (1938), after its long run on Broadway, became the most popular play of the century in amateur theaters; until recently it was being performed somewhere in the world, and often in several places simultaneously, on every night of every year. That helps to explain the neglect of Wilder by literary critics, who are inclined to feel that such popularity must be only too well deserved.

Another reason why critics have failed to discuss his work is that it cannot be placed in any category that includes the work of other contemporary writers. Born in 1897, Wilder belongs to the same age group as Faulkner, Hemingway, Fitzgerald, Hart Crane, and Edmund Wilson, but it would be hard to name qualities that he shares with any of these, or with their successors. His work is untimely in a spectacular fashion. Indeed, he comes close to denying the existence of time when he denies its essential attribute, which is that of being irreversible. "It is only in appearance that time is a river," he says. "It is rather a vast landscape and it is the eye of the beholder that moves." Since human nature is unchanging, anything that once happened might happen again. "There are no Golden Ages and no Dark Ages. There is the oceanlike monotony of the generations of men under the alternations of fair and foul weather."

That same comparison of humanity with the unchanging ocean can be found in Emerson, who says, "Society is a wave. The wave moves onward, but the water of which it is composed does not." There are many Emersonian notes in Wilder's novels, though they do not appear to be echoes. One of them is the habit, passed on to his characters, of speaking in aphorisms. Thus, a character says in ***The Eighth Day,*** "Suffering is like money, Mr. Tolland. It circulates from hand to hand. We pass on what we take in." The style there is Emerson's, and elsewhere many of the ideas are close to his. One example is Wilder's belief in the influence exerted by heroes of the sort that Emerson calls Representative Men. John Ashley and his children are such heroes; they bear, as it were, a sign on their foreheads; and Wilder leads us to infer that perhaps a change is coming at last; that these are the new men and women of ***The Eighth Day.***

He likes to write about the Ashleys; they arouse his narrative verve and his gift for inventing new situations; but he is not blind to their faults. In one of his comments on them, he seems to be making a wry statement about himself. "Readers recognized his voice," he says of young

Roger, the newspaperman, ". . . . reasonable without being argumentative, earnest without being ponderous, and always brief. It was the voice of ethical persuasion. Finally his admirers and enemies found relief in the formula that he was 'old-fashioned.' He seemed to speak for the America of one's grandparents." I do not know what place Wilder's work will occupy in the America of our great-grandchildren. I do know that it is different from anyone else's work—as is proved once again by ***The Eighth Day***—and that our present literature would be appreciably poorer without that earnest but never ponderous voice. (pp. 1-2)

Malcolm Cowley, "A Unique Case," in The Washington Post, *April 2, 1967, pp. 1-2.*

Donald Haberman (essay date 1967)

[*Haberman is an American educator and critic. In the following excerpt from his study* The Plays of Thornton Wilder *(1967), he discusses how Wilder manipulates time and space through his use of language and staging techniques.*]

Knowing that he can never have it (and probably that he does not really want it), the American still gazes wistfully at the European's identification with time and place. Norman Holmes Pearson has described the American writer's longing for community as "the desire to belong, not so much to any particular society as to a spiritual fellowship which unites men with each other" ["The American Writer and the Feeling for Community" in *Some American Studies*]. Wilder more generally contrasted the European with the American [in "Toward an American Language," *Atlantic,* July, 1952]:

> "I am I," says the European, "because the immemorial repetitions of my country's way of life surround me. I know them and they know me."
>
> An American can have no such stabilizing relation to any one place, nor to any one community, nor to any one moment in time.

The European understands his time and place literally; the American tries to realize his life in terms of an idea. His community is located in the imagination.

Wilder's lifelong traveling from place to place has encouraged him to regard geography as essentially without any real influence on identity. But his is the American experience—Sartre has called our cities mere camps, temporary and fragile—exaggerated. Time also has a special meaning for Wilder. In 1954 he wrote [in his essay **"Joyce and the Modern Novel"**]:

> After I'd graduated from college I was sent to Europe to study archaeology. One day our class in Rome was taken out into the country to dig up a bit of the Etruscan world, a street. Once thousands of persons had walked it. The rut was very deep. Those who have uncovered such a spot are never the same again.
>
> Now in the 20th Century, we all have something of the mind of an archaeologist. The other centuries knew that many people had lived and died a long while ago, and they knew there were many people living on the earth. But the invention of the printing press . . . had made these realizations far more actual. Now everybody knows them, not as something you learn in school and recite to one another, but "in their bones"—that millions and billions have lived and died. The extent of this enlarged realization alters the whole view of life.

Wilder's first novel, ***The Cabala,*** literally translated into plot what the archaeologist finds, by exposing at once several important layers in the history of Rome. John Keats lives alongside a Renaissance princess, whose son embodies some of the spirit of classical Rome, and the actual time of the novel is sometime during the first quarter of the twentieth century. This view of the simultaneous presentness of all the past Wilder had encountered already as early as his days at Oberlin where a teacher, Charles Wager, told him, "Every great work was written this morning."

Yet if Wilder feels these problems as an American, he feels them as strongly as a man who wants to write for the stage. In **"Some Thoughts on Playwriting,"** he contrasted the novel with the play:

> The novel is a past reported in the present. On the stage it is always now. This confers upon the action an increased vitality which the novelist longs in vain to incorporate into his work. . . .
>
> *A play is what takes place.*
>
> *A novel is what one person tells us took place.*

Gertrude Stein's book *The Geographical History of America,* for which Wilder wrote the introduction, helped Wilder to understand his own experience in the light of all experience. In 1935 he wrote to Gertrude Stein:

> What a book! I mean What a book! I've been living for a month with ever-increasing intensity on the conceptions of Human Nature and the Human Mind, and on the relations of Masterpieces to their apparent subject matter. Those things, yes and identity, have become cell and marrow in me and now at last I have more about them. . . .
>
> Yes, I'm crazy about America. And you did that to me, too.
>
> [*The Flowers of Friendship,* edited by Donald Gallup]

If Wilder was crazy about America, it was not simply patriotic feeling. In the *Time* magazine cover story in [January 12] 1953, he is quoted as saying about *The Geographical History:*

> Human nature, she [Gertrude Stein] said, clings to identity, to location in time and place. The human mind has no identity; it gazes at pure existing and pure creating, and "it knows what it knows when it knows it." It can be found in masterpieces, for masterpieces alone report the ever-unfolding and the boundless Now. But it can also be found in America, which was brought up to believe in boundlessness. America's very ge-

> ography, said Stein, is "an invitation to wander."

All great literature of the past, myths, and history are meaningful and belong to the present of twentieth-century America despite their apparently ephemeral and particularizing characters. In fact, what is particular about them is lost as Americans struggle to make the "masterpieces" their own; it is as though all the past were one great American myth. This is another way of expressing Professor Pearson's "spiritual fellowship which unites men with each other," as opposed to a "particular society." The history of Europe, for example, is real for Americans, but in the sense that a myth is real: what it says is addressed to the Human Mind; the events themselves are relevant only insofar as they convey meaning.

Gertrude Stein's Human Nature and the Human Mind are related to Wilder's idea of "each tiny occasion of the daily life and the vast stretches of time and place." He told the *Paris Review* interviewer:

> ***The Skin of Our Teeth,*** which takes five thousand years to go by, is really a way of trying to make sense out of the multiplicity of the human race and its affections.
>
> So that I see myself making an effort to find the dignity in the trivial of our daily life, against those preposterous stretches which seem to rob it of any such dignity; and the validity of each individual's emotion
> [*Writers at Work,* edited by Malcolm Cowley].

Human Nature in ***Our Town*** is found in each of the small events located in turn-of-the-century New England and in ***The Skin of Our Teeth*** in the events of a particular suburban family, but because of the peculiar style of generalized presentation of "pure existing and pure creating," that is, the absence or the confusion of time and place, it results in an appeal to the Human Mind. Wilder learned from Gertrude Stein that the qualities most characteristically American are those most appealing to the Human Mind.

Wilder paid part of his debt to Gertrude Stein in ***Our Town.*** Throughout the play he constantly reminds the audience that what they are witnessing happened a long time ago. Grover's Corners, New Hampshire, never existed except as a dreamy bucolic idyll that is desired but not realized. The Stage Manager helps convey the nostalgia through memory when he says, "First automobile's going to come along in about five years—belonged to banker Cartwright." When Mrs. Gibbs appears on stage for the first time, the Stage Manager says:

> Mrs. Gibbs died first—long time ago, in fact. She went out to visit her daughter, Rebecca, who married an insurance man in Canton, Ohio, and died there—pneumonia—but her body was brought back here. She's up in the cemetery there now—in with a whole mess of Gibbses and Herseys—she was Julia Hersey 'fore she married.

After the newspaper boy, Joe Crowell, goes offstage:

> Want to tell you something about that boy Joe Crowell there. Joe was awful bright—graduated from high school here, head of his class. So he got a scholarship to Massachusetts Tech. Graduated head of his class there, too. It was all wrote up in the Boston paper at the time. Goin' to be a great engineer, Joe was. But the war broke out and he died in France.—All that education for nothing.

Mrs. Gibbs is one of the many Herseys and Gibbses, before and after her, as she lies in the cemetery. The same is true of Joe Crowell. He is one of the many whose promise was wasted in catastrophe, whether natural or manmade, although perhaps Joe is seen more as a sacrifice than as a waste, for presumably he died defending the things represented by the best in ***Our Town.***

The glimpses of future time—that is, time after the action of the play but before the time of the audience—reminders that what happens is actually time past, are more than inverse flashbacks. They represent, like the sudden return on the wedding day to George's proposal to Emily, a consistent and deliberate rearrangement of time. The logic that dominates the play has little relation to the progression of historical time, although Wilder reminds the audience that as individuals they must all finally submit to the tyranny of that historical time. Partly Wilder relies on this confusion, as with the interruption by the proposal, to prevent the ordinariness of subject matter from seeming uninteresting. More importantly, however, the interruption of events without having any of them reach a conclusion—George never really gets around to proposing to Emily—prevents them, and their place as one in a great number, from being overlooked. They are never one part of a sequence, but always stand out in their own separateness.

The reminder of time past seems to work directly in opposition to Wilder's idea of the stage's eternal *now;* however, as memory it moves with a logic all its own and exists as present time. He said in 1952 in a magazine article **"The American Loneliness"** [in the *Atlantic,* August, 1952], "Time is something we create, we call into being, not something we submit to—an order outside us." By recalling past time, Wilder has, in the three acts of his play, created his own time separate from that time of the audience which ticks away each minute. He has presented in recognizable sequence birth, marriage, and death, events analogous to the cycle of life of any member of the audience. But the sequence—particularly its end in death—gives the events a special poignancy, and the events achieve a meaning beyond the sequence. Each event in the life of Emily Webb is single and unimportant, but more, each event is also part of a universe too vast to imagine. The repeated shifts in time are reminders that all parts of life's sequence are in operation for any number of people at any time. It is the force of memory that is always in the present tense. This memory, juggling all the events at once like a circus performer, keeps the action in the eternal *now* on stage. Wilder offers memory as the real thing, feeling that it has a greater value than the actual experience. Witnessing the past with all the advantages of hindsight but without the power to change anything dramatizes the anguish of the inadequacy of life.

Emily in the third act, when she is dead, sees beyond mortality the continuity of life. The audience, too, should see themselves as having a place in a great continuum. When the Stage Manager says that those people who dig up the bank's cornerstone will know more about the people of ***Our Town*** "than the Treaty of Versailles and the Lindbergh flight," he is saying the same thing as Emily in a different way—that the events of history have to do with time, but the *real* life of the people is immortal. "Yet [in Babylon] every night all those families sat down to supper, and the smoke went up the chimney—same as here." Although the dead forget, and however inadequate humanity may be, life goes on eternally in the same old way.

For ***The Skin of Our Teeth,*** Wilder devised a single complex time from three distinct points of measurement, sometimes shifting from one to the other, sometimes fusing them with one another. The first and simplest use of time is that which measures the events of the Antrobus family, living as any suburban family in the United States of the mid-twentieth century. This is the family of numberless situation comedies. Along with this artificial present time is historical time—the family through history. So that the past might gain an even greater relevance to the present, Wilder exploited the stage time, the two hours it takes the play to be performed, by having the actors pretend to be actors who are performing a play. Underlying these is a thematic progression, like the birth to death of ***Our Town.*** The first disaster the Antrobus family encounters is purely physical and from outside, the Ice Age. The flood of the second act is also physical and from outside, but with the implication that it results from some sort of moral failing on man's part. The third and least comic, war, is exclusively man's effort to destroy himself. Yet each time man has it within his power to retrieve his situation from destruction at the last moment and to begin again.

In the first act, Moses, one of the refugees from the approaching glacier, questions Mrs. Antrobus about her family: "I understand you had two sons." She turns to the audience: "Abel, Abel, my son, my son, Abel, my son, Abel, Abel, my son." The pain of the loss of children to parents complexly superimposed on murder or fratricide, really the same things in a view that regards man as a single family, is deftly and movingly expressed through the cultural memory of Cain and Abel and further of David and Absalom. The mood of complicated sorrows is interrupted at once by a comic shriek from Sabina in the kitchen. The comedy prevents Mrs. Antrobus from appearing simply a maudlin bore, but it is to the point, for Sabina has seen Henry, or Cain, the other son, throw a stone at a neighbor's boy. Although Sabina is funny, what she sees—"And it looked to me like stark murder"—is horrifying enough; man never seems to have learned very much from his past mistakes.

Again when the Antrobus family, re-enacting the story of Noah at Atlantic City, are climbing aboard the ark, Henry is nowhere to be found. Mrs. Antrobus on the boardwalk frantically calls him, and then in desperation, switching from the name Henry, she calls Cain. Henry suddenly appears. The substitution of names and the almost magical appearance of Henry combine to make a frightening piece of stage business, Mrs. Antrobus, the incarnation of selfless mother love, refuses to leave without Henry, who is everything that is disgusting and detestable in man. Not only is Henry loved in spite of his wickedness, but because man is not human without being evil, Henry must go along into the ark. There is even some relief in the audience as the lost child is found; "Here I am, mama," he says brightly. That he is called by love suggests an aspect in man almost too private and sinister to be presented any other way but fictionally, if it is not to be sentimental or false.

In Act III the audience sees the culmination of Henry's career. Sabina, now the returning camp-follower, attempts to force Mrs. Antrobus and Gladys to recognize that Henry is the enemy. Upon his return, however, Henry is given one of the two baked potatoes being saved for Mr. Antrobus and is nourished back to health despite his unchanged ways. He snarls, "The first thing to do is to burn up those old books; it's the ideas he [Antrobus] gets out of those old books . . . that makes the whole world so you can't live in it." At best, Moses and Homer are refugees and the Muses a pathetic singing troupe in America. Although on the fringes, they are there available to us in our need. Henry, a book-burner, would destroy them utterly. Antrobus, his father, is also hated. "I'll kill him so fast. I've spent seven years trying to find him; the others I've killed were just substitutes." Wilder has called up the Oedipal father-son competition, but it is not the usual Freudian cliché. Henry's urge is to self-destruction, to tear from himself all that is best and most productive in the past history of mankind. Here is the answer to Mrs. Antrobus' call to him from the boardwalk. He is all evil in all time, retained and *cherished* in the family unit. The audience can expect nothing different.

Having the characters in the play played by actors who are also characters in the play permits Wilder to speak directly and in a somewhat didactic manner to the audience, much as the Stage Manager does in ***Our Town.*** As actors miss their cues and are taken ill, as Sabina refuses to say her lines and confides in the audience in the character of the actress Miss Somerset, and as the scenery totters out of place, the play, like the human race, seems on the point of collapse. But it, too, will get through by the skin of its teeth. The contretemps in the play's production show that the past lives not only in the present of the family Antrobus but also in the present and the future of each member of the audience; the past is inescapable.

In only one place does the shifting from the particular reality of the Antrobus family to a reality beyond it become obtrusive. After the war Antrobus and Henry struggle together, and their fight develops into a "real" one between the two actors. Wilder felt compelled to provide for these actors psychological explanations for their behavior. It is unfortunate that Sabina should be the spokesman in this scene for the common-sense view that evil needs no psychologizing, for she has been consistently discredited throughout the play, and there is no reason to believe her now. The explanation is unconvincing, a refugee from a social worker's report, with about the same validity and dramatic value. The scene is an even greater surprise since

Wilder has always assiduously avoided dependence on the clinic.

The three levels of time are completed in the speeches of the hours and extended both backward and forward by the circular structure of the play. In an article about Joyce in 1954 Wilder wrote about books that are not read, using those of Rousseau as examples.

> Did you ever read Rousseau's *Émile* or *La Nouvelle Héloïse*? I never did—but I can pretty well believe that all of us, whether we know it or not, have been in large part formed by them. Every century has its underground books which have permeated thought. Often they have been transmitted through relatively few readers. I believe those two great books of Rousseau are shaping us still—though many of us will probably never read them
>
> **["Joyce and the Modern Novel"]**.

The speeches of the hours, a device Wilder had used ten years earlier in ***Pullman Car Hiawatha,*** demonstrate his belief that the past is alive all around us. History, of whatever sort, is the really important world in which we all live. (pp. 54-62)

In ***The Merchant of Yonkers,*** Wilder employed the machinery of farce to effect the ground of timelessness and the absence of a particularized place. Farce is necessarily artificial, and no one need believe in its actuality. Only the truth it presents is important. The characters are stock characters and are not limited by any time. By definition the action of farce is based on an absurd premise, which is, however, developed logically. Having its bases in the imagination, or Human Mind, which ranges with complete freedom, the comic imagination shows us the vast human possibilities that can be ours if only we have the mind and strength to make them so. To be sure, the possibilities are not always pleasant, as for example the plays of Molière. Both the writer and the audience of comedy are in the position of God, for it is they who manipulate, who laugh at, who contain all the actions of the characters moving before them. Jokes and references may be topical, and they may stale with the passage of time; but the action of comedy is timeless because it, like the American, is insubmissive to anything outside it. The comic spirit of ***The Merchant of Yonkers*** presents the individual existing, related to totality, and freed from obedience to destiny.

Wilder's accomplishment in the willful manipulation of time and space largely went unperceived. Most critics saw ***Our Town*** as a nostalgic tribute to the good years before World War I in America, carefully limiting its time and place. ***The Merchant of Yonkers*** was regarded as a failure, having as its only redeeming feature the setting and costumes designed by Boris Aronson. ***The Skin of Our Teeth*** might have corrected the false view of Wilder's skill, but a large part of its audience felt, or at least proclaimed, that the play was mad and incomprehensible. People by no means ill educated or stupid who saw the original production will claim still, whenever the play is mentioned, that they did not understand a single word of it. Amazingly enough, this attitude is contradicted by those who almost immediately found it simple-minded. In fact, neither attitude is reasonable.

Wilder offered suggestions for staging the play:

> At various moments the play superficially resembles other modes, but never thoroughly and never for long: "dream plays"; German expressionism; a comic strip; musical comedy turns. Its prevailing and unifying character is Old Fashioned American Stock Company Theatre.
>
> So the walls are frankly "flats" that ripple when a draft hits them. To be consistent, I should be willing that the Atlantic City boardwalk be one of those vaudeville drops. . . .
>
> A cyclorama has been suggested for the back of the stage; but I have never seen a cyclorama that did not suggest "beauty" of the poetic drama type. I cannot see how background from which the refugees emerge in Act One and the humble not-quite-sublime representatives of the Philosopher-Hours parade in front of in Act Three could be better represented than by the same brick walls and steam-pipes that were used in ***Our Town.***
>
> However, while the Antrobuses' sitting-room should have the character of a stage-setting from an old-fashioned stock company play, I do not mean that it should be dismal or dull.
>
> ["Author's Suggestions for Staging the Play," Yale Collection of American Literature].

The "prevailing and unifying character" of the old-fashioned American stock company play was also the manner intended for ***The Merchant of Yonkers.*** In ***The Skin of Our Teeth,*** however, it undergoes a change resulting from the other modes which are superimposed.

When Wilder was at the American Academy in Rome in 1920-1921, a German had lent him several German expressionist plays by Georg Kaiser, Fritz von Unruh, Oskar Kokoschka, Walter Hasenclever, and Carl Sternheim. Wilder, perhaps too modestly, perhaps to cross the trail with a red herring, says that he does not remember them and that his knowledge of German then was not sufficiently great that he could have got much from them. However, his interest in expressionist theater techniques was undoubtedly strengthened by his play-going marathon in Germany in 1928. But most important to him as lessons was Dreiser's *Plays of the Natural and the Supernatural.* The plays in this peculiar volume exhibit the arbitrarily arranged reality and dreamlike atmosphere characteristic of expressionism.

The imaginative presentation of human behavior patterns as in a dream Wilder employed most forcefully at the conclusion of Act II of ***The Skin of Our Teeth.*** The scene is Atlantic City. The characters in this act come closest to being like the characters in a comic strip. They are larger than life, and they have a naïve mythic quality. After Antrobus has succumbed to Sabina, after Mrs. Antrobus has tossed into the sea her letter in which are written "all the things that a woman knows," after Gladys is exposed in red stockings, and after it is revealed that Henry has again hit a man with a stone, the almost-but-not-quite-real At-

Wilder and director Max Reinhardt discussing the script of The Merchant of Yonkers, *1938.*

lantic City dissolves. Lights begin to flash and whirl unpleasantly. A "high whistling noise begins." All the animals are described as appearing in pairs. Loud thunder is heard. Antrobus tries in vain to speak to the radio audience. The conveners snake-dance across the stage while a voice from the bingo parlor calls the numbers and letters of the game and Esmeralda frighteningly pronounces doom to them all. Throughout, Mrs. Antrobus calls Henry Cain.

In this mad scene Wilder deserts recognizable reality first of all because such a removal from what is familiar dramatizes best the collapse of the Antrobus world. A realistic scene of destruction could only appear rather mild and perhaps even silly. Secondly, the nightmare on stage, from which the Antrobus family escapes by fleeing through the aisles of the theater, is a representation of the disintegration of man's moral and emotional world. This inner world is mysterious and cannot satisfactorily be represented according to traditional Aristotelian logic. It demands the arbitrary logic of the imagination. The flying scenery, suggested, according to Wilder, by the performances of Olsen and Johnson's *Hellzapoppin'*, is more than comic stage business. The shakiness of the world on stage suggests, even beyond the impermanence of the theatrical representation, the more sinister idea of the impermanence of the particular details of life. Beginning with the fall of Antrobus, or Adam, everything that depended on their faith, the static stability of Eden, is removed and must be recreated.

Mood, so important to the dramaturgy of expressionism, is also used by Wilder, first in ***Our Town*** and then in ***The Skin of Our Teeth.*** Near the conclusion of Act II of ***Our Town,*** many events are viewed as happening simultaneously: first the choir rehearsal with George and Emily talking from their windows across the lawn; then the choir with George talking with his father; finally the ladies returning from choir rehearsal with the speeches of Dr. and Mrs. Gibbs, George and Rebecca, and Mr. Webb and Emily. These events appear slight if they are considered separately, but together they become meaningful, especially after they are summed up in Rebecca's speech about the letter addressed to Jane Crofut. They are given their place in the mind of God. The moonlight, although no attempt is made to reproduce it, is repeatedly described by the characters. This moonlight, which the audience must work to create, combined with the singing of the choir, establishes a mood or feeling which the audience is nearly powerless to resist. Just as with the umbrellas at the funeral in the third act, this mood so prepares the audience for the correct response that the actors must play their parts with the greatest simplicity, keeping limited any display of emotion. If the actors force the scene, it topples into sentimental weeping and reduces the meaning to particularity, although what Wilder has prepared is honest sentiment and a carefully generalized portrayal.

Almost identical effects are created in ***The Skin of Our Teeth.*** At the conclusion of the first act, to encourage the audience to accept the danger to the entire human group, Wilder has the refugees sing "Jingle Bells" and then "Tenting Tonight." These songs, like the hymns in ***Our Town,*** are part of the childhood of the audience. The response to the songs, therefore, is automatically an emotional one. The singing colors whatever happens on stage. This primitive emotional reaction is emphasized by the passages in Greek and Hebrew. The foreign words recited dramatically, precisely because the audience do not understand their meaning, touch something in the audience that is deeper than rational argument could go. In a memo, presumably to the director, Elia Kazan, Wilder wrote:

> I earnestly hope you retain the speeches in Greek and Hebrew even if it is bold and may puzzle a portion of the audience, for those who get it, it will be a value so deep-reaching that it will be worth the risk. And I think that with the additional support to the scene of the cold-suspense . . . the passage will sustain.

Unfortunately Wilder's plea was not heeded, and the speeches did not appear in the original New York production.

Although both expressionism and Wilder's use of it are based on an ideal vision, expressionism's ideal moves away from ordinary reality and finds its form in situations dependent on the will of the writer. The vision is communicated through what are recognizably artificial situations. Wilder is equally artificial, but most prominently in the area of his stagecraft. By eliminating clichés of staging, he is able to offer the clichés of life as one kind of truth. He learned technique from expressionism, but ultimately he rejected expressionism's vision of the world as being too specialized.

In his major plays Wilder has consistently sought to emphasize those aspects of the stage involved in pretense. The success of such pretense is peculiar to the theater because of the audience. Sabina, who has protested that she had been unable to understand a single word of ***The Skin of Our Teeth,*** wonderingly confesses in the first act, "Now that you audience are listening to this, too, I understand it a little better." He has returned theatrical conventions to their rightful position in order to emphasize the idea of imitation and to capture "not verisimilitude but reality" [as stated in his ***Three Plays***]. This reality, whose time is always *now* and whose place is always *here,* clarifies and enlarges the endless repetition of human experience. More important, it provides a way to explain the peculiar life of twentieth-century people. (pp. 68-73)

Donald Haberman, in his The Plays of Thornton Wilder: A Critical Study, *Wesleyan University Press, 1967, 162 p.*

M. C. Kuner (essay date 1972)

[Kuner is an American dramatist and critic. In the following excerpt from her biographical and critical study Thornton Wilder: The Bright and the Dark, *she discusses Wilder's development of a distinctly American artistic vision, commenting on the literary influences and philosophical concerns that inform his writing.]*

One of the most persistent specters that haunts a writer is his fear of going stale: to the end of his life Charles Dickens was hounded by the thought that his inspiration might dry up—and with it his income. The twentieth-century writer suffers from a more exaggerated form of the same disease: over-photographed, over-interviewed, over-quoted, pressured to reveal the subject matter or even the title of his next book before the critical ink has been spilled over his last one; understandably concerned with his rating on the best-seller list (which often affects the sale of his novel or play to the films); driven to produce not only because of the need to express himself as an artist but also to prove, perhaps unconsciously, to a publicity-oriented world that he is still a name to be reckoned with, for nothing can be more obsolescent than last year's reputation—all these considerations force an author to some kind of self-examination after he has achieved his first real success. How much truer this is when, two years after he has climbed to the top of the literary tree he is toppled by the arrows of critical displeasure. As we have seen, the charges of reviewers like Michael Gold forced Wilder to an evaluation of this phase of his career and, in many ways, changed it. Two other forces certainly combined to direct his efforts in another direction, and, as always with Wilder, they came in the form of new ideas. It is true that every writer is more or less susceptible to the currents of his times, but it is not until Wilder has thoroughly absorbed a concept, has apprehended it intellectually rather than emotionally, that it can have any effect on his work.

Wilder's two-year visit to Europe and his study of its theaters served him well in several ways. As he was beginning to think seriously about writing for the stage and had clearly indicated in all his own work, whether fiction or drama, that he was not interested in realism as a means of expression, he was forced to consider what approach he might take so that he could give his ideas their proper setting. In the late 1920's—and, indeed, even before that—Europe had abandoned the realism that had swept across the literary scene nearly three-quarters of a century before and was experimenting with novel techniques. Wilder was to derive inspiration from them, since they meshed neatly with his own notions: what he had to learn was to adapt the methods to his own needs.

It was probably also an excellent idea for him to put distance between himself and his native land: people and situations can often be seen more clearly when not viewed at close range. If Hemingway preferred to see a place before he wrote about it, Wilder appeared to deal with it more effectively after he had left and then returned to it. When, in 1931, he published his first volume of short plays, the themes of which were completely American, he was obviously looking at his country with fresh eyes.

Finally, and perhaps most important of all, the next five

years, which attached him to the University of Chicago, plunged him into a kind of world—both academic and social—that he had not known before; and from that intellectual experience he was able to draw enough material to occupy him until the outbreak of World War II.

Just as Jean-Paul Sartre was to influence Wilder's thinking in later years, Gertrude Stein at this time contributed a great deal to his search for the right techniques. Of course, *what* a writer says ultimately dictates the form he chooses: it is not really possible to separate style from content. But when the artist is as tradition-conscious as Wilder, when he is always looking for a design that will impose some kind of order on chaos, it is safe to assume that he will be deeply interested in any concepts that can help him realize his goals. Gertrude Stein's theories, as the correspondence between them indicates, made enough of an impression on Wilder to cause him to translate them into his own terms.

That he was beginning himself to move in the direction of a discovery that would culminate in ***Our Town*** is apparent when we consider his first book of this second period. ***The Long Christmas Dinner,*** published in 1931, was a collection of six short plays, all of them worthy of being staged (unlike those in ***The Angel That Troubled the Waters***) and largely American in theme. In addition, one element that had marred ***The Cabala,*** the uneasy marriage between fantasy and reality, was less troublesome in this volume, for Wilder had by now learned how to handle the mixture.

Three of the plays in the volume might be described as conventional in technique. ***Queens of France,*** which is set in the New Orleans of 1869, is essentially the story of a confidence man, a lawyer, who encourages lonely women to offer proof of their royal birth so that they can claim the title of Queen of France. One of his clients is a spinster schoolteacher, one a housewife, one a cocotte. Although their lives are totally different in every way, they all become willing victims of the lawyer's game because the excitement of proving that they are really glamorous, beautiful people gives their lives some color. As the play ends the lawyer is busily fleecing still another "royal" client; the irony is, their lives would not be so drab, they would not need this artificially created excitement if they would realize that the simple state of being alive has a wonder all its own. If, as Thoreau maintained, "most men lead lives of quiet desperation," it is because, as Wilder sees it, they don't appreciate the magic of human existence. In ***Our Town*** Emily is to enlarge on this idea in a poignant speech after she is dead.

Love and How to Cure It has a London background: Soho, in 1895. A young undergraduate is in love with a music-hall dancer, who rejects him. Breaking into the theater, Arthur Warburton flourishes a gun at Linda, threatening to shoot her if she will not marry him. But Joey, the comedian, slyly empties the gun and makes it clear to Arthur that people who go around shooting others for love really only love themselves. At that moment the young man understands that Linda has never been touched by passion. She is interested only in her dancing. As with James Blair of ***The Cabala,*** love is—and perhaps always will be, because of her nature—beyond her experience.

A far better play than these two, although Wilder thought poorly enough of it to drop it from the reprinted volume, is ***Such Things Only Happen in Books.*** It is a variation on the idea in ***Queens of France***—that people dismiss details because they do not appreciate their rich contribution to life—but it is told in a way that suggests Wilder was, at the same time, poking gentle fun at himself. John, a young novelist, lives in a quiet New Hampshire village with his wife, Gabrielle. (In this play the time is the present.) When the curtain goes up they present a picture of domestic bliss: they are both sitting in the library of their home, John playing solitaire, Gabrielle sewing. John is convinced that in life "most people live along without plots. In fiction (like cards) you have to adjust the cards to make a plot." On the whole, books are seen as "a quiet, harmless fraud about life." But as the play progresses, all sorts of strange information can be gleaned. The servant, Katie, has been tended by a doctor after she poured boiling water on herself by accident while she was washing her brother's clothes. As it turns out, her brother is a criminal she has been hiding in that very house for the past three months. Other details come to light—including the fact that John's devoted wife is the mistress of the doctor. But John is aware of none of this. When his wife mischievously points out that he is growing careless in his game of solitaire, he observes petulantly, "I certainly see all the moves that are to be seen. You don't expect me to look under the cards, do you?" John is as blind to the events of his surroundings as the powder-room attendant of Katherine Brush's short story, "Night Club": while horrendous crises are disrupting the lives of the women who wander in and out of the powder-room, Mrs. Brady is too busy reading *True Story* and *True Romances* to appreciate what is happening. Having eyes, they see not; having ears, they hear not. And they, too, miss the wonder of the human experience.

But it is with the characterization and the dramatic effectiveness that Wilder achieves a creditable growth. If the characters are not memorable, they are at least believable. And the practical demands of the theater are met in these plays, too: they are not so amorphous or philosophical as to evaporate when the curtain rises. Best of all, the dialogue is quite different from Wilder's earlier efforts: it *sounds* like the language of ordinary, everyday people. And it is speakable—actable. Yet what makes this volume impressive is the treatment he accords the three remaining plays.

The Long Christmas Dinner, which gives the collection its name, is a study in one of Wilder's favorite subjects—obsessions, if you will—time. In an article written some twenty years later, Wilder was to relate this preoccupation to America itself. After noting that the European is what he is because he is familiar with the "immemorial repetitions of [his] country's way of life" as it surrounds him, Wilder adds, "An American can have no such stabilizing relation to any one place, nor to any one community, nor to any one moment in time."

Whether because of its size, geographical position, historical antecedents, or technological skill, this country, when compared with older civilizations, has always reflected a more transient society and a more accelerated life rhythm.

Buildings in large cities, for example, are put up and pulled down seemingly overnight. Members of a lower economic bracket in America can raise themselves by hard work far more easily and quickly than their counterparts in Europe, where class lines are more tightly drawn. The result is a shifting landscape and a shifting population unlike that of the rest of the Western world, encouraging still further change and, sometimes, rootlessness.

Wilder was influenced not only by this environment but by his reading of the French philosopher Henri Bergson, whose theory of time, utilized by many late nineteenth century writers, offered an intellectual challenge to the once-accepted stability of the universe. According to this concept, there is in reality no past, present, or future, since all are one. For instance, suppose you ask the time of a passerby at a particular moment; in the interval it takes him to look at his watch—which registers, say, 2:15 P.M.—and give you an answer, a second has already passed. Another example: an out-of-town friend is staying at a hotel in your city for perhaps a week. You make an appointment to call on that friend at a certain hour. When you knock at the door, you know that behind it you will find a familiar face. Eight days later, if you were to knock at that same hotel-room door, a stranger would open it. And all because time has passed. This new assessment of time, added to Wilder's experiences as a student of archaeology (someone in the world of "now" digging up the remnants of a civilization of "then"), exerted an enormous influence on his thinking.

Finally, Wilder's peripatetic childhood and its exposure to many different, exotic cultures made space inconsequential, for it became easier, thanks to twentieth-century travel, to move from place to place, and easiest of all to let the imagination become the real scene-shifter. ***The Long Christmas Dinner*** asks the audience to recognize that "ninety years are to be traversed in this play, which represents in accelerated motion ninety Christmas dinners in the Bayard household."

As in ***Our Town,*** the play is concerned with the daily routine of average people. The major preoccupations are with birth, marriage, sickness, old age, and death. Wilder fixes the play in "real" time, as the title suggests, by choosing Christmas as the focal point: it is an occasion that unites most families, it has the feeling of a ritual (tradition), and, of course, it does have (or should) a religious significance. The family in this play gathers around the table, representing the present; at one end of the stage is a door, indicating birth, at the other end a portal, indicating death. The process of aging is shown very simply by the use of wigs and shawls. And, as in ***Our Town,*** the properties are kept to a minimum: the characters pantomime eating and in every way supply an imaginative, unrealistic counterpoint to the real events of the story.

There is, in fact, no story. Mother Bayard, sitting at the table with her family, remembers the Indians who were part of the early American experience. After a while she says she feels tired, rises, and walks out—toward the portal of death. Cousin Brandon puts on a white wig; a perambulator is wheeled on stage from the opposite portal—life ebbs and flows. The son Roderick gets up and moves toward the portal of death, then returns, for, as we can imagine, his illness has not proved fatal. Finally he, too, must go—but he makes his exit with astonishment, as if he can't grasp why. Another baby is wheeled across the stage toward the portal of death: it never had the chance to grow up and take its place at the table. And another generation now sits in the parental place, some of them using the very phrases their mothers and fathers had used when they were young. A middle-aged man reflects that the war is not a bad thing, since it releases the poisons that collect in nations; but *his* son is drafted, and rises and walks toward the portal of death, tossing aside his white wig, for he did not grow old on his way to that final door. Another son disappears from the scene because he is a rebel against his family and runs off to China. Finally only old cousin Ermengarde is left, and as she moves toward the door the play ends.

A good deal of the dialogue consists of repetition, another device that Wilder was to make use of in future plays, particularly after Gertrude Stein had explained her belief in its effectiveness as a means of underscoring the cycle of life. The repetition at times verges on monotony: after listening to a Christmas sermon one of the Bayard wives remarks, "Lovely, I cried and cried." The next generation is to say exactly the same thing. Since almost a century passes in the course of this play and yet nothing actually "happens," we are confronted by the dramatic contrast between eternity and finiteness. One effect is to make us feel as though we have boarded a train that originated further back and that we will leave when our time comes; but the train will go hurtling on, disgorging future passengers and taking on still others, but never stopping for long.

The Happy Journey to Trenton and Camden makes use of the flow of time and also introduces a Stage Manager, who will function importantly in ***Our Town*** and ***The Skin of Our Teeth.*** We are told that "no scenery is required in this play," while the Stage Manager, holding a script in front of him, tells us what the minor characters have to say, very much in the manner of his successor in ***Our Town.*** Again, nothing much "happens." The Kirby family, lower middle class Americans, take a drive in a car that is really four chairs. (Wilder returns to this device in his cycle of plays ***The Seven Ages of Man:*** a father and his children in **"Childhood"** make just such a trip.) At the beginning the children are occupied in the ordinary way: the boy, Arthur, is playing marbles; his sister, Caroline, is chattering with her friends. During the course of the trip the family engages in purely trivial activities: they eat hot dogs, admire the billboards, stop at a gas station, admire the scenery. And the language they speak is unpretentious, unadorned, even unintellectual. But we are not allowed to believe in their "reality" for long, since the Stage Manager interrupts from time to time and reminds us that they are only actors performing a role. It is this device of placing them at a distance that keeps them from sounding sentimental or uninteresting.

Bertolt Brecht, a German playwright who began his career in Berlin in the 1920's, had developed a concept of theater that insisted emotional moments should be interrupted by constant reminders to the audience that they were watching only an illusion of life: there was to be no attempt at copying "reality." He called this idea *Verfremdung,* or "Alienation," and its purpose was to instruct the public rather than to encourage it to wallow in sentiment. But long before Brecht popularized this theory, Wilder was experimenting along similar lines. In this respect he was not an innovator, of course; nor was Brecht entirely. Both had been strongly influenced by the Expressionistic movement that grew up in Germany after World War I (there the goal was a didactic theater in which the theme or "message" was more important than the characters, who were drawn as abstracts, while the tightly knit plot was discarded in favor of episodic scenes). Wilder had enough of a sense of the future to realize that some new treatment of ideas had to be employed in the theater if it was not to die of sameness and stodginess. Possibly the most important aspect of the Kirbys' "happy journey" is the reason for it, which we do not really discover until the end. Mrs. Kirby wants to visit her married daughter, but this is no ordinary visit: she comes to comfort the young woman because her baby has died at birth: "God thought best, dear. God thought best. We don't understand why. We just go on, honey, doin' our business." So argued Captain Alvarez, trying to give solace to Estaban, grieving for his dead twin brother; so believed the pre-Christian Captain Philocles in ***The Woman of Andros.*** Basically, Wilder's philosophy remained unchanged; what altered was his perception of how to display it.

The most original and ambitious play in the volume is ***Pullman Car Hiawatha.*** Again a Stage Manager is present, but this time Wilder searches for universal types rather than particular members of a family. Consequently there is only one couple on the train—Philip and Harriet; the other passengers are a Maiden Lady, a Doctor, A Woman of Fifty, Two Engineers, a Porter, and an Insane Woman. The train, naturally, is a symbol not only of movement in space but of passage of time as it roars to its destination, and of course it is one of Wilder's favorite devices for indicating rootlessness. As in ***Our Town,*** the Stage Manager tells us about the car on its way to Chicago: he is very definite about the time, which is December 21, 1930. He invites the audience to listen to the other characters as they think; then actors enter, representing towns, fields, villages (including Grover's Corners of future fame). Others representing tramps, mechanics, passengers, come by, describing places in America and events that have occurred. Finally Time itself makes its appearance: the Minutes are gossips, the Hours are philosophers, the Years theologians. The Planets join them, speaking no words, only uttering vague sounds. At the end the archangels Michael and Gabriel board the train: they have come to fetch Harriet, who is dying. At first she refuses to accompany them; then she bids good-bye to the town, the shops, the wallpaper (this is certainly Emily of ***Our Town***), and slips away. As the play closes, the train, now in the Chicago depot, is boarded by attendants who begin to clean the cars. And so the cycle of life—and death—goes.

To dramatize further the concept of the circle of life, Wilder gives to the Hours dialogue taken from the great philosophers. Spinoza's words are quoted by one, observing that the "common occurrences of daily life are vain and futile." Plato is quoted by another, "How will a man choose the ruler that shall rule over him: Will he not choose a man who has first established order in himself. . . ?" The quote from Aristotle notes that quality called divine which man possesses sometimes but God has always. And the passage concludes with the quote from Genesis concerning the creation of Heaven and Earth and the command "Let there be light." Greek and Jew, classical source and Biblical, pre-Christian and post-Christian world, all blend and harmonize. But only when there is a sense of order. Therefore, although the death of Harriet is sad, that too is part of the natural order. It is even sadder that the Insane Woman, who has moments of lucidity that would shame a sane person, wishes to go with Gabriel and Michael in Harriet's place; but she cannot, for it is not her time but Harriet's that has come. And that is a further sign that the pattern exists, even though it is incomprehensible to us.

The Happy Journey will be developed more fully in ***Our Town,*** when, in effect, the Kirby family of the shorter play is studied in depth. And **Pullman Car Hiawatha** will blossom into ***The Skin of Our Teeth,*** with its use of philosophy, theology, literature, history, and the entire panorama of the cosmos. Although the earlier plays have both charm and interest, they are in a way blueprints for Wilder's two major theater pieces. Meanwhile, the simplicity and "realism" of the dialogue in ***The Long Christmas Dinner*** was carried over into his next work: his translation of *Lucrèce,* from the French of André Obey, attempted a language that was modern and unadorned. Wilder was a great admirer of Obey, who was not only a playwright but an actor and the manager of a troupe in Paris called the Compagnie de Quinze. And there was much in Obey's style that attracted Wilder's interest: like a number of outstanding French dramatists, Obey found nothing "escapist" in using material based on the classics. Obey was also to deal with Biblical themes in his play *Noé,* in which he concerns himself with the story of the Flood, the Ark, and Divine Justice. Indirectly, his character of Noah was to serve as a model for Mr. Antrobus in ***The Skin of Our Teeth.***

Since Wilder had shown such an affinity for the themes of antiquity, it is probable that the story of the rape of Lucrèce suggested to audiences another occasion for more of his beautiful prose. They seemed disconcerted by the translation's simplicity (Wilder had obviously abandoned his study of Cardinal Newman for his exploration of Jonathan Swift, whose sarcastic personality must have been in many ways antipathetic to him). Despite an outstanding cast headed by Katharine Cornell as Lucrèce, Brian Aherne as Tarquin, Blanche Yurka as First Narrator, and Brenda Forbes as Marina; despite sets and costumes by Robert Edmond Jones, music by Deems Taylor, and direction by Guthrie McClintic, the play, which opened at the Belasco Theatre on December 20, 1932, was not successful. For the next three years Wilder occupied himself working on another novel and learning more and more, as he put it, from the teachings of Gertrude Stein. For one of Wilder's most attractive qualities is that while he is perfectly capable of dropping into the lecturer's manner when he is talking to others (no doubt a carry-over from his former teaching days), his avidity for fresh ideas and new horizons makes him a perpetual student in the best sense. And Miss Stein, who dearly loved the role of mentor, must have been enchanted by his deference and admiration. At a party, when Picasso read his own verse, Wilder obligingly translated from Spanish into French for Miss Stein. They visited each other constantly; they even spoke of writing a book together: she was to supply the plot, he the words. (In the end she wrote the book, *Ida,* herself.) They exchanged long letters when they were apart; he wrote introductions to her books. And from this exposure to her ideas Wilder was able to sort out his own.

In some ways her point of view merely coincided with, or confirmed, his. Her concept of religion was very similar to Wilder's. As he was later to point out, "Religion, as Miss Stein uses the term, has very little to do with cults and dogmas, particularly in America. . . . Religion is what a person knows—knows beyond knowing, knows beyond anyone's power to teach him." In ***Our Town*** the Stage Manager expresses his convictions about the poets (and the saints) who understand instinctively the miracle of living. Again, it is obvious that in writing ***The Long Christmas Dinner*** Wilder was not deeply interested in character in a psychological sense: he was far more interested in what the character represented symbolically. Whereas the realistic playwright tried to draw a recognizable, particular portrait and from that point give it universal application, Wilder tried the reverse: he began with the universal and from it derived the particular. This technique was Brecht's also, but it would be equally fair to say that the unknown author of the fifteenth-century play *Everyman* probably had the same aim in mind. Therefore Gertrude Stein's insistence that characters have more life and effectiveness when they are imagined (she cites Vasari and Plutarch, who brought vividness to the biographies they wrote simply by stating the facts and letting the reader's fancy provide the rest), struck a responsive chord in Wilder, who had reached the same conclusion himself.

But in two areas she did contribute a great deal to his work. After the critical hostility accorded ***The Woman of Andros,*** Wilder was clearly concerned about finding a subject that would please him without sounding as though it were escapist. His rediscovery of America coincided with Miss Stein's *Geographical History of America,* a shrewd appraisal of its weaknesses and strengths. In a letter he told her his opinion of her book, for which he was to write the introduction:

> What a book! I mean what a book! I've been living for a month with ever-increasing intensity on the conceptions of Human Nature and the Human Mind, and on the relations of Masterpieces to their apparent subject matter. Those things . . . have become cell and marrow in me. . . . Yes, I'm crazy about America. And you did that to me, too.

While Wilder was liberating himself from the elegances of Walter Pater and George Moore—two British writers known for their rarified style—and abandoning the hothouse prose of ***The Woman of Andros*** in favor of a simpler expression, as demonstrated by ***The Long Christmas Dinner,*** Gertrude Stein reminded him that "melody should be a by-product it should never be an end in itself. . . . " What she was advocating, of course, was an end to imitation and to consciously "pretty" writing, and a blending of form with content. He left off copying writers of another age and another country because he realized that the European sense of space, time, and identity were unlike the American: "Those senses are not ours and the American people and American writers have long been engaged in reshaping the inherited language to express modes of apprehension." Gertrude Stein's observation that it is "something strictly American to conceive a space that is filled with moving" reinforced Wilder's discovery. He could admit, finally, that "elevation and intensity are not solely and inseparably associated with noble images. . . . The United States is a middle class nation and has widened and broadened and deepened the concepts of the wide and the broad and the deep without diminishing the concept of the high." Gertrude Stein wanted language to do something and so stay alive; Wilder, following her lead, renounced the influence of older British writers, seeing in the new freedom and the search for a diction that would express the present the quality that made America unique: the openness of its society. . . . (pp. 94-111)

Heaven's My Destination, written in 1935 but set in the American Midwest of 1930, derived its title, Wilder tells us, from a doggerel verse of the day; children wrote it in their schoolbooks, filling in the blank places:

> — is my name;
> America's my nation;
> — is my dwelling place
> And Heaven's my destination.

For the epigraph of the novel Wilder uses a statement made by Chrysis in ***The Woman of Andros:*** "Of all the forms of genius, goodness has the longest awkward age." For Wilder believes that living is itself an art and that, like art, it requires a kind of genius. . . . (p. 112)

The novel [***Heaven's My Destination***] confused a number of critics when it first appeared. Wilder himself noted that some thought it was the portrait of a saint, others believed it was a satire on a ridiculous fool. Still others suggested it was some kind of a joke and took Wilder to task for being frivolous at such a moment in America's history. Sigmund Freud, who had been overwhelmed with admiration for ***The Bridge of San Luis Rey,*** was revolted by ***Heaven's My Destination;*** he did not understand why Wilder wanted to write a book about an "American fanatic" and threw the book away in anger. But Gertrude Stein loved it. She was quite right.

Perhaps one reason why the book is so memorable, particularly when compared with the "angry" novels of those times, is that Wilder based his major character on a real person, or rather, on real people. He tells us that George Brush had about him a little of Gene Tunney (who also carried classics around and passionately loved literature); a little of Wilder's brother, Amos; a little of Wilder's father, who was a strict Calvinist, a letter-of-the-religious-law man; and a little of Wilder himself. He looked on the book as an effort to come to terms with his background (not only Calvinism, but the missionary schools in China and the religious atmosphere at Oberlin), and concluded,

"The comic spirit is given to us in order that we may analyze, weigh and clarify things in us which nettle us, or which we are outgrowing or trying to reshape." While all the elements that had interested him in previous books are here—the classical tradition, humanism, intuitive faith, the meaning of life, the search for a pattern—they are leavened by a marvelous objectivity that recognizes the plight of the human condition; but in its moment of greatest anguish it recognizes also the absurdity—a technique Chekhov would have appreciated and admired. The earnestness is balanced by a humor not often found in Wilder.

Ultimately, the success he achieved with the character of George raises another question: whether Wilder might not have been wiser to concentrate more on the real and the particular rather than on the symbolic and the universal. But he had made his choice in the latter direction, and from that choice, three years later, in January of 1938, came ***Our Town.***

A few years after ***Our Town*** was produced Wilder drew up some principles that, he believed, defined the drama. They serve so admirably as the backbone for all his plays that they make a useful introduction to them.

Wilder stressed, first of all, the fact that the theater was an art that demanded many collaborators and therefore needed intervening "executants"—that is, actors, directors, and designers upon whom the interpretation would depend. Thus he mentioned a production of *The Merchant of Venice* that was played with a maximum of sympathy for Shylock; yet Wilder himself recalled a performance he had seen in which the great French actor Fermin Gémier presented Shylock as a vengeful and hysterical buffoon, while Portia was a *gamine* from the Paris streets. Both points of view are equally interesting, both equally valid. Therefore, for Wilder,

> Characterization in a play is like a blank check which the dramatist accords to the actor for him to fill in—not entirely blank, for a number of indications of individuality are already there, but to a far less definite and absolute degree than in the novel. . . . The dramatist's principal interest being the movement of the story, he is willing to resign the more detailed aspects of characterization to the actor. . . .

Although his example of *The Merchant* does not really prove his case, for Shylock is not an abstract but a very sharply drawn character, the argument tells us something about Wilder's notion of theatrical characterization. Just as he rejected the realism of the depression-oriented novel, he rejected the realism of detailed portraiture such as O'Neill was giving the American theater in plays like *Desire Under the Elms.* Brecht had reduced his characters to deliberate symbols in order to enhance the political beliefs he held; Wilder used the same means to clarify his religious beliefs. In any theater that is essentially didactic the characters are obviously less important than the message.

Another theory that Wilder propounded was that the action in a play "takes place in a perpetual present time. . . . Novels are written in the past tense. . . . On the stage it is always now." In addition, the novel has the advantage of an omniscient author who can tell his readers facts that the other characters do not know; on a stage everything must be presented between the characters. Wilder pointed out that the Greek Chorus performed just such a function in the theater, and he believed that the modern playwright had to find an equivalent—as he was to do in supplying the Stage Manager for ***Our Town.*** A play thus provided with a Stage Narrator attains a kind of timelessness, for the narrator can be part of the play's momentary action and yet be a commentator on what has happened in the past; or he can look into the future and tell the audience what he sees, for he is both enclosed in finite time and stands beyond, outside it. Finally, if he can move back and forth in time so freely, he must be aware of the repetitions of history and the ideas that flow from one century to the next, and so he becomes a transmitter of myth, legend, allegory. In such a theater the characters are analogous not to the planets, which "wander," but to the stars, which are fixed; while the background or setting, like the earth itself, moves in time.

Observing that the theater is a world of pretense, Wilder enumerated such conventions as the playing of women's roles by men in the Greek (and Elizabethan) age; the use of metric speech, although in life people do not speak verse; the reliance on masks and other devices. And he argued that these conventions did not spring from naiveté but from the vitality of the public imagination: they provoked the audience into participating instead of having all the work done for them by the dramatist. Even more important, in Wilder's estimation, the action was thereby raised from the specific to the general. In Shakespeare's world Juliet was not a "real" girl living in a "real" house cluttered with "real" furnishings; she was played by a boy on a bare stage and so became not a particular person but all the star-crossed heroines who have ever lived and who will live in the future. By Wilder's definition, theatrical pretense is absolutely essential to reinforce his theories of time.

Because drama is a collective experience, in Wilder's words, because it appeals to the "group-mind," it has about it the excitement of a festival, a coming together to celebrate an event. And so ritual must be part of drama in some fashion. It may be based on a typical evening during a particular season of the year, like ***The Long Christmas Dinner.*** The details of the ritual are not important, but it must have enough familiarity about it to be recognizable as a convention to the audience. Equally, the material must be broad enough in scope to reach a large number of people *simultaneously,* and this need demands a subject-matter that is common to ordinary experience.

Our Town is, therefore, the blossoming of Wilder's theories. Emily and George are types rather than individuals, outlines rather than photographs. Although the play begins in America's past (between 1901 and 1913), it deals with the future, too. For in the end, Emily, having died, comes back to visit Grover's Corners; she exists simultaneously in all three pockets of time. The Stage Manager constantly reminds us of the make-believe quality of the play by asking us to imagine this or that prop; he himself plays different roles in addition to his own; he is not limited by sex, since he takes the part of Mrs. Morgan as well as of other men in the town; and from time to time he comments on the weather or the state of the world, lectures to the audience, and interprets the actions of the characters for us. Wilder even succeeds in supplying us with ritual: the hum of activity that makes up everyday life. One might almost say that brushing one's teeth or one's hair is a ritual; Wilder picks up moments like these to affirm that all of us are bound together in one vast chain, because we all share certain common thoughts and actions. There is a moment in James Joyce's *Portrait of the Artist* when Stephen thinks about God, who, he knows, is called "Dieu" in French, and God can always tell the nationality of the boy praying to Him by the language that is used. The mere idea of a French boy offering a simple prayer to "Dieu" (whose real name is God anyway, Stephen asserts), while at the same time an Irish boy is praying in *his* own language and so on across the universe, is enough to give Stephen a headache, for where does infinity end? But it is exactly this feeling that Wilder is after: we are all one in the One. (pp. 123-28)

M. C. Kuner, in her Thornton Wilder: The Bright and the Dark, *Thomas Y. Crowell Company, 1972, 226 p.*

Granville Hicks (review date 21 October 1973)

[*Hicks was an American literary critic whose famous study* The Great Tradition: An Interpretation of American Literature since the Civil War *(1933) established him as one of the foremost marxist critics in the United States. After 1939, however,Hicks denounced communist ideology, which he called a "hopelessly narrow way of judging literature," and in his later years rejected ideological approaches to literary criticism. In the following review, he assesses* Theophilus North.]

Of the eight eminent writers of the twenties and thirties about whom Malcolm Cowley writes in "A Second Flowering," only one is still alive, Thornton Wilder. Wilder survives not merely as a man but also as a writer. In 1962, when he was 65, he retired to the Arizona desert to meditate upon a novel, which became ***The Eighth Day*** (1967) and won a National Book Award. Now, in his 77th year, he has another book, ***Theophilus North,*** which might conceivably equal the popularity of his second book and first best seller, now half a century old, ***The Bridge of San Luis Rey.***

From the beginning each of Wilder's books has been a new departure. ***The Eighth Day,*** a combination of mystery story and family chronicle, differed from anything he had previously written in tone, narrative method and setting. ***Theophilus North*** takes off in an even more surprising direction. Although it is fair enough, as such things go, for the publisher to call it a novel, a term more and more loosely used, it is a novel made up of closely related short stories. So far as I can remember, Wilder has published no short stories in the past, though many short plays, and so once more we find him at work in a medium that is new to him. The stories, moreover, as stories, are adroit, amusing and altogether successful in an old-fashioned way.

The principal unifying factor is Theophilus North, who is both narrator and hero. Like T. Wilder, T. North was born in Wisconsin in 1897, the son of an influential newspaper editor, and received part of his education in China, his father being Consul General in Hong Kong and Shanghai. He spent a year during World War I in the Coast Artillery and returned to Yale to get his A.B. in 1920. He —the pronoun still refers to either T. Wilder or T. North—taught for some years at a private school in New Jersey and took his M.A. at Princeton. But outward characteristics of this order often seem to play a small part in Wilder's work, and it may be that the resemblances here are part of some game with which Wilder is amusing himself. At any rate it is clear that the novel, or whatever you choose to call it, is not autobiographical in any important way. Whether in some subtler sense North stands for Wilder is a harder question to dispose of.

Wilder's plan for a collection of closely related stories requires an approximate unity of time and place, and it is further necessary that North, in order to perform his dual role, must be able to observe and participate in a variety of actions on several social levels. Wilder solves the problems with an ingenuity that is concealed by his offhand manner. Having settled by chance in Newport, Rhode Island, in the summer of 1926, after giving up his job in the New Jersey prep school, North supports himself by teaching tennis to boys and girls and by reading in any of several languages to people who need his services. Soon he knows the city well, and comes to believe that in Newport, as in Schliemann's Troy, there are nine cities. He sees most frequently the inhabitants of the sixth city, the very rich, and those of the seventh, their servants, and strongly prefers the latter to the former. In general, though he makes something of the nine cities, sociohistorical generalizations are not Theophilus's primary interests, nor are they Wilder's.

There are a dozen incidents in which Theophilus proves helpful to inhabitants of Newport. His specialty is saving marriages and smoothing the course of true love, but he also practices his own brand of exorcism on a haunted house, thwarts the avaricious heirs of a gifted old man, saves a young man from being the victim of a talent for what North calls "calligraphic mimicry," helps a legless boy live up to his potentialities and eases the passing of the venerable Tante Liselotte. Although at the outset Theophilus announces his desire to keep to himself and not be involved in the life of Newport, he turns out to be a habitual Good Samaritan, or perhaps one might compare him to an uncommonly conscientious and imaginative Boy Scout.

Sometimes Theophilus does his good deed by means of a trick that might have been employed by O. Henry, but the trick always turns out to have deeper implications than O. Henry would have given it. In "Diana Bell," for instance, Theophilus prevents Diana from eloping by giving her and her lover opportunity to bore one another. Wilder tells the story with humor and gusto, but Theophilus is concerned with more than the snobbish wishes of Diana's parents, and he has something to say about incompatibility. In the same way a little common sense is enough to dispose of the neurotic symptoms of the aging but by no means moribund Dr. Bosworth; a large part of his trouble, however, is what Theophilus calls "the death watch," the vigilance of heirs to speed a rich relative on his path to the grave, and that is harder to deal with. In a couple of stories literature plays an important part in North's therapy, and in others he is—or at any rate appears to his neighbors to be—a faith healer. (Like Hawthorne, Wilder makes ambiguous use of the supernatural.)

Wilder's tone remains consistently lively, is often comic, and the book is extraordinarily entertaining. There are those, I have no doubt, who will call it corny, and sometimes it comes recklessly close to sentimentality—as ***Our Town*** does, or, for that matter, ***The Skin of Our Teeth*** and ***The Matchmaker.*** (Theophilus sometimes makes me think of Dolly Levi.) Occasionally, I admit, I felt that a story might have been written for some woman's magazine, perhaps one that flourished about 1826. But in spite of an excess of sweetness now and then and some obvious manipulation for the sake of happy endings, the stories hold the reader in a firm grip.

It might be enough to say that the book is fun to read and let the matter rest there, but Wilder's works as a rule have multiple meanings, and I have a persistent sense that these stories are saying something, though not in a loud voice. According to Cowley, Wilder describes himself as "fundamentally a happy person." Cowley continues: "He likes to find the goodness or greatness in people and books. He is optimistic by instinct, in the fashion of an older America." At the same time there is in his makeup a tough streak of pessimism. ***The Bridge of San Luis Rey*** was widely believed to carry a message of consolation and hope, which is probably why it sold so well, but in the end of Brother Juniper's examination of the lives of the victims of the bridge's fall he can conclude only that there was "perhaps an intention."

In ***The Eighth Day,*** when Dr. Gillies is asked to speak to the inhabitants of Coaltown on Dec. 31, 1899, the eve of a new century, he describes to them in flamboyant terms the wonderful age that is coming. But Wilder breaks in to inform the reader: "Dr. Gillies was lying for all he was worth. He had no doubt that the coming century would be too direful to contemplate—that is to say, like all the other centuries." He lies because of the young men in the audience: "It is the duty of old men to lie to the young. Let these encounter their own disillusions. We strengthen our souls, when young, on hope; the strength we acquire enables us later to endure despair as a Roman should."

If Wilder is an optimist, his opportunism operates only in the short run, for his view of man's fate is by no means cheerful. But he does see that there are happy passages along life's way, and he seems to believe that we should make the most of them, not merely in the sense of seizing the day but also as experiences to be taken into account in our judgment of the human condition.

What Theophilus North learns in Newport is that most people could be happier than they are, and experimentation teaches him that sometimes he can improve their lot. His first name proclaims that he is a lover of God, but we see him as one who loves his fellow man which—as Leigh Hunt observed—may be the same thing. As for the second name, it may be a reminder of the cold wind of skepticism. It is like Wilder that he should celebrate 50 years of distinguished writing by producing a book that is gayer in spirit than anything he had previously written, that generously displays his varied talents and that asks more questions than it answers.

It might be argued that Theophilus is what some critics would call a Jesus-figure. He heals the sick after his own fashion, and his deeds attract a large following. Members of the establishment denounce him for stirring up the people. But I don't want to push this as far as it might be pushed. It is more useful to suggest that Theophilus in various complicated ways fulfilled his early ambition to be a saint. He lists saintliness first among the nine ambitions that he held at one time or another in his youth. Eventually he abandoned this ambition as beyond him, but all his ambitions influenced his life. "The past and the future are always *present* within us." (pp. 1, 16)

Granville Hicks, in a review of "Theophilus North," in The New York Times Book Review, *October 21, 1973, pp. 1, 16.*

[What] I seek everywhere is the mask under which human beings conceal their unhappiness.

Thornton Wilder, as quoted by André Maurois in his* A Private Universe, *D. Appleton and Company, 1932.

W. D. Maxwell-Mahon (essay date May 1978)

[*In the following essay, Maxwell-Mahon discusses Wilder's novels, asserting that his later fiction "declined into mediocrity."*]

The publication of Thornton Wilder's novel ***The Woman of Andros*** in 1930 elicited unfavourable comment from many American readers. Set in Greece just before the birth of Christ, Wilder's adaptation of a classical comedy by Terence was regarded as not only irrelevant to, but deliberately evasive of, the domestic crisis that had followed the Wall Street crash. What had pre-Christian Greece and a dying hetaera to do with America in the Depression? Michael Gold; a critic with Marxist sympathies, was indignant:

> Is this the speech of a pioneering continent? . . . Where are the cotton mills? Where are the child slaves of the beetfields? Where are the stockbroker suicides, the labor racketeers, or passion and death of the coalminers? . . . Is Mr. Wilder a Swede or a Greek, or is he an American?
>
> (The New Republic, *LXVI, October 22nd, 1930, pp. 266-7*).

Gold's insistence that Wilder produce novels of social realism depicting a particular class was generally dismissed as political ideology thinly disguised as literary criticism. His questioning of Wilder's racial consciousness, however, found (and still finds) considerable support. Yet the basic premise is the same in both cases: the function of art is utilitarian. And in both cases, the consequences of this Benthamite notion are artistically disastrous. Critics who demand that a writer use his craft to foster a sense of national identity in his readers are restricting the creative imagination just as much as those who insist that he preach political dogma. It was because of such a limiting imperative, I would suggest, that Thornton Wilder's fiction declined into mediocrity.

Wilder's early fiction was strongly influenced by the New Humanism of Irving Babbitt and Paul More. These academics, both Harvard men, reacted against the naturalism prevailing in contemporary life and literature by stressing the ethical side of human behaviour and the dualism of man and nature. Wilder, like T. S. Eliot, was attracted by the religious and rational aspect of the movement. Another factor of germinal influence on Wilder's creative thought was the period he spent during 1920 in Rome. Greek and Roman culture had been among the subjects he studied at Yale, and after graduating from that university in 1919 he received a scholarship enabling him to join the archaeological team of the American Academy at Rome for a year. Participation in the excavation of an Etruscan street made the past a vivid actuality for Wilder, helping to establish the transcendental approach to social and evolutionary change that critics see as a basic feature of his work. The conjunction of past and present in a Roman setting provided inspiration for writing ***The Cabala*** (1926), the first of his novels.

The Cabala takes its name from the small coterie of French and Italian aristocrats whose social intrigues in Rome after the First World War are the subject-matter of the novel. These aristocrats have considerable influence, but the use of their power seems eminently futile; with complete disregard, or perhaps total unawareness, of the actualities of modern life, they intrigue for the restoration of the Bourbon monarchy and the divine right of kings. At the end of the novel, however, their real nature is revealed and this calls for a re-adjustment of opinion about their activities.

The current debate, in particular among structuralist critics, about the function of a *persona* in literature has a bearing on the narrative mode of ***The Cabala.*** Generally speaking, in allowing the narrator Samuele to take on the rôle of implied author, Wilder anticipates Gerard Genette's conception of the 'pseudo-diegetic voice'. The omniscient Samuele, a young American spending a year in Rome, is both commentator on, and confidant of, the members of the Cabala. He is also a character in his own right, and the change that takes place in his moral perspective is basic to the humanistic argument of the novel.

At the beginning of ***The Cabala,*** Wilder sets about creating its prevailing atmosphere of immateriality and timelessness. The spirit of Virgil is evoked on numerous occasions by references to the Italy he had known and loved. The Cabala itself is said to be 'medieval' in pursuing what the rest of the world discarded centuries ago; the members, who try to reverse the normal order of night and day routine, have the reputation of being 'supernatural'. The sense of existing out of time, of other-worldliness, is also conveyed by the account of the dying poet. Occupying poor lodgings near the Spanish Steps with a water-colourist friend, he is visited by Samuele and another American, Blair. The real identity of the unnamed poet becomes apparent during his sick-bed conversation with Samuele:

> 'Will you promise me something? My things weren't good enough; they were just beginning to be better. When I am dead I want you to make sure that Francis does what he promised. There must be no name on my grave. Just write: "Here lies one whose name was writ in water." '
>
> There was a noise in the next room. Blair had returned with the water-colourist. We withdrew. The poet was too sick to see us again, and when I came back from the country he had died and his fame had begun to spread over the whole world.

In the wider context of Wilder's writing, this description of the death of John Keats introduces two recurrent themes: the revival of the dead through a shared culture and civilisation, and the preservation of every experience in the continuum of space and time.

Wilder is very like Henry James in the contrast he draws between sophisticated, amoral, Continentals and naïve, morally self-assured, Americans. Of necessity, Samuele is more sensitive than the rest of his countrymen to the finer shades of European life surrounding him. He is delighted to receive an invitation to the Renaissance villa of Mlle de Morfontaine; his musings as he sits at the dinner-table with members of the Cabala have a double irony in view of the novel's surprise ending:

> I had assumed that the conversation of the Cabala in camera would be vertiginous. If I anticipated the wit and eloquence of its table-talk I dreaded their gradual discovery that I was tongue-tied or doltish. When, therefore, the conversation at last broke forth I had the mixed sensation of discovering that it was not unlike that of a house party on the Hudson. 'Wait,' I told myself, 'they will warm up. Or perhaps it is my presence here that prevents them from being at their best.' I recalled the literary tradition that the gods of antiquity had not died but still drifted about the earth shorn of the greatest part of their glory.

Samuele's disappointment in the Cabala is matched by their disappointment in him. He seemed the ideal person to reform the licentious Marcantonio, son of the Duchess d'Aquilanera. Young Americans, the Duchess says to Samuele, are so different from young Italians: 'You are *vielles filles;* you are as temperate as I do not know what.' Again, the ending of the novel gives a retrospective irony to Samuele's situation. Of all things, he promises to discipline Marcantonio by training him for the forthcoming Olympic Games. This crack-brained scheme, which originates with Marcantonio himself, only serves to build up unsatisfied sexual urges that find their outlet when the young Italian seduces or is seduced by (one is never sure which) his half-sister. His subsequent suicide may suggest that he is a victim of a guilt-complex. But Marcantonio dies because he can find nothing to live by. The outburst that follows the lecture on the evils of the flesh given by Samuele emphasizes this hopeless state: 'I hate them all', Marcantonio cries. 'I hate it. There's no end to it all. What shall I do?'

Despite its disastrous consequences, Samuele's attempt to reform Marcantonio by turning him into an Italian version of an all-American college boy is basically humanitarian. Samuele responds sympathetically to the warm Italian temperament; this sympathy is strongly evoked by the plight of Alix, the Princess d'Espoli. It appears inevitable that the Princess should be attracted to James Blair in her search for satisfying love-affairs. Two more different people would be hard to find. Alix is characterised by a strain of 'heartbroken frivolity', the outcome of an arranged and unhappy marriage, that is indissolubly linked with life itself. Blair has neither the capacity nor the will to embrace the spirit of human love:

> The fact is that quite early James Blair had been frightened by life (in a way which the Princess, in a moment of misery and inspiration, was to divine later with the cry: What kind of a stupid mother could he have had?) and had for ever after bent upon books the floodtides of his energy. At times his scholarship resembled panic; he acted as though he feared that raising his eyes from the page he would view the world, or his share in the world, dissolving in ruin.

That Alix should turn to the modern equivalent of a soothsayer for guidance in pursuing Blair is particularly appropriate in view of her hidden nature and fatalistic convictions. Finally reduced to utter despair and more than a little insane, she exemplifies the truth of the adage that even the gods cannot command love: it comes freely or not at all.

The most subtle and intricate relationship that Samuele finds himself witness to is that between the Cardinal Vaini and Mademoiselle Marie-Astrée-Luce de Morfontaine. Religion is the source of this attachment, for the Cardinal is a professional cleric and Astrée-Luce is an amateur saint. For the Cabala in general and Astrée-Luce in particular, the Cardinal has the status of a latter-day St Augustine. His reputation has been established through missionary work in China and he sets the seal on this reputation by refusing high office at Rome on his return from the East. He aspires to nothing higher than breeding rabbits and cultivating roses. Such humility! Such otherworldliness! What nobody realises is that the Cardinal has lost his faith:

> As he said later, he should have died at the moment of leaving his work in China. The eight years that had elapsed since then had been a dream of increasing confusion. Living is fighting, and away from the field the most frightening changes were taking place in his mind. Faith is fighting, and now that he was no longer fighting he couldn't find his faith anywhere.

Having lost his own faith, the Cardinal sets about destroying that of Astrée-Luce. It is devil's work and easily undertaken for the devout creature is completely lacking in intelligence. The scene in which she is devastated by the logic of the argument proving the non-existence of a teleological universe and a beneficent Deity introduces another of Wilder's fundamental themes. The immediate result of the Cardinal's rhetorical victory is cathartic; Astrée-Luce is convinced that he is Satan himself, and the shot she fires at him from a revolver signals the end of her blind trust in her God. The shot also has the effect of shocking the Cardinal out of his apostasy. 'Murder was child's play compared to what he had done.' The restoration of his faith, and of his attachment to Astrée-Luce, then begins; but the Cabala has lost its spell and its disintegration follows.

Our acceptance of imaginative realism, Coleridge said, depends on that willing suspension of disbelief for the moment which constitutes poetic faith. Certainly the reader's poetic faith is severely tested by the closing chapters of Wilder's first novel. Miss Grier, an ever-present but unobtrusive character, reveals the secret of the Cabala to Samuele:

> 'Well, first you must know, Samuele, that the gods of antiquity did not die with the arrival of Christianity. What are you smiling at?'
>
> 'You're adorable. You have resolved to make your explanation last for ever. I asked about the Cardinal and you have gone back to Jupiter. What became of the gods of antiquity?'
>
> 'Naturally when they began to lose worshippers they began to lose some of their divine attributes. They even found themselves able to die if they wanted to. But when one of them died his godhead was passed on to someone else; no sooner is Saturn dead than some man somewhere feels a new personality descending upon him like a straitjacket, do you see?'

If Wilder had left the novel to end like this, fantasy and reality could have been accommodated in satirical intent. But he overplays his hand. Sailing back to America, Samuele is given the power of materialising the spirit of Virgil with whom he discusses the meaning of what he has experienced in Rome. He is left with the rather trite advice to 'seek out some city that is young' and learn to live there.

The analysis of, and quotations from, ***The Cabala*** help to illustrate the predominate features of Wilder's fiction. He provides sets of character-sketches rather than integrated studies of human personalities in a growth situation. The characters are, in fact, occasions for presenting some ethical or moral dilemma of general significance. He follows the Aristotelian concept of the well-made plot, with the result that cause and effect are seen to operate in close inter-dependence; this does not, however, preclude the open-ending that leaves the thematic questions unanswered. His style is aphoristic and at times gnomic; his tone is urbane and the feeling humorously ironic.

Wilder's novels are linked together not only through the fundamental enquiry into the nature of human existence and the ethics of behaviour, but also by the way a statement in one book is taken up and enlarged upon in another. For instance, in ***The Cabala*** we find the following comment:

> . . . there is a certain spiritual law that requires our tragic coincidences. Which of us has not felt it? Take no precautions.

A specific example of tragic coincidence forms the basis of plot and theme in his next novel, ***The Bridge of San Luis Rey*** (1927). The opening sentence of the book places the situation before us with incisive brevity:

> On Friday noon, July the twentieth, 1714, the finest bridge in all Peru broke and precipitated five travellers into the gulf below.

Why *those* travellers? And why at *that* particular moment? These are the questions that exercise the mind of Brother Juniper, a Franciscan friar who saw the five 'gesticulating ants' plunge to their death. He commits the cardinal error of attempting to find a rational answer for the irrational, to resolve the very nature of the Supreme Being according to logical principles. Faith, so Wilder argues in this novel, cannot be reduced to an act of pure reason. One believes in the purpose of God or not. There is no question of the sincerity of Brother Juniper's faith; he clings to it with heroic perseverance even when he is burnt at the stake by the Inquisition for cataloging examples of tragic coincidences:

> He sat in his cell that last night trying to seek in his own life the pattern that had escaped him in five others. He was not rebellious. He was willing to lay down his life for the purity of the Church, but he longed for one voice somewhere to testify for him that his intention, at least, had been for faith; he thought there was no one in the world who believed him. But the next morning in all that crowd and sunlight there were many who believed for he was much loved.

In a sense, then, Brother Juniper has confirmed faith in the tragic conclusion to his investigations. Perhaps this was a Divine intention?

The first and last chapters of ***The Bridge of San Luis Rey*** are respectively entitled: 'Perhaps an Accident' and 'Perhaps an Intention'. Spanning these two pillars is the narrative structure composed of the descriptions of the lives of those who perished when the bridge collapses. These descriptions, veritable case-histories, may be supposed to come from the great book about coincidence for which Brother Juniper was burnt alive. They trace the pattern of cause and effect that brings each person to a particular place at the same time. In this connection, the critic Rex Burbank recalls a remark that Wilder made in Berlin during 1931 when interviewed by Walther Tritsch: 'It is the magic unity of purpose and chance, of destiny and accident', he said, 'that I have tried to describe in my books'.

The Marquesa de Montemayor, the first of the five victims to be analysed in ***The Bridge of San Luis Rey,*** is thought to have her prototype in Mme de Sévigné, the seventeenth-century French writer famous for her letters. The determining factor in the Marquesa's behaviour is love for her daughter Clara. The extreme possessiveness of this love is the cause of Clara's departure for Europe to marry a Spanish nobleman. There at least she can be herself. The Marquesa, whose subsequent drunken and bedraggled state makes her an object of derision in Lima, realizes full well that she is responsible for Clara's flight; but she can do nothing to lessen her possessiveness:

> And then on that green balcony a strange warfare would shake the hideous old lady, a singularly futile struggle against a temptation to which she would never have the opportunity of succumbing.

The temptation against which the Marquesa struggles is the urge, which can never be realised, to force Clara to love her against her will and to ask forgiveness for not doing so in the past.

Shortly before each of the five victims reaches the bridge he or she has a moment of self-revelation. In the case of the Marquesa, it occurs when she finds the letter written by her young servant Pepita to the Abbess of the Convent from which she had come originally. In reading this letter, the Marquesa is struck by the complete unselfishness with which the child speaks of her longing to return to her 'dear mother in God' and her willingness to bear the separation if it is the Abbess's wish. Confronted by the letter, Pepita declares it is bad: 'It wasn't . . . it wasn't . . . brave.' The extent of her own selfish moral cowardice overwhelms the Marquesa. It is in this chastened mood that she approaches her destiny:

> She opened the door upon her balcony and looked at the great tiers of stars that glittered above the Andes. Throughout the hours of the night, though there had been few to hear it, the whole sky had been loud with the singing of these constellations. Then she took a candle into the next room and looked at Pepita as she slept, and pushed back the damp hair from the girl's face.
>
> 'Let me live now,' she whispered. 'Let me begin again.'
>
> Two days later they started back to Lima, and while crossing the bridge of San Luis Rey the accident which we know befell them.

From what has already been said, it should begin to be clear that the novel has a specific pattern of human relationships that constitute its plot. Two people bound strongly to each other through personal or family ties are separated, and the separation brings to one or other the suffering necessary for a radical change in attitude and activity. We see this pattern or plot-structure in the account of Camila Perichole, a character drawn from Prosper Merimée's *La Carosse du Saint Sacré.* As the leading actress of Lima, Camila or 'La Perichole' enjoys the favours of the nobility. She owes her position originally, however, not to her acting skill but to the care and affection of the rascally Uncle Pio. He is the Svengali who has trained her in her profession; as a result, their relationship becomes as close, if not closer, than that of father and daughter:

> She could find no fault in him and she was sturdily loyal. They loved one another deeply but

> without passion. He respected the slight nervous shadow that crossed her face when he came too near to her. But there arose out of this denial itself the perfume of a tenderness, that ghost of passion which, in the most unexpected relationship, can make even a whole lifetime devoted to irksome duty pass like a gracious dream.

The lack of passion in Camila's relationship with Uncle Pio is more than made up for by her numerous love affairs. To a certain extent these *divertissements* become just that in the overall structure of the plot; they distract attention from the development of the tragic issues. Nevertheless, they provide reasons for the emotional crises in the lives of some of the other characters. The alienation between Camila and Uncle Pio is attributable to her determination to be the centre, not of the stage, but of a salon where she will be surrounded by her admirers. In such a social theatre, he is not necessary. Separation intensifies Uncle Pio's affection for Camila, and the chance to express this increased devotion comes when her beauty is ravaged by smallpox and she lives in seclusion with her son, little Don Jaime. He offers to take the child to live with him for a year in Lima, to teach him all that a gentleman should know about fencing and music and Latin. The culmination of this act of love is reached when Uncle Pio and his charge set out for Lima:

> He carried him on his shoulder. As they drew near to the bridge of San Luis Rey, Jaime tried to conceal his shame, for he knew that one of those moments was coming that separated him from other people. He was especially ashamed because Uncle Pio had just overtaken a friend of his, a sea-captain. And just as they got to the bridge he spoke to an old lady who was travelling with a little girl. Uncle Pio said that when they had crossed the bridge they would sit down and rest, but it turned out not to be necessary.

Camila's sexual wiles make her a decisive factor in the lives of Manuel and Esteban, foundlings who had been abandoned at the door of the convent run by the Abbess. The affection between these young men is that of David and Jonathan. They are inseparable—at least until Camila enters their lives. She uses Manuel as a letter-writer to her numerous lovers, and as a result of her beauty and the task of expressing her sentiments, he becomes infatuated. To complicate matters, Esteban has also fallen in love with Camila. The young men vie with each other in self-sacrifice to ensure that neither suffers from this *contretemps.* Manuel's death from blood-poisoning leaves Esteban inconsolable. His attachment to Manuel is so complete that he identifies himself with the dead man; hence his attempted suicide. Esteban is given the chance of a new life by the sea-captain whom Uncle Pio stops to talk to on reaching the bridge. The plan is that Captain Alvarado and Esteban will embark on a ship bound for the Continent:

> They started for Lima. When they reached the bridge of San Luis Rey the Captain descended to the stream below in order to supervise the passage of some merchandise, but Esteban crossed by the bridge and fell with it.

The question to be answered at the end of the novel is related to Wilder's general philosophy: how are human affairs managed? By God or by man himself? Wilder appears to be drawing parallels in ***The Bridge of San Luis Rey*** between the conflict of spirit and flesh and the conflict between chance and purpose. Or so Rex Burbank suggests. There does appear to be a certain dialecticism at work in the narrative, but to argue that it is the fundamental issue is to ignore the final words of the Abbess. Talking to Clara on the latter's return to Lima years after the tragedy, her thoughts go back to the eternal debate on God's will and the way it is fulfilled:

> 'Even now,' she thought, 'almost no one remembers Esteban and Pepita but myself. Camila alone remembers her Uncle Pio and her son; this woman, her mother. But soon we shall die and all memory of those five will have left the earth, and we ourselves shall be loved for a while and forgotten. But the love will have been enough; all those impulses of love return to the love that made them. Even memory is not necessary for love. There is a land of the living and a land of the dead, and the bridge is love, the only survival, the only meaning.'

Most critics see ***The Bridge of San Luis Rey*** as Wilder's best novel. But a case for this distinction can be made out for ***The Woman of Andros*** (1930), the novel that caused so much controversy in the America of the Depression. In ***The Cabala,*** Wilder had glanced at the problem for the young of finding something to live by. This problem is dealt with in full in ***The Woman of Andros.*** The opening of the novel has the compressed thought and feeling so typical of Wilder's most effective writing:

> The earth sighed as it turned in its course; the shadow of night crept gradually along the Mediterranean, and Asis was left in darkness. The great cliff that was one day to be called Gibraltar held for a long time a gleam of red and orange, while across from it the mountains of Atlas showed deep blue pockets in their shining sides. The caves that surround the Neapolitan gulf fell into a profounder shade, each giving forth from the darkness its chiming or its booming sound. Triumph had passed from Greece and wisdom from Egypt, but with the coming on of night they seemed to regain their lost honours, and the land that was soon to be called Holy prepared in the dark its wonderful burden.

Wilder used Terence's play *Andria,* which in turn was based on two comedies by Menander, for the basic plot and the characters of his novel. In itself this is of small interest, but taken in the wider context of Wilder's work it shows his utilization of classical culture as a frame of reference or imaginative background. Furthermore, the brevity and simplicity of the plot-situation that he borrowed and reversed from the comic to the tragic is admirably suited to his particular style and expression. In short, structure and medium are perfectly suited to each other in ***The Woman of Andros.***

The novel presents the fundamental situation almost as if Wilder were following Freytag's well-known 'pyramid' construction for a five-act play. Simo's son Pamphilus is supposed to be preparing to marry Chremes' daughter, Philomena. Instead he has become a regular visitor to the symposia of the woman of Andros, Chrysis. Naturally, Chremes is most indignant as he watches the opportunity of strengthening family position frittered away; the people of the island of Brynos, the locale of the story, are annoyed at the 'imported' notions the hetaera is disseminating among their sons. Chremes describes the goings-on to Simo, but fails to get the response he wants:

> She has twelve or fifteen of them to dinner every seven or eight days—the unmarried ones, of course. They lie about on couches and eat odd food and talk. Presently she rises and recites; she can recite whole tragedies without the book. She is very strict with the young men, apparently. She makes them pronounce all the Attic accents, they eat in the Athenian mode, drinking toasts and wearing garlands, and each in turn is elected King of the Banquet. And at the close hot towels are passed around for them to wipe their hands on.

Chremes has some grounds for complaint. Naturally, one does not like to see young men initiated into the mysteries of life by a professional prostitute. Chrysis justifies her educational programme, however, by recalling that Plato had said the true philosophers are the young men of their age. 'Not,' she would add, 'because they do it very well, but because they rush upon ideas with their whole soul.' Her method of instruction is psychologically and aesthetically calculated to make the greatest impression, for she clothes her ideas in the imaginative form of fables. When the discussion turns on the way poets mislead their readers by representing life as always heroic, she tells her young guests of the hero who had served Zeus well and who, after his death, asked to return to earth for a day. The request was granted on condition that the young man should be both participant and onlooker, both the person who lives again the happiest day he had known and who sees that day in the total context of his life. Wilder was to use this sort of fantasy with memorable results in his play ***Our Town*** (1938). In ***The Woman of Andros*** the moral of Chrysis's fable is brought out in the description of a past and present awareness existing unconsciously side by side. The hero sees that the living too are dead, that we only become alive momentarily:

> It was Chrysis's reiterated theory of life that all human beings—save a few mysterious exceptions who seemed to be in possession of some secret from the gods—merely endured the slow misery of existence, hiding as best they could their consternation that life had no wonderful surprises after all, and that its most difficult burden was the incommunicability of love.

The effect of Chrysis's fable on Pamphilus is to give him more understanding of the grey lives of his parents—and to make him fear the same fate. 'How does one live?' he asked the bright sky. 'What does one do first?'

For all that she labours to prepare her 'sheep', as she calls the young men, for the business of living, Chrysis herself has difficulty finding something permanent to live by. In part, she gives a meaning to her existence through the preparations for, and conduct of, symposia; in part, she derives consolation from becoming a saviour for a small group of social outcasts and unfortunates that she gathers round her. Her unhappiness, for she bears sorrow within her as other women bear the fruit of their womb, is increased by her love for Pamphilus. There can be no realisation of this love, not merely because Chrysis is a prostitute (though that is a great stumbling block), but because Pamphilus has fallen in love with her young sister, Glycerium. The resolution of Chrysis's unhappiness is tragic; she discovers that she is slowly dying of cancer. Her last remarks to Pamphilus express everything that was worthwhile in her life and in Greek humanitarianism:

> Then raising herself on one elbow she breathed in anguish: 'Perhaps we shall meet somewhere beyond life when all these pains shall have been removed. I think the gods have some mystery still in store for us. But if we do not, let me say now . . . ' her hands opened and closed upon the clothes that covered her, ' . . . I want to say to someone . . . that I have known the worst that the world can do to me, and that nevertheless I praise the world and all living. All that is, is well. Remember some day, remember me as one who loved all things and accepted from the gods all things, the bright and the dark. And you do likewise. Farewell.'

The final events of the novel, which include the acceptance of the pregnant Glycerium by Pamphilus's family and the death of her infant in child-birth, pale into insignificance in the light of this magnificent testimony. Wilder brings his story back to its starting point, placing the end symbolically in the beginning, with a description of the rain falling over the Mediterranean countries after a long drought:

> On the sea the helmsman suffered the downpour, and on the high pastures the shepherd turned and drew his cloak closer about him. In the hills the long-dried steam-beds began to fill again and the noise of water falling from level to level, warring with the stones in the way, filled the gorges. But behind the thick beds of clouds the moon soared radiantly bright, shining upon Italy and its smoking mountains. And in the East the stars shone tranquilly down upon the land that was soon to be called Holy and that even then was preparing its precious burden.

Wilder's next novel, ***Heaven's My Destination*** (1935), is set in the American Midwest during the Depression. He thus answered critics who assailed him for not paying his due to his country. He did not, however, provide them with a *tranche de vie* in the manner of Steinbeck or Sinclair Lewis. Instead, he gave his attention to the American mania for revivalist activities, for the public testimony of personal salvation. The fact that his father and mother were children of clergymen and that his brother was a Divinity teacher warrants mention as the novel has autobiographical touches.

In their anxiety to welcome Wilder back into the fold of true-blood Americans, critics rather fall over themselves in deciding what he had in mind when writing ***Heaven's My Destination.*** Some argue that his intention is fiercely satirical, that he belongs in spirit to Voltaire and Nathaniel West whose *Candide* and *A Cool Million* respectively mock those obsessed with unrealistic notions of right conduct. Other critics find Wilder's novel either allegorical or anagogical or both. George Brush, the salesman for a textbook publisher who features as the hero, then becomes the spirit of American innocence plagued by the transported evils of the Old World; he is also seen as an exponent of American fundamentalism, with its goal of combining good business with sure salvation. Wilder himself was left somewhat bewildered by these interpretations; he said to Ross Parmenter in 1938: 'My last novel was written as objectively as it could be done and the result has been that people tell me that it has meant to them things as diverse as a Pilgrim's Progress of the religious life and an extreme sneering at sacred things, the portrait of a saint on the one hand and a ridiculous fool jeered at by the author on the other' (Quoted by Burbank, R.: *Thornton Wilder,* Boston, 1961).

From what is actually said and described in ***Heaven's My Destination,*** it seems reasonable to infer that Wilder wrote in satirical vein however objective he might have been about the details of evangelism and its American manifestation. His hero is dedicated to the task of reforming society (which means every person he meets) by pointing out the evils of smoking, drinking, sexual intercourse, and bank accounts. The memory of the girl he had made pregnant during his college days adds fuel to the fire of his missionary zeal; he is quite oblivious of the indifference with which she regards this peccadillo—but then he also didn't notice she was a drug addict. Girls are not Brush's strong point! When introduced to Miss Mississippi Corey by her father—'the sweetest and snappiest little homegirl in Oklahoma'—he explains to her his ideals of womanhood:

> 'Now, out of all my study I've drawn up a few rules for girls. Can I tell them to you? You might get to be a really nice girl if you worked on these rules.' Her hand fluttered to her mouth, a gesture which he took for consent. 'In the first place, always be simple in what you do. Never laugh loud, for instance, and never make unnecessary movements with your hands and eyes. A lot of girls never get married because they have no friend to tell them that. In the second place, of course, never drink liquor or smoke. When girls do that, it's hard to recognize them for girls. And third and most important . . . '
>
> At this point Mississippi Corey had hysterics.

Despite the effectiveness of various comic scenes, ***Heaven's My Destination*** seldom rises above a pleasing romp in the Bible Belt. Its restrictive range has a lot to do with the character of Brush. He is at times unbelievably ignorant of the common facts of life and the reader's sympathy remains disengaged. Furthermore, he does not develop any real self-understanding for all that he appears to have become more rational at the end of the novel. Consequently, his experiences soon become episodic and could conceivably go on for ever. Lastly, the social milieu that forms the background to the novel offers too little scope for Wilder's cultured sensibility. He was, and always remained, a European cosmopolitan.

Wilder returned to classical antiquity with ***The Ides of March*** (1948), a novel that offers parallels between the dictatorship of Julius Caesar and Mussolini. Wilder's military service in Italy during World War II, together with his residence in Rome during the 1920's, gave him a firsthand acquaintance with the historical background to his subject. But his basic concern was not with the politics of power but existentialism. At this time, the germinal influences on his thought were the writings of Jean-Paul Sartre and Heidegger, and the result can be seen in his study of Julius Caesar's last days. The form and content of ***The Ides of March*** consist of letters, documents, reports, and pamphlets supposedly written by Caesar and his contemporaries. Some liberties have been taken with the sequence of events, but the general chronology is historically correct; by imaginative insight of considerable subtlety and acumen, Wilder creates the effect of an immediate and living experience.

Wilder with friends in Chicago, 1936.

Caesar's letters to his friend Lucius Mamilius Turrinus, blinded and crippled by the Belgians in the Gallic Wars, contain the essence of his ethical and metaphysical ideas. We have an early intimation of his existentialistic outlook in the first of these letters. Caesar writes:

> I must be certain that in no corner of my being there lingers the recognition that there is a possibility of a mind in and behind the universe which influences our minds and actions. If I acknowledge the possibility of one such mystery, all the other mysteries come flooding back: there are the Gods who have taught us what is excellent and who are watching us; there are our souls which are infused in us at birth and which outlive our death; there are the rewards and punishments which furnish a meaning to our slightest action.

Because of his position as political and religious head of

the State, Caesar is the greatest of all Roman slaves. He has no liberty but that of responsibility for the welfare of those he governs, and he glories in his paradoxical situation. Apart from his loss of personal liberty, he is in constant danger of becoming something other than himself—of becoming what the people think he is. Consequently, his thoughts about statecraft and ethics are inextricably bound up with the problem of Being and non-Being.

Wilder is able to engage our sympathies for Caesar not only through the exposition of his inner nature but also through sustaining the dramatic tension of the plot. We know that Caesar is to be struck down by assassins, that he will never live to achieve his ambitions. But so does Caesar. If there is one thing of which he is certain, it is that he will be murdered. Letters and documents that come into his hands show that he has every reason to fear the worst. Yet his courage never deserts him; the letter to Turrinus in which he confronts death might well have been written by Chrysis, the woman of Andros:

> I can now appraise at a glance those who have not yet foreseen their death. I know them for the children they are. They think by evading its contemplation they are enhancing the savour of life. The reverse is true; only those who have grasped their non-being are capable of praising the sunlight.

The Eighth Day (1967) was Wilder's penultimate novel. The long interval separating this work from the previous one is of some consequence as ***The Eighth Day*** is the longest of all Wilder's fictional writings. The length is disadvantageous since Wilder is at his best when confining himself to succinct and aphoristic statement. From his point of view, perhaps, there is justification for combining several novels in one in order to provide a comprehensive coverage of his theme. This theme appears to be the regeneration of the Ashley family; in reality it is the genesis of the spirit of Americanism. Wilder finally came to grips with the sort of novel he was expected to write and the result is far from satisfactory.

The Prologue to ***The Eighth Day*** provides the clue to its title. Dr Gillies, one of Wilder's *personae,* addresses a gathering of townsfolk at Coaltown, Illinois, on New Year's Eve, 1899:

> 'Nature never sleeps. The process of life never stands still. The creation has not come to an end. The Bible says that God created man on the sixth day and rested but each of those days was many millions of years long. That day of rest must have been a short one. Man is not an end but a beginning. We are at the beginning of the second week. We are children of the eighth day.'

The 'we' in this speech may be taken to represent the American people. Wilder's representatives of the people are, firstly, the Kangeheelas, the Indian tribe dispossessed of their land by the early settlers, and secondly, the Ashley and Lansing families who are the descendants of those settlers. The weaving together of the destinies of these two groups constitutes the plot of the novel; its story begins with a celebrated murder case:

> In the early summer of 1902 John Barrington Ashley of Coaltown, a small mining centre in southern Illinois, was tried for the murder of Breckenridge Lansing, also of Coaltown. He was found guilty and sentenced to death. Five days later, at one in the morning of Tuesday, July 22, he escaped from his guards on a train that was carrying him to his execution.

The rescue of Ashley by six unknown, masked, men and the fresh evidence that eventually leads to his acquital are mysteries only solved at the end of the novel. The main interest lies in the transformation of Ashley's character during his flight to South America and the development of the characters of the children he is forced to leave behind him. The necessity for a change of heart and mind in the case of Ashley is stressed by one of Wilder's authorial statements, in which the novel abounds, that he 'had lived without fear and without judgement.' He has to be shown, in short, how to estimate the human relationship between members of society and the value of self-knowledge. 'Ashley was a man of faith and did not know it'; he has to learn what it is he trusts in and why.

One of the difficulties in reading ***The Eighth Day*** is the shifting focus on Ashley and his son, Roger. Perhaps the shift should be seen as an attempt deliberately to blur the distinction between the two characters and make them seem a composite picture of an American. Roger has, however, a marked individuality of his own. 'Everybody liked him and he liked nobody,' says Wilder; then later: 'He was loved and he loved no one.' In the development of his character, Roger grows in compassion for the underprivileged and oppressed among whom he struggles to earn a living in Chicago during 1902-05. As he is in turn waiter, hospital orderly, and newspaper reporter, he 'was being drawn into the human community by thoughts of the dying, the banished, and the unborn.'

Roger's sister Lily, the eldest and most interesting of the three Ashley girls, is a match for him in strength of character. Although single-minded in her rise to world-wide fame as a singer and defiant of society in bearing and raising her illegitimate child, she is utterly unself-centred. Her plans are for a city of children on the shores of a lake in Switzerland where racial discrimination and class distinction will not exist. Wilder seems to be combining the ideal city of St Augustine with the living principle of St Paul in this vision: a city of God in which faith, hope, and charity reign supreme.

The history of the Lansing family in ***The Eighth Day*** is more supplementary than complementary to that of the Ashleys. Nevertheless, the account of Eustacia and her husband Breckenridge contains some of the finest writing in the book. This is particularly so towards the end of their unhappy relationship, when Breckenridge lies seriously ill in Coaltown. His sense of failure, and of guilt at the callous treatment of his wife and son, George, turn him into a devil of spite and vindictiveness. His tormenting of Eustacia eventually has a cathartic effect and he is resurrected, as it were, in the knowledge of her self-sacrifice for him. As is so often the case in Wilder's novels, this moment of revelation is followed swiftly by death as he is shot down, supposedly by John Ashley. To those who might think that the sufferings of Eustacia and her children are, like those of Ashley and his family, still lacking in purpose, Wilder, through the medium of Dr Gillies, replies with the message not only of the novel but of his abiding philosophy: 'We keep on saying that we "live our lives". Shucks; life lives us.'

Of Wilder's last novel ***Theophilus North*** (1973), which was published two years before his death, the most that can be said is that it touches the nadir of his fiction. Set in the 1920's, the account of Theophilus North's ministration to the unhappy and disillusioned of Newport, Rhode Island, is at the level of Gissing's *The Private Papers of Henry Ryecroft*—pontifical, sentimental, and tutelary. Wilder appears to be re-living many of the fantasies he had as a young man; these are given an air of respectibility by linking them with Freudian psychology; the 'nine life ambitions' are materialised by way of the various characters with whom North comes into contact after he resigns his job to spend all his time searching for a meaningful life. Predictably, he finds this meaning in the self-abnegation of helping others to find it. Perhaps Wilder was writing a sequel to ***Heaven's My Destination*** and presenting us with the sort of man George Brush should have been. But this sort of man, despite his noble deeds (or because of them), is the shadow and not the substance of his creator. (pp. 35-44)

W. D. Maxwell-Mahon, "The Novels of Thornton Wilder," in Unisa English Studies, *Vol. XVI, No. 1, May, 1978, pp. 35-44.*

Harry Levin (review date 21 November 1985)

[*Levin is an American educator and critic who has published studies on subjects ranging from Renaissance culture to the contemporary novel, and is noted for his interest in the relationship between literature and society. In the following review, Levin discusses Wilder's career, his personality, his views on art, and his approach to writing as depicted in* The Journals of Thornton Wilder, 1939-1961 *and Gilbert A. Harrison's biography* The Enthusiast: A Life of Thornton Wilder (*1985*).]

In 1949 the bicentennial of Goethe's birth was celebrated by an international symposium at Aspen, Colorado. What other American man of letters at the time, if not Thornton Wilder, could have met so well that cosmopolitan occasion? His topic was the Goethean ideal of world literature, which he proceeded to demonstrate by translating the German and Spanish addresses of Albert Schweitzer and José Ortega y Gasset. Wilder had attended a German school in China, when his father was serving as consul there. Later on, after graduating from Yale, he had spent a year of classical studies at the American Academy in Rome. Nicolà Chiaromonte characterized him as "the only contemporary American writer who is literate in the European sense, . . . the humanistic sense." Some of his compatriots regarded Wilder as being all too literary, too widely traveled and highly cultivated, for his own good as a writer. On that score he was stridently attacked, despite his popularity and geniality, from two very different points of view.

The first attack came as a polemical review of ***The Woman of Andros*** (1930) by a communist hatchet man, Michael Gold. From the immediate standpoint of relevance to the class struggle, this novel seemed to him unduly slight, unconscionably precious, and inhibited by the genteel tradition. Like its predecessors, the quasi-Proustian ***Cabala*** (1926) and the Pulitzer Prize-winning ***Bridge of San Luis Rey*** (1927), it dealt with exotic settings, religious subtleties, and feelings—symbolized by the broken bridge—of unrequited love. Wilder's good-humored response to the attack took the form of a picaresque sally into the Depression, ***Heaven's My Destination*** (1935), caricaturing his own high-mindedness through the divagations of an evangelical traveling salesman, not excluding the proverbial misadventure with a farmer's daughter. Turning toward the theater, Wilder became more and more involved with domestic and quotidian themes. Except in his historical pastiche, ***The Ides of March*** (1948), with its simulated letters from Caesar, Cicero, and Catullus, he managed to live down the smell of the lamp.

The second attack on Wilder purported to be an exposure. He was accused by two Joycean devotees, Joseph Campbell and Henry Morton Robinson, of having plagiarized from *Finnegans Wake* in his cosmic comedy, ***The Skin of Our Teeth*** (1942). Wilder, a far more perceptive reader of Joyce than his accusers, had made no secret of his devotion. Perhaps his Roman training had instilled in him a palimpsestic approach to literature. The most vivid character in ***The Bridge of San Luis Rey*** is modeled on Madame de Sévigné, while his English title, ***The Woman of Andros,*** acknowledges its Latin source in the *Andria* of Terence. If ***The Matchmaker*** (revised by Wilder from his ***Merchant of Yonkers***) was originally derived from J. N. Nestroy's *Einen Jux will er sich machen,* that Viennese extravaganza had in turn been based upon the Victorian farce of John Oxenford, *A Day Well Spent*—in a cumulative process of transposition that would later adapt to music and reach the screen with *Hello, Dolly!*

Today we are more conscious of, and less self-conscious about, what has come to be known as intertextuality. Wilder was hardly less preoccupied than Joyce had been with the *da capo* recurrence of things, thematic as well as textual. Both of them, after harking back to prehistoric monsters and tribal bards, looked ahead through war years toward survival. Both embodied their universals in a family pattern, varying as the Earwickers of Dublin did from the Antrobuses of suburban New Jersey. But drama, much more readily than prose fiction, can generalize about the human race. By striking the box set and opening the stage, Wilder rejected naturalism and revived the morality play: *Everyman, Mankind.* As for womankind, he argued, on stage all could be represented by one, "a timeless individualized Symbol." Sabina could be maid-of-all-work, beauty queen, reincarnation of Lilith, the eternal Other Woman, and also Tallulah Bankhead creating the part while rebelling against it in lines supplied by the playwright.

"The supranational subject is mine—" he noted in self-appraisal, "the individual in the all-time." And yet, in order to be individualized, the subject had to be localized. In ***Our Town*** (1938) we were told about a letter addressed to "Jane Crofut; the Crofut Farm; Grover's Corners; Sutton County; New Hampshire; United States of America; Continent of North America; Western Hemisphere; the Earth; the Solar System; the Universe; the Mind of God." Here Wilder may again have been borrowing from Joyce, for Stephen Dedalus similarly orientates himself in *A Portrait of the Artist as a Young Man.* But Stephen was echoing a traditional schoolboy formula, after all, and the variance means more to us than the parallel between his Dublin and Jane's Grover's Corners. Wilder's allegory of life cycles is fleshed out in the local colors of Main Street. Generalities are vernacularized through his Middle American dialogue. Indeed this fastidious stylist, not unlike Flaubert, had an especially sensitive ear for the *cliché juste.*

But Wilder remained, with Goethe, ever curious about the telescopic view about man's place in nature and in history. Hence it is not surprising if we remember him—warmly—in paradoxical images: as the homespun classicist, the backslapping aesthete, the familial bachelor, the gregarious recluse, the folksy citizen of the world. Equally at ease in the classroom and backstage, he acted out the American dilemma of society and solitude: in his case, of innumerable friendships ranging from Gene Tunney to Gertrude Stein and periodic withdrawals to undisclosed retreats, where much of his creative work was accomplished in the utmost privacy. He was a personality in the sense that Henry James was and that William Faulkner, apart from his writing, was not. In the sense that Hemingway and Fitzgerald were strained and egocentric personalities, his was a mellow and generous temperament. The fact that he was haunted by the ghost of a stillborn twin brother might have had something to do with his psychic duality.

That personal identification with otherness inclined him to be something of an actor, and consequently he was more in his element as a dramatist than as a novelist. He was also somewhat inclined by descent and conscience to play the preacher, while doctrinally more attuned to Kierkegaard than to Calvin. Moreover, he had started out in, and often reverted to, the role of a teacher. It was therefore not surprising when his own persona, charged with so many interests and ideas, tended to outshine his dramatis personae. Much of this went into his prolific and many-sided correspondence, which unquestionably deserves to be collected and published. It is fortunate that voluminous journals, kept by him off and on for more than fifty years, have been preserved among his papers and manuscripts in the Beinecke Library at Yale. A central selection from them has . . . appeared [in ***The Journals of Thornton Wilder, 1939-1961***] under the authoritative editorship of Donald Gallup, who is both Wilder's literary executor and the leading bibliographer of modern American literature.

Mr. Gallup has given us "rather more than one-third" of the material spanning a twenty-two-year period in Wilder's later life. The unifying principle among these thoughtful jottings, dated mostly from hotel rooms in both hemispheres, seems manifest in an entry from 1940: "Now that I am thinking of becoming a critic. . . . " Not that the critical diarist has abandoned his imaginative undertakings, though the record is missing between 1941 and 1948—an interval that witnessed the emergence of ***The Skin of Our Teeth*** and ***The Ides of March,*** and included Wilder's three-year wartime service in the United States Military Intelligence. The diaries teem with embryonic projects, few of which were carried through gestation. The main completed exception was ***The Alcestiad,*** a Wilderesque reworking of the resurrection myth still best remembered through Euripides' *Alcestis.* After years of interrupted tinkering, it became the least successful of Wilder's works, both as a play and afterward as an opera libretto.

The perpetual work-in-progress to which these notes return most frequently, and from which two finished scenes are appended to Gallup's book, is *The Emporium.* The notion of Americanizing Kafka by dramatizing his alluring and off-putting Castle as a metropolitan department store, and by turning his bewildered protagonist into a Horatio Alger hero—this was one of Wilder's more engaging premises. But inspiration was always much easier for him than realization. Mocking the conventions and planning the surprises made it all the harder. He was worried by his happy endings and held up by his last acts. The pageant-like conclusion to ***The Skin of Our Teeth*** was contrived and anti-climactic; ***The Bridge of San Luis Rey*** had the peculiar advantage of beginning with the catastrophe and then looking backward to explore the meaning of its five victims' lives. Wilder's journals, like James's prefaces, take us into the writer's confidence, confront us with his technical problems, and suggest angles for their solution.

There are some lively comments on fellow dramatists—O'Neill, Claudel, Anouilh, Büchner, the Greeks—along with occasional discussions of the other arts, notably music and film; but the volume's most sustained and valuable contribution lies in its series of observations on major novelists. These knowledgeable insights can be sharply aphoristic. Thus Thomas Mann, though respectfully cited, is termed "that ponderously signpost-planting author." André Gide's outlook is skeptically described as "the sincere desire to be sincere of one who cannot be so." Discriminating admiration for James is qualified by this stricture: "Never was there a greater fuss-budget of a novelist, continually intruding his view of the case precisely under the pretense of withholding it." And, though Wilder gradually learned to appreciate Faulkner, he maintained a temperamental and cultural distance: "It is as though we were hearing the fall of the House of Atreus told by a voice that was feverish and shrill, scandal-mongering-nosey, and a little prurient."

The pungency of such remarks, set down by a fellow craftsman and not primarily for publication, is warranted by their professionalism. Further animadversions throw unaccustomed light upon novels by Cervantes, Stendhal, Dickens, Gogol, Tolstoy, Camus, and Genet. But Wilder's criticism was increasingly focused upon the classics of the American Renaissance, which he had undertaken to reconsider as Charles Eliot Norton Professor of Poetry at Harvard in 1950-1951. Many of the pages in his journals are taken up with preliminary sketches for the six public lectures or with after-thoughts and outlines for the book that was to be organized around them. [In a footnote, the critic adds: It was never completed. Three of the lectures were published in the *Atlantic Monthly* (1952) and, with some revision, in Wilder's posthumous collection, ***American Characteristics and Other Essays*** (1979).] The assignment, which he characteristically viewed as an opportunity to deliver "lay sermons," stimulated his flair for comparing national characteristics and his quest for psychological archetypes. On the premise that "the central figure of the superior works of our literature is Everyman," he typified the difference between our culture and all others in a personification named Tom Everage—that everyday average man, so unlike Thornton Wilder.

He was at his best in treating authors as individuals, who faced their common task—and his—of "American Symbol-Making." Under his trenchant analysis Poe and Whitman stand out; Emerson subsides into "odd doubletalk," Thoreau into "idiosyncratic exaggeration"; and Melville gets shipwrecked before and after his unique triumph in *Moby-Dick.* Hawthorne is most severely judged, perhaps because he comes closest to Wilder as a fabulist and moralist.

> For Hawthorne, the basic sin which he claims to hold before our eyes is: resorting to the head rather than to the heart. Yet an obsession on his part is that sex is sin. But sex is nearer the heart than the head, and N. H. is at once entangled in a series of contradictions which make havoc throughout his book [*The Scarlet Letter*].

Hester Prynne is unfavorably contrasted with Anna Karenina and Goethe's Gretchen:

> Gretchen [in *Faust*] and Anna Karenina are broken by society and by their lovers but not by their poets; Hester is disavowed by her creator, who reserves for her only the cold justification that—had she been less "impure"—she might have launched a crusade for bettering the world's understanding of women.

As an auditor of Wilder's Norton Lectures, I can attest that they were polished performances, all but ready for publication as first presented. But, having fallen dangerously "in love with the Norton book," he went on elaborating drafts, prolonging revisions, and accumulating reservations until it turned into an albatross. He would produce no "writing of the category imaginative narration" for sixteen years. Nor could it be claimed that his two septuagenarian novels, ***The Eighth Day*** (1967) and ***Theophilus North*** (1973) lived up to his earlier achievement.

"That didactic-expository year at Harvard," he would explain to himself, " . . . brought into focus those modes of thinking that are disturbingly incompatible with what I gropingly call symbolization." Yet, when he responded to that call from Cambridge, he had already been deeply immersed in two abstruse hobbies involving scholarly research. One was his "compulsive infatuation" with the exegesis of *Finnegans Wake,* a "narcotic" inducing the illusion of an ersatz creativity, which he would subsequently renounce. As if this were not demanding enough, the other hobby was not simply the baroque Spanish drama of Lope de Vega; it was, more specifically, the problem of dating his 450 extant plays, and thereby charting his chronological development. "Fun, fun, fun," Wilder chortles, at the prospect of putting together a learned article; but the 1198 journal pages of notes on Lope remain unpublished. At all events, they show—as do the Joycean marginalia—how easily the artist in Wilder could be sidetracked, even before the roadblock of "the Nortons."

He had reached the point where personality flourished at the expense of artistic practice. Given his generosity as well as his curiosity, he could offer little resistance to the social distractions coming his way: testimonial dinners, honorary degrees, polyglot speeches, UNESCO conferences, trips to Hollywood, unremitting other travels in the US and abroad, lunch with *Bundeskanzler* Adenauer and dinner with mystagogic Gurdjieff—not to mention the unstinted and unrecorded attention he gave to friends everywhere. In setting his career into perspective, these journals can be usefully supplemented by the sympathetic biography of Gilbert A. Harrison [*The Enthusiast: A Life of Thornton Wilder*]. The fullest study yet to appear, this has the merit of drawing richly on firsthand impressions and associations, though the documentation could be more precise and various minor errors could be corrected. The range of Wilder's knowledge and acquaintance would strain the awareness of almost any biographer. Yet for all his friendly gestures and outgoing traits, Wilder's protean activities helped him to retain the elusiveness of an essentially private man.

If he felt at home anywhere, it would have been in academic communities (his successive home towns were Madison, Berkeley, Oberlin, and New Haven). Mr. Harrison informs us that Wilder's "happiest years"—years productive of ***Heaven's My Destination***—were those of his professorship at the University of Chicago during the 1930s, when he was in his thirties. He was in his fifties during the year that led to what Mr. Harrison calls "his Harvard breakdown." He did, in fact, collapse and spend a month in the hospital, having been victimized—partly by his own good nature—into accepting too many invitations. However, it was not unusual for the Norton Professor to teach one regular college course—and this is what prompted the journal's brilliant entries upon the rereading of certain novels. His colleague in the course, John H. Finley, aptly delineated the figure he cut: Wilder "knew everybody, did everything, had marvelous social gifts, was very American, almost folksy, . . . cheerful and talkative as a village—and as isolated."

Mr. Harrison had access to Wilder's journals, and has included tantalizing excerpts from them that have not been reproduced in the Gallup edition. These omissions seem to result from an editorial policy which excludes "most passages of introspection and self-analysis." Yet such passages would constitute the core of the most interesting writers' journals, and Wilder as a reader would probably have been most interested in them. Consider, for example, five pages printed by Harrison under Wilder's heading, "A Look-Around My Situation," written at Saint-Jean-de-Luz in the spring of his climacteric year, 1950. Gallup's one-page extract covers merely his itinerary and agenda. But this was arrived at, in context, through painful self-searching, a recoil from the sociable whirl, and a statement about the author's "removedness from the writings." Surely the final paragraph ought to be quoted:

> One last word: The disarray in my psychic life which was perhaps caused by the uprooting which was the war and which has been so advanced by the even deeper immersion in the "false positions" I have recounted, have [*sic*] one still more harmful result. All these activities have been *flights from seriousness.* I am deep in *dilettantism.* Even my apparent preoccupation with deeply serious matters, e.g., the reading of Kierkegaard, is superficial and doubly superficial because it pretends to be searching. Gradually, gradually I must resume my, my own meditation on the only things that can reawaken any writing I have to do. I must gaze directly at the boundless misery of the human situation, collective and individual.

It should be clear that there is nothing at all discreditable in this momentary confession. Nor should it be held against Wilder that he never actually succeeded in carrying out this uneasy resolve. On the contrary, and regardless of any outcome, his self-doubts do great credit to the virtues that he possessed in abundance: modesty, conscientiousness, and high standards. His dissatisfaction with dilettantism (dilettantism in depth?) bespeaks the professional. If he worried so over his departures from seriousness, he must have been a truly serious man. Cheerfulness kept breaking in, and his ebullient manner made it all too easy for his contemporaries to set him down as an incorrigible optimist—or, in Mr. Harrison's ambiguous epithet, an enthusiast. But, though he commented knowingly on *Don Quixote,* he was not quixotic himself. Ultimately he never allowed his bookish idealism or his comic ingenuity to derange his oceanic awe before the tragic realities that bound our daily existence. (pp. 31-4)

> *Harry Levin, "Global Villager," in* The New York Review of Books, *Vol. XXXII, No. 18, November 21, 1985, pp. 31-4.*

Frederic Raphael (review date 14 March 1986)

[*Raphael is an American novelist, short story writer, critic, dramatist, and screenwriter. In the following review, he presents a mixed assessment of* The Journals of Thornton Wilder 1939-1961, *commenting that "it is an odd experience to be both bored and exhilarated by the same volume."*]

Thornton Wilder was, as the cant has it, a one-off. The only Pulitzer Prize-winner for both fiction and theatre, he achieved early popularity with ***The Bridge of San Luis Rey*** and consolidated it with the folksy experimentalism of ***Our Town*** and ***The Skin of Our Teeth*** (by far the better play). He was also an intellectual, a peripatetic visiting professor, but never a full-blown academic. His characteristic resting place seems to have been between two stools. Well-read in several languages, he was evidently a lively, opinionated talker, *sans complexes* when it came to big issues or big names (his put-downs of Gide and Faulkner are unmaliciously mordant). The climax, or climacteric, of his career as a literary pundit came with an invitation to deliver the Norton Lectures at Harvard in 1950-51. He was no stranger to the podium, being much solicited and finding it hard to say no. (It may or may not be significant that, among his *obiter dicta,* he attributes to the homosexual a chronic need to be propositioned.) In the event, Harvard made more demands on him than he could well meet. He took exaggerated pains over the preparation of his material, on "The American Literary Heritage", but lecturing alarmed him. "If one had really good ideas," he remarks, "that would be the worst use one could put them to, and appallingly damaging to the lecturer." The damage he suffered was partly psychic, partly physical: he undertook an additional undergraduate course, after the death of F. O. Mathiessen, and was exhausted by the combined demands.

His Cambridge fiasco, as his admired Stendhal might have termed it, inflicted an obscure hurt (Henry James too was a familiar spirit) and Wilder appears never fully to have recovered. He published two more novels, neither of them as accessibly innovative as ***The Ides of March*** (1948), and revised ***The Merchant of Yonkers*** into ***The Matchmaker,*** whence was derived *Hello, Dolly!,* but he became increasingly stalled among projects he never finished or might better never have started. *The Emporium,* of which we have two lame scenes here, was conceived as a homage to Kafka's *The Castle,* as its incomplete state suggests.

His ***Journal*** was perhaps a way of keeping busy without having to face critics or the public; so far from being an uninhibited private record, its sententious garrulity suggests a man of philosophical temper and literary curiosity who despairs of arriving at publishable conclusions. Wilder's sister, in an affectionate but slightly unreliable introduction (***The Woman of Andros*** is *not* set on "the Greek island of that name"), tells of coming downstairs at night to find her brother in the library. "Thornton", she said, "is there anything you want?" "No", he answered, "I'm just looking—looking for a book that hasn't been written." In view of the *fausses couches* listed here, the missing volume may well have been one of his own.

The lineaments of Dr Casaubon were perhaps always present. Wilder was a compulsive compiler of *fichiers.* If his finished work was often cannily terse, his researches into Lope de Vega (whose myriad plays he was determined to tabulate chronologically) and *Finnegans Wake* filled thousands of pages, and many weeks, with no palpable results. Joyce's example may be responsible for a belief that the Big Subject had to be Everyman, a dubious proposition which alienated him from the particular without ever yielding the universal. Books, rather than life itself, stimulated his imagination: his second novel, ***The Cabala,*** is Proustian and the characters of Doña Clara and Doña Maria, in ***The Bridge of San Luis Rey,*** are clearly founded on Madame de Sévigné and her overestimated daughter, about whom he is still writing almost thirty years later. These ***Journals,*** sourly construed, could be said to be those of an intellectual fidget, unduly given to self-exhortation in the style of James's "à l'oeuvre, mon bon", and to lucubrations of questionable value:

> The position that man is incurably wicked and can only be saved by supernatural intervention

> may well be taken as a complete negativism unless the doctrine of supernatural intervention be seen as an indirect symbolic statement of an element in human nature itself equally interpretable as purely human activity for finding his subjective and his social harmony.

Since the editor, Donald Gallup, declares that he has cut the entries by two-thirds, it is sometimes hard to imagine what he has spared us. However, one fears that the omission of "passages of introspection and self-analysis, including dreams" may have excised material germane to getting a fix on Wilder's elusive character. Given the relevance of dreams to his dramatic method, the personae (and plots) of his unwilled reveries might be of more than casual interest. As it is, we are victims of a double vigilance: the author himself decided that his ***Journal*** should contain no

> descriptions of the Holy Week ceremonies at Valladolid; no account of the conversations with the Max Beerbohms; of the weekend at Notley [Abbey, home of the then Oliviers] and the parties at Sibyl [Colefax]'s . . . I am able to guard myself against writing here for "show", for parade, for "audience".

In view of the quality of the anecdotes which slip through his self-denying blockade, this general rigour is to be deplored. If we could do without those subtle reservations about narrative method in *The Wings of the Dove,* what could be more delicious than the story of André Gide asking a rich young man to lunch and then (since avarice, not lust, was his abiding sin) foisting the bill on his guest, with the womanish excuse, "C'est plus fort que moi"?

There are some excellent epigrams ("Success is paralyzing only to those who have never wished for anything else") and some that are less than excellent ("Conjunctions are the sinews of prose, or its wheels"), and many passages of shrewd and unpretentious intelligence, but it cannot be said that these ***Journals*** sustain the level of, say, Henry de Montherlant's *Carnets* or even Gide's own disingenuous *Journal.* Perhaps it is simply that Wilder winced too much at his own reflections to make a neat Narcissus. He declares that his pages are meant only to serve as "school of writing, as *four*—oven, furnace". But doesn't the notion that they were never intended for publication founder on that translation of "*four*"? It can scarcely have been done for his own benefit. He might have written better for himself if he had faced candidly that no writer composes *in vacuo* and that he nearly always writes better if he admits it. Lack of style is not evidence of a private language.

The editing is punctilious, but peccable. "*Il pauro*" is painful and I doubt if "Estregona" is, as Mr Gallup suggests, a misprint for "Estremadura". Since Wilder was on a trip to Málaga at the time of the entry, "Estepona" seems a likelier reading. Equally, "Alhambra Hotel" should surely be "Alhambra Palace Hotel", where the musicians switched to Chopin in order to gratify the visiting Stravinsky. Several rather odd locutions pass without editorial sanction, which avoids a plethora of pedantic (*sic*)s but excites uncertainty about the quality of the transcription. The ***Journals*** are at once tiresome and stimulating; it is an odd experience to be both bored and exhilarated by the same volume, but Wilder's ambiguous nature might have relished the idea of startling a reader to sleep.

Frederic Raphael, "Memoirs of an Intellectual Fidget," in The Times Literary Supplement, *No. 4328, March 14, 1986, p. 281.*

David Castronovo (essay date 1986)

[*In the following excerpt from his study* Thornton Wilder *(1986), American critic Castronovo views* The Skin of Our Teeth *as a serious drama that bears a resemblance to the experimental works of Luigi Pirandello, Bertolt Brecht, and James Joyce.*]

Measuring Wilder's progress as a dramatist inevitably involves placing ***The Skin of Our Teeth*** beside ***Our Town:*** the works invite comparison not only because of their ambitiousness but more importantly because of strong thematic affinities. Both concern American families struggling with implacable fate and their own smallness: Emily and George and their parents and Mr. and Mrs. Antrobus and their children experience joy and dread as they contend not only with the localized social problems of American life, but more importantly with the churnings of the universe. The macrocosmic references in both plays—to planets, vast numbers, ideas that hover around mortal lives—are an unmistakable sign that Wilder remains obsessed by the ways ordinary lives in Grover's Corners or Excelsior, New Jersey, take their place in a universal design. But for all this similarity in cosmic subject matter, there is a very considerable difference in the dramatic visions of the plays. The last act of ***Our Town*** takes place in a graveyard—its epiphanies are tragic, but its affirmations about stars and striving are so much inauthentic rhetoric grafted onto a great play. Unfortunately for those who seek easy contrasts with ***The Skin of Our Teeth,*** the later play—for all its brio and broad humor—is not essentially comic, although a wide variety of comic and humorous strategies are used in the very serious, emotionally wrenching drama about the struggle to transcend the disasters of nature, human society, and the warped human self. Act III situates the family in a war-ravaged home with Gladys as an unwed mother, Henry filled with fascistic rage, and Sabina anxious to become a good self-absorbed American citizen ready for a peacetime prosperity of movies and fun. Mr. Antrobus is ready to start putting the world together again, but he is old and tired and has had many setbacks. This is, hardly comic—and in its matter-of-fact look at what men and women wind up with, it is hardly the complacent vision that repelled Mary McCarthy when she reviewed the play [in the *Partisan Review* in 1938]. ***The Skin of Our Teeth*** is not about the fat of the land: what's in view for man is grinding struggle, close calls with total destruction, and the permanent fact of human violence and selfishness.

This theme of human struggle and limited achievement comes to us in the form of three loosely constructed, elliptical acts. Never a writer of well-made plays, Wilder has now brought his own episodic technique to a pitch of dizzy perfection. From his ***Journals*** we learn that Wilder considered that he was "shattering the ossified conventions" of realistic drama in order to let his "generalized beings" emerge.

Act I, set in Excelsior, New Jersey, has about as much logic and verisimilitude as a vaudeville skit. Using the Brechtian strategy of screen projections and announcements, Wilder surveys the "News Events of the World." Mostly the reports concern the extreme cold, the wall of ice moving south, and the scene in the home of George Antrobus. It is six o'clock and "the master not home yet"; Sabina—the sexy maid who sometimes steps out of her part to complain about the play—is parodying the chit-chat that often opens a realistic well-made play: "If anything happened to him, we would certainly be inconsolable and have to move into a less desirable residential district." The dramatic movement—never Wilder's strong point—involves waiting for Antrobus, contending with the cold, disciplining a dinosaur and a mastodon, receiving Antrobus's messages about surviving ("burn everything except Shakespeare"), and living in a typical bickering American family; Maggie Antrobus—unlike her inventive, intellectual, progressive husband—is instinctual and practical. Her children, Henry and Gladys, are emblems of violence and sexuality: the boy has obviously killed his brother with a stone; the girl has trouble keeping her dress down. When their father arrives home—with a face like that of a Keystone Cop, a tendency to pinch Sabina, and a line of insults that sounds like W. C. Fields, the plot moves a bit more swiftly. He asks the dinosaur to leave and receives Homer and Moses into the house. As the act ends, the family of man is trying to conserve its ideas and knowledge—including the alphabet and arithmetic; it has also accepted "the refugees"—the Greek poet and the Hebrew lawgiver. The fire of civilization is alive, and members of the audience are asked to pass up chairs to keep it going.

Act II has the glitz of Atlantic City and the continuing problem of Mr. Antrobus dealing with the disasters of terrestrial life, the fact of his own sexuality, and the gnawing obligations of a father and husband. Once again, in the style of Brecht's epic theater, an announcer comments on screen projections—"Fun at the Beach" and the events of the convocation of "the Ancient and Honorable Order of Mammals." The plot is jumpier than ever—Miss Lily Sabina Fairweather, Miss Atlantic City 1942, tries to seduce Antrobus; a fortune-teller squawks about coming rains; Mrs. Antrobus bickers with the children, champions the idea of the family, and protests against Antrobus's breaking of his marriage promise; Antrobus, ashamed of himself at last, shepherds his flock and an assortment of animals into a boat.

Dealing with the effects of war, Act III is a powerful ending to this play about surviving. The wild and often inspired stage gimmickry of the first two acts has given way to the darkened stage and the ravaged Antrobus home. The emotions become more concentrated, the actions and efforts seem less scattered, the people's situations reach us as both tragedy and the inevitable business of men and women enduring. A play that seemed to be in revolt against realistic character representation, psychological probing, and the fine shadings of nineteenth-century drama, explodes into a moving exploration of personalities as they face the modern world. Deeply affected by the suffering of the war, the family members come into focus as human beings rather than emblems. Henry, the linchpin of this act about war and violence, explains himself for the first time and becomes more than a stick figure. Resentful about having "anybody over me" he has turned himself into a fascist as a way of mastering the authorities—his father, especially—who oppressed him. His truculence, fierce selfishness, and horrible individualism make him both a believable neurotic and a distillation of brutal resentment. Sabina, the temptress who has competed with Mrs. Antrobus for the attention of George, also comes alive as an individual. Driven to depression and cynicism by the hardship of the war, she pronounces that people "have a right to grab what they can find." As "just an ordinary girl" who doesn't mind dealing in black-market goods to pay for a night at the movies, she represents Wilder's honest appraisal of what suffering often does to people. Antrobus—the principle of light, reason, and progress in the play—also has his moments of depression. He yearns for simple relief: "Just a desire to settle down; to slip into the old grooves and keep the neighbors from walking over my lawn." But somehow a pile of old tattered books, brought to life by passages from Spinoza, Plato, and Aristotle delivered by stand-in actors, rekindles the desire "to start building." Self-interest, complacency, despair, and violence coexist with intellectual aspirations and energies to begin again: although outnumbered by ordinarily self-involved and extraordinarily violent people, Antrobus can still go on. Despite the fact that the play ends, as it began, with "the world at sixes and sevens," there is still the principle of the family in Mrs. Antrobus's words and the desire to create the future from the past in Mr. Antrobus's reverence for Plato and technology.

The styles of this play are as various as modern literature and the twentieth-century stage. Not at all austere or carefully crafted, the drama is a brilliant jumble of Pirandello, Joyce, and epic theater.

Once again Wilder employs the manner, and the basic outlook, of *Six Characters in Search of an Author.* Sabina and Henry, particularly, make us aware that they are performing, that their parts are not entirely to their liking, and that they want to convey something about themselves that the theater does not have the means to express. Just as Pirandello's actors distort the story of a tragic family, Wilder's script does not always allow Sabina to tell about her truths or Henry to explain his real-life motivations. Like Pirandello's agonized daughter-figure, Henry insists on the brutal truth of his situation and interrupts the flow of the action to cry out against the false representation that he is given by the playwright. The management of the stage business in ***The Skin of Our Teeth*** is another reminder of Pirandello's theater. The awkward, clumsy matter of props and their arrangement leads us back to *Six Characters* and its arguments about where people should stand, what a room was like, and how people should look. Wilder delights in offering us not only a drama of survival, but also the laborious process of making a play—the scaffolding of a work of art is just as much his subject as the work itself. The stops and starts, the interruptions and localized quarrels of the actors, the puncturing of the whole theatrical illusion by the reality of actors who have become sick from some food and need to be replaced: such ploys carry through Wilder's theme of struggle and endurance, but also suggest the impact of Pirandello's artfully disordered dramas. Wilder's debt to Pirandello does not end with stage technique. The vision of the play—Antrobus beginning again and the family ready "to go on for ages and ages yet"—has most often been traced to Joyce's *Finnegans Wake:* Wilder himself acknowledged this partial debt in the midst of the brouhaha about his "plagiarism." Other influences were overlooked. Pirandello's tragic and tormented family in *Six Characters* goes offstage only to find another theater in which to play out its drama: in a mood of guarded optimism, this is precisely what the Antrobus family is about to do. Sabina reports that they are on their way.

The Skin of Our Teeth also becomes a more enjoyable and intelligible theatrical experience when it is placed beside Bertolt Brecht's epic-theater works. The staging, character presentation, themes, and generalizing power bear an important relationship to Brecht's experiments in the 1930s. Without having to argue for direct influences, one still can see a great deal about Wilder's techniques and idea by placing them in apposition to a work like *Mother Courage.* Since both plays take place in time of war, employ epic exaggeration, explore violence and selfishness, and take an unadorned look at what suffering does to people, it is not unreasonable to view them together. *Mother Courage* was also written three years before ***The Skin of Our Teeth,*** a fact that is not without significance considering Wilder's close touch with the currents of twentieth-century literature. Yet whether he was influenced directly or not, the affinities are strong. As pieces of stagecraft, both plays employ a large historical sweep and present material in a nonrealistic manner; Brecht's play of the Thirty Years War and Wilder's play of civilization's disaster both reach for large generalizations about man's durability and defects. The works do this essentially didactic job by means of screen projections, announcers, jagged episodic plots, and characters who are often stereotypical or emblematic. Wilder's third act overcomes Brecht's relentless detachment from his characters, but even here—as we sympathize with Sabina and Henry—we are not in a theater where the individual psyche is the main concern. Wilder is more involved with the process of learning, the hope of progress, and the impediments in human nature and culture than with the individuality of his people. In this he is one with Brecht, a writer who studies the harshness of civilization and the brutality of ordinary folk. Sabina's selfish, compromising, essentially amoral view of the human struggle for survival is like nothing so much as Mother Courage's matter-of-fact attitude toward suffering and willingness to hitch up her wagon and do business after her children are dead. Wilder has humanized and intellectualized this savage world, but he essentially works with its terrifying ingredients. Even Antrobus, the beacon light of the three acts, is tainted by the lust, a cynicism, cheapness, and hypocrisy that Brecht saw as the central features of bourgeois life. While Antrobus brings his noble and selfish impulses into a unity, he is still like Humanity as described by Brecht in *Saint Joan of the Stockyards:*

> Humanity! Two souls abide
> Within thy breast!
> Do not set either one aside:
> To live with both is best!
> Be torn apart with constant care!
> Be two in one! Be here, be there!
> Hold the low one, hold the high one—
> Hold the straight one, hold the sly one—
> Hold the pair!

During the period when Wilder was working on ***The Skin of Our Teeth,*** the influence of *Finnegans Wake* was also taking effect on his vision. In his correspondence with Edmund Wilson in 1940 and 1941 Wilder gave his own version of the Joyce connection and offered a perspective on his imagination that is more wide-ranging than Robinson and Campbell's detective work. Wilder explained to Wilson [in his letter of January 13, 1940] that the *Wake* was a book with "a figure in the carpet": the design, he argued, was to be discovered in Joyce's anal eroticism; the great conundrum of modern literature was all about "order, neatness, single-minded economy of means." Whether or not this is a reductive interpretation of Joyce, the "discovery" tells us something about Wilder's mind, points to his own career as a preserver of other people's motifs, and suggests a possible explanation for his constant borrowings in ***The Skin.*** Wilder claimed [in a June 15, 1940 letter to Wilson] that he felt a joyous "relief" as he understood Joyce's psychic and literary strategies; each interpreter of these remarks (and of Wilder's *Wake* obsessions) will have to decide what they are revealing. But the present study of Wilder's imagination offers this material as another example of his loving accumulation of ideas and patterns. The letters are a way of coming to terms with his own nature.

Writing to Wilson, Wilder spoke of the *Wake* as embodying "the neurotic's frenzy to tell and not tell." Tell what? the reader might ask. Once again, this remark might be turned on Wilder's own work-in-progress: there are at least two of Wilder's recurring anxieties in the new play—resentment and guilt felt by a son *and* fear of civilization's destruction. His play, Wilder told Wilson [in a letter dated June 16, 1940], was meant to dramatize "the end of the world in comic strip." On one level the description matched Joyce's remarks that *Finnegans Wake* is "a farce of dustiny." But Wilder's readers cannot help recalling the disaster of ***The Bridge,*** the end of the patrician world in ***The Cabala,*** the declining pagan world in ***The Woman of Andros. The Skin of Our Teeth*** may be seen as both a Joyce-burdened work and the latest version of Wilder's anxieties about violence and the collapse of Western culture. (pp. 99-107)

David Castronovo, in his Thornton Wilder, *Ungar, 1986, 174 p.*

Patricia R. Schroeder (essay date 1989)

[*In the following excerpt from her critical study* The Presence of the Past in Modern American Drama *(1989), Schroeder discusses Wilder's dramatic treatment of the concepts of time and history.*]

At first glance, Thornton Wilder's stage past may seem to

Wilder with his mother and sisters in 1928. Left to right: Isabel, Thornton, Wilder's mother Isabella, and Janet.

have only a tenuous connection with that of other twentieth-century American playwrights. For O'Neill, Miller, and Williams, the past is present in the memories of the characters; exposition therefore assumes a major dramatic role in their plays. Yet Wilder's work does share his compatriots' concern with portraying time's passage on the stage, although his emphasis is somewhat different. On Wilder's stage, time's passing is most often obvious to us but unnoticed by the characters, even as it shapes their lives and changes the world they inhabit.

In a 1956 essay entitled "The Man Who Abolished Time" [published in the October issue of *Saturday Review*], Malcolm Cowley pointed out Wilder's pervasive interest in the effects of time. According to Cowley, Wilder's guiding principle and recurring theme is that *"Everything that happened might happen anywhere and will happen again."* As a result of this principle, says Cowley, Wilder continually experiments with time in his novels and his plays, "foreshortening time" to emphasize the repeated patterns of history. Cowley's essay is a landmark, since it offers one of the first analyses of Wilder's perennial experiments with time. Yet Cowley's assessment (both in the 1956 article and in an expanded version published in 1973) is somewhat misleading, suggesting that Wilder holds a "disregard for history" and even that he "denies the importance of time."

It would be more accurate to say that Wilder's *characters* deny the importance of time; they do their best to preserve inherited patterns—annual Christmas dinners, familiar wedding ceremonies—designed to stave off the changes that time inevitably, if imperceptibly, brings with it. Yet to the spectators of a Wilder play, time passes quickly and visibly: characters grow gray before our eyes, and the Ice Age is immediately followed by World War II. With the exception of some very early plays, time is rarely "abolished" on Wilder's stage; rather, it becomes an actual theatrical presence.

This difference between time as it passes and time as characters perceive it is at the heart of Wilder's dramatic experiments; one might even call it the central conflict of his plays. For Wilder was aware that time passes at different rates, depending on who is measuring the pace. For a geologist, centuries count as nothing; for an archeologist or a historian, time collapses; for a lover in the presence of the beloved, an hour can pass unnoticed, yet to one who must wait, that same hour can seem interminable. Rather than focusing his theatrical experiments on methods of exposition, then, Wilder concentrated on depicting the profound and inescapable effects of time as well as the many perspectives available to measure its passing.

Throughout his career Wilder devised, recovered, and adapted stage techniques that produce a double vision of past and present, that demonstrate the role of the individual moment in creating the repeated patterns of history. The playwright described his problem in this way [in his Preface to ***Three Plays***]:

> Every person who has ever lived has lived an unbroken succession of unique occasions. Yet the more one is aware of individuality in experience (innumerable! innumerable!) the more one becomes attentive to what these disparate moments have in common, to repetitive patterns. As an artist (or listener or beholder) which "truth" do you prefer—that of the isolated occasion, or that which includes or resumes the innumerable? Which truth is more worth telling?

Wilder's plays suggest that he found *both* truths worth telling, and his dramatic experiments all contribute to his expressing them simultaneously. He continually adjusted stage time to portray situations both as "disparate moments" and also as contributors to "repetitive patterns." By presenting, as he said of ***The Skin of Our Teeth,*** "two times at once," he was able to proclaim the intrinsic significance of each moment and simultaneously to explore the place of the moment, once past, in shaping the unfolding patterns of history.

Wilder's very first published plays (***The Angel That Troubled the Waters,*** 1928) suggest both his willingness to experiment with stage time and the early difficulties he faced in creating a temporally flexible dramatic form; many of these plays, in fact, do "abolish" time in just the way Cowley described. The form the young Wilder employed—and Wilder admits to having begun experimenting with these plays while still a high school student—was the three-minute play for three actors, a literary form that, according to the playwright's "Forward" to the volume, "satisfies my desire for compression." Despite the immaturity of the three-minute plays themselves, this impulse toward compression led the young Wilder to experiment with the telescoping of time, thereby allowing his three minutes of stage time to incorporate many of the general patterns of history. The three-minute form became an early proving ground for the playwright who would later collapse the past into the present to stage the life of an entire village, and who would include the Ice Age, the Deluge, and a world war in a single three-act play.

The majority of these three-minute plays explore competing visions of time through one simple technique: they divorce well-known characters from their usual environments and force them to function in different times or in unfamiliar contexts. In one play Mozart, worrying over his poverty and despairing of a commission, is interrupted in his practical considerations by a commission from Death. Here, the concerns of the earthly world and human time contrast with those of the spiritual world and eternity, implying their concurrent but conflicting demands for our attention. Another play presents the death of Childe Roland, whose dying prayer to the Blessed Virgin is answered not by the Queen of Heaven he addresses, but by three mystical queens in a mythic dark tower, entrance to the underworld of a time period and a system of beliefs different from those he invokes.

In another play from this collection, entitled ***Proserpina and the Devil,*** Wilder's instinct for compression takes on an added dimension as he first conflates the traditions of classical mythology with those of Christianity and then inserts them into a seventeenth-century Venetian marionette show. On this puppet stage, the Lake of Wrath serves as the River Styx, Noah's Ark as Charon's barge, Pluto as Satan, Hermes as the Archangel Gabriel, and "a handsome Italian matron" in stiff brocade as Demeter. Wilder's interest in the repeated cycles of time is apparent here in this interchanging of mythic and religious figures in the more recent—although still historical—context of seventeenth-century Italy. His abridgement of time also demonstrates the ways in which the details of a workaday routine—represented in the play by the difficulties of the puppeteers, or the "matter of pins and hooks-and-eyes" that prevents Proserpina's rescue—can obscure the interaction of larger contexts, which shape and are shaped by the event itself.

In one three-minute play, ***Fanny Otcott,*** Wilder explores with some success both his interest in competing perspectives and his concern for the interaction between historical patterns and particular moments. ***Fanny Otcott*** is structurally different from its companion pieces in two important ways. Unlike many of the other plays, which present only the static meditations of ready-made mythic or historic figures, ***Fanny Otcott*** contains an evolving plot. The climax occurs when Fanny recognizes the possibilities afforded by conflicting interpretations of events past and present. In addition, in ***Fanny Otcott*** Wilder focuses his inquiries on one character's view of her personal past and so emphasizes both individual perception and the particular moment with an immediacy unmatched in the volume.

Against the backdrop of an Arthurian tower—a reminder that Fanny's situation has often been repeated through history—the aging actress Fanny Otcott sorts out her souvenirs—"in short, her past." Enter George, her long-ago lover and now a bishop, whose memories of his former "association" with Fanny are very different from her own. What Fanny remembers with tenderness and delight—"It was like hawthorn-buds and meadow larks and Mr. Handel's Water-music"—George recalls as "a distressing spot on my conscience." The play ends as Fanny dismisses the illusory memory world she has so long inhabited and resolves to rejoice in present life rather than in recollections of the past.

This is the earliest clear-cut instance in Wilder's dramatic canon of a dilemma his later plays insist upon: Fanny cannot seize the day if she insists on burying it with memories, but neither can she recognize the ultimate importance of the present moment if she isolates it from its place in the developing patterns of her life. The validity of the concept by which she has lived—that is, her interpretation of her affair with George—is called into question by George's conflicting recollections, and the possibility that contradictory patterns can emerge from a single event becomes clear to her. Fanny now recognizes that her own perception of a single past episode has shaped her entire past, present, and future. Although this recognition affirms the intrinsic significance of both that defining moment and her unique perception of it, it simultaneously suggests that the importance of a particular moment is undiscoverable until that moment has been absorbed into a larger context. By the end of this short play Fanny achieves a new awareness, as she seizes the present moment of the play—her disappointing reunion with George—to alter both her understanding of the past and the development of her future. She learns that living in the past obscures the value of the present.

Fanny's final recognition that an individual's interpretation of the past is the past that matters most seems to parallel a growing awareness of Wilder's. Throughout his next ten years of technical exploration with the one-act form, Wilder would continue to examine the invasion of the present by past decisions and the distance in time needed to see the effects of such decisions—the central dilemma that would inform all his formal experiments and culminate in the achievement of ***Our Town.***

The young Wilder's precocious creativity in presenting stage time as both flexible and variable is evident in his three-minute plays, but their obviously contrived form produced insoluble problems as well. The interesting devices Wilder was learning to employ in these plays most often have lyric rather than dramatic effects, and the brief moments of the plays usually remain static, lacking climax or direction. By abolishing time, these plays demonstrate the young Wilder's tendency to "experiment with form before he had troubled to think up an adequate plot."

Wilder's youthful digressions from traditional dramatic form are easy to understand, however, in the light of the overly plotted, inflexible dramatic models available to an aspiring young playwright in 1920s America. As described in the first chapter, the American stage at that time (with a few notable exceptions) was deeply entrenched in a formal realism much too rigid to have supported the overlapping temporal perspectives that interested Wilder. Like Eugene O'Neill, Wilder lamented the reductive vision of time demanded by the proscenium stage. In Wilder's view, the playwrights and producers of the conventionally realistic theatre had "shut the play up into a museum showcase"; they had "loaded the stage with specific objects," each of which

> fixes and narrows the action to one moment in time and place. . . . When you emphasize *place* in the theatre, you drag down and limit and harness time to it. You thrust the action back into the past time, whereas it is precisely the glory of the stage that it is always "now" there.

By rejecting its pretenses, the drama had forfeited its ability to telescope time, remaining content to mirror events significant only at a certain moment. On the proscenium stage, where time was "harnessed" to place, the past could no longer collide with the present in diverse and unexpected ways.

The problems confronting the young Wilder were thus manifold: formal realism had atrophied contemporary dramatic form, and his own three-minute plays were structurally weak, in one sense even evading the issue of stage time. How, then, was he to develop a form suitable for embodying conflicting visions of time? In his classical education Wilder found a partial answer to this question [in his essay "Some Thoughts on Playwriting]; he discovered that

> the history of the theatre shows us that in its greatest ages the stage employed the greatest number of conventions. The stage is fundamental pretense and it thrives on the acceptance of that fact and in the multiplication of additional pretenses.

If few twentieth-century American playwrights had been able to develop new conventions for expressing contemporary attitudes toward time's passing, at least some of the drama's old vitality could be restored by rejuvenating its old conventions. Wilder therefore turned to the drama of past centuries and foreign countries. If the dramatic models available to him were incompatible with his design, then he would find alternative models.

As William A. Scally has noted [in "Modern Return to Medieval Drama," in *The Many Forms of Drama*], Wilder borrowed techniques for presenting "cyclic history" from the British medieval mystery plays. Other eras and other places provided other models. In the works of the Elizabethans, Wilder discovered the freedom that antimimetic staging could produce; as he says of *Romeo and Juliet:*

> When the play is staged as Shakespeare intended it, the bareness of the stage releases the events from the particular and the experience of Juliet partakes of that of all girls in love, in every time, place, and language. **["Some Thoughts on Playwriting"]**

In the works of the Japanese Noh dramatists, in which an actor's circling the stage represents a long journey and the passage of much time, Wilder discovered a similar freedom. And like O'Neill, who had recognized in the works of the new German expressionist playwrights a method for depicting a subjective reality, Wilder found in the expressionists and particularly in Bertolt Brecht some contemporary methods for breaking down the outdated verisimilitude, with its linear relationship between past and present, of the proscenium stage.

Wilder's theatrical debt to Brecht has attracted much critical attention. Wilder's thematic interests are very different from Brecht's—"humanistic" rather than "Marxist," to borrow a pair of convenient, albeit reductive, labels—but his methods of staging and his exuberant theatricality partake heavily of Brecht's own. Like Brecht, who exaggerates theatrical gestures and emphasizes conventions to produce his notorious "alienation effect," Wilder frequently uses an intrusive Stage Manager, self-conscious characters, and a disregard for chronological time; like Brecht, Wilder insists on the reality of theatre as theatre. For Wilder, however, the separate reality of theatre does not necessarily impose distance between audience and character; rather, it establishes the equal validity of multiple temporal contexts. By combining Brechtian theatricality, Elizabethan flexibility of space, and expressionistic distortions of time and perspective, Wilder synthesized a form that permitted him to portray concurrent yet rival perspectives on the passage of time.

Despite his enormous creativity in adapting techniques and developing a plastic dramatic form, Wilder himself minimized his own importance in rejuvenating the American theatre. As he expressed it [in his preface to ***Three Plays***]: his experiments with dramatic form were mere stepping-stones for more talented playwrights:

> The theatre has lagged behind the other arts in finding the "new ways" to express how men and women feel in our time. I am not one of the new dramatists we are looking for. I wish I were. I hope I have played a part in preparing the way for them. I am not an innovator but a rediscoverer of forgotten goods and a remover of obtrusive bric-a-brac.

Here, Wilder seems to have underestimated the importance of his particular moment (or imagination) in both absorbing and shaping general historical patterns—in this case, the inherited pattern of dramatic form. He was, in fact, a consummate innovator, the novelty of his mature work apparent in his new uses and original syntheses of restored techniques.

Before Wilder could effectively "unharness" stage time in full-length plays, however, he experimented with rival visions of time in one-act plays. These plays demonstrate the variety of techniques he had recovered to depict both the impact of time's passage and the many ways of viewing it.

Wilder returned from his 1928 lecture tour of Europe armed with an entire new arsenal of antimimetic techniques, prepared to attack the reductive vision of the realistic stage. He proposed to bombard that "abject realism" which he saw as "deeply in earnest, every detail is true, but the whole finally tumbles to the ground—true but without significance" ["Preface" to ***Our Town*** in ***American Characteristics and Other Essays***]. The variety of the experiments in ***The Long Christmas Dinner and Other Plays in One Act*** attests to the vigor of his attack.

The difference between time as it passes and time as characters perceive it is at the heart of Wilder's dramatic experiments; one might even call it the central conflict of his plays.

—Patricia R. Schroeder

The title play of the volume dramatizes the interaction between passing moments and repeated patterns; it also demonstrates Wilder's maturing techniques for depicting rather than merely repudiating stage time. ***The Long Christmas Dinner*** presents a single occasion—the Bayard family's annual Christmas dinner—that evolves into a larger pattern of inherited traditions as it is repeated yearly. The ninety years of annual Christmas dinners pass in a continuum, unbroken by act divisions, scenery changes, or other abrupt transitions of the formally realistic stage. Characters simply enter the dining room when they are born or marry into the family and exit when they move away or die. In effect, the ninety-year cycle of repeated ritual becomes, on the stage, only one event, with one setting, one action—in short, one long, unbroken Christmas dinner despite the gradual alterations in its component parts. In this way, the present includes the past, each dinner is all dinners, and the particular moment expands to encompass the entire historical pattern.

As time passes and the play progresses, however, the participants at the dinner change: the baby carriage that stands near the table is eventually replaced by an adult actor, who later expresses the passage of even more time by donning a gray wig. As each character matures, he or she inherits a new role within the family hierarchy and reshapes that role according to his or her individual responses to it. The passage of time is thus linked to the inevitability of change: although the reenactment of certain familial roles by successive characters implies continuity of the pattern, the joys and griefs of each character are immediate, unprecedented, and contribute in unique ways to the development of that pattern.

Within this cycle of evolution and repetition, some things change and some endure. The circular structure of the play emphasizes repetition: ***The Long Christmas Dinner*** begins and ends with the reflections of an elderly woman—in each case called "Mother Bayard" by the members of her family—on enjoying her first Christmas dinner in her grown child's new home. Each woman's outlook on her Christmas dinner party is unique, however, and these differences in detail affirm each character's role in shaping the inherited rituals. The rituals themselves endure, but they change by retaining the imprint of each character who has enacted them.

In other instances this change is emphasized, as the patterns and beliefs of one generation are modified by the next. Charles' assertion that "time certainly goes by very fast in a great new country like this" is refuted by his impatient son Roderick, who claims: "Time passes so slowly here that it stands still, that's what's the trouble. . . . I'm going somewhere where time passes." Here, Roderick shares his father's confusion of time with place but disagrees about the rate at which it passes. And in a number of instances throughout the play, a single, familial role—mother, sister, cousin—is filled successively by characters from different generations and demonstrates explicitly the mutually shaping effects of repeated patterns and individual responses, of past history and present moments.

In ***The Long Christmas Dinner*** Wilder successfully dramatized the past as a shifting yet essential part of the present; the characters may modify the patterns they have inherited, but the patterns continue to direct their actions. The wonder felt by each character at a repeated, special event—the birth of a baby, a twig wrapped in ice ("You almost never see that," we are told on four separate occasions—3, 10, 13, 25)—illustrates Wilder's vision of an event as both an individual experience and a part of a larger context, apparent only through time. And because the form of the play depicts the restructuring through time of a single, repeated event, the passage of time becomes a felt experience as well as a central theme. The play beautifully illustrates both the concern for the past Wilder shared with his compatriots and the differences from them engendered by his interest in competing temporal contexts.

Other plays in this volume explore the effects of time in quite different ways and demonstrate the real flexibility that Wilder was now bringing to the stage. While in ***The Long Christmas Dinner*** Wilder compressed nearly a century of Bayard family history into one half-hour of stage time and so provided a sweeping retrospective viewpoint, in ***Pullman Car Hiawatha*** he employed an opposite strategy. The play presents a total cross-section, from personal detail to cosmic context, of a single moment in time—the moment of Harriet's death. By halting time to focus on one event, Wilder is able to dramatize concurrent but conflicting temporal contexts.

The most obvious context is human time—the time of Harriet's life, which is now at an end. What life has meant to Harriet becomes clear in her farewell speech:

> Goodbye, 1312 Ridgewood Avenue, Oaksbury, Illinois. I hope I remember all its steps and doors and wallpapers forever. Goodbye, Emerson Grammar School on the corner of Forbush Avenue and Wherry Street. Goodbye, Miss Walker and Miss Cramer who taught me English and Miss Matthewson who taught me Biology. Goodbye, First Congregational Church on the corner of Meyerson Avenue and Sixth Street and Dr. McReady and Mrs. McReady and Julia. Goodbye, Papa and Mama.

Seen from this unique, retrospective viewpoint, time passes imperceptibly in an accumulation of details with significance only for the person involved. And while Harriet's farewell speech is clearly meant to move us, Wilder nevertheless takes pains in this play to show that the perspective of memory is limited, and that other time frames impart different sorts of meaning.

This becomes apparent through the actions of the Stage Manager. At the moment of Harriet's death, the Stage Manager breaks into the action and abruptly enlarges the prevailing viewpoint:

> All right. So much for the inside of the car. That'll be enough of that for the present. Now for its position geographically, astronomically, theologically considered.
>
> Pullman Car Hiawatha, ten minutes of ten. December twenty-first, 1930. All ready.

This sudden shift from the living and dying inside the train to conditions exterior to it forces us to acknowledge alternative ways of viewing the action. The moving train passes through a variety of contexts as it travels through an ever-changing landscape and through numerous systems for measuring time. By shifting the focus away from Harriet, the Stage Manager forces us to accept the limits of a human perspective on time.

Despite the convergence of these general contexts at the moment of Harriet's death, however, life on the Pullman Car Hiawatha is given an emphasis equal, within the framework of this play, to that given the local geography, the weather, and the stars; Harriet's death is in no way trivialized. In fact, none of the larger systems for measuring time—astronomical, geological, meteorological, theological—imparted nearly so much meaning to Harriet's life as did the domestic details she remembers. The Stage Manager's final action underscores the importance of particular human vision in both generating and acknowledging systems for measuring time. Although his role as central intelligence has permitted him to view all time frames equally as they converge, in his final action he chooses a limited and local perspective from which to view events. He abandons his managerial role and closes out the play as the particularly clumsy passenger in Upper Berth Five.

Despite his implication in ***Pullman Car Hiawatha*** that the individual or the local point of view provides the best vantage point from which to assess the importance of events, in ***The Happy Journey from Trenton to Camden*** the playwright explores the perils of maintaining too limited a perspective. In technique, this play is similar to its companion pieces: as in ***The Long Christmas Dinner,*** time is compressed, and a three-hour car trip takes only about fifteen minutes of stage time; as in ***Pullman Car Hiawatha,*** the characters ride an imaginary vehicle moving through time and space, represented on the stage only by a few suggestive boards and four chairs. This play differs from the others, however, in that it offers no temporal perspective between the uniquely personal and the eternal. Lacking intermediary contexts—such as the repeated family roles of the Bayards or the "geographical, meteorological, and astronomical" considerations through which the Pullman Car Hiawatha passes on its way to eternity—the daily routines of the Kirbys seem petty and inconsequential.

Early in their journey, the Kirbys must stop to allow a funeral procession to pass, and when they reach their destination we learn that the convalescent daughter they have traveled to visit has lost a newborn child. The twin deaths in the play are thus set in relief against the details of Kirby family life, and their response to the deaths illustrates their single-mindedness: despite the mysteries of death and afterlife, life must continue, the chicken must be roasted for dinner, and the loss of Beulah's child must not interfere with the functioning of the family unit. As Ma Kirby tells her daughter, "God thought best. We don't understand why. We just go on, honey, doin' our business." Unlike ***The Long Christmas Dinner,*** which spans nearly a century, or ***Pullman Car Hiawatha,*** which includes representatives of the entire galaxy, the world presented in ***The Happy Journey*** is totally grounded in the present. By the end of the play Ma Kirby's habitual recitation of proverbial wisdom becomes a rather annoying drone, and the colossal backdrop of eternity against which the Kirbys continue their homely activities serves only to diminish their importance.

The Happy Journey thus presents a vision of the world that is almost as narrow as that of the realistic stage Wilder eschewed. Yet the unconventional staging—reminiscent of the Elizabethan methods that Wilder admired—does offer us a new way of observing the limitations of such an artificially confined perspective.

In recovering forgotten conventions to compose the plays in this volume, Wilder developed an impressive array of antimimetic techniques. When transferred to his full-length plays, these techniques allowed Wilder to portray time as something that moves in diverse ways and the past as something always encapsulated in the present, despite the limited and varying vantage points from which it can be viewed.

In an early preface to ***Our Town*** (written with the play in 1938, but not published until 1979), Wilder uses an intriguing metaphor to explain the play's multiple ways of viewing time. He had tried to present, as he said [in his "Preface" to the play], "the life of the village against the life of the stars." ***Our Town*** does present "the life of the village," with its cyclic, daily patterns and its locally shared assumptions, enacted in loving detail by the inhabitants of Grover's Corners. The larger eternal patterns represented by "the life of the stars" also play a significant part in the action, as questions about birth, death, and afterlife occasionally interrupt the diurnality of the action, especially when introduced directly to the audience by the Stage Manager. As a result of these conflicting yet concurrent methods of portraying life on the stage, the audience is continually forced to select, from among several points in time, a place to stand and view the action.

The necessity of such a choice is dramatized in act 3, when Emily returns posthumously to Grover's Corners to relive her twelfth birthday. At this point Emily, now dead, is largely the product of all she has been; her parents, her girlhood relationship with George, her life as a farm wife have all combined to color her perceptions and form her identity. She cannot, therefore, be again what she once was, and her now mature reliving of her twelfth birthday demonstrates explicitly—both to her and to the audience—the impossibility of recovering the past or of unraveling the patterns of life once they have been woven. The value of a seemingly trivial moment (in this case, Emily's birthday) is thus seen from the twofold perspective of past and present: the first demonstrates the moment's importance in developing the pattern of a lifetime; the second proclaims its intrinsic worth as something fleeting and unrepeatable.

This twofold interpretation of a present moment is offered throughout the play by the Stage Manager, who operates within two worlds—that of the production and that of the play—at once. His very first speech demonstrates his ability to function in both contexts, as he introduces the cast of players and the inhabitants of Grover's Corners almost simultaneously. In his role as a theatrical device, the Stage Manager single-handedly runs the show: he acts as a living playbill, he describes and prepares the imaginary set, he directs the actors, and he often interrupts the play to comment on the future significance of an action just presented. By intruding in this way between the audience and the characters, he permits us to share his double vision of present and future (which Emily achieves only after her death in the third act) from the very beginning of the play.

Early in the play the Stage Manager offers us our first choice of time frames, and the response we must inevitably make directs our attention to the importance of the present moment. The Stage Manager allows us to eavesdrop on a conversation between the town's current paper boy, Joe Crowell, and Dr. Gibbs, as both go about their early morning routines:

> DR. GIBBS. Anything serious goin' on in the world since Wednesday?
>
> JOE CROWELL, JR. Yessir. My schoolteacher, Miss Foster, 's getting married to a fella over in Concord.

This brief interchange between neighbors establishes the importance of community events and also indicates the limited perspective of a Grover's Corners youth, to whom the marriage of a teacher has national significance. The Stage Manager, however, in an attempt to broaden the temporal viewpoint, stops the action to reveal Joe's future:

> Want to tell you something about that boy Joe Crowell there. Joe was awful bright—graduated from high school here, head of his class. So he got a scholarship to Massachusetts Tech. Graduated head of his class there, too. It was all wrote up in the Boston paper at the time. Goin' to be a great engineer, Joe was. But the war broke out and he died in France.—All that education for nothing.

The Stage Manager clearly has the ability to foretell the future, but his balanced viewpoint offers only a part of the picture. Within the pattern of world war, Joe's education was, certainly, meaningless, but within the pattern of life in Grover's Corners, Joe's academic accomplishment stands out as a significant achievement in his short life and a model of success in his community. The Stage Manager's timeless perspective would rob Joe of his achievements, but attention to the actual moment of Joe's success would preserve them. Evidently much of the dignity and value of daily life depends on a limited temporal perspective, one that disregards the formation of larger patterns and focuses on the present moment.

The Stage Manager's awareness of the future does not always blind him to the benefits of attending to the present, however; in fact, he often shrinks his own extended frame of reference by presenting the immediate impact of a moment along with its historical significance. That he does value immediacy is clearly evident when he presents the drug store scene, in which George and Emily first recognize their love for one another. The Stage Manager introduces the event by interrupting George and Emily's wedding and placing the drug store scene within the general context of "Love and Marriage" (the title of the second act):

> Now I have to interrupt again here. You see, we want to know how all this began—this wedding, this plan to spend a lifetime together. I'm awfully interested in how big things like that begin. You know how it is: you're twenty-one or twenty-two and you make some decisions; then whissh! you're seventy: you've been a lawyer for fifty years, and that white-haired lady at your side has eaten over fifty thousand meals with you. How do such things begin?

After establishing the drug store incident as a "big thing" in forming the pattern of George and Emily's future, however, the Stage Manager reminds us in an unabashed appeal to our emotions of some of the special properties intrinsic to the moment itself, qualities that are immediate and understandable only from a short-term perspective:

> George and Emily are going to show you now the conversation that they had when they first knew that . . . that . . . as the saying goes . . . they were meant for each other. But before they do I want you to remember what it was like to have been very young. And particularly the days when you were first in love: when you were like a person sleepwalking, and you didn't quite see the street you were in, and didn't quite hear everything that was said to you. You're just a little bit crazy. Will you remember that, please?

The Stage Manager's direct commentary on the number

of ways one can view this scene is not his most important contribution to it, however; he also emphasizes the moment by shifting it from its ordinary dramatic context. In a formally realistic play, this meeting between George and Emily would have been a focal point in time, a traditional, second-act "recognition scene." By interrupting thc present day of the action (that is, George and Emily's wedding day) to introduce the recognition scene in a flashback, out of temporal sequence, he stresses the magic of the moment itself, outside any larger pattern, isolated in time. Furthermore, by modifying standard three-act form and presenting incidents nonsequentially, he repeats a familiar pattern (here, traditional dramatic form) by altering one of its components (the formally realistic handling of stage time). In this way he recapitulates in a theatrical context the constant reevaluating of particular moments in terms of developing patterns that the characters enact in the alternative world of Grover's Corners.

But even this theatrical exemplification of the play's thematic patterns is not always specific enough to ensure our attention to the moment at hand. It demands the Stage Manager's continued presence in a world outside that of the action and so implies that present action cannot display its own worth. To counteract this suggestion and so emphasize even more completely the value of the moment in a world of multiple temporal frameworks, the Stage Manager occasionally renounces his ability to foresee the future and becomes, at least temporarily, an ordinary citizen of Grover's Corners. In the recognition scene he jumps from his role as Stage Manager to become, with the addition of a pair of spectacles, the proprietor of Morgan's drug store. George and Emily's discussion there is important not only for the pattern of future events and family and community relationships it initiates (and which the Stage Manager describes), but also for the excitement and emotional impact of the moment itself (which Mr. Morgan shares and cheerfully approves). By alternating his all-knowing theatrical role with that of a specific character, the Stage Manager is able to study historical patterns and also to participate in momentary events. In this way he embodies the tensions that continually inform ***Our Town.***

The importance of a particular moment is demonstrated so compellingly in this recognition in part because of the groundwork laid for it in act 1. The real "action" of act 1 is extremely limited: we are shown a community of simple characters performing their daily, habitual tasks. The act builds up no conflict, no potential clash between antagonists. In fact, if act 1 has any relationship to traditional dramatic form it is in the repetition of details and the circularity of daily activities that, by suggesting perpetual reenactment, expose the past while depicting the present. The act moves placidly through the events of a typical Grover's Corners day: predawn newspaper deliveries and the children's breakfast give way to stringing beans and baseball practice, which in turn make way for the evening meal and the smell of heliotrope in a moonlit garden. The circularity of these events is underscored by direct references to the life cycle, including the babies born in the first few minutes of the act and the impending death of Simon Stimson (choir master and genteel town drunk) at the end.

This finely focused attention to repeated detail and specific moments characterizes both the first and second acts of ***Our Town.*** Act 3, however, reverses the emphasis of the first two acts, as the death of Emily forces us to notice the larger perspectives of life and death, with only occasional references to the routines of "Daily Life" or the inherited patterns of "Love and Marriage." Just as the value of the moment was challenged in the first two acts by intermittent references to the necessity of a historical perspective, so in this act the larger temporal perspective is challenged by the local, immediate point of view that preceded it. This contrast is emphasized in the Stage Manager's opening soliloquy, in which he says:

> Now, there are some things we all know, but we don't take'm out and look at'm very often. We all know that *something* is eternal, and that something has to do with human beings. All the greatest people ever lived have been telling us that for five thousand years and yet you'd be surprised how people are always losing hold of it. There's something way down deep that's eternal about every human being.

In this way, the Stage Manager directs our attention away from the individual moments of life to the eternal importance of every individual. This time, however, he includes the audience specifically in his analysis. In describing the changes in Grover's Corners since act 2, he points not to stage left or stage right (as he did in act 1), but directly into the audience to locate the scene of the action. From the mountaintop cemetery on which he now stands—implying the more distanced, perhaps more elevated perspective he commands—the members of the audience become the living citizens of Grover's Corners. Because of our previous attention to (and eventual inclusion in) the daily moments of Grover's Corners, we are now offered a richer and more immediate understanding of the universal and the timeless.

In accordance with this reversal of emphasis in act 3, the structure of the act is also somewhat different from that of the first two. The present action of act 3 is interrupted by an important scene presented out of sequence, out of its usual place in the context of chronological time, as was that of act 2; the return to Emily's twelfth birthday in act 3, however, is more than a mere flashback, since this time Emily shares our retrospective view. Instead of merely acting out a scene for us, conscious only of the present, in act 3 Emily is painfully aware of the future significance of the events she relives. The resultant dramatic irony allows her to acknowledge the value of each fleeting moment and to lament her current inability to recapture it. Her double perspective on her own life forces her tormented question, "Do human beings ever realize life while they live it?—every, every minute?"

The routines of daily life that began acts 1 and 2 are thus relegated to this past scene in act 3, since the routines of daily life are now merely a cherished memory for Emily, framed within the boundaries of eternity. As she enters the kitchen for breakfast on her birthday morning, Emily is immediately bombarded with details she had either forgotten or never even noticed. Her new awareness of her past obliviousness causes her great pain. "I can't look at everything hard enough," she cries as she observes that her mother had once been young and remembers a long-forgotten childhood gift from George. Her new double perspective permits her to see not only that each moment of life is priceless, but also, as Simon Stimson tells her, that to be alive is to "move about in a cloud of ignorance; to go up and down trampling the feelings of those . . . of those about you. To spend and waste time as though you had a million years."

The value of memory thus seems both a blessing and a curse: it enables Emily finally to appreciate the defining details of her own ended life, but it also illuminates the human inability to recognize the important moments of life until they have passed. Emily's double perspective allows her to see the multiple time frames at work during her life, and to recognize that the most limited of these is the one for which she will grieve most. In an echo of Harriet's farewell to life in ***Pullman Car Hiawatha,*** Emily addresses time and enumerates the details that she now sees as having been most significant in defining her identity on earth:

> Good-by, Good-by, world. Good-by, Grover's Corners . . . Mama and Papa. Good-by to clocks ticking . . . and Mama's sunflowers. And food and coffee. And new-ironed dresses and hot baths . . . and sleeping and waking up. Oh, earth, you're too wonderful for anybody to realize you.

The ultimate value of a timeless perspective, it seems, is the insight it can afford into the value of the particular moment. Emily's return to the graveyard places the final emphasis on the importance of specific events and unrepeatable moments in a world crowded with competing temporal contexts, as she resumes her place within that peaceful void, the solitary context of eternity. There, the details of life gradually fade from the memories of the graveyard inhabitants (like Mrs. Gibbs, who can no longer remember the names of the stars), and the characters, cut off from the concerns and routines of daily living, drift away from life itself. As the Stage Manager tells us:

> You know as well as I do that the dead don't stay interested in us living people for very long. Gradually, gradually, they lose hold of the earth . . . and the ambitions they had . . . and the things they suffered . . . and the people they loved. They get weaned away from the earth. . . .

Life in ***Our Town,*** finally, consists of a multitude of interacting systems for evaluating time, from those of the village to those of the stars. The ones that most clearly define and enrich life, however, are those that distract, disorder, and confuse the inhabitants and so protect them from death's timeless void: the ones composed of each character's ambitions and sufferings and joys, of significant details, of a limited perspective, and of cherished, particular events. The unusual structure of the play successfully embodies Wilder's ambition to "represent the Act in Eternity"—that is, to depict the importance of each fleeting moment within the ever-expanding boundaries of time.

In ***Our Town,*** Wilder employed firsthand what he saw in the Elizabethans: that a simply staged play could universalize the particular without denying the impact of individual moments. But Wilder was also interested, as his early plays show, in the changes that time brings, in the patterns that time creates from seemingly isolated present moments. In ***The Skin of Our Teeth*** Wilder used an overt theatricalism akin to Brecht's to demonstrate the importance of passing moments in unfolding history, regardless of the limited perspective of an individual acting at a given time.

From the opening of ***The Skin of Our Teeth,*** the audience is bombarded with an array of conflicting details; we cannot locate the characters in a specific time or place because both keep changing. The curtain does not even rise as the play begins but rather becomes a projection screen for slides of the daily "News Events of the World." In this curious newscast, the scrubwomen who clean the theatre are pictured and introduced, allowing the world of the theatre and the production to intrude into the world of the performance before the action can even begin. Another news item advertises a wedding ring currently in the theatre's lost and found, inscribed "To Eva from Adam. Genesis II:18," and so invokes a wider set of contexts—historical, temporal, biblical. The ring will be returned to its owner only with proper identification, however, and so the world of legal documents and credentials encroaches upon the context of theatre, the contexts of love and marriage, and the contexts of time and religion. The limitations of all these perspectives are made clear by the next slide: a wall of ice that "has not yet been satisfactorily explained" is disrupting communication and pushing a cathedral—monument of human aspirations—from Montreal to Vermont.

Contexts continue to overlap at this unprecedented rate throughout the play. In this way, Wilder once again poses the question that Emily had asked in ***Our Town:*** how is it possible to assess the value of the present until it has become part of the past, part of a pattern recognizable only through time? In ***The Skin of Our Teeth,*** once again, Wilder suggests the near impossibility of doing so.

Wilder draws attention to this concern primarily by collapsing temporal distinctions: the Ice Age in act 1 turns into both the antediluvian world and the New Jersey boardwalk in act 2, only to become a twentieth-century postwar city in act 3. Within this multitemporal framework, repeated patterns are emphasized because everybody assumes multiple identities. Henry Antrobus is four thousand years old, but a little boy; Sabina is a scullery maid, boardwalk beauty queen, camp follower, and Sabine woman, all at the same time. George Antrobus has recently "discovered" the wheel, a detail that defines George as a prehistoric man, an inventor, an explorer, or perhaps all three; he lives in the suburbs (conveniently located near a church, a school, and an A & P), a context that locates him in modern New Jersey; he has been a gardener (Adam?) but left the position "under circumstances which have been variously reported" (111); and he is a veteran of foreign wars, symbol of the omnipresent human conflict inevitably produced by competing contexts. Like the Bayards in ***The Long Christmas Dinner,*** who enact repeated but changing familial roles, the Antrobus family of ***The Skin of Our Teeth*** demonstrate the continuity of all human experience, throughout all time.

Within this palimpsest of competing chronologies and perspectives, every action of the characters is in some undetermined way important and in some way influences the course of events or the evolution of human beings. No present action can be seen as trivial in a world where George's decision to put the family pets out overnight leads to the extinction of the mammoth and the dinosaur, and where the audience's passing their chairs up to the stage can help "save the human race." From the beginning of the play, then, we are faced, as are the characters, with a universe of overlapping time frames, in which any event or any decision can have undreamed-of repercussions, and in which the significance of each moment becomes clear only when that moment has been engulfed by the past.

A play enacting multiple eras and embodying competing temporal viewpoints is not, of course, reducible to any simple thematic coherence; no one interpretation of an event or a moment ever seems sufficient in ***The Skin of Our Teeth.*** This becomes abundantly clear during the rehearsal scene, when Mr. Fitzpatrick, the stage manager, interrupts the play to rehearse some last-minute understudies (supposedly the cleaning crew of the theatre) because several of the actors have become ill. This rehearsal scene obviously underscores the importance of time in the play, since the passing hours of evening are depicted as characters quoting philosophers' thoughts. While explaining the scene to the audience, Mr. Fitzpatrick mentions that the personification of time doesn't "mean anything. It's just a kind of poetic effect." The actress Miss Somerset, however, vehemently disagrees: "Not mean anything! Why, it certainly does. . . . I think it means that when people are asleep they have all those lovely thoughts, much better than when they're awake." And Ivy, Miss Somerset's maid, presents yet another analysis of the playwright's device:

> The author meant that—just like the hours and stars go over our heads at night, in the same way the ideas and thoughts of the great men are in the air around us all the time and they're working on us, even when we don't know it.

The irony of all these conflicts of interpretation is apparent in the passage from Spinoza (otherwise known as "Nine o'clock"), which asserts that "all the objects of my desire and fear were in themselves nothing good nor bad save insofar as the mind was affected by them." In short, the subject of the scene is that the meanings of things can be determined only from an individual point of view and in the fullness of time; the action of the scene and the disagreement between the characters serve principally to dramatize the alternative perspectives that passing time demands.

Competing time frames and perspectives are thus much more than virtuoso technical devices in ***The Skin of Our Teeth;*** they are an actual subject of the play. ***The Skin of Our Teeth*** offers us, finally, a glimpse at the unlimited (if sometimes unrecognized) possibilities inherent in a world of rival contexts. What makes those possibilities recognizable in the pluralistic world of the play is Wilder's telescoping of stage time: by providing retrospective and future viewpoints simultaneously with an immediate one, Wilder demonstrates the value of the moment in creating history.

In Thornton Wilder's two major full-length plays as well as in a number of his shorter ones, he stressed the importance of each present moment, each choice, in determining as yet unrecognizable historical patterns. Whether his technique for expressing such a theme included the intermingling of historical eras, the achronological rendering of stage time, or the presentation of events on an unlocalized, unbounded stage, it always typified his "effort to find the dignity in the trivial of our daily life, against those preposterous stretches which seem to rob it of any dignity" [as Wilder stated in an interview in *Writers at Work: The Paris Review Interviews*]. One is always aware, when watching a Wilder play, that present moments play a starring role in determining what will become the past.

What I hope is clear by now is that Wilder's contributions to American drama are not so different from those of his more frequently studied compatriots. He shares their awareness of the past's multiple relationships with the present, and he shares their interest in developing conventions to explore those relationships. Like O'Neill, Wilder began his career by exploding the proscenium stage and ended by exploiting that explosion, inviting the audience to share the experiences of his characters. Like Miller, he asserts that each moment, each choice, is part of a larger pattern; the difference here is that Miller focuses on the specific pattern of causation, while Wilder refuses to limit his perspectives at all. And like Williams, Wilder experiments with dramatic conventions to portray "two times at once," even though Williams's interest in the double vision of remembered time and chronological time is narrower in scope than Wilder's collapsing of eras.

In the light of Wilder's constant attempts to reconcile the particular moment with the larger forces of history, it seems fitting that his own place in the American drama should be assessed not only by the specific events that are the plays themselves, but also by their place in creating modern dramatic form. In part because of Wilder's "rediscovery of forgotten goods" and his combination of diverse elements into a flexible vehicle for expressing contemporary concerns, the American drama has moved away from the confines of formal realism to become an arena of evolving possibilities. In short, the "disparate moment" that is Thornton Wilder's dramatic canon has forever altered the "repetitive pattern" of inherited dramatic form. (pp. 53-75)

Patricia R. Schroeder, "Thornton Wilder: Disparate Moments and Repetitive Patterns," in her The Presence of the Past in Modern American Drama, *Fairleigh Dickinson University Press, 1989, pp. 53-75.*

FURTHER READING

Biography

Bryer, Jackson R., ed. *Conversations with Thornton Wilder.* Jackson: University Press of Mississippi, 1992, 130 p.

Collection of interviews with Wilder.

Kuner, M. C. *Thornton Wilder: The Bright and the Dark.* New York: Thomas Y. Crowell Company, 1972, 226 p.

Biographical and critical study of Wilder's career.

Wilder, Amos Niven. *Thornton Wilder and His Public.* Philadelphia: Fortress Press, 1980, 102 p.

Amos Niven Wilder, Thornton Wilder's older brother, presents a biographical perspective on Thornton Wilder's works, discusses their critical and popular reception, and examines their significance in American culture.

Criticism

Atkinson, Brooks. "Mr. Wilder's Roman Fantasia." *The New York Times Book Review* (22 February 1948): 1, 30.

Reviews *The Ides of March,* emphasizing the work's philosophical and scholarly qualities.

———. "The Skin of His Teeth." *The Critic* XXV, No. 6 (June-July 1967): 73-4.

Negative review of *The Eighth Day.*

Blackmur, R. P. "A Psychogenic Goodness." *The Nation* CXL, No. 3630 (30 January 1935): 135-36.

Negative review of *Heaven's My Destination,* commenting on Wilder's artistic limitations.

Borish, E. "Thornton Wilder—Novelist: A Re-Examination." *Revue des langues vivantes* XXXVII, No. 2 (1971): 152-59.

Discusses Wilder's early works, arguing that although Wilder was not part of the popular literary tradition of the 1920s, he wrote "in the tradition of the outstanding novels of American literary history."

Broyard, Anatole. "Fairy Tales for Adults." *The New York Times* (24 October 1973): 45.

Praises *Theophilus North* and emphasizes Wilder's sentimentality.

Campbell, Joseph, and Robinson, Henry Morton. "The Skin of Whose Teeth?" *The Saturday Review of Literature* XXV, No. 51 (19 December 1942): 3-4.

Discusses parallels between *The Skin of Our Teeth* and Joyce's *Finnegans Wake.*

Canby, Henry Seidel. "Praise All Living." *The Saturday Review of Literature* VI, No. 32 (1 March 1930): 771-72.

Reviews *The Woman of Andros* and comments on Wilder's approach to writing fiction.

———. "A Baptist Don Quixote." *The Saturday Review of Literature,* XI, No. 25 (5 January 1935): 405, 411.

Reviews *Heaven's My Destination,* characterizing Wilder's novels as "moral apologues, skillfully disguised as story telling."

Carter, John. "Mr. Wilder's *Bridge of San Luis Rey* Is a Metaphysical Study of Love." *The New York Times Book Review* (27 November 1927): 7.

Positive review of the novel's realistic elements.

Davis, Elmer. "Caesar's Last Months." *The Saturday Review of Literature* XXXI, No. 8 (21 February 1948): 11-12.

Praises Wilder's fictional treatment of history in *The Ides of March.*

Dean, Alexander. "Our Town on the Stage." *The Yale Review* XXVII, No. 4 (June 1938): 836-38.

Lauds Wilder's use of revolutionary staging techniques in *Our Town.*

DeMott, Benjamin. "Old-Fashioned Innovator." *The New York Times Book Review* (2 April 1967): 1, 51-3.

Mixed review of *The Eighth Day* in which DeMott discusses the conventional and "unfashionable" aspects of Wilder's writing.

Frank, Waldo. "Thornton Wilder: 'Moment of the Dolls'." *The New Leader* XXXI, No. 16 (17 April 1948): 10.

Reviews *The Ides of March,* praising Wilder's fictional treatment of seemingly remote and unrealistic subjects.

Goldstone, Richard. "Wilder, Studying and Studied." *The Antioch Review,* XXVII, No. 2 (Summer 1967): 264-69.

Positive review of *The Eighth Day,* focusing on Wilder's treatment of American culture.

Guthrie, Tyrone. "The World of Thornton Wilder." *The New York Times Magazine* (27 November 1955): 26-7, 64-8.

Overview of Wilder's career as a dramatist.

Hazlitt, Henry. "Communist Criticism." *The Nation* CXXXI, No. 3412 (26 November 1930): 583-84.

Defends Wilder in response to Michael Gold's scathing review in the 22 October 1930 issue of *New Republic.*

Henderson, Philip. "Thornton Wilder." In his *The Novel Today: Studies in Contemporary Attitudes,* pp. 137-41. London: John Lane the Bodley Head, 1936.

A brief, negative assessment of Wilder's early novels.

Kauffmann, Stanley. "Thornton Wilder." *The New Republic* 156, No. 14 (8 April 1967): 26, 45-6.

Scathing review of *The Eighth Day* wherein Kauffman contemplates the highs and lows of Wilder's career.

Marshall, Margaret, and McCarthy, Mary. "Our Critics, Right or Wrong." *The Nation* CXLI, No. 3668 (23 October 1935): 468-69, 472.

Discusses the critical reception of Wilder's early novels.

Mosel, Tad. "The Moment *Writing* Comes in Sight." *The Kenyon Review* VIII, No. 2 (Spring 1986): 126-30.

Comments on Wilder's writing process as revealed in *The Journals of Thornton Wilder, 1939-1961.*

Nichols, Lewis. "Gnashing Teeth: A Note on the Current Uproar Caused by Thornton Wilder's Play." *The New York Times* XCII, No. 31,023 (3 January 1943): 1.

Considers *The Skin of Our Teeth* an important play, asserting that the controversy surrounding the work is a positive sign of interest in the theater.

Porter, David. "Alcestis Reborn." *The Carleton Miscellany* XVIII, No. 2 (Summer 1980): 219-22.

Favorable assessment of *The Alcestiad,* emphasizing the influence of Greek myth in Wilder's writing.

Scott, Winfield Townley. "*Our Town* and the Golden Veil." *The Virginia Quarterly Review* 29, No. 1 (Winter 1953): 103-17.

A positive appraisal of *Our Town,* asserting that Wilder's "evident purpose was to dramatize the common essentials of the lives of average people."

Sievers, W. David. "Freudian Fraternity of the Thirties: Thornton Wilder." In his *Freud on Broadway: A History of Psychoanalysis and the American Drama,* pp. 255-61. New York: Cooper Square Publishers, 1970.

Discusses the influence of Joyce's *Finnegans Wake* on *The Skin of our Teeth,* commenting: "the state of saturation with Joyce in which the play was written has harmed it in certain ways."

Smith, Harrison. "The Skin of Whose Teeth: Part II." *The Saturday Review of Literature,* XXV, No. 52 (26 December 1942): 12.

Examines the controversy surrounding allusions to *Finnegans Wake* in *The Skin of Our Teeth.*

Starrett, Vincent. "Best Loved Books: Wilder's *The Bridge of San Luis Rey,* One of the Most Original Novels of Our Time." *Chicago Sunday Tribune* (1 August 1954): Sec. 4, p. 2.

Positive review of *The Bridge of San Luis Rey,* asserting that Wilder is "one of the most sensitive and civilized of contemporary American artists."

Toohey, John L. *"The Skin of Our Teeth."* In his *The Pulitzer Prize Plays,* pp. 186-94. New York: The Citadel Press, 1967.

Discusses critical responses to the original production of *The Skin of Our Teeth.*

Willson, Lawrence. "The Question of Wilder." *The Sewanee Review* XCV, No. 1 (Winter 1987): 162-68.

Relates memories of Wilder, commenting on the writer's personality and views on literature.

Additional coverage of Wilder's life and career is contained in the following sources published by Gale Research: *Authors in the News,* Vol. 2; *Contemporary Authors,* Vols. 61-64 (obit.), Vols. 13-16 (rev. ed.); *Contemporary Authors New Revision Series,* Vol. 40; *Contemporary Literary Criticism,* Vols. 1, 5, 6, 10, 15, 35; *DISCovering Authors; Drama Criticism,* Vol. 1; *Dictionary of Literary Biography,* Vols. 4, 7, 9; *Major 20th-Century Writers;* and *World Literature Criticism.*

Marguerite Young

1909-

(Full name Marguerite Vivian Young) American novelist, poet, and nonfiction writer.

The following entry provides an overview of Young's career.

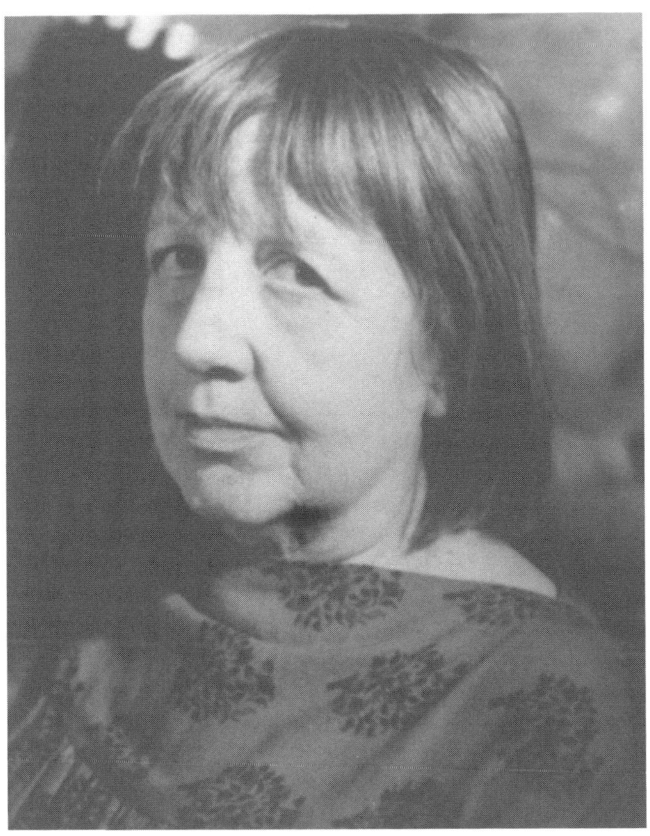

INTRODUCTION

Best known for her epic-length novel *Miss MacIntosh, My Darling,* Young uses stream-of-consciousness narrative techniques to explore such philosophical and metaphysical concerns as the nature of illusion and reality, the source of human endurance, and the meaning of dreams and hallucinations. Young has remarked: "All of my writing is about the recognition that there is no single reality. But the beauty of it is that you nevertheless go on, walking towards utopia, which may not exist, on a bridge which might end before you reach the other side." Critical perceptions of her works have been mixed; while some critics fault her style as obfuscated and cumbersome, others applaud her use of descriptive and lyrical prose to explore complex themes.

Born in Indianapolis, Indiana, Young was cared for by her maternal grandmother for most of her childhood. She attended Indiana and Butler universities, and received her B. A. in English and French in 1930. While at the University of Chicago, where she earned a master's degree in English in 1936, Young found employment reading the works of William Shakespeare to a wealthy woman who was bedridden due to an addiction to opium. Young's association with this woman greatly influenced her interest in dreams and the effects of opium on perception, which she incorporated into her writing style and subject matter. Although she never earned her PhD, Young was a doctoral candidate at the University of Iowa, where she studied philosophy and English. During this time she became deeply interested in the theories of such philosophers as John Locke, David Hume, and William James. Young has received numerous awards, including the Guggenheim Fellowship in 1948 and the Rockefeller Fellowship in 1954. She has also taught at such institutions as Indiana University, the University of Iowa, and Columbia University.

Young wrote two poetry collections early in her career. *Prismatic Ground,* which Young herself has stated claims "no particular distinction," received little critical attention. *Moderate Fable* garnered some success for its thematic and stylistic complexity. J. F. Nims has stated that in this work Young is "concerned with such weighty themes as perfection, flaw, time, probability, reality and illusion." Young expands upon these themes in *Angel in the Forest: A Fairy Tale of Two Utopias,* in which she details the rise and fall of two utopian societies that once existed in New Harmony, Indiana. The Rappites, a German religious group headed by the tyrannical Father Rapp, were eventually taken over by the short-lived Owenite society, who, led by Robert Owen, adhered to a belief system that included ideals of freedom, humanism, and socialism. Some critics faulted Young for omitting and obscuring historical facts and details in *Angel in the Forest,* and found her lyrical prose style unsuitable for the subject matter. Nevertheless, many critics extolled Young's innovative use of language in *Angel in the Forest.* Marianne Hauser, for example, commented: "Only an artist of her stature can afford to clothe her keen realistic, nudist deductions in the glittering brocades of such a baroque, unreal, out-of-this-world fantasy."

Young spent nearly twenty years writing her 1,198 page novel *Miss MacIntosh, My Darling,* a work which chronicles Vera Cartwheel's search for her childhood nursemaid, Miss MacIntosh, who is thought to have drowned. The work is filled with characters consumed by various obsessions and beliefs, all of which are revealed as false or misleading. Even Miss MacIntosh herself, who Vera remembers as an intelligent, voluptuous woman with flaming red hair, is revealed to be a confused woman who hid her baldness with a red wig and concealed the fact that she had only one breast. Some critics have faulted Young's treatment of illusory reality in *Miss MacIntosh* as evasive and disordered, while others have applauded Young for mastering a prose style that complements and illuminates her themes. William Goyen commented: "Her style is the very theme itself. We must read this major American work as a passionate affirmation of the snares of its own vision; as an obsessive probing of that vision until its obscure interior turns outward and allows itself to be looked at fearlessly, revealing its very terrible nature."

PRINCIPAL WORKS

Prismatic Ground (poetry) 1937
Moderate Fable (poetry) 1944
Angel in the Forest: A Fairy Tale of Two Utopias (nonfiction) 1945
Miss MacIntosh, My Darling (novel) 1965

CRITICISM

Jessica Nelson North (review date November 1937)

[*In the following review, North provides a positive assessment of* Prismatic Ground.]

The Muse, disgusted in an age barren of most things poetic, has lately turned her back on lyric poetry to give us a spate of something else. But when one is wallowing in a deep of stream-lined streams of consciousness, to find a book of clear-voiced lyrics is a treat. It is like looking up between skyscrapers at the Dipper in the night sky.

As frequently, distinction is achieved in ***Prismatic Ground*** by ignoring the trend of fashion. The poems in the book are not personal, except as they reflect an individual mind. They are objective and varied—arranged carefully so that each lyric stands by itself instead of blurring into a sequence of similar thought. This, I think, is proper in a book of short poems of irregular lengths and varying motifs. Like beads on a string, they make a unity, but may be counted off separately, enjoyed and remembered alone.

The author's main trick of craftsmanship is a Katherine Mansfield way of making the tiny thing momentous by surrounding it with subtleties of connotation implied but never stated. Picking her way with sure but delicate footsteps among all sorts of fragile images, she leads us through plenty to starvation and makes us like it. Meanwhile we find ourselves by a miracle grown so small we can look up through waving grasses to the immensities of butterflies' wings, glow-worms, wild crab-apples, blue field-mice, and all earth's obscure and humble creatures.

> In Lilliput where
> The night is a firefly
> And the wild grasses curve
> Obscuring the sky . . .
> . . . . .
>
> In Lilliput
> The lady died.

and all things being relative, a death in miniature seems here as important as a holocaust.

The author's main trick of craftsmanship is a Katherine Mansfield way of making the tiny thing momentous by surrounding it with subtleties of connotation implied but never stated. Picking her way with sure but delicate footsteps among all sorts of fragile images, she leads us through plenty to starvation and makes us like it.

—Jessica Nelson North

This method has its dangers. Sometimes the deliberate search for esoteric properties shows through the lines. There is a limit to the number of odd and beautiful things one may use in a poem. If Miss Young sometimes gets caught with a surplus, however, she has illustrious apologies and examples in the work of Léonie Adams and Elinor Wylie. It is necessary to be adroit, to dilute the concrete with metaphysics, to use the brittle and temporal not for itself, but only to suggest the imperishable and eternal. This, the author of ***Prismatic Ground*** has learned:

> Chiselled immaculate in sunlight, heavy
> With waxen leaves and clear-cut bloom,
> Yet by the moon drift persuaded, the pear tree
> Has branched in shadows through her room.
>
> So thick is the flower of the wild white bough
> Mirrored in her still sleeping now,
> No one can tell which is the tree
> Of bloom reflected, which is she.

Occasionally, in these poems, there is a technical sleight-of-hand which leads the reader to expect regularity in rhyme or rhythm and gives him neither. The result is not disappointment, but an amused surprise:

> Indeed the populace is largely
> Composed of fowl and creatures
> Four-footed. It would seem to me
> Small for heaven's fires. . . .

In another book, Marguerite Young will probably be more sparing in her use of legend and fantasy. Perhaps she will become an artificer less like Cellini and more like Da Vinci. If she keeps her queer magic her readers will follow her happily out of Lilliput into a larger country. (pp. 109-11)

Jessica Nelson North, "Lilliput," in Poetry, *Vol. LI, No. 11, November, 1937, pp. 109-11.*

Wylie Sypher (review date Fall 1944)

[*Sypher is an American educator and critic. In the following excerpt, he asserts Young's talent in* Moderate Fable, *but suggests that her poetry seldom progresses from conceptual to contemplative.*]

If Miss Young is "external," she accomplishes quite different effects. She still lingers on prismatic ground in the sense that the purely conceptual tension of many of her poems [in ***Moderate Fable***] is relatively too great; that is, she writes a poetry of ideas rather than a thoughtful or meditative poetry. Having moved from an earlier concern [in ***Prismatic Ground***] with the local to an interplanetary point of view that entails some sacrifice of humanity, she is much concerned with themes of space, time, process, illusion and reality. These could well lead, as they do in Auden, to contemplative verse; in her case they frequently remain on the level of the conceptual rather than speculative, as in **"The Responsibility of Parentage."** The serious danger is cleverness and a polymath obscurity. To be sure, this very reliance upon the cerebral makes possible some of the most successful poems—**"That Chance," "A Crystal Principle," "A High Subjectivity."** C. Day Lewis expected that poetry would increasingly assimilate the science of the century. Miss Young does not entirely fulfill this expectation; she cultivates astonishment and seems to presume that a large subject makes a large poem. She is at her best (which is very nimble) whenever the language of the sense interpenetrates the language of concept, resulting in genuinely metaphysical equivalence of mind and flesh:

. . . and valid in being therefore
And beautiful, the escape from each simple of
total
Is the heartbeat thief, mistake, flaw
Permitting his purple eye and whitened skull.

In spite of the pressure behind **"Null Class"** or **"Farewell at the Station"** or **"At the Cinema"** the tension of the verse, with its density and glitter of metaphor, is usually on the surface—the sort of intensity that one feels in mosaics, hard, Byzantine, rigidly iconographic. Undeniably Miss Young can also be subtle—

The idea of the universe is inconclusive
As albino nuns with partridge eyes and silk lash-
es,
As choirs of widows veiled in snowlight . . .

Although she might well abandon Hopkins-like mannerisms, the cadences are very artful. This second volume of strangely exciting poetry puts her talent beyond question. (pp. 463-64)

Wylie Sypher, "Between Shall-I and I-Will," in Partisan Review, *Vol. XI, No. 4, Fall, 1944, pp. 463-66.*

Jeremy Ingalls (review date January 1945)

[*Ingalls is an American poet, short story writer, editor, and critic. In the following review, she praises the subtlety and intricacy of Young's poetry in* Moderate Fable, *noting her ability to address philosophic concerns.*]

Marguerite Young's ***Moderate Fable*** presents, from the title page to the last of forty-three poems, a philosophic argument, a lively contribution to the history of ideas. To underline the fact that—before and since the years of the *Rigveda*—effective poetry has made and can make such a contribution I am impelled by certain recurring inadequacies of published comment not only on Marguerite Young but also on the work of Auden, Marianne Moore, Muriel Rukeyser, Karl Shapiro, Wallace Stevens, and other poets who stand in the forum of debate in our time. Auden's "wit," Marianne Moore's "counted syllables," Muriel Rukeyser's "experiments in form," Shapiro's "masculine" style, Stevens' "grace," Marguerite Young's "procession of animals" have been exploited to the disservice of the inquiry which their individual devices of expression are designed to assist . . . the debate on the whole nature of man's experience. Without presuming to catalogue the debaters in their individual positions, we can observe, nevertheless, that they are vigorously occupied by the venerable problems of the world of the will and the world of the mind.

Marguerite Young examines the world of the mind from the Berkeleyan position she reaffirms in **"Bishop Berkeley of Cloyne,"** one of the final and one of the finest poems in the sequence. Her procedure is indicated by the book's title. ***Moderate Fable*** moves within the reasonable, i.e. *moderate,* limits of human knowing; and is a talk or invention involving the supernatural, also involving the use of animals as signs for human beings, with the added implication that the whole substance inquired into may be fictitious, the full significance of the word *fable.* The subtlety and intricacy of her verse matches the tradition of [George] Berkeley himself, among the subtlest of metaphysicians. Her book is a competent and beautiful gloss upon Berkeley's *Common Place Book,* following its methods of examining the Berkeleyan principle—existence as conscious spirit and the objects (ideas) of which such spirit is conscious—through its aspects, applications, and possible objections.

Marguerite Young's most powerful single poem, **"The Whales,"** placed appropriately just beyond the center of the series, demonstrates the dilemma of the human mind which cannot *know* beyond the arbitrary signs provided in its own experience. So the southern whale who, driven by memory, comes sometimes again to sleep "in a river or sheltered cove," is incapable of comprehending "the vision unreasoned in his mind," the sense-signs meaningful to the creatures of the land. As man against the universe beyond the signals of his sense experience grows bewildered or gropes in irrelevant analogies, so the real and allegorical whale is separated from "an inland of that famed time." We stand locked within the barrier signs of our own consciousness . . .

a green immensity divides from us
The fable of butterflies in a lane of dust.

The history of ideas in our time is particularly marked by the consciousness that our devices for discussing the world, from higher mathematics to theology, are arbitrary signs which operate contingent to "reality," but are not "reality." In this sense, aspects of the Berkeleyan position are valid for argument and material for poetry, the operation of "figures" for the apprehension of reality. We are concerned with "the cardinal points of a dissolving compass," as in **"That Apple Was Mental."** We have thought of the white rats . . .

> Does God with diamond eyes look down on these
> For the purposes of what intrinsic studies?

Astrophysics and the physics of the atom conclude as in the poem, **"That Chance"** . . .

> There is no complete probable
> But deviation from the law
> In lonely items of the real.

Marguerite Young is a secure and exquisite—I use the word advisedly—artist in the expression of the mind's "confusion" . . .

> the lean crow buried by the sexton beetles
> Is from the mating of stars a strange result . . .

observing that "the idea of the universe is inconclusive"; fearing **"Death By Rarity"** . . .

> that rarity overwhelming all marvelous
> Names of birds whose names are poems
> And the rarity of this so personal blood
> Sleet in the golden vein.

Her poles of thought are marked by the title poem, an analogy of the impossible wedding of earth and that-not-of-earth, and by the conclusion of **"Bishop Berkeley,"**

> May God, the Bishop Berkeley said, be real
> And not postulated merely as our theory
> Like blowing cherry trees, myself, and John the Baptist.

Unlike many philosophers constructing schemata on the Berkeleyan principle, Miss Young, in dealing with his theory of cognition, does not ignore his theory of spiritual intuition.

Of Marguerite Young's distinguished position among the younger poets, of her memorable lines, of her chromatic and flexible verse forms, those who have followed these poems separately, in the magazines, are already aware. Since ***Prismatic Ground*** in 1937, her skill has developed steadily. Now that the organic unity of her new poems is established, she stands firmly among the mature poets whose art serves expertly the search for wisdom. (pp. 215-18)

Jeremy Ingalls, "Bishop Berkeley and the Whales," in Poetry, *Vol. LXV, No. IV, January, 1945, pp. 215-18.*

Isaac Rosenfeld (review date Fall 1945)

[*Rosenfeld was an American novelist, short story writer, and critic whose works include* An Age of Enormity: Life and Writing in the Forties and Fifties *(1962), a posthumously published collection of criticism. In the following review of* Angel in the Forest, *he notes Young's ability to introduce "literary and descriptive elements into predominantly analytical disciplines," thereby "displacing the more traditional, particularly the historical, modes of analysis."*]

To my mind, the significance of Miss Young's book lies in its extension of literature to other fields. The introduction of literary and descriptive elements into predominantly analytical disciplines has had the effect of displacing the more traditional, particularly the historical, modes of analysis—as in philosophy, through the activity of the existentialists. ***Angel in the Forest*** seems to be a step in this direction, at least in so far as it shows that history, too, can be ahistorical.

The facts of history and of literature are the same, as far as facts go; the facts of poetry, all the better, are even superior to those of history, for they are more typical—which is an old truth with a modern moral, (at any rate, one that is winning wide respect) namely, that the imagination is also a *Forschungsmittel* into the nature of man. So far there is no cause for conflict because the trained imagination, harnessed to a task, is always welcome, even in some academic circles. It is when the imagination becomes a thing in itself, as literal in its claims as it is in poetry that the trouble begins, for then one must sublimate one perspective or the other, the poetic or the historical one, genius, as a rule, not being there to combine the two. So it is with this "Fairy Tale of Two Utopias."

The facts are that Father Rapp, leader of a German religious sect, established a celibate community, dictatorial and unreasonable, at Harmony, Indiana, along the banks of the Wabash, and met with a qualified but considerable worldly success, although he and his disciples expected the world to end in 1842 and kept their backs turned against it. The site of the Rapp community, together with buildings and installations, was taken over by Robert Owen and his followers who met with no success whatsoever, although they were oriented toward the world, freedom, humanity and the new science of society, socialism, the rational order. I dare say Miss Young's research was extensive. The life in both utopias is well documented, particularly Robert Owen's, whose English background, furthermore, is fully covered. All the essentials of an historical account are to be found in the book: the facts, characters, ideologies, atmospheres, the mysticism and the enthusiasm, the crucial events, and of course the social forces and movements without which a history reads like a mere succession of stills. And yet the most important thing of all is missing—the simple sense of history, of time passing and past, accumulated and running out. Everything is concentrated into an ever-present moment, a bright eternal now. The pitch of sensibility is raised to the point where only the actual experiencing subject could feel so much, undergo such a long series of fresh sensations and be so dazzled by it all. There is no time for generalization, for detachment reached after an assortment of the facts; no time to stop elaborating the texture and find the pattern of the threads. Analysis, social commentary, evaluation, one's personal position must all be sublimated to the literary act, embodied and rendered in the text, as in a naturalistic novel. Insight is indispensable, but there is no single, natural place for it; it must therefore be maintained at every point along the way, with the result that it becomes a strained virtue whose effect is lost through dispersal. There is no real intellectual climax in the book.

The same method of elaboration of irrelevancies interferes with the development of ***Angel in the Forest*** as a literary work. Thus the scene in which Father Rapp castrates and thereby kills his son for breaking the rule of celibacy is set down in a paragraph that has no more weight than the writing which describes the hop-fields along the river. It is done in the same manner, one style prevailing everywhere—a cataloguing of rhythmical units: "Nakedness, a howling, a grovelling, a mute repentance as the body learns its master, self-mastery. . . . Unfortunately," continues the paragraph, "this was no mere flogging but emasculation, and the victim died, crying like a stuck pig—somewhere in the neighborhood of the piggery." An elaborate understatement, lost among its kind.

The feeling for literature is there, and all the credentials of writing. But it is a literary method made up completely of writing—good writing, certainly; original, the images clearly struck, the irony and the wit implicit in the words and the words well chosen; and yet it is a literature of sensibility, without drama and without structure, a porridge of highly polished rice.

I do not want to appear to be condemning this method entirely. Its imaginative intention is of the very highest, and it is all to Marguerite Young's credit as a poet to have seen that her two utopias call for its application. After all the social studies have been made there remains something compelling to sheer poetic speculation in the old story of reason failing, unreason winning out. We may even find a pathetic charm in the naiveté and simplicity of prescientific socialism—a charm that distracts us momentarily from the disquietude we feel over our presumably wiser, modern hopes. But what is it that lends that other charm, more like an evil, to irrationalism? What is its essential religious secret, what, perhaps, its truth? And why, after all the disenchantment, does the simplicity of the humanitarian ideal, the enlightenment, remain the only possible earthly kingdom?

Miss Young is wise about such matters. There is nothing pat in her approach, no formula, no indiscreet commitment to regret. She allows the initial mystery to stand after making, for what it's worth, her original effort to clear it up. But hers is a wisdom without thesis—the inexpensive kind. (pp. 551-53)

Isaac Rosenfeld, "The Forest and the Trees," in Partisan Review, *Vol. XII, No. 4, Fall, 1945, pp. 551-53.*

Marianne Hauser (review date Spring 1946)

[*Hauser is a French-born American novelist, short story writer, and critic. In the following review of* Angel in the Forest, *she extols Young's literary style and her talent for expressing the real and fantastic in everyday life.*]

In ***Angel in the Forest,*** Marguerite Young has found a strikingly regional subject matter, one transcending regionalism, to express both her wit and fantasy to the fullest, to illuminate the American scene with vision. Her region is nearly that of, though it purports to be concerned pre-eminently with the Indiana corn field and the cultural factors diversely at play there, the lost Atlantis, the city of Campanella, other marvelous matters. The dual intention, reality and unreality, is made clear from the first page—when you cross the Wabash to that land by a "creaking ferry," the other passengers being only two blind mules. Here, myth extends its many branches like an octopus, along with the filling station, along with hollyhocks and "spinsters numerous as hollyhocks." The subtitle, ***A Fairy Tale of Two Utopias,*** is thus a meaningful indication of surrealistic and realistic events in a pattern of infinite motion. New Harmony, Indiana village, laboratory, and nameless graveyard of man's aspiration for the ideal happiness, both social and individual, both of heaven and earth, becomes, under Miss Young's eyes, the one gloomy, the other prismatic, a spectacle of the world at large, contradictory as the human soul, even more contradictory, since it takes in harsh aspects other than the soul—for instance, the climate, its extremes of hot and cold. A view of life as homely as that of James Whitcomb Riley, Hoosier poet, is combined with a view of life as unhomely as that of Swedenborg or Bishop Berkeley of Cloyne, John Locke's mind, born into the world as a blank page—here frequently discussed—takes on the wild, eccentric coloration of E. T. A. Hoffmann, German fairy tale writer. There are all kinds of conspiracies going on within a text which escapes its boundaries.

"What dream among dreams," Marguerite Young asks, "is reality?" Such a question sets the key for the entire procedure.

At the beginning of the last century, two divers dreams, ancient in origin, converged on the banks of the Wabash far away, Father Rapp's golden New Jerusalem, a city foursquare as measured by the burnished reed—both Biblical reed and Jimson weed which grow today in a still unlegislated country; and Robert Owen's equally unrealizable rectangular community of reason. Father Rapp, founder of the first Utopia, a Scriptural communism, promised bliss eternal in heaven, "when this green earth should be destroyed by violence, by poisonous hailstones." Robert Owen, his successor, founder of the second Utopia in a village deserted by the Rappites, made the more difficult promise of bliss eternal on earth, which paradoxically enough was very gray in his era, though he held it to be indestructible. For Father Rapp, the earth was in its springtime—for Robert Owen, the earth was in its autumn. The Owenites had not even enough energy to harvest the hops in that field where, so short a time back, the angel Gabriel had promised that men should be a "confluence of bright sunbeams." The Owenites were easily discouraged, having no angel. Father Rapp, long-bearded patriarch from cloudy Wurtemberg, a businessman *par excellence,* both "mystic and murderer," planned for his not-too-distant heaven by means of hard labor, the whiskey trade, strictly enforced celibacy on all but pigs, sheep, goats, the animal kingdom (on which celibacy Lord Byron watching from afar, wrote a caustic canto, "Don Juan"). Robert Owen, father of the British labor movement and many societies for the real advancement of the human race, visualized an Eden of Children, such as he had established at New Lanark cotton mills, shorter and shorter working hours, mental independence, a triumph over all mythologies. The Devil (perhaps in league with the shades of Father Rapp and company) was preparing "a hole deep in the polar ice to swallow Robert Owen's soul," according to one of the many popular rhymes on the subject of elysium.

Both Utopias failed dismally—Rapp's being a financial success but a spiritual loss, Robert Owen's being a financial loss though, in the last analysis, perhaps not a spiritual loss. The paradox suggests a poem of Browning's. At any rate, the exodus of the Rappites was followed by the disintegration of the Owenite settlement before it was hardly established in what was perhaps "a fatal atmosphere." For instance, the germs of malaria had already been released. Our heroes are not, in fact, Rapp and Owen—but populations, inclusive of the Rappite hens and roosters who dwelt outside Utopia, inclusive of the community of drunks which built its citadel at the gates of Owenite Utopia, inclusive even of "the little goat who, in 1940, cried and cried with its fleece caught on a thorn bough." All that remained of New Harmony, in 1940, was human nature and the spectre of two enchanting dreams which, Jehovah's and Rousseau's, could not pass away. An angel's footprints in stone, the maze where the Rappites had wandered, the black locust trees which the Rappites had left standing as their most macabre monument. Of the Owenites, fewer relics, fewer monuments, since their contribution to society had to do with legislation and government in all nations. Of the Owenites, only the golden rain trees which were to cast their shadows over "a new moral world," when there should be neither crime nor punishment—not one sentient creature crying.

> Utopias of the past seemed, in spite of their shade trees, not so tangible, finally, as Miss Hobbie and Miss Duckie, old sisters carrying their feather pillows to the show where the seats were hard to set on—sneaking in to see Clark Gable. All mankind seemed not so real as one lonely, frostbitten character, like the man who died with his feet in the ashes of the cold stove last winter, or was it winter before last?

People were still betting on imaginary horses—like those at the race track at Dade Park, like those of the Apocalypse, too. Roosevelt was a white man riding on a white horse. Hitler was a brown man riding on a brown horse.

In fact, the phantasmagoria of life persisted, above and beyond the crystalizations of lost Utopias.

Marguerite Young does not relate the dilemma of two Utopias for the sake of an easy maxim. Life is viewed in its irrational diversity, and no judgment is passed. The narrator of an epic, cosmic and psychic, she speaks and sings her tale, words and visions rising and falling with the rhythm of life, which has, she implies, more agents, seen and unseen, than can be mentioned in even this spacious contest. We must consider, for example, in considering

---

***Angel In the Forest* is too vivacious to be written down as "rare," for the few only. Nothing is here esoteric or invented for the sake of invention. Every figure is human or the project of the human imagination, of the greatest consequence in ordinary life, partaking, too, of that life.**

—Marianne Hauser

New Harmony—whether the whale swallowed Jonah or Jonah swallowed the whale—the effects of such translucent matter on the present fluctuation of Wall Street. We must consider the woman "who buried her baby, no bigger than her hand, in a hollow tree stump, filled with old cocoons and autumn leaves." When she came back next spring, they all were gone. From the shadows who people New Harmony in 1940, from "the walking dead," rise, by subtle, implicit innuendo, the living shapes and voices of a still persistent past, bevies of kings, emperors, clowns, cotton lords, cotton workers. Human progress is shown in many shapes, through Father Rapp's golden rose of Micah, to be enjoyed only by the dead, through Robert Owen's toy pyramids which represented, he said, the edifice of human society at that date, his toy blocks which represented human society when it should be conducted according to the light of reason only. "Alas, however, for the best of plans! We are all, finally, perhaps the best of us, mistaken human beings, like our human life, which may be another mistake, due to the aboriginal whirlwind." Father Rapp spent his old age as a millionaire growing peach trees. Robert Owen spent his old age discoursing with those spirit voices whose existence he had previously denied, in arguments with Coleridge at Manchester.

The law of perpetual change is expressed in Indiana's shifting landscape, one of many symbols. "For thousands of years, what is now the state of Indiana was a vast plain of granitic rock covered by a deep, salt, tideless sea." When man arises at last, he is "already old and corrupt, like the earth before him—a creature with a history." There was "never a first dawn"—"never a pristine Eden but that where the ants performed their marriage flight and lost their wings"—a statement which profoundly expresses the basic conception of the cost of life. In juxtaposition with the lost sea of Indiana, we witness moments no less ghostly, drawn from the largesse of time and space: old, deaf, blind, dreaming George III, playing a harpsichord or rather a series of harpsichords—or barking like a mad dog at Windsor; the unacknowledged death of Anne Brontë in a seaside hotel; the Pope of Rome dressed as the Pope's valet and become, by this shift in costume, God's truest representative on earth; the fat Emperor of Russia, entertaining "a cancerous tutor or a ballet dancer from another sphere," Abraham Lincoln, Queen Victoria, Frances Wright, Audubon, Raffinesque, John Quincy Adams, Coleridge, Shelley, many other notables; indeed, many disrelated people and events drawn into a complex system which seems, in each instant, unity.

Values fluctuate; effects may precede cause; there is the fact of chaos, negative and positive. There is always a question mark and what Marguerite Young calls "a joker in the philosophic pack." She does not see life as, in fact, a given system. Yet by doubting each accepted value, each norm, each convention, by examining the fragments and splinters, she creates out of a manifold diversity of impressions and artistic unity, a roundness of strange beauty, a most distinguished work of art. Her vision is, for all its strangeness, not wilfully solipsistic, the refuge of an unfounded individualism. As evidenced by her poetry, ***Moderate Fable,*** a fable moderate because it omits narcissism, her thinking has been conditioned by philosophers—Democritus, for example, Locke, William James, many others to whom she makes, indeed, a constant though unobtrusive reference. Fewer idealists than skeptics. She has humanized, however, the unhuman fable. What may in ***Angel in the Forest*** appear to the unschooled or biased reader a singular display of mental acrobatics for their own sake must seem, to the schooled, the generous, the end-result of amoral mental discipline. Only an artist of her stature can afford to clothe her keen, realistic, nudist deductions in the glittering brocades of such a baroque, unreal, out-of-this-world fantasy. She philosophizes with her tongue in her cheek.

To combine cold, unsentimental thinking with quick, lively tragicomedy, the commonplace like the old outhouse with beautifully mad imagery like "the asexual angel Gabriel in a hop field"—therein lies the genius of the adventuresome performance. The book is, as so many critics have pointed out, "wild," perhaps because made up of "wild" data, angels, drunks. The writing seems free of literary scheming, too, as if the writer needed no sly skill. Readers looking for neatly swept sidewalks, road signs, traffic lights, will find themselves engulfed in a precolonial wilderness, a fertile abundance of many-faced trees and flowers—in the hollow of every tree, a man, on every treetop, an angel. If there is in Miss Young's book a "too-much," as the more literal minded may argue, it is the "too-much" of the Renaissance imagination which delighted in excesses, the "too-much" of a modernist Rabelais, a John Webster. The writing, from first to last, shows a dynamic force, stronger than the neat rules of literary perfection. It is a piece of banal, sacred life, not anemic. (And some of our most gifted writers suffer from anemia, perhaps because they have made the mistake of worshipping perfection, the one thing never worshipped by Marguerite Young, who writes: "Our perfection is our death.")

It is just because of its unusual range of experience that ***Angel in the Forest*** may appeal to many diverse readers as Utopia, as mock Biblical, as Americana, as essay on human character. The book is too vivacious to be written down as "rare," for the few only. Nothing is here esoteric or invented for the sake of invention. Every figure is human or the project of the human imagination, of the greatest consequence in ordinary life, partaking, too, of that life. As to the angel Gabriel, for example (and he is another barefoot boy on Wall Street)—

> Evolved out of ether and air, tears and sorrow, an angel stood in the hop field. He was big, massive, corpulent. He carried a rainbow on his back. . . . He was taller than an oak full grown, and of a diameter exceeding the oak, the beech, the sassafras. . . . He was grass and fire and homely as an old shoe. He was a farmer with a golden book in his hand. . . . His voice was like the river Wabash, loud and wild, rolling between the buff-colored hills.

Perhaps Miss Young agrees, to some extent, with the crucial angel she despises. Like Voltaire in *Candide,* like Dr. Johnson in *Rasselas,* she affirms that this is not the best of all possible worlds, that there is no perfect happiness attainable. Yet even this formula fails—for it is Shelley's bright hair, the ghost of Shelley, Robert Owen's friend, who rides in the wind with Robert Owen on his last journey of man's redemption from crime and punishment. Perhaps the drama is still going on?

Indeed, it is a very grim fairy tale Marguerite Young has written—grim and glorious. (pp. 343-48)

*Marianne **Hauser,** "The Dual Intention," in* The Sewanee Review, *Vol. LIV, No. 2, Spring, 1946, pp. 343-48.*

Granville Hicks (review date 11 September 1965)

[*Hicks was an American literary critic whose famous study* The Great Tradition: An Interpretation of American Literature since the Civil War *(1933) established him as the foremost advocate of Marxist critical thought in Depression-era America. After 1939, Hicks sharply denounced communist ideology, and in his later years adopted a less ideological posture in critical matters. In the following review, he lauds Young's skill in "elaborating an idea or a figure of speech or a visual detail" in* Miss MacIntosh, My Darling, *but observes that her method of presenting dream states without providing "fixed points of reference" detracts from the effectiveness and clarity of her narrative.*]

In his essay in *The Living Novel* John Brooks wrote: "I would even venture the opinion—in the face, I admit, of overwhelming evidence of all kinds to the contrary—that no one who sets himself any standards to speak of and actually finishes a novel, even a bad or skimpy one, can be a completely unadmirable person." What, then, are we to make of a woman who spends nineteen years in writing a novel of 1,198 king-size pages, each one of which displays imaginative power and conscientious craftsmanship? What, in short, are we to assume about Marguerite Young, whose ***Miss MacIntosh, My Darling*** has just been published? Are we not compelled to say that she is not merely admirable but heroic on an Amazonian scale?

It is not easy to give even a rough idea of the novel. The narrator (some of the time) is Vera Cartwheel, who, as we meet her, is on a bus somewhere in the Middle West, looking for her beloved and vanished nursemaid, Miss MacIntosh.

> Long years, drifting without other purpose, I had searched for that hale companion of my lost childhood, no one but a fusty, busty old nursemaid, very simple-minded, very simple, the salt of common sense, her red hair gleaming to show that quick temper she always had, that impatience with which she would dismiss all shades and phantoms, even herself should she become one, for self-pity was not her meat, not her drink.

(We are to learn, hundreds of pages further on, that Miss MacIntosh's bustiness, red hair, and common sense are all false.)

Vera tells a little about her childhood in a decayed mansion on the New England coast, with her mother, who was living out her life in an opium trance; but she soon returns to the bus and her traveling companions, all of whom are acting out fantasies of their own. We go backwards and forwards, learning more about Miss MacIntosh and Vera's mother. Then there is the mother's friend and lawyer, Mr. Spitzer, a man of wide interests and strange capacities, whose adventures occupy some twenty chapters. In the midst of Mr. Spitzer's story—if that word may be used—we have a longish passage about Mrs. Cartwheel's Cousin Hannah, a suffragette of legendary accomplishments. Eventually we get back to the bus and to a set of new characters, particularly the eternally pregnant Esther Longtree. In two rather hasty chapters Vera tells of her mother's death and her own happy encounter with the stone-deaf man.

The book is one long, very long, dream made up of dreams within dreams within dreams. It is not a novel in any ordinary sense but a series of improvisations, of fantastic variations on a single theme. The author, expressing the views of Mr. Spitzer, says: "Life was a dream, and death was another dream, and even a dream was a dream . . . " We read of "the master of illusion and sleight of hand," "phantasms of life and death," "unceasing duplicity," "ambiguities and ambivalences," "illusions compounding illusions," "inscrutable silence," "delusive surfaces," "cities of dubieties," "the spectre of the spectre, the dream of the dream," "the great, asymmetrical, and inarticulate chaos."

There are constantly recurring symbols: the sea, fire, music, pigeons, seagulls, ice, life-sized chessmen, a black rooster, twins, blindness, deafness, and countless others. (What a field day for the academic critics of the future!) Many of the sentences are so long that quotation is difficult, but let me cite a relatively uninvolved passage:

> The cats had always been insolent, even when the old lady was alive—and after the old lady's death, they had seemed to know they owned the place—or so Mr. Spitzer had thought when, returning from the funeral parlor where he had identified the corpse and left a bouquet of flowers, he had hesitantly called to leave his engraved calling card, to pay, in fact, his respects to the new owners. There had been cats sitting upon satin pillows in the drawing room, cats walking about like flower-faced sibyls, cats purring at Mr. Spitzer's feet, cats on pedestals, cats swinging in hammocks. There had been a great white cat standing at the top of the marble stairway—less fearful than the raven might have been, certainly, yet giving Mr. Spitzer quite a start. There had been cats' eyes gleaming like gooseberries in the shadows, enigmatic faces of delicacy and disdain. A cat had walked up and down on the piano keys, playing a little tune from the works of one of the more obscure eighteenth-century musical composers.

The whimsical note is not common, but the inventiveness is. Miss Young has a great gift for elaborating an idea or a figure of speech or a visual detail. She is a poet, of course, and she writes like one. In fact, the work as a whole reminds me of one of Conrad Aiken's long poems—"Senlin," say, or "The Pilgrimage of Festus"—rather than any novel I can think of. As with Aiken, the hypnotic use of language creates an hallucinatory effect suited to the events—or non-events—that are being described.

But why 1,198 pages? There is no intrinsic reason that I can see why the novel could not be shorter—or longer. Miss Young, it seems, could go on forever, and there are moments when the reader has a feeling that that is just what she is doing. There is no getting around it—reading the book is a chore. My admiration for Miss Young's literary powers carried me through five or six hundred pages, but from there on, though there were many episodes that caught my interest, I had to rely heavily on sheer determination.

It has been said often enough that life is a dream, and many serious and talented writers have occupied themselves with the presentation of dream states. But for practical purposes we do have to make a distinction between sleeping and being awake. The horror of Kafka's novels come from the fact that his hero has a sense of what is real and rational and feels that he is the victim of hallucinations. In ***Miss MacIntosh*** there are no fixed points of reference; everyone in the book might perfectly well be a character in somebody else's dream. The reader is lost in a sea of dreams, and more than once I felt that I was going down for the last time. But Miss Young is heroic, and so, by George, is her publisher. (pp. 35-6)

Granville Hicks, "Adrift on a Sea of Dreams," in The Saturday Review, *New York, Vol. XLVIII, No. 37, September 11, 1965, pp. 35-6.*

William Goyen (review date 12 September 1965)

[*Goyen is an American short story writer, biographer, poet, novelist, playwright, and critic. In the following review of* Miss MacIntosh, My Darling, *he commends Young's prose style and depiction of American life, characterizing the novel as "a work of stunning magnitude and beauty."*]

Marguerite Young's titanic novel [***Miss MacIntosh, My Darling***] has been in slow generation for more than 17 years. During this period, published sections of it have signaled, like surface bubbles, the dynamism of the submerged whole. Now it appears before us on 1,198 pages. What we behold is a mammoth epic, a massive fable, a picaresque journey, a Faustian quest and a work of stunning magnitude and beauty.

Miss MacIntosh, an old, drowned woman, is "reality" to Vera Cartwheel, whose tidal monologue relates her search for that reality. Broken-nosed, bald-headed Miss MacIntosh was a "plainly sensible woman" who spoke in proverbs and axioms to her young charge. She was nursemaid to the voyager-narrator, whose mother languishes in grandiose dreams under opium in a baroque New England seaside house among imaginary guests and companions whom she "dreams." Miss MacIntosh is unadorned, barebreasted fact; the uncovered pate of reality; illusion stripped of its wig, its false bosom. She comes from the real ground of the Midwest, from What Cheer, Iowa.

Vera Cartwheel's very environment is illusion, delusion, fantasy. She struggles against "dreaming" people; but when she turns from what is illusion she encounters only illusion again. "What shall we do when, fleeing from illusion we are confronted by illusion? When falling from illusion, we fall into illusion?" cries out Vera Cartwheel as she voyages through a kind of drowned world, seeking her darling, truth. For when Miss MacIntosh walks into the sea one day, leaving her aspects and articles upon the shore—her wig, her false breast, her old mackintosh, her black umbrella—Vera Cartwheel begins a search for her drowned reality which was, in ironic effect, illusion.

The story of the novel is simply this, and it is created by Vera Cartwheel's journey to rediscover "Miss MacIntosh," whose drowning was never certified. Vera returns, by bus, to the region of her own beginnings, to the Wabash Valley country of Indiana. There, in a desolate hotel, she begins, among nightmare people who are lost in delusion and whom she believes she is "dreaming" quite as her mother did, the search for Miss MacIntosh, the elusive and unanswering.

This is the theme and ground of this sweeping, swelling and inexhaustibly breeding fiction, which pulls behind it, on and on, page after page, loads and burdens of images proliferating images; precise cataloguings; inventories and enumerations of facts, plants, hats, heraldries, geographies, birds, rivers, cities ancient and modern, kings and dynasties and archeologies. It breaks into conceits, images, metaphors, preclosities, bizareeries. Concrete character detail elaborates into huge metaphors, into musicalizations, rhapsodies, repetitively rolling and resounding and doubling back upon themselves in an oceanic tumult.

The book's mysterious readability is effected through enchantment and hypnosis. Its force is cumulative; its method is amassment, as in the great styles of Joyce or Hermann Broch or Melville or Faulkner, where reference and context become muddled through constant and compulsive tormenting of basic obsessive themes.

Miss Young's initial cords are baldness, musical annotation, pregnancy (false and real), drug taking. As these real states and actions become surreal in the characters' experience, the novel swells into several enormous and extended expositions or these cords, composed around four major characters: Miss MacIntosh; Catherine Cartwheel, the narrator's "poor dreaming mother"; Mr. Spitzer, loyal companion and nightly visitor to Catherine Cartwheel, composer of unheard, unwritten music and twin brother to a dead gambler with whose identity he is confounded; and one of the most extraordinary characters in American literature, Esther Longtree, a voluptuous, rosy-fleshed waitress in a Wabash Valley cafe who is cursed by an "everlasting, lonely pregnancy." Miss Young's blazing flight of meditation upon Esther Longtree's situation—false life, stillbirth—dominates and empowers the latter section of the novel, and in a soaring revelation brings the whole work to a stopping-point on this theme at the end of nearly 1,200 pages.

The fluent, seminal passages, grounded on these four beings and their basic significance, are so procreative and so fertile that they spurt forth in some of the richest, most expressive, most original and exhaustively revealing passages of prose that this reader has experienced in a long time. Lesser sequences, leafing out like a water plant, explore the submerged lives, aberrations, "dreams" of several other vivid and haunting personages. These include Weed, the Christian Hangman, upon whose human function and life-situation Miss Young configures a fantastic shape of meaning; ghostly Dr. Justice O'Leary, who delivers imaginary pregnant women of imaginary babies; Mr. Bonebreaker, an antic Bible salesman who might have married Miss MacIntosh had he not discovered on their Wedding Eve that she was bald and had but one breast. In these sections the humor is folk, slapstick, Chaplinesque, melodramatic and Satanic. For ***Miss MacIntosh, My Darling*** is as often mischievously funny and devilishly humorous as it is incantatory and operatic.

Rarely does American fiction break out into fullness of song, into the force and vigor of increase, of organic embellishment. Rather it has shrunk, or dieted itself, into smaller, safer cries and statements, well-formed and studied representations of human experience, or taken refuge in areas of special experience—the work of the Burroughses and Selbys and Mailers and others. In ***Miss MacIntosh, My Darling*** we have come upon a strong, deep loudness, a full-throated outcry, a literature of expanse and daring that makes most of our notable male writers look like a motorcycle gang trying to prove a kind of literary masculinity.

What might appear to be an ornateness of style for its own sake—an overindulgence of language, an excess of descriptive ornamentation—is Miss Young's method of relentlessly examining the complexities of her characters and themes. Her style is the very theme itself. We must read this major American work as a passionate affirmation of the snares of its own vision; as an obsessive probing of that vision until its obscure interior turns outward and allows itself to be looked at fearlessly, revealing its very terrible nature. We must see it as an organic growth of literary materials that express life; as controlled sense of the natural vitality of image and metaphor related to the organic life they express and enlarge.

For ***Miss MacIntosh, My Darling,*** soaring into the universal, has rooted itself in the American reality. It involves and depends on the basic and traditional American literary themes: smalltown, childhood memory, homesickness, nostalgia for the past, the sense and the diction of region. The novel is, in this writer's judgment, one of the most arresting literary achievements in our last 20 years. Marguerite Young has found, surely, instinctively and in her own time, her grand metaphor; and it glistens and radiates and *exists* in this colossal shape as hard and as concrete as truth itself. It is a masterwork.

She has been lurking, like one of her own "dreamed" characters in search of themselves, on the edge of American literature and letters for many years, ominous, shadowy, emerging. She has arrived and her arrival must be proclaimed.

William Goyen, "A Fable of Illusion and Reality," in The New York Times Book Review, *September 12, 1965, p. 5.*

Bernard Bergonzi (review date 25 November 1965)

[*An English novelist, scholar, and essayist, Bergonzi has written extensively on the works of H. G. Wells, T. S. Eliot, and other major figures in twentieth-century literature. In the following excerpt, he faults the repetitious nature of* Miss MacIntosh, My Darling *and states that the work lacks development of characters and ideas.*]

If I were Charles Scribner's Sons I think that I would be feeling pretty nervous about publishing a first novel that took seventeen years to write, came to 3449 pages of typescript, and, in book form, weighs three-and-a-quarter pounds. Hence, doubtless, the unusual volume of publicity material that accompanied the review copy of ***Miss MacIntosh, My Darling,*** including a photograph of Miss Young delivering that mighty pile of typescript, and two pages of advance comments on the novel, all of them, in principle, favorable, ranging from the full-throated ecstatic to the mildly approbatory. The idea is, I suppose, to present this novel as an immediate "classic," with the underlying implication: "This has *got* to be a work of great literary genius (or else why have we sunk so much capital into it?)." Such faith in a really rather outlandish product is admirable and even touching; but I think they are right to feel nervous.

We are told in the blurb that ***Miss MacIntosh, My Darling*** is "poetic," a sinister word in such a context, since it implies that we are being shunted off the regular streets of novelistic traffic into a special region where verbal rhapsodizing and a lack of vertebrate structure replace the customary qualities of fiction. Nor does it have much to do with poetry in the fullest sense; not, at least, as the modern reader understands poetry: the description "poetic," I would suggest, should be reserved for those novels that possess, in addition to their other qualities, an unusual accuracy and sensitivity of language, not necessarily in a lyrical way, which brings the style into play in the content of the novel: *Ulysses* is the supreme example.

Miss Young, however, is "poetic" in a bad sense; in love with words, certainly, but given to endless verbal doodling, the infinitely repetitious elaboration of a single idea over dozens of pages at a time. The prodigious length of her book is not the result of an excess of content, the proliferation of characters and events of the usual jumbo-sized fictional saga: quite simply, it is because her principle of composition is never to use one word if fifteen thousand will do instead. Still, one must be as fair as possible. There can be no doubt that Miss Young does have genuine gifts for the creation of fiction and, in particular, for the writing of evocative imagistic prose. There are some interesting people concealed in the dark resounding caverns of her book, or rather floating about in the timeless void of the memories of Vera Cartwheel, the narrator of the story, whom we meet in the first chapter traveling on a bus one dark night, somewhere in the Middle West, searching for her long lost nursemaid, Miss MacIntosh. There is Vera's mother, Catherine Cartwheel, known as the "opium lady," who spends her days, bedridden and subject to hallucinations, in a great lonely house on the New England coast; Catherine is visited from time to time by her lawyer, Joachim Spitzer, a shy man who wanted to be a composer of music, and who is obsessed by memories of his sportsman brother, Peron, who has committed suicide. A very lengthy section of the book describes the life and death of Cousin Hannah, a formidable Bostonian lady who was a pioneer suffragette and famous explorer. Another long section near the end of the book is about the tribulations of a girl called Esther Longtree, who constantly manifests the symptoms of pregnancy without being pregnant. Above all, there is Miss MacIntosh, bald, austere, eccentric, devoted, whom Miss Young wants to place in the My Most Unforgettable Character class. She looms impressively through parts of the story but is rendered with such obsessive over-elaboration that the cumulative effect reminded me of Dylan Thomas's phrase: "this for her is a monstrous image blindly / magnified out of praise."

Having revealed these characters, Miss Young does virtually nothing with them; they merely exist, separately embalmed in the author's memories, without dramatic contact. In all this novel's many hundreds of pages there is hardly any dialogue. The only significant exception to this occurs at about page 900, where we are told of Miss MacIntosh's abortive love affair, in the remote past, with Mr. Bonebreaker, a Chicago evangelist, which is vigorously and even entertainingly rendered. Some ruthless editorial surgery at this point might have produced a fragment of good fiction. But it is, presumably, pointless to attack Miss Young for not providing something she was not interested in providing. The novel offers a "poetic" rather than a dramatic interest, in intention at least, and we must not complain if the handful of characters disappear for hundreds of pages at a time in a dense verbal goulash.

So the novel stands or falls by its language alone. For short stretches Miss Young's prose, as I have indicated, does have a certain lyrical and evocative power. But the stretches are rarely short, and the kind of prose-poetry which works in brief paragraphs—as for instance in Rimbaud's *Illuminations*—becomes intolerable when protracted over an infinity of pages. Nor, for that matter, are Miss Young's images particularly arresting; she relies very heavily on those traditional properties of the brooding northern imagination which occur so often in literary works with a Gothic tinge: ghosts, angels, snow, fog, darkness, stars, mirrors, ice, rain, moons, seagulls, clouds, the sea. Rimbaud and Dylan Thomas got a good deal of mileage out of them and although they can be described as some of the perdurable archetypes of the human imagination, Miss Young makes very conventional use of them. Here is a specimen of her writing:

> Ah, all bee-hive cities were flooded as were the sunken islands of this earth and coffins of flame enclosing secret stars, bells of silver, bells of gold in seas of ringing bells, bells of the sea ringing earth, bells ringing the bell-ringers in lonely towers, crowns of ivory under the waves, crowns of silver where the waves leaped and roared like lions with golden wreathed mouths, crowns of gold, many-eyed wings of snow-white peacocks clashing their windy tails with atonal music in gardens of snow, gardens under the earth, comets crumbling into fireflies in drowned gardens and lights on sunken porches and swollen insect lights in sunken roads, honeycomb lights of skyscrapers bisected by drifting clouds and snow-crowned, many-headed mountain tops like sleeping kings and queens and drifting white umbrellas and black umbrellas bellowing like church bells and the life-sized chessmen who had walked on squares of black and gold as if this life had been designed by reason and not by love, dead love . . .

And so on, for many more lines, until the sentence finally slithers to a reluctant conclusion. As Dr. Johnson remarked of Ossian, "A man might write such stuff for ever, if he would but abandon his mind to it." (pp. 34-5)

Bernard Bergonzi, "Queen for a Day," in The New York Review of Books, *Vol. V, No. 8, November 25, 1965, pp. 34-5.*

Marianne Hauser (review date Autumn 1967)

[*In the following review, Hauser lauds the thematic and stylistic complexity of* Miss MacIntosh, My Darling, *which she describes as "a masterful, exhilarating work of art, a saga of America, a classic."*]

Twenty years have gone by since the publication of Marguerite Young's ***Angel in the Forest: A Fairy Tale of Two Utopias.*** The author, already known for her poetry, revealed herself as a brilliant prose writer, a unique chronicler of her native Indiana. Now with ***Miss MacIntosh, My Darling*** she has given us her first novel: a masterful, exhilarating work of art, a saga of America, a classic.

It is a leviathan novel, constructed on many spheres of dream and reality. A young girl, Vera Cartwheel, sets out on a bus journey in search of her old nursemaid, a spinster from What Cheer, Iowa. The journey on the bus, most prosaic of vehicles, becomes a journey backwards through time as Vera relives her childhood or adolescence. And the American landscape, viewed from the bus window, swells forth into the landscape of the soul.

Vera, daughter of an opium-addicted mother "more beautiful than angels of light", remembers the ornate New England house by the sea, the ghost-filled room where the mother lay drugged and dreaming, she too engaged in a timeless journey along diverging roads or river beds. By her bedside, a frequent visitor, old fat Mr. Spitzer, contains within himself the crucial dream, he being perhaps his own dead twin brother, the gambler Peron Spitzer whom she loves. In the opium lady's universe, as indeed in the author's, the dead are no less of the existing world than are the living, or those who never lived. Even inanimate objects, a drug bottle, a chandelier, are endowed with life by the mother, and accepted or rejected as her guests.

The themes explored in ***Angel in the Forest***—time, life, and death dreamed or real—soar through the novel and burst into an exuberant display of stars and starfish, butterflies, lutes, frogs; lost suffragette skirts, roulette wheels; other marvels. A kaleidoscopic imagery animates Miss Young's plot and sends her characters through surprising metamorphoses. Nothing is static here, least of all death. The novel is as crowded with people as the London streets in Hogarth's etchings. Yet while her men and women, bawdy, funny or tragic, robust or tortured, act out their human destiny, they also relate to the gods and goddesses of ancient myth. Their essential being is in God's dream, or in the dream of the opium lady.

It is the opium lady who will always put a question mark behind the truth. "My mother," Vera recalls, "pretended that the real was the dream, that the dream was the real." But was her mother pretending? In the extraordinary world of Vera's childhood, Miss MacIntosh seemed to be the only rational person, a fount of knowledge and authority, the epitome of common sense, as sensible and common as an old shoe. However, as Vera's mother noticed, "Sometimes the phantom was fact, but the fact was another phantom."

Certainly there is a matter-of-fact Miss MacIntosh with "water-colored eyes" and red hair, a no-nonsense governess, pronouncer of solid truths: "He is bare whom virtue hath not clothed . . . this world is very naked indeed and one swallow does not make a summer, and a thin meadow is soon mowed, and winter is summer's heir, and the night is no man's friend, and the night is filled with darkness."

But one night, as Vera enters her nursemaid's room, she finds a different Miss MacIntosh, one who is hairless, defenseless.

> Where her head should be there was another moon, cold and dented and shining, seeming to float upon the waves of corrugated darkness. . . . She stepped out from behind the curtain which, blowing like a shroud or torn sail, had concealed her head, and I saw her head, that great dome, that sphere devoid of being, saw that there was something missing from the mortal woman, that all was not right, for she was bald. She was bald as the egg or as the rock where nothing grows.

She seems to Vera "a monstrous stranger". And in a scene of unforgettable horror: " . . . she was someone else and moving toward me with an attitude of strange, fearful beseechment in the darkness crossed by moonlight as if, of course, she was familiar to me, and she had known me for many years. . . . " After screaming at the nightmare:

"Miss MacIntosh, you are a man!", Vera strikes at her with a riding crop, "that bare unflowering branch in my bony hand . . . ".

The nursemaid's red wig flares up throughout the narration, recurrent symbol of a mask which hides the supposedly naked truth. Nothing is absolutc. The truth is another mask, and Vera discovers many other Miss MacIntoshes, her darling being indeed the multiple phantom of love, pursued by all of us and never captured. There is the comical Miss MacIntosh, roaring "Heave ho, my hearties!" like an old salt; standing in a tidal pool in a voluminous bathing costume and black helmet, holding aloft an umbrella. And upon these vivid manifestations of one old spinster, there lies as in a double exposure the mystery of her disappearance as she vanished, leaving no forwarding address but the cold sea—"her clothes strewn on that lonely beach . . . the great tides roaring like lions where she had walked alone, her broken black umbrella beating like a bird's wounded wing at the edge of the sea which had returned it . . . ". The flight or death of Vera's love—a surrealist reversal of the birth of Venus—becomes Vera's guilty obsession. " . . . who but I had killed her?" she asks, unable to blame God or nature.

Oceanic imagery and sounds pervade a novel whose structure is that of a great symphony, whose incantations lend magic even to an old broken umbrella. If Mr. Spitzer's music is silent music, written perhaps for the deaf ear alone, the music of ***Miss MacIntosh, My Darling*** is never silent, striking brilliant notes from rocks and stars and from those unplayed compositions of Mr. Spitzer, who wonders if he shouldn't have been a lawyer "to a long-haired sea medusa who kept not this calendar of earth and who registered not the gradations between sleeping and waking or the finer hairs or the boundaries between life and death. . . . ". The sea medusa, Mr. Spitzer's ideal client, is but one symbol of his eternal love, the opium lady, white goddess, sleeping beauty who ages suddenly and dies when she leaves her bed.

The novel resounds with the folklore of many countries and ancestors, even those whose history is preserved only on bone and fossil. A pageant of figures, legendary or real, files through the chapters: the frog in his various guises of prince, musician, devouring toad; chessmen, the hangman, the blind man, the deaf man finally, he who "heard with his eyes" and in whose arms Vera finds sexual love and reality or another phantom.

Marguerite Young employs mythology not as a fashionable device to embroider her story, but as a searchlight, directed upon the darker reaches of our ancestral memory, our soul. Her reversal from black to white and white to black is part of our common heritage. Her black coachman with his fearsome coach and fiery-eyed horses—spectre of terror in German and American ghost stories—is conjured up again and again in his grisly magnificence—the coachman for whom we all wait and who waits for us. He might be black, with alabaster horses, or white, with black horses. He might be the unseen coachman "with the star shining through him"; and Mr. Spitzer, the wrong passenger in the wrong carriage, hears "the horses' hooves upon the resonant clouds, and the coachman was a skeleton". Mr. Spitzer's high silk hat casts a shadow "like the coachman's hat". The coach and the coachman's whip point toward death. Even the child Vera had attacked her bald nursemaid, her love, with the riding crop in her "bony hand".

Within the chiaroscuro of fable, Marguerite Young's characters assume a vitality unequalled in recent novels. There is Cousin Hannah, prototype of the suffragette, Bostonian sky rider, mountain climber, explorer, and surely one of the most fiercely individual women in literature. There is Esther Longtree, a deeply tragic, deeply comic figure, forever swollen with imaginary pregnancies, imaginary infanticides. She can move the reader to tears or to wild laughter, this mule-faced waitress of the Greasy Spoon, who has the last word in the book: "Owt to luntsch. Bee bak in a whale."

It should be emphasized that ***Miss MacIntosh, My Darling*** could have been written only in America, by an American. It is a highly original creation. But it did not come out of a sterile bell jar. Its roots are in the literary soil of America. Are not the Spitzer twins at least distant cousins of Mark Twain's twins, one of whom was drowned in his bath? Miss Young's mirror images relate to Hawthorne's beautiful youths romping in front of a mirror which reflects the caperings of grotesque seniles. Her political hangman, perfectionist in his grim field, brings to mind the awful ironies of Bitter Bierce. And her expeditions into the turnabouts of reality and illusion, good and evil, echo her spiritual ancestor Herman Melville.

Other echoes sound through ***Miss MacIntosh,*** those of Don Quixote, his dual dream; those of Bishop Berkeley of Cloyne whose world view Marguerite Young expresses in a sublime poetic aside: "God, if there is a God, cannot know everything, any more than Mrs. Hogden-Fogden could, poor soul. There must be at least one small, warped flower growing, I believe, contrary to the ideal of unity, outside the consciousness of God, outside his field . . . and that would be the crucial flower, of course, the important one." (pp. 731-34)

Marianne Hauser, "The Crucial Flower," in The Sewanee Review, *Vol. LXXV, No. 4, Autumn, 1967, pp. 731-34.*

Marguerite Young with Ellen G. Friedman and Miriam Fuchs (interview date 23 March 1988)

[*In the following interview, which was conducted in 1988 and first published in Fall 1989, Young discusses her approach to writing, criticism of her works, and her literary influences.*]

[*Friedman and Fuchs*]: *You have been writing for more than half a century. Although your two books of poetry* **Prismatic Ground** *and* **Moderate Fable** *were published a few years apart, there were twenty years between* **Angel in the Forest** *and* **Miss MacIntosh, My Darling.** *There will be about twenty-five years between* **Miss MacIntosh** *and your forthcoming work on Eugene Debs. Do these long intervals represent major changes in the direction of your thought?*

[Young]: No. All the books I have written have been one book, from the beginning. The first poem I ever wrote, about loss, when I was five years old, expressed the themes of everything I would ever write. My early volumes of poetry, ***Prismatic Ground*** and ***Moderate Fable,*** also express a sense of loss. And ***Angel in the Forest,*** examining the nineteenth-century communities of Father George Rapp and Robert Owen's socialist experiment in New Harmony, Indiana, is about abandoned utopias. I would say my theme has always been paradise lost, always the lost cause, the lost leader, the lost utopia. ***Miss MacIntosh, My Darling*** carries on this theme because Miss MacIntosh, with the loss of her wig, shows herself to be the orphaned angel, the asexual angel, neither male nor female, unable to live without her mask of illusions. Losing those illusions, she showed herself to be the denuded character every person would be if confronted with the loss of their illusions as she was. She is the central character with all the spokes of other characters radiating out from her. I always thought of Miss MacIntosh as the center of the wheel, the hub, then the spokes as the subsidiary, secondary characters, and the wheel as endlessly expanding like a universe. I never alter my style in anything I write. My Debs book is as poetic as ***Miss MacIntosh,*** but balladry rather than epic.

You have strong political views. Have critics recognized them, or have the poetic qualities and eccentric characters in your writing diverted critics from your sociopolitical points? Does **Miss MacIntosh, My Darling** *show a social conscience?*

Some of the reviewers recognized the social and political implications of ***Miss MacIntosh, My Darling.*** It isn't that Miss MacIntosh has a social conscience, but the book does. If you understand hallucination and illusion, you don't blindly follow any leader. You must know if the person is sane or insane and so on, over the abyss. Mr. Spitzer's adventures and the passages on the little frog musician investigate the nature of illusion, and if there is no certain reality, the idea of following a leader must be scrutinized. Some of the poetic writers who insert passages of realism in their texts have no underlying philosophy to uphold them and revert to realism. I don't believe there can be a poetic novel without political consciousness. I have a strong political conscience, and the Debs book shows this as well.

Why do you project reality as tenuous?

When you have examined all the illusions of life and know that there isn't any reality, but you nevertheless go on, then you are a mature human being. You accept the idea that it is all mask and illusion and that people are in disguise. You see the crumbling of reality and you accept it. The reason I had Esther Longtree in ***Miss MacIntosh, My Darling*** marry the little bond salesman was that he was the most demented person of all. The reason Vera married the stone-deaf man was that she could not marry a perfect being. She had to marry a flawed creature because she knew that all creatures are flawed, but out of the flaw may come the universe. Like the crystal flaw that is in ***Moderate Fable,*** my book of poems. Because it was imperfect it came into being.

How do you counter critics who accuse you of excessive fantasy?

I never fantasized or invented a thing, not one thing. I knew every single thing I ever wrote about—I knew the opium lady of ***Miss MacIntosh, My Darling*** and Cousin Hannah, the alter ego of the opium lady if she had been set loose in the world. A lawyer I once knew told me of a strange case, a suffragette who had never married. After her death, he opened her trunk and discovered fifty wedding gowns. I used this material to create Cousin Hannah, the suffragette and adventurer of foreign lands, particularly the East. I enjoyed writing about Cousin Hannah. Had I left out her section, I could have done a lot of other things, but when the dream came into being, I always pursued it. I had read the histories of mountain climbers, of suffragette captains, of travelers to the Middle East. I've read all the books about them like Lady Duckworthy, all the ladies who went to the Middle East. I'd like to go myself. I didn't invent anything in my book. I didn't need to.

Why is Miss MacIntosh not merely bald, but missing a breast and other things as well?

Because everything is lost. Remember that after she had her breast amputated she went to work in a bowling alley? A place where she could get herself killed? She lost everything, her hair, her love, her brother, her identity.

How did you decide to write about New Harmony, Indiana, the location of **Angel in the Forest?**

My mother lived there, and one day I bumped into a group of coal miners from the Ozarks, wandering coal miners living a gypsy life, like in John Steinbeck's *Grapes of Wrath.* I started to speak with these coal miners, and became very interested in them. It was because of these coal miners that I decided to write about New Harmony. ***Angel in the Forest*** is based upon social consciousness. Every real book is, no matter what the subject. A good writer cannot avoid having social consciousness. I don't mean this about small pieces of writing, but about a big book. If it's a big book, there has to be more than one undertow. In ***Miss MacIntosh,*** for example, there are many novels, novellas, and short stories. There's Mr. Spitzer's story and that of Esther Longtree, who is the mother of us all, I would say, quoting Gertrude Stein. Esther is Mr. Spitzer's feminine counterpart. A close friend of mine once called Esther's section a song of songs, a song of songs of schizophrenia. Esther doesn't know whether you are alive or dead, whether you were born or she only dreamed that you were born. Every dead butterfly is her baby. With every empty cocoon something of her is lost. I have four or five other novellas as well.

Is this material that you omitted from **Miss MacIntosh, My Darling?**

Yes, this is material I hope to bring out. One piece is based on the fact that when Mr. Spitzer asks for something in a store, he always gets it and never wants it. He would say, "Do you have a town clock?" And the man would say, "Yes, we do." No matter what ridiculous thing, he was just asking. Then Mr. Spitzer would be weighted with it. He would have to buy something he absolutely did not want because he was always asking for things. Another piece is about Mr. Spitzer's efforts to get to King of Prussia, Pennsylvania, where he heard that an elderly lady had the pony which had never grown old, that once belonged to Queen Victoria. It's a quest for something that cannot be found. My editor at Scribner's liked the novellas very much and wanted to publish them. I always wanted to go over them again. When I started to write about New Harmony, the utopia, I was inspired to do so by an account of a flour miller who tried to pass on his thumbmark to his son. That cannot be done, and the son ended by committing suicide. I wrote a short story about it, but it was not successful at all, it was too difficult to do, I don't know why. I have put that flour miller and this thumb into ***Miss MacIntosh, My Darling*** somewhere. In fact, I've put that flour miller and his thumb into everything I've ever written since. Just maybe a reference to it—it's the thing I never could write, the idea of identity and passage of the soul.

Does the idea of passage function in **Miss MacIntosh, My Darling,** *in which a specific object will reappear as another object? For instance, a coin becomes a drachma, which becomes a black poker chip elsewhere in the text. Are these clues towards solving a mystery?*

They are references to transmutation and transmigration, to metempsychosis, resurrection, loss of identity, change of function—and of definitions of money.

You knew Harriet Monroe, Gertrude Stein, Anais Nin, Djuna Barnes, and many others. Did you travel to Paris in the twenties?

No, I wish I had. I never had a nickel. The first money I ever had was when I received an award from the American Association of University Women. John Crowe Ransom wrote to me from Ohio, saying "Are you in New York yet?" He knew I would go to New York, and I did.

Did you resent the fact that male writers experimenting in fiction and poetry received a great deal of attention while the women were neglected?

Not at the time. It never occurred to me because I always believed that many great writers were women—Kay Boyle, Katherine Anne Porter, Christina Stead, Katherine Mansfield, Anna Kavan, Jane Bowles. Jane Bowles, whom I'd met, was quite a success around the time of *Two Serious Ladies.* I never thought of myself as either a woman or a man. I thought of myself as a person who was born to be a writer, who was doomed to be a writer. But after ***Miss MacIntosh, My Darling*** was published, I found I was the victim of some brutal male reviewers. "If she had gotten married she never would have *done* this," they would write. Like Kay Boyle, whose work I'm wild about, I could have married, written a book with every baby, a baby with every book. There were also some cruel reviews by women, but the tone of the male reviewers, sometimes hysterical, was different. I have suffered, but I don't want to name names—but there have been men who have seemed to want to destroy me or my writing, men I don't even know. At this point, however, I must say that some men, particularly William Goyen, wrote me beautiful reviews. Still, I think there is a rage against women. I've come to see that now although at the time I did not notice it. I was preoccupied with my teaching and my writing. I would teach from nine to four, sleep an hour, and write from six until midnight, night after night. I realize now, incidentally, that ***Miss MacIntosh, My Darling*** would have sold many more copies if I had published one volume at a time.

I believe that all my work explores the human desire or obsession for utopia, and the structure of all my works is the search for utopias lost and rediscovered. . . . All my writing is about the recognition that there is no single reality. But the beauty of it is that you nevertheless go on, walking towards utopia, which may not exist, on a bridge which might end before you reach the other side.

—Marguerite Young

In **Miss MacIntosh, My Darling** *you show a keen awareness of male/female dichotomies. Sometimes a male becomes a woman or a woman becomes a man. Why?*

It's spiritual. Body—soul—and clothing, with the profound influence upon me of William James and Saint Augustine in *The City of God.* The multiple and the pagan feeling, instead of the monolithic reality that Miss MacIntosh tried to assume but did not succeed at. The pagan reality.

Why did you decide to write a biography of Eugene Debs?

If you knew all I knew about utopia, you would ask why not Debs. He talked to the simplest of people with poems and images—from *The Arabian Nights* and Poe's "The Raven," from *Don Quixote,* from Dickens. His speech was beautiful. I didn't choose Debs. He chose me.

When I finished ***Miss MacIntosh, My Darling,*** Mark Van Doren asked me, "If someone gave you a choice of writer for a biography, who would it be?" I had had one glass of champagne, which is fatal for me. Otherwise I probably would have said Dreiser, whom I love, and almost wouldn't speak to anyone who ever attacked him. But I reverted to my childhood and said James Whitcomb Riley. And Van Doren jumped to his feet screaming, "That's what I hoped you would say." If you know anything about James Whitcomb Riley, you know that Little Orphan Annie is one of the most fantastic characters who ever lived in America before Charlie Chaplin. Riley and Debs were drinking companions. It was through their conversations about how to get to paradise or utopia that I became more and more involved with Debs. I stopped working on Riley to write a short book on Debs, and it has turned out to be 2400 pages, three volumes of 800 pages each. My book on Riley is almost finished. So I have four books ready. The more I think about Riley, the greater my appreciation is. Riley was one of the key spirits of Debs's life, one of the five most interesting people Debs ever knew. The first and foremost was James Whitcomb Riley. There are reasons for that.

Miss MacIntosh *is nearly 1200 pages, and your Debs book will be 2400 pages. This means you are writing, in your lifetime, only a few works. Do you regret this?*

I didn't realize that the Debs project would be so long. I wrote a short book on Debs, and the publisher said I should turn it into an epic. In my Debs biography, I break down the categories of poetry and prose. In fact, these categories belong not to writers, but to critics. I think the category between fiction and non-fiction is nothing. The poetry of non-fiction is as fabulous as any poetry you could ever write in fiction. Poets have greatly influenced me. The only difference between the novel as poem and the lyric as poem is the difference in length.

And the distinctions between fiction and biography?

I don't find any.

You have said that Sinclair Lewis and Theodore Dreiser are two of your favorite writers, yet your own style is not at all like theirs. Can you explain this?

Just as I do not want my students to imitate my style, I admire authors who write differently from me. Lewis and Dreiser didn't try to write in a poetic style. I had referred to Sinclair Lewis's America in the first pages of ***Angel in the Forest,*** and then I met Lewis in the bar of the Algonquin Hotel in New York City. A man with red hair came crawling toward me, screaming and crawling along the bar. He said, "Marguerite Young, you are my favorite author." I said, "I? And who are you?" He said something like "I get so damned tired of my imitators. You showed another America, real and beautiful, but baroque and bizarre." That's why he liked me. I think most people don't like others who, without a voice of their own, emulate the other. I certainly don't want anybody just to pick up my thoughts and hand them back to me.

What other writers do you admire?

There are many writers I admire, Laurence Sterne, Edgar Allan Poe, Victor Hugo. I was devoted to W. H. Auden. I loved Dylan Thomas, William Carlos Williams, and Wallace Stevens. I love James Merrill's poems and his short novels. Ambrose Bierce. Vachel Lindsay, I like, and I knew his sister quite well. I love the work of Kay Boyle and Christina Stead. I once spent a wonderful week in New York with Christina, who knew everything surreal there is to know about life. I knew Anais Nin, who called me after I had been away for a few years. She was seeking help because at that time no one would give her a decent review. She was made fun of. I prefer *Collages* of all her work. That's what she intended—a new kind of writing, but she did not live to do it. I like Gertrude Stein, and spent two weeks with her at the University of Chicago. I like her. She did not influence me in any way, but she wrote a novel called *Marguerite* in which she explained me. She wasn't writing about me, she just defined the meaning of the name Marguerite, and it was true of everything she wrote about me. No, I like Gertrude Stein and Alice B. Toklas, and all those people, and I knew Harriet Monroe. Of the contemporaries, I read Toni Morrison's work and the short stories of Cynthia Ozick. I believe that Ozick, like me, has been influenced by William James. When I read people I know if they have read their William James. Their Henry James too, but especially their William James. I admire T. S. Eliot, though he did not influence me as people like to think.

What about the echoes of Eliot in **Miss MacIntosh, My Darling?**

There are no echoes of Eliot. There are echoes of the things that influenced him. At the University of Chicago I majored in epic literature of the world and studied the material that Eliot had studied. I studied Dante, Milton, Lucretius, Locke, Fourier, Darwin, Owen, and many others. I did not need to go to Eliot. My references, for instance, to crabs come from—I forget now—but I think from Danish folklore, not from Eliot. I love Eliot's work, don't get me wrong, but I resent people who say I echo Eliot.

Who did influence you directly?

I studied with Robert Morss Lovett, the great professor of epic literature. Another important influence was Ronald S. Crane, a professor of aesthetics at the University of Chicago. I was in his class, and we read *Tom Jones* thirteen times, doing an intricate study of its structure. Nothing could have been more valuable for my own writing, although it was one time more than I cared to read *Tom Jones.*

Some reviewers have criticized your non-realistic style for being poetic, repetitive, almost obsessive. Have you altered your style from one book to another?

No. I have never altered my style in anything I've written. My Debs biography is as poetic as ***Miss MacIntosh, My Darling,*** but it is more of a ballad while ***Miss MacIntosh*** is an epic. I would never write realistic prose. I don't like people who try to write in a poetic style, but in the course of their book abandon it for realism, and weave back and forth like drunkards between the surreal and the real. I think that the style is the writing, a beautiful sense of style. And if you don't have it, it doesn't matter what you write, it doesn't really make any difference. I'm not speaking of realistic novels now, but of the pseudo-poetic novel or short story. I'm quite sure that most writers would sustain real poetry if they could, but it takes devotion and talent. I've been willing to go for years without publishing. That's been my career.

Have you always viewed yourself as an experimentalist writer?

I see myself as traditional even though I know you see my work as experimental. I don't really consider Sterne, Joyce, and Proust experimental either because the tradition of their writing goes back a long way. Traditional. The Grand Tradition. Clear back to *Don Quixote.* I never decided to write in a "new way" at all. It's realism that's fairly new. Is it experimental to have been influenced by the Bible? By Saint Augustine?

But you don't write about Saint Augustine. Studying your style, people would think of Joyce's Ulysses, *for instance.*

But I was not influenced by Joyce although he's a great writer, and I love his work. I was influenced by Saint Augustine. The books that did influence me were *Tristram Shandy* and Gogol's *Dead Souls,* Dickens and Poe.

Are you saying that your goal wasn't to break tradition, to alter the narrative line?

No. Theological, historical, philosophical—I'm as much influenced by Joseph Smith and the Mormons as I am, more so, than by Eliot. Actually, I'm much more influenced by the poetry of the Mormons.

If you believe that your writing is traditional, why does **Miss MacIntosh, My Darling** *have no beginning, middle or end?*

Because life has no beginning, middle or end.

You tell your students to follow their obsessions to their ultimate conclusions. What is your own obsession?

Absolutely, that is what I tell them. If you don't have obsessions, don't write. Debs was obsessed. James Whitcomb Riley was obsessed. And my characters are obsessed. The personages in the Debs book are obsessed, including Emma Goldman and Margaret Anderson. I have hundreds of characters . . . I had a book, which was stolen, the art of the life of the character, in which you present a whole life in three or four pages. I used that method. I'm obsessed. My first attempt to write about Robert Owen was in the form of poetry. Then I turned it into a blank verse poem, but I discovered that I couldn't fit in all the facts, which are fabulous. I decided to rewrite it a third time, still retaining every image I had already written in the first two versions. My published volume, ***Angel in the Forest,*** contains all the other versions. I think that Mark Van Doren recognized this obsession in me when, in his introduction to ***Angel in the Forest,*** he described the intensity of my efforts to capture illusion as an "unkillable concern."

Will you describe your obsession?

I believe that all my work explores the human desire or obsession for utopia, and the structure of all my works is the search for utopias lost and rediscovered. This is true of ***Miss MacIntosh, My Darling, Moderate Fable, Prismatic Ground, Angel in the Forest,*** and my Debs manuscript. All my writing is about the recognition that there is no single reality. But the beauty of it is that you nevertheless go on, walking towards utopia, which may not exist, on a bridge which might end before you reach the other side. (pp. 147-54)

Marguerite Young, Ellen G. Friedman, and Miriam Fuchs, in an interview in The Review of Contemporary Fiction, *Vol. 9, No. 3, Fall, 1989, pp. 147-54.*

Miriam Fuchs (essay date Fall 1989)

[*In the following essay, Fuchs surveys Young's works, focusing on their utopian themes, and on Young's status as an experimental writer.*]

On one of the 1198 pages of Marguerite Young's ***Miss MacIntosh, My Darling,*** a character is declared to be "not of this margin, canon, text" but an "apocryphal firefly shining far beyond the edge.. . . . " In the vast spaces beyond the canonical, the apocryphal creature flourishes, dubiously and miraculously. Undaunted by the slippage from traditional logic, Young's narrative sweeps the firefly into pinnacles, descends it into lagoons, spirals interstellar space, and plummets to the narrow site where a flyleaf is stuck between two small texts, whose pages instantly unfurl into holy "testaments."

Like her apocryphal firefly, Marguerite Young flourishes outside the strictures of the canon, beyond its margins as well. As an experimental writer, who is also a woman—whose style is labyrinthine enough to withstand all but the most tenacious of readers—she is twice removed from "mainstream" American fiction. William Goyen's 1965 review of ***Miss MacIntosh, My Darling*** as "a work of stunning magnitude and beauty," one of "the richest, most expressive, most original" works of the century, did little to ensure its reputation [*New York Times Book Review,* 12 September 1965]. Erika Duncan, in her essay written for [*The Review of Contemporary Fiction's* Fall 1989] issue, calls Young's work "an epic elegy for all creation" and Steven Shaviro, also in [*The Review of Contemporary Fiction's* Fall 1989] issue, declares ***Miss MacIntosh, My Darling*** "as carefully and deliberately crafted as any great twentieth-century work." For Anna Balakian, Young is "one of the most innovative novelists of our time . . . to this part of the century what Gertrude Stein may have been to the beginning, but so much more *human,* more poetic, visionary" [Letter to Miriam Fuchs, 26 April 1988]. Despite assessments such as these, Young remains a solitary writer, unsanctioned by the canon and neglected by critics. Moving from the early poetry of ***Prismatic Ground*** (1937) and ***Moderate Fable*** (1944) to the historical poetic narrative of ***Angel in the Forest*** (1945) to the stunning epic lyricism of ***Miss MacIntosh, My Darling*** (1965), Young is currently working on two ambitious projects: a biography of James Whitcomb Riley and a three-volume biography of Eugene Victor Debs. Regarding these biographical texts as a subtle and natural shift in her writing, Young insists, in her interview in this issue, that the unblemished lines which distinguish poetry, prose, fiction, non-fiction, realism, fabulation and experimentalism belong "not to writers, but to critics," because "the poetry of non-fiction is as fabulous as any poetry [I] could ever write in fiction."

All of Young's works, whatever category readers choose for them, are utopian in the sense that each one recognizes the universal struggle for ideality and the impossibility of reaching it. Ensuring that her characters fail, and filling her utopias with losses, Young preserves the interfusion as well as the resulting *con*fusion of their efforts. With each loss, however, comes the dignity—and privilege—of surviving, a partial success, which is the only success that Young recognizes. As her characters and historical figures pursue what ultimately is, and must forever be chimerical, she records failure after failure: jobs bungled, messages confused, appointments forgotten, distances miscalculated. And loss after loss: lost leaders, lost causes, lost lovers, lost paradises, and specifically in ***Angel in the Forest,*** the abandoned utopian communities of George Rapp and Robert Owen in nineteenth-century America. Loss occurs early in Young's texts. At the start of ***Angel in the Forest,*** efforts to establish a new moral order are declared unsuccessful, their evocation laden with the "memory of failure"—"cobwebbed and insubstantial" like the dilapidated country ten-cent store that stands precariously where Rapp's "New Jerusalem" once prospered in New Harmony, Indiana. The title character of ***Miss MacIntosh, My Darling*** walks off into the frigid Atlantic waters, leaving behind a corset, a frazzled red wig, and a pair of glassless spectacles.

Young believes that all attempts—individual or communal—towards harmony and completion must, of necessity, be imperfect and incomplete, falling finally into disharmony and fragmentation. But she refuses to settle for anything *other* than fragmentation. "More complete in their incompletion than if they had been whole," her characters' broken and fleeting visions shatter conventions of Western logic so persistently and so utterly that they become, particularly in ***Miss MacIntosh, My Darling,*** the routine affairs of each day's work. For Young, nothing is factitious but the cultural-historical practice of declaring authenticity by subjecting phenomena to the constraints of binary logic. Cousin Hannah and Catherine Cartwheel, the hallucinating women of ***Miss MacIntosh, My Darling,*** and its befuddled Mr. Spitzer (who believes he is his own twin brother, not himself), as well as the utopian visionaries and materialistic socialists of ***Angel in the Forest*** share the grandeur, and the bewilderment of the imagination, releasing the fine line between the quixotic and the real. But Young insists there is no fine line, "no algebra of the human spirit, no bone-setting of the bones . . . no reunion of broken parts. . . ." "Life was imagination, even to the last tenth" although she provocatively warns, "one did not know which tenth the last tenth was . . ." (***Miss MacIntosh***).

If the "last tenth" can be propelled towards infinity, nothing lies beyond the final tenth to delimit and define it. Young's world is therefore precarious, in perpetual danger of collapsing into a void, but breathtaking as it spirals into psychic and spatial immensities. Using characters like Mr. Spitzer, who totters at the edge of a skyscraper window, poised to take one more step into the hallway, and Cousin Hannah, who pirouettes in the concert hall of her hallucinating mind—both gloriously insensible to their "limitations"—Young defies centuries of Western thought, characterized by Nietzsche, Bataille, Derrida, and others as the dialectical tension between masculine and feminine, intellect and emotion, order and chaos. This decision means, for Young, that her multitudes of losses are not defined by her few instances of "gain." The absence of one does not imply the presence of the other, since both circulate and interpenetrate, surging beyond all fixed formulas of binary relationship.

In her interview for this issue [see excerpt above], Young calls her story of a flour miller who tries to pass his thumbprint on to his son the piece that she never could write. Acknowledging her "failure" to complete this story that comes at the end of ***Angel in the Forest,*** Young has worked the flour miller into each of her subsequent manuscripts. Of course, each time she writes in one text what she could not write in another, she writes it. And because she does not tell the whole story, or simply uses fragments (the "whole" version being the illusion), it is not ever finished. Thus, Young's reminder to herself that creation is always flawed is synonymous with her enacting the flaw. Like the undertaker in ***Angel in the Forest*** who warns that "Nobody [can] remove the flaws from the universe without destroying the universe," Young wants us to accept, even embrace, scraps of knowledge that seem not to fit and phenomena we cannot rationalize. Her work topples the edifice of genre and ignores the imperatives of logic; as nonadmissive material comes crashing out, Young gathers it into "tremblings, flashings, coruscatings of sparks," in other words, into the broken visions of her characters, each vision failing even as it is conceived.

Except for the communal experiments presented in ***Angel in the Forest,*** Young's utopias are often "without site." Since "every soul is the other soul," and "every face . . . the other face," nothing is singular or in oppositional relation to anything else. Young describes each phenomenon as if it is the other—simultaneously and eternally coexisting. Her characters are also mutable, never completely themselves since individuation is impossible, and therefore never quite the "Other." Hélène Cixous advocates a similar conception of character to countermand what she calls its "fetishization" in most works of fiction [*New Literary History,* 1974]. The traditional "I" marks a privileged, unbreachable self: "an 'I' who is a *whole* subject . . . conscious [and] knowable" is also "the enunciatory 'I,' *express[ing] himself* in the text . . . in the name of some reality principle . . . to which the text is subordinated." Aligning the circumscribed character with the privileged hero and the voice of masculine authority, complicit with classical reasoning, Cixous explains that *"le personnage"* of fiction should designate more than a single person. It should shatter "the homogeneity of the ego" and spread itself "in every possible direction, into every possible contradiction, transegoistically." This off-centered subjectivity frees the text to interrogate binary categories which, for Cixous, indicate mastery and subjugation, man and woman, the private and the political. Thus, literature may function as cultural critique, and writers as "poets of subversion."

Young also critiques the old dichotomies—in sentences that she thrusts forward in crescendo and casts back in diminuendo. Vera Cartwheel explains how her mother Catherine, a wealthy opium addict who never leaves her bed, conceives of subjectivity:

> The personal pronoun I did not always mean, of course, the same being or thing to my mother. How often, eating an apple, had she said—I am eating myself? How often had she said—I am a cloud eating the moon—I am eating an hourglass—I am eating a door knob? How often had she warned a hallucinatory or even a real visitor not to be seated in a golden fourteenth-century

> chair set upon a floor of clouds—for she was the chair, and she might crumble into the glittering stardust? She was the divan, the mirror, the lamp, the rug, all of which might suddenly move away in the evening light, leaving a bare room. . . . She was Brooklyn Bridge, dissolving when a rose petal fell. . . . She was everybody and the rose petal, too, the cause of this dissolution which was this creation, and she was the street lamp beaming through the fog like one great pearl, a sarcophagus enclosing the moon's flame. . . . And if she was everybody and everything, how could she be she and live, for what was her personal identity among so many transshifting objects and flickering shadows, and how should she walk where the landscape moved like waves?

Catherine's "hallucinations" play themselves over, but never play themselves out, for Young's prose resists resolution and refuses to settle on a unitary or coherent subject. In sumptuous passages like this which continue for chapters at a time, Young doubles, quadruples, septuples her images, expanding character into what Cixous would call a "fabulous opera." Ordinary people in ***Miss MacIntosh, My Darling*** see through opaque surfaces and hear music beyond the range of human perception. Catherine and Hannah dream each other's dreams so profoundly that Mr. Spitzer, who watches over them, decides they do not need to meet after so much psychic intimacy. Catherine sees sable snow, Esther Longtree is eternally pregnant, Mr. Spitzer hears a violin performance that is so exquisite he trembles in rapture to the "nuances of difference between the premonitory passages. . . ." Although the musician uses an imaginary bow on an imaginary violin, Mr. Spitzer knows immediately the name of the musical selection and is amazed at the man's technical proficiency. The world these characters travel, nearly unrepresentable, is a vast interspace of sense, intellect, prescience and faith. What they lose is considerable—certainty, proportion, worldly ambition. But without a hierarchy for assigning relative values or declaring what is bogus, what they gain may be infinite.

Quixotic figures appear in Young's first volume of poetry, ***Prismatic Ground,*** published in 1937 by Macmillan. Comprised for the most part of short lyrical verses and organized by fairly regular rhyme schemes, these poems (some of which appeared in magazines like the *New Republic* and *Poetry*) show Young's early interest in heroes, prophets, and obscure dreamers. Magellan, the "intrepid explorer" who circumnavigated the globe, and Daniel from the Old Testament, interpreting dreams and foretelling the future, are "lesser" than heroic, and the recognition of weakness makes their courage all the more striking. In the poem **"Lesser Magellan,"** the Holy Grail which inspires Magellan is more sparkle than sacred, "amethyst / Shadows of a shut door," "a bag of saffron" and perfumes of the East. But despite less than exalted aspirations, Magellan sails where " . . . no one had gone, / Where mists rise to dim / The silver apples of dawn . . ." Daniel, too, less than perfect, speaks for himself "As a matter of record." He agrees on his heroics, "But as time wears on, I am inclined / To believe I was but stoical, / A creature with a stubborn mind," and thus no more or less than most of humanity. As their codified histories are opened to interrogation and adjustment, their stories, like all of Young's stories, are not quite complete, their achievements underscoring their limitations.

Young dramatizes heroes but focuses also on the smallest of natural phenomena, finding universal lessons in each particular. The poem broadly and figuratively entitled **"Sky of Grasses"** converges on a tiny "fitful spider." Other phenomena include a single falling leaf, a cricket's "timorous sound," creatures so small that "one word could blow [them] apart / like dust . . ." (**"The Visit"**). But as Young swings from the minute to the gargantuan in ***Miss MacIntosh, My Darling,*** in ***Prismatic Ground*** she collapses the heavens and the skies to a size "smaller than the faint far sound / Of a seed pod shaking the grey ground." "In faint words only, / In tremulous sound, / In syllables softly / Blown to the ground" (**"Departing Song"**), Young locates her faith and her loves—in the space where the individual senses merge, where words are falling leaves, and dimension is sound.

Even in these early graceful lyrics, Young peels at her subjects' borders, diffusing their details and questioning their singular form. The pear tree in the poem **"Whorl,"** whose branches are "Chiselled immaculate in sunlight," dissolves by "moon drift" into mysterious and shifting silhouettes. As the branches span further and further, reaching into a woman's room, the tree, the blooms, and the sleeper are a shimmering configuration of reflections and shadows, more psychic than visual. In **"Minnows and a Monster,"** unfathomable mysteries are invoked by the fractured surface of water and reflected moonlight. The speaker flings out a fishnet ("delicate meshes") and waits for his "catch"—not a fish, however, but "Catches of dreaming, dreaming," an "eerie being," an "enigma gleaming . . ." Like many of Young's images, the fisherman's catch belongs neither to the water nor the sky, but to the commingling of both. Prismatic and luminescent, the volume's poetry, initially focusing on individual images, gradually yields a panorama of nature that is diaphanous, "silken bound," shimmering with reflected surfaces.

In the seven years between ***Prismatic Ground*** and ***Moderate Fable,*** Young published individual poems in such places as *Southern Review, Kenyon Review, Poetry,* and *Horizon,* at the same time working on ***Angel in the Forest.*** A fortuitous series of events, which Young has recounted in an interview with Charles Ruas, galvanized her energies and resulted, first, in her moving from the Midwest to New York City and, second, in the publication of both ***Moderate Fable*** and ***Angel in the Forest***. Young was approached by a stranger, a talent scout for the publisher Reynal and Hitchcock, one night during a snowstorm in Iowa City. Parting gladly with two manuscripts—one poetry, the other prose—she was surprised to receive a call from the man the next morning, telling her that he was recommending the publication of ***Moderate Fable*** and that a decision on the other manuscript would be made very soon. Young was also notified at the same time that she had won a substantial fellowship from the American Association of University Women. Within forty-eight hours, she had left the Midwest for New York City, where she has lived ever since. The day Young arrived in New York, she learned that ***Angel in the Forest*** had been accepted for publication. As Young tells it, she had "two books coming out, and they both came out together. I received the votes for best nonfiction of the year and also for best poetry from the National Academy of Arts and Letters." She received the award for ***Moderate Fable.***

Titles in ***Moderate Fable*** such as **"Failing Perspective," "Figures of Space," "Null Class,"** and **"That Apple Was Mental"** show Young moving into spaces that were banished from pictorial representation since the Renaissance. Ignoring the schemata of the centralized vanishing point and interrupting the seamless progression from foreground to background, Young maneuvers into areas where perspective "fails." She draws away from the chiseled images of ***Prismatic Ground*** and slides past their exacting borders or penetrates their interiors until they extend towards infinity. In **"Crystal Principle"** she finds "a pattern even in anomalies." In **"A High Subjectivity"** she explores the "negative magnitude" of the universe; in **"Failing Perspective,"** the "Discrepant elements not always visible." Able to "see" what Western perspective has obscured, Young can thus conceive of what has been unrepresentable. Looking for the object that resists classification, she asks in **"That Apple Was Mental":** "Can a real thing, invisible, be coloration of / Mental, and inaudible a sound of congruent harpers / harping?" The poem entitled **"That Chance"** plumbs the spaces of an anti-Newtonian universe where laws of gravity do not apply. The only singular law is that which governs the multiplicity of chance: "There is no absolute, / There is no complete probable / But deviation from the law / In lonely items of the real."

Following the exception, Young favors the "noun which has no corresponding entity in space," for example, the unicorn and "the spider—webbed angel." Anomalous, improbable, and thus exquisite, creatures like the giraffe, the nighthawk, the deer-footed mouse, albino nuns with partridge eyes and phenomena like the flytrap flower run through the poetry to humble and remind us that if ever we thought the earth arches toward perfection, it surely does not: "And in this confusion," she says in **"That Cloud,"** "is our only existence possible." Her poem about a giraffe, a creature who survives "beyond the curve of probable," is a gentle, affectionate tribute to all that is superfluous, irrelevant, inappropriate, and inefficient—in other words, to all of Young's visionaries and hallucinators:

> Tower of misalliance, a vain and vexed
> But relevant mistake, and scheme of all our flaws,
> Giraffe in the low-lying woods of the acacia
> Dwelling outside the curve of probables
>
> Nor Aristotelian, but irrational with eyes of mute,
> Creation whose lean head is telescope
> And whose existence is entirely mental state
> And absolute of ever waning hope,
>
> He is beautiful, he is like the oblique daughters of
> Jerusalem, he is the exaggerated mood
> When man perceived upon angelic dark
> A ladder erected to the golden cloud . . .
>
> (from **"The Giraffe"**)

The giraffe is reminiscent of characters like the blind portrait painter and the crippled dancer who, enacting their "untenable dreams," attract Mr. Spitzer to the city, where in ***Miss MacIntosh, My Darling*** he can witness their miraculous but precarious success. Disparaged or shunned by others, they are the "dispossessed," the culture's misfits and imperceptible heroes. Like her scrutinizing Mr. Spitzer, Young is drawn to dreamers and political idealists, particularly to those who acknowledge the contradictions and impossibility of their projects and then proceed to work at them interminably. ***Angel in the Forest*** is Young's tribute to and account of the indefatigable idealists Father George Rapp and Robert Owen. In 1814 Rapp established a community in New Harmony based on celibacy and scriptural communism, which had considerable economic success. Rapp sold the property in 1825 to Owen, who founded another utopian community based on principles of rationalism and materialistic socialism. That both of these communities ultimately failed is beside the point; that both existed for a time despite the odds, and in their failings, caused inhabitants to break away and establish other communities is far more relevant—the social reverberations of failure being their improbable success.

As Young collapses the old binary distinctions, and with them the ontic status of any phenomenon, the definition of "real"—and thus of the non-real or the utopian—fluctuates. Young plays with the "real," attributing meaning by amplifying the possibilities. Vera Cartwheel in ***Miss MacIntosh, My Darling*** illustrates the process: "there was only one definition of reality, that it was real, real as my mother's opium dreams of scallop boats and the feet of satyrs . . . real as the sea which had no surf line, and real as that rock which was perched upon an angel's wing. Whatever one found was real was real . . . and even the unreal things were real, even those who were ignored, rejected, despised, abandoned, unloved, perhaps even unknown, never of fruit or flower." Nearing a definition as well as postponing it, Vera approaches Derrida's sense of *difference* as she finds traces of meaning through the continuous displacement of signifiers, and thus enforces multiple signification. A phenomenon designated as "utopia" has no "real," intrinsic, stable meaning; nor does it acquire meaning in binary opposition to other phenomena such as "reality" or "society." Instead, utopia is constituted by all of its manifestations, acquiring tentative and variable meanings through succession. The more failures Young chronicles in ***Angel in the Forest*** the more ubiquitous utopia appears. When the Owenite community in New Harmony, Indiana (the same location as the earlier Rappite experiment), founders, inhabitants leave to establish other utopias, some only a few miles away, others as far as Cincinnati. It is the continual displacement of utopias that assigns meaning to the word; each attempt to establish a utopia is the formation of one more blighted star in the "planetary system" of utopias.

Recalling to Charles Ruas the three versions through which ***Angel in the Forest*** passed before it was ready for publication, Young noted the palimpsestic qualities of the manuscript. She wrote the first ***Angel in the Forest*** as a series of sixty ballads, which depicted New Harmony but omitted its history. She rewrote the manuscript in blank verse, but still could not incorporate all the "facts and figures" she had discovered while doing extensive research. Rewriting again, this time in prose, Young was able to suffuse the text with "everything I had written in the two poetic versions. It was the prose variation that took me about three years. I used all those images. I wanted to write a poetic prose." A compilation of individual portraits and collective histories, ***Angel in the Forest*** is also evocative and poetic narrative. Despite the unitary form in which ***Angel in the Forest*** was published, the images from other *Angels* are embedded in every page, suggesting—as Young does in all her writing—that finality and completion can never be achieved. Like the "process" of utopia, which is the passage from one utopian configuration to another, creation is infinite, with each attempt imperfectly contained in every other attempt. A difficult lesson for the political utopians to learn is that "what lies beyond this shifting world must be shifting, too."

If the shifting and the variable are the only "truths" worth seeking, precisely because they cannot be represented in a final form, any character's belief that he has finally witnessed perfection is erroneous. Robert Dale, for example, insists that the greatest happiness of his life occurred at the moment his ship headed for New Harmony was blocked by ice. All was instantly frozen: "as if the earth had returned to its first condition, a Parmenidean quietude, all crystal, stainless, and perfect, without wind, without motion." But for Young there must always be a flaw. It is the flaw that makes the utopia, the flaw that heightens the crystal, and Dale's observation is yet another mistake of another utopian in ***Angel in the Forest.***

Focused on what they presume to be "real," the twentieth-century inhabitants of New Harmony, which is no longer an experimental community, lack the impulse for utopian achievement; the barber sharpens his hone, the waitress talks of leaving. The owner of the only theater in town recalls the week he played *Lost Horizon* as "a hell on earth for him." Watching the 1937 movie, the farmers find "no sense in the damn thing, Shangri-la, how could there be snow one minute and warm sunlight . . . the next, just by turning a corner—or how [could] a man eighty-five years old have all his teeth in his head, like that lama in a monastery, Sam Jaffe." The town's flour miller, whose story Young says she has never finished, speaks convincingly for all that the farmers cannot see because it cannot be clearly represented; it has no single signifier. Despite all apparent similitude of flour millers, all dressed alike, and of all flour and all wheat, Young's miller knows that there are essential differences. But the fissure which separates flour millers is "so slight that nobody can name it, nobody can catch hold of it"—even though it spews forth multitudes—"as many flours as there are millers." Preferring to see something "that is at least possible," the farmers are alike in that they have no affinity for the utopian dream. But if flours are different, Young suggests that farmers are different, and sooner or later one, then others, will have an itch, "so slight that nobody can name it," and the struggle for the dream will begin again.

The "no-place" of utopia that unravels in ***Angel in the Forest*** as a series of "some places," becomes in ***Miss MacIntosh, My Darling*** an "everyplace." With few delineated settings, the landscape is encompassing but vague. Vera's early explanation that there is "no landscape but the soul's, and that is the inexactitude, the ever shifting and the distant" blurs distinctions of inner and outer, locating the physical landscape in the abstraction of the soul, which sets the image reeling into other fleeting images. A utopia of language, ***Miss MacIntosh, My Darling*** treats what we do not know to exist as though it exists, pursuing it until it does exist—textually—in defiance of such principles as mimesis, resemblance, logical signification.

If every soul is the other soul, then every book is the other book, and ***Miss MacIntosh, My Darling*** is the other utopia, the one which spins loose of politics and history and, enjoying the freedom of what Barthes calls "the paradisiac text . . . a heterology by plenitude," exercises "every kind of linguistic pleasure [*The Pleasure of the Text,* 1975]." Pulling the signifier from the signified, and locating her utopia in the passage that once connected them, Young finds its dimensions to be incalculable. Mr. Spitzer serves as executor to Cousin Hannah's estate. A meticulous lawyer, he has always "assessed, investigated, measured," making lists and double-checking them with other lists to be certain there is "no missing factor or sign." He enters Cousin Hannah's house prepared to sort out her things, expecting finally to "establish her identity" and be done with his fetishization for the "whole," "knowable" Hannah. But even in death she thwarts his compulsion for order and mastery. Hannah has left behind forty locked trunks. Fumbling like a mad locksmith in search of the "master" key, Mr. Spitzer looks in vain for the single "open sesame," but resigns himself to the necessity for forty different keys, thus forty different "entrances" to Hannah's posthumous self:

> Although he had counted forty lids and forty keys, he had found that there was always one lid more than there was a key, one key more than there was a lid, one star more, one star less, and so he was left with that key which fitted no lock, that lock which fitted no key or body, perhaps this star, perhaps those mysteries which could not be solved. . . .
>
> There had been these seas of silk spun by martyred cocoons, silks so delicate that they might be drawn for miles through a wedding ring like clouds through the golden hoop of the absent moon . . . laces which seemed to melt, to dissolve at a touch, ribbons crumbling into fog and bands of silk disintegrating into dust and silks flowing into water as if water were their counterpart. . . . He had been trapped by wedding gowns winding around his feet like seas, seas of hissing silks, skirts hemmed by marsh flowers, skirts blowing like waves, skirts drifting around his head or over his head like the sails of boats, short trains and long trains, tents of cobweb where one fire burned like the eye of this mystery, skirts like glacial snow drifting from a ledge

> of stone, skirts which were shrouds, skirts like the white umbrellas floating over him, carousels of brides where no bride was unless it was himself with these waters winding around his heart. . . .

Opening the trunks, he discovers a plenitude of riches, images, fabrics, a mix of metaphor and metamorphics which, in spreading itself everywhere, subverts his authority and resists his desire to shut each trunk. Rich in contradictions, the sentences blur gender, create disproportionate relations, and propel figurative language to nearly unimaginable levels.

A text in which a blind conductor leads a mute orchestra to resounding applause, ***Miss MacIntosh, My Darling*** absorbs and transforms its numerous deaths and suffering into a paradise of miracles. Young knows that all of our attempts towards ideality will fail. But the reward of those failures is the gift of knowledge, the ability to perceive the beauty of "unearthly music," which Young calls "music of passage from here to there, now to then." Infinite passage is infinite potential, and by offering no final destination, no single epiphany, Young breaks off ***Miss MacIntosh, My Darling*** perhaps reluctantly and certainly abruptly, gesturing that 1198 pages are not enough to contain her utopia.

Like the flawed heroes of ***Prismatic Ground,*** the exquisite creatures of ***Moderate Fable,*** and the visionaries and idealists of ***Angel in the Forest,*** the idiosyncratic cast of characters in ***Miss MacIntosh, My Darling*** evinces Young's belief, which like a palimpsest is expressed, then expressed again in each of her works. In whatever genres she writes, and however she blurs their borders, Young insists that the end can never be the end. There is always something unaccounted for, some infinitesimal detail that disturbs the universe, and causes all of its utopians to dream. (pp. 166-76)

Miriam Fuchs, "Marguerite Young's Utopias: 'The Most Beautiful Music [They] Had Never Heard'," in The Review of Contemporary Fiction, *Vol. 9, No. 3, Fall, 1989, pp. 166-76.*

Susan Strehle (essay date Fall 1989)

[In the following essay, Strehle asserts that the narrative structure of Miss MacIntosh, My Darling *"replaces historical time with the time of female subjectivity."]*

In an essay titled "Women's Time," Julia Kristeva suggests that "female subjectivity would seem to provide a specific measure that essentially retains *repetition* and *eternity* from among the multiple modalities of time known through the history of civilizations." Linked on the one hand to "cycles, gestation, the eternal recurrence of a biological rhythm which conforms to that of nature" and on the other hand to "a monumental temporality," "all-encompassing and infinite like imaginary space," women's time not only differs from, but poses problems for the time of history: "time as project, teleology, linear and prospective unfolding." Linear and historical time, Kristeva observes, is also "that of language considered as the enunciation of sentences (noun + verb; topic-comment; beginning-ending)" and by extension that of traditional narratives founded on the construction of a linear and complete history [*The Kristeva Reader,* 1986].

One distinctive achievement of Marguerite Young's ***Miss MacIntosh, My Darling*** (1965) is its narration from within women's time of the experience of various characters estranged from history. At every level, ranging from its non-linear syntax to its repetitive explorations of characters and incidents to its larger formal inversion of linear plot—and, more broadly, to its emphasis on mental and emotional activities occurring in the time of repetition and eternity—this novel replaces historical time with the time of female subjectivity. The result is an expansive, monumental novel of 1198 pages, written over eighteen years and utterly lacking the succinctness and clarity of teleological narratives whose parts relate progressively to each other and to the ending that draws time and plots to static completion. The result is also an "unreadable" novel that roused as much condemnation as praise in initial reviews and that subsequently sank into relative obscurity among critics of postmodern fiction, though it has maintained an underground readership. Reviewers objected, predictably, to the novel's expansive length and style: "it is overwritten, frothy, often artificial, and annoying . . . it drowns the reader in its deadening pursuit of how to make every ten words count for one" [Catharine Hughes, *America,* October 2, 1965]; for another reviewer, it is "simply a huge, badly written, apparently not edited, undisciplined spilling out of words," marred by "unsorted elements, complicated movements, insoluble obscurity [J.M. Edelstein, *New Republic,* 2 October 1965.]." The language of these complaints reveals a preference for the linear spare "naturalness" of history, with its disciplined sorting of elements and its implicit assertion that all mysteries are soluble. History has become the time natural to civilized beings, including reviewers, whose values and expectations are conditioned by and condition the production of novelistic histories. In this context, Young's novel can only appear "artificial," in the pejorative sense, and out of control, "undisciplined."

Young chooses and controls her narrative strategies with care, of course—they are simply not the strategies of conventional novels because her goal is not the production of distinctive life histories set in external, causal, historical time. Rather, she explores the unconscious, the inner subjectivities of characters who lack the singular and definitive identity that comes from and enables a place in history, and who are defined instead through overlapping doubts, dreams, questions and uncertainties. These characters have multiple, divided and contradictory imaginations of themselves; they appear in the novel in loosely configured patterns of repetition, opposition, and variation on similar themes. In an important passage in the first chapter, Young develops—first through a series of questions, for the narrator shares the habits of inquiry and doubt—a sense of the subjective unity of life for characters whose quirky eccentricity makes them feel isolated and seem divided from any larger community. But they are closely related by the omniscient narrative eye which sees, beneath the singularity of surface, the resemblances of heart and soul:

> Who knew even his own divided heart? Who knew all hearts as his own? Among beings strange to each other, those divided by the long roarings of time, of space, those who have never met or, when they meet, have not recognized as their own the other heart and that heart's weaknesses, have turned stonily away, would there not be, in the vision of some omniscient eye, a web of spidery logic establishing the most secret relationships, deep calling to deep, illuminations of the eternal darkness, recognitions in the night world of voyager dreams . . . all souls as one and united? Every heart is the other heart. Every soul is the other soul. Every face is the other face. The individual is the one illusion.

The novel proceeds on this faith to expose the "web of spidery logic" relating characters' subjective depths to each other and to a vision of life itself unified at the level of eternal or monumental time.

Each of Young's characters is a dreamer and a doubter; all inhabit the ahistorical night world of fluid yearning rather than the daytime world of projective striving and accomplishment. "The theme of the book," Young knew from the outset, "would be an inquest into the illusions individuals suffer from." The narrator, Vera Cartwheel, has been raised in a palatial, isolated house on the Atlantic coast. Her mother, an opium addict, took to bed and the world of dreams when Vera was very young; Catherine entertains imaginary callers and imagines life, sometimes quite accurately, from within a drugged dream. Mr. Joaquin Spitzer is her only real visitor; a lawyer and composer of silent music, he has loved her and managed her practical affairs for years, but she prefers his mercurial twin brother Peron, who committed suicide years before. Miss MacIntosh, hired by Mr. Spitzer as a nursemaid /governess when Vera is seven, urges practical common sense and an engagement with reality on the child. Then, when Vera is fourteen, she discovers that Miss MacIntosh's reality is stranger than her mother's opium dreams: Miss MacIntosh is bald, hairless from birth, lonely, lesbian, and far more original than the maxims she has spouted from Poor Richard's Almanac would suggest. The discovery of love in the month that follows is also an awakening to loss and death, for Miss MacIntosh disappears, drowning herself for no single reason in the ocean. Years pass; Vera leaves home and goes searching for Miss MacIntosh—or for the principle of reality, transfigured by love, she represents. As the novel opens, Vera rides a bus to the Midwest; the characters and events of her youth emerge in flashback, though given the importance placed on memory and imagination, they dominate the first 942 pages of the novel, and the bus arrives at its destination, a small Indiana town, on page 948. During the journey, the long-haired bus driver and fellow passengers Madge, pregnant, fearful and lonely, and her husband Homer, sleepy and oblivious, emerge as characters commenting on the same themes of illusion and reality, dream and imagination, mothers and children. In the last section of the novel, Vera hears the stories of Doc, the town's aged, dreaming obstetrician who has only imaginary babies to deliver, and Esther Longtree, a cross-eyed waitress who, having strangled her firstborn, mulatto infant, remains always pregnant with imaginary babies. Then, in the last six pages, Vera meets the stone-deaf man, falls in love with him, conceives a child, and looks forward to an imminent marriage.

This plot evokes linear and historical expectations in several ways, but frustrates and displaces them at every turn. Formally, Vera's story is a sort of bildungsroman, the coming to maturity of a protagonist who encounters a sequential series of eccentric characters, each caught in illusions that comment on and instruct Vera's progress. Moreover, once Miss MacIntosh has awakened her, Vera takes off on a quest, placing the plot as a sort of romance—and as Northrup Frye reminds us [in *Anatomy of Criticism,* 1957], "the romance is naturally a sequential and processional form" leading through a series of adventures to a conflict between hero and enemy. In this way, then, the historical expectations of the bildungsroman meet the transhistorical, mythic—but still essentially linear—expectations of romance, both of which focus on the sequential series of enlightening moments that should, formally, culminate in knowledge, identity, and exaltation. Young, however, invokes these models of linear "progress" ironically. She subverts them, replacing the sequential with the simultaneous, the linear with the recurrent, chronology with duration. As a bildungsroman, Vera's story is oddly diffuse; Vera disappears for several hundred pages, little of her own experience appears in the novel, and though it ends in her approaching marriage, it does not culminate in her assumption of a stable or definable identity. Her quest proceeds ironically through the stage of the "perilous journey"—the long bus ride—but includes no "adventures" of the traditional sort. In the absence of the agnostic assumption that hero and villain can come into determinate conflict, or even that self and other can be defined as different (for "Every heart is the other heart"), the dialectical progress of the romance toward synthesis becomes impossible. In fact, plot itself becomes, at least in a traditional sense, impossible: the protagonist of Anne Tyler's *The Accidental Tourist* carries ***Miss MacIntosh, My Darling*** on planes because "It had the advantage of being plotless, as far as he could tell, but invariably interesting, so he could dip into it at random."

Young writes a lush, image-laden, circling prose that, as those reviewers who admired the novel saw, enacts and doubles her themes. In particular, her syntax abandons the linear model identified by Kristeva as basic to the historical conception of language, creating a unique and daring mode of feminine writing. Young repeats, develops, supplements, as if no signifier could fix meaning in any determinate way, as if the process of creating were approximate and the signified always deferred. Describing her month of knowing Miss MacIntosh, whom she can never clearly identify, Vera writes: "Where there was only water, the firmament laid upon the firmament, I should remember her as the lonely heart of all, even as she had been in that last month where the old values had shifted before my eyes, the old certainties had been broken and like the waves wandering and tossed as the sorrows of the human heart were enlarged beyond nature." This "where" that places the subject of the sentence becomes less rather than more determinate as the assertion unfolds: in some future

"I should remember her" as she was in the past, but between the unlocated past and future, the elided and absent present makes time in the sense of external history disappear, while the repetitive acts of consciousness place Vera and her story in women's time. And where, exactly, was there only water, firmament on firmament? At the very beginning of Genesis, before the spirit of God moves on the face of the waters to decree those divisions between Heaven, earth and seas—in short, before the advent of the patriarchal Word that crystalizes solid identity out of maternal fluidity and flux. Learning Miss MacIntosh, Vera relearns that maternal time and space, which is also the unseeded but fertile womb in which Esther Longtree creates her children and the darkened room in which Catherine Cartwheel entertains her callers. In the month Vera spends knowing Miss MacIntosh, lonely heart and matriarch of this feminine creative space, old values shift, old certainties break, and in place of predictable facts about external nature, Vera turns inward, to learn the enormous sorrows of the human heart. The dry land brought forth by the Word disappears, together with the old values and certainties erected upon it, as these become "like the waves wandering and tossed." In the heart, another dark interior chamber relegated by tradition to women, the fluid and the repetitive merge to sustain life. Young's novel comes from this heart, with its recurrent biological rhythms and its inescapable connections to women's subjective life.

The patriarchal Word has its comic representative in the novel: Titus Bonebreaker, Bible salesman, distributor of religious tracts and sidewalk preacher of salvation. A loud and incessant speaker for things metaphysical and teleological, Bonebreaker presses the Word on Miss MacIntosh, urging her to repent for sins she has not committed, and he gives her his own word, declaring an extravagant love that does not see her and proposing a marriage that does not take place. Aggressively and symbolically male—in their single embrace, Miss MacIntosh feels an embarrassing "protuberance between them"—Bonebreaker stands in sharp contrast to those characters who inhabit women's time. Bonebreaker speaks for the time of history, projective striving and culmination: "The end of time was always at hand, but Mr. Bonebreaker, nonetheless punctual, was always consulting his great, open-faced watch which did not lose a moment. . . . Every minute counted for Mr. Bonebreaker." He turns time to account, speaking ceaselessly to disseminate the Word of the impending end of time. But Mr. Bonebreaker's word is not good: when Miss MacIntosh reveals herself to him, showing her baldness and her missing breast, he turns and runs. Where he should, she thinks, speak words of acceptance, he is for once entirely speechless.

While women's time, as it guides Young's text, calls up an awareness of the unity of subjective life, enabling the process of "deep calling to deep," historical time as represented in Mr. Bonebreaker emphasizes instead the agonistic—conquest and conversion—that can only break bones. Mr. Bonebreaker's flight ends Miss MacIntosh's flirtation with history. Though she keeps his watch and his phallic black umbrella, though she cites the almanac in praise of the constructive use of time, she teaches Vera an ahistorical view of time and history. Vera learns from her the timeless, "essential loneliness of each," and her suicide shows Vera that death is not a single culmination and end of time but an ongoing, echoing loss: "Yet once more, Miss MacIntosh, my darling, and once more . . . yet once more, oh, my darling, washed by seas as the old sheep dog barks on and on." Miss MacIntosh is Vera's darling because she both starts and symbolizes Vera's recognition of her alliance with other women, and more generally with other beings who suffer isolation amid the accidents of history. Miss MacIntosh, bald reality become beautiful through this kinship of the heart and soul, allows Vera to recognize at the outset that "Every heart is the other heart," and enables her to marry that other heart at the end.

To explore a vision of life unified in the recurrent and monumental modalities of women's time is the goal and project of the novel; it is also the source of its strangeness, its experimental strategies, and of its absence from the emerging canon of postmodern epical fiction. ***Miss MacIntosh, My Darling*** differs from the epic narratives produced by contemporary men whose importance has been far more broadly established by critical studies; unlike Thomas Pynchon, John Barth, Robert Coover or Don DeLillo, Marguerite Young does not pack in the facts, data, information and news of the century. There are no elections, wars or depressions in Young's novel, no recent developments in politics or economics. The various actions are not set in any specified year. The New England coastal location where the novel begins is not identified by state or city, and the town in Indiana where the novel ends is not named. These choices, too, dissolve history. Seen in the context of its deliberate and consistent emphasis on telling women's time, Young's novel merits a closer look by a wider scholarly audience. (pp. 177-82)

Susan Strehle, "Telling Women's Time: 'Miss MacIntosh, My Darling'," in The Review of Contemporary Fiction, *Vol. 9, No. 3, Fall, 1989, pp. 177-182.*

Steven Shaviro (essay date Spring 1990)

[In the following essay, Shaviro discusses the thematic and stylistic complexity of Miss MacIntosh, My Darling, *maintaining that the work "has not yet been allowed into the canon or accorded a firm place in contemporary literature" because "[w]e simply have not yet learned how to read [it]."]*

Marguerite Young's only published novel, ***Miss MacIntosh, My Darling,*** occupies a singular place in recent American fiction. Despite all the recent re-evaluations of work by women writers, Young's book has not yet been allowed into the canon or accorded a firm place in contemporary literature. This lack of recognition is considered here to be a backhanded testimony to the novel's beauty, uniqueness, and strength. I suggest further that one sign of the importance of this text is its refusal to conform to our usual paradigms of either modernism or postmodernism. We simply have not yet learned how to read ***Miss MacIntosh, My Darling.***

Young's novel is daunting for several reasons. First is the sheer length of the book: 1,198 pages of dense prose. Second, the reader is overwhelmed by the exorbitance of Young's language—the long, paratactic sentences; the echoing and redundancy; the repetitions with subtle differences; the infinite variations; and the thick materiality of the words on the page. In addition, and perhaps most troubling for the critic accustomed to "metafictional" games, there is Young's admirable refusal to fetishize craft and form. Although ***Miss MacIntosh, My Darling*** is as formally intricate and deliberately crafted as any great twentieth-century work, it denies its readers the comfort of approaching it from the point of view that is satisfied with cataloguing allusions, tracing cross-references, and unraveling self-reflexive structures. ***Miss MacIntosh*** cannot be reduced to the totality of a linguistic structure or contained within the self-assured mastery of an authorial presence. It manifests an exacerbated self-consciousness, but one that is never self-confirming or self-enclosed. It moves out into the chaos and multiplicity of the world, rather than folding back upon itself to assert its own constitutive quality as language or consciousness. The result is that one cannot read ***Miss MacIntosh, My Darling*** without literally being overwhelmed and carried away, for its aesthetic effect is to multiply and intensify passions rather than to shape and contain them. The novel's pleonastic excess undermines the reader's endeavors to maintain critical distance and control.

If we enter into the labyrinthine language of ***Miss MacIntosh, My Darling,*** we quickly discover that there is nothing solid to hold onto—there are no obvious points of reference and no guideposts to show us the way. Our initial sense of disorientation is much the same as that experienced by Vera Cartwheel, the narrator: "There was now no landscape but the soul's, and that is the inexactitude, the ever shifting and the distant. . . . My life had been made up of just these disrelated, delusive images hovering only for a moment at the margin of consciousness, then passing like ships in the night, even ships manned by dead helmsmen, by ghostly crews, by one's own soul at large." Everything in this book is "disrelated, delusive," marginal, and fluctuating. ***Miss MacIntosh, My Darling*** is a novel without a center or a present. The soul is always "at large," never at home with itself.

Young's book is a delirious phantasmagoria of memories that cannot be recaptured and expectations that cannot be realized. It is an epic lament of loss and disappointment, perpetually in flight, moving at once toward an impossible future and an unregainable past. Lyrical expression proliferates throughout the novel in innumerable modes of puzzlement, nostalgia, anger, anguish, exhilaration, and despair. These outbursts indicate the priority of passion (or pathos) over character (or ethos).

The novel's language creates a continual falling apart of any possibility of internal coherence. ***Miss MacIntosh, My Darling*** is a nomadic text. Images proliferate and circulate at so rapid a pace that they are uprooted from any possibility of symbolic correspondence or of synecdochic participation in some deeper realm of essences. The novel is articulated horizontally rather than vertically, in the form of a quantitative accumulation of imagery with continual shifts of focus rather than that of a systematic series of distinctions based upon a rigid hierarchical organization. The richness of the novel defies objectification—nothing is ever merely what it seems; nothing is simply given once and for all. But this richness is immanent and not transcendent, realized in incessant metamorphoses rather than being anchored in archetypal meanings. There are no essences or fixed principles behind the restless flux of appearances. Within the novel, Mr. Spitzer stands out as the main seeker after symbolic harmonies and ultimate correspondences. But he is condemned never to find the resolution he seeks, not even in that finality of silence—that ground and zero degree of all symbols—that is death.

There is another reason for the book's rejection of symbolic correspondences. Whereas the logic and organization of most modernist and post-modernist texts are predominantly spatial, those of ***Miss MacIntosh*** are profoundly temporal. Time is crucial to every articulation of the book, although this is not a time of narrative progression or organic development. Rather, the book deploys a temporality of infinite windings and detours, one that is not centered in a present and that is nonlinear and nonteleological. This is so, first, because the novel is largely given over to the narrator's memories. In addition, one of Vera's discoveries is that memory itself is scarcely an accurate guide: "Memory is surrounded by the unknown, the void, and there is so much that we have not heard, much that we have not seen. Memory sometimes provides the one flower more than ever blossomed. Memory sometimes omits the only flower there really was. . . . Perhaps, in retrospection, every lost event must be changed by the illumination larger than that of any instant, larger than life." Since events are always lost and memory is never a simple representation of the past, the novel must hazard a mode of telling that cannot transcend or free itself from time, which is forever bound by temporal restrictions and yet ignores or violates the conventional laws of simultaneity and succession.

In the back-and-forth movement between Vera's narration of her journey to Indiana and her reminiscences of her childhood by the New England seashore, and in the slippage from her own experiences to the inner lives of the other characters, a variety of temporal rhythms is put into play—a multiplicity of durations (in a Bergsonian sense) that coexist and yet remain radically incompatible with one another and irreducible to any common measure. Everything is subjected to a complex temporal scansion; for this reason, it becomes difficult to isolate punctual events. Instead, most of the novel takes place in a kind of global, rhetorically amplified, and continually expanding or contracting imperfect tense. Actions are habitual and indefinitely repeatable, spread over vast periods of time without precise beginnings and endings; yet these actions are already relegated to the past, which is long over. This irrevocable "pastness" is a function less of the fact that Vera is remembering a vanished life than of the novel's overall focus upon moments never realized in any present; on forgotten secrets and futile, unfinished gestures; on lost opportunities and disappointed anticipations—"so many buried hopes, so many exhausted feelings which he [Mr. Spitzer] still must feel, even in retrospect." The time of progressive action and resolution is revoked, but any hope (such as Mr. Spitzer entertains) of escaping or negating the ravages of time is also denied.

In this suspension, the different characters live—or find it impossible to live—in different rhythms and experience vastly different cycles of expectation and disappointment. The simplest case is that of Vera's mother, the Opium Lady, whose hallucinations return with mechanical regularity (and even conform to the arbitrary order of the alphabet). But each of the other characters is similarly—if more complexly—defined by patterns of recurrence and temporal stasis, by transformations that deny them the repose of a fixed identity and yet lead nowhere. Against such a background, even the rare events that radically alter the shape of things (most notably, Vera's discovery of Miss MacIntosh's secret) cannot be narrated in a straightforward manner. These temporal turning points are themselves not punctual: they are slowly elaborated, in obsessive detail and at great length, only to be interrupted by other layers upon layers of reminiscences, not to be picked up again until many chapters later (the account of Vera's breakfast with Miss MacIntosh is dropped after page 298 and does not resume until page 859).

The narration of ***Miss MacIntosh, My Darling*** thus encompasses a plurality of different temporalities; it moves at wildly varying velocities. It gives an impression at once of rapid metamorphosis (on the level of individual images and their transformation), of slow alteration and development (on the level of the long, intricate, fluctuating sentences and paragraphs), and of recurrence or stasis (on the level of chapters, each of which establishes a single level of intensity focused upon a particular character, perspective, or situation). Even this stasis is the consequence of a mode of organization that is temporal rather than spatial.

Miss MacIntosh, My Darling **is a delirious phantasmagoria of memories that cannot be recaptured and expectations that cannot be realized. It is an epic lament of loss and disappointment, perpetually in flight, moving at once toward an impossible future and an unregainable past.**

—Steven Shaviro

The multiple temporal organization of ***Miss MacIntosh, My Darling*** thus is radically opposed to the spatializing premises of the (generally male) modernist aesthetic. Modernist writers such as Joyce and Pound—and their postmodern metafictional successors—work by orchestrating discontinuous fragments into a complex formal structure. The creative mind exerts its pressure against the refractoriness of reality. The process of shaping and spatially articulating an initially heterogeneous material generates a new kind of unity, a new totalization. For the traditional assumption of pregiven coherence on the side of what is represented or signified, modernism substitutes an active "phallic" overdetermination on the part of the signifier. Nothing could be further from the affective (and a-phallic) aesthetic of Young's writing. Although ***Miss MacIntosh*** does not assume an organic or pre-given unity, it is not organized around fragments. It is characterized instead by a delirious hypercontinuity of discourse. It does not unify disparate elements in a willful imposition from above; rather, it subtly differentiates within this immanent continuity, developing and making explicit its inchoate potentialities in a series of movements that well up from below. The plurality thus realized resists all pressures of totalization. No hierarchical organization, no distribution of oppositions and differences, no formal or phallic articulation is sufficient to contain it. The multiple and material specificity of the book's discourse is not a function of the ideality of a transcendental signifier.

This point about form can be restated in more general terms. Young's art is not one of fragments precisely because, for her, fragmentation is not a danger or a problem. In contrast to the elitist male modernist writers, she does not feel any compulsion to struggle against the chaos and democratic ferment of modern life; in contrast to so many postmodernist writers, she does not regard the decenteredness of contemporary existence with blankness, self-protective irony, or thinly disguised nostalgia. Rather than imposing ideas of order or mourning their absence, Young offers us a text that revels in the flux and confusion of immanent experience. In the deepest sense, order and disorder cannot really be opposed. The delirious multiplication of codes, axioms, and structuring principles is perhaps the most profound experience of chaos. "[T]he search for life, for love, for truth that does not fail" is what leads Vera Cartwheel into labyrinths of isolation, insanity, and illusion.

Every character in ***Miss MacIntosh, My Darling*** has his or her own fantasy of order, and every one of these fantasies ends in failure. The book is strewn with confusion, despair, and suicide; the one American myth absent from this very American book is the myth of success. But this very proliferation of fantasies, and of their inevitable frustrations and failures, constitutes the unmasterable plurality of the real. ***Miss MacIntosh, My Darling*** celebrates the bizarreness and intransigence of schizoid dislocation and deluded passion. It locates the beauty and materiality of the real in all that which is most improbable, outlandish, unsuccessful, or contradictory. This is why Young can proudly describe her novel as "the Song of Songs of schizophrenia" (see Charles Ruas, *Conversations with American Writers,* New York: McGraw-Hill, 1986, 121). The delirious aestheticism of her novel seems to cultivate and celebrate multiple errors—the mistaken and endlessly proliferating passions—for their own sakes.

These multiple perspectives are mutually contradictory and mutually exclusive: they never coalesce into one. What is "real" for Young is radical plurality—and not any possibility of the reduction of the many to a common measure. It is remarkable that there is virtually no conversation, no dialogue, anywhere in ***Miss MacIntosh, My Dar-***

ling. There are only monologues, each of which remains firmly entrenched in its own singularity. This is what accounts for Vera Cartwheel's special place in the book. As the narrator, her role is to transcribe these multiple singularities without normalizing or totalizing them. She is the recipient and the recorder, the ideal listener to those delirious discourses that the other characters direct at nobody in particular. She hears—or overhears—everyone else's confessions, but the communication is never reciprocal. At one point, Vera wistfully remarks that "I could have confessed much to Esther Longtree if she had been as much interested in my confessions as I had been in hers," but such is obviously not the case. Esther, like nearly all the other characters, is incapable of listening. Vera listens, but she can only address the reader. (It is significant that Vera ends up marrying a talkative but "stone deaf man," to whose bizarre declamations she can only tacitly respond, "I spelled out my name upon my lover's hand, for surely a woman must find some way by which to talk to the silence that she loved".) Vera's unique position at the point of interference of all these monologues allows her not to transcend or resolve the confusion, but to come to terms with—to accept and even delight in—the impossibility of so doing. In a world of failed desires, Vera is the only one who comes to realize the impossibility either of achieving one's fantasies or of ceasing to desire and to project them. She ultimately finds not "an ultimate harmony" opposed to chaos and built on solid ground, but "the beautiful malignancy of the ocean, of always moving waters like the dreams sweeping over the dreams."

In this pluralistic world of dreams and failures, Miss MacIntosh holds a special place. She is the pivot around whom the book turns, the lost object of Vera's desire. She appeals to Vera because the refusal of fantasy is itself the most powerful and seductive fantasy. If the monotonous variety of her mother's opium dreams seems "arid" to Vera, then conversely nothing seems richer, more fascinating, or more disturbing than Miss MacIntosh's quintessential nudity. Miss MacIntosh's ostensible rejection of imagination, her belief only in the literal, is grotesquely and beautifully embodied in her (dissimulated) baldness. Her bald skull—together with her amputated breast—*is* the reduction that she continually preaches: the bedrock of the purely literal, of a sterile world without imagination, "that sphere devoid of being . . . the rock where nothing grows." Yet such a literalization, inscribed in Miss MacIntosh's very flesh, is something that she cannot bear, that she can only seek to deny. It reduces her not to the common or the essential, but to a point of extreme uncategorizable singularity: "her face was as absolutely impersonal and expressionless as a face may be and still be human, and she was this monster moving toward me in the darkness."

Encountered in her chamber in the moonlight, without her red wig, Miss MacIntosh is shorn of all her distinguishing characteristics and even of a decidable gender. But this lack of definition, as of expression, absolutely particularizes her; it makes her an exceptional monstrosity rather than a human commonplace. Such nudity, such bare actuality, is the zero degree of fantasy—its extremity or its starting point, but not its negation. What is most actual is what is most fantastic. The simplicity Miss MacIntosh preaches cannot be adequated to the "essential baldness" that she nakedly embodies. A disguise is required to transform her actual barrenness into a representation of the plain and the straightforward, to invest her with that clearminded vigor that utterly scorns disguises. Thus, Miss MacIntosh's gospel of hard work, plain facts, and common sense is as excessive, self-deluded, and dependent upon illusion as any opium dream or utopian extravagance could possibly be. Her vociferous denial of the imaginary is itself an imaginary construct. Her unintended lesson to Vera is that "mediocrity has also its power to crumble into the most phantasmagoric dream that man has dreamed."

This is why there can be no opposition between the fantastic and the real. The real is embedded in the imaginary and not opposed to it; every actuality is discovered—or even produced—by a proliferation of fantasies, a movement of desire. This production is not contradicted by the fact that all desires are disappointed, all fantasies unrealized. If every apparent real is infected by unreality, this also means that the unreality of failure and disappointment is perfectly real in its own right. ***Miss MacIntosh, My Darling*** grants its own degree of actuality to everything that can be experienced or imagined. A delusion, a hallucination is a real event. There is a specific positive reality even to those things that are lost or absent:

> One still must accept that reality one found, no matter what it was or was not. For there was only one definition of reality, that it was real, real as my mother's opium dreams of scallop boats and the feet of satyrs and sails upon the waves, real as Mr. Spitzer's brother who might be the musician or the gambler, real as Miss MacIntosh's sand-colored face which had no hairline, real as a sea which had no surf-line, and real as that rock which was perched upon an angel's wing. Whatever one found was real was real, everyone I ever knew had said or in one way or another had proved, and even the unreal things were real, even those which were ignored, rejected, despised, abandoned, unloved, perhaps even unknown, never of fruit or flower.

This recovery of despised and forgotten realities is perhaps the most impressive achievement of Young's novel. The assertion that reality has to be imagined is not an idealistic one, for it is conditioned by an extreme sense of fatality. The reality that we imagine is not the one we choose, but the one by which we are constrained. It is composed not of our impositions, but of our failures. If the real is a hallucination, it is one of which we are the victims and the products, not the creators. The various characters do not possess their fantasies so much as they are possessed by them. I am tempted to apply to Young's novel the Wittgensteinian formula that Harold Bloom uses to describe Emerson: solipsism, when pushed to a sufficiently extreme point, becomes identical with absolute realism. In the case of ***Miss MacIntosh, My Darling,*** however, this solipsism-turned-realism, this terrifying sense of fatality, is that of all the characters and cannot be imputed to a single (authorial) consciousness. We are left with a multitude of failed constructions of the real, of experiences of disappointment, absence, and loss. The novel consists of nothing but illusions, yet it records nothing but disillusion. It swarms with an incredibly rich and various life, yet it is continually haunted by death. Death seems to permeate every moment, every extravagance, every desire, and every encounter.

Thus, Vera's discovery of Miss MacIntosh's baldness seems to lead inexorably to the latter's suicide. Even at the moment of revelation, Vera understands that what she has discovered is a kind of death: "I should hold to every moment as if I lived with a dying man, and I should protect her from her knowledge of herself"; and again, "I had never loved her in this life, and I might love her only in this death—when she was no more or when she had faded into all that she protested against, when she herself should be the phantom of a dead love, a face no one quite remembered." To violate Miss MacIntosh in her nakedness, to confront her with the evidence of her delirious singularity, is already to have killed her—and therefore is not to be able to forget her. Vera is condemned to love Miss MacIntosh and to have lost her, to love her precisely to the extent that she has lost her. Vera is eternally bound to her nursemaid's "impersonal and expressionless" figure, just as Cousin Hannah is forever haunted by her lost beloved, the woman she abandoned long ago on the mountaintop. Even more strangely, Mr. Spitzer is bound to his own absence, to that identical twin brother whose death seems to be his own. Mr. Spitzer is implicated in his own non-being, which is put into question to the outrageous extent that he is unable even to determine which of the two twins he is.

In all these cases, nothing can compensate for the blankness of loss because loss is not something that can be characterized or interpreted in any way. "Ah, what image was there of his love which had no image?" Death has no image; it is, Mr. Spitzer feels, a terrible mistake, but one that can never be rectified. This is why death is always at work, even (or especially) when it is ignored or denied: "for no matter how inclusive he tried to be, there was a factor missing, something beyond the encompassing of all." Death is this excess, this "factor missing" that our plans are never able to include but that haunts every fantasy and every projection precisely because it is absent.

To be alive is thus to be subject to a death, a fatality, whose insistence one must both mimic and evade. Each character in the book is defined by a particular fatality: for Vera's mother, it is the opium bottle (which she names Mr. Res Tacamah); for Esther Longtree, it is her body, the physical being that expands and contracts, enduring so many imaginary pregnancies. Mr. Spitzer's fatality is his resemblance to his vanished brother; Miss MacIntosh's is her baldness. Such a fatality determines both the positive existence of a character and its limit or point of destruction. The characters in this novel are defined by their passions; but the moment of a passion's greatest intensity is that at which it spends itself, or turns against itself, or encounters its own death. Thus, Miss MacIntosh's mania for simplicity is a consequence or an expression of her baldness, but for her actually to confront that baldness is to die. This is so for nearly all the characters: the utopian moment at which their fantasies are given body is also the instant at which they are destroyed. They are all essentially in the situation of the violinist who is as "afraid of music as of death," and who is fired from the orchestra after twenty years of flawless simulation of violin playing, when his bow touches the strings for the first and only time.

The characters are thus forever split against themselves. They continually strive to defer the realization of their dreams, even though it is only these dreams that impel them. They seek to postpone the fatal encounters in which they can alone be defined. But they evade the finality of death only at the price of assuming the burden of dying at every instant within their lives. Esther can never actually give birth, as she would negate her eternal pregnancy by doing so. Instead, she must endure a multitude of interrupted births, the stillborn whose little corpses she strews across the landscape. Similarly, Vera's mother defers her life through drugs in order thereby to defer that life's consequences, which are the pain of love and, ultimately, old age and death. In the endless but sterile multiplications of her dreams, nothing is lost, and the dead always return; but this only marks the extent to which everything she experiences or imagines has already been taken from her and is always already subtended by death. Mr. Spitzer, for his part, seems to have lost the very possibility of death; he questions it interminably, and he sets it adrift in oceans of doubt and skepticism and an inability to act. Yet the undecidability of his death is only the countereffect of his "having died, even in this sad life time, so many fugitive deaths, having so often rehearsed his ultimate passage."

The extraordinary characters who populate the byways and digressions of ***Miss MacIntosh, My Darling*** thus lead lives without growth or progression and die deaths without finality. They are continually subject to death and continually occupied with evading it. Even suicide is not a conclusion: it is because Miss MacIntosh has vanished that Vera is condemned forever to look for her. Thus, nothing can ever come to an end in this novel—there is no ultimate achievement but only the incessant repetitions of obsession. The chord that would complete our harmonies, and for which Mr. Spitzer spends his life searching, is always already lost. But this perpetual inconclusion is the very life of passion the novel recounts. If there is no all-encompassing harmony, there is also no final cadence and, hence, no return to silence. Young's novel is not concerned with first and last things but with all the points in between, which are actually far more intense and important. ***Miss MacIntosh, My Darling*** burrows into the most intimate, hidden moments of women's and men's lives; it obsessively focuses upon, and draws out to amazing lengths, those traumatic and yet all-too-fleeting moments of transition that actually define human experience. It rejects ultimates or fixed states, the better to trace the painful movements of becoming. Young explores the relation of consciousness to what it is not able to dominate and conserve: to death, to pregnancy and birth, to the failure to die or to be born or to give birth, to blindness and deafness and other instances of deprivation, to change and loss, to frustrated or unexpressed passion, to lost loves and deluded ambitions. Passion is necessarily bound to loss, if only because it cannot guarantee or even predict its outcome.

It is thus in terms of loss and ignorance that, at the end of the novel, Vera describes her own pregnancy: "I do not know the night in which I conceived as I do not know the night in which I was conceived. My pearls were lost, were strewn upon the ground like strings of hailstones which had melted in the summer clouds or like dews which had fallen from the heavens, and never would I find my pearls in the morning light, never even look for them." ***Miss MacIntosh, My Darling*** explores and populates the obscure spaces of this evanescent night of the passions. It does not recover what has been lost but—more important—enters into the very heart of loss itself. Young's book is dedicated to "all dead loves and all remembered things," to the lost chords and interrupted births that exceed any measure of achievement or possession. (pp. 213-22)

Steven Shaviro, "Lost Chords and Interrupted Births: Marguerite Young's Exorbitant Vision," in Critique: Studies in Contemporary Fiction, *Vol. XXXI, No. 3, Spring, 1990, pp. 213-22.*

FURTHER READING

Biography

Duncan, Erika. "The Literary Life—and How It's Lived: A Reminiscence with Marguerite Young." *Book Forum* III, No. 3 (1977): 426-35.

Duncan, one of Young's former students, details Young's personal life and offers her impression of Young as a teacher.

Criticism

Burke, Kenneth. "The Work of Regeneration." *The Kenyon Review* VII, No. 4 (Autumn 1945): 696-700

Characterizes *Angel in the Forest* as a "meditative" work that inspires profound thought.

Duncan, Erika. "Variations on Infinity: An Epic Elegy for All of Creation." *The Review of Contemporary Fiction* 9, No. 3 (Fall 1989): 183-87.

Illustrates how Young uses complex narrative structures to explore psychological and philosophical issues in her works.

Edelstein, J. M. "Miss MacIntosh, Her Darling." *The New Republic* 153, No. 14 (2 October 1965): 28-9.

Negative assessment of *Miss MacIntosh, My Darling,* which Edelstein asserts is comprised of "unsorted elements, complicated movements, insoluble obscurity—all to the detriment of artistic moderation."

"Glug." *Newsweek* LXVI, No. 11 (13 September 1965): 90.

Responds negatively to *Miss MacIntosh, My Darling,* commenting: "Miss Young's elephantine novel is a real bramble. Everything about it is excessive, overripe, plummy, 'feminine.' As to narrative—well, forget it."

Shaik, Fatima. "*Miss MacIntosh, My Darling:* Poetry of the Subconscious." *The Review of Contemporary Fiction* 9, No. 3 (Fall 1989): 188-90.

Explains how Young uses poetic language in *Miss MacIntosh, My Darling* to explore the subconscious mind.

Shaviro, Steven. "Exorbitance and Death: Marguerite Young's Vision." *The Review of Contemporary Fiction* 9, No. 3 (Fall 1989): 191-97.

Attempts to "define the singularity of [*Miss MacIntosh, My Darling*] in relation to the English-language modernist canon."

"New Harmonists." *The Times Literary Supplement,* No. 3,394 (16 March 1967): 221.

Maintains that *Angel in the Forest* contains many inaccuracies and irrelevant details, and lacks character development.

Zinnes, Harriet. "Miss MacIntosh, Mythic and Real." *Prairie Schooner* XXXIX (1966): 361-63.

Offers praise for Young's narrative style and treatment of reality and fantasy in *Miss MacIntosh, My Darling.* Zinnes observes: "This is a novel that is the history of the self of our time, tortured by dream and reality alike, burdened with the flesh and the dream, seeking both, desiring both and seeking in each the other."

Additional coverage of Young's life and career is contained in the following sources published by Gale Research: *Contemporary Authors,* Vols. 13-16 and *Contemporary Authors Permanent Series,* Vol. 1

☐ Contemporary Literary Criticism

Indexes

Literary Criticism Series
Cumulative Author Index
Cumulative Nationality Index

How to Use This Index

The main references

Calvino, Italo
1923-1985.....**CLC 5, 8, 11, 22, 33, 39, 73; SSC 3**

list all author entries in the following Gale Literary Criticism series:

BLC = *Black Literature Criticism*
CLC = *Contemporary Literary Criticism*
CLR = *Children's Literature Review*
CMLC = *Classical and Medieval Literature Criticism*
DA = *DISCovering Authors*
DC = *Drama Criticism*
HLC = *Hispanic Literature Criticism*
LC = *Literature Criticism from 1400 to 1800*
NCLC = *Nineteenth-Century Literature Criticism*
PC = *Poetry Criticism*
SSC = *Short Story Criticism*
TCLC = *Twentieth-Century Literary Criticism*
WLC = *World Literature Criticism, 1500 to the Present*

The cross-references

See also CANR 23; CA 85-88;
obituary CA 116

list all author entries in the following Gale biographical and literary sources:

AAYA = *Authors & Artists for Young Adults*
AITN = *Authors in the News*
BEST = *Bestsellers*
BW = *Black Writers*
CA = *Contemporary Authors*
CAAS = *Contemporary Authors Autobiography Series*
CABS = *Contemporary Authors Bibliographical Series*
CANR = *Contemporary Authors New Revision Series*
CAP = *Contemporary Authors Permanent Series*
CDALB = *Concise Dictionary of American Literary Biography*
CDBLB = *Concise Dictionary of British Literary Biography*
DLB = *Dictionary of Literary Biography*
DLBD = *Dictionary of Literary Biography Documentary Series*
DLBY = *Dictionary of Literary Biography Yearbook*
HW = *Hispanic Writers*
JRDA = *Junior DISCovering Authors*
MAICYA = *Major Authors and Illustrators for Children and Young Adults*
MTCW = *Major 20th-Century Writers*
SAAS = *Something about the Author Autobiography Series*
SATA = *Something about the Author*
YABC = *Yesterday's Authors of Books for Children*

Literary Criticism Series Cumulative Author Index

Antoine, Marc
See Proust, (Valentin-Louis-George-Eugene-) Marcel

Antoninus, Brother
See Everson, William (Oliver)

Antonioni, Michelangelo 1912- ..... **CLC 20**
See also CA 73-76

Antschel, Paul 1920-1970....... **CLC 10, 19**
See also Celan, Paul
See also CA 85-88; CANR 33; MTCW

Anwar, Chairil 1922-1949 .... **TCLC 22**
See also CA 121

Apollinaire, Guillaume .. **TCLC 3, 8, 51; PC 7**
See also Kostrowitzki, Wilhelm Apollinaris de

Appelfeld, Aharon 1932- .... **CLC 23, 47**
See also CA 112; 133

Apple, Max (Isaac) 1941-........ **CLC 9, 33**
See also CA 81-84; CANR 19; DLB 130

Appleman, Philip (Dean) 1926-..... **CLC 51**
See also CA 13-16R; CAAS 18; CANR 6, 29

Appleton, Lawrence
See Lovecraft, H(oward) P(hillips)

Apteryx
See Eliot, T(homas) S(tearns)

Apuleius, (Lucius Madaurensis)
125(?)-175(?) .... **CMLC 1**

Aquin, Hubert 1929-1977.......... **CLC 15**
See also CA 105; DLB 53

Aragon, Louis 1897-1982........ **CLC 3, 22**
See also CA 69-72; 108; CANR 28; DLB 72; MTCW

Arany, Janos 1817-1882......... **NCLC 34**

Arbuthnot, John 1667-1735.......... **LC 1**
See also DLB 101

Archer, Herbert Winslow
See Mencken, H(enry) L(ouis)

Archer, Jeffrey (Howard) 1940- .... **CLC 28**
See also BEST 89:3; CA 77-80; CANR 22

Archer, Jules 1915- .... **CLC 12**
See also CA 9-12R; CANR 6; SAAS 5; SATA 4

Archer, Lee
See Ellison, Harlan

Arden, John 1930- .... **CLC 6, 13, 15**
See also CA 13-16R; CAAS 4; CANR 31; DLB 13; MTCW

Arenas, Reinaldo
1943-1990 .... **CLC 41; HLC**
See also CA 124; 128; 133; HW

Arendt, Hannah 1906-1975 .... **CLC 66**
See also CA 17-20R; 61-64; CANR 26; MTCW

Aretino, Pietro 1492-1556 .... **LC 12**

Arghezi, Tudor.................... **CLC 80**
See also Theodorescu, Ion N.

Arguedas, Jose Maria
1911-1969 .... **CLC 10, 18**
See also CA 89-92; DLB 113; HW

Argueta, Manlio 1936-............ **CLC 31**
See also CA 131; HW

Ariosto, Ludovico 1474-1533......... **LC 6**

Aristides
See Epstein, Joseph

Aristophanes
450B.C.-385B.C.... **CMLC 4; DA; DC 2**

Arlt, Roberto (Godofredo Christophersen)
1900-1942 .... **TCLC 29; HLC**
See also CA 123; 131; HW

Armah, Ayi Kwei 1939-.... **CLC 5, 33; BLC**
See also BW; CA 61-64; CANR 21; DLB 117; MTCW

Armatrading, Joan 1950-.......... **CLC 17**
See also CA 114

Arnette, Robert
See Silverberg, Robert

Arnim, Achim von (Ludwig Joachim von Arnim) 1781-1831 .... **NCLC 5**
See also DLB 90

Arnim, Bettina von 1785-1859.... **NCLC 38**
See also DLB 90

Arnold, Matthew
1822-1888 ..... **NCLC 6, 29; DA; PC 5; WLC**
See also CDBLB 1832-1890; DLB 32, 57

Arnold, Thomas 1795-1842 ...... **NCLC 18**
See also DLB 55

Arnow, Harriette (Louisa) Simpson
1908-1986 .... **CLC 2, 7, 18**
See also CA 9-12R; 118; CANR 14; DLB 6; MTCW; SATA 42, 47

Arp, Hans
See Arp, Jean

Arp, Jean 1887-1966............... **CLC 5**
See also CA 81-84; 25-28R; CANR 42

Arrabal
See Arrabal, Fernando

Arrabal, Fernando 1932- ... **CLC 2, 9, 18, 58**
See also CA 9-12R; CANR 15

Arrick, Fran..................... **CLC 30**

Artaud, Antonin 1896-1948 ..... **TCLC 3, 36**
See also CA 104

Arthur, Ruth M(abel) 1905-1979.... **CLC 12**
See also CA 9-12R; 85-88; CANR 4; SATA 7, 26

Artsybashev, Mikhail (Petrovich)
1878-1927 .... **TCLC 31**

Arundel, Honor (Morfydd)
1919-1973 .... **CLC 17**
See also CA 21-22; 41-44R; CAP 2; SATA 4, 24

Asch, Sholem 1880-1957 .... **TCLC 3**
See also CA 105

Ash, Shalom
See Asch, Sholem

Ashbery, John (Lawrence)
1927- ...... **CLC 2, 3, 4, 6, 9, 13, 15, 25, 41, 77**
See also CA 5-8R; CANR 9, 37; DLB 5; DLBY 81; MTCW

Ashdown, Clifford
See Freeman, R(ichard) Austin

Ashe, Gordon
See Creasey, John

Ashton-Warner, Sylvia (Constance)
1908-1984 .... **CLC 19**
See also CA 69-72; 112; CANR 29; MTCW

Asimov, Isaac
1920-1992 ...... **CLC 1, 3, 9, 19, 26, 76**
See also BEST 90:2; CA 1-4R; 137; CANR 2, 19, 36; CLR 12; DLB 8; DLBY 92; JRDA; MAICYA; MTCW; SATA 1, 26, 74

Astley, Thea (Beatrice May)
1925- .... **CLC 41**
See also CA 65-68; CANR 11, 43

Aston, James
See White, T(erence) H(anbury)

Asturias, Miguel Angel
1899-1974 .... **CLC 3, 8, 13; HLC**
See also CA 25-28; 49-52; CANR 32; CAP 2; DLB 113; HW; MTCW

Atares, Carlos Saura
See Saura (Atares), Carlos

Atheling, William
See Pound, Ezra (Weston Loomis)

Atheling, William, Jr.
See Blish, James (Benjamin)

Atherton, Gertrude (Franklin Horn)
1857-1948 .... **TCLC 2**
See also CA 104; DLB 9, 78

Atherton, Lucius
See Masters, Edgar Lee

Atkins, Jack
See Harris, Mark

Atticus
See Fleming, Ian (Lancaster)

Atwood, Margaret (Eleanor)
1939- ..... **CLC 2, 3, 4, 8, 13, 15, 25, 44; DA; PC 8; SSC 2; WLC**
See also BEST 89:2; CA 49-52; CANR 3, 24, 33; DLB 53; MTCW; SATA 50

Aubigny, Pierre d'
See Mencken, H(enry) L(ouis)

Aubin, Penelope 1685-1731(?)........ **LC 9**
See also DLB 39

Auchincloss, Louis (Stanton)
1917- .... **CLC 4, 6, 9, 18, 45**
See also CA 1-4R; CANR 6, 29; DLB 2; DLBY 80; MTCW

Auden, W(ystan) H(ugh)
1907-1973 ...... **CLC 1, 2, 3, 4, 6, 9, 11, 14, 43; DA; PC 1; WLC**
See also CA 9-12R; 45-48; CANR 5; CDBLB 1914-1945; DLB 10, 20; MTCW

Audiberti, Jacques 1900-1965 ...... **CLC 38**
See also CA 25-28R

Auel, Jean M(arie) 1936-.......... **CLC 31**
See also AAYA 7; BEST 90:4; CA 103; CANR 21

Auerbach, Erich 1892-1957 .... **TCLC 43**
See also CA 118

Augier, Emile 1820-1889 .... **NCLC 31**

August, John
See De Voto, Bernard (Augustine)

Augustine, St. 354-430........... **CMLC 6**

Aurelius
See Bourne, Randolph S(illiman)

Baroja (y Nessi), Pio
1872-1956 . . . . **TCLC 8; HLC**
See also CA 104

Baron, David
See Pinter, Harold

Baron Corvo
See Rolfe, Frederick (William Serafino Austin Lewis Mary)

Barondess, Sue K(aufman)
1926-1977 . . . . **CLC 8**
See also Kaufman, Sue
See also CA 1-4R; 69-72; CANR 1

Baron de Teive
See Pessoa, Fernando (Antonio Nogueira)

Barres, Maurice 1862-1923 . . . . **TCLC 47**
See also DLB 123

Barreto, Afonso Henrique de Lima
See Lima Barreto, Afonso Henrique de

Barrett, (Roger) Syd 1946- . . . . **CLC 35**
See also Pink Floyd

Barrett, William (Christopher)
1913-1992 . . . . **CLC 27**
See also CA 13-16R; 139; CANR 11

Barrie, J(ames) M(atthew)
1860-1937 . . . . **TCLC 2**
See also CA 104; 136; CDBLB 1890-1914; CLR 16; DLB 10; MAICYA; YABC 1

Barrington, Michael
See Moorcock, Michael (John)

Barrol, Grady
See Bograd, Larry

Barry, Mike
See Malzberg, Barry N(athaniel)

Barry, Philip 1896-1949 . . . . **TCLC 11**
See also CA 109; DLB 7

Bart, Andre Schwarz
See Schwarz-Bart, Andre

Barth, John (Simmons)
1930- . . . . . . **CLC 1, 2, 3, 5, 7, 9, 10, 14, 27, 51; SSC 10**
See also AITN 1, 2; CA 1-4R; CABS 1; CANR 5, 23; DLB 2; MTCW

Barthelme, Donald
1931-1989 . . . . . . **CLC 1, 2, 3, 5, 6, 8, 13, 23, 46, 59; SSC 2**
See also CA 21-24R; 129; CANR 20; DLB 2; DLBY 80, 89; MTCW; SATA 7, 62

Barthelme, Frederick 1943- . . . . **CLC 36**
See also CA 114; 122; DLBY 85

Barthes, Roland (Gerard)
1915-1980 . . . . **CLC 24**
See also CA 130; 97-100; MTCW

Barzun, Jacques (Martin) 1907- . . . . **CLC 51**
See also CA 61-64; CANR 22

Bashevis, Isaac
See Singer, Isaac Bashevis

Bashkirtseff, Marie 1859-1884 . . . **NCLC 27**

Basho
See Matsuo Basho

Bass, Kingsley B., Jr.
See Bullins, Ed

Bass, Rick 1958- . . . . **CLC 79**
See also CA 126

Bassani, Giorgio 1916- . . . . **CLC 9**
See also CA 65-68; CANR 33; DLB 128; MTCW

Bastos, Augusto (Antonio) Roa
See Roa Bastos, Augusto (Antonio)

Bataille, Georges 1897-1962 . . . . **CLC 29**
See also CA 101; 89-92

Bates, H(erbert) E(rnest)
1905-1974 . . . . **CLC 46; SSC 10**
See also CA 93-96; 45-48; CANR 34; MTCW

Bauchart
See Camus, Albert

Baudelaire, Charles
1821-1867 . . . . . **NCLC 6, 29; DA; PC 1; WLC**

Baudrillard, Jean 1929- . . . . **CLC 60**

Baum, L(yman) Frank 1856-1919 . . . **TCLC 7**
See also CA 108; 133; CLR 15; DLB 22; JRDA; MAICYA; MTCW; SATA 18

Baum, Louis F.
See Baum, L(yman) Frank

Baumbach, Jonathan 1933- . . . . . . **CLC 6, 23**
See also CA 13-16R; CAAS 5; CANR 12; DLBY 80; MTCW

Bausch, Richard (Carl) 1945- . . . . . . **CLC 51**
See also CA 101; CAAS 14; CANR 43; DLB 130

Baxter, Charles 1947- . . . . **CLC 45, 78**
See also CA 57-60; CANR 40; DLB 130

Baxter, George Owen
See Faust, Frederick (Schiller)

Baxter, James K(eir) 1926-1972 . . . . **CLC 14**
See also CA 77-80

Baxter, John
See Hunt, E(verette) Howard, Jr.

Bayer, Sylvia
See Glassco, John

Beagle, Peter S(oyer) 1939- . . . . **CLC 7**
See also CA 9-12R; CANR 4; DLBY 80; SATA 60

Bean, Normal
See Burroughs, Edgar Rice

Beard, Charles A(ustin)
1874-1948 . . . . **TCLC 15**
See also CA 115; DLB 17; SATA 18

Beardsley, Aubrey 1872-1898 . . . . . **NCLC 6**

Beattie, Ann
1947- . . . . **CLC 8, 13, 18, 40, 63; SSC 11**
See also BEST 90:2; CA 81-84; DLBY 82; MTCW

Beattie, James 1735-1803 . . . . **NCLC 25**
See also DLB 109

Beauchamp, Kathleen Mansfield 1888-1923
See Mansfield, Katherine
See also CA 104; 134; DA

Beaumarchais, Pierre-Augustin Caron de
1732-1799 . . . . **DC 4**

Beauvoir, Simone (Lucie Ernestine Marie Bertrand) de
1908-1986 . . . . **CLC 1, 2, 4, 8, 14, 31, 44, 50, 71; DA; WLC**
See also CA 9-12R; 118; CANR 28; DLB 72; DLBY 86; MTCW

Becker, Jurek 1937- . . . . **CLC 7, 19**
See also CA 85-88; DLB 75

Becker, Walter 1950- . . . . **CLC 26**

Beckett, Samuel (Barclay)
1906-1989 . . . . . . **CLC 1, 2, 3, 4, 6, 9, 10, 11, 14, 18, 29, 57, 59; DA; WLC**
See also CA 5-8R; 130; CANR 33; CDBLB 1945-1960; DLB 13, 15; DLBY 90; MTCW

Beckford, William 1760-1844 . . . . **NCLC 16**
See also DLB 39

Beckman, Gunnel 1910- . . . . **CLC 26**
See also CA 33-36R; CANR 15; CLR 25; MAICYA; SAAS 9; SATA 6

Becque, Henri 1837-1899 . . . . **NCLC 3**

Beddoes, Thomas Lovell
1803-1849 . . . . **NCLC 3**
See also DLB 96

Bedford, Donald F.
See Fearing, Kenneth (Flexner)

Beecher, Catharine Esther
1800-1878 . . . . **NCLC 30**
See also DLB 1

Beecher, John 1904-1980 . . . . **CLC 6**
See also AITN 1; CA 5-8R; 105; CANR 8

Beer, Johann 1655-1700 . . . . **LC 5**

Beer, Patricia 1924- . . . . **CLC 58**
See also CA 61-64; CANR 13; DLB 40

Beerbohm, Henry Maximilian
1872-1956 . . . . **TCLC 1, 24**
See also CA 104; DLB 34, 100

Begiebing, Robert J(ohn) 1946- . . . . . **CLC 70**
See also CA 122; CANR 40

Behan, Brendan
1923-1964 . . . . **CLC 1, 8, 11, 15, 79**
See also CA 73-76; CANR 33; CDBLB 1945-1960; DLB 13; MTCW

Behn, Aphra
1640(?)-1689 . . . . **LC 1; DA; DC 4; WLC**
See also DLB 39, 80, 131

Behrman, S(amuel) N(athaniel)
1893-1973 . . . . **CLC 40**
See also CA 13-16; 45-48; CAP 1; DLB 7, 44

Belasco, David 1853-1931 . . . . **TCLC 3**
See also CA 104; DLB 7

Belcheva, Elisaveta 1893- . . . . **CLC 10**

Beldone, Phil "Cheech"
See Ellison, Harlan

Beleno
See Azuela, Mariano

Belinski, Vissarion Grigoryevich
1811-1848 . . . . **NCLC 5**

Belitt, Ben 1911- . . . . **CLC 22**
See also CA 13-16R; CAAS 4; CANR 7; DLB 5

Bell, James Madison
1826-1902 . . . . **TCLC 43; BLC**
See also BW; CA 122; 124; DLB 50

Bell, Madison (Smartt) 1957- . . . . . . **CLC 41**
See also CA 111; CANR 28

Bell, Marvin (Hartley) 1937- . . . . . **CLC 8, 31**
See also CA 21-24R; CAAS 14; DLB 5; MTCW

Bell, W. L. D.
See Mencken, H(enry) L(ouis)

Bellamy, Atwood C.
See Mencken, H(enry) L(ouis)

Bellamy, Edward 1850-1898 ...... **NCLC 4**
See also DLB 12

Bellin, Edward J.
See Kuttner, Henry

Belloc, (Joseph) Hilaire (Pierre)
1870-1953 .... **TCLC 7, 18**
See also CA 106; DLB 19, 100; YABC 1

Belloc, Joseph Peter Rene Hilaire
See Belloc, (Joseph) Hilaire (Pierre)

Belloc, Joseph Pierre Hilaire
See Belloc, (Joseph) Hilaire (Pierre)

Belloc, M. A.
See Lowndes, Marie Adelaide (Belloc)

Bellow, Saul
1915- ...... **CLC 1, 2, 3, 6, 8, 10, 13, 15, 25, 33, 34, 63, 79; DA; SSC 14; WLC**
See also AITN 2; BEST 89:3; CA 5-8R; CABS 1; CANR 29; CDALB 1941-1968; DLB 2, 28; DLBD 3; DLBY 82; MTCW

Belser, Reimond Karel Maria de
1929- .... **CLC 14**

Bely, Andrey .... **TCLC 7**
See also Bugayev, Boris Nikolayevich

Benary, Margot
See Benary-Isbert, Margot

Benary-Isbert, Margot 1889-1979... **CLC 12**
See also CA 5-8R; 89-92; CANR 4; CLR 12; MAICYA; SATA 2, 21

Benavente (y Martinez), Jacinto
1866-1954 .... **TCLC 3**
See also CA 106; 131; HW; MTCW

Benchley, Peter (Bradford)
1940- .... **CLC 4, 8**
See also AITN 2; CA 17-20R; CANR 12, 35; MTCW; SATA 3

Benchley, Robert (Charles)
1889-1945 .... **TCLC 1**
See also CA 105; DLB 11

Benedikt, Michael 1935- .... **CLC 4, 14**
See also CA 13-16R; CANR 7; DLB 5

Benet, Juan 1927-................ **CLC 28**
See also CA 143

Benet, Stephen Vincent
1898-1943 .... **TCLC 7; SSC 10**
See also CA 104; DLB 4, 48, 102; YABC 1

Benet, William Rose 1886-1950 ... **TCLC 28**
See also CA 118; DLB 45

Benford, Gregory (Albert) 1941-.... **CLC 52**
See also CA 69-72; CANR 12, 24; DLBY 82

Bengtsson, Frans (Gunnar)
1894-1954 .... **TCLC 48**

Benjamin, David
See Slavitt, David R(ytman)

Benjamin, Lois
See Gould, Lois

Benjamin, Walter 1892-1940...... **TCLC 39**

Benn, Gottfried 1886-1956......... **TCLC 3**
See also CA 106; DLB 56

Bennett, Alan 1934- .... **CLC 45, 77**
See also CA 103; CANR 35; MTCW

Bennett, (Enoch) Arnold
1867-1931 .... **TCLC 5, 20**
See also CA 106; CDBLB 1890-1914; DLB 10, 34, 98

Bennett, Elizabeth
See Mitchell, Margaret (Munnerlyn)

Bennett, George Harold 1930-
See Bennett, Hal
See also BW; CA 97-100

Bennett, Hal .... **CLC 5**
See also Bennett, George Harold
See also DLB 33

Bennett, Jay 1912-............... **CLC 35**
See also AAYA 10; CA 69-72; CANR 11, 42; JRDA; SAAS 4; SATA 27, 41

Bennett, Louise (Simone)
1919- .... **CLC 28; BLC**
See also DLB 117

Benson, E(dward) F(rederic)
1867-1940 .... **TCLC 27**
See also CA 114; DLB 135

Benson, Jackson J. 1930-.......... **CLC 34**
See also CA 25-28R; DLB 111

Benson, Sally 1900-1972 .... **CLC 17**
See also CA 19-20; 37-40R; CAP 1; SATA 1, 27, 35

Benson, Stella 1892-1933......... **TCLC 17**
See also CA 117; DLB 36

Bentham, Jeremy 1748-1832 ..... **NCLC 38**
See also DLB 107

Bentley, E(dmund) C(lerihew)
1875-1956 .... **TCLC 12**
See also CA 108; DLB 70

Bentley, Eric (Russell) 1916-....... **CLC 24**
See also CA 5-8R; CANR 6

Beranger, Pierre Jean de
1780-1857 .... **NCLC 34**

Berger, Colonel
See Malraux, (Georges-)Andre

Berger, John (Peter) 1926- ...... **CLC 2, 19**
See also CA 81-84; DLB 14

Berger, Melvin H. 1927- .... **CLC 12**
See also CA 5-8R; CANR 4; CLR 32; SAAS 2; SATA 5

Berger, Thomas (Louis)
1924- .... **CLC 3, 5, 8, 11, 18, 38**
See also CA 1-4R; CANR 5, 28; DLB 2; DLBY 80; MTCW

Bergman, (Ernst) Ingmar
1918- .... **CLC 16, 72**
See also CA 81-84; CANR 33

Bergson, Henri 1859-1941 .... **TCLC 32**

Bergstein, Eleanor 1938- .... **CLC 4**
See also CA 53-56; CANR 5

Berkoff, Steven 1937-............. **CLC 56**
See also CA 104

Bermant, Chaim (Icyk) 1929- ...... **CLC 40**
See also CA 57-60; CANR 6, 31

Bern, Victoria
See Fisher, M(ary) F(rances) K(ennedy)

Bernanos, (Paul Louis) Georges
1888-1948 .... **TCLC 3**
See also CA 104; 130; DLB 72

Bernard, April 1956- .... **CLC 59**
See also CA 131

Bernhard, Thomas
1931-1989 .... **CLC 3, 32, 61**
See also CA 85-88; 127; CANR 32; DLB 85, 124; MTCW

Berrigan, Daniel 1921-............. **CLC 4**
See also CA 33-36R; CAAS 1; CANR 11, 43; DLB 5

Berrigan, Edmund Joseph Michael, Jr.
1934-1983
See Berrigan, Ted
See also CA 61-64; 110; CANR 14

Berrigan, Ted..................... **CLC 37**
See also Berrigan, Edmund Joseph Michael, Jr.
See also DLB 5

Berry, Charles Edward Anderson 1931-
See Berry, Chuck
See also CA 115

Berry, Chuck..................... **CLC 17**
See also Berry, Charles Edward Anderson

Berry, Jonas
See Ashbery, John (Lawrence)

Berry, Wendell (Erdman)
1934- .... **CLC 4, 6, 8, 27, 46**
See also AITN 1; CA 73-76; DLB 5, 6

Berryman, John
1914-1972 ...... **CLC 1, 2, 3, 4, 6, 8, 10, 13, 25, 62**
See also CA 13-16; 33-36R; CABS 2; CANR 35; CAP 1; CDALB 1941-1968; DLB 48; MTCW

Bertolucci, Bernardo 1940- .... **CLC 16**
See also CA 106

Bertrand, Aloysius 1807-1841 .... **NCLC 31**

Bertran de Born c. 1140-1215 ..... **CMLC 5**

Besant, Annie (Wood) 1847-1933 ... **TCLC 9**
See also CA 105

Bessie, Alvah 1904-1985........... **CLC 23**
See also CA 5-8R; 116; CANR 2; DLB 26

Bethlen, T. D.
See Silverberg, Robert

Beti, Mongo................. **CLC 27; BLC**
See also Biyidi, Alexandre

Betjeman, John
1906-1984 .... **CLC 2, 6, 10, 34, 43**
See also CA 9-12R; 112; CANR 33; CDBLB 1945-1960; DLB 20; DLBY 84; MTCW

Bettelheim, Bruno 1903-1990 ...... **CLC 79**
See also CA 81-84; 131; CANR 23; MTCW

Betti, Ugo 1892-1953 .... **TCLC 5**
See also CA 104

Betts, Doris (Waugh) 1932-.... **CLC 3, 6, 28**
See also CA 13-16R; CANR 9; DLBY 82

Bevan, Alistair
See Roberts, Keith (John Kingston)

Beynon, John
See Harris, John (Wyndham Parkes Lucas) Beynon

Bialik, Chaim Nachman 1873-1934 .... **TCLC 25**

Bickerstaff, Isaac
See Swift, Jonathan

Bidart, Frank 1939- .... **CLC 33**
See also CA 140

Bienek, Horst 1930- .... **CLC 7, 11**
See also CA 73-76; DLB 75

Bierce, Ambrose (Gwinett) 1842-1914(?) .... **TCLC 1, 7, 44; DA; SSC 9; WLC**
See also CA 104; 139; CDALB 1865-1917; DLB 11, 12, 23, 71, 74

Billings, Josh
See Shaw, Henry Wheeler

Billington, Rachel 1942- .... **CLC 43**
See also AITN 2; CA 33-36R

Binyon, T(imothy) J(ohn) 1936- .... **CLC 34**
See also CA 111; CANR 28

Bioy Casares, Adolfo 1914- .... **CLC 4, 8, 13; HLC**
See also CA 29-32R; CANR 19, 43; DLB 113; HW; MTCW

Bird, C.
See Ellison, Harlan

Bird, Cordwainer
See Ellison, Harlan

Bird, Robert Montgomery 1806-1854 .... **NCLC 1**

Birney, (Alfred) Earle 1904- .... **CLC 1, 4, 6, 11**
See also CA 1-4R; CANR 5, 20; DLB 88; MTCW

Bishop, Elizabeth 1911-1979 ...... **CLC 1, 4, 9, 13, 15, 32; DA; PC 3**
See also CA 5-8R; 89-92; CABS 2; CANR 26; CDALB 1968-1988; DLB 5; MTCW; SATA 24

Bishop, John 1935- .... **CLC 10**
See also CA 105

Bissett, Bill 1939- .... **CLC 18**
See also CA 69-72; CANR 15; DLB 53; MTCW

Bitov, Andrei (Georgievich) 1937- ... **CLC 57**
See also CA 142

Biyidi, Alexandre 1932-
See Beti, Mongo
See also BW; CA 114; 124; MTCW

Bjarme, Brynjolf
See Ibsen, Henrik (Johan)

Bjornson, Bjornstjerne (Martinius) 1832-1910 .... **TCLC 7, 37**
See also CA 104

Black, Robert
See Holdstock, Robert P.

Blackburn, Paul 1926-1971 ...... **CLC 9, 43**
See also CA 81-84; 33-36R; CANR 34; DLB 16; DLBY 81

Black Elk 1863-1950 .... **TCLC 33**

Black Hobart
See Sanders, (James) Ed(ward)

Blacklin, Malcolm
See Chambers, Aidan

Blackmore, R(ichard) D(oddridge) 1825-1900 .... **TCLC 27**
See also CA 120; DLB 18

Blackmur, R(ichard) P(almer) 1904-1965 .... **CLC 2, 24**
See also CA 11-12; 25-28R; CAP 1; DLB 63

Black Tarantula, The
See Acker, Kathy

Blackwood, Algernon (Henry) 1869-1951 .... **TCLC 5**
See also CA 105

Blackwood, Caroline 1931- .... **CLC 6, 9**
See also CA 85-88; CANR 32; DLB 14; MTCW

Blade, Alexander
See Hamilton, Edmond; Silverberg, Robert

Blaga, Lucian 1895-1961 .... **CLC 75**

Blair, Eric (Arthur) 1903-1950
See Orwell, George
See also CA 104; 132; DA; MTCW; SATA 29

Blais, Marie-Claire 1939- .... **CLC 2, 4, 6, 13, 22**
See also CA 21-24R; CAAS 4; CANR 38; DLB 53; MTCW

Blaise, Clark 1940- .... **CLC 29**
See also AITN 2; CA 53-56; CAAS 3; CANR 5; DLB 53

Blake, Nicholas
See Day Lewis, C(ecil)
See also DLB 77

Blake, William 1757-1827 ..... **NCLC 13, 37; DA; WLC**
See also CDBLB 1789-1832; DLB 93; MAICYA; SATA 30

Blasco Ibanez, Vicente 1867-1928 .... **TCLC 12**
See also CA 110; 131; HW; MTCW

Blatty, William Peter 1928- .... **CLC 2**
See also CA 5-8R; CANR 9

Bleeck, Oliver
See Thomas, Ross (Elmore)

Blessing, Lee 1949- .... **CLC 54**

Blish, James (Benjamin) 1921-1975 .... **CLC 14**
See also CA 1-4R; 57-60; CANR 3; DLB 8; MTCW; SATA 66

Bliss, Reginald
See Wells, H(erbert) G(eorge)

Blixen, Karen (Christentze Dinesen) 1885-1962
See Dinesen, Isak
See also CA 25-28; CANR 22; CAP 2; MTCW; SATA 44

Bloch, Robert (Albert) 1917- .... **CLC 33**
See also CA 5-8R; CANR 5; DLB 44; SATA 12

Blok, Alexander (Alexandrovich) 1880-1921 .... **TCLC 5**
See also CA 104

Blom, Jan
See Breytenbach, Breyten

Bloom, Harold 1930- .... **CLC 24**
See also CA 13-16R; CANR 39; DLB 67

Bloomfield, Aurelius
See Bourne, Randolph S(illiman)

Blount, Roy (Alton), Jr. 1941- ..... **CLC 38**
See also CA 53-56; CANR 10, 28; MTCW

Bloy, Leon 1846-1917 .... **TCLC 22**
See also CA 121; DLB 123

Blume, Judy (Sussman) 1938- ... **CLC 12, 30**
See also AAYA 3; CA 29-32R; CANR 13, 37; CLR 2, 15; DLB 52; JRDA; MAICYA; MTCW; SATA 2, 31

Blunden, Edmund (Charles) 1896-1974 .... **CLC 2, 56**
See also CA 17-18; 45-48; CAP 2; DLB 20, 100; MTCW

Bly, Robert (Elwood) 1926- .... **CLC 1, 2, 5, 10, 15, 38**
See also CA 5-8R; CANR 41; DLB 5; MTCW

Bobette
See Simenon, Georges (Jacques Christian)

Boccaccio, Giovanni 1313-1375
See also SSC 10

Bochco, Steven 1943- .... **CLC 35**
See also CA 124; 138

Bodenheim, Maxwell 1892-1954 ... **TCLC 44**
See also CA 110; DLB 9, 45

Bodker, Cecil 1927- .... **CLC 21**
See also CA 73-76; CANR 13; CLR 23; MAICYA; SATA 14

Boell, Heinrich (Theodor) 1917-1985
See Boll, Heinrich (Theodor)
See also CA 21-24R; 116; CANR 24; DA; DLB 69; DLBY 85; MTCW

Boerne, Alfred
See Doeblin, Alfred

Bogan, Louise 1897-1970 ..... **CLC 4, 39, 46**
See also CA 73-76; 25-28R; CANR 33; DLB 45; MTCW

Bogarde, Dirk .... **CLC 19**
See also Van Den Bogarde, Derek Jules Gaspard Ulric Niven
See also DLB 14

Bogosian, Eric 1953- .... **CLC 45**
See also CA 138

Bograd, Larry 1953- .... **CLC 35**
See also CA 93-96; SATA 33

Boiardo, Matteo Maria 1441-1494 .... **LC 6**

Boileau-Despreaux, Nicolas 1636-1711 .... **LC 3**

Boland, Eavan (Aisling) 1944- ... **CLC 40, 67**
See also CA 143; DLB 40

Boll, Heinrich (Theodor) 1917-1985 .... **CLC 2, 3, 6, 9, 11, 15, 27, 39, 72; WLC**
See also Boell, Heinrich (Theodor)
See also DLB 69; DLBY 85

Bolt, Lee
See Faust, Frederick (Schiller)

Bolt, Robert (Oxton) 1924- .... **CLC 14**
See also CA 17-20R; CANR 35; DLB 13; MTCW

Bomkauf
See Kaufman, Bob (Garnell)

Breslin, Jimmy .... **CLC 4, 43**
See also Breslin, James
See also AITN 1

Bresson, Robert 1907- .... **CLC 16**
See also CA 110

Breton, Andre 1896-1966 . . . **CLC 2, 9, 15, 54**
See also CA 19-20; 25-28R; CANR 40; CAP 2; DLB 65; MTCW

Breytenbach, Breyten 1939(?)- . . **CLC 23, 37**
See also CA 113; 129

Bridgers, Sue Ellen 1942- .... **CLC 26**
See also AAYA 8; CA 65-68; CANR 11, 36; CLR 18; DLB 52; JRDA; MAICYA; SAAS 1; SATA 22

Bridges, Robert (Seymour) 1844-1930 .... **TCLC 1**
See also CA 104; CDBLB 1890-1914; DLB 19, 98

Bridie, James .... **TCLC 3**
See also Mavor, Osborne Henry
See also DLB 10

Brin, David 1950- .... **CLC 34**
See also CA 102; CANR 24; SATA 65

Brink, Andre (Philippus) 1935- .... **CLC 18, 36**
See also CA 104; CANR 39; MTCW

Brinsmead, H(esba) F(ay) 1922- .... **CLC 21**
See also CA 21-24R; CANR 10; MAICYA; SAAS 5; SATA 18

Brittain, Vera (Mary) 1893(?)-1970 .... **CLC 23**
See also CA 13-16; 25-28R; CAP 1; MTCW

Broch, Hermann 1886-1951 .... **TCLC 20**
See also CA 117; DLB 85, 124

Brock, Rose
See Hansen, Joseph

Brodkey, Harold 1930- .... **CLC 56**
See also CA 111; DLB 130

Brodsky, Iosif Alexandrovich 1940-
See Brodsky, Joseph
See also AITN 1; CA 41-44R; CANR 37; MTCW

Brodsky, Joseph .... **CLC 4, 6, 13, 36, 50**
See also Brodsky, Iosif Alexandrovich

Brodsky, Michael Mark 1948- ..... **CLC 19**
See also CA 102; CANR 18, 41

Bromell, Henry 1947- .... **CLC 5**
See also CA 53-56; CANR 9

Bromfield, Louis (Brucker) 1896-1956 .... **TCLC 11**
See also CA 107; DLB 4, 9, 86

Broner, E(sther) M(asserman) 1930- .... **CLC 19**
See also CA 17-20R; CANR 8, 25; DLB 28

Bronk, William 1918- .... **CLC 10**
See also CA 89-92; CANR 23

Bronstein, Lev Davidovich
See Trotsky, Leon

Bronte, Anne 1820-1849 .... **NCLC 4**
See also DLB 21

Bronte, Charlotte 1816-1855 . . . **NCLC 3, 8, 33; DA; WLC**
See also CDBLB 1832-1890; DLB 21

Bronte, (Jane) Emily 1818-1848 .... **NCLC 16, 35; DA; PC 8; WLC**
See also CDBLB 1832-1890; DLB 21, 32

Brooke, Frances 1724-1789 .... **LC 6**
See also DLB 39, 99

Brooke, Henry 1703(?)-1783 .... **LC 1**
See also DLB 39

Brooke, Rupert (Chawner) 1887-1915 .... **TCLC 2, 7; DA; WLC**
See also CA 104; 132; CDBLB 1914-1945; DLB 19; MTCW

Brooke-Haven, P.
See Wodehouse, P(elham) G(renville)

Brooke-Rose, Christine 1926- ...... **CLC 40**
See also CA 13-16R; DLB 14

Brookner, Anita 1928- ...... **CLC 32, 34, 51**
See also CA 114; 120; CANR 37; DLBY 87; MTCW

Brooks, Cleanth 1906- .... **CLC 24**
See also CA 17-20R; CANR 33, 35; DLB 63; MTCW

Brooks, George
See Baum, L(yman) Frank

Brooks, Gwendolyn 1917- ...... **CLC 1, 2, 4, 5, 15, 49; BLC; DA; PC 7; WLC**
See also AITN 1; BW; CA 1-4R; CANR 1, 27; CDALB 1941-1968; CLR 27; DLB 5, 76; MTCW; SATA 6

Brooks, Mel .... **CLC 12**
See also Kaminsky, Melvin
See also DLB 26

Brooks, Peter 1938- .... **CLC 34**
See also CA 45-48; CANR 1

Brooks, Van Wyck 1886-1963 ...... **CLC 29**
See also CA 1-4R; CANR 6; DLB 45, 63, 103

Brophy, Brigid (Antonia) 1929- .... **CLC 6, 11, 29**
See also CA 5-8R; CAAS 4; CANR 25; DLB 14; MTCW

Brosman, Catharine Savage 1934- .... **CLC 9**
See also CA 61-64; CANR 21

Brother Antoninus
See Everson, William (Oliver)

Broughton, T(homas) Alan 1936- ... **CLC 19**
See also CA 45-48; CANR 2, 23

Broumas, Olga 1949- .... **CLC 10, 73**
See also CA 85-88; CANR 20

Brown, Charles Brockden 1771-1810 .... **NCLC 22**
See also CDALB 1640-1865; DLB 37, 59, 73

Brown, Christy 1932-1981 .... **CLC 63**
See also CA 105; 104; DLB 14

Brown, Claude 1937- .... **CLC 30; BLC**
See also AAYA 7; BW; CA 73-76

Brown, Dee (Alexander) 1908- . . **CLC 18, 47**
See also CA 13-16R; CAAS 6; CANR 11; DLBY 80; MTCW; SATA 5

Brown, George
See Wertmueller, Lina

Brown, George Douglas 1869-1902 .... **TCLC 28**

Brown, George Mackay 1921- .... **CLC 5, 48**
See also CA 21-24R; CAAS 6; CANR 12, 37; DLB 14, 27; MTCW; SATA 35

Brown, (William) Larry 1951- ...... **CLC 73**
See also CA 130; 134

Brown, Moses
See Barrett, William (Christopher)

Brown, Rita Mae 1944- ..... **CLC 18, 43, 79**
See also CA 45-48; CANR 2, 11, 35; MTCW

Brown, Roderick (Langmere) Haig-
See Haig-Brown, Roderick (Langmere)

Brown, Rosellen 1939- .... **CLC 32**
See also CA 77-80; CAAS 10; CANR 14

Brown, Sterling Allen 1901-1989 .... **CLC 1, 23, 59; BLC**
See also BW; CA 85-88; 127; CANR 26; DLB 48, 51, 63; MTCW

Brown, Will
See Ainsworth, William Harrison

Brown, William Wells 1813-1884 .... **NCLC 2; BLC; DC 1**
See also DLB 3, 50

Browne, (Clyde) Jackson 1948(?)- ... **CLC 21**
See also CA 120

Browning, Elizabeth Barrett 1806-1861 ..... **NCLC 1, 16; DA; PC 6; WLC**
See also CDBLB 1832-1890; DLB 32

Browning, Robert 1812-1889 .... **NCLC 19; DA; PC 2**
See also CDBLB 1832-1890; DLB 32; YABC 1

Browning, Tod 1882-1962 .... **CLC 16**
See also CA 141; 117

Bruccoli, Matthew J(oseph) 1931- . . **CLC 34**
See also CA 9-12R; CANR 7; DLB 103

Bruce, Lenny .... **CLC 21**
See also Schneider, Leonard Alfred

Bruin, John
See Brutus, Dennis

Brulls, Christian
See Simenon, Georges (Jacques Christian)

Brunner, John (Kilian Houston) 1934- .... **CLC 8, 10**
See also CA 1-4R; CAAS 8; CANR 2, 37; MTCW

Brutus, Dennis 1924- .... **CLC 43; BLC**
See also BW; CA 49-52; CAAS 14; CANR 2, 27, 42; DLB 117

Bryan, C(ourtlandt) D(ixon) B(arnes) 1936- .... **CLC 29**
See also CA 73-76; CANR 13

Bryan, Michael
See Moore, Brian

Bryant, William Cullen 1794-1878 .... **NCLC 6; DA**
See also CDALB 1640-1865; DLB 3, 43, 59

Bryusov, Valery Yakovlevich 1873-1924 .... **TCLC 10**
See also CA 107

Buchan, John 1875-1940 .... **TCLC 41**
See also CA 108; DLB 34, 70; YABC 2

Buchanan, George 1506-1582 .... **LC 4**

Buchheim, Lothar-Guenther 1918- . . . **CLC 6**
See also CA 85-88

Buchner, (Karl) Georg
1813-1837 . . . . **NCLC 26**

Buchwald, Art(hur) 1925- . . . . **CLC 33**
See also AITN 1; CA 5-8R; CANR 21; MTCW; SATA 10

Buck, Pearl S(ydenstricker)
1892-1973 . . . . **CLC 7, 11, 18; DA**
See also AITN 1; CA 1-4R; 41-44R; CANR 1, 34; DLB 9, 102; MTCW; SATA 1, 25

Buckler, Ernest 1908-1984. . . . . **CLC 13**
See also CA 11-12; 114; CAP 1; DLB 68; SATA 47

Buckley, Vincent (Thomas)
1925-1988 . . . . **CLC 57**
See also CA 101

Buckley, William F(rank), Jr.
1925- . . . . **CLC 7, 18, 37**
See also AITN 1; CA 1-4R; CANR 1, 24; DLBY 80; MTCW

Buechner, (Carl) Frederick
1926- . . . . **CLC 2, 4, 6, 9**
See also CA 13-16R; CANR 11, 39; DLBY 80; MTCW

Buell, John (Edward) 1927- . . . . **CLC 10**
See also CA 1-4R; DLB 53

Buero Vallejo, Antonio 1916- . . . **CLC 15, 46**
See also CA 106; CANR 24; HW; MTCW

Bufalino, Gesualdo 1920(?)- . . . . **CLC 74**

Bugayev, Boris Nikolayevich 1880-1934
See Bely, Andrey
See also CA 104

Bukowski, Charles
1920-1994 . . . . **CLC 2, 5, 9, 41, 82**
See also CA 17-20R; CANR 40; DLB 5, 130; MTCW

Bulgakov, Mikhail (Afanas'evich)
1891-1940 . . . . **TCLC 2, 16**
See also CA 105

Bulgya, Alexander Alexandrovich
1901-1956 . . . . **TCLC 53**
See also Fadeyev, Alexander
See also CA 117

Bullins, Ed 1935- . . . . **CLC 1, 5, 7; BLC**
See also BW; CA 49-52; CAAS 16; CANR 24; DLB 7, 38; MTCW

Bulwer-Lytton, Edward (George Earle Lytton)
1803-1873 . . . . **NCLC 1**
See also DLB 21

Bunin, Ivan Alexeyevich
1870-1953 . . . . **TCLC 6; SSC 5**
See also CA 104

Bunting, Basil 1900-1985. . . . **CLC 10, 39, 47**
See also CA 53-56; 115; CANR 7; DLB 20

Bunuel, Luis 1900-1983 . . **CLC 16, 80; HLC**
See also CA 101; 110; CANR 32; HW

Bunyan, John 1628-1688 . . **LC 4; DA; WLC**
See also CDBLB 1660-1789; DLB 39

Burford, Eleanor
See Hibbert, Eleanor Alice Burford

Burgess, Anthony
CLC 1, 2, 4, 5, 8, 10, 13, 15, 22, 40, 62, 81
See also Wilson, John (Anthony) Burgess
See also AITN 1; CDBLB 1960 to Present; DLB 14

Burke, Edmund
1729(?)-1797 . . . . **LC 7; DA; WLC**
See also DLB 104

Burke, Kenneth (Duva)
1897-1993 . . . . **CLC 2, 24**
See also CA 5-8R; 143; CANR 39; DLB 45, 63; MTCW

Burke, Leda
See Garnett, David

Burke, Ralph
See Silverberg, Robert

Burney, Fanny 1752-1840 . . . . **NCLC 12**
See also DLB 39

Burns, Robert
1759-1796 . . . . . . **LC 3; DA; PC 6; WLC**
See also CDBLB 1789-1832; DLB 109

Burns, Tex
See L'Amour, Louis (Dearborn)

Burnshaw, Stanley 1906- . . . . . **CLC 3, 13, 44**
See also CA 9-12R; DLB 48

Burr, Anne 1937- . . . . **CLC 6**
See also CA 25-28R

Burroughs, Edgar Rice
1875-1950 . . . . **TCLC 2, 32**
See also CA 104; 132; DLB 8; MTCW; SATA 41

Burroughs, William S(eward)
1914- . . . . **CLC 1, 2, 5, 15, 22, 42, 75; DA; WLC**
See also AITN 2; CA 9-12R; CANR 20; DLB 2, 8, 16; DLBY 81; MTCW

Burton, Richard F. 1821-1890. . . . **NCLC 42**
See also DLB 55

Busch, Frederick 1941- . . . **CLC 7, 10, 18, 47**
See also CA 33-36R; CAAS 1; DLB 6

Bush, Ronald 1946- . . . . **CLC 34**
See also CA 136

Bustos, F(rancisco)
See Borges, Jorge Luis

Bustos Domecq, H(onorio)
See Bioy Casares, Adolfo; Borges, Jorge Luis

Butler, Octavia E(stelle) 1947- . . . . . **CLC 38**
See also BW; CA 73-76; CANR 12, 24, 38; DLB 33; MTCW

Butler, Robert Olen (Jr.) 1945-. . . . . **CLC 81**
See also CA 112

Butler, Samuel 1612-1680 . . . . **LC 16**
See also DLB 101, 126

Butler, Samuel
1835-1902 . . . . . . **TCLC 1, 33; DA; WLC**
See also CA 104; CDBLB 1890-1914; DLB 18, 57

Butler, Walter C.
See Faust, Frederick (Schiller)

Butor, Michel (Marie Francois)
1926- . . . . **CLC 1, 3, 8, 11, 15**
See also CA 9-12R; CANR 33; DLB 83; MTCW

Buzo, Alexander (John) 1944- . . . . . . **CLC 61**
See also CA 97-100; CANR 17, 39

Buzzati, Dino 1906-1972 . . . . **CLC 36**
See also CA 33-36R

Byars, Betsy (Cromer) 1928- . . . . **CLC 35**
See also CA 33-36R; CANR 18, 36; CLR 1, 16; DLB 52; JRDA; MAICYA; MTCW; SAAS 1; SATA 4, 46

Byatt, A(ntonia) S(usan Drabble)
1936- . . . . **CLC 19, 65**
See also CA 13-16R; CANR 13, 33; DLB 14; MTCW

Byrne, David 1952-. . . . . **CLC 26**
See also CA 127

Byrne, John Keyes 1926-. . . . . **CLC 19**
See also Leonard, Hugh
See also CA 102

Byron, George Gordon (Noel)
1788-1824 . . . . . . **NCLC 2, 12; DA; WLC**
See also CDBLB 1789-1832; DLB 96, 110

C.3.3.
See Wilde, Oscar (Fingal O'Flahertie Wills)

Caballero, Fernan 1796-1877. . . . . **NCLC 10**

Cabell, James Branch 1879-1958 . . . **TCLC 6**
See also CA 105; DLB 9, 78

Cable, George Washington
1844-1925 . . . . **TCLC 4; SSC 4**
See also CA 104; DLB 12, 74

Cabral de Melo Neto, Joao 1920- . . . **CLC 76**

Cabrera Infante, G(uillermo)
1929- . . . . **CLC 5, 25, 45; HLC**
See also CA 85-88; CANR 29; DLB 113; HW; MTCW

Cade, Toni
See Bambara, Toni Cade

Cadmus
See Buchan, John

Caedmon fl. 658-680. . . . . **CMLC 7**

Caeiro, Alberto
See Pessoa, Fernando (Antonio Nogueira)

Cage, John (Milton, Jr.) 1912- . . . . . **CLC 41**
See also CA 13-16R; CANR 9

Cain, G.
See Cabrera Infante, G(uillermo)

Cain, Guillermo
See Cabrera Infante, G(uillermo)

Cain, James M(allahan)
1892-1977 . . . . **CLC 3, 11, 28**
See also AITN 1; CA 17-20R; 73-76; CANR 8, 34; MTCW

Caine, Mark
See Raphael, Frederic (Michael)

Calasso, Roberto 1941- . . . . **CLC 81**
See also CA 143

Calderon de la Barca, Pedro
1600-1681 . . . . **LC 23; DC 3**

Caldwell, Erskine (Preston)
1903-1987 . . . . **CLC 1, 8, 14, 50, 60**
See also AITN 1; CA 1-4R; 121; CAAS 1; CANR 2, 33; DLB 9, 86; MTCW

Caldwell, (Janet Miriam) Taylor (Holland)
1900-1985 . . . . **CLC 2, 28, 39**
See also CA 5-8R; 116; CANR 5

Calhoun, John Caldwell 1782-1850 .... **NCLC 15**
See also DLB 3

Calisher, Hortense 1911- .... **CLC 2, 4, 8, 38**
See also CA 1-4R; CANR 1, 22; DLB 2; MTCW

Callaghan, Morley Edward 1903-1990 .... **CLC 3, 14, 41, 65**
See also CA 9-12R; 132; CANR 33; DLB 68; MTCW

Calvino, Italo 1923-1985 ..... **CLC 5, 8, 11, 22, 33, 39, 73; SSC 3**
See also CA 85-88; 116; CANR 23; MTCW

Cameron, Carey 1952- .... **CLC 59**
See also CA 135

Cameron, Peter 1959- .... **CLC 44**
See also CA 125

Campana, Dino 1885-1932 .... **TCLC 20**
See also CA 117; DLB 114

Campbell, John W(ood, Jr.) 1910-1971 .... **CLC 32**
See also CA 21-22; 29-32R; CANR 34; CAP 2; DLB 8; MTCW

Campbell, Joseph 1904-1987 .... **CLC 69**
See also AAYA 3; BEST 89:2; CA 1-4R; 124; CANR 3, 28; MTCW

Campbell, (John) Ramsey 1946- .... **CLC 42**
See also CA 57-60; CANR 7

Campbell, (Ignatius) Roy (Dunnachie) 1901-1957 .... **TCLC 5**
See also CA 104; DLB 20

Campbell, Thomas 1777-1844 .... **NCLC 19**
See also DLB 93

Campbell, Wilfred .... **TCLC 9**
See also Campbell, William

Campbell, William 1858(?)-1918
See Campbell, Wilfred
See also CA 106; DLB 92

Campos, Alvaro de
See Pessoa, Fernando (Antonio Nogueira)

Camus, Albert 1913-1960 .... **CLC 1, 2, 4, 9, 11, 14, 32, 63, 69; DA; DC 2; SSC 9; WLC**
See also CA 89-92; DLB 72; MTCW

Canby, Vincent 1924- .... **CLC 13**
See also CA 81-84

Cancale
See Desnos, Robert

Canetti, Elias 1905- ...... **CLC 3, 14, 25, 75**
See also CA 21-24R; CANR 23; DLB 85, 124; MTCW

Canin, Ethan 1960- .... **CLC 55**
See also CA 131; 135

Cannon, Curt
See Hunter, Evan

Cape, Judith
See Page, P(atricia) K(athleen)

Capek, Karel 1890-1938 ..... **TCLC 6, 37; DA; DC 1; WLC**
See also CA 104; 140

Capote, Truman 1924-1984 ...... **CLC 1, 3, 8, 13, 19, 34, 38, 58; DA; SSC 2; WLC**
See also CA 5-8R; 113; CANR 18; CDALB 1941-1968; DLB 2; DLBY 80, 84; MTCW

Capra, Frank 1897-1991 .... **CLC 16**
See also CA 61-64; 135

Caputo, Philip 1941- .... **CLC 32**
See also CA 73-76; CANR 40

Card, Orson Scott 1951- .... **CLC 44, 47, 50**
See also CA 102; CANR 27; MTCW

Cardenal (Martinez), Ernesto 1925- .... **CLC 31; HLC**
See also CA 49-52; CANR 2, 32; HW; MTCW

Carducci, Giosue 1835-1907 .... **TCLC 32**

Carew, Thomas 1595(?)-1640 .... **LC 13**
See also DLB 126

Carey, Ernestine Gilbreth 1908- .... **CLC 17**
See also CA 5-8R; SATA 2

Carey, Peter 1943- .... **CLC 40, 55**
See also CA 123; 127; MTCW

Carleton, William 1794-1869 ...... **NCLC 3**

Carlisle, Henry (Coffin) 1926- ...... **CLC 33**
See also CA 13-16R; CANR 15

Carlsen, Chris
See Holdstock, Robert P.

Carlson, Ron(ald F.) 1947- .... **CLC 54**
See also CA 105; CANR 27

Carlyle, Thomas 1795-1881 .. **NCLC 22; DA**
See also CDBLB 1789-1832; DLB 55

Carman, (William) Bliss 1861-1929 .... **TCLC 7**
See also CA 104; DLB 92

Carnegie, Dale 1888-1955 .... **TCLC 53**

Carossa, Hans 1878-1956 .... **TCLC 48**
See also DLB 66

Carpenter, Don(ald Richard) 1931- .... **CLC 41**
See also CA 45-48; CANR 1

Carpentier (y Valmont), Alejo 1904-1980 .... **CLC 8, 11, 38; HLC**
See also CA 65-68; 97-100; CANR 11; DLB 113; HW

Carr, Emily 1871-1945 .... **TCLC 32**
See also DLB 68

Carr, John Dickson 1906-1977 ...... **CLC 3**
See also CA 49-52; 69-72; CANR 3, 33; MTCW

Carr, Philippa
See Hibbert, Eleanor Alice Burford

Carr, Virginia Spencer 1929- .... **CLC 34**
See also CA 61-64; DLB 111

Carrier, Roch 1937- .... **CLC 13, 78**
See also CA 130; DLB 53

Carroll, James P. 1943(?)- .... **CLC 38**
See also CA 81-84

Carroll, Jim 1951- .... **CLC 35**
See also CA 45-48; CANR 42

Carroll, Lewis .... **NCLC 2; WLC**
See also Dodgson, Charles Lutwidge
See also CDBLB 1832-1890; CLR 2, 18; DLB 18; JRDA

Carroll, Paul Vincent 1900-1968 .... **CLC 10**
See also CA 9-12R; 25-28R; DLB 10

Carruth, Hayden 1921- .... **CLC 4, 7, 10, 18**
See also CA 9-12R; CANR 4, 38; DLB 5; MTCW; SATA 47

Carson, Rachel Louise 1907-1964 ... **CLC 71**
See also CA 77-80; CANR 35; MTCW; SATA 23

Carter, Angela (Olive) 1940-1992 ...... **CLC 5, 41, 76; SSC 13**
See also CA 53-56; 136; CANR 12, 36; DLB 14; MTCW; SATA 66; SATA-Obit 70

Carter, Nick
See Smith, Martin Cruz

Carver, Raymond 1938-1988 ... **CLC 22, 36, 53, 55; SSC 8**
See also CA 33-36R; 126; CANR 17, 34; DLB 130; DLBY 84, 88; MTCW

Cary, (Arthur) Joyce (Lunel) 1888-1957 .... **TCLC 1, 29**
See also CA 104; CDBLB 1914-1945; DLB 15, 100

Casanova de Seingalt, Giovanni Jacopo 1725-1798 .... **LC 13**

Casares, Adolfo Bioy
See Bioy Casares, Adolfo

Casely-Hayford, J(oseph) E(phraim) 1866-1930 .... **TCLC 24; BLC**
See also CA 123

Casey, John (Dudley) 1939- .... **CLC 59**
See also BEST 90:2; CA 69-72; CANR 23

Casey, Michael 1947- .... **CLC 2**
See also CA 65-68; DLB 5

Casey, Patrick
See Thurman, Wallace (Henry)

Casey, Warren (Peter) 1935-1988 ... **CLC 12**
See also CA 101; 127

Casona, Alejandro .... **CLC 49**
See also Alvarez, Alejandro Rodriguez

Cassavetes, John 1929-1989 .... **CLC 20**
See also CA 85-88; 127

Cassill, R(onald) V(erlin) 1919- ... **CLC 4, 23**
See also CA 9-12R; CAAS 1; CANR 7; DLB 6

Cassity, (Allen) Turner 1929- .... **CLC 6, 42**
See also CA 17-20R; CAAS 8; CANR 11; DLB 105

Castaneda, Carlos 1931(?)- .... **CLC 12**
See also CA 25-28R; CANR 32; HW; MTCW

Castedo, Elena 1937- .... **CLC 65**
See also CA 132

Castedo-Ellerman, Elena
See Castedo, Elena

Castellanos, Rosario 1925-1974 .... **CLC 66; HLC**
See also CA 131; 53-56; DLB 113; HW

Castelvetro, Lodovico 1505-1571 ..... **LC 12**

Castiglione, Baldassare 1478-1529 ... **LC 12**

Castle, Robert
See Hamilton, Edmond

Castro, Guillen de 1569-1631 .... **LC 19**

Castro, Rosalia de 1837-1885 ..... **NCLC 3**

Ch'ien Chung-shu 1910- . . . . **CLC 22**
See also CA 130; MTCW

Child, L. Maria
See Child, Lydia Maria

Child, Lydia Maria 1802-1880 . . . . **NCLC 6**
See also DLB 1, 74; SATA 67

Child, Mrs.
See Child, Lydia Maria

Child, Philip 1898-1978 . . . . **CLC 19, 68**
See also CA 13-14; CAP 1; SATA 47

Childress, Alice
1920- . . . . **CLC 12, 15; BLC; DC 4**
See also AAYA 8; BW; CA 45-48; CANR 3, 27; CLR 14; DLB 7, 38; JRDA; MAICYA; MTCW; SATA 7, 48

Chislett, (Margaret) Anne 1943- . . . . **CLC 34**

Chitty, Thomas Willes 1926- . . . . **CLC 11**
See also Hinde, Thomas
See also CA 5-8R

Chomette, Rene Lucien 1898-1981 . . **CLC 20**
See also Clair, Rene
See also CA 103

Chopin, Kate . . . . **TCLC 5, 14; DA; SSC 8**
See also Chopin, Katherine
See also CDALB 1865-1917; DLB 12, 78

Chopin, Katherine 1851-1904
See Chopin, Kate
See also CA 104; 122

Chretien de Troyes
c. 12th cent. - . . . . **CMLC 10**

Christie
See Ichikawa, Kon

Christie, Agatha (Mary Clarissa)
1890-1976 . . . . . . **CLC 1, 6, 8, 12, 39, 48**
See also AAYA 9; AITN 1, 2; CA 17-20R; 61-64; CANR 10, 37; CDBLB 1914-1945; DLB 13, 77; MTCW; SATA 36

Christie, (Ann) Philippa
See Pearce, Philippa
See also CA 5-8R; CANR 4

Christine de Pizan 1365(?)-1431(?) . . . . **LC 9**

Chubb, Elmer
See Masters, Edgar Lee

Chulkov, Mikhail Dmitrievich
1743-1792 . . . . **LC 2**

Churchill, Caryl 1938- . . . . **CLC 31, 55**
See also CA 102; CANR 22; DLB 13; MTCW

Churchill, Charles 1731-1764 . . . . **LC 3**
See also DLB 109

Chute, Carolyn 1947- . . . . **CLC 39**
See also CA 123

Ciardi, John (Anthony)
1916-1986 . . . . **CLC 10, 40, 44**
See also CA 5-8R; 118; CAAS 2; CANR 5, 33; CLR 19; DLB 5; DLBY 86; MAICYA; MTCW; SATA 1, 46, 65

Cicero, Marcus Tullius
106B.C.-43B.C. . . . . **CMLC 3**

Cimino, Michael 1943- . . . . **CLC 16**
See also CA 105

Cioran, E(mil) M. 1911- . . . . **CLC 64**
See also CA 25-28R

Cisneros, Sandra 1954- . . . . . . **CLC 69; HLC**
See also AAYA 9; CA 131; DLB 122; HW

Clair, Rene . . . . **CLC 20**
See also Chomette, Rene Lucien

Clampitt, Amy 1920- . . . . **CLC 32**
See also CA 110; CANR 29; DLB 105

Clancy, Thomas L., Jr. 1947-
See Clancy, Tom
See also CA 125; 131; MTCW

Clancy, Tom . . . . **CLC 45**
See also Clancy, Thomas L., Jr.
See also AAYA 9; BEST 89:1, 90:1

Clare, John 1793-1864 . . . . **NCLC 9**
See also DLB 55, 96

Clarin
See Alas (y Urena), Leopoldo (Enrique Garcia)

Clark, Al C.
See Goines, Donald

Clark, (Robert) Brian 1932- . . . . **CLC 29**
See also CA 41-44R

Clark, Eleanor 1913- . . . . **CLC 5, 19**
See also CA 9-12R; CANR 41; DLB 6

Clark, J. P.
See Clark, John Pepper
See also DLB 117

Clark, John Pepper 1935- . . . . **CLC 38; BLC**
See also Clark, J. P.
See also BW; CA 65-68; CANR 16

Clark, M. R.
See Clark, Mavis Thorpe

Clark, Mavis Thorpe 1909- . . . . **CLC 12**
See also CA 57-60; CANR 8, 37; CLR 30; MAICYA; SAAS 5; SATA 8, 74

Clark, Walter Van Tilburg
1909-1971 . . . . **CLC 28**
See also CA 9-12R; 33-36R; DLB 9; SATA 8

Clarke, Arthur C(harles)
1917- . . . . . . **CLC 1, 4, 13, 18, 35; SSC 3**
See also AAYA 4; CA 1-4R; CANR 2, 28; JRDA; MAICYA; MTCW; SATA 13, 70

Clarke, Austin 1896-1974 . . . . **CLC 6, 9**
See also CA 29-32; 49-52; CAP 2; DLB 10, 20

Clarke, Austin C(hesterfield)
1934- . . . . **CLC 8, 53; BLC**
See also BW; CA 25-28R; CAAS 16; CANR 14, 32; DLB 53, 125

Clarke, Gillian 1937- . . . . **CLC 61**
See also CA 106; DLB 40

Clarke, Marcus (Andrew Hislop)
1846-1881 . . . . **NCLC 19**

Clarke, Shirley 1925- . . . . **CLC 16**

Clash, The . . . . **CLC 30**
See also Headon, (Nicky) Topper; Jones, Mick; Simonon, Paul; Strummer, Joe

Claudel, Paul (Louis Charles Marie)
1868-1955 . . . . **TCLC 2, 10**
See also CA 104

Clavell, James (duMaresq)
1925- . . . . **CLC 6, 25**
See also CA 25-28R; CANR 26; MTCW

Cleaver, (Leroy) Eldridge
1935- . . . . **CLC 30; BLC**
See also BW; CA 21-24R; CANR 16

Cleese, John (Marwood) 1939- . . . . . **CLC 21**
See also Monty Python
See also CA 112; 116; CANR 35; MTCW

Cleishbotham, Jebediah
See Scott, Walter

Cleland, John 1710-1789 . . . . **LC 2**
See also DLB 39

Clemens, Samuel Langhorne 1835-1910
See Twain, Mark
See also CA 104; 135; CDALB 1865-1917; DA; DLB 11, 12, 23, 64, 74; JRDA; MAICYA; YABC 2

Cleophil
See Congreve, William

Clerihew, E.
See Bentley, E(dmund) C(lerihew)

Clerk, N. W.
See Lewis, C(live) S(taples)

Cliff, Jimmy . . . . **CLC 21**
See also Chambers, James

Clifton, (Thelma) Lucille
1936- . . . . **CLC 19, 66; BLC**
See also BW; CA 49-52; CANR 2, 24, 42; CLR 5; DLB 5, 41; MAICYA; MTCW; SATA 20, 69

Clinton, Dirk
See Silverberg, Robert

Clough, Arthur Hugh 1819-1861 . . **NCLC 27**
See also DLB 32

Clutha, Janet Paterson Frame 1924-
See Frame, Janet
See also CA 1-4R; CANR 2, 36; MTCW

Clyne, Terence
See Blatty, William Peter

Cobalt, Martin
See Mayne, William (James Carter)

Coburn, D(onald) L(ee) 1938- . . . . . . **CLC 10**
See also CA 89-92

Cocteau, Jean (Maurice Eugene Clement)
1889-1963 . . . . **CLC 1, 8, 15, 16, 43; DA; WLC**
See also CA 25-28; CANR 40; CAP 2; DLB 65; MTCW

Codrescu, Andrei 1946- . . . . **CLC 46**
See also CA 33-36R; CANR 13, 34

Coe, Max
See Bourne, Randolph S(illiman)

Coe, Tucker
See Westlake, Donald E(dwin)

Coetzee, J(ohn) M(ichael)
1940- . . . . **CLC 23, 33, 66**
See also CA 77-80; CANR 41; MTCW

Coffey, Brian
See Koontz, Dean R(ay)

Cohen, Arthur A(llen)
1928-1986 . . . . **CLC 7, 31**
See also CA 1-4R; 120; CANR 1, 17, 42; DLB 28

Cohen, Leonard (Norman)
1934- . . . . **CLC 3, 38**
See also CA 21-24R; CANR 14; DLB 53; MTCW

Cohen, Matt 1942- . . . . **CLC 19**
See also CA 61-64; CAAS 18; CANR 40; DLB 53

Cohen-Solal, Annie 19(?)- . . . . **CLC 50**

Colegate, Isabel 1931- . . . . **CLC 36**
See also CA 17-20R; CANR 8, 22; DLB 14; MTCW

Coleman, Emmett
See Reed, Ishmael

Coleridge, Samuel Taylor
1772-1834 . . . . **NCLC 9; DA; WLC**
See also CDBLB 1789-1832; DLB 93, 107

Coleridge, Sara 1802-1852 . . . . **NCLC 31**

Coles, Don 1928- . . . . **CLC 46**
See also CA 115; CANR 38

Colette, (Sidonie-Gabrielle)
1873-1954 . . . . . . **TCLC 1, 5, 16; SSC 10**
See also CA 104; 131; DLB 65; MTCW

Collett, (Jacobine) Camilla (Wergeland)
1813-1895 . . . . **NCLC 22**

Collier, Christopher 1930- . . . . **CLC 30**
See also CA 33-36R; CANR 13, 33; JRDA; MAICYA; SATA 16, 70

Collier, James L(incoln) 1928- . . . . . **CLC 30**
See also CA 9-12R; CANR 4, 33; JRDA; MAICYA; SATA 8, 70

Collier, Jeremy 1650-1726 . . . . **LC 6**

Collins, Hunt
See Hunter, Evan

Collins, Linda 1931- . . . . **CLC 44**
See also CA 125

Collins, (William) Wilkie
1824-1889 . . . . **NCLC 1, 18**
See also CDBLB 1832-1890; DLB 18, 70

Collins, William 1721-1759 . . . . **LC 4**
See also DLB 109

Colman, George
See Glassco, John

Colt, Winchester Remington
See Hubbard, L(afayette) Ron(ald)

Colter, Cyrus 1910- . . . . **CLC 58**
See also BW; CA 65-68; CANR 10; DLB 33

Colton, James
See Hansen, Joseph

Colum, Padraic 1881-1972 . . . . **CLC 28**
See also CA 73-76; 33-36R; CANR 35; MAICYA; MTCW; SATA 15

Colvin, James
See Moorcock, Michael (John)

Colwin, Laurie (E.)
1944-1992 . . . . **CLC 5, 13, 23**
See also CA 89-92; 139; CANR 20; DLBY 80; MTCW

Comfort, Alex(ander) 1920- . . . . **CLC 7**
See also CA 1-4R; CANR 1

Comfort, Montgomery
See Campbell, (John) Ramsey

Compton-Burnett, I(vy)
1884(?)-1969 . . . . . . **CLC 1, 3, 10, 15, 34**
See also CA 1-4R; 25-28R; CANR 4; DLB 36; MTCW

Comstock, Anthony 1844-1915 . . . . **TCLC 13**
See also CA 110

Conan Doyle, Arthur
See Doyle, Arthur Conan

Conde, Maryse . . . . **CLC 52**
See also Boucolon, Maryse

Condon, Richard (Thomas)
1915- . . . . **CLC 4, 6, 8, 10, 45**
See also BEST 90:3; CA 1-4R; CAAS 1; CANR 2, 23; MTCW

Congreve, William
1670-1729 . . . **LC 5, 21; DA; DC 2; WLC**
See also CDBLB 1660-1789; DLB 39, 84

Connell, Evan S(helby), Jr.
1924- . . . . **CLC 4, 6, 45**
See also AAYA 7; CA 1-4R; CAAS 2; CANR 2, 39; DLB 2; DLBY 81; MTCW

Connelly, Marc(us Cook)
1890-1980 . . . . **CLC 7**
See also CA 85-88; 102; CANR 30; DLB 7; DLBY 80; SATA 25

Connor, Ralph . . . . **TCLC 31**
See also Gordon, Charles William
See also DLB 92

Conrad, Joseph
1857-1924 . . . . **TCLC 1, 6, 13, 25, 43; DA; SSC 9; WLC**
See also CA 104; 131; CDBLB 1890-1914; DLB 10, 34, 98; MTCW; SATA 27

Conrad, Robert Arnold
See Hart, Moss

Conroy, Pat 1945-. . . . . **CLC 30, 74**
See also AAYA 8; AITN 1; CA 85-88; CANR 24; DLB 6; MTCW

Constant (de Rebecque), (Henri) Benjamin
1767-1830 . . . . **NCLC 6**
See also DLB 119

Conybeare, Charles Augustus
See Eliot, T(homas) S(tearns)

Cook, Michael 1933- . . . . **CLC 58**
See also CA 93-96; DLB 53

Cook, Robin 1940- . . . . **CLC 14**
See also BEST 90:2; CA 108; 111; CANR 41

Cook, Roy
See Silverberg, Robert

Cooke, Elizabeth 1948- . . . . **CLC 55**
See also CA 129

Cooke, John Esten 1830-1886 . . . . . **NCLC 5**
See also DLB 3

Cooke, John Estes
See Baum, L(yman) Frank

Cooke, M. E.
See Creasey, John

Cooke, Margaret
See Creasey, John

Cooney, Ray . . . . **CLC 62**

Cooper, Henry St. John
See Creasey, John

Cooper, J. California. . . . . **CLC 56**
See also BW; CA 125

Cooper, James Fenimore
1789-1851 . . . . **NCLC 1, 27**
See also CDALB 1640-1865; DLB 3; SATA 19

Coover, Robert (Lowell)
1932- . . . . **CLC 3, 7, 15, 32, 46**
See also CA 45-48; CANR 3, 37; DLB 2; DLBY 81; MTCW

Copeland, Stewart (Armstrong)
1952- . . . . **CLC 26**
See also Police, The

Coppard, A(lfred) E(dgar)
1878-1957 . . . . **TCLC 5**
See also CA 114; YABC 1

Coppee, Francois 1842-1908 . . . . . . **TCLC 25**

Coppola, Francis Ford 1939- . . . . **CLC 16**
See also CA 77-80; CANR 40; DLB 44

Corbiere, Tristan 1845-1875 . . . . . **NCLC 43**

Corcoran, Barbara 1911- . . . . **CLC 17**
See also CA 21-24R; CAAS 2; CANR 11, 28; DLB 52; JRDA; SATA 3

Cordelier, Maurice
See Giraudoux, (Hippolyte) Jean

Corelli, Marie 1855-1924 . . . . **TCLC 51**
See also Mackay, Mary
See also DLB 34

Corman, Cid . . . . **CLC 9**
See also Corman, Sidney
See also CAAS 2; DLB 5

Corman, Sidney 1924-
See Corman, Cid
See also CA 85-88

Cormier, Robert (Edmund)
1925- . . . . **CLC 12, 30; DA**
See also AAYA 3; CA 1-4R; CANR 5, 23; CDALB 1968-1988; CLR 12; DLB 52; JRDA; MAICYA; MTCW; SATA 10, 45

Corn, Alfred 1943- . . . . **CLC 33**
See also CA 104; DLB 120; DLBY 80

Cornwell, David (John Moore)
1931- . . . . **CLC 9, 15**
See also le Carre, John
See also CA 5-8R; CANR 13, 33; MTCW

Corrigan, Kevin . . . . **CLC 55**

Corso, (Nunzio) Gregory 1930- . . . **CLC 1, 11**
See also CA 5-8R; CANR 41; DLB 5, 16; MTCW

Cortazar, Julio
1914-1984 . . . . . . **CLC 2, 3, 5, 10, 13, 15, 33, 34; HLC; SSC 7**
See also CA 21-24R; CANR 12, 32; DLB 113; HW; MTCW

Corwin, Cecil
See Kornbluth, C(yril) M.

Cosic, Dobrica 1921- . . . . **CLC 14**
See also CA 122; 138

Costain, Thomas B(ertram)
1885-1965 . . . . **CLC 30**
See also CA 5-8R; 25-28R; DLB 9

Costantini, Humberto
1924(?)-1987 . . . . **CLC 49**
See also CA 131; 122; HW

Costello, Elvis 1955-. . . . . **CLC 21**

Cotter, Joseph S. Sr.
See Cotter, Joseph Seamon Sr.

Cotter, Joseph Seamon Sr.
1861-1949 . . . . **TCLC 28; BLC**
See also BW; CA 124; DLB 50

Couch, Arthur Thomas Quiller
See Quiller-Couch, Arthur Thomas

Coulton, James
See Hansen, Joseph

Couperus, Louis (Marie Anne) 1863-1923 . . . . **TCLC 15**
See also CA 115

Court, Wesli
See Turco, Lewis (Putnam)

Courtenay, Bryce 1933- . . . . **CLC 59**
See also CA 138

Courtney, Robert
See Ellison, Harlan

Cousteau, Jacques-Yves 1910- . . . . . . **CLC 30**
See also CA 65-68; CANR 15; MTCW; SATA 38

Coward, Noel (Peirce) 1899-1973 . . . . **CLC 1, 9, 29, 51**
See also AITN 1; CA 17-18; 41-44R; CANR 35; CAP 2; CDBLB 1914-1945; DLB 10; MTCW

Cowley, Malcolm 1898-1989 . . . . **CLC 39**
See also CA 5-8R; 128; CANR 3; DLB 4, 48; DLBY 81, 89; MTCW

Cowper, William 1731-1800 . . . . **NCLC 8**
See also DLB 104, 109

Cox, William Trevor 1928- . . . **CLC 9, 14, 71**
See also Trevor, William
See also CA 9-12R; CANR 4, 37; DLB 14; MTCW

Cozzens, James Gould 1903-1978 . . . . **CLC 1, 4, 11**
See also CA 9-12R; 81-84; CANR 19; CDALB 1941-1968; DLB 9; DLBD 2; DLBY 84; MTCW

Crabbe, George 1754-1832 . . . . **NCLC 26**
See also DLB 93

Craig, A. A.
See Anderson, Poul (William)

Craik, Dinah Maria (Mulock) 1826-1887 . . . . **NCLC 38**
See also DLB 35; MAICYA; SATA 34

Cram, Ralph Adams 1863-1942 . . . . **TCLC 45**

Crane, (Harold) Hart 1899-1932 . . . . **TCLC 2, 5; DA; PC 3; WLC**
See also CA 104; 127; CDALB 1917-1929; DLB 4, 48; MTCW

Crane, R(onald) S(almon) 1886-1967 . . . . **CLC 27**
See also CA 85-88; DLB 63

Crane, Stephen (Townley) 1871-1900 . . . . **TCLC 11, 17, 32; DA; SSC 7; WLC**
See also CA 109; 140; CDALB 1865-1917; DLB 12, 54, 78; YABC 2

Crase, Douglas 1944- . . . . **CLC 58**
See also CA 106

Crashaw, Richard 1612(?)-1649 . . . . . . **LC 24**
See also DLB 126

Craven, Margaret 1901-1980 . . . . **CLC 17**
See also CA 103

Crawford, F(rancis) Marion 1854-1909 . . . . **TCLC 10**
See also CA 107; DLB 71

Crawford, Isabella Valancy 1850-1887 . . . . **NCLC 12**
See also DLB 92

Crayon, Geoffrey
See Irving, Washington

Creasey, John 1908-1973 . . . . **CLC 11**
See also CA 5-8R; 41-44R; CANR 8; DLB 77; MTCW

Crebillon, Claude Prosper Jolyot de (fils) 1707-1777 . . . . **LC 1**

Credo
See Creasey, John

Creeley, Robert (White) 1926- . . . . . **CLC 1, 2, 4, 8, 11, 15, 36, 78**
See also CA 1-4R; CAAS 10; CANR 23, 43; DLB 5, 16; MTCW

Crews, Harry (Eugene) 1935- . . . . **CLC 6, 23, 49**
See also AITN 1; CA 25-28R; CANR 20; DLB 6; MTCW

Crichton, (John) Michael 1942- . . . . **CLC 2, 6, 54**
See also AAYA 10; AITN 2; CA 25-28R; CANR 13, 40; DLBY 81; JRDA; MTCW; SATA 9

Crispin, Edmund . . . . **CLC 22**
See also Montgomery, (Robert) Bruce
See also DLB 87

Cristofer, Michael 1945(?)- . . . . **CLC 28**
See also CA 110; DLB 7

Croce, Benedetto 1866-1952 . . . . . . **TCLC 37**
See also CA 120

Crockett, David 1786-1836 . . . . **NCLC 8**
See also DLB 3, 11

Crockett, Davy
See Crockett, David

Croker, John Wilson 1780-1857 . . **NCLC 10**
See also DLB 110

Crommelynck, Fernand 1885-1970 . . **CLC 75**
See also CA 89-92

Cronin, A(rchibald) J(oseph) 1896-1981 . . . . **CLC 32**
See also CA 1-4R; 102; CANR 5; SATA 25, 47

Cross, Amanda
See Heilbrun, Carolyn G(old)

Crothers, Rachel 1878(?)-1958 . . . . . **TCLC 19**
See also CA 113; DLB 7

Croves, Hal
See Traven, B.

Crowfield, Christopher
See Stowe, Harriet (Elizabeth) Beecher

Crowley, Aleister . . . . **TCLC 7**
See also Crowley, Edward Alexander

Crowley, Edward Alexander 1875-1947
See Crowley, Aleister
See also CA 104

Crowley, John 1942- . . . . **CLC 57**
See also CA 61-64; CANR 43; DLBY 82; SATA 65

Crud
See Crumb, R(obert)

Crumarums
See Crumb, R(obert)

Crumb, R(obert) 1943- . . . . **CLC 17**
See also CA 106

Crumbum
See Crumb, R(obert)

Crumski
See Crumb, R(obert)

Crum the Bum
See Crumb, R(obert)

Crunk
See Crumb, R(obert)

Crustt
See Crumb, R(obert)

Cryer, Gretchen (Kiger) 1935- . . . . . . **CLC 21**
See also CA 114; 123

Csath, Geza 1887-1919 . . . . **TCLC 13**
See also CA 111

Cudlip, David 1933- . . . . **CLC 34**

Cullen, Countee 1903-1946 . . . . . . **TCLC 4, 37; BLC; DA**
See also BW; CA 108; 124; CDALB 1917-1929; DLB 4, 48, 51; MTCW; SATA 18

Cum, R.
See Crumb, R(obert)

Cummings, Bruce F(rederick) 1889-1919
See Barbellion, W. N. P.
See also CA 123

Cummings, E(dward) E(stlin) 1894-1962 . . . . . . **CLC 1, 3, 8, 12, 15, 68; DA; PC 5; WLC 2**
See also CA 73-76; CANR 31; CDALB 1929-1941; DLB 4, 48; MTCW

Cunha, Euclides (Rodrigues Pimenta) da 1866-1909 . . . . **TCLC 24**
See also CA 123

Cunningham, E. V.
See Fast, Howard (Melvin)

Cunningham, J(ames) V(incent) 1911-1985 . . . . **CLC 3, 31**
See also CA 1-4R; 115; CANR 1; DLB 5

Cunningham, Julia (Woolfolk) 1916- . . . . **CLC 12**
See also CA 9-12R; CANR 4, 19, 36; JRDA; MAICYA; SAAS 2; SATA 1, 26

Cunningham, Michael 1952- . . . . **CLC 34**
See also CA 136

Cunninghame Graham, R(obert) B(ontine) 1852-1936 . . . . **TCLC 19**
See also Graham, R(obert) B(ontine) Cunninghame
See also CA 119; DLB 98

Currie, Ellen 19(?)- . . . . **CLC 44**

Curtin, Philip
See Lowndes, Marie Adelaide (Belloc)

Curtis, Price
See Ellison, Harlan

Cutrate, Joe
See Spiegelman, Art

Czaczkes, Shmuel Yosef
See Agnon, S(hmuel) Y(osef Halevi)

D. P.
See Wells, H(erbert) G(eorge)

de la Roche, Mazo 1879-1961 ...... **CLC 14**
See also CA 85-88; CANR 30; DLB 68; SATA 64

Delbanco, Nicholas (Franklin) 1942- .... **CLC 6, 13**
See also CA 17-20R; CAAS 2; CANR 29; DLB 6

del Castillo, Michel 1933- .... **CLC 38**
See also CA 109

Deledda, Grazia (Cosima) 1875(?)-1936 .... **TCLC 23**
See also CA 123

Delibes, Miguel .... **CLC 8, 18**
See also Delibes Setien, Miguel

Delibes Setien, Miguel 1920-
See Delibes, Miguel
See also CA 45-48; CANR 1, 32; HW; MTCW

DeLillo, Don 1936- ..... **CLC 8, 10, 13, 27, 39, 54, 76**
See also BEST 89:1; CA 81-84; CANR 21; DLB 6; MTCW

de Lisser, H. G.
See De Lisser, Herbert George
See also DLB 117

De Lisser, Herbert George 1878-1944 .... **TCLC 12**
See also de Lisser, H. G.
See also CA 109

Deloria, Vine (Victor), Jr. 1933-.... **CLC 21**
See also CA 53-56; CANR 5, 20; MTCW; SATA 21

Del Vecchio, John M(ichael) 1947- .... **CLC 29**
See also CA 110; DLBD 9

de Man, Paul (Adolph Michel) 1919-1983 .... **CLC 55**
See also CA 128; 111; DLB 67; MTCW

De Marinis, Rick 1934- .... **CLC 54**
See also CA 57-60; CANR 9, 25

Demby, William 1922- .... **CLC 53; BLC**
See also BW; CA 81-84; DLB 33

Demijohn, Thom
See Disch, Thomas M(ichael)

de Montherlant, Henry (Milon)
See Montherlant, Henry (Milon) de

de Natale, Francine
See Malzberg, Barry N(athaniel)

Denby, Edwin (Orr) 1903-1983..... **CLC 48**
See also CA 138; 110

Denis, Julio
See Cortazar, Julio

Denmark, Harrison
See Zelazny, Roger (Joseph)

Dennis, John 1658-1734............ **LC 11**
See also DLB 101

Dennis, Nigel (Forbes) 1912-1989.... **CLC 8**
See also CA 25-28R; 129; DLB 13, 15; MTCW

De Palma, Brian (Russell) 1940-.... **CLC 20**
See also CA 109

De Quincey, Thomas 1785-1859 ... **NCLC 4**
See also CDBLB 1789-1832; DLB 110

Deren, Eleanora 1908(?)-1961
See Deren, Maya
See also CA 111

Deren, Maya .... **CLC 16**
See also Deren, Eleanora

Derleth, August (William) 1909-1971 .... **CLC 31**
See also CA 1-4R; 29-32R; CANR 4; DLB 9; SATA 5

de Routisie, Albert
See Aragon, Louis

Derrida, Jacques 1930-............ **CLC 24**
See also CA 124; 127

Derry Down Derry
See Lear, Edward

Dersonnes, Jacques
See Simenon, Georges (Jacques Christian)

Desai, Anita 1937- .... **CLC 19, 37**
See also CA 81-84; CANR 33; MTCW; SATA 63

de Saint-Luc, Jean
See Glassco, John

de Saint Roman, Arnaud
See Aragon, Louis

Descartes, Rene 1596-1650 .... **LC 20**

De Sica, Vittorio 1901(?)-1974 ..... **CLC 20**
See also CA 117

Desnos, Robert 1900-1945........ **TCLC 22**
See also CA 121

Destouches, Louis-Ferdinand 1894-1961 .... **CLC 9, 15**
See also Celine, Louis-Ferdinand
See also CA 85-88; CANR 28; MTCW

Deutsch, Babette 1895-1982 .... **CLC 18**
See also CA 1-4R; 108; CANR 4; DLB 45; SATA 1, 33

Devenant, William 1606-1649 .... **LC 13**

Devkota, Laxmiprasad 1909-1959 .... **TCLC 23**
See also CA 123

De Voto, Bernard (Augustine) 1897-1955 .... **TCLC 29**
See also CA 113; DLB 9

De Vries, Peter 1910-1993 .... **CLC 1, 2, 3, 7, 10, 28, 46**
See also CA 17-20R; 142; CANR 41; DLB 6; DLBY 82; MTCW

Dexter, Martin
See Faust, Frederick (Schiller)

Dexter, Pete 1943- .... **CLC 34, 55**
See also BEST 89:2; CA 127; 131; MTCW

Diamano, Silmang
See Senghor, Leopold Sedar

Diamond, Neil 1941- .... **CLC 30**
See also CA 108

di Bassetto, Corno
See Shaw, George Bernard

Dick, Philip K(indred) 1928-1982 .... **CLC 10, 30, 72**
See also CA 49-52; 106; CANR 2, 16; DLB 8; MTCW

Dickens, Charles (John Huffam) 1812-1870 ...... **NCLC 3, 8, 18, 26; DA**
See also CDBLB 1832-1890; DLB 21, 55, 70; JRDA; MAICYA; SATA 15

Dickey, James (Lafayette) 1923- .... **CLC 1, 2, 4, 7, 10, 15, 47**
See also AITN 1, 2; CA 9-12R; CABS 2; CANR 10; CDALB 1968-1988; DLB 5; DLBD 7; DLBY 82; MTCW

Dickey, William 1928- .... **CLC 3, 28**
See also CA 9-12R; CANR 24; DLB 5

Dickinson, Charles 1951- .... **CLC 49**
See also CA 128

Dickinson, Emily (Elizabeth) 1830-1886 .. **NCLC 21; DA; PC 1; WLC**
See also CDALB 1865-1917; DLB 1; SATA 29

Dickinson, Peter (Malcolm) 1927- .... **CLC 12, 35**
See also AAYA 9; CA 41-44R; CANR 31; CLR 29; DLB 87; JRDA; MAICYA; SATA 5, 62

Dickson, Carr
See Carr, John Dickson

Dickson, Carter
See Carr, John Dickson

Didion, Joan 1934- ..... **CLC 1, 3, 8, 14, 32**
See also AITN 1; CA 5-8R; CANR 14; CDALB 1968-1988; DLB 2; DLBY 81, 86; MTCW

Dietrich, Robert
See Hunt, E(verette) Howard, Jr.

Dillard, Annie 1945-............ **CLC 9, 60**
See also AAYA 6; CA 49-52; CANR 3, 43; DLBY 80; MTCW; SATA 10

Dillard, R(ichard) H(enry) W(ilde) 1937- .... **CLC 5**
See also CA 21-24R; CAAS 7; CANR 10; DLB 5

Dillon, Eilis 1920-................ **CLC 17**
See also CA 9-12R; CAAS 3; CANR 4, 38; CLR 26; MAICYA; SATA 2, 74

Dimont, Penelope
See Mortimer, Penelope (Ruth)

Dinesen, Isak .... **CLC 10, 29; SSC 7**
See also Blixen, Karen (Christentze Dinesen)

Ding Ling .... **CLC 68**
See also Chiang Pin-chin

Disch, Thomas M(ichael) 1940-... **CLC 7, 36**
See also CA 21-24R; CAAS 4; CANR 17, 36; CLR 18; DLB 8; MAICYA; MTCW; SAAS 15; SATA 54

Disch, Tom
See Disch, Thomas M(ichael)

d'Isly, Georges
See Simenon, Georges (Jacques Christian)

Disraeli, Benjamin 1804-1881 .. **NCLC 2, 39**
See also DLB 21, 55

Ditcum, Steve
See Crumb, R(obert)

Dixon, Paige
See Corcoran, Barbara

Dixon, Stephen 1936-............. **CLC 52**
See also CA 89-92; CANR 17, 40; DLB 130

Evan, Evin
See Faust, Frederick (Schiller)

Evans, Evan
See Faust, Frederick (Schiller)

Evans, Marian
See Eliot, George

Evans, Mary Ann
See Eliot, George

Evarts, Esther
See Benson, Sally

Everett, Percival
See Everett, Percival L.

Everett, Percival L. 1956- .... **CLC 57**
See also CA 129

Everson, R(onald) G(ilmour)
1903- .... **CLC 27**
See also CA 17-20R; DLB 88

Everson, William (Oliver)
1912- .... **CLC 1, 5, 14**
See also CA 9-12R; CANR 20; DLB 5, 16; MTCW

Evtushenko, Evgenii Aleksandrovich
See Yevtushenko, Yevgeny (Alexandrovich)

Ewart, Gavin (Buchanan)
1916- .... **CLC 13, 46**
See also CA 89-92; CANR 17; DLB 40; MTCW

Ewers, Hanns Heinz 1871-1943 ... **TCLC 12**
See also CA 109

Ewing, Frederick R.
See Sturgeon, Theodore (Hamilton)

Exley, Frederick (Earl)
1929-1992 .... **CLC 6, 11**
See also AITN 2; CA 81-84; 138; DLBY 81

Eynhardt, Guillermo
See Quiroga, Horacio (Sylvestre)

Ezekiel, Nissim 1924-............. **CLC 61**
See also CA 61-64

Ezekiel, Tish O'Dowd 1943- .... **CLC 34**
See also CA 129

Fadeyev, A.
See Bulgya, Alexander Alexandrovich

Fadeyev, Alexander.............. **TCLC 53**
See also Bulgya, Alexander Alexandrovich

Fagen, Donald 1948-.............. **CLC 26**

Fainzilberg, Ilya Arnoldovich 1897-1937
See Ilf, Ilya
See also CA 120

Fair, Ronald L. 1932-............. **CLC 18**
See also BW; CA 69-72; CANR 25; DLB 33

Fairbairns, Zoe (Ann) 1948- .... **CLC 32**
See also CA 103; CANR 21

Falco, Gian
See Papini, Giovanni

Falconer, James
See Kirkup, James

Falconer, Kenneth
See Kornbluth, C(yril) M.

Falkland, Samuel
See Heijermans, Herman

Fallaci, Oriana 1930-............. **CLC 11**
See also CA 77-80; CANR 15; MTCW

Faludy, George 1913-............. **CLC 42**
See also CA 21-24R

Faludy, Gyoergy
See Faludy, George

Fanon, Frantz 1925-1961..... **CLC 74; BLC**
See also BW; CA 116; 89-92

Fanshawe, Ann .... **LC 11**

Fante, John (Thomas) 1911-1983 ... **CLC 60**
See also CA 69-72; 109; CANR 23; DLB 130; DLBY 83

Farah, Nuruddin 1945-....... **CLC 53; BLC**
See also CA 106; DLB 125

Fargue, Leon-Paul 1876(?)-1947 ... **TCLC 11**
See also CA 109

Farigoule, Louis
See Romains, Jules

Farina, Richard 1936(?)-1966 .... **CLC 9**
See also CA 81-84; 25-28R

Farley, Walter (Lorimer)
1915-1989 .... **CLC 17**
See also CA 17-20R; CANR 8, 29; DLB 22; JRDA; MAICYA; SATA 2, 43

Farmer, Philip Jose 1918-....... **CLC 1, 19**
See also CA 1-4R; CANR 4, 35; DLB 8; MTCW

Farquhar, George 1677-1707 .... **LC 21**
See also DLB 84

Farrell, J(ames) G(ordon)
1935-1979 .... **CLC 6**
See also CA 73-76; 89-92; CANR 36; DLB 14; MTCW

Farrell, James T(homas)
1904-1979 .... **CLC 1, 4, 8, 11, 66**
See also CA 5-8R; 89-92; CANR 9; DLB 4, 9, 86; DLBD 2; MTCW

Farren, Richard J.
See Betjeman, John

Farren, Richard M.
See Betjeman, John

Fassbinder, Rainer Werner
1946-1982 .... **CLC 20**
See also CA 93-96; 106; CANR 31

Fast, Howard (Melvin) 1914- ...... **CLC 23**
See also CA 1-4R; CAAS 18; CANR 1, 33; DLB 9; SATA 7

Faulcon, Robert
See Holdstock, Robert P.

Faulkner, William (Cuthbert)
1897-1962 ..... **CLC 1, 3, 6, 8, 9, 11, 14, 18, 28, 52, 68; DA; SSC 1; WLC**
See also AAYA 7; CA 81-84; CANR 33; CDALB 1929-1941; DLB 9, 11, 44, 102; DLBD 2; DLBY 86; MTCW

Fauset, Jessie Redmon
1884(?)-1961 .... **CLC 19, 54; BLC**
See also BW; CA 109; DLB 51

Faust, Frederick (Schiller)
1892-1944(?) .... **TCLC 49**
See also CA 108

Faust, Irvin 1924-................. **CLC 8**
See also CA 33-36R; CANR 28; DLB 2, 28; DLBY 80

Fawkes, Guy
See Benchley, Robert (Charles)

Fearing, Kenneth (Flexner)
1902-1961 .... **CLC 51**
See also CA 93-96; DLB 9

Fecamps, Elise
See Creasey, John

Federman, Raymond 1928- ...... **CLC 6, 47**
See also CA 17-20R; CAAS 8; CANR 10, 43; DLBY 80

Federspiel, J(uerg) F. 1931-........ **CLC 42**

Feiffer, Jules (Ralph) 1929-.... **CLC 2, 8, 64**
See also AAYA 3; CA 17-20R; CANR 30; DLB 7, 44; MTCW; SATA 8, 61

Feige, Hermann Albert Otto Maximilian
See Traven, B.

Fei-Kan, Li
See Li Fei-kan

Feinberg, David B. 1956-.......... **CLC 59**
See also CA 135

Feinstein, Elaine 1930-............ **CLC 36**
See also CA 69-72; CAAS 1; CANR 31; DLB 14, 40; MTCW

Feldman, Irving (Mordecai) 1928-.... **CLC 7**
See also CA 1-4R; CANR 1

Fellini, Federico 1920-1993 .... **CLC 16**
See also CA 65-68; 143; CANR 33

Felsen, Henry Gregor 1916- .... **CLC 17**
See also CA 1-4R; CANR 1; SAAS 2; SATA 1

Fenton, James Martin 1949-....... **CLC 32**
See also CA 102; DLB 40

Ferber, Edna 1887-1968........... **CLC 18**
See also AITN 1; CA 5-8R; 25-28R; DLB 9, 28, 86; MTCW; SATA 7

Ferguson, Helen
See Kavan, Anna

Ferguson, Samuel 1810-1886..... **NCLC 33**
See also DLB 32

Ferling, Lawrence
See Ferlinghetti, Lawrence (Monsanto)

Ferlinghetti, Lawrence (Monsanto)
1919(?)- .... **CLC 2, 6, 10, 27; PC 1**
See also CA 5-8R; CANR 3, 41; CDALB 1941-1968; DLB 5, 16; MTCW

Fernandez, Vicente Garcia Huidobro
See Huidobro Fernandez, Vicente Garcia

Ferrer, Gabriel (Francisco Victor) Miro
See Miro (Ferrer), Gabriel (Francisco Victor)

Ferrier, Susan (Edmonstone)
1782-1854 .... **NCLC 8**
See also DLB 116

Ferrigno, Robert 1948(?)-.......... **CLC 65**
See also CA 140

Feuchtwanger, Lion 1884-1958 ..... **TCLC 3**
See also CA 104; DLB 66

Feydeau, Georges (Leon Jules Marie)
1862-1921 .... **TCLC 22**
See also CA 113

Ficino, Marsilio 1433-1499 .... **LC 12**

Fiedeler, Hans
See Doeblin, Alfred

Fiedler, Leslie A(aron) 1917- .... **CLC 4, 13, 24**
See also CA 9-12R; CANR 7; DLB 28, 67; MTCW

Field, Andrew 1938- .... **CLC 44**
See also CA 97-100; CANR 25

Field, Eugene 1850-1895 .... **NCLC 3**
See also DLB 23, 42; MAICYA; SATA 16

Field, Gans T.
See Wellman, Manly Wade

Field, Michael .... **TCLC 43**

Field, Peter
See Hobson, Laura Z(ametkin)

Fielding, Henry 1707-1754 .... **LC 1; DA; WLC**
See also CDBLB 1660-1789; DLB 39, 84, 101

Fielding, Sarah 1710-1768 .... **LC 1**
See also DLB 39

Fierstein, Harvey (Forbes) 1954- ... **CLC 33**
See also CA 123; 129

Figes, Eva 1932- .... **CLC 31**
See also CA 53-56; CANR 4; DLB 14

Finch, Robert (Duer Claydon) 1900- .... **CLC 18**
See also CA 57-60; CANR 9, 24; DLB 88

Findley, Timothy 1930- .... **CLC 27**
See also CA 25-28R; CANR 12, 42; DLB 53

Fink, William
See Mencken, H(enry) L(ouis)

Firbank, Louis 1942-
See Reed, Lou
See also CA 117

Firbank, (Arthur Annesley) Ronald 1886-1926 .... **TCLC 1**
See also CA 104; DLB 36

Fisher, M(ary) F(rances) K(ennedy) 1908-1992 .... **CLC 76**
See also CA 77-80; 138

Fisher, Roy 1930- .... **CLC 25**
See also CA 81-84; CAAS 10; CANR 16; DLB 40

Fisher, Rudolph 1897-1934 .... **TCLC 11; BLC**
See also BW; CA 107; 124; DLB 51, 102

Fisher, Vardis (Alvero) 1895-1968.... **CLC 7**
See also CA 5-8R; 25-28R; DLB 9

Fiske, Tarleton
See Bloch, Robert (Albert)

Fitch, Clarke
See Sinclair, Upton (Beall)

Fitch, John IV
See Cormier, Robert (Edmund)

Fitgerald, Penelope 1916- .... **CLC 61**

Fitzgerald, Captain Hugh
See Baum, L(yman) Frank

FitzGerald, Edward 1809-1883 .... **NCLC 9**
See also DLB 32

Fitzgerald, F(rancis) Scott (Key) 1896-1940 ...... **TCLC 1, 6, 14, 28; DA; SSC 6; WLC**
See also AITN 1; CA 110; 123; CDALB 1917-1929; DLB 4, 9, 86; DLBD 1; DLBY 81; MTCW

Fitzgerald, Penelope 1916- ...... **CLC 19, 51**
See also CA 85-88; CAAS 10; DLB 14

Fitzgerald, Robert (Stuart) 1910-1985 .... **CLC 39**
See also CA 1-4R; 114; CANR 1; DLBY 80

FitzGerald, Robert D(avid) 1902-1987 .... **CLC 19**
See also CA 17-20R

Fitzgerald, Zelda (Sayre) 1900-1948 .... **TCLC 52**
See also CA 117; 126; DLBY 84

Flanagan, Thomas (James Bonner) 1923- .... **CLC 25, 52**
See also CA 108; DLBY 80; MTCW

Flaubert, Gustave 1821-1880 .... **NCLC 2, 10, 19; DA; SSC 11; WLC**
See also DLB 119

Flecker, (Herman) James Elroy 1884-1915 .... **TCLC 43**
See also CA 109; DLB 10, 19

Fleming, Ian (Lancaster) 1908-1964 .... **CLC 3, 30**
See also CA 5-8R; CDBLB 1945-1960; DLB 87; MTCW; SATA 9

Fleming, Thomas (James) 1927- .... **CLC 37**
See also CA 5-8R; CANR 10; SATA 8

Fletcher, John Gould 1886-1950 ... **TCLC 35**
See also CA 107; DLB 4, 45

Fleur, Paul
See Pohl, Frederik

Flooglebuckle, Al
See Spiegelman, Art

Flying Officer X
See Bates, H(erbert) E(rnest)

Fo, Dario 1926- .... **CLC 32**
See also CA 116; 128; MTCW

Fogarty, Jonathan Titulescu Esq.
See Farrell, James T(homas)

Folke, Will
See Bloch, Robert (Albert)

Follett, Ken(neth Martin) 1949- .... **CLC 18**
See also AAYA 6; BEST 89:4; CA 81-84; CANR 13, 33; DLB 87; DLBY 81; MTCW

Fontane, Theodor 1819-1898 ..... **NCLC 26**
See also DLB 129

Foote, Horton 1916- .... **CLC 51**
See also CA 73-76; CANR 34; DLB 26

Foote, Shelby 1916- .... **CLC 75**
See also CA 5-8R; CANR 3; DLB 2, 17

Forbes, Esther 1891-1967 .... **CLC 12**
See also CA 13-14; 25-28R; CAP 1; CLR 27; DLB 22; JRDA; MAICYA; SATA 2

Forche, Carolyn (Louise) 1950- ..... **CLC 25**
See also CA 109; 117; DLB 5

Ford, Elbur
See Hibbert, Eleanor Alice Burford

Ford, Ford Madox 1873-1939 .... **TCLC 1, 15, 39**
See also CA 104; 132; CDBLB 1914-1945; DLB 34, 98; MTCW

Ford, John 1895-1973 .... **CLC 16**
See also CA 45-48

Ford, Richard 1944- .... **CLC 46**
See also CA 69-72; CANR 11

Ford, Webster
See Masters, Edgar Lee

Foreman, Richard 1937- .... **CLC 50**
See also CA 65-68; CANR 32

Forester, C(ecil) S(cott) 1899-1966 .... **CLC 35**
See also CA 73-76; 25-28R; SATA 13

Forez
See Mauriac, Francois (Charles)

Forman, James Douglas 1932- ...... **CLC 21**
See also CA 9-12R; CANR 4, 19, 42; JRDA; MAICYA; SATA 8, 70

Fornes, Maria Irene 1930- ...... **CLC 39, 61**
See also CA 25-28R; CANR 28; DLB 7; HW; MTCW

Forrest, Leon 1937- .... **CLC 4**
See also BW; CA 89-92; CAAS 7; CANR 25; DLB 33

Forster, E(dward) M(organ) 1879-1970 ..... **CLC 1, 2, 3, 4, 9, 10, 13, 15, 22, 45, 77; DA; WLC**
See also AAYA 2; CA 13-14; 25-28R; CAP 1; CDBLB 1914-1945; DLB 34, 98; DLBD 10; MTCW; SATA 57

Forster, John 1812-1876 .... **NCLC 11**

Forsyth, Frederick 1938- ...... **CLC 2, 5, 36**
See also BEST 89:4; CA 85-88; CANR 38; DLB 87; MTCW

Forten, Charlotte L. .... **TCLC 16; BLC**
See also Grimke, Charlotte L(ottie) Forten
See also DLB 50

Foscolo, Ugo 1778-1827 .... **NCLC 8**

Fosse, Bob .... **CLC 20**
See also Fosse, Robert Louis

Fosse, Robert Louis 1927-1987
See Fosse, Bob
See also CA 110; 123

Foster, Stephen Collins 1826-1864 .... **NCLC 26**

Foucault, Michel 1926-1984 .... **CLC 31, 34, 69**
See also CA 105; 113; CANR 34; MTCW

Fouque, Friedrich (Heinrich Karl) de la Motte 1777-1843 .... **NCLC 2**
See also DLB 90

Fournier, Henri Alban 1886-1914
See Alain-Fournier
See also CA 104

Fournier, Pierre 1916- .... **CLC 11**
See also Gascar, Pierre
See also CA 89-92; CANR 16, 40

Fowles, John 1926- .... **CLC 1, 2, 3, 4, 6, 9, 10, 15, 33**
See also CA 5-8R; CANR 25; CDBLB 1960 to Present; DLB 14; MTCW; SATA 22

Fox, Paula 1923- . . . . **CLC 2, 8**
See also AAYA 3; CA 73-76; CANR 20, 36; CLR 1; DLB 52; JRDA; MAICYA; MTCW; SATA 17, 60

Fox, William Price (Jr.) 1926- . . . . . **CLC 22**
See also CA 17-20R; CANR 11; DLB 2; DLBY 81

Foxe, John 1516(?)-1587 . . . . **LC 14**

Frame, Janet . . . . **CLC 2, 3, 6, 22, 66**
See also Clutha, Janet Paterson Frame

France, Anatole . . . . **TCLC 9**
See also Thibault, Jacques Anatole Francois
See also DLB 123

Francis, Claude 19(?)- . . . . **CLC 50**

Francis, Dick 1920- . . . . **CLC 2, 22, 42**
See also AAYA 5; BEST 89:3; CA 5-8R; CANR 9, 42; CDBLB 1960 to Present; DLB 87; MTCW

Francis, Robert (Churchill)
1901-1987 . . . . **CLC 15**
See also CA 1-4R; 123; CANR 1

Frank, Anne(lies Marie)
1929-1945 . . . . **TCLC 17; DA; WLC**
See also CA 113; 133; MTCW; SATA 42

Frank, Elizabeth 1945- . . . . **CLC 39**
See also CA 121; 126

Franklin, Benjamin
See Hasek, Jaroslav (Matej Frantisek)

Franklin, Benjamin 1706-1790. . . **LC 25; DA**
See also CDALB 1640-1865; DLB 24, 43, 73

Franklin, (Stella Maraia Sarah) Miles
1879-1954 . . . . **TCLC 7**
See also CA 104

Fraser, Antonia (Pakenham)
1932- . . . . **CLC 32**
See also CA 85-88; MTCW; SATA 32

Fraser, George MacDonald 1925- . . . . **CLC 7**
See also CA 45-48; CANR 2

Fraser, Sylvia 1935- . . . . **CLC 64**
See also CA 45-48; CANR 1, 16

Frayn, Michael 1933- . . . . . . **CLC 3, 7, 31, 47**
See also CA 5-8R; CANR 30; DLB 13, 14; MTCW

Fraze, Candida (Merrill) 1945- . . . . . **CLC 50**
See also CA 126

Frazer, J(ames) G(eorge)
1854-1941 . . . . **TCLC 32**
See also CA 118

Frazer, Robert Caine
See Creasey, John

Frazer, Sir James George
See Frazer, J(ames) G(eorge)

Frazier, Ian 1951- . . . . **CLC 46**
See also CA 130

Frederic, Harold 1856-1898. . . . . . **NCLC 10**
See also DLB 12, 23

Frederick, John
See Faust, Frederick (Schiller)

Frederick the Great 1712-1786 . . . . . . **LC 14**

Fredro, Aleksander 1793-1876. . . . . **NCLC 8**

Freeling, Nicolas 1927- . . . . **CLC 38**
See also CA 49-52; CAAS 12; CANR 1, 17; DLB 87

Freeman, Douglas Southall
1886-1953 . . . . **TCLC 11**
See also CA 109; DLB 17

Freeman, Judith 1946- . . . . **CLC 55**

Freeman, Mary Eleanor Wilkins
1852-1930 . . . . **TCLC 9; SSC 1**
See also CA 106; DLB 12, 78

Freeman, R(ichard) Austin
1862-1943 . . . . **TCLC 21**
See also CA 113; DLB 70

French, Marilyn 1929- . . . . . . **CLC 10, 18, 60**
See also CA 69-72; CANR 3, 31; MTCW

French, Paul
See Asimov, Isaac

Freneau, Philip Morin 1752-1832 . . **NCLC 1**
See also DLB 37, 43

Freud, Sigmund 1856-1939 . . . . **TCLC 52**
See also CA 115; 133; MTCW

Friedan, Betty (Naomi) 1921- . . . . . . **CLC 74**
See also CA 65-68; CANR 18; MTCW

Friedman, B(ernard) H(arper)
1926- . . . . **CLC 7**
See also CA 1-4R; CANR 3

Friedman, Bruce Jay 1930- . . . . **CLC 3, 5, 56**
See also CA 9-12R; CANR 25; DLB 2, 28

Friel, Brian 1929- . . . . **CLC 5, 42, 59**
See also CA 21-24R; CANR 33; DLB 13; MTCW

Friis-Baastad, Babbis Ellinor
1921-1970 . . . . **CLC 12**
See also CA 17-20R; 134; SATA 7

Frisch, Max (Rudolf)
1911-1991 . . . . . **CLC 3, 9, 14, 18, 32, 44**
See also CA 85-88; 134; CANR 32; DLB 69, 124; MTCW

Fromentin, Eugene (Samuel Auguste)
1820-1876 . . . . **NCLC 10**
See also DLB 123

Frost, Frederick
See Faust, Frederick (Schiller)

Frost, Robert (Lee)
1874-1963 . . . . **CLC 1, 3, 4, 9, 10, 13, 15, 26, 34, 44; DA; PC 1; WLC**
See also CA 89-92; CANR 33; CDALB 1917-1929; DLB 54; DLBD 7; MTCW; SATA 14

Froude, James Anthony
1818-1894 . . . . **NCLC 43**
See also DLB 18, 57

Froy, Herald
See Waterhouse, Keith (Spencer)

Fry, Christopher 1907- . . . . **CLC 2, 10, 14**
See also CA 17-20R; CANR 9, 30; DLB 13; MTCW; SATA 66

Frye, (Herman) Northrop
1912-1991 . . . . **CLC 24, 70**
See also CA 5-8R; 133; CANR 8, 37; DLB 67, 68; MTCW

Fuchs, Daniel 1909-1993 . . . . **CLC 8, 22**
See also CA 81-84; 142; CAAS 5; CANR 40; DLB 9, 26, 28

Fuchs, Daniel 1934- . . . . **CLC 34**
See also CA 37-40R; CANR 14

Fuentes, Carlos
1928- . . . . . . **CLC 3, 8, 10, 13, 22, 41, 60; DA; HLC; WLC**
See also AAYA 4; AITN 2; CA 69-72; CANR 10, 32; DLB 113; HW; MTCW

Fuentes, Gregorio Lopez y
See Lopez y Fuentes, Gregorio

Fugard, (Harold) Athol
1932- . . . . **CLC 5, 9, 14, 25, 40, 80; DC 3**
See also CA 85-88; CANR 32; MTCW

Fugard, Sheila 1932- . . . . **CLC 48**
See also CA 125

Fuller, Charles (H., Jr.)
1939- . . . . **CLC 25; BLC; DC 1**
See also BW; CA 108; 112; DLB 38; MTCW

Fuller, John (Leopold) 1937- . . . . **CLC 62**
See also CA 21-24R; CANR 9; DLB 40

Fuller, Margaret . . . . **NCLC 5**
See also Ossoli, Sarah Margaret (Fuller marchesa d')

Fuller, Roy (Broadbent)
1912-1991 . . . . **CLC 4, 28**
See also CA 5-8R; 135; CAAS 10; DLB 15, 20

Fulton, Alice 1952- . . . . **CLC 52**
See also CA 116

Furphy, Joseph 1843-1912. . . . . **TCLC 25**

Fussell, Paul 1924- . . . . **CLC 74**
See also BEST 90:1; CA 17-20R; CANR 8, 21, 35; MTCW

Futabatei, Shimei 1864-1909 . . . . . . **TCLC 44**

Futrelle, Jacques 1875-1912 . . . . . . **TCLC 19**
See also CA 113

G. B. S.
See Shaw, George Bernard

Gaboriau, Emile 1835-1873 . . . . . . **NCLC 14**

Gadda, Carlo Emilio 1893-1973 . . . . **CLC 11**
See also CA 89-92

Gaddis, William
1922- . . . . **CLC 1, 3, 6, 8, 10, 19, 43**
See also CA 17-20R; CANR 21; DLB 2; MTCW

Gaines, Ernest J(ames)
1933- . . . . **CLC 3, 11, 18; BLC**
See also AITN 1; BW; CA 9-12R; CANR 6, 24, 42; CDALB 1968-1988; DLB 2, 33; DLBY 80; MTCW

Gaitskill, Mary 1954- . . . . **CLC 69**
See also CA 128

Galdos, Benito Perez
See Perez Galdos, Benito

Gale, Zona 1874-1938 . . . . **TCLC 7**
See also CA 105; DLB 9, 78

Galeano, Eduardo (Hughes) 1940- . . . **CLC 72**
See also CA 29-32R; CANR 13, 32; HW

Galiano, Juan Valera y Alcala
See Valera y Alcala-Galiano, Juan

Gallagher, Tess 1943- . . . . **CLC 18, 63**
See also CA 106; DLB 120

Gallant, Mavis
1922- . . . . **CLC 7, 18, 38; SSC 5**
See also CA 69-72; CANR 29; DLB 53; MTCW

Gill, Patrick
See Creasey, John

Gilliam, Terry (Vance) 1940- .... **CLC 21**
See also Monty Python
See also CA 108; 113; CANR 35

Gillian, Jerry
See Gilliam, Terry (Vance)

Gilliatt, Penelope (Ann Douglass)
1932-1993 .... **CLC 2, 10, 13, 53**
See also AITN 2; CA 13-16R; 141; DLB 14

Gilman, Charlotte (Anna) Perkins (Stetson)
1860-1935 .... **TCLC 9, 37; SSC 13**
See also CA 106

Gilmour, David 1949- .... **CLC 35**
See also Pink Floyd
See also CA 138

Gilpin, William 1724-1804 .... **NCLC 30**

Gilray, J. D.
See Mencken, H(enry) L(ouis)

Gilroy, Frank D(aniel) 1925- .... **CLC 2**
See also CA 81-84; CANR 32; DLB 7

Ginsberg, Allen
1926- ...... **CLC 1, 2, 3, 4, 6, 13, 36, 69; DA; PC 4; WLC 3**
See also AITN 1; CA 1-4R; CANR 2, 41; CDALB 1941-1968; DLB 5, 16; MTCW

Ginzburg, Natalia
1916-1991 .... **CLC 5, 11, 54, 70**
See also CA 85-88; 135; CANR 33; MTCW

Giono, Jean 1895-1970 .... **CLC 4, 11**
See also CA 45-48; 29-32R; CANR 2, 35; DLB 72; MTCW

Giovanni, Nikki
1943- ...... **CLC 2, 4, 19, 64; BLC; DA**
See also AITN 1; BW; CA 29-32R; CAAS 6; CANR 18, 41; CLR 6; DLB 5, 41; MAICYA; MTCW; SATA 24

Giovene, Andrea 1904- .... **CLC 7**
See also CA 85-88

Gippius, Zinaida (Nikolayevna) 1869-1945
See Hippius, Zinaida
See also CA 106

Giraudoux, (Hippolyte) Jean
1882-1944 .... **TCLC 2, 7**
See also CA 104; DLB 65

Gironella, Jose Maria 1917- .... **CLC 11**
See also CA 101

Gissing, George (Robert)
1857-1903 .... **TCLC 3, 24, 47**
See also CA 105; DLB 18, 135

Giurlani, Aldo
See Palazzeschi, Aldo

Gladkov, Fyodor (Vasilyevich)
1883-1958 .... **TCLC 27**

Glanville, Brian (Lester) 1931- ...... **CLC 6**
See also CA 5-8R; CAAS 9; CANR 3; DLB 15; SATA 42

Glasgow, Ellen (Anderson Gholson)
1873(?)-1945 .... **TCLC 2, 7**
See also CA 104; DLB 9, 12

Glassco, John 1909-1981 .... **CLC 9**
See also CA 13-16R; 102; CANR 15; DLB 68

Glasscock, Amnesia
See Steinbeck, John (Ernst)

Glasser, Ronald J. 1940(?)- .... **CLC 37**

Glassman, Joyce
See Johnson, Joyce

Glendinning, Victoria 1937- .... **CLC 50**
See also CA 120; 127

Glissant, Edouard 1928- .... **CLC 10, 68**

Gloag, Julian 1930- .... **CLC 40**
See also AITN 1; CA 65-68; CANR 10

Gluck, Louise (Elisabeth)
1943- .... **CLC 7, 22, 44, 81**
See also Glueck, Louise
See also CA 33-36R; CANR 40; DLB 5

Glueck, Louise
See also Gluck, Louise (Elisabeth)
See also DLB 5

Gobineau, Joseph Arthur (Comte) de
1816-1882 .... **NCLC 17**
See also DLB 123

Godard, Jean-Luc 1930- .... **CLC 20**
See also CA 93-96

Godden, (Margaret) Rumer 1907- ... **CLC 53**
See also AAYA 6; CA 5-8R; CANR 4, 27, 36; CLR 20; MAICYA; SAAS 12; SATA 3, 36

Godoy Alcayaga, Lucila 1889-1957
See Mistral, Gabriela
See also CA 104; 131; HW; MTCW

Godwin, Gail (Kathleen)
1937- .... **CLC 5, 8, 22, 31, 69**
See also CA 29-32R; CANR 15, 43; DLB 6; MTCW

Godwin, William 1756-1836 ...... **NCLC 14**
See also CDBLB 1789-1832; DLB 39, 104

Goethe, Johann Wolfgang von
1749-1832 .... **NCLC 4, 22, 34; DA; PC 5; WLC 3**
See also DLB 94

Gogarty, Oliver St. John
1878-1957 .... **TCLC 15**
See also CA 109; DLB 15, 19

Gogol, Nikolai (Vasilyevich)
1809-1852 .... **NCLC 5, 15, 31; DA; DC 1; SSC 4; WLC**

Goines, Donald
1937(?)-1974 .... **CLC 80; BLC**
See also AITN 1; BW; CA 124; 114; DLB 33

Gold, Herbert 1924- .... **CLC 4, 7, 14, 42**
See also CA 9-12R; CANR 17; DLB 2; DLBY 81

Goldbarth, Albert 1948- .... **CLC 5, 38**
See also CA 53-56; CANR 6, 40; DLB 120

Goldberg, Anatol 1910-1982 .... **CLC 34**
See also CA 131; 117

Goldemberg, Isaac 1945- .... **CLC 52**
See also CA 69-72; CAAS 12; CANR 11, 32; HW

Golden Silver
See Storm, Hyemeyohsts

Golding, William (Gerald)
1911-1993 .... **CLC 1, 2, 3, 8, 10, 17, 27, 58, 81; DA; WLC**
See also AAYA 5; CA 5-8R; 141; CANR 13, 33; CDBLB 1945-1960; DLB 15, 100; MTCW

Goldman, Emma 1869-1940 .... **TCLC 13**
See also CA 110

Goldman, Francisco 1955- .... **CLC 76**

Goldman, William (W.) 1931- .... **CLC 1, 48**
See also CA 9-12R; CANR 29; DLB 44

Goldmann, Lucien 1913-1970 ...... **CLC 24**
See also CA 25-28; CAP 2

Goldoni, Carlo 1707-1793 .... **LC 4**

Goldsberry, Steven 1949- .... **CLC 34**
See also CA 131

Goldsmith, Oliver
1728-1774 .... **LC 2; DA; WLC**
See also CDBLB 1660-1789; DLB 39, 89, 104, 109; SATA 26

Goldsmith, Peter
See Priestley, J(ohn) B(oynton)

Gombrowicz, Witold
1904-1969 .... **CLC 4, 7, 11, 49**
See also CA 19-20; 25-28R; CAP 2

Gomez de la Serna, Ramon
1888-1963 .... **CLC 9**
See also CA 116; HW

Goncharov, Ivan Alexandrovich
1812-1891 .... **NCLC 1**

Goncourt, Edmond (Louis Antoine Huot) de
1822-1896 .... **NCLC 7**
See also DLB 123

Goncourt, Jules (Alfred Huot) de
1830-1870 .... **NCLC 7**
See also DLB 123

Gontier, Fernande 19(?)- .... **CLC 50**

Goodman, Paul 1911-1972 .... **CLC 1, 2, 4, 7**
See also CA 19-20; 37-40R; CANR 34; CAP 2; DLB 130; MTCW

Gordimer, Nadine
1923- .... **CLC 3, 5, 7, 10, 18, 33, 51, 70; DA**
See also CA 5-8R; CANR 3, 28; MTCW

Gordon, Adam Lindsay
1833-1870 .... **NCLC 21**

Gordon, Caroline
1895-1981 .... **CLC 6, 13, 29**
See also CA 11-12; 103; CANR 36; CAP 1; DLB 4, 9, 102; DLBY 81; MTCW

Gordon, Charles William 1860-1937
See Connor, Ralph
See also CA 109

Gordon, Mary (Catherine)
1949- .... **CLC 13, 22**
See also CA 102; DLB 6; DLBY 81; MTCW

Gordon, Sol 1923- .... **CLC 26**
See also CA 53-56; CANR 4; SATA 11

Gordone, Charles 1925- .... **CLC 1, 4**
See also BW; CA 93-96; DLB 7; MTCW

Gorenko, Anna Andreevna
See Akhmatova, Anna

Gorky, Maxim .... **TCLC 8; WLC**
See also Peshkov, Alexei Maximovich

Goryan, Sirak
See Saroyan, William

Gosse, Edmund (William)
1849-1928 .... **TCLC 28**
See also CA 117; DLB 57

Grimble, Reverend Charles James
See Eliot, T(homas) S(tearns)

Grimke, Charlotte L(ottie) Forten 1837(?)-1914
See Forten, Charlotte L.
See also BW; CA 117; 124

Grimm, Jacob Ludwig Karl 1785-1863 .... **NCLC 3**
See also DLB 90; MAICYA; SATA 22

Grimm, Wilhelm Karl 1786-1859 .. **NCLC 3**
See also DLB 90; MAICYA; SATA 22

Grimmelshausen, Johann Jakob Christoffel von 1621-1676 .... **LC 6**

Grindel, Eugene 1895-1952
See Eluard, Paul
See also CA 104

Grossman, David 1954- .... **CLC 67**
See also CA 138

Grossman, Vasily (Semenovich) 1905-1964 .... **CLC 41**
See also CA 124; 130; MTCW

Grove, Frederick Philip .... **TCLC 4**
See also Greve, Felix Paul (Berthold Friedrich)
See also DLB 92

Grubb
See Crumb, R(obert)

Grumbach, Doris (Isaac) 1918- .... **CLC 13, 22, 64**
See also CA 5-8R; CAAS 2; CANR 9, 42

Grundtvig, Nicolai Frederik Severin 1783-1872 .... **NCLC 1**

Grunge
See Crumb, R(obert)

Grunwald, Lisa 1959-............. **CLC 44**
See also CA 120

Guare, John 1938- .... **CLC 8, 14, 29, 67**
See also CA 73-76; CANR 21; DLB 7; MTCW

Gudjonsson, Halldor Kiljan 1902-
See Laxness, Halldor
See also CA 103

Guenter, Erich
See Eich, Guenter

Guest, Barbara 1920-............. **CLC 34**
See also CA 25-28R; CANR 11; DLB 5

Guest, Judith (Ann) 1936- .... **CLC 8, 30**
See also AAYA 7; CA 77-80; CANR 15; MTCW

Guild, Nicholas M. 1944-.......... **CLC 33**
See also CA 93-96

Guillemin, Jacques
See Sartre, Jean-Paul

Guillen, Jorge 1893-1984.......... **CLC 11**
See also CA 89-92; 112; DLB 108; HW

Guillen (y Batista), Nicolas (Cristobal) 1902-1989 ..... **CLC 48, 79; BLC; HLC**
See also BW; CA 116; 125; 129; HW

Guillevic, (Eugene) 1907-.......... **CLC 33**
See also CA 93-96

Guillois
See Desnos, Robert

Guiney, Louise Imogen 1861-1920 .... **TCLC 41**
See also DLB 54

Guiraldes, Ricardo (Guillermo) 1886-1927 .... **TCLC 39**
See also CA 131; HW; MTCW

Gunn, Bill .... **CLC 5**
See also Gunn, William Harrison
See also DLB 38

Gunn, Thom(son William) 1929- .... **CLC 3, 6, 18, 32, 81**
See also CA 17-20R; CANR 9, 33; CDBLB 1960 to Present; DLB 27; MTCW

Gunn, William Harrison 1934(?)-1989
See Gunn, Bill
See also AITN 1; BW; CA 13-16R; 128; CANR 12, 25

Gunnars, Kristjana 1948-.......... **CLC 69**
See also CA 113; DLB 60

Gurganus, Allan 1947-............ **CLC 70**
See also BEST 90:1; CA 135

Gurney, A(lbert) R(amsdell), Jr. 1930- .... **CLC 32, 50, 54**
See also CA 77-80; CANR 32

Gurney, Ivor (Bertie) 1890-1937... **TCLC 33**

Gurney, Peter
See Gurney, A(lbert) R(amsdell), Jr.

Gustafson, Ralph (Barker) 1909-.... **CLC 36**
See also CA 21-24R; CANR 8; DLB 88

Gut, Gom
See Simenon, Georges (Jacques Christian)

Guthrie, A(lfred) B(ertram), Jr. 1901-1991 .... **CLC 23**
See also CA 57-60; 134; CANR 24; DLB 6; SATA 62; SATA-Obit 67

Guthrie, Isobel
See Grieve, C(hristopher) M(urray)

Guthrie, Woodrow Wilson 1912-1967
See Guthrie, Woody
See also CA 113; 93-96

Guthrie, Woody.................. **CLC 35**
See also Guthrie, Woodrow Wilson

Guy, Rosa (Cuthbert) 1928-........ **CLC 26**
See also AAYA 4; BW; CA 17-20R; CANR 14, 34; CLR 13; DLB 33; JRDA; MAICYA; SATA 14, 62

Gwendolyn
See Bennett, (Enoch) Arnold

H. D. .... **CLC 3, 8, 14, 31, 34, 73; PC 5**
See also Doolittle, Hilda

Haavikko, Paavo Juhani 1931- .... **CLC 18, 34**
See also CA 106

Habbema, Koos
See Heijermans, Herman

Hacker, Marilyn 1942- .... **CLC 5, 9, 23, 72**
See also CA 77-80; DLB 120

Haggard, H(enry) Rider 1856-1925 .... **TCLC 11**
See also CA 108; DLB 70; SATA 16

Haig, Fenil
See Ford, Ford Madox

Haig-Brown, Roderick (Langmere) 1908-1976 .... **CLC 21**
See also CA 5-8R; 69-72; CANR 4, 38; CLR 31; DLB 88; MAICYA; SATA 12

Hailey, Arthur 1920- .... **CLC 5**
See also AITN 2; BEST 90:3; CA 1-4R; CANR 2, 36; DLB 88; DLBY 82; MTCW

Hailey, Elizabeth Forsythe 1938-... **CLC 40**
See also CA 93-96; CAAS 1; CANR 15

Haines, John (Meade) 1924-....... **CLC 58**
See also CA 17-20R; CANR 13, 34; DLB 5

Haldeman, Joe (William) 1943-..... **CLC 61**
See also CA 53-56; CANR 6; DLB 8

Haley, Alex(ander Murray Palmer) 1921-1992 .... **CLC 8, 12, 76; BLC; DA**
See also BW; CA 77-80; 136; DLB 38; MTCW

Haliburton, Thomas Chandler 1796-1865 .... **NCLC 15**
See also DLB 11, 99

Hall, Donald (Andrew, Jr.) 1928- .... **CLC 1, 13, 37, 59**
See also CA 5-8R; CAAS 7; CANR 2; DLB 5; SATA 23

Hall, Frederic Sauser
See Sauser-Hall, Frederic

Hall, James
See Kuttner, Henry

Hall, James Norman 1887-1951 ... **TCLC 23**
See also CA 123; SATA 21

Hall, (Marguerite) Radclyffe 1886(?)-1943 .... **TCLC 12**
See also CA 110

Hall, Rodney 1935- .... **CLC 51**
See also CA 109

Halliday, Michael
See Creasey, John

Halpern, Daniel 1945-............ **CLC 14**
See also CA 33-36R

Hamburger, Michael (Peter Leopold) 1924- .... **CLC 5, 14**
See also CA 5-8R; CAAS 4; CANR 2; DLB 27

Hamill, Pete 1935-.............. **CLC 10**
See also CA 25-28R; CANR 18

Hamilton, Clive
See Lewis, C(live) S(taples)

Hamilton, Edmond 1904-1977....... **CLC 1**
See also CA 1-4R; CANR 3; DLB 8

Hamilton, Eugene (Jacob) Lee
See Lee-Hamilton, Eugene (Jacob)

Hamilton, Franklin
See Silverberg, Robert

Hamilton, Gail
See Corcoran, Barbara

Hamilton, Mollie
See Kaye, M(ary) M(argaret)

Hamilton, (Anthony Walter) Patrick 1904-1962 .... **CLC 51**
See also CA 113; DLB 10

Hamilton, Virginia 1936-.......... **CLC 26**
See also AAYA 2; BW; CA 25-28R; CANR 20, 37; CLR 1, 11; DLB 33, 52; JRDA; MAICYA; MTCW; SATA 4, 56

Hazlitt, William 1778-1830 ...... **NCLC 29**
See also DLB 110

Hazzard, Shirley 1931- .... **CLC 18**
See also CA 9-12R; CANR 4; DLBY 82; MTCW

Head, Bessie 1937-1986... **CLC 25, 67; BLC**
See also BW; CA 29-32R; 119; CANR 25; DLB 117; MTCW

Headon, (Nicky) Topper 1956(?)- ... **CLC 30**
See also Clash, The

Heaney, Seamus (Justin)
1939- .... **CLC 5, 7, 14, 25, 37, 74**
See also CA 85-88; CANR 25; CDBLB 1960 to Present; DLB 40; MTCW

Hearn, (Patricio) Lafcadio (Tessima Carlos)
1850-1904 .... **TCLC 9**
See also CA 105; DLB 12, 78

Hearne, Vicki 1946- .... **CLC 56**
See also CA 139

Hearon, Shelby 1931-............. **CLC 63**
See also AITN 2; CA 25-28R; CANR 18

Heat-Moon, William Least .... **CLC 29**
See also Trogdon, William (Lewis)
See also AAYA 9

Hebbel, Friedrich 1813-1863..... **NCLC 43**
See also DLB 129

Hebert, Anne 1916- .... **CLC 4, 13, 29**
See also CA 85-88; DLB 68; MTCW

Hecht, Anthony (Evan)
1923- .... **CLC 8, 13, 19**
See also CA 9-12R; CANR 6; DLB 5

Hecht, Ben 1894-1964 .... **CLC 8**
See also CA 85-88; DLB 7, 9, 25, 26, 28, 86

Hedayat, Sadeq 1903-1951........ **TCLC 21**
See also CA 120

Heidegger, Martin 1889-1976 ...... **CLC 24**
See also CA 81-84; 65-68; CANR 34; MTCW

Heidenstam, (Carl Gustaf) Verner von
1859-1940 .... **TCLC 5**
See also CA 104

Heifner, Jack 1946- .... **CLC 11**
See also CA 105

Heijermans, Herman 1864-1924 ... **TCLC 24**
See also CA 123

Heilbrun, Carolyn G(old) 1926-..... **CLC 25**
See also CA 45-48; CANR 1, 28

Heine, Heinrich 1797-1856 .... **NCLC 4**
See also DLB 90

Heinemann, Larry (Curtiss) 1944- .. **CLC 50**
See also CA 110; CANR 31; DLBD 9

Heiney, Donald (William)
1921-1993 .... **CLC 9**
See also CA 1-4R; 142; CANR 3

Heinlein, Robert A(nson)
1907-1988 ...... **CLC 1, 3, 8, 14, 26, 55**
See also CA 1-4R; 125; CANR 1, 20; DLB 8; JRDA; MAICYA; MTCW; SATA 9, 56, 69

Helforth, John
See Doolittle, Hilda

Hellenhofferu, Vojtech Kapristian z
See Hasek, Jaroslav (Matej Frantisek)

Heller, Joseph
1923- .... **CLC 1, 3, 5, 8, 11, 36, 63; DA; WLC**
See also AITN 1; CA 5-8R; CABS 1; CANR 8, 42; DLB 2, 28; DLBY 80; MTCW

Hellman, Lillian (Florence)
1906-1984 ...... **CLC 2, 4, 8, 14, 18, 34, 44, 52; DC 1**
See also AITN 1, 2; CA 13-16R; 112; CANR 33; DLB 7; DLBY 84; MTCW

Helprin, Mark 1947- ..... **CLC 7, 10, 22, 32**
See also CA 81-84; DLBY 85; MTCW

Helyar, Jane Penelope Josephine 1933-
See Poole, Josephine
See also CA 21-24R; CANR 10, 26

Hemans, Felicia 1793-1835 ...... **NCLC 29**
See also DLB 96

Hemingway, Ernest (Miller)
1899-1961 .... **CLC 1, 3, 6, 8, 10, 13, 19, 30, 34, 39, 41, 44, 50, 61, 80; DA; SSC 1; WLC**
See also CA 77-80; CANR 34; CDALB 1917-1929; DLB 4, 9, 102; DLBD 1; DLBY 81, 87; MTCW

Hempel, Amy 1951- .... **CLC 39**
See also CA 118; 137

Henderson, F. C.
See Mencken, H(enry) L(ouis)

Henderson, Sylvia
See Ashton-Warner, Sylvia (Constance)

Henley, Beth .... **CLC 23**
See also Henley, Elizabeth Becker
See also CABS 3; DLBY 86

Henley, Elizabeth Becker 1952-
See Henley, Beth
See also CA 107; CANR 32; MTCW

Henley, William Ernest
1849-1903 .... **TCLC 8**
See also CA 105; DLB 19

Hennissart, Martha
See Lathen, Emma
See also CA 85-88

Henry, O......... **TCLC 1, 19; SSC 5; WLC**
See also Porter, William Sydney

Henry, Patrick 1736-1799 .... **LC 25**

Henryson, Robert 1430(?)-1506(?).... **LC 20**

Henry VIII 1491-1547 .... **LC 10**

Henschke, Alfred
See Klabund

Hentoff, Nat(han Irving) 1925- ..... **CLC 26**
See also AAYA 4; CA 1-4R; CAAS 6; CANR 5, 25; CLR 1; JRDA; MAICYA; SATA 27, 42, 69

Heppenstall, (John) Rayner
1911-1981 .... **CLC 10**
See also CA 1-4R; 103; CANR 29

Herbert, Frank (Patrick)
1920-1986 .... **CLC 12, 23, 35, 44**
See also CA 5 '-56; 118; CANR 5, 43; DLB 8; MTCW; SATA 9, 37, 47

Herbert, George 1593-1633 .... **LC 24; PC 4**
See also CDBLB Before 1660; DLB 126

Herbert, Zbigniew 1924- .... **CLC 9, 43**
See also CA 89-92; CANR 36; MTCW

Herbst, Josephine (Frey)
1897-1969 .... **CLC 34**
See also CA 5-8R; 25-28R; DLB 9

Hergesheimer, Joseph
1880-1954 .... **TCLC 11**
See also CA 109; DLB 102, 9

Herlihy, James Leo 1927-1993 ...... **CLC 6**
See also CA 1-4R; 143; CANR 2

Hermogenes fl. c. 175- .... **CMLC 6**

Hernandez, Jose 1834-1886...... **NCLC 17**

Herrick, Robert 1591-1674 ..... **LC 13; DA**
See also DLB 126

Herring, Guilles
See Somerville, Edith

Herriot, James 1916- .... **CLC 12**
See also Wight, James Alfred
See also AAYA 1; CANR 40

Herrmann, Dorothy 1941- .... **CLC 44**
See also CA 107

Herrmann, Taffy
See Herrmann, Dorothy

Hersey, John (Richard)
1914-1993 .... **CLC 1, 2, 7, 9, 40, 81**
See also CA 17-20R; 140; CANR 33; DLB 6; MTCW; SATA 25; SATA-Obit 76

Herzen, Aleksandr Ivanovich
1812-1870 .... **NCLC 10**

Herzl, Theodor 1860-1904 .... **TCLC 36**

Herzog, Werner 1942- .... **CLC 16**
See also CA 89-92

Hesiod c. 8th cent. B.C.- .... **CMLC 5**

Hesse, Hermann
1877-1962 .... **CLC 1, 2, 3, 6, 11, 17, 25, 69; DA; SSC 9; WLC**
See also CA 17-18; CAP 2; DLB 66; MTCW; SATA 50

Hewes, Cady
See De Voto, Bernard (Augustine)

Heyen, William 1940- .... **CLC 13, 18**
See also CA 33-36R; CAAS 9; DLB 5

Heyerdahl, Thor 1914-........... **CLC 26**
See also CA 5-8R; CANR 5, 22; MTCW; SATA 2, 52

Heym, Georg (Theodor Franz Arthur)
1887-1912 .... **TCLC 9**
See also CA 106

Heym, Stefan 1913- .... **CLC 41**
See also CA 9-12R; CANR 4; DLB 69

Heyse, Paul (Johann Ludwig von)
1830-1914 .... **TCLC 8**
See also CA 104; DLB 129

Hibbert, Eleanor Alice Burford
1906-1993 .... **CLC 7**
See also BEST 90:4; CA 17-20R; 140; CANR 9, 28; SATA 2; SATA-Obit 74

Higgins, George V(incent)
1939- .... **CLC 4, 7, 10, 18**
See also CA 77-80; CAAS 5; CANR 17; DLB 2; DLBY 81; MTCW

Higginson, Thomas Wentworth
1823-1911 .... **TCLC 36**
See also DLB 1, 64

Highet, Helen
See MacInnes, Helen (Clark)

Highsmith, (Mary) Patricia 1921- . . . . **CLC 2, 4, 14, 42**
See also CA 1-4R; CANR 1, 20; MTCW

Highwater, Jamake (Mamake) 1942(?)- . . . . **CLC 12**
See also AAYA 7; CA 65-68; CAAS 7; CANR 10, 34; CLR 17; DLB 52; DLBY 85; JRDA; MAICYA; SATA 30, 32, 69

Hijuelos, Oscar 1951- . . . . . . **CLC 65; HLC**
See also BEST 90:1; CA 123; HW

Hikmet, Nazim 1902(?)-1963. . . . . . . **CLC 40**
See also CA 141; 93-96

Hildesheimer, Wolfgang 1916-1991 . . . . **CLC 49**
See also CA 101; 135; DLB 69, 124

Hill, Geoffrey (William) 1932- . . . . **CLC 5, 8, 18, 45**
See also CA 81-84; CANR 21; CDBLB 1960 to Present; DLB 40; MTCW

Hill, George Roy 1921- . . . . **CLC 26**
See also CA 110; 122

Hill, John
See Koontz, Dean R(ay)

Hill, Susan (Elizabeth) 1942- . . . . **CLC 4**
See also CA 33-36R; CANR 29; DLB 14; MTCW

Hillerman, Tony 1925-. . . . . **CLC 62**
See also AAYA 6; BEST 89:1; CA 29-32R; CANR 21, 42; SATA 6

Hillesum, Etty 1914-1943 . . . . **TCLC 49**
See also CA 137

Hilliard, Noel (Harvey) 1929-. . . . . . **CLC 15**
See also CA 9-12R; CANR 7

Hillis, Rick 1956-. . . . . **CLC 66**
See also CA 134

Hilton, James 1900-1954 . . . . **TCLC 21**
See also CA 108; DLB 34, 77; SATA 34

Himes, Chester (Bomar) 1909-1984 . . . . **CLC 2, 4, 7, 18, 58; BLC**
See also BW; CA 25-28R; 114; CANR 22; DLB 2, 76; MTCW

Hinde, Thomas . . . . **CLC 6, 11**
See also Chitty, Thomas Willes

Hindin, Nathan
See Bloch, Robert (Albert)

Hine, (William) Daryl 1936- . . . . **CLC 15**
See also CA 1-4R; CAAS 15; CANR 1, 20; DLB 60

Hinkson, Katharine Tynan
See Tynan, Katharine

Hinton, S(usan) E(loise) 1950- . . . . **CLC 30; DA**
See also AAYA 2; CA 81-84; CANR 32; CLR 3, 23; JRDA; MAICYA; MTCW; SATA 19, 58

Hippius, Zinaida . . . . **TCLC 9**
See also Gippius, Zinaida (Nikolayevna)

Hiraoka, Kimitake 1925-1970
See Mishima, Yukio
See also CA 97-100; 29-32R; MTCW

Hirsch, E(ric) D(onald), Jr. 1928-. . . **CLC 79**
See also CA 25-28R; CANR 27; DLB 67; MTCW

Hirsch, Edward 1950- . . . . **CLC 31, 50**
See also CA 104; CANR 20, 42; DLB 120

Hitchcock, Alfred (Joseph) 1899-1980 . . . . **CLC 16**
See also CA 97-100; SATA 24, 27

Hitler, Adolf 1889-1945. . . . . **TCLC 53**
See also CA 117

Hoagland, Edward 1932- . . . . **CLC 28**
See also CA 1-4R; CANR 2, 31; DLB 6; SATA 51

Hoban, Russell (Conwell) 1925- . . **CLC 7, 25**
See also CA 5-8R; CANR 23, 37; CLR 3; DLB 52; MAICYA; MTCW; SATA 1, 40

Hobbs, Perry
See Blackmur, R(ichard) P(almer)

Hobson, Laura Z(ametkin) 1900-1986 . . . . **CLC 7, 25**
See also CA 17-20R; 118; DLB 28; SATA 52

Hochhuth, Rolf 1931-. . . . . **CLC 4, 11, 18**
See also CA 5-8R; CANR 33; DLB 124; MTCW

Hochman, Sandra 1936-. . . . . **CLC 3, 8**
See also CA 5-8R; DLB 5

Hochwaelder, Fritz 1911-1986. . . . . . **CLC 36**
See also CA 29-32R; 120; CANR 42; MTCW

Hochwalder, Fritz
See Hochwaelder, Fritz

Hocking, Mary (Eunice) 1921- . . . . . **CLC 13**
See also CA 101; CANR 18, 40

Hodgins, Jack 1938-. . . . . **CLC 23**
See also CA 93-96; DLB 60

Hodgson, William Hope 1877(?)-1918 . . . . **TCLC 13**
See also CA 111; DLB 70

Hoffman, Alice 1952-. . . . . **CLC 51**
See also CA 77-80; CANR 34; MTCW

Hoffman, Daniel (Gerard) 1923- . . . . **CLC 6, 13, 23**
See also CA 1-4R; CANR 4; DLB 5

Hoffman, Stanley 1944-. . . . . **CLC 5**
See also CA 77-80

Hoffman, William M(oses) 1939- . . . **CLC 40**
See also CA 57-60; CANR 11

Hoffmann, E(rnst) T(heodor) A(madeus) 1776-1822 . . . . **NCLC 2; SSC 13**
See also DLB 90; SATA 27

Hofmann, Gert 1931-. . . . . **CLC 54**
See also CA 128

Hofmannsthal, Hugo von 1874-1929 . . . . **TCLC 11; DC 4**
See also CA 106; DLB 81, 118

Hogan, Linda 1947- . . . . **CLC 73**
See also CA 120

Hogarth, Charles
See Creasey, John

Hogg, James 1770-1835. . . . . **NCLC 4**
See also DLB 93, 116

Holbach, Paul Henri Thiry Baron 1723-1789 . . . . **LC 14**

Holberg, Ludvig 1684-1754 . . . . **LC 6**

Holden, Ursula 1921-. . . . . **CLC 18**
See also CA 101; CAAS 8; CANR 22

Holderlin, (Johann Christian) Friedrich 1770-1843 . . . . **NCLC 16; PC 4**

Holdstock, Robert
See Holdstock, Robert P.

Holdstock, Robert P. 1948-. . . . . **CLC 39**
See also CA 131

Holland, Isabelle 1920- . . . . **CLC 21**
See also CA 21-24R; CANR 10, 25; JRDA; MAICYA; SATA 8, 70

Holland, Marcus
See Caldwell, (Janet Miriam) Taylor (Holland)

Hollander, John 1929-. . . . . . **CLC 2, 5, 8, 14**
See also CA 1-4R; CANR 1; DLB 5; SATA 13

Hollander, Paul
See Silverberg, Robert

Holleran, Andrew 1943(?)-. . . . . **CLC 38**

Hollinghurst, Alan 1954-. . . . . **CLC 55**
See also CA 114

Hollis, Jim
See Summers, Hollis (Spurgeon, Jr.)

Holmes, John
See Souster, (Holmes) Raymond

Holmes, John Clellon 1926-1988. . . . **CLC 56**
See also CA 9-12R; 125; CANR 4; DLB 16

Holmes, Oliver Wendell 1809-1894 . . . . **NCLC 14**
See also CDALB 1640-1865; DLB 1; SATA 34

Holmes, Raymond
See Souster, (Holmes) Raymond

Holt, Victoria
See Hibbert, Eleanor Alice Burford

Holub, Miroslav 1923-. . . . . **CLC 4**
See also CA 21-24R; CANR 10

Homer c. 8th cent. B.C.- . . . . . **CMLC 1; DA**

Honig, Edwin 1919- . . . . **CLC 33**
See also CA 5-8R; CAAS 8; CANR 4; DLB 5

Hood, Hugh (John Blagdon) 1928- . . . . **CLC 15, 28**
See also CA 49-52; CAAS 17; CANR 1, 33; DLB 53

Hood, Thomas 1799-1845. . . . . **NCLC 16**
See also DLB 96

Hooker, (Peter) Jeremy 1941-. . . . . . **CLC 43**
See also CA 77-80; CANR 22; DLB 40

Hope, A(lec) D(erwent) 1907- . . . . **CLC 3, 51**
See also CA 21-24R; CANR 33; MTCW

Hope, Brian
See Creasey, John

Hope, Christopher (David Tully) 1944- . . . . **CLC 52**
See also CA 106; SATA 62

Hopkins, Gerard Manley 1844-1889 . . . . **NCLC 17; DA; WLC**
See also CDBLB 1890-1914; DLB 35, 57

Hopkins, John (Richard) 1931-. . . . . . **CLC 4**
See also CA 85-88

Hopkins, Pauline Elizabeth 1859-1930 . . . . **TCLC 28; BLC**
See also CA 141; DLB 50

Hopkinson, Francis 1737-1791 . . . . . . **LC 25**
See also DLB 31

Hopley-Woolrich, Cornell George 1903-1968
See Woolrich, Cornell
See also CA 13-14; CAP 1

Horatio
See Proust, (Valentin-Louis-George-Eugene-) Marcel

Horgan, Paul 1903- . . . . **CLC 9, 53**
See also CA 13-16R; CANR 9, 35; DLB 102; DLBY 85; MTCW; SATA 13

Horn, Peter
See Kuttner, Henry

Hornem, Horace Esq.
See Byron, George Gordon (Noel)

Horovitz, Israel 1939- . . . . **CLC 56**
See also CA 33-36R; DLB 7

Horvath, Odon von
See Horvath, Oedoen von
See also DLB 85, 124

Horvath, Oedoen von 1901-1938. . . **TCLC 45**
See also Horvath, Odon von
See also CA 118

Horwitz, Julius 1920-1986. . . . . **CLC 14**
See also CA 9-12R; 119; CANR 12

Hospital, Janette Turner 1942-. . . . . **CLC 42**
See also CA 108

Hostos, E. M. de
See Hostos (y Bonilla), Eugenio Maria de

Hostos, Eugenio M. de
See Hostos (y Bonilla), Eugenio Maria de

Hostos, Eugenio Maria
See Hostos (y Bonilla), Eugenio Maria de

Hostos (y Bonilla), Eugenio Maria de 1839-1903 . . . . **TCLC 24**
See also CA 123; 131; HW

Houdini
See Lovecraft, H(oward) P(hillips)

Hougan, Carolyn 1943- . . . . **CLC 34**
See also CA 139

Household, Geoffrey (Edward West) 1900-1988 . . . . **CLC 11**
See also CA 77-80; 126; DLB 87; SATA 14, 59

Housman, A(lfred) E(dward) 1859-1936 . . . . . . **TCLC 1, 10; DA; PC 2**
See also CA 104; 125; DLB 19; MTCW

Housman, Laurence 1865-1959 . . . . . **TCLC 7**
See also CA 106; DLB 10; SATA 25

Howard, Elizabeth Jane 1923- . . . **CLC 7, 29**
See also CA 5-8R; CANR 8

Howard, Maureen 1930- . . . . . **CLC 5, 14, 46**
See also CA 53-56; CANR 31; DLBY 83; MTCW

Howard, Richard 1929- . . . . . . **CLC 7, 10, 47**
See also AITN 1; CA 85-88; CANR 25; DLB 5

Howard, Robert Ervin 1906-1936 . . . **TCLC 8**
See also CA 105

Howard, Warren F.
See Pohl, Frederik

Howe, Fanny 1940- . . . . **CLC 47**
See also CA 117; SATA 52

Howe, Julia Ward 1819-1910 . . . . . **TCLC 21**
See also CA 117; DLB 1

Howe, Susan 1937-. . . . . **CLC 72**
See also DLB 120

Howe, Tina 1937-. . . . . **CLC 48**
See also CA 109

Howell, James 1594(?)-1666 . . . . **LC 13**

Howells, W. D.
See Howells, William Dean

Howells, William D.
See Howells, William Dean

Howells, William Dean 1837-1920 . . . . **TCLC 7, 17, 41**
See also CA 104; 134; CDALB 1865-1917; DLB 12, 64, 74, 79

Howes, Barbara 1914- . . . . **CLC 15**
See also CA 9-12R; CAAS 3; SATA 5

Hrabal, Bohumil 1914-. . . . . **CLC 13, 67**
See also CA 106; CAAS 12

Hsun, Lu . . . . **TCLC 3**
See also Shu-Jen, Chou

Hubbard, L(afayette) Ron(ald) 1911-1986 . . . . **CLC 43**
See also CA 77-80; 118; CANR 22

Huch, Ricarda (Octavia) 1864-1947 . . . . **TCLC 13**
See also CA 111; DLB 66

Huddle, David 1942- . . . . **CLC 49**
See also CA 57-60; DLB 130

Hudson, Jeffrey
See Crichton, (John) Michael

Hudson, W(illiam) H(enry) 1841-1922 . . . . **TCLC 29**
See also CA 115; DLB 98; SATA 35

Hueffer, Ford Madox
See Ford, Ford Madox

Hughart, Barry 1934-. . . . . **CLC 39**
See also CA 137

Hughes, Colin
See Creasey, John

Hughes, David (John) 1930- . . . . **CLC 48**
See also CA 116; 129; DLB 14

Hughes, (James) Langston 1902-1967 . . . . . **CLC 1, 5, 10, 15, 35, 44; BLC; DA; DC 3; PC 1; SSC 6; WLC**
See also BW; CA 1-4R; 25-28R; CANR 1, 34; CDALB 1929-1941; CLR 17; DLB 4, 7, 48, 51, 86; JRDA; MAICYA; MTCW; SATA 4, 33

Hughes, Richard (Arthur Warren) 1900-1976 . . . . **CLC 1, 11**
See also CA 5-8R; 65-68; CANR 4; DLB 15; MTCW; SATA 8, 25

Hughes, Ted 1930- . . . . **CLC 2, 4, 9, 14, 37; PC 7**
See also CA 1-4R; CANR 1, 33; CLR 3; DLB 40; MAICYA; MTCW; SATA 27, 49

Hugo, Richard F(ranklin) 1923-1982 . . . . **CLC 6, 18, 32**
See also CA 49-52; 108; CANR 3; DLB 5

Hugo, Victor (Marie) 1802-1885 . . **NCLC 3, 10, 21; DA; WLC**
See also DLB 119; SATA 47

Huidobro, Vicente
See Huidobro Fernandez, Vicente Garcia

Huidobro Fernandez, Vicente Garcia 1893-1948 . . . . **TCLC 31**
See also CA 131; HW

Hulme, Keri 1947- . . . . **CLC 39**
See also CA 125

Hulme, T(homas) E(rnest) 1883-1917 . . . . **TCLC 21**
See also CA 117; DLB 19

Hume, David 1711-1776. . . . . **LC 7**
See also DLB 104

Humphrey, William 1924- . . . . **CLC 45**
See also CA 77-80; DLB 6

Humphreys, Emyr Owen 1919-. . . . . **CLC 47**
See also CA 5-8R; CANR 3, 24; DLB 15

Humphreys, Josephine 1945-. . . . **CLC 34, 57**
See also CA 121; 127

Hungerford, Pixie
See Brinsmead, H(esba) F(ay)

Hunt, E(verette) Howard, Jr. 1918- . . . . **CLC 3**
See also AITN 1; CA 45-48; CANR 2

Hunt, Kyle
See Creasey, John

Hunt, (James Henry) Leigh 1784-1859 . . . . **NCLC 1**

Hunt, Marsha 1946-. . . . . **CLC 70**
See also CA 143

Hunt, Violet 1866-1942 . . . . **TCLC 53**

Hunter, E. Waldo
See Sturgeon, Theodore (Hamilton)

Hunter, Evan 1926- . . . . **CLC 11, 31**
See also CA 5-8R; CANR 5, 38; DLBY 82; MTCW; SATA 25

Hunter, Kristin (Eggleston) 1931-. . . **CLC 35**
See also AITN 1; BW; CA 13-16R; CANR 13; CLR 3; DLB 33; MAICYA; SAAS 10; SATA 12

Hunter, Mollie 1922-. . . . . **CLC 21**
See also McIlwraith, Maureen Mollie Hunter
See also CANR 37; CLR 25; JRDA; MAICYA; SAAS 7; SATA 54

Hunter, Robert (?)-1734. . . . . **LC 7**

Hurston, Zora Neale 1903-1960 . . . . **CLC 7, 30, 61; BLC; DA; SSC 4**
See also BW; CA 85-88; DLB 51, 86; MTCW

Huston, John (Marcellus) 1906-1987 . . . . **CLC 20**
See also CA 73-76; 123; CANR 34; DLB 26

Hustvedt, Siri 1955-. . . . . **CLC 76**
See also CA 137

Hutten, Ulrich von 1488-1523. . . . . . . **LC 16**

Huxley, Aldous (Leonard) 1894-1963 . . . . . **CLC 1, 3, 4, 5, 8, 11, 18, 35, 79; DA; WLC**
See also CA 85-88; CDBLB 1914-1945; DLB 36, 100; MTCW; SATA 63

Huysmans, Charles Marie Georges 1848-1907
See Huysmans, Joris-Karl
See also CA 104

Huysmans, Joris-Karl . . . . **TCLC 7**
See also Huysmans, Charles Marie Georges
See also DLB 123

Hwang, David Henry 1957- . . . . **CLC 55; DC 4**
See also CA 127; 132

Hyde, Anthony 1946- . . . . **CLC 42**
See also CA 136

Hyde, Margaret O(ldroyd) 1917- . . . **CLC 21**
See also CA 1-4R; CANR 1, 36; CLR 23; JRDA; MAICYA; SAAS 8; SATA 1, 42, 76

Hynes, James 1956(?)- . . . . **CLC 65**

Ian, Janis 1951- . . . . **CLC 21**
See also CA 105

Ibanez, Vicente Blasco
See Blasco Ibanez, Vicente

Ibarguengoitia, Jorge 1928-1983 . . . . **CLC 37**
See also CA 124; 113; HW

Ibsen, Henrik (Johan) 1828-1906 . . . . **TCLC 2, 8, 16, 37, 52; DA; DC 2; WLC**
See also CA 104; 141

Ibuse Masuji 1898-1993 . . . . **CLC 22**
See also CA 127; 141

Ichikawa, Kon 1915- . . . . **CLC 20**
See also CA 121

Idle, Eric 1943- . . . . **CLC 21**
See also Monty Python
See also CA 116; CANR 35

Ignatow, David 1914- . . . . . . **CLC 4, 7, 14, 40**
See also CA 9-12R; CAAS 3; CANR 31; DLB 5

Ihimaera, Witi 1944- . . . . **CLC 46**
See also CA 77-80

Ilf, Ilya . . . . **TCLC 21**
See also Fainzilberg, Ilya Arnoldovich

Immermann, Karl (Lebrecht) 1796-1840 . . . . **NCLC 4**
See also DLB 133

Inclan, Ramon (Maria) del Valle
See Valle-Inclan, Ramon (Maria) del

Infante, G(uillermo) Cabrera
See Cabrera Infante, G(uillermo)

Ingalls, Rachel (Holmes) 1940- . . . . . **CLC 42**
See also CA 123; 127

Ingamells, Rex 1913-1955 . . . . **TCLC 35**

Inge, William Motter 1913-1973 . . . . **CLC 1, 8, 19**
See also CA 9-12R; CDALB 1941-1968; DLB 7; MTCW

Ingelow, Jean 1820-1897 . . . . **NCLC 39**
See also DLB 35; SATA 33

Ingram, Willis J.
See Harris, Mark

Innaurato, Albert (F.) 1948(?)- . . **CLC 21, 60**
See also CA 115; 122

Innes, Michael
See Stewart, J(ohn) I(nnes) M(ackintosh)

Ionesco, Eugene 1912- . . . . **CLC 1, 4, 6, 9, 11, 15, 41; DA; WLC**
See also CA 9-12R; MTCW; SATA 7

Iqbal, Muhammad 1873-1938 . . . . . **TCLC 28**

Ireland, Patrick
See O'Doherty, Brian

Iron, Ralph
See Schreiner, Olive (Emilie Albertina)

Irving, John (Winslow) 1942- . . . . **CLC 13, 23, 38**
See also AAYA 8; BEST 89:3; CA 25-28R; CANR 28; DLB 6; DLBY 82; MTCW

Irving, Washington 1783-1859 . . . . **NCLC 2, 19; DA; SSC 2; WLC**
See also CDALB 1640-1865; DLB 3, 11, 30, 59, 73, 74; YABC 2

Irwin, P. K.
See Page, P(atricia) K(athleen)

Isaacs, Susan 1943- . . . . **CLC 32**
See also BEST 89:1; CA 89-92; CANR 20, 41; MTCW

Isherwood, Christopher (William Bradshaw) 1904-1986 . . . . **CLC 1, 9, 11, 14, 44**
See also CA 13-16R; 117; CANR 35; DLB 15; DLBY 86; MTCW

Ishiguro, Kazuo 1954- . . . . . . **CLC 27, 56, 59**
See also BEST 90:2; CA 120; MTCW

Ishikawa Takuboku 1886(?)-1912 . . . . **TCLC 15**
See also CA 113

Iskander, Fazil 1929- . . . . **CLC 47**
See also CA 102

Ivan IV 1530-1584 . . . . **LC 17**

Ivanov, Vyacheslav Ivanovich 1866-1949 . . . . **TCLC 33**
See also CA 122

Ivask, Ivar Vidrik 1927-1992 . . . . **CLC 14**
See also CA 37-40R; 139; CANR 24

Jackson, Daniel
See Wingrove, David (John)

Jackson, Jesse 1908-1983 . . . . **CLC 12**
See also BW; CA 25-28R; 109; CANR 27; CLR 28; MAICYA; SATA 2, 29, 48

Jackson, Laura (Riding) 1901-1991
See Riding, Laura
See also CA 65-68; 135; CANR 28; DLB 48

Jackson, Sam
See Trumbo, Dalton

Jackson, Sara
See Wingrove, David (John)

Jackson, Shirley 1919-1965 . . . . . **CLC 11, 60; DA; SSC 9; WLC**
See also AAYA 9; CA 1-4R; 25-28R; CANR 4; CDALB 1941-1968; DLB 6; SATA 2

Jacob, (Cyprien-)Max 1876-1944 . . . **TCLC 6**
See also CA 104

Jacobs, Jim 1942- . . . . **CLC 12**
See also CA 97-100

Jacobs, W(illiam) W(ymark) 1863-1943 . . . . **TCLC 22**
See also CA 121; DLB 135

Jacobsen, Jens Peter 1847-1885 . . **NCLC 34**

Jacobsen, Josephine 1908- . . . . **CLC 48**
See also CA 33-36R; CAAS 18; CANR 23

Jacobson, Dan 1929- . . . . **CLC 4, 14**
See also CA 1-4R; CANR 2, 25; DLB 14; MTCW

Jacqueline
See Carpentier (y Valmont), Alejo

Jagger, Mick 1944- . . . . **CLC 17**

Jakes, John (William) 1932- . . . . **CLC 29**
See also BEST 89:4; CA 57-60; CANR 10, 43; DLBY 83; MTCW; SATA 62

James, Andrew
See Kirkup, James

James, C(yril) L(ionel) R(obert) 1901-1989 . . . . **CLC 33**
See also BW; CA 117; 125; 128; DLB 125; MTCW

James, Daniel (Lewis) 1911-1988
See Santiago, Danny
See also CA 125

James, Dynely
See Mayne, William (James Carter)

James, Henry 1843-1916 . . . . . . **TCLC 2, 11, 24, 40, 47; DA; SSC 8; WLC**
See also CA 104; 132; CDALB 1865-1917; DLB 12, 71, 74; MTCW

James, Montague (Rhodes) 1862-1936 . . . . **TCLC 6**
See also CA 104

James, P. D. . . . . **CLC 18, 46**
See also White, Phyllis Dorothy James
See also BEST 90:2; CDBLB 1960 to Present; DLB 87

James, Philip
See Moorcock, Michael (John)

James, William 1842-1910 . . . . . **TCLC 15, 32**
See also CA 109

James I 1394-1437 . . . . **LC 20**

Jameson, Anna 1794-1860 . . . . **NCLC 43**
See also DLB 99

Jami, Nur al-Din 'Abd al-Rahman 1414-1492 . . . . **LC 9**

Jandl, Ernst 1925- . . . . **CLC 34**

Janowitz, Tama 1957- . . . . **CLC 43**
See also CA 106

Jarrell, Randall 1914-1965 . . . . **CLC 1, 2, 6, 9, 13, 49**
See also CA 5-8R; 25-28R; CABS 2; CANR 6, 34; CDALB 1941-1968; CLR 6; DLB 48, 52; MAICYA; MTCW; SATA 7

Jarry, Alfred 1873-1907 . . . . **TCLC 2, 14**
See also CA 104

Jarvis, E. K.
See Bloch, Robert (Albert); Ellison, Harlan; Silverberg, Robert

Jeake, Samuel, Jr.
See Aiken, Conrad (Potter)

Jean Paul 1763-1825 . . . . **NCLC 7**

Jeffers, (John) Robinson 1887-1962 .... **CLC 2, 3, 11, 15, 54; DA; WLC**
See also CA 85-88; CANR 35; CDALB 1917-1929; DLB 45; MTCW

Jefferson, Janet
See Mencken, H(enry) L(ouis)

Jefferson, Thomas 1743-1826 .... **NCLC 11**
See also CDALB 1640-1865; DLB 31

Jeffrey, Francis 1773-1850....... **NCLC 33**
See also DLB 107

Jelakowitch, Ivan
See Heijermans, Herman

Jellicoe, (Patricia) Ann 1927- ...... **CLC 27**
See also CA 85-88; DLB 13

Jen, Gish .... **CLC 70**
See also Jen, Lillian

Jen, Lillian 1956(?)-
See Jen, Gish
See also CA 135

Jenkins, (John) Robin 1912- .... **CLC 52**
See also CA 1-4R; CANR 1; DLB 14

Jennings, Elizabeth (Joan) 1926- .... **CLC 5, 14**
See also CA 61-64; CAAS 5; CANR 8, 39; DLB 27; MTCW; SATA 66

Jennings, Waylon 1937-........... **CLC 21**

Jensen, Johannes V. 1873-1950.... **TCLC 41**

Jensen, Laura (Linnea) 1948- ...... **CLC 37**
See also CA 103

Jerome, Jerome K(lapka) 1859-1927 .... **TCLC 23**
See also CA 119; DLB 10, 34, 135

Jerrold, Douglas William 1803-1857 .... **NCLC 2**

Jewett, (Theodora) Sarah Orne 1849-1909 .... **TCLC 1, 22; SSC 6**
See also CA 108; 127; DLB 12, 74; SATA 15

Jewsbury, Geraldine (Endsor) 1812-1880 .... **NCLC 22**
See also DLB 21

Jhabvala, Ruth Prawer 1927- .... **CLC 4, 8, 29**
See also CA 1-4R; CANR 2, 29; MTCW

Jiles, Paulette 1943-........... **CLC 13, 58**
See also CA 101

Jimenez (Mantecon), Juan Ramon 1881-1958 .... **TCLC 4; HLC; PC 7**
See also CA 104; 131; DLB 134; HW; MTCW

Jimenez, Ramon
See Jimenez (Mantecon), Juan Ramon

Jimenez Mantecon, Juan
See Jimenez (Mantecon), Juan Ramon

Joel, Billy .... **CLC 26**
See also Joel, William Martin

Joel, William Martin 1949-
See Joel, Billy
See also CA 108

John of the Cross, St. 1542-1591 .... **LC 18**

Johnson, B(ryan) S(tanley William) 1933-1973 .... **CLC 6, 9**
See also CA 9-12R; 53-56; CANR 9; DLB 14, 40

Johnson, Benj. F. of Boo
See Riley, James Whitcomb

Johnson, Benjamin F. of Boo
See Riley, James Whitcomb

Johnson, Charles (Richard) 1948- .... **CLC 7, 51, 65; BLC**
See also BW; CA 116; CAAS 18; CANR 42; DLB 33

Johnson, Denis 1949-............. **CLC 52**
See also CA 117; 121; DLB 120

Johnson, Diane 1934-........ **CLC 5, 13, 48**
See also CA 41-44R; CANR 17, 40; DLBY 80; MTCW

Johnson, Eyvind (Olof Verner) 1900-1976 .... **CLC 14**
See also CA 73-76; 69-72; CANR 34

Johnson, J. R.
See James, C(yril) L(ionel) R(obert)

Johnson, James Weldon 1871-1938 .... **TCLC 3, 19; BLC**
See also BW; CA 104; 125; CDALB 1917-1929; CLR 32; DLB 51; MTCW; SATA 31

Johnson, Joyce 1935-............. **CLC 58**
See also CA 125; 129

Johnson, Lionel (Pigot) 1867-1902 .... **TCLC 19**
See also CA 117; DLB 19

Johnson, Mel
See Malzberg, Barry N(athaniel)

Johnson, Pamela Hansford 1912-1981 .... **CLC 1, 7, 27**
See also CA 1-4R; 104; CANR 2, 28; DLB 15; MTCW

Johnson, Samuel 1709-1784 .... **LC 15; DA; WLC**
See also CDBLB 1660-1789; DLB 39, 95, 104

Johnson, Uwe 1934-1984 .... **CLC 5, 10, 15, 40**
See also CA 1-4R; 112; CANR 1, 39; DLB 75; MTCW

Johnston, George (Benson) 1913- ... **CLC 51**
See also CA 1-4R; CANR 5, 20; DLB 88

Johnston, Jennifer 1930-........... **CLC 7**
See also CA 85-88; DLB 14

Jolley, (Monica) Elizabeth 1923- ... **CLC 46**
See also CA 127; CAAS 13

Jones, Arthur Llewellyn 1863-1947
See Machen, Arthur
See also CA 104

Jones, D(ouglas) G(ordon) 1929-.... **CLC 10**
See also CA 29-32R; CANR 13; DLB 53

Jones, David (Michael) 1895-1974 .... **CLC 2, 4, 7, 13, 42**
See also CA 9-12R; 53-56; CANR 28; CDBLB 1945-1960; DLB 20, 100; MTCW

Jones, David Robert 1947-
See Bowie, David
See also CA 103

Jones, Diana Wynne 1934- .... **CLC 26**
See also CA 49-52; CANR 4, 26; CLR 23; JRDA; MAICYA; SAAS 7; SATA 9, 70

Jones, Edward P. 1950-........... **CLC 76**
See also CA 142

Jones, Gayl 1949-.......... **CLC 6, 9; BLC**
See also BW; CA 77-80; CANR 27; DLB 33; MTCW

Jones, James 1921-1977.... **CLC 1, 3, 10, 39**
See also AITN 1, 2; CA 1-4R; 69-72; CANR 6; DLB 2; MTCW

Jones, John J.
See Lovecraft, H(oward) P(hillips)

Jones, LeRoi .... **CLC 1, 2, 3, 5, 10, 14**
See also Baraka, Amiri

Jones, Louis B. .... **CLC 65**
See also CA 141

Jones, Madison (Percy, Jr.) 1925- ... **CLC 4**
See also CA 13-16R; CAAS 11; CANR 7

Jones, Mervyn 1922- .... **CLC 10, 52**
See also CA 45-48; CAAS 5; CANR 1; MTCW

Jones, Mick 1956(?)- .... **CLC 30**
See also Clash, The

Jones, Nettie (Pearl) 1941- .... **CLC 34**
See also CA 137

Jones, Preston 1936-1979 .... **CLC 10**
See also CA 73-76; 89-92; DLB 7

Jones, Robert F(rancis) 1934- .... **CLC 7**
See also CA 49-52; CANR 2

Jones, Rod 1953- .... **CLC 50**
See also CA 128

Jones, Terence Graham Parry 1942- .... **CLC 21**
See also Jones, Terry; Monty Python
See also CA 112; 116; CANR 35; SATA 51

Jones, Terry
See Jones, Terence Graham Parry
See also SATA 67

Jones, Thom 1945(?)-............. **CLC 81**

Jong, Erica 1942-.......... **CLC 4, 6, 8, 18**
See also AITN 1; BEST 90:2; CA 73-76; CANR 26; DLB 2, 5, 28; MTCW

Jonson, Ben(jamin) 1572(?)-1637 .... **LC 6; DA; DC 4; WLC**
See also CDBLB Before 1660; DLB 62, 121

Jordan, June 1936-.......... **CLC 5, 11, 23**
See also AAYA 2; BW; CA 33-36R; CANR 25; CLR 10; DLB 38; MAICYA; MTCW; SATA 4

Jordan, Pat(rick M.) 1941- .... **CLC 37**
See also CA 33-36R

Jorgensen, Ivar
See Ellison, Harlan

Jorgenson, Ivar
See Silverberg, Robert

Josipovici, Gabriel 1940- .... **CLC 6, 43**
See also CA 37-40R; CAAS 8; DLB 14

Joubert, Joseph 1754-1824 .... **NCLC 9**

Jouve, Pierre Jean 1887-1976...... **CLC 47**
See also CA 65-68

Joyce, James (Augustine Aloysius) 1882-1941 . . . . . . **TCLC 3, 8, 16, 35; DA; SSC 3; WLC**
See also CA 104; 126; CDBLB 1914-1945; DLB 10, 19, 36; MTCW

Jozsef, Attila 1905-1937. . . . . **TCLC 22**
See also CA 116

Juana Ines de la Cruz 1651(?)-1695 . . . **LC 5**

Judd, Cyril
See Kornbluth, C(yril) M.; Pohl, Frederik

Julian of Norwich 1342(?)-1416(?) . . . . **LC 6**

Just, Ward (Swift) 1935- . . . . **CLC 4, 27**
See also CA 25-28R; CANR 32

Justice, Donald (Rodney) 1925- . . **CLC 6, 19**
See also CA 5-8R; CANR 26; DLBY 83

Juvenal c. 55-c. 127 . . . . **CMLC 8**

Juvenis
See Bourne, Randolph S(illiman)

Kacew, Romain 1914-1980
See Gary, Romain
See also CA 108; 102

Kadare, Ismail 1936- . . . . **CLC 52**

Kadohata, Cynthia. . . . . **CLC 59**
See also CA 140

Kafka, Franz 1883-1924 . . . . **TCLC 2, 6, 13, 29, 47, 53; DA; SSC 5; WLC**
See also CA 105; 126; DLB 81; MTCW

Kahn, Roger 1927- . . . . **CLC 30**
See also CA 25-28R; SATA 37

Kain, Saul
See Sassoon, Siegfried (Lorraine)

Kaiser, Georg 1878-1945 . . . . **TCLC 9**
See also CA 106; DLB 124

Kaletski, Alexander 1946- . . . . **CLC 39**
See also CA 118; 143

Kalidasa fl. c. 400- . . . . **CMLC 9**

Kallman, Chester (Simon) 1921-1975 . . . . **CLC 2**
See also CA 45-48; 53-56; CANR 3

Kaminsky, Melvin 1926-
See Brooks, Mel
See also CA 65-68; CANR 16

Kaminsky, Stuart M(elvin) 1934- . . . **CLC 59**
See also CA 73-76; CANR 29

Kane, Paul
See Simon, Paul

Kane, Wilson
See Bloch, Robert (Albert)

Kanin, Garson 1912-. . . . . **CLC 22**
See also AITN 1; CA 5-8R; CANR 7; DLB 7

Kaniuk, Yoram 1930-. . . . . **CLC 19**
See also CA 134

Kant, Immanuel 1724-1804 . . . . . . **NCLC 27**
See also DLB 94

Kantor, MacKinlay 1904-1977 . . . . . . **CLC 7**
See also CA 61-64; 73-76; DLB 9, 102

Kaplan, David Michael 1946- . . . . . . **CLC 50**

Kaplan, James 1951- . . . . **CLC 59**
See also CA 135

Karageorge, Michael
See Anderson, Poul (William)

Karamzin, Nikolai Mikhailovich 1766-1826 . . . . **NCLC 3**

Karapanou, Margarita 1946- . . . . **CLC 13**
See also CA 101

Karinthy, Frigyes 1887-1938 . . . . . . **TCLC 47**

Karl, Frederick R(obert) 1927- . . . . . **CLC 34**
See also CA 5-8R; CANR 3

Kastel, Warren
See Silverberg, Robert

Kataev, Evgeny Petrovich 1903-1942
See Petrov, Evgeny
See also CA 120

Kataphusin
See Ruskin, John

Katz, Steve 1935- . . . . **CLC 47**
See also CA 25-28R; CAAS 14; CANR 12; DLBY 83

Kauffman, Janet 1945-. . . . . **CLC 42**
See also CA 117; CANR 43; DLBY 86

Kaufman, Bob (Garnell) 1925-1986 . . . . **CLC 49**
See also BW; CA 41-44R; 118; CANR 22; DLB 16, 41

Kaufman, George S. 1889-1961 . . . . . **CLC 38**
See also CA 108; 93-96; DLB 7

Kaufman, Sue . . . . **CLC 3, 8**
See also Barondess, Sue K(aufman)

Kavafis, Konstantinos Petrou 1863-1933
See Cavafy, C(onstantine) P(eter)
See also CA 104

Kavan, Anna 1901-1968 . . . . . . **CLC 5, 13, 82**
See also CA 5-8R; CANR 6; MTCW

Kavanagh, Dan
See Barnes, Julian

Kavanagh, Patrick (Joseph) 1904-1967 . . . . **CLC 22**
See also CA 123; 25-28R; DLB 15, 20; MTCW

Kawabata, Yasunari 1899-1972 . . . . **CLC 2, 5, 9, 18**
See also CA 93-96; 33-36R

Kaye, M(ary) M(argaret) 1909-. . . . . **CLC 28**
See also CA 89-92; CANR 24; MTCW; SATA 62

Kaye, Mollie
See Kaye, M(ary) M(argaret)

Kaye-Smith, Sheila 1887-1956. . . . . **TCLC 20**
See also CA 118; DLB 36

Kaymor, Patrice Maguilene
See Senghor, Leopold Sedar

Kazan, Elia 1909-. . . . . **CLC 6, 16, 63**
See also CA 21-24R; CANR 32

Kazantzakis, Nikos 1883(?)-1957 . . . . **TCLC 2, 5, 33**
See also CA 105; 132; MTCW

Kazin, Alfred 1915- . . . . **CLC 34, 38**
See also CA 1-4R; CAAS 7; CANR 1; DLB 67

Keane, Mary Nesta (Skrine) 1904-
See Keane, Molly
See also CA 108; 114

Keane, Molly. **CLC 31**
See also Keane, Mary Nesta (Skrine)

Keates, Jonathan 19(?)- . . . . **CLC 34**

Keaton, Buster 1895-1966 . . . . **CLC 20**

Keats, John 1795-1821 . . . **NCLC 8; DA; PC 1; WLC**
See also CDBLB 1789-1832; DLB 96, 110

Keene, Donald 1922- . . . . **CLC 34**
See also CA 1-4R; CANR 5

Keillor, Garrison. . . . . **CLC 40**
See also Keillor, Gary (Edward)
See also AAYA 2; BEST 89:3; DLBY 87; SATA 58

Keillor, Gary (Edward) 1942-
See Keillor, Garrison
See also CA 111; 117; CANR 36; MTCW

Keith, Michael
See Hubbard, L(afayette) Ron(ald)

Keller, Gottfried 1819-1890. . . . . . . **NCLC 2**
See also DLB 129

Kellerman, Jonathan 1949- . . . . **CLC 44**
See also BEST 90:1; CA 106; CANR 29

Kelley, William Melvin 1937- . . . . . . **CLC 22**
See also BW; CA 77-80; CANR 27; DLB 33

Kellogg, Marjorie 1922-. . . . . **CLC 2**
See also CA 81-84

Kellow, Kathleen
See Hibbert, Eleanor Alice Burford

Kelly, M(ilton) T(erry) 1947-. . . . . . . **CLC 55**
See also CA 97-100; CANR 19, 43

Kelman, James 1946- . . . . **CLC 58**

Kemal, Yashar 1923- . . . . **CLC 14, 29**
See also CA 89-92

Kemble, Fanny 1809-1893 . . . . **NCLC 18**
See also DLB 32

Kemelman, Harry 1908-. . . . . **CLC 2**
See also AITN 1; CA 9-12R; CANR 6; DLB 28

Kempe, Margery 1373(?)-1440(?) . . . . . **LC 6**

Kempis, Thomas a 1380-1471 . . . . **LC 11**

Kendall, Henry 1839-1882. . . . . . . **NCLC 12**

Keneally, Thomas (Michael) 1935- . . . . . . **CLC 5, 8, 10, 14, 19, 27, 43**
See also CA 85-88; CANR 10; MTCW

Kennedy, Adrienne (Lita) 1931- . . . . **CLC 66; BLC**
See also BW; CA 103; CABS 3; CANR 26; DLB 38

Kennedy, John Pendleton 1795-1870 . . . . **NCLC 2**
See also DLB 3

Kennedy, Joseph Charles 1929-. . . . . . **CLC 8**
See also Kennedy, X. J.
See also CA 1-4R; CANR 4, 30, 40; SATA 14

Kennedy, William 1928-. . . **CLC 6, 28, 34, 53**
See also AAYA 1; CA 85-88; CANR 14, 31; DLBY 85; MTCW; SATA 57

Kennedy, X. J.. **CLC 42**
See also Kennedy, Joseph Charles
See also CAAS 9; CLR 27; DLB 5

Kent, Kelvin
See Kuttner, Henry

Kenton, Maxwell
See Southern, Terry

L'Amour, Louis (Dearborn) 1908-1988 . . . . **CLC 25, 55**
See also AITN 2; BEST 89:2; CA 1-4R; 125; CANR 3, 25, 40; DLBY 80; MTCW

Lampedusa, Giuseppe (Tomasi) di . . . **TCLC 13**
See also Tomasi di Lampedusa, Giuseppe

Lampman, Archibald 1861-1899 . . **NCLC 25**
See also DLB 92

Lancaster, Bruce 1896-1963. . . . . **CLC 36**
See also CA 9-10; CAP 1; SATA 9

Landau, Mark Alexandrovich
See Aldanov, Mark (Alexandrovich)

Landau-Aldanov, Mark Alexandrovich
See Aldanov, Mark (Alexandrovich)

Landis, John 1950- . . . . **CLC 26**
See also CA 112; 122

Landolfi, Tommaso 1908-1979. . . **CLC 11, 49**
See also CA 127; 117

Landon, Letitia Elizabeth 1802-1838 . . . . **NCLC 15**
See also DLB 96

Landor, Walter Savage 1775-1864 . . . . **NCLC 14**
See also DLB 93, 107

Landwirth, Heinz 1927-
See Lind, Jakov
See also CA 9-12R; CANR 7

Lane, Patrick 1939- . . . . **CLC 25**
See also CA 97-100; DLB 53

Lang, Andrew 1844-1912 . . . . **TCLC 16**
See also CA 114; 137; DLB 98; MAICYA; SATA 16

Lang, Fritz 1890-1976 . . . . **CLC 20**
See also CA 77-80; 69-72; CANR 30

Lange, John
See Crichton, (John) Michael

Langer, Elinor 1939- . . . . **CLC 34**
See also CA 121

Langland, William 1330(?)-1400(?) . . . . **LC 19; DA**

Langstaff, Launcelot
See Irving, Washington

Lanier, Sidney 1842-1881 . . . . **NCLC 6**
See also DLB 64; MAICYA; SATA 18

Lanyer, Aemilia 1569-1645 . . . . **LC 10**

Lao Tzu . . . . **CMLC 7**

Lapine, James (Elliot) 1949- . . . . **CLC 39**
See also CA 123; 130

Larbaud, Valery (Nicolas) 1881-1957 . . . . **TCLC 9**
See also CA 106

Lardner, Ring
See Lardner, Ring(gold) W(ilmer)

Lardner, Ring W., Jr.
See Lardner, Ring(gold) W(ilmer)

Lardner, Ring(gold) W(ilmer) 1885-1933 . . . . **TCLC 2, 14**
See also CA 104; 131; CDALB 1917-1929; DLB 11, 25, 86; MTCW

Laredo, Betty
See Codrescu, Andrei

Larkin, Maia
See Wojciechowska, Maia (Teresa)

Larkin, Philip (Arthur) 1922-1985 . . . . **CLC 3, 5, 8, 9, 13, 18, 33, 39, 64**
See also CA 5-8R; 117; CANR 24; CDBLB 1960 to Present; DLB 27; MTCW

Larra (y Sanchez de Castro), Mariano Jose de 1809-1837 . . . . **NCLC 17**

Larsen, Eric 1941- . . . . **CLC 55**
See also CA 132

Larsen, Nella 1891-1964 . . . . . **CLC 37; BLC**
See also BW; CA 125; DLB 51

Larson, Charles R(aymond) 1938-. . . **CLC 31**
See also CA 53-56; CANR 4

Latham, Jean Lee 1902-. . . . . **CLC 12**
See also AITN 1; CA 5-8R; CANR 7; MAICYA; SATA 2, 68

Latham, Mavis
See Clark, Mavis Thorpe

Lathen, Emma . . . . **CLC 2**
See also Hennissart, Martha; Latsis, Mary J(ane)

Lathrop, Francis
See Leiber, Fritz (Reuter, Jr.)

Latsis, Mary J(ane)
See Lathen, Emma
See also CA 85-88

Lattimore, Richmond (Alexander) 1906-1984 . . . . **CLC 3**
See also CA 1-4R; 112; CANR 1

Laughlin, James 1914- . . . . **CLC 49**
See also CA 21-24R; CANR 9; DLB 48

Laurence, (Jean) Margaret (Wemyss) 1926-1987 . . **CLC 3, 6, 13, 50, 62; SSC 7**
See also CA 5-8R; 121; CANR 33; DLB 53; MTCW; SATA 50

Laurent, Antoine 1952- . . . . **CLC 50**

Lauscher, Hermann
See Hesse, Hermann

Lautreamont, Comte de 1846-1870 . . . . **NCLC 12; SSC 14**

Laverty, Donald
See Blish, James (Benjamin)

Lavin, Mary 1912- . . . . . . **CLC 4, 18; SSC 4**
See also CA 9-12R; CANR 33; DLB 15; MTCW

Lavond, Paul Dennis
See Kornbluth, C(yril) M.; Pohl, Frederik

Lawler, Raymond Evenor 1922- . . . . **CLC 58**
See also CA 103

Lawrence, D(avid) H(erbert Richards) 1885-1930 . . . . **TCLC 2, 9, 16, 33, 48; DA; SSC 4; WLC**
See also CA 104; 121; CDBLB 1914-1945; DLB 10, 19, 36, 98; MTCW

Lawrence, T(homas) E(dward) 1888-1935 . . . . **TCLC 18**
See also Dale, Colin
See also CA 115

Lawrence of Arabia
See Lawrence, T(homas) E(dward)

Lawson, Henry (Archibald Hertzberg) 1867-1922 . . . . **TCLC 27**
See also CA 120

Lawton, Dennis
See Faust, Frederick (Schiller)

Laxness, Halldor . . . . **CLC 25**
See also Gudjonsson, Halldor Kiljan

Layamon fl. c. 1200- . . . . **CMLC 10**

Laye, Camara 1928-1980 . . . **CLC 4, 38; BLC**
See also BW; CA 85-88; 97-100; CANR 25; MTCW

Layton, Irving (Peter) 1912- . . . . . **CLC 2, 15**
See also CA 1-4R; CANR 2, 33, 43; DLB 88; MTCW

Lazarus, Emma 1849-1887. . . . . **NCLC 8**

Lazarus, Felix
See Cable, George Washington

Lazarus, Henry
See Slavitt, David R(ytman)

Lea, Joan
See Neufeld, John (Arthur)

Leacock, Stephen (Butler) 1869-1944 . . . . **TCLC 2**
See also CA 104; 141; DLB 92

Lear, Edward 1812-1888 . . . . **NCLC 3**
See also CLR 1; DLB 32; MAICYA; SATA 18

Lear, Norman (Milton) 1922- . . . . . . **CLC 12**
See also CA 73-76

Leavis, F(rank) R(aymond) 1895-1978 . . . . **CLC 24**
See also CA 21-24R; 77-80; MTCW

Leavitt, David 1961- . . . . **CLC 34**
See also CA 116; 122; DLB 130

Leblanc, Maurice (Marie Emile) 1864-1941 . . . . **TCLC 49**
See also CA 110

Lebowitz, Fran(ces Ann) 1951(?)- . . . . **CLC 11, 36**
See also CA 81-84; CANR 14; MTCW

le Carre, John . . . . **CLC 3, 5, 9, 15, 28**
See also Cornwell, David (John Moore)
See also BEST 89:4; CDBLB 1960 to Present; DLB 87

Le Clezio, J(ean) M(arie) G(ustave) 1940- . . . . **CLC 31**
See also CA 116; 128; DLB 83

Leconte de Lisle, Charles-Marie-Rene 1818-1894 . . . . **NCLC 29**

Le Coq, Monsieur
See Simenon, Georges (Jacques Christian)

Leduc, Violette 1907-1972. . . . . **CLC 22**
See also CA 13-14; 33-36R; CAP 1

Ledwidge, Francis 1887(?)-1917 . . . **TCLC 23**
See also CA 123; DLB 20

Lee, Andrea 1953- . . . . **CLC 36; BLC**
See also BW; CA 125

Lee, Andrew
See Auchincloss, Louis (Stanton)

Lee, Don L. . . . . **CLC 2**
See also Madhubuti, Haki R.

Lee, George W(ashington) 1894-1976 . . . . **CLC 52; BLC**
See also BW; CA 125; DLB 51

Lee, (Nelle) Harper
1926- .... **CLC 12, 60; DA; WLC**
See also CA 13-16R; CDALB 1941-1968; DLB 6; MTCW; SATA 11

Lee, Julian
See Latham, Jean Lee

Lee, Larry
See Lee, Lawrence

Lee, Lawrence 1941-1990.......... **CLC 34**
See also CA 131; CANR 43

Lee, Manfred B(ennington)
1905-1971 .... **CLC 11**
See also Queen, Ellery
See also CA 1-4R; 29-32R; CANR 2

Lee, Stan 1922-.................. **CLC 17**
See also AAYA 5; CA 108; 111

Lee, Tanith 1947-................ **CLC 46**
See also CA 37-40R; SATA 8

Lee, Vernon...................... **TCLC 5**
See also Paget, Violet
See also DLB 57

Lee, William
See Burroughs, William S(eward)

Lee, Willy
See Burroughs, William S(eward)

Lee-Hamilton, Eugene (Jacob)
1845-1907 .... **TCLC 22**
See also CA 117

Leet, Judith 1935- .... **CLC 11**

Le Fanu, Joseph Sheridan
1814-1873 .... **NCLC 9; SSC 14**
See also DLB 21, 70

Leffland, Ella 1931- .... **CLC 19**
See also CA 29-32R; CANR 35; DLBY 84; SATA 65

Leger, Alexis
See Leger, (Marie-Rene Auguste) Alexis Saint-Leger

Leger, (Marie-Rene Auguste) Alexis Saint-Leger 1887-1975........ **CLC 11**
See also Perse, St.-John
See also CA 13-16R; 61-64; CANR 43; MTCW

Leger, Saintleger
See Leger, (Marie-Rene Auguste) Alexis Saint-Leger

Le Guin, Ursula K(roeber)
1929- .... **CLC 8, 13, 22, 45, 71; SSC 12**
See also AAYA 9; AITN 1; CA 21-24R; CANR 9, 32; CDALB 1968-1988; CLR 3, 28; DLB 8, 52; JRDA; MAICYA; MTCW; SATA 4, 52

Lehmann, Rosamond (Nina)
1901-1990 .... **CLC 5**
See also CA 77-80; 131; CANR 8; DLB 15

Leiber, Fritz (Reuter, Jr.)
1910-1992 .... **CLC 25**
See also CA 45-48; 139; CANR 2, 40; DLB 8; MTCW; SATA 45; SATA-Obit 73

Leimbach, Martha 1963-
See Leimbach, Marti
See also CA 130

Leimbach, Marti .... **CLC 65**
See also Leimbach, Martha

Leino, Eino .... **TCLC 24**
See also Loennbohm, Armas Eino Leopold

Leiris, Michel (Julien) 1901-1990... **CLC 61**
See also CA 119; 128; 132

Leithauser, Brad 1953-............ **CLC 27**
See also CA 107; CANR 27; DLB 120

Lelchuk, Alan 1938-............... **CLC 5**
See also CA 45-48; CANR 1

Lem, Stanislaw 1921-........ **CLC 8, 15, 40**
See also CA 105; CAAS 1; CANR 32; MTCW

Lemann, Nancy 1956-............. **CLC 39**
See also CA 118; 136

Lemonnier, (Antoine Louis) Camille
1844-1913 .... **TCLC 22**
See also CA 121

Lenau, Nikolaus 1802-1850...... **NCLC 16**

L'Engle, Madeleine (Camp Franklin)
1918- .... **CLC 12**
See also AAYA 1; AITN 2; CA 1-4R; CANR 3, 21, 39; CLR 1, 14; DLB 52; JRDA; MAICYA; MTCW; SAAS 15; SATA 1, 27, 75

Lengyel, Jozsef 1896-1975.......... **CLC 7**
See also CA 85-88; 57-60

Lennon, John (Ono)
1940-1980 .... **CLC 12, 35**
See also CA 102

Lennox, Charlotte Ramsay
1729(?)-1804 .... **NCLC 23**
See also DLB 39

Lentricchia, Frank (Jr.) 1940-...... **CLC 34**
See also CA 25-28R; CANR 19

Lenz, Siegfried 1926-............. **CLC 27**
See also CA 89-92; DLB 75

Leonard, Elmore (John, Jr.)
1925- .... **CLC 28, 34, 71**
See also AITN 1; BEST 89:1, 90:4; CA 81-84; CANR 12, 28; MTCW

Leonard, Hugh
See Byrne, John Keyes
See also DLB 13

Leopardi, (Conte) Giacomo (Talegardo Francesco di Sales Save
1798-1837 .... **NCLC 22**

Le Reveler
See Artaud, Antonin

Lerman, Eleanor 1952-............. **CLC 9**
See also CA 85-88

Lerman, Rhoda 1936-............. **CLC 56**
See also CA 49-52

Lermontov, Mikhail Yuryevich
1814-1841 .... **NCLC 5**

Leroux, Gaston 1868-1927........ **TCLC 25**
See also CA 108; 136; SATA 65

Lesage, Alain-Rene 1668-1747........ **LC 2**

Leskov, Nikolai (Semyonovich)
1831-1895 .... **NCLC 25**

Lessing, Doris (May)
1919- ..... **CLC 1, 2, 3, 6, 10, 15, 22, 40; DA; SSC 6**
See also CA 9-12R; CAAS 14; CANR 33; CDBLB 1960 to Present; DLB 15; DLBY 85; MTCW

Lessing, Gotthold Ephraim
1729-1781 .... **LC 8**
See also DLB 97

Lester, Richard 1932-............. **CLC 20**

Lever, Charles (James)
1806-1872 .... **NCLC 23**
See also DLB 21

Leverson, Ada 1865(?)-1936(?) .... **TCLC 18**
See also Elaine
See also CA 117

Levertov, Denise
1923- ...... **CLC 1, 2, 3, 5, 8, 15, 28, 66**
See also CA 1-4R; CANR 3, 29; DLB 5; MTCW

Levi, Jonathan.................... **CLC 76**

Levi, Peter (Chad Tigar) 1931-..... **CLC 41**
See also CA 5-8R; CANR 34; DLB 40

Levi, Primo
1919-1987 .... **CLC 37, 50; SSC 12**
See also CA 13-16R; 122; CANR 12, 33; MTCW

Levin, Ira 1929- .... **CLC 3, 6**
See also CA 21-24R; CANR 17; MTCW; SATA 66

Levin, Meyer 1905-1981 .... **CLC 7**
See also AITN 1; CA 9-12R; 104; CANR 15; DLB 9, 28; DLBY 81; SATA 21, 27

Levine, Norman 1924-............ **CLC 54**
See also CA 73-76; CANR 14; DLB 88

Levine, Philip 1928-.. **CLC 2, 4, 5, 9, 14, 33**
See also CA 9-12R; CANR 9, 37; DLB 5

Levinson, Deirdre 1931-........... **CLC 49**
See also CA 73-76

Levi-Strauss, Claude 1908- .... **CLC 38**
See also CA 1-4R; CANR 6, 32; MTCW

Levitin, Sonia (Wolff) 1934- .... **CLC 17**
See also CA 29-32R; CANR 14, 32; JRDA; MAICYA; SAAS 2; SATA 4, 68

Levon, O. U.
See Kesey, Ken (Elton)

Lewes, George Henry
1817-1878 .... **NCLC 25**
See also DLB 55

Lewis, Alun 1915-1944............ **TCLC 3**
See also CA 104; DLB 20

Lewis, C. Day
See Day Lewis, C(ecil)

Lewis, C(live) S(taples)
1898-1963 ..... **CLC 1, 3, 6, 14, 27; DA; WLC**
See also AAYA 3; CA 81-84; CANR 33; CDBLB 1945-1960; CLR 3, 27; DLB 15, 100; JRDA; MAICYA; MTCW; SATA 13

Lewis, Janet 1899-............... **CLC 41**
See also Winters, Janet Lewis
See also CA 9-12R; CANR 29; CAP 1; DLBY 87

Lewis, Matthew Gregory
1775-1818 .... **NCLC 11**
See also DLB 39

Lewis, (Harry) Sinclair 1885-1951 ..... **TCLC 4, 13, 23, 39; DA; WLC**
See also CA 104; 133; CDALB 1917-1929; DLB 9, 102; DLBD 1; MTCW

Lewis, (Percy) Wyndham 1884(?)-1957 .... **TCLC 2, 9**
See also CA 104; DLB 15

Lewisohn, Ludwig 1883-1955...... **TCLC 19**
See also CA 107; DLB 4, 9, 28, 102

Lezama Lima, Jose 1910-1976 ... **CLC 4, 10**
See also CA 77-80; DLB 113; HW

L'Heureux, John (Clarke) 1934-.... **CLC 52**
See also CA 13-16R; CANR 23

Liddell, C. H.
See Kuttner, Henry

Lie, Jonas (Lauritz Idemil) 1833-1908(?) .... **TCLC 5**
See also CA 115

Lieber, Joel 1937-1971............. **CLC 6**
See also CA 73-76; 29-32R

Lieber, Stanley Martin
See Lee, Stan

Lieberman, Laurence (James) 1935- .... **CLC 4, 36**
See also CA 17-20R; CANR 8, 36

Lieksman, Anders
See Haavikko, Paavo Juhani

Li Fei-kan 1904-................. **CLC 18**
See also CA 105

Lifton, Robert Jay 1926-.......... **CLC 67**
See also CA 17-20R; CANR 27; SATA 66

Lightfoot, Gordon 1938-........... **CLC 26**
See also CA 109

Lightman, Alan P. 1948- .... **CLC 81**
See also CA 141

Ligotti, Thomas 1953- .... **CLC 44**
See also CA 123

Liliencron, (Friedrich Adolf Axel) Detlev von 1844-1909 .... **TCLC 18**
See also CA 117

Lima, Jose Lezama
See Lezama Lima, Jose

Lima Barreto, Afonso Henrique de 1881-1922 .... **TCLC 23**
See also CA 117

Limonov, Eduard.................. **CLC 67**

Lin, Frank
See Atherton, Gertrude (Franklin Horn)

Lincoln, Abraham 1809-1865..... **NCLC 18**

Lind, Jakov .... **CLC 1, 2, 4, 27, 82**
See also Landwirth, Heinz
See also CAAS 4

Lindbergh, Anne (Spencer) Morrow 1906- .... **CLC 82**
See also CA 17-20R; CANR 16; MTCW; SATA 33

Lindsay, David 1878-1945 .... **TCLC 15**
See also CA 113

Lindsay, (Nicholas) Vachel 1879-1931 .... **TCLC 17; DA; WLC**
See also CA 114; 135; CDALB 1865-1917; DLB 54; SATA 40

Linke-Poot
See Doeblin, Alfred

Linney, Romulus 1930- .... **CLC 51**
See also CA 1-4R; CANR 40

Linton, Eliza Lynn 1822-1898.... **NCLC 41**
See also DLB 18

Li Po 701-763.................. **CMLC 2**

Lipsius, Justus 1547-1606 .... **LC 16**

Lipsyte, Robert (Michael) 1938- .... **CLC 21; DA**
See also AAYA 7; CA 17-20R; CANR 8; CLR 23; JRDA; MAICYA; SATA 5, 68

Lish, Gordon (Jay) 1934-.......... **CLC 45**
See also CA 113; 117; DLB 130

Lispector, Clarice 1925-1977....... **CLC 43**
See also CA 139; 116; DLB 113

Littell, Robert 1935(?)- .... **CLC 42**
See also CA 109; 112

Little, Malcolm 1925-1965
See Malcolm X
See also BW; CA 125; 111; DA; MTCW

Littlewit, Humphrey Gent.
See Lovecraft, H(oward) P(hillips)

Litwos
See Sienkiewicz, Henryk (Adam Alexander Pius)

Liu E 1857-1909................ **TCLC 15**
See also CA 115

Lively, Penelope (Margaret) 1933- .... **CLC 32, 50**
See also CA 41-44R; CANR 29; CLR 7; DLB 14; JRDA; MAICYA; MTCW; SATA 7, 60

Livesay, Dorothy (Kathleen) 1909- .... **CLC 4, 15, 79**
See also AITN 2; CA 25-28R; CAAS 8; CANR 36; DLB 68; MTCW

Livy c. 59B.C.-c. 17 .... **CMLC 11**

Lizardi, Jose Joaquin Fernandez de 1776-1827 .... **NCLC 30**

Llewellyn, Richard .... **CLC 7**
See also Llewellyn Lloyd, Richard Dafydd Vivian
See also DLB 15

Llewellyn Lloyd, Richard Dafydd Vivian 1906-1983 .... **CLC 80**
See also Llewellyn, Richard
See also CA 53-56; 111; CANR 7; SATA 11, 37

Llosa, (Jorge) Mario (Pedro) Vargas
See Vargas Llosa, (Jorge) Mario (Pedro)

Lloyd Webber, Andrew 1948-
See Webber, Andrew Lloyd
See also AAYA 1; CA 116; SATA 56

Llull, Ramon c. 1235-c. 1316..... **CMLC 12**

Locke, Alain (Le Roy) 1886-1954 .... **TCLC 43**
See also BW; CA 106; 124; DLB 51

Locke, John 1632-1704 .... **LC 7**
See also DLB 101

Locke-Elliott, Sumner
See Elliott, Sumner Locke

Lockhart, John Gibson 1794-1854 .... **NCLC 6**
See also DLB 110, 116

Lodge, David (John) 1935-......... **CLC 36**
See also BEST 90:1; CA 17-20R; CANR 19; DLB 14; MTCW

Loennbohm, Armas Eino Leopold 1878-1926
See Leino, Eino
See also CA 123

Loewinsohn, Ron(ald William) 1937- .... **CLC 52**
See also CA 25-28R

Logan, Jake
See Smith, Martin Cruz

Logan, John (Burton) 1923-1987..... **CLC 5**
See also CA 77-80; 124; DLB 5

Lo Kuan-chung 1330(?)-1400(?)...... **LC 12**

Lombard, Nap
See Johnson, Pamela Hansford

London, Jack.. **TCLC 9, 15, 39; SSC 4; WLC**
See also London, John Griffith
See also AITN 2; CDALB 1865-1917; DLB 8, 12, 78; SATA 18

London, John Griffith 1876-1916
See London, Jack
See also CA 110; 119; DA; JRDA; MAICYA; MTCW

Long, Emmett
See Leonard, Elmore (John, Jr.)

Longbaugh, Harry
See Goldman, William (W.)

Longfellow, Henry Wadsworth 1807-1882 .... **NCLC 2; DA**
See also CDALB 1640-1865; DLB 1, 59; SATA 19

Longley, Michael 1939- .... **CLC 29**
See also CA 102; DLB 40

Longus fl. c. 2nd cent. - .... **CMLC 7**

Longway, A. Hugh
See Lang, Andrew

Lopate, Phillip 1943- .... **CLC 29**
See also CA 97-100; DLBY 80

Lopez Portillo (y Pacheco), Jose 1920- .... **CLC 46**
See also CA 129; HW

Lopez y Fuentes, Gregorio 1897(?)-1966 .... **CLC 32**
See also CA 131; HW

Lorca, Federico Garcia
See Garcia Lorca, Federico

Lord, Bette Bao 1938- .... **CLC 23**
See also BEST 90:3; CA 107; CANR 41; SATA 58

Lord Auch
See Bataille, Georges

Lord Byron
See Byron, George Gordon (Noel)

Lord Dunsany .... **TCLC 2**
See also Dunsany, Edward John Moreton Drax Plunkett

Lorde, Audre (Geraldine) 1934-1992 .... **CLC 18, 71; BLC**
See also BW; CA 25-28R; 142; CANR 16, 26; DLB 41; MTCW

Lord Jeffrey
See Jeffrey, Francis

Lorenzo, Heberto Padilla
See Padilla (Lorenzo), Heberto

Loris
See Hofmannsthal, Hugo von

Loti, Pierre .... **TCLC 11**
See also Viaud, (Louis Marie) Julien
See also DLB 123

Louie, David Wong 1954- .... **CLC 70**
See also CA 139

Louis, Father M.
See Merton, Thomas

Lovecraft, H(oward) P(hillips)
1890-1937 .... **TCLC 4, 22; SSC 3**
See also CA 104; 133; MTCW

Lovelace, Earl 1935-.............. **CLC 51**
See also CA 77-80; CANR 41; DLB 125; MTCW

Lovelace, Richard 1618-1657........ **LC 24**
See also DLB 131

Lowell, Amy 1874-1925 .... **TCLC 1, 8**
See also CA 104; DLB 54

Lowell, James Russell 1819-1891 .. **NCLC 2**
See also CDALB 1640-1865; DLB 1, 11, 64, 79

Lowell, Robert (Traill Spence, Jr.)
1917-1977 ... **CLC 1, 2, 3, 4, 5, 8, 9, 11, 15, 37; DA; PC 3; WLC**
See also CA 9-12R; 73-76; CABS 2; CANR 26; DLB 5; MTCW

Lowndes, Marie Adelaide (Belloc)
1868-1947 .... **TCLC 12**
See also CA 107; DLB 70

Lowry, (Clarence) Malcolm
1909-1957 .... **TCLC 6, 40**
See also CA 105; 131; CDBLB 1945-1960; DLB 15; MTCW

Lowry, Mina Gertrude 1882-1966
See Loy, Mina
See also CA 113

Loxsmith, John
See Brunner, John (Kilian Houston)

Loy, Mina .... **CLC 28**
See also Lowry, Mina Gertrude
See also DLB 4, 54

Loyson-Bridet
See Schwob, (Mayer Andre) Marcel

Lucas, Craig 1951-............... **CLC 64**
See also CA 137

Lucas, George 1944-.............. **CLC 16**
See also AAYA 1; CA 77-80; CANR 30; SATA 56

Lucas, Hans
See Godard, Jean-Luc

Lucas, Victoria
See Plath, Sylvia

Ludlam, Charles 1943-1987..... **CLC 46, 50**
See also CA 85-88; 122

Ludlum, Robert 1927- .... **CLC 22, 43**
See also AAYA 10; BEST 89:1, 90:3; CA 33-36R; CANR 25, 41; DLBY 82; MTCW

Ludwig, Ken...................... **CLC 60**

Ludwig, Otto 1813-1865.......... **NCLC 4**
See also DLB 129

Lugones, Leopoldo 1874-1938 ..... **TCLC 15**
See also CA 116; 131; HW

Lu Hsun 1881-1936 .... **TCLC 3**

Lukacs, George .... **CLC 24**
See also Lukacs, Gyorgy (Szegeny von)

Lukacs, Gyorgy (Szegeny von) 1885-1971
See Lukacs, George
See also CA 101; 29-32R

Luke, Peter (Ambrose Cyprian)
1919- .... **CLC 38**
See also CA 81-84; DLB 13

Lunar, Dennis
See Mungo, Raymond

Lurie, Alison 1926-........ **CLC 4, 5, 18, 39**
See also CA 1-4R; CANR 2, 17; DLB 2; MTCW; SATA 46

Lustig, Arnost 1926-.............. **CLC 56**
See also AAYA 3; CA 69-72; SATA 56

Luther, Martin 1483-1546........... **LC 9**

Luzi, Mario 1914-................ **CLC 13**
See also CA 61-64; CANR 9; DLB 128

Lynch, B. Suarez
See Bioy Casares, Adolfo; Borges, Jorge Luis

Lynch, David (K.) 1946-........... **CLC 66**
See also CA 124; 129

Lynch, James
See Andreyev, Leonid (Nikolaevich)

Lynch Davis, B.
See Bioy Casares, Adolfo; Borges, Jorge Luis

Lyndsay, SirDavid 1490-1555 .... **LC 20**

Lynn, Kenneth S(chuyler) 1923-.... **CLC 50**
See also CA 1-4R; CANR 3, 27

Lynx
See West, Rebecca

Lyons, Marcus
See Blish, James (Benjamin)

Lyre, Pinchbeck
See Sassoon, Siegfried (Lorraine)

Lytle, Andrew (Nelson) 1902-...... **CLC 22**
See also CA 9-12R; DLB 6

Lyttelton, George 1709-1773........ **LC 10**

Maas, Peter 1929- .... **CLC 29**
See also CA 93-96

Macaulay, Rose 1881-1958 ..... **TCLC 7, 44**
See also CA 104; DLB 36

Macaulay, Thomas Babington
1800-1859 .... **NCLC 42**
See also CDBLB 1832-1890; DLB 32, 55

MacBeth, George (Mann)
1932-1992 .... **CLC 2, 5, 9**
See also CA 25-28R; 136; DLB 40; MTCW; SATA 4; SATA-Obit 70

MacCaig, Norman (Alexander)
1910- .... **CLC 36**
See also CA 9-12R; CANR 3, 34; DLB 27

MacCarthy, (Sir Charles Otto) Desmond
1877-1952 .... **TCLC 36**

MacDiarmid, Hugh..... **CLC 2, 4, 11, 19, 63**
See also Grieve, C(hristopher) M(urray)
See also CDBLB 1945-1960; DLB 20

MacDonald, Anson
See Heinlein, Robert A(nson)

Macdonald, Cynthia 1928-...... **CLC 13, 19**
See also CA 49-52; CANR 4; DLB 105

MacDonald, George 1824-1905..... **TCLC 9**
See also CA 106; 137; DLB 18; MAICYA; SATA 33

Macdonald, John
See Millar, Kenneth

MacDonald, John D(ann)
1916-1986 .... **CLC 3, 27, 44**
See also CA 1-4R; 121; CANR 1, 19; DLB 8; DLBY 86; MTCW

Macdonald, John Ross
See Millar, Kenneth

Macdonald, Ross..... **CLC 1, 2, 3, 14, 34, 41**
See also Millar, Kenneth
See also DLBD 6

MacDougal, John
See Blish, James (Benjamin)

MacEwen, Gwendolyn (Margaret)
1941-1987 .... **CLC 13, 55**
See also CA 9-12R; 124; CANR 7, 22; DLB 53; SATA 50, 55

Machado (y Ruiz), Antonio
1875-1939 .... **TCLC 3**
See also CA 104; DLB 108

Machado de Assis, Joaquim Maria
1839-1908 .... **TCLC 10; BLC**
See also CA 107

Machen, Arthur................... **TCLC 4**
See also Jones, Arthur Llewellyn
See also DLB 36

Machiavelli, Niccolo 1469-1527 .. **LC 8; DA**

MacInnes, Colin 1914-1976...... **CLC 4, 23**
See also CA 69-72; 65-68; CANR 21; DLB 14; MTCW

MacInnes, Helen (Clark)
1907-1985 .... **CLC 27, 39**
See also CA 1-4R; 117; CANR 1, 28; DLB 87; MTCW; SATA 22, 44

Mackay, Mary 1855-1924
See Corelli, Marie
See also CA 118

Mackenzie, Compton (Edward Montague)
1883-1972 .... **CLC 18**
See also CA 21-22; 37-40R; CAP 2; DLB 34, 100

Mackenzie, Henry 1745-1831 .... **NCLC 41**
See also DLB 39

Mackintosh, Elizabeth 1896(?)-1952
See Tey, Josephine
See also CA 110

MacLaren, James
See Grieve, C(hristopher) M(urray)

Mac Laverty, Bernard 1942-....... **CLC 31**
See also CA 116; 118; CANR 43

MacLean, Alistair (Stuart)
1922-1987 .... **CLC 3, 13, 50, 63**
See also CA 57-60; 121; CANR 28; MTCW; SATA 23, 50

Mariner, Scott
See Pohl, Frederik

Marinetti, Filippo Tommaso 1876-1944 .... **TCLC 10**
See also CA 107; DLB 114

Marivaux, Pierre Carlet de Chamblain de 1688-1763 .... **LC 4**

Markandaya, Kamala .... **CLC 8, 38**
See also Taylor, Kamala (Purnaiya)

Markfield, Wallace 1926-........... **CLC 8**
See also CA 69-72; CAAS 3; DLB 2, 28

Markham, Edwin 1852-1940 ...... **TCLC 47**
See also DLB 54

Markham, Robert
See Amis, Kingsley (William)

Marks, J
See Highwater, Jamake (Mamake)

Marks-Highwater, J
See Highwater, Jamake (Mamake)

Markson, David M(errill) 1927- .... **CLC 67**
See also CA 49-52; CANR 1

Marley, Bob...................... **CLC 17**
See also Marley, Robert Nesta

Marley, Robert Nesta 1945-1981
See Marley, Bob
See also CA 107; 103

Marlowe, Christopher 1564-1593 ..... **LC 22; DA; DC 1; WLC**
See also CDBLB Before 1660; DLB 62

Marmontel, Jean-Francois 1723-1799 .... **LC 2**

Marquand, John P(hillips) 1893-1960 .... **CLC 2, 10**
See also CA 85-88; DLB 9, 102

Marquez, Gabriel (Jose) Garcia...... **CLC 68**
See also Garcia Marquez, Gabriel (Jose)

Marquis, Don(ald Robert Perry) 1878-1937 .... **TCLC 7**
See also CA 104; DLB 11, 25

Marric, J. J.
See Creasey, John

Marrow, Bernard
See Moore, Brian

Marryat, Frederick 1792-1848 .... **NCLC 3**
See also DLB 21

Marsden, James
See Creasey, John

Marsh, (Edith) Ngaio 1899-1982 .... **CLC 7, 53**
See also CA 9-12R; CANR 6; DLB 77; MTCW

Marshall, Garry 1934-............ **CLC 17**
See also AAYA 3; CA 111; SATA 60

Marshall, Paule 1929- .... **CLC 27, 72; BLC; SSC 3**
See also BW; CA 77-80; CANR 25; DLB 33; MTCW

Marsten, Richard
See Hunter, Evan

Martha, Henry
See Harris, Mark

Martin, Ken
See Hubbard, L(afayette) Ron(ald)

Martin, Richard
See Creasey, John

Martin, Steve 1945-.............. **CLC 30**
See also CA 97-100; CANR 30; MTCW

Martin, Violet Florence 1862-1915 .... **TCLC 51**

Martin, Webber
See Silverberg, Robert

Martindale, Patrick Victor
See White, Patrick (Victor Martindale)

Martin du Gard, Roger 1881-1958 .... **TCLC 24**
See also CA 118; DLB 65

Martineau, Harriet 1802-1876.... **NCLC 26**
See also DLB 21, 55; YABC 2

Martines, Julia
See O'Faolain, Julia

Martinez, Jacinto Benavente y
See Benavente (y Martinez), Jacinto

Martinez Ruiz, Jose 1873-1967
See Azorin; Ruiz, Jose Martinez
See also CA 93-96; HW

Martinez Sierra, Gregorio 1881-1947 .... **TCLC 6**
See also CA 115

Martinez Sierra, Maria (de la O'LeJarraga) 1874-1974 .... **TCLC 6**
See also CA 115

Martinsen, Martin
See Follett, Ken(neth Martin)

Martinson, Harry (Edmund) 1904-1978 .... **CLC 14**
See also CA 77-80; CANR 34

Marut, Ret
See Traven, B.

Marut, Robert
See Traven, B.

Marvell, Andrew 1621-1678 .... **LC 4; DA; WLC**
See also CDBLB 1660-1789; DLB 131

Marx, Karl (Heinrich) 1818-1883 .... **NCLC 17**
See also DLB 129

Masaoka Shiki.................. **TCLC 18**
See also Masaoka Tsunenori

Masaoka Tsunenori 1867-1902
See Masaoka Shiki
See also CA 117

Masefield, John (Edward) 1878-1967 .... **CLC 11, 47**
See also CA 19-20; 25-28R; CANR 33; CAP 2; CDBLB 1890-1914; DLB 10; MTCW; SATA 19

Maso, Carole 19(?)- .... **CLC 44**

Mason, Bobbie Ann 1940- .... **CLC 28, 43, 82; SSC 4**
See also AAYA 5; CA 53-56; CANR 11, 31; DLBY 87; MTCW

Mason, Ernst
See Pohl, Frederik

Mason, Lee W.
See Malzberg, Barry N(athaniel)

Mason, Nick 1945-............... **CLC 35**
See also Pink Floyd

Mason, Tally
See Derleth, August (William)

Mass, William
See Gibson, William

Masters, Edgar Lee 1868-1950 ...... **TCLC 2, 25; DA; PC 1**
See also CA 104; 133; CDALB 1865-1917; DLB 54; MTCW

Masters, Hilary 1928- .... **CLC 48**
See also CA 25-28R; CANR 13

Mastrosimone, William 19(?)-...... **CLC 36**

Mathe, Albert
See Camus, Albert

Matheson, Richard Burton 1926- ... **CLC 37**
See also CA 97-100; DLB 8, 44

Mathews, Harry 1930-.......... **CLC 6, 52**
See also CA 21-24R; CAAS 6; CANR 18, 40

Mathias, Roland (Glyn) 1915-...... **CLC 45**
See also CA 97-100; CANR 19, 41; DLB 27

Matsuo Basho 1644-1694............ **PC 3**

Mattheson, Rodney
See Creasey, John

Matthews, Greg 1949- .... **CLC 45**
See also CA 135

Matthews, William 1942-.......... **CLC 40**
See also CA 29-32R; CAAS 18; CANR 12; DLB 5

Matthias, John (Edward) 1941-...... **CLC 9**
See also CA 33-36R

Matthiessen, Peter 1927- .... **CLC 5, 7, 11, 32, 64**
See also AAYA 6; BEST 90:4; CA 9-12R; CANR 21; DLB 6; MTCW; SATA 27

Maturin, Charles Robert 1780(?)-1824 .... **NCLC 6**

Matute (Ausejo), Ana Maria 1925- .... **CLC 11**
See also CA 89-92; MTCW

Maugham, W. S.
See Maugham, W(illiam) Somerset

Maugham, W(illiam) Somerset 1874-1965 ...... **CLC 1, 11, 15, 67; DA; SSC 8; WLC**
See also CA 5-8R; 25-28R; CANR 40; CDBLB 1914-1945; DLB 10, 36, 77, 100; MTCW; SATA 54

Maugham, William Somerset
See Maugham, W(illiam) Somerset

Maupassant, (Henri Rene Albert) Guy de 1850-1893 .... **NCLC 1, 42; DA; SSC 1; WLC**
See also DLB 123

Maurhut, Richard
See Traven, B.

Mauriac, Claude 1914-............. **CLC 9**
See also CA 89-92; DLB 83

Mauriac, Francois (Charles) 1885-1970 .... **CLC 4, 9, 56**
See also CA 25-28; CAP 2; DLB 65; MTCW

Mavor, Osborne Henry 1888-1951
See Bridie, James
See also CA 104

Maxwell, William (Keepers, Jr.) 1908- . . . . **CLC 19**
See also CA 93-96; DLBY 80

May, Elaine 1932- . . . . **CLC 16**
See also CA 124; 142; DLB 44

Mayakovski, Vladimir (Vladimirovich) 1893-1930 . . . . **TCLC 4, 18**
See also CA 104

Mayhew, Henry 1812-1887 . . . . . . **NCLC 31**
See also DLB 18, 55

Maynard, Joyce 1953- . . . . **CLC 23**
See also CA 111; 129

Mayne, William (James Carter) 1928- . . . . **CLC 12**
See also CA 9-12R; CANR 37; CLR 25; JRDA; MAICYA; SAAS 11; SATA 6, 68

Mayo, Jim
See L'Amour, Louis (Dearborn)

Maysles, Albert 1926- . . . . **CLC 16**
See also CA 29-32R

Maysles, David 1932- . . . . **CLC 16**

Mazer, Norma Fox 1931- . . . . **CLC 26**
See also AAYA 5; CA 69-72; CANR 12, 32; CLR 23; JRDA; MAICYA; SAAS 1; SATA 24, 67

Mazzini, Guiseppe 1805-1872 . . . . **NCLC 34**

McAuley, James Phillip 1917-1976 . . . . **CLC 45**
See also CA 97-100

McBain, Ed
See Hunter, Evan

McBrien, William Augustine 1930- . . . . **CLC 44**
See also CA 107

McCaffrey, Anne (Inez) 1926- . . . . . . **CLC 17**
See also AAYA 6; AITN 2; BEST 89:2; CA 25-28R; CANR 15, 35; DLB 8; JRDA; MAICYA; MTCW; SAAS 11; SATA 8, 70

McCann, Arthur
See Campbell, John W(ood, Jr.)

McCann, Edson
See Pohl, Frederik

McCarthy, Charles, Jr. 1933-
See McCarthy, Cormac
See also CANR 42

McCarthy, Cormac . . . . **CLC 4, 57**
See also McCarthy, Charles, Jr.
See also DLB 6

McCarthy, Mary (Therese) 1912-1989 . . . **CLC 1, 3, 5, 14, 24, 39, 59**
See also CA 5-8R; 129; CANR 16; DLB 2; DLBY 81; MTCW

McCartney, (James) Paul 1942- . . . . **CLC 12, 35**

McCauley, Stephen (D.) 1955- . . . . . **CLC 50**
See also CA 141

McClure, Michael (Thomas) 1932- . . . . **CLC 6, 10**
See also CA 21-24R; CANR 17; DLB 16

McCorkle, Jill (Collins) 1958- . . . . . . **CLC 51**
See also CA 121; DLBY 87

McCourt, James 1941- . . . . **CLC 5**
See also CA 57-60

McCoy, Horace (Stanley) 1897-1955 . . . . **TCLC 28**
See also CA 108; DLB 9

McCrae, John 1872-1918 . . . . **TCLC 12**
See also CA 109; DLB 92

McCreigh, James
See Pohl, Frederik

McCullers, (Lula) Carson (Smith) 1917-1967 . . . . **CLC 1, 4, 10, 12, 48; DA; SSC 9; WLC**
See also CA 5-8R; 25-28R; CABS 1, 3; CANR 18; CDALB 1941-1968; DLB 2, 7; MTCW; SATA 27

McCulloch, John Tyler
See Burroughs, Edgar Rice

McCullough, Colleen 1938(?)- . . . . . . **CLC 27**
See also CA 81-84; CANR 17; MTCW

McElroy, Joseph 1930- . . . . **CLC 5, 47**
See also CA 17-20R

McEwan, Ian (Russell) 1948- . . . **CLC 13, 66**
See also BEST 90:4; CA 61-64; CANR 14, 41; DLB 14; MTCW

McFadden, David 1940- . . . . **CLC 48**
See also CA 104; DLB 60

McFarland, Dennis 1950- . . . . **CLC 65**

McGahern, John 1934- . . . . **CLC 5, 9, 48**
See also CA 17-20R; CANR 29; DLB 14; MTCW

McGinley, Patrick (Anthony) 1937- . . . . **CLC 41**
See also CA 120; 127

McGinley, Phyllis 1905-1978 . . . . . . **CLC 14**
See also CA 9-12R; 77-80; CANR 19; DLB 11, 48; SATA 2, 24, 44

McGinniss, Joe 1942- . . . . **CLC 32**
See also AITN 2; BEST 89:2; CA 25-28R; CANR 26

McGivern, Maureen Daly
See Daly, Maureen

McGrath, Patrick 1950- . . . . **CLC 55**
See also CA 136

McGrath, Thomas (Matthew) 1916-1990 . . . . **CLC 28, 59**
See also CA 9-12R; 132; CANR 6, 33; MTCW; SATA 41; SATA-Obit 66

McGuane, Thomas (Francis III) 1939- . . . . **CLC 3, 7, 18, 45**
See also AITN 2; CA 49-52; CANR 5, 24; DLB 2; DLBY 80; MTCW

McGuckian, Medbh 1950- . . . . **CLC 48**
See also CA 143; DLB 40

McHale, Tom 1942(?)-1982 . . . . **CLC 3, 5**
See also AITN 1; CA 77-80; 106

McIlvanney, William 1936- . . . . **CLC 42**
See also CA 25-28R; DLB 14

McIlwraith, Maureen Mollie Hunter
See Hunter, Mollie
See also SATA 2

McInerney, Jay 1955- . . . . **CLC 34**
See also CA 116; 123

McIntyre, Vonda N(eel) 1948- . . . . . **CLC 18**
See also CA 81-84; CANR 17, 34; MTCW

McKay, Claude . . . . . **TCLC 7, 41; BLC; PC 2**
See also McKay, Festus Claudius
See also DLB 4, 45, 51, 117

McKay, Festus Claudius 1889-1948
See McKay, Claude
See also BW; CA 104; 124; DA; MTCW; WLC

McKuen, Rod 1933- . . . . **CLC 1, 3**
See also AITN 1; CA 41-44R; CANR 40

McLoughlin, R. B.
See Mencken, H(enry) L(ouis)

McLuhan, (Herbert) Marshall 1911-1980 . . . . **CLC 37**
See also CA 9-12R; 102; CANR 12, 34; DLB 88; MTCW

McMillan, Terry (L.) 1951- . . . . . **CLC 50, 61**
See also CA 140

McMurtry, Larry (Jeff) 1936- . . . . **CLC 2, 3, 7, 11, 27, 44**
See also AITN 2; BEST 89:2; CA 5-8R; CANR 19, 43; CDALB 1968-1988; DLB 2; DLBY 80, 87; MTCW

McNally, T. M. 1961- . . . . **CLC 82**

McNally, Terrence 1939- . . . . . . **CLC 4, 7, 41**
See also CA 45-48; CANR 2; DLB 7

McNamer, Deirdre 1950- . . . . **CLC 70**

McNeile, Herman Cyril 1888-1937
See Sapper
See also DLB 77

McPhee, John (Angus) 1931- . . . . . . **CLC 36**
See also BEST 90:1; CA 65-68; CANR 20; MTCW

McPherson, James Alan 1943- . . . . **CLC 19, 77**
See also BW; CA 25-28R; CAAS 17; CANR 24; DLB 38; MTCW

McPherson, William (Alexander) 1933- . . . . **CLC 34**
See also CA 69-72; CANR 28

McSweeney, Kerry . . . . **CLC 34**

Mead, Margaret 1901-1978 . . . . **CLC 37**
See also AITN 1; CA 1-4R; 81-84; CANR 4; MTCW; SATA 20

Meaker, Marijane (Agnes) 1927-
See Kerr, M. E.
See also CA 107; CANR 37; JRDA; MAICYA; MTCW; SATA 20, 61

Medoff, Mark (Howard) 1940- . . . **CLC 6, 23**
See also AITN 1; CA 53-56; CANR 5; DLB 7

Meged, Aharon
See Megged, Aharon

Meged, Aron
See Megged, Aharon

Megged, Aharon 1920- . . . . **CLC 9**
See also CA 49-52; CAAS 13; CANR 1

Mehta, Ved (Parkash) 1934- . . . . **CLC 37**
See also CA 1-4R; CANR 2, 23; MTCW

Melanter
See Blackmore, R(ichard) D(oddridge)

Melikow, Loris
See Hofmannsthal, Hugo von

Melmoth, Sebastian
See Wilde, Oscar (Fingal O'Flahertie Wills)

Nessi, Pio Baroja y
See Baroja (y Nessi), Pio

Nestroy, Johann 1801-1862 ...... **NCLC 42**
See also DLB 133

Neufeld, John (Arthur) 1938- ...... **CLC 17**
See also CA 25-28R; CANR 11, 37; MAICYA; SAAS 3; SATA 6

Neville, Emily Cheney 1919- .... **CLC 12**
See also CA 5-8R; CANR 3, 37; JRDA; MAICYA; SAAS 2; SATA 1

Newbound, Bernard Slade 1930-
See Slade, Bernard
See also CA 81-84

Newby, P(ercy) H(oward)
1918- .... **CLC 2, 13**
See also CA 5-8R; CANR 32; DLB 15; MTCW

Newlove, Donald 1928- .... **CLC 6**
See also CA 29-32R; CANR 25

Newlove, John (Herbert) 1938- ..... **CLC 14**
See also CA 21-24R; CANR 9, 25

Newman, Charles 1938- .... **CLC 2, 8**
See also CA 21-24R

Newman, Edwin (Harold) 1919- .... **CLC 14**
See also AITN 1; CA 69-72; CANR 5

Newman, John Henry
1801-1890 .... **NCLC 38**
See also DLB 18, 32, 55

Newton, Suzanne 1936- .... **CLC 35**
See also CA 41-44R; CANR 14; JRDA; SATA 5

Nexo, Martin Andersen
1869-1954 .... **TCLC 43**

Nezval, Vitezslav 1900-1958 ...... **TCLC 44**
See also CA 123

Ng, Fae Myenne 1957(?)- .... **CLC 81**

Ngema, Mbongeni 1955- .... **CLC 57**
See also CA 143

Ngugi, James T(hiong'o) .... **CLC 3, 7, 13**
See also Ngugi wa Thiong'o

Ngugi wa Thiong'o 1938- ..... **CLC 36; BLC**
See also Ngugi, James T(hiong'o)
See also BW; CA 81-84; CANR 27; DLB 125; MTCW

Nichol, B(arrie) P(hillip)
1944-1988 .... **CLC 18**
See also CA 53-56; DLB 53; SATA 66

Nichols, John (Treadwell) 1940- .... **CLC 38**
See also CA 9-12R; CAAS 2; CANR 6; DLBY 82

Nichols, Leigh
See Koontz, Dean R(ay)

Nichols, Peter (Richard)
1927- .... **CLC 5, 36, 65**
See also CA 104; CANR 33; DLB 13; MTCW

Nicolas, F. R. E.
See Freeling, Nicolas

Niedecker, Lorine 1903-1970 .... **CLC 10, 42**
See also CA 25-28; CAP 2; DLB 48

Nietzsche, Friedrich (Wilhelm)
1844-1900 .... **TCLC 10, 18**
See also CA 107; 121; DLB 129

Nievo, Ippolito 1831-1861 .... **NCLC 22**

Nightingale, Anne Redmon 1943-
See Redmon, Anne
See also CA 103

Nik.T.O.
See Annensky, Innokenty Fyodorovich

Nin, Anais
1903-1977 ...... **CLC 1, 4, 8, 11, 14, 60; SSC 10**
See also AITN 2; CA 13-16R; 69-72; CANR 22; DLB 2, 4; MTCW

Nissenson, Hugh 1933- .... **CLC 4, 9**
See also CA 17-20R; CANR 27; DLB 28

Niven, Larry .... **CLC 8**
See also Niven, Laurence Van Cott
See also DLB 8

Niven, Laurence Van Cott 1938-
See Niven, Larry
See also CA 21-24R; CAAS 12; CANR 14; MTCW

Nixon, Agnes Eckhardt 1927- ...... **CLC 21**
See also CA 110

Nizan, Paul 1905-1940 .... **TCLC 40**
See also DLB 72

Nkosi, Lewis 1936- .... **CLC 45; BLC**
See also BW; CA 65-68; CANR 27

Nodier, (Jean) Charles (Emmanuel)
1780-1844 .... **NCLC 19**
See also DLB 119

Nolan, Christopher 1965- .... **CLC 58**
See also CA 111

Norden, Charles
See Durrell, Lawrence (George)

Nordhoff, Charles (Bernard)
1887-1947 .... **TCLC 23**
See also CA 108; DLB 9; SATA 23

Norfolk, Lawrence 1963- .... **CLC 76**

Norman, Marsha 1947- .... **CLC 28**
See also CA 105; CABS 3; CANR 41; DLBY 84

Norris, Benjamin Franklin, Jr.
1870-1902 .... **TCLC 24**
See also Norris, Frank
See also CA 110

Norris, Frank
See Norris, Benjamin Franklin, Jr.
See also CDALB 1865-1917; DLB 12, 71

Norris, Leslie 1921- .... **CLC 14**
See also CA 11-12; CANR 14; CAP 1; DLB 27

North, Andrew
See Norton, Andre

North, Anthony
See Koontz, Dean R(ay)

North, Captain George
See Stevenson, Robert Louis (Balfour)

North, Milou
See Erdrich, Louise

Northrup, B. A.
See Hubbard, L(afayette) Ron(ald)

North Staffs
See Hulme, T(homas) E(rnest)

Norton, Alice Mary
See Norton, Andre
See also MAICYA; SATA 1, 43

Norton, Andre 1912- .... **CLC 12**
See also Norton, Alice Mary
See also CA 1-4R; CANR 2, 31; DLB 8, 52; JRDA; MTCW

Norway, Nevil Shute 1899-1960
See Shute, Nevil
See also CA 102; 93-96

Norwid, Cyprian Kamil
1821-1883 .... **NCLC 17**

Nosille, Nabrah
See Ellison, Harlan

Nossack, Hans Erich 1901-1978 ..... **CLC 6**
See also CA 93-96; 85-88; DLB 69

Nosu, Chuji
See Ozu, Yasujiro

Nova, Craig 1945- .... **CLC 7, 31**
See also CA 45-48; CANR 2

Novak, Joseph
See Kosinski, Jerzy (Nikodem)

Novalis 1772-1801 .... **NCLC 13**
See also DLB 90

Nowlan, Alden (Albert) 1933-1983 .. **CLC 15**
See also CA 9-12R; CANR 5; DLB 53

Noyes, Alfred 1880-1958 .... **TCLC 7**
See also CA 104; DLB 20

Nunn, Kem 19(?)- .... **CLC 34**

Nye, Robert 1939- .... **CLC 13, 42**
See also CA 33-36R; CANR 29; DLB 14; MTCW; SATA 6

Nyro, Laura 1947- .... **CLC 17**

Oates, Joyce Carol
1938- ...... **CLC 1, 2, 3, 6, 9, 11, 15, 19, 33, 52; DA; SSC 6; WLC**
See also AITN 1; BEST 89:2; CA 5-8R; CANR 25; CDALB 1968-1988; DLB 2, 5, 130; DLBY 81; MTCW

O'Brien, E. G.
See Clarke, Arthur C(harles)

O'Brien, Edna
1936- ... **CLC 3, 5, 8, 13, 36, 65; SSC 10**
See also CA 1-4R; CANR 6, 41; CDBLB 1960 to Present; DLB 14; MTCW

O'Brien, Fitz-James 1828-1862 ... **NCLC 21**
See also DLB 74

O'Brien, Flann .... **CLC 1, 4, 5, 7, 10, 47**
See also O Nuallain, Brian

O'Brien, Richard 1942- .... **CLC 17**
See also CA 124

O'Brien, Tim 1946- .... **CLC 7, 19, 40**
See also CA 85-88; CANR 40; DLBD 9; DLBY 80

Obstfelder, Sigbjoern 1866-1900 ... **TCLC 23**
See also CA 123

O'Casey, Sean
1880-1964 .... **CLC 1, 5, 9, 11, 15**
See also CA 89-92; CDBLB 1914-1945; DLB 10; MTCW

O'Cathasaigh, Sean
See O'Casey, Sean

Ochs, Phil 1940-1976 .... **CLC 17**
See also CA 65-68

Pepys, Samuel
1633-1703 . . . . **LC 11; DA; WLC**
See also CDBLB 1660-1789; DLB 101

Percy, Walker
1916-1990 . . . . **CLC 2, 3, 6, 8, 14, 18, 47, 65**
See also CA 1-4R; 131; CANR 1, 23; DLB 2; DLBY 80, 90; MTCW

Perec, Georges 1936-1982 . . . . **CLC 56**
See also CA 141; DLB 83

Pereda (y Sanchez de Porrua), Jose Maria de
1833-1906 . . . . **TCLC 16**
See also CA 117

Pereda y Porrua, Jose Maria de
See Pereda (y Sanchez de Porrua), Jose Maria de

Peregoy, George Weems
See Mencken, H(enry) L(ouis)

Perelman, S(idney) J(oseph)
1904-1979 . . . **CLC 3, 5, 9, 15, 23, 44, 49**
See also AITN 1, 2; CA 73-76; 89-92; CANR 18; DLB 11, 44; MTCW

Peret, Benjamin 1899-1959 . . . . **TCLC 20**
See also CA 117

Peretz, Isaac Loeb 1851(?)-1915 . . . **TCLC 16**
See also CA 109

Peretz, Yitzkhok Leibush
See Peretz, Isaac Loeb

Perez Galdos, Benito 1843-1920 . . . **TCLC 27**
See also CA 125; HW

Perrault, Charles 1628-1703 . . . . **LC 2**
See also MAICYA; SATA 25

Perry, Brighton
See Sherwood, Robert E(mmet)

Perse, St.-John . . . . **CLC 4, 11, 46**
See also Leger, (Marie-Rene Auguste) Alexis Saint-Leger

Peseenz, Tulio F.
See Lopez y Fuentes, Gregorio

Pesetsky, Bette 1932- . . . . **CLC 28**
See also CA 133; DLB 130

Peshkov, Alexei Maximovich 1868-1936
See Gorky, Maxim
See also CA 105; 141; DA

Pessoa, Fernando (Antonio Nogueira)
1888-1935 . . . . **TCLC 27; HLC**
See also CA 125

Peterkin, Julia Mood 1880-1961 . . . . **CLC 31**
See also CA 102; DLB 9

Peters, Joan K. 1945- . . . . **CLC 39**

Peters, Robert L(ouis) 1924- . . . . **CLC 7**
See also CA 13-16R; CAAS 8; DLB 105

Petofi, Sandor 1823-1849 . . . . **NCLC 21**

Petrakis, Harry Mark 1923- . . . . **CLC 3**
See also CA 9-12R; CANR 4, 30

Petrarch 1304-1374 . . . . **PC 8**

Petrov, Evgeny . . . . **TCLC 21**
See also Kataev, Evgeny Petrovich

Petry, Ann (Lane) 1908- . . . . . . **CLC 1, 7, 18**
See also BW; CA 5-8R; CAAS 6; CANR 4; CLR 12; DLB 76; JRDA; MAICYA; MTCW; SATA 5

Petursson, Halligrimur 1614-1674 . . . . **LC 8**

Philipson, Morris H. 1926- . . . . **CLC 53**
See also CA 1-4R; CANR 4

Phillips, David Graham
1867-1911 . . . . **TCLC 44**
See also CA 108; DLB 9, 12

Phillips, Jack
See Sandburg, Carl (August)

Phillips, Jayne Anne 1952- . . . . . **CLC 15, 33**
See also CA 101; CANR 24; DLBY 80; MTCW

Phillips, Richard
See Dick, Philip K(indred)

Phillips, Robert (Schaeffer) 1938- . . . **CLC 28**
See also CA 17-20R; CAAS 13; CANR 8; DLB 105

Phillips, Ward
See Lovecraft, H(oward) P(hillips)

Piccolo, Lucio 1901-1969 . . . . **CLC 13**
See also CA 97-100; DLB 114

Pickthall, Marjorie L(owry) C(hristie)
1883-1922 . . . . **TCLC 21**
See also CA 107; DLB 92

Pico della Mirandola, Giovanni
1463-1494 . . . . **LC 15**

Piercy, Marge
1936- . . . . **CLC 3, 6, 14, 18, 27, 62**
See also CA 21-24R; CAAS 1; CANR 13, 43; DLB 120; MTCW

Piers, Robert
See Anthony, Piers

Pieyre de Mandiargues, Andre 1909-1991
See Mandiargues, Andre Pieyre de
See also CA 103; 136; CANR 22

Pilnyak, Boris . . . . **TCLC 23**
See also Vogau, Boris Andreyevich

Pincherle, Alberto 1907-1990 . . . **CLC 11, 18**
See also Moravia, Alberto
See also CA 25-28R; 132; CANR 33; MTCW

Pinckney, Darryl 1953- . . . . **CLC 76**
See also CA 143

Pindar 518B.C.-446B.C. . . . . **CMLC 12**

Pineda, Cecile 1942- . . . . **CLC 39**
See also CA 118

Pinero, Arthur Wing 1855-1934 . . . **TCLC 32**
See also CA 110; DLB 10

Pinero, Miguel (Antonio Gomez)
1946-1988 . . . . **CLC 4, 55**
See also CA 61-64; 125; CANR 29; HW

Pinget, Robert 1919- . . . . **CLC 7, 13, 37**
See also CA 85-88; DLB 83

Pink Floyd . . . . **CLC 35**
See also Barrett, (Roger) Syd; Gilmour, David; Mason, Nick; Waters, Roger; Wright, Rick

Pinkney, Edward 1802-1828 . . . . . **NCLC 31**

Pinkwater, Daniel Manus 1941- . . . . **CLC 35**
See also Pinkwater, Manus
See also AAYA 1; CA 29-32R; CANR 12, 38; CLR 4; JRDA; MAICYA; SAAS 3; SATA 46

Pinkwater, Manus
See Pinkwater, Daniel Manus
See also SATA 8

Pinsky, Robert 1940- . . . . **CLC 9, 19, 38**
See also CA 29-32R; CAAS 4; DLBY 82

Pinta, Harold
See Pinter, Harold

Pinter, Harold
1930- . . . . . **CLC 1, 3, 6, 9, 11, 15, 27, 58, 73; DA; WLC**
See also CA 5-8R; CANR 33; CDBLB 1960 to Present; DLB 13; MTCW

Pirandello, Luigi
1867-1936 . . . . . . **TCLC 4, 29; DA; WLC**
See also CA 104

Pirsig, Robert M(aynard)
1928- . . . . **CLC 4, 6, 73**
See also CA 53-56; CANR 42; MTCW; SATA 39

Pisarev, Dmitry Ivanovich
1840-1868 . . . . **NCLC 25**

Pix, Mary (Griffith) 1666-1709 . . . . **LC 8**
See also DLB 80

Pixerecourt, Guilbert de
1773-1844 . . . . **NCLC 39**

Plaidy, Jean
See Hibbert, Eleanor Alice Burford

Planche, James Robinson
1796-1880 . . . . **NCLC 42**

Plant, Robert 1948- . . . . **CLC 12**

Plante, David (Robert)
1940- . . . . **CLC 7, 23, 38**
See also CA 37-40R; CANR 12, 36; DLBY 83; MTCW

Plath, Sylvia
1932-1963 . . . . . **CLC 1, 2, 3, 5, 9, 11, 14, 17, 50, 51, 62; DA; PC 1; WLC**
See also CA 19-20; CANR 34; CAP 2; CDALB 1941-1968; DLB 5, 6; MTCW

Plato 428(?)B.C.-348(?)B.C. . . . **CMLC 8; DA**

Platonov, Andrei . . . . **TCLC 14**
See also Klimentov, Andrei Platonovich

Platt, Kin 1911- . . . . **CLC 26**
See also CA 17-20R; CANR 11; JRDA; SAAS 17; SATA 21

Plick et Plock
See Simenon, Georges (Jacques Christian)

Plimpton, George (Ames) 1927- . . . . . **CLC 36**
See also AITN 1; CA 21-24R; CANR 32; MTCW; SATA 10

Plomer, William Charles Franklin
1903-1973 . . . . **CLC 4, 8**
See also CA 21-22; CANR 34; CAP 2; DLB 20; MTCW; SATA 24

Plowman, Piers
See Kavanagh, Patrick (Joseph)

Plum, J.
See Wodehouse, P(elham) G(renville)

Plumly, Stanley (Ross) 1939- . . . . . . **CLC 33**
See also CA 108; 110; DLB 5

Plumpe, Friedrich Wilhelm
1888-1931 . . . . **TCLC 53**
See also CA 112

Poe, Edgar Allan
1809-1849 . . . . . **NCLC 1, 16; DA; PC 1; SSC 1; WLC**
See also CDALB 1640-1865; DLB 3, 59, 73, 74; SATA 23

Poet of Titchfield Street, The
See Pound, Ezra (Weston Loomis)

Pohl, Frederik 1919- . . . . **CLC 18**
See also CA 61-64; CAAS 1; CANR 11, 37; DLB 8; MTCW; SATA 24

Poirier, Louis 1910-
See Gracq, Julien
See also CA 122; 126

Poitier, Sidney 1927- . . . . **CLC 26**
See also BW; CA 117

Polanski, Roman 1933- . . . . **CLC 16**
See also CA 77-80

Poliakoff, Stephen 1952- . . . . **CLC 38**
See also CA 106; DLB 13

Police, The . . . . **CLC 26**
See also Copeland, Stewart (Armstrong); Summers, Andrew James; Sumner, Gordon Matthew

Pollitt, Katha 1949- . . . . **CLC 28**
See also CA 120; 122; MTCW

Pollock, (Mary) Sharon 1936- . . . . . . **CLC 50**
See also CA 141; DLB 60

Pomerance, Bernard 1940- . . . . **CLC 13**
See also CA 101

Ponge, Francis (Jean Gaston Alfred)
1899-1988 . . . . **CLC 6, 18**
See also CA 85-88; 126; CANR 40

Pontoppidan, Henrik 1857-1943 . . . **TCLC 29**

Poole, Josephine . . . . **CLC 17**
See also Helyar, Jane Penelope Josephine
See also SAAS 2; SATA 5

Popa, Vasko 1922- . . . . **CLC 19**
See also CA 112

Pope, Alexander
1688-1744 . . . . **LC 3; DA; WLC**
See also CDBLB 1660-1789; DLB 95, 101

Porter, Connie (Rose) 1959(?)- . . . . . **CLC 70**
See also CA 142

Porter, Gene(va Grace) Stratton
1863(?)-1924 . . . . **TCLC 21**
See also CA 112

Porter, Katherine Anne
1890-1980 . . . . . . **CLC 1, 3, 7, 10, 13, 15, 27; DA; SSC 4**
See also AITN 2; CA 1-4R; 101; CANR 1; DLB 4, 9, 102; DLBY 80; MTCW; SATA 23, 39

Porter, Peter (Neville Frederick)
1929- . . . . **CLC 5, 13, 33**
See also CA 85-88; DLB 40

Porter, William Sydney 1862-1910
See Henry, O.
See also CA 104; 131; CDALB 1865-1917; DA; DLB 12, 78, 79; MTCW; YABC 2

Portillo (y Pacheco), Jose Lopez
See Lopez Portillo (y Pacheco), Jose

Post, Melville Davisson
1869-1930 . . . . **TCLC 39**
See also CA 110

Potok, Chaim 1929- . . . . **CLC 2, 7, 14, 26**
See also AITN 1, 2; CA 17-20R; CANR 19, 35; DLB 28; MTCW; SATA 33

Potter, Beatrice
See Webb, (Martha) Beatrice (Potter)
See also MAICYA

Potter, Dennis (Christopher George)
1935- . . . . **CLC 58**
See also CA 107; CANR 33; MTCW

Pound, Ezra (Weston Loomis)
1885-1972 . . . . . . **CLC 1, 2, 3, 4, 5, 7, 10, 13, 18, 34, 48, 50; DA; PC 4; WLC**
See also CA 5-8R; 37-40R; CANR 40; CDALB 1917-1929; DLB 4, 45, 63; MTCW

Povod, Reinaldo 1959- . . . . **CLC 44**
See also CA 136

Powell, Anthony (Dymoke)
1905- . . . . **CLC 1, 3, 7, 9, 10, 31**
See also CA 1-4R; CANR 1, 32; CDBLB 1945-1960; DLB 15; MTCW

Powell, Dawn 1897-1965 . . . . **CLC 66**
See also CA 5-8R

Powell, Padgett 1952- . . . . **CLC 34**
See also CA 126

Powers, J(ames) F(arl)
1917- . . . . **CLC 1, 4, 8, 57; SSC 4**
See also CA 1-4R; CANR 2; DLB 130; MTCW

Powers, John J(ames) 1945-
See Powers, John R.
See also CA 69-72

Powers, John R. . . . . **CLC 66**
See also Powers, John J(ames)

Pownall, David 1938- . . . . **CLC 10**
See also CA 89-92; CAAS 18; DLB 14

Powys, John Cowper
1872-1963 . . . . **CLC 7, 9, 15, 46**
See also CA 85-88; DLB 15; MTCW

Powys, T(heodore) F(rancis)
1875-1953 . . . . **TCLC 9**
See also CA 106; DLB 36

Prager, Emily 1952- . . . . **CLC 56**

Pratt, E(dwin) J(ohn)
1883(?)-1964 . . . . **CLC 19**
See also CA 141; 93-96; DLB 92

Premchand . . . . **TCLC 21**
See also Srivastava, Dhanpat Rai

Preussler, Otfried 1923- . . . . **CLC 17**
See also CA 77-80; SATA 24

Prevert, Jacques (Henri Marie)
1900-1977 . . . . **CLC 15**
See also CA 77-80; 69-72; CANR 29; MTCW; SATA 30

Prevost, Abbe (Antoine Francois)
1697-1763 . . . . **LC 1**

Price, (Edward) Reynolds
1933- . . . . **CLC 3, 6, 13, 43, 50, 63**
See also CA 1-4R; CANR 1, 37; DLB 2

Price, Richard 1949- . . . . **CLC 6, 12**
See also CA 49-52; CANR 3; DLBY 81

Prichard, Katharine Susannah
1883-1969 . . . . **CLC 46**
See also CA 11-12; CANR 33; CAP 1; MTCW; SATA 66

Priestley, J(ohn) B(oynton)
1894-1984 . . . . **CLC 2, 5, 9, 34**
See also CA 9-12R; 113; CANR 33; CDBLB 1914-1945; DLB 10, 34, 77, 100; DLBY 84; MTCW

Prince 1958(?)- . . . . **CLC 35**

Prince, F(rank) T(empleton) 1912- . . **CLC 22**
See also CA 101; CANR 43; DLB 20

Prince Kropotkin
See Kropotkin, Peter (Aleksieevich)

Prior, Matthew 1664-1721 . . . . **LC 4**
See also DLB 95

Pritchard, William H(arrison)
1932- . . . . **CLC 34**
See also CA 65-68; CANR 23; DLB 111

Pritchett, V(ictor) S(awdon)
1900- . . . . **CLC 5, 13, 15, 41; SSC 14**
See also CA 61-64; CANR 31; DLB 15; MTCW

Private 19022
See Manning, Frederic

Probst, Mark 1925- . . . . **CLC 59**
See also CA 130

Prokosch, Frederic 1908-1989 . . . . **CLC 4, 48**
See also CA 73-76; 128; DLB 48

Prophet, The
See Dreiser, Theodore (Herman Albert)

Prose, Francine 1947- . . . . **CLC 45**
See also CA 109; 112

Proudhon
See Cunha, Euclides (Rodrigues Pimenta) da

Proulx, E. Annie 1935- . . . . **CLC 81**

Proust, (Valentin-Louis-George-Eugene-) Marcel
1871-1922 . . . **TCLC 7, 13, 33; DA; WLC**
See also CA 104; 120; DLB 65; MTCW

Prowler, Harley
See Masters, Edgar Lee

Prus, Boleslaw . . . . **TCLC 48**
See also Glowacki, Aleksander

Pryor, Richard (Franklin Lenox Thomas)
1940- . . . . **CLC 26**
See also CA 122

Przybyszewski, Stanislaw
1868-1927 . . . . **TCLC 36**
See also DLB 66

Pteleon
See Grieve, C(hristopher) M(urray)

Puckett, Lute
See Masters, Edgar Lee

Puig, Manuel
1932-1990 . . . **CLC 3, 5, 10, 28, 65; HLC**
See also CA 45-48; CANR 2, 32; DLB 113; HW; MTCW

Purdy, Al(fred Wellington)
1918- . . . . **CLC 3, 6, 14, 50**
See also CA 81-84; CAAS 17; CANR 42; DLB 88

Purdy, James (Amos)
1923- . . . . **CLC 2, 4, 10, 28, 52**
See also CA 33-36R; CAAS 1; CANR 19; DLB 2; MTCW

Pure, Simon
See Swinnerton, Frank Arthur

Pushkin, Alexander (Sergeyevich)
1799-1837 . . . . . **NCLC 3, 27; DA; WLC**
See also SATA 61

P'u Sung-ling 1640-1715 . . . . **LC 3**

Putnam, Arthur Lee
See Alger, Horatio, Jr.

Puzo, Mario 1920- . . . . **CLC 1, 2, 6, 36**
See also CA 65-68; CANR 4, 42; DLB 6; MTCW

Pym, Barbara (Mary Crampton) 1913-1980 . . . . **CLC 13, 19, 37**
See also CA 13-14; 97-100; CANR 13, 34; CAP 1; DLB 14; DLBY 87; MTCW

Pynchon, Thomas (Ruggles, Jr.) 1937- . . . . . **CLC 2, 3, 6, 9, 11, 18, 33, 62, 72; DA; SSC 14; WLC**
See also BEST 90:2; CA 17-20R; CANR 22; DLB 2; MTCW

Q
See Quiller-Couch, Arthur Thomas

Qian Zhongshu
See Ch'ien Chung-shu

Qroll
See Dagerman, Stig (Halvard)

Quarrington, Paul (Lewis) 1953- . . . . **CLC 65**
See also CA 129

Quasimodo, Salvatore 1901-1968 . . . **CLC 10**
See also CA 13-16; 25-28R; CAP 1; DLB 114; MTCW

Queen, Ellery . . . . **CLC 3, 11**
See also Dannay, Frederic; Davidson, Avram; Lee, Manfred B(ennington); Sturgeon, Theodore (Hamilton); Vance, John Holbrook

Queen, Ellery, Jr.
See Dannay, Frederic; Lee, Manfred B(ennington)

Queneau, Raymond 1903-1976 . . . . **CLC 2, 5, 10, 42**
See also CA 77-80; 69-72; CANR 32; DLB 72; MTCW

Quevedo, Francisco de 1580-1645 . . . . **LC 23**

Quiller-Couch, Arthur Thomas 1863-1944 . . . . **TCLC 53**
See also CA 118; DLB 135

Quin, Ann (Marie) 1936-1973 . . . . **CLC 6**
See also CA 9-12R; 45-48; DLB 14

Quinn, Martin
See Smith, Martin Cruz

Quinn, Simon
See Smith, Martin Cruz

Quiroga, Horacio (Sylvestre) 1878-1937 . . . . **TCLC 20; HLC**
See also CA 117; 131; HW; MTCW

Quoirez, Francoise 1935- . . . . **CLC 9**
See also Sagan, Francoise
See also CA 49-52; CANR 6, 39; MTCW

Raabe, Wilhelm 1831-1910 . . . . **TCLC 45**
See also DLB 129

Rabe, David (William) 1940- . . . **CLC 4, 8, 33**
See also CA 85-88; CABS 3; DLB 7

Rabelais, Francois 1483-1553 . . . . **LC 5; DA; WLC**

Rabinovitch, Sholem 1859-1916
See Aleichem, Sholom
See also CA 104

Radcliffe, Ann (Ward) 1764-1823 . . **NCLC 6**
See also DLB 39

Radiguet, Raymond 1903-1923 . . . . **TCLC 29**
See also DLB 65

Radnoti, Miklos 1909-1944 . . . . **TCLC 16**
See also CA 118

Rado, James 1939- . . . . **CLC 17**
See also CA 105

Radvanyi, Netty 1900-1983
See Seghers, Anna
See also CA 85-88; 110

Raeburn, John (Hay) 1941- . . . . **CLC 34**
See also CA 57-60

Ragni, Gerome 1942-1991 . . . . **CLC 17**
See also CA 105; 134

Rahv, Philip . . . . **CLC 24**
See also Greenberg, Ivan

Raine, Craig 1944- . . . . **CLC 32**
See also CA 108; CANR 29; DLB 40

Raine, Kathleen (Jessie) 1908- . . . **CLC 7, 45**
See also CA 85-88; DLB 20; MTCW

Rainis, Janis 1865-1929 . . . . **TCLC 29**

Rakosi, Carl . . . . **CLC 47**
See also Rawley, Callman
See also CAAS 5

Raleigh, Richard
See Lovecraft, H(oward) P(hillips)

Rallentando, H. P.
See Sayers, Dorothy L(eigh)

Ramal, Walter
See de la Mare, Walter (John)

Ramon, Juan
See Jimenez (Mantecon), Juan Ramon

Ramos, Graciliano 1892-1953 . . . . . **TCLC 32**

Rampersad, Arnold 1941- . . . . **CLC 44**
See also CA 127; 133; DLB 111

Rampling, Anne
See Rice, Anne

Ramuz, Charles-Ferdinand 1878-1947 . . . . **TCLC 33**

Rand, Ayn 1905-1982 . . . . . . **CLC 3, 30, 44, 79; DA; WLC**
See also AAYA 10; CA 13-16R; 105; CANR 27; MTCW

Randall, Dudley (Felker) 1914- . . . . **CLC 1; BLC**
See also BW; CA 25-28R; CANR 23; DLB 41

Randall, Robert
See Silverberg, Robert

Ranger, Ken
See Creasey, John

Ransom, John Crowe 1888-1974 . . . . **CLC 2, 4, 5, 11, 24**
See also CA 5-8R; 49-52; CANR 6, 34; DLB 45, 63; MTCW

Rao, Raja 1909- . . . . **CLC 25, 56**
See also CA 73-76; MTCW

Raphael, Frederic (Michael) 1931- . . . . **CLC 2, 14**
See also CA 1-4R; CANR 1; DLB 14

Ratcliffe, James P.
See Mencken, H(enry) L(ouis)

Rathbone, Julian 1935- . . . . **CLC 41**
See also CA 101; CANR 34

Rattigan, Terence (Mervyn) 1911-1977 . . . . **CLC 7**
See also CA 85-88; 73-76; CDBLB 1945-1960; DLB 13; MTCW

Ratushinskaya, Irina 1954- . . . . **CLC 54**
See also CA 129

Raven, Simon (Arthur Noel) 1927- . . . . **CLC 14**
See also CA 81-84

Rawley, Callman 1903-
See Rakosi, Carl
See also CA 21-24R; CANR 12, 32

Rawlings, Marjorie Kinnan 1896-1953 . . . . **TCLC 4**
See also CA 104; 137; DLB 9, 22, 102; JRDA; MAICYA; YABC 1

Ray, Satyajit 1921-1992 . . . . **CLC 16, 76**
See also CA 114; 137

Read, Herbert Edward 1893-1968 . . . . **CLC 4**
See also CA 85-88; 25-28R; DLB 20

Read, Piers Paul 1941- . . . . . . **CLC 4, 10, 25**
See also CA 21-24R; CANR 38; DLB 14; SATA 21

Reade, Charles 1814-1884 . . . . **NCLC 2**
See also DLB 21

Reade, Hamish
See Gray, Simon (James Holliday)

Reading, Peter 1946- . . . . **CLC 47**
See also CA 103; DLB 40

Reaney, James 1926- . . . . **CLC 13**
See also CA 41-44R; CAAS 15; CANR 42; DLB 68; SATA 43

Rebreanu, Liviu 1885-1944 . . . . **TCLC 28**

Rechy, John (Francisco) 1934- . . . . **CLC 1, 7, 14, 18; HLC**
See also CA 5-8R; CAAS 4; CANR 6, 32; DLB 122; DLBY 82; HW

Redcam, Tom 1870-1933 . . . . **TCLC 25**

Reddin, Keith . . . . **CLC 67**

Redgrove, Peter (William) 1932- . . . . **CLC 6, 41**
See also CA 1-4R; CANR 3, 39; DLB 40

Redmon, Anne . . . . **CLC 22**
See also Nightingale, Anne Redmon
See also DLBY 86

Reed, Eliot
See Ambler, Eric

Reed, Ishmael 1938- . . . **CLC 2, 3, 5, 6, 13, 32, 60; BLC**
See also BW; CA 21-24R; CANR 25; DLB 2, 5, 33; DLBD 8; MTCW

Reed, John (Silas) 1887-1920 . . . . . . **TCLC 9**
See also CA 106

Reed, Lou . . . . **CLC 21**
See also Firbank, Louis

Reeve, Clara 1729-1807 . . . . **NCLC 19**
See also DLB 39

Reid, Christopher (John) 1949- . . . . . **CLC 33**
See also CA 140; DLB 40

Reid, Desmond
See Moorcock, Michael (John)

Reid Banks, Lynne 1929-
See Banks, Lynne Reid
See also CA 1-4R; CANR 6, 22, 38; CLR 24; JRDA; MAICYA; SATA 22, 75

Reilly, William K.
See Creasey, John

Reiner, Max
See Caldwell, (Janet Miriam) Taylor (Holland)

Reis, Ricardo
See Pessoa, Fernando (Antonio Nogueira)

Remarque, Erich Maria
1898-1970 . . . . **CLC 21; DA**
See also CA 77-80; 29-32R; DLB 56; MTCW

Remizov, A.
See Remizov, Aleksei (Mikhailovich)

Remizov, A. M.
See Remizov, Aleksei (Mikhailovich)

Remizov, Aleksei (Mikhailovich)
1877-1957 . . . . **TCLC 27**
See also CA 125; 133

Renan, Joseph Ernest
1823-1892 . . . . **NCLC 26**

Renard, Jules 1864-1910 . . . . **TCLC 17**
See also CA 117

Renault, Mary . . . . **CLC 3, 11, 17**
See also Challans, Mary
See also DLBY 83

Rendell, Ruth (Barbara) 1930- . . **CLC 28, 48**
See also Vine, Barbara
See also CA 109; CANR 32; DLB 87; MTCW

Renoir, Jean 1894-1979 . . . . **CLC 20**
See also CA 129; 85-88

Resnais, Alain 1922- . . . . **CLC 16**

Reverdy, Pierre 1889-1960 . . . . **CLC 53**
See also CA 97-100; 89-92

Rexroth, Kenneth
1905-1982 . . . . . . **CLC 1, 2, 6, 11, 22, 49**
See also CA 5-8R; 107; CANR 14, 34; CDALB 1941-1968; DLB 16, 48; DLBY 82; MTCW

Reyes, Alfonso 1889-1959 . . . . **TCLC 33**
See also CA 131; HW

Reyes y Basoalto, Ricardo Eliecer Neftali
See Neruda, Pablo

Reymont, Wladyslaw (Stanislaw)
1868(?)-1925 . . . . **TCLC 5**
See also CA 104

Reynolds, Jonathan 1942- . . . . **CLC 6, 38**
See also CA 65-68; CANR 28

Reynolds, Joshua 1723-1792 . . . . **LC 15**
See also DLB 104

Reynolds, Michael Shane 1937- . . . . **CLC 44**
See also CA 65-68; CANR 9

Reznikoff, Charles 1894-1976 . . . . **CLC 9**
See also CA 33-36; 61-64; CAP 2; DLB 28, 45

Rezzori (d'Arezzo), Gregor von
1914- . . . . **CLC 25**
See also CA 122; 136

Rhine, Richard
See Silverstein, Alvin

Rhodes, Eugene Manlove
1869-1934 . . . . **TCLC 53**

R'hoone
See Balzac, Honore de

Rhys, Jean
1890(?)-1979 . . . . **CLC 2, 4, 6, 14, 19, 51**
See also CA 25-28R; 85-88; CANR 35; CDBLB 1945-1960; DLB 36, 117; MTCW

Ribeiro, Darcy 1922- . . . . **CLC 34**
See also CA 33-36R

Ribeiro, Joao Ubaldo (Osorio Pimentel)
1941- . . . . **CLC 10, 67**
See also CA 81-84

Ribman, Ronald (Burt) 1932- . . . . **CLC 7**
See also CA 21-24R

Ricci, Nino 1959- . . . . **CLC 70**
See also CA 137

Rice, Anne 1941- . . . . **CLC 41**
See also AAYA 9; BEST 89:2; CA 65-68; CANR 12, 36

Rice, Elmer (Leopold)
1892-1967 . . . . **CLC 7, 49**
See also CA 21-22; 25-28R; CAP 2; DLB 4, 7; MTCW

Rice, Tim 1944- . . . . **CLC 21**
See also CA 103

Rich, Adrienne (Cecile)
1929- . . . . **CLC 3, 6, 7, 11, 18, 36, 73, 76; PC 5**
See also CA 9-12R; CANR 20; DLB 5, 67; MTCW

Rich, Barbara
See Graves, Robert (von Ranke)

Rich, Robert
See Trumbo, Dalton

Richards, David Adams 1950- . . . . . . **CLC 59**
See also CA 93-96; DLB 53

Richards, I(vor) A(rmstrong)
1893-1979 . . . . **CLC 14, 24**
See also CA 41-44R; 89-92; CANR 34; DLB 27

Richardson, Anne
See Roiphe, Anne Richardson

Richardson, Dorothy Miller
1873-1957 . . . . **TCLC 3**
See also CA 104; DLB 36

Richardson, Ethel Florence (Lindesay)
1870-1946
See Richardson, Henry Handel
See also CA 105

Richardson, Henry Handel . . . . **TCLC 4**
See also Richardson, Ethel Florence (Lindesay)

Richardson, Samuel
1689-1761 . . . . **LC 1; DA; WLC**
See also CDBLB 1660-1789; DLB 39

Richler, Mordecai
1931- . . . . **CLC 3, 5, 9, 13, 18, 46, 70**
See also AITN 1; CA 65-68; CANR 31; CLR 17; DLB 53; MAICYA; MTCW; SATA 27, 44

Richter, Conrad (Michael)
1890-1968 . . . . **CLC 30**
See also CA 5-8R; 25-28R; CANR 23; DLB 9; MTCW; SATA 3

Riddell, J. H. 1832-1906 . . . . **TCLC 40**

Riding, Laura . . . . **CLC 3, 7**
See also Jackson, Laura (Riding)

Riefenstahl, Berta Helene Amalia 1902-
See Riefenstahl, Leni
See also CA 108

Riefenstahl, Leni . . . . **CLC 16**
See also Riefenstahl, Berta Helene Amalia

Riffe, Ernest
See Bergman, (Ernst) Ingmar

Riley, James Whitcomb
1849-1916 . . . . **TCLC 51**
See also CA 118; 137; MAICYA; SATA 17

Riley, Tex
See Creasey, John

Rilke, Rainer Maria
1875-1926 . . . . **TCLC 1, 6, 19; PC 2**
See also CA 104; 132; DLB 81; MTCW

Rimbaud, (Jean Nicolas) Arthur
1854-1891 . . . . . **NCLC 4, 35; DA; PC 3; WLC**

Rinehart, Mary Roberts
1876-1958 . . . . **TCLC 52**
See also CA 108

Ringmaster, The
See Mencken, H(enry) L(ouis)

Ringwood, Gwen(dolyn Margaret) Pharis
1910-1984 . . . . **CLC 48**
See also CA 112; DLB 88

Rio, Michel 19(?)- . . . . **CLC 43**

Ritsos, Giannes
See Ritsos, Yannis

Ritsos, Yannis 1909-1990 . . . . . **CLC 6, 13, 31**
See also CA 77-80; 133; CANR 39; MTCW

Ritter, Erika 1948(?)- . . . . **CLC 52**

Rivera, Jose Eustasio 1889-1928 . . . **TCLC 35**
See also HW

Rivers, Conrad Kent 1933-1968 . . . . . . **CLC 1**
See also BW; CA 85-88; DLB 41

Rivers, Elfrida
See Bradley, Marion Zimmer

Riverside, John
See Heinlein, Robert A(nson)

Rizal, Jose 1861-1896 . . . . **NCLC 27**

Roa Bastos, Augusto (Antonio)
1917- . . . . **CLC 45; HLC**
See also CA 131; DLB 113; HW

Robbe-Grillet, Alain
1922- . . . . . . **CLC 1, 2, 4, 6, 8, 10, 14, 43**
See also CA 9-12R; CANR 33; DLB 83; MTCW

Robbins, Harold 1916- . . . . **CLC 5**
See also CA 73-76; CANR 26; MTCW

Robbins, Thomas Eugene 1936-
See Robbins, Tom
See also CA 81-84; CANR 29; MTCW

Robbins, Tom . . . . **CLC 9, 32, 64**
See also Robbins, Thomas Eugene
See also BEST 90:3; DLBY 80

Robbins, Trina 1938- . . . . **CLC 21**
See also CA 128

Roberts, Charles G(eorge) D(ouglas) 1860-1943 . . . . **TCLC 8**
See also CA 105; CLR 33; DLB 92; SATA 29

Roberts, Kate 1891-1985 . . . . **CLC 15**
See also CA 107; 116

Roberts, Keith (John Kingston) 1935- . . . . **CLC 14**
See also CA 25-28R

Roberts, Kenneth (Lewis) 1885-1957 . . . . **TCLC 23**
See also CA 109; DLB 9

Roberts, Michele (B.) 1949- . . . . **CLC 48**
See also CA 115

Robertson, Ellis
See Ellison, Harlan; Silverberg, Robert

Robertson, Thomas William 1829-1871 . . . . **NCLC 35**

Robinson, Edwin Arlington 1869-1935 . . . . **TCLC 5; DA; PC 1**
See also CA 104; 133; CDALB 1865-1917; DLB 54; MTCW

Robinson, Henry Crabb 1775-1867 . . . . **NCLC 15**
See also DLB 107

Robinson, Jill 1936- . . . . **CLC 10**
See also CA 102

Robinson, Kim Stanley 1952- . . . . . . **CLC 34**
See also CA 126

Robinson, Lloyd
See Silverberg, Robert

Robinson, Marilynne 1944- . . . . **CLC 25**
See also CA 116

Robinson, Smokey . . . . **CLC 21**
See also Robinson, William, Jr.

Robinson, William, Jr. 1940-
See Robinson, Smokey
See also CA 116

Robison, Mary 1949- . . . . **CLC 42**
See also CA 113; 116; DLB 130

Rod, Edouard 1857-1910 . . . . **TCLC 52**

Roddenberry, Eugene Wesley 1921-1991
See Roddenberry, Gene
See also CA 110; 135; CANR 37; SATA 45

Roddenberry, Gene . . . . **CLC 17**
See also Roddenberry, Eugene Wesley
See also AAYA 5; SATA-Obit 69

Rodgers, Mary 1931- . . . . **CLC 12**
See also CA 49-52; CANR 8; CLR 20; JRDA; MAICYA; SATA 8

Rodgers, W(illiam) R(obert) 1909-1969 . . . . **CLC 7**
See also CA 85-88; DLB 20

Rodman, Eric
See Silverberg, Robert

Rodman, Howard 1920(?)-1985 . . . . . **CLC 65**
See also CA 118

Rodman, Maia
See Wojciechowska, Maia (Teresa)

Rodriguez, Claudio 1934- . . . . **CLC 10**
See also DLB 134

Roelvaag, O(le) E(dvart) 1876-1931 . . . . **TCLC 17**
See also CA 117; DLB 9

Roethke, Theodore (Huebner) 1908-1963 . . . . . . **CLC 1, 3, 8, 11, 19, 46**
See also CA 81-84; CABS 2; CDALB 1941-1968; DLB 5; MTCW

Rogers, Thomas Hunton 1927- . . . . . **CLC 57**
See also CA 89-92

Rogers, Will(iam Penn Adair) 1879-1935 . . . . **TCLC 8**
See also CA 105; DLB 11

Rogin, Gilbert 1929- . . . . **CLC 18**
See also CA 65-68; CANR 15

Rohan, Koda . . . . **TCLC 22**
See also Koda Shigeyuki

Rohmer, Eric . . . . **CLC 16**
See also Scherer, Jean-Marie Maurice

Rohmer, Sax . . . . **TCLC 28**
See also Ward, Arthur Henry Sarsfield
See also DLB 70

Roiphe, Anne Richardson 1935- . . . **CLC 3, 9**
See also CA 89-92; DLBY 80

Rojas, Fernando de 1465-1541 . . . . . . **LC 23**

Rolfe, Frederick (William Serafino Austin Lewis Mary) 1860-1913. . . . . . **TCLC 12**
See also CA 107; DLB 34

Rolland, Romain 1866-1944. . . . . . . **TCLC 23**
See also CA 118; DLB 65

Rolvaag, O(le) E(dvart)
See Roelvaag, O(le) E(dvart)

Romain Arnaud, Saint
See Aragon, Louis

Romains, Jules 1885-1972 . . . . **CLC 7**
See also CA 85-88; CANR 34; DLB 65; MTCW

Romero, Jose Ruben 1890-1952 . . . **TCLC 14**
See also CA 114; 131; HW

Ronsard, Pierre de 1524-1585 . . . . **LC 6**

Rooke, Leon 1934- . . . . **CLC 25, 34**
See also CA 25-28R; CANR 23

Roper, William 1498-1578 . . . . **LC 10**

Roquelaure, A. N.
See Rice, Anne

Rosa, Joao Guimaraes 1908-1967 . . . **CLC 23**
See also CA 89-92; DLB 113

Rosen, Richard (Dean) 1949- . . . . **CLC 39**
See also CA 77-80

Rosenberg, Isaac 1890-1918. . . . . . . **TCLC 12**
See also CA 107; DLB 20

Rosenblatt, Joe . . . . **CLC 15**
See also Rosenblatt, Joseph

Rosenblatt, Joseph 1933-
See Rosenblatt, Joe
See also CA 89-92

Rosenfeld, Samuel 1896-1963
See Tzara, Tristan
See also CA 89-92

Rosenthal, M(acha) L(ouis) 1917- . . . **CLC 28**
See also CA 1-4R; CAAS 6; CANR 4; DLB 5; SATA 59

Ross, Barnaby
See Dannay, Frederic

Ross, Bernard L.
See Follett, Ken(neth Martin)

Ross, J. H.
See Lawrence, T(homas) E(dward)

Ross, Martin
See Martin, Violet Florence
See also DLB 135

Ross, (James) Sinclair 1908- . . . . **CLC 13**
See also CA 73-76; DLB 88

Rossetti, Christina (Georgina) 1830-1894 . . . **NCLC 2; DA; PC 7; WLC**
See also DLB 35; MAICYA; SATA 20

Rossetti, Dante Gabriel 1828-1882 . . . . **NCLC 4; DA; WLC**
See also CDBLB 1832-1890; DLB 35

Rossner, Judith (Perelman) 1935- . . . . **CLC 6, 9, 29**
See also AITN 2; BEST 90:3; CA 17-20R; CANR 18; DLB 6; MTCW

Rostand, Edmond (Eugene Alexis) 1868-1918 . . . . **TCLC 6, 37; DA**
See also CA 104; 126; MTCW

Roth, Henry 1906- . . . . **CLC 2, 6, 11**
See also CA 11-12; CANR 38; CAP 1; DLB 28; MTCW

Roth, Joseph 1894-1939. . . . . **TCLC 33**
See also DLB 85

Roth, Philip (Milton) 1933- . . . . . . **CLC 1, 2, 3, 4, 6, 9, 15, 22, 31, 47, 66; DA; WLC**
See also BEST 90:3; CA 1-4R; CANR 1, 22, 36; CDALB 1968-1988; DLB 2, 28; DLBY 82; MTCW

Rothenberg, Jerome 1931- . . . . **CLC 6, 57**
See also CA 45-48; CANR 1; DLB 5

Roumain, Jacques (Jean Baptiste) 1907-1944 . . . . **TCLC 19; BLC**
See also BW; CA 117; 125

Rourke, Constance (Mayfield) 1885-1941 . . . . **TCLC 12**
See also CA 107; YABC 1

Rousseau, Jean-Baptiste 1671-1741 . . . **LC 9**

Rousseau, Jean-Jacques 1712-1778 . . . . **LC 14; DA; WLC**

Roussel, Raymond 1877-1933 . . . . . **TCLC 20**
See also CA 117

Rovit, Earl (Herbert) 1927- . . . . **CLC 7**
See also CA 5-8R; CANR 12

Rowe, Nicholas 1674-1718. . . . . **LC 8**
See also DLB 84

Rowley, Ames Dorrance
See Lovecraft, H(oward) P(hillips)

Rowson, Susanna Haswell 1762(?)-1824 . . . . **NCLC 5**
See also DLB 37

Roy, Gabrielle 1909-1983. . . . . . . **CLC 10, 14**
See also CA 53-56; 110; CANR 5; DLB 68; MTCW

Rozewicz, Tadeusz 1921- . . . . **CLC 9, 23**
See also CA 108; CANR 36; MTCW

Ruark, Gibbons 1941- . . . . **CLC 3**
See also CA 33-36R; CANR 14, 31; DLB 120

Rubens, Bernice (Ruth) 1923- . . . **CLC 19, 31**
See also CA 25-28R; CANR 33; DLB 14; MTCW

Rudkin, (James) David 1936- ...... **CLC 14**
See also CA 89-92; DLB 13

Rudnik, Raphael 1933-............. **CLC 7**
See also CA 29-32R

Ruffian, M.
See Hasek, Jaroslav (Matej Frantisek)

Ruiz, Jose Martinez .... **CLC 11**
See also Martinez Ruiz, Jose

Rukeyser, Muriel
1913-1980 .... **CLC 6, 10, 15, 27**
See also CA 5-8R; 93-96; CANR 26; DLB 48; MTCW; SATA 22

Rule, Jane (Vance) 1931-.......... **CLC 27**
See also CA 25-28R; CAAS 18; CANR 12; DLB 60

Rulfo, Juan 1918-1986.... **CLC 8, 80; HLC**
See also CA 85-88; 118; CANR 26; DLB 113; HW; MTCW

Runeberg, Johan 1804-1877...... **NCLC 41**

Runyon, (Alfred) Damon
1884(?)-1946 .... **TCLC 10**
See also CA 107; DLB 11, 86

Rush, Norman 1933-............. **CLC 44**
See also CA 121; 126

Rushdie, (Ahmed) Salman
1947- .... **CLC 23, 31, 55**
See also BEST 89:3; CA 108; 111; CANR 33; MTCW

Rushforth, Peter (Scott) 1945- ..... **CLC 19**
See also CA 101

Ruskin, John 1819-1900.......... **TCLC 20**
See also CA 114; 129; CDBLB 1832-1890; DLB 55; SATA 24

Russ, Joanna 1937-............... **CLC 15**
See also CA 25-28R; CANR 11, 31; DLB 8; MTCW

Russell, George William 1867-1935
See A. E.
See also CA 104; CDBLB 1890-1914

Russell, (Henry) Ken(neth Alfred)
1927- .... **CLC 16**
See also CA 105

Russell, Willy 1947-............. **CLC 60**

Rutherford, Mark .... **TCLC 25**
See also White, William Hale
See also DLB 18

Ruyslinck, Ward
See Belser, Reimond Karel Maria de

Ryan, Cornelius (John) 1920-1974 ... **CLC 7**
See also CA 69-72; 53-56; CANR 38

Ryan, Michael 1946- .... **CLC 65**
See also CA 49-52; DLBY 82

Rybakov, Anatoli (Naumovich)
1911- .... **CLC 23, 53**
See also CA 126; 135

Ryder, Jonathan
See Ludlum, Robert

Ryga, George 1932-1987 .... **CLC 14**
See also CA 101; 124; CANR 43; DLB 60

S. S.
See Sassoon, Siegfried (Lorraine)

Saba, Umberto 1883-1957 .... **TCLC 33**
See also DLB 114

Sabatini, Rafael 1875-1950 .... **TCLC 47**

Sabato, Ernesto (R.)
1911- .... **CLC 10, 23; HLC**
See also CA 97-100; CANR 32; HW; MTCW

Sacastru, Martin
See Bioy Casares, Adolfo

Sacher-Masoch, Leopold von
1836(?)-1895 .... **NCLC 31**

Sachs, Marilyn (Stickle) 1927- ..... **CLC 35**
See also AAYA 2; CA 17-20R; CANR 13; CLR 2; JRDA; MAICYA; SAAS 2; SATA 3, 68

Sachs, Nelly 1891-1970 .... **CLC 14**
See also CA 17-18; 25-28R; CAP 2

Sackler, Howard (Oliver)
1929-1982 .... **CLC 14**
See also CA 61-64; 108; CANR 30; DLB 7

Sacks, Oliver (Wolf) 1933- .... **CLC 67**
See also CA 53-56; CANR 28; MTCW

Sade, Donatien Alphonse Francois Comte
1740-1814 .... **NCLC 3**

Sadoff, Ira 1945-.................. **CLC 9**
See also CA 53-56; CANR 5, 21; DLB 120

Saetone
See Camus, Albert

Safire, William 1929-............ **CLC 10**
See also CA 17-20R; CANR 31

Sagan, Carl (Edward) 1934-........ **CLC 30**
See also AAYA 2; CA 25-28R; CANR 11, 36; MTCW; SATA 58

Sagan, Francoise .... **CLC 3, 6, 9, 17, 36**
See also Quoirez, Francoise
See also DLB 83

Sahgal, Nayantara (Pandit) 1927-... **CLC 41**
See also CA 9-12R; CANR 11

Saint, H(arry) F. 1941- .... **CLC 50**
See also CA 127

St. Aubin de Teran, Lisa 1953-
See Teran, Lisa St. Aubin de
See also CA 118; 126

Sainte-Beuve, Charles Augustin
1804-1869 .... **NCLC 5**

Saint-Exupery, Antoine (Jean Baptiste Marie Roger) de 1900-1944 ... **TCLC 2; WLC**
See also CA 108; 132; CLR 10; DLB 72; MAICYA; MTCW; SATA 20

St. John, David
See Hunt, E(verette) Howard, Jr.

Saint-John Perse
See Leger, (Marie-Rene Auguste) Alexis Saint-Leger

Saintsbury, George (Edward Bateman)
1845-1933 .... **TCLC 31**
See also DLB 57

Sait Faik .... **TCLC 23**
See also Abasiyanik, Sait Faik

Saki .... **TCLC 3; SSC 12**
See also Munro, H(ector) H(ugh)

Salama, Hannu 1936-............ **CLC 18**

Salamanca, J(ack) R(ichard)
1922- .... **CLC 4, 15**
See also CA 25-28R

Sale, J. Kirkpatrick
See Sale, Kirkpatrick

Sale, Kirkpatrick 1937- .... **CLC 68**
See also CA 13-16R; CANR 10

Salinas (y Serrano), Pedro
1891(?)-1951 .... **TCLC 17**
See also CA 117; DLB 134

Salinger, J(erome) D(avid)
1919- ...... **CLC 1, 3, 8, 12, 55, 56; DA; SSC 2; WLC**
See also AAYA 2; CA 5-8R; CANR 39; CDALB 1941-1968; CLR 18; DLB 2, 102; MAICYA; MTCW; SATA 67

Salisbury, John
See Caute, David

Salter, James 1925- .... **CLC 7, 52, 59**
See also CA 73-76; DLB 130

Saltus, Edgar (Everton)
1855-1921 .... **TCLC 8**
See also CA 105

Saltykov, Mikhail Evgrafovich
1826-1889 .... **NCLC 16**

Samarakis, Antonis 1919- .... **CLC 5**
See also CA 25-28R; CAAS 16; CANR 36

Sanchez, Florencio 1875-1910..... **TCLC 37**
See also HW

Sanchez, Luis Rafael 1936-........ **CLC 23**
See also CA 128; HW

Sanchez, Sonia 1934-......... **CLC 5; BLC**
See also BW; CA 33-36R; CANR 24; CLR 18; DLB 41; DLBD 8; MAICYA; MTCW; SATA 22

Sand, George
1804-1876 ...... **NCLC 2, 42; DA; WLC**
See also DLB 119

Sandburg, Carl (August)
1878-1967 .... **CLC 1, 4, 10, 15, 35; DA; PC 2; WLC**
See also CA 5-8R; 25-28R; CANR 35; CDALB 1865-1917; DLB 17, 54; MAICYA; MTCW; SATA 8

Sandburg, Charles
See Sandburg, Carl (August)

Sandburg, Charles A.
See Sandburg, Carl (August)

Sanders, (James) Ed(ward) 1939- ... **CLC 53**
See also CA 13-16R; CANR 13; DLB 16

Sanders, Lawrence 1920- .... **CLC 41**
See also BEST 89:4; CA 81-84; CANR 33; MTCW

Sanders, Noah
See Blount, Roy (Alton), Jr.

Sanders, Winston P.
See Anderson, Poul (William)

Sandoz, Mari(e Susette)
1896-1966 .... **CLC 28**
See also CA 1-4R; 25-28R; CANR 17; DLB 9; MTCW; SATA 5

Saner, Reg(inald Anthony) 1931- .... **CLC 9**
See also CA 65-68

Sannazaro, Jacopo 1456(?)-1530 ...... **LC 8**

Sansom, William 1912-1976....... **CLC 2, 6**
See also CA 5-8R; 65-68; CANR 42; MTCW

Santayana, George 1863-1952..... **TCLC 40**
See also CA 115; DLB 54, 71

Scum
See Crumb, R(obert)

Scumbag, Little Bobby
See Crumb, R(obert)

Seabrook, John
See Hubbard, L(afayette) Ron(ald)

Sealy, I. Allan 1951- .... **CLC 55**

Search, Alexander
See Pessoa, Fernando (Antonio Nogueira)

Sebastian, Lee
See Silverberg, Robert

Sebastian Owl
See Thompson, Hunter S(tockton)

Sebestyen, Ouida 1924- .... **CLC 30**
See also AAYA 8; CA 107; CANR 40; CLR 17; JRDA; MAICYA; SAAS 10; SATA 39

Secundus, H. Scriblerus
See Fielding, Henry

Sedges, John
See Buck, Pearl S(ydenstricker)

Sedgwick, Catharine Maria
1789-1867 .... **NCLC 19**
See also DLB 1, 74

Seelye, John 1931- .... **CLC 7**

Seferiades, Giorgos Stylianou 1900-1971
See Seferis, George
See also CA 5-8R; 33-36R; CANR 5, 36; MTCW

Seferis, George .... **CLC 5, 11**
See also Seferiades, Giorgos Stylianou

Segal, Erich (Wolf) 1937- .... **CLC 3, 10**
See also BEST 89:1; CA 25-28R; CANR 20, 36; DLBY 86; MTCW

Seger, Bob 1945- .... **CLC 35**

Seghers, Anna .... **CLC 7**
See also Radvanyi, Netty
See also DLB 69

Seidel, Frederick (Lewis) 1936- ..... **CLC 18**
See also CA 13-16R; CANR 8; DLBY 84

Seifert, Jaroslav 1901-1986 ..... **CLC 34, 44**
See also CA 127; MTCW

Sei Shonagon c. 966-1017(?) ...... **CMLC 6**

Selby, Hubert, Jr. 1928- ..... **CLC 1, 2, 4, 8**
See also CA 13-16R; CANR 33; DLB 2

Selzer, Richard 1928- .... **CLC 74**
See also CA 65-68; CANR 14

Sembene, Ousmane
See Ousmane, Sembene

Senancour, Etienne Pivert de
1770-1846 .... **NCLC 16**
See also DLB 119

Sender, Ramon (Jose)
1902-1982 .... **CLC 8; HLC**
See also CA 5-8R; 105; CANR 8; HW; MTCW

Seneca, Lucius Annaeus
4B.C.-65 .... **CMLC 6**

Senghor, Leopold Sedar
1906- .... **CLC 54; BLC**
See also BW; CA 116; 125; MTCW

Serling, (Edward) Rod(man)
1924-1975 .... **CLC 30**
See also AITN 1; CA 65-68; 57-60; DLB 26

Serna, Ramon Gomez de la
See Gomez de la Serna, Ramon

Serpieres
See Guillevic, (Eugene)

Service, Robert
See Service, Robert W(illiam)
See also DLB 92

Service, Robert W(illiam)
1874(?)-1958 ...... **TCLC 15; DA; WLC**
See also Service, Robert
See also CA 115; 140; SATA 20

Seth, Vikram 1952- .... **CLC 43**
See also CA 121; 127; DLB 120

Seton, Cynthia Propper
1926-1982 .... **CLC 27**
See also CA 5-8R; 108; CANR 7

Seton, Ernest (Evan) Thompson
1860-1946 .... **TCLC 31**
See also CA 109; DLB 92; JRDA; SATA 18

Seton-Thompson, Ernest
See Seton, Ernest (Evan) Thompson

Settle, Mary Lee 1918- .... **CLC 19, 61**
See also CA 89-92; CAAS 1; DLB 6

Seuphor, Michel
See Arp, Jean

Sevigne, Marie (de Rabutin-Chantal) Marquise de 1626-1696 .... **LC 11**

Sexton, Anne (Harvey)
1928-1974 .... **CLC 2, 4, 6, 8, 10, 15, 53; DA; PC 2; WLC**
See also CA 1-4R; 53-56; CABS 2; CANR 3, 36; CDALB 1941-1968; DLB 5; MTCW; SATA 10

Shaara, Michael (Joseph Jr.)
1929-1988 .... **CLC 15**
See also AITN 1; CA 102; DLBY 83

Shackleton, C. C.
See Aldiss, Brian W(ilson)

Shacochis, Bob .... **CLC 39**
See also Shacochis, Robert G.

Shacochis, Robert G. 1951-
See Shacochis, Bob
See also CA 119; 124

Shaffer, Anthony (Joshua) 1926- .... **CLC 19**
See also CA 110; 116; DLB 13

Shaffer, Peter (Levin)
1926- .... **CLC 5, 14, 18, 37, 60**
See also CA 25-28R; CANR 25; CDBLB 1960 to Present; DLB 13; MTCW

Shakey, Bernard
See Young, Neil

Shalamov, Varlam (Tikhonovich)
1907(?)-1982 .... **CLC 18**
See also CA 129; 105

Shamlu, Ahmad 1925- .... **CLC 10**

Shammas, Anton 1951- .... **CLC 55**

Shange, Ntozake
1948- .... **CLC 8, 25, 38, 74; BLC; DC 3**
See also AAYA 9; BW; CA 85-88; CABS 3; CANR 27; DLB 38; MTCW

Shanley, John Patrick 1950- .... **CLC 75**
See also CA 128; 133

Shapcott, Thomas William 1935- ... **CLC 38**
See also CA 69-72

Shapiro, Jane .... **CLC 76**

Shapiro, Karl (Jay) 1913- .. **CLC 4, 8, 15, 53**
See also CA 1-4R; CAAS 6; CANR 1, 36; DLB 48; MTCW

Sharp, William 1855-1905 .... **TCLC 39**

Sharpe, Thomas Ridley 1928-
See Sharpe, Tom
See also CA 114; 122

Sharpe, Tom .... **CLC 36**
See also Sharpe, Thomas Ridley
See also DLB 14

Shaw, Bernard .... **TCLC 45**
See also Shaw, George Bernard

Shaw, G. Bernard
See Shaw, George Bernard

Shaw, George Bernard
1856-1950 .... **TCLC 3, 9, 21; DA; WLC**
See also Shaw, Bernard
See also CA 104; 128; CDBLB 1914-1945; DLB 10, 57; MTCW

Shaw, Henry Wheeler
1818-1885 .... **NCLC 15**
See also DLB 11

Shaw, Irwin 1913-1984 .... **CLC 7, 23, 34**
See also AITN 1; CA 13-16R; 112; CANR 21; CDALB 1941-1968; DLB 6, 102; DLBY 84; MTCW

Shaw, Robert 1927-1978 .... **CLC 5**
See also AITN 1; CA 1-4R; 81-84; CANR 4; DLB 13, 14

Shaw, T. E.
See Lawrence, T(homas) E(dward)

Shawn, Wallace 1943- .... **CLC 41**
See also CA 112

Sheed, Wilfrid (John Joseph)
1930- .... **CLC 2, 4, 10, 53**
See also CA 65-68; CANR 30; DLB 6; MTCW

Sheldon, Alice Hastings Bradley
1915(?)-1987
See Tiptree, James, Jr.
See also CA 108; 122; CANR 34; MTCW

Sheldon, John
See Bloch, Robert (Albert)

Shelley, Mary Wollstonecraft (Godwin)
1797-1851 .... **NCLC 14; DA; WLC**
See also CDBLB 1789-1832; DLB 110, 116; SATA 29

Shelley, Percy Bysshe
1792-1822 .... **NCLC 18; DA; WLC**
See also CDBLB 1789-1832; DLB 96, 110

Shepard, Jim 1956- .... **CLC 36**
See also CA 137

Shepard, Lucius 1947- .... **CLC 34**
See also CA 128; 141

Shepard, Sam
1943- .... **CLC 4, 6, 17, 34, 41, 44**
See also AAYA 1; CA 69-72; CABS 3; CANR 22; DLB 7; MTCW

Shepherd, Michael
See Ludlum, Robert

Sherburne, Zoa (Morin) 1912- . . . . . . **CLC 30**
See also CA 1-4R; CANR 3, 37; MAICYA; SATA 3

Sheridan, Frances 1724-1766 . . . . **LC 7**
See also DLB 39, 84

Sheridan, Richard Brinsley 1751-1816 . . . **NCLC 5; DA; DC 1; WLC**
See also CDBLB 1660-1789; DLB 89

Sherman, Jonathan Marc . . . . **CLC 55**

Sherman, Martin 1941(?)- . . . . **CLC 19**
See also CA 116; 123

Sherwin, Judith Johnson 1936- . . . **CLC 7, 15**
See also CA 25-28R; CANR 34

Sherwood, Frances 1940- . . . . **CLC 81**

Sherwood, Robert E(mmet) 1896-1955 . . . . **TCLC 3**
See also CA 104; DLB 7, 26

Shiel, M(atthew) P(hipps) 1865-1947 . . . . **TCLC 8**
See also CA 106

Shiga, Naoya 1883-1971 . . . . **CLC 33**
See also CA 101; 33-36R

Shimazaki Haruki 1872-1943
See Shimazaki Toson
See also CA 105; 134

Shimazaki Toson . . . . **TCLC 5**
See also Shimazaki Haruki

Sholokhov, Mikhail (Aleksandrovich) 1905-1984 . . . . **CLC 7, 15**
See also CA 101; 112; MTCW; SATA 36

Shone, Patric
See Hanley, James

Shreve, Susan Richards 1939- . . . . . . **CLC 23**
See also CA 49-52; CAAS 5; CANR 5, 38; MAICYA; SATA 41, 46

Shue, Larry 1946-1985 . . . . **CLC 52**
See also CA 117

Shu-Jen, Chou 1881-1936
See Hsun, Lu
See also CA 104

Shulman, Alix Kates 1932- . . . . . . **CLC 2, 10**
See also CA 29-32R; CANR 43; SATA 7

Shuster, Joe 1914- . . . . **CLC 21**

Shute, Nevil . . . . **CLC 30**
See also Norway, Nevil Shute

Shuttle, Penelope (Diane) 1947- . . . . . **CLC 7**
See also CA 93-96; CANR 39; DLB 14, 40

Sidney, Mary 1561-1621 . . . . **LC 19**

Sidney, Sir Philip 1554-1586 . . . . **LC 19; DA**
See also CDBLB Before 1660

Siegel, Jerome 1914- . . . . **CLC 21**
See also CA 116

Siegel, Jerry
See Siegel, Jerome

Sienkiewicz, Henryk (Adam Alexander Pius) 1846-1916 . . . . **TCLC 3**
See also CA 104; 134

Sierra, Gregorio Martinez
See Martinez Sierra, Gregorio

Sierra, Maria (de la O'LeJarraga) Martinez
See Martinez Sierra, Maria (de la O'LeJarraga)

Sigal, Clancy 1926- . . . . **CLC 7**
See also CA 1-4R

Sigourney, Lydia Howard (Huntley) 1791-1865 . . . . **NCLC 21**
See also DLB 1, 42, 73

Siguenza y Gongora, Carlos de 1645-1700 . . . . **LC 8**

Sigurjonsson, Johann 1880-1919 . . . **TCLC 27**

Sikelianos, Angelos 1884-1951 . . . . **TCLC 39**

Silkin, Jon 1930- . . . . **CLC 2, 6, 43**
See also CA 5-8R; CAAS 5; DLB 27

Silko, Leslie Marmon 1948- . . . . **CLC 23, 74; DA**
See also CA 115; 122

Sillanpaa, Frans Eemil 1888-1964 . . . **CLC 19**
See also CA 129; 93-96; MTCW

Sillitoe, Alan 1928- . . . . **CLC 1, 3, 6, 10, 19, 57**
See also AITN 1; CA 9-12R; CAAS 2; CANR 8, 26; CDBLB 1960 to Present; DLB 14; MTCW; SATA 61

Silone, Ignazio 1900-1978 . . . . **CLC 4**
See also CA 25-28; 81-84; CANR 34; CAP 2; MTCW

Silver, Joan Micklin 1935- . . . . **CLC 20**
See also CA 114; 121

Silver, Nicholas
See Faust, Frederick (Schiller)

Silverberg, Robert 1935- . . . . **CLC 7**
See also CA 1-4R; CAAS 3; CANR 1, 20, 36; DLB 8; MAICYA; MTCW; SATA 13

Silverstein, Alvin 1933- . . . . **CLC 17**
See also CA 49-52; CANR 2; CLR 25; JRDA; MAICYA; SATA 8, 69

Silverstein, Virginia B(arbara Opshelor) 1937- . . . . **CLC 17**
See also CA 49-52; CANR 2; CLR 25; JRDA; MAICYA; SATA 8, 69

Sim, Georges
See Simenon, Georges (Jacques Christian)

Simak, Clifford D(onald) 1904-1988 . . . . **CLC 1, 55**
See also CA 1-4R; 125; CANR 1, 35; DLB 8; MTCW; SATA 56

Simenon, Georges (Jacques Christian) 1903-1989 . . . . **CLC 1, 2, 3, 8, 18, 47**
See also CA 85-88; 129; CANR 35; DLB 72; DLBY 89; MTCW

Simic, Charles 1938- . . . **CLC 6, 9, 22, 49, 68**
See also CA 29-32R; CAAS 4; CANR 12, 33; DLB 105

Simmons, Charles (Paul) 1924- . . . . . **CLC 57**
See also CA 89-92

Simmons, Dan 1948- . . . . **CLC 44**
See also CA 138

Simmons, James (Stewart Alexander) 1933- . . . . **CLC 43**
See also CA 105; DLB 40

Simms, William Gilmore 1806-1870 . . . . **NCLC 3**
See also DLB 3, 30, 59, 73

Simon, Carly 1945- . . . . **CLC 26**
See also CA 105

Simon, Claude 1913- . . . . **CLC 4, 9, 15, 39**
See also CA 89-92; CANR 33; DLB 83; MTCW

Simon, (Marvin) Neil 1927- . . . . **CLC 6, 11, 31, 39, 70**
See also AITN 1; CA 21-24R; CANR 26; DLB 7; MTCW

Simon, Paul 1942(?)- . . . . **CLC 17**
See also CA 116

Simonon, Paul 1956(?)- . . . . **CLC 30**
See also Clash, The

Simpson, Harriette
See Arnow, Harriette (Louisa) Simpson

Simpson, Louis (Aston Marantz) 1923- . . . . **CLC 4, 7, 9, 32**
See also CA 1-4R; CAAS 4; CANR 1; DLB 5; MTCW

Simpson, Mona (Elizabeth) 1957- . . . **CLC 44**
See also CA 122; 135

Simpson, N(orman) F(rederick) 1919- . . . . **CLC 29**
See also CA 13-16R; DLB 13

Sinclair, Andrew (Annandale) 1935- . . . . **CLC 2, 14**
See also CA 9-12R; CAAS 5; CANR 14, 38; DLB 14; MTCW

Sinclair, Emil
See Hesse, Hermann

Sinclair, Iain 1943- . . . . **CLC 76**
See also CA 132

Sinclair, Iain MacGregor
See Sinclair, Iain

Sinclair, Mary Amelia St. Clair 1865(?)-1946
See Sinclair, May
See also CA 104

Sinclair, May . . . . **TCLC 3, 11**
See also Sinclair, Mary Amelia St. Clair
See also DLB 36, 135

Sinclair, Upton (Beall) 1878-1968 . . . . . . **CLC 1, 11, 15, 63; DA; WLC**
See also CA 5-8R; 25-28R; CANR 7; CDALB 1929-1941; DLB 9; MTCW; SATA 9

Singer, Isaac
See Singer, Isaac Bashevis

Singer, Isaac Bashevis 1904-1991 . . . . **CLC 1, 3, 6, 9, 11, 15, 23, 38, 69; DA; SSC 3; WLC**
See also AITN 1, 2; CA 1-4R; 134; CANR 1, 39; CDALB 1941-1968; CLR 1; DLB 6, 28, 52; DLBY 91; JRDA; MAICYA; MTCW; SATA 3, 27; SATA-Obit 68

Singer, Israel Joshua 1893-1944 . . . **TCLC 33**

Singh, Khushwant 1915- . . . . **CLC 11**
See also CA 9-12R; CAAS 9; CANR 6

Sinjohn, John
See Galsworthy, John

Sinyavsky, Andrei (Donatevich) 1925- . . . . **CLC 8**
See also CA 85-88

Sirin, V.
See Nabokov, Vladimir (Vladimirovich)

Sissman, L(ouis) E(dward)
1928-1976 .... **CLC 9, 18**
See also CA 21-24R; 65-68; CANR 13; DLB 5

Sisson, C(harles) H(ubert) 1914-..... **CLC 8**
See also CA 1-4R; CAAS 3; CANR 3; DLB 27

Sitwell, Dame Edith
1887-1964 .... **CLC 2, 9, 67; PC 3**
See also CA 9-12R; CANR 35; CDBLB 1945-1960; DLB 20; MTCW

Sjoewall, Maj 1935-............... **CLC 7**
See also CA 65-68

Sjowall, Maj
See Sjoewall, Maj

Skelton, Robin 1925-............. **CLC 13**
See also AITN 2; CA 5-8R; CAAS 5; CANR 28; DLB 27, 53

Skolimowski, Jerzy 1938-......... **CLC 20**
See also CA 128

Skram, Amalie (Bertha)
1847-1905 .... **TCLC 25**

Skvorecky, Josef (Vaclav)
1924-................. **CLC 15, 39, 69**
See also CA 61-64; CAAS 1; CANR 10, 34; MTCW

Slade, Bernard................. **CLC 11, 46**
See also Newbound, Bernard Slade
See also CAAS 9; DLB 53

Slaughter, Carolyn 1946-.......... **CLC 56**
See also CA 85-88

Slaughter, Frank G(ill) 1908- ...... **CLC 29**
See also AITN 2; CA 5-8R; CANR 5

Slavitt, David R(ytman) 1935-.... **CLC 5, 14**
See also CA 21-24R; CAAS 3; CANR 41; DLB 5, 6

Slesinger, Tess 1905-1945 .... **TCLC 10**
See also CA 107; DLB 102

Slessor, Kenneth 1901-1971........ **CLC 14**
See also CA 102; 89-92

Slowacki, Juliusz 1809-1849 ..... **NCLC 15**

Smart, Christopher 1722-1771........ **LC 3**
See also DLB 109

Smart, Elizabeth 1913-1986........ **CLC 54**
See also CA 81-84; 118; DLB 88

Smiley, Jane (Graves) 1949- .... **CLC 53, 76**
See also CA 104; CANR 30

Smith, A(rthur) J(ames) M(arshall)
1902-1980 .... **CLC 15**
See also CA 1-4R; 102; CANR 4; DLB 88

Smith, Betty (Wehner) 1896-1972... **CLC 19**
See also CA 5-8R; 33-36R; DLBY 82; SATA 6

Smith, Charlotte (Turner)
1749-1806 .... **NCLC 23**
See also DLB 39, 109

Smith, Clark Ashton 1893-1961 .... **CLC 43**
See also CA 143

Smith, Dave................... **CLC 22, 42**
See also Smith, David (Jeddie)
See also CAAS 7; DLB 5

Smith, David (Jeddie) 1942-
See Smith, Dave
See also CA 49-52; CANR 1

Smith, Florence Margaret
1902-1971 .... **CLC 8**
See also Smith, Stevie
See also CA 17-18; 29-32R; CANR 35; CAP 2; MTCW

Smith, Iain Crichton 1928- .... **CLC 64**
See also CA 21-24R; DLB 40

Smith, John 1580(?)-1631 .... **LC 9**

Smith, Johnston
See Crane, Stephen (Townley)

Smith, Lee 1944-.............. **CLC 25, 73**
See also CA 114; 119; DLBY 83

Smith, Martin
See Smith, Martin Cruz

Smith, Martin Cruz 1942-......... **CLC 25**
See also BEST 89:4; CA 85-88; CANR 6, 23, 43

Smith, Mary-Ann Tirone 1944-..... **CLC 39**
See also CA 118; 136

Smith, Patti 1946- .... **CLC 12**
See also CA 93-96

Smith, Pauline (Urmson)
1882-1959 .... **TCLC 25**

Smith, Rosamond
See Oates, Joyce Carol

Smith, Sheila Kaye
See Kaye-Smith, Sheila

Smith, Stevie.............. **CLC 3, 8, 25, 44**
See also Smith, Florence Margaret
See also DLB 20

Smith, Wilbur A(ddison) 1933-..... **CLC 33**
See also CA 13-16R; CANR 7; MTCW

Smith, William Jay 1918-.......... **CLC 6**
See also CA 5-8R; DLB 5; MAICYA; SATA 2, 68

Smith, Woodrow Wilson
See Kuttner, Henry

Smolenskin, Peretz 1842-1885.... **NCLC 30**

Smollett, Tobias (George) 1721-1771 .. **LC 2**
See also CDBLB 1660-1789; DLB 39, 104

Snodgrass, W(illiam) D(e Witt)
1926- .... **CLC 2, 6, 10, 18, 68**
See also CA 1-4R; CANR 6, 36; DLB 5; MTCW

Snow, C(harles) P(ercy)
1905-1980 .... **CLC 1, 4, 6, 9, 13, 19**
See also CA 5-8R; 101; CANR 28; CDBLB 1945-1960; DLB 15, 77; MTCW

Snow, Frances Compton
See Adams, Henry (Brooks)

Snyder, Gary (Sherman)
1930- .... **CLC 1, 2, 5, 9, 32**
See also CA 17-20R; CANR 30; DLB 5, 16

Snyder, Zilpha Keatley 1927- ...... **CLC 17**
See also CA 9-12R; CANR 38; CLR 31; JRDA; MAICYA; SAAS 2; SATA 1, 28, 75

Soares, Bernardo
See Pessoa, Fernando (Antonio Nogueira)

Sobh, A.
See Shamlu, Ahmad

Sobol, Joshua..................... **CLC 60**

Soderberg, Hjalmar 1869-1941 .... **TCLC 39**

Sodergran, Edith (Irene)
See Soedergran, Edith (Irene)

Soedergran, Edith (Irene)
1892-1923 .... **TCLC 31**

Softly, Edgar
See Lovecraft, H(oward) P(hillips)

Softly, Edward
See Lovecraft, H(oward) P(hillips)

Sokolov, Raymond 1941-........... **CLC 7**
See also CA 85-88

Solo, Jay
See Ellison, Harlan

Sologub, Fyodor .... **TCLC 9**
See also Teternikov, Fyodor Kuzmich

Solomons, Ikey Esquir
See Thackeray, William Makepeace

Solomos, Dionysios 1798-1857 ... **NCLC 15**

Solwoska, Mara
See French, Marilyn

Solzhenitsyn, Aleksandr I(sayevich)
1918- ...... **CLC 1, 2, 4, 7, 9, 10, 18, 26, 34, 78; DA; WLC**
See also AITN 1; CA 69-72; CANR 40; MTCW

Somers, Jane
See Lessing, Doris (May)

Somerville, Edith 1858-1949 ...... **TCLC 51**
See also DLB 135

Somerville & Ross
See Martin, Violet Florence; Somerville, Edith

Sommer, Scott 1951- .... **CLC 25**
See also CA 106

Sondheim, Stephen (Joshua)
1930- .... **CLC 30, 39**
See also CA 103

Sontag, Susan 1933-... **CLC 1, 2, 10, 13, 31**
See also CA 17-20R; CANR 25; DLB 2, 67; MTCW

Sophocles
496(?)B.C.-406(?)B.C..... **CMLC 2; DA; DC 1**

Sorel, Julia
See Drexler, Rosalyn

Sorrentino, Gilbert
1929- .... **CLC 3, 7, 14, 22, 40**
See also CA 77-80; CANR 14, 33; DLB 5; DLBY 80

Soto, Gary 1952-........ **CLC 32, 80; HLC**
See also AAYA 10; CA 119; 125; DLB 82; HW; JRDA

Soupault, Philippe 1897-1990 ...... **CLC 68**
See also CA 116; 131

Souster, (Holmes) Raymond
1921- .... **CLC 5, 14**
See also CA 13-16R; CAAS 14; CANR 13, 29; DLB 88; SATA 63

Southern, Terry 1926- .... **CLC 7**
See also CA 1-4R; CANR 1; DLB 2

Southey, Robert 1774-1843 .... **NCLC 8**
See also DLB 93, 107; SATA 54

Southworth, Emma Dorothy Eliza Nevitte
1819-1899 .... **NCLC 26**

Sutro, Alfred 1863-1933 . . . . **TCLC 6**
See also CA 105; DLB 10

Sutton, Henry
See Slavitt, David R(ytman)

Svevo, Italo . . . . **TCLC 2, 35**
See also Schmitz, Aron Hector

Swados, Elizabeth 1951- . . . . **CLC 12**
See also CA 97-100

Swados, Harvey 1920-1972 . . . . **CLC 5**
See also CA 5-8R; 37-40R; CANR 6; DLB 2

Swan, Gladys 1934- . . . . **CLC 69**
See also CA 101; CANR 17, 39

Swarthout, Glendon (Fred)
1918-1992 . . . . **CLC 35**
See also CA 1-4R; 139; CANR 1; SATA 26

Sweet, Sarah C.
See Jewett, (Theodora) Sarah Orne

Swenson, May
1919-1989 . . . . **CLC 4, 14, 61; DA**
See also CA 5-8R; 130; CANR 36; DLB 5; MTCW; SATA 15

Swift, Augustus
See Lovecraft, H(oward) P(hillips)

Swift, Graham 1949- . . . . **CLC 41**
See also CA 117; 122

Swift, Jonathan
1667-1745 . . . . **LC 1; DA; WLC**
See also CDBLB 1660-1789; DLB 39, 95, 101; SATA 19

Swinburne, Algernon Charles
1837-1909 . . . . . . **TCLC 8, 36; DA; WLC**
See also CA 105; 140; CDBLB 1832-1890; DLB 35, 57

Swinfen, Ann . . . . **CLC 34**

Swinnerton, Frank Arthur
1884-1982 . . . . **CLC 31**
See also CA 108; DLB 34

Swithen, John
See King, Stephen (Edwin)

Sylvia
See Ashton-Warner, Sylvia (Constance)

Symmes, Robert Edward
See Duncan, Robert (Edward)

Symonds, John Addington
1840-1893 . . . . **NCLC 34**
See also DLB 57

Symons, Arthur 1865-1945 . . . . **TCLC 11**
See also CA 107; DLB 19, 57

Symons, Julian (Gustave)
1912- . . . . **CLC 2, 14, 32**
See also CA 49-52; CAAS 3; CANR 3, 33; DLB 87; DLBY 92; MTCW

Synge, (Edmund) J(ohn) M(illington)
1871-1909 . . . . **TCLC 6, 37; DC 2**
See also CA 104; 141; CDBLB 1890-1914; DLB 10, 19

Syruc, J.
See Milosz, Czeslaw

Szirtes, George 1948- . . . . **CLC 46**
See also CA 109; CANR 27

Tabori, George 1914- . . . . **CLC 19**
See also CA 49-52; CANR 4

Tagore, Rabindranath
1861-1941 . . . . **TCLC 3, 53; PC 8**
See also CA 104; 120; MTCW

Taine, Hippolyte Adolphe
1828-1893 . . . . **NCLC 15**

Talese, Gay 1932- . . . . **CLC 37**
See also AITN 1; CA 1-4R; CANR 9; MTCW

Tallent, Elizabeth (Ann) 1954- . . . . . **CLC 45**
See also CA 117; DLB 130

Tally, Ted 1952- . . . . **CLC 42**
See also CA 120; 124

Tamayo y Baus, Manuel
1829-1898 . . . . **NCLC 1**

Tammsaare, A(nton) H(ansen)
1878-1940 . . . . **TCLC 27**

Tan, Amy 1952- . . . . **CLC 59**
See also AAYA 9; BEST 89:3; CA 136; SATA 75

Tandem, Felix
See Spitteler, Carl (Friedrich Georg)

Tanizaki, Jun'ichiro
1886-1965 . . . . **CLC 8, 14, 28**
See also CA 93-96; 25-28R

Tanner, William
See Amis, Kingsley (William)

Tao Lao
See Storni, Alfonsina

Tarassoff, Lev
See Troyat, Henri

Tarbell, Ida M(inerva)
1857-1944 . . . . **TCLC 40**
See also CA 122; DLB 47

Tarkington, (Newton) Booth
1869-1946 . . . . **TCLC 9**
See also CA 110; 143; DLB 9, 102; SATA 17

Tarkovsky, Andrei (Arsenyevich)
1932-1986 . . . . **CLC 75**
See also CA 127

Tartt, Donna 1964(?)- . . . . **CLC 76**
See also CA 142

Tasso, Torquato 1544-1595 . . . . **LC 5**

Tate, (John Orley) Allen
1899-1979 . . . . **CLC 2, 4, 6, 9, 11, 14, 24**
See also CA 5-8R; 85-88; CANR 32; DLB 4, 45, 63; MTCW

Tate, Ellalice
See Hibbert, Eleanor Alice Burford

Tate, James (Vincent) 1943- . . . **CLC 2, 6, 25**
See also CA 21-24R; CANR 29; DLB 5

Tavel, Ronald 1940- . . . . **CLC 6**
See also CA 21-24R; CANR 33

Taylor, Cecil Philip 1929-1981 . . . . . **CLC 27**
See also CA 25-28R; 105

Taylor, Edward 1642(?)-1729. . . . **LC 11; DA**
See also DLB 24

Taylor, Eleanor Ross 1920- . . . . **CLC 5**
See also CA 81-84

Taylor, Elizabeth 1912-1975 . . . **CLC 2, 4, 29**
See also CA 13-16R; CANR 9; MTCW; SATA 13

Taylor, Henry (Splawn) 1942- . . . . . . **CLC 44**
See also CA 33-36R; CAAS 7; CANR 31; DLB 5

Taylor, Kamala (Purnaiya) 1924-
See Markandaya, Kamala
See also CA 77-80

Taylor, Mildred D. . . . . **CLC 21**
See also AAYA 10; BW; CA 85-88; CANR 25; CLR 9; DLB 52; JRDA; MAICYA; SAAS 5; SATA 15, 70

Taylor, Peter (Hillsman)
1917- . . . . . . **CLC 1, 4, 18, 37, 44, 50, 71; SSC 10**
See also CA 13-16R; CANR 9; DLBY 81; MTCW

Taylor, Robert Lewis 1912- . . . . **CLC 14**
See also CA 1-4R; CANR 3; SATA 10

Tchekhov, Anton
See Chekhov, Anton (Pavlovich)

Teasdale, Sara 1884-1933. . . . . **TCLC 4**
See also CA 104; DLB 45; SATA 32

Tegner, Esaias 1782-1846. . . . . **NCLC 2**

Teilhard de Chardin, (Marie Joseph) Pierre
1881-1955 . . . . **TCLC 9**
See also CA 105

Temple, Ann
See Mortimer, Penelope (Ruth)

Tennant, Emma (Christina)
1937- . . . . **CLC 13, 52**
See also CA 65-68; CAAS 9; CANR 10, 38; DLB 14

Tenneshaw, S. M.
See Silverberg, Robert

Tennyson, Alfred
1809-1892 . . **NCLC 30; DA; PC 6; WLC**
See also CDBLB 1832-1890; DLB 32

Teran, Lisa St. Aubin de . . . . **CLC 36**
See also St. Aubin de Teran, Lisa

Teresa de Jesus, St. 1515-1582 . . . . . . **LC 18**

Terkel, Louis 1912-
See Terkel, Studs
See also CA 57-60; CANR 18; MTCW

Terkel, Studs . . . . **CLC 38**
See also Terkel, Louis
See also AITN 1

Terry, C. V.
See Slaughter, Frank G(ill)

Terry, Megan 1932- . . . . **CLC 19**
See also CA 77-80; CABS 3; CANR 43; DLB 7

Tertz, Abram
See Sinyavsky, Andrei (Donatevich)

Tesich, Steve 1943(?)-. . . . . **CLC 40, 69**
See also CA 105; DLBY 83

Teternikov, Fyodor Kuzmich 1863-1927
See Sologub, Fyodor
See also CA 104

Tevis, Walter 1928-1984 . . . . **CLC 42**
See also CA 113

Tey, Josephine. . . . . **TCLC 14**
See also Mackintosh, Elizabeth
See also DLB 77

Thackeray, William Makepeace 1811-1863 .... **NCLC 5, 14, 22, 43; DA; WLC**
See also CDBLB 1832-1890; DLB 21, 55; SATA 23

Thakura, Ravindranatha
See Tagore, Rabindranath

Tharoor, Shashi 1956- .... **CLC 70**
See also CA 141

Thelwell, Michael Miles 1939- ..... **CLC 22**
See also CA 101

Theobald, Lewis, Jr.
See Lovecraft, H(oward) P(hillips)

Theodorescu, Ion N. 1880-1967
See Arghezi, Tudor
See also CA 116

Theriault, Yves 1915-1983 .... **CLC 79**
See also CA 102; DLB 88

Theroux, Alexander (Louis) 1939- .... **CLC 2, 25**
See also CA 85-88; CANR 20

Theroux, Paul (Edward) 1941- .... **CLC 5, 8, 11, 15, 28, 46**
See also BEST 89:4; CA 33-36R; CANR 20; DLB 2; MTCW; SATA 44

Thesen, Sharon 1946- .... **CLC 56**

Thevenin, Denis
See Duhamel, Georges

Thibault, Jacques Anatole Francois 1844-1924
See France, Anatole
See also CA 106; 127; MTCW

Thiele, Colin (Milton) 1920- .... **CLC 17**
See also CA 29-32R; CANR 12, 28; CLR 27; MAICYA; SAAS 2; SATA 14, 72

Thomas, Audrey (Callahan) 1935- .... **CLC 7, 13, 37**
See also AITN 2; CA 21-24R; CANR 36; DLB 60; MTCW

Thomas, D(onald) M(ichael) 1935- .... **CLC 13, 22, 31**
See also CA 61-64; CAAS 11; CANR 17; CDBLB 1960 to Present; DLB 40; MTCW

Thomas, Dylan (Marlais) 1914-1953 ... **TCLC 1, 8, 45; DA; PC 2; SSC 3; WLC**
See also CA 104; 120; CDBLB 1945-1960; DLB 13, 20; MTCW; SATA 60

Thomas, (Philip) Edward 1878-1917 .... **TCLC 10**
See also CA 106; DLB 19

Thomas, Joyce Carol 1938- .... **CLC 35**
See also BW; CA 113; 116; CLR 19; DLB 33; JRDA; MAICYA; MTCW; SAAS 7; SATA 40

Thomas, Lewis 1913-1993 .... **CLC 35**
See also CA 85-88; 143; CANR 38; MTCW

Thomas, Paul
See Mann, (Paul) Thomas

Thomas, Piri 1928- .... **CLC 17**
See also CA 73-76; HW

Thomas, R(onald) S(tuart) 1913- .... **CLC 6, 13, 48**
See also CA 89-92; CAAS 4; CANR 30; CDBLB 1960 to Present; DLB 27; MTCW

Thomas, Ross (Elmore) 1926- ...... **CLC 39**
See also CA 33-36R; CANR 22

Thompson, Francis Clegg
See Mencken, H(enry) L(ouis)

Thompson, Francis Joseph 1859-1907 .... **TCLC 4**
See also CA 104; CDBLB 1890-1914; DLB 19

Thompson, Hunter S(tockton) 1939- .... **CLC 9, 17, 40**
See also BEST 89:1; CA 17-20R; CANR 23; MTCW

Thompson, James Myers
See Thompson, Jim (Myers)

Thompson, Jim (Myers) 1906-1977(?) .... **CLC 69**
See also CA 140

Thompson, Judith .... **CLC 39**

Thomson, James 1700-1748 .... **LC 16**

Thomson, James 1834-1882 ...... **NCLC 18**

Thoreau, Henry David 1817-1862 ...... **NCLC 7, 21; DA; WLC**
See also CDALB 1640-1865; DLB 1

Thornton, Hall
See Silverberg, Robert

Thurber, James (Grover) 1894-1961 ... **CLC 5, 11, 25; DA; SSC 1**
See also CA 73-76; CANR 17, 39; CDALB 1929-1941; DLB 4, 11, 22, 102; MAICYA; MTCW; SATA 13

Thurman, Wallace (Henry) 1902-1934 .... **TCLC 6; BLC**
See also BW; CA 104; 124; DLB 51

Ticheburn, Cheviot
See Ainsworth, William Harrison

Tieck, (Johann) Ludwig 1773-1853 .... **NCLC 5**
See also DLB 90

Tiger, Derry
See Ellison, Harlan

Tilghman, Christopher 1948(?)- ..... **CLC 65**

Tillinghast, Richard (Williford) 1940- .... **CLC 29**
See also CA 29-32R; CANR 26

Timrod, Henry 1828-1867 .... **NCLC 25**
See also DLB 3

Tindall, Gillian 1938- .... **CLC 7**
See also CA 21-24R; CANR 11

Tiptree, James, Jr. .... **CLC 48, 50**
See also Sheldon, Alice Hastings Bradley
See also DLB 8

Titmarsh, Michael Angelo
See Thackeray, William Makepeace

Tocqueville, Alexis (Charles Henri Maurice Clerel Comte) 1805-1859..... **NCLC 7**

Tolkien, J(ohn) R(onald) R(euel) 1892-1973 .... **CLC 1, 2, 3, 8, 12, 38; DA; WLC**
See also AAYA 10; AITN 1; CA 17-18; 45-48; CANR 36; CAP 2; CDBLB 1914-1945; DLB 15; JRDA; MAICYA; MTCW; SATA 2, 24, 32

Toller, Ernst 1893-1939 .... **TCLC 10**
See also CA 107; DLB 124

Tolson, M. B.
See Tolson, Melvin B(eaunorus)

Tolson, Melvin B(eaunorus) 1898(?)-1966 .... **CLC 36; BLC**
See also BW; CA 124; 89-92; DLB 48, 76

Tolstoi, Aleksei Nikolaevich
See Tolstoy, Alexey Nikolaevich

Tolstoy, Alexey Nikolaevich 1882-1945 .... **TCLC 18**
See also CA 107

Tolstoy, Count Leo
See Tolstoy, Leo (Nikolaevich)

Tolstoy, Leo (Nikolaevich) 1828-1910 ...... **TCLC 4, 11, 17, 28, 44; DA; SSC 9; WLC**
See also CA 104; 123; SATA 26

Tomasi di Lampedusa, Giuseppe 1896-1957
See Lampedusa, Giuseppe (Tomasi) di
See also CA 111

Tomlin, Lily .... **CLC 17**
See also Tomlin, Mary Jean

Tomlin, Mary Jean 1939(?)-
See Tomlin, Lily
See also CA 117

Tomlinson, (Alfred) Charles 1927- .... **CLC 2, 4, 6, 13, 45**
See also CA 5-8R; CANR 33; DLB 40

Tonson, Jacob
See Bennett, (Enoch) Arnold

Toole, John Kennedy 1937-1969 .... **CLC 19, 64**
See also CA 104; DLBY 81

Toomer, Jean 1894-1967 ...... **CLC 1, 4, 13, 22; BLC; PC 7; SSC 1**
See also BW; CA 85-88; CDALB 1917-1929; DLB 45, 51; MTCW

Torley, Luke
See Blish, James (Benjamin)

Tornimparte, Alessandra
See Ginzburg, Natalia

Torre, Raoul della
See Mencken, H(enry) L(ouis)

Torrey, E(dwin) Fuller 1937- .... **CLC 34**
See also CA 119

Torsvan, Ben Traven
See Traven, B.

Torsvan, Benno Traven
See Traven, B.

Torsvan, Berick Traven
See Traven, B.

Torsvan, Berwick Traven
See Traven, B.

Torsvan, Bruno Traven
See Traven, B.

Urmuz
See Codrescu, Andrei

Ustinov, Peter (Alexander) 1921- .... **CLC 1**
See also AITN 1; CA 13-16R; CANR 25; DLB 13

v
See Chekhov, Anton (Pavlovich)

Vaculik, Ludvik 1926- .... **CLC 7**
See also CA 53-56

Valenzuela, Luisa 1938-... **CLC 31; SSC 14**
See also CA 101; CANR 32; DLB 113; HW

Valera y Alcala-Galiano, Juan
1824-1905 .... **TCLC 10**
See also CA 106

Valery, (Ambroise) Paul (Toussaint Jules)
1871-1945 .... **TCLC 4, 15**
See also CA 104; 122; MTCW

Valle-Inclan, Ramon (Maria) del
1866-1936 .... **TCLC 5; HLC**
See also CA 106; DLB 134

Vallejo, Antonio Buero
See Buero Vallejo, Antonio

Vallejo, Cesar (Abraham)
1892-1938 .... **TCLC 3; HLC**
See also CA 105; HW

Valle Y Pena, Ramon del
See Valle-Inclan, Ramon (Maria) del

Van Ash, Cay 1918- .... **CLC 34**

Vanbrugh, Sir John 1664-1726 ...... **LC 21**
See also DLB 80

Van Campen, Karl
See Campbell, John W(ood, Jr.)

Vance, Gerald
See Silverberg, Robert

Vance, Jack .... **CLC 35**
See also Vance, John Holbrook
See also DLB 8

Vance, John Holbrook 1916-
See Queen, Ellery; Vance, Jack
See also CA 29-32R; CANR 17; MTCW

Van Den Bogarde, Derek Jules Gaspard Ulric Niven 1921-
See Bogarde, Dirk
See also CA 77-80

Vandenburgh, Jane .... **CLC 59**

Vanderhaeghe, Guy 1951- .... **CLC 41**
See also CA 113

van der Post, Laurens (Jan) 1906- ... **CLC 5**
See also CA 5-8R; CANR 35

van de Wetering, Janwillem 1931- .. **CLC 47**
See also CA 49-52; CANR 4

Van Dine, S. S. .... **TCLC 23**
See also Wright, Willard Huntington

Van Doren, Carl (Clinton)
1885-1950 .... **TCLC 18**
See also CA 111

Van Doren, Mark 1894-1972..... **CLC 6, 10**
See also CA 1-4R; 37-40R; CANR 3; DLB 45; MTCW

Van Druten, John (William)
1901-1957 .... **TCLC 2**
See also CA 104; DLB 10

Van Duyn, Mona (Jane)
1921- .... **CLC 3, 7, 63**
See also CA 9-12R; CANR 7, 38; DLB 5

Van Dyne, Edith
See Baum, L(yman) Frank

van Itallie, Jean-Claude 1936-....... **CLC 3**
See also CA 45-48; CAAS 2; CANR 1; DLB 7

van Ostaijen, Paul 1896-1928 ..... **TCLC 33**

Van Peebles, Melvin 1932- ...... **CLC 2, 20**
See also BW; CA 85-88; CANR 27

Vansittart, Peter 1920-............ **CLC 42**
See also CA 1-4R; CANR 3

Van Vechten, Carl 1880-1964 ...... **CLC 33**
See also CA 89-92; DLB 4, 9, 51

Van Vogt, A(lfred) E(lton) 1912-..... **CLC 1**
See also CA 21-24R; CANR 28; DLB 8; SATA 14

Varda, Agnes 1928- .... **CLC 16**
See also CA 116; 122

Vargas Llosa, (Jorge) Mario (Pedro)
1936- .... **CLC 3, 6, 9, 10, 15, 31, 42; DA; HLC**
See also CA 73-76; CANR 18, 32, 42; HW; MTCW

Vasiliu, Gheorghe 1881-1957
See Bacovia, George
See also CA 123

Vassa, Gustavus
See Equiano, Olaudah

Vassilikos, Vassilis 1933-......... **CLC 4, 8**
See also CA 81-84

Vaughn, Stephanie................. **CLC 62**

Vazov, Ivan (Minchov)
1850-1921 .... **TCLC 25**
See also CA 121

Veblen, Thorstein (Bunde)
1857-1929 .... **TCLC 31**
See also CA 115

Vega, Lope de 1562-1635........... **LC 23**

Venison, Alfred
See Pound, Ezra (Weston Loomis)

Verdi, Marie de
See Mencken, H(enry) L(ouis)

Verdu, Matilde
See Cela, Camilo Jose

Verga, Giovanni (Carmelo)
1840-1922 .... **TCLC 3**
See also CA 104; 123

Vergil 70B.C.-19B.C. .... **CMLC 9; DA**

Verhaeren, Emile (Adolphe Gustave)
1855-1916 .... **TCLC 12**
See also CA 109

Verlaine, Paul (Marie)
1844-1896 .... **NCLC 2; PC 2**

Verne, Jules (Gabriel)
1828-1905 .... **TCLC 6, 52**
See also CA 110; 131; DLB 123; JRDA; MAICYA; SATA 21

Very, Jones 1813-1880........... **NCLC 9**
See also DLB 1

Vesaas, Tarjei 1897-1970.......... **CLC 48**
See also CA 29-32R

Vialis, Gaston
See Simenon, Georges (Jacques Christian)

Vian, Boris 1920-1959 .... **TCLC 9**
See also CA 106; DLB 72

Viaud, (Louis Marie) Julien 1850-1923
See Loti, Pierre
See also CA 107

Vicar, Henry
See Felsen, Henry Gregor

Vicker, Angus
See Felsen, Henry Gregor

Vidal, Gore
1925- ..... **CLC 2, 4, 6, 8, 10, 22, 33, 72**
See also AITN 1; BEST 90:2; CA 5-8R; CANR 13; DLB 6; MTCW

Viereck, Peter (Robert Edwin)
1916- .... **CLC 4**
See also CA 1-4R; CANR 1; DLB 5

Vigny, Alfred (Victor) de
1797-1863 .... **NCLC 7**
See also DLB 119

Vilakazi, Benedict Wallet
1906-1947 .... **TCLC 37**

Villiers de l'Isle Adam, Jean Marie Mathias Philippe Auguste Comte
1838-1889 .... **NCLC 3; SSC 14**
See also DLB 123

Vincent, Gabrielle a pseudonym...... **CLC 13**
See also CA 126; CLR 13; MAICYA; SATA 61

Vinci, Leonardo da 1452-1519....... **LC 12**

Vine, Barbara .... **CLC 50**
See also Rendell, Ruth (Barbara)
See also BEST 90:4

Vinge, Joan D(ennison) 1948-...... **CLC 30**
See also CA 93-96; SATA 36

Violis, G.
See Simenon, Georges (Jacques Christian)

Visconti, Luchino 1906-1976....... **CLC 16**
See also CA 81-84; 65-68; CANR 39

Vittorini, Elio 1908-1966...... **CLC 6, 9, 14**
See also CA 133; 25-28R

Vizinczey, Stephen 1933-.......... **CLC 40**
See also CA 128

Vliet, R(ussell) G(ordon)
1929-1984 .... **CLC 22**
See also CA 37-40R; 112; CANR 18

Vogau, Boris Andreyevich 1894-1937(?)
See Pilnyak, Boris
See also CA 123

Vogel, Paula A(nne) 1951-......... **CLC 76**
See also CA 108

Voight, Ellen Bryant 1943-........ **CLC 54**
See also CA 69-72; CANR 11, 29; DLB 120

Voigt, Cynthia 1942- .... **CLC 30**
See also AAYA 3; CA 106; CANR 18, 37, 40; CLR 13; JRDA; MAICYA; SATA 33, 48

Voinovich, Vladimir (Nikolaevich)
1932- .... **CLC 10, 49**
See also CA 81-84; CAAS 12; CANR 33; MTCW

Voltaire
1694-1778 ... **LC 14; DA; SSC 12; WLC**

Wasserstein, Wendy
1950- .... **CLC 32, 59; DC 4**
See also CA 121; 129; CABS 3

Waterhouse, Keith (Spencer)
1929- .... **CLC 47**
See also CA 5-8R; CANR 38; DLB 13, 15; MTCW

Waters, Roger 1944-.............. **CLC 35**
See also Pink Floyd

Watkins, Frances Ellen
See Harper, Frances Ellen Watkins

Watkins, Gerrold
See Malzberg, Barry N(athaniel)

Watkins, Paul 1964-.............. **CLC 55**
See also CA 132

Watkins, Vernon Phillips
1906-1967 .... **CLC 43**
See also CA 9-10; 25-28R; CAP 1; DLB 20

Watson, Irving S.
See Mencken, H(enry) L(ouis)

Watson, John H.
See Farmer, Philip Jose

Watson, Richard F.
See Silverberg, Robert

Waugh, Auberon (Alexander) 1939- .. **CLC 7**
See also CA 45-48; CANR 6, 22; DLB 14

Waugh, Evelyn (Arthur St. John)
1903-1966 ...... **CLC 1, 3, 8, 13, 19, 27, 44; DA; WLC**
See also CA 85-88; 25-28R; CANR 22; CDBLB 1914-1945; DLB 15; MTCW

Waugh, Harriet 1944- .... **CLC 6**
See also CA 85-88; CANR 22

Ways, C. R.
See Blount, Roy (Alton), Jr.

Waystaff, Simon
See Swift, Jonathan

Webb, (Martha) Beatrice (Potter)
1858-1943 .... **TCLC 22**
See also Potter, Beatrice
See also CA 117

Webb, Charles (Richard) 1939-...... **CLC 7**
See also CA 25-28R

Webb, James H(enry), Jr. 1946-.... **CLC 22**
See also CA 81-84

Webb, Mary (Gladys Meredith)
1881-1927 .... **TCLC 24**
See also CA 123; DLB 34

Webb, Mrs. Sidney
See Webb, (Martha) Beatrice (Potter)

Webb, Phyllis 1927-.............. **CLC 18**
See also CA 104; CANR 23; DLB 53

Webb, Sidney (James)
1859-1947 .... **TCLC 22**
See also CA 117

Webber, Andrew Lloyd............. **CLC 21**
See also Lloyd Webber, Andrew

Weber, Lenora Mattingly
1895-1971 .... **CLC 12**
See also CA 19-20; 29-32R; CAP 1; SATA 2, 26

Webster, John 1579(?)-1634(?) .... **DC 2**
See also CDBLB Before 1660; DA; DLB 58; WLC

Webster, Noah 1758-1843 .... **NCLC 30**

Wedekind, (Benjamin) Frank(lin)
1864-1918 .... **TCLC 7**
See also CA 104; DLB 118

Weidman, Jerome 1913-............ **CLC 7**
See also AITN 2; CA 1-4R; CANR 1; DLB 28

Weil, Simone (Adolphine)
1909-1943 .... **TCLC 23**
See also CA 117

Weinstein, Nathan
See West, Nathanael

Weinstein, Nathan von Wallenstein
See West, Nathanael

Weir, Peter (Lindsay) 1944- .... **CLC 20**
See also CA 113; 123

Weiss, Peter (Ulrich)
1916-1982 .... **CLC 3, 15, 51**
See also CA 45-48; 106; CANR 3; DLB 69, 124

Weiss, Theodore (Russell)
1916- .... **CLC 3, 8, 14**
See also CA 9-12R; CAAS 2; DLB 5

Welch, (Maurice) Denton
1915-1948 .... **TCLC 22**
See also CA 121

Welch, James 1940- .... **CLC 6, 14, 52**
See also CA 85-88; CANR 42

Weldon, Fay
1933(?)- .... **CLC 6, 9, 11, 19, 36, 59**
See also CA 21-24R; CANR 16; CDBLB 1960 to Present; DLB 14; MTCW

Wellek, Rene 1903- .... **CLC 28**
See also CA 5-8R; CAAS 7; CANR 8; DLB 63

Weller, Michael 1942- .... **CLC 10, 53**
See also CA 85-88

Weller, Paul 1958-............... **CLC 26**

Wellershoff, Dieter 1925-.......... **CLC 46**
See also CA 89-92; CANR 16, 37

Welles, (George) Orson
1915-1985 .... **CLC 20, 80**
See also CA 93-96; 117

Wellman, Mac 1945- .... **CLC 65**

Wellman, Manly Wade 1903-1986 .. **CLC 49**
See also CA 1-4R; 118; CANR 6, 16; SATA 6, 47

Wells, Carolyn 1869(?)-1942 ...... **TCLC 35**
See also CA 113; DLB 11

Wells, H(erbert) G(eorge)
1866-1946 .... **TCLC 6, 12, 19; DA; SSC 6; WLC**
See also CA 110; 121; CDBLB 1914-1945; DLB 34, 70; MTCW; SATA 20

Wells, Rosemary 1943-............ **CLC 12**
See also CA 85-88; CLR 16; MAICYA; SAAS 1; SATA 18, 69

Welty, Eudora
1909- ...... **CLC 1, 2, 5, 14, 22, 33; DA; SSC 1; WLC**
See also CA 9-12R; CABS 1; CANR 32; CDALB 1941-1968; DLB 2, 102; DLBY 87; MTCW

Wen I-to 1899-1946 .... **TCLC 28**

Wentworth, Robert
See Hamilton, Edmond

Werfel, Franz (V.) 1890-1945 ...... **TCLC 8**
See also CA 104; DLB 81, 124

Wergeland, Henrik Arnold
1808-1845 .... **NCLC 5**

Wersba, Barbara 1932-............ **CLC 30**
See also AAYA 2; CA 29-32R; CANR 16, 38; CLR 3; DLB 52; JRDA; MAICYA; SAAS 2; SATA 1, 58

Wertmueller, Lina 1928- .... **CLC 16**
See also CA 97-100; CANR 39

Wescott, Glenway 1901-1987....... **CLC 13**
See also CA 13-16R; 121; CANR 23; DLB 4, 9, 102

Wesker, Arnold 1932- .... **CLC 3, 5, 42**
See also CA 1-4R; CAAS 7; CANR 1, 33; CDBLB 1960 to Present; DLB 13; MTCW

Wesley, Richard (Errol) 1945-....... **CLC 7**
See also BW; CA 57-60; CANR 27; DLB 38

Wessel, Johan Herman 1742-1785 .... **LC 7**

West, Anthony (Panther)
1914-1987 .... **CLC 50**
See also CA 45-48; 124; CANR 3, 19; DLB 15

West, C. P.
See Wodehouse, P(elham) G(renville)

West, (Mary) Jessamyn
1902-1984 .... **CLC 7, 17**
See also CA 9-12R; 112; CANR 27; DLB 6; DLBY 84; MTCW; SATA 37

West, Morris L(anglo) 1916-..... **CLC 6, 33**
See also CA 5-8R; CANR 24; MTCW

West, Nathanael
1903-1940 .... **TCLC 1, 14, 44**
See also CA 104; 125; CDALB 1929-1941; DLB 4, 9, 28; MTCW

West, Owen
See Koontz, Dean R(ay)

West, Paul 1930- .... **CLC 7, 14**
See also CA 13-16R; CAAS 7; CANR 22; DLB 14

West, Rebecca 1892-1983 .. **CLC 7, 9, 31, 50**
See also CA 5-8R; 109; CANR 19; DLB 36; DLBY 83; MTCW

Westall, Robert (Atkinson)
1929-1993 .... **CLC 17**
See also CA 69-72; 141; CANR 18; CLR 13; JRDA; MAICYA; SAAS 2; SATA 23, 69; SATA-Obit 75

Westlake, Donald E(dwin)
1933- .... **CLC 7, 33**
See also CA 17-20R; CAAS 13; CANR 16

Westmacott, Mary
See Christie, Agatha (Mary Clarissa)

Weston, Allen
See Norton, Andre

Wetcheek, J. L.
See Feuchtwanger, Lion

Wetering, Janwillem van de
See van de Wetering, Janwillem

Wetherell, Elizabeth
See Warner, Susan (Bogert)

Whalen, Philip 1923- . . . . **CLC 6, 29**
See also CA 9-12R; CANR 5, 39; DLB 16

Wharton, Edith (Newbold Jones) 1862-1937 . . . . . . **TCLC 3, 9, 27, 53; DA; SSC 6; WLC**
See also CA 104; 132; CDALB 1865-1917; DLB 4, 9, 12, 78; MTCW

Wharton, James
See Mencken, H(enry) L(ouis)

Wharton, William (a pseudonym) . . . . **CLC 18, 37**
See also CA 93-96; DLBY 80

Wheatley (Peters), Phillis 1754(?)-1784 . . . . **LC 3; BLC; DA; PC 3; WLC**
See also CDALB 1640-1865; DLB 31, 50

Wheelock, John Hall 1886-1978 . . . . **CLC 14**
See also CA 13-16R; 77-80; CANR 14; DLB 45

White, E(lwyn) B(rooks) 1899-1985 . . . . **CLC 10, 34, 39**
See also AITN 2; CA 13-16R; 116; CANR 16, 37; CLR 1, 21; DLB 11, 22; MAICYA; MTCW; SATA 2, 29, 44

White, Edmund (Valentine III) 1940- . . . . **CLC 27**
See also AAYA 7; CA 45-48; CANR 3, 19, 36; MTCW

White, Patrick (Victor Martindale) 1912-1990 . . **CLC 3, 4, 5, 7, 9, 18, 65, 69**
See also CA 81-84; 132; CANR 43; MTCW

White, Phyllis Dorothy James 1920-
See James, P. D.
See also CA 21-24R; CANR 17, 43; MTCW

White, T(erence) H(anbury) 1906-1964 . . . . **CLC 30**
See also CA 73-76; CANR 37; JRDA; MAICYA; SATA 12

White, Terence de Vere 1912- . . . . . . **CLC 49**
See also CA 49-52; CANR 3

White, Walter F(rancis) 1893-1955 . . . . **TCLC 15**
See also White, Walter
See also CA 115; 124; DLB 51

White, William Hale 1831-1913
See Rutherford, Mark
See also CA 121

Whitehead, E(dward) A(nthony) 1933- . . . . **CLC 5**
See also CA 65-68

Whitemore, Hugh (John) 1936- . . . . . **CLC 37**
See also CA 132

Whitman, Sarah Helen (Power) 1803-1878 . . . . **NCLC 19**
See also DLB 1

Whitman, Walt(er) 1819-1892 . . . . . **NCLC 4, 31; DA; PC 3; WLC**
See also CDALB 1640-1865; DLB 3, 64; SATA 20

Whitney, Phyllis A(yame) 1903- . . . . **CLC 42**
See also AITN 2; BEST 90:3; CA 1-4R; CANR 3, 25, 38; JRDA; MAICYA; SATA 1, 30

Whittemore, (Edward) Reed (Jr.) 1919- . . . . **CLC 4**
See also CA 9-12R; CAAS 8; CANR 4; DLB 5

Whittier, John Greenleaf 1807-1892 . . . . **NCLC 8**
See also CDALB 1640-1865; DLB 1

Whittlebot, Hernia
See Coward, Noel (Peirce)

Wicker, Thomas Grey 1926-
See Wicker, Tom
See also CA 65-68; CANR 21

Wicker, Tom . . . . **CLC 7**
See also Wicker, Thomas Grey

Wideman, John Edgar 1941- . . . . **CLC 5, 34, 36, 67; BLC**
See also BW; CA 85-88; CANR 14, 42; DLB 33

Wiebe, Rudy (Henry) 1934- . . . **CLC 6, 11, 14**
See also CA 37-40R; CANR 42; DLB 60

Wieland, Christoph Martin 1733-1813 . . . . **NCLC 17**
See also DLB 97

Wieners, John 1934- . . . . **CLC 7**
See also CA 13-16R; DLB 16

Wiesel, Elie(zer) 1928- . . . . **CLC 3, 5, 11, 37; DA**
See also AAYA 7; AITN 1; CA 5-8R; CAAS 4; CANR 8, 40; DLB 83; DLBY 87; MTCW; SATA 56

Wiggins, Marianne 1947- . . . . **CLC 57**
See also BEST 89:3; CA 130

Wight, James Alfred 1916-
See Herriot, James
See also CA 77-80; SATA 44, 55

Wilbur, Richard (Purdy) 1921- . . . . **CLC 3, 6, 9, 14, 53; DA**
See also CA 1-4R; CABS 2; CANR 2, 29; DLB 5; MTCW; SATA 9

Wild, Peter 1940- . . . . **CLC 14**
See also CA 37-40R; DLB 5

Wilde, Oscar (Fingal O'Flahertie Wills) 1854(?)-1900 . . . . **TCLC 1, 8, 23, 41; DA; SSC 11; WLC**
See also CA 104; 119; CDBLB 1890-1914; DLB 10, 19, 34, 57; SATA 24

Wilder, Billy . . . . **CLC 20**
See also Wilder, Samuel
See also DLB 26

Wilder, Samuel 1906-
See Wilder, Billy
See also CA 89-92

Wilder, Thornton (Niven) 1897-1975 . . . . . . **CLC 1, 5, 6, 10, 15, 35, 82; DA; DC 1; WLC**
See also AITN 2; CA 13-16R; 61-64; CANR 40; DLB 4, 7, 9; MTCW

Wilding, Michael 1942- . . . . **CLC 73**
See also CA 104; CANR 24

Wiley, Richard 1944- . . . . **CLC 44**
See also CA 121; 129

Wilhelm, Kate . . . . **CLC 7**
See also Wilhelm, Katie Gertrude
See also CAAS 5; DLB 8

Wilhelm, Katie Gertrude 1928-
See Wilhelm, Kate
See also CA 37-40R; CANR 17, 36; MTCW

Wilkins, Mary
See Freeman, Mary Eleanor Wilkins

Willard, Nancy 1936- . . . . **CLC 7, 37**
See also CA 89-92; CANR 10, 39; CLR 5; DLB 5, 52; MAICYA; MTCW; SATA 30, 37, 71

Williams, C(harles) K(enneth) 1936- . . . . **CLC 33, 56**
See also CA 37-40R; DLB 5

Williams, Charles
See Collier, James L(incoln)

Williams, Charles (Walter Stansby) 1886-1945 . . . . **TCLC 1, 11**
See also CA 104; DLB 100

Williams, (George) Emlyn 1905-1987 . . . . **CLC 15**
See also CA 104; 123; CANR 36; DLB 10, 77; MTCW

Williams, Hugo 1942- . . . . **CLC 42**
See also CA 17-20R; DLB 40

Williams, J. Walker
See Wodehouse, P(elham) G(renville)

Williams, John A(lfred) 1925- . . . . **CLC 5, 13; BLC**
See also BW; CA 53-56; CAAS 3; CANR 6, 26; DLB 2, 33

Williams, Jonathan (Chamberlain) 1929- . . . . **CLC 13**
See also CA 9-12R; CAAS 12; CANR 8; DLB 5

Williams, Joy 1944- . . . . **CLC 31**
See also CA 41-44R; CANR 22

Williams, Norman 1952- . . . . **CLC 39**
See also CA 118

Williams, Tennessee 1911-1983 . . . . . **CLC 1, 2, 5, 7, 8, 11, 15, 19, 30, 39, 45, 71; DA; DC 4; WLC**
See also AITN 1, 2; CA 5-8R; 108; CABS 3; CANR 31; CDALB 1941-1968; DLB 7; DLBD 4; DLBY 83; MTCW

Williams, Thomas (Alonzo) 1926-1990 . . . . **CLC 14**
See also CA 1-4R; 132; CANR 2

Williams, William C.
See Williams, William Carlos

Williams, William Carlos 1883-1963 . . . . **CLC 1, 2, 5, 9, 13, 22, 42, 67; DA; PC 7**
See also CA 89-92; CANR 34; CDALB 1917-1929; DLB 4, 16, 54, 86; MTCW

Williamson, David (Keith) 1942- . . . . **CLC 56**
See also CA 103; CANR 41

Williamson, Jack . . . . **CLC 29**
See also Williamson, John Stewart
See also CAAS 8; DLB 8

Williamson, John Stewart 1908-
See Williamson, Jack
See also CA 17-20R; CANR 23

Willie, Frederick
See Lovecraft, H(oward) P(hillips)

Wylie, Elinor (Morton Hoyt) 1885-1928 .... **TCLC 8**
See also CA 105; DLB 9, 45

Wylie, Philip (Gordon) 1902-1971... **CLC 43**
See also CA 21-22; 33-36R; CAP 2; DLB 9

Wyndham, John
See Harris, John (Wyndham Parkes Lucas) Beynon

Wyss, Johann David Von 1743-1818 .... **NCLC 10**
See also JRDA; MAICYA; SATA 27, 29

Yakumo Koizumi
See Hearn, (Patricio) Lafcadio (Tessima Carlos)

Yanez, Jose Donoso
See Donoso (Yanez), Jose

Yanovsky, Basile S.
See Yanovsky, V(assily) S(emenovich)

Yanovsky, V(assily) S(emenovich) 1906-1989 .... **CLC 2, 18**
See also CA 97-100; 129

Yates, Richard 1926-1992 ..... **CLC 7, 8, 23**
See also CA 5-8R; 139; CANR 10, 43; DLB 2; DLBY 81, 92

Yeats, W. B.
See Yeats, William Butler

Yeats, William Butler 1865-1939 ..... **TCLC 1, 11, 18, 31; DA; WLC**
See also CA 104; 127; CDBLB 1890-1914; DLB 10, 19, 98; MTCW

Yehoshua, A(braham) B. 1936- .... **CLC 13, 31**
See also CA 33-36R; CANR 43

Yep, Laurence Michael 1948- ...... **CLC 35**
See also AAYA 5; CA 49-52; CANR 1; CLR 3, 17; DLB 52; JRDA; MAICYA; SATA 7, 69

Yerby, Frank G(arvin) 1916-1991 .... **CLC 1, 7, 22; BLC**
See also BW; CA 9-12R; 136; CANR 16; DLB 76; MTCW

Yesenin, Sergei Alexandrovich
See Esenin, Sergei (Alexandrovich)

Yevtushenko, Yevgeny (Alexandrovich) 1933- .... **CLC 1, 3, 13, 26, 51**
See also CA 81-84; CANR 33; MTCW

Yezierska, Anzia 1885(?)-1970 ..... **CLC 46**
See also CA 126; 89-92; DLB 28; MTCW

Yglesias, Helen 1915-........... **CLC 7, 22**
See also CA 37-40R; CANR 15; MTCW

Yokomitsu Riichi 1898-1947 ...... **TCLC 47**

Yonge, Charlotte (Mary) 1823-1901 .... **TCLC 48**
See also CA 109; DLB 18; SATA 17

York, Jeremy
See Creasey, John

York, Simon
See Heinlein, Robert A(nson)

Yorke, Henry Vincent 1905-1974 ... **CLC 13**
See also Green, Henry
See also CA 85-88; 49-52

Young, Al(bert James) 1939- .... **CLC 19; BLC**
See also BW; CA 29-32R; CANR 26; DLB 33

Young, Andrew (John) 1885-1971 .... **CLC 5**
See also CA 5-8R; CANR 7, 29

Young, Collier
See Bloch, Robert (Albert)

Young, Edward 1683-1765 .... **LC 3**
See also DLB 95

Young, Marguerite 1909-.......... **CLC 82**
See also CA 13-16; CAP 1

Young, Neil 1945-................ **CLC 17**
See also CA 110

Yourcenar, Marguerite 1903-1987 .... **CLC 19, 38, 50**
See also CA 69-72; CANR 23; DLB 72; DLBY 88; MTCW

Yurick, Sol 1925-................. **CLC 6**
See also CA 13-16R; CANR 25

Zabolotskii, Nikolai Alekseevich 1903-1958 .... **TCLC 52**
See also CA 116

Zamiatin, Yevgenii
See Zamyatin, Evgeny Ivanovich

Zamyatin, Evgeny Ivanovich 1884-1937 .... **TCLC 8, 37**
See also CA 105

Zangwill, Israel 1864-1926........ **TCLC 16**
See also CA 109; DLB 10, 135

Zappa, Francis Vincent, Jr. 1940-1993
See Zappa, Frank
See also CA 108; 143

Zappa, Frank..................... **CLC 17**
See also Zappa, Francis Vincent, Jr.

Zaturenska, Marya 1902-1982.... **CLC 6, 11**
See also CA 13-16R; 105; CANR 22

Zelazny, Roger (Joseph) 1937- ..... **CLC 21**
See also AAYA 7; CA 21-24R; CANR 26; DLB 8; MTCW; SATA 39, 57

Zhdanov, Andrei A(lexandrovich) 1896-1948 .... **TCLC 18**
See also CA 117

Zhukovsky, Vasily 1783-1852 .... **NCLC 35**

Ziegenhagen, Eric................. **CLC 55**

Zimmer, Jill Schary
See Robinson, Jill

Zimmerman, Robert
See Dylan, Bob

Zindel, Paul 1936- .... **CLC 6, 26; DA**
See also AAYA 2; CA 73-76; CANR 31; CLR 3; DLB 7, 52; JRDA; MAICYA; MTCW; SATA 16, 58

Zinov'Ev, A. A.
See Zinoviev, Alexander (Aleksandrovich)

Zinoviev, Alexander (Aleksandrovich) 1922- .... **CLC 19**
See also CA 116; 133; CAAS 10

Zoilus
See Lovecraft, H(oward) P(hillips)

Zola, Emile (Edouard Charles Antoine) 1840-1902 ...... **TCLC 1, 6, 21, 41; DA; WLC**
See also CA 104; 138; DLB 123

Zoline, Pamela 1941-............. **CLC 62**

Zorrilla y Moral, Jose 1817-1893.. **NCLC 6**

Zoshchenko, Mikhail (Mikhailovich) 1895-1958 .... **TCLC 15**
See also CA 115

Zuckmayer, Carl 1896-1977........ **CLC 18**
See also CA 69-72; DLB 56, 124

Zuk, Georges
See Skelton, Robin

Zukofsky, Louis 1904-1978 .... **CLC 1, 2, 4, 7, 11, 18**
See also CA 9-12R; 77-80; CANR 39; DLB 5; MTCW

Zweig, Paul 1935-1984......... **CLC 34, 42**
See also CA 85-88; 113

Zweig, Stefan 1881-1942 .... **TCLC 17**
See also CA 112; DLB 81, 118

CLC Cumulative Nationality Index

CHILEAN

CHINESE

COLOMBIAN

CUBAN

CZECHOSLOVAKIAN

DANISH

DUTCH

EGYPTIAN

ENGLISH

ESTONIAN

FIJIAN

FINNISH

FRENCH

CLC-82 Title Index

ISBN 0-8103-4990-6
90000
9 780810 349902